THE NAGEL EDITION

חומש קורן לב לדעת
THE KOREN LEV LADAAT ḤUMASH

ספר במדבר
BEMIDBAR/NUMBERS

KOREN

THE NAGEL EDITION

חומש קורן לב לדעת
THE KOREN LEV LADAAT ḤUMASH

BEMIDBAR / NUMBERS

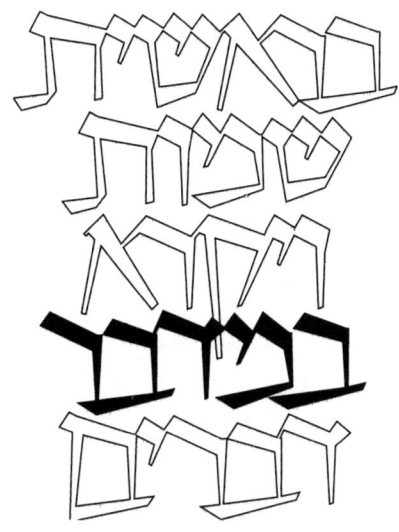

TORAH TRANSLATION BY
Rabbi Lord Jonathan Sacks זצ״ל

COMMENTARIES BY
Rabbi Shlomo Einhorn, Executive Editor
and Rabbi Dr. Zvi Grumet, Senior Editor

•

KOREN PUBLISHERS JERUSALEM

The Koren Lev Ladaat Ḥumash
Volume 4: Bemidbar
First Edition, 2023

Koren Publishers Jerusalem Ltd.
POB 4044, Jerusalem 9104001, ISRAEL
POB 8531, New Milford, CT, 06776, USA

www.korenpub.com

Torah Translation © 2021, Estate of Jonathan Sacks, from the Magerman Edition of the Koren Tanakh
Koren Tanakh Font ©1962, 2023 Koren Publishers Jerusalem Ltd.
Commentary © Koren Publishers Jerusalem Ltd.

Considerable research and expense have gone into the creation of this publication.
Unauthorized copying may be considered *geneivat da'at* and breach of copyright law.
No part of this publication (content or design, including use of the Koren fonts)
may be reproduced, stored in a retrieval system or transmitted in any form or by any
means electronic, mechanical, photocopying or otherwise, without the prior written
permission of the publisher, except in the case of brief quotations
embedded in critical articles or reviews.

The creation of this work was made possible with the generous support of the Jewish Book Trust Inc.

Printed in PRC

ISBN 978-965-7766-29-3

YAHBEM04

THE NAGEL EDITION
OF THE KOREN YOUNG ADULT ḤUMASH LEV LADAAT
IS DEDICATED TO THE MEMORY OF

Jack M. Nagel z"l
ר' יעקב אלימלך ז"ל

A beloved husband, devoted father, adoring grandfather and great-grandfather.
A true Visionary, who survived the Shoah, and whose philosophy was
to deal compassionately and kindly with all people.
His love for Torah and being a mensch guided him throughout his life.
He believed Education was the key to Jewish survival, and he made it his life's mission
to enrich the Los Angeles community with all aspects of Jewish scholarship and culture.
He established and remained committed to many yeshivot and Centers of Jewish
Learning throughout the United States and in his cherished homeland, Israel.

He had great faith, great heart, and great courage and was blessed
together with his Eshet Chayil, our Mother Gitta,
to leave a legacy of Tzedaka, Chesed and Emunah.

מרבה תורה מרבה חיים. מרבה צדקה מרבה שלום.
"The more Torah, the more life. The more charity, the more peace." (Avot 2:8)

Dedicated with love by his children:

Dr. Ronnie and Cheryl Nagel	Los Angeles, California, USA
Esther and Dr. Paul Lerer	Englewood, New Jersey, USA
David and Marnie Nagel	Los Angeles, California, USA
Careena and Drew Parker	Englewood, New Jersey, USA
And his devoted wife, Dr. Gitta Nagel	Los Angeles, California, USA

CONTENTS

מבוא	ix	Preface
הקדמה	x	Introduction

ספר במדבר		**SEFER BEMIDBAR**
במדבר	1	Bemidbar
נשא	33	Naso
בהעלתך	77	Behaalotekha
שלח	117	Shelaḥ
קרח	149	Koraḥ
חקת	179	Ḥukat
בלק	207	Balak
פינחס	241	Pinḥas
מטות	273	Mattot
מסעי	303	Masei

ספר ויקרא עם רש״י	331	**SEFER BEMIDBAR WITH RASHI**
הפטרות וקריאות נוספות	471	**HAFTAROT AND SPECIAL READINGS**
נספח – פרשני התורה	513	Appendix – The Classic Commentators

PUBLISHER'S PREFACE

"דור לדור ישבח מעשיך" (תהלים קמה, ד)

"One generation will praise Your works to the next…" (Psalms 145:4)

It is with gratitude and a certain ambition that we introduce this volume of **THE NAGEL EDITION OF THE KOREN LEV LADAAT ḤUMASH**, a Ḥumash designed to encourage connection, reflection, and learning of our foundation stone, the Torah.

The connection between Jewish young adults and the Torah is critical. Our children must learn the text of the Ḥumash and the classical commentators who have illuminated difficult passages. But it is just as important – and all-too-often neglected – that the student or young adult engage emotionally and experientially with the text. How does the Torah give them a prism to view the world around them? The need for this deeper, spiritual interaction gives rise to the name of this edition: **Lev Ladaat: The Understanding Heart**. For our ambition is that every Jew engage with the Torah and incorporate its values into his or her daily life, not just as an academic exercise.

It is with this ambition that Koren Publishers Jerusalem has created this edition, designed for high school students and young adults in synagogue *minyanim*. Since 1962, the Koren Tanakh has been recognized for its textual accuracy and innovative graphic design. We have remained committed to these qualities, and we have recently had the privilege of enriching the Ḥumash text with the eloquent English translation of one of the most articulate and original Jewish thinkers of our time, Rabbi Lord Jonathan Sacks, *zt"l*.

It is with gratitude that we acknowledge Rabbi Sacks for this exceptional translation of the Torah. And our thanks are no less due to Rabbi Shlomo Einhorn, from whose fertile imagination and broad educational experience the concept for this Young Adult Ḥumash sprang. Likewise to Rabbi Dr. Zvi Grumet, whose intimate knowledge of the Ḥumash and its commentaries has enriched these pages inestimably. And to Caryn Meltz, our Managing Editor, who brought it all together into a handsome and useful edition. And finally, to the team of translators, editors, and typesetters – Rabbi Yedidya Naveh, Rabbi Jonathan Mishkin, Suri Brand, Ilana Sobel, Carolyn Budow Ben-David, Rina Ben-Gal, Efrat Gross, and Avichai Gamdani – who made the volume a reality.

None of this would have been possible without the support and detailed involvement of the Nagel Family of California and New Jersey, who understood both the ambitions and methods of this edition. **THE NAGEL EDITION OF THE KOREN LEV LADAAT ḤUMASH** is dedicated to the memory of Jack Nagel, *z"l*, who was an exceptional community leader. He and his beloved wife Gitta have enabled so much of Jewish life in the Los Angeles community, especially in the area of Jewish education: *yeshivot*, high schools, and so much more. Surviving the Holocaust and making a new life for himself and family, Jack's was an exemplary Jewish life, combining *Torah im derekh eretz*. Koren is honored to be associated with his memory.

On behalf of all our *rabbanim*, scholars, and designers, we thank the Nagel Family. And to the many thousands of readers, in this and future generations: We are forever in your debt.

We hope the use of this Ḥumash will bring Jews closer and closer to the Torah and all the good it represents.

Matthew Miller, Publisher
Jerusalem, 5783 (2023)

EDITOR'S INTRODUCTION

What if there were no more bookstores left on Earth? What if we woke up to discover that the written word had been almost eliminated? This is the frightening possibility we confront when we visit "The Last Bookstore" in downtown Los Angeles. The Last Bookstore takes the guise of a survival shelter where all of Earth's great books are sold, in case there may one day be no other places to find books. I once had the opportunity to spend some time there, and I found my way to a Bible, which included a commentary for teenagers. It roused my curiosity – why is there no edition of the Ḥumash directed toward young adults? Ought we be simply waiting for young Jewish people to come to the Torah, instead of bringing the Torah to them?

Some might say that teens aren't interested in the Ḥumash. They are mistaken. For twenty-two years I have been teaching young adults, and I have always found them to be as hungry for knowledge and connection as any other group. Whenever I look past a student's distracted veneer and genuinely engage them with some profound thought, it opens a reservoir of dialogue that I could not have found elsewhere.

With social media and technology becoming a constant part of our lives, our need for real and deep connection has only grown stronger. The Torah, we know, is an עֵץ חַיִּים הִיא לַמַּחֲזִיקִים בָּהּ – a tree of life for all who hold on to it.

Putting together a project like this Ḥumash is complex. It's very easy to slip into anachronistic concepts aimed at grabbing attention. But we owe more to ourselves; we are hungry for substantive and truly thought-provoking conversations.

To you, our young adults, we now offer this Ḥumash. Will you use it? Will you allow it to guide you? When you are having a hard day and the walls seem to close in on you, will you pick this Torah up and let it lift you up? Will you let God into your life? We find Him in these words.

Why do we study Torah?

- *The Torah is a blueprint of the universe*, starting at the beginning – Bereshit. The Midrash teaches that God "looked into the Torah and created a world." Do we want to understand the world? "We should look at where it came from."

- *How to practice Judaism.* Torah teaches us how to live as Jews. It teaches us how to practice our Judaism. The Gemara teaches: "תַּלְמוּד גָּדוֹל, שֶׁהַתַּלְמוּד מֵבִיא לִידֵי מַעֲשֶׂה" – learning is great in that it moves us to action. I love the word *halakha*, which denotes Jewish Law. It means to walk. We can't walk in the ways of Judaism unless we know the *halakha*.

- *The values of Judaism.* The Torah guides us not only in how to practice Judaism's laws but, at times more importantly, how to live its values. The emphasis that our people places on charity, education, visiting the sick – it's all derived from the sensibilities of the Torah.

- *To help us do battle.* The sages interpret the wars described in the Torah as symbolic of our struggle against the *yetzer hara*, our evil inclination. Our shadow side is cunning. We have only one weapon against it, says the Gemara in Kiddushin: Torah study.

- *It is our oxygen, our life force.* The Gemara in Berakhot teaches us that just as a fish cannot live without water, so too we cannot exist without Torah. There isn't an example of a Jewish community that has thrived and flourished over multiple generations without a love and appreciation for producing Torah.

- *Crisis management.* Think about what enabled Yosef to survive trauma after trauma in Egypt? What made him so resilient? What did Yosef have that allowed him to survive? Rashi tells us that before he was thrown into the pit, Yosef would spend his time with Yaakov, studying the Torah taught by Shem and Ever. Shem and Ever were survivors. They had endured the flood and the generation of the dispersion. Deep down, Yaakov knew that Yosef would need this Torah.

- *To develop a relationship with God.* Part of our mission in this world is to cleave to the Almighty. Through a relationship with God one learns what it means to be a proper human being. We enter into a relationship with our Father in Heaven by learning His word.

◂ It's the

- *It's the great equalizer.* Rav Boruch Ber, the great rosh yeshiva, is quoted to have once said that Torah is the great equalizer. A child starting sixth grade could learn Bava Metzia, as though it's the most basic and simple piece of the Gemara. But at the same time, it's one of the hardest parts of the Talmud, challenging even the most advanced scholars. Torah is accessible to everyone at all levels.
- *It's your story.* Project years ahead and imagine bringing your spouse back to the house of your parents. While you're cleaning up the house, you find your old yearbook. You can't wait to share it with the person that you love. Why are you so excited? Because you are going to share the story of your life. That's why we open up the Torah. Our entire legacy is there; where we came from, what we went through, where our customs come from, and where our identity has come from.
- *And finally: It's your way out.* Imagine you are lost in a maze. You cannot find the way out. Suddenly, you're told by the maze keeper, who stands above the maze, that there is one way out. It's the simplest way of all – the way that you came in. Retrace your steps, and that's how you'll find a way out. The Jews have survived the Shoah and have rebuilt a remarkable edifice called the State of Israel. We have done amazing things in America and around the world. We have built *yeshivot* filled to the brim with students. But we also find ourselves at a crossroads, facing multiple challenges. God's guidance for us is: Retrace your steps. Figure out where you became lost, because that will tell us how to get through the maze of life. That's why we need the Torah.

With all these ideas in mind, we have designed this Ḥumash in such a way as to maximize the student's opportunity for reflection, connection, and learning. In addition to Rabbi Lord Jonathan Sacks's beautiful new translation of the Torah, we have included several different commentaries to add meaning to your journey:

WISDOM OF THE HEART: This commentary is designed to make you think critically about the stories, laws, and poetry in the Torah and how they relate to your life. It often includes a question about your own experiences and opinions.

THE CLASSIC COMMENTATORS: This section begins with a guiding issue or question and brings two or three classic commentaries from Jewish history who have offered answers. Compare the answers given by the different commentaries. With whom do you agree? These are followed by *Questions for Thought*, which push you to read the commentaries more closely and find hidden ideas below the surface.

TEXTUAL SKILLS: These questions encourage you to read the text of the Torah more closely. The exact ways words and phrases appear carry tremendous meaning, and by paying attention to details we can make ourselves better readers.

QUICK BITES: This section provides a brief thought about the Torah that we can take with us out of the classroom and share with family and friends. It can be a jumping-off point for a deeper conversation.

EXPLORING HASHKAFA: This essay at the end of most *parashot* deals with a "big idea" that challenges us as Jews in the modern world. It is not meant to give us easy answers, but to help us learn to think in creative ways about complex questions.

I write these words with profound gratitude to God. It is my hope that this project brings about a deeper love and understanding of God among the Jewish people.

It is an honor to work on this project together with Koren Publishers. Their professionalism, responsibility to tradition, and keen sense of style have made this a truly wonderful experience. Thank you to Matthew Miller and all the talented and hardworking editorial staff at Koren.

Thank you to my wonderful school and community, Yeshivat Yavneh, where many of these teachings were first developed and shared with teenagers.

Thank you to my wife, Shira. We were standing on the shore of the Mediterranean Sea when you held a rough draft of this Ḥumash in your hand. You looked at me and said: "This project must happen."

◀ Thank you

Thank you to my parents and family who continue to encourage, praise, and support my work.

Thank you to the Nagel family. The connection between our families goes back over sixty years, and our bond of Torah began with a family *ḥavura* on Wilshire Boulevard. Together with Jack, of blessed memory, we completed Sanhedrin and then began Bava Batra. It has been an exceptional privilege, and I have the *zekhut* of continuing this tradition with the family. This work was made possible by the incredible family vision gifted to the Nagels by Jack and Gitta. To Dr. Ronnie, Esther, David, and Careena, my blessing is that the merit of this project may stand for your whole family's long life and health. May we continue to follow your trailblazing path, as together we celebrate this very historic moment – *The Koren Lev Ladaat Ḥumash.*

Rabbi Shlomo Einhorn
Executive Editor

פרשת במדבר
PARASHAT BEMIDBAR

> "Wilderness. The word itself is music."
> Edward Abbey

The date: One month after the inauguration of the *Mishkan*, the traveling Tabernacle.

The travels are about to begin, not only of the *Mishkan*, but of the entire nation and its mission. Little did those people know that their travels would become a template for the wanderings of Jews for millennia. Internal fighting, external enemies, and self-doubt become our adversaries, and yet each makes us stronger. The Wandering Jew becomes the Learning Jew, learning from experiences. They learned from their experiences, we learn from our ours, and we can learn from theirs too.

PARASHAT BEMIDBAR

> **1:1–16** Toward the beginning of Benei Yisrael's second year in the wilderness, God commands Moshe to count all of Benei Yisrael, which he does together with Aharon. They are given twelve assistants – one notable from each tribe.

1 1 The LORD spoke to Moshe in the Sinai Desert, in the Tent of Meeting, on the first of the second 2 month, in the second year since their coming out from the land of Egypt. He said: "Take a census of the entire community of Israel by their clans and their ancestral houses, 3 listing every male by name individually, twenty years of age and upward: everyone in Israel who is capable of active service. You and Aharon shall number them by their 4 divisions. And one man from each tribe shall join you in the task, each the head of his 5 ancestral house. These are the names of the men who will assist you: from Reuven, 6/7 Elitzur son of Shedeiur; from Shimon, Shelumiel son of Tzurishadai; from Yehuda, 8/9 Naḥshon son of Aminadav; from Yissakhar, Netanel son of Tzuar; from Zevulun, Eliav 10 son of Ḥelon. For the sons of Yosef: from Efrayim, Elishama son of Amihud; from 11/12 Menashe, Gamliel son of Pedatzur. From Binyamin, Avidan son of Gidoni; from Dan, 13/14 Aḥiezer son of Amishadai; from Asher, Pagiel son of Okhran; from Gad, Elyasaf son 15/16 of Deuel; and from Naftali, Aḥira son of Einan." These were the ones chosen from the community, princes of their ancestral tribes; they are the heads of Israel's clans.

QUESTIONS FOR THOUGHT
- Regarding what do Rashbam and Sforno agree?
- What is the basic disagreement between them?
- Can you find a verse from the daily *tefilla* which would support one of those two positions?
- In what way is Ibn Ezra's explanation very different from the other two?

TEXTUAL SKILLS

1. Notice which of the twelve tribes is omitted. Did God explain why that tribe has no representative?

2. Look at the names of the representatives of the tribes. What do you notice?

WISDOM OF THE HEART

According to a midrash, the Torah was given in three ways: fire, water, and wilderness. That suggests that Torah is meant to be engaged on three levels. The first is fire, passion. Encountering Torah is more than simply an intellectual pursuit; it is meant to engage us personally – and we are meant to engage it passionately. The second is water, fluidity. Liquid fills all the nooks and crannies; it can adapt to any shape. Torah can be meaningful in every place, every generation, every society, and every type of learner. Finally, there is wilderness, which represents the need to strip away preconceived notions and prejudices, about others and about ourselves.

Which encounter would you like to experience with Torah? Fire, water, or wilderness?

פרשת במדבר

א וַיְדַבֵּר יְהוָה אֶל־מֹשֶׁה בְּמִדְבַּר סִינַי בְּאֹהֶל מוֹעֵד בְּאֶחָד לַחֹדֶשׁ
ב הַשֵּׁנִי בַּשָּׁנָה הַשֵּׁנִית לְצֵאתָם מֵאֶרֶץ מִצְרַיִם לֵאמֹר: שְׂאוּ
אֶת־רֹאשׁ כָּל־עֲדַת בְּנֵי־יִשְׂרָאֵל לְמִשְׁפְּחֹתָם לְבֵית אֲבֹתָם
ג בְּמִסְפַּר שֵׁמוֹת כָּל־זָכָר לְגֻלְגְּלֹתָם: מִבֶּן עֶשְׂרִים שָׁנָה וָמַעְלָה
כָּל־יֹצֵא צָבָא בְּיִשְׂרָאֵל תִּפְקְדוּ אֹתָם לְצִבְאֹתָם אַתָּה וְאַהֲרֹן:
ד וְאִתְּכֶם יִהְיוּ אִישׁ אִישׁ לַמַּטֶּה אִישׁ רֹאשׁ לְבֵית־אֲבֹתָיו הוּא:
ה וְאֵלֶּה שְׁמוֹת הָאֲנָשִׁים אֲשֶׁר יַעַמְדוּ אִתְּכֶם לִרְאוּבֵן אֱלִיצוּר
ו בֶּן־שְׁדֵיאוּר: לְשִׁמְעוֹן שְׁלֻמִיאֵל בֶּן־צוּרִישַׁדָּי: לִיהוּדָה נַחְשׁוֹן
ז בֶּן־עַמִּינָדָב: לְיִשָּׂשכָר נְתַנְאֵל בֶּן־צוּעָר: לִזְבוּלֻן אֱלִיאָב
ח בֶּן־חֵלֹן: לִבְנֵי יוֹסֵף לְאֶפְרַיִם אֱלִישָׁמָע בֶּן־עַמִּיהוּד לִמְנַשֶּׁה
ט גַּמְלִיאֵל בֶּן־פְּדָהצוּר: לְבִנְיָמִן אֲבִידָן בֶּן־גִּדְעֹנִי: לְדָן אֲחִיעֶזֶר
י בֶּן־עַמִּישַׁדָּי: לְאָשֵׁר פַּגְעִיאֵל בֶּן־עָכְרָן: לְגָד אֶלְיָסָף בֶּן־דְּעוּאֵל:
יא לְנַפְתָּלִי אֲחִירַע בֶּן־עֵינָן: אֵלֶּה קְרִיאֵי הָעֵדָה נְשִׂיאֵי מַטּוֹת קְרוּאֵי

CLASSIC COMMENTATORS

Why was there a need to count *Benei Yisrael* – weren't they counted as they left Egypt, only thirteen months earlier?

אבן עזרא

לתקן הדגלים, ואיך יסעו ואיך יחנו בעבור המקדש.

IBN EZRA

The Israelites were counted for the purpose of arranging the flags, and to determine the distribution of the people for traveling in concert with the Tabernacle.

רשב״ם

לפי שמעתה צריכים ללכת לארץ ישראל, ובני עשרים ראוים לצאת בצבא המלחמה.

RASHBAM

At this point the nation was preparing to enter the land of Israel. This meant that men age twenty and above had to be organized for battle.

ר׳ עובדיה ספורנו

לסדרם שיכנסו לארץ מיד, "איש על דגלו" בלתי מלחמה אלא שיפנו האומות מפניה.

RABBI OVADYA SFORNO

The goal of the census was to arrange the nation for immediate entry into the land of Israel, each man according to his banner. Hopefully the nation would be able to take the land without a fight; the inhabitants of Canaan would flee in fright before them.

17/18 Moshe and Aharon took these men, those who had been marked out by name, and they convened the entire community on the first day of the second month. And the people declared themselves by their clans and their ancestral houses. All those over
19 twenty years old were counted individually by name, as the Lord had commanded
20 Moshe; so it was that he counted them in the Sinai Desert. The children of Reuven, Yisrael's firstborn – his descendants by their clans and their ancestral families – the tally of their names, each male aged twenty years and above: everyone capable of active service, all
21 counted individually – those counted from the tribe of Reuven numbered 46,500.
22 Of the children of Shimon – his descendants by their clans and their ancestral families – the tally of their names, each male aged twenty years and above: everyone capable
23 of active service, all counted individually – those counted from the tribe of Shimon numbered 59,300.
24 Of the children of Gad – his descendants by their clans and their ancestral families – the tally of their names, each male aged twenty years and above: everyone capable of
25 active service, all counted individually – those counted from the tribe of Gad numbered 45,650.
26 Of the children of Yehuda – his descendants by their clans and their ancestral families – the tally of their names, each male aged twenty years and above: everyone capable of active
27 service, all counted individually – those counted from the tribe of Yehuda numbered 74,600.
28 Of the children of Yissakhar – his descendants by their clans and their ancestral families – the tally of their names, each male aged twenty years and above: everyone
29 capable of active service, all counted individually – those counted from the tribe of Yissakhar numbered 54,400.

CLASSIC COMMENTATORS

Benei Yisrael were counted in Exodus 38:26, and their number there was identical (!) to their number here. How can that possibly be?

רמב״ן
RAMBAN

יותר נכון שנאמר שכן אירע מעשה ... מתו מהם הרבה ... כנוהג שבעולם ובני עשרים משלימים שנתם מתשרי ועד אייר, ואירע הדבר שהיו המשלימים כמניין המתים.

The correct interpretation of this phenomenon is that in the months between Tishrei and Iyar, many Israelites died. However, the number of youths who turned twenty in that same period, and who were now included in the census, was exactly the same as the total of expired citizens.

ר׳ יצחק שמואל רג׳יו
RABBI ISAAC SAMUEL REGGIO

וזה פלא גדול ... אות על היות האומה מושגחת בהנהגה למעלה ממנהג התולדות והטבע.

This represents an astounding wonder, and testifies to the fact that Israel was governed by celestial and unnatural providence.

יז אֲבוֹתָ֔ם רָאשֵׁ֥י אַלְפֵ֖י יִשְׂרָאֵ֥ל הֵֽם: וַיִּקַּ֤ח מֹשֶׁה֙ וְאַהֲרֹ֔ן אֵ֥ת
יח הָאֲנָשִׁ֣ים הָאֵ֑לֶּה אֲשֶׁ֥ר נִקְּב֖וּ בְּשֵׁמֹֽת: וְאֵ֨ת כָּל־הָעֵדָ֜ה הִקְהִ֗ילוּ
בְּאֶחָד֙ לַחֹ֣דֶשׁ הַשֵּׁנִ֔י וַיִּתְיַֽלְד֥וּ עַל־מִשְׁפְּחֹתָ֖ם לְבֵ֣ית אֲבֹתָ֑ם
יט בְּמִסְפַּ֣ר שֵׁמ֗וֹת מִבֶּ֨ן עֶשְׂרִ֥ים שָׁנָ֛ה וָמַ֖עְלָה לְגֻלְגְּלֹתָֽם: כַּאֲשֶׁ֛ר
כ צִוָּ֥ה יְהוָ֖ה אֶת־מֹשֶׁ֑ה וַֽיִּפְקְדֵ֖ם בְּמִדְבַּ֥ר סִינָֽי: ‏ וַיִּהְי֤וּ ‏ שני

בְנֵֽי־רְאוּבֵ֥ן בְּכֹ֣ר יִשְׂרָאֵ֗ל תּוֹלְדֹתָ֛ם לְמִשְׁפְּחֹתָ֖ם לְבֵ֣ית אֲבֹתָ֑ם
בְּמִסְפַּ֤ר שֵׁמוֹת֙ לְגֻלְגְּלֹתָ֔ם כָּל־זָכָ֗ר מִבֶּ֨ן עֶשְׂרִ֥ים שָׁנָ֖ה וָמַ֑עְלָה
כא כֹּ֖ל יֹצֵ֥א צָבָֽא: פְּקֻדֵיהֶ֖ם לְמַטֵּ֣ה רְאוּבֵ֑ן שִׁשָּׁ֧ה וְאַרְבָּעִ֛ים אֶ֖לֶף
וַחֲמֵ֥שׁ מֵאֽוֹת:

כב לִבְנֵ֣י שִׁמְע֗וֹן תּוֹלְדֹתָ֛ם לְמִשְׁפְּחֹתָ֖ם לְבֵ֣ית אֲבֹתָ֑ם פְּקֻדָ֗יו בְּמִסְפַּ֤ר
שֵׁמוֹת֙ לְגֻלְגְּלֹתָ֔ם כָּל־זָכָ֗ר מִבֶּ֨ן עֶשְׂרִ֥ים שָׁנָ֖ה וָמַ֑עְלָה כֹּ֖ל יֹצֵ֥א
כג צָבָֽא: פְּקֻדֵיהֶ֖ם לְמַטֵּ֣ה שִׁמְע֑וֹן תִּשְׁעָ֧ה וַחֲמִשִּׁ֛ים אֶ֖לֶף וּשְׁלֹ֥שׁ
מֵאֽוֹת:

כד לִבְנֵ֣י גָ֔ד תּוֹלְדֹתָ֛ם לְמִשְׁפְּחֹתָ֖ם לְבֵ֣ית אֲבֹתָ֑ם בְּמִסְפַּ֣ר שֵׁמ֗וֹת
כה מִבֶּ֨ן עֶשְׂרִ֥ים שָׁנָ֛ה וָמַ֖עְלָה כֹּ֖ל יֹצֵ֥א צָבָֽא: פְּקֻדֵיהֶ֖ם לְמַטֵּ֣ה גָ֑ד
חֲמִשָּׁ֧ה וְאַרְבָּעִ֛ים אֶ֖לֶף וְשֵׁ֥שׁ מֵא֖וֹת וַחֲמִשִּֽׁים:

כו לִבְנֵ֣י יְהוּדָ֔ה תּוֹלְדֹתָ֛ם לְמִשְׁפְּחֹתָ֖ם לְבֵ֣ית אֲבֹתָ֑ם בְּמִסְפַּ֣ר שֵׁמֹ֗ת
כז מִבֶּ֨ן עֶשְׂרִ֥ים שָׁנָ֛ה וָמַ֖עְלָה כֹּ֖ל יֹצֵ֥א צָבָֽא: פְּקֻדֵיהֶ֖ם לְמַטֵּ֣ה יְהוּדָ֑ה
אַרְבָּעָ֧ה וְשִׁבְעִ֛ים אֶ֖לֶף וְשֵׁ֥שׁ מֵאֽוֹת:

כח לִבְנֵ֣י יִשָּׂשכָ֔ר תּוֹלְדֹתָ֛ם לְמִשְׁפְּחֹתָ֖ם לְבֵ֣ית אֲבֹתָ֑ם בְּמִסְפַּ֣ר
כט שֵׁמֹ֗ת מִבֶּ֨ן עֶשְׂרִ֥ים שָׁנָ֛ה וָמַ֖עְלָה כֹּ֖ל יֹצֵ֥א צָבָֽא: פְּקֻדֵיהֶ֖ם לְמַטֵּ֣ה
יִשָּׂשכָ֑ר אַרְבָּעָ֧ה וַחֲמִשִּׁ֛ים אֶ֖לֶף וְאַרְבַּ֥ע מֵאֽוֹת:

30 Of the children of Zevulun – his descendants by their clans and their ancestral families – the tally of their names, each male aged twenty years and above: everyone capable
31 of active service, all counted individually – those counted from the tribe of Zevulun numbered 57,400.
32 Of the children of Yosef: of the children of Efrayim – his descendants by their clans and their ancestral families – the tally of their names, each male aged twenty years and
33 above: everyone capable of active service, all counted individually – those counted from the tribe of Efrayim numbered 40,500.
34 Of the children of Menashe – his descendants by their clans and their ancestral families – the tally of their names, each male aged twenty years and above: everyone
35 capable of active service, all counted individually – those counted from the tribe of Menashe numbered 32,200.
36 Of the children of Binyamin – his descendants by their clans and their ancestral families – the tally of their names, each male aged twenty years and above: everyone
37 capable of active service, all counted individually – those counted from the tribe of Binyamin numbered 35,400.
38 Of the children of Dan – his descendants by their clans and their ancestral families – the tally of their names, each male aged twenty years and above: everyone capable of
39 active service, all counted individually – those counted from the tribe of Dan numbered 62,700.
40 Of the children of Asher – his descendants by their clans and their ancestral families – the tally of their names, each male aged twenty years and above: everyone capable of active
41 service, all counted individually – those counted from the tribe of Asher numbered 41,500.
42 The children of Naftali – his descendants by their clans and their ancestral families – the tally of their names, each male aged twenty years and above: everyone capable of active
43 service, all counted individually – those counted from the tribe of Naftali numbered 53,400.

QUESTIONS FOR THOUGHT

- In what way are the approaches of Ramban and R. Reggio similar? In what way are they dramatically different?
- Which of these approaches do you find most rational? Why? Which do you find most inspiring? Why?

TEXTUAL SKILLS

1. What is odd about the order in which the tribes are counted?

2. What do you find interesting about the relative sizes of the tribes?

ל לִבְנֵ֣י זְבוּלֻ֔ן תּוֹלְדֹתָ֥ם לְמִשְׁפְּחֹתָ֖ם לְבֵ֣ית אֲבֹתָ֑ם בְּמִסְפַּ֣ר שֵׁמֹ֗ת

לא מִבֶּ֨ן עֶשְׂרִ֤ים שָׁנָה֙ וָמַ֔עְלָה כֹּ֖ל יֹצֵ֣א צָבָֽא: פְּקֻדֵיהֶ֖ם לְמַטֵּ֣ה זְבוּלֻ֑ן שִׁבְעָ֧ה וַחֲמִשִּׁ֛ים אֶ֖לֶף וְאַרְבַּ֥ע מֵאֽוֹת:

לב לִבְנֵ֣י יוֹסֵ֔ף לִבְנֵ֣י אֶפְרַ֔יִם תּוֹלְדֹתָ֥ם לְמִשְׁפְּחֹתָ֖ם לְבֵ֣ית אֲבֹתָ֑ם

לג בְּמִסְפַּ֣ר שֵׁמֹ֗ת מִבֶּ֨ן עֶשְׂרִ֤ים שָׁנָה֙ וָמַ֔עְלָה כֹּ֖ל יֹצֵ֣א צָבָֽא: פְּקֻדֵיהֶ֖ם לְמַטֵּ֣ה אֶפְרָ֑יִם אַרְבָּעִ֥ים אֶ֖לֶף וַחֲמֵ֥שׁ מֵאֽוֹת:

לד לִבְנֵ֣י מְנַשֶּׁ֔ה תּוֹלְדֹתָ֥ם לְמִשְׁפְּחֹתָ֖ם לְבֵ֣ית אֲבֹתָ֑ם בְּמִסְפַּ֣ר שֵׁמֹ֗ת

לה מִבֶּ֨ן עֶשְׂרִ֤ים שָׁנָה֙ וָמַ֔עְלָה כֹּ֖ל יֹצֵ֣א צָבָֽא: פְּקֻדֵיהֶ֖ם לְמַטֵּ֣ה מְנַשֶּׁ֑ה שְׁנַ֧יִם וּשְׁלֹשִׁ֛ים אֶ֖לֶף וּמָאתָֽיִם:

לו לִבְנֵ֣י בִנְיָמִ֔ן תּוֹלְדֹתָ֥ם לְמִשְׁפְּחֹתָ֖ם לְבֵ֣ית אֲבֹתָ֑ם בְּמִסְפַּ֣ר שֵׁמֹ֗ת

לז מִבֶּ֨ן עֶשְׂרִ֤ים שָׁנָה֙ וָמַ֔עְלָה כֹּ֖ל יֹצֵ֣א צָבָֽא: פְּקֻדֵיהֶ֖ם לְמַטֵּ֣ה בִנְיָמִ֑ן חֲמִשָּׁ֧ה וּשְׁלֹשִׁ֛ים אֶ֖לֶף וְאַרְבַּ֥ע מֵאֽוֹת:

לח לִבְנֵ֣י דָ֔ן תּוֹלְדֹתָ֥ם לְמִשְׁפְּחֹתָ֖ם לְבֵ֣ית אֲבֹתָ֑ם בְּמִסְפַּ֣ר שֵׁמֹ֗ת

לט מִבֶּ֨ן עֶשְׂרִ֤ים שָׁנָה֙ וָמַ֔עְלָה כֹּ֖ל יֹצֵ֣א צָבָֽא: פְּקֻדֵיהֶ֖ם לְמַטֵּ֣ה דָ֑ן שְׁנַ֧יִם וְשִׁשִּׁ֛ים אֶ֖לֶף וּשְׁבַ֥ע מֵאֽוֹת:

מ לִבְנֵ֣י אָשֵׁ֔ר תּוֹלְדֹתָ֥ם לְמִשְׁפְּחֹתָ֖ם לְבֵ֣ית אֲבֹתָ֑ם בְּמִסְפַּ֣ר שֵׁמֹ֗ת

מא מִבֶּ֨ן עֶשְׂרִ֤ים שָׁנָה֙ וָמַ֔עְלָה כֹּ֖ל יֹצֵ֣א צָבָֽא: פְּקֻדֵיהֶ֖ם לְמַטֵּ֣ה אָשֵׁ֑ר אֶחָ֧ד וְאַרְבָּעִ֛ים אֶ֖לֶף וַחֲמֵ֥שׁ מֵאֽוֹת:

מב בְּנֵ֣י נַפְתָּלִ֔י תּוֹלְדֹתָ֥ם לְמִשְׁפְּחֹתָ֖ם לְבֵ֣ית אֲבֹתָ֑ם בְּמִסְפַּ֣ר שֵׁמֹ֗ת

מג מִבֶּ֨ן עֶשְׂרִ֤ים שָׁנָה֙ וָמַ֔עְלָה כֹּ֖ל יֹצֵ֣א צָבָֽא: פְּקֻדֵיהֶ֖ם לְמַטֵּ֣ה נַפְתָּלִ֑י שְׁלֹשָׁ֧ה וַחֲמִשִּׁ֛ים אֶ֖לֶף וְאַרְבַּ֥ע מֵאֽוֹת:

44 These were the ones counted by Moshe, Aharon, and the twelve princes of Israel, one
45 from each ancestral house. Thus the total number of the Israelites counted, by their ancestral houses, aged twenty years and above – everyone in Israel capable of active
46
47 service – was 603,550. The ancestral house of the Levites, however, was not counted among them.
48
49 For the Lord had spoken to Moshe and said, "You shall not count the tribe of Levi,
50 nor take a census of them among the Israelites. Instead, you shall appoint the Levites over the Tabernacle of the Testimony, over all its utensils and all that belongs to it. For they are to carry the Tabernacle and all its utensils; they are to tend to it, and around
51 the Tabernacle they shall encamp. When the Tabernacle is to move onward, the Levites shall take it down, and when the Tabernacle is to encamp, the Levites shall erect it.
52 Any outsider who draws close to it shall be put to death. The Israelites shall encamp in
53 their respective camps, each by his own banner, in his division. But the Levites shall encamp around the Tabernacle of the Testimony, so that fury does not engulf the community of the Israelites; the Levites shall keep watch faithfully over the Tabernacle of
54 the Testimony." The Israelites did so; all that the Lord had commanded Moshe, they fulfilled.

QUESTIONS FOR THOUGHT

- Which of the commentaries understands the omission of Levi as a technical matter?
- What important information is missing from both explanations?
- If the instruction to omit Levi didn't come until *after* the count was over, why didn't Moshe count them earlier?

TEXTUAL SKILLS

1. In verses 44–47, notice the repeated use of the word כל. What do you think it is trying to say?
2. In this passage, the root פ-ק-ד appears seven times, but with two different meanings! What are those two different meanings?

WISDOM OF THE HEART

The Torah already noted that the Levites camped around the *Mishkan*. Why did it have to mention this again? R. Naftali Tzvi Yehuda Berlin answers that that there are two aspects to the position of the camp of Levi. One is that the Levites surrounded the *Mishkan* as an honor guard. The second is that the camp of Levi served an important function – as a buffer between *Benei Yisrael* and the *Mishkan*. It is one thing for people to make mistakes and sin, but it is quite another to do so directly in the presence of God. The placement of Levi ensured that the Divine Presence dwelling among the people would be a source of blessing, not disaster.

Is there a difference between doing something wrong privately and doing it when you know people are watching?

מד אֵ֣לֶּה הַפְּקֻדִ֡ים אֲשֶׁר֩ פָּקַ֨ד מֹשֶׁ֤ה וְאַהֲרֹן֙ וּנְשִׂיאֵ֣י יִשְׂרָאֵ֔ל שְׁנֵ֥ים עָשָׂ֖ר
מה אִ֑ישׁ אִישׁ־אֶחָ֥ד לְבֵית־אֲבֹתָ֖יו הָיֽוּ: וַיִּֽהְי֛וּ כׇּל־פְּקוּדֵ֥י בְנֵֽי־יִשְׂרָאֵ֖ל
לְבֵ֣ית אֲבֹתָ֑ם מִבֶּ֨ן עֶשְׂרִ֤ים שָׁנָה֙ וָמַ֔עְלָה כׇּל־יֹצֵ֥א צָבָ֖א בְּיִשְׂרָאֵֽל:
מו וַיִּֽהְיוּ֙ כׇּל־הַפְּקֻדִ֔ים שֵׁשׁ־מֵא֥וֹת אֶ֖לֶף וּשְׁלֹ֣שֶׁת אֲלָפִ֑ים וַחֲמֵ֥שׁ מֵא֖וֹת
מז וַחֲמִשִּֽׁים: וְהַלְוִיִּ֖ם לְמַטֵּ֣ה אֲבֹתָ֑ם לֹ֥א הׇתְפָּקְד֖וּ בְּתוֹכָֽם:
מח וַיְדַבֵּ֥ר יְהֹוָ֖ה אֶל־מֹשֶׁ֥ה לֵּאמֹֽר: אַ֣ךְ אֶת־מַטֵּ֤ה לֵוִי֙ לֹ֣א תִפְקֹ֔ד
מט
נ וְאֶת־רֹאשָׁ֖ם לֹ֣א תִשָּׂ֑א בְּת֖וֹךְ בְּנֵ֥י יִשְׂרָאֵֽל: וְאַתָּ֡ה הַפְקֵ֣ד אֶת־
הַלְוִיִּם֩ עַל־מִשְׁכַּ֨ן הָעֵדֻ֜ת וְעַ֣ל כׇּל־כֵּלָיו֮ וְעַ֣ל כׇּל־אֲשֶׁר־לוֹ֒ הֵ֜מָּה
יִשְׂא֣וּ אֶת־הַמִּשְׁכָּ֗ן וְאֶת־כׇּל־כֵּלָ֔יו וְהֵ֖ם יְשָׁרְתֻ֑הוּ וְסָבִ֥יב לַמִּשְׁכָּ֖ן
נא יַחֲנֽוּ: וּבִנְסֹ֣עַ הַמִּשְׁכָּ֗ן יוֹרִ֤ידוּ אֹתוֹ֙ הַלְוִיִּ֔ם וּבַחֲנֹת֙ הַמִּשְׁכָּ֔ן יָקִ֖ימוּ
נב אֹת֣וֹ הַלְוִיִּ֑ם וְהַזָּ֥ר הַקָּרֵ֖ב יוּמָֽת: וְחָנ֖וּ בְּנֵ֣י יִשְׂרָאֵ֑ל אִ֧ישׁ עַֽל־
נג מַחֲנֵ֛הוּ וְאִ֥ישׁ עַל־דִּגְל֖וֹ לְצִבְאֹתָֽם: וְהַלְוִיִּ֞ם יַחֲנ֤וּ סָבִיב֙ לְמִשְׁכַּ֣ן
הָעֵדֻ֔ת וְלֹא־יִהְיֶ֣ה קֶ֔צֶף עַל־עֲדַ֖ת בְּנֵ֣י יִשְׂרָאֵ֑ל וְשָׁמְרוּ֙ הַלְוִיִּ֔ם
נד אֶת־מִשְׁמֶ֖רֶת מִשְׁכַּ֥ן הָעֵדֽוּת: וַֽיַּעֲשׂ֖וּ בְּנֵ֣י יִשְׂרָאֵ֑ל כְּ֠כֹ֠ל אֲשֶׁ֨ר
צִוָּ֧ה יְהֹוָ֛ה אֶת־מֹשֶׁ֖ה כֵּ֥ן עָשֽׂוּ:

CLASSIC COMMENTATORS

Why was Levi not counted together with *Benei Yisrael*?

IBN EZRA — אבן עזרא

The tribe of Levi was tallied separately from the rest of Israel. Because they were invested with the responsibility of the Tabernacle, they were not sent out to war.

כי פקודת המשכן עליהם, על כן לא יצאו בצבא.

RABBI YOSEF BEKHOR SHOR — ר' יוסף בכור שור

Levites were counted according to a different criterion than everybody else. Whereas the men of the other tribes were included in the census once they turned twenty years old, those in Levi were counted when they were one month, and, separately, when they were thirty years old.

שלא היה מניינם שוה, שאלו נמנו מבן עשרים והלוים מבן חדש ומבן שלשים.

> **2:1–34** *The camp of Benei Yisrael was organized into four flanks, each flank consisting of three tribes, one of which was designated the leader. The first flank was led by Yehuda (in the east), the second by Reuven (in the south), the third by Efrayim (in the west), and the fourth by Dan (in the north). Every tribe had an identifying flag distinguished by its color and an image. Levi did not camp with the other tribes but formed its own camp, with four flanks arranged as an inner ring – a buffer between Benei Yisrael and the Mishkan, which was at the heart of the camp.*

2 1-2 The LORD spoke to Moshe and Aharon: "The Israelites shall camp, each by his banner, the ensign of his ancestral house, positioned around the Tent of Meeting at a distance. 3 Camping to the east, toward the sunrise, shall be the divisions under the banner of 4 Yehuda. The leader of Yehuda's descendants is Naḥshon son of Aminadav. And his 5 division numbers 74,600. Camping next to them shall be the tribe of Yissakhar. The 6 leader of Yissakhar's descendants is Netanel son of Tzuar. And his division numbers 7 54,400. Then the tribe of Zevulun. The leader of Zevulun's descendants is Eliav son 8-9 of Ḥelon. His division numbers 57,400. The total number in Yehuda's camp, in their 10 divisions, is 186,400. They shall be the first to set out. The divisions under the banner of Reuven's camp shall be to the south. The leader of Reuven's descendants is Elitzur 11-12 son of Shedeiur. And his division numbers 46,500. Camping next to them shall be the tribe of Shimon. The leader of Shimon's descendants is Shelumiel son of Tzurishadai. 13-14 His division numbers 59,300. Then the tribe of Gad: the leader of Gad's descendants is

---

QUESTIONS FOR THOUGHT

- The Talmud Yerushalmi quotes a debate about whether *Benei Yisrael* traveled in the same square formation as they camped or if they traveled in a line. Which of these opinions seems to be indicated by each of the above commentaries?
- How would each opinion explain verse 17?
- Which opinion seems to be more logical? Which seems to fit the text of the Torah best? (Note: See Num. 10:11–28!)

TEXTUAL SKILLS

1. Can you figure out why the flanks were organized as they were? For example, why were Yissakhar and Zevulun attached to Yehuda, and why were Shimon and Gad attached to Reuven, etc.?
2. There are two roots which stand out because they are repeated so frequently in this chapter – one appears nineteen times and the other appears twenty times! What are they? What do you think the Torah is trying to convey through their repeated use?
3. Find another two roots, one which appears seven times and the other which appears eight times. What is the connection between these two?
4. Compare 2:33 with 1:47. Can you explain the reason for the difference between them? Why do you think that the Torah needed to write this a second time?

ב

שלישי

א וַיְדַבֵּ֣ר יהו֔ה אֶל־מֹשֶׁ֥ה וְאֶל־אַהֲרֹ֖ן לֵאמֹֽר: ב אִ֣ישׁ עַל־דִּגְל֤וֹ בְאֹתֹת֙ לְבֵ֣ית אֲבֹתָ֔ם יַחֲנ֖וּ בְּנֵ֣י יִשְׂרָאֵ֑ל מִנֶּ֕גֶד סָבִ֥יב לְאֹֽהֶל־מוֹעֵ֖ד יַחֲנֽוּ: ג וְהַחֹנִים֙ קֵ֣דְמָה מִזְרָ֔חָה דֶּ֛גֶל מַחֲנֵ֥ה יְהוּדָ֖ה לְצִבְאֹתָ֑ם וְנָשִׂיא֙ לִבְנֵ֣י יְהוּדָ֔ה נַחְשׁ֖וֹן בֶּן־עַמִּֽינָדָֽב: ד וּצְבָא֖וֹ וּפְקֻדֵיהֶ֑ם אַרְבָּעָ֧ה וְשִׁבְעִ֛ים אֶ֖לֶף וְשֵׁ֥שׁ מֵאֽוֹת: ה וְהַחֹנִ֥ים עָלָ֖יו מַטֵּ֣ה יִשָּׂשכָ֑ר וְנָשִׂיא֙ לִבְנֵ֣י יִשָּׂשכָ֔ר נְתַנְאֵ֖ל בֶּן־צוּעָֽר: ו וּצְבָא֖וֹ וּפְקֻדָ֑יו אַרְבָּעָ֧ה וַחֲמִשִּׁ֛ים אֶ֖לֶף וְאַרְבַּ֥ע מֵאֽוֹת: ז מַטֵּ֖ה זְבוּלֻ֑ן וְנָשִׂיא֙ לִבְנֵ֣י זְבוּלֻ֔ן אֱלִיאָ֖ב בֶּן־חֵלֹֽן: ח וּצְבָא֖וֹ וּפְקֻדָ֑יו שִׁבְעָ֧ה וַחֲמִשִּׁ֛ים אֶ֖לֶף וְאַרְבַּ֥ע מֵאֽוֹת: ט כָּל־הַפְּקֻדִ֞ים לְמַחֲנֵ֣ה יְהוּדָ֗ה מְאַ֨ת אֶ֜לֶף וּשְׁמֹנִ֥ים אֶ֛לֶף וְשֵֽׁשֶׁת־אֲלָפִ֥ים וְאַרְבַּע־מֵא֖וֹת לְצִבְאֹתָ֑ם רִאשֹׁנָ֖ה יִסָּֽעוּ: דֶּ֣גֶל מַחֲנֵ֧ה רְאוּבֵ֛ן תֵּימָ֖נָה לְצִבְאֹתָ֑ם י וְנָשִׂיא֙ לִבְנֵ֣י רְאוּבֵ֔ן אֱלִיצ֖וּר בֶּן־שְׁדֵיאֽוּר: יא וּצְבָא֖וֹ וּפְקֻדָ֑יו שִׁשָּׁ֧ה וְאַרְבָּעִ֛ים אֶ֖לֶף וַחֲמֵ֥שׁ מֵאֽוֹת: יב וְהַחוֹנִ֥ם עָלָ֖יו מַטֵּ֣ה שִׁמְע֑וֹן וְנָשִׂיא֙ לִבְנֵ֣י שִׁמְע֔וֹן שְׁלֻמִיאֵ֖ל בֶּן־צוּרִֽישַׁדָּֽי: יג וּצְבָא֖וֹ וּפְקֻדֵיהֶ֑ם תִּשְׁעָ֧ה וַחֲמִשִּׁ֛ים אֶ֖לֶף וּשְׁלֹ֥שׁ מֵאֽוֹת: יד וּמַטֵּ֖ה גָּ֑ד וְנָשִׂיא֙ לִבְנֵ֣י גָ֔ד

CLASSIC COMMENTATORS

The setup of the camp of *Benei Yisrael* is clear. The setup of their travel is not.

RASHI — רש״י

During the marches the entire nation maintained the formation which they observed when they settled down. Each group of three was assigned a specific side of the national camp.

הליכתן כחנייתן, כל דגל מהלך לרוח הקבועה לו.

RASHBAM — רשב״ם

Two companies – each comprising three tribes – marched at the front of the nation. These were followed by the Tabernacle and the Levites. Bringing up the rear were the final two banners, with the remaining six tribes.

שני דגלים נוסעים תחילה, ואחר כן המשכן והלוים, ואחר כן שני דגלים אחרונים.

¹⁵
¹⁶ Elyasaf son of Reuel. And his division numbers 45,650. The total number in Reuven's
¹⁷ camp, in their divisions, is 186,400. They shall set out second. And the Tent of Meeting and the Levite camp shall set out in the midst of the camps. All shall set out as they
¹⁸ encamp, each in his own place under his banner. The divisions under the banner of Efrayim shall be to the west. The leader of Efrayim's descendants is Elishama son of
¹⁹
²⁰ Amihud. And his division numbers 40,500. Next to them shall be the tribe of Menashe.
²¹ The leader of Menashe's descendants is Gamliel son of Pedatzur. His division numbers
²² 32,200. Then the tribe of Binyamin: the leader of Binyamin's descendants is Avidan son
²³
²⁴ of Gidoni. His division numbers 35,400. The total number of men in Efrayim's camp,
²⁵ in their divisions, is 108,100. They shall set out third. The divisions under the banner of Dan shall be to the north. The leader of Dan's descendants is Aḥiezer son of Amishadai.
²⁶
²⁷ His division numbers 62,700. Camping next to them shall be the tribe of Asher. The
²⁸ leader of Asher's descendants is Pagiel son of Okhran. His division numbers 41,500.
²⁹
³⁰ Then the tribe of Naftali: the leader of Naftali's descendants is Aḥira son of Einan. His
³¹ division numbers 53,400. The total number in Dan's camp, in their divisions, is 157,600. They shall set out last, by their banners."

WISDOM OF THE HEART

Have you ever noticed or heard that some people are very strict with mitzvot when at home in their communities but make all sorts of leniencies when they are traveling and there is no one else around? Verse 17 says כאשר יחנו כן יסעו, meaning that they should travel just like they camp. Rabbi Yekutiel Yehuda Teitelbaum, author of *Yetev Lev*, comments that this verse could be understood as a warning against that practice. If our beliefs are genuine and our practice authentic, then there should be no difference at all between what we do when we are around others or when we are alone. True religion is transparent, and our insides should match what we show to others.

How do you think you might change if you lived in a world where people could read what you were actually thinking?

טו אֱלִיסָף בֶּן־דְּעוּאֵל: וּצְבָאוֹ וּפְקֻדֵיהֶם חֲמִשָּׁה וְאַרְבָּעִים אֶלֶף
טז וְשֵׁשׁ מֵאוֹת וַחֲמִשִּׁים: כָּל־הַפְּקֻדִים לְמַחֲנֵה רְאוּבֵן מְאַת אֶלֶף וְאֶחָד וַחֲמִשִּׁים אֶלֶף וְאַרְבַּע־מֵאוֹת וַחֲמִשִּׁים לְצִבְאֹתָם וּשְׁנִיִּם
יז יִסָּעוּ: וְנָסַע אֹהֶל־מוֹעֵד מַחֲנֵה הַלְוִיִּם בְּתוֹךְ הַמַּחֲנֹת
יח כַּאֲשֶׁר יַחֲנוּ כֵּן יִסָּעוּ אִישׁ עַל־יָדוֹ לְדִגְלֵיהֶם: דֶּגֶל מַחֲנֵה אֶפְרַיִם לְצִבְאֹתָם יָמָּה וְנָשִׂיא לִבְנֵי אֶפְרַיִם אֱלִישָׁמָע בֶּן־
יט עַמִּיהוּד: וּצְבָאוֹ וּפְקֻדֵיהֶם אַרְבָּעִים אֶלֶף וַחֲמֵשׁ מֵאוֹת: וְעָלָיו
כ מַטֵּה מְנַשֶּׁה וְנָשִׂיא לִבְנֵי מְנַשֶּׁה גַּמְלִיאֵל בֶּן־פְּדָהצוּר: וּצְבָאוֹ
כב וּפְקֻדֵיהֶם שְׁנַיִם וּשְׁלֹשִׁים אֶלֶף וּמָאתָיִם: וּמַטֵּה בִּנְיָמִן וְנָשִׂיא
כג לִבְנֵי בִנְיָמִן אֲבִידָן בֶּן־גִּדְעֹנִי: וּצְבָאוֹ וּפְקֻדֵיהֶם חֲמִשָּׁה וּשְׁלֹשִׁים
כד אֶלֶף וְאַרְבַּע מֵאוֹת: כָּל־הַפְּקֻדִים לְמַחֲנֵה אֶפְרַיִם מְאַת אֶלֶף
כה וּשְׁמֹנַת־אֲלָפִים וּמֵאָה לְצִבְאֹתָם וּשְׁלִשִׁים יִסָּעוּ: דֶּגֶל מַחֲנֵה דָן צָפֹנָה לְצִבְאֹתָם וְנָשִׂיא לִבְנֵי דָן אֲחִיעֶזֶר בֶּן־עַמִּישַׁדָּי:
כו וּצְבָאוֹ וּפְקֻדֵיהֶם שְׁנַיִם וְשִׁשִּׁים אֶלֶף וּשְׁבַע מֵאוֹת: וְהַחֹנִים
כח עָלָיו מַטֵּה אָשֵׁר וְנָשִׂיא לִבְנֵי אָשֵׁר פַּגְעִיאֵל בֶּן־עָכְרָן: וּצְבָאוֹ
כט וּפְקֻדֵיהֶם אֶחָד וְאַרְבָּעִים אֶלֶף וַחֲמֵשׁ מֵאוֹת: וּמַטֵּה נַפְתָּלִי
ל וְנָשִׂיא לִבְנֵי נַפְתָּלִי אֲחִירַע בֶּן־עֵינָן: וּצְבָאוֹ וּפְקֻדֵיהֶם שְׁלֹשָׁה
לא וַחֲמִשִּׁים אֶלֶף וְאַרְבַּע מֵאוֹת: כָּל־הַפְּקֻדִים לְמַחֲנֵה דָן מְאַת אֶלֶף וְשִׁבְעָה וַחֲמִשִּׁים אֶלֶף וְשֵׁשׁ מֵאוֹת לָאַחֲרֹנָה יִסְעוּ לְדִגְלֵיהֶם:

32 These were the numbers of the Israelites by their ancestral houses. The total number
33 in the camps by their divisions was 603,550. As the Lord had commanded Moshe, the
34 Levites were not counted among the other Israelites. And so the Israelites did all that
the Lord had commanded Moshe. Thus they camped by their banners, and thus they
set out, each amid his clan and his ancestral house.

The Israelite camp

לב אֵלֶּה פְּקוּדֵי בְנֵי־יִשְׂרָאֵל לְבֵית אֲבֹתָם כָּל־פְּקוּדֵי הַמַּחֲנֹת לְצִבְאֹתָם שֵׁשׁ־מֵאוֹת אֶלֶף וּשְׁלֹשֶׁת אֲלָפִים וַחֲמֵשׁ מֵאוֹת וַחֲמִשִּׁים: לג וְהַלְוִיִּם לֹא הָתְפָּקְדוּ בְּתוֹךְ בְּנֵי יִשְׂרָאֵל כַּאֲשֶׁר צִוָּה יְהֹוָה אֶת־מֹשֶׁה: לד וַיַּעֲשׂוּ בְּנֵי יִשְׂרָאֵל כְּכֹל אֲשֶׁר־צִוָּה יְהֹוָה אֶת־מֹשֶׁה כֵּן־חָנוּ לְדִגְלֵיהֶם וְכֵן נָסָעוּ אִישׁ לְמִשְׁפְּחֹתָיו עַל־בֵּית אֲבֹתָיו:

QUICK BITE

According to a midrash, the four flags representing the four flanks of the camp each had a unique image – the face of a human, a lion, an ox, or an eagle. Ibn Ezra notices that this is similar to the description of Yeḥezkel's vision (Ezek. ch. 1), suggesting that the real intent of the midrash is to describe *Benei Yisrael* as a living embodiment of God's chariot.

When *Benei Yisrael* are counted and organized, they are counted first as individuals, then as parts of families. Those families are identified as belonging to tribes, and each of those tribes belongs to a flank. The four flanks together surround the core of the camp, the *Mishkan*, where God's presence dwells in the middle of the camp. Every one of us stands as an individual; every one of us counts by ourself. At the same time, none of us lives in a vacuum.

We are not islands. We all exist as part of something bigger, in fact, as part of a series of concentric rings of bigger things. Our families, our friends, our communities each contribute something to our very identities, and we can lean on them.

At the center of the camp stands the *Mishkan*, which defines the character of the camp. It is what makes this nation different. Each one of us is like the camp of *Benei Yisrael*. Each of us has our secret core which defines us, and into which we do not allow others in. It remains covered in layers of protection. But each of us is also our own *kohen gadol*. We can go into our inner core and clean it out, do some things to correct ourselves, without anyone else seeing or knowing. When we do that, not only are we better, but the world around us changes for the better too.

BEMIDBAR | CHAPTER 3

> **3:1–4** *Aharon had four sons, all of whom were anointed as kohanim. Nadav and Avihu, two of the sons, died childless during the inauguration of the Mishkan. The remaining two, Elazar and Itamar, functioned as kohanim during Aharon's lifetime.*

3 1 These were the descendants of Aharon and Moshe at the time when the LORD spoke 2 to Moshe at Mount Sinai. The names of Aharon's sons were Nadav, the firstborn, 3 Avihu, Elazar, and Itamar. These were the names of Aharon's sons, the anointed priests, 4 ordained for priestly service. But Nadav and Avihu died before the LORD when, before the LORD, they offered unauthorized fire in the Wilderness of Sinai; they had had no sons. And Elazar and Itamar served as priests while their father Aharon lived.

QUESTIONS FOR THOUGHT

- Which of these commentaries finds a simple answer based on reading the entire chapter?
- Rashi and R. Hirsch each highlight a special characteristic of Moshe. Which characteristic does each one highlight?
- Which of these commentaries explain why Moshe's children are *never* mentioned explicitly?
- How do you think that any of these commentaries could be relevant to children of contemporary rabbis?

TEXTUAL SKILLS

1. This passage is introduced with the words *ve'eleh toledot*. That phrase is used only thirteen times in all of Tanakh, eleven of which are in Genesis. This is the only other appearance in the Torah, but it does appear one other time in Tanakh. Where is that?
2. This is the third time (out of four) that the deaths of Nadav and Avihu are mentioned in the Torah.

WISDOM OF THE HEART

This passage opens by letting us know that we are about to hear the *toledot* of Aharon and Moshe, and yet Moshe's children are never mentioned. Rav Soloveitchik comments:

> We are all acquainted with the *akeda* that Avraham performed, but we do not pay sufficient attention to an *akeda* that was carried out by Moshe. Moshe's *akeda* was perhaps more awesome and terrifying than Avraham's. After Avraham puts Yitzḥak on the altar, the angel says, "Take him home." Avraham did not have to go through with this. Moshe never experienced this satisfaction – in his case, the Ribono Shel Olam requested and received his sacrifice (Lev. 10:1–2, 15:1).

The sacrifice that Rav Soloveitchik points to is that Moshe apparently needed to lose his family, separating from his wife (according to a midrash) and perhaps even from his children. His complete dedication and perpetual availability to both God and the people demanded that he not be encumbered by other responsibilities or even relationships. That supreme sacrifice, however, is never demanded of or even approved for anyone else; it is an expression of Moshe's uniqueness. The Talmud describes the *tanna* ben Azzai, who was so entranced by Torah that he could not imagine marrying. Ben Azzai died young, and some suggest that it was because he removed himself from the normal daily activities which God entrusts to us.

במדבר | פרק ג

ג א וְאֵלֶּה תּוֹלְדֹת אַהֲרֹן וּמֹשֶׁה בְּיוֹם דִּבֶּר יְהֹוָה אֶת־מֹשֶׁה בְּהַר סִינָי: ב וְאֵלֶּה שְׁמוֹת בְּנֵי־אַהֲרֹן הַבְּכֹר ׀ נָדָב וַאֲבִיהוּא אֶלְעָזָר וְאִיתָמָר: ג אֵלֶּה שְׁמוֹת בְּנֵי אַהֲרֹן הַכֹּהֲנִים הַמְּשֻׁחִים אֲשֶׁר־מִלֵּא יָדָם לְכַהֵן: ד וַיָּמָת נָדָב וַאֲבִיהוּא לִפְנֵי יְהֹוָה בְּהַקְרִבָם אֵשׁ זָרָה לִפְנֵי יְהֹוָה בְּמִדְבַּר סִינַי וּבָנִים לֹא־הָיוּ לָהֶם וַיְכַהֵן אֶלְעָזָר וְאִיתָמָר עַל־פְּנֵי אַהֲרֹן אֲבִיהֶם:

רביעי

CLASSIC COMMENTATORS

Based on the opening words of this passage, we expect to hear about the children of both Moshe and Aharon, yet we only hear about Aharon's.

רש״י

RASHI

ואינו מזכיר אלא בני אהרן, ונקראו תולדות משה לפי שלימדן תורה, מלמד שכל המלמד את בן חברו תורה, מעלה עליו הכתוב כאילו ילדו.

The text promises to introduce the descendants of both Aharon and Moshe and yet it then lists only the sons of Aharon! Since Moshe taught Torah to his four nephews, they were considered his descendants as well. We learn from here that if an individual educates somebody else's child, the text treats the teacher as the pupil's own parent.

ר׳ יוסף בכור שור

RABBI YOSEF BEKHOR SHOR

כלומר: הכהנים והלוים. ומונה בני אהרן תחילה, שהם כהנים, ואחר כך משה ושאר הלוים. דמשפחת העמרמי שהוא מונה בתוך הלוים (במדבר ג׳:כ״ז) זהו משה ובניו, שהרי לא היו לעמרם בנים אחרים כי אם משה ואהרן, ובני אהרן כבר נמנו בפני עצמם.

The text now discusses the priests and the Levites. It begins by listing the sons of Aharon, who represented the priests. These are followed by Moshe and the rest of the Levites. For the clan of Amram, which is tallied among the Levites (in Num. 3:27), this includes Moshe and his sons. After all, Moshe and Aharon were the only sons born to their father Amram, and the sons of Aharon had already been counted.

ר׳ שמשון רפאל הירש

RABBI SAMSON RAPHAEL HIRSCH

על אף שהכתוב מזכיר גם את תולדות משה, בניו לא ניקבו בשמות. שכן בפרקים אלה על הפקודים, רק המחזיקים במשרה ציבורית - נשיאים או כהנים - נקראו בשמם. אך זה משה האיש לא עטה על בניו את גלימת המשרה; הוא הניח אותם להיעלם בהמון העם, ללא כל תואר או ציון מיוחד.

Even though the text suggests that it will list the descendants of Moshe, his sons are not mentioned by name. This is because in the present chapters only the names of individuals who held public office – that is, the chieftains, or the priests – are specified. Moshe did not grant his sons any official positions, but allowed them to disappear into the anonymity of the nation. They held no title nor produced any notable achievement.

BEMIDBAR | CHAPTER 3

5/6 The Lord said to Moshe, "Bring close the tribe of Levi and set them before Aharon
7 the priest to assist him. They shall keep his charge and that of the whole community
8 at the Tent of Meeting, carrying out the service of the Tabernacle. Theirs shall be the charge of all the utensils of the Tent of Meeting, and they shall keep, too, the charge
9 of the Israelites by performing the service of the Tabernacle. Give the Levites over to Aharon and his sons; they among the Israelites are to be dedicated wholly to him.
10 Appoint Aharon and his sons to attend to the priestly duties; any outsider who draws close will die."
11/12 And the Lord spoke to Moshe: "In place of the firstborn, the first to emerge from every womb among the Israelites, I have taken the Levites from among the Israelites; the
13 Levites shall be Mine, for all the firstborn are Mine. On the day I struck down all the firstborn in Egypt, I consecrated every firstborn in Israel to Myself, man and animal. They are to be Mine; I am the Lord."

RABBI SAMSON RAPHAEL HIRSCH / ר׳ שמשון רפאל הירש

Even though the service in the Temple was transferred from the Israelites' firstborn sons to the Levites, that did not mean that the sanctity of the firstborn sons entirely lapsed; these men remained holy, and dedicated to the Lord. The only practical effect of this substitution was that the Israelites' firstborn sons no longer served as the nation's representatives in the Tabernacle. Nevertheless, their position within their individual families remained the same, and they stood as the leaders among their brothers in connection with God.

בהעברת העבודה במקדש מהבכורות ללוויים, לא פוסקת קדושת הבכורות. על אף העברה זו, הם עדיין מוקדשים לה׳. ההעברה רק מבטלת את מעמדם כנציגי האומה במקדש, אולם מעמדם בתוך המשפחה נותר על כנו, והם ממשיכים לייצג את קניין המשפחה לה׳.

QUESTIONS FOR THOUGHT

- In what way are the explanations of Rashi and Bekhor Shor similar? In what way are they different?
- In what way are the explanations of Ibn Ezra and R. Hirsch similar? What interesting understanding does R. Hirsch add?
- Can you think of sources which would support one of the two positions on whether Levi was a supplement to or a replacement for the firstborns?

WISDOM OF THE HEART

The word משמרת, describing the role of the Levites as protectors, is used both in verse 7 and in verse 8. Ibn Ezra explains that the first describes the need to ensure that the sacrifices of the people are protected, while the second speaks about the importance of making sure that the Mishkan and its utensils are kept safe from encroachment by non-kohanim. Those two represent two different ways of serving God: סור מרע – staying away from the bad; and עשה טוב – making sure to do good. The combination creates a healthy balance between our love and fear of God.

Which do you find more challenging – to refrain from bad things or to be active in doing positive ones?

ה וַיְדַבֵּר יהוה אֶל־מֹשֶׁה לֵּאמֹר: הַקְרֵב אֶת־מַטֵּה לֵוִי וְהַעֲמַדְתָּ
ז אֹתוֹ לִפְנֵי אַהֲרֹן הַכֹּהֵן וְשֵׁרְתוּ אֹתוֹ: וְשָׁמְרוּ אֶת־מִשְׁמַרְתּוֹ
וְאֶת־מִשְׁמֶרֶת כָּל־הָעֵדָה לִפְנֵי אֹהֶל מוֹעֵד לַעֲבֹד אֶת־עֲבֹדַת
ח הַמִּשְׁכָּן: וְשָׁמְרוּ אֶת־כָּל־כְּלֵי אֹהֶל מוֹעֵד וְאֶת־מִשְׁמֶרֶת בְּנֵי
ט יִשְׂרָאֵל לַעֲבֹד אֶת־עֲבֹדַת הַמִּשְׁכָּן: וְנָתַתָּה אֶת־הַלְוִיִּם לְאַהֲרֹן
י וּלְבָנָיו נְתוּנִם נְתוּנִם הֵמָּה לוֹ מֵאֵת בְּנֵי יִשְׂרָאֵל: וְאֶת־אַהֲרֹן
וְאֶת־בָּנָיו תִּפְקֹד וְשָׁמְרוּ אֶת־כְּהֻנָּתָם וְהַזָּר הַקָּרֵב יוּמָת:
יא וַיְדַבֵּר יהוה אֶל־מֹשֶׁה לֵּאמֹר: וַאֲנִי הִנֵּה לָקַחְתִּי אֶת־הַלְוִיִּם
מִתּוֹךְ בְּנֵי יִשְׂרָאֵל תַּחַת כָּל־בְּכוֹר פֶּטֶר רֶחֶם מִבְּנֵי יִשְׂרָאֵל
יג וְהָיוּ לִי הַלְוִיִּם: כִּי לִי כָּל־בְּכוֹר בְּיוֹם הַכֹּתִי כָל־בְּכוֹר בְּאֶרֶץ
מִצְרַיִם הִקְדַּשְׁתִּי לִי כָל־בְּכוֹר בְּיִשְׂרָאֵל מֵאָדָם עַד־בְּהֵמָה לִי
יִהְיוּ אֲנִי יהוה:

CLASSIC COMMENTATORS

Is God taking Levi in addition to the firstborns or as a replacement for them?

רש״י

ואני מהיכן זכיתי בהן מתוך בני ישראל – שיהו ישראל שוכרין אותם לשירות שלי? על ידי הבכורות זכיתי בהן, ולקחתים תמורתם.

RASHI

Says the Almighty: And why have I acquired the Levites from among all of the groups within Israel? Why should the Israelites pay this tribe to serve Me? I took the Levites for Myself as a substitute for Israel's firstborns.

אבן עזרא

כי גם הבכורים לי הם.

IBN EZRA

For all of the firstborns belong to Me as well.

ר׳ יוסף בכור שור

ולפי הפשט נראה: שאותם שמשמשין במשכן אינם ראוין לנחלה, כדי שלא יתנו עסק רק בעבודת הקב״ה, שיהו זריזין ומלומדין בה. ובכור נוטל פי שנים בנחלה, ולפיכך לקח הקב״ה לוים במקומן, וצוה שלא יתנו להם נחלה.

RABBI YOSEF BEKHOR SHOR

According to the straightforward meaning of the text it appears that those individuals who serve in the Tabernacle do not deserve a share in the land. These men are not granted parcels of land, so that they will devote themselves exclusively to the service of the Holy One, blessed be He. The Levites must work eagerly and expertly in this task. The firstborn son receives double the portion of land, which is why God substituted the Levites for the firstborns and commanded that they not be given any land.

Bemidbar | Chapter 3

> **3:14–39** *Levites were counted from the age of one month. They were divided into three families: Gershon, Kehat, and Merari. Gershon's job was to handle all of the fabrics of Mishkan (except the parokhet, which separated between the kodesh and the kodesh hakodashim); Kehat was responsible for the vessels and the parokhet; and Merari was in charge of the walls and the supporting posts.*

14 Then the Lord spoke to Moshe in the Sinai Desert: "Count the Levites by their ances-
15 tral houses and their clans. Count every male a month old or more." So Moshe counted
16 them at the Lord's word as he was commanded. These were the names of Levi's sons:
17 Gershon, Kehat, and Merari. These were the names of Gershon's sons with their clans:
18 Livni and Shimi. Kehat's sons with their clans: Amram, Yitzhar, Ḥevron, and Uziel.
19 Merari's sons with their clans: Maḥli and Mushi. These were the Levite clans by their
20 ancestral houses. Gershon encompassed the clans of Livni and Shimi; these were the
21 Gershonite clans. Their total number of males a month old and upward was 7,500. The
22 Gershonite families were to camp behind the Tabernacle to the west. And the leader
23 of the Gershonite families was Elyasaf son of Lael. The charge of the sons of Gershon
24 at the Tent of Meeting was the Tabernacle and the tent, its covering, the screen at the
25

The families of Levi camping around the *Mishkan*

יד וַיְדַבֵּר יהוה אֶל־מֹשֶׁה בְּמִדְבַּר סִינַי לֵאמֹר: פְּקֹד אֶת־בְּנֵי לֵוִי לְבֵית אֲבֹתָם לְמִשְׁפְּחֹתָם כָּל־זָכָר מִבֶּן־חֹדֶשׁ וָמַעְלָה תִּפְקְדֵם: טז וַיִּפְקֹד אֹתָם מֹשֶׁה עַל־פִּי יהוה כַּאֲשֶׁר צֻוָּה: וַיִּהְיוּ־אֵלֶּה בְנֵי־לֵוִי בִּשְׁמֹתָם גֵּרְשׁוֹן וּקְהָת וּמְרָרִי: יח וְאֵלֶּה שְׁמוֹת בְּנֵי־גֵרְשׁוֹן לְמִשְׁפְּחֹתָם לִבְנִי וְשִׁמְעִי: יט וּבְנֵי קְהָת לְמִשְׁפְּחֹתָם עַמְרָם וְיִצְהָר חֶבְרוֹן וְעֻזִּיאֵל: כ וּבְנֵי מְרָרִי לְמִשְׁפְּחֹתָם מַחְלִי וּמוּשִׁי אֵלֶּה הֵם מִשְׁפְּחֹת הַלֵּוִי לְבֵית אֲבֹתָם: כא לְגֵרְשׁוֹן מִשְׁפַּחַת הַלִּבְנִי וּמִשְׁפַּחַת הַשִּׁמְעִי אֵלֶּה הֵם מִשְׁפְּחֹת הַגֵּרְשֻׁנִּי: כב פְּקֻדֵיהֶם בְּמִסְפַּר כָּל־זָכָר מִבֶּן־חֹדֶשׁ וָמָעְלָה פְּקֻדֵיהֶם שִׁבְעַת אֲלָפִים וַחֲמֵשׁ מֵאוֹת: כג מִשְׁפְּחֹת הַגֵּרְשֻׁנִּי אַחֲרֵי הַמִּשְׁכָּן יַחֲנוּ יָמָּה: וּנְשִׂיא בֵית־אָב לַגֵּרְשֻׁנִּי אֶלְיָסָף בֶּן־לָאֵל: וּמִשְׁמֶרֶת בְּנֵי־גֵרְשׁוֹן בְּאֹהֶל מוֹעֵד

חמישי

CLASSIC COMMENTATORS

Members of the other tribes were counted from the age of twenty, yet those from Levi were counted from the age of one month. This discrepancy puzzled the commentators.

רשב״ם

לפי שהיו באים לפטור את הבכורות שחייבין פדיון מבן חדש ומעלה, לכן גם מניינם מבן חדש.

RASHBAM

The Levites are counted from the age of one month because they act as substitutes for the firstborn Israelites, who must be redeemed at that age.

ר' יוסף בכור שור

שיצאו מכלל נפלים.

RABBI YOSEF BEKHOR SHOR

By the age of one month, it is clear that a child will survive infancy.

ר' שמשון רפאל הירש

הלויים נמנים מבן חודש ומעלה...הדבר מראה, שייעודם כלויים כולל הרבה יותר מאשר עשייה גרידא של העבודה ... שהמפקד מבן חודש ומעלה קשור לייעוד כללי יותר, אשר יש בו מעבר לשירות מעשי זה. על כרחך זהו ייעוד שאפילו צעיר לימים עשוי להיות כשר לעבוד בו; על כל פנים, זה חייב להיות ייעוד שהאדם זקוק לחינוך לקראתו משחר ילדותו ונערותו ואילך.

RABBI SAMSON RAPHAEL HIRSCH

The Levites were counted when they were but one month old, which shows that they were designated for more than just the Tabernacle service. The Levites of such a young age were chosen for something other than actual ritual labor. They were selected, trained, and educated during their childhood and youth.

26 entrance to the Tent of Meeting, the curtains of the courtyard, the screen at the entrance to the courtyard surrounding the Tabernacle and altar, and its ropes – and all the service
27 related to these. Kehat encompassed the clans of Amram, Yitzhar, Ḥevron, and Uziel;
28 these were the Kohatite clans. Their total number of males a month old and upward
29 was 8,600; these kept the charge of the Sanctuary. The Kohatite families were to camp
30 on the south side of the Tabernacle. The leader of the ancestral house of the Kohatite
31 families was Elitzafan son of Uziel. Their charge was the Ark, the table, the candelabrum, the altars, and the sacred utensils used in their service, and the screen and everything
32 pertaining to it. Chief of the leaders of the Levites was Elazar son of Aharon the priest;
33 he was appointed over those responsible for keeping charge of the Sanctuary. Merari
34 encompassed the clans of Maḥli and Mushi; these were the Merarite families. The total
35 number of their males a month old and upward was 6,200. The leader of the ancestral house of the Merarite families was Tzuriel son of Aviḥayil; and they were to camp on
36 the north side of the Tabernacle. The Merarites were appointed to take care of the
37 frames, bars, posts, and bases of the Tabernacle, all its utensils and accessories, as well
38 as the posts of the surrounding courtyard with their bases, pegs, and ropes. Those who were to camp to the east of the Tabernacle in front of the Tent of Meeting toward the sunrise were Moshe, Aharon, and his sons. They were charged, on the Israelites' behalf, to keep faithful watch over the Sanctuary. Any outsider who drew close would die.
39 The total number of Levites counted by Moshe and Aharon at the LORD's command,

---

QUESTIONS FOR THOUGHT

- Both Rashbam and Bekhor Shor offer practical explanations for the unique way that Levi was counted, but they disagree on what that practicality is. What are their opinions about what that practical element is?
- R. Hirsch offers a completely different explanation. According to him, why is Levi counted from the age of one month?
- In what way can R. Hirsch's explanation be broadened so that it is relevant for every family in *Am Yisrael* (not just Levi) and in every era (not just when there is a *Mishkan*)?

WISDOM OF THE HEART

Ramban suggests that Levi was not unusually small; rather, the other tribes were unusually large. Levi's size was what we would expect with normal reproduction rates. The other tribes, however, had unusually high reproduction rates because of the special blessing God gave them as a result of the hard work they endured in Egypt. Levi, exempt from that burden (according to a midrash), was not blessed like the others. As the mishna (Avot 5:23) says, לפום צערא אגרא, the reward matches the suffering. This is true in our lives as well. The more we put in, the more we take out. Or, as Einstein famously said, genius is 1 percent inspiration and 99 percent perspiration.

Which builds your self-esteem more – winning a game in which you have to prove your ability or winning one based purely on luck?

כו הַמִּשְׁכָּ֤ן וְהָאֹ֙הֶל֙ מִכְסֵ֔הוּ וּמָסַ֕ךְ פֶּ֖תַח אֹ֣הֶל מוֹעֵֽד: וְקַלְעֵ֣י הֶֽחָצֵ֗ר וְאֶת־מָסַךְ֙ פֶּ֣תַח הֶֽחָצֵ֔ר אֲשֶׁ֧ר עַל־הַמִּשְׁכָּ֛ן וְעַל־הַמִּזְבֵּ֖חַ סָבִ֑יב וְאֵת֙ מֵֽיתָרָ֔יו לְכֹ֖ל עֲבֹדָתֽוֹ: וְלִקְהָ֕ת מִשְׁפַּ֣חַת

כז הָֽעַמְרָמִ֗י וּמִשְׁפַּ֙חַת֙ הַיִּצְהָרִ֔י וּמִשְׁפַּ֙חַת֙ הַֽחֶבְרֹנִ֔י וּמִשְׁפַּ֖חַת הָֽעָזִּֽיאֵלִ֑י אֵ֥לֶּה הֵ֖ם מִשְׁפְּחֹ֥ת הַקְּהָתִֽי:

כח בְּמִסְפַּר֙ כָּל־זָכָ֔ר מִבֶּן־חֹ֖דֶשׁ וָמָ֑עְלָה שְׁמֹנַ֤ת אֲלָפִים֙ וְשֵׁ֣שׁ מֵא֔וֹת שֹׁמְרֵ֖י מִשְׁמֶ֥רֶת הַקֹּֽדֶשׁ:

כט מִשְׁפְּחֹ֥ת בְּנֵֽי־קְהָ֖ת יַחֲנ֑וּ עַ֛ל יֶ֥רֶךְ הַמִּשְׁכָּ֖ן תֵּימָֽנָה:

ל וּנְשִׂ֥יא בֵֽית־אָ֖ב לְמִשְׁפְּחֹ֣ת הַקְּהָתִ֑י אֶלִיצָפָ֖ן בֶּן־עֻזִּיאֵֽל:

לא וּמִשְׁמַרְתָּ֗ם הָאָרֹ֤ן וְהַשֻּׁלְחָן֙ וְהַמְּנֹרָ֣ה וְהַֽמִּזְבְּחֹ֔ת וּכְלֵ֣י הַקֹּ֔דֶשׁ אֲשֶׁ֥ר יְשָׁרְת֖וּ בָּהֶ֑ם וְהַ֨מָּסָ֔ךְ וְכֹ֖ל עֲבֹדָתֽוֹ:

לב וּנְשִׂיא֙ נְשִׂיאֵ֣י הַלֵּוִ֔י אֶלְעָזָ֖ר בֶּן־אַהֲרֹ֣ן הַכֹּהֵ֑ן פְּקֻדַּ֕ת שֹׁמְרֵ֖י מִשְׁמֶ֥רֶת הַקֹּֽדֶשׁ:

לג לִמְרָרִ֕י מִשְׁפַּ֙חַת֙ הַמַּחְלִ֔י וּמִשְׁפַּ֖חַת הַמּוּשִׁ֑י אֵ֥לֶּה הֵ֖ם מִשְׁפְּחֹ֥ת מְרָרִֽי:

לד וּפְקֻֽדֵיהֶם֙ בְּמִסְפַּ֣ר כָּל־זָכָ֔ר מִבֶּן־חֹ֖דֶשׁ וָמָ֑עְלָה שֵׁ֥שֶׁת אֲלָפִ֖ים וּמָאתָֽיִם:

לה וּנְשִׂ֤יא בֵֽית־אָב֙ לְמִשְׁפְּחֹ֣ת מְרָרִ֔י צוּרִיאֵ֖ל בֶּן־אֲבִיחָ֑יִל עַ֣ל יֶ֧רֶךְ הַמִּשְׁכָּ֛ן יַחֲנ֖וּ צָפֹֽנָה:

לו וּפְקֻדַּ֣ת מִשְׁמֶ֔רֶת בְּנֵ֖י מְרָרִ֑י קַרְשֵׁי֙ הַמִּשְׁכָּ֔ן וּבְרִיחָ֖יו וְעַמֻּדָ֣יו וַאֲדָנָ֑יו וְכָ֨ל־כֵּלָ֔יו וְכֹ֖ל עֲבֹדָתֽוֹ:

לז וְעַמֻּדֵ֧י הֶֽחָצֵ֛ר סָבִ֖יב וְאַדְנֵיהֶ֑ם וִֽיתֵדֹתָ֖ם וּמֵֽיתְרֵיהֶֽם:

לח וְהַחֹנִ֣ים לִפְנֵ֣י הַמִּשְׁכָּ֡ן קֵ֣דְמָה לִפְנֵי֩ אֹֽהֶל־מוֹעֵ֨ד ׀ מִזְרָ֜חָה מֹשֶׁ֣ה ׀ וְאַהֲרֹ֣ן וּבָנָ֗יו שֹֽׁמְרִים֙ מִשְׁמֶ֣רֶת הַמִּקְדָּ֔שׁ לְמִשְׁמֶ֖רֶת בְּנֵ֣י יִשְׂרָאֵ֑ל וְהַזָּ֥ר הַקָּרֵ֖ב יוּמָֽת:

לט כָּל־פְּקוּדֵ֨י הַלְוִיִּ֜ם אֲשֶׁר֩ פָּקַ֨ד מֹשֶׁ֧ה וְֽאַהֲרֹ֛ן עַל־פִּ֥י יְהוָ֖ה לְמִשְׁפְּחֹתָ֑ם כָּל־זָכָ֕ר

40 by their clans, all the males a month old and upward, was 22,000. Then the LORD said to Moshe, "Count all the firstborn Israelite males a month of age and upward, taking
41 a census of their names. Take the Levites for Me – I am the LORD – in place of all the firstborn of the Israelites, and the livestock of the Levites in place of all the firstborn
42 of the Israelites' livestock." So Moshe counted all the firstborn of the Israelites, as the
43 LORD had commanded him. The total number of firstborn males a month of age and upward, the full tally of their names, was 22,273.
44 Then the LORD spoke to Moshe: "Take the Levites in place of all the firstborn of Israel,
45 and the livestock of the Levites in place of their livestock. The Levites shall be Mine;
46 I am the LORD. As for the redemption of the 273 firstborn Israelites who exceed the
47 number of the Levites, collect five shekel for each, according to the Sanctuary weight – a
48 shekel being twenty gerah. Give the money to Aharon and his sons as a redemption for
49 the additional Israelites." Moshe took the redemption money from those who were over
50 and above those redeemed by the Levites; from the firstborn of the Israelites he took
51 silver weighing 1,365 shekel by the Sanctuary weight. Moshe gave the redemption money to Aharon and his sons, at the LORD's word, as the LORD had commanded Moshe.

CLASSIC COMMENTATORS

The firstborns were sanctified as *Benei Yisrael* left Egypt (Ex. 13:1, 13). What was their status during the year since they left Egypt?

RAMBAN

רמב"ן

הנה הבכורים נתקדשו להיותם לשם מעת שצוה קדש לי כל בכור ... ולא נפדו עד הנה שעדיין לא נאמר למי יהיה הפדיון, כי עתה הוא שנתקדשו הכהנים ... והנה הם עומדים בקדושתם סתם. ויתכן שהיתה בהם עבודת הקרבנות.

The firstborn Israelite men were sanctified from the point that God declared their state of holiness in Egypt. They were not redeemed before the present stage, since God had not announced who their substitute would be. It was only now that the *kohanim* were chosen to replace them. Thus all along the firstborn sons possessed a general holiness, and it is possible that they were involved in the sacrificial service.

QUESTIONS FOR THOUGHT

- Ramban offers two different suggestions for the status of the firstborns during that first year. What are they?
- Based on what we know about the first year since the exodus, which of those makes more sense?
- What is the connection between swapping Levites for the firstborns and the redemption money going to the *kohanim*?

WISDOM OF THE HEART

Rambam says at the end of *Hilkhot Shemitta Veyovel* that anyone, even if not from Levi, who dedicates himself completely to the service of God will have their basic needs taken care of by God the way Levi's were.

What do you think it means to be "completely dedicated" to the service of God?

מ וַיֹּאמֶר יְהֹוָה שׁשׁי מִבֶּן־חֹדֶשׁ וָמַעְלָה שְׁנַיִם וְעֶשְׂרִים אָלֶף:
אֶל־מֹשֶׁה פְּקֹד כׇּל־בְּכֹר זָכָר לִבְנֵי יִשְׂרָאֵל מִבֶּן־חֹדֶשׁ וָמָעְלָה
מא וְשָׂא אֵת מִסְפַּר שְׁמֹתָם: וְלָקַחְתָּ אֶת־הַלְוִיִּם לִי אֲנִי יְהֹוָה תַּחַת
כׇּל־בְּכֹר בִּבְנֵי יִשְׂרָאֵל וְאֵת בֶּהֱמַת הַלְוִיִּם תַּחַת כׇּל־בְּכוֹר בְּבֶהֱמַת
מב בְּנֵי יִשְׂרָאֵל: וַיִּפְקֹד מֹשֶׁה כַּאֲשֶׁר צִוָּה יְהֹוָה אֹתוֹ אֶת־כׇּל־בְּכֹר
מג בִּבְנֵי יִשְׂרָאֵל: וַיְהִי כׇל־בְּכוֹר זָכָר בְּמִסְפַּר שֵׁמֹת מִבֶּן־חֹדֶשׁ וָמַעְלָה
לִפְקֻדֵיהֶם שְׁנַיִם וְעֶשְׂרִים אֶלֶף שְׁלֹשָׁה וְשִׁבְעִים וּמָאתָיִם:
מד וַיְדַבֵּר יְהֹוָה אֶל־מֹשֶׁה לֵּאמֹר: קַח אֶת־הַלְוִיִּם תַּחַת כׇּל־בְּכוֹר
מה בִּבְנֵי יִשְׂרָאֵל וְאֶת־בֶּהֱמַת הַלְוִיִּם תַּחַת בְּהֶמְתָּם וְהָיוּ־לִי הַלְוִיִּם
אֲנִי יְהֹוָה: וְאֵת פְּדוּיֵי הַשְּׁלֹשָׁה וְהַשִּׁבְעִים וְהַמָּאתָיִם הָעֹדְפִים
מו עַל־הַלְוִיִּם מִבְּכוֹר בְּנֵי יִשְׂרָאֵל: וְלָקַחְתָּ חֲמֵשֶׁת חֲמֵשֶׁת שְׁקָלִים
מז לַגֻּלְגֹּלֶת בְּשֶׁקֶל הַקֹּדֶשׁ תִּקָּח עֶשְׂרִים גֵּרָה הַשָּׁקֶל: וְנָתַתָּה
מח הַכֶּסֶף לְאַהֲרֹן וּלְבָנָיו פְּדוּיֵי הָעֹדְפִים בָּהֶם: וַיִּקַּח מֹשֶׁה אֵת
מט כֶּסֶף הַפִּדְיוֹם מֵאֵת הָעֹדְפִים עַל פְּדוּיֵי הַלְוִיִּם: מֵאֵת בְּכוֹר בְּנֵי
נ יִשְׂרָאֵל לָקַח אֶת־הַכָּסֶף חֲמִשָּׁה וְשִׁשִּׁים וּשְׁלֹשׁ מֵאוֹת וָאָלֶף
נא בְּשֶׁקֶל הַקֹּדֶשׁ: וַיִּתֵּן מֹשֶׁה אֶת־כֶּסֶף הַפְּדֻיִם לְאַהֲרֹן וּלְבָנָיו
עַל־פִּי יְהֹוָה כַּאֲשֶׁר צִוָּה יְהֹוָה אֶת־מֹשֶׁה:

TEXTUAL SKILLS

1. When Rambam lists the mitzva to redeem the firstborn, he ignores this passage and cites Numbers 18:15 as the source. Why?
2. The Torah says that just like the firstborn males of *Benei Yisrael* were redeemed "one-for-one" (only the "extras" were redeemed for money), the firstborn animals were redeemed by the animals of the Levites (Num. 3:41). The question posed is if this was a "wholesale" redemption, as a package deal, or if the redemption of the firstborn animals was similar to the redemption of the people in which each was accounted for. How do you know?

4:1–14 *Moving the Mishkan required intricate coordination and choreography. Aharon and his sons packed the inner vessels as well as the outer altar, and each was wrapped in at least two coverings (see chart below). The accessories which accompanied each of the vessels were placed into the same "package" as the vessel itself, but were sometimes placed in their own internal wrapping.*

Vessel	Coverings	Accessories
Ark	parokhet, tekhelet-dyed wool, taḥash skin	no accessories
Table	tekhelet-dyed wool, taḥash skin	red-dyed wool
Candelabrum	tekhelet-dyed wool, taḥash skin	no separate wrapping
Inner (golden) altar	tekhelet-dyed wool, taḥash skin	tekhelet-dyed wool
Outer (bronze) altar	purple-dyed wool, taḥash skin	no separate wrapping

4 1,2 The LORD spoke to Moshe and Aharon: "Take a census of the Kohatites among the 3 Levites, by their families and their ancestral houses, from thirty to fifty years old: all 4 those able to go into service to perform the work of the Tent of Meeting. This will be the 5 service of the Kohatites in the Tent of Meeting: the most sacred objects; when the camp is about to set out, Aharon and his sons shall come and take down the screening curtain 6 and cover the Ark of the Testimony with it. Then they shall put over it a covering of fine 7 leather, and over that a cloth of pure blue, and then they shall insert its poles. On the table of the showbread they shall spread a blue cloth, and on it place the bowls, spoons, jars, and the libation pitchers; and the bread of the Presence shall be on it constantly. 8 They shall spread over them a scarlet cloth, and then cover it with a covering of fine

---

QUESTIONS FOR THOUGHT

- Which of the commentaries fits the words of the Torah best?
- The other commentator, who does not fit the words as well, offers an explanation for his position. What explanation does he offer?
- Which of these two commentaries do you think makes the most sense? Why?
- In what way is the first covering for the Ark different from all the others?

TEXTUAL SKILLS

1. The order in which the families of Levi were counted (3:14–20) is different from the order in which their work is described (ch. 4). Try to explain the order for each listing.
2. Can you offer an explanation for the order in which the vessels of the *Mishkan* were packed?
3. Which one of the vessels was placed on carrying poles (rather than placing the poles into the vessel)?

במדבר | פרק ד

שביעי

א וַיְדַבֵּ֣ר יְהוָ֔ה אֶל־מֹשֶׁ֥ה וְאֶל־אַהֲרֹ֖ן לֵאמֹֽר: נָשֹׂ֗א אֶת־רֹאשׁ֙ בְּנֵ֣י
ב קְהָ֔ת מִתּ֖וֹךְ בְּנֵ֣י לֵוִ֑י לְמִשְׁפְּחֹתָ֖ם לְבֵ֥ית אֲבֹתָֽם: מִבֶּ֨ן שְׁלֹשִׁ֤ים
ג שָׁנָה֙ וָמַ֔עְלָה וְעַ֖ד בֶּן־חֲמִשִּׁ֣ים שָׁנָ֑ה כָּל־בָּא֙ לַצָּבָ֔א לַעֲשׂ֥וֹת
ד מְלָאכָ֖ה בְּאֹ֥הֶל מוֹעֵֽד: זֹ֛את עֲבֹדַ֥ת בְּנֵי־קְהָ֖ת בְּאֹ֣הֶל מוֹעֵ֑ד
ה קֹ֖דֶשׁ הַקֳּדָשִֽׁים: וּבָ֨א אַהֲרֹ֤ן וּבָנָיו֙ בִּנְסֹ֣עַ הַֽמַּחֲנֶ֔ה וְהוֹרִ֕דוּ אֵ֖ת
ו פָּרֹ֣כֶת הַמָּסָ֑ךְ וְכִ֨סּוּ־בָ֔הּ אֵ֖ת אֲרֹ֥ן הָעֵדֻֽת: וְנָתְנ֣וּ עָלָ֗יו כְּסוּי֙ ע֣וֹר
תַּ֔חַשׁ וּפָרְשׂ֧וּ בֶֽגֶד־כְּלִ֛יל תְּכֵ֖לֶת מִלְמָ֑עְלָה וְשָׂמ֖וּ בַּדָּֽיו: וְעַ֣ל ׀
ז שֻׁלְחַ֣ן הַפָּנִ֗ים יִפְרְשׂוּ֮ בֶּ֣גֶד תְּכֵלֶת֒ וְנָתְנ֣וּ עָ֠לָ֠יו אֶת־הַקְּעָרֹ֤ת וְאֶת־
הַכַּפֹּת֙ וְאֶת־הַמְּנַקִּיֹּ֔ת וְאֵ֖ת קְשׂ֣וֹת הַנָּ֑סֶךְ וְלֶ֥חֶם הַתָּמִ֖יד עָלָ֥יו
ח יִהְיֶֽה: וּפָרְשׂ֣וּ עֲלֵיהֶ֗ם בֶּ֚גֶד תּוֹלַ֣עַת שָׁנִ֔י וְכִסּ֣וּ אֹת֔וֹ בְּמִכְסֵ֖ה ע֣וֹר

CLASSIC COMMENTATORS

As opposed to the other vessels, which had two coverings – one for honor and a *taḥash* skin to protect it from the elements – the Ark had an additional one, made of *tekhelet*-dyed wool. The commentaries debate whether this third covering, described in verse 6, was on top of the *taḥash* skin or underneath it.

IBN EZRA

אבן עזרא

In my opinion they had already spread the covering of *tekhelet*-dyed wool above the screen covering. [That is, the *taḥash* skin was placed above the *tekhelet* material.]

והנכון בעיני שפירושו: וכבר פרשו בגד כליל תכלת מלמעלה לפרכת המסך.

RAMBAN

רמב"ן

Due to the importance of the Ark, the *taḥash* skin was not visible at all after it was spread over the vessel. For first the Ark was covered by the screening curtain, and then over both items was laid the *taḥash* skin to protect these from the desert rains. Covering these three objects together was the layer of *tekhelet*-dyed wool, so that this glorious covering which resembled the pure heavens could be seen by all. Whereas, all of the other vessels, namely the table, the candelabrum, and the altars, were covered by *taḥash* skins as their top layers.

ונתנו עליו כסוי עור תחש – בעבור מעלת הארון לא היה נראה עליו כסוי עור תחש, אבל היו מכסים אותו בפרוכת שהוא המסך לו, ומכסים את שניהם במכסה עור תחש בעבור הגשמים, ופורשים על הכל בגד כליל תכלת מלמעלה, שיהיה נראה עליו הבגד הנכבד שהוא כעין השמים לטוהר. אבל שאר כל הכלים, השלחן והמנורה והמזבחות, היה נראה עליהם מלמעלה מכסה עור תחש.

9 leather; and then they shall insert its poles. They shall take a blue cloth and cover the
10 candelabrum and its lamps, tongs, pans, and all the oil vessels used in its service. Then they must put it and all its utensils into a covering of fine leather, and place them on a
11 carrying frame. They shall spread a blue cloth on the golden altar, and cover it with a
12 covering of fine leather; and then they shall insert its poles. Then they shall take all the service utensils, with which they serve in the Sanctuary, put them into a blue cloth, cover
13 them with a covering of fine leather, and place them on a carrying frame. They shall
14 remove the ashes from the altar and spread a purple cloth over it. Then they shall place upon it all the special implements with which they serve there – the pans, the forks, the shovels, the basins, and all the altar's utensils – and spread over it all a covering of

---

WISDOM OF THE HEART

In describing how the vessels of the *Mishkan* were covered, the Torah usually mentions the vessel first (such as the Ark or the table) and then the covering which is used. When it comes to the candelabrum, however, the order is reversed – the Torah first mentions the covering of *tekhelet* and only afterward that it is used to cover the candelabrum (see v. 9). R. Naftali Tzvi Yehuda Berlin suggests that the candelabrum represents deep Torah learning, while its *tekhelet* covering represents God's careful supervision over the people. People who are deeply involved in Torah learning often come up with new ideas and insights, and when they do there is a temptation for them to take credit for those insights. The Torah wants to make sure that those learning Torah don't get too arrogant about what they've found, and so insists on first mentioning God's supervision. Even though we would never have come to those insights without the hard work and the talents that we bring, we are reminded that there is divine guidance and inspiration even in the things we think that we created.

Is it arrogant to believe that God blessed us with certain talents? Does humility demand that we believe that we are worthless, nothing more than the fulfillment of God's wishes?

The poles on the Ark were different from the poles used for carrying the other vessels; the poles on the Ark were permanently affixed to the Ark, never to be removed. One rabbi suggested that since the Ark represents the place where God's presence "dwelt," the Torah wanted us to remember that we can never take God's presence among us for granted. If we don't act properly then He could leave at any time. This is similar to the message God gives to Shlomo when the *Beit Hamikdash* is inaugurated (I Kings 9:2–9): no matter who we are or how much we've done, we can never be complacent about God's presence being among us.

ט תַּחַשׁ וְשָׂמוּ אֶת־בַּדָּיו: וְלָקְחוּ ׀ בֶּגֶד תְּכֵלֶת וְכִסּוּ אֶת־מְנֹרַת
הַמָּאוֹר וְאֶת־נֵרֹתֶיהָ וְאֶת־מַלְקָחֶיהָ וְאֶת־מַחְתֹּתֶיהָ וְאֵת כָּל־
י כְּלֵי שַׁמְנָהּ אֲשֶׁר יְשָׁרְתוּ־לָהּ בָּהֶם: וְנָתְנוּ אֹתָהּ וְאֶת־כָּל־כֵּלֶיהָ
יא אֶל־מִכְסֵה עוֹר תָּחַשׁ וְנָתְנוּ עַל־הַמּוֹט: וְעַל ׀ מִזְבַּח הַזָּהָב
יִפְרְשׂוּ בֶּגֶד תְּכֵלֶת וְכִסּוּ אֹתוֹ בְּמִכְסֵה עוֹר תָּחַשׁ וְשָׂמוּ אֶת־
יב בַּדָּיו: וְלָקְחוּ אֶת־כָּל־כְּלֵי הַשָּׁרֵת אֲשֶׁר יְשָׁרְתוּ־בָם בַּקֹּדֶשׁ
וְנָתְנוּ אֶל־בֶּגֶד תְּכֵלֶת וְכִסּוּ אוֹתָם בְּמִכְסֵה עוֹר תַּחַשׁ וְנָתְנוּ
יג עַל־הַמּוֹט: וְדִשְּׁנוּ אֶת־הַמִּזְבֵּחַ וּפָרְשׂוּ עָלָיו בֶּגֶד אַרְגָּמָן: וְנָתְנוּ
עָלָיו אֶת־כָּל־כֵּלָיו אֲשֶׁר יְשָׁרְתוּ עָלָיו בָּהֶם אֶת־הַמַּחְתֹּת אֶת־
הַמִּזְלָגֹת וְאֶת־הַיָּעִים וְאֶת־הַמִּזְרָקֹת כֹּל כְּלֵי הַמִּזְבֵּחַ וּפָרְשׂוּ

QUICK BITE

The Talmud (Ḥullin 24a) notices that while our text (4:3) identifies the work of the Levites as beginning at age thirty, a later text (8:24) states that they are to start at age twenty-five. The answer offered in the Talmud is they begin their training at age twenty-five but don't start working until age thirty. The Talmud then states that from here we learn that if a student hasn't shown success after five years then it is unlikely that they will ever show success. R. Elyashiv comments that this statement does not suggest that we should give up on the student who does not show success. Quite the contrary; we need to continue teaching, and the student needs to continue learning. But it does mean that even as we continue to teach we need to adjust our expectations.

Not every student will be a star, and that is okay; each will find his or her own way to shine.

Read the description of the covering of the Ark and try to imagine it. The *kohanim* remove the *parokhet* from the poles and carefully move it, without looking at the Ark, so that it eventually covers the Ark. The *kodesh hakodashim* is never dismantled, it is shrunk under the *parokhet* until it is concentrated to include just the Ark. The Divine Presence is never gone. When it is time to rebuild, that miniaturized *kodesh hakodashim* gets expanded back into its full size, and the rest of the *Mishkan* follows.

4:15–20 *Once the vessels were wrapped, the family of Kehat could carry them. Their job was particularly dangerous; if they touched those vessels directly or even looked at the vessels being wrapped they were liable to die.*

15 fine leather, and then insert its poles. When Aharon and his sons have finished covering the Sanctuary and all the furnishings of the Sanctuary, when the camp is ready to set out, then the Kohatites shall come to carry them; but they must not touch the sacred objects lest they die. These are what the Kohatites must carry for the Tent of Meeting.

16 The responsibility of Elazar son of Aharon the priest is for the lighting oil, the fragrant incense, the daily grain offering, and the anointing oil. He is also responsible for the whole Tabernacle and all that is in it, for the Sanctuary and all its utensils."

17
18 Again the Lord spoke to Moshe and Aharon: "Do not let the tribe of the clans of Kehat
19 be cut off from among the Levites. So that they may live and not die when they come close to the most sacred things, they must do this: let Aharon and his sons go in and
20 assign each man his duties and what he must carry; but they themselves must not go in and watch while the holy things are being covered, for they would die."

מלאכת מחשבת

כי כל השוכן בשפע ההצלחות ביותר הוא מוכן אל הנפילה, אל הפורענות...
... הייתה גדולה בני קהת שמשא הארון וכלי הקודש, ומכל מקום, כדי שלא ירום לבבם בגאוה על זה ולא ימותו, נתן להם הקדוש ברוך הוא ... שאינם רשאים לשאת כי אם אחר שאהרן ובניו יכסו את הקודש ... ואמר "אל תכריתו את שבט משפחות הקהתי" רצונו: אין ראוי שייכרתו הקהתים בעונש הגאווה ורום הלבב בהתנשאם על הלויים ... בזאת שאהרן ובניו יבואו ושמו אותם איש איש על עבודתו ועל משאו ובאלה ילמדו מידת הענווה לעבוד ולשרת אהרן ובניו, ולא ימותו בגאוותם וזדון ליבם להשתרר על אחיהם גם השתרר.

MELEKHET MAḤASHEVET

Any individual who is fortunate to enjoy the bounty of success is actually at risk of failure and descent into punishment. The men of the Kehat family were given the highest task, carrying the Ark and the other sacred vessels. Hence it was critical to help them avoid becoming proud and haughty in their position, an attitude which could prove fatal to a Levite caught up in his pride. Thus the Holy One, blessed be He, mandated that before the Levites could begin their transport duties, Aharon and his sons had to cover the sacred items entrusted to their cousins. This is what the text means when it warns, "Do not let the tribe of the clans of Kehat be cut off from among the Levites" – do not allow these men to be punished for letting their self-importance control their behavior. Aharon and his sons should therefore detail precisely what the Kehatites' job should be, while the guidance of the *kohanim* trained these Levites to humbly serve the priestly class.

QUESTIONS FOR THOUGHT

- Abarbanel understands that seeing the vessels is not the ultimate problem. What would be the ultimate problem for him? Notice that in his last line he makes a vague reference to Exodus 19:21. How does the reference to the verse from Exodus support his explanation here?
- Both the *Melekhet Maḥashevet* and R. Hirsch understand that seeing the vessels would do bad things to the person who sees them, but they disagree as to what that bad thing is. What are their respective opinions about this?
- Which of the above explanations could possibly suggest why seeing the vessels would be punishable by death?
- Which of the above explanations do you think could be applicable or meaningful today?

טו עָלָיו כְּסוּי עוֹר תַּחַשׁ וְשָׂמוּ בַדָּיו: וְכִלָּה אַהֲרֹן־וּבָנָיו לְכַסֹּת אֶת־הַקֹּדֶשׁ וְאֶת־כָּל־כְּלֵי הַקֹּדֶשׁ בִּנְסֹעַ הַמַּחֲנֶה וְאַחֲרֵי־כֵן יָבֹאוּ בְנֵי־קְהָת לָשֵׂאת וְלֹא־יִגְּעוּ אֶל־הַקֹּדֶשׁ וָמֵתוּ אֵלֶּה מַשָּׂא

טז בְנֵי־קְהָת בְּאֹהֶל מוֹעֵד: וּפְקֻדַּת אֶלְעָזָר ׀ בֶּן־אַהֲרֹן הַכֹּהֵן שֶׁמֶן הַמָּאוֹר וּקְטֹרֶת הַסַּמִּים וּמִנְחַת הַתָּמִיד וְשֶׁמֶן הַמִּשְׁחָה פְּקֻדַּת כָּל־הַמִּשְׁכָּן וְכָל־אֲשֶׁר־בּוֹ בְּקֹדֶשׁ וּבְכֵלָיו:

מפטיר ד

יז וַיְדַבֵּר יְהֹוָה אֶל־מֹשֶׁה וְאֶל־אַהֲרֹן לֵאמֹר: אַל־תַּכְרִיתוּ אֶת־ יח שֵׁבֶט מִשְׁפְּחֹת הַקְּהָתִי מִתּוֹךְ הַלְוִיִּם: וְזֹאת ׀ עֲשׂוּ לָהֶם וְחָיוּ וְלֹא יָמֻתוּ בְּגִשְׁתָּם אֶת־קֹדֶשׁ הַקֳּדָשִׁים אַהֲרֹן וּבָנָיו יָבֹאוּ וְשָׂמוּ כ אוֹתָם אִישׁ אִישׁ עַל־עֲבֹדָתוֹ וְאֶל־מַשָּׂאוֹ: וְלֹא־יָבֹאוּ לִרְאוֹת כְּבַלַּע אֶת־הַקֹּדֶשׁ וָמֵתוּ:

CLASSIC COMMENTATORS

What is so bad about the family of Kehat seeing the vessels?

אברבנאל

וזאת עשו להם - רצונו לומר בעבורם, ויחיו ולא ימותו בכרת בגשתם אל קודש הקודשים, כי נפש האדם בגשתו אל הקודש תכסוף לראות חוץ מגבולו, ולכן אתם צריכים לכסות ולהעלים, כדי שלא ימותו בהרסם לראות.

ר' שמשון רפאל הירש

כוונתו היא שכלי הקודש לא יהיו בעיני נושאיהם דברים שישיגום משיגי הגוף בלבד, אלא שיהיו להם דברים שבמחשבה ושבהם ובמוסמל בהם ימלאו רוחם ונפשם. חדירתם זו בעיני רוחם ושכלם למהותם של כלי הקודש שנמסרו לשמירתם היא היא החלק העיקרי של תפקידם, ואילו היו משׂחים הבטתם החושנית, הסתכלותם בעיני בשר, בכלי הקודש בזמן כיסויים, היה נפגם ואף מתחלל מלוא תפקידם זה.

ABARBANEL

The Levites were required to follow a strict protocol to prevent them from dying through excision when they approached the Holy of Holies. For when a person comes close to something sacred, it is only natural for him to want to see what lies beyond the border of permissibility. This is why the *kohanim* were commanded to cover and conceal the vessels, lest the Levites exceed their mandate and be killed.

RABBI SAMSON RAPHAEL HIRSCH

It was important that the sacred vessels not be viewed as purely physical objects whose purpose could be discerned through the usual human senses. These items had a symbolic and spiritual character whose meaning required intellectual capacity to grasp. The primary task of the men entrusted with the care of the utensils was to probe their souls and their minds to understand what exactly it was they were transporting. Therefore, had the people of Kehat relied on their sense of sight as they focused on their job, they would have missed, or indeed profaned, the entire nature of their mission.

EXPLORING HASHKAFA
Unity and Diversity

You don't have to read too far in the book of Numbers to get the sense that tribes are important. Every tribe is counted and every tribal leader is mentioned – and that is just in the first chapter! Most of that information is repeated as the tribes are organized into the camps in chapter 2. As we go through the book we are confronted with this again and again. The scouts sent to check out the land represent the twelve tribes. People, both good and bad, are identified not only by their father's names but by their tribes, and at the end of the book, forty years later, the land is divided. Moreover, there are multiple stories affirming just how important those affiliations were. Just so you shouldn't think that this is something new in the book of Numbers, there are many indications of this already in the beginning of Exodus, and there is a beautiful midrash regarding the crossing through the Sea of Reeds which describes the sea splitting into twelve lanes separated by transparent walls. It is fair to say that one of the primary ways people identified themselves was by their tribe, and the Torah is interested in preserving this.

At the same time, the Torah wishes to strengthen a national identity. Those tribes need to be forged into a cohesive unit. There is a famous midrash describing *Benei Yisrael* as camping at the foot of Mount Sinai "as a single person with a single heart." The organization of the camp around the *Mishkan* in this *parasha* is a powerful move designed to strengthen that sense of national unity around a single focus. Many stories in this book emphasize that the fate of the whole nation is tied into the actions of the few, regardless of which tribe they come from.

The dual emphasis, tribal identity and national identity, becomes evident again as we continue beyond the Torah. The book of Joshua presents the nation working as a single entity to conquer the land. Once the land is divided and settled and we move into the book of Judges, the picture changes, as it seems that, with rare exceptions, each tribe must fend for itself. That reverses again when we get to the book of Samuel, where the focus on establishing a monarchy reinforces the need for national identity and unity.

Why is tribal identity important? Looking at the blessings given both by Yaakov and Moshe at the end of their lives it becomes clear that different tribes represent different strengths. The strength of the whole is enhanced when we recognize, develop, and appreciate the strengths of the different subgroups. It is like an orchestra, which can play great music only if the violinists are excellent at playing violin and the trumpeters are great at blowing the trumpet. The strength of *Am Yisrael* relies on the strengths of the different groups within it and on the maintenance of those identities as distinct.

Over the course of the years there have various attempts to unify *Am Yisrael* by blurring differences. The text for *tefilla* known as *Nusaḥ Sepharad* initially emerged as the result of a mystical effort to bring the Messiah by uniting Ashkenazic and Sephardic Jews around a single siddur. That failed, as both the Ashkenazim and the Sepharadim rejected it, insisting on maintaining their distinct ways of prayer. Later attempts by the Chief Rabbinate in Israel to create a unified text (known as *Nusaḥ Aḥid* and distributed to soldiers) never caught on among the general public.

Maintaining the distinctiveness and differences of different groups within the Jewish people respects the plurality of traditions that have developed over the years and through the dispersions to various parts of the world. That constitutes a great strength. At the same time, great care must be taken to make sure that those differences do not become sources of delegitimization, division, enmity, or power struggle. That would turn a potential great strength into a devastating weakness. To paraphrase Rabbi Jonathan Sacks, maintaining the dignity of our differences builds our individual identities, affirms the identities of those who are different from us, and ensures that we can work together as a nation.

פרשת נשא
PARASHAT NASO

"Success means that we go to sleep at night knowing that
our talents and abilities were used in a way that serves others."
Marianne Williamson

With the completion of the structure of the camp with its concentric rings – *Benei Yisrael* in the outer ring, the Levites in the second ring, and the *Mishkan* at the center – and before continuing with the inauguration of the *Mishkan*, the Torah introduces a series of mitzvot organized in a different set of circles. Beginning with the outer ring, we send the impure people out of the camp and learn to treat the *ger*, who lives on the outskirts, with respect. We then move inward, to the level of the family, with the mitzva of *sota*, to help restore trust between a couple. Then we move to the level of the individual, the *nazir*, who is seeking an inner peace. When we finish preparing camp, the family, and the individual, then the blessing of the *kohen* can truly radiate outward.

PARASHAT NASO

> **4:21–28** The job of the family of Gershon was to carry and take care of all the fabrics in the Mishkan – from the cloths surrounding the courtyard, to the cloths which served as the gateways to the Mishkan, and to the cloths composing its ceiling.

4:21–22 Then the Lord spoke to Moshe: "Take a census too of the Gershonites, by their clans **23** and their ancestral houses, from thirty years old to fifty: all who go into service to carry **24** out the work of the Tent of Meeting. This will be the service of the clans of Gershon, **25** serving and carrying: they shall carry the curtains of the Tabernacle and the Tent of Meeting, its covering, the covering of fine leather that is over it, the screen at the **26** entrance to the Tent of Meeting, the hangings for the courtyard, the curtain for the entrance of the gate to the courtyard around the Tabernacle and the altar, and their ropes, together with all the utensils for their service and everything made for them; **27** and they will serve. All the carrying and service of the Gershonites shall be performed at Aharon and his sons' command; you shall assign to their charge all that they are to **28** carry. This is the service of the families of the Gershonites for the Tent of Meeting. Their

---

ר׳ יוסף בכור שור

לפי שגרשון גדול לבני לוי, דכתיב גרשון קהת ומררי, וגם במנין מבן חודש נמנו בני גרשון ראשונה (במדבר ג׳:י״ז). ובזה המנין בני קהת ראשונה ... לפי שכאן לעבודת הקודש מנאן, ועיקר העבודה לבני קהת, הארון והשלחן והמנורה והמזבחות ... ולכך כתיב נשא את ראש בני גרשון גם הם - אף על פי שצויתי למנות בני קהת ראשונה.

RABBI YOSEF BEKHOR SHOR

Gershon was the oldest of Levi's three sons, as the verse states, "Levi's sons were Gershon, Kehat, and Merari" (Gen. 46:11). Furthermore, in the census of the Levites, taken of males who were at least a month old, the people of Gershon were tabulated first. Whereas, in the present census, which counted the Levites from the age of thirty and up, the Kehat clan was counted first. This is because the current survey was for the purpose of the sacred service, and that was performed primarily by the Kehatites. It was they who were required to transport the Ark, the table, the candelabrum, and the two altars. This is why the text states to also count the men of Gershon, even though God has commanded that the members of Kehat be reckoned first.

QUESTIONS FOR THOUGHT

- Both commentaries understand that the word "also" refers back to the early *naso* for the family of Kehat, meaning, that just like Moshe was to *naso* the Kehatites, so too should he *naso* the Gershonites. What else do both commentaries agree upon, especially regarding Kehat?
- One commentary understands that Kehat was listed first in this count for practical reasons, while the other says that it was for a different reason. Which one says that it was for practical reasons? What is the "other" reason suggested by the other commentary?

פרשת נשא

כב וַיְדַבֵּר יְהוָה אֶל־מֹשֶׁה לֵּאמֹר: נָשֹׂא אֶת־רֹאשׁ בְּנֵי גֵרְשׁוֹן גַּם־הֵם לְבֵית אֲבֹתָם לְמִשְׁפְּחֹתָם: מִבֶּן שְׁלֹשִׁים שָׁנָה וָמַעְלָה עַד בֶּן־חֲמִשִּׁים שָׁנָה תִּפְקֹד אוֹתָם כָּל־הַבָּא לִצְבֹא צָבָא לַעֲבֹד עֲבֹדָה בְּאֹהֶל מוֹעֵד: זֹאת עֲבֹדַת מִשְׁפְּחֹת הַגֵּרְשֻׁנִּי לַעֲבֹד וּלְמַשָּׂא: וְנָשְׂאוּ אֶת־יְרִיעֹת הַמִּשְׁכָּן וְאֶת־אֹהֶל מוֹעֵד מִכְסֵהוּ וּמִכְסֵה הַתַּחַשׁ אֲשֶׁר־עָלָיו מִלְמָעְלָה וְאֶת־מָסַךְ פֶּתַח אֹהֶל מוֹעֵד: וְאֵת קַלְעֵי הֶחָצֵר וְאֶת־מָסַךְ ׀ פֶּתַח ׀ שַׁעַר הֶחָצֵר אֲשֶׁר עַל־הַמִּשְׁכָּן וְעַל־הַמִּזְבֵּחַ סָבִיב וְאֵת מֵיתְרֵיהֶם וְאֶת־כָּל־כְּלֵי עֲבֹדָתָם וְאֵת כָּל־אֲשֶׁר יֵעָשֶׂה לָהֶם וְעָבָדוּ: עַל־פִּי אַהֲרֹן וּבָנָיו תִּהְיֶה כָּל־עֲבֹדַת בְּנֵי הַגֵּרְשֻׁנִּי לְכָל־מַשָּׂאָם וּלְכֹל עֲבֹדָתָם וּפְקַדְתֶּם עֲלֵהֶם בְּמִשְׁמֶרֶת אֵת כָּל־מַשָּׂאָם: זֹאת עֲבֹדַת מִשְׁפְּחֹת בְּנֵי הַגֵּרְשֻׁנִּי בְּאֹהֶל מוֹעֵד וּמִשְׁמַרְתָּם בְּיַד

CLASSIC COMMENTATORS

God commands Moshe to *naso* (translated here as "Take a census of") the family of Kehat, as well as the family of Gershon. For Gershon the Torah says to also (in this translation indicated by the word "too") *naso* the family of Gershon. This one word, "also," caught the attention of some of the commentaries.

RABBI SAMSON RAPHAEL HIRSCH

The text first orders that a census be taken of the men of Kehat, despite the fact that Gershon was Levi's firstborn son. The men of Kehat were addressed first, because packing up the *Mishkan*'s sacred utensils and transmitting them to the Levites were paramount among all of the transporting tasks. The Torah now turns its attention to counting the Gershon family and establishing their job. Thus the phrase *gam hem* (they also) relates back to the first census of the Kehat clan. The term shows that the earlier mention of Kehat was not meant to discriminate against Gershon.

ר׳ שמשון רפאל הירש

מניין בני קהת בא ראשון בכתוב. ואף על פי שגרשון היה הבכור, היה צורך לעסוק תחילה בבני קהת שכן ... הייתה עטיפת ומסירת הכלים המקודשים ביותר של המקדש קודמת לכל דבר אחר. עתה מזכיר הכתוב את מניין בני גרשון וקובע את תפקידם. תיבות "גם הם" מתייחסות לאותו מניין ראשון של בני קהת. הן מורות שהקדמת בני קהת לא נועדה להפלות לרעה את בני גרשון. ושמא משום כך נאמר "גם" כאן.

BEMIDBAR | CHAPTER 4

NASO | 36

4:29–49 *The family of Merari, which is responsible for the heavy lifting in carrying the Mishkan, is counted last. They focus on the poles, beams, and planks that support all the fabrics. The passage concludes with the actual counting of the families:*

Kehat	2750
Gershon	2630
Merari	3200
Total:	**8580**

29 charge will be under the authority of Itamar son of Aharon the priest. As for the sons
30 of Merari, you shall number them by their clans and ancestral houses, from thirty years
31 old to fifty, all who go into service to carry out the work of the Tent of Meeting. This is what they are charged to carry as the whole of their service in the Tent of Meeting:
32 the boards of the Tabernacle, its crossbars, its posts, its sockets; and the posts of the surrounding courtyard with their sockets, pegs, and ropes, together with all their furnishings and everything for their service. You shall assign each object by name to the
33 man charged with carrying it. This is the service of the families of the Merarites, the whole of their service for the Tent of Meeting, under the authority of Itamar son of
34 Aharon the priest." So Moshe and Aharon and the leaders of the community counted
35 the Kohatites by their clans and their ancestral houses, from thirty years old to fifty,
36 all who went into the service of the Tent of Meeting; and those numbered by their

מלבי"ם

שיקרא שם מיוחד לכל כלי כלי שהם ממונים לשאתו, שהיו רושמים על קרשי המשכן לידע איזה בן זוגו, וכל קרש היה ניתן במקום שזכה בו בפעם הראשונה, ועל כן ציוה לייחד שם לכל אחד, ולייחד מי הממונה לנשאו, וגם עליהם היה איתמר ממונה.

MALBIM

Itamar was told to assign a "name" [a label] to each of the utensils that the Levites were required to transport. To do this, each of the *Mishkan* boards was marked so that it was clear which board went with which. Consequently, the sequence in which these planks was erected was always the same. This is why God commanded Itamar to provide a name for each object, and to establish which specific Levite was responsible for any given board.

ר' שמשון רפאל הירש

גם החלקים שהופקדו ביד בני מררי [חלקי המבנה המעמידים את המשכן], הינם בעלי משמעות סמלית. לפיכך בעת שאתם מוסרים חלקים אלה, עליכם להזכירם בשמותיהם, המורים על משמעותם.

RABBI SAMSON RAPHAEL HIRSCH

Even the pieces that were carried by the Merari family – those parts used to erect the *Mishkan* – possessed symbolic significance. God therefore told Itamar: when you hand over these objects to the Levites, make sure to identify them by name, so that their purpose will be enunciated.

QUESTIONS FOR THOUGHT

- Ramban understands the instruction very differently from the other two commentaries. What does he say that "assign by name" means?
- According to the different commentaries, why does the Torah say that this needed to be done for Merari's job but not for the jobs of the other families of Levi?
- Between Malbim and R. Hirsch, one says that identifying the items serves a practical purpose, and the other understands that it serves a different purpose. What is the practical purpose, and what is the other purpose? Match up those commentaries with the opinions.

אִיתָמָ֕ר בֶּֽן־אַהֲרֹ֖ן הַכֹּהֵֽן: ס בְּנֵ֣י מְרָרִ֔י לְמִשְׁפְּחֹתָ֥ם כט
לְבֵית־אֲבֹתָ֖ם תִּפְקֹ֥ד אֹתָֽם: מִבֶּן֩ שְׁלֹשִׁ֨ים שָׁנָ֜ה וָמַ֗עְלָה וְעַ֛ד ל
בֶּן־חֲמִשִּׁ֥ים שָׁנָ֖ה תִּפְקְדֵ֑ם כָּל־הַבָּא֙ לַצָּבָ֔א לַעֲבֹ֕ד אֶת־עֲבֹדַ֖ת
אֹ֥הֶל מוֹעֵֽד: וְזֹאת֙ מִשְׁמֶ֣רֶת מַשָּׂאָ֔ם לְכָל־עֲבֹדָתָ֖ם בְּאֹ֣הֶל מוֹעֵ֑ד לא
קַרְשֵׁי֙ הַמִּשְׁכָּ֔ן וּבְרִיחָ֖יו וְעַמּוּדָ֥יו וַאֲדָנָֽיו: וְעַמּוּדֵי֩ הֶֽחָצֵ֨ר סָבִ֜יב לב
וְאַדְנֵיהֶ֗ם וִיתֵֽדֹתָם֙ וּמֵ֣יתְרֵיהֶ֔ם לְכָל־כְּלֵיהֶ֔ם וּלְכֹ֖ל עֲבֹדָתָ֑ם
וּבְשֵׁמֹ֣ת תִּפְקְד֔וּ אֶת־כְּלֵ֖י מִשְׁמֶ֥רֶת מַשָּׂאָֽם: זֹ֣את עֲבֹדַ֗ת לג
מִשְׁפְּחֹת֙ בְּנֵ֣י מְרָרִ֔י לְכָל־עֲבֹדָתָ֖ם בְּאֹ֣הֶל מוֹעֵ֑ד בְּיַד֙ אִֽיתָמָ֔ר
בֶּֽן־אַהֲרֹ֖ן הַכֹּהֵֽן: וַיִּפְקֹ֨ד מֹשֶׁ֧ה וְאַהֲרֹ֛ן וּנְשִׂיאֵ֥י הָעֵדָ֖ה אֶת־בְּנֵ֣י לד
הַקְּהָתִ֑י לְמִשְׁפְּחֹתָ֖ם וּלְבֵ֥ית אֲבֹתָֽם: מִבֶּ֨ן שְׁלֹשִׁ֥ים שָׁנָ֛ה וָמַ֖עְלָה לה
וְעַ֣ד בֶּן־חֲמִשִּׁ֣ים שָׁנָ֑ה כָּל־הַבָּא֙ לַצָּבָ֔א לַעֲבֹדָ֖ה בְּאֹ֥הֶל מוֹעֵֽד:
וַיִּהְי֥וּ פְקֻדֵיהֶ֖ם לְמִשְׁפְּחֹתָ֑ם אַלְפַּ֕יִם שְׁבַ֥ע מֵא֖וֹת וַחֲמִשִּֽׁים: לו

CLASSIC COMMENTATORS

The Torah says that for Merari, the items to be carried should be assigned by name. What does that mean, and why is that necessary?

RAMBAN

Itamar was instructed to assign the vessels to individuals who would carry them, as the verse states, "All those over twenty years old were counted individually by name" (1:18). Thus, turning to a particular Levite, the *kohen* would say: You, so-and-so, are responsible for carrying this number of boards. To another man he would demand: It is your job to carry this number of crossbars or pillars. Itamar was very specific – he did not simply tell the entire group of Merarites that they were obligated to transport the boards, sockets, and pillars, and then let them distribute the materials among themselves. This detail is mentioned with regard to the people of Merari, because the objects given to them were the heaviest. As such, these men might have tried to lessen their own burdens by foisting some of their items on their fellow Levites. [To avoid this shifting around, every man was told exactly what he had to take.] But in fact, Itamar similarly approached the members of Kehat and Gershon, with the same attention.

רמב״ן

שיפקוד ביד כל איש במספר שמות לגולגלותם כלי משאם, יאמר: איש פלוני ישא מן הקרשים כך במספר, ולפלוני מן הבריחים או העמודים כך במספר, לא שיצוה בני מררי בכללם ישאו כל הקרשים והאדנים והעמודים. והזכיר זה תחלה בבני מררי בעבור כובד משאם, אולי יקל כל אחד מהם ממשאו, ויטיל על חברו, והוא הדין גם בבני קהת וגרשון.

37 clans were 2,750. These were the ones numbered from the clans of Kehat, all who served in the Tent of Meeting, whom Moshe and Aharon numbered at the LORD's command
38 through Moshe. Those numbered of the Gershonites, by their families and ancestral
39 houses, from thirty years old to fifty: all who went into the service of the Tent of
40 Meeting – those numbered by their clans and ancestral houses were 2,630. These were
41 the ones numbered from the families of the Gershonites, all who served in the Tent of
42 Meeting, whom Moshe and Aharon numbered at the command of the LORD. Those
43 numbered from the clans of the Merarites, by their clans and ancestral houses, from
44 thirty years old to fifty, all who went into the service of the Tent of Meeting – those
45 numbered by their clans were 3,200. These were the ones numbered from the clans of the Merarites, whom Moshe and Aharon numbered at the LORD's command through
46 Moshe. All the Levites, whom Moshe, Aharon, and the leaders of Israel numbered by
47 their clans and ancestral houses, from thirty years old to fifty: all who entered to do the
48 work of service and the work of carrying relating to the Tent of Meeting – those num-
49 bered were 8,580. At the command of the LORD they were listed, and by the authority of Moshe, each according to his service and to what he was to carry; thus was each one numbered as the LORD had commanded Moshe.

WISDOM OF THE HEART

Rav Shmuel Borenstein, the second Rebbe of Sokhatchov and author of *Shem Mishemuel*, suggests that there are three ways to deal with our negative impulses (known as our *yetzer hara*), which are represented by the three families of Levi. Kehat (meaning to knock out) suggests that we not allow negative thoughts to even enter our minds. Gershon (meaning to chase away) is for when those thoughts have already entered, and we must then banish them. Merari (from the language of bitterness) is the bitter inner battle when we can't simply block those impulses.

How do you handle desires to do things which you know are wrong?

The Torah counts each family of Levi separately, and then gives the total (v. 46). A midrash comments that the Torah is emphasizing that even though some of the families had more "important" jobs than the others, they are all considered equal before God, as they are all serving Him, each in their own way. R. Tzvi Elimelech Shapiro, the Rebbe of Dinov, suggests that this should be a model for all of us. Every one of us has a different role to play – some more prominent or respected than others. Nonetheless, in God's eyes we are the same, and the "team" needs even those who play seemingly minor roles.

לו אֵ֣לֶּה פְקוּדֵ֞י מִשְׁפְּחֹ֣ת הַקְּהָתִ֗י כׇּל־הָעֹבֵ֖ד בְּאֹ֣הֶל מוֹעֵ֑ד אֲשֶׁ֨ר
לז פָּקַ֥ד מֹשֶׁ֛ה וְאַהֲרֹ֖ן עַל־פִּ֥י יְהֹוָ֖ה בְּיַד־מֹשֶֽׁה׃ ◆ וּפְקוּדֵ֞י שני
לח בְּנֵ֣י גֵרְשׁ֗וֹן לְמִשְׁפְּחוֹתָ֖ם וּלְבֵ֣ית אֲבֹתָֽם׃ מִבֶּן֩ שְׁלֹשִׁ֨ים שָׁנָ֜ה
וָמַ֗עְלָה וְעַ֛ד בֶּן־חֲמִשִּׁ֥ים שָׁנָ֖ה כׇּל־הַבָּא֙ לַצָּבָ֔א לַעֲבֹדָ֖ה בְּאֹ֥הֶל
לט מוֹעֵֽד׃ וַיִּהְי֣וּ פְקֻדֵיהֶ֔ם לְמִשְׁפְּחֹתָ֖ם לְבֵ֣ית אֲבֹתָ֑ם אַלְפַּ֖יִם וְשֵׁ֥שׁ
מ מֵא֖וֹת וּשְׁלֹשִֽׁים׃ אֵ֣לֶּה פְקוּדֵ֗י מִשְׁפְּחֹת֙ בְּנֵ֣י גֵרְשׁ֔וֹן כׇּל־הָעֹבֵ֖ד
מא בְּאֹ֣הֶל מוֹעֵ֑ד אֲשֶׁ֨ר פָּקַ֥ד מֹשֶׁ֛ה וְאַהֲרֹ֖ן עַל־פִּ֥י יְהֹוָֽה׃ וּפְקוּדֵ֗י
מב מִשְׁפְּחֹ֛ת בְּנֵ֥י מְרָרִ֖י לְמִשְׁפְּחֹתָ֑ם לְבֵ֣ית אֲבֹתָֽם׃ מִבֶּן֩ שְׁלֹשִׁ֨ים
שָׁנָ֜ה וָמַ֗עְלָה וְעַ֛ד בֶּן־חֲמִשִּׁ֥ים שָׁנָ֖ה כׇּל־הַבָּא֙ לַצָּבָ֔א לַעֲבֹדָ֖ה
מג בְּאֹ֣הֶל מוֹעֵֽד׃ וַיִּהְי֣וּ פְקֻדֵיהֶ֔ם לְמִשְׁפְּחֹתָ֑ם שְׁלֹ֥שֶׁת אֲלָפִ֖ים
מד וּמָאתָֽיִם׃ אֵ֣לֶּה פְקוּדֵ֗י מִשְׁפְּחֹ֙ת֙ בְּנֵ֣י מְרָרִ֔י אֲשֶׁ֨ר פָּקַ֥ד מֹשֶׁ֛ה
מה וְאַהֲרֹ֖ן עַל־פִּ֥י יְהֹוָ֖ה בְּיַד־מֹשֶֽׁה׃ כׇּל־הַפְּקֻדִ֡ים אֲשֶׁר֩ פָּקַ֨ד מֹשֶׁ֤ה
וְאַהֲרֹן֙ וּנְשִׂיאֵ֣י יִשְׂרָאֵ֔ל אֶת־הַלְוִיִּ֖ם לְמִשְׁפְּחֹתָ֖ם וּלְבֵ֥ית אֲבֹתָֽם׃
מו מִבֶּ֨ן שְׁלֹשִׁ֤ים שָׁנָה֙ וָמַ֔עְלָה וְעַ֛ד בֶּן־חֲמִשִּׁ֥ים שָׁנָ֖ה כׇּל־הַבָּ֗א
מז לַעֲבֹ֨ד עֲבֹדַ֧ת עֲבֹדָ֛ה וַעֲבֹדַ֥ת מַשָּׂ֖א בְּאֹ֥הֶל מוֹעֵֽד׃ וַיִּהְי֖וּ פְקֻדֵיהֶ֑ם
מח שְׁמֹנַ֣ת אֲלָפִ֔ים וַחֲמֵ֥שׁ מֵא֖וֹת וּשְׁמֹנִֽים׃ עַל־פִּ֨י יְהֹוָ֜ה פָּקַ֤ד אוֹתָם֙
מט בְּיַד־מֹשֶׁ֔ה אִ֥ישׁ אִ֛ישׁ עַל־עֲבֹדָת֖וֹ וְעַל־מַשָּׂא֑וֹ וּפְקֻדָ֕יו אֲשֶׁר־
צִוָּ֥ה יְהֹוָ֖ה אֶת־מֹשֶֽׁה׃

TEXTUAL SKILLS

1. The introduction to the counting of Kehat begins with the word *naso* (literally meaning to lift up; translated here as "Take a census"). That same word is used to introduce the counting of Gershon but is absent for Merari. Can you find an explanation?

2. Compare the size of the tribe of Levi as counted in chapter 3 with the size of the tribe as counted in chapter 4. What do you notice as being unusual?

Bemidbar | Chapter 5

5:1–4 *Individuals afflicted with any of three different kinds of impurity, each of which can be spread beyond the affected person, must be sent out of the camp of Benei Yisrael.*

5 ¹ Then the LORD spoke to Moshe: "Command the Israelites to send away from the camp ² anyone who has an impure blight, or has had a discharge, or anyone made impure by ³ contact with the dead. Male or female, you must send them away – send them away outside the camp, so that they do not defile their camps, in the midst of which I dwell." ⁴ The Israelites did so: outside the camp they sent them. As the LORD spoke to Moshe, so the Israelites did.

TEXTUAL SKILLS

1. In these four verses there are two words which capture the focus of the passage, each of which appears four times. What are they?

2. The word אל in verse 3 seems extra. How does its presence change the meaning of what comes afterward?

WISDOM OF THE HEART

According to a midrash, the command to send the three types of impure people outside the camp is a hint to the three sins which the Talmud identifies as causing the first exile: sexual immorality, murder, and idolatry. R. Shlomo Ephraim Luntschitz, in his commentary *Keli Yakar*, wonders about the connection between these mitzvot and the Talmud. How do you jump from merely sending people out of the camp to actual exile of the whole people? He explains that this portion of the Torah is written immediately after establishing the camp with the *Mishkan* at the center. The entire purpose of this organization was to place God's Presence at the center of the camp, but the presence of these kinds of impurities – generated by different kinds of sins – would chase God's Presence away. To retain God's Presence we need to purify the camp. What the midrash is trying to explain is what happens when we don't do that, when we retain these people among us and tolerate their behavior. Simply, God's Presence disappears, and when the Divine Presence goes into exile so do we.

There are two approaches to dealing with people who don't meet communal standards. One is to exclude them from the community, whereas the other is to reach out to them and try to draw them closer, raising them up. Which do you think is appropriate for your community? Would your answer change if these were people you didn't like, or if they were your siblings?

QUICK BITE

R. Avraham Sofer, in his *Ketav Sofer*, writes that even without a special command from God, *Benei Yisrael* would have sent these three types of impure people from the camp. After all, their impurity can spread, and they would want to keep themselves from contracting impurity. Nonetheless, the Torah goes out of its way to tell us that they did as God instructed them. Verse 4 even says twice that they did as God instructed them – once at the beginning and again at the end. He suggests that the Torah is emphasizing that they did so not for their own personal reasons, but only because they were instructed to do so.

במדבר | פרק ה

שלישי

ה א וַיְדַבֵּ֥ר יְהֹוָ֖ה אֶל־מֹשֶׁ֥ה לֵּאמֹֽר: ב צַ֚ו אֶת־בְּנֵ֣י יִשְׂרָאֵ֔ל וִֽישַׁלְּחוּ֙ מִן־הַֽמַּחֲנֶ֔ה כׇּל־צָר֖וּעַ וְכׇל־זָ֑ב וְכֹ֖ל טָמֵ֥א לָנָֽפֶשׁ: ג מִזָּכָ֤ר עַד־נְקֵבָה֙ תְּשַׁלֵּ֔חוּ אֶל־מִח֥וּץ לַֽמַּחֲנֶ֖ה תְּשַׁלְּח֑וּם וְלֹ֤א יְטַמְּאוּ֙ אֶת־מַ֣חֲנֵיהֶ֔ם אֲשֶׁ֥ר אֲנִ֖י שֹׁכֵ֥ן בְּתוֹכָֽם: ד וַיַּֽעֲשׂוּ־כֵן֙ בְּנֵ֣י יִשְׂרָאֵ֔ל וַיְשַׁלְּח֣וּ אוֹתָ֔ם אֶל־מִח֖וּץ לַֽמַּחֲנֶ֑ה כַּאֲשֶׁ֨ר דִּבֶּ֤ר יְהֹוָה֙ אֶל־מֹשֶׁ֔ה כֵּ֥ן עָשׂ֖וּ בְּנֵ֥י יִשְׂרָאֵֽל:

CLASSIC COMMENTATORS

After four chapters of counting *Benei Yisrael*, organizing them, and setting up the work of Levi, the Torah abruptly starts talking about something different. The commentaries try to explain why this command suddenly appears.

RASHBAM — רשב״ם

After the Torah has discussed the arrangement of the camp and the way in which the tribes are to be set up, it now demands that impure individuals be expelled from the community.

לאחר שנסדרו ונקבעו סדר המחנות וחנייתן, הוצרך לומר שילוח טמאים מן המחנות.

RABBI YOSEF BEKHOR SHOR — ר׳ יוסף בכור שור

Said God to Israel: Since My Divine Presence dwells among you while the nation is encamped around the *Mishkan* like angels, it is imperative to cleanse your camp from impure people.

דמאחר ששכינה ביניכם ואתם חונים סביב המשכן כמלאכים, צריכים אתם לטהר מחניכם מן הטמאים.

RAMBAN — רמב״ן

Once the *Mishkan* was erected, God commanded the people to remove any impure men and women from the camp. This would ensure the sanctity of the congregation, which in turn would make the place suitable to host the Divine Presence.

אחר שהקים את המשכן, צוה בשלוח הטמאים מן המחנה, שיהיה המחנה קדוש וראוי שתשרה בו שכינה.

QUESTIONS FOR THOUGHT

- Regarding what do all three commentaries agree?
- What do Bekhor Shor and Ramban add to what Rashbam says? Can you find a support for the positions of Bekhor Shor and Ramban from within the text?
- What is the difference between the opinions of Bekhor Shor and Ramban? Which of these positions does the text seem to support more?
- Is this a command to throw undesirables out of the community or to temporarily ban people who have done undesirable acts? Which of those two positions do you think would help to build a healthy community?

Bemidbar | Chapter 5

> **5:5–10** *This enigmatic passage describes a situation where someone commits a sin that requires payment to a person. That payment is accompanied by a twenty-five percent surcharge and an* אשם *offering. If the intended recipient dies before payment is made, then the payment is made to a kohen.*

5 And the Lord spoke to Moshe: "Tell the Israelites: When one man or woman commits
6
7 any sin against another, breaking faith with the Lord and incurring guilt, then he or she shall confess the sin committed and make restitution, adding a fifth to its value, and
8 giving it all to the one whom he has wronged. But if there is no relative to whom restitution can be made for the wrong, the restitution for that wrong shall go to the Lord, to the priest, in addition to the ram of atonement by which atonement is made on his
9 behalf. All gifts the Israelites present to the priest as sacred offerings shall be his. Each
10 priest's sacred offerings will be his; whatever anyone gives him shall be his."

TEXTUAL SKILLS

1. There is another passage in the Torah describing a similar law, but dealing with theft from a native member of *Benei Yisrael* (Lev. 5:20–26). What similarities in language can you find between the two passages?
2. Why do you think that this law is written here, rather than next to its companion in Leviticus?
3. Notice that the Torah switches between singular and plural to describe the sinner here.
4. What phrase appears three times in verses 9–10?

WISDOM OF THE HEART

The requirement to confess is an essential part of any process of repentance; why does the Torah identify it here as a requirement specifically for someone who steals? R. Yitzhak Meir Alter, founder of the Ger dynasty, suggests that stealing is at the root of all sin. After all, God placed each one of us in the world with a specific plan, a purpose. When we violate that purpose or don't fulfill it we are stealing from God. That's why the Torah specified it for stealing – it is the paradigm for all sin.

Do you think that there are predetermined missions for each of us, or does God want us to figure out for ourselves what we should be striving to accomplish in our lives?

QUICK BITE

R. Avraham Saba, in *Tzeror Hamor*, wants to know why the laws dealing with sin and confession are listed immediately after the laws dealing with impurity. He suggests that the laws of impurity deal with what happens when our bodies become defiled; that is something that everyone understands. The Torah wants us to understand that sin defiles our soul. The way to purify our body is through immersion in a mikve; the way to purify our soul is through acknowledging and accepting responsibility for our sins.

במדבר | פרק ה

ה וַיְדַבֵּר יְהוָה אֶל־מֹשֶׁה לֵּאמֹר: דַּבֵּר אֶל־בְּנֵי יִשְׂרָאֵל אִישׁ אוֹ־אִשָּׁה כִּי יַעֲשׂוּ מִכָּל־חַטֹּאת הָאָדָם לִמְעֹל מַעַל בַּיהוָה וְאָשְׁמָה הַנֶּפֶשׁ הַהִוא:
ז וְהִתְוַדּוּ אֶת־חַטָּאתָם אֲשֶׁר עָשׂוּ וְהֵשִׁיב אֶת־אֲשָׁמוֹ בְּרֹאשׁוֹ וַחֲמִישִׁתוֹ יֹסֵף עָלָיו וְנָתַן לַאֲשֶׁר אָשַׁם לוֹ: וְאִם־
ח אֵין לָאִישׁ גֹּאֵל לְהָשִׁיב הָאָשָׁם אֵלָיו הָאָשָׁם הַמּוּשָׁב לַיהוָה לַכֹּהֵן מִלְּבַד אֵיל הַכִּפֻּרִים אֲשֶׁר יְכַפֶּר־בּוֹ עָלָיו: וְכָל־תְּרוּמָה
ט לְכָל־קָדְשֵׁי בְנֵי־יִשְׂרָאֵל אֲשֶׁר־יַקְרִיבוּ לַכֹּהֵן לוֹ יִהְיֶה: וְאִישׁ
י אֶת־קֳדָשָׁיו לוֹ יִהְיוּ אִישׁ אֲשֶׁר־יִתֵּן לַכֹּהֵן לוֹ יִהְיֶה:

CLASSIC COMMENTATORS

According to rabbinic tradition, this passage discusses a case in which someone stole from a *ger* and, when challenged, denied under oath that he had stolen. The person later regretted his actions, and so must repay the theft, add a fine and offer an אשם for lying under oath. If the *ger* dies before payment is made, and he has no living relatives, then the payment is made to the *kohen* on duty. As part of the process for the thief, the Torah says there is a confession (v. 7). Is that confession a precondition for punishment or an independent obligation?

רש"י

והתודו – לימד שאינו חייב חומש ואשם על פי עדים עד שיודה בדבר.

RASHI

The thief is obligated to pay the fifth and to bring the אשם sacrifice only if he admits his infraction, and not if he was reported by witnesses.

רלב"ג

והתודו את חטאתם אשר עשו, למדנו שחייב החוטא להתודות על חטאו, ואף על פי שכבר נענש עליו.

RALBAG

We learn from here that the individual must confess his sinful behavior, even if he has already been punished for it.

ר' יצחק רג'יו

רצונו לומר, לא די במה שמתחרט בלבו אבל יתודה בפה לעין כל.

RABBI ISAAC SAMUEL REGGIO

It is not enough for the thief to regret his actions in his heart; he must offer a verbal admission in front of everybody.

QUESTIONS FOR THOUGHT

- Between Rashi and Ralbag, which of them says that the confession is a precondition and which says that it is an obligation? How would each of them translate the letter *vav* at the beginning of the first word in verse 7?
- According to the commentary who says that the confession is a precondition, without which there is no obligation to pay the fine or bring the אשם, why would someone voluntarily take on an additional obligation?
- What does R. Reggio add that the other two commentaries do not include? Why do you think that might be important?

11,12 The Lord spoke to Moshe: "Speak to the Israelites and tell them: If any man's wife goes
13 astray and is unfaithful to him; if another man has sexual relations with her, and this happens without the husband's knowledge because she defiled herself in secret, there
14 were no witness against her, and she was not caught in the act – if a fit of jealousy overcomes him, making him jealous over his wife who has defiled herself, or a fit of jealousy
15 overcomes him, making him jealous over his wife who has not defiled herself – then the man shall bring his wife to the priest together with the prescribed offering for her, one-tenth of an ephah of barley flour. He shall not pour oil on it or place frankincense upon it, for it is a grain offering of jealousy, a grain offering of remembrance, calling
16 attention to a wrong. The priest shall bring the woman close and have her stand before
17 the Lord. He shall then take sacred water in an earthenware vessel, and pick up some
18 earth from the floor of the Tabernacle and place it in the water. He shall have the woman stand before the Lord, and loosen the hair of the woman's head, placing on her palms the grain offering of remembrance, the grain offering of jealousy. His hand shall hold

---

ר' שמשון רפאל הירש

בפרשה הקודמת שימשה לשון "מעילה" ללמדנו, שהיחסים החברתיים בין אדם לחבירו קדושים אף הם לה'. גם כאן משמשת לשון "מעילה" ללמדנו שקשר הנישואין בין איש לאשתו קדוש הוא לה'.

RABBI SAMSON RAPHAEL HIRSCH

The term *me'ila* appears in the previous passage to teach that proper conduct between Israelites is considered a sacred achievement in the eyes of the Lord. In the present context too, the word signifies that God considers a healthy marriage to be a holy union.

QUESTIONS FOR THOUGHT

- According to Ralbag, what do the two passages have in common? What is different between them?
- According to R. Hirsch, what do the two passages have in common?
- Which of the two commentaries above might you use in preparing to speak at a celebration for a newly married couple? Why would you choose that one?

TEXTUAL SKILLS

1. What root appears four (!) times in verse 14?
2. Notice how the two halves of verse 14 are exactly parallel, except for one critical word.

WISDOM OF THE HEART

Many are troubled by the process of *sota*. Rav Yaakov Kaminetzky understands that the process of the *sota* was designed not as a punishment but as a way for a woman to prove her innocence to her husband, which could seem all but impossible. Perhaps, as Ramban points out, that is why this is the only mitzva that relies on a miracle – God is prepared to step in to help facilitate that process.

ה רביעי וַיְדַבֵּ֥ר יְהֹוָ֖ה אֶל־מֹשֶׁ֥ה לֵּאמֹֽר: דַּבֵּר֙ אֶל־בְּנֵ֣י יִשְׂרָאֵ֔ל וְאָמַרְתָּ֖ א
אֲלֵהֶ֑ם אִ֣ישׁ אִ֗ישׁ כִּֽי־תִשְׂטֶ֤ה אִשְׁתּוֹ֙ וּמָעֲלָ֥ה ב֖וֹ מָֽעַל: וְשָׁכַ֨ב ב
אִ֤ישׁ אֹתָהּ֙ שִׁכְבַת־זֶ֔רַע וְנֶעְלַם֙ מֵעֵינֵ֣י אִישָׁ֔הּ וְנִסְתְּרָ֖ה וְהִ֣יא
נִטְמָ֑אָה וְעֵד֙ אֵ֣ין בָּ֔הּ וְהִ֖וא לֹ֥א נִתְפָּֽשָׂה: וְעָבַ֨ר עָלָ֧יו רֽוּחַ־קִנְאָ֛ה יד
וְקִנֵּ֥א אֶת־אִשְׁתּ֖וֹ וְהִ֣וא נִטְמָ֑אָה אוֹ־עָבַ֨ר עָלָ֤יו רֽוּחַ־קִנְאָה֙ וְקִנֵּ֣א
אֶת־אִשְׁתּ֔וֹ וְהִ֖יא לֹ֥א נִטְמָֽאָה: וְהֵבִ֨יא הָאִ֣ישׁ אֶת־אִשְׁתּוֹ֮ אֶל־ טו
הַכֹּהֵן֒ וְהֵבִ֤יא אֶת־קׇרְבָּנָהּ֙ עָלֶ֔יהָ עֲשִׂירִ֥ת הָאֵיפָ֖ה קֶ֣מַח שְׂעֹרִ֑ים
לֹֽא־יִצֹ֨ק עָלָ֜יו שֶׁ֗מֶן וְלֹֽא־יִתֵּ֤ן עָלָיו֙ לְבֹנָ֔ה כִּֽי־מִנְחַ֤ת קְנָאֹת֙ ה֔וּא
מִנְחַ֥ת זִכָּר֖וֹן מַזְכֶּ֥רֶת עָוֺֽן: וְהִקְרִ֥יב אֹתָ֖הּ הַכֹּהֵ֑ן וְהֶֽעֱמִדָ֖הּ לִפְנֵ֥י טז
יְהֹוָֽה: וְלָקַ֧ח הַכֹּהֵ֛ן מַ֥יִם קְדֹשִׁ֖ים בִּכְלִי־חָ֑רֶשׂ וּמִן־הֶֽעָפָ֗ר אֲשֶׁ֤ר יז
יִהְיֶה֙ בְּקַרְקַ֣ע הַמִּשְׁכָּ֔ן יִקַּ֥ח הַכֹּהֵ֖ן וְנָתַ֥ן אֶל־הַמָּֽיִם: וְהֶעֱמִ֨יד יח
הַכֹּהֵ֥ן אֶת־הָֽאִשָּׁה֮ לִפְנֵ֣י יְהֹוָה֒ וּפָרַע֙ אֶת־רֹ֣אשׁ הָֽאִשָּׁ֔ה וְנָתַ֣ן
עַל־כַּפֶּ֗יהָ אֵ֚ת מִנְחַ֣ת הַזִּכָּר֔וֹן מִנְחַ֥ת קְנָאֹ֖ת הִ֑וא וּבְיַ֤ד הַכֹּהֵן֙

CLASSIC COMMENTATORS

The commentators notice that the passage of the *sota* describes her actions as *me'ila* (usually used to describe getting personal benefit from something sanctified for the *Mishkan*), just like the previous passage describes the violation as *me'ila*. Is there are anything more to this, which might explain why the *sota* appears at this point in the text?

RALBAG

The case of the *sota* is juxtaposed to the previous passage because the whole purpose of the procedure is to resolve friction and quarrels within a household. That is the same goal inherent in the previous topic, removing strife from within *Benei Yisrael*. Indeed, establishing peace between a husband and wife takes precedence over striving for sound relations among neighbors.

רלב״ג

הנה סמך זאת הפרשה לפרשה הקודמת שהיה תכליתה להסיר קטטה ומחלוקת מישראל בכללם, כי זאת הפרשה היא להסיר הקטטה מן הבית. והנה שלום הבית קודם לשלום העם.

19 the bitter water that gives rise to a curse. And the priest shall administer an oath to her, saying to the woman, 'If no man has had sexual relations with you, and if you have not gone astray, letting yourself be defiled while married to your husband, may your
20 innocence be established by this bitter, cursing water. But if you have gone astray while married to your husband, and if you have let yourself be defiled and a man other than
21 your husband has had relations with you' – the priest shall here put the woman under the oath of the curse, and say to her – 'the Lord make you a curse and an oath among
22 your people, when the Lord makes your thigh sag and your belly swell; may this curse-causing water enter your intestines and make your belly swell and your thigh
23 sag.' And the woman shall say, 'Amen, Amen.' Then the priest shall write these curses
24 on a scroll and wash them off into the bitter water. He shall make the woman drink the bitter water that causes a curse, and the curse-causing water will enter into her

---

RAMBAN

רמב״ן

והנה אין בכל משפטי התורה דבר תלוי בנס זולתי הענין הזה, שהוא פלא ונס קבוע שיעשה בישראל בהיותם רובם עושים רצונו של מקום, כי הוא חפץ למען צדקו ליסר את הנשים שלא תעשינה כזמת יתר העמים, ולנקות ישראל מן הממזרות שיהיו ראויין להשרות שכינתו בתוכם.

Throughout the length and breadth of the Torah's laws, the case of the *sota* represents the sole example of a miracle being used to determine the truth of a matter. This wonder is available to the people of Israel when the majority of the populace is living according to the rules of the Almighty. For it is God's desire to teach the nation's women to avoid the licentiousness practiced within the gentile cultures. It is also crucial to cleanse Israel from children born of unlawful unions. If this is achieved, the nation will be worthy of accommodating the Divine Presence.

QUESTIONS FOR THOUGHT

- What does each of the above commentaries identify as the unique feature of the *sota* ritual?
- According to each, why did the Torah distinguish the *sota* ritual this way?

WISDOM OF THE HEART

There is a well-known question of why the passage of the *sota* is situated next to that of the *nazir*. Equally well-known is the Gemara's answer, that someone who sees a *sota* should refrain from drinking wine. That seems like a strange conclusion. How is someone else's marital problem related to my personal habit? Perhaps the Talmud is trying to tell us that issues of trust and mistrust don't happen in a vacuum – the entire society must look at itself and ask if the kinds of behaviors it has been engaging in or endorsing are playing a role in creating the kind of culture which would cause husbands and wives to fall into such a deep cycle of mistrust.

Think about your own circle of friends. What kind of values are you and your circle fostering? Are you happy with those? Can you influence those values positively?

במדבר | פרק ה

יט יִהְיוּ מֵי הַמָּרִים הַמְאָרְרִים: וְהִשְׁבִּיעַ אֹתָהּ הַכֹּהֵן וְאָמַר אֶל־הָאִשָּׁה אִם־לֹא שָׁכַב אִישׁ אֹתָךְ וְאִם־לֹא שָׂטִית טֻמְאָה תַּחַת
כ אִישֵׁךְ הִנָּקִי מִמֵּי הַמָּרִים הַמְאָרְרִים הָאֵלֶּה: וְאַתְּ כִּי שָׂטִית תַּחַת אִישֵׁךְ וְכִי נִטְמֵאת וַיִּתֵּן אִישׁ בָּךְ אֶת־שְׁכָבְתּוֹ מִבַּלְעֲדֵי
כא אִישֵׁךְ: וְהִשְׁבִּיעַ הַכֹּהֵן אֶת־הָאִשָּׁה בִּשְׁבֻעַת הָאָלָה וְאָמַר הַכֹּהֵן לָאִשָּׁה יִתֵּן יְהוָה אוֹתָךְ לְאָלָה וְלִשְׁבֻעָה בְּתוֹךְ עַמֵּךְ בְּתֵת
כב יְהוָה אֶת־יְרֵכֵךְ נֹפֶלֶת וְאֶת־בִּטְנֵךְ צָבָה: וּבָאוּ הַמַּיִם הַמְאָרְרִים הָאֵלֶּה בְּמֵעַיִךְ לַצְבּוֹת בֶּטֶן וְלַנְפִּל יָרֵךְ וְאָמְרָה הָאִשָּׁה אָמֵן ׀
כג אָמֵן: וְכָתַב אֶת־הָאָלֹת הָאֵלֶּה הַכֹּהֵן בַּסֵּפֶר וּמָחָה אֶל־מֵי
כד הַמָּרִים: וְהִשְׁקָה אֶת־הָאִשָּׁה אֶת־מֵי הַמָּרִים הַמְאָרְרִים וּבָאוּ

TEXTUAL SKILLS

1. In the previous passage the Torah states twice that the *kohen* presents the woman "before the Lord." What is the *kohen* actually doing when he has "the woman stand before the Lord?"

2. Are you familiar with another story in the Torah involving a sinner who is made to drink water that has some kind of powder added to it? In what ways are these stories similar? In what ways are they very different?

CLASSIC COMMENTATORS

The ritual of the *sota* is quite strange. The commentaries point out some of its unique features and why they are so significant.

RABBI SAMSON RAPHAEL HIRSCH

It is important to note that the present passage emphasizes again and again that it is the *kohen* who administers each step of the *sota* procedure. What this means is that the matter of the suspected wife is not handled by the courts, but is addressed by the *Mikdash* officials. Of course, the *kohen* is the agent and the representative of the *Mikdash*; God shows Himself as the founder of that center and as the guarantor of its demands. This is why the name of the Lord is employed in the ritual, and the impending punishment is to be administered by God Himself. It is He who distributes life and bestows blessing. For the ultimate purpose of this process is not the destruction of the sinner, but the promised preservation of modesty within the community. Nothing less than the salvation of Israel relies on the establishment and maintenance of modesty.

ר׳ שמשון רפאל הירש

יש לשים לב, שלאורך כל פרשה זו חוזר הכתוב ואומר כמה פעמים שהכהן הוא העושה את סדר המעשים האלה. סדר זה אינו מעשה בית דין אלא פניה למקדש. הכהן הוא שליחו וניצגו של המקדש, וה' יראה עצמו כמיסדו וכערב לדרישותיו. משום כך נזכר כאן גם שם ה': הפורענות צפויה מאת ה', אשר באהבתו חולק חיים וברכה. שכן תכליתו הסופית של סדר זה אינה אובדן החוטא; אלא להבטיח ולקיים את הצניעות, אשר בה תלויים ישועת ישראל וברכתו.

> **5:25–31** *The kohen offers the* מנחה *brought by the husband, and the woman drinks the water. If she is guilty, then her belly will swell and her "thigh will sag." If she is innocent, her name will be cleared and she will be blessed with a child.*

25 and turn bitter. The priest shall take the grain offering of jealousy from the woman's
26 hand, wave the grain offering before the Lord, and bring it close to the altar. Then the priest shall take a handful of the grain offering as a token, and burn it on the altar, after
27 which he shall make the woman drink the water. He having given her the water to drink, then, if she has let herself be defiled and behaved unfaithfully toward her husband, the curse-causing water will turn bitter, her belly will swell, her thigh will sag, and the
28 woman will become a curse among her people. But if the woman has not let herself be
29 defiled and is pure, then she shall be cleared and will conceive children." This is the law for cases of jealousy, when a woman goes astray with someone in place of her husband
30 and becomes defiled, or when a fit of jealousy overcomes a man and he grows jealous over his wife. He shall have the woman stand before the Lord, and the priest will deal
31 with her as all this law prescribes. No guilt will attach to the husband, but the woman in question will bear the punishment of her offense.

- Rav Joseph B. Soloveitchik once explained that the *sota* ritual was a revolution in the ancient world, as it gave an accused woman an opportunity to clear her name. This was in contrast to other cultures where, for example, the accused woman was thrown into the water with stones tied to her feet – if she floated, then it was a sign of her innocence. Which of the above commentaries says something similar?
- In the story leading up to the man bringing his wife to the *kohen*, what did the man and the woman each do which could have been done differently to avoid this scene?

TEXTUAL SKILLS

1. The word used to describe what happens to the woman's belly if she is guilty, צבה, appears three times in all of Tanakh – and all three are in the context of the *sota*. Can you offer an explanation as to why the Torah would use a word which is nearly impossible to define to describe what happens to the guilty *sota*?

2. Notice how the description of the waters changes multiple times throughout the entire description of the *sota* ritual.

WISDOM OF THE HEART

The very last verse says that when the *sota* is proven innocent, her husband will also be cleared of sin. What sin did he commit? Many of the commentaries, such as Rashbam, suggest that this entire process involves many layers of sin, one of which is the husband bringing his wife to undergo this ordeal. Ralbag takes this even further, suggesting that the man also needs to atone for his part in the breakdown of trust, especially since his accusation turned out to be false. If there is a breakdown in trust that is so severe, the husband and wife must engage in a tremendous amount of soul-searching to figure out how things went so wrong, and hard work to figure out how to rebuild a trusting relationship.

במדבר | פרק ה

כה בָהּ הַמַּיִם הַמְאָרְרִים לְמָרִים: וְלָקַח הַכֹּהֵן מִיַּד הָאִשָּׁה אֵת מִנְחַת הַקְּנָאֹת וְהֵנִיף אֶת־הַמִּנְחָה לִפְנֵי יהוה וְהִקְרִיב אֹתָהּ אֶל־הַמִּזְבֵּחַ: כו וְקָמַץ הַכֹּהֵן מִן־הַמִּנְחָה אֶת־אַזְכָּרָתָהּ וְהִקְטִיר הַמִּזְבֵּחָה וְאַחַר יַשְׁקֶה אֶת־הָאִשָּׁה אֶת־הַמָּיִם: כז וְהִשְׁקָהּ אֶת־הַמַּיִם וְהָיְתָה אִם־נִטְמְאָה וַתִּמְעֹל מַעַל בְּאִישָׁהּ וּבָאוּ בָהּ הַמַּיִם הַמְאָרְרִים לְמָרִים וְצָבְתָה בִטְנָהּ וְנָפְלָה יְרֵכָהּ וְהָיְתָה הָאִשָּׁה לְאָלָה בְּקֶרֶב עַמָּהּ: כח וְאִם־לֹא נִטְמְאָה הָאִשָּׁה וּטְהֹרָה הִוא וְנִקְּתָה וְנִזְרְעָה זָרַע: כט זֹאת תּוֹרַת הַקְּנָאֹת אֲשֶׁר תִּשְׂטֶה אִשָּׁה תַּחַת אִישָׁהּ וְנִטְמָאָה: ל אוֹ אִישׁ אֲשֶׁר תַּעֲבֹר עָלָיו רוּחַ קִנְאָה וְקִנֵּא אֶת־אִשְׁתּוֹ וְהֶעֱמִיד אֶת־הָאִשָּׁה לִפְנֵי יהוה וְעָשָׂה לָהּ הַכֹּהֵן אֵת כָּל־הַתּוֹרָה הַזֹּאת: לא וְנִקָּה הָאִישׁ מֵעָוֺן וְהָאִשָּׁה הַהִוא תִּשָּׂא אֶת־עֲוֺנָהּ:

CLASSIC COMMENTATORS

In the final verse of the entire *sota* saga, the Torah states that the man will be cleansed of his sin. To what sin is the Torah referring?

RASHBAM — רשב״ם

For this man refused to tolerate his wife having relations with another man. Had the husband remained silent in such a circumstance, he would not be cleansed from sin, for in fact, his wife would be forbidden to him from that point on.

שלא סבל אשתו להיות מזנה תחתיו. ואילו שתק לא היה מנוקה מעון, שהיא אסורה לו.

RALBAG — רלב״ג

The husband is cleansed of the sin of suspecting his wife of infidelity. For this experience has removed that suspicion from his heart.

האיש ההוא ינקה מעון על החשד שהיה חושד אשתו, כי זה הדבר יסיר החשד ההוא מלבו.

QUESTIONS FOR THOUGHT

- According to one of the commentaries, the husband's speaking up is similar to Leviticus 19:17, although neither makes this comparison explicitly. Which commentary is that, and how is it similar?

BEMIDBAR | CHAPTER 6

NASO | 50

> **6:1–8** *Any person, man or woman, who decides to declare themselves a nazir must refrain from consuming any grape products, must not cut their hair, and must refrain from contact with a corpse – even that of a mother or father.*

6 1 Then the Lord spoke to Moshe: "Speak to the Israelites. Say: When a man or a woman
2
3 takes a special vow, the vow of a nazirite, to separate him or herself to the Lord, he must separate himself from wine and strong drink. He must drink neither vinegar made from wine nor vinegar made from any other strong drink, nor may he drink any juice made
4 with grapes, nor eat fresh grapes or raisins. All the days of his separation he must not
5 eat anything that comes from the grapevine, from seed to skin. All the days of his separation vow, no razor shall touch his head. Until the completion of the time for which he separated himself to the Lord, he shall be holy, and must let the locks of his hair grow
6 long. All the days of his separation to the Lord, he must not come near a dead body.
7 Even for his father or mother or brother or sister, if they die, he must not defile himself,
8 for his vow of separation to his God is on his head. All the days of his separation he is

---

ר' שמשון רפאל הירש

גידול שער ראשו מציין שהוא הגביל את עצמו לחוגו שלו; ובכך מבטא הנזיר את העובדה שהוא הקדיש את עצמו "לאלקיו" ... בדומה לכך, הציץ על מצח הכהן הגדול קרוי "נזר הקדש".

RABBI SAMSON RAPHAEL HIRSCH

When a *nazir* allows their hair to grow long, that is an announcement that the individual has withdrawn into themselves. As such, the *nazir* expresses they have sanctified and dedicated themselves to God. In a similar way, the gold headband worn by the *kohen gadol* is referred to as the *nezer hakodesh* – the sacred diadem.

QUESTIONS FOR THOUGHT

- Regarding what do Ibn Ezra and Ibn Kaspi agree?
- In what way are their explanations different?
- What similarity is there between the interpretations of Ibn Kaspi and R. Hirsch?
- How does the next verse (v. 8) support the opinion of R. Hirsch?
- Which of the commentaries is closest to the translation here?

WISDOM OF THE HEART

At first glance it would seem that the *nazir* has greater sanctity than a *kohen*, since the *nazir* is not even permitted to become impure even if his parents, siblings, or children die, which is permitted to a *kohen*. R. Avraham Borenstein, author of *Avnei Nezer*, suggests that since the sanctity of the *kohen* comes from his family, he is allowed to violate that sanctity to honor his family. The sanctity of the *nazir*, however, is independent of outside sources, and therefore cannot be violated. R. Yehuda Leib Alter, in his *Sefat Emet*, adds that this demonstrates the power of the individual will – it can propel us beyond our natural limitations.

Have you encountered people whose willpower brought them to success that nobody ever believed they would achieve? What do you think is the source of that willpower?

במדבר | פרק ו

א וַיְדַבֵּר יְהוָה אֶל־מֹשֶׁה לֵּאמֹר: דַּבֵּר אֶל־בְּנֵי יִשְׂרָאֵל וְאָמַרְתָּ
אֲלֵהֶם אִישׁ אוֹ־אִשָּׁה כִּי יַפְלִא לִנְדֹּר נֶדֶר נָזִיר לְהַזִּיר לַיהוָה:
ג מִיַּיִן וְשֵׁכָר יַזִּיר חֹמֶץ יַיִן וְחֹמֶץ שֵׁכָר לֹא יִשְׁתֶּה וְכָל־מִשְׁרַת
ד עֲנָבִים לֹא יִשְׁתֶּה וַעֲנָבִים לַחִים וִיבֵשִׁים לֹא יֹאכֵל: כֹּל יְמֵי נִזְרוֹ
ה מִכֹּל אֲשֶׁר יֵעָשֶׂה מִגֶּפֶן הַיַּיִן מֵחַרְצַנִּים וְעַד־זָג לֹא יֹאכֵל: כָּל־יְמֵי
נֶדֶר נִזְרוֹ תַּעַר לֹא־יַעֲבֹר עַל־רֹאשׁוֹ עַד־מְלֹאת הַיָּמִם אֲשֶׁר־
ו יַזִּיר לַיהוָה קָדֹשׁ יִהְיֶה גַּדֵּל פֶּרַע שְׂעַר רֹאשׁוֹ: כָּל־יְמֵי הַזִּירוֹ
ז לַיהוָה עַל־נֶפֶשׁ מֵת לֹא יָבֹא: לְאָבִיו וּלְאִמּוֹ לְאָחִיו וּלְאַחֹתוֹ לֹא־
ח יִטַּמָּא לָהֶם בְּמֹתָם כִּי נֵזֶר אֱלֹהָיו עַל־רֹאשׁוֹ: כֹּל יְמֵי נִזְרוֹ קָדֹשׁ

CLASSIC COMMENTATORS

In verse 7 the Torah explains that the *nazir* may not become defiled by a corpse, because "the *nezer* of his God is on his head." While it is translated here as "for his vow of separation to his God is on his head," the commentaries debate what that phrase means.

IBN EZRA

According to some commentators, the term *nazir* derives from the word *nezer*, an approach based on the verse, "the *nezer* [crown] of his God is on his head." Such an interpretation is perhaps the straightforward meaning here. Recognize that most human beings are slaves to their physical desires. Whereas, the supreme individual, the one who deserves to wear a crown of glory on his head, is the man or woman who is not at all tempted by passions.

RABBI YOSEF IBN KASPI

The *nazir* is said to wear the great crown of God on his head because his undertaking separates him from other important figures and indeed from the nation as a whole. Now the ever-present sign that the *nazir* is a significant personality is the growth of the person's hair. The excessive hair serves to distinguish the *nazir* from the community, just like a crown identifies the king as exceptional.

אבן עזרא

ויש אומרים: כי מלת נזיר מגזרת: נזר, ועדותם כי נזר אלהיו על ראשו, ואיננו רחוק. ודע כי כל בני אדם עובדי תאות העולם, והמלך באמת, שיש לו נזר ועטרת ממלכות בראשו, כל מי שהוא חפשי מן התאות.

ר' יוסף אבן כספי

נקרא העטרה אשר בראש המלך והגדול נזר, להיות הענין ההוא מבדיל בינו ובין שאר השרים והעם. והנה הסימן הקיים הנראה לכל לזה הנזיר הוא גדל שער ראשו, אם כן זה לו הוד מבדיל בראשו כמו הנזר בראש המלך.

6:9–21 If a nazir accidentally becomes defiled by contact with a corpse, then after he is purified he needs to bring three offerings, a חטאת, an עולה, and an אשם, and then he restarts his period of nezirut from the beginning. When the period of nezirut is completed, he must bring an עולה, a חטאת, and a שלמים offering, and he must cut his hair, which is burnt along with the שלמים. After that his nezirut is completed, and he may return to his normal activities.

9 holy to the Lord. If someone dies suddenly beside him, defiling his consecrated head, he shall shave his head on the day of his purification; on the seventh day he shall shave
10 it. Then, on the eighth day, he shall bring two turtledoves or two young pigeons to the
11 priest, to the entrance of the Tent of Meeting. The priest will offer one as a purification offering and the other as a burnt offering, and make atonement for him for the guilt he incurred through contact with the dead body. He shall consecrate his head anew
12 on that day. He must rededicate himself to the Lord for the full term of his vow, and bring a yearling lamb as a guilt offering. The former days are discounted because his

רמב״ן

וטעם החטאת ... כי האיש הזה חוטא נפשו במלאת הנזירות, כי הוא עתה נזיר מקדושתו ועבודת השם, וראוי היה לו שיזיר לעולם ויעמוד כל ימיו נזיר וקדוש לאלהיו, כענין שאמר (עמוס ב:יא) "ואקים מבניכם לנביאים ומבחוריכם לנזירים", השוה אותו הכתוב לנביא, וכדכתיב (פסוק ח') "כל ימי נזרו קדוש הוא לה׳", והנה הוא צריך כפרה בשובו להיטמא בתאוות העולם.

RAMBAN

The reason that a *nazir* is obligated to bring a חטאת (purification offering) is that he is actually sinning when he ends his term of *nezirut*. It is then that he retreats from the life of sanctity and service of God that he had embraced. In fact, it would have been appropriate for the individual to remain a *nazir* for the rest of his life as a man dedicated to his God. Thus the prophet states, "I raised up into prophets some of your sons and into nazirites some of your young men" (Amos 2:11), thereby comparing the *nazir* to the prophet. Our passage also declares, "All the days of his separation he is holy to the Lord" (Num. 6:8). Thus, the person requires atonement when he returns to a life of impurity and the world of desire.

תורת העולה

אמר הרמב״ם כי רפואת הנפש כרפואת הגוף... צריך להדריך עצמו בהיפך מידותיו הרעות עד שיעמוד על המיצוע במידות (=בדרך האמצעית), שהוא הטוב בכל דבר ... וזהו ענין הנזיר, כי אם נזיר מטעם שראה שנטה אל תאוות העולם, צריך להפריש עצמו אל קצה האחרון השני בהרחקה גדולה - עד שירגיל עצמו לעמוד אחר כך בדרך המיצוע. ולפיכך אמרה התורה "קדוש יהיה (ה'), כי עיקר קדושתו של נזיר יהיה לעתיד אחר השלמת ימי נזרו, שיעמוד אז בעניין מיצוע, לא בשעת נדרו, שאז חטא ולזה נאמר (י״א) "וכיפר עליו מאשר חטא..." כי הרחקת הנזיר הוא רע מצד עצמו, מאחר שכל הקצוות רעות; ולא נצטווה עליו הנזיר אלא לתכלית טוב, שיעמוד על המיצוע.

TORAT HA'OLAH

According to the Rambam, fixing the soul is as important as healing the body.... An individual must train himself to control and suppress his negative desires until he guides his character toward the golden mean. That is the ideal policy in all matters.... Such is the ultimate purpose of the *nazir*. Should a person recognize that he is attracted to the passions this world has to offer, he must force himself to embrace the complete opposite extreme of abstinence, so that in the end he can locate himself in the middle of partial indulgence. This is why the Torah characterization of the *nazir* is "he is holy to the Lord": the aim is for the individual to attain sanctity for the future, long after his term as a *nazir* has ended. Whereas, while he is actually living like a *nazir* the person is considered to be a sinner, as the verse states, "and make atonement for him for the guilt he incurred" (Num. 6:11). For the distance that a *nazir* places between himself and the community, and between himself and the permitted pleasures of life is not a positive thing – all extremes are negative. The Torah commands and tolerates the phenomenon of *nezirut* only in order to assist a man or a woman to reach the middle path of behavior.

ט הוּא לַיהוָה וְכִי־יָמוּת מֵת עָלָיו בְּפֶתַע פִּתְאֹם וְטִמֵּא רֹאשׁ נִזְרוֹ
י וְגִלַּח רֹאשׁוֹ בְּיוֹם טָהֳרָתוֹ בַּיּוֹם הַשְּׁבִיעִי יְגַלְּחֶנּוּ: וּבַיּוֹם הַשְּׁמִינִי
יָבִא שְׁתֵּי תֹרִים אוֹ שְׁנֵי בְּנֵי יוֹנָה אֶל־הַכֹּהֵן אֶל־פֶּתַח אֹהֶל מוֹעֵד:
יא וְעָשָׂה הַכֹּהֵן אֶחָד לְחַטָּאת וְאֶחָד לְעֹלָה וְכִפֶּר עָלָיו מֵאֲשֶׁר
יב חָטָא עַל־הַנָּפֶשׁ וְקִדַּשׁ אֶת־רֹאשׁוֹ בַּיּוֹם הַהוּא: וְהִזִּיר לַיהוָה
אֶת־יְמֵי נִזְרוֹ וְהֵבִיא כֶּבֶשׂ בֶּן־שְׁנָתוֹ לְאָשָׁם וְהַיָּמִים הָרִאשֹׁנִים

CLASSIC COMMENTATORS

The very concept of *nezirut* is the subject of a major debate. On the one hand the Torah calls him holy (v. 8) with the "crown of his God on his head" (v. 7), while on the other hand he must bring a חטאת – usually understood as a purification offering, when he completes his *nezirut*. Is being a *nazir* something that the Torah is in favor of or something of which the Torah disapproves?

RAMBAM

Now an individual might be tempted to argue: Since the emotions of jealousy, lust, desire for honor, and other such passions lead a person down a dark path and end up killing him, it would be best for me were I to avoid all temptation, and distance myself from all desire. Such an individual might then refuse to eat any meat or drink any wine. He will neglect to marry a wife and disdain a home with comfortable furnishings. Instead of wearing beautiful clothes, this ascetic will dress himself in sackcloth and coarse wool, like the priests of idolatrous cultures do. But this too is a nasty approach to life, and one is forbidden to follow it. One who adopts this sort of outlook is labeled a sinner, as the verse regarding the *nazir* states, "and make atonement for him for the guilt he incurred through contact with the dead body" (Num. 6:11). Commenting on the phenomenon of the *nazir*, our Sages proclaim: Although this person has abstained only from wine, he is nevertheless referred to as a sinner; how much more is one held in contempt for forswearing all of life's pleasures. As such, the Sages insist that a person is permitted to repudiate only those things which the Torah lists in this regard. One must not take vows or oaths forbidding to himself or herself things that are otherwise allowed. Say the Sages: Does the Torah not prohibit enough items and activities for you, that you are seeking new restrictions for your life? Similarly, it is wrong for people to fast frequently. Regarding this entire approach to life, Shlomo has written, "Do not be too righteous, and do not seek more wisdom, for why should you become desolate?" (Eccl. 7:16).

רמב״ם

שֶׁמָּא יֹאמַר הָאָדָם: "הוֹאִיל וְהַקִּנְאָה וְהַתַּאֲוָה וְהַכָּבוֹד וְכַיּוֹצֵא בָהֶם דֶּרֶךְ רָעָה הֵן וּמוֹצִיאִין אֶת הָאָדָם מִן הָעוֹלָם, אֶפְרֹשׁ מֵהֶן בְּיוֹתֵר וְאֶתְרַחֵק לַצַּד הָאַחֲרוֹן", עַד שֶׁלֹּא יֹאכַל בָּשָׂר וְלֹא יִשְׁתֶּה יַיִן וְלֹא יִשָּׂא אִשָּׁה וְלֹא יֵשֵׁב בְּדִירָה נָאָה וְלֹא יִלְבַּשׁ מַלְבּוּשׁ נָאֶה אֶלָּא הַשַּׂק וְהַצֶּמֶר הַקָּשֶׁה וְכַיּוֹצֵא בָּהֶן, כְּגוֹן כֹּהֲנֵי הָעוֹבְדֵי כוֹכָבִים, גַּם זֶה דֶּרֶךְ רָעָה הִיא וְאָסוּר לֵילֵךְ בָּהּ. הַמְהַלֵּךְ בְּדֶרֶךְ זוֹ נִקְרָא חוֹטֵא, שֶׁהֲרֵי הוּא אוֹמֵר בְּנָזִיר "וְכִפֶּר עָלָיו מֵאֲשֶׁר חָטָא עַל הַנֶּפֶשׁ", אָמְרוּ חֲכָמִים: וּמָה אִם נָזִיר שֶׁלֹּא פֵּרַשׁ אֶלָּא מִן הַיַּיִן צָרִיךְ כַּפָּרָה – הַמּוֹנֵעַ עַצְמוֹ מִכָּל דָּבָר וְדָבָר עַל אַחַת כַּמָּה וְכַמָּה, לְפִיכָךְ צִוּוּ חֲכָמִים שֶׁלֹּא יִמְנַע אָדָם עַצְמוֹ אֶלָּא מִדְּבָרִים שֶׁמְּנָעַתּוּ הַתּוֹרָה בִּלְבַד, וְלֹא יְהֵא אוֹסֵר עַצְמוֹ בִּנְדָרִים וּבִשְׁבוּעוֹת עַל דְּבָרִים הַמֻּתָּרִים. כָּךְ אָמְרוּ חֲכָמִים: לֹא דַּיֶּךָ מַה שֶּׁאָסְרָה תּוֹרָה, אֶלָּא שֶׁאַתָּה אוֹסֵר עָלֶיךָ דְּבָרִים אֲחֵרִים?! וּבִכְלָל הַזֶּה אֵלּוּ שֶׁמִּתְעַנִּין תָּמִיד אֵינָם בְּדֶרֶךְ טוֹבָה, וְאָסְרוּ חֲכָמִים שֶׁיְּהֵא אָדָם מְסַגֵּף עַצְמוֹ בְּתַעֲנִית. וְעַל כָּל הַדְּבָרִים הָאֵלּוּ וְכַיּוֹצֵא בָּהֶן צִוָּה שְׁלֹמֹה וְאָמַר "אַל תְּהִי צַדִּיק הַרְבֵּה וְאַל תִּתְחַכַּם יוֹתֵר לָמָּה תִּשּׁוֹמֵם" (קֹהֶלֶת ז:טז).

13 separation was defiled. This is the law of the nazirite: On the day that the term of his nazirite vow is completed, he shall be brought to the entrance to the Tent of Meeting.
14 He shall present his offering to the Lord: one male yearling lamb without blemish for a burnt offering, one yearling ewe lamb without blemish for a purification offering, one
15 ram without blemish for a peace offering, and a basket of unleavened bread, loaves of fine flour mixed with olive oil, and unleavened wafers smeared with olive oil, along with
16 their grain offering and libations. The priest shall present these before the Lord and
17 offer up his purification offering and his burnt offering. He shall then offer the ram as a sacrifice, a peace offering to the Lord, together with the basket of unleavened bread.
18 The priest shall also offer his grain offering and his libation. The nazirite shall shave his consecrated hair at the entrance to the Tent of Meeting and take the hair of his conse-
19 crated head and place it on the fire beneath the peace offering. The priest shall take the boiled foreleg of the ram, one unleavened loaf from the basket, and one unleavened wafer, and place them on the hands of the nazirite after he has shaved his consecrated
20 head. The priest shall wave them as a wave offering before the Lord. It is a sacred gift for the priest, together with the breast of the wave offering and the thigh of the upraised
21 gift. After this the nazirite may drink wine." This is the law of the nazirite who vows offerings to the Lord as a nazirite. Whatever he can afford further and vows to give, beyond what the law of the nazirite obliges him to, that too shall he fulfill.

TEXTUAL SKILLS

1. Verses 19–20 describe a process during the offerings in which the *nazir* takes an active part. Find the description in the process of *sota* which is similar.
2. The normal process when there are multiple offerings is that the חטאת precedes the עולה, and that is even true when a *nazir*'s period of *nezirut* is broken by impurity (see v. 11). In what order does the Torah describe these offerings when the *nezirut* comes to its successful completion?

WISDOM OF THE HEART

R. Shlomo Ephraim Luntschitz, in his *Keli Yakar*, suggests an innovative reason for the requirement that a *nazir* bring an atonement offering. A person who becomes a *nazir* was obviously lacking something prior to doing so, or he would not have chosen a painful path of self-denial. Little was he aware that the painful path is filled with minefields, as the more restrictions we have the greater our desire to violate them. A healthier approach would have been to find a source of joy and to find a way to get closer to God through an injection of positive energy that would spread throughout the entire self, rather than through a path of suffering, which ultimately makes us associate our relationship with God with pain.

Can you understand why someone might think that the way to get closer to God is by denying themselves certain pleasures? How would you envision a different way to accomplish the same thing?

יג וְזֹאת תּוֹרַת הַנָּזִיר בְּיוֹם מְלֹאת יְמֵי נִזְרוֹ יָבִיא אֹתוֹ אֶל־פֶּתַח אֹהֶל מוֹעֵד: יד וְהִקְרִיב אֶת־קָרְבָּנוֹ לַיהוה כֶּבֶשׂ בֶּן־שְׁנָתוֹ תָמִים אֶחָד לְעֹלָה וְכַבְשָׂה אַחַת בַּת־שְׁנָתָהּ תְּמִימָה לְחַטָּאת וְאַיִל־אֶחָד תָּמִים לִשְׁלָמִים: טו וְסַל מַצּוֹת סֹלֶת חַלֹּת בְּלוּלֹת בַּשֶּׁמֶן וּרְקִיקֵי מַצּוֹת מְשֻׁחִים בַּשָּׁמֶן וּמִנְחָתָם וְנִסְכֵּיהֶם: טז וְהִקְרִיב הַכֹּהֵן לִפְנֵי יהוה וְעָשָׂה אֶת־חַטָּאתוֹ וְאֶת־עֹלָתוֹ: יז וְאֶת־הָאַיִל יַעֲשֶׂה זֶבַח שְׁלָמִים לַיהוה עַל סַל הַמַּצּוֹת וְעָשָׂה הַכֹּהֵן אֶת־מִנְחָתוֹ וְאֶת־נִסְכּוֹ: יח וְגִלַּח הַנָּזִיר פֶּתַח אֹהֶל מוֹעֵד אֶת־רֹאשׁ נִזְרוֹ וְלָקַח אֶת־שְׂעַר רֹאשׁ נִזְרוֹ וְנָתַן עַל־הָאֵשׁ אֲשֶׁר־תַּחַת זֶבַח הַשְּׁלָמִים: יט וְלָקַח הַכֹּהֵן אֶת־הַזְּרֹעַ בְּשֵׁלָה מִן־הָאַיִל וְחַלַּת מַצָּה אַחַת מִן־הַסַּל וּרְקִיק מַצָּה אֶחָד וְנָתַן עַל־כַּפֵּי הַנָּזִיר אַחַר הִתְגַּלְּחוֹ אֶת־נִזְרוֹ: כ וְהֵנִיף אוֹתָם הַכֹּהֵן תְּנוּפָה לִפְנֵי יהוה קֹדֶשׁ הוּא לַכֹּהֵן עַל חֲזֵה הַתְּנוּפָה וְעַל שׁוֹק הַתְּרוּמָה וְאַחַר יִשְׁתֶּה הַנָּזִיר יָיִן: כא זֹאת תּוֹרַת הַנָּזִיר אֲשֶׁר יִדֹּר קָרְבָּנוֹ לַיהוה עַל־נִזְרוֹ מִלְּבַד אֲשֶׁר־תַּשִּׂיג יָדוֹ כְּפִי נִדְרוֹ אֲשֶׁר יִדֹּר כֵּן יַעֲשֶׂה עַל תּוֹרַת נִזְרוֹ:

QUESTIONS FOR THOUGHT

- According to Ramban, what ideal does the concept of the *nazir* represent?
- What about the *nazir* does Rambam find so objectionable?
- If the idea is so objectionable, why does the Torah allow it? *Torat Ha'olah* (Rama) tries to answer the question. What answer does he offer?
- Do you think that the Torah wants us to enjoy the permitted pleasures of this world or to separate ourselves from them? Which of those two paths would bring you to a higher appreciation of God?

6:22–27 *The kohanim are instructed to bless the people with a triple blessing, following a precise formulation. God promises His blessing.*

22 The LORD spoke to Moshe: "Tell Aharon and his sons: This is how you are to bless the
23
24 Israelites. Say to them: 'May the LORD bless you and watch over you. May the LORD
25
26 make His face shine upon you and be gracious to you. May the LORD raise His face
27 toward you and grant you peace.' They shall set My name upon the Israelites, and I will

---

TEXTUAL SKILLS

1. Notice the progression in the blessings, both in the number of words in each and in the numbers of letters in each.
2. An aspect of the blessing which appears twice describes God's "face" being directed at the people as a source of blessing. Leviticus 17:10, 20:5–6, 26:17 all describe God's face directed at *Benei Yisrael* as something negative. Can you find a pattern of when it is considered positive and when it is something to avoid?

WISDOM OF THE HEART

The last line of the blessing of the *kohanim* asks God to show favoritism toward *Benei Yisrael*, literally, for God to "raise His face" toward us. This conflicts with Deuteronomy 10:17, where one of the descriptions of God is that He does not show favoritism, He does not "raise His face" toward us. R. Samson Raphael Hirsch points out that there is a difference between "raising His face" and "raising His face toward" someone. The first, which God doesn't do and which the Torah forbids judges to do, is to show favoritism toward one party in a dispute. The second one, however, the one mentioned in the blessing of the *kohanim*, is the opposite of what is described in the *tokhaḥa*, in which God "hides His face" from us. It means that God pays attention to us, every one of us individually and to all of us as a group. There is no greater blessing than to know that God cares about us and lets us know that He does.

Popular wisdom says that the most important thing you can give in a relationship is the feeling that you genuinely care about the other person, whether a friend, spouse, or other family member. Do you agree or disagree? Can you think of specific examples?

QUICK BITE

There are two blessings which conclude with the word אהבה, love. One is the blessing issued by the *kohanim*; the other is the blessing immediately before the *Shema*. There is a beautiful idea which connects them. The blessing issued by the *kohanim* must come from a place of love, as any blessing given by one person to another is based on profound love and caring. That blessing, however, is not the climax, it only prepares for the climax – the blessing given by God to the Jewish people as a result. The blessing just before the *Shema* operates similarly. We describe God's love for *Benei Yisrael*, choosing to give them the Torah. That blessing, however, is not the climax, but the preparation for the climax – our declaration of our love for God in the *Shema*. God's love for us inspires us to be able to reciprocate.

בְּמִדְבַּר | פרק ו

כב וַיְדַבֵּ֥ר יְהֹוָ֖ה אֶל־מֹשֶׁ֥ה לֵּאמֹֽר: דַּבֵּ֤ר אֶֽל־אַהֲרֹן֙ וְאֶל־בָּנָ֣יו לֵאמֹ֔ר
כד כֹּ֥ה תְבָרְכ֖וּ אֶת־בְּנֵ֣י יִשְׂרָאֵ֑ל אָמ֖וֹר לָהֶֽם: יְבָרֶכְךָ֥ יְהֹוָ֖ה
כה וְיִשְׁמְרֶֽךָ: יָאֵ֨ר יְהֹוָ֧ה ׀ פָּנָ֛יו אֵלֶ֖יךָ וִֽיחֻנֶּֽךָּ: יִשָּׂ֨א
כו יְהֹוָ֤ה ׀ פָּנָיו֙ אֵלֶ֔יךָ וְיָשֵׂ֥ם לְךָ֖ שָׁלֽוֹם: וְשָׂמ֥וּ אֶת־שְׁמִ֖י

CLASSIC COMMENTATORS

The command for the *kohanim* to bless the people is quite puzzling, and some find it troubling. Why does God need the *kohanim* in order to bless the people?

RAV MOSHE ALSHIKH

When the *kohanim* bless the people of Israel, "They shall set My name upon the Israelites, and I will bless them" (Num. 6:27). This means that the *kohanim* prime the masses to receive God's blessing, and prepare them for God's influence. This would not happen if God blessed the nation directly; then the name of the Lord would not be bestowed upon Israel in anticipation of God's involvement.

רב משה אלשי״ך

והטעם, כי הנה על ידי כך "ושמו את שמי על בני ישראל" – הם מכוונים אותם לקבל הברכה ומשפיעים עליהם, מה שאין כן בדברם עמו יתברך "ברכם ה'" – אין אתם משימים שם ה' על ישראל לכוונה אליו.

RABBI SAMSON RAPHAEL HIRSCH

Initially, the *kohanim* and their blessing are passive mechanisms. They become active only once they are called upon by the congregation to proclaim their blessing. It is the power of the community which summons the *kohanim* and activates their benediction. Thus, it is from within the throats of the *kohanim* that the nation blesses itself in the manner commanded by God.

ר׳ שמשון רפאל הירש

הכהנים וברכתם מכשירים נפעלים הם, רק אחרי היקראם על ידי הקהל, הם אומרים את הברכה, אשר בא כוח הקהל מקריא אותה לפניהם: כך באמת מתוך גרונם של הכהנים מברך הקהל את עצמו בברכה שציווה ה׳.

RABBI ISAAC SAMUEL REGGIO

God informs the *kohanim* that they are not actually the true vehicle that confers the blessing upon Israel. Their task is to pronounce the requested blessings with their mouths, whereupon God will honor their appeal.

ר׳ יצחק שמואל רג׳יו

לא אתם המברכים האמתיים ומשפיעים ברכה לישראל אלא אתם תאמרו ורק תוציאו הדברים בפה ואני אמלא משאלותיכם.

QUESTIONS FOR THOUGHT

- Which of the above commentaries actually answers the question above directly?
- In what way do Alshikh and R. Reggio say precisely the opposite of each other?
- Rambam points out that it is important that the person calling out the words to the *kohanim* not be a *kohen*, but one of the people. Which of the above commentaries would be supported by this ruling of Rambam?
- Think about the role of the *kohanim* as described until now in Numbers. Why do you think that the Torah might conclude the focus on the *kohanim* by giving this particular mitzva?
- Do you think that *kohanim* have a special power to bless? Do you think that any individual has a special power to bless, or does God bless whom He chooses without the intervention of humans?

BEMIDBAR | CHAPTER 7 NASO | 58

7 1 bless them." On the day when Moshe finished establishing the Tabernacle, he anointed
2 it and consecrated it. He anointed and consecrated the altar, too, and all its utensils. And the princes of Israel, leaders of their ancestral houses, drew close. They were the princes
3 of the tribes, the ones who had directed the census. And they brought their offerings before the Lord: six covered wagons and twelve oxen – a wagon for every two leaders,
4 and for each one an ox. They presented them before the Tabernacle. The Lord said
5 to Moshe, "Accept these from them and use them for service in the Tent of Meeting.
6 Give them to the Levites, to each according to his service." Moshe took the wagons
7 and the oxen, and he gave them to the Levites. He gave two wagons and four oxen to
8 the Gershonites as their service required. He gave four wagons and eight oxen to the
9 Merarites for their service under the supervision of Itamar son of Aharon the priest. But to the Kohatites he gave none, for their responsibility was for the sacred articles that

ר' שמשון רפאל הירש

"צב" נמצא גם בספר ישעיהו (סו:כ), כדבר המשמש להובלה... "צב" קרוב באופן הגייתו ל"סבב", וכנראה שהוא מורה על המחיצות המקיפות את כל צדדי העגלה, והמגִנות על האנשים או החפצים הנמצאים בעגלה. החלקים שמהם הורכב המשכן לא היו מכוסים בעת שהועמסו על העגלות; ולפיכך היה צורך בכיסוי על העגלות.

RABBI SAMSON RAPHAEL HIRSCH

The term *tzav* appears also in Isaiah (66:20), where it refers to a method of transport.... Meanwhile the word *tzav* resembles the term *savav* [surrounding] and suggests the canvas that encircles the sides of a wagon. This serves to protect the people and the objects which are being carried inside the vehicle. For the parts of the *Mishkan* structure were not wrapped in any kind of tarpaulin before being loaded onto the wagons. Therefore the carriage itself had to be covered.

QUESTIONS FOR THOUGHT

- Both Ibn Ezra and R. Hirsch use the same verse from Isaiah, but they come to very different conclusions about what the word means. Which of those two do you think does a better job of explaining why that word is used here?
- *Ho'il Moshe* explains that they are wagons with a "swollen belly," meaning that the underside is low to the ground because it is overloaded. Rashbam has a different derivation of the word. Both seem to try to find a meaning based on context – the fact that this word is used earlier in Numbers. What context did each of them find in Numbers to help them draw their conclusions about what the word means?

TEXTUAL SKILLS

1. What phrase appears to be repeated in verse 1? Can you find a reason for the repetition?
2. The Torah identifies that these tribal princes were the same as those mentioned in chapter 1, who assisted in the census. Which of those events took place first, the census or the dedication of the *Mishkan*?

WISDOM OF THE HEART

According to a midrash, Moshe was hesitant to take the offerings of the tribal princes until God instructed him explicitly. The items they donated were not on the list that God gave to Moshe at the beginning of the project; with the shadow of the golden calf hanging over the people Moshe wanted to make sure that nothing would go beyond God's exact instructions.

במדבר | פרק ז

א וַיְהִי בְּיוֹם כַּלּוֹת חמישי עַל־בְּנֵי יִשְׂרָאֵל וַאֲנִי אֲבָרֲכֵם:
מֹשֶׁה לְהָקִים אֶת־הַמִּשְׁכָּן וַיִּמְשַׁח אֹתוֹ וַיְקַדֵּשׁ אֹתוֹ וְאֶת־
כָּל־כֵּלָיו וְאֶת־הַמִּזְבֵּחַ וְאֶת־כָּל־כֵּלָיו וַיִּמְשָׁחֵם וַיְקַדֵּשׁ אֹתָם:
ב וַיַּקְרִיבוּ נְשִׂיאֵי יִשְׂרָאֵל רָאשֵׁי בֵּית אֲבֹתָם הֵם נְשִׂיאֵי הַמַּטֹּת
הֵם הָעֹמְדִים עַל־הַפְּקֻדִים: ג וַיָּבִיאוּ אֶת־קָרְבָּנָם לִפְנֵי יהוה
שֵׁשׁ־עֶגְלֹת צָב וּשְׁנֵי־עָשָׂר בָּקָר עֲגָלָה עַל־שְׁנֵי הַנְּשִׂאִים וְשׁוֹר
לְאֶחָד וַיַּקְרִיבוּ אוֹתָם לִפְנֵי הַמִּשְׁכָּן: ד וַיֹּאמֶר יהוה אֶל־מֹשֶׁה
לֵּאמֹר: ה קַח מֵאִתָּם וְהָיוּ לַעֲבֹד אֶת־עֲבֹדַת אֹהֶל מוֹעֵד וְנָתַתָּה
אוֹתָם אֶל־הַלְוִיִּם אִישׁ כְּפִי עֲבֹדָתוֹ: ו וַיִּקַּח מֹשֶׁה אֶת־הָעֲגָלֹת
וְאֶת־הַבָּקָר וַיִּתֵּן אוֹתָם אֶל־הַלְוִיִּם: ז אֵת ׀ שְׁתֵּי הָעֲגָלֹת וְאֵת
אַרְבַּעַת הַבָּקָר נָתַן לִבְנֵי גֵרְשׁוֹן כְּפִי עֲבֹדָתָם: ח וְאֵת ׀ אַרְבַּע
הָעֲגָלֹת וְאֵת שְׁמֹנַת הַבָּקָר נָתַן לִבְנֵי מְרָרִי כְּפִי עֲבֹדָתָם בְּיַד
אִיתָמָר בֶּן־אַהֲרֹן הַכֹּהֵן: ט וְלִבְנֵי קְהָת לֹא נָתָן כִּי־עֲבֹדַת הַקֹּדֶשׁ

CLASSIC COMMENTATORS

The word צב is used in verse 3. That word appears only one other time in all of Tanakh, and the meaning there is unclear. The commentaries debate its meaning here.

IBN EZRA — אבן עזרא

In the verse, "on horseback and on chariot, on *tzabbim*, mules, dromedaries" (Isaiah 66:20), the term refers to a type of ox harnessed to wagons.

כמו: "ובצבים ובפרדים" (ישעיהו סו:כ), מין ממיני השורים מושכין העגלות.

RASHBAM — רשב״ם

It seems to me that the word *tzav* relates to the fact that these wagons are intended to be used by the army [*tzava*] to cover great distances.

ונראה בעיני: עגלות העשויות להלוך בצבא ובדרכים רחוקים.

HO'IL MOSHE — הואיל משה

The Torah describes covered wagons whose bellies swell [*tzava*].

עגלות מכוסות שבטנן צבה.

BEMIDBAR | CHAPTER 7

NASO

> **7:10–17** *The tribal princes brought individual offerings in honor of the dedication of the altar. The first to bring was Naḥshon son of Aminadav, head of the tribe of Yehuda.*

10 had to be carried on their shoulders. The princes presented their dedication offering for the altar at the time when it was anointed. The princes brought their offerings before
11 the altar. The LORD said to Moshe, "Each day one prince is to bring close his offering
12 for the dedication of the altar." The one who presented his offering on the first day was
13 Naḥshon son of Aminadav, from the tribe of Yehuda. His offering was one silver bowl weighing one hundred and thirty shekel and one silver basin weighing seventy shekel according to the Sanctuary weight, both filled with fine flour mixed with oil for a grain
14
15 offering; one golden spoon weighing ten shekel, full of incense; one young bull, one
16 ram, and one yearling sheep for a burnt offering; one goat for a purification offering;
17 and for the peace sacrifice two oxen, five rams, five male goats, and five yearling sheep. This was the offering of Naḥshon son of Aminadav.

QUESTIONS FOR THOUGHT

- According to Ramban, why did the leaders initially bring the wagons and the oxen?
- Which of the commentaries understands that they initially planned to bring two separate offerings?
- Why do you think that they would bring both a joint offering and individual ones? Can you think of a similar practice which happens regularly in Jewish life?

TEXTUAL SKILLS

1. The timing of these offerings is described in verse 10. Notice how it is different from the timing described later in verse 88.
2. Notice which tribe is the first to bring the offering.
3. Notice that there appears to be much repetition in verses 10–11.

WISDOM OF THE HEART

On each of the seven days of the dedication of the *Mishkan* it was assembled in the morning and disassembled in the evening, and was used only for the special inaugural offerings; God's presence didn't appear until the inaugural period was over, on the eighth day. Rav Dovid Feinstein points out that the only way to get to that eighth day is to first go through the first seven. The rising again and again after each falling is a necessary component of growth and of moving forward.

How do we know when we are supposed to continue trying, despite the setbacks, and when we are supposed to accept the reality that the result we are looking to achieve might not be possible for us and we must accept our limitations?

עֲלֵהֶ֣ם בַּכָּתֵ֔ף יִשָּֽׂאוּ׃ וַיַּקְרִ֣יבוּ הַנְּשִׂאִ֗ים אֵ֚ת חֲנֻכַּ֣ת הַמִּזְבֵּ֔חַ בְּי֖וֹם הִמָּשַׁ֣ח אֹת֑וֹ וַיַּקְרִ֧יבוּ הַנְּשִׂיאִ֛ם אֶת־קָרְבָּנָ֖ם לִפְנֵ֥י הַמִּזְבֵּֽחַ׃

יא וַיֹּ֥אמֶר יְהֹוָ֖ה אֶל־מֹשֶׁ֑ה נָשִׂ֨יא אֶחָ֜ד לַיּ֗וֹם נָשִׂ֤יא אֶחָד֙ לַיּ֔וֹם יַקְרִ֨יבוּ֙ אֶת־קָרְבָּנָ֔ם לַחֲנֻכַּ֖ת הַמִּזְבֵּֽחַ׃

יב וַיְהִ֗י הַמַּקְרִ֛יב בַּיּ֥וֹם הָרִאשׁ֖וֹן אֶת־קָרְבָּנ֑וֹ נַחְשׁ֥וֹן בֶּן־עַמִּינָדָ֖ב לְמַטֵּ֥ה יְהוּדָֽה׃

יג וְקָרְבָּנ֞וֹ קַֽעֲרַת־כֶּ֣סֶף אַחַ֗ת שְׁלֹשִׁ֣ים וּמֵאָה֮ מִשְׁקָלָהּ֒ מִזְרָ֤ק אֶחָד֙ כֶּ֔סֶף שִׁבְעִ֥ים שֶׁ֖קֶל בְּשֶׁ֣קֶל הַקֹּ֑דֶשׁ שְׁנֵיהֶ֣ם ׀ מְלֵאִ֗ים סֹ֛לֶת בְּלוּלָ֥ה בַשֶּׁ֖מֶן לְמִנְחָֽה׃

יד כַּ֥ף אַחַ֛ת עֲשָׂרָ֥ה זָהָ֖ב מְלֵאָ֥ה קְטֹֽרֶת׃

טו פַּ֣ר אֶחָ֞ד בֶּן־בָּקָ֗ר אַ֧יִל אֶחָ֛ד כֶּֽבֶשׂ־אֶחָ֥ד בֶּן־שְׁנָת֖וֹ לְעֹלָֽה׃

טז שְׂעִיר־עִזִּ֥ים אֶחָ֖ד לְחַטָּֽאת׃

יז וּלְזֶ֣בַח הַשְּׁלָמִים֮ בָּקָ֣ר שְׁנַ֒יִם֒ אֵילִ֤ם חֲמִשָּׁה֙ עַתֻּדִ֣ים חֲמִשָּׁ֔ה כְּבָשִׂ֥ים בְּנֵֽי־שָׁנָ֖ה חֲמִשָּׁ֑ה זֶ֛ה קָרְבַּ֥ן נַחְשׁ֖וֹן בֶּן־עַמִּינָדָֽב׃

CLASSIC COMMENTATORS

It seems as though the tribal princes brought two different offerings, one a joint offering and the other individual ones.

RASHI

After the princes offered the wagons and the oxen for transporting the *Mishkan*, they were eager to donate sacrifices for the dedication of the altar.

RAMBAN

The tribal princes "brought their offerings before the Lord: six covered wagons" (Num. 7:3), meaning six large carriages to transport their sacrifices, "and twelve oxen" to pull those vehicles. Now the princes brought these wagons loaded with their sacrificial animals "before the Tabernacle," whereupon God commanded Moshe, "Accept these from them" (7:5) – take everything they have brought. The intention was that the wagons and the beasts that were not meant for offerings were to be used "for service in the Tent of Meeting." Subsequently, these men removed their offerings from the wagon beds, and brought them toward the altar.... The Lord ordered that "Each day one prince is to bring close his offering for the dedication of the altar" (7:11).

רש״י

לאחר שהתנדבו העגלות והבקר לשאת המשכן, נתנו לבם להתנדב קרבנות על המזבח לחנכו.

רמב״ן

ויתכן שנפרש ויביאו את קרבנם לה׳ שש עגלות צב - שש עגלות גדולות נושאות קרבניהם, ושנים עשר בקר - מושכים העגלות, והנה הביאו העגלות מלאות והבקר לפני המשכן, והשם צוה את משה: קח מאתם הכל, והיו העגלות והבקר שאינם לקרבן לעבוד את עבודת אהל מועד (ז:ה). ואחר כך לקחו הנשיאים את קרבניהם מעל העגלות, ויקריבו אותם לפני המזבח, והשם צוה: נשיא אחד ליום יקריבו (ז:י״א).

7:18–89 On each of the first twelve days of the dedication of the Mishkan a different tribal leader brought an individual offering representing his tribe, and all were identical. Meanwhile, Moshe would enter to hear God's message, which he heard coming from above the kaporet and from between the two cherubim.

18
19 On the second day Netanel son of Tzuar, prince of Yissakhar, presented his offering. He presented as his offering one silver bowl weighing one hundred and thirty shekel and one silver basin weighing seventy shekel according to the Sanctuary weight, both filled
20 with fine flour mixed with oil for a grain offering; one golden spoon weighing ten shekel,
21
22 full of incense; one young bull, one ram, and one yearling sheep for a burnt offering; one
23 goat for a purification offering; and for the peace sacrifice two oxen, five rams, five male goats, and five yearling sheep. This was the offering of Netanel son of Tzuar.

RAMBAN

The Holy One, blessed be He, honors those who revere Him. As such, God wished to mention each of the tribal princes by name, to list their sacrifices, and to specify which day their offerings were submitted. It would have been disrespectful for the Torah to say on the first day, "This was the offering of Naḥshon son of Aminadav," and subsequently to merely summarize the gifts of the other princes by saying, "So-and-so also brought what the first fellow offered." The final summary of the donations emphasizes that God considered all of the gifts to be of equal value.

רמב"ן

והנכון בטעם הכתוב, כי הקב"ה חולק כבוד ליראיו... רצה להזכירם בשמם ובפרט קרבניהם ולהזכיר יומו של כל אחד, לא שיזכיר ויכבד את הראשון ויאמר "זה קרבן נחשון בן עמינדב", ויאמר "וכן הקריבו הנשיאים איש איש יומו", כי יהיה זה קיצור בכבוד האחרים, ואחרי כן חזר וכללם להגיד שהיו שקולים לפניו.

QUESTIONS FOR THOUGHT

- The midrash understands that the offerings were identical, but also dramatically different from each prince. What does that mean?
- Do Ibn Kaspi and Ramban agree with the midrash, that the offerings were dramatically different, or disagree?
- Ibn Kaspi and Ramban disagree as to who this extensive repetition is meant to benefit. What does each of them say?

TEXTUAL SKILLS

1. In what order do the tribal leaders bring their offerings?
2. Compare verse 12, introducing Naḥshon's offering, with the parallel verses introducing the offering of the other tribal leaders (18, 24, 30, 36, etc.). What differences do you find?

יט בַּיּוֹם֙ הַשֵּׁנִ֔י הִקְרִ֖יב נְתַנְאֵ֣ל בֶּן־צוּעָ֑ר נְשִׂ֖יא יִשָּׂשכָֽר: הִקְרִ֨ב אֶת־קָרְבָּנ֜וֹ קַֽעֲרַת־כֶּ֣סֶף אַחַ֗ת שְׁלֹשִׁ֣ים וּמֵאָה֮ מִשְׁקָלָהּ֒ מִזְרָ֤ק אֶחָד֙ כֶּ֔סֶף שִׁבְעִ֣ים שֶׁ֔קֶל בְּשֶׁ֖קֶל הַקֹּ֑דֶשׁ שְׁנֵיהֶ֣ם ׀ מְלֵאִ֗ים סֹ֛לֶת בְּלוּלָ֥ה בַשֶּׁ֖מֶן לְמִנְחָֽה: כ כַּ֥ף אַחַ֛ת עֲשָׂרָ֥ה זָהָ֖ב מְלֵאָ֥ה קְטֹֽרֶת: כא פַּ֣ר אֶחָ֞ד בֶּן־בָּקָ֗ר אַ֧יִל אֶחָ֛ד כֶּֽבֶשׂ־אֶחָ֥ד בֶּן־שְׁנָת֖וֹ לְעֹלָֽה: כב שְׂעִיר־עִזִּ֥ים אֶחָ֖ד לְחַטָּֽאת: כג וּלְזֶ֣בַח הַשְּׁלָמִים֮ בָּקָ֣ר שְׁנַ֒יִם֒ אֵילִ֤ם חֲמִשָּׁה֙ עַתּוּדִ֣ים חֲמִשָּׁ֔ה כְּבָשִׂ֥ים בְּנֵֽי־שָׁנָ֖ה חֲמִשָּׁ֑ה זֶ֛ה קָרְבַּ֥ן נְתַנְאֵ֖ל בֶּן־צוּעָֽר:

CLASSIC COMMENTATORS

Why does the Torah need to repeat the details of each of the offerings when they are absolutely identical, word for word? Would it not have been simpler to write it once and then simply list the names of each of the tribal leaders who brought it?

BEMIDBAR RABBA

Even though each set of sacrifices was identical to all the others, the princes intended for their items to symbolize great and important matters, and each individual brought these objects according to his own thoughts.

במדבר רבה

אף על פי שקרבן שוה הקריבו כולם, על דברים גדולים הקריבו וכל אחד ואחד הקריבו לפי דעתו.

RABBI YOSEF IBN KASPI

The Torah discusses a matter at length when it is addressing the masses rather than individuals. We find such an example in the narrative following the construction of the *Mishkan*. Similarly, the text provides great detail when it first commands that this center be built. This is why the Torah spends so much time listing the particulars of the donations to the *Mishkan* by the nation and its leaders. The reader gets the sense of the grandness of these gifts by the fact that the text lists their specifics over and over. Contributing to this understanding is the summary that appears at the end of the story, "All this was the dedication offering from the princes of Israel for the altar at the time it was anointed: There were twelve silver bowls, twelve silver basins, and twelve golden spoons" (Num. 7:84).

ר' יוסף אבן כספי

אריכות לשון נמצא ברוב בספר תורתנו במה שהוא נתלה בענין שכוונתו הראשונה הוא להמון העם ולא ליחידים. ולכן זה הסיפור שהוא הנמשך אחרי בנין המשכן ... הנה כמו שאריכו הדברים בבנין המשכן תחילה בציווי הראשון, ואחר בסיפור מעשהו ואחר בהקמתו, נמשך לו ... התנדבות העם וראשיהם לחנוכת אותו הבית הנכבד; לכן האריך בסיפור פרטי זאת הנדבה המופלגת. ואנחנו בכללנו נרגיש בהפלגתה בכפילת סיפורה פעמים רבות ורבות, וגם בחיבור סכום מספרה באחרית הסיפור כמו שיעשה באמרו (פסוק פ"ד) "זאת חנוכת המזבח ... מאת נשיאי ישראל קערות כסף שתים עשרה, מזרקי כסף שנים עשר...".

24,25 On the third day came Eliav son of Ḥelon, prince of the Zebulunites: His offering was one silver bowl weighing one hundred and thirty shekel and one silver basin weighing seventy shekel according to the Sanctuary weight, both filled with fine flour mixed with 26,27 oil for a grain offering; one golden spoon weighing ten shekel, full of incense; one young 28 bull, one ram, and one yearling sheep for a burnt offering; one goat for a purification 29 offering; and for the peace sacrifice two oxen, five rams, five male goats, and five yearling sheep. This was the offering of Eliav son of Ḥelon.

30,31 On the fourth day came Elitzur son of Shedeiur, prince of the Reubenites: His offering was one silver bowl weighing one hundred and thirty shekel and one silver basin weighing seventy shekel according to the Sanctuary weight, both filled with fine flour mixed 32,33 with oil for a grain offering; one golden spoon weighing ten shekel, full of incense; one 34 young bull, one ram, and one yearling sheep for a burnt offering; one goat for a purifi- 35 cation offering; and for the peace sacrifice two oxen, five rams, five male goats, and five yearling sheep. This was the offering of Elitzur son of Shedeiur.

36,37 On the fifth day came Shelumiel son of Tzurishadai, prince of the Simeonites: His offering was one silver bowl weighing one hundred and thirty shekel and one silver basin weighing seventy shekel according to the Sanctuary weight, both filled with fine

---

WISDOM OF THE HEART

The extreme repetition of the daily offerings of the tribal princes – a detailed listing for each of the twelve heads, using the same exact words for each – demands our attention. According to a midrash, although the offerings were identical, the intention of each of the tribal leaders was different. That suggests that intent can have a profound impact on the nature of the offering, so that even though they looked identical on the surface they were actually very different. This can be helpful when we apply it to our experiences, like *tefilla*. We say the same *Amida* three times a day, six days a week. The words almost never change. But if our intentions are different, then each prayer becomes its own unique entity, even though on the surface it looks the same. Perhaps even more amazing is that we can be in a room with dozens or hundreds of others people, each saying the same words, but each having a unique and individual experience of *tefilla*.

In your own tefilla, you might want to consider taking a moment each day before you start and decide to focus on a different blessing to concentrate on. You will quickly discover how every tefilla in a week can turn out to be different.

The Torah describes the dedication of the *Mishkan* in three different places, each with its own focus. R. Ezra Bick suggests that the one at the end of Exodus features Moshe's role in bringing the *Mishkan* to completion. The second story, in the beginning of Leviticus, focuses on the *kohanim* – their roles and their personal sacrifices. The third, in Numbers, places the emphasis on the distributed leadership of *Benei Yisrael* as illustrated by the special role played by the tribal leaders.

כה בַּיּוֹם֙ הַשְּׁלִישִׁ֔י נָשִׂ֖יא לִבְנֵ֣י זְבוּלֻ֑ן אֱלִיאָ֖ב בֶּן־חֵלֹֽן: קָרְבָּנ֞וֹ קַֽעֲרַת־
כֶּ֣סֶף אַחַ֗ת שְׁלֹשִׁ֣ים וּמֵאָה֮ מִשְׁקָלָהּ֒ מִזְרָ֤ק אֶחָד֙ כֶּ֔סֶף שִׁבְעִ֥ים
שֶׁ֖קֶל בְּשֶׁ֣קֶל הַקֹּ֑דֶשׁ שְׁנֵיהֶ֣ם ׀ מְלֵאִ֗ים סֹ֛לֶת בְּלוּלָ֥ה בַשֶּׁ֖מֶן
כו לְמִנְחָֽה: כַּ֥ף אַחַ֛ת עֲשָׂרָ֥ה זָהָ֖ב מְלֵאָ֥ה קְטֹֽרֶת: פַּ֣ר אֶחָ֞ד בֶּן־
כז בָּקָ֗ר אַ֧יִל אֶחָ֛ד כֶּֽבֶשׂ־אֶחָ֥ד בֶּן־שְׁנָת֖וֹ לְעֹלָֽה: שְׂעִיר־עִזִּ֥ים
כח אֶחָ֖ד לְחַטָּֽאת: וּלְזֶ֣בַח הַשְּׁלָמִים֮ בָּקָ֣ר שְׁנַ֒יִם֒ אֵילִ֤ם חֲמִשָּׁה֙
כט עַתֻּדִ֣ים חֲמִשָּׁ֔ה כְּבָשִׂ֥ים בְּנֵֽי־שָׁנָ֖ה חֲמִשָּׁ֑ה זֶ֛ה קָרְבַּ֥ן אֱלִיאָ֖ב
בֶּן־חֵלֹֽן:

ל בַּיּוֹם֙ הָרְבִיעִ֔י נָשִׂ֖יא לִבְנֵ֣י רְאוּבֵ֑ן אֱלִיצ֖וּר בֶּן־שְׁדֵיאֽוּר: קָרְבָּנ֞וֹ
לא קַֽעֲרַת־כֶּ֣סֶף אַחַ֗ת שְׁלֹשִׁ֣ים וּמֵאָה֮ מִשְׁקָלָהּ֒ מִזְרָ֤ק אֶחָד֙ כֶּ֔סֶף
שִׁבְעִ֥ים שֶׁ֖קֶל בְּשֶׁ֣קֶל הַקֹּ֑דֶשׁ שְׁנֵיהֶ֣ם ׀ מְלֵאִ֗ים סֹ֛לֶת בְּלוּלָ֥ה
לב בַשֶּׁ֖מֶן לְמִנְחָֽה: כַּ֥ף אַחַ֛ת עֲשָׂרָ֥ה זָהָ֖ב מְלֵאָ֥ה קְטֹֽרֶת: פַּ֣ר אֶחָ֞ד
לג בֶּן־בָּקָ֗ר אַ֧יִל אֶחָ֛ד כֶּֽבֶשׂ־אֶחָ֥ד בֶּן־שְׁנָת֖וֹ לְעֹלָֽה: שְׂעִיר־עִזִּ֥ים
לד אֶחָ֖ד לְחַטָּֽאת: וּלְזֶ֣בַח הַשְּׁלָמִים֮ בָּקָ֣ר שְׁנַ֒יִם֒ אֵילִ֤ם חֲמִשָּׁה֙
לה עַתֻּדִ֣ים חֲמִשָּׁ֔ה כְּבָשִׂ֥ים בְּנֵֽי־שָׁנָ֖ה חֲמִשָּׁ֑ה זֶ֛ה קָרְבַּ֥ן אֱלִיצ֖וּר
בֶּן־שְׁדֵיאֽוּר:

לו בַּיּוֹם֙ הַֽחֲמִישִׁ֔י נָשִׂ֖יא לִבְנֵ֣י שִׁמְע֑וֹן שְׁלֻֽמִיאֵ֖ל בֶּן־צוּרִֽישַׁדָּֽי:
לז קָרְבָּנ֞וֹ קַֽעֲרַת־כֶּ֣סֶף אַחַ֗ת שְׁלֹשִׁ֣ים וּמֵאָה֮ מִשְׁקָלָהּ֒ מִזְרָ֤ק אֶחָד֙

QUICK BITE

The word **מדבר**, in verse 89, is written with unusual vowels, suggesting to Rashi that it needs to be read as describing God speaking with Himself, which Moshe overhears. R. Meir Druck saw this as a metaphor for all communication. Before you speak with someone else, imagine you saying those things to yourself. How would you react if someone said those things to you? Only then should you allow yourself to have others "overhear" your message to them.

38 flour mixed with oil for a grain offering; one golden spoon weighing ten shekel, full
39 of incense; one young bull, one ram, and one yearling sheep for a burnt offering; one
40
41 goat for a purification offering; and for the peace sacrifice two oxen, five rams, five male goats, and five yearling sheep. This was the offering of Shelumiel son of Tzurishadai.
42
43 On the sixth day came Elyasaf son of Deuel, prince of the Gadites: His offering was one silver bowl weighing one hundred and thirty shekel and one silver basin weighing seventy shekel according to the Sanctuary weight, both filled with fine flour mixed with
44
45 oil for a grain offering; one golden spoon weighing ten shekel, full of incense; one young
46 bull, one ram, and one yearling sheep for a burnt offering; one goat for a purification
47 offering; and for the peace sacrifice two oxen, five rams, five male goats, and five yearling sheep. This was the offering of Elyasaf son of Deuel.
48
49 On the seventh day came Elishama son of Amihud, prince of the Efraimites: His offering was one silver bowl weighing one hundred and thirty shekel and one silver basin weighing seventy shekel according to the Sanctuary weight, both filled with fine flour mixed
50
51 with oil for a grain offering; one golden spoon weighing ten shekel, full of incense; one
52 young bull, one ram, and one yearling sheep for a burnt offering; one goat for a purifi-
53 cation offering; and for the peace sacrifice two oxen, five rams, five male goats, and five yearling sheep. This was the offering of Elishama son of Amihud.

כֶּ֣סֶף שִׁבְעִ֣ים שֶׁ֔קֶל בְּשֶׁ֖קֶל הַקֹּ֑דֶשׁ שְׁנֵיהֶ֣ם ׀ מְלֵאִ֗ים סֹ֛לֶת בְּלוּלָ֥ה בַשֶּׁ֖מֶן לְמִנְחָֽה: כַּ֥ף אַחַ֛ת עֲשָׂרָ֥ה זָהָ֖ב מְלֵאָ֥ה קְטֹֽרֶת: פַּ֣ר אֶחָ֞ד בֶּן־בָּקָ֗ר אַ֧יִל אֶחָ֛ד כֶּֽבֶשׂ־אֶחָ֥ד בֶּן־שְׁנָת֖וֹ לְעֹלָֽה: שְׂעִיר־עִזִּ֥ים אֶחָ֖ד לְחַטָּֽאת: וּלְזֶ֣בַח הַשְּׁלָמִים֮ בָּקָ֣ר שְׁנַ֒יִם֒ אֵילִ֤ם חֲמִשָּׁה֙ עַתּוּדִ֣ים חֲמִשָּׁ֔ה כְּבָשִׂ֥ים בְּנֵֽי־שָׁנָ֖ה חֲמִשָּׁ֑ה זֶ֛ה קָרְבַּ֥ן שְׁלֻֽמִיאֵ֖ל בֶּן־צוּרִֽישַׁדָּֽי:

בַּיּוֹם֙ הַשִּׁשִּׁ֔י נָשִׂ֖יא לִבְנֵ֣י גָ֑ד אֶלְיָסָ֖ף בֶּן־דְּעוּאֵֽל: קָרְבָּנ֞וֹ קַעֲרַת־כֶּ֣סֶף אַחַ֗ת שְׁלֹשִׁ֣ים וּמֵאָה֮ מִשְׁקָלָהּ֒ מִזְרָ֤ק אֶחָד֙ כֶּ֔סֶף שִׁבְעִ֥ים שֶׁ֖קֶל בְּשֶׁ֣קֶל הַקֹּ֑דֶשׁ שְׁנֵיהֶ֣ם ׀ מְלֵאִ֗ים סֹ֛לֶת בְּלוּלָ֥ה בַשֶּׁ֖מֶן לְמִנְחָֽה: כַּ֥ף אַחַ֛ת עֲשָׂרָ֥ה זָהָ֖ב מְלֵאָ֥ה קְטֹֽרֶת: פַּ֣ר אֶחָ֞ד בֶּן־בָּקָ֗ר אַ֧יִל אֶחָ֛ד כֶּֽבֶשׂ־אֶחָ֥ד בֶּן־שְׁנָת֖וֹ לְעֹלָֽה: שְׂעִיר־עִזִּ֥ים אֶחָ֖ד לְחַטָּֽאת: וּלְזֶ֣בַח הַשְּׁלָמִים֮ בָּקָ֣ר שְׁנַ֒יִם֒ אֵילִ֤ם חֲמִשָּׁה֙ עַתּוּדִ֣ים חֲמִשָּׁ֔ה כְּבָשִׂ֥ים בְּנֵֽי־שָׁנָ֖ה חֲמִשָּׁ֑ה זֶ֛ה קָרְבַּ֥ן אֶלְיָסָ֖ף בֶּן־דְּעוּאֵֽל:

בַּיּוֹם֙ הַשְּׁבִיעִ֔י נָשִׂ֖יא לִבְנֵ֣י אֶפְרָ֑יִם אֱלִֽישָׁמָ֖ע בֶּן־עַמִּיהֽוּד: קָרְבָּנ֞וֹ קַעֲרַת־כֶּ֣סֶף אַחַ֗ת שְׁלֹשִׁ֣ים וּמֵאָה֮ מִשְׁקָלָהּ֒ מִזְרָ֤ק אֶחָד֙ כֶּ֔סֶף שִׁבְעִ֥ים שֶׁ֖קֶל בְּשֶׁ֣קֶל הַקֹּ֑דֶשׁ שְׁנֵיהֶ֣ם ׀ מְלֵאִ֗ים סֹ֛לֶת בְּלוּלָ֥ה בַשֶּׁ֖מֶן לְמִנְחָֽה: כַּ֥ף אַחַ֛ת עֲשָׂרָ֥ה זָהָ֖ב מְלֵאָ֥ה קְטֹֽרֶת: פַּ֣ר אֶחָ֞ד בֶּן־בָּקָ֗ר אַ֧יִל אֶחָ֛ד כֶּֽבֶשׂ־אֶחָ֥ד בֶּן־שְׁנָת֖וֹ לְעֹלָֽה: שְׂעִיר־עִזִּ֥ים אֶחָ֖ד לְחַטָּֽאת: וּלְזֶ֣בַח הַשְּׁלָמִים֮ בָּקָ֣ר שְׁנַ֒יִם֒ אֵילִ֤ם חֲמִשָּׁה֙ עַתּוּדִ֣ים חֲמִשָּׁ֔ה כְּבָשִׂ֥ים בְּנֵֽי־שָׁנָ֖ה חֲמִשָּׁ֑ה זֶ֛ה קָרְבַּ֥ן אֱלִֽישָׁמָ֖ע בֶּן־עַמִּיהֽוּד:

⁵⁴ ⁵⁵ On the eighth day came Gamliel son of Pedahtzur, prince of the Manassites: His offering was one silver bowl weighing one hundred and thirty shekel and one silver basin weighing seventy shekel according to the Sanctuary weight, both filled with fine flour mixed ⁵⁶ ⁵⁷ with oil for a grain offering; one golden spoon weighing ten shekel, full of incense; one ⁵⁸ young bull, one ram, and one yearling sheep for a burnt offering; one goat for a purifi- ⁵⁹ cation offering; and for the peace sacrifice two oxen, five rams, five male goats, and five yearling sheep. This was the offering of Gamliel son of Pedahtzur.

⁶⁰ ⁶¹ On the ninth day came Avidan son of Gidoni, prince of the Benjaminites: His offering was one silver bowl weighing one hundred and thirty shekel and one silver basin weighing seventy shekel according to the Sanctuary weight, both filled with fine flour mixed ⁶² ⁶³ with oil for a grain offering; one golden spoon weighing ten shekel, full of incense; one ⁶⁴ young bull, one ram, and one yearling sheep for a burnt offering; one goat for a purifi- ⁶⁵ cation offering; and for the peace sacrifice two oxen, five rams, five male goats, and five yearling sheep. This was the offering of Avidan son of Gidoni.

⁶⁶ ⁶⁷ On the tenth day came Aḥiezer son of Amishadai, prince of the Danites: His offering was one silver bowl weighing one hundred and thirty shekel and one silver basin weighing seventy shekel according to the Sanctuary weight, both filled with fine flour mixed with ⁶⁸ ⁶⁹ oil for a grain offering; one golden spoon weighing ten shekel, full of incense; one young ⁷⁰ bull, one ram, and one yearling sheep for a burnt offering; one goat for a purification ⁷¹ offering; and for the peace sacrifice two oxen, five rams, five male goats, and five yearling sheep. This was the offering of Aḥiezer son of Amishadai.

| נה | בַּיּוֹם֙ הַשְּׁמִינִ֔י נָשִׂ֖יא לִבְנֵ֣י מְנַשֶּׁ֑ה גַּמְלִיאֵ֖ל בֶּן־פְּדָהצֽוּר: קָרְבָּנ֞וֹ קַעֲרַת־כֶּ֣סֶף אַחַ֗ת שְׁלֹשִׁ֣ים וּמֵאָה֮ מִשְׁקָלָהּ֒ מִזְרָ֤ק אֶחָד֙ כֶּ֔סֶף שִׁבְעִ֥ים שֶׁ֖קֶל בְּשֶׁ֣קֶל הַקֹּ֑דֶשׁ שְׁנֵיהֶ֣ם ׀ מְלֵאִ֗ים סֹ֛לֶת בְּלוּלָ֥ה
| נו | בַשֶּׁ֖מֶן לְמִנְחָֽה: כַּ֥ף אַחַ֛ת עֲשָׂרָ֥ה זָהָ֖ב מְלֵאָ֥ה קְטֹֽרֶת: פַּ֣ר אֶחָ֞ד
| נז | בֶּן־בָּקָ֗ר אַ֧יִל אֶחָ֛ד כֶּֽבֶשׂ־אֶחָ֥ד בֶּן־שְׁנָת֖וֹ לְעֹלָֽה: שְׂעִיר־עִזִּ֥ים
| נח | אֶחָ֖ד לְחַטָּֽאת: וּלְזֶ֣בַח הַשְּׁלָמִים֮ בָּקָ֣ר שְׁנַ֒יִם֒ אֵילִ֤ם חֲמִשָּׁה֙
| נט | עַתֻּדִ֣ים חֲמִשָּׁ֔ה כְּבָשִׂ֥ים בְּנֵֽי־שָׁנָ֖ה חֲמִשָּׁ֑ה זֶ֛ה קָרְבַּ֥ן גַּמְלִיאֵ֖ל בֶּן־פְּדָהצֽוּר:
| ס | בַּיּוֹם֙ הַתְּשִׁיעִ֔י נָשִׂ֖יא לִבְנֵ֣י בִנְיָמִ֑ן אֲבִידָ֖ן בֶּן־גִּדְעֹנִֽי: קָרְבָּנ֞וֹ קַֽעֲרַת־כֶּ֣סֶף אַחַ֗ת שְׁלֹשִׁ֣ים וּמֵאָה֮ מִשְׁקָלָהּ֒ מִזְרָ֤ק אֶחָד֙ כֶּ֔סֶף שִׁבְעִ֥ים שֶׁ֖קֶל
| סא | בְּשֶׁ֣קֶל הַקֹּ֑דֶשׁ שְׁנֵיהֶ֣ם ׀ מְלֵאִ֗ים סֹ֛לֶת בְּלוּלָ֥ה בַשֶּׁ֖מֶן לְמִנְחָֽה: כַּ֥ף
| סב | אַחַ֛ת עֲשָׂרָ֥ה זָהָ֖ב מְלֵאָ֥ה קְטֹֽרֶת: פַּ֣ר אֶחָ֞ד בֶּן־בָּקָ֗ר אַ֧יִל אֶחָ֛ד
| סג | כֶּֽבֶשׂ־אֶחָ֥ד בֶּן־שְׁנָת֖וֹ לְעֹלָֽה: שְׂעִיר־עִזִּ֥ים אֶחָ֖ד לְחַטָּֽאת: וּלְזֶ֣בַח
| סד סה | הַשְּׁלָמִים֮ בָּקָ֣ר שְׁנַ֒יִם֒ אֵילִ֤ם חֲמִשָּׁה֙ עַתֻּדִ֣ים חֲמִשָּׁ֔ה כְּבָשִׂ֥ים בְּנֵֽי־שָׁנָ֖ה חֲמִשָּׁ֑ה זֶ֛ה קָרְבַּ֥ן אֲבִידָ֖ן בֶּן־גִּדְעֹנִֽי:
| סו | בַּיּוֹם֙ הָעֲשִׂירִ֔י נָשִׂ֖יא לִבְנֵ֣י דָ֑ן אֲחִיעֶ֖זֶר בֶּן־עַמִּֽישַׁדָּֽי: קָרְבָּנ֞וֹ קַֽעֲרַת־כֶּ֣סֶף אַחַ֗ת שְׁלֹשִׁ֣ים וּמֵאָה֮ מִשְׁקָלָהּ֒ מִזְרָ֤ק אֶחָד֙ כֶּ֔סֶף שִׁבְעִ֥ים שֶׁ֖קֶל
| סז | בְּשֶׁ֣קֶל הַקֹּ֑דֶשׁ שְׁנֵיהֶ֣ם ׀ מְלֵאִ֗ים סֹ֛לֶת בְּלוּלָ֥ה בַשֶּׁ֖מֶן לְמִנְחָֽה: כַּ֥ף
| סח | אַחַ֛ת עֲשָׂרָ֥ה זָהָ֖ב מְלֵאָ֥ה קְטֹֽרֶת: פַּ֣ר אֶחָ֞ד בֶּן־בָּקָ֗ר אַ֧יִל אֶחָ֛ד
| סט | כֶּֽבֶשׂ־אֶחָ֥ד בֶּן־שְׁנָת֖וֹ לְעֹלָֽה: שְׂעִיר־עִזִּ֥ים אֶחָ֖ד לְחַטָּֽאת: וּלְזֶ֣בַח
| ע עא | הַשְּׁלָמִים֮ בָּקָ֣ר שְׁנַ֒יִם֒ אֵילִ֤ם חֲמִשָּׁה֙ עַתֻּדִ֣ים חֲמִשָּׁ֔ה כְּבָשִׂ֥ים בְּנֵֽי־שָׁנָ֖ה חֲמִשָּׁ֑ה זֶ֛ה קָרְבַּ֥ן אֲחִיעֶ֖זֶר בֶּן־עַמִּֽישַׁדָּֽי:

72 On the eleventh day came Pagiel son of Okhran, prince of the Asherites: His offering
73 was one silver bowl weighing one hundred and thirty shekel and one silver basin weighing seventy shekel according to the Sanctuary weight, both filled with fine flour mixed
74 with oil for a grain offering; one golden spoon weighing ten shekel, full of incense; one
75
76 young bull, one ram, and one yearling sheep for a burnt offering; one goat for a purifi-
77 cation offering; and for the peace sacrifice two oxen, five rams, five male goats, and five yearling sheep. This was the offering of Pagiel son of Okhran.
78 On the twelfth day came Aḥira son of Einan, prince of the Naftalites: His offering was
79 one silver bowl weighing one hundred and thirty shekel and one silver basin weighing seventy shekel according to the Sanctuary weight, both filled with fine flour mixed with
80 oil for a grain offering; one golden spoon weighing ten shekel, full of incense; one young
81
82 bull, one ram, and one yearling sheep for a burnt offering; one goat for a purification
83 offering; and for the peace sacrifice two oxen, five rams, five male goats, and five yearling sheep. This was the offering of Aḥira son of Einan.
84 All this was the dedication offering from the princes of Israel for the altar at the time it was anointed: There were twelve silver bowls, twelve silver basins, and twelve golden
85 spoons, each silver bowl weighing one hundred and thirty shekel and each basin seventy shekel – so all the silver in the utensils weighed two thousand four hundred shekel
86 according to the Sanctuary weight. There were twelve gold spoons full of incense weighing ten shekel each according to the Sanctuary weight – so all the gold of the spoons

שביעי

עב בְּיוֹם֙ עַשְׁתֵּ֣י עָשָׂ֣ר י֔וֹם נָשִׂ֖יא לִבְנֵ֣י אָשֵׁ֑ר פַּגְעִיאֵ֖ל בֶּן־עָכְרָֽן:
עג קָרְבָּנ֞וֹ קַֽעֲרַת־כֶּ֣סֶף אַחַ֗ת שְׁלֹשִׁ֣ים וּמֵאָה֮ מִשְׁקָלָהּ֒ מִזְרָ֤ק אֶחָד֙ כֶּ֔סֶף שִׁבְעִ֥ים שֶׁ֖קֶל בְּשֶׁ֣קֶל הַקֹּ֑דֶשׁ שְׁנֵיהֶ֣ם ׀ מְלֵאִ֗ים סֹ֛לֶת בְּלוּלָ֥ה
עד בַשֶּׁ֖מֶן לְמִנְחָֽה: כַּ֥ף אַחַ֛ת עֲשָׂרָ֥ה זָהָ֖ב מְלֵאָ֥ה קְטֹֽרֶת: פַּ֣ר אֶחָ֞ד
עה
עו בֶּן־בָּקָ֗ר אַ֧יִל אֶחָ֛ד כֶּֽבֶשׂ־אֶחָ֥ד בֶּן־שְׁנָת֖וֹ לְעֹלָֽה: שְׂעִיר־עִזִּ֥ים
עז אֶחָ֖ד לְחַטָּֽאת: וּלְזֶ֣בַח הַשְּׁלָמִים֮ בָּקָ֣ר שְׁנַ֒יִם֒ אֵילִ֤ם חֲמִשָּׁה֙ עַתּוּדִ֣ים חֲמִשָּׁ֔ה כְּבָשִׂ֥ים בְּנֵֽי־שָׁנָ֖ה חֲמִשָּׁ֑ה זֶ֛ה קָרְבַּ֥ן פַּגְעִיאֵ֖ל בֶּן־עָכְרָֽן:

עח בְּיוֹם֙ שְׁנֵ֣ים עָשָׂ֣ר י֔וֹם נָשִׂ֖יא לִבְנֵ֣י נַפְתָּלִ֑י אֲחִירַ֖ע בֶּן־עֵינָֽן: קָרְבָּנ֞וֹ
עט קַֽעֲרַת־כֶּ֣סֶף אַחַ֗ת שְׁלֹשִׁ֣ים וּמֵאָה֮ מִשְׁקָלָהּ֒ מִזְרָ֤ק אֶחָד֙ כֶּ֔סֶף שִׁבְעִ֥ים שֶׁ֖קֶל בְּשֶׁ֣קֶל הַקֹּ֑דֶשׁ שְׁנֵיהֶ֣ם ׀ מְלֵאִ֗ים סֹ֛לֶת בְּלוּלָ֥ה
פא בַשֶּׁ֖מֶן לְמִנְחָֽה: כַּ֥ף אַחַ֛ת עֲשָׂרָ֥ה זָהָ֖ב מְלֵאָ֥ה קְטֹֽרֶת: פַּ֣ר אֶחָ֞ד
פב בֶּן־בָּקָ֗ר אַ֧יִל אֶחָ֛ד כֶּֽבֶשׂ־אֶחָ֥ד בֶּן־שְׁנָת֖וֹ לְעֹלָֽה: שְׂעִיר־עִזִּ֥ים
פג אֶחָ֖ד לְחַטָּֽאת: וּלְזֶ֣בַח הַשְּׁלָמִים֮ בָּקָ֣ר שְׁנַ֒יִם֒ אֵילִ֤ם חֲמִשָּׁה֙ עַתּוּדִ֣ים חֲמִשָּׁ֔ה כְּבָשִׂ֥ים בְּנֵֽי־שָׁנָ֖ה חֲמִשָּׁ֑ה זֶ֛ה קָרְבַּ֥ן אֲחִירַ֖ע בֶּן־עֵינָֽן:

פד זֹ֣את ׀ חֲנֻכַּ֣ת הַמִּזְבֵּ֗חַ בְּיוֹם֙ הִמָּשַׁ֣ח אֹת֔וֹ מֵאֵ֖ת נְשִׂיאֵ֣י יִשְׂרָאֵ֑ל קַֽעֲרֹ֨ת כֶּ֜סֶף שְׁתֵּ֣ים עֶשְׂרֵ֗ה מִזְרְקֵי־כֶ֨סֶף֙ שְׁנֵ֣ים עָשָׂ֔ר כַּפּ֥וֹת זָהָ֖ב
פה שְׁתֵּ֥ים עֶשְׂרֵֽה: שְׁלֹשִׁ֣ים וּמֵאָ֗ה הַקְּעָרָ֤ה הָֽאַחַת֙ כֶּ֔סֶף וְשִׁבְעִ֖ים הַמִּזְרָ֣ק הָֽאֶחָ֑ד כֹּ֚ל כֶּ֣סֶף הַכֵּלִ֔ים אַלְפַּ֥יִם וְאַרְבַּע־מֵא֖וֹת בְּשֶׁ֥קֶל
פו הַקֹּֽדֶשׁ: כַּפּוֹת֩ זָהָ֨ב שְׁתֵּֽים־עֶשְׂרֵ֜ה מְלֵאֹ֣ת קְטֹ֗רֶת עֲשָׂרָ֨ה

87 weighed one hundred and twenty shekel. The total number of the animals for the burnt offerings was twelve bulls, twelve rams, and twelve yearling sheep, along with their grain
88 offerings. There were also twelve goats for the purification offerings. The total number of all the animals for the peace sacrifices was twenty-four bulls, sixty rams, sixty goats, and sixty yearling sheep. This was the dedication offering for the altar after it was anointed.
89 When Moshe entered the Tent of Meeting to speak with the Lord, he would hear the Voice speaking to him from above the cover over the Ark of the Covenant, from between the two cherubim. Thus did He speak to him.

פז הַכַּף בְּשֶׁקֶל הַקֹּדֶשׁ כָּל־זְהַב הַכַּפּוֹת עֶשְׂרִים וּמֵאָה: כָּל־הַבָּקָר מפטיר
לְעֹלָה שְׁנֵים עָשָׂר פָּרִים אֵילִם שְׁנֵים־עָשָׂר כְּבָשִׂים בְּנֵי־שָׁנָה
פח שְׁנֵים עָשָׂר וּמִנְחָתָם וּשְׂעִירֵי עִזִּים שְׁנֵים עָשָׂר לְחַטָּאת: וְכֹל
בְּקַר ׀ זֶבַח הַשְּׁלָמִים עֶשְׂרִים וְאַרְבָּעָה פָּרִים אֵילִם שִׁשִּׁים
עַתֻּדִים שִׁשִּׁים כְּבָשִׂים בְּנֵי־שָׁנָה שִׁשִּׁים זֹאת חֲנֻכַּת הַמִּזְבֵּחַ
פט אַחֲרֵי הִמָּשַׁח אֹתוֹ: וּבְבֹא מֹשֶׁה אֶל־אֹהֶל מוֹעֵד לְדַבֵּר אִתּוֹ
וַיִּשְׁמַע אֶת־הַקּוֹל מִדַּבֵּר אֵלָיו מֵעַל הַכַּפֹּרֶת אֲשֶׁר עַל־אֲרֹן
הָעֵדֻת מִבֵּין שְׁנֵי הַכְּרֻבִים וַיְדַבֵּר אֵלָיו:

MORE QUICK BITES

- **6:9** If a *nazir* becomes impure as a result of contact with a human corpse he must wait until he is pure and then restart his period of being a *nazir*. There is a powerful message in this. When you encounter an obstacle, when you stumble and fall, when you fail – don't let that get you down. You can overcome, you can succeed. Learn from your mistakes, pick yourself up, and start again – with a greater chance of getting closer to success.

- **7:14** One of the offerings was a spoon, a כף, which weighed ten shekel of gold. R. Meir of Premishlan offered a hasidic reading of the verse. The כף, he suggested, was from כפוף, meaning to be bent over or humble; the ten-shekel weight is represented by the letter *yud* (whose numerical value is ten), and in a Yiddish pronunciation sounded like the word for a Jew, a Yid. When a Jew comes before God with humility (bent over, like the spoon), then in God's eyes he is like gold.

EXPLORING HASHKAFA
MIRACLES AND MAGIC?

There are many layers of difficulty in understanding the process of the *sota*. One of those is highlighted by Ramban, who points out that there is no other mitzva in the Torah whose fulfillment is dependent on miraculous intervention. He is referring, of course, not to the process of dealing with the accused woman but to what happens at the end – the water that she drinks will bear miraculous consequences, either negative or positive, depending on whether she was guilty or not. This raises an important question about the role of miracles in Judaism.

When we look through Tanakh it is clear that miracles play a central role – from God's intervention in Sodom to the plagues in Egypt, from the manna in the wilderness to water flowing from a rock, from the sun standing still for Yehoshua to wondrous feats performed by Eliyahu and Elisha. And while Rambam plays down the importance of miracles as a basis of faith, they nonetheless seem to play a significant role in Tanakh.

When we move past Tanakh, however, the picture gets more complicated. The Talmud has multiple stories of miracles performed by various *tanna'im* and *amora'im*, like Ḥoni Hame'agel who made it rain just the right amount and R. Ḥanina ben Dosa who made vinegar burn as cleanly as olive oil. On the other hand, many Sages were unhappy with the idea of people playing God. Shimon ben Shataḥ was tempted to put Ḥoni into banishment for his actions, and both the Talmud Bavli and the Yerushalmi include unpleasant accounts describing Ḥoni's death.

The debate about magic, and with it the ability to manipulate the world via mystical acts, continued throughout the generations. There are those like Rambam, who believe that there is no such thing as magic, that humans have no ability to perform miracles, and that all accounts describing such things are either metaphors or descriptions of very talented masters of illusion. One extreme articulation of this position argues that belief in magic is stupid, and the reason the Torah forbids it is that it is forbidden to be stupid! Others argue that humans do have the ability to manipulate things in the world, but it is forbidden, as that is supposed to be reserved for God alone. A deeper portrayal of this position makes the point that God wants us to accept His authority in the world, and that if we want to change things it must be through Him, not to "do an end-run" around God and undermine Him. This is expressed in the story in the Talmud regarding Ḥoni's grandson, Abba Ḥilkiya, to whom people turned every time there was a drought, rather than turning to God.

The debates continued long after the Talmud and are still very present today. For example, should halakha include considerations of Kabbala and mysticism? They cover a wide range of practices, from cutting fingernails to choosing an etrog, from the appropriate time for *tefilla* to throwing bread into the water on Rosh Hashana. It all boils down to a few core questions. Is it okay with God if we find ways to "hack the system"? Do we believe that the "hacks" work or not, and if they do, are they permitted or not? What kind of relationship does God want to have with us, and what kind or relationship do we want to have with God?

פרשת בהעלתך
PARASHAT BEHAALOTEKHA

> "It is not the critic who counts, not the man who points out how the strong man stumbled or where the doer of deeds could have done better. The credit belongs to the man who is actually in the arena; whose face is marred by the dust and sweat and blood."
> Theodore Roosevelt

This *parasha* is split in the middle, marked by two inverted letters that separate the two halves and frame the pivotal section in the middle. The first half of the *parasha* prepares *Benei Yisrael* for the final leg of what supposed to be a brief journey from Egypt to the Promised Land. The *menora* lights up the *Mishkan*, which is in the center of the camp; the rest of the people are organized neatly and follow the precise instructions announced through the silver trumpets. And just to make the connection back to the exodus from Egypt even clearer, *Benei Yisrael* reenacts the Pesaḥ. And then everything changes. The trip takes too long; the food is boring; Moshe experiences a crisis moment in his leadership. What else could possibly go wrong?

PARASHAT BEHAALOTEKHA

8 ¹ And the Lord spoke to Moshe: "Speak to Aharon; say to him: When you raise up the ² lamps, the seven lamps shall light the space in front of the candelabrum." Aharon did ³ so; he mounted the lamps toward the front of the candelabrum as the Lord had com- ⁴ manded Moshe. This is how the lampstand was made: of hammered gold, hammered from its base to its flowers. According to the vision that the Lord had shown Moshe, so was the lampstand made.

ר' יוסף בכור שור

לפי שדיבר בהקמת המשכן ובחנוכתו, ואין בית בנוי וראוי לבא שם הארון עד שידליקו לו את הנר, ויבשמו לו את הבית, והבישום כבר נעשה על ידי נשיאים, שהביאו כפות מליאות קטורת, ועתה מדבר בהדלקת הנרות.

RABBI YOSEF BEKHOR SHOR

The Torah had previously been describing the erection and the inauguration of the *Mishkan*. And it would not have been appropriate for the Ark to be positioned inside the Holy of Holies before the lamps had been kindled within the structure. Furthermore, the incense too had to first be burned, a task that the princes had taken care of. These men had each donated pans full of incense, as listed in chapter 7. Thus, the text now mentions the lighting of the candelabrum.

QUESTIONS FOR THOUGHT

- Regarding what do all of the commentaries above agree?
- Which of the commentaries see this instruction as related to the previous verse, and which see it as connected to the entire previous chapter?
- Abarbanel understands that this instruction clarifies the relative roles of Moshe and Aharon. What are those roles, and how do they connect?
- Ibn Ezra and Bekhor Shor agree that this instruction is not about Aharon. Which aspect of the *Mishkan* and its function does each of them think that this instruction emphasizes?
- Which of the above commentaries do you think could be relevant for contemporary synagogues? In what way would that relevance be expressed?

WISDOM OF THE HEART

Noting that the instruction for Aharon to light the *menora* immediately follows the listing of the gifts of the tribal princes, a midrash suggests that Aharon was feeling bad that he was not included in those offerings, and that God consoled him by indicating that his role in lighting the *menora* was greater than theirs. Ramban explains this midrash as a reference to the Hasmoneans, who were able to light the *menora* many hundreds of years later in the re-inauguration of the *Beit Hamikdash* in the story of Ḥanukka. R. Akiva Tatz, wondering why that second inauguration was considered greater than this first one, suggests that it is because the re-inauguration came as a result of much hard work and a long uphill battle. We only really appreciate what we work hard for, and when we have to struggle to achieve it then our achievement has greater lasting power.

What examples from your own life can you think of in which you worked really hard to attain something?

פרשת בהעלתך

ח א וַיְדַבֵּר יְהוָה אֶל־מֹשֶׁה לֵּאמֹר: דַּבֵּר אֶל־אַהֲרֹן וְאָמַרְתָּ אֵלָיו ח
בְּהַעֲלֹתְךָ אֶת־הַנֵּרֹת אֶל־מוּל פְּנֵי הַמְּנוֹרָה יָאִירוּ שִׁבְעַת
הַנֵּרוֹת: וַיַּעַשׂ כֵּן אַהֲרֹן אֶל־מוּל פְּנֵי הַמְּנוֹרָה הֶעֱלָה נֵרֹתֶיהָ ג
כַּאֲשֶׁר צִוָּה יְהוָה אֶת־מֹשֶׁה: וְזֶה מַעֲשֵׂה הַמְּנֹרָה מִקְשָׁה זָהָב ד
עַד־יְרֵכָהּ עַד־פִּרְחָהּ מִקְשָׁה הִוא כַּמַּרְאֶה אֲשֶׁר הֶרְאָה יְהוָה
אֶת־מֹשֶׁה כֵּן עָשָׂה אֶת־הַמְּנֹרָה:

CLASSIC COMMENTATORS

The commentaries are puzzled by the placement of the instruction to light the lamps here. Doesn't it belong back in Exodus, where the construction of the *Mishkan* is described, or in Leviticus, where the functioning of the *Mishkan* is detailed?

IBN EZRA — אבן עזרא

ונסמכה זאת הפרשה להורות, כי הדבור היה גם בלילה, כי שם הנר דלוק ולא יכבה.

This discussion of the candelabrum is juxtaposed to the previous section [the end of chapter 7, which reads, "When Moshe entered the Tent of Meeting to speak with the Lord, he would hear the Voice speaking to him" (Num. 7:89)] in order to teach that God communicated to Moshe at night as well as during the day. For the lamps burned continuously and were never extinguished.

ABARBANEL — אברבנאל

ויהיה הענין בסמיכות הפרשיות שבעבור שזכר למעלה שבבא משה אל אהל מועד וישמע את הקול אבל אהרן לא הי' שומע אותו לכן סמך לזה שיצוה את אהרן על הדלקת הנרות במנורה אשר בהיכל הקדש כדי להודיע שאהרן וגם בניו יכנסו בהיכל בכל יום בבקר ובערב להדליק את הנרות ועם כל זה לא ישמע אהרן את הקול שיהיה שומע משה. גם משה היה נכנס שם פעמים בלילה לשמוע את דברי ה' והי' ההיכל מאיר מנרות המנורה להיישיר דרכו של משה בבאו אל קדש הקדשים לשמוע נבואתו וזהו סמיכות הפרשיות האלה נאה ומתישב.

According to the description in the previous chapter, when Moshe entered the Tent of Meeting he was privileged to hear the voice of God, whereas Aharon was incapable of discerning that communication. Therefore, God now commanded Moshe to tell Aharon to light the lamps of the candelabrum within the holy Sanctuary, meaning that he and his sons were to enter the chamber every morning and evening to perform that task. Nevertheless, Aharon would not be privy to the voice that Moshe was allowed to hear. At times, Moshe would enter the *Mishkan* at night to receive God's message. Thus, the inside of the structure was illuminated so that the prophet could see where he was going as he approached the Holy of Holies. This explains the sequence of the passages in the Torah.

5
6 The LORD spoke to Moshe: "Take the Levites from among the Israelites and purify
7 them. This is what you shall do to them to purify them: Sprinkle upon them the water of
   purification, and have them shave their whole bodies and wash their clothes; then they
8 will be purified. They shall take a young bull with its grain offering of fine flour mixed
9 with oil. You, meanwhile, shall take a second young bull for a purification offering. You
   shall bring the Levites before the Tent of Meeting and assemble all the community of
10 Israel. Then you shall bring the Levites forward before the LORD, and the Israelites
11 shall lay their hands upon the Levites. Aharon shall then present the Levites before
   the LORD like a wave offering from the Israelites, so that they may perform the LORD's
12 service. The Levites shall then lay their hands upon the heads of the bulls, and Aharon
   shall offer one as a purification offering and the other as a burnt offering to the LORD,
13 to make atonement for the Levites. You shall have the Levites stand before Aharon
14 and his sons, and then present them like a wave offering to the LORD. Thus you shall
   separate the Levites from among the other Israelites; the Levites shall become Mine.
15 After that, the Levites shall enter to perform the service of the Tent of Meeting, once

---

QUESTIONS FOR THOUGHT

- One of the commentaries understands that they need to be physically separated from the rest of *Benei Yisrael*, a second understands that they need to be inspired to take on their new positions, and a third understands that the phrase means to prepare to start the process. Match these opinions with the commentaries above.
- Look at the context of verse 6 and of the entire passage. Which of the commentaries seems to best fit each of those contexts?

TEXTUAL SKILLS

1. The process of inaugurating the Levites includes the requirement that they shave their entire bodies. Where else in the Torah do we encounter this requirement?
2. As part of the inauguration, *Benei Yisrael* had to lean their hands on the Levites. This is similar to the requirement for a person to lean their hands on an offering (Lev. 1–4). Can you find a connection between them?

WISDOM OF THE HEART

As part of their induction, the Levites were required to shave all their body hair. This reminds us of the person afflicted with צרעת, who was also required to shave their body as part of the purification process. R. Moshe Sternbuch suggests that their induction included some disagreeable elements precisely because the job of the Levite was not all glory; there was a lot of unpleasant, hard work. Perhaps it could be suggested that shaving all the body hair essentially restores the person to the way they were when they were born. The person with צרעת needs to be "reborn" as a healthy person who has been cured. The Levites needed to be reborn as they entered a completely new status.

Every so often we enter a new stage of life – starting first grade or high school, or starting a new job. What kinds of things do you do which reflect that this is a new start?

במדבר | פרק ח

ו וַיְדַבֵּר יְהוָה אֶל־מֹשֶׁה לֵּאמֹר: קַח אֶת־הַלְוִיִּם מִתּוֹךְ בְּנֵי
ז יִשְׂרָאֵל וְטִהַרְתָּ אֹתָם: וְכֹה־תַעֲשֶׂה לָהֶם לְטַהֲרָם הַזֵּה עֲלֵיהֶם
מֵי חַטָּאת וְהֶעֱבִירוּ תַעַר עַל־כָּל־בְּשָׂרָם וְכִבְּסוּ בִגְדֵיהֶם
ח וְהִטֶּהָרוּ: וְלָקְחוּ פַּר בֶּן־בָּקָר וּמִנְחָתוֹ סֹלֶת בְּלוּלָה בַשָּׁמֶן
ט וּפַר־שֵׁנִי בֶן־בָּקָר תִּקַּח לְחַטָּאת: וְהִקְרַבְתָּ אֶת־הַלְוִיִּם לִפְנֵי
י אֹהֶל מוֹעֵד וְהִקְהַלְתָּ אֶת־כָּל־עֲדַת בְּנֵי יִשְׂרָאֵל: וְהִקְרַבְתָּ
אֶת־הַלְוִיִּם לִפְנֵי יְהוָה וְסָמְכוּ בְנֵי־יִשְׂרָאֵל אֶת־יְדֵיהֶם עַל־
יא הַלְוִיִּם: וְהֵנִיף אַהֲרֹן אֶת־הַלְוִיִּם תְּנוּפָה לִפְנֵי יְהוָה מֵאֵת בְּנֵי
יב יִשְׂרָאֵל וְהָיוּ לַעֲבֹד אֶת־עֲבֹדַת יְהוָה: וְהַלְוִיִּם יִסְמְכוּ אֶת־יְדֵיהֶם
עַל רֹאשׁ הַפָּרִים וַעֲשֵׂה אֶת־הָאֶחָד חַטָּאת וְאֶת־הָאֶחָד עֹלָה
יג לַיהוָה לְכַפֵּר עַל־הַלְוִיִּם: וְהַעֲמַדְתָּ אֶת־הַלְוִיִּם לִפְנֵי אַהֲרֹן וְלִפְנֵי
יד בָנָיו וְהֵנַפְתָּ אֹתָם תְּנוּפָה לַיהוָה: וְהִבְדַּלְתָּ אֶת־הַלְוִיִּם מִתּוֹךְ
טו בְּנֵי יִשְׂרָאֵל וְהָיוּ לִי הַלְוִיִּם: וְאַחֲרֵי־כֵן יָבֹאוּ הַלְוִיִּם לַעֲבֹד שני

CLASSIC COMMENTATORS

God commands Moshe to "take the Levites." What does it mean for them to be taken?

RASHI — רש"י

Persuade them to undertake this preparation by telling them: How fortunate and privileged you are to serve the Almighty!

קחם בדברים: אשריכם שתזכו להיות שמשים למקום.

IBN EZRA — אבן עזרא

At that time the Levites were all mixed up among the rest of the tribes. Indeed, before the nation moved on from Mount Sinai, everybody lived together.

כי מעורבין היו, וכן כל השבטים קודם שיסעו מהר סיני.

RABBI ISAAC SAMUEL REGGIO — ר' יצחק שמואל רג'יו

The command is now issued regarding the training and preparation of the Levites for their new task. They were to undergo purification and atonement.

בא עתה לצוות איך יחנכם וימלא את ידם, וזה בטהר אותם ובכפר עליהם.

16 you have purified them and presented them as a wave offering. They are wholly given over to Me from among the Israelites. I have taken them for Myself in place of the
17 first to emerge from every womb, the firstborn of all the Israelites. For all the firstborn among the Israelites, man and beast alike, are Mine; on the day that I struck down the
18 firstborn in Egypt, I consecrated them to Myself. But I have now taken the Levites in
19 place of all the firstborn among the Israelites, and I have given the Levites to Aharon and his sons from among the Israelites, to perform the service of the Israelites in the Tent of Meeting and to make atonement for the Israelites, so that no plague will come
20 among the Israelites for drawing too close to the Sanctuary." Moshe, Aharon, and all the community of Israel did this for the Levites; all that the Lord commanded Moshe
21 with regard to the Levites, so the Israelites did. The Levites purified themselves and washed their clothes. Aharon presented them as a wave offering before the Lord, and
22 made atonement for them in order to purify them. And after that, the Levites went in to perform their service in the Tent of Meeting before Aharon and his sons. As the Lord

---

RABBI SAMSON RAPHAEL HIRSCH ר׳ שמשון רפאל

הרחקת בני ישראל מן המקדש היא המשך של ההגבלה שנצטוותה בסיני.

The people of Israel were required to maintain their distance from the *Mishkan*, just as they were warned not to approach Mount Sinai before the revelation.

QUESTIONS FOR THOUGHT

- Which of the commentaries understands that the Levites were chosen in order to avoid a plague?
- Which understands that the choice of the Levites is the reason that a plague would come if a non-Levite approached the *Mishkan*?
- Which understands that the reason for the plague long predates the choice of the Levites?

TEXTUAL SKILLS

1. Notice similarities between: the first half of verse 16 and 3:9; the second half of verse 16 and 3:12; and verse 17 and 3:13. What differences can you find between them?
2. Notice which word is doubled both in verse 16 and in verse 19.

WISDOM OF THE HEART

In the *Beit Hamikdash*, the Levites were singers and musicians. The significance of music is highlighted by a passage in Sanhedrin (94a) which states that King Ḥizkiyahu could have been the Messiah if only he had sung in response to God's miracles. It is not surprising that the experience in the *Beit Hamikdash* was accompanied by music, which elevates the spirit, and it is also no surprise that music plays an important role in *tefilla* in general.

What types of music do you find uplifting? Do you think that there should be guidelines for what kind of music is introduced into public tefilla in the synagogue?

טז אֶת־אֹהֶל מוֹעֵד וְטִהַרְתָּ אֹתָם וְהֵנַפְתָּ אֹתָם תְּנוּפָה: כִּי נְתֻנִים
נְתֻנִים הֵמָּה לִי מִתּוֹךְ בְּנֵי יִשְׂרָאֵל תַּחַת פִּטְרַת כָּל־רֶחֶם בְּכוֹר
יז כֹּל מִבְּנֵי יִשְׂרָאֵל לָקַחְתִּי אֹתָם לִי: כִּי לִי כָל־בְּכוֹר בִּבְנֵי יִשְׂרָאֵל
בָּאָדָם וּבַבְּהֵמָה בְּיוֹם הַכֹּתִי כָל־בְּכוֹר בְּאֶרֶץ מִצְרַיִם הִקְדַּשְׁתִּי
יח אֹתָם לִי: וָאֶקַּח אֶת־הַלְוִיִּם תַּחַת כָּל־בְּכוֹר בִּבְנֵי יִשְׂרָאֵל:
יט וָאֶתְּנָה אֶת־הַלְוִיִּם נְתֻנִים ׀ לְאַהֲרֹן וּלְבָנָיו מִתּוֹךְ בְּנֵי יִשְׂרָאֵל
לַעֲבֹד אֶת־עֲבֹדַת בְּנֵי־יִשְׂרָאֵל בְּאֹהֶל מוֹעֵד וּלְכַפֵּר עַל־בְּנֵי
יִשְׂרָאֵל וְלֹא יִהְיֶה בִּבְנֵי יִשְׂרָאֵל נֶגֶף בְּגֶשֶׁת בְּנֵי־יִשְׂרָאֵל אֶל־
כ הַקֹּדֶשׁ: וַיַּעַשׂ מֹשֶׁה וְאַהֲרֹן וְכָל־עֲדַת בְּנֵי־יִשְׂרָאֵל לַלְוִיִּם כְּכֹל
אֲשֶׁר־צִוָּה יְהוָה אֶת־מֹשֶׁה לַלְוִיִּם כֵּן־עָשׂוּ לָהֶם בְּנֵי יִשְׂרָאֵל:
כא וַיִּתְחַטְּאוּ הַלְוִיִּם וַיְכַבְּסוּ בִּגְדֵיהֶם וַיָּנֶף אַהֲרֹן אֹתָם תְּנוּפָה
כב לִפְנֵי יְהוָה וַיְכַפֵּר עֲלֵיהֶם אַהֲרֹן לְטַהֲרָם: וְאַחֲרֵי־כֵן בָּאוּ הַלְוִיִּם
לַעֲבֹד אֶת־עֲבֹדָתָם בְּאֹהֶל מוֹעֵד לִפְנֵי אַהֲרֹן וְלִפְנֵי בָנָיו כַּאֲשֶׁר

CLASSIC COMMENTATORS

God says that the purpose of the Levites doing the work is to prevent a plague from affecting *Benei Yisrael*. Why would there be a plague?

RABBI YOSEF BEKHOR SHOR

If the Israelites' firstborns were to serve in the *Mishkan*, the nation would be stricken with a plague. Since it is unlikely that a firstborn's father and grandfather were both firstborns, this firstborn would not have been trained within his family in the proper service procedures. As such, the firstborn would not possess the expertise necessary to do the job, and the Holy One, blessed be He, would unleash a plague as a result.

RABBI OVADYA SFORNO

The strangers who approach the *Mishkan* will sin by doing so, and the Levites who permit them access will sin as well. God will therefore hold the entire congregation culpable.

ר׳ יוסף בכור שור

שאם היו הבכורים עובדים - היה בהם נגף, שהרי הבכור לא היה אביו בכור ולא אבי אביו, ושמא לא הורגלו בעבודה. וכשבא זה לעבודה לא היה בקי ונזהר, ויעשה שלא כהוגן, ויגפנו הקב״ה.

ר׳ עובדיה ספורנו

שבזה יחטאו הזרים הנגשים, והלוים שיניחו את הזרים לגשת, ויתחייבו כולם.

8:23–26 *Levites are inducted into service at the age of twenty-five and remain in service until the age of fifty.*

23 had commanded Moshe regarding the Levites, so they did for them. And the LORD
24 spoke to Moshe: "The Levites: From twenty-five years upward they shall go into the
25 service of the Tent of Meeting. At fifty years old they shall retire from the service and
26 serve no longer. They may assist their fellow Levites in carrying out their duties in the Tent of Meeting, but shall not perform the service itself. This is how you shall conduct the Levites with regard to their duties."

RAMBAN

ועל דרך הפשט: הנמנים ביד משה ואהרן היו מבן שלשים שנה ומעלה, והם אשר הפקיד אותם איש איש על עבודתו ועל משאו (במדבר ד׳:מ״ט), אבל בכאן צוה כי כל אשר ידע בעצמו שבא לכלל עשרים וחמש שנה יהיה כשר לעבודה, ויבא בכל אות נפשו לעבוד עמהם ולסייעם בעבודה, אבל לא יהיה פקיד נגיד על עבודה ידועה.

Here is the straightforward meaning of the text: The Levites above the age of thirty who were tallied by Moshe and Aharon were assigned, "each according to his service and to what he was to carry" (Num. 4:49). Whereas, in the current passage God allows all Levites who themselves know they are at least twenty-five to join in the service [even though Moshe did not officially include them in his census]. Any such individuals who feel the desire to participate in the tasks associated with the *Mishkan* are permitted to do so, and to assist the *kohanim* in their holy work. Still, these unrecorded Levites could not be put in charge of a particular department.

QUESTIONS FOR THOUGHT

- According to Rashbam, what happens to the Levites after age fifty?
- What makes Ramban's suggestion so unusual?
- Between Rashi and Rashbam, which seems to fit more closely with the words in the Torah? Why do you think so?
- Which of the above explanations do you think shows the greatest understanding of and sensitivity to human nature? Why do you think so?
- If you were running a company and looking to hire qualified employees, what could you learn from each of the above commentaries to help you make decisions about hiring, training, and promoting people?

WISDOM OF THE HEART

The Torah dictates a mandatory retirement age for Levites. After age fifty there are a variety of things that they can do, but they can no longer do any of the primary work assigned to the Levites. Almost as a metaphor, the Talmud says that they may lock up the gates of the *Beit Hamikdash* at the end of the day. Notice that it does not say that they can open the gates, as these are Levites who are closing their careers. R. Soloveitchik was once asked about Psalms 90:10: "The span of our life is seventy years – perhaps eighty, if we are strong." The Hebrew word used for strong is *gevurot*, which usually means the ability to exercise self-control, to hold back. The questioner asked what kind of *gevura* is associated with being eighty. He responded with a powerful message. The *gevura* of being eighty is the ability to accept that we can no longer do what we were able to do at seventy or sixty or fifty. That requires a tremendous amount of restraint, an incredible degree of accepting limitations.

When is it good to accept our limitations as opposed to trying to overcome them?

כג צִוָּה יְהוָה אֶת־מֹשֶׁה עַל־הַלְוִיִּם כֵּן עָשׂוּ לָהֶם: וַיְדַבֵּר
כד יְהוָה אֶל־מֹשֶׁה לֵּאמֹר: זֹאת אֲשֶׁר לַלְוִיִּם מִבֶּן חָמֵשׁ וְעֶשְׂרִים
כה שָׁנָה וָמַעְלָה יָבוֹא לִצְבֹא צָבָא בַּעֲבֹדַת אֹהֶל מוֹעֵד: וּמִבֶּן
כו חֲמִשִּׁים שָׁנָה יָשׁוּב מִצְּבָא הָעֲבֹדָה וְלֹא יַעֲבֹד עוֹד: וְשֵׁרֵת
אֶת־אֶחָיו בְּאֹהֶל מוֹעֵד לִשְׁמֹר מִשְׁמֶרֶת וַעֲבֹדָה לֹא יַעֲבֹד
כָּכָה תַּעֲשֶׂה לַלְוִיִּם בְּמִשְׁמְרֹתָם:

TEXTUAL SKILLS

1. What key word appears three times in this short passage?
2. In verse 26 there are two roots which each appear twice and may be designed to create a contrast. What are those two words and what contrast is being set up?

CLASSIC COMMENTATORS

Earlier (4:3, 4:23, and 4:30) the Torah identified the induction age for Levites as thirty years, yet here the Torah identifies it as twenty-five years. How are we to resolve this contradiction?

RASHI

How can we reconcile this statement with an earlier verse which states, "from thirty to fifty years old: all those able to go into service to perform the work of the Tent of Meeting" (4:3)? When a Levite turns twenty-five years old he enrolls to study the laws of the service, and he spends five years preparing for that task. The Levite then starts the actual work when he becomes thirty years old.

רש"י

ובמקום אחר הוא אומר: מבן שלשים שנה (במדבר ד':ג'), הא כיצד? בן עשרים וחמש בא ללמוד הלכות עבודה, ולומד חמש שנים, ובן שלשים עובד.

RASHBAM

Our verse introduces a new commandment that the Torah has yet to discuss. In *Parashat Bemidbar* (Num. 4:1–20) and in *Parashat Naso* (4:23–49) we find the instruction from the Holy One, blessed be He, to tally the Levites between the ages of thirty and fifty. These are the men who will serve in the spiritual center and who are responsible for transporting its components during Israel's travels. Now, however, the text begins to describe the Levites' additional role, to guard the *Mishkan*. Once an individual reaches the age of twenty five, he is still too young to be entrusted with carrying the vessels and other objects of the Sanctuary, but he is the right age to be given guard duty for the sacred items. Similarly, a man of fifty might be too old to haul the heavy parts of the *Mishkan*, but he is still able to join his brethren in watching over the holy vessels and the precincts of the *Mishkan*.

רשב"ם

בפרשת מדבר סיני (במדבר ד':א'-כ') ובפרשת נשא (במדבר ד':כ"ג-מ"ט) ציוה הקב"ה למנותם מבן שלשים שנה עד בן חמשים שנה, לעבוד ולמשא, לשאת את המשכן. ועתה בפרשה זו בא לפרש מצות עבודת משמרת משכן, אשר חמש שנים לפני השלשים שנה, שאינו ראוי למשא, יהי ראוי ומצווה לשמירת משכן וכליו. ומבן חמשים ומעלה, שאינו ראוי לעבודת משא, יהא מצווה לעבודת שמירה.

9 1 The Lord spoke to Moshe in the Sinai Desert in the first month of the second year after
2 they had left Egypt: "Let the Israelites offer the Passover sacrifice at its appointed time.
3 On the fourteenth day of this month in the afternoon you shall offer it at its appointed
4 time. Bring it in accordance with all its decrees and laws." And so Moshe instructed
5 the Israelites to offer the Passover sacrifice. On the afternoon of the fourteenth day of
the first month they offered the Passover sacrifice in the Sinai Desert. Just as the Lord
6 commanded Moshe, so the Israelites did. But there were people who were impure
because of contact with the dead, and they were unable to offer the Passover sacrifice on
7 that day. That very day they approached Moshe and Aharon: "We have become impure
because of contact with the dead," these people said to him, "but must we be debarred
8 from presenting the Lord's offering at its appointed time among all the Israelites?" "Wait,"
Moshe replied, "and let me hear what the Lord commands concerning you."

ר׳ עובדיה ספורנו

מלבד מה שעשו בשמיני למלואים וחנוכת הנשיאים יעשו גם כן את הפסח, שלא יפטרו ממנו בשביל שמחת המצוות שקיימו, כמו שקרה בבנין בית ראשון שספרו רבותינו ז״ל שבטל שלמה את יום הכפורים בשמחת חנוכת הבית.

RABBI OVADYA SFORNO

In addition to the celebrations that the people of Israel undertook on the eighth day of the inauguration of the *Mishkan*, and the presentations of the tribal princes, it was imperative for the nation to observe the Pesaḥ as well. This festival was not to be ignored in the face of the other commandments which the Israelites were busy fulfilling. That was exactly what happened when Shlomo dedicated the First Temple. According to our Sages, of blessed memory, the king canceled the commemoration of Yom Kippur that year in honor of the rejoicing that had gripped the nation at the completion of the Temple.

QUESTIONS FOR THOUGHT

- Both Ramban and Sforno agree that this first year was a special case. What do they each think is the reason that this year was special? What do you think each would say about the following year – would it need a special instruction? Why or why not?
- According to Ramban, if God hadn't planned for them to observe the Pesaḥ until they go to the Promised Land, what changed that made God now decide that they should do it in the wilderness?

TEXTUAL SKILLS

1. Where else in the Torah do we find that Moshe does not know how to proceed and consults with God?
2. Look at the date on which this chapter begins and compare it to the date which appears in 1:1. Can you figure out the chronological order of the first nine chapters of Numbers? (See also the events described in chapter 3 and chapter 8.)

WISDOM OF THE HEART

The people who were excluded from the Pesaḥ could easily have skipped it – they were exempt. But they didn't take the easy way out; they were not looking for ways out of their responsibilities, but rather looking for a way in. In their merit we have the mitzva of *Pesaḥ Sheni*, the only "make-up" mitzva.

What characteristic describes people who are looking for ways in?

במדבר | פרק ט

שלישי

א וַיְדַבֵּ֨ר יְהֹוָ֤ה אֶל־מֹשֶׁה֙ בְמִדְבַּר־סִינַ֔י בַּשָּׁנָ֤ה הַשֵּׁנִית֙ לְצֵאתָ֣ם מֵאֶ֣רֶץ מִצְרַ֔יִם בַּחֹ֥דֶשׁ הָרִאשׁ֖וֹן לֵאמֹֽר׃ ב וְיַעֲשׂ֧וּ בְנֵי־יִשְׂרָאֵ֛ל אֶת־הַפָּ֖סַח בְּמוֹעֲדֽוֹ׃ ג בְּאַרְבָּעָ֣ה עָשָׂר־י֠וֹם בַּחֹ֨דֶשׁ הַזֶּ֜ה בֵּ֧ין הָעַרְבַּ֛יִם תַּעֲשׂ֥וּ אֹת֖וֹ בְּמוֹעֲד֑וֹ כְּכׇל־חֻקֹּתָ֥יו וּכְכׇל־מִשְׁפָּטָ֖יו תַּעֲשׂ֥וּ אֹתֽוֹ׃ ד וַיְדַבֵּ֥ר מֹשֶׁ֛ה אֶל־בְּנֵ֥י יִשְׂרָאֵ֖ל לַעֲשֹׂ֥ת הַפָּֽסַח׃ ה וַיַּעֲשׂ֣וּ אֶת־הַפֶּ֡סַח בָּרִאשׁ֡וֹן בְּאַרְבָּעָה֩ עָשָׂ֨ר י֥וֹם לַחֹ֛דֶשׁ בֵּ֥ין הָעַרְבַּ֖יִם בְּמִדְבַּ֣ר סִינָ֑י כְּ֠כֹ֠ל אֲשֶׁ֨ר צִוָּ֤ה יְהֹוָה֙ אֶת־מֹשֶׁ֔ה כֵּ֥ן עָשׂ֖וּ בְּנֵ֥י יִשְׂרָאֵֽל׃ ו וַיְהִ֣י אֲנָשִׁ֗ים אֲשֶׁ֨ר הָי֤וּ טְמֵאִים֙ לְנֶ֣פֶשׁ אָדָ֔ם וְלֹא־יָכְל֥וּ לַעֲשֹׂת־הַפֶּ֖סַח בַּיּ֣וֹם הַה֑וּא וַיִּקְרְב֞וּ לִפְנֵ֥י מֹשֶׁ֛ה וְלִפְנֵ֥י אַהֲרֹ֖ן בַּיּ֥וֹם הַהֽוּא׃ ז וַ֠יֹּאמְר֠וּ הָאֲנָשִׁ֤ים הָהֵ֙מָּה֙ אֵלָ֔יו אֲנַ֥חְנוּ טְמֵאִ֖ים לְנֶ֣פֶשׁ אָדָ֑ם לָ֣מָּה נִגָּרַ֗ע לְבִלְתִּ֨י הַקְרִ֜ב אֶת־קׇרְבַּ֤ן יְהֹוָה֙ בְּמֹ֣עֲד֔וֹ בְּת֖וֹךְ בְּנֵ֥י יִשְׂרָאֵֽל׃ ח וַיֹּ֥אמֶר אֲלֵהֶ֖ם מֹשֶׁ֑ה עִמְד֣וּ וְאֶשְׁמְעָ֔ה מַה־יְצַוֶּ֥ה יְהֹוָ֖ה לָכֶֽם׃

CLASSIC COMMENTATORS

God already commanded *Benei Yisrael* to observe the Pesaḥ, after the exodus (Ex. 12:24–27). Why is there a need to repeat the instruction just one year later?

RAMBAN / רמב״ן

ויתכן שהוצרך למצוה הזו בעבור שלא נצטוו מתחלה בעשיית פסח דורות אלא בארץ (שמות י״ב:כ״ה) ... ועכשיו רצה הקב״ה וצוה שיעשו אותו כדי שתהיה זכר שגאולתם והנסים שנעשו להם ולאבותיהם נעתק להם מן האבות הרואים לבניהם, ובניהם לבניהם, ובניהם לדור אחר.

Perhaps the Torah now reiterates the commandment to observe the Pesaḥ because the initial instruction regarding future generations seems geared to a time when the nation dwells in the land of Israel. Thus the verse states, "When you enter the land the Lord will give you as He has promised, you shall keep this ceremony" (Ex. 12:25). However, now the Holy One, blessed be He, expresses His desire for the people to celebrate the Passover as a remembrance of their redemption from Egypt. As such, they should recall the attendant miracles which God performed for them and for their ancestors during that ordeal. It was critical for the generation which lived through the exodus to recount to their children what they had witnessed and experienced. This information is to be transmitted year after year in every era for all eternity.

> **9:9–14** If someone misses observing the Pesaḥ because he is impure or too far from the mikdash, then he may do so one month later. But anyone who neglects to observe the Pesaḥ in its proper time and is neither impure nor too distant from the mikdash will receive the consequence of כרת.

9
10 And the Lord spoke to Moshe: "Tell the Israelites: When any of you or your future descendants are impure because of contact with the dead, or away on a journey, they
11 may still offer a Passover sacrifice to the Lord. They shall offer it in the afternoon of the fourteenth day of the second month; then shall they eat it with unleavened bread and
12 bitter herbs. They shall not leave any of it over until morning, nor shall they break any of its bones. They shall offer it in compliance with all the rules of the Passover sacrifice.
13 But anyone who is ritually pure and not on a journey, but still fails to offer the Passover sacrifice, that person shall be severed from his people, because he did not offer the
14 Lord's sacrifice at its appointed time; he will bear his guilt. If there is a migrant living among you and he offers a Passover sacrifice to the Lord, he shall do so in compliance

Num. 15:15–30). Why do you think that might be necessary for these mitzvot? Do you think that a *ger* would find that inclusion reassuring or off-putting?

TEXTUAL SKILLS

1. Are you familiar with any other mitzva in the Torah for which there is an opportunity to make it up if someone misses performing it?

2. Note: verse 7 and verse 13 are the only references in the entire Tanakh that identify the Pesaḥ as a *korban*, a sacrifice!

WISDOM OF THE HEART

Anyone who is "far away" from the place where the sacrifices are offered is permitted to come on *Pesaḥ Sheni*, exactly one month later, to bring the offering then. According to Rabbi Eliezer (whose opinion is ultimately rejected by the Gemara but quoted by Rashi), "far away doesn't really mean far away; even if the person was right outside the entrance of the *Beit Hamikdash* they can become exempt. That sounds odd – why would someone who is right outside the door be exempt? What is preventing them from entering that they would be considered "far away"?

R. Yehezkel of Kozmir suggests that sometimes in our minds we feel that we aren't ready for something, whether because we feel unworthy or for some other reason. R. Eliezer understands that psychological barriers are very real.

Are there times that you feel yourself blocked emotionally, perhaps by some kind of fear, from doing something that you'd really like to do? How do you think you could get past those blocks?

QUICK BITE

Some people have a custom to eat matza on *Pesaḥ Sheni*, echoing Pesaḥ itself. R. Yaakov Emden writes that he was taught that when *Benei Yisrael* left Egypt, the food (matza) they brought with them lasted one month, until what would later become *Pesaḥ Sheni*. The custom commemorates the last day of eating matza before the manna began to fall.

ט וַיְדַבֵּר יהוה אֶל־מֹשֶׁה לֵּאמֹר: דַּבֵּר אֶל־בְּנֵי יִשְׂרָאֵל לֵאמֹר אִישׁ אִישׁ כִּי־יִהְיֶה טָמֵא | לָנֶפֶשׁ אוֹ בְדֶרֶךְ רְחֹקָה לָכֶם אוֹ יא לְדֹרֹתֵיכֶם וְעָשָׂה פֶסַח לַיהוה: בַּחֹדֶשׁ הַשֵּׁנִי בְּאַרְבָּעָה עָשָׂר יב יוֹם בֵּין הָעַרְבַּיִם יַעֲשׂוּ אֹתוֹ עַל־מַצּוֹת וּמְרֹרִים יֹאכְלֻהוּ: לֹא־יַשְׁאִירוּ מִמֶּנּוּ עַד־בֹּקֶר וְעֶצֶם לֹא יִשְׁבְּרוּ־בוֹ כְּכָל־חֻקַּת הַפֶּסַח יג יַעֲשׂוּ אֹתוֹ: וְהָאִישׁ אֲשֶׁר־הוּא טָהוֹר וּבְדֶרֶךְ לֹא־הָיָה וְחָדַל לַעֲשׂוֹת הַפֶּסַח וְנִכְרְתָה הַנֶּפֶשׁ הַהִוא מֵעַמֶּיהָ | כִּי קָרְבַּן יהוה יד לֹא הִקְרִיב בְּמֹעֲדוֹ חֶטְאוֹ יִשָּׂא הָאִישׁ הַהוּא: וְכִי־יָגוּר אִתְּכֶם גֵּר וְעָשָׂה פֶסַח לַיהוה כְּחֻקַּת הַפֶּסַח וּכְמִשְׁפָּטוֹ כֵּן יַעֲשֶׂה חֻקָּה

CLASSIC COMMENTATORS

The Torah already told us that a *ger* is included in the Pesaḥ (Ex. 12:48). Why is there a need to repeat it in the context of *Pesaḥ Sheni*?

RABBI YOSEF BEKHOR SHOR
ר' יוסף בכור שור

A *ger* too must delay his celebration of Pesaḥ until the second iteration of the festival should he be impure on the first date, or distant from the *Mishkan* when it begins.

וכי יגור אתכם גר – גם הוא ידחה לפסח שני, אם הוא טמא מת בראשון או בדרך רחוקה.

RAMBAN
רמב"ן

This verse serves as a commandment to the *ger* to observe the Passover sacrifice in the wilderness just as the Israelites are ordered to do.

וכי יגור אתכם גר – לצוות הגרים בפסח זה של מדבר, כאשר יצוה בו לישראל.

RALBAG
רלב"ג

A *ger* who was not an Israelite at the time that Pesaḥ was celebrated was not obligated to observe the festival then. However, if he joins the nation during the month following Pesaḥ, he is required to keep *Pesaḥ Sheni*.

וכי יגור אתכם גר ועשה פסח לה' – רוצה לומר פסח שני, כיון שלא נתחייב בראשון, שהרי לא היה גר בראשון ולא נתחייב בו.

QUESTIONS FOR THOUGHT

- According to each of the above commentaries, why might we have thought that the *ger* would be excluded?
- Which of those arguments, about the theoretical exclusion of the *ger*, seems to make the most sense to you?
- In what way is Ralbag's explanation very different from the explanations of the other two?
- There are a few select mitzvot for which the Torah makes special mention of the *ger* (Ex. 20:10; Lev. 16:29, 17:8–15, 18:26, 20:2, 24:22;

9:15–23 *When the Mishkan was finally completed it was covered by a cloud by day which appeared to be on fire at night. When the cloud moves, Benei Yisrael break camp and follow it; when it stops, Benei Yisrael encamp.*

15 with all its rules and laws. You shall have one law for migrant and native born alike." On the day when the Tabernacle was erected, the cloud covered the Tabernacle, the Tent of the Testimony, and from evening until morning it hung over the Tabernacle with the
16 appearance of fire. It was always there; the cloud covered the Tent, appearing at night as
17 fire. Whenever the cloud rose above the Tent, the Israelites would set out, and wherever
18 the cloud settled, the Israelites would encamp. At the Lord's command, the Israelites set out, and at the Lord's command they would encamp; for as long as the cloud rested
19 on the Tabernacle, they continued to camp there. Even when the cloud lingered over the Tabernacle for many days, the Israelites kept the Lord's charge and did not jour-
20 ney on. Sometimes the cloud would be over the Tabernacle for just a few days; at the Lord's command they would camp, and at the Lord's command they would set out.
21 Sometimes the cloud stayed only from evening to morning, and in the morning it rose,
22 and they set out. Day or night, they would set out when the cloud rose. Whether it was two days, or a month, or for many days together, the Israelites would camp as long as the cloud rested over the Tabernacle, and would not move on. They journeyed only when
23 the cloud rose. At the Lord's command they camped, and at the Lord's command they set out. And they kept the Lord's charge, the Lord's word through Moshe.

WISDOM OF THE HEART

When stating that *Benei Yisrael* did not travel when the divine cloud was stationed over the *Mishkan*, the Torah adds that "they kept the Lord's charge," meaning that they were protecting or guarding something dedicated to God. What was that, and why would it be dependent on their traveling or not? R. Pinchas Halevi Horowitz, in his commentary *Panim Yafot*, offers a beautiful interpretation. When we are busy with our daily lives, running to work or school – or in the case of *Benei Yisrael*, packing and unpacking during their travels – then we become preoccupied with the nitty-gritty of daily life and can't properly focus on building our characters and our spiritual cores. It is for that reason that it was only when they did not travel that they were able to focus on "the Lord's charge," the responsibility to develop themselves spiritually.

How, in our very busy lives today, can we carve out time and headspace to dedicate ourselves for a time to developing our spiritual side?

QUICK BITE

Nobody told *Benei Yisrael* not to travel when the cloud stood still; they just didn't. Imagine a young child in a large mall holding on to their mother for dear life, fearful of losing her.

טו אַחַת יִהְיֶה לָכֶם וְלַגֵּר וּלְאֶזְרַח הָאָֽרֶץ: וּבְיוֹם֙ הָקִ֣ים *רביעי*
אֶת־הַמִּשְׁכָּ֗ן כִּסָּ֤ה הֶֽעָנָן֙ אֶת־הַמִּשְׁכָּ֔ן לְאֹ֖הֶל הָעֵדֻ֑ת וּבָעֶ֜רֶב יִהְיֶ֧ה
טז עַל־הַמִּשְׁכָּ֛ן כְּמַרְאֵה־אֵ֖שׁ עַד־בֹּֽקֶר: כֵּ֚ן יִהְיֶ֣ה תָמִ֔יד הֶעָנָ֖ן יְכַסֶּ֑נּוּ
יז וּמַרְאֵה־אֵ֖שׁ לָֽיְלָה: וּלְפִ֞י הֵעָל֤וֹת הֶֽעָנָן֙ מֵעַ֣ל הָאֹ֔הֶל וְאַ֣חֲרֵי
כֵ֔ן יִסְע֖וּ בְּנֵ֣י יִשְׂרָאֵ֑ל וּבִמְק֗וֹם אֲשֶׁ֤ר יִשְׁכָּן־שָׁם֙ הֶֽעָנָ֔ן שָׁ֥ם יַחֲנ֖וּ
יח בְּנֵ֥י יִשְׂרָאֵֽל: עַל־פִּ֣י יְהֹוָ֗ה יִסְעוּ֙ בְּנֵ֣י יִשְׂרָאֵ֔ל וְעַל־פִּ֥י יְהֹוָ֖ה יַחֲנ֑וּ
יט כָּל־יְמֵ֗י אֲשֶׁ֨ר יִשְׁכֹּ֧ן הֶעָנָ֛ן עַל־הַמִּשְׁכָּ֖ן יַחֲנֽוּ: וּבְהַאֲרִ֧יךְ הֶֽעָנָ֛ן
עַל־הַמִּשְׁכָּ֖ן יָמִ֣ים רַבִּ֑ים וְשָֽׁמְר֧וּ בְנֵי־יִשְׂרָאֵ֛ל אֶת־מִשְׁמֶ֥רֶת יְהֹוָ֖ה
כ וְלֹ֥א יִסָּֽעוּ: וְיֵ֞שׁ אֲשֶׁ֨ר יִהְיֶ֧ה הֶֽעָנָ֛ן יָמִ֥ים מִסְפָּ֖ר עַל־הַמִּשְׁכָּ֑ן עַל־
כא פִּ֤י יְהֹוָה֙ יַחֲנ֔וּ וְעַל־פִּ֥י יְהֹוָ֖ה יִסָּֽעוּ: וְיֵ֞שׁ אֲשֶׁר־יִהְיֶ֤ה הֶֽעָנָן֙ מֵעֶ֣רֶב
עַד־בֹּ֔קֶר וְנַעֲלָ֧ה הֶעָנָ֛ן בַּבֹּ֖קֶר וְנָסָ֑עוּ א֚וֹ יוֹמָ֣ם וָלַ֔יְלָה וְנַעֲלָ֥ה הֶעָנָ֖ן
כב וְנָסָֽעוּ: אֽוֹ־יֹמַ֜יִם אוֹ־חֹ֣דֶשׁ אֽוֹ־יָמִ֗ים בְּהַאֲרִ֨יךְ הֶעָנָ֤ן עַל־הַמִּשְׁכָּן֙
לִשְׁכֹּ֣ן עָלָ֔יו יַחֲנ֥וּ בְנֵֽי־יִשְׂרָאֵ֖ל וְלֹ֣א יִסָּ֑עוּ וּבְהֵעָלֹת֖וֹ יִסָּֽעוּ: עַל־פִּ֤י
כג יְהֹוָה֙ יַחֲנ֔וּ וְעַל־פִּ֥י יְהֹוָ֖ה יִסָּ֑עוּ אֶת־מִשְׁמֶ֤רֶת יְהֹוָה֙ שָׁמָ֔רוּ עַל־פִּ֥י
יְהֹוָ֖ה בְּיַד־מֹשֶֽׁה:

TEXTUAL SKILLS

1. There are a number of key words which appear multiple times in this passage – עָנָן, נָסַע, מִשְׁכָּן, חנה. There is also a three-word phrase that appears repeatedly and captures the essence of the message of the passage. Can you find it? What do you think it is trying to convey?

2. The central verse of the passage, verse 19, divides the passage into two halves, each with a different focus. Find the focus of each half.

3. Look carefully at the language used to describe the travels and encampments. Does the Torah say that they were instructed to follow the cloud or that they chose to follow it? What difference would that make?

BEMIDBAR | CHAPTER 10   BEHAALOTEKHA | 92

10:1–10 *Moshe is to fashion two silver trumpets for signaling the people to travel, set up camp, or rally for battle. They are also blown as accompaniment to the holiday offerings.*

10 1 The Lord spoke to Moshe: "Make two silver trumpets; make them of hammered
2 metal. Use them for summoning the community and for having the camps set out.
3 When both are blown with a long note, the entire community shall assemble before
4 you at the entrance to the Tent of Meeting. If only one is blown, the princes, leaders of
5 Israel's divisions, shall assemble before you. When you blow a series of short blasts, the
6 camps on the east side shall march, and when you blow a second series of short blasts, the camps on the south side will march; thus shall a series of short blasts signal them
7 to move on. To assemble the community, blow a long blast, not a series of short blasts.
8 Aharon's sons the priests shall blow the trumpets. This shall be for you an everlasting
9 decree throughout your generations. When you go to war against an enemy who is attacking you in your land, you shall blow short blasts on the trumpets to be remem-
10 bered before the Lord your God, to be delivered from your enemies. And on your days of rejoicing, your festivals and New Moons, you shall blow the trumpets over your burnt offerings and your peace offerings. They will be a reminder of you before your God. I am the Lord your God."

QUESTIONS FOR THOUGHT

- According to Ibn Ezra, what power is apparently given to Moshe which he did not have earlier?
- According to Malbim, if the camp moves because of the cloud, what is the purpose of the trumpets?
- To what extent should we wait for God to signal to us what to do in our lives, and to what extent should we take initiative?

TEXTUAL SKILLS

1. What are the two different kinds of trumpet sounds that the Torah describes?
2. Notice that verse 2 introduces the entire passage, which has two halves. Try to match the two halves of the passage with the two halves of verse 2.

WISDOM OF THE HEART

The Torah identifies the two silver trumpets as שתי חצצרות. The Maggid of Mezeritch suggests that this word is a contraction of חצי, meaning "half," and צורות, meaning "forms," so that the phrase שתי חצצרות would yield the meaning of two halves of a whole. Many decisions we have to make in life demand that we balance two opposing values, both of which are worthwhile. Do I value absolute truth or kindness? Justice or compassion? The answer is yes to both; finding our path is about learning to maintain both values while nonetheless coming to a decision and carving a way forward. These trumpets were used by Moshe in a leadership role; more than anyone, thoughtful leaders need to balance all the different considerations and constituencies in order to navigate their people to a better place.

במדבר | פרק י

א וַיְדַבֵּ֥ר יְהֹוָ֖ה אֶל־מֹשֶׁ֥ה לֵּאמֹֽר׃ ב עֲשֵׂ֣ה לְךָ֗ שְׁתֵּי֙ חֲצֽוֹצְרֹ֣ת כֶּ֔סֶף מִקְשָׁ֖ה תַּעֲשֶׂ֣ה אֹתָ֑ם וְהָי֤וּ לְךָ֙ לְמִקְרָ֣א הָֽעֵדָ֔ה וּלְמַסַּ֖ע אֶת־הַֽמַּחֲנֽוֹת׃ ג וְתָקְע֖וּ בָּהֵ֑ן וְנֽוֹעֲד֤וּ אֵלֶ֙יךָ֙ כָּל־הָ֣עֵדָ֔ה אֶל־פֶּ֖תַח אֹ֥הֶל מוֹעֵֽד׃ ד וְאִם־בְּאַחַ֖ת יִתְקָ֑עוּ וְנֽוֹעֲד֤וּ אֵלֶ֙יךָ֙ הַנְּשִׂיאִ֔ים רָאשֵׁ֖י אַלְפֵ֥י יִשְׂרָאֵֽל׃ ה וּתְקַעְתֶּ֖ם תְּרוּעָ֑ה וְנָֽסְעוּ֙ הַֽמַּחֲנ֔וֹת הַחֹנִ֖ים קֵֽדְמָה׃ ו וּתְקַעְתֶּ֤ם תְּרוּעָה֙ שֵׁנִ֔ית וְנָֽסְעוּ֙ הַֽמַּחֲנ֔וֹת הַחֹנִ֖ים תֵּימָ֑נָה תְּרוּעָ֥ה יִתְקְע֖וּ לְמַסְעֵיהֶֽם׃ ז וּבְהַקְהִ֖יל אֶת־הַקָּהָ֑ל תִּתְקְע֖וּ וְלֹ֥א תָרִֽיעוּ׃ ח וּבְנֵ֤י אַהֲרֹן֙ הַכֹּ֣הֲנִ֔ים יִתְקְע֖וּ בַּחֲצֹֽצְר֑וֹת וְהָי֥וּ לָכֶ֛ם לְחֻקַּ֥ת עוֹלָ֖ם לְדֹרֹֽתֵיכֶֽם׃ ט וְכִֽי־תָבֹ֨אוּ מִלְחָמָ֜ה בְּאַרְצְכֶ֗ם עַל־הַצַּר֙ הַצֹּרֵ֣ר אֶתְכֶ֔ם וַהֲרֵעֹתֶ֖ם בַּחֲצֹֽצְרֹ֑ת וֲנִזְכַּרְתֶּ֗ם לִפְנֵי֙ יְהֹוָ֣ה אֱלֹֽהֵיכֶ֔ם וְנוֹשַׁעְתֶּ֖ם מֵאֹיְבֵיכֶֽם׃ י וּבְי֨וֹם שִׂמְחַתְכֶ֥ם וּֽבְמוֹעֲדֵיכֶם֮ וּבְרָאשֵׁ֣י חָדְשֵׁיכֶם֒ וּתְקַעְתֶּ֣ם בַּחֲצֹֽצְרֹ֗ת עַ֚ל עֹלֹ֣תֵיכֶ֔ם וְעַ֖ל זִבְחֵ֣י שַׁלְמֵיכֶ֑ם וְהָי֨וּ לָכֶ֤ם לְזִכָּרוֹן֙ לִפְנֵ֣י אֱלֹֽהֵיכֶ֔ם אֲנִ֖י יְהֹוָ֥ה אֱלֹהֵיכֶֽם׃

CLASSIC COMMENTATORS

The previous chapter clearly articulates that the people moved when the cloud lifted from the *Mishkan*, yet here there seems to be another factor, the trumpets. What is the relationship between the lifting of the cloud and the signaling with the trumpets?

IBN EZRA

When a תרועה is sounded, the tribes under the banner of Yehuda are to break camp and travel, even while the cloud still hovers above the *Mishkan*.

MALBIM

God now tells the nation that in addition to the sign of the cloud, which communicates when the nation should move or stop, the trumpets will provide a complementary system of signals. These instruments were used to gather the congregation together, as well as to indicate the moment when each group of tribes was to set forth on the next leg of their journey.

אבן עזרא

ואם היתה תרועה – יסע דגל מחנה יהודה, אף על פי שהענן על המשכן.

מלבי״ם

אמר לו שחוץ ממה שיהיה להם אות אל הנסיעה ע״י הענן תעשה עוד אות על ידי חצוצרות בשגם שהחצוצרות היו משמשים גם למקרא העדה, ולסדר אימת וזמן של נסיעת כל דגל בפני עצמו.

11 On the twentieth day of the second month in the second year, the cloud rose above
12 the Tabernacle of the Covenant. The Israelites set out on their journey from the Sinai
13 Desert, and the cloud came to rest in the Wilderness of Paran. For the first time, at
14 the Lord's command through Moshe, they set out. The divisions of Yehuda's camp
   set out first, under their banner. Leading that division was Naḥshon son of Aminadav.
15/16 Netanel son of Tzuar was in charge of the division of the tribe of Yissakhar. Eliav
17 son of Ḥelon was in charge of the division of the tribe of Zevulun. The Tabernacle
   was taken down, and the Gershonites and the Merarites, who carried it, set out.
18 The divisions of the camp of Reuven set out next, under their banner. Leading that
19 division was Elitzur son of Shedeiur. Shelumiel son of Tzurishadai was in charge of the
20 division of the tribe of Shimon. Elyasaf son of Deuel was in charge of the division of
21 the tribe of Gad. Then the Kohatites, who carried the sacred objects, set out. By the
22 time they arrived, the Tabernacle would have been erected. The divisions of the camp
   of Efrayim set out next, under their banner. Leading that division was Elishama son of
23 Amihud. Gamliel son of Pedahtzur was in charge of the division of the tribe of Menashe.
24/25 Avidan son of Gidoni was in charge of the division of the tribe of Binyamin. Then, at
   the rear of the whole camp, the divisions of the camp of Dan set out under their banner.
26 Leading that division was Aḥiezer son of Amishadai. Pagiel son of Okhran was in charge
27 of the division of the tribe of Asher. Aḥira son of Einan was in charge of the division of
28 the tribe of Naftali. This was the order in which the Israelites set out in their divisions.

ר' עובדיה ספורנו

כאשר יחנו – שכשיגיע מחצית כל הדגלים יהיה המשכן מוקם לגמרי באמצע כולם, כי תיכף אחר דגל ראובן נסעו הקהתים נושאי המקדש... ובכן היה אז כולו באמצע כל המחנות גם בעת המסע.

RABBI OVADYA SFORNO

When the second half of the nation arrived at the new campsite, they found that the *Mishkan* had already been assembled in the middle of the latest location. This is because once the camp of Reuven [and his accompanying tribes] left on their journey [after the trio of Yehuda tribes], the clan of Kehat followed with their transport of the Sanctuary vessels.... As such, the entire *Mishkan* remained in the middle of the camp both when the nation camped and when Israel traveled through the wilderness.

QUESTIONS FOR THOUGHT

- How would Rashi explain the description we have in this chapter?
- How would Sforno explain the earlier verse (2:17)?
- Which of these approaches makes more sense to you? Why?

WISDOM OF THE HEART

Dan took up the rear position in the camp, making sure that there were no stragglers. This was a fulfillment of Yaakov's blessing that Dan would take care of their brothers and sisters.

חמישי

יא וַיְהִ֞י בַּשָּׁנָ֧ה הַשֵּׁנִ֛ית בַּחֹ֥דֶשׁ הַשֵּׁנִ֖י בְּעֶשְׂרִ֣ים בַּחֹ֑דֶשׁ נַעֲלָה֙ הֶֽעָנָ֔ן
יב מֵעַ֖ל מִשְׁכַּ֣ן הָעֵדֻֽת: וַיִּסְע֥וּ בְנֵֽי־יִשְׂרָאֵ֖ל לְמַסְעֵיהֶ֑ם מִמִּדְבַּ֣ר
יג סִינָ֔י וַיִּשְׁכֹּ֥ן הֶעָנָ֖ן בְּמִדְבַּ֥ר פָּארָֽן: וַיִּסְע֖וּ בָּרִאשֹׁנָ֑ה עַל־פִּ֥י יְהֹוָ֖ה
יד בְּיַד־מֹשֶֽׁה: וַיִּסַּ֞ע דֶּ֣גֶל מַחֲנֵ֧ה בְנֵֽי־יְהוּדָ֛ה בָּרִאשֹׁנָ֖ה לְצִבְאֹתָ֑ם
טו וְעַ֨ל־צְבָא֔וֹ נַחְשׁ֖וֹן בֶּן־עַמִּֽינָדָֽב: וְעַ֨ל־צְבָ֔א מַטֵּ֖ה בְּנֵ֣י יִשָּׂשכָ֑ר
טז נְתַנְאֵ֖ל בֶּן־צוּעָֽר: וְעַ֨ל־צְבָ֔א מַטֵּ֖ה בְּנֵ֣י זְבוּלֻ֑ן אֱלִיאָ֖ב בֶּן־חֵלֹֽן:
יז וְהוּרַ֖ד הַמִּשְׁכָּ֑ן וְנָסְע֤וּ בְנֵֽי־גֵרְשׁוֹן֙ וּבְנֵ֣י מְרָרִ֔י נֹשְׂאֵ֖י הַמִּשְׁכָּֽן:
יח וְנָסַ֗ע דֶּ֛גֶל מַחֲנֵ֥ה רְאוּבֵ֖ן לְצִבְאֹתָ֑ם וְעַ֨ל־צְבָא֔וֹ אֱלִיצ֖וּר בֶּן־
יט שְׁדֵיאֽוּר: וְעַ֨ל־צְבָ֔א מַטֵּ֖ה בְּנֵ֣י שִׁמְע֑וֹן שְׁלֻֽמִיאֵ֖ל בֶּן־צוּרִֽישַׁדָּֽי:
כ וְעַ֨ל־צְבָ֖א מַטֵּ֣ה בְנֵי־גָ֑ד אֶלְיָסָ֖ף בֶּן־דְּעוּאֵֽל: וְנָסְעוּ֙ הַקְּהָתִ֔ים
כא כב נֹשְׂאֵ֣י הַמִּקְדָּ֑שׁ וְהֵקִ֥ימוּ אֶת־הַמִּשְׁכָּ֖ן עַד־בֹּאָֽם: וְנָסַ֗ע דֶּ֛גֶל מַחֲנֵ֥ה
כג בְנֵי־אֶפְרַ֖יִם לְצִבְאֹתָ֑ם וְעַ֨ל־צְבָא֔וֹ אֱלִישָׁמָ֖ע בֶּן־עַמִּיהֽוּד: וְעַ֨ל־
כד צְבָ֔א מַטֵּ֖ה בְּנֵ֣י מְנַשֶּׁ֑ה גַּמְלִיאֵ֖ל בֶּן־פְּדָהצֽוּר: וְעַ֨ל־צְבָ֔א מַטֵּ֖ה
כה בְּנֵ֣י בִנְיָמִ֑ן אֲבִידָ֖ן בֶּן־גִּדְעוֹנִֽי: וְנָסַ֗ע דֶּ֛גֶל מַחֲנֵ֥ה בְנֵי־דָ֖ן מְאַסֵּ֣ף
לְכָל־הַֽמַּחֲנֹ֖ת לְצִבְאֹתָ֑ם וְעַ֨ל־צְבָא֔וֹ אֲחִיעֶ֖זֶר בֶּן־עַמִּֽישַׁדָּֽי:
כו וְעַ֨ל־צְבָ֔א מַטֵּ֖ה בְּנֵ֣י אָשֵׁ֑ר פַּגְעִיאֵ֖ל בֶּן־עָכְרָֽן: וְעַ֨ל־צְבָ֔א מַטֵּ֖ה
כז כח בְּנֵ֣י נַפְתָּלִ֑י אֲחִירַ֖ע בֶּן־עֵינָֽן: אֵ֛לֶּה מַסְעֵ֥י בְנֵֽי־יִשְׂרָאֵ֖ל לְצִבְאֹתָ֑ם

CLASSIC COMMENTATORS

The Torah earlier (2:17) indicated that they were to travel the same way that they camped. The commentaries debate how to reconcile that description with the one we have here.

RASHI

During the marches the entire nation maintained the formation that they observed when they encamped. Each group of three was assigned a specific side of the national camp.

רש״י

הליכתן כחנייתן, כל דגל מהלך לרוח הקבועה לו.

29 Moshe said to Ḥovav son of Reuel the Midianite, Moshe's father-in-law, "We are setting out to the place that the Lord said He would give us. Come with us and we will be
30 good to you, for the Lord has promised good things to Israel." But he replied, "I will
31 not come; I must go back to my own land and my own people." "Please do not leave us," said Moshe, "for you know where we should camp in the wilderness; you would be
32 our eyes. If you come with us, whatever good the Lord does for us, we will do for you."
33 They journeyed from the Lord's mountain for three days; and the Ark of the Lord's
34 Covenant went ahead of them for those three days to find a resting place for them. The
35 Lord's cloud was over them by day as they journeyed from the camp. When the Ark set out, Moshe would say, "Arise, Lord; let Your enemies be scattered, and Your foes
36 flee before You." When it came to rest, he would say, "Bring back, O Lord, the myriad thousands of Israel."

QUESTIONS FOR THOUGHT

- Which of the commentaries understands that the word והיית is to be understood as relating to things that happened in the past, and which understands that it is to be read as pointing to the future?
- If this is meant to convince Ḥovav to go with *Benei Yisrael*, which of these explanations do you think offers the most convincing reason for him to accompany them?
- Which of these commentaries do you think tries to understand this incident as part of the series of discussions in this chapter relating to the travels of *Benei Yisrael*?

TEXTUAL SKILLS

1. Ḥovav says that he would prefer to go to his *eretz* and his *moledet*. Where in Genesis do those words take on special prominence?
2. Is Ḥovav Moshe's father-in-law or brother-in-law?
3. What phrase appears twice in verse 33?

WISDOM OF THE HEART

The two verses at the center of the *parasha* are literally bracketed in the text by two instances of an inverted letter *nun*. According to one opinion in the Talmud, the two verses in the middle are considered to be their own book. R. Soloveitchik explains that these two verses describe the ideal scenario: the Ark moves, and the enemies flee; the Ark rests, and *Benei Yisrael* are secure in their place. God's plan was for the conquest of the Promised Land to be easy, smooth, and bloodless. The Ark would lead the way, the Canaanites would flee, and *Benei Yisrael* would usher in the Messianic Age. That's the ideal version, the version of the two verses. Instead we have the version that actually happened, filled with complications, ups and downs, and failures alongside successes, the version we are still experiencing today. Why did the ideal version fail to happen? It was because of the problems we begin to read about immediately after the ideal, bracketed passage.

Sometimes we make plans and we think that they are perfect. But they rarely work out exactly as we wanted. How can we turn those unfortunate turns of events into successes?

כט וַיֹּאמֶר מֹשֶׁה לְחֹבָב בֶּן־רְעוּאֵל הַמִּדְיָנִי חֹתֵן מֹשֶׁה נֹסְעִים ׀ אֲנַחְנוּ אֶל־הַמָּקוֹם אֲשֶׁר אָמַר יְהֹוָה אֹתוֹ אֶתֵּן לָכֶם לְכָה אִתָּנוּ וְהֵטַבְנוּ לָךְ כִּי־יְהֹוָה דִּבֶּר־טוֹב עַל־יִשְׂרָאֵל:
ל וַיֹּאמֶר אֵלָיו לֹא אֵלֵךְ כִּי אִם־אֶל־אַרְצִי וְאֶל־מוֹלַדְתִּי אֵלֵךְ:
לא וַיֹּאמֶר אַל־נָא תַּעֲזֹב אֹתָנוּ כִּי ׀ עַל־כֵּן יָדַעְתָּ חֲנֹתֵנוּ בַּמִּדְבָּר וְהָיִיתָ לָּנוּ לְעֵינָיִם: לב וְהָיָה כִּי־תֵלֵךְ עִמָּנוּ וְהָיָה ׀ הַטּוֹב הַהוּא אֲשֶׁר יֵיטִיב יְהֹוָה עִמָּנוּ וְהֵטַבְנוּ לָךְ: לג וַיִּסְעוּ מֵהַר יְהֹוָה דֶּרֶךְ שְׁלֹשֶׁת יָמִים וַאֲרוֹן בְּרִית־יְהֹוָה נֹסֵעַ לִפְנֵיהֶם דֶּרֶךְ שְׁלֹשֶׁת יָמִים לָתוּר לָהֶם מְנוּחָה: לד וַעֲנַן יְהֹוָה עֲלֵיהֶם יוֹמָם בְּנָסְעָם מִן־הַמַּחֲנֶה: ׆ לה וַיְהִי בִּנְסֹעַ הָאָרֹן וַיֹּאמֶר מֹשֶׁה קוּמָה ׀ יְהֹוָה וְיָפֻצוּ אֹיְבֶיךָ וְיָנֻסוּ מְשַׂנְאֶיךָ מִפָּנֶיךָ: לו וּבְנֻחֹה יֹאמַר שׁוּבָה יְהֹוָה רִבְבוֹת אַלְפֵי יִשְׂרָאֵל: ׆

CLASSIC COMMENTATORS

After Ḥovav declines Moshe's invitation, Moshe tries to convince him to come. One phrase Moshe uses is וְהָיִיתָ לָּנוּ לְעֵינָיִם. It is not at all clear what he means.

RABBI YOSEF KARA   ר׳ יוסף קרא

Said Moshe to Ḥovav: You can illuminate our eyes with the sound advice that you provide, as an earlier verse states, "Now listen to me, let me advise you; and may God be with you" (Ex. 18:19).

והיית מאיר עינינו בעיצה טובה ונכונה שנתת לנו, דכתיב: עתה שמע בקולי איעצך (שמות י״ח:י״ט).

IBN EZRA   אבן עזרא

Said Moshe to Ḥovav: Come with us and be our eyes as you show us the way through the wilderness.

לכה אתנו והיה לנו לעינים – להראות הדרך.

RABBI YOSEF BEKHOR SHOR   ר׳ יוסף בכור שור

Said Moshe to Ḥovav: Everyone who sees you escorting us through the desert will say that you abandoned your country and your home because you understood that the Holy One, blessed be He, is with us. Therefore, all the other nations will be afraid to contend with us or to challenge us on the battlefield.

שיאמרו הרואים אותך עמנו: לא לחינם הניח זה ארצו ומקומו, אם לא שראה שהקב״ה עמהם, ויראו להזדקק לנו ולהלחם עמנו.

BEMIDBAR | CHAPTER 11

11 1 The people began to rail bitterly in the LORD's presence. And the LORD heard and was incensed; fire from the LORD blazed against them, consuming at the edge of the camp.
2 The people cried out to Moshe – Moshe prayed to the LORD – and the fire subsided.
3 And so that place was named Tavera, because the LORD's fire had blazed against them.
4 The rabble in their midst began to have strong cravings, and once again the Israelites
5 began to weep, saying, "Who will give us meat to eat? We remember the fish we ate in Egypt at no cost, the cucumbers, and the melons, and the leeks, and the onions, and
6 the garlic. But now our throats are dry. There is nothing at all but this manna to look at."
7 The manna was like coriander seed, and like bdellium in color. The people went around
8 gathering it. Then they would grind it in a mill or crush it in a mortar. They cooked it
9 in a pot and they made cakes from it; it tasted like cakes made with oil. When the dew

---

ר' אנשלמה אשטרוק

המזונות בודאי הן מספקים להם ברווח ובחינם, כי איך יעבידו בפרך וברב עבודה ונפש יבשה אין כל.

RABBI SHLOMO ASTRUC

The Egyptians obviously supplied the Israelites with great quantities of free food. If they had not done so, the oppressors would hardly have been able to insist that the malnourished Hebrews continue slaving away for them.

QUESTIONS FOR THOUGHT

- In what way are the explanations of Ramban and R. Astruc similar? In what subtle way are they different?
- According to Abarbanel, in what way was the manna similar to the fish that the Israelites ate in Egypt? How does that affect our understanding of their complaint?
- In what way is Ibn Ezra's comment different from all the others? What does his comment imply in terms of what it meant to be a slave in Egypt?

TEXTUAL SKILLS

1. There are two different stories in this passage. Can you identify them? Are they connected? What do you think the connection is?
2. There are three highly unusual words in this passage. One (in v. 1) appears only twice in all of Tanakh, another (in v. 4) appears only once in all of Tanakh, and a third (in v. 8) also appears only twice in Tanakh.

WISDOM OF THE HEART

According to a midrash, the manna could take on any taste that the people wanted. If so, then why did *Benei Yisrael* complain about the food they were missing? After all, they could have simply thought of the tastes they desired. R. Shlomo Aviner suggests that that was precisely the problem. When you can have anything you want, then nothing tastes good, nothing is special, nothing excites you. The Talmud says that nobody leaves this world with even half of their desires fulfilled. Perhaps that is a blessing.

Imagine that your parents always gave you anything that you asked for – no questions asked, no hesitation. How would that make you feel?

א וַיְהִ֤י הָעָם֙ כְּמִתְאֹ֣נְנִ֔ים רַ֖ע בְּאָזְנֵ֣י יְהוָ֑ה וַיִּשְׁמַ֤ע יְהוָה֙ וַיִּ֣חַר אַפּ֔וֹ
ב וַתִּבְעַר־בָּם֙ אֵ֣שׁ יְהוָ֔ה וַתֹּ֖אכַל בִּקְצֵ֥ה הַֽמַּחֲנֶֽה: וַיִּצְעַ֥ק הָעָ֖ם
ג אֶל־מֹשֶׁ֑ה וַיִּתְפַּלֵּ֤ל מֹשֶׁה֙ אֶל־יְהוָ֔ה וַתִּשְׁקַ֖ע הָאֵֽשׁ: וַיִּקְרָ֛א שֵֽׁם־
ד הַמָּק֥וֹם הַה֖וּא תַּבְעֵרָ֑ה כִּֽי־בָעֲרָ֥ה בָ֖ם אֵ֥שׁ יְהוָֽה: וְהָֽאסַפְסֻף֙
אֲשֶׁ֣ר בְּקִרְבּ֔וֹ הִתְאַוּ֖וּ תַּאֲוָ֑ה וַיָּשֻׁ֣בוּ וַיִּבְכּ֗וּ גַּ֚ם בְּנֵ֣י יִשְׂרָאֵ֔ל וַיֹּ֣אמְר֔וּ
ה מִ֥י יַאֲכִלֵ֖נוּ בָּשָֽׂר: זָכַ֨רְנוּ֙ אֶת־הַדָּגָ֔ה אֲשֶׁר־נֹאכַ֥ל בְּמִצְרַ֖יִם חִנָּ֑ם
אֵ֣ת הַקִּשֻּׁאִ֗ים וְאֵת֙ הָֽאֲבַטִּחִ֔ים וְאֶת־הֶחָצִ֥יר וְאֶת־הַבְּצָלִ֖ים
ו וְאֶת־הַשּׁוּמִֽים: וְעַתָּ֛ה נַפְשֵׁ֥נוּ יְבֵשָׁ֖ה אֵ֣ין כֹּ֑ל בִּלְתִּ֖י אֶל־הַמָּ֥ן
ז עֵינֵֽינוּ: וְהַמָּ֕ן כִּזְרַע־גַּ֖ד ה֑וּא וְעֵינ֖וֹ כְּעֵ֥ין הַבְּדֹֽלַח: שָׁ֩טוּ֩ הָעָ֨ם
ח וְלָֽקְט֜וּ וְטָחֲנ֣וּ בָרֵחַ֗יִם א֤וֹ דָכוּ֙ בַּמְּדֹכָ֔ה וּבִשְּׁלוּ֙ בַּפָּר֔וּר וְעָשׂ֥וּ
ט אֹת֖וֹ עֻג֑וֹת וְהָיָ֣ה טַעְמ֔וֹ כְּטַ֖עַם לְשַׁ֥ד הַשָּֽׁמֶן: וּבְרֶ֧דֶת הַטַּ֛ל עַל־

CLASSIC COMMENTATORS

As part of the people's complaint about the manna they recall the fish that they ate in Egypt at no cost. Did the Egyptians really give them free fish?

אבן עזרא

בזול, כאילו היא חינם.

IBN EZRA

The Egyptians sold the Israelites fish at a low cost, which made it seem that they were getting the food for free.

רמב״ן

כי היו הדייגים המצרים מעבידין אותם למשוך הדגים שנאחזים במצודה ובמכמורות, והיו נותנים להם מן הדגים כמנהג כל פורשי מכמורת.

RAMBAN

The Egyptian fishermen enslaved the Hebrews and forced them to haul up the nets and traps that were full of fish. As compensation for their labor, the Israelites were given a percentage of the catch, as is customary.

אברבנאל

והיה זה לפי שנהר נילוס יוצא ומתפשט וכל אחד מהמצרים היה חופר גומא שהיה מתמלא מהיאור, וכשהנהר שב למקומו, היו נשארים הדגים בחפירות ההם, ובזה הדרך היו אוכלים אותם חינם.

ABARBANEL

It was usual for the Nile River to overflow its banks and to flow over the countryside. When this was about to happen, the Egyptians would dig pits for themselves which would fill up with the streaming water. Then, when the water returned to its place, the people would simply empty these holes of the fish that had become trapped there. This is how the Israelites ended up with free fish.

11:10–15 *Distressed by the complaints, Moshe tells God that he cannot deal with the people alone – and if that is what God wants of him, he would prefer to die.*

10 fell over the camp at night, the manna would fall upon that. Moshe heard the people weeping clan by clan, each one at his tent's opening. The Lord's anger blazed intensely,
11 and Moshe was distressed. "Why have You treated Your servant so badly?" asked Moshe of the Lord. "Why have I found so little favor in Your sight that You lay all the burden of
12 this people upon me? Was it I who conceived all this people? Was it I who gave birth to them all, that You should say to me, 'Carry them in your bosom, as a nursemaid carries
13 a baby,' to the land that You swore to their fathers? Where am I to get meat to give all
14 this people when they come wailing to me, 'Give us meat to eat'? I cannot bear all this
15 people alone; the burden is too heavy for me. If this is how You treat me, kill me now, if I find any favor in Your sight, and let me not see my own misery."

- Which word appears twice in the comment of Bekhor Shor? What point is he trying to make? According to Bekhor Shor, in what way is Moshe's comment similar to David's declaration in II Samuel 24:14?
- Which commentary do you think presents the most realistic portrayal of Moshe's crisis?
- Which commentary do you think reflects the most meaningful expression of a good leader?

TEXTUAL SKILLS

1. Moshe asks God if it is his responsibility to act as the people's nursemaid. The word for nursemaid is אומן, which actually refers to a male nursemaid. That term appears only two other times in Tanakh – Isaiah 49:23 and Esther 2:7.
2. Compare Moshe's reaction to the complaint about food to his reaction to the first story in this chapter.
3. The word למה appears twice in verse 11. Find the differences between them.
4. How many topics does Moshe raise in his complaint to God?

WISDOM OF THE HEART

Moshe walks through the camp and hears the people crying, "clan by clan, each one at his tent's opening." R. Moshe Sofer, also known as *Ḥatam Sofer*, comments that this was particularly troubling because they were not concerned for each other, but only for their own families, their own tents, their own clans. The strength of the people is when they take care of each other, not when they selfishly turn inward. The story is told of Mayer Amschel Rothschild, founder of the banking dynasty, who showed his five sons his open hand. "Look at each finger," he said. "How easy would it be to break it?" Then he clenched his fist. "And now?" As he spread his sons geographically to establish branches of his bank, he instructed them to act as a family unit and work in unison.

Being a member of a team requires extra work and dedication, but increases our capacity to succeed and brings out the best in us. Is there a point at which our individual needs outweigh our responsibilities to the team?

הַמַּחֲנֶה לַיְלָה יֵרֵד הַמָּן עָלָיו: וַיִּשְׁמַע מֹשֶׁה אֶת־הָעָם בֹּכֶה לְמִשְׁפְּחֹתָיו אִישׁ לְפֶתַח אָהֳלוֹ וַיִּחַר־אַף יהוה מְאֹד וּבְעֵינֵי מֹשֶׁה רָע: וַיֹּאמֶר מֹשֶׁה אֶל־יהוה לָמָה הֲרֵעֹתָ לְעַבְדֶּךָ וְלָמָּה לֹא־מָצָתִי חֵן בְּעֵינֶיךָ לָשׂוּם אֶת־מַשָּׂא כָּל־הָעָם הַזֶּה עָלָי: הֶאָנֹכִי הָרִיתִי אֵת כָּל־הָעָם הַזֶּה אִם־אָנֹכִי יְלִדְתִּיהוּ כִּי־תֹאמַר אֵלַי שָׂאֵהוּ בְחֵיקֶךָ כַּאֲשֶׁר יִשָּׂא הָאֹמֵן אֶת־הַיֹּנֵק עַל הָאֲדָמָה אֲשֶׁר נִשְׁבַּעְתָּ לַאֲבֹתָיו: מֵאַיִן לִי בָּשָׂר לָתֵת לְכָל־הָעָם הַזֶּה כִּי־יִבְכּוּ עָלַי לֵאמֹר תְּנָה־לָּנוּ בָשָׂר וְנֹאכֵלָה: לֹא־אוּכַל אָנֹכִי לְבַדִּי לָשֵׂאת אֶת־כָּל־הָעָם הַזֶּה כִּי כָבֵד מִמֶּנִּי: וְאִם־כָּכָה ׀ אַתְּ־עֹשָׂה לִּי הָרְגֵנִי נָא הָרֹג אִם־מָצָאתִי חֵן בְּעֵינֶיךָ וְאַל־אֶרְאֶה בְּרָעָתִי:

CLASSIC COMMENTATORS

In his final line, Moshe tells God that he would prefer to die than ואל אראה ברעתי. The commentaries debate what this Hebrew phrase means and what it refers to.

RABBI YOSEF BEKHOR SHOR — ר' יוסף בכור שור
Moshe claims that he would rather die by the hand of God than continue to suffer and languish under the abuse of the people.
כי מוטב לי למות בידך ולא להיות מתנוונה והולך בידם.

ABARBANEL — אברבנאל
Moshe fears that he will become embarrassed by his inability to lead the nation or give them what they demand.
שלא אתבייש לעיניהם ולא אוכל להנהיגם ולתת צרכם כפי שאלתם.

RABBI OVADYA SFORNO — ר' עובדיה ספורנו
The dissolution of his stewardship would be more difficult for Moshe than his actual death.
ברעת חסרון ההנהגה המסובבת בגללי, כי זה יהיה קשה עלי מן המות.

QUESTIONS FOR THOUGHT

- According to each of the commentaries, whose fate was Moshe concerned about?
- In what way is it difficult to fit Sforno's interpretation into Moshe's words? How does Sforno try to deal with that?

11:16–20 God instructs Moshe to gather seventy elders who will assist him in leading and managing the people. He also directs Moshe to tell the people that He will provide them with meat – every day for a full month.

16 Then the Lord said to Moshe, "Gather for Me seventy of Israel's elders, whom you know to be the people's elders and officers, and bring them to the Tent of Meeting. Let
17 them stand there with you. I will come down and speak with you there, and I will take some of the spirit that is on you and place it upon them; they will share the burden
18 of the people with you, and you will not have to bear it alone. And say to the people: Consecrate yourselves for tomorrow; you will then have meat to eat, for you have been wailing in the presence of the Lord, 'Who will give us meat to eat? It was better for us
19 in Egypt.' The Lord will give you meat, and you will eat. You will eat it not just for one
20 day, or two days, or five, or ten, or twenty days, but for a whole month, until it comes out at your nostrils and becomes nauseating to you; for you have rejected the Lord who is

---

- In what way could this be similar to the announcement of Aharon as Moshe's assistant (Ex. 4:14–16)?
- Does encouraging young stars strengthen or weaken a leader? Explain

TEXTUAL SKILLS

1. Match up God's two messages to Moshe with Moshe's two complaints in the previous passage.
2. In what ways are God's description of the delivery of meat (vv. 19–20) similar to and different from the description of the travels of *Benei Yisrael* (9:21–22)?
3. Notice that in Exodus (chs. 16–18) we have a series of stories about manna, meat (specifically, quail), Moshe's father-in-law, and distributed leadership (Yitro's suggestion to establish a judicial system). There is a parallel series of stories on the same topics in Numbers 10–11 (although in a different order).

WISDOM OF THE HEART

Some conflicts are "zero-sum games" – there is a limited amount of a resource available and the winner gets it. Often, however, a skilled negotiator can figure out how to transform the conflict into a win-win situation, in which cooperation actually increases the resources available and everyone ends up better off. Rashi uses the example of lighting candles – lighting a second candle using the flame of the first doesn't diminish the light of the first; rather, it increases the available light. Such was the prophecy granted the seventy elders. The flame of prophecy burning inside Moshe ignited them, and as a result there was greater light and insight for all of *Benei Yisrael*.

What kind of personality or attitude does it require for a person who once held a unique position to embrace and encourage the idea of many people being empowered to do what they once did alone? How do you think such an attitude can be cultivated?

במדבר | פרק יא | בהעלתך

טז וַיֹּאמֶר יְהֹוָה אֶל־מֹשֶׁה אֶסְפָה־לִּי שִׁבְעִים אִישׁ מִזִּקְנֵי יִשְׂרָאֵל אֲשֶׁר יָדַעְתָּ כִּי־הֵם זִקְנֵי הָעָם וְשֹׁטְרָיו וְלָקַחְתָּ אֹתָם אֶל־אֹהֶל מוֹעֵד וְהִתְיַצְּבוּ שָׁם עִמָּךְ: יז וְיָרַדְתִּי וְדִבַּרְתִּי עִמְּךָ שָׁם וְאָצַלְתִּי מִן־הָרוּחַ אֲשֶׁר עָלֶיךָ וְשַׂמְתִּי עֲלֵיהֶם וְנָשְׂאוּ אִתְּךָ בְּמַשָּׂא הָעָם וְלֹא־תִשָּׂא אַתָּה לְבַדֶּךָ: יח וְאֶל־הָעָם תֹּאמַר הִתְקַדְּשׁוּ לְמָחָר וַאֲכַלְתֶּם בָּשָׂר כִּי בְּכִיתֶם בְּאָזְנֵי יְהֹוָה לֵאמֹר מִי יַאֲכִלֵנוּ בָּשָׂר כִּי־טוֹב לָנוּ בְּמִצְרָיִם וְנָתַן יְהֹוָה לָכֶם בָּשָׂר וַאֲכַלְתֶּם: יט לֹא יוֹם אֶחָד תֹּאכְלוּן וְלֹא יוֹמָיִם וְלֹא | חֲמִשָּׁה יָמִים וְלֹא עֲשָׂרָה יָמִים וְלֹא עֶשְׂרִים יוֹם: כ עַד | חֹדֶשׁ יָמִים עַד אֲשֶׁר־יֵצֵא מֵאַפְּכֶם וְהָיָה לָכֶם לְזָרָא יַעַן כִּי־מְאַסְתֶּם אֶת־יְהֹוָה אֲשֶׁר בְּקִרְבְּכֶם וַתִּבְכּוּ

CLASSIC COMMENTATORS

God tells Moshe that the seventy elders will also have God's spirit rest upon them. The word used to describe the process is ואצלתי, and the commentaries debate its meaning.

RASHI — רש״י
כתרגומו: ואירבי.
The verb should be understood as the Aramaic renders it: *vaarabei* – I will enhance.

IBN EZRA — אבן עזרא
אקח מאשר אצלך.
God tells Moshe that He will siphon off from him some of His spirit.

RABBI YOSEF BEKHOR SHOR — ר׳ יוסף בכור שור
איני רוצה לתת להם רוח אחר אלא משלך, כדי שיהיו טפלין לך.
Said God: I do not want to give them a spirit other than from you, so that they will be subordinate to you.

QUESTIONS FOR THOUGHT

- According to which of the commentaries is Moshe's prophecy diminished by his sharing of "God's spirit" with them?
- Which of the commentaries understands that God is describing a process which makes the elders' prophecy dependent on Moshe's?
- Does Rashi agree with one of the other two commentaries, or does he have a third understanding?

21 among you and have come wailing in His presence, 'Why ever did we leave Egypt?'" But Moshe said, "Here I am among six hundred thousand men on foot, and You say, 'I will
22 give them meat to eat for a whole month'! If whole flocks and herds were slaughtered for them, would there be enough? If all the fish of the sea were caught for them, would there be enough?!"
23 The LORD said to Moshe, "Does the LORD's hand fall short? Soon you shall see whether
24 what I say comes true or not." Moshe went out and told the people what the LORD had said. He gathered seventy of the people's elders and had them stand surrounding the
25 Tent. Then the LORD came down in the cloud and spoke to him, and took some of the spirit that was upon him and placed it on the seventy elders. When the spirit rested

---

ר׳ עובדיה ספורנו

הצאן ובקר ישחט להם ומצא להם – איך יספיק זה להסיר תלונותם, מאחר שאינם שואלים בשר אלא כדי לנסות... הלא אין ספק שכמו שנסו בזה ינסו במאכלים זולת זה לאין תכלית.

RABBI OVADYA SFORNO

When Moshe protests to God, "If whole flocks and herds were slaughtered for them, would there be enough?" (Num. 11:22), what he means is: even such an abundance of meat would not quell the Israelites' complaints. For they are really only demanding flesh in order to test God.... And it is certain that just as the people have challenged God with regard to meat, so will they think of other foods that they want to ask for. There will be no end to the matter.

QUESTIONS FOR THOUGHT

- In what way are the commentaries of Ibn Ezra and Ramban similar? Regarding what detail do they disagree?
- What other big question does R. Hirsch's explanation answer?
- Sforno shifts the focus of Moshe's comment from God to the people. What important psychological insight does Sforno offer?
- Do you think that great religious thinkers are those who have good answers to difficult questions, or is their greatness in the kinds of questions they ask?

WISDOM OF THE HEART

It sounds like Moshe is questioning God's ability to provide meat for the people. This bothered the commentators throughout the ages. Is it really possible that Moshe doubted God's ability? Many creative answers have been offered – Moshe thought that God should not perform a miracle, Moshe was convinced that God had no intention of performing a miracle, Moshe didn't consider birds as meat – but there is one that stands out in that it does not seek for ways to "explain away" the question. R. Yosef Ibn Kaspi says that this is not the first time that Moshe has challenged God (he started at the burning bush), nor should we expect it to be the last. But there is a huge difference between doubting God and challenging Him. Moshe's challenging was an attempt to clarify, to understand God's plan. That kind of challenging is welcomed and encouraged – what kind of teacher would not want their students to really understand?

There are examples of questions which are not welcomed, like the question in the Haggada attributed to the wicked son. What distinguishes legitimate questions from ones which are considered unacceptable?

במדבר | פרק יא

כא לְפָנָיו לֵאמֹר לָמָה זֶּה יְצָאנוּ מִמִּצְרָיִם: וַיֹּאמֶר מֹשֶׁה שֵׁשׁ־מֵאוֹת אֶלֶף רַגְלִי הָעָם אֲשֶׁר אָנֹכִי בְּקִרְבּוֹ וְאַתָּה אָמַרְתָּ בָּשָׂר אֶתֵּן

כב לָהֶם וְאָכְלוּ חֹדֶשׁ יָמִים: הֲצֹאן וּבָקָר יִשָּׁחֵט לָהֶם וּמָצָא לָהֶם אִם אֶת־כָּל־דְּגֵי הַיָּם יֵאָסֵף לָהֶם וּמָצָא לָהֶם:

כג וַיֹּאמֶר יְהוָה אֶל־מֹשֶׁה הֲיַד יְהוָה תִּקְצָר עַתָּה תִרְאֶה הֲיִקְרְךָ

כד דְבָרִי אִם־לֹא: וַיֵּצֵא מֹשֶׁה וַיְדַבֵּר אֶל־הָעָם אֵת דִּבְרֵי יְהוָה וַיֶּאֱסֹף שִׁבְעִים אִישׁ מִזִּקְנֵי הָעָם וַיַּעֲמֵד אֹתָם סְבִיבֹת הָאֹהֶל:

כה וַיֵּרֶד יְהוָה ׀ בֶּעָנָן וַיְדַבֵּר אֵלָיו וַיָּאצֶל מִן־הָרוּחַ אֲשֶׁר עָלָיו וַיִּתֵּן עַל־שִׁבְעִים אִישׁ הַזְּקֵנִים וַיְהִי כְּנוֹחַ עֲלֵיהֶם הָרוּחַ וַיִּתְנַבְּאוּ

CLASSIC COMMENTATORS

Moshe seems to question God's ability to provide meat for an entire month. The commentaries are disturbed by this – did Moshe think that God was not capable of doing that?

אבן עזרא
משה לא ידע, בעבור שידע שהשם לא יחדש אות או מופת כי אם להצדיק נביאיו.

IBN EZRA
Moshe did not know that God was willing to create a new sign or wonder in order to satisfy the people's demands. He believed that God performed such miracles only for the sake of bolstering the claims of a prophet.

רמב״ן
כאשר יעשה השם אותות ומופתים לישראל חסד הם מאתו, וכלם לטוב להם ... אבל עתה, כשאמר לו שיתן להם שאלתם ויאכלו בשר עד אשר יצא מאפכם והיה לכם לזרא (במדבר י"א:כ'), ידע משה שלא יהיה אות מאת השם לבראת להם בשר. הבין משה שלא יהיה זה בנס מאתו יתברך, ועל כן שאל כמתמיה: מה יעשה להם בדרך הארץ.

RAMBAN
When God performs signs and wonders on Israel's behalf, these are acts of kindness and are executed for the benefit of the people.... But now, God announced His intention to honor the masses' request and they would eat meat until it comes out of their nostrils and becomes nauseating to them. When he heard this, Moshe realized that God's provision of meat would not be executed in a miraculous manner. Hence he wondered how God would feed the people through natural means.

ר' שמשון רפאל הירש
משה היה יכול להבין מכך, שעצם מינוי הזקנים הוא האמצעי להספקת צרכי העם, ושהוא – משה – בעזרת עמיתיו החדשים יטפל בהאכלת העם. היה לו מקום להניח שפרנסת העם תהיה התפקיד הראשון שבו ישתתפו עמו שבעים הזקנים ... ומכאן תמיהתו.

RABBI SAMSON RAPHAEL HIRSCH
Moshe might have concluded that the appointment of the seventy elders would be the means by which the people's demands would be fulfilled, and that with the help of his new colleagues he would deal with the Israelites' dietary requests. Perhaps Moshe imagined that the first task of this new group was to feed the masses. This is why Moshe was so surprised at God's announcement.

BEMIDBAR | CHAPTER 11

> **11:26–30** *Two men, Eldad and Meidad, are not among the seventy who go with Moshe out of the camp, but they nonetheless also experience prophecy. Yehoshua is distressed by this and suggests that Moshe lock them up, but Moshe does not think that their prophecy poses any kind of a problem.*

26 upon them, they prophesied – but they did not do so again. Two men, one named Eldad and the other Meidad, had remained in the camp, yet the spirit rested upon them. Though they were among those listed, they had not gone out to the Tent – and they
27 spoke prophecy in the camp. A young man ran and told Moshe, "Eldad and Meidad are
28 speaking prophecy in the camp!" Yehoshua son of Nun, who had been Moshe's disciple
29 since his youth, said, "My lord Moshe, stop them!" But Moshe replied, "Are you jealous for me? Would that all the Lord's people were prophets, that the Lord would put His
30 spirit upon them all!" And Moshe returned to the camp together with the elders of Israel.

רש"י

וישארו שני אנשים - מאותן שנבחרו, אמרו: אין אנו כדיים לגדולה זו. והמה בכתובים - במבוררין לסנהדרין. ונכתבו כולם נקובים בשמות ועל ידי גורל, לפי שהחשבון עולה לשנים עשר שבטים ששה לכל שבט ושבט, חוץ משני שבטים שאין מגיע אליהם אלא חמשה חמשה. אמר משה: אין שבט שומע לי לפחות משבטו זקן אחד. מה עשה? נטל שבעים ושנים פתקים וכתב על שבעים: זקן, ועל שנים: חלק. עמד ובירד ששה מכל שבט והיו שבעים ושנים. אמר להם: בואו וטלו פיתקיכם מתוך קלפי, מי שעלה בידו חלק אמר לו: המקום לא חפץ בך.

RASHI

"Two men…had remained in the camp" – Two of the chosen men remained, saying: we are not worthy of this honor.

"Though they were among those listed" – Eldad and Meidad were among the individuals chosen to participate in the Sanhedrin [the supreme court of seventy elders]. Now, how were these men picked? Seventy-two men who were eligible to receive prophecy had their names written down, and the group of seventy was chosen by a lottery. [Thus the names of Eldad and Meidad were originally on the list of possible elders.] For in order to reach the requisite number of seventy men, ten of the tribes could contribute six elders, but the remaining two tribes would be allowed only five representatives each. Moshe well knew that none of the tribes would agree to send just five individuals to this body. How did he solve the predicament? He began with seventy-two tickets, and wrote the word "elder" on seventy of them, leaving the final two cards blank. He then took the seventy-two suitable candidates – six from each tribe – and asked them each to draw a ticket by lottery. If a man picked out a card that said, "elder" he would be sanctified. Whereas, if he removed a blank card, Moshe would say to him: God does not wish you to participate.

QUESTIONS FOR THOUGHT

- According to each of the opinions in the Talmud, were Eldad and Meidad more worthy or less worthy than the other seventy elders?
- Which opinion does Rashi seem to follow?

TEXTUAL SKILLS

1. From these verses, where does it seem likely the Tent of Meeting is located? See also Exodus 33:7–11.
2. There are five characters in this scene – Eldad, Meidad, Moshe, Yehoshua, and …?
3. Verses 25 and 26 both have a phrase that begins with the word ויתנבאו. Compare how the phrases end differently in those two verses.

במדבר | פרק יא

כו וְלֹ֣א יָסָ֑פוּ: וַיִּשָּׁאֲר֣וּ שְׁנֵֽי־אֲנָשִׁ֣ים ׀ בַּֽמַּחֲנֶ֗ה שֵׁ֣ם הָאֶחָ֣ד ׀ אֶלְדָּ֡ד וְשֵׁם֩ הַשֵּׁנִ֨י מֵידָ֜ד וַתָּ֧נַח עֲלֵיהֶ֣ם הָר֗וּחַ וְהֵ֙מָּה֙ בַּכְּתֻבִ֔ים וְלֹ֥א

כז יָצְא֖וּ הָאֹ֑הֱלָה וַיִּֽתְנַבְּא֖וּ בַּֽמַּחֲנֶֽה: וַיָּ֣רָץ הַנַּ֔עַר וַיַּגֵּ֥ד לְמֹשֶׁ֖ה

כח וַיֹּאמַ֑ר אֶלְדָּ֣ד וּמֵידָ֔ד מִֽתְנַבְּאִ֖ים בַּֽמַּחֲנֶֽה: וַיַּ֜עַן יְהוֹשֻׁ֣עַ בִּן־נ֗וּן

כט מְשָׁרֵ֥ת מֹשֶׁ֛ה מִבְּחֻרָ֖יו וַיֹּאמַ֑ר אֲדֹנִ֥י מֹשֶׁ֖ה כְּלָאֵֽם: וַיֹּ֧אמֶר ל֣וֹ מֹשֶׁ֗ה הַֽמְקַנֵּ֥א אַתָּ֖ה לִ֑י וּמִ֨י יִתֵּ֜ן כָּל־עַ֤ם יְהֹוָה֙ נְבִיאִ֔ים כִּֽי־יִתֵּ֧ן

ל יְהֹוָ֛ה אֶת־רוּח֖וֹ עֲלֵיהֶֽם: וַיֵּאָסֵ֥ף מֹשֶׁ֖ה אֶל־הַֽמַּחֲנֶ֑ה ה֖וּא וְזִקְנֵ֥י

שביעי

CLASSIC COMMENTATORS

The story of Eldad and Meidad is obscure. Who are they? What are they doing? Is their prophecy something good or bad?

SANHEDRIN 17A

"And there remained two men in the camp" (Num. 11:26). Some say that their names remained in the box from which they drew the lots…. At the time that the Holy One, Blessed be He, said to Moshe: "Gather for Me seventy of Israel's elders" (11:16), Moshe said: How shall I do that? If I pick six men from each of the tribes, I will have a total of seventy-two, which will be two more than we need. But if I select just five from each tribe, that will give a body of sixty elders, which is ten fewer than what God instructed. And if I choose six from some tribes and five from other tribes, that will create enmity between the tribes. What did Moshe do? He chose six candidates from every tribe and then brought out seventy-two tickets. On seventy of these slips he wrote, "elder," but left two of the cards blank. He rolled them up, placed them in the box, and called them to pick from the box. For each who drew a slip that said, "elder," Moshe said: "Heaven has sanctified you for this position." Whereas, if a man drew a blank slip, Moshe said: "The Omnipresent did not choose you; what can I do?…" Rabbi Shimon explained the verse differently: Eldad and Meidad remained in the camp. When the Holy One, Blessed be He, said to Moshe: "Gather for Me seventy elders," Eldad and Meidad said: "We do not deserve that level of greatness." Said the Holy One, blessed be He: "Since you humbled yourselves, I will add even more honor to your greatness. And how did God elevate these two individuals? All the other elders prophesied once and stopped, but these two prophesied and did not stop.

סנהדרין יז עמוד א

"וישארו שני אנשים במחנה". יש אומרים: בקלפי נשתיירו, שבשעה שאמר לו הקדוש ברוך הוא למשה: "אספה לי שבעים איש…" אמר משה: "כיצד אעשה? אברור ששה מכל שבט ושבט - נמצאו שנים יתרים. אברור חמשה מכל שבט - נמצאו עשרה חסרים. אברור ששה משבט זה וחמשה משבט זה - הריני מטיל קנאה בין השבטים". מה עשה? בירר ששה ששה והביא שבעים ושנים פתקין, על שבעים כתב "זקן" ושנים הניח חלק. גללן ונתן בקלפי. אמר להם: "בואו וטלו פתקיכם". כל מי שעלה בידו "זקן" אמר: "כבר קידשך שמים". מי שעלה בידו חלק, אמר לו: "המקום לא חפץ בך, אני מה אעשה לך?"… ר' שמעון אומר: במחנה נשתיירו. בשעה שאמר לו הקדוש ברוך הוא למשה "אספה לי שבעים איש…" אמרו אלדד ומידד: "אין אנו ראויים לאותה גדולה". אמר הקדוש ברוך הוא: "הואיל ומיעטתם עצמכם, הריני מוסיף גדולה על גדולתכם". ומה גדולה הוסיף להם? - שהנביאים כולם נתנבאו ופסקו - והם נתנבאו ולא פסקו!

31 Then a wind from the LORD sprang up, sweeping quail in from the sea and letting them fall near the camp, about a day's journey on one side and a day's journey on the other,
32 around the camp and piled up two cubits above the ground. All that day, all night, and all the next day, the people went out and gathered quail. Even those who gathered least gathered ten omer, and they spread them out all around the camp. While the meat was
33 still between their teeth, before it was eaten, the LORD's anger blazed against the people,
34 and the LORD struck the people with a very great plague. The place was named Kivrot
35 HaTaava, because there they buried the people who had craved. And from Kivrot HaTaava the people journeyed to Ḥatzerot, and at Ḥatzerot they stayed.

מלבי״ם

והטעם בזה שהשם הודיע למשה שיאכלו חדש ימים שזה יהיה לו למופת שלא בקשו בשר בעבור תאותם לבד, רק בעבור מרדם בה׳, ומשה הגיד להם שיהיה להם בשר חדש ימים. ולפי זה לא היה להם לאסוף ממנו הרבה מאד, אחר שידעו שימצא שם כל ימי החדש, ויוכלו לקחת ממנו בכל יום כפי הצורך לא להקדים לאסוף ממנו על הרבה ימים... ועל כן הכה בהם תיכף.

MALBIM

When God informed Moshe that Israel would enjoy a diet of flesh for thirty days, that was meant as a sign for the people. For the nation had demanded meat not only in order to satisfy their craving for the food; they were also intent on rebelling against the LORD. That was when Moshe told the masses that they would be fed meat for thirty days. This meant that when the quail arrived the people would not need to gather the birds in great quantities – Moshe assured them that the supply would continue for a full month. Thus, every day they would be able to collect as much meat as they wanted without having to think about their future consumption needs.... And yet, upon the availability of the quail, the people went out and collected the birds for the entire day, all through the succeeding night, and throughout the next day as well. Because of this gluttony God struck the nation at the end of the second day.

QUESTIONS FOR THOUGHT

- According to Malbim, what was the sin that caused God to strike them immediately?
- On how many different points does R. Reggio disagree with Malbim?
- Which of these two commentaries portrays God's actions in a more favorable light? Explain!

WISDOM OF THE HEART

Moshe names the place where the incident with the meat took place Kivrot HaTaava, literally, "the burial places of desire." It seems to make sense, because many people died there as a result of their cravings. We could, however, understand it very differently, as the place where they buried their desires. Sometimes we profoundly want something. We can't rest until we get it; it becomes a consuming obsession. And then, when we get it, it doesn't seem so interesting or desirable anymore. It was the wanting to get it which drove us, not the wanting to actually have it and enjoy it. They wanted the meat so much, and when it came they couldn't control themselves. But then, as the Torah describes, they moved on from there. They learned their lesson; they buried their desires.

Can you tell within yourself when your craving is for the object of your desire and when it is just an obsession with getting it?

לא יִשְׂרָאֵל: וְרוּחַ נָסַע ׀ מֵאֵת יְהוָה וַיָּגָז שַׂלְוִים מִן־הַיָּם וַיִּטֹּשׁ עַל־הַמַּחֲנֶה כְּדֶרֶךְ יוֹם כֹּה וּכְדֶרֶךְ יוֹם כֹּה סְבִיבוֹת הַמַּחֲנֶה

לב וּכְאַמָּתַיִם עַל־פְּנֵי הָאָרֶץ: וַיָּקָם הָעָם כָּל־הַיּוֹם הַהוּא וְכָל־הַלַּיְלָה וְכֹל ׀ יוֹם הַמָּחֳרָת וַיַּאַסְפוּ אֶת־הַשְּׂלָו הַמַּמְעִיט אָסַף

לג עֲשָׂרָה חֳמָרִים וַיִּשְׁטְחוּ לָהֶם שָׁטוֹחַ סְבִיבוֹת הַמַּחֲנֶה: הַבָּשָׂר עוֹדֶנּוּ בֵּין שִׁנֵּיהֶם טֶרֶם יִכָּרֵת וְאַף יְהוָה חָרָה בָעָם וַיַּךְ יְהוָה

לד בָּעָם מַכָּה רַבָּה מְאֹד: וַיִּקְרָא אֶת־שֵׁם־הַמָּקוֹם הַהוּא קִבְרוֹת

לה הַתַּאֲוָה כִּי־שָׁם קָבְרוּ אֶת־הָעָם הַמִּתְאַוִּים: מִקִּבְרוֹת הַתַּאֲוָה נָסְעוּ הָעָם חֲצֵרוֹת וַיִּהְיוּ בַּחֲצֵרוֹת:

TEXTUAL SKILLS

1. Even though they are spelled identically, the word חֲמָרִים (v. 32) is very different from the word חֲמֹרִים (Gen. 45:23). What does each mean? (Bonus: Compare them to Ex. 8:10 – what do they have in common?)

2. Earlier in this chapter (v. 3) this place was named Tavera (Burning). Which name stuck? (Hint: Look at 33:16–17)

3. Notice how this story opens with the three words אסף, תאוה, and בשר (v. 4) and closes with these same words (vv. 32–34)!

CLASSIC COMMENTATORS

The Torah seems to indicate that God struck people down immediately, as soon as they started to eat. Didn't He say that they would be able to eat for an entire month?

ר' יצחק שמואל רג"ו

אין פירושו שביום הראשון באכלם ממנו מתו בו ... אלא בסוף השלשים יום היה זה, כי ה' ברוך הוא אינו חפץ בהשחתת בריותיו, ואף על פי שחטאו חטאה גדולה לאמר למה זה יצאנו ממצרים, רצה להאריך אפו עד חדש ימים, אולי כשיאכלו ממנו לשבעה ימים או יומיים ינחמו על רעתם ... ואילו הפסיקו טרם מלאת חדש ימים לא היו נענשים, אבל לא עשו כן.

RABBI ISAAC SAMUEL REGGIO

The text does not imply that the people died on the first day that they received the meat, but rather at the end of the thirtieth day. For the Lord has no interest in the destruction of His creatures, sinful though they may be. And even though Israel had the temerity to complain, "Why did God take us out of that Egyptian paradise?" the Almighty still held His fury in abeyance for a full month. God hoped that perhaps the Israelites, having had their fill of meat after a week or two, would repent from their wickedness....Had the nation seen the error of their ways before the thirty days elapsed, they would not have been punished. Unfortunately, they did not do so.

12:1–9 *Miriam and Aharon speak about Moshe, discussing both his prophecy and his wife. God rebukes them for not recognizing Moshe's uniqueness, specifically regarding his prophecy.*

12 1 Once, Miriam and Aharon spoke against Moshe because of his Kushite wife; he had
2 married a Kushite woman. "Has the Lord spoken only through Moshe?" they said.
3 "Has He not spoken through us also?" The Lord heard this. Now the man Moshe was
4 very humble, more so than any other man on earth. And suddenly the Lord said to Moshe and Aharon and Miriam: "All three of you, come out to the Tent of Meeting."
5 So the three of them went. The Lord came down in a column of cloud, and, standing at the entrance to the Tent, called, "Aharon and Miriam." The two of them came
6 forward. The Lord said: "Now listen to My words: When there is a prophet among
7 you, I make Myself known to him in a vision, I speak to him in a dream. Not so
8 with Moshe My servant: he is trusted in all My House: With him I speak mouth to mouth, clearly, never in riddles. He sees the Lord's form. Why, then, are you not
9 afraid to speak against My servant Moshe?" The Lord's anger flared against them;

ר' יוסף אבן כספי

RABBI YOSEF IBN KASPI

והיה הענין כן: כי משה אחרי נשאו צפורה לקח אשה כושית על צפורה לסבה שידע הוא ע"ה. ואין לשאול טעמים בפעולותיו כי בודאי מחכמה עשה זה... אבל בעבור שלא נזכר זה, עתה בעבור שלא נבהל באומרו: על אודות האשה הכושית אשר לקח, בעבור שלא שמענו זה מעולם, אמר אחר זה: כי אשה כושית לקח. כאלו אמר: דעו שאשה כושית לקח, ואם לא נזכר עדיין, ועליה דברו אלה.

After Moshe married Tzipora, he married a second woman – an Ethiopian – for reasons that only he knew. There is no point in questioning Moshe's motives, for he surely acted wisely in this matter.... Although in the start of the verse Miriam and Aharon are said to speak about Moshe's Kushite wife, the text then emphasizes that Moshe "had married a Kushite woman," because this information had not previously been supplied. It is as if the narrator is stating: be aware that Moshe had married an Ethiopian woman, even though no mention had yet been made of her. This was the sister-in-law whom the two siblings were discussing.

QUESTIONS FOR THOUGHT

- Rashi and Ibn Kaspi disagree as to who the Ethiopian wife is. What does each one say?
- Which of these explanations fits the words of the Torah better?
- Which of these has a better explanation of the connection between the two topics that Miriam and Aharon speak about?
- How can you explain the fact that God rebukes Miriam and Aharon for challenging Moshe's prophecy, but says nothing about their raising the issue of his wife?

WISDOM OF THE HEART

Moshe's humility stands at the center of this story. R. Aharon Kotler explains that humility doesn't mean that you think you're worthless; that's just low self-esteem. Humility is understanding that your talents are a gift from God and recognizing that your achievements should drive you to desire to do even more.

במדבר | פרק יב

א וַתְּדַבֵּ֨ר מִרְיָ֤ם וְאַהֲרֹן֙ בְּמֹשֶׁ֔ה עַל־אֹד֛וֹת הָאִשָּׁ֥ה הַכֻּשִׁ֖ית אֲשֶׁ֣ר
ב לָקָ֑ח כִּֽי־אִשָּׁ֥ה כֻשִׁ֖ית לָקָֽח: וַיֹּאמְר֗וּ הֲרַ֤ק אַךְ־בְּמֹשֶׁה֙ דִּבֶּ֣ר יְהֹוָ֔ה
ג הֲלֹ֖א גַּם־בָּ֣נוּ דִבֵּ֑ר וַיִּשְׁמַ֖ע יְהֹוָֽה: וְהָאִ֥ישׁ מֹשֶׁ֖ה עָנָ֣יו מְאֹ֑ד מִכֹּל֙
ד הָֽאָדָ֔ם אֲשֶׁ֖ר עַל־פְּנֵ֥י הָאֲדָמָֽה: וַיֹּ֨אמֶר יְהֹוָ֜ה פִּתְאֹ֗ם
אֶל־מֹשֶׁ֤ה וְאֶֽל־אַהֲרֹן֙ וְאֶל־מִרְיָ֔ם צְא֥וּ שְׁלָשְׁתְּכֶ֖ם אֶל־אֹ֣הֶל
ה מוֹעֵ֑ד וַיֵּצְא֖וּ שְׁלָשְׁתָּֽם: וַיֵּ֤רֶד יְהֹוָה֙ בְּעַמּ֣וּד עָנָ֔ן וַֽיַּעֲמֹ֖ד פֶּ֣תַח
ו הָאֹ֑הֶל וַיִּקְרָא֙ אַהֲרֹ֣ן וּמִרְיָ֔ם וַיֵּצְא֖וּ שְׁנֵיהֶֽם: וַיֹּ֖אמֶר שִׁמְעוּ־נָ֣א
דְבָרָ֑י אִם־יִֽהְיֶה֙ נְבִ֣יאֲכֶ֔ם יְהֹוָ֔ה בַּמַּרְאָה֙ אֵלָ֣יו אֶתְוַדָּ֔ע בַּחֲל֖וֹם
ז אֲדַבֶּר־בּֽוֹ: לֹא־כֵ֖ן עַבְדִּ֣י מֹשֶׁ֑ה בְּכָל־בֵּיתִ֖י נֶאֱמָ֥ן הֽוּא: פֶּ֣ה אֶל־
ח פֶּ֞ה אֲדַבֶּר־בּ֗וֹ וּמַרְאֶה֙ וְלֹ֣א בְחִידֹ֔ת וּתְמֻנַ֥ת יְהֹוָ֖ה יַבִּ֑יט וּמַדּ֨וּעַ֙
ט לֹ֤א יְרֵאתֶם֙ לְדַבֵּ֣ר בְּעַבְדִּ֖י בְמֹשֶֽׁה: וַיִּֽחַר־אַ֧ף יְהֹוָ֛ה בָּ֖ם וַיֵּלַֽךְ:

CLASSIC COMMENTATORS

Miriam and Aharon speak about two topics that seem to be unconnected – his Ethiopian wife and his prophecy. Are they linked at all?

RASHI

Rabbi Natan explained: Miriam was standing next to Tzipora when the message came to Moshe, "Eldad and Meidad are speaking prophecy in the camp!" (11:27), whereupon Tzipora muttered: How unfortunate for the wives of those two who have now attained the status of prophets; for the men will soon be leaving their wives just like my husband has separated from me. That was when Miriam learned of Moshe's marital situation, which she then related to Aharon.

"His Kushite wife" – The adjective means that everybody talked about Tzipora's beauty; whoever saw her admitted that her good looks were as obvious as the blackness of a Kushite.

"Because of his Kushite wife" – They spoke about the fact that Moshe divorced his wife.

רש״י

רבי נתן אומר: מרים היתה בצד צפורה בשעה שנאמר למשה אלדד ומידד מתנבאים במחנה, כיון ששמעה צפורה אמרה: אוי לנשותיהן של אלו אם הם נזקקים לנבואה שיהיו פורשין מנשותיהן כדרך שפירש בעלי ממני, ומשם ידעה מרים והגידה לאהרן.

האשה הכשית: מגיד שהכל מודים ביפיה כשם שהכל מודים בשחרותו של כושי.

ד״ה על אדות האשה: על אודות גירושיה.

BEMIDBAR | CHAPTER 12   BEHAALOTEKHA

> **12:10–16** When God finishes speaking with Miriam and Aharon, Miriam is afflicted with צרעת. Aharon asks Moshe to pray on her behalf, which he does. God insists that there must be a consequence for her action, and that she needs to go through the seven-day purification process from צרעת before she can be welcomed back into the camp. The nation waits for her to return before moving on to their next destination, Ḥatzerot.

10 and He departed. When the cloud withdrew from the Tent, Miriam had been struck with an impure blight, white as snow. Aharon turned toward Miriam and saw that she
11 was blighted. Aharon said to Moshe, "Please, my lord, do not hold against us the sin
12 that we have foolishly committed! Let her not be like a stillborn child emerging from
13 its mother's womb with half its flesh eaten away!" And Moshe cried out to the Lord, "Please, God, heal her now!"
14 But the Lord said to Moshe: "If her father had spat in her face, would she not be shamed for seven days? Let her be shut out of the camp for seven days; after that, she may be
15 brought back." So Miriam was shut out of the camp for seven days, and the people
16 did not move on until Miriam was brought back. After that, the people set out from Ḥatzerot and encamped in the Wilderness of Paran.

QUESTIONS FOR THOUGHT

- Which of the above commentaries understands that Aharon is referring to Moshe, and which understands that he is referring to Miriam?
- What difference would it make if he were referring to Moshe or to Miriam?
- Which part of the verse seems to be challenging for both commentaries to make sense of?

TEXTUAL SKILLS

1. Notice that Aharon uses the imagery of a mother while God invokes the image of a father.
2. Notice that Miriam is not the first member of this family to be afflicted with צרעת.
3. Moshe's prayer (v. 13) is the shortest prayer in Tanakh. Notice that it is structured as A-B-C-B-A.

WISDOM OF THE HEART

God calls to Moshe, Aharon, and Miriam to go out to the Tent of Meeting, but as soon as they get there He sends Aharon and Miriam out to explain to them just how different Moshe and his prophecy are from them and their experiences of prophecy. Why does He call them to the Tent of Meeting if He is going to call them outside right away? Perhaps it is to drive home the point. Moshe's prophecy is unique, and only he can go into the Tent of Meeting to speak with God freely. If they think that they are the same as him and that they can also go to the Tent of Meeting, they are mistaken. How do they learn that? By getting thrown out of the Tent of Meeting while only Moshe is allowed to remain.

How do you feel when someone else attains a position that you thought you should have received? Sometimes we overestimate our own abilities or under-appreciate another person's talents. Is it possible that the person who did get the position really was better suited for it?

במדבר | פרק יב

י וְהֶעָנָן סָר מֵעַל הָאֹהֶל וְהִנֵּה מִרְיָם מְצֹרַעַת כַּשָּׁלֶג וַיִּפֶן אַהֲרֹן
אֶל־מִרְיָם וְהִנֵּה מְצֹרָעַת: יא וַיֹּאמֶר אַהֲרֹן אֶל־מֹשֶׁה בִּי אֲדֹנִי אַל־
נָא תָשֵׁת עָלֵינוּ חַטָּאת אֲשֶׁר נוֹאַלְנוּ וַאֲשֶׁר חָטָאנוּ: יב אַל־נָא
תְהִי כַּמֵּת אֲשֶׁר בְּצֵאתוֹ מֵרֶחֶם אִמּוֹ וַיֵּאָכֵל חֲצִי בְשָׂרוֹ: יג וַיִּצְעַק
מֹשֶׁה אֶל־יְהוָה לֵאמֹר אֵל נָא רְפָא נָא לָהּ:

מפטיר יד וַיֹּאמֶר יְהוָה אֶל־מֹשֶׁה וְאָבִיהָ יָרֹק יָרַק בְּפָנֶיהָ הֲלֹא תִכָּלֵם
שִׁבְעַת יָמִים תִּסָּגֵר שִׁבְעַת יָמִים מִחוּץ לַמַּחֲנֶה וְאַחַר תֵּאָסֵף:
טו וַתִּסָּגֵר מִרְיָם מִחוּץ לַמַּחֲנֶה שִׁבְעַת יָמִים וְהָעָם לֹא נָסַע
עַד־הֵאָסֵף מִרְיָם: טז וְאַחַר נָסְעוּ הָעָם מֵחֲצֵרוֹת וַיַּחֲנוּ בְּמִדְבַּר
פָּארָן:

CLASSIC COMMENTATORS

The word תהי, in verse 12, can mean either "her" or "you" (masculine). Aharon uses it in his plea for Moshe to heal Miriam. What does it mean and what is he trying to say?

RASHBAM

Said Aharon to Moshe: for your own sake and honor, do not let yourself be like a dead man. How might Moshe be like that? Since Moshe and Miriam emerged from the same womb, when the sister suffers, it is as though the punishment extends to Moshe as well. As such, it would be to Moshe's personal benefit to pray for Miriam's recovery.

RABBI YOSEF BEKHOR SHOR

Said Aharon to Moshe: do not allow Miriam to remain like an infant who emerges half dead from the womb. That is, if an infant is born with צרעת, meaning that their flesh is partially eaten away by contagion, they can never be healed from that condition. The צרעת becomes their legacy. However, Miriam's state was not congenital but was imposed upon her as a punishment. As such, prayer and repentance could effect a change in her situation. This is why Aharon begged Moshe to plead to God on their sister's behalf so that she would be cured.

רשב״ם

אל נא תהי כמת – כלומר: לכבודך ובשבילך, אל נא תהיה אתה בעצמך כמת. והיאך? מי שהוא ממעיו, מרחם אמו של אחיו שהוא חי, הרי נאכל חצי בשרו – של חי. כלומר: מאחר שנולדה מרים מרחם אמו של משה, והיא מתה, הרי נאכל חצי בשרו של משה.

ר׳ יוסף בכור שור

אל נא תהי כמת – אל נא תהי מרים כמת, אשר בצאתו מרחם אמו ויאכל חצי בשרו. כלומר: צרעת הבאה מתולדתו, שכשיוצא מבטן אמו, בשרו מת ונאכל ולקוי, ואין דרכו להרפא לעולם, כי תולדתו הוא. אבל זה הלקוי, אינו תולדתה, אלא על ידי חטא בא לה, ועל ידי תפילה ותשובה דין הוא שילך. ולפיכך: התפלל עליה ותחיה המכה.

MORE QUICK BITES

- **8:2** The Torah writes that Aharon did as he was instructed; he lit the lamps as God said. Isn't this unnecessary? Why would the Torah need to tell us that Aharon did as he was told? R. Isaac Samuel Reggio suggests that even though any *kohen* can do the lighting, Aharon made it his business to do it every day. Sometimes, it is desirable to follow the mishna in Pirkei *Avot* (2:5) which instructs us to take up responsibility when there is nobody else around who will do so. That implies that when there are others around who could perform a task just as well, then there is no need for us to take the responsibility (and the glory), since the job will get done anyway. Perhaps R. Reggio is suggesting that it can be worthwhile to stick to what you started, even if it is a humble act that anyone else can do, because it demonstrates that you do not hold yourself as being "too good" or "too important" to do the "little" things.

- **8:24** The Torah describes the work of the Levites as לצבוא צבא, language usually reserved for army service. When you think about an army, it consists of many individuals organized into units, working together in a coordinated manner and following the direction of a commander. When the Torah describes creation (Gen. 2:1), it talks about the צבא of the heavens and the צבא of the earth, referring to all the different things which were created, categorized, and organized, and all of which follow the direction of a Supreme Commander. Similarly the Levites were organized into different families that worked in parallel to each other, and they were carefully organized and followed the direction of their commander. Seeing all the parts of Levi working would have been like watching a carefully choreographed dance or the workings of a perfectly tuned watch. That alone helped to create not only a sense of dignity in the *Mishkan*, but also a sense of beauty.

- **11:10** Moshe complains that he is not *Benei Yisrael*'s parent; hence, he could not handle taking care of their needs. The implication is that if he would have been their parent, he would have found the inner resources to handle whatever they would dish out.

- **12:13** The Ḥafetz Ḥayyim notices that the Torah does not say that Moshe prayed, rather, that he cried out to God. He understands from this that the essence of prayer is an outburst arising from what is deep inside our soul. The deeper the source of our prayer, the farther the prayer goes.

EXPLORING HASHKAFA
Humility

Of all the personal characteristics God could have chosen to highlight about Moshe, God identifies humility. "The man Moshe was very humble, more so than any other man on earth." Not Moshe's courage, caring, or even his unparalleled prophecy. His humility.

The significance of humility was picked up by Rambam. Rambam's concept of the "golden path" states that in every personal trait we should strive for the middle – to be neither too lenient nor too strict, neither too generous nor too stingy (*Hilkhot De'ot* 1). He makes two exceptions, however, one of which is humility. "It's not enough to be somewhat humble; he should be exceedingly so" (*Hilkhot De'ot* 2:3).

What does it mean to be humble? Rabbi Lord Jonathan Sacks describes it like this:

> Humility is not what it is sometimes taken to be – a low estimate of oneself. That is false or counterfeit humility. True humility is mindlessness of self. An *anav* (the biblical word used in this chapter) is one who never thinks about himself because he has more important things to think about. I once heard someone say about a religious leader: "He took God so seriously that he didn't need to take himself seriously at all."

Some of this would seem to conflict with contemporary values of self-esteem and personal dignity. In fact, it seems to conflict with rabbinic proclamations about the dignity, uniqueness, even the majesty of humanity. "Man is beloved because he was created in the Divine image" (*Pirkei Avot* 3:14). The notion of humans being partners with God, so central to understanding the beginning of Genesis and the responsibility of *Benei Yisrael*, also seem to be at odds with the emphasis on extreme humility.

Rav Soloveitchik grappled with this tension in numerous writings. He describes a push-pull relationship between humanity's need for greatness and the demand for humility, a relationship which tries to maintain both the majesty of the human being and our humility:

> In the very movement where *kedusha* exults, "I am near God, I am a great being," it decrees its defeat. Being close to God awakens in me the desire to be closer yet, and that itself informs me that complete fulfillment of my desire is impossible, because I am but a small being. I am near God because I am great; I am not as near as I would want to be, because I am small. (*Shiurei Harav*, 1974)

Perhaps the very uniqueness of humanity is that it can recognize its greatness, and despite that still strive for humility.

פרשת שלח
PARASHAT SHELAḤ

> "Hard choices, easy life. Easy choices, hard life."
> Jerzy Gregorek

On the cusp of entering the Promised Land, a great leader sends twelve great men – with Divine approval – to scout the land. Sounds like a perfect mission, right? What could go wrong? The land is wonderful, they report, but unconquerable. One brave man and then another try to stop the revolt which ensues, but to no avail. What went wrong? How could it? How do you recover when your dream is lost?

PARASHAT SHELAḤ

13 ¹ Then the L ORD spoke to Moshe: "Send out men to scout the land of Canaan, which I am going to give to the Israelites, one man from each of their ancestral tribes, each a ³ leader among them." So Moshe sent them at the L ORD's command from the Wilderness ⁴ of Paran. They were all leading men among the Israelites. These were their names: from ⁵ the tribe of Reuven, Shamua son of Zakur; from the tribe of Shimon, Shafat son of Ḥori; ⁶⁄⁷ from the tribe of Yehuda, Kalev son of Yefuneh; from the tribe of Yissakhar, Yigal son of ⁸⁄⁹ Yosef; from the tribe of Efrayim, Hoshe'a son of Nun; from the tribe of Binyamin, Palti ¹⁰⁄¹¹ son of Rafu; from the tribe of Zevulun, Gadiel son of Sodi; from the tribe of Yosef, from ¹² the tribe of Menashe, Gadi son of Susi; from the tribe of Dan, Amiel son of Gemali; ¹³⁄¹⁴ from the tribe of Asher, Setur son of Mikhael; from the tribe of Naftali, Naḥbi son of ¹⁵⁄¹⁶ Vofsi; from the tribe of Gad, Geuel son of Makhi. These were the names of the men Moshe sent to scout the land. And Moshe named Hoshe'a son of Nun Yehoshua.

רמב״ן

והיה במנהג שישלחו שנים אנשים מרגלים חרש לאמר, וישלחום מקצתם, וה' היודע עתידות ציוהו שישלח איש אחד איש אחד מכל מטות ישראל ושיהיו הנשיאים שבהם, כי חפץ ה' שיהיו שוים בעניין כל הגדולים, אולי יזכרו וישובו אל ה'.

RAMBAN

It would have been a better strategy for Moshe to have sent two spies secretly to the land of Canaan, meaning that only some of the tribes would have been represented. But the L ORD, who knows all future events, commanded Moshe to send one scout from each tribe, and furthermore, that these men be men be princes of their clans. In this way all of the leadership would be equally involved in this enterprise, and that would perhaps cause them to remember the L ORD and to return to Him.

ר' עובדיה ספורנו

שלח לך אנשים: אל תניח שישלחום הם, כמו שאמרו לעשות באומרם "נשלחה אנשים לפנינו" (דברים א':כ"ב), שמא ישלחו הדיוטות בלתי מכירים שבח הארץ, ויספרו בגנותה.

RABBI OVADYA SFORNO

God instructed Moshe to select the scouts rather than allow the tribes to choose their own representatives, lest they send simple men who did not appreciate the land's special quality and would report on its faults.

QUESTIONS FOR THOUGHT

- Regarding what important question do all of the above commentaries agree?
- Which of the above commentaries understands that God thought it was a bad idea to send scouts?
- In what way are Rashi's and Ramban's explanations diametrically opposite?
- Do you believe that God regularly places obstacles in our way to see if we fail, or that God tries to make sure that we succeed?

TEXTUAL SKILLS

1. Notice the order of the tribes listed. Can you explain it?
2. Notice what is different about the description for the tribe of Menashe.
3. What is odd about verse 16?

פרשת שלח

יג א וַיְדַבֵּ֥ר יְהֹוָ֖ה אֶל־מֹשֶׁ֥ה לֵּאמֹֽר׃ ב שְׁלַח־לְךָ֣ אֲנָשִׁ֗ים וְיָתֻ֙רוּ֙ אֶת־אֶ֣רֶץ כְּנַ֔עַן אֲשֶׁר־אֲנִ֥י נֹתֵ֖ן לִבְנֵ֣י יִשְׂרָאֵ֑ל אִ֣ישׁ אֶחָד֩ אִ֨ישׁ אֶחָ֜ד לְמַטֵּ֤ה אֲבֹתָיו֙ תִּשְׁלָ֔חוּ כֹּ֖ל נָשִׂ֥יא בָהֶֽם׃ ג וַיִּשְׁלַ֨ח אֹתָ֥ם מֹשֶׁ֛ה מִמִּדְבַּ֥ר פָּארָ֖ן עַל־פִּ֣י יְהֹוָ֑ה כֻּלָּ֣ם אֲנָשִׁ֔ים רָאשֵׁ֥י בְנֵֽי־יִשְׂרָאֵ֖ל הֵֽמָּה׃ ד וְאֵ֖לֶּה שְׁמוֹתָ֑ם לְמַטֵּ֣ה רְאוּבֵ֔ן שַׁמּ֖וּעַ בֶּן־זַכּֽוּר׃ ה לְמַטֵּ֣ה שִׁמְע֔וֹן שָׁפָ֖ט בֶּן־חוֹרִֽי׃ ו לְמַטֵּ֣ה יְהוּדָ֔ה כָּלֵ֖ב בֶּן־יְפֻנֶּֽה׃ ז לְמַטֵּ֣ה יִשָּׂשכָ֔ר יִגְאָ֖ל בֶּן־יוֹסֵֽף׃ ח לְמַטֵּ֥ה אֶפְרָ֖יִם הוֹשֵׁ֥עַ בִּן־נֽוּן׃ ט לְמַטֵּ֣ה בִנְיָמִ֔ן פַּלְטִ֖י בֶּן־רָפֽוּא׃ י לְמַטֵּ֣ה זְבוּלֻ֔ן גַּדִּיאֵ֖ל בֶּן־סוֹדִֽי׃ יא לְמַטֵּ֥ה יוֹסֵ֖ף לְמַטֵּ֣ה מְנַשֶּׁ֑ה גַּדִּ֖י בֶּן־סוּסִֽי׃ יב לְמַטֵּ֣ה דָ֔ן עַמִּיאֵ֖ל בֶּן־גְּמַלִּֽי׃ יג לְמַטֵּ֣ה אָשֵׁ֔ר סְת֖וּר בֶּן־מִיכָאֵֽל׃ יד לְמַטֵּ֣ה נַפְתָּלִ֔י נַחְבִּ֖י בֶּן־וׇפְסִֽי׃ טו לְמַטֵּ֣ה גָ֔ד גְּאוּאֵ֖ל בֶּן־מָכִֽי׃ טז אֵ֚לֶּה שְׁמ֣וֹת הָֽאֲנָשִׁ֔ים אֲשֶׁר־שָׁלַ֥ח מֹשֶׁ֖ה לָת֣וּר אֶת־הָאָ֑רֶץ וַיִּקְרָ֥א מֹשֶׁ֛ה לְהוֹשֵׁ֥עַ בִּן־נ֖וּן יְהוֹשֻֽׁעַ׃

CLASSIC COMMENTATORS

The text here indicates that it was God's idea to send the scouts. When Moshe retells the story in Deuteronomy (1:21–23), he presents it as the people's idea. Whose idea was it, and was it a bad idea?

RASHI

God said to Moshe: I am not commanding you to do so, but if you want, send spies. Initially it was the people who came to Moshe and requested the mission, as the verse states, "Then all of you drew close to me and said, 'Let us send men ahead of us to explore the land'" (Deut. 1:22). At that point Moshe consulted with God, who said: I have already guaranteed the Israelites that the land is a good one. I'll give them an opportunity to stumble into sin over the spies.

רש״י

שלח לך: לדעתך, אני איני מצוה לך, אם תרצה שלח, לפי שבאו ישראל ואמרו (דברים א׳:כ״ב) "נשלחה אנשים לפנינו", ומשה נמלך בשכינה. אמר: אני אמרתי להם שהיא טובה... חייהם שאני נותן להם מקום לטעות בדברי המרגלים.

BEMIDBAR | CHAPTER 13　　　　　　　　　　　　　　　　　　　　　SHELAḤ | 120

17 When Moshe sent them to scout the land of Canaan, he told them, "Ascend there into
18 the Negev; then go up into the hill country. See what the land is like. Are the people who
19 live there strong or weak, few or many? Is the land in which they live a good place or bad?
20 Are the cities in which they live open or fortified? Is the soil rich or poor? Are there trees
   in it or not? Take courage and bring back some of the fruit of the land" – it was the season
21 of the first ripe grapes. So they went up and scouted the land from the Wilderness of
22 Tzin to Reḥov, near Levo Ḥamat. They went up through the Negev and came to Ḥevron,
   where Aḥiman, Sheshai, and Talmai, descendants of Anak, were dwelling. Ḥevron had
23 been built seven years before the Egyptian city of Tzoan. Then they came to the Eshkol
   Ravine and there they cut down a vine branch, and on it one cluster of grapes, which
   they carried on a pole between two men. They also took some pomegranates and figs.
24 That place was named the Eshkol Ravine, because of the cluster that the Israelites cut

העמק דבר

לא הלכו כולם ביחד, אלא חילקו את הארץ לשנים שנים, על כן נשלמה הליכתם בארבעים יום. ומעתה מדבר הכתוב בשנים שעלו בנגב, והמה כלב ועוד אחד. ויבא עד חברון - אחד מהם והוא כלב בא בתוך העיר והמבצר. והשני ירא ליכנס לעיר מפני אימת בני הענק, וגם במבצר קשה לנוס אם תהא השעה צריכה. אבל האחד בא בלי פחד וגם ראה את ילידי הענק ולא חת מפני כל.

HAAMEK DAVAR

Actually, the twelve men did not travel through the country all together, but split up into pairs. That was how they managed to cover the entire territory in forty days. The present verse refers to only one who went to Ḥevron, which was Kalev, who entered the city and its fortress. The other one who was supposed to travel with him was too afraid of the descendants of the giant to approach the town, plus it would have been difficult to quickly escape the citadel had the need arisen. But Kalev was unafraid, even when he saw the giant's children.

QUESTIONS FOR THOUGHT

- Regarding what do Rashi and *Haamek Davar* agree? On what do they have a strong disagreement?
- Do you think that the explanation of *Haamek Davar* is closer to that of Rashi or R. Hirsch? Why do you think that?
- Rashi makes assumptions, both about Kalev and the other scouts. What are those assumptions? Do the other commentaries agree or disagree?
- When things don't go as planned, does that necessarily mean that the plans were flawed?

TEXTUAL SKILLS

1. Look carefully at Moshe's instructions. The order seems to be confused. Can you explain it?

2. What phrase in verse 22 seems out of place?

WISDOM OF THE HEART

Moshe instructs the scouts to check out the land and the people who live on it. That's a strange description; where else would they have been living? Apparently, the same land could be good for some people and but bad for others. During most of our exile, the land of Israel produced very little for the people who lived on it. Something about the relationship just wasn't right. When *Benei Yisrael* returned, both the swamps and the deserts began to bloom.

במדבר | פרק יג

יז וַיִּשְׁלַח אֹתָם מֹשֶׁה לָתוּר אֶת־אֶרֶץ כְּנָעַן וַיֹּאמֶר אֲלֵהֶם עֲלוּ
זֶה בַּנֶּגֶב וַעֲלִיתֶם אֶת־הָהָר: וּרְאִיתֶם אֶת־הָאָרֶץ מַה־הִוא
וְאֶת־הָעָם הַיֹּשֵׁב עָלֶיהָ הֶחָזָק הוּא הֲרָפֶה הַמְעַט הוּא אִם־רָב:
יט וּמָה הָאָרֶץ אֲשֶׁר־הוּא יֹשֵׁב בָּהּ הֲטוֹבָה הִוא אִם־רָעָה וּמָה
כ הֶעָרִים אֲשֶׁר־הוּא יוֹשֵׁב בָּהֵנָּה הַבְּמַחֲנִים אִם בְּמִבְצָרִים: וּמָה
הָאָרֶץ הַשְּׁמֵנָה הִוא אִם־רָזָה הֲיֵשׁ־בָּהּ עֵץ אִם־אַיִן וְהִתְחַזַּקְתֶּם
כא וּלְקַחְתֶּם מִפְּרִי הָאָרֶץ וְהַיָּמִים יְמֵי בִּכּוּרֵי עֲנָבִים: ▸ וַיַּעֲלוּ וַיָּתֻרוּ   שני
כב אֶת־הָאָרֶץ מִמִּדְבַּר־צִן עַד־רְחֹב לְבֹא חֲמָת: וַיַּעֲלוּ בַנֶּגֶב וַיָּבֹא
עַד־חֶבְרוֹן וְשָׁם אֲחִימַן שֵׁשַׁי וְתַלְמַי יְלִידֵי הָעֲנָק וְחֶבְרוֹן שֶׁבַע
כג שָׁנִים נִבְנְתָה לִפְנֵי צֹעַן מִצְרָיִם: וַיָּבֹאוּ עַד־נַחַל אֶשְׁכֹּל וַיִּכְרְתוּ
מִשָּׁם זְמוֹרָה וְאֶשְׁכּוֹל עֲנָבִים אֶחָד וַיִּשָּׂאֻהוּ בַמּוֹט בִּשְׁנָיִם וּמִן־
כד הָרִמֹּנִים וּמִן־הַתְּאֵנִים: לַמָּקוֹם הַהוּא קָרָא נַחַל אֶשְׁכּוֹל עַל

CLASSIC COMMENTATORS

All the descriptions of the actions of the scouts are in plural, except for one – ויבא עד חברון – he came to Ḥevron (v. 22). How are we to understand that?

רש״י

כלב לבדו הלך שם, ונשתטח על קברי אבות שלא יהא ניסת לחביריו להיות בעצתם.

RASHI

Kalev [the scout from the tribe of Yehuda] was the only one of the team to travel to Ḥevron. When he got there he prostrated himself in prayer on the graves of the patriarchs, asking God for help in resisting the influence of his colleagues.

ר׳ שמשון רפאל הירש

לדעתנו, "ויעלו" וכן גם "ויבא" מתייחסים לכל השליחים יחד. "ויבא" בא בלשון יחיד, להורות שהם הלכו יחד והגיעו עד חברון – כאיש אחד בלב אחד. "הם עלו מן הדרום, וכולם כאחד הגיעו לחברון".

RABBI SAMSON RAPHAEL HIRSCH

In my opinion, all of the verbs used to describe this mission, including "So they went up" (13:21) and "he came [to Ḥevron]" (13:22) refer to the entire group of twelve scouts. And the reason that the latter example appears in the singular form is to emphasize that the team arrived in Ḥevron together, as a single unit fulfilling their mission as one.

BEMIDBAR | CHAPTER 13   SHELAḤ | 122

> **13:25–29** *The scouts return from their mission and report to Moshe, Aharon, and the entire nation. They display the fruit and report that the land is excellent but unconquerable – there are giants and fortified cities as well as feared nations like the Amorites and Amalek.*

25,26 there. They returned from scouting the land when forty days had passed. As soon as they arrived they came to Moshe and Aharon and to all the community of Israel at Kadesh in the Wilderness of Paran, and brought their report to them and to all the community,
27 and showed them the fruit of the land. They told Moshe, "We came to the land you sent
28 us to, and it is indeed flowing with milk and with honey, and this is its fruit. But the people who live in the land are fierce, and the cities are fortified and very large indeed. We
29 even saw the descendants of Anak there. In the Negev region, Amalek lives; the Hittites, Jebusites, and Amorites live in the hill country, and the Canaanites live by the sea and by

רלב״ג

אילו היו מספרים זה תחילה למשה ולאהרן, כמו שהיה ראוי, לא היה מתחדש מפני דיבתם מה שאירע מן הרע, שכבר היה נקל למשה ולאהרן לישב לבם שיסמכו בה׳ יתעלה; עם שיהושע וכלב היו מחזיקים את ידיהם. אבל הם השיבו אותם את כל העדה, ובזה הניאו לב העם בדרך שלא יכלו לתקן עותתם.

RALBAG

Had the scouts reported directly to Moshe and Aharon as they should have done, their findings would not have been widely known across the nation, and the utter breakdown in trust would not have occurred. For Moshe and Aharon would have been able to handily respond to the spies' hesitation; they would have restored their colleagues' faith in the Lord. Furthermore, Yehoshua and Kalev could have succeeded in encouraging the rest of their team that all was not lost. However, the twelve men appeared before the entire people of Israel and ended up instilling fear in the hearts of the masses in a way that could not be undone.

QUESTIONS FOR THOUGHT

- Try using your own words to restate each of the three opinions above.
- Which of the three explanations do you think presents the most convincing argument for why the scouts' report was considered so sinful?
- All three explanations assume that the scouts conspired to offer a negative report. Can you imagine an alternate explanation that does not presume that their intention was evil?

WISDOM OF THE HEART

The scouts stayed in the land for forty days. The number forty can be found throughout the Torah: the flood lasted forty days; Moshe stayed on the mountain for forty days; a person who violates a biblical prohibition gets forty lashes; and as a result of this incident *Benei Yisrael* end up spending forty years in the wilderness. The number forty represents birth or rebirth, an opportunity for re-creation. The flood was God's re-creation of the world, giving it a new start. Moshe's forty days on the mountain turned him into a different man – he came down with his face glowing. The forty lashes are intended to prompt the person to re-create himself, from a brazen sinner to a regular citizen. The forty years in the wilderness were an opportunity for the people to re-create themselves – into a nation that was ready to take on the challenge of conquering and settling the Promised Land.

If you could re-create some aspect of yourself, what would you choose to focus on? What's holding you back from trying?

במדבר | פרק יג

כה אֶשְׁכּוֹל אֲשֶׁר־כָּרְתוּ מִשָּׁם בְּנֵי יִשְׂרָאֵל: וַיָּשֻׁבוּ מִתּוּר
כו הָאָרֶץ מִקֵּץ אַרְבָּעִים יוֹם: וַיֵּלְכוּ וַיָּבֹאוּ אֶל־מֹשֶׁה וְאֶל־אַהֲרֹן
וְאֶל־כָּל־עֲדַת בְּנֵי־יִשְׂרָאֵל אֶל־מִדְבַּר פָּארָן קָדֵשָׁה וַיָּשִׁיבוּ
כז אוֹתָם דָּבָר וְאֶת־כָּל־הָעֵדָה וַיַּרְאוּם אֶת־פְּרִי הָאָרֶץ: וַיְסַפְּרוּ־לוֹ
וַיֹּאמְרוּ בָּאנוּ אֶל־הָאָרֶץ אֲשֶׁר שְׁלַחְתָּנוּ וְגַם זָבַת חָלָב וּדְבַשׁ
כח הִוא וְזֶה־פִּרְיָהּ: אֶפֶס כִּי־עַז הָעָם הַיֹּשֵׁב בָּאָרֶץ וְהֶעָרִים בְּצֻרוֹת
כט גְּדֹלֹת מְאֹד וְגַם־יְלִדֵי הָעֲנָק רָאִינוּ שָׁם: עֲמָלֵק יוֹשֵׁב בְּאֶרֶץ
הַנֶּגֶב וְהַחִתִּי וְהַיְבוּסִי וְהָאֱמֹרִי יוֹשֵׁב בָּהָר וְהַכְּנַעֲנִי יוֹשֵׁב עַל־

CLASSIC COMMENTATORS

It seems like the scouts completed their mission as instructed – we would not have expected them to lie. Why, then, are they blamed and considered to have committed a terrible sin?

RAMBAN

Because Moshe asked the men to find out whether the land contained rich or poor soil, the scouts reported that the earth of Canaan is fertile and that "it is indeed flowing with milk and with honey" (13:27). Secondly, since the spies were told to determine whether the place was covered with trees or not, they illustrated the point by returning with fruit from such plants. Recognize that throughout this whole description the twelve said nothing but the truth; they honestly answered the questions that had been put to them. It was therefore correct for the scouts to state that the Canaanites were strong and that they lived in protected cities – they were tasked with providing an accurate analysis of the challenges facing Israel in their conquest. Hadn't Moshe told them to find out: "Are the people who live there strong or weak?... Are the cities in which they live open or fortified?" (13:18–19)? Nevertheless, the transgression of the scouts lay in their use of the word "but" (v. 28). That lone term betrayed their fear that Israel's undertaking would be difficult, if not impossible to achieve.

רמב״ן

בעבור שציוה אותם לראות השמנה היא אם רזה, השיבו לו כי היא שמנה וגם זבת חלב ודבש היא, ועל שאלתו, היש בה עץ אם אין, השיבו לו: וזה פריה, כי כן ציוה אותם להראותו. והנה בכל זה אמרו אמת, והשיבו על מה שנצטוו. והיה להם לאמר, שהעם היושב עליה עז והערים בצורות, כי יש להם להשיב אמרי אמת לשולחם, כי כן ציוה אותם "החזק הוא הרפה הבמחנים אם במבצרים", אבל רשעם במלת "אפס", שהיא מורה על דבר אפס ונמנע מן האדם שאי אפשר בשום עניין.

RABBI ISAAC SAMUEL REGGIO

In his instructions to the scouts, Moshe first asked that they investigate the people and afterward that they check out the land. However, because the spies were committed to discouraging the nation and to denigrating the land of Israel, they switched the order; they opened their report with some praise about the land, but then expanded their report when reporting about the difficult inhabitants.

ר' יצחק שמואל רג'יו

והנה משה שאל להם תחילה על עניין העם ואחר כך על עניין הארץ, אולם המרגלים שהיה בדעתם להניא את לב העם ולספר בגנות הארץ התחילו בעניין הארץ וסיפרו בשבחה ... ואחר כך הרחיבו בשאול פיהם בעניין גנותה.

> **13:30–14:4** *Kalev tries to reassure the people that they can capture the land, but the other scouts demoralize Benei Yisrael by describing all the people of the land as giants and the land as one that devours its inhabitants. The people cry, wishing that they had died In Egypt or in the wilderness, rather than face seeing their families slaughtered in battle. Some even call to appoint a new leader and return to Egypt.*

30 the Jordan." But Kalev silenced the people around Moshe and said, "Let us go up at once
31 and take possession of it, for certainly we are able." The men who had gone up with him
32 said, "We cannot go up against those people, for they are stronger than us." So they gave the Israelites an adverse report of the land that they had scouted: "The land which we have journeyed through and scouted is a land that consumes its inhabitants; the people
33 we saw in it were tall and broad to a man. There we saw the Nefilim – the descendants of Anak are from the Nefilim. We looked to our own eyes like grasshoppers, and so
14 1 we were in theirs." All the community lifted their heads and cried out – that night
2 the people wept. And all the Israelites railed against Moshe and Aharon; all the community said to them, "If only we had died in Egypt, if only we had died in this
3 wilderness! Why is the Lord bringing us as far as this land only to fall by the sword? Our wives and children will be made plunder. Would it not be better for us to go back
4 to Egypt?" So they said to one another, "Let us appoint a leader and go back to Egypt."

- Which of the above commentaries needs to add information that the text does not provide in order for them to write their explanation?

TEXTUAL SKILLS

1. The grammatical form of the beginning of verse 30 is called past-perfect, meaning that it describes something which already happened. How does that affect the way we understand the flow of who said what, and when they said it?
2. Compare what the scouts are reported as saying here with their earlier report.

WISDOM OF THE HEART

Some people live with fear, seeing only the dark side. Others are optimistic and live with hope. Kalev saw the same thing that the other scouts did, but he lived with hope. There is a tale of two shoe sales reps who travel to a third-world country in search of new business opportunities. One calls his wife the moment he lands, telling her, "Honey, I'm coming back home. There's no hope. Nobody here is wearing shoes, so there's no one to sell to." He boards the next flight home. The second calls his wife and says, "Honey, you wouldn't believe what I found here. There is so much opportunity. No one here is wearing shoes. I can sell to the whole country!"

Do you think that someone can change from being a pessimist to an optimist? How can they make that happen?

במדבר | פרק יד

לּ הַיָּם וְעַל יַד הַיַּרְדֵּן: וַיַּהַס כָּלֵב אֶת־הָעָם אֶל־מֹשֶׁה וַיֹּאמֶר עָלֹה
לא נַעֲלֶה וְיָרַשְׁנוּ אֹתָהּ כִּי־יָכוֹל נוּכַל לָהּ: וְהָאֲנָשִׁים אֲשֶׁר־עָלוּ עִמּוֹ
לב אָמְרוּ לֹא נוּכַל לַעֲלוֹת אֶל־הָעָם כִּי־חָזָק הוּא מִמֶּנּוּ: וַיֹּצִיאוּ
דִּבַּת הָאָרֶץ אֲשֶׁר תָּרוּ אֹתָהּ אֶל־בְּנֵי יִשְׂרָאֵל לֵאמֹר הָאָרֶץ
אֲשֶׁר עָבַרְנוּ בָהּ לָתוּר אֹתָהּ אֶרֶץ אֹכֶלֶת יוֹשְׁבֶיהָ הִוא וְכָל־הָעָם
לג אֲשֶׁר־רָאִינוּ בְתוֹכָהּ אַנְשֵׁי מִדּוֹת: וְשָׁם רָאִינוּ אֶת־הַנְּפִילִים
בְּנֵי עֲנָק מִן־הַנְּפִלִים וַנְּהִי בְעֵינֵינוּ כַּחֲגָבִים וְכֵן הָיִינוּ בְּעֵינֵיהֶם:
יד א וַתִּשָּׂא כָּל־הָעֵדָה וַיִּתְּנוּ אֶת־קוֹלָם וַיִּבְכּוּ הָעָם בַּלַּיְלָה הַהוּא:
ב וַיִּלֹּנוּ עַל־מֹשֶׁה וְעַל־אַהֲרֹן כֹּל בְּנֵי יִשְׂרָאֵל וַיֹּאמְרוּ אֲלֵהֶם כָּל־
הָעֵדָה לוּ־מַתְנוּ בְּאֶרֶץ מִצְרַיִם אוֹ בַּמִּדְבָּר הַזֶּה לוּ־מָתְנוּ: וְלָמָה
ג יְהֹוָה מֵבִיא אֹתָנוּ אֶל־הָאָרֶץ הַזֹּאת לִנְפֹּל בַּחֶרֶב נָשֵׁינוּ וְטַפֵּנוּ
ד יִהְיוּ לָבַז הֲלוֹא טוֹב לָנוּ שׁוּב מִצְרָיְמָה: וַיֹּאמְרוּ אִישׁ אֶל־אָחִיו

CLASSIC COMMENTATORS

The scouts say that they saw themselves as grasshoppers and that the people of the land saw them the same way. How do they know how the people of the land saw them?

RASHI

The scouts knew this because they heard the Canaanites saying to each other: Look! There are ants walking through our vineyards which resemble men!

רש״י

וכן היינו בעיניהם – שְׁמַעֲנוּם אוֹמְרִים זֶה לָזֶה: נְמָלִים יֵשׁ בַּכֶּרֶם כַּאֲנָשִׁים.

RABBI OVADYA SFORNO

The scouts said: Because the Canaanites viewed us as grasshoppers, or as even smaller insects, they considered us no threat at all to them. That explains why they did not bother to react to our presence – it would have been demeaning to them to waste any effort swatting us away.

ר׳ עובדיה ספורנו

וכן היינו בעיניהם – כחגבים או פחות מזה, ובשביל זה לא קמו עלינו, כי לא החשיבו אותנו ויבז בעיניהם להרע לנו.

QUESTIONS FOR THOUGHT

- According to each of the above commentaries, what was the source of the information the scouts reported here?
- According to Sforno, about whom does that report actually provide meaningful information to us as readers?

5 Moshe and Aharon fell facedown before all the assembled community of Israel.
6 Yehoshua son of Nun and Kalev son of Yefuneh, who were among those who scouted
7 the land, tore their clothes and said before the entire community of Israel: "The land
8 we journeyed through and scouted is a very, very good land. If the Lord favors us, He will bring us into this land, a land flowing with milk and with honey, and He will give
9 it to us. Do not rebel against the Lord, and do not be afraid of the people of the land, for they are no more than bread for us. They have been stripped of their protection
10 and the Lord is with us. Do not be afraid of them!" The community, all, threatened to stone them to death – but then the Lord's glory was revealed to all the Israelites at the Tent of Meeting.

רמב״ן

ירמזו לשרי מעלה שאין אומה נופלת עד שנופל שר שלה כתחלה ... יאמר: כבר סר הכח אשר בצלו יחיו הגוים, וה׳ המשפיל אותם אתנו.

RAMBAN
Yehoshua and Kalev here allude to the Canaanites' guardian angel, for a nation can be conquered only if its protective angel is taken down first.... Thus the two scouts maintain that the protection under which these nations typically thrive has been removed, and the Lord has lowered these people before Israel.

הואיל משה

עד הנה היו הכנעני תחת צל שדי שגזר בחכמתו [בברית בין הבתרים – בראשית ט״ו:ט״ז] לקיימם, אבל עתה שלם עונם ובא הקץ ולהורישם וסר צלם מעליהם כי אין עוד רצון האל לקיימם.

HO'IL MOSHE
Yehoshua and Kalev explain that for centuries the Canaanite nations had enjoyed the protection God assured them when He decreed in the covenant between the pieces (Gen. 15:16) that these people would remain temporarily untouchable. However, now the land's inhabitants have sinned sufficiently that God will no longer defend them, so Israel can conquer the country.

QUESTIONS FOR THOUGHT

- Which of the above commentaries understands that the "shade" protecting them refers to their psychological state and not to some supernatural force?
- Bekhor Shor and *Ho'il Moshe* seem to say very similar things. Find two important differences between their explanations.
- In what way are Rashi's and Ramban's explanations similar?
- Which commentary tries to fit its explanation into the two words which follow, וה׳ אתנו?
- Which of these explanations do you think would have been most likely used by Yehoshua and Kalev to try to convince *Benei Yisrael*?

WISDOM OF THE HEART

Yehoshua and Kalev, as they try to convince *Benei Yisrael* not to be afraid, mention that "the shadow" of the Canaanites has left. R. Samson Raphael Hirsch explains that people on the low moral and spiritual ground hide in the shadows, and it is the darkness which shrouds them which generates fear. When people with high ethical and religious principles expose them, when they shine a light on the situation and expose those hiding in the darkness, then it becomes clear that there is no reasonable justification for fear. So much of our energies are spent on thinking that others have that which we don't. When we peel away the masks, we often realize how much of what we thought they had was just a show.

נְתְנָה רֹאשׁ וְנָשׁוּבָה מִצְרָיְמָה: וַיִּפֹּל מֹשֶׁה וְאַהֲרֹן עַל־פְּנֵיהֶם ה
לִפְנֵי כָּל־קְהַל עֲדַת בְּנֵי יִשְׂרָאֵל: וִיהוֹשֻׁעַ בִּן־נוּן וְכָלֵב בֶּן־יְפֻנֶּה ו
מִן־הַתָּרִים אֶת־הָאָרֶץ קָרְעוּ בִּגְדֵיהֶם: וַיֹּאמְרוּ אֶל־כָּל־עֲדַת ז
בְּנֵי־יִשְׂרָאֵל לֵאמֹר הָאָרֶץ אֲשֶׁר עָבַרְנוּ בָהּ לָתוּר אֹתָהּ טוֹבָה
הָאָרֶץ מְאֹד מְאֹד: אִם־חָפֵץ בָּנוּ יְהֹוָה וְהֵבִיא אֹתָנוּ אֶל־הָאָרֶץ ח *שלישי*
הַזֹּאת וּנְתָנָהּ לָנוּ אֶרֶץ אֲשֶׁר־הִוא זָבַת חָלָב וּדְבָשׁ: אַךְ בַּיהֹוָה ט
אַל־תִּמְרֹדוּ וְאַתֶּם אַל־תִּירְאוּ אֶת־עַם הָאָרֶץ כִּי לַחְמֵנוּ הֵם
סָר צִלָּם מֵעֲלֵיהֶם וַיהֹוָה אִתָּנוּ אַל־תִּירָאֻם: וַיֹּאמְרוּ כָּל־הָעֵדָה י
לִרְגּוֹם אֹתָם בָּאֲבָנִים וּכְבוֹד יְהֹוָה נִרְאָה בְּאֹהֶל מוֹעֵד אֶל־כָּל־
בְּנֵי יִשְׂרָאֵל:

CLASSIC COMMENTATORS

Part of the argument used by Yehoshua and Kalev to the people includes a phrase which literally means, "their shade has moved from them." What does that mean?

RASHI
רש"י

Yehoshua and Kalev argued: All of the Canaanites' protection and strength has disappeared, for the righteous individuals among them have died. This refers specifically to Iyyov, whose merits shielded his neighbors from harm [like shade does].

מגינם וחזקם, כשרים שבהם מתו, איוב שהיה מגן עליהם.

RASHBAM
רשב"ם

Yehoshua and Kalev claimed that the Canaanites lacked any kind of shield to protect them. Indeed, they said, from the moment that God dried up the waters of the Sea of Reeds, all of the land's inhabitants were cringing in fear at the prospect of Israel's invasion. We find such a reaction in Raḥav's description to Yehoshua's scouts (Josh. 2:9–11).

אין להם מחסה לחסות בו, כי כבר נמוגו כל יושבי ארץ מפנינו משעה שהוביש ים סוף כמו שאמרה רחב הזונה (יהושע ב':ט'-י"א).

RABBI YOSEF BEKHOR SHOR
ר' יוסף בכור שור

Yehoshua and Kalev boasted: Although the Holy One, blessed be He, usually provides protective shade to all of humanity, in the current instance He has lifted that shield. This has left the Canaanites vulnerable to us, for God is devoted to assisting us in taking the land.

הקב"ה, שהוא צל ושומר לכל הבריות, סר מעליהם והפקירם לנו והוא איתנו לעזרתנו.

> **14:11–19** *God threatens to destroy the nation and begin afresh with a new nation. Moshe defends the people, arguing that to destroy them would be a desecration of God's name.*

11 The Lord said to Moshe, "How long will these people provoke Me? How long will
12 they fail to have faith in Me in spite of all the signs I have performed among them? I will strike them with a plague now and disinherit them, and make you into a nation
13 greater and mightier than they." But Moshe said to the Lord, "The Egyptians will hear
14 about it, for by Your power You brought this people up from among them, and they will tell the inhabitants of this land. They have heard that You, Lord, are among these people, that You, Lord, are seen face-to-face, that Your cloud stands over them, that
15 You go before them in a pillar of cloud by day and in a pillar of fire by night. If You kill
16 this people like a single man, the nations that have heard of Your fame will say, 'It was because the Lord was unable to bring this people into the land He swore to them; that
17 is why He slaughtered them in the wilderness.' So now, let my Lord's power be great,
18 as You declared when You said: 'The Lord is slow to anger and abounding in kindness, forgiving sin and rebellion, though He does not acquit the guilty, but holds the descendants to account for the sins of the fathers; children and grandchildren to the third and
19 fourth generation.' Please – pardon the sin of this people in Your great kindness, as You

---

QUESTIONS FOR THOUGHT

- Both Rashbam and Ralbag use context to support explain Moshe's argument. Which of them understands that it is connected to the previous verses and which understands that it is connected to the verses which follow?
- When do you think a leader's authority is strengthened – when he uses the power he has or when he refrains from using it?

TEXTUAL SKILLS

1. Compare Moshe's defense of *Benei Yisrael* here (vv. 13–16) to his defense after the golden calf (Ex. 32:12). In what ways are they similar? In what ways are they different?

2. Look at the language at the end of verse 12. Where in Genesis do you find similar language?

WISDOM OF THE HEART

Watch two children in a schoolyard, or two nations flexing their muscles – they each think that power is the ability to crush the other. Moshe's argument with God challenges that very notion. God's power would not be revealed by His destruction of *Benei Yisrael*; rather, it would show weakness, the need to assert power. Power rests in the ability to forgive, for only the truly strong can afford to forgive. The thirteen attributes of God's mercy do not illustrate weakness, but testify to His greatness.

What makes it difficult to back down from a confrontation with someone else?

במדבר | פרק יד

יא וַיֹּאמֶר יהוה אֶל־מֹשֶׁה עַד־אָנָה יְנַאֲצֻנִי הָעָם הַזֶּה וְעַד־אָנָה
יב לֹא־יַאֲמִינוּ בִי בְּכֹל הָאֹתוֹת אֲשֶׁר עָשִׂיתִי בְּקִרְבּוֹ: אַכֶּנּוּ בַדֶּבֶר
יג וְאוֹרִשֶׁנּוּ וְאֶעֱשֶׂה אֹתְךָ לְגוֹי־גָּדוֹל וְעָצוּם מִמֶּנּוּ: וַיֹּאמֶר מֹשֶׁה
אֶל־יהוה וְשָׁמְעוּ מִצְרַיִם כִּי־הֶעֱלִיתָ בְכֹחֲךָ אֶת־הָעָם הַזֶּה
יד מִקִּרְבּוֹ: וְאָמְרוּ אֶל־יוֹשֵׁב הָאָרֶץ הַזֹּאת שָׁמְעוּ כִּי־אַתָּה יהוה
בְּקֶרֶב הָעָם הַזֶּה אֲשֶׁר־עַיִן בְּעַיִן נִרְאָה ׀ אַתָּה יהוה וַעֲנָנְךָ
עֹמֵד עֲלֵהֶם וּבְעַמֻּד עָנָן אַתָּה הֹלֵךְ לִפְנֵיהֶם יוֹמָם וּבְעַמּוּד
טו אֵשׁ לָיְלָה: וְהֵמַתָּה אֶת־הָעָם הַזֶּה כְּאִישׁ אֶחָד וְאָמְרוּ הַגּוֹיִם
טז אֲשֶׁר־שָׁמְעוּ אֶת־שִׁמְעֲךָ לֵאמֹר: מִבִּלְתִּי יְכֹלֶת יהוה לְהָבִיא
אֶת־הָעָם הַזֶּה אֶל־הָאָרֶץ אֲשֶׁר־נִשְׁבַּע לָהֶם וַיִּשְׁחָטֵם בַּמִּדְבָּר:
יז וְעַתָּה יִגְדַּל־נָא כֹּחַ אֲדֹנָי כַּאֲשֶׁר דִּבַּרְתָּ לֵאמֹר: יהוה אֶרֶךְ
יח אַפַּיִם וְרַב־חֶסֶד נֹשֵׂא עָוֹן וָפָשַׁע וְנַקֵּה לֹא יְנַקֶּה פֹּקֵד עֲוֹן אָבוֹת
יט עַל־בָּנִים עַל־שִׁלֵּשִׁים וְעַל־רִבֵּעִים: סְלַח־נָא לַעֲוֹן הָעָם הַזֶּה
כְּגֹדֶל חַסְדֶּךָ וְכַאֲשֶׁר נָשָׂאתָה לָעָם הַזֶּה מִמִּצְרַיִם וְעַד־הֵנָּה:

CLASSIC COMMENTATORS

After arguing that destroying the people would desecrate God's name, Moshe offers a suggestion to glorify His name (v. 17). How does he propose that would help?

RASHBAM — רשב"ם

יגדל נא כח – להאריך אפך.

Moshe pleaded to God: Will You not demonstrate Your great power of restraint by suppressing Your anger?

RALBAG — רלב"ג

ראוי שתשמר מלעשות מה שיביא האנשים לחשוב שידך תקצר מעשות אשר ייעדת מהטוב לעמך.

Said Moshe: You should avoid doing anything that might cause Your detractors to claim You are incapable of fulfilling Your promises to Your nation.

BEMIDBAR | CHAPTER 14 — SHELAḤ

> **14:20–25** *God agrees to forgive the nation, but there will still be consequences: with the exception of Kalev, the generation that left Egypt and witnessed God's miracles will not get to see the land. God instructs Moshe to lead the people on their new travels, away from the Promised Land and into the wilderness.*

20 have forgiven this people from the time of Egypt until now." And the Lord said, "I have
21 forgiven them at your word. Yet as surely as I live and as the Lord's glory fills the whole
22 earth, none of those who have seen My glory and the signs I performed in Egypt and
23 in the wilderness, and have tested Me these ten times and not obeyed Me, shall see the
24 land I swore to their fathers. None of those who have provoked Me will see it. But My servant Kalev, because he was filled with a different spirit and has followed Me wholeheartedly – him I will bring into the land he came to, and his descendants will inherit
25 it. The Amalekites and Canaanites are living in the valleys; so turn tomorrow and head for the wilderness by way of the Sea of Reeds."

TEXTUAL SKILLS

1. What is the connection between God forgiving the people (v. 20) and His glory filling the earth (v. 21)?
2. Notice that the root נ-א-ץ opens God's response to the popular rebellion (v. 11) and closes His response (v. 23).
3. Who would we have expected to have been mentioned in verse 24 but is not?
4. Notice the similarity between verse 25 and 13:29.

WISDOM OF THE HEART

God identifies Kalev as having a "different spirit" – he had his own rhythm, marched to his own beat. As humans we are torn between two competing impulses. On the one hand we have the need to fit in, to be part of a group. We seek companionship with like-minded people; it provides a much-needed sense of belonging, reassuring us that we are not alone. On the other hand, we want to be individuals. Each of us is different, unique. We want to be recognized for who we are and don't want others to dictate our likes and dislikes, our attitudes and behaviors. The two competing needs – to fit in and to be different – are constantly at battle. Sometimes one wins and other times the other gains the upper hand, but they never disappear. The great challenge is to figure out when it is right to go with the flow, and when it is preferable to resist the pressure and stand up for what we deeply believe in.

Which impulse is more dominant in your life right now – to belong to a group or to stand out as an individual? In which areas do you prefer to belong, and in which do you prefer to highlight your uniqueness?

QUICK BITE

In the story of Sedom, Avraham asks God if the city would be saved in merit of the presence of even ten righteous men. We have to ask: in a city as evil as Sedom, what could ten righteous men accomplish? Perhaps it has nothing to do with what they could accomplish. Rather, perhaps even the fact that someone could stand up and identify something as being wrong is enough to build hope that there is a possibility for change. Such is Kalev's brave stand. He accomplishes nothing, but the very fact that he can stand up gives God hope for the future of the people.

כא וַיֹּ֣אמֶר יְהוָ֔ה סָלַ֖חְתִּי כִּדְבָרֶֽךָ׃ וְאוּלָ֖ם חַי־אָ֑נִי וְיִמָּלֵ֥א כְבוֹד־יְהוָ֖ה
כב אֶת־כָּל־הָאָֽרֶץ׃ כִּ֣י כָל־הָאֲנָשִׁ֗ים הָרֹאִ֤ים אֶת־כְּבֹדִי֙ וְאֶת־אֹ֣תֹתַ֔י
אֲשֶׁר־עָשִׂ֥יתִי בְמִצְרַ֖יִם וּבַמִּדְבָּ֑ר וַיְנַסּ֣וּ אֹתִ֗י זֶ֚ה עֶ֣שֶׂר פְּעָמִ֔ים וְלֹ֥א
כג שָׁמְע֖וּ בְּקוֹלִֽי׃ אִם־יִרְאוּ֙ אֶת־הָאָ֔רֶץ אֲשֶׁ֥ר נִשְׁבַּ֖עְתִּי לַאֲבֹתָ֑ם
כד וְכָל־מְנַאֲצַ֖י לֹ֥א יִרְאֽוּהָ׃ וְעַבְדִּ֣י כָלֵ֗ב עֵ֣קֶב הָֽיְתָ֞ה ר֤וּחַ אַחֶ֙רֶת֙
עִמּ֔וֹ וַיְמַלֵּ֖א אַחֲרָ֑י וַהֲבִֽיאֹתִ֗יו אֶל־הָאָ֙רֶץ֙ אֲשֶׁר־בָּ֣א שָׁ֔מָּה וְזַרְע֖וֹ
כה יוֹרִשֶֽׁנָּה׃ וְהָעֲמָלֵקִ֥י וְהַכְּנַעֲנִ֖י יוֹשֵׁ֣ב בָּעֵ֑מֶק מָחָ֗ר פְּנ֨וּ וּסְע֥וּ לָכֶ֛ם
הַמִּדְבָּ֖ר דֶּ֥רֶךְ יַם־סֽוּף׃

CLASSIC COMMENTATORS

As part of God's decision to deny entry into the land to the generation that left Egypt, He declares that they tested Him ten times. What are those times?

RASHI — רש״י

Israel challenged Him twice at the sea, twice with regard to the manna (Ex., ch. 16), and twice tested God's ability to feed them before God ultimately brought quail. All ten tests of God are listed in tractate Arakhin (15a).

שנים בים, שנים במן, שנים בשליו, כולהו כדאיתנהו במסכת ערכין (בבלי ערכין טו).

IBN EZRA — אבן עזרא

The term "ten" should not be taken literally; it suggests "many." The Torah uses this figure because it culminates a series of numbers [that is, the end of single digits], and represents the first in a series of totals [that is, the tens].

הטעם, רבים. והזכיר עשר בעבור היותו סך חשבון, כי הוא סוף האחדים וראש העשרות.

RASHBAM — רשב״ם

God does not refer to ten individual tests, but means that Israel has challenged Him on multiple occasions. We find a similar use of the term in the verse, "Your father cheated me, changing my wages ten times" (Gen. 31:7), and in the verse, "When I cut off your supply of bread, ten women shall bake bread in a single oven" (Lev. 26:26).

עשר פעמים - הרבה, כמו: עשרת מונים (בראשית ל״א:ז׳), ואפו עשר נשים (ויקרא כ״ו:כ״ו).

QUESTIONS FOR THOUGHT

- What is the basic disagreement between Rashi and Rashbam?
- What does Ibn Ezra add that Rashbam doesn't address?
- Do you think that the above approaches to explaining this verse could be applied to other places in the Torah where numbers are mentioned? Why or why not?
- Look at Avot 5:4. Which of the above opinions do you think would be supported by that mishna?

14:26–35 *God tells Moshe and Aharon that everyone above the age of twenty will die in the wilderness and not go to the Promised Land, with the exception of Kalev and Yehoshua. The people will remain in the wilderness for forty years, and only the next generation will enter the land.*

26
27 Then the Lord spoke to Moshe and Aharon: "How long shall this wicked community keep railing against Me? I have heard the Israelites' complaints with which they rail
28 against Me. Tell them: 'As surely as I live,' says the Lord, 'I will do to you the very
29 thing I heard you say. In this wilderness your corpses will fall, all of your number, all those listed in the census, from twenty years old and upward: all those who have railed
30 against Me. None of you will enter the land that I promised to settle you in, except for
31 Kalev son of Yefuneh and Yehoshua son of Nun. I will bring in Your children, whom you
32 said would be taken captive, and they will know the land you rejected. But as for you,
33 your corpses will fall in this wilderness. Your children will shepherd in the wilderness for forty years, suffering for your faithlessness until the last of your corpses lies here in
34 the wilderness. For the number of the days in which you scouted the land, forty days, you shall bear your sins – for every day a year: forty years. You will know what it is to
35 oppose Me. I, the Lord, have spoken.' This will I do to this entire wicked community that has gathered together against Me. In this wilderness they shall come to their end,

QUESTIONS FOR THOUGHT

- Read through this entire passage carefully. What support can you find for the above opinions?
- Why would it make a difference who the intended audience is?

TEXTUAL SKILLS

1. Compare this passage with verses 21–24. What similarities and differences do you find?
2. Where else in Numbers did we find a special status for people aged twenty and up?
3. What word appears three times in verse 27?

WISDOM OF THE HEART

For each of the forty days the scouts were in the land building their opposition to entering the land, *Benei Yisrael* were to spend a year in the wilderness building their desire to enter the land. R. Moshe Sofer points out that the power of good outweighs the power of the bad. If one day of sin could bring about a year of punishment, just imagine what one day of mitzvot could accomplish.

QUICK BITE

In verse 35 there are two different words with exactly the same letters but with a slight difference in the order, ימתו and יתמו. R. Zev of Zhitomir points out that this demonstrates the power of our words – a single word, or even a single letter, can change a person's life.

רביעי	כו וַיְדַבֵּ֣ר יְהֹוָ֔ה אֶל־מֹשֶׁ֥ה וְאֶֽל־אַהֲרֹ֖ן לֵאמֹֽר: עַד־מָתַ֗י לָעֵדָ֤ה הָֽרָעָה֙ הַזֹּ֔את אֲשֶׁ֛ר הֵ֥מָּה מַלִּינִ֖ים עָלָ֑י אֶת־תְּלֻנּ֞וֹת בְּנֵ֣י יִשְׂרָאֵ֗ל
כח	אֲשֶׁ֨ר הֵ֧מָּה מַלִּינִ֛ים עָלַ֖י שָׁמָֽעְתִּי: אֱמֹ֣ר אֲלֵהֶ֗ם חַי־אָ֨נִי֙ נְאֻם־
כט	יְהֹוָ֔ה אִם־לֹ֕א כַּאֲשֶׁ֥ר דִּבַּרְתֶּ֖ם בְּאָזְנָ֑י כֵּ֖ן אֶֽעֱשֶׂ֥ה לָכֶֽם: בַּמִּדְבָּ֣ר הַ֠זֶּ֠ה יִפְּל֨וּ פִגְרֵיכֶ֜ם וְכָל־פְּקֻדֵיכֶם֙ לְכָל־מִסְפַּרְכֶ֔ם מִבֶּ֛ן עֶשְׂרִ֥ים
ל	שָׁנָ֖ה וָמָ֑עְלָה אֲשֶׁ֥ר הֲלִֽינֹתֶ֖ם עָלָֽי: אִם־אַתֶּם֙ תָּבֹ֣אוּ אֶל־הָאָ֔רֶץ אֲשֶׁ֤ר נָשָׂ֨אתִי֙ אֶת־יָדִ֔י לְשַׁכֵּ֥ן אֶתְכֶ֖ם בָּ֑הּ כִּ֚י אִם־כָּלֵ֣ב בֶּן־יְפֻנֶּ֔ה
לא	וִיהוֹשֻׁ֖עַ בִּן־נֽוּן: וְטַ֨פְּכֶ֔ם אֲשֶׁ֥ר אֲמַרְתֶּ֖ם לָבַ֣ז יִהְיֶ֑ה וְהֵבֵיאתִ֣י
לב	אֹתָ֔ם וְיָֽדְעוּ֙ אֶת־הָאָ֔רֶץ אֲשֶׁ֥ר מְאַסְתֶּ֖ם בָּֽהּ: וּפִגְרֵיכֶ֖ם אַתֶּ֑ם
לג	יִפְּל֖וּ בַּמִּדְבָּ֥ר הַזֶּֽה: וּ֠בְנֵיכֶ֠ם יִהְי֨וּ רֹעִ֤ים בַּמִּדְבָּר֙ אַרְבָּעִ֣ים שָׁנָ֔ה
לד	וְנָשְׂא֖וּ אֶת־זְנוּתֵיכֶ֑ם עַד־תֹּ֥ם פִּגְרֵיכֶ֖ם בַּמִּדְבָּֽר: בְּמִסְפַּ֨ר הַיָּמִ֜ים אֲשֶׁר־תַּרְתֶּ֣ם אֶת־הָאָרֶץ֮ אַרְבָּעִ֣ים יוֹם֒ י֣וֹם לַשָּׁנָ֞ה י֣וֹם לַשָּׁנָ֗ה
לה	תִּשְׂאוּ֙ אֶת־עֲוֺנֹ֣תֵיכֶ֔ם אַרְבָּעִ֖ים שָׁנָ֑ה וִידַעְתֶּ֖ם אֶת־תְּנוּאָתִֽי: אֲנִ֣י יְהֹוָה֮ דִּבַּ֒רְתִּי֒ אִם־לֹ֣א ׀ זֹ֣את אֶֽעֱשֶׂ֗ה לְכָל־הָעֵדָ֤ה הָֽרָעָה֙ הַזֹּ֔את

CLASSIC COMMENTATORS

God says that an עדה רעה has been railing against Him and tells Moshe to inform them of their punishment. To whom is God referring as an עדה רעה?

RASHI
רש״י
God refers here to the ten sinful spies.
לעדה הרעה – אילו עשרת המרגלים.

HAAMEK DAVAR
העמק דבר
God refers to the nation's leaders.
הכוונה על כל ראשי העם.

HO'IL MOSHE
הואיל משה
The present phrase should be understood as it is used throughout the passage, namely as referring to the entire nation and not specifically to the scouts.
כמשמעו בכל הפרשה, עדת ישראל ולא המרגלים.

36 and there they shall die." So the men Moshe sent to scout the land, and who came back and caused all the community to rail against him by giving an adverse report of the
37 land – those men who gave the adverse report of the land died by a plague before the
38 Lord. And only Yehoshua son of Nun and Kalev son of Yefuneh remained alive of all
39 those men who went to scout the land. When Moshe reported these words to all the
40 Israelites, the people were overcome with grief. They rose early the next morning and climbed up to the heights of the hill country, saying, "We are ready to go up to the place
41 that the Lord spoke of; we were wrong." But Moshe said, "Why are you transgressing
42 the Lord's command? It will not work. Do not go up; the Lord is not with you. Do not
43 be struck down by your enemies. Ahead of you are the Amalekites and Canaanites, and you will fall by the sword. Because you have turned away from following the Lord, the
44 Lord will not be with you." Defiantly, they went up to the heights of the hill country.
45 Neither the Ark of the Lord's Covenant nor Moshe left the camp. And the Amalekites and Canaanites who lived in that hill country came down, and fought them, and crushed them, all the way to Ḥorma.

QUESTIONS FOR THOUGHT

- Why do you think *Haamek Davar* rejects R. Reggio's explanation?
- Can you find a proof from elsewhere in the Torah that would support either of these positions?

TEXTUAL SKILLS

1. The word דבה appears three times in this story to describe the story told by the scouts. What verb is consistently associated with it? Compare this to Genesis 37:2, the only other place where דבה appears in the Torah.
2. Notice how similar Moshe's message (vv. 42–43) is to that of the scouts (13:31). What is the most important difference between them?
3. The word ויעפילו appears (in a different form) only one other time in Tanakh (Hab. 2:4).

WISDOM OF THE HEART

If the sin of the people was that they were afraid to enter the land, then why didn't God accept their repentance when they pulled themselves together to go and try to conquer it? Abarbanel explains that their sin was that they didn't trust God to help them conquer the land. When they decided to try the next day, it wasn't because they suddenly trusted God but because they trusted their own might and power. That is not repentance. The Baal Shem Tov adds that they never acknowledged their sin, only that God thought that they had sinned.

When someone apologizes for something that hurt you, what do you want to hear in that apology? How do you think you should apologize when your behavior hurt someone else?

לו הַנּוֹעָדִים עָלַי בַּמִּדְבָּר הַזֶּה יִתַּמּוּ וְשָׁם יָמֻתוּ: וְהָאֲנָשִׁים אֲשֶׁר־
שָׁלַח מֹשֶׁה לָתוּר אֶת־הָאָרֶץ וַיָּשֻׁבוּ וילונו עָלָיו אֶת־כָּל־הָעֵדָה וַיִּלּוֹנוּ
לְהוֹצִיא דִבָּה עַל־הָאָרֶץ: וַיָּמֻתוּ הָאֲנָשִׁים מוֹצִאֵי דִבַּת־הָאָרֶץ
לח רָעָה בַּמַּגֵּפָה לִפְנֵי יהוה: וִיהוֹשֻׁעַ בִּן־נוּן וְכָלֵב בֶּן־יְפֻנֶּה חָיוּ
לט מִן־הָאֲנָשִׁים הָהֵם הַהֹלְכִים לָתוּר אֶת־הָאָרֶץ: וַיְדַבֵּר מֹשֶׁה
אֶת־הַדְּבָרִים הָאֵלֶּה אֶל־כָּל־בְּנֵי יִשְׂרָאֵל וַיִּתְאַבְּלוּ הָעָם מְאֹד:
מ וַיַּשְׁכִּמוּ בַבֹּקֶר וַיַּעֲלוּ אֶל־רֹאשׁ־הָהָר לֵאמֹר הִנֶּנּוּ וְעָלִינוּ אֶל־
הַמָּקוֹם אֲשֶׁר־אָמַר יהוה כִּי חָטָאנוּ: וַיֹּאמֶר מֹשֶׁה לָמָּה זֶּה אַתֶּם
מא עֹבְרִים אֶת־פִּי יהוה וְהִוא לֹא תִצְלָח: אַל־תַּעֲלוּ כִּי אֵין יהוה
מב בְּקִרְבְּכֶם וְלֹא תִּנָּגְפוּ לִפְנֵי אֹיְבֵיכֶם: כִּי הָעֲמָלֵקִי וְהַכְּנַעֲנִי שָׁם
לִפְנֵיכֶם וּנְפַלְתֶּם בֶּחָרֶב כִּי־עַל־כֵּן שַׁבְתֶּם מֵאַחֲרֵי יהוה וְלֹא־
מג יִהְיֶה יהוה עִמָּכֶם: וַיַּעְפִּלוּ לַעֲלוֹת אֶל־רֹאשׁ הָהָר וַאֲרוֹן בְּרִית־
מד יהוה וּמֹשֶׁה לֹא־מָשׁוּ מִקֶּרֶב הַמַּחֲנֶה: וַיֵּרֶד הָעֲמָלֵקִי וְהַכְּנַעֲנִי
מה הַיֹּשֵׁב בָּהָר הַהוּא וַיַּכּוּם וַיַּכְּתוּם עַד־הַחָרְמָה:

CLASSIC COMMENTATORS

Why did God not accept the decision of those who decided to conquer the land without hesitation as constituting repentance?

RABBI ISAAC SAMUEL REGGIO
The Lord reads the hearts of man and knew that at this moment the people had lost faith in Him. Israel no longer believed in the covenant, and they made an effort to approach the land only because the deaths of the scouts terrified them.

ר' יצחק שמואל רג'יו
ה' יראה ללבב וידע שלבם לא נכון עמו ולא נאמנו בבריתו ורק פחדו בראותם מיתת המרגלים.

HAAMEK DAVAR
Even though it is usually commendable to repent for sinful behavior by correcting the original transgression, that does not hold true when the correction itself is a violation of God's will.

העמק דבר
אף על גב שטוב לתקן החטא בדבר שחטא, אבל לא במקום שהתשובה עצמה גם כן נגד דבר ה'.

BEMIDBAR | CHAPTER 15

SHELAḤ | 136

> **15:1–16** When Benei Yisrael will reach the Promised Land and someone will bring either a נדבה (freewill offering) or a חגיגה (festival animal offering), it needs to be accompanied by a מנחה (grain offering) and a נסך (libation of wine). These rules apply equally to native-born members of Benei Yisrael and to those who join them.
>
> | Animal | מנחה | נסך |
> |---|---|---|
> | Sheep | 1/10 ephah of flour mixed with 1/4 hin olive oil | 1/4 hin wine |
> | Ram | 2/10 ephah of flour mixed with 1/3 hin olive oil | 1/3 hin wine |
> | Bull | 3/10 ephah of flour mixed with 1/2 hin olive oil | 1/2 hin wine |
>
> **Note:** Ephah (dry measure) ≈ 25 liters; hin (liquid measure) ≈ 4 liters.

15 ¹,² The Lord spoke to Moshe: "Speak to the Israelites. Say: When you come to the land that ³ I am giving you to live in, and you present a fire offering from the herd or from the flock for a pleasing aroma to the Lord – whether it be a burnt offering or a sacrifice to fulfill a ⁴ spoken vow, or brought as a freewill offering, or a festival offering – the one who brings this offering to the Lord shall bring with it a grain offering of a tenth of a measure of fine ⁵ flour mixed with a quarter of a hin of oil, and with the burnt offering or the sacrifice, a ⁶ quarter of a hin of wine as a libation for every lamb. In the case of a ram, you shall bring a grain offering of two-tenths of a measure of fine flour mixed with a third of a hin of oil. ⁷ You shall also offer a third of a hin of wine as a libation, for a pleasing aroma to the Lord. ⁸ If, however, you offer an animal from the herd as a burnt offering or as a sacrifice to fulfill ⁹ a spoken vow, or as a peace offering to the Lord, then you shall bring with each animal ¹⁰ a grain offering of three-tenths of a measure of fine flour mixed with half a hin of oil. You shall also offer half a hin of wine as a libation; it is a fire offering, a pleasing aroma to the ¹¹,¹² Lord. So shall it be with each ox, each ram, and with any sheep or goat. However many ¹³ you offer, you shall do the same for each. Every native-born person, presenting a fire ¹⁴ offering as a pleasing aroma to the Lord, shall perform them in this way. And whensoever, through the generations, a migrant joins you or lives among you, and he too prepares a ¹⁵ fire offering for a pleasing aroma to the Lord, he shall do just as you do. There shall be one law for the congregation: as for you, so for any migrant. It shall be an eternal decree ¹⁶ throughout the generations: you and the migrant shall be the same before the Lord. One law and one rule for you and for the migrant who lives among you."

QUESTIONS FOR THOUGHT

- Why do you think that these requirements are to be instituted only after *Benei Yisrael* enter the land?
- Why do you think that the Torah specifies that these requirements apply to the *ger* as well? (Notice how many times the word גר appears in the final three verses of this passage.)

שלח | פרק טו

טו א וַיְדַבֵּ֥ר יהוה אֶל־מֹשֶׁ֥ה לֵּאמֹֽר: ב דַּבֵּר֙ אֶל־בְּנֵ֣י יִשְׂרָאֵ֔ל וְאָמַרְתָּ֖ אֲלֵהֶ֑ם כִּ֣י תָבֹ֗אוּ אֶל־אֶ֙רֶץ֙ מֽוֹשְׁבֹ֣תֵיכֶ֔ם אֲשֶׁ֥ר אֲנִ֖י נֹתֵ֥ן לָכֶֽם: ג וַעֲשִׂיתֶ֨ם אִשֶּׁ֤ה לַֽיהוה֙ עֹלָ֣ה אוֹ־זֶ֔בַח לְפַלֵּא־נֶ֙דֶר֙ א֣וֹ בִנְדָבָ֔ה א֖וֹ בְּמֹעֲדֵיכֶ֑ם לַעֲשׂ֞וֹת רֵ֤יחַ נִיחֹ֙חַ֙ לַֽיהוה מִן־הַבָּקָ֖ר א֥וֹ מִן־הַצֹּֽאן: ד וְהִקְרִ֛יב הַמַּקְרִ֥יב קָרְבָּנ֖וֹ לַֽיהוה מִנְחָה֙ סֹ֣לֶת עִשָּׂר֔וֹן בָּל֕וּל בִּרְבִעִ֥ית הַהִ֖ין שָֽׁמֶן: ה וְיַ֤יִן לַנֶּ֙סֶךְ֙ רְבִיעִ֣ית הַהִ֔ין תַּעֲשֶׂ֥ה עַל־הָעֹלָ֖ה א֣וֹ לַזָּ֑בַח לַכֶּ֖בֶשׂ הָאֶחָֽד: ו א֤וֹ לָאַ֙יִל֙ תַּעֲשֶׂ֣ה מִנְחָ֔ה סֹ֖לֶת שְׁנֵ֣י עֶשְׂרֹנִ֑ים בְּלוּלָ֥ה בַשֶּׁ֖מֶן שְׁלִשִׁ֥ית הַהִֽין: ז וְיַ֥יִן לַנֶּ֖סֶךְ שְׁלִשִׁ֣ית הַהִ֑ין תַּקְרִ֥יב רֵֽיחַ־נִיחֹ֖חַ לַֽיהוה: ח וְכִֽי־תַעֲשֶׂ֥ה בֶן־בָּקָ֖ר עֹלָ֣ה אוֹ־זָ֑בַח לְפַלֵּא־נֶ֥דֶר אֽוֹ־שְׁלָמִ֖ים לַֽיהוה: ט וְהִקְרִ֤יב עַל־בֶּן־הַבָּקָר֙ מִנְחָ֔ה סֹ֖לֶת שְׁלֹשָׁ֣ה עֶשְׂרֹנִ֑ים בָּל֥וּל בַּשֶּׁ֖מֶן חֲצִ֥י הַהִֽין: י וְיַ֛יִן תַּקְרִ֥יב לַנֶּ֖סֶךְ חֲצִ֣י הַהִ֑ין אִשֵּׁ֥ה רֵֽיחַ־נִיחֹ֖חַ לַֽיהוה: יא כָּ֣כָה יֵעָשֶׂ֗ה לַשּׁוֹר֙ הָֽאֶחָ֔ד א֖וֹ לָאַ֣יִל הָאֶחָ֑ד אֽוֹ־לַשֶּׂ֥ה בַכְּבָשִׂ֖ים א֥וֹ בָעִזִּֽים: יב כַּמִּסְפָּ֖ר אֲשֶׁ֣ר תַּעֲשׂ֑וּ כָּ֛כָה תַּעֲשׂ֥וּ לָאֶחָ֖ד כְּמִסְפָּרָֽם: יג כָּל־הָאֶזְרָ֥ח יַעֲשֶׂה־כָּ֖כָה אֶת־אֵ֑לֶּה לְהַקְרִ֛יב אִשֵּׁ֥ה רֵֽיחַ־נִיחֹ֖חַ לַֽיהוה: יד וְכִֽי־יָגוּר֩ אִתְּכֶ֨ם גֵּ֜ר א֤וֹ אֲשֶֽׁר־בְּתוֹכְכֶם֙ לְדֹרֹ֣תֵיכֶ֔ם וְעָשָׂ֛ה אִשֵּׁ֥ה רֵֽיחַ־נִיחֹ֖חַ לַֽיהוה כַּאֲשֶׁ֥ר תַּעֲשׂ֖וּ כֵּ֥ן יַעֲשֶֽׂה: טו הַקָּהָ֕ל חֻקָּ֥ה אַחַ֛ת לָכֶ֖ם וְלַגֵּ֣ר הַגָּ֑ר חֻקַּ֤ת עוֹלָם֙ לְדֹרֹ֣תֵיכֶ֔ם כָּכֶ֛ם כַּגֵּ֥ר יִהְיֶ֖ה לִפְנֵ֥י יהוה: טז תּוֹרָ֥ה אַחַ֛ת וּמִשְׁפָּ֥ט אֶחָ֖ד יִהְיֶ֣ה לָכֶ֑ם וְלַגֵּ֖ר הַגָּ֥ר אִתְּכֶֽם:

חמישי appears beside verse 8
יד appears at top right

QUICK BITE

The description of the wine libations describes the combination of the offering and the libation as a רֵיחַ נִיחוֹחַ, a "pleasing aroma" to God, five times! The pairing of the offering and the produce of the land of Israel transforms the offering into one which especially pleasing to God.

> **15:17–31** When Benei Yisrael reach the Promised Land, they are to take ḥalla from the dough they make from the local wheat. This ḥalla has a status similar to תרומה, meaning that it must be eaten in purity by a kohen. If Benei Yisrael sin because of a mistaken ruling by their leaders, there is a public offering of a bull as an עולה and a goat as a חטאת, accompanied by their appropriate מנחה and נסך offerings. If, however, an individual sins accidentally, the sin can be atoned for via a חטאת offering of a goat. But if the sin is done intentionally, whether from a native member of Benei Yisrael or someone who joined the people, the sinner will be cut off from the nation.

17–18 The LORD spoke to Moshe: "Speak to the Israelites. Say: When you come to the land
19 to which I am bringing you, and eat the bread of the land, you shall set some aside as
20 an offering to the LORD. As the first portion of your kneading, you shall set aside a loaf
21 as an offering, like the offering you present from the threshing floor. You shall present to the LORD an offering from the first of your kneading throughout your generations.
22 If, without intention, you fail to perform any of these commandments that the LORD
23 gave to Moshe, anything that the LORD has commanded you through Moshe from the
24 day the LORD commanded it and onward – in all generations to come – if it is done unintentionally by the community, the entire community must offer one bull from the herd as a burnt offering, a pleasing aroma to the LORD, with its prescribed grain
25 offering and libation, and one goat as a purification offering. The priest shall then make atonement for all the community of Israel and they will be forgiven, because it was an accidental failing, and because they brought their sacrifice, a fire offering to the LORD
26 and the purification offering for their error before the LORD. The community of Israel and the migrants living among them will all be forgiven, because all the people acted in

---

RAMBAN

The meaning of this passage is not entirely clear.... The obligation described here with regard to communal error is fundamentally different than that which is described in *Parashat Vayikra*. In the earlier text, the people are required to bring a bull for a חטאת, whereas here the Torah mandates a bull for an עולה and a goat for a חטאת. To explain this discrepancy, our Sages (Horayot 8a) maintain that our text deals with the inadvertent commission of idolatry by the congregation.... In fact the straightforward meaning of the current section refers to the sacrifice owed by those people who might lead lives as unintentional apostates. On an individual level this could refer to a person who has joined one of the gentile nations and accepted their practices in all matters, expressing no interest whatsoever in living a Jewish existence. This might result, for example, if a child was abducted and raised among gentiles. On a communal level this might occur if a society comes to believe that the significance and the binding nature of the Torah have lapsed and that Judaism was never meant to be eternal.

רמב״ן

הפרשה הזו סתומה במשמעה ... והנה חיוב הקרבן הזה בשגגת העדה משונה מן הקרבן האמור בפרשת ויקרא, כי שם חייב להביא פר לחטאת וכאן פר לעולה ושעיר לחטאת, על כן הוצרכו רבותינו לומר (בבלי הוריות ח) שזה הקרבן על שגגת העדה בעבודה זרה.... והנה זה כפי משמעו הוא קרבן המשומד לכל התורה בשוגג, כגון ההולך ונדבק לאחת מן האומות לעשות כהם ולא ירצה להיות בכלל ישראל כלל. ויהיה כל זה בשוגג, כגון שיהיה יחיד בתינוק שנשבה לבין הגוים, ובקהל, כגון שיחשבו שכבר עבר זמן התורה ולא היתה לדורות עולם.

במדבר | פרק טו

ששי

יח וַיְדַבֵּר יהוה אֶל־מֹשֶׁה לֵּאמֹר: דַּבֵּר אֶל־בְּנֵי יִשְׂרָאֵל וְאָמַרְתָּ
יט אֲלֵהֶם בְּבֹאֲכֶם אֶל־הָאָרֶץ אֲשֶׁר אֲנִי מֵבִיא אֶתְכֶם שָׁמָּה: וְהָיָה
כ בַּאֲכָלְכֶם מִלֶּחֶם הָאָרֶץ תָּרִימוּ תְרוּמָה לַיהוה: רֵאשִׁית עֲרִסֹתֵכֶם
כא חַלָּה תָּרִימוּ תְרוּמָה כִּתְרוּמַת גֹּרֶן כֵּן תָּרִימוּ אֹתָהּ: מֵרֵאשִׁית
כב עֲרִסֹתֵיכֶם תִּתְּנוּ לַיהוה תְּרוּמָה לְדֹרֹתֵיכֶם: וְכִי תִשְׁגּוּ
וְלֹא תַעֲשׂוּ אֵת כָּל־הַמִּצְוֹת הָאֵלֶּה אֲשֶׁר־דִּבֶּר יהוה אֶל־מֹשֶׁה:
כג אֵת כָּל־אֲשֶׁר צִוָּה יהוה אֲלֵיכֶם בְּיַד־מֹשֶׁה מִן־הַיּוֹם אֲשֶׁר
כד צִוָּה יהוה וָהָלְאָה לְדֹרֹתֵיכֶם: וְהָיָה אִם מֵעֵינֵי הָעֵדָה נֶעֶשְׂתָה
לִשְׁגָגָה וְעָשׂוּ כָל־הָעֵדָה פַּר בֶּן־בָּקָר אֶחָד לְעֹלָה לְרֵיחַ נִיחֹחַ
לַיהוה וּמִנְחָתוֹ וְנִסְכּוֹ כַּמִּשְׁפָּט וּשְׂעִיר־עִזִּים אֶחָד לְחַטָּת:
כה וְכִפֶּר הַכֹּהֵן עַל־כָּל־עֲדַת בְּנֵי יִשְׂרָאֵל וְנִסְלַח לָהֶם כִּי־שְׁגָגָה
הִוא וְהֵם הֵבִיאוּ אֶת־קָרְבָּנָם אִשֶּׁה לַיהוה וְחַטָּאתָם לִפְנֵי יהוה
כו עַל־שִׁגְגָתָם: וְנִסְלַח לְכָל־עֲדַת בְּנֵי יִשְׂרָאֵל וְלַגֵּר הַגָּר בְּתוֹכָם כִּי

CLASSIC COMMENTATORS

The middle of this passage (vv. 22–26) discusses a sin done accidentally by the public after receiving misdirection from its leadership. The commentaries are bothered by the fact that this was already discussed (Lev. 4:13–21), and there the Torah requires a bull as a חטאת whereas here the Torah requires a bull as an עולה followed by a goat as a חטאת.

IBN EZRA   אבן עזרא

The present text describes a sin committed in error by neglecting to fulfill a positive command

וזה החטא הוא שלא עשו מה שצוה לעשות, והוא שוגג.

27 error. If it is an individual who sins inadvertently, he shall offer a year-old female goat as
28 a purification offering. The priest shall make atonement before the LORD for the person
29 who sinned inadvertently, to atone for his sin, and he will be forgiven. There shall be one law for one who inadvertently commits a sin, whether he is a native-born Israelite
30 or a migrant living among them. However, if a person commits a sin high-handedly, whether he is native born or a migrant, he reviles the LORD and shall be severed from
31 the people. Because he despises the LORD's word and violates His commandments, he will be severed utterly and must bear his guilt."

WISDOM OF THE HEART

There is a difference between the mitzva of giving תרומה and מעשר on the one hand, and giving *halla* to the *kohen* on the other. The mitzvot of תרומה and מעשר apply only to produce of the land of Israel; farmers outside the land are exempt. By contrast, the mitzva of *halla* was activated upon entry into the land, and once it was activated, *halla* must be given to the *kohen* regardless of where the wheat was grown or the dough was kneaded. Many commentaries point out that the distinction is based on a slight difference in the way the Torah introduces these mitzvot. While most of the mitzvot that are dependent on the land are introduced by the phrase כי תבואו אל הארץ (when you arrive in the land), the mitzva of *halla* is introduced by the phrase בבואכם אל הארץ (as you enter the land). R. Moshe Feinstein explains that there is a rationale for the distinction as well: תרומה and מעשר are only given after the produce has ripened and been harvested. It is the product of a process which has come to completion, like the entry into the land. When that process has been broken however, like by exile, then the mitzva does not apply. By contrast, the obligation to give *halla* comes into force as soon as the dough is kneaded, even before baking. It represents our hope that the process will end well. That is why we are to give *halla* even when we are not in the land, when our process has not yet come to completion. *Halla* represents our hope and conviction that the process will be completed successfully, that we will be redeemed.

Is hope the result of faith, of a positive attitude, of a blindness to reality, or of something else?

QUICK BITES

One of the mitzvot discussed here describes what happens when the entire community sins as a result of being misled by the leaders. Many have wondered why this is introduced here – why was it not discussed in Leviticus, together with the rest of the offerings brought as a result of sin? R. Samson Raphael Hirsch offers an interesting approach. He suggests that this relates directly to the story which occupies the bulk of this *parasha*, in which a group of leaders – ten out of twelve – mislead the people into rejecting the Promised Land and rebelling against God's gift. It is for that reason that this mitzva was saved for here.

The produce of the land of Israel is special. It has its own sanctity, so much so that some of it must be given to the *kohanim* and the Levites, or eaten next to the Temple, or even given to the poor. R. Moshe Sofer says that farmers harvesting the land can actually feel the sanctity in their hands.

כז לְכָל־הָעָם בִּשְׁגָגָה: וְאִם־נֶפֶשׁ אַחַת תֶּחֱטָא בִשְׁגָגָה שביעי
כח וְהִקְרִיבָה עֵז בַּת־שְׁנָתָהּ לְחַטָּאת: וְכִפֶּר הַכֹּהֵן עַל־הַנֶּפֶשׁ הַשֹּׁגֶגֶת בְּחֶטְאָה בִשְׁגָגָה לִפְנֵי יהוה לְכַפֵּר עָלָיו וְנִסְלַח לוֹ:
כט הָאֶזְרָח בִּבְנֵי יִשְׂרָאֵל וְלַגֵּר הַגָּר בְּתוֹכָם תּוֹרָה אַחַת יִהְיֶה לָכֶם
ל לָעֹשֶׂה בִּשְׁגָגָה: וְהַנֶּפֶשׁ אֲשֶׁר־תַּעֲשֶׂה ׀ בְּיָד רָמָה מִן־הָאֶזְרָח וּמִן־הַגֵּר אֶת־יהוה הוּא מְגַדֵּף וְנִכְרְתָה הַנֶּפֶשׁ הַהִוא מִקֶּרֶב
לא עַמָּהּ: כִּי דְבַר־יהוה בָּזָה וְאֶת־מִצְוָתוֹ הֵפַר הִכָּרֵת ׀ תִּכָּרֵת הַנֶּפֶשׁ הַהִוא עֲוֺנָה בָהּ:

QUESTIONS FOR THOUGHT

- According to Ibn Ezra, what makes the sin described here different from the one described in Leviticus?
- Ramban offers two different explanations. Which of those do you think fits the words of the text better?
- In what way can Ramban's second explanation be especially meaningful in contemporary Jewish life? How about Ibn Ezra's?
- Why do you think the Torah placed these passages – ḥalla, the offerings for a communal sin, and the offering for an individual sin – immediately following the story of the scouts?

TEXTUAL SKILLS

1. Which word appears seven times in verses 19–21?
2. Find two parallels between the passage regarding ḥalla and the previous one dealing with the מנחה and נסך offerings.
3. In the section of verses 17–31, discussing personal sin, there are two words, each central to understanding this passage, and each of which appears three times. There is also another word, also central to the passage, which appears four times! Find those words.
4. The term יד רמה is used in verse 30, apparently to describe someone who does something intentionally. It appears two other times in the Torah: Exodus 14:8 and Numbers 33:3. What can we learn from the other places it is used, to help us understand what kind of sin the Torah is describing here?

BEMIDBAR | CHAPTER 15

SHELAḤ | 142

> **15:32–36** *While Benei Yisrael are in the wilderness they catch a man gathering wood on Shabbat. He is brought to Moshe and Aharon. Unsure of what his punishment should be, they place him under guard until God instructs that he be stoned to death.*

32 When the Israelites were in the wilderness, they encountered a man gathering wood
33 on the Sabbath. Those who found him gathering wood brought him before Moshe and
34 Aharon, and before the whole community, and he was placed in custody, because it had
35 not been specified what should be done to him. And the LORD said to Moshe, "The man shall be put to death. The whole community must stone him outside the camp."
36 And so, as the LORD had commanded Moshe, the whole community took him outside the camp and stoned him to death.

רמב״ן

ולפרשה הזאת סמך אחריה ענין המקושש כי היה בזמן הזה אחר מעשה המרגלים על דרך הפשט. וזה טעם ויהיו בני ישראל במדבר - כי בהתאחר שם העם בגזרה הנזכרת היה המאורע הזה.

RAMBAN

The straightforward meaning of the juxtaposition is that the case of the wood gatherer occurred after the debacle of the scouts. This explains why the Torah states that Israel was in the wilderness – they tarried there as a punishment for the rebellion.

QUESTIONS FOR THOUGHT

- Three of the above commentaries connect this with what came previously. Which commentary connects it with what the Torah speaks about afterward?
- In what way is Ramban's explanation very different from all of the others?
- What is surprising about the commentary of *Haamek Davar*? How would the explanation he brings help to explain a puzzling statement made in 27:3?
- Look at verses 2, 17, and 32. Do you see a connection between them? If so, which of the above commentaries do you think that this connection supports?

WISDOM OF THE HEART

This incident involving the person gathering wood on Shabbat is strange. Why would he do this, at this time, and in such a public manner? And why would he not be named, like all the other major violators in the wilderness? Perhaps even stranger is that one opinion in the Talmud identifies the person as Tzelofḥad, the man whose daughters ask for their father's portion in the land. Maharsha, in his comment on that gemara, suggests that Tzelofḥad did this intentionally. After the decree that *Benei Yisrael* would not enter the land, many people thought that they were no longer obligated in mitzvot. Tzelofḥad engages in a deliberate and very public violation of Shabbat so that he would get caught and put to death to prove that the mitzvot were still binding. That's why his daughters later proudly identify him as the man who died as a result of his sin – it was a sin that they could be proud of, and for that reason his name deserved to be maintained in its connection to the land.

> **Every once in a while we hear in the news about someone who sacrificed his life to promote or defend a cause. Is that something which you think should be celebrated and honored, or discouraged?**

לב וַיִּהְיוּ בְנֵי־יִשְׂרָאֵל בַּמִּדְבָּר וַיִּמְצְאוּ אִישׁ מְקֹשֵׁשׁ עֵצִים בְּיוֹם
לג הַשַּׁבָּת: וַיַּקְרִיבוּ אֹתוֹ הַמֹּצְאִים אֹתוֹ מְקֹשֵׁשׁ עֵצִים אֶל־מֹשֶׁה
לד וְאֶל־אַהֲרֹן וְאֶל כָּל־הָעֵדָה: וַיַּנִּיחוּ אֹתוֹ בַּמִּשְׁמָר כִּי לֹא פֹרַשׁ
לה מַה־יֵּעָשֶׂה לוֹ: וַיֹּאמֶר יְהֹוָה אֶל־מֹשֶׁה מוֹת יוּמַת
לו הָאִישׁ רָגוֹם אֹתוֹ בָאֲבָנִים כָּל־הָעֵדָה מִחוּץ לַמַּחֲנֶה: וַיֹּצִיאוּ
אֹתוֹ כָּל־הָעֵדָה אֶל־מִחוּץ לַמַּחֲנֶה וַיִּרְגְּמוּ אֹתוֹ בָּאֲבָנִים וַיָּמֹת
כַּאֲשֶׁר צִוָּה יְהֹוָה אֶת־מֹשֶׁה:

CLASSIC COMMENTATORS

The commentaries are puzzled as to why this brief story about the violation of Shabbat is told here and why it is prefaced by telling us that it happened in the wilderness.

אבן עזרא

בעבור שנשאו קול כל העדה (במדבר י״ד:א׳) וחטאו, ונסלח להם בעבור תפלת משה, אמר: וכי תשגו ולא תעשו (שם ט״ו:כ״ב), ... ובסוף: והנפש אשר תעשה ביד רמה (שם ט״ו:ל׳) רמז למעשיהם. והזכיר דבר המקושש כי עשה ביד רמה.

ר׳ יוסף בכור שור

ויהיו בני ישראל במדבר – כמו שנגזר עליהם שלא יכנסו לארץ.

העמק דבר

כמו שכתבו התוספות בבבא בתרא (קיט ע״ב) בשם מדרש, שהמקושש נתכוון לשם שמים, דישראל סברו שאין התורה נוהגת אלא בארץ ישראל ... ומשעה שנגזר עליהם להיות ארבעים שנה במדבר ולהיות גולים ממקום למקום, היה להם דין גלות ... כסבורים שפטורים ממצוות עד שיבואו לארץ ישראל. ולזה בא המקושש להראות שימיתו אותו על חילול שבת. משום הכי כתיב ״ויהיו בני ישראל במדבר״, שזה גרם את מעשה המקושש.

IBN EZRA

Since the entire nation sinned (14:1) and were forgiven as a result of Moshe's prayer, the Torah now describes what to do when the nation sins "without intention, you fail to perform..." (15:22). That section concludes with a discussion of an individual who "commits a sin high-handedly" (15:30), meaning brazenly, which was an allusion to the rebellion of the previous chapter. That is why the story of the wood gatherer is inserted here, because he acted brazenly.

RABBI YOSEF BEKHOR SHOR

The text emphasizes that this incident took place in the wilderness after God decreed that Israel would not enter Canaan.

HAAMEK DAVAR

According to Tosafot's comments on Bava Batra (119b), which cite the midrash, this individual who gathered the wood had noble intentions for his actions. Since the people of Israel believed that the Torah laws would apply only once the nation crossed into the land, he sacrificed his life to demonstrate that this was not so.... Now as soon as God decreed that the Israelites were to wander for forty days in the desert, they were considered to have been exiled from their homeland.... The masses therefore thought that in the meantime they were exempt from the commandments they had been taught. Hence this man decided to show everybody else that he would be executed for violating the laws of the Sabbath. This is why the text states that Israel was in the wilderness when they discovered the gatherer – it was the nation's banishment to the desert that led to his willful transgression of God's rule.

BEMIDBAR | CHAPTER 15   SHELAḤ | 144

> **15:37–41** *Four-cornered garments are required to have fringes – tzitzit – added to each of the corners, and one of the strings on each corner should be of tekhelet. Those fringes are to serve as visual reminders of God's commandments, so that we not automatically follow the desires of our eyes and our hearts.*

37–38 The Lord said to Moshe: "Speak to the Israelites; tell them to make fringes on the corners of their garments throughout the generations. To the fringe on each corner they
39 should attach a blue cord. And this shall be your fringe: seeing it, you shall remember all the Lord's commands and keep them. You will not then go astray, following the
40 lusts of your heart or of your eyes. This is to remind you to keep all My commands, to
41 remain holy to your God. I am the Lord your God, who brought you out of Egypt to be your God. I am the Lord your God."

TEXTUAL SKILLS

1. These fringes are called tzitzit, literally meaning things to look at. Where in the Torah is there the singular version of that word, ציץ?
2. Notice that the last verse opens and closes with the same phrase.
3. Which words, phrases, or images in this passage remind you of the *kohen gadol* or of Leviticus?
4. Read the passage carefully. Is it written as if God is speaking or as if Moshe is?

WISDOM OF THE HEART

Clothes are an important marker of who we are. Some people wear uniforms, and certain kinds of jewelry identify a person as belonging to a group. Think about how head coverings can easily identify someone as being part of a particular culture. Servants are marked by the clothes they wear, as are their bosses and masters. As Rav Soloveitchik points out, as part of the process of leaving Egypt, *Benei Yisrael* need to leave behind their servant clothing, which God now replaces with clothes of royalty. *Tekhelet* was very difficult to produce, and therefore very expensive. There were times in history that it was forbidden for anyone but royalty to have *tekhelet* in their garments. The mitzva to have a string of *tekhelet* declares *Benei Yisrael* to be royalty. It lifts them from their slavery in Egypt to an elevated status as God's people. Rav Soloveitchik further suggests that the white strings of the tzitzit reflect clarity, rational thinking. By contrast, the blue reflects the seas and the heavens, each of them mysterious, endless, and incomprehensible. The insignia of *Benei Yisrael*, the blue and white, reflects the blending of the rational and the mysterious grandeur, both of which are necessary for religious life.

> **Do you sometimes find yourself torn between what makes sense logically and what feels right emotionally? Which of those tends to win?**

QUICK BITE

Many of the Hasidic masters stress that giving up, losing hope, is a grave injustice that we do to ourselves, especially if we lose hope because of the mistakes that we've made. The Seer of Lublin, commenting on the verse of the Torah instructing us not to follow our hearts and our eyes, suggests that the Torah is telling us that even if we already followed our hearts and made serious mistakes, we should not simply continue what we are doing and give up hope of fixing ourselves.

במדבר | פרק טו

לח וַיֹּאמֶר יְהוָה אֶל־מֹשֶׁה לֵּאמֹר: דַּבֵּר אֶל־בְּנֵי יִשְׂרָאֵל וְאָמַרְתָּ אֲלֵהֶם וְעָשׂוּ לָהֶם צִיצִת עַל־כַּנְפֵי בִגְדֵיהֶם לְדֹרֹתָם וְנָתְנוּ עַל־צִיצִת הַכָּנָף פְּתִיל תְּכֵלֶת: לט וְהָיָה לָכֶם לְצִיצִת וּרְאִיתֶם אֹתוֹ וּזְכַרְתֶּם אֶת־כָּל־מִצְוֹת יְהוָה וַעֲשִׂיתֶם אֹתָם וְלֹא תָתוּרוּ אַחֲרֵי לְבַבְכֶם וְאַחֲרֵי עֵינֵיכֶם אֲשֶׁר־אַתֶּם זֹנִים אַחֲרֵיהֶם: מ לְמַעַן תִּזְכְּרוּ וַעֲשִׂיתֶם אֶת־כָּל־מִצְוֹתָי וִהְיִיתֶם קְדֹשִׁים לֵאלֹהֵיכֶם: מא אֲנִי יְהוָה אֱלֹהֵיכֶם אֲשֶׁר הוֹצֵאתִי אֶתְכֶם מֵאֶרֶץ מִצְרַיִם לִהְיוֹת לָכֶם לֵאלֹהִים אֲנִי יְהוָה אֱלֹהֵיכֶם:

מפטיר

CLASSIC COMMENTATORS

How do tzitzit help us to remember the mitzvot?

רש״י

שמנין גימטריא של ציצית שש מאות, ושמונה חוטין וחמשה קשרין הרי תרי״ג.

RASHI

You shall remember all of the Lord's commands: You will make this association because the numerical value of the term tzitzit is six hundred, there are eight strings on each of the garment's corners, and each set of strings is tied with five knots, (for a total of 613).

ר׳ יוסף בכור שור

שאינו נעשה אלא לזכירה, וכשרואה זאת המצוה, זוכר ונותן לב לשמור המצות. כי הציצית כמו חותם שבכסותו, שעושין לעבד סימן שהוא משועבד לרבו, וכשרואים ישראל זוכרים שהם משועבדים להקב״ה, ועליהם לקיים כל מצוותיו.

RABBI YOSEF BEKHOR SHOR

The purpose of the fringes is to remind those who see them to observe the gamut of the Torah's commandments. The tzitzit thereby resemble a badge that is sewn onto a servant's clothes to identify him as being indentured to a particular master. Thus, when the Israelites look at their tzitzit they recall that they are subservient to the Holy One, blessed be He, and as such are bound to keep His law.

QUESTIONS FOR THOUGHT

- Imagine that instead of tzitzit with a string of *tekhelet*, the Torah had instructed us to wear a purple bracelet. According to which of the commentaries would this bracelet not have worked the same way that tzitzit do as a reminder of the mitzvot?
- Bekhor Shor offers what could be understood as two different explanations. What is the difference between the two?
- In the time of the Torah, a four-cornered garment was standard clothing. Today it is not. Do you think that the special four-cornered garment worn today to fulfill this mitzva works better, worse, or the same as a reminder of the mitzvot?

MORE QUICK BITES

- **13:25** Many things described by the scouts as obstacles were real concerns. Kalev's call of "Let us go up" didn't address any of the real issues. R. Kalonymus Kalman Shapiro, the Rebbe of Piacesna, says that the core issue was one of faith. The scouts had declared that their fear had overcome them; Kalev's counterclaim was that God could deal with all the obstacles, and if they believed it then He would.

- **13:33** The scouts described that the local people saw them like grasshoppers. They could not possibly have known how others viewed them; the most they could know is how they saw themselves. That report revealed their own insecurity, a fatal flaw for someone entrusted with any kind of important task. Until Roger Bannister ran the mile in under four minutes nobody thought that it was possible, and because everyone believed that it was impossible – it was impossible. He did it, and it suddenly became possible; today many people have breached that barrier.

- **14:11** God's threat to start all over again with Moshe founding a new nation is not an empty one. In the flood, God started creation all over again and started humanity with a single family from the world before.

EXPLORING HASHKAFA
The Specialness of the Land

What is it that makes the land of Israel special?

For the halakhist, the answer is simple. It is special because it has more mitzvot attached to it. Living in the land and on it provides more opportunities for sanctifying our lives on a daily basis, even via the fruits and vegetables that we eat.

For the more mystically minded, the land itself is infused with a potential for spirituality which simply doesn't exist elsewhere. R. Yehuda Halevi describes this in the *Kuzari*, saying simply that some lands are better for growing grapes, others olives, and others wheat. This land is better for spirituality. That is why, he suggests, that prophecy is possible only in the land, because of the land's inherent nature.

Ramban, also a mystic, develops this idea in two different directions. In the first, he portrays the land in almost human terms. It has a persona; there are things it can and cannot tolerate. Put idolatry or immorality into the land, and it will spit it out, the same way that your body will vomit out food that it senses is incompatible. In his other approach, the land has a unique relationship with the people designed to live in it. It will temporarily tolerate others living there, but will not flourish unless it is united with its special nation. Ramban goes so far as to suggest that mitzvot performed outside the land are nothing more than practice for when the Jewish people are reunited with it – it is only there that mitzvot take on their fullest meaning.

For the rationalist, the land is special because God chose it for the chosen people. There is nothing intrinsically different about it; God could have chosen any other land, but it was this land which was chosen. It is similar to the reality that we don't get to choose our parents or (in most cases) our children – the fact that they are our parents or children is what makes them special. This is the land of the history of the Jewish people, the land of their destiny.

For the pragmatic philosopher, the land of Israel was chosen because of its centrality on the planet. Certainly in the ancient world, it was the intersection of civilization on three continents. Since God chose the Jewish people to impact on all of humanity, the headquarters would need to be in the most central place on earth.

Whether you understand the land of Israel through a halakhic, mystical, rational, or pragmatic lens, it was and remains the only homeland the Jewish people have had. It is home.

פרשת קרח
PARASHAT KORAḤ

"We can agree to disagree, but we don't need to be disagreeable."
John Wooden

Koraḥ. A democratic revolutionary, dangerous anarchist, or power-hungry potential dictator? How do we know? Who would support Koraḥ today if he stood up to what could have been perceived as a nepotistic, closed circle of leaders who concentrated the key positions of power in a single family? How does Moshe stand up to the first direct challenge to his leadership?

PARASHAT KORAḤ

16 1 Koraḥ, son of Yitzhar son of Kehat son of Levi, together with Datan and Aviram sons of
2 Eliav and On son of Pelet – descendants of Reuven – took two hundred fifty Israelite
3 men, leaders of the community, chosen from the assembly, men of repute, and confronted Moshe and Aharon together. They said to them, "You have gone too far. All the community is holy, every one of them, and the Lord is in their midst. Why then do
4 you set yourselves above the Lord's people?" When Moshe heard this, he fell upon his

---

RAMBAN

The Levites rebelled against Moshe because Koraḥ fumed over the appointment of his cousin Elitzafan, as our Rabbis maintain. Koraḥ was also jealous of Aharon's position.... Now during Israel's sojourn in the wilderness they experienced no real calamity. Even the incident of the golden calf, which represented a serious and infamous transgression, resulted in the deaths of a relatively small percentage of the population. This was thanks to the prayers of Moshe which saved the people from utter calamity.... Thus the Israelites loved Moshe as a kindred spirit to themselves, and followed all of his instructions. Had any individual dared to revolt against Moshe he would have been summarily stoned by the masses. This is why Koraḥ accepted Aharon's selection as High Priest, and the firstborn did not complain when they were replaced by the Levites. The nation obliged Moshe regarding all of his actions. However, when the nation arrived in the Wilderness of Paran (in 12:1), disastrous events began to happen. Some people were burned at Tavera from the fire of the Lord [11:3], while many other citizens perished at Kivrot HaTaava [11:34]. Furthermore, during the debacle of the scouts, Moshe did not petition God on behalf of his people to nullify the Almighty's decree. Subsequently the tribal representatives all died in a plague before the Lord, and God declared that the entire nation would perish in the wilderness. All of this soured the nation's attitudes toward their leader, and they began to believe that their misfortunes were due to Moshe's words.... Thus the present complaints against Moshe surfaced now, after the punishment had been pronounced because of the scouts.

רמב״ן

והנכון במורדים שבעם קרח על נשיאות אליצפן כמאמר רבותינו וקנא גם באהרן... והנה ישראל בהיותם במדבר סיני לא אירע להם שום רעה, כי גם בדבר העגל שהיה החטא גדול ומפורסם היו המתים מועטים ונצלו בתפלתו של משה... והנה היו אוהבים אותו כנפשם ושומעין אליו, ואלו היה אדם מורד במשה בזמן ההוא היו העם סוקלין אותו, ולכן סבל קרח גדולת אהרן... אבל בבואם אל מדבר פארן, ונשרפו באש תבערה ומתו בקברות התאוה רבים, וכאשר חטאו במרגלים לא התפלל משה עליהם ולא בטל הגזרה מהם, ומתו נשיאי כל השבטים במגפה לפני י״י ונגזר על כל העם שיתמו במדבר ושם ימותו, אז היה נפש כל העם מרה, והיו אומרים בלבם כי יבאו להם בדברי משה תקלות... וזה טעם תלונתם הנה במקום הזה אחר גזרת המרגלים מיד.

QUESTIONS FOR THOUGHT

- Each of the commentaries ties Koraḥ's rebellion to an earlier trigger in Numbers. What events does each identify?
- Both Rashi and Ibn Ezra choose contexts which seem to be far removed from this incident. Why do you think they did that?
- What is the difference between the jealousy identified by Rashi and that identified by Ibn Ezra?
- What is the strength of Ramban's explanation?
- According to all of the explanations, whose position does Koraḥ want?

פרשת קרח

טז
א וַיִּקַּ֣ח קֹ֔רַח בֶּן־יִצְהָ֥ר בֶּן־קְהָ֖ת בֶּן־לֵוִ֑י וְדָתָ֨ן וַאֲבִירָ֜ם בְּנֵ֣י
ב אֱלִיאָ֗ב וְא֛וֹן בֶּן־פֶּ֖לֶת בְּנֵ֣י רְאוּבֵֽן: וַיָּקֻ֨מוּ֙ לִפְנֵ֣י מֹשֶׁ֔ה וַאֲנָשִׁ֥ים
מִבְּנֵֽי־יִשְׂרָאֵ֖ל חֲמִשִּׁ֣ים וּמָאתָ֑יִם נְשִׂיאֵ֥י עֵדָ֛ה קְרִאֵ֥י מוֹעֵ֖ד
ג אַנְשֵׁי־שֵֽׁם: וַיִּקָּהֲל֞וּ עַל־מֹשֶׁ֣ה וְעַל־אַהֲרֹ֗ן וַיֹּאמְר֣וּ אֲלֵהֶם֮
רַב־לָכֶם֒ כִּ֤י כָל־הָֽעֵדָה֙ כֻּלָּ֣ם קְדֹשִׁ֔ים וּבְתוֹכָ֖ם יְהֹוָ֑ה וּמַדּ֥וּעַ
ד תִּֽתְנַשְּׂא֖וּ עַל־קְהַ֥ל יְהֹוָֽה: וַיִּשְׁמַ֣ע מֹשֶׁ֔ה וַיִּפֹּ֖ל עַל־פָּנָֽיו:

TEXTUAL SKILLS

1. The term used to describe the action taken by Moshe's challengers is **להקהל על** (v. 3). That same expression is used many times in the Torah (see, for example, Ex. 32:1; Num. 17:7, 20:2). In what way is this term different from the very similar **להקהל** (without **על** – see, for example, Ex. 35:1; Lev. 8:4; Num. 1:18)?

2. This is neither the first nor the last time in the book of Numbers that Moshe falls on his face. What do these three incidents have in common?

CLASSIC COMMENTATORS

What sparked Koraḥ's rebellion and why did it happen now?

RASHI

Now what possessed Koraḥ to pick a fight with Moshe? He resented the fact that Moshe had chosen their cousin, Elitzafan son of Uziel, as head of the Kehat family [as reported in Num. 3:30], at God's command. Said Koraḥ: My father Yitzhar was one of four – as the verse states, "The sons of Kehat were Amram, Yitzhar, Ḥevron, and Uziel" (Ex. 6:18). Now Amram was the eldest brother and his two sons seized the top positions in the nation: the kingship and the high priesthood. But would it not have been fair for the next highest office to be delegated to the family of the second son, namely my father Yitzhar? And yet, Moshe designated the son of Uziel – the youngest of the four brothers – as prince of the Kehat clan! Because of that, I will challenge Moshe and nullify his appointment.

IBN EZRA

These Levites resented the fact that they had been made subservient to Aharon and his sons, as an earlier verse (Num. 8:19) attests.

רש״י

מה ראה קרח לחלוק עם משה? נתקנא על נשיאותו של אליצפן בן עוזיאל (במדבר ג׳:ל׳) שמינהו משה נשיא על בני קהת על פי הדיבר. אמר: אחי אבא ארבעה היו, בני קהת עמרם ויצהר חברון ועוזיאל (שמות ו׳:י״ח) עמרם הבכור נטלו שני בניו גדולה, אחד מלך ואחד כהן גדול, מי ראוי ליטול את שנייה לא אני שאני בן יצהר שהוא שיני לעמרם, והוא מינה את בן אחיו הקטן מכולם, הריני חולק עליו ומבטל את דבריו.

אבן עזרא

הלוים קשרו עליו בעבור היותם נתונים לאהרן ולבניו (במדבר ח׳:י״ט).

BEMIDBAR | CHAPTER 16 — KORAḤ

> **16:5–11** Moshe issues a challenge to Koraḥ and his followers: Let each of them prepare a firepan (censer) with the incense offering, and on the following day God will choose whom He wants as the sanctified one. Moshe also speaks with Koraḥ, imploring him not to focus his ire at Aharon or seek the role of kohen, but rather to be content with the fact that he was a Levite, identified by God for a special role.

5 face. Then he spoke to Koraḥ and all his company. "In the morning," he said, "the Lord will make known who is His and who is holy, and will bring that one close to Him. The
6 one He chooses will be the one He will allow to come close. Do this: Let Koraḥ and
7 his company take censers. Tomorrow light fire in them and place incense upon them before the Lord. The man whom the Lord chooses – he is holy. It is you, sons of Levi,
8 who have gone too far!" Moshe said to Koraḥ, "Listen now, you sons of Levi. Is it not
9 enough for you that the God of Israel has separated you from the Israelite community, enabling you to come close to Him, to serve in the Lord's Tabernacle, and stand in the
10 presence of the community to minister to them? He has brought you, and with you all
11 your fellow Levites, to be close to Him, and yet you seek the priesthood also? And so you and all your company have assembled to defy the Lord. Aharon – who is he that

TEXTUAL SKILLS

1. Try to match Moshe's response to Koraḥ's complaint. Which parts of Moshe's response address Koraḥ's complaint and which do not?
2. Koraḥ complained to Moshe, רב לכם, meaning "you have too much." What is Moshe's response?
3. In verse 8, what is the conflict between the first half of the verse and the second half?

WISDOM OF THE HEART

Moshe says to Koraḥ, "Is it not enough for you that the God of Israel has separated you…" Listen carefully to Moshe's words. It was not he who chose himself, or he who set aside the tribe of Levi, but God. If we understand that it is God who gives us our mission, then there is no reason for jealousy. Everyone gets what is appropriate for them.

How do we know today that what we are doing is actually God's choice for us? Don't we have a role in choosing our path?

QUICK BITES

Every person created is unique and has a unique contribution to make to the world. One of the most difficult things in life is to figure out what our individual, distinct contribution is. R. Meir Schlesinger once commented that the most important prayer for anyone studying Torah is ותן חלקנו בתורתך, "Give us our portion in Torah." Every individual, he said, has a unique portion of the Torah which is theirs. The challenge is to discover what that portion is.

Rav Soloveitchik noted that in some sense Koraḥ's claim that all of *Benei Yisrael* were holy is correct. All of *Benei Yisrael* share a sanctity by virtue of being members of the people. Koraḥ's error was in not recognizing individual sources of uniqueness and sanctity – creativity, initiative, originality – which go beyond the communal.

ה וַיְדַבֵּ֨ר אֶל־קֹ֜רַח וְאֶֽל־כָּל־עֲדָתוֹ֮ לֵאמֹר֒ בֹּ֠קֶר וְיֹדַ֨ע יְהֹוָ֧ה אֶת־
אֲשֶׁר־ל֛וֹ וְאֶת־הַקָּד֖וֹשׁ וְהִקְרִ֣יב אֵלָ֑יו וְאֵ֛ת אֲשֶׁ֥ר יִבְחַר־בּ֖וֹ יַקְרִ֥יב
ו אֵלָֽיו: זֹ֖את עֲשׂ֑וּ קְחוּ־לָכֶ֣ם מַחְתּ֔וֹת קֹ֖רַח וְכָל־עֲדָתֽוֹ: וּתְנ֣וּ
ז בָהֵ֣ן ׀ אֵ֡שׁ וְשִׂימוּ֩ עֲלֵיהֶ֨ן ׀ קְטֹ֜רֶת לִפְנֵ֤י יְהֹוָה֙ מָחָ֔ר וְהָיָ֗ה הָאִ֛ישׁ
ח אֲשֶׁר־יִבְחַ֥ר יְהֹוָ֖ה ה֣וּא הַקָּד֑וֹשׁ רַב־לָכֶ֖ם בְּנֵ֥י לֵוִֽי: וַיֹּ֥אמֶר
ט מֹשֶׁ֖ה אֶל־קֹ֑רַח שִׁמְעוּ־נָ֖א בְּנֵ֥י לֵוִֽי: הַמְעַ֣ט מִכֶּ֗ם כִּֽי־הִבְדִּיל֩
אֱלֹהֵ֨י יִשְׂרָאֵ֤ל אֶתְכֶם֙ מֵעֲדַ֣ת יִשְׂרָאֵ֔ל לְהַקְרִ֥יב אֶתְכֶ֖ם אֵלָ֑יו
י לַעֲבֹ֗ד אֶת־עֲבֹדַת֙ מִשְׁכַּ֣ן יְהֹוָ֔ה וְלַעֲמֹ֛ד לִפְנֵ֥י הָעֵדָ֖ה לְשָׁרְתָֽם: וַיַּקְרֵב֙ אֹֽתְךָ֔ וְאֶת־כָּל־אַחֶ֥יךָ בְנֵי־לֵוִ֖י אִתָּ֑ךְ וּבִקַּשְׁתֶּ֖ם גַּם־כְּהֻנָּֽה:
יא לָכֵ֗ן אַתָּה֙ וְכָל־עֲדָ֣תְךָ֔ הַנֹּעָדִ֖ים עַל־יְהֹוָ֑ה וְאַהֲרֹ֣ן מַה־ה֔וּא כִּ֥י

CLASSIC COMMENTATORS

Moshe suggests a "test" for the position of *kohen gadol* involving bringing the incense offering outside of the precincts of the *Mishkan*. Did he think of this himself, or did God instruct him to do it?

RAMBAN

רמב"ן

Moshe himself conceived of this plan to offer the incense. He trusted that God would endorse this test.

והנה משה מעצמו חשב המחשבה הזאת של הקטרת ... ובטח משה כי השם מקיים דבר עבדו.

HAAMEK DAVAR

העמק דבר

Moshe fell on his face in prayer, and while he was in that meditative state he received divine inspiration. He then knew how to respond to the rebellious crowd.

ויפול על פניו – לתפלה ... ובין כך השיג רוח הקודש וידע להשיב דבר.

QUESTIONS FOR THOUGHT

- What do you think prompted Ramban to suggest his interpretation? In light of Koraḥ's accusation against Moshe, why is this interpretation ironic?
- Why do you think *Haamek Davar* rejects Ramban's position?
- Do you think that it is acceptable or problematic to "force" God to do something in order to demonstrate a point to the public?
- In what way is this story similar to that of Eliyahu on Mount Carmel (I Kings 18)?

12 you should have grievances against him?" After this, Moshe sent for Datan and Aviram,
13 sons of Eliav. But they said, "We will not come up. Is it not enough that you have brought us out of a land flowing with milk and with honey to kill us in the desert, that you insist
14 on lording it over us? And more: you have not brought us to a land flowing with milk and with honey, nor have you given us an inheritance of cropland and vineyard. Would
15 you pull out these people's eyes?! We will not come up!" Moshe became very angry and said to the Lord, "Pay no attention to their offering. I have not taken a single donkey from them, nor have I wronged any one of them."
16 Moshe said to Koraḥ, "You and your entire company shall appear before the Lord
17 tomorrow: you, they, and Aharon. Each one shall take his censer, place incense upon it, and present it before the Lord, each holding his censer, two hundred fifty censers
18 in all, and you and Aharon likewise with yours." Each took his censer, placed fire in it, put incense upon it, and stood at the entrance to the Tent of Meeting, as did Moshe
19 and Aharon. Koraḥ gathered all his company against them to the entrance to the Tent

רמב״ן

ואינו נכון בעיני שיהיה על הקטרת, לפי שעל דתן ואבירם הוא אומר כן, שחרה לו על דבריהם, והם לא היו בתוך העדה הנועדים להקטיר קטרת.

RAMBAN

It does not seem to me that Moshe is referring here to the incense that was slated to be offered the following day. This is because Moshe is speaking about Datan and Aviram, who had angered him with their accusations. And these men were not included within the group scheduled to burn the incense.

ר׳ עובדיה ספורנו

אל תפן אל שום מין קרבן שיקריבו לכפר עליהם... וזה כי איני מוחל על עלבוני, ואין למחול להם בלעדי זה.

RABBI OVADYA SFORNO

Moshe pleaded with God to reject any sacrifice that his opponents might offer to atone for their behavior.... Moshe thereby refused to forgive the offense these men had caused, and so he argued that God could not accept any atonement without the prophet's forgiveness.

QUESTIONS FOR THOUGHT

- What is the main difference between Rashi's explanation and Ibn Ezra's?
- Is Sforno's understanding closer to Rashi's or to Ibn Ezra's?
- Whose explanation is Ramban rejecting?
- In what ways are Moshe's comments in verse 15 similar to and different from I Samuel 12:3 and I Kings 18:36–37?

WISDOM OF THE HEART

Moshe asks God not to accept the offering of the rebels. The Midrash suggests that this offering is not referring to the special incense which he had proposed as a challenge but to some role that they had in the daily offering in the *Mishkan*. The Lubavitch Rebbe explains that the communal offering does not belong to any individual – it belongs to the collective, the entire community. This is so much so, that if the *kohen* processing it has idolatrous intentions it does not invalidate the offering, because the *kohen* has no greater portion than anyone else.

במדבר | פרק טז | קרח

יב תְּלוּנוּ עָלָיו: וַיִּשְׁלַח מֹשֶׁה לִקְרֹא לְדָתָן וְלַאֲבִירָם בְּנֵי אֱלִיאָב תְּלִינוּ
יג וַיֹּאמְרוּ לֹא נַעֲלֶה: הַמְעַט כִּי הֶעֱלִיתָנוּ מֵאֶרֶץ זָבַת חָלָב וּדְבַשׁ
יד לַהֲמִיתֵנוּ בַּמִּדְבָּר כִּי־תִשְׂתָּרֵר עָלֵינוּ גַּם־הִשְׂתָּרֵר: אַף לֹא ‏‎ שני
אֶל־אֶרֶץ זָבַת חָלָב וּדְבַשׁ הֲבִיאֹתָנוּ וַתִּתֶּן־לָנוּ נַחֲלַת שָׂדֶה
וָכָרֶם הַעֵינֵי הָאֲנָשִׁים הָהֵם תְּנַקֵּר לֹא נַעֲלֶה: וַיִּחַר לְמֹשֶׁה
טו מְאֹד וַיֹּאמֶר אֶל־יהוה אַל־תֵּפֶן אֶל־מִנְחָתָם לֹא חֲמוֹר אֶחָד
טז מֵהֶם נָשָׂאתִי וְלֹא הֲרֵעֹתִי אֶת־אַחַד מֵהֶם: וַיֹּאמֶר מֹשֶׁה אֶל־
קֹרַח אַתָּה וְכָל־עֲדָתְךָ הֱיוּ לִפְנֵי יהוה אַתָּה וָהֵם וְאַהֲרֹן מָחָר:
יז וּקְחוּ ׀ אִישׁ מַחְתָּתוֹ וּנְתַתֶּם עֲלֵיהֶם קְטֹרֶת וְהִקְרַבְתֶּם לִפְנֵי
יהוה אִישׁ מַחְתָּתוֹ חֲמִשִּׁים וּמָאתַיִם מַחְתֹּת וְאַתָּה וְאַהֲרֹן אִישׁ
יח מַחְתָּתוֹ: וַיִּקְחוּ אִישׁ מַחְתָּתוֹ וַיִּתְּנוּ עֲלֵיהֶם אֵשׁ וַיָּשִׂימוּ עֲלֵיהֶם
יט קְטֹרֶת וַיַּעַמְדוּ פֶּתַח אֹהֶל מוֹעֵד וּמֹשֶׁה וְאַהֲרֹן: וַיַּקְהֵל עֲלֵיהֶם
קֹרַח אֶת־כָּל־הָעֵדָה אֶל־פֶּתַח אֹהֶל מוֹעֵד וַיֵּרָא כְבוֹד־יהוה

CLASSIC COMMENTATORS

After Datan and Aviram's sharp words, Moshe asks God not to accept their מנחה. To what מנחה is Moshe referring?

רש״י / **RASHI**

לפי פשוטו: הקטרת שהם מקריבים לפניך מחר אל תפן אליה.

According to the straightforward meaning, this refers to the incense that Moshe's opponents were to sacrifice to God on the following day. Moshe asked God not to accept those offerings.

אבן עזרא / **IBN EZRA**

כבר פירשתי כי העלה והמנחה מארכת האף על הרשעים, ודתן ואבירם היו אנשים גדולים, והקריבו מנחה קודם זה המעשה.

I have already explained that the sacrifice of an עולה or a מנחה serve to suspend punishment against the wicked. Now because Datan and Aviram were important personages, they had brought a מנחה before this episode.

BEMIDBAR | CHAPTER 16 — KORAḤ

> **16:20–27** *God threatens to immediately annihilate all those Koraḥ has gathered to observe, but Moshe and Aharon plead that the onlookers should not be punished because of the evil of the leaders. God therefore tells Moshe to instruct the onlookers to separate themselves from Koraḥ, Datan, and Aviram, lest they all be consumed together. The crowd disperses when Moshe warns them, but Datan and Aviram stand defiantly with their families outside of their tents.*

20 of Meeting. Then the glory of the Lord was revealed to the entire community. The
21 Lord spoke to Moshe and Aharon: "Separate yourselves from this community and
22 let Me consume them in a moment." They fell on their faces and said, "God, the God of the spirit of all flesh, if one man sins, will You rage against the entire community?"
23/24 The Lord spoke to Moshe: "Tell the community to move away from the dwellings of
25 Koraḥ, Datan, and Aviram." Moshe rose and went to Datan and Aviram. Israel's elders
26 followed him. He spoke to the community, saying: "Turn away now from the tents of these wicked men. Do not touch anything of theirs, lest you be swept away for all their
27 sins." So they moved away from around the dwellings of Koraḥ, Datan, and Aviram. Datan and Aviram came out and stood at the openings of their tents with their wives,

משך חכמה — MESHEKH ḤOKHMA

זה היה שעת זעמו של הקב"ה ... לכן הודיעם שרגע זה הוא זועם וחיים ברצונו.

At this moment the rage of the Holy One, blessed be He, was stirring. As such God warned that everybody's life was in danger should His fury be released.

QUESTIONS FOR THOUGHT

- What is the difference between the opinions of Ramban and R. Hirsch?
- Which commentary doesn't think that God ever intended to kill the masses of people for their role?
- Which commentary understands that God's intention was to save the people from imminent disaster?
- Rashi (Ex. 12:22) writes that once permission is given to the destructive force to destroy, it does not distinguish between the righteous and the guilty. Which commentary here says something similar?
- Do you think that bystanders bear some responsibility for crimes that they witness? Why or why not? Which of these commentaries make comments that are related to this question?

TEXTUAL SKILLS

1. Where else in the Torah can you find an argument similar to the one made by Moshe and Aharon in verse 22?
2. Notice the similarity between verse 22 and 27:16.
3. Notice the contrast between verse 25 and verse 12.

WISDOM OF THE HEART

God tells Moshe and Aharon to separate themselves from the evil עדה, the corrupt community. Hillel, in a famous mishna (Avot 2:4), tells us not to separate from the community. Community can have a powerful influence on how we conduct ourselves and even on how we think. With that in mind, we need to decide which community we want to part of, so that it has a positive impact on us, and which communities we need to stay away from.

What makes it difficult to pull ourselves away from a group which we know is bad for us?

שלישי כ אֶל־כׇּל־הָעֵדָה: וַיְדַבֵּר יְהֹוָה אֶל־מֹשֶׁה וְאֶל־אַהֲרֹן
כא לֵאמֹר: הִבָּדְלוּ מִתּוֹךְ הָעֵדָה הַזֹּאת וַאֲכַלֶּה אֹתָם כְּרָגַע: וַיִּפְּלוּ
עַל־פְּנֵיהֶם וַיֹּאמְרוּ אֵל אֱלֹהֵי הָרוּחֹת לְכׇל־בָּשָׂר הָאִישׁ אֶחָד
כג יֶחֱטָא וְעַל כׇּל־הָעֵדָה תִּקְצֹף: וַיְדַבֵּר יְהֹוָה אֶל־מֹשֶׁה
כד לֵּאמֹר: דַּבֵּר אֶל־הָעֵדָה לֵאמֹר הֵעָלוּ מִסָּבִיב לְמִשְׁכַּן־קֹרַח
כה דָּתָן וַאֲבִירָם: וַיָּקׇם מֹשֶׁה וַיֵּלֶךְ אֶל־דָּתָן וַאֲבִירָם וַיֵּלְכוּ אַחֲרָיו
כו זִקְנֵי יִשְׂרָאֵל: וַיְדַבֵּר אֶל־הָעֵדָה לֵאמֹר סוּרוּ נָא מֵעַל אׇהֳלֵי
הָאֲנָשִׁים הָרְשָׁעִים הָאֵלֶּה וְאַל־תִּגְּעוּ בְּכׇל־אֲשֶׁר לָהֶם פֶּן־
כז תִּסָּפוּ בְּכׇל־חַטֹּאתָם: וַיֵּעָלוּ מֵעַל מִשְׁכַּן־קֹרַח דָּתָן וַאֲבִירָם
מִסָּבִיב וְדָתָן וַאֲבִירָם יָצְאוּ נִצָּבִים פֶּתַח אׇהֳלֵיהֶם וּנְשֵׁיהֶם

CLASSIC COMMENTATORS

Why would God have threatened to kill all of the people who gathered around if they were not directly involved in the rebellion against Moshe and Aharon?

RAMBAN

רמב״ן

Korah summoned the entire community and bragged that it was on behalf of their honor that he was challenging Moshe. This claim appealed to the people, who all gathered to see if in fact God would approve of Korah's defiance.... Because the nation entertained the proposition of Moshe being replaced, they too deserved to be destroyed.

אז קרא קרח לכל העדה ואמר להם כי בכבוד כולם הוא מקנא, וייטב הדבר בעיניהם ונקהלו כלם לראות אולי יישר בעיני האלהים ... הנה נתחייבו כלייה שהיו מהרהרים אחרי רבם.

KELI YAKAR

כלי יקר

It seems unlikely that God ever planned to punish those individuals who had not sinned against Him. Rather, God's threat to "consume the community" was directed at Korah's company alone. However, Moshe misunderstood the warning and thought that God intended to destroy the nation. This is because the text reports, "Korah gathered all the community together."

קרוב לשמוע שגם מתחילה לא עלתה על דעתו יתברך להעניש הבלתי חוטאים אלא שעל עדת קרח אמר כן, ומשה הבין שעל כל עדת ישראל אמר כן לפי שכבר נאמר "ויקהל עליהם קרח את כל העדה."

RABBI SAMSON RAPHAEL HIRSCH

ר׳ שמשון רפאל הירש

As I have already written, the very presence of the Israelite people during this spectacle served to grant support and legitimacy to Korah's cause. This made the nation complicit in the rebellion against Moshe.

כפי שכבר הערנו על פסוק יט, בעצם היותם שם, הם עמדו לצדו של קרח. לפיכך גם הם היו שותפים לחטא.

28 children, and infants. Moshe said, "By this you will know that the Lord sent me to do
29 these deeds; it was not my idea. If all these men die as others do, and share the common
30 fate of all humanity, then the Lord has not sent me. But if the Lord creates something entirely new, so that the ground opens its mouth and swallows them and all they have, and they go down alive to Sheol, then you will know that these men have provoked
31 the Lord." As soon as he had finished speaking these words, the ground beneath them
32 split open. The earth opened its mouth and swallowed them and their households, with
33 all the people who pertained to Koraḥ and all their possessions – they and all that was theirs descended alive to Sheol – the earth closed over them – and they perished from
34 the midst of the assembly. At their cry, all the Israelites around them fled, for they said,
35 "The earth could swallow us." And fire came forth from the Lord and consumed the

אבן עזרא

יש אומרים: שהיא תורה על המצא מה שלא היה. וכבר פירשתי שאין המלה רק מגזרת: ובָרָא אותהן (יחזקאל כ״ג:מ״ז), וכבר נבקעו מדינות רבות וירדו הדרים בה שאלה, והנה פירושה כטעם: גזירה.

IBN EZRA

Some commentators maintain that the term בריאה refers to a new creation that has never existed before. But I have already explained that the word derives from the verb "cut down" as in the verse, "and cut them down [*uvareh*] with their swords" (Ezek. 23:47). Indeed, many lands have been split open and their inhabitants have been sent downward to their deaths. Hence the term בריאה connotes a cutting or fissure.

QUESTIONS FOR THOUGHT

- According to Ibn Ezra, what makes this sign significant?
- According to Ramban, the use of the word בריאה adds greatly to the significance of the sign. What does it add?
- What proof could Ramban bring to support his opinion from verse 33?
- Rambam (*Shemoneh Perakim*, ch. 8) writes that all the supernatural miracles that ever happened or that ever will happen were planned in advance during the six days of creation and built into the nature of those things which eventually seemed to change miraculously. Does Rambam agree with Ibn Ezra or Ramban?

TEXTUAL SKILLS

1. Where did the Torah earlier use the image of the ground opening up to swallow people?
2. The language used in the beginning of verse 35 is in a tense called past perfect, meaning, that it already happened. When do you think the fire came from God to consume those who brought the incense?

WISDOM OF THE HEART

The Rebbe of Lelov suggests that the unique death of Koraḥ and his clan – being swallowed by the earth – was to ensure that they, and their sin, should never be forgotten.

Can you think of other situations in which it could be important to remember the way a person died, not just how they lived?

כח וּבְנֵיהֶ֖ם וְטַפָּ֑ם: וַיֹּאמֶר֮ מֹשֶׁה֒ בְּזֹאת֙ תֵּֽדְע֔וּן כִּֽי־יְהוָ֣ה שְׁלָחַ֔נִי
כט לַעֲשׂ֕וֹת אֵ֖ת כָּל־הַמַּעֲשִׂ֣ים הָאֵ֑לֶּה כִּי־לֹ֖א מִלִּבִּֽי: אִם־כְּמ֤וֹת
כָּל־הָֽאָדָם֙ יְמֻת֣וּן אֵ֔לֶּה וּפְקֻדַּת֙ כָּל־הָ֣אָדָ֔ם יִפָּקֵ֖ד עֲלֵיהֶ֑ם לֹ֥א
ל יְהוָ֖ה שְׁלָחָֽנִי: וְאִם־בְּרִיאָ֞ה יִבְרָ֣א יְהוָ֗ה וּפָצְתָ֨ה הָאֲדָמָ֤ה אֶת־פִּ֨יהָ֙
וּבָלְעָ֤ה אֹתָם֙ וְאֶת־כָּל־אֲשֶׁ֣ר לָהֶ֔ם וְיָרְד֥וּ חַיִּ֖ים שְׁאֹ֑לָה וִֽידַעְתֶּ֗ם
לא כִּ֧י נִֽאֲצ֛וּ הָאֲנָשִׁ֥ים הָאֵ֖לֶּה אֶת־יְהוָֽה: וַיְהִי֙ כְּכַלֹּת֔וֹ לְדַבֵּ֕ר אֵ֥ת
לב כָּל־הַדְּבָרִ֖ים הָאֵ֑לֶּה וַתִּבָּקַ֥ע הָאֲדָמָ֖ה אֲשֶׁ֥ר תַּחְתֵּיהֶֽם: וַתִּפְתַּ֤ח
הָאָ֨רֶץ֙ אֶת־פִּ֔יהָ וַתִּבְלַ֥ע אֹתָ֖ם וְאֶת־בָּֽתֵּיהֶ֑ם וְאֵ֤ת כָּל־הָֽאָדָם֙
לג אֲשֶׁ֣ר לְקֹ֔רַח וְאֵ֖ת כָּל־הָרְכֽוּשׁ: וַיֵּרְד֨וּ הֵ֜ם וְכָל־אֲשֶׁ֥ר לָהֶ֛ם חַיִּ֖ים
לד שְׁאֹ֑לָה וַתְּכַ֤ס עֲלֵיהֶם֙ הָאָ֔רֶץ וַיֹּאבְד֖וּ מִתּ֥וֹךְ הַקָּהָֽל: וְכָל־יִשְׂרָאֵ֗ל
לה אֲשֶׁ֥ר סְבִיבֹתֵיהֶ֖ם נָ֣סוּ לְקֹלָ֑ם כִּ֣י אָֽמְר֔וּ פֶּן־תִּבְלָעֵ֖נוּ הָאָֽרֶץ: וְאֵ֥שׁ
יָצְאָ֖ה מֵאֵ֣ת יְהוָ֑ה וַתֹּ֗אכַל אֵ֣ת הַחֲמִשִּׁ֤ים וּמָאתַ֨יִם֙ אִ֔ישׁ מַקְרִיבֵ֖י

CLASSIC COMMENTATORS

When Moshe presents his case to the people, he identifies the opening of the ground as a בריאה. What does that mean and why is it important?

RAMBAN

The term refers to something that has been created out of nothing. The word בריאה is the only word available in Hebrew to express such a concept. Now even though the splitting open of the ground is not a new creation, the earth opening a "mouth" and swallowing people certainly is unprecedented. For when an earthquake causes the ground to rupture, an event which is not uncommon, the land remains cracked open and the crevices left open eventually fill with water forming lakes. But for the earth to open and close right afterward, like a person who opens his mouth to swallow and closes it right afterward, that appeared for the first time, like a new creation.

רמב״ן

והנכון: שתאמר על המצא הדבר מאין, כי אין אצלנו בלשון הקדש מורה על זה זולתי המלה הזאת. אבל הענין כי בקיעת האדמה אינה בריאה מחודשת, אבל פתיחת הארץ את פיה לבלוע היא חידוש לא נהיה מעולם. כי כאשר תבקע האדמה כמו שנעשה פעמים רבים ברעש הנקרא זלזלה, תשאר פתוחה, גם ימלא הנקע מים ויעשה כאגמים, אבל שתפתח ותסגר מיד כאדם הפותח פיו לבלוע ויסגור אותו אחרי בלעו, זה דבר נתחדש ביום ההוא, כאלו הוא נברא מאין.

BEMIDBAR | CHAPTER 17 KORAḤ | 160

> **17:1–8** *Even though the firepans are used for the unauthorized incense, they are nonetheless considered sanctified. As such, God instructs Moshe to collect them and use them to copper-plate the altar as a sign for Benei Yisrael to remember the prohibition against a non-kohen performing the service in the Mikdash. The next day, the people complain that Moshe and Aharon are responsible for many deaths, so Moshe and Aharon retreat to the Tent of Meeting.*

17 1 two hundred fifty men who were offering incense. Then the LORD spoke to Moshe:
2 "Tell Elazar son of Aharon the priest to remove the censers from the fire, for they have
3 become holy. Scatter the burning coals far and wide. And the censers of those who committed a mortal sin – make them into hammered plates as a covering for the altar. Having been offered before the LORD, they have become holy. And they will be a sign
4 for the Israelites." Elazar the priest took the bronze censers that the men consumed by
5 fire had presented, and hammered them into a covering for the altar, as the LORD had said to him through Moshe – a reminder for the Israelites that no outsider, no one not descended from Aharon, should offer incense before the LORD, and become like Koraḥ and his company.
6 The next day the entire Israelite community complained to Moshe and Aharon, "You
7 have killed the LORD's people!" As the community assembled against Moshe and Aharon, they turned toward the Tent of Meeting. A cloud was covering it, and the glory of the
8/9 LORD appeared. Moshe and Aharon came to the front of the Tent of Meeting. And the

---

AKEDAT YITZḤAK   עקדת יצחק

Once the firepans were offered before the LORD in order to verify what was true and what was false, the implements were dedicated as a sign for the nation of Israel. For, something which is used to negate and refute the opponents of sanctity is undoubtedly holy itself.

כי במה שהקריבו המחתות לפני ה' לברר בם האמת מהשקר נתקדשו להיות לאות לבני ישראל, כי הדבר המחליש והמבטל את המתנגד לקודש – קודש הוא בלי ספק.

QUESTIONS FOR THOUGHT

- Ramban offers two very different explanations. According to each one, who sanctified the firepans, and for what were they sanctified?
- In what way is the explanation of *Akedat Yitzḥak* dramatically different from Ramban's first explanation?
- Can you imagine an equivalent in contemporary society of any of the three interpretations above?

WISDOM OF THE HEART

The Talmud (Sanhedrin 110a) understands verse 5 as meaning to teach us to avoid prolonging discord. Ḥazon Ish explains that this is true even when we believe that we are right. It is important to understand that discord is different from debate, which is a central feature of Jewish learning. Debate is about discovering truth; discord occurs when the debate turns into personal animosity.

Do you sometimes sense that people continue to argue even when they know that they are wrong, just so that they can claim victory?

במדבר | פרק יז

יז א וַיְדַבֵּ֥ר יְהֹוָ֖ה אֶל־מֹשֶׁ֥ה לֵּאמֹֽר: אֱמֹ֨ר ב אֶל־אֶלְעָזָ֜ר בֶּן־אַהֲרֹ֣ן הַכֹּהֵ֗ן וְיָרֵ֤ם אֶת־הַמַּחְתֹּת֙ מִבֵּ֣ין הַשְּׂרֵפָ֔ה וְאֶת־הָאֵ֖שׁ זְרֵה־הָ֑לְאָה כִּ֖י קָדֵֽשׁוּ: אֵ֡ת מַחְתּוֹת֩ הַֽחַטָּאִ֨ים הָאֵ֜לֶּה ג בְּנַפְשֹׁתָ֗ם וְעָשׂ֨וּ אֹתָ֜ם רִקֻּעֵ֤י פַחִים֙ צִפּ֣וּי לַמִּזְבֵּ֔חַ כִּֽי־הִקְרִיבֻ֥ם לִפְנֵֽי־יְהֹוָ֖ה וַיִּקְדָּ֑שׁוּ וְיִֽהְי֥וּ לְא֖וֹת לִבְנֵ֥י יִשְׂרָאֵֽל: וַיִּקַּ֞ח אֶלְעָזָ֣ר ד הַכֹּהֵ֗ן אֵ֚ת מַחְתּ֣וֹת הַנְּחֹ֔שֶׁת אֲשֶׁ֥ר הִקְרִ֖יבוּ הַשְּׂרֻפִ֑ים וַֽיְרַקְּע֖וּם צִפּ֣וּי לַמִּזְבֵּֽחַ: זִכָּר֞וֹן לִבְנֵ֣י יִשְׂרָאֵ֗ל לְ֠מַ֠עַן אֲשֶׁ֨ר לֹֽא־יִקְרַ֜ב אִ֣ישׁ ה זָ֗ר אֲ֠שֶׁ֠ר לֹ֣א מִזֶּ֤רַע אַהֲרֹן֙ ה֔וּא לְהַקְטִ֥יר קְטֹ֖רֶת לִפְנֵ֣י יְהֹוָ֑ה וְלֹֽא־יִהְיֶ֤ה כְקֹ֙רַח֙ וְכַ֣עֲדָת֔וֹ כַּאֲשֶׁ֨ר דִּבֶּ֧ר יְהֹוָ֛ה בְּיַד־מֹשֶׁ֖ה לֽוֹ:

וַיִּלֹּ֜נוּ כׇּל־עֲדַ֤ת בְּנֵֽי־יִשְׂרָאֵל֙ מִֽמׇּחֳרָ֔ת עַל־מֹשֶׁ֥ה וְעַֽל־אַהֲרֹ֖ן לֵאמֹ֑ר ו אַתֶּ֥ם הֲמִתֶּ֖ם אֶת־עַ֥ם יְהֹוָֽה: וַיְהִ֗י בְּהִקָּהֵ֤ל הָעֵדָה֙ עַל־מֹשֶׁ֣ה ז וְעַֽל־אַהֲרֹ֔ן וַיִּפְנוּ֙ אֶל־אֹ֣הֶל מוֹעֵ֔ד וְהִנֵּ֥ה כִסָּ֖הוּ הֶעָנָ֑ן וַיֵּרָ֖א כְּב֥וֹד יְהֹוָֽה: וַיָּבֹ֥א מֹשֶׁ֛ה וְאַהֲרֹ֖ן אֶל־פְּנֵ֥י אֹ֥הֶל מוֹעֵֽד: ח

רביעי וַיְדַבֵּ֥ר

CLASSIC COMMENTATORS

How could the firepans, used as a challenge to Aharon, be considered sanctified?

RAMBAN

One possibility is that since the incense offerings were brought following Moshe's instruction, the pans became sanctified once they were used since they all intended the incense for God. They believed that since Moshe authorized it, God would respond to their incense by bringing fire, hence the firepans became service utensils in the Tent of Meeting forever. However, I think that it is more correct to explain that God is declaring that once these objects were brought before Him, He consecrated them as a sign and remembrance for the people of Israel.

רמב״ן

כי בעבור שעשו כן על פי משה היו קדש, כי הם הקדישו אותם לשמים על פיו. חשבו שיענה אותם האלהים באש, ותהיינה המחתות האלה כלי שרת באהל מועד לעולם. והנכון בעיני, כי יאמר הכתוב כי הקריבום לפני ה׳ ויקדשו להיות לאות לבני ישראל, כלומר: אני הקדשתי אותם מעת שהקריבו אותם לפני, כדי שיהיו לאות לבני ישראל.

10 LORD spoke to Moshe: "Get away from this community; let Me consume them in an
11 instant." They fell on their faces, and Moshe said to Aharon, "Take the censer, put fire from the altar into it, place incense upon it, and go quickly to the community and make atonement for them. Fury has come forth from the LORD; the plague has
12 begun." Aharon took it as Moshe said and ran into the midst of the assembly, for the plague had already begun among the people. He offered incense and made atonement
13 for the people; he stood between the dead and the living, and the plague was halted;
14/15 14,700 died from that plague, in addition to those who died on account of Koraḥ. And Aharon returned to Moshe at the entrance to the Tent of Meeting – for the plague had stopped.

ר' יוסף אבן כספי

הנה לא היה בזה למשה תשובה דרך התנצלות כמו שהיה לו למטה, כי בכאן כולם התנועעו בשוה כי מת קרח המדיח, וכולם נקהלו בתחלת ההערה, לכן מתו קהל רב מהם, ולא מצא משה רפואה במניעה רק לחסר מהרעה כיכלתו.

RABBI YOSEF IBN KASPI

Moshe could not offer a defense as he had before, since now the entire nation was equally upset that the instigator Koraḥ had died and they all assembled against him. Moshe could not have prevented the plague, but did what he could to minimize it.

העמק דבר

בתפלתם הועילו שלא יהיה "כרגע", אלא כעין מגפה על ידי מלאך המשחית כמו שהיה בימי דוד, והיה נמשך על כל פנים איזה עת, ולא נפלו כולם כאיש אחד. ומשום הכי היתה שהות לעשות סגולת הקטורת.

HAAMEK DAVAR

The prayer of Moshe and Aharon succeeded in that the nation was not consumed in an instant. Rather, the punishment was dispatched in the form of a plague carried out by the destructive angel, as it later would be in the era of King David. This plague lasted for some period of time, which meant that the victims did not all die at the same time. As a result, there was time for the incense to stop the plague.

QUESTIONS FOR THOUGHT

- How does each of the above commentaries understand what Moshe and Aharon are trying to accomplish by falling on their faces?
- How does each understand the function of the incense in this scene?
- Which of these commentaries do you think offers the best explanation of how this scene serves as a response to the people's complaint that Moshe and Aharon were killing God's people (v. 6)?

WISDOM OF THE HEART

Various midrashim suggest a pre-story to Koraḥ's rebellion. One version describes Koraḥ as asking Moshe whether a house filled with Torah scrolls requires a mezuza, and in another he poses the question whether a garment made completely of *tekhelet* still requires tzitzit. R. Soloveitchik describes these as a common-sense rebellion against the Torah – things that according to ordinary logic don't seem to make sense. R. Soloveitchik explains that every discipline has its own internal logic, even its own internal language. Using the language or the logic from one to discuss another leads to great confusion and distorted results. Torah also has its own internal logic and language, and that is what Koraḥ missed.

Do you think that the Torah should make sense to people who are not "insiders" to the system? Why or why not?

במדבר | פרק יז

יְהוָה אֶל־מֹשֶׁה לֵּאמֹר: הֵרֹמּוּ מִתּוֹךְ הָעֵדָה הַזֹּאת וַאֲכַלֶּה
אֹתָם כְּרָגַע וַיִּפְּלוּ עַל־פְּנֵיהֶם: וַיֹּאמֶר מֹשֶׁה אֶל־אַהֲרֹן קַח
אֶת־הַמַּחְתָּה וְתֶן־עָלֶיהָ אֵשׁ מֵעַל הַמִּזְבֵּחַ וְשִׂים קְטֹרֶת וְהוֹלֵךְ
מְהֵרָה אֶל־הָעֵדָה וְכַפֵּר עֲלֵיהֶם כִּי־יָצָא הַקֶּצֶף מִלִּפְנֵי יְהוָה
הֵחֵל הַנָּגֶף: וַיִּקַּח אַהֲרֹן כַּאֲשֶׁר ׀ דִּבֶּר מֹשֶׁה וַיָּרָץ אֶל־תּוֹךְ
הַקָּהָל וְהִנֵּה הֵחֵל הַנֶּגֶף בָּעָם וַיִּתֵּן אֶת־הַקְּטֹרֶת וַיְכַפֵּר עַל־
הָעָם: וַיַּעֲמֹד בֵּין־הַמֵּתִים וּבֵין הַחַיִּים וַתֵּעָצַר הַמַּגֵּפָה: וַיִּהְיוּ
הַמֵּתִים בַּמַּגֵּפָה אַרְבָּעָה עָשָׂר אֶלֶף וּשְׁבַע מֵאוֹת מִלְּבַד הַמֵּתִים
עַל־דְּבַר־קֹרַח: וַיָּשָׁב אַהֲרֹן אֶל־מֹשֶׁה אֶל־פֶּתַח אֹהֶל מוֹעֵד
וְהַמַּגֵּפָה נֶעֱצָרָה:

CLASSIC COMMENTATORS

Earlier (16:22), faced with an impending decree from God, Moshe and Aharon defend the people from God's threat. Here they are silent as they fall on their faces. While they then spring into action, many people have already died. How are we to understand their actions and what they accomplished?

ר׳ שמשון רפאל הירש

אמר ה׳ למשה: אם רצונכם בכך, הסירו עצמכם מהם, ואכלה את ההמונים המתקוממים עליכם. אך משה ואהרן לא סרו; אלא נפלו על פניהם לפני ה׳ ... הם לא תבעו את מות אלה שפגעו בהם ... אלא אהרן רץ אל תוך הקהל שכבר נידון למוות, נתן ביטוי להתמסרות לה׳ בלב ונפש בקטורת העולה אל ה׳, וכך עמד בין המתים והחיים כשליח כפרה וישועה. בכך הראה אהרן לעם את טיבו האמיתי ואת טיבה האמיתי של שליחותו: לפדות ולנצח את המוות.

RABBI SAMSON RAPHAEL HIRSCH

The Lord said to Moshe: If you so desire, remove yourselves from the presence of the nation and I will destroy the masses who are rebelling against you. However, Moshe and Aharon would not separate themselves from their charges, but instead fell on their faces in anguish before the Lord.... The leaders were interested in the deaths of only the people who had sinned against them.... And yet, Aharon ran into the midst of the nation, which had already been condemned to die, and, lighting the incense on fire before God, he expressed his wholehearted devotion to the Almighty. The High Priest then remained standing among the living and the dying as an emissary of atonement and salvation. Aharon thereby demonstrated to the nation the true nature of his calling: to redeem the people and to triumph over death.

17:16–21 *God instructs Moshe to gather a staff from the leaders of each of the tribes, plus one from Aharon, and place them in the Tent of Meeting in front of the Ark. The staff of the person whom God chooses as the kohen gadol will flower, and this should settle the question of God's choice for kohen gadol. Moshe gathers the staffs.*

16/17 Then the LORD spoke to Moshe: "Speak to the Israelites and take from them twelve staffs, one for each ancestral house, from all the leaders of their ancestral houses. Write
18 each man's name on his staff, and on Levi's staff write Aharon's name, for there shall be
19 one staff for the head of each ancestral house. Place them in the Tent of Meeting in front
20 of the Ark of the Covenant, where I meet with you. The staff of the man I choose – that will give flower. Thus I will rid myself of the incessant railings of the Israelites against
21 you." Moshe spoke to the Israelites, and each of their leaders gave him a staff, one for each leader, according to their ancestral houses, twelve staffs with Aharon's staff among

---

QUESTIONS FOR THOUGHT

- Regarding what do Ramban and *Haamek Davar* agree?
- Why does *Haamek Davar* think that this incident should be the exception in which thirteen tribes are represented?
- Where in Genesis can we find the idea that a clan with twelve heads of families represents the model for building a nation?

TEXTUAL SKILLS

1. In Numbers there are many places where we find representatives for each of the tribes. In what ways is this time different?

2. Notice how many times the word מטה appears in the passage beginning with verse 16 and ending in verse 24.

WISDOM OF THE HEART

A number of midrashim identify some of those who joined Korah's rebellion and even died in that rebellion as the princes of the tribes listed in the beginning of Numbers. These are the princes who assisted Moshe in the counting of *Benei Yisrael* and who brought offerings for the inauguration of the *Mishkan*. One midrash even identifies Naḥshon son of Aminadav, the heroic leader of the tribe of Yehuda, who according to midrashic tradition leapt into the sea even before it split, demonstrating his faith in God. This raises the question of what message these midrashim are trying to covey. R. Isaiah Horowitz, author of *Shenei Luḥot Habrit*, suggests that the Midrash is trying to teach us that even great people can make terrible mistakes. It reminds us of the mishna (Avot 2:4) in which Hillel warns us not to be complacent or overconfident, until our final day. Perhaps we could add that these were people in positions of particular status and authority – they were second only to Moshe. The taste of power can be very enticing, and like with money, when one develops a craving for it that appetite can never be satiated. Korah offered them what they could not refuse – a chance to seek even more power. For some, that temptation is irresistible, and the midrashim want to warn us against that temptation in our own lives.

How do you think that people can prepare themselves to overcome the inevitable cycle of wanting more? Are there times when we would not want to break that cycle?

במדבר | פרק יז

יז וַיְדַבֵּר יְהוָה אֶל־מֹשֶׁה לֵּאמְר: דַּבֵּר ׀ אֶל־בְּנֵי יִשְׂרָאֵל וְקַח חמישי
מֵאִתָּם מַטֶּה מַטֶּה לְבֵית אָב מֵאֵת כָּל־נְשִׂיאֵהֶם לְבֵית אֲבֹתָם
יח שְׁנֵים עָשָׂר מַטּוֹת אִישׁ אֶת־שְׁמוֹ תִּכְתֹּב עַל־מַטֵּהוּ: וְאֵת שֵׁם
אַהֲרֹן תִּכְתֹּב עַל־מַטֵּה לֵוִי כִּי מַטֶּה אֶחָד לְרֹאשׁ בֵּית אֲבוֹתָם:
יט וְהִנַּחְתָּם בְּאֹהֶל מוֹעֵד לִפְנֵי הָעֵדוּת אֲשֶׁר אִוָּעֵד לָכֶם שָׁמָּה:
כ וְהָיָה הָאִישׁ אֲשֶׁר אֶבְחַר־בּוֹ מַטֵּהוּ יִפְרָח וַהֲשִׁכֹּתִי מֵעָלַי אֶת־
תְּלֻנּוֹת בְּנֵי יִשְׂרָאֵל אֲשֶׁר הֵם מַלִּינִם עֲלֵיכֶם: וַיְדַבֵּר מֹשֶׁה כא
אֶל־בְּנֵי יִשְׂרָאֵל וַיִּתְּנוּ אֵלָיו ׀ כָּל־נְשִׂיאֵיהֶם מַטֶּה לְנָשִׂיא אֶחָד
מַטֶּה לְנָשִׂיא אֶחָד לְבֵית אֲבֹתָם שְׁנֵים עָשָׂר מַטּוֹת וּמַטֵּה

CLASSIC COMMENTATORS

Was Aharon's staff included in the twelve, or was it in addition to the twelve?

RAMBAN

Aharon's staff was among the twelve specimens that were collected. For the text does not say that Moshe should take a staff from the ancestral House of Levi and write Aharon's name upon it. Rather, Aharon's staff was included in the twelve, while the descendants of Yosef were considered as a single tribe. The reason for this is that the tribes of Israel are always tallied as twelve.

HAAMEK DAVAR

It seems that Aharon's staff was in addition to the twelve others. This was so even though Israel is always treated as comprising just twelve tribes, and whenever Levi is counted among them, the two Yosef tribes are combined into one, as Ramban points out. Nevertheless, that principle does not apply here. For whichever one of the tribes was selected for the priesthood, that group would necessarily stand apart from the others, whereupon the two tribes of Menashe and Efrayim would complete the required dozen. And if, for example, Efrayim had been chosen to produce the High Priest, that tribe would have been removed from the group, and its partner Menashe would have been the twelfth on the list. This in fact was the entire point of the demonstration: to determine which of the thirteen tribes would be the preferred clan and no longer be counted among the twelve tribes constituting the ordinary Israelites.

רמב״ן

מטה אהרן הוא בי״ב, כי לא אמר ותקח מטה לבית לוי ותכתוב עליו שם אהרן, אבל הוא במניין הנזכר, והנה לא נחשב יוסף רק לשבט אחד. והטעם, כי לא יימנו שבטי ישראל לעולם רק שנים עשר.

העמק דבר

משמע חוץ ממטה אהרן, ואף על פי דלעולם לא נמנו אלא י״ב שבטים, ובמקום שנמנה שבט לוי לא נמנה יוסף אלא לאחד, כמו שכתב הרמב״ן – מכל מקום כאן לא שייך זה הכלל, שהרי אם היה נבחר שבט אחר מי שהוא, היה אותו השבט יוצא ממניין השבטים, ושבט אפרים ומנשה היו משלימים מניין י״ב. ואם היה נבחר שבט אפרים לחוד, היה הוא יוצא, ומנשה ולוי בכלל י״ב. וזה באו המטות להורות, איזה שבט מי״ג שבטים הוא נבחר ולא יהיה נמנה בכלל שבטי ישראל.

²²⁻²³ them. Moshe placed the staffs before the Lord in the Tent of the Testimony. And the following day Moshe entered the Tent of the Testimony, and Aharon's staff, representing the House of Levi, had given flower. It had budded, produced blossoms, and was
²⁴ now bearing almonds. Moshe brought out all the staffs from before the Lord to all the Israelites. They saw. And each man took back his staff.
²⁵ Then the Lord said to Moshe, "Put back Aharon's staff in front of the Ark of the Covenant to serve as a sign to rebels so that their railings against Me end, and they will
²⁶ not die." Moshe did so. As the Lord commanded him, so he did.
²⁷ The Israelites said to Moshe, "We are going to die. We are lost; all of us are lost.
²⁸ Whoever approaches the Lord's Tabernacle is to die. Will we die out completely?"

מלבי"ם / MALBIM

עתה שראו הפלא הזה נכנס בלבם האימה והפחד ממשכן ה' והשוכן בו ונתנו אל לבם הלא הם בסכנה תמיד אם יתקרבו אל המקדש יותר מדאי ימותו ועל זה אמרו הן גוענו אבדנו – במות קרח ועדתו, וכן כלנו אבדנו – בעת יצא הנגף שהיתה הגזרה על כלם.

The wonder of the blooming staff instilled in the hearts of the people a reverence for the Lord's Tabernacle, and fear of the One who dwells within it. The terror now gripped the nation that they remained in certain and mortal danger should they ever dare to approach the holy Sanctuary. Thus they proclaim, "We are going to die. We are lost," referring to Koraḥ and his followers being snuffed out, and "all of us are lost," referring to the plague that was unleashed as a decree against them.

QUESTIONS FOR THOUGHT

- One of the above commentaries thinks that the people only now appreciated the danger of approaching the *Mishkan*; a second suggests that they only now understood that God had selected the tribe of Levi and Aharon as His servants; a third understands that the effects were cumulative. Match up these opinions with the commentaries.
- In theory, *Benei Yisrael* should have become fearful earlier – when Datan and Aviram were swallowed by the earth, or when Koraḥ's people were burned by a heavenly flame, or after the plague. Which of the commentaries do you think offers a better explanation of why only now they are afraid?
- In his commentary, Rabbi Samson Raphael Hirsch adds the following: "In their fear, they express the narrow and dangerous bridge that every Jew should feel when it comes to the holy places. Everyone should want to get close, but must not get too close!" What do you think R. Hirsch understands to be the danger of getting "too close" in today's world, where there is no Temple? Is it possible to be "too devoted" to God?

WISDOM OF THE HEART

Keli Yakar cites a tradition that not only did Aharon's staff began to sprout, but everything in the *Mishkan* did, except the staffs of the other leaders. The author explains the symbolism: The flowering of Aharon's staff demonstrated that he was essential to the *Mishkan* and its function. The lack of buds on the other staffs demonstrated that they were disconnected from the *Mishkan*.

How do you think that religious institutions today can demonstrate that their purpose is to provide life and goodness?

קרח

כב אַהֲרֹ֖ן בְּת֥וֹךְ מַטּוֹתָֽם׃ וַיַּנַּ֥ח מֹשֶׁ֛ה אֶת־הַמַּטֹּ֖ת לִפְנֵ֣י יְהֹוָ֑ה בְּאֹ֖הֶל
כג הָעֵדֻֽת׃ וַיְהִ֣י מִֽמׇּחֳרָ֗ת וַיָּבֹ֤א מֹשֶׁה֙ אֶל־אֹ֣הֶל הָעֵד֔וּת וְהִנֵּ֛ה פָּרַ֥ח
מַטֵּֽה־אַהֲרֹ֖ן לְבֵ֣ית לֵוִ֑י וַיֹּ֤צֵֽא פֶ֙רַח֙ וַיָּ֣צֵֽץ צִ֔יץ וַיִּגְמֹ֖ל שְׁקֵדִֽים׃
כד וַיֹּצֵ֨א מֹשֶׁ֤ה אֶת־כׇּל־הַמַּטֹּת֙ מִלִּפְנֵ֣י יְהֹוָ֔ה אֶֽל־כׇּל־בְּנֵ֖י יִשְׂרָאֵ֑ל
וַיִּרְא֥וּ וַיִּקְח֖וּ אִ֥ישׁ מַטֵּֽהוּ׃
כה וַיֹּ֨אמֶר יְהֹוָ֜ה אֶל־מֹשֶׁ֗ה הָשֵׁ֞ב אֶת־מַטֵּ֤ה אַהֲרֹן֙ לִפְנֵ֣י הָעֵד֔וּת ששי
לְמִשְׁמֶ֥רֶת לְא֖וֹת לִבְנֵי־מֶ֑רִי וּתְכַ֧ל תְּלוּנֹּתָ֛ם מֵעָלַ֖י וְלֹ֥א יָמֻֽתוּ׃
כו וַיַּ֖עַשׂ מֹשֶׁ֑ה כַּאֲשֶׁ֨ר צִוָּ֧ה יְהֹוָ֛ה אֹת֖וֹ כֵּ֥ן עָשָֽׂה׃
כז וַיֹּֽאמְרוּ֙ בְּנֵ֣י יִשְׂרָאֵ֔ל אֶל־מֹשֶׁ֖ה לֵאמֹ֑ר הֵ֥ן גָּוַ֛עְנוּ אָבַ֖דְנוּ
כח כֻּלָּ֥נוּ אָבָֽדְנוּ׃ כֹּ֣ל הַקָּרֵ֧ב ׀ הַקָּרֵ֛ב אֶל־מִשְׁכַּ֥ן יְהֹוָ֖ה יָמ֑וּת

CLASSIC COMMENTATORS

What did *Benei Yisrael* realize from the test of the staffs?

ABARBANEL

When the people of Israel witnessed the test of the staffs they knew and understood one thing with certainty: that the Lord had chosen the tribe of Levi in general, and had chosen Aharon and his family in particular for the office of the High Priest. Now, after the fact, the people believed that Koraḥ and his company had died because they had approached and touched sacred objects. Thus the nation complains to Moshe, "We are going to die. We are lost; all of us are lost…. Will we die out completely?" What they meant was: look at the variety of ways in which Israelites have been killed!

RABBI SAMSON RAPHAEL HIRSCH

All of these incidents, which culminate with the testimony of Aharon's staff, successfully achieve their purpose. The nation now accepts without a doubt that only Aharon and the Levites are ever permitted to approach the Tabernacle. It is also now evident that this restriction has been imposed by the Lord Himself.

אברבנאל

אחרי שראו בחינת המקלות הכירו וידעו שבחר השם בשבט הלוי בכלל ואהרן בפרט ובזרעו לענין הכהונה הגדולה וחשבו למפרע שקרח ועדתו מתו לפי שנתקרבו לדברים המקודשים ונגעו בהם ולכן אמרו למשה הן גוענו אבדנו כלנו אבדנו, האם תמנו לגוע, רצונם לומר, בכמה מינים אבדנו וגוענו במדבר הזה.

ר' שמשון רפאל הירש

כל המאורעות האלה – אשר הגיעו לפסגתם בעדות מטה אהרן – השיגו את מטרתם. העם הבינו שרק בני אהרן והלויים רשאים לקרב אל המקדש, ושהגבלה זו נטוותה על ידי ה'.

18 1 The LORD said to Aharon: "You, your sons, and your ancestral house shall bear any guilt connected with the Sanctuary, and you and your sons will bear any guilt connected 2 with your priesthood. Bring with you also your brothers from the tribe of Levi, your father's tribe. Let them join you and minister to you and your sons before the Tent of 3 the Testimony. They shall discharge their duties to you and to the Tent as a whole, but they must not draw close to the utensils of the Sanctuary or the altar, or both they and 4 you will die. They will join you in discharging the duties of the Tent of Meeting for all 5 the service of the Tent; no outsider shall draw near you. You shall discharge the duties 6 of the Sanctuary and the altar, so that fury may never again fall upon the Israelites. I have singled out your brothers, the Levites, from among the Israelites as a gift to you, 7 dedicated to the LORD to perform the service of the Tent of Meeting. You and your sons shall take care to perform the duties of your priesthood in all matters pertaining to the altar and inside the curtain. I give you your priestly service as a gift, but any outsider who draws close will die."

QUESTIONS FOR THOUGHT

- According to Rashi and R. Hirsch, who is giving the gift?
- How would each explain why this description is used here, as God's response to the cries of *Benei Yisrael* at the end of chapter 17?
- Which of the two commentaries fits better in the context of the death penalty for *kohanim* if non-*kohanim* approach the *Mikdash*?
- Which of the two fits better in the context of the death penalty for non-*kohanim* who approach the *Mikdash*?

TEXTUAL SKILLS

1. This passage is very similar to Numbers 3:5–10 and 8:16–19. How many similarities can you find?
2. In what ways are these passages different?
3. Find at least two links between this passage and the story of Koraḥ.

WISDOM OF THE HEART

The root שמר, meaning to guard or protect, appears many times in this passage. The *kohanim* have to guard the holy places and holy items. The Levites are to assist the *kohanim* in that special task. There is an interesting relationship between the Jewish people and the things we hold sacred, a relationship which is sometimes described as symbiotic, meaning that each of the parties involved benefits. We protect the things we value – the *Mishkan* and its vessels, the Torah, education for our children, our national and religious institutions, and more. But the relationship is not unidirectional. These things protect us as well. They preserve our identity and our personal and national souls. As Aḥad Ha'am, a prominent Zionist thinker, said: "More than the Jew has kept the Shabbat, Shabbat has kept the Jew."

What sacred Jewish institutions would you put at the top of your priority list to preserve and protect?

במדבר | פרק יח

יח א וַיֹּאמֶר יהוה אֶל־אַהֲרֹן אַתָּה הַאַם תַּמְנוּ לִגְוֺעַ: וּבָנֶיךָ וּבֵית־אָבִיךָ אִתָּךְ תִּשְׂאוּ אֶת־עֲוֺן הַמִּקְדָּשׁ וְאַתָּה ב וּבָנֶיךָ אִתָּךְ תִּשְׂאוּ אֶת־עֲוֺן כְּהֻנַּתְכֶם: וְגַם אֶת־אַחֶיךָ מַטֵּה לֵוִי שֵׁבֶט אָבִיךָ הַקְרֵב אִתָּךְ וְיִלָּווּ עָלֶיךָ וִישָׁרְתוּךָ וְאַתָּה ג וּבָנֶיךָ אִתָּךְ לִפְנֵי אֹהֶל הָעֵדֻת: וְשָׁמְרוּ מִשְׁמַרְתְּךָ וּמִשְׁמֶרֶת כָּל־הָאֹהֶל אַךְ אֶל־כְּלֵי הַקֹּדֶשׁ וְאֶל־הַמִּזְבֵּחַ לֹא יִקְרָבוּ וְלֹא־ ד יָמֻתוּ גַם־הֵם גַּם־אַתֶּם: וְנִלְווּ עָלֶיךָ וְשָׁמְרוּ אֶת־מִשְׁמֶרֶת אֹהֶל ה מוֹעֵד לְכֹל עֲבֹדַת הָאֹהֶל וְזָר לֹא־יִקְרַב אֲלֵיכֶם: וּשְׁמַרְתֶּם אֵת מִשְׁמֶרֶת הַקֹּדֶשׁ וְאֵת מִשְׁמֶרֶת הַמִּזְבֵּחַ וְלֹא־יִהְיֶה עוֹד קֶצֶף ו עַל־בְּנֵי יִשְׂרָאֵל: וַאֲנִי הִנֵּה לָקַחְתִּי אֶת־אֲחֵיכֶם הַלְוִיִּם מִתּוֹךְ בְּנֵי יִשְׂרָאֵל לָכֶם מַתָּנָה נְתֻנִים לַיהוה לַעֲבֹד אֶת־עֲבֹדַת אֹהֶל ז מוֹעֵד: וְאַתָּה וּבָנֶיךָ אִתְּךָ תִּשְׁמְרוּ אֶת־כְּהֻנַּתְכֶם לְכָל־דְּבַר הַמִּזְבֵּחַ וּלְמִבֵּית לַפָּרֹכֶת וַעֲבַדְתֶּם עֲבֹדַת מַתָּנָה אֶתֵּן אֶת־כְּהֻנַּתְכֶם וְהַזָּר הַקָּרֵב יוּמָת:

CLASSIC COMMENTATORS

The Torah (v. 7) describes the work of the *kohanim* as עֲבֹדַת מַתָּנָה, work that is a gift. How can work be a gift?

RASHI
God has given the priests responsibility for the *Mishkan* service as a gift to them.

רש"י
במתנה נתתיה לכם.

RABBI SAMSON RAPHAEL HIRSCH
The text characterizes the priestly duties in the *Mishkan* as work which is a gift since it demands labors of devotion and self-sacrifice.... Indeed, the purpose of the work in the Temple procedures is to teach people to dedicate themselves completely to the divine mission.

ר' שמשון רפאל הירש
הכתוב מאפיין את עבודות הכוהנים במקדש כ"עבודת מתנה", עבודה של מסירות והתמסרות ... הנה תכלית העבודה במקדש היא ללמדנו מסירת כל עצמותנו.

> **18:8–14** *Kohanim have not only increased responsibility, but also special rights. These include the right to receive portions of offerings in the holiest category, called kodesh hakodashim (which must be eaten only by the kohen and only in the precincts of the Mikdash), תרומה from olives, grapes, and grain (which may be eaten by the kohen and his immediate family), the first fruits [bikkurim], and items identified as ḥerem.*

8 The Lord spoke to Aharon: "I place in your charge the offerings made to Me, all the sacred gifts of the Israelites. I give them to you and your sons as an anointed right; this
9 is an everlasting decree. This is what belongs to you among the holiest offerings, from the fire: all their offerings, their grain offerings, their purification offerings, and their guilt offerings. The holiest offerings that they bring to Me will be yours and your sons'.
10 You shall eat them in the way of the holiest things. All your males may eat it; it is holy
11 to you. This too will be yours: as an everlasting statute I give the upraised gifts of all the Israelites' wave offerings to you, together with your sons and daughters. Anyone
12 who is ritually pure in your household may eat of them. All the best of the oil, wine,
13 and grain, the choice produce that they give to the Lord, I give to you. The first fruits of all that is in their land that they bring to the Lord will be yours. Anyone who is
14 pure in your household may eat it. Everything that is set aside in Israel shall be yours.

- Regarding what do all of the above commentaries agree?
- Look at Exodus 24:9–11. How do you think that it could be relevant to this debate?

TEXTUAL SKILLS

1. It is a little unusual for God to begin a communication with the word ואני, "and I…" Look at a few other examples (Gen. 6:17, 9:19; Ex. 7:3, 14:17) to get a sense of how it is used and what it might mean here.
2. When describing those things which may be eaten by the kohen's family, the Torah adds one important requirement (vv. 11, 13). What is that?
3. Many of these "gifts" to the *kohanim*, including additional specifics, were mentioned in Leviticus, chapter 7. Why do you think it was important for the Torah mention them again in this context?

WISDOM OF THE HEART

The Torah uses two words to describe the portions which go to the *kohanim*: one is חֵלֶב, meaning the fattest or the best, and the other is ביכורים, meaning the first. People sometimes have a tendency to do only the minimum when they are required to do something. Take taxes, for example. Who wouldn't want to pay fewer taxes? Even though those taxes pay for the police and fire departments, road and bridge maintenance, public education, ensuring care for the poor, and so much more, we would always prefer that someone else foot the bill. It would be easy to imagine that people obligated to give their produce to a *kohen* wouldn't necessarily give their best. After all, they might think, why should he get better produce than me? Why should he get before me? Yet that is exactly what the Torah requires – that we give the *kohen* the first and the best. In doing so, we recognize the special role that the *kohen* has – a role that nobody else can replace.

Why do you think that today we have a hard time appreciating the specialness of the kohen?

במדבר | פרק יח

ח וַיְדַבֵּר יְהוָה אֶל־אַהֲרֹן וַאֲנִי הִנֵּה נָתַתִּי לְךָ אֶת־מִשְׁמֶרֶת תְּרוּמֹתָי לְכָל־קָדְשֵׁי בְנֵי־יִשְׂרָאֵל לְךָ נְתַתִּים לְמָשְׁחָה וּלְבָנֶיךָ לְחָק־עוֹלָם: ט זֶה־יִהְיֶה לְךָ מִקֹּדֶשׁ הַקֳּדָשִׁים מִן־הָאֵשׁ כָּל־קָרְבָּנָם לְכָל־מִנְחָתָם וּלְכָל־חַטָּאתָם וּלְכָל־אֲשָׁמָם אֲשֶׁר יָשִׁיבוּ לִי קֹדֶשׁ קָדָשִׁים לְךָ הוּא וּלְבָנֶיךָ: י בְּקֹדֶשׁ הַקֳּדָשִׁים תֹּאכְלֶנּוּ כָּל־זָכָר יֹאכַל אֹתוֹ קֹדֶשׁ יִהְיֶה־לָּךְ: יא וְזֶה־לְּךָ תְּרוּמַת מַתָּנָם לְכָל־תְּנוּפֹת בְּנֵי יִשְׂרָאֵל לְךָ נְתַתִּים וּלְבָנֶיךָ וְלִבְנֹתֶיךָ אִתְּךָ לְחָק־עוֹלָם כָּל־טָהוֹר בְּבֵיתְךָ יֹאכַל אֹתוֹ: יב כֹּל חֵלֶב יִצְהָר וְכָל־חֵלֶב תִּירוֹשׁ וְדָגָן רֵאשִׁיתָם אֲשֶׁר־יִתְּנוּ לַיהוָה לְךָ נְתַתִּים: יג בִּכּוּרֵי כָּל־אֲשֶׁר בְּאַרְצָם אֲשֶׁר־יָבִיאוּ לַיהוָה לְךָ יִהְיֶה כָּל־טָהוֹר בְּבֵיתְךָ יֹאכְלֶנּוּ: יד כָּל־חֵרֶם בְּיִשְׂרָאֵל לְךָ יִהְיֶה:

CLASSIC COMMENTATORS

The Torah writes (v. 10) that the portions of the holiest offerings are eaten by the *kohanim* in the *kodesh hakodashim*, the inner sanctum of the *Mikdash*. Could this possibly be true?

RASHI — רש"י

We learn from here that the holiest types of sacrifices may be eaten only in the Tabernacle courtyard, and only by male priests.

לימד על קדשי הקדשים שאין נאכלין אלא בעזרה ולזכרי כהונה.

IBN EZRA — אבן עזרא

These may be eaten even in the most holy of places, namely the Tent of Meeting. This is referred to as the "Holy of Holies" relative to the Tabernacle courtyard.

אפילו בקדש הקדשים שהוא אהל מועד, ונקרא קדש קדשים כנגד חצר המשכן.

RAMBAN — רמב"ן

These items must be eaten in a state approximating the Holy of Holies…that is, they should be consumed with the highest degree of sanctity.

שתאכלנו בקדושת קדש הקדשים ... שתהיה אכילתך בהם בקדושה חמורה.

QUESTIONS FOR THOUGHT

- Which of the above commentaries fits the words of the Torah best?
- Which of the above commentaries seems to make the most logical sense?

> **18:15–32** *All firstborn sheep, goats, or cows are offered as sacrifices, and the kohen gets a portion of them, which he may eat with his family. Other firstborn animals, as well as firstborn sons, are redeemed for five shekels. The Levites, who assist the kohanim in serving as a buffer between the Mikdash and Benei Yisrael, receive one-tenth of the agricultural produce, but they must give one-tenth of what they receive to the kohen. Neither the kohen nor the Levite receives an agricultural portion of the Promised Land.*

15 All the first to emerge from the womb of any creature, human or animal, that is offered to the Lord shall be yours. You must, however, redeem firstborn boys and the firstborn
16 of impure animals. Their redemption price from the age of one month shall be set at five
17 shekel of silver according to the Sanctuary weight: twenty gerah per shekel. You must not redeem the firstborn of an ox, sheep, or goat; they are sacred. You must dash their
18 blood on the altar and send their fat up in smoke for a pleasing aroma to the Lord. But their meat is yours. It shall be yours like the breast of the wave offering and the right
19 thigh. All the sacred gifts that the Israelites raise up to the Lord I give to you, your sons, and your daughters as an everlasting statute. It is an everlasting covenant of salt before
20 the Lord, for you and for your descendants." The Lord said to Aharon: "You will have no inheritance in their land, nor shall you have any share among them. I am your share,
21 your inheritance, among the Israelites. And I give to the Levites all tithes in Israel as an inheritance in return for the service they perform, the service in the Tent of Meeting.
22 From now the Israelites shall no longer come close to the Tent of Meeting, or they will
23 incur guilt and die. Instead, the Levites will perform the service of the Tent of Meeting, and they will bear responsibility for their own sins; this is an everlasting decree through

---

HAAMEK DAVAR | העמק דבר

Said God to Aharon: Your benefit is the service of the Lord and immersion in the Torah. For there is no greater love than devotion to the Almighty and the pursuit of Torah study.

הנאתך הוא בעבודת ה׳ ובשקידת התורה, ואין אהבה כאהבת ה׳ ואהבת התורה.

QUESTIONS FOR THOUGHT

- In what way is the opinion of Bekhor Shor different from the other two?
- Ralbag and *Haamek Davar* seem very similar. What is an important difference between them?
- Which of the above fits the text of the Torah best?
- Rambam (*Shemitta VeYovel* 13:12) writes that Levi was separated out to serve God and teach His righteous path to the masses, and he quotes Deuteronomy 33:10 as his source. With which of the above commentaries does Rambam agree, if any?

טו כׇּל־פֶּטֶר רֶחֶם לְכׇל־בָּשָׂר אֲשֶׁר־יַקְרִיבוּ לַיהֹוָה בָּאָדָם וּבַבְּהֵמָה יִהְיֶה־לָּךְ אַךְ ׀ פָּדֹה תִפְדֶּה אֵת בְּכוֹר הָאָדָם וְאֵת בְּכוֹר־הַבְּהֵמָה הַטְּמֵאָה תִּפְדֶּה:

טז וּפְדוּיָו מִבֶּן־חֹדֶשׁ תִּפְדֶּה בְּעֶרְכְּךָ כֶּסֶף חֲמֵשֶׁת שְׁקָלִים בְּשֶׁקֶל הַקֹּדֶשׁ עֶשְׂרִים גֵּרָה הוּא:

יז אַךְ בְּכוֹר־שׁוֹר אוֹ־בְכוֹר כֶּשֶׂב אוֹ־בְכוֹר עֵז לֹא תִפְדֶּה קֹדֶשׁ הֵם אֶת־דָּמָם תִּזְרֹק עַל־הַמִּזְבֵּחַ וְאֶת־חֶלְבָּם תַּקְטִיר אִשֶּׁה לְרֵיחַ נִיחֹחַ לַיהֹוָה:

יח וּבְשָׂרָם יִהְיֶה־לָּךְ כַּחֲזֵה הַתְּנוּפָה וּכְשׁוֹק הַיָּמִין לְךָ יִהְיֶה:

יט כֹּל ׀ תְּרוּמֹת הַקֳּדָשִׁים אֲשֶׁר יָרִימוּ בְנֵי־יִשְׂרָאֵל לַיהֹוָה נָתַתִּי לְךָ וּלְבָנֶיךָ וְלִבְנֹתֶיךָ אִתְּךָ לְחׇק־עוֹלָם בְּרִית מֶלַח עוֹלָם הִוא לִפְנֵי יְהֹוָה לְךָ וּלְזַרְעֲךָ אִתָּךְ:

כ וַיֹּאמֶר יְהֹוָה אֶל־אַהֲרֹן בְּאַרְצָם לֹא תִנְחָל וְחֵלֶק לֹא־יִהְיֶה לְךָ בְּתוֹכָם אֲנִי חֶלְקְךָ וְנַחֲלָתְךָ בְּתוֹךְ בְּנֵי יִשְׂרָאֵל:

שביעי

כא וְלִבְנֵי לֵוִי הִנֵּה נָתַתִּי כׇּל־מַעֲשֵׂר בְּיִשְׂרָאֵל לְנַחֲלָה חֵלֶף עֲבֹדָתָם אֲשֶׁר־הֵם עֹבְדִים אֶת־עֲבֹדַת אֹהֶל מוֹעֵד:

כב וְלֹא־יִקְרְבוּ עוֹד בְּנֵי יִשְׂרָאֵל אֶל־אֹהֶל מוֹעֵד לָשֵׂאת חֵטְא לָמוּת:

כג וְעָבַד הַלֵּוִי הוּא אֶת־עֲבֹדַת אֹהֶל מוֹעֵד וְהֵם יִשְׂאוּ עֲוֺנָם חֻקַּת עוֹלָם לְדֹרֹתֵיכֶם וּבְתוֹךְ בְּנֵי יִשְׂרָאֵל לֹא

CLASSIC COMMENTATORS

God tells Aharon that He is their portion (v. 20), so they do not need a portion of the land. What is the primary job of the Levites and the *kohanim* that not having to grow food frees them to do?

RABBI YOSEF BEKHOR SHOR — ר׳ יוסף בכור שור

The priests will therefore be available to carry out the service.

ולכך תהיה תהיה פנוי לשמור משמרת.

RALBAG — רלב״ג

The priests will have plenty of time to study Torah and to promote awareness of their Creator.

ויהיה להם הפנאי לעסוק בתורה ולהזכיר את בוראם.

24 all your generations. But among the Israelites they will not inherit land, because I have given as an inheritance to the Levites the tithe of the Israelites which they have lifted up to the LORD as an upraised gift. That is why I have said of them that they shall have no land inheritance among the Israelites."
25/26 The LORD spoke to Moshe: "Speak to the Levites and say to them: When you receive from the Israelites the tithe that I have given you from them as your inheritance, you
27 shall lift up a tenth of it as an offering to the LORD, a tithe of the tithe. It will be considered your own upraised gift, like the grain of the threshing floor or the flow from the
28 winepress. So shall you set aside an offering to the LORD from all the tithes that you take from the Israelites, and you shall give it as an upraised gift to the LORD for Aharon
29 the priest. From all your gifts, you shall set aside an offering to the LORD; of each the
30 finest portion shall be consecrated. Say to the Levites: When you have presented the best portion of it, it will be reckoned to you as the yield of the threshing floor and the
31 winepress. You and your household may eat of it anywhere, because this is your pay-
32 ment for your service in the Tent of Meeting. You will not bear guilt for it once you have separated out the finest portion; then you will not be profaning the sacred offerings of the Israelites, and will not die."

WISDOM OF THE HEART

The Rebbe of Zidichov makes an interesting observation. When we take food and give it to the *kohen*, the rest of the food doesn't get jealous that it wasn't sanctified. Choosing one portion rather than another doesn't indicate that it is necessarily better, just that it has a different purpose to serve. We can apply this idea to ourselves as well. Some of us are better at making money, others at interpersonal relationships, and still others at spiritual achievements. Every one of us has different gifts with different responsibilities and functions. That doesn't make us intrinsically more important or less important than anyone else. When we understand what our special role is, there is no reason for jealousy. Figuring that out, however, can be a great challenge.

What helps you overcome feelings of jealousy?

QUICK BITE

Salt, a requirement for all animal offerings, has a unique quality: it never spoils and is, in fact, used as a preservative. R. Yisrael of Chortkov probes salt's uniqueness a little further. Salt has great value in bringing out the flavors in other foods. Perhaps for that reason it was chosen as a requirement for offerings – it brings out the best in the sacrifices, and reminds us that we should strive to do the same.

כד יִנְחֲל֖וּ נַחֲלָֽה: כִּי֩ אֶת־מַעְשַׂ֨ר בְּנֵֽי־יִשְׂרָאֵ֜ל אֲשֶׁ֨ר יָרִ֤ימוּ לַֽיהֹוָה֙ תְּרוּמָ֔ה נָתַ֥תִּי לַלְוִיִּ֖ם לְנַֽחֲלָ֑ה עַל־כֵּן֙ אָמַ֣רְתִּי לָהֶ֔ם בְּת֨וֹךְ֙ בְּנֵ֣י יִשְׂרָאֵ֔ל לֹ֥א יִנְחֲל֖וּ נַֽחֲלָֽה:

יז כה וַיְדַבֵּ֥ר יְהֹוָ֖ה אֶל־מֹשֶׁ֥ה לֵּאמֹֽר: כו וְאֶל־הַלְוִיִּ֤ם תְּדַבֵּר֙ וְאָֽמַרְתָּ֣ אֲלֵהֶ֔ם כִּֽי־תִ֠קְח֠וּ מֵאֵ֨ת בְּנֵֽי־יִשְׂרָאֵ֜ל אֶת־הַֽמַּעֲשֵׂ֗ר אֲשֶׁ֨ר נָתַ֧תִּי לָכֶ֛ם מֵֽאִתָּ֖ם בְּנַחֲלַתְכֶ֑ם וַהֲרֵמֹתֶ֤ם מִמֶּ֨נּוּ֙ תְּרוּמַ֣ת יְהֹוָ֔ה מַעֲשֵׂ֖ר מִן־הַֽמַּעֲשֵֽׂר: כז וְנֶחְשַׁ֥ב לָכֶ֖ם תְּרֽוּמַתְכֶ֑ם כַּדָּגָן֙ מִן־הַגֹּ֔רֶן וְכַֽמְלֵאָ֖ה מִן־הַיָּֽקֶב: כח כֵּ֣ן תָּרִ֤ימוּ גַם־אַתֶּם֙ תְּרוּמַ֣ת יְהֹוָ֔ה מִכֹּל֙ מַעְשְׂרֹ֣תֵיכֶ֔ם אֲשֶׁ֣ר תִּקְח֔וּ מֵאֵ֖ת בְּנֵ֣י יִשְׂרָאֵ֑ל וּנְתַתֶּ֤ם מִמֶּ֨נּוּ֙ אֶת־תְּרוּמַ֣ת יְהֹוָ֔ה לְאַהֲרֹ֖ן הַכֹּהֵֽן: כט מִכֹּל֙ מַתְּנֹ֣תֵיכֶ֔ם תָּרִ֕ימוּ אֵ֖ת כׇּל־תְּרוּמַ֣ת יְהֹוָ֑ה מִכׇּל־חֶלְבּ֔וֹ אֶֽת־מִקְדְּשׁ֖וֹ מִמֶּֽנּוּ: מפטיר ל וְאָמַרְתָּ֖ אֲלֵהֶ֑ם בַּהֲרִֽימְכֶ֤ם אֶת־חֶלְבּוֹ֙ מִמֶּ֔נּוּ וְנֶחְשַׁב֙ לַלְוִיִּ֔ם כִּתְבוּאַ֥ת גֹּ֖רֶן וְכִתְבוּאַ֥ת יָֽקֶב: לא וַאֲכַלְתֶּ֤ם אֹתוֹ֙ בְּכׇל־מָק֔וֹם אַתֶּ֖ם וּבֵֽיתְכֶ֑ם כִּֽי־שָׂכָ֥ר הוּא֙ לָכֶ֔ם חֵ֖לֶף עֲבֹֽדַתְכֶ֖ם בְּאֹ֥הֶל מוֹעֵֽד: לב וְלֹא־תִשְׂא֤וּ עָלָיו֙ חֵ֔טְא בַּהֲרִֽימְכֶ֥ם אֶת־חֶלְבּ֖וֹ מִמֶּ֑נּוּ וְאֶת־קׇדְשֵׁ֧י בְנֵֽי־יִשְׂרָאֵ֛ל לֹ֥א תְחַלְּל֖וּ וְלֹ֥א תָמֽוּתוּ:

TEXTUAL SKILLS

1. The word **נחלה** appears eight times in this passage, but it refers to two very different things. What are they?

2. Verses 15–16 discuss the mitzva to redeem the firstborn. Compare this with the earlier passage discussing redemption in 3:44–51. Why do you think that there is a need for both discussions? In what ways are they very different?

3. There are two times Torah speaks about salt in the context of the *Mikdash* and identifies it with the word **ברית**, covenant: verse 19 here and Leviticus 2:13. In what ways are they different?

MORE QUICK BITES

- **16:1** R. Moshe Sofer observes that Koraḥ's name was the same as one of Esav's sons (Gen. 36:14). Building on this he suggests that how we are identified, both by others and by ourselves, has a profound impact on how we act and who we become.

- **17:11** Moshe and Aharon fall on their faces. Rabbeinu Baḥya sees this as a source for the custom to "fall on our faces" when reciting *Taḥanun*. Just as Moshe and Aharon did so because they sensed the Divine Presence, we too have that capacity after the pinnacle of our prayer.

EXPLORING HASHKAFA
Debate and the Search for Truth

On the face of it, Koraḥ makes a valid point. It looks like corruption when the key leadership positions are all in one family. In that light, Moshe's response – which involves a show of power and many deaths – seems like it is out of place. Would it not have been appropriate to have a discussion, even a debate? After all, is our tradition not based on a culture of debate? That culture is so deeply enshrined that one passage in the Talmud describes a debate between Beit Hillel and Beit Shamai which lasted for three years, after which a Heavenly voice declared, "these and those are the words of the Living God!"

Much has been written about the concept of "these and those" (known in Hebrew as אלו ואלו דברי אלהים חיים), and it is clear that it has been applied in almost every sphere of Jewish learning – halakha, Jewish philosophy and belief, Tanakh, and more. There are very, very few things about which there is no room for diversity, discussion, and debate. If so, then what was so offensive about Koraḥ's argument?

The two above examples, Koraḥ on the one hand and Beit Hillel – Beit Shamai on the other, are contrasted to each other by a mishna (Avot 5:21). "Any dispute for the sake of Heaven will have enduring value, but any dispute not for the sake of Heaven will not have enduring value. What is an example of a dispute for the sake of Heaven? The dispute between Hillel and Shamai. What is an example of a dispute which is not for the sake of Heaven? The dispute of Koraḥ and all his company."

R. Menaḥem Meiri explains the distinction. A dispute for the sake of Heaven is one in which the goal is to seek truth. The other type is when the sides want to win, regardless of what the truth may be or what means they use to get there. Watch arguments. Does one person concede points made by the other or just change the topic to counter-attack about something else? Do the people involved argue respectfully or do they call each other names or use insults, put-downs, and other rhetoric devices to make the other side feel bad? Is there a personal motive involved?

It is valuable, in our own lives, to think about the arguments we have. What role does our ego play? And just as important, what do we want to accomplish? Are we looking to win, or to solve a problem? Debates for the sake of Heaven do not have to go away, but they should allow us to live with our disagreements, and with the people with whom we disagree.

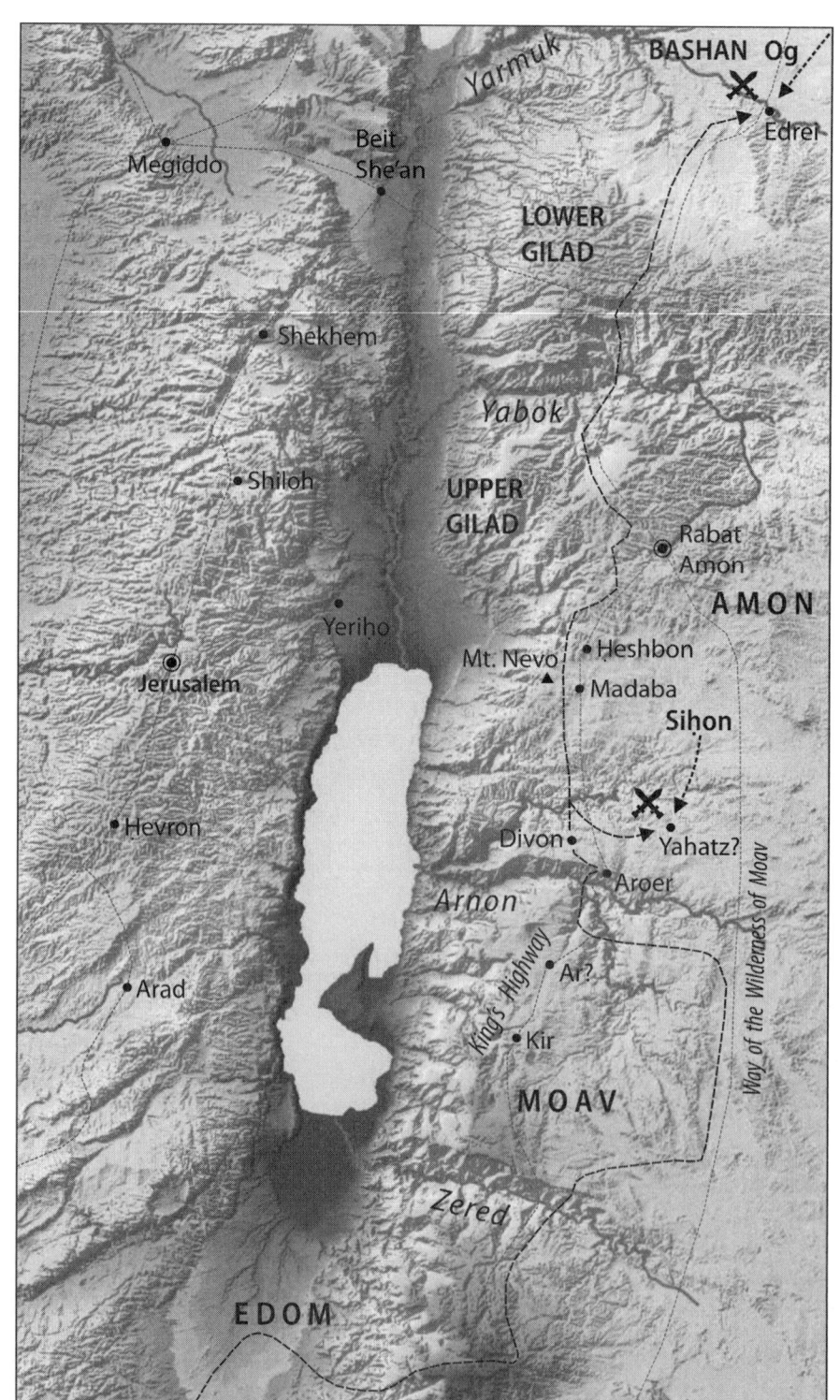

The eastern side of the Jordan Valley, where *Benei Yisrael* traveled and fought on the final leg of their journey to the Promised Land.

פרשת חקת
PARASHAT ḤUKAT

"It is only through mystery and madness that the soul is revealed."
Thomas Moore

R. Yisrael Meir Alter, author of *Ḥidushei Harim*, once met the Rebbe of Radzimin on Shabbat *Parashat Ḥukat* and saw that he was sad. With concern, R. Alter asked what was wrong. The Rebbe responded: "Every year, when we get to this *parasha*, I am distraught. How could it be that the very people who witnessed the splitting of the sea and the giving of the Torah on Mount Sinai were the same people who sank so far in their rebellion against God?"

PARASHAT ḤUKAT

> **19:1–22** The purification process for anyone who becomes impure as a result of contact with a corpse involves being sprinkled with water into which was placed the ashes of a red cow along with a branch of cedar wood, hyssop, and red-dyed wool. The red cow is not a sacrifice, but is slaughtered and burnt whole outside of the camp. Any kohen involved in the processing of the red cow becomes impure and has to immerse in a mikve. Purification is necessary even for someone who was in the tent of the corpse, for someone who encountered a corpse in the open, and even for unsealed vessels in the tent of the deceased. It requires being sprinkled with the special water on the third day and the seventh day after contamination, followed by immersion in a mikve. Anyone who is not purified and nonetheless has contact with the Mishkan or with sanctified items receives the punishment of karet.

19 ¹ The LORD spoke to Moshe and Aharon: "This is the decree of the Law that the LORD ² commands. Tell the Israelites to bring you a cow, completely red, without blemish, on ³ which no yoke has been laid. Give this to Elazar the priest; it shall be taken outside the ⁴ camp and slaughtered in his presence. Elazar the priest shall take some of its blood with ⁵ his finger and sprinkle it seven times toward the front of the Tent of Meeting. The cow shall then be burned in front of him; its skin, flesh, and blood shall be burned, together ⁶ with its dung. The priest shall take cedarwood, hyssop, and scarlet cloth and throw them ⁷ into the fire where the cow is burning. Then the priest shall wash his clothes and bathe his body in water. Afterward he may enter the camp, but he will remain impure until ⁸ that evening. The one who burned it shall wash his clothes in water and bathe his body ⁹ in water, but he too will remain impure until evening. Meanwhile, one who is pure shall gather up the ashes of the cow and place them outside the camp in a pure place. And they shall be kept by the Israelite community for the water of lustration, as a purification

---

QUESTIONS FOR THOUGHT

- Can you think of a reason why the Torah would want to specifically include Elazar or exclude Aharon in the processing of the red cow?
- A mishna (Para 3:5) lists all the different red cows processed, including some done by the High Priest. How do you think Rashi might explain that mishna?

TEXTUAL SKILLS

1. Notice that the items added to the water are also used for the purification of the person afflicted with צרעת (Lev. 14:4).
2. Twice the Torah describes the punishment for someone who violated the *Mishkan*, in verses 13 and 20. What is missing both times?
3. What verb does the Torah use to describe the process of purification?

פרשת חקת

יט א וַיְדַבֵּר יהוה אֶל־מֹשֶׁה וְאֶל־אַהֲרֹן לֵאמֹר: זֹאת חֻקַּת הַתּוֹרָה אֲשֶׁר־צִוָּה יהוה לֵאמֹר דַּבֵּר ׀ אֶל־בְּנֵי יִשְׂרָאֵל וְיִקְחוּ אֵלֶיךָ פָרָה אֲדֻמָּה תְּמִימָה אֲשֶׁר אֵין־בָּהּ מוּם אֲשֶׁר לֹא־עָלָה עָלֶיהָ עֹל: ג וּנְתַתֶּם אֹתָהּ אֶל־אֶלְעָזָר הַכֹּהֵן וְהוֹצִיא אֹתָהּ אֶל־מִחוּץ לַמַּחֲנֶה וְשָׁחַט אֹתָהּ לְפָנָיו: ד וְלָקַח אֶלְעָזָר הַכֹּהֵן מִדָּמָהּ בְּאֶצְבָּעוֹ וְהִזָּה אֶל־נֹכַח פְּנֵי אֹהֶל־מוֹעֵד מִדָּמָהּ שֶׁבַע פְּעָמִים: ה וְשָׂרַף אֶת־הַפָּרָה לְעֵינָיו אֶת־עֹרָהּ וְאֶת־בְּשָׂרָהּ וְאֶת־דָּמָהּ עַל־פִּרְשָׁהּ יִשְׂרֹף: ו וְלָקַח הַכֹּהֵן עֵץ אֶרֶז וְאֵזוֹב וּשְׁנִי תוֹלָעַת וְהִשְׁלִיךְ אֶל־תּוֹךְ שְׂרֵפַת הַפָּרָה: ז וְכִבֶּס בְּגָדָיו הַכֹּהֵן וְרָחַץ בְּשָׂרוֹ בַּמַּיִם וְאַחַר יָבֹא אֶל־הַמַּחֲנֶה וְטָמֵא הַכֹּהֵן עַד־הָעָרֶב: ח וְהַשֹּׂרֵף אֹתָהּ יְכַבֵּס בְּגָדָיו בַּמַּיִם וְרָחַץ בְּשָׂרוֹ בַּמָּיִם וְטָמֵא עַד־הָעָרֶב: ט וְאָסַף ׀ אִישׁ טָהוֹר אֵת אֵפֶר הַפָּרָה וְהִנִּיחַ מִחוּץ לַמַּחֲנֶה בְּמָקוֹם טָהוֹר וְהָיְתָה לַעֲדַת בְּנֵי־יִשְׂרָאֵל לְמִשְׁמֶרֶת

CLASSIC COMMENTATORS

The Torah repeatedly highlights that it is Elazar, Aharon's son, who is to be involved in the slaughtering of the red cow. Is that a one-time rule or does it establish the rule for the future?

רש״י — **RASHI**
מצותה בסגן.
This teaches that the deputy High Priest is charged with this commandment.

רמב״ן — **RAMBAN**
הוראת שעה היתה בפרה הראשונה שתהיה באלעזר.
Elazar's participation was a temporary measure regarding the first red cow.

רלב״ג — **RALBAG**
למדנו מזה שהפרה נעשית בין בכהן גדול בין בכהן הדיוט.
We learn from Elazar's involvement that this procedure can be conducted by either the High Priest or a common kohen.

10 offering. The one who gathers the ashes of the cow shall likewise wash his clothes but remains impure until evening. This shall be an everlasting decree for the Israelites and
11 for any migrant living among them. Whoever touches the dead body of any person shall
12 be impure for seven days. He must purify himself with the water on the third and seventh days to become pure. If he does not purify himself on the third and seventh days,
13 he will not be pure. Whoever touches a corpse of a person who has died, and fails to purify himself, defiles the Lord's Tabernacle. He shall be severed from Israel because, since the water of lustration was not sprinkled on him, he remains impure; his impurity
14 is still with him. This is the law: when a person dies in a tent, whoever enters that tent
15 and whoever is in it shall remain impure for seven days. Any open vessel not sealed
16 with a cover shall be impure. Anyone in the open field who touches a person killed by the sword, or who died naturally, or a human bone or a grave, shall be impure for seven
17 days. For this impure person they shall take some of the ashes of the burnt purification
18 offering, and place living water along with it into a vessel. A person who is pure shall then take hyssop, dip it into the water, and sprinkle it on the tent, on all the vessels, on the people who were there, and on anyone who touched the bone, the slain person, or
19 any other corpse, or a grave. On the third day and seventh day the person who is pure shall sprinkle it on the one who is impure, thus purifying him on the seventh day. He
20 shall then wash his clothes and immerse in water, and at evening he will be pure. Anyone who becomes impure and fails to purify himself shall be severed from the assembly, for he has defiled the Lord's Sanctuary. Since water of lustration was not sprinkled on
21 him, he is impure. This is an everlasting decree for them. The one who sprinkles the water of lustration shall wash his own clothes. Anyone who had contact with the water
22 of lustration shall remain impure until evening. Anything the impure person touches is rendered impure, and one who touches him remains impure until evening."

WISDOM OF THE HEART

We live in an era in which so much of our private lives is available in the public sphere. Some of the Torah's laws, like those concerning the red cow, are exactly the opposite. Any understanding of them remains hidden from us, private. There is special beauty in those things which are kept out of the public eye; it's what makes them special.

Which would you prefer – a world in which no part of our private lives is available publicly or one in which everything is available publicly?

לְמֵי נִדָּה חַטָּאת הִוא: י וְכִבֶּס הָאֹסֵף אֶת־אֵפֶר הַפָּרָה אֶת־בְּגָדָיו וְטָמֵא עַד־הָעָרֶב וְהָיְתָה לִבְנֵי יִשְׂרָאֵל וְלַגֵּר הַגָּר בְּתוֹכָם לְחֻקַּת עוֹלָם: הַנֹּגֵעַ בְּמֵת לְכָל־נֶפֶשׁ אָדָם וְטָמֵא שִׁבְעַת יָמִים: יא הוּא יִתְחַטָּא־בוֹ בַּיּוֹם הַשְּׁלִישִׁי וּבַיּוֹם הַשְּׁבִיעִי יִטְהָר וְאִם־לֹא יִתְחַטָּא בַּיּוֹם הַשְּׁלִישִׁי וּבַיּוֹם הַשְּׁבִיעִי לֹא יִטְהָר: יב כָּל־הַנֹּגֵעַ בְּמֵת בְּנֶפֶשׁ הָאָדָם אֲשֶׁר־יָמוּת וְלֹא יִתְחַטָּא אֶת־מִשְׁכַּן יְהוָה טִמֵּא וְנִכְרְתָה הַנֶּפֶשׁ הַהִוא מִיִּשְׂרָאֵל כִּי מֵי נִדָּה לֹא־זֹרַק עָלָיו טָמֵא יִהְיֶה עוֹד טֻמְאָתוֹ בוֹ: יג זֹאת הַתּוֹרָה אָדָם כִּי־יָמוּת בְּאֹהֶל כָּל־הַבָּא אֶל־הָאֹהֶל וְכָל־אֲשֶׁר בָּאֹהֶל יִטְמָא שִׁבְעַת יָמִים: יד וְכֹל כְּלִי פָתוּחַ אֲשֶׁר אֵין־צָמִיד פָּתִיל עָלָיו טָמֵא הוּא: טו וְכֹל אֲשֶׁר־יִגַּע עַל־פְּנֵי הַשָּׂדֶה בַּחֲלַל־חֶרֶב אוֹ בְמֵת אוֹ־בְעֶצֶם אָדָם אוֹ בְקָבֶר יִטְמָא שִׁבְעַת יָמִים: טז וְלָקְחוּ לַטָּמֵא מֵעֲפַר שְׂרֵפַת הַחַטָּאת וְנָתַן עָלָיו מַיִם חַיִּים אֶל־כֶּלִי: יז **שני** וְלָקַח אֵזוֹב וְטָבַל בַּמַּיִם אִישׁ טָהוֹר וְהִזָּה עַל־הָאֹהֶל וְעַל־כָּל־הַכֵּלִים וְעַל־הַנְּפָשׁוֹת אֲשֶׁר הָיוּ־שָׁם וְעַל־הַנֹּגֵעַ בַּעֶצֶם אוֹ בֶחָלָל אוֹ בַמֵּת אוֹ בַקָּבֶר: יח וְהִזָּה הַטָּהֹר עַל־הַטָּמֵא בַּיּוֹם הַשְּׁלִישִׁי וּבַיּוֹם הַשְּׁבִיעִי וְחִטְּאוֹ בַּיּוֹם הַשְּׁבִיעִי וְכִבֶּס בְּגָדָיו וְרָחַץ בַּמַּיִם וְטָהֵר בָּעָרֶב: יט וְאִישׁ אֲשֶׁר־יִטְמָא וְלֹא יִתְחַטָּא וְנִכְרְתָה הַנֶּפֶשׁ הַהִוא מִתּוֹךְ הַקָּהָל כִּי אֶת־מִקְדַּשׁ יְהוָה טִמֵּא מֵי נִדָּה לֹא־זֹרַק עָלָיו טָמֵא הוּא: כ וְהָיְתָה לָּהֶם לְחֻקַּת עוֹלָם וּמַזֵּה מֵי־הַנִּדָּה יְכַבֵּס בְּגָדָיו וְהַנֹּגֵעַ בְּמֵי הַנִּדָּה יִטְמָא עַד־הָעָרֶב: כא וְכֹל אֲשֶׁר־יִגַּע־בּוֹ הַטָּמֵא יִטְמָא וְהַנֶּפֶשׁ הַנֹּגַעַת תִּטְמָא עַד־הָעָרֶב: כב

BEMIDBAR | CHAPTER 20 — ḤUKAT | 184

> **20:1–6** *Miriam dies in the Wilderness of Tzin, and there is no water. The people challenge Moshe for bringing them to a place where nothing grows and there is no water. Moshe and Aharon go to the Tent of Meeting, where they fall on their faces and God appears to them.*

20 1 The Israelites, all the community, arrived at the Wilderness of Tzin in the first month, 2 and the people stayed at Kadesh. There Miriam died and was buried. And there was 3 no water for the community, and together they confronted Moshe and Aharon. The people contended with Moshe: "If only we had died when our brothers died before 4 the Lord! Why have you brought the Lord's assembly into this wilderness only for us 5 and our livestock to die here? Why did you take us up out of Egypt to bring us to this dreadful place with no grain, no figs, no vines or pomegranates – there is no water to 6 drink!" Moshe and Aharon went away from the assembly to the entrance of the Tent of Meeting. They fell on their faces, and the Lord's glory was revealed to them.

QUESTIONS FOR THOUGHT

- According to *Harekhasim Levika*, even events which are listed right next to each other did not necessarily happen in rapid sequence, but could have been separated by a significant amount of time. How would that affect our understanding of the connection between verses 1 and 2? With whom is he disagreeing in making this claim?
- *Harekhasim Levika* spreads the events in the wilderness over the entire forty-year period, while Ibn Ezra concentrates them in either the first year or the last year. Which of those do you think makes more sense? Why?
- What difference would it make in our understanding if the story in which Moshe loses the right to enter the land happened in the fortieth year or sometime in the middle of those forty years?

TEXTUAL SKILLS

1. In what ways is the complaint here similar to and different from the one in 14:2?
2. In verse 5 the people complain that Moshe did not bring them to a place which grows figs, grapes, or pomegranates. God had promised a land of milk and honey. From where did they get the idea that the land would have figs, grapes, and pomegranates?

WISDOM OF THE HEART

Once again, it is the basic needs of the people which, when not met, bring them to challenge their leaders. Psychologist Abraham Maslow proposed that people's needs can be categorized and ordered. There are low-level, basic, survival-oriented needs, like food, water and safety; middle-level needs like the need to belong, to be loved, and to be respected; and then there are the highest-level needs, like the need to understand, to appreciate beauty, and to feel life is meaningful. If one's basic needs aren't met, it is nearly impossible to strive for higher ones. The lack of water experienced by *Benei Yisrael* is so basic that to satisfy their need they would have been prepared to lose everything they had worked for during the past forty years. When we see someone with a need, it is important for us to understand how to fulfill those basic needs before we can try to bring the person higher.

במדבר | פרק כ | חקת

א וַיָּבֹאוּ בְנֵי־יִשְׂרָאֵל כָּל־הָעֵדָה מִדְבַּר־צִן בַּחֹדֶשׁ הָרִאשׁוֹן וַיֵּשֶׁב הָעָם בְּקָדֵשׁ וַתָּמָת שָׁם מִרְיָם וַתִּקָּבֵר שָׁם: ב וְלֹא־הָיָה מַיִם לָעֵדָה וַיִּקָּהֲלוּ עַל־מֹשֶׁה וְעַל־אַהֲרֹן: ג וַיָּרֶב הָעָם עִם־מֹשֶׁה וַיֹּאמְרוּ לֵאמֹר וְלוּ גָוַעְנוּ בִּגְוַע אַחֵינוּ לִפְנֵי יְהֹוָה: ד וְלָמָה הֲבֵאתֶם אֶת־קְהַל יְהֹוָה אֶל־הַמִּדְבָּר הַזֶּה לָמוּת שָׁם אֲנַחְנוּ וּבְעִירֵנוּ: ה וְלָמָה הֶעֱלִיתֻנוּ מִמִּצְרַיִם לְהָבִיא אֹתָנוּ אֶל־הַמָּקוֹם הָרָע הַזֶּה לֹא ׀ מְקוֹם זֶרַע וּתְאֵנָה וְגֶפֶן וְרִמּוֹן וּמַיִם אַיִן לִשְׁתּוֹת: ו וַיָּבֹא מֹשֶׁה וְאַהֲרֹן מִפְּנֵי הַקָּהָל אֶל־פֶּתַח אֹהֶל מוֹעֵד וַיִּפְּלוּ עַל־פְּנֵיהֶם וַיֵּרָא כְבוֹד־יְהֹוָה אֲלֵיהֶם:

CLASSIC COMMENTATORS

The Torah describes this story as happening in the first month. In what year after the exodus did this story happen?

RASHI
רש"י
ולא היה מים לעדה - מכאן שכל ארבעים שנה היה להם הבאר בזכות מרים.

We learn from here that during Israel's forty-year sojourn in the wilderness they drew water from a well thanks to Miriam's merit.

IBN EZRA
אבן עזרא
בחדש הראשון - בשנת המ'. והנה אין בתורה כלל שום מעשה או נבואה רק בשנה הראשונה ובשנת הארבעים.

Miriam died in the first month of the fortieth year. Indeed, all of the events reported in the latter four books of the Torah took place either in the first or the fortieth year of the nation's history.

HAREKHASIM LEVIKA
הרכסים לבקעה
בשנה השנית מיד אחר המעפילים עשה משה כאשר נצטוה ונסעו מקדש ברנע ... ונעו ונדו אנה ואנה ... ובתוך אותן השנים אירע מעשה קרח ובאו לקדש מדבר צין בשנת העשרים או סמוך לה. ומיתת מרים, אף שנסמכה לביאת קדש, אין הכרח שהמעשים תכופים ... וכן חוסר המים אין הכרח לפי פשוטו לומר שהיה סמוך למיתתה ... וגם אין מצוה ממצות התורה לומר שמעשה הסלע בשנת הארבעים.

In the second year, immediately after the debacle of the spies and the futile attempt to march on the land, Moshe did as God commanded and led the people away from Kadesh Barnea…. Following that, the nation wandered here and there in the wilderness…and during that period Koraḥ rebelled against Moshe. Thus Israel arrived at the Wilderness of Tzin sometime around year twenty. Hence even though Miriam's death is mentioned in conjunction with Kadesh, those two events did not necessarily happen at the same time…. Similarly, there is no real need to say that Israel suffered their dearth of water around the time that Miriam died. Finally, there is no commandment to believe that the incident of the rock happened in the fortieth year.

⁷⁸ And the Lord spoke to Moshe: "Take the staff, you and your brother Aharon, and assemble the community. Speak to the rock before their eyes and it will give forth water. You shall bring forth water for them from the rock, giving the community and their
⁹ animals to drink." Moshe took the staff from before the Lord, as He had commanded
¹⁰ him. And Moshe and Aharon gathered the assembly together before the rock. He said to
¹¹ them, "Listen now, rebels! Shall we produce water for you from this rock?" Then Moshe raised his hand and struck the rock twice with his staff. Water gushed out, and the com-
¹² munity and their animals drank. But the Lord said to Moshe and Aharon, "Because you did not put your trust in Me to demonstrate My holiness in the Israelites' eyes, you shall
¹³ not bring this assembly into the land that I am giving them." These were the waters of Meriva, where the Israelites quarreled with the Lord and where He showed them His

---

מנחה בלולה

חטא משה מפורסם בפסוק "ויבוא משה ואהרן מפני הקהל אל פתח אהל מועד". כי תמורת שהיה להם להוכיח את ישראל ולעמוד בפרץ באמור להם: "מדוע תריבו את ה'?" ... נסתרו אל פתח אוהל מועד כמו בורחים.

MINHA BELULA

The text identifies the leaders' transgression when it states, "Moshe and Aharon went away from the assembly to the entrance of the Tent of Meeting" (20:6). Their job at that moment was to rebuke Israel and exclaim: why are you provoking the Lord? Instead of doing that, they secluded themselves in the entrance of the Tent of Meeting, as if they were trying to escape the demands of the people.

QUESTIONS FOR THOUGHT

- Each of the above commentaries is very concerned with a phrase in verse 12 and relates to it. What is that phrase, and why is it so important to them all?
- In what way is the explanation of *Minha Belula* different from the other two?
- Which of the above explanations could explain why Aharon is also punished?
- According to each of the above, is Moshe's sin a personal one or one of leadership? Why might that make a difference?

TEXTUAL SKILLS

1. Compare Moshe's language in verse 10 with 17:25.
2. This is the second time a place involving water is called מריבה. Compare this to the first one, in Exodus 17:1.

WISDOM OF THE HEART

It's easy to believe that we are completely in charge of our lives. It's just as easy to believe that we cannot control anything. Traditional Jewish belief maintains that neither is true – we direct much of our life, but God has a hand in it as well. The only question is what the balance is. According to R. Shmuel Bornstein, in *Shem Mishmuel*, by hitting the rock Moshe made it seem like everything can be controlled by people, and that was the wrong message.

How much do you think that God controls your life? What does that mean in terms of your responsibility? Would you prefer that your life be more in God's hands or less?

חקת | פרק כ

שלישי /שני/

ח וַיְדַבֵּ֥ר יְהֹוָ֖ה אֶל־מֹשֶׁ֥ה לֵּאמֹֽר: קַ֣ח אֶת־הַמַּטֶּ֗ה וְהַקְהֵ֤ל אֶת־
הָעֵדָה֙ אַתָּה֙ וְאַהֲרֹ֣ן אָחִ֔יךָ וְדִבַּרְתֶּ֧ם אֶל־הַסֶּ֛לַע לְעֵינֵיהֶ֖ם וְנָתַ֣ן
מֵימָ֑יו וְהוֹצֵאתָ֨ לָהֶ֥ם מַ֙יִם֙ מִן־הַסֶּ֔לַע וְהִשְׁקִיתָ֥ אֶת־הָעֵדָ֖ה
ט וְאֶת־בְּעִירָֽם: וַיִּקַּ֥ח מֹשֶׁ֛ה אֶת־הַמַּטֶּ֖ה מִלִּפְנֵ֣י יְהֹוָ֑ה כַּאֲשֶׁ֖ר
י צִוָּֽהוּ: וַיַּקְהִ֜לוּ מֹשֶׁ֧ה וְאַהֲרֹ֛ן אֶת־הַקָּהָ֖ל אֶל־פְּנֵ֣י הַסָּ֑לַע וַיֹּ֣אמֶר
לָהֶ֔ם שִׁמְעוּ־נָא֙ הַמֹּרִ֔ים הֲמִן־הַסֶּ֣לַע הַזֶּ֔ה נוֹצִ֥יא לָכֶ֖ם מָֽיִם:
יא וַיָּ֨רֶם מֹשֶׁ֜ה אֶת־יָד֗וֹ וַיַּ֧ךְ אֶת־הַסֶּ֛לַע בְּמַטֵּ֖הוּ פַּעֲמָ֑יִם וַיֵּצְא֣וּ מַ֣יִם
רַבִּ֔ים וַתֵּ֥שְׁתְּ הָעֵדָ֖ה וּבְעִירָֽם: וַיֹּ֣אמֶר יְהֹוָה֮ אֶל־מֹשֶׁ֣ה
יב וְאֶֽל־אַהֲרֹן֒ יַ֚עַן לֹא־הֶאֱמַנְתֶּ֣ם בִּ֔י לְהַ֨קְדִּישֵׁ֔נִי לְעֵינֵ֖י בְּנֵ֣י יִשְׂרָאֵ֑ל
לָכֵ֗ן לֹ֤א תָבִ֙יאוּ֙ אֶת־הַקָּהָ֣ל הַזֶּ֔ה אֶל־הָאָ֖רֶץ אֲשֶׁר־נָתַ֥תִּי לָהֶֽם:
יג הֵ֚מָּה מֵ֣י מְרִיבָ֔ה אֲשֶׁר־רָב֥וּ בְנֵֽי־יִשְׂרָאֵ֖ל אֶת־יְהֹוָ֑ה וַיִּקָּדֵ֖שׁ
בָּֽם:

CLASSIC COMMENTATORS

What was so terrible about what Moshe did, that he deserves such a harsh punishment?

RABBEINU ḤANANEL

ר׳ חננאל

Moshe and Aharon's sin lay in their boast, "Shall we produce water for you from this rock?" What they should have said was: The Lord will produce water for you from this rock!... The people might therefore have believed that the leaders used some secret wisdom of theirs to extract the water. This is what God meant when He said, "You did not…demonstrate My holiness."

החטא הוא אמרם "המן הסלע הזה נוציא לכם מים", וראוי שיאמרו: "יוציא ה' לכם מים"... ואולי חשבו העם כי משה ואהרן בחכמתם הוציאו להם מים מן הסלע הזה, וזהו "לא קידשתם אותי".

RAMBAM

רמב״ם

Moshe and Aharon forgot that they were not dealing with simpletons.... Even the most inferior among the Israelites' women held a degree of prophecy equal to that of Yeḥezkel son of Buzi.... Their every action and word would be observed by the nation. Thus, when the Israelites saw that Moshe and Aharon had lost their temper, the people thought: since Moshe is angry at us, that must mean that God Himself is enraged that we have asked for water. And yet, there is no evidence in the text that the Almighty found Israel's request at all inappropriate, or that God was now displeased at the nation.

שלא היה מדבר עם עמי הארץ... אבל עם קהל שהקטנה שבנשיהם הייתה כיחזקאל בן בוזי... וכל מה שיאמר או יעשה, יבחנוהו. וכאשר ראוהו שהתרגז, אמרו: "...לולא ידע שהאלוהים התאנף בנו על דרישת המים, ושאנחנו הכעסנוהו, יתברך, לא היה מתרגז". ואנו לא מצאנו לשם יתברך שהתרגז או שכעס בדברו אליו בעניין הזה.

14 holiness. Moshe sent messengers from Kadesh to the king of Edom: "This is what your
15 brother Israel says: 'You know all the hardship we have encountered, how our ancestors went down to Egypt and lived in Egypt for a long time. And the Egyptians oppressed
16 us and our forebears, and we cried out to the LORD. He heard our voice, sent a messenger, and He brought us out of Egypt. Now here we are in Kadesh, a town adjoining
17 your border. Please, let us pass through your land. We will not pass through any field or vineyard, nor will we drink water from any well. We will go along the King's Highway and not turn from it to the right or the left until we have passed through your territory.'"
18 But Edom said to him, "You shall not pass through, or I will come out against you with
19 the sword." The Israelites said, "We will keep to the beaten track. If we or our livestock drink any of your water, we will pay for it. It is such a small matter; we only want to pass
20 through on foot." But they said, "You will not pass through." And Edom came out against
21 them with a large fighting force, heavily armed. Edom refused to let Israel pass through their territory, and Israel turned away.

ר' יוסף בכור שור
היו ישראל מפתים אותם בדברים, כאדם שמספר לפני אהבו וקרובו תלאותיו ומספר לו מאורעיו, לפי שישים אל לבו וירחם עליו.

RABBI YOSEF BEKHOR SHOR
Israel was trying to elicit the sympathy the Edomites, like an individual who catalogues all of his travails in front of his friends and relatives hoping to elicit their sympathy.

QUESTIONS FOR THOUGHT

- Using a single word for each, what emotion does each of the commentaries suggest that Moshe is trying to evoke in Edom?
- Based on what they write here, how do you think each would explain why Moshe mentions the fact that God heard their cries and saved them?
- According to Rashi's explanation, what might be the danger of Moshe's approach to Edom?
- What do you think you should do when you have a history with someone of an unpleasant encounter but you need to speak with them?

TEXTUAL SKILLS

1. Moshe is the second person in the Torah to send מלאכים to a long-lost brother, recounting a tale of exile and freedom. Who was the first? In what other ways are these stories similar?

2. There are two different "roads" that Moshe offers to travel on as he requests to pass through. Find the names of those two roads.

WISDOM OF THE HEART

When we are down on our luck we often turn to others – family and friends – for help. But when things go well for us, we sometimes forget those who may be less fortunate. As *Benei Yisrael* enter the final leg of their journey guided by God, they are feeling confident in their path and their mission. Nonetheless, they turn to Edom and reach out to a long-lost brother. R. Yonatan Eybeschutz suggests that we have much to learn from Moshe reaching out to Edom.

חקת | פרק כ

יד וַיִּשְׁלַ֨ח מֹשֶׁ֧ה מַלְאָכִ֛ים מִקָּדֵ֖שׁ אֶל־מֶ֣לֶךְ אֱד֑וֹם *רביעי* יח
כֹּ֤ה אָמַר֙ אָחִ֣יךָ יִשְׂרָאֵ֔ל אַתָּ֣ה יָדַ֔עְתָּ אֵ֥ת כָּל־הַתְּלָאָ֖ה אֲשֶׁ֥ר
מְצָאָֽתְנוּ: טו וַיֵּרְד֤וּ אֲבֹתֵ֙ינוּ֙ מִצְרַ֔יְמָה וַנֵּ֥שֶׁב בְּמִצְרַ֖יִם יָמִ֣ים רַבִּ֑ים
וַיָּרֵ֥עוּ לָ֛נוּ מִצְרַ֖יִם וְלַאֲבֹתֵֽינוּ: טז וַנִּצְעַ֤ק אֶל־יְהוָה֙ וַיִּשְׁמַ֣ע קֹלֵ֔נוּ
וַיִּשְׁלַ֣ח מַלְאָ֔ךְ וַיֹּצִאֵ֖נוּ מִמִּצְרָ֑יִם וְהִנֵּה֙ אֲנַ֣חְנוּ בְקָדֵ֔שׁ עִ֖יר קְצֵ֥ה
גְבוּלֶֽךָ: יז נַעְבְּרָה־נָּ֣א בְאַרְצֶ֗ךָ לֹ֤א נַעֲבֹר֙ בְּשָׂדֶ֣ה וּבְכֶ֔רֶם וְלֹ֥א
נִשְׁתֶּ֖ה מֵ֣י בְאֵ֑ר דֶּ֧רֶךְ הַמֶּ֣לֶךְ נֵלֵ֗ךְ לֹ֤א נִטֶּה֙ יָמִ֣ין וּשְׂמֹ֔אול עַ֥ד
אֲשֶֽׁר־נַעֲבֹ֖ר גְּבֻלֶֽךָ: יח וַיֹּ֤אמֶר אֵלָיו֙ אֱד֔וֹם לֹ֥א תַעֲבֹ֖ר בִּ֑י פֶּן־בַּחֶ֖רֶב
אֵצֵ֥א לִקְרָאתֶֽךָ: יט וַיֹּאמְר֨וּ אֵלָ֥יו בְּנֵֽי־יִשְׂרָאֵ֜ל בַּֽמְסִלָּ֣ה נַעֲלֶ֗ה וְאִם־
מֵימֶ֤יךָ נִשְׁתֶּה֙ אֲנִ֣י וּמִקְנַ֔י וְנָתַתִּ֖י מִכְרָ֑ם רַ֥ק אֵין־דָּבָ֖ר בְּרַגְלַ֥י
אֶֽעֱבֹֽרָה: כ וַיֹּ֖אמֶר לֹ֣א תַעֲבֹ֑ר וַיֵּצֵ֤א אֱדוֹם֙ לִקְרָאת֔וֹ בְּעַ֥ם כָּבֵ֖ד
וּבְיָ֥ד חֲזָקָֽה: כא וַיְמָאֵ֣ן ׀ אֱד֗וֹם נְתֹן֙ אֶת־יִשְׂרָאֵ֔ל עֲבֹ֖ר בִּגְבֻל֑וֹ וַיֵּ֥ט
יִשְׂרָאֵ֖ל מֵעָלָֽיו:

CLASSIC COMMENTATORS

Moshe's message to Edom begins with a brief description of *Benei Yisrael's* suffering. Why does he tell them all of this?

RASHI

רש"י

אחיך ישראל – מה ראה להזכיר לו כאן אחוה, אלא אמר לו: אחים אנחנו בני אברהם, שנאמר לו: כי גר יהיה זרעך (בראשית ט"ו:י"ג), ועל שנינו היה אותו החוב לפרוע. אתה ידעת את כל התלאה – לפיכך פירש אביכם מעל אבינו, וילך אל ארץ מפני יעקב אחיו (בראשית ל"ו:ו'), מפני השטר חוב המוטל עליהם, והטילו על יעקב.

Your brother Israel: Why did Moshe remind Edom of their familial connection to Israel? Said Moshe to his counterpart: Both of our peoples descend from Avraham, who was told, "your descendants will be migrants in a land not their own" (Gen. 15:13), so that both of our nations should have suffered that fate. You know all the hardship we have encountered: It was due to your ancestor Esav's reluctance to endure the cost of obtaining the land, that he separated himself from our patriarch Yaakov, as the verse states, "and he moved to another region, away from his brother Yaakov" (Gen. 36:6). Esav abdicated the duty that had been imposed on both brothers, and left Yaakov to suffer it alone.

20:22–29 *As Benei Yisrael begin the final leg of their trip to the Promised Land, God tells Moshe and Aharon to prepare for Aharon's imminent death and to ready Aharon's son Elazar to take his place as High Priest. On Mount Hor, Aharon is to remove his special clothes and Elazar is to be dressed in them. Moshe does as instructed. When Aharon dies, the entire nation mourns him for thirty days.*

22 They set out from Kadesh, and all the Israelite community arrived at Mount Hor.
23 There at Mount Hor, by the border of the land of Edom, the Lord said to Moshe and
24 Aharon, "Aharon is to be gathered to his people. He shall not enter the land that I have given to the Israelites, because you disobeyed My command at the waters of Meriva.
25/26 Take Aharon and his son Elazar, and bring them up onto Mount Hor. Strip Aharon of his vestments and put them on his son Elazar. There will Aharon be gathered in and he
27 will die." Moshe did as the Lord commanded. They ascended Mount Hor in the sight
28 of all the community. Moshe stripped Aharon of his vestments and put them on his son Elazar. And there, Aharon died, at the top of the mountain; and Moshe and Elazar
29 came down from the mountain. When all the community saw that Aharon had perished,

TEXTUAL SKILLS

1. This is the second event in this *parasha* which happens literally "before the eyes" (לְעֵינֵי) of the community. What is the first? Is there a connection between them?
2. This is the fourth time in this book that Elazar, son of Aharon, is featured (and the second time in this *parasha*).
3. The expression to be "gathered unto his people" (יֵאָסֵף אֶל עַמָּיו), describing death, is used for only six people in all of Tanakh: Avraham, Yitzḥak, Yishmael, Yaakov, Aharon, and Moshe.

Can you find the other places?

WISDOM OF THE HEART

When God tells Moshe to remove Aharon's clothing, He adds immediately that Aharon's son Elazar should be dressed in them. One of the greatest achievements a person can hope to accomplish is to know that the legacy they worked for is being carried beyond, and especially if it is his own children who are carrying on that legacy. That is not something which should be taken for granted, especially since another great gift parents want to leave their children is the ability to become their own people, independent and able to make their own decisions.

How can parents navigate the balance between wanting their legacy to continue and wanting their children to be autonomous decision-makers? How can their children navigate that same balance of respect for their parents and their values on the one hand and their own independence on the other?

QUICK BITE

In preparing for Aharon's death, God tells Moshe to remove Aharon's priestly clothing. Money, glory, and honor do not accompany us into the next world. The legacy of our actions, however – whether we helped to make this world a better place than the one we found when we entered – lives on long beyond our own lives.

חקת | פרק כ

כב וַיִּסְעוּ מִקָּדֵשׁ וַיָּבֹאוּ בְנֵי־יִשְׂרָאֵל כָּל־הָעֵדָה הֹר הָהָר: וַיֹּאמֶר ⟨חמישי /שלישי/⟩
יְהֹוָה אֶל־מֹשֶׁה וְאֶל־אַהֲרֹן בְּהֹר הָהָר עַל־גְּבוּל אֶרֶץ־אֱדוֹם
כג לֵאמֹר: יֵאָסֵף אַהֲרֹן אֶל־עַמָּיו כִּי לֹא יָבֹא אֶל־הָאָרֶץ אֲשֶׁר
כד נָתַתִּי לִבְנֵי יִשְׂרָאֵל עַל אֲשֶׁר־מְרִיתֶם אֶת־פִּי לְמֵי מְרִיבָה: קַח
כה אֶת־אַהֲרֹן וְאֶת־אֶלְעָזָר בְּנוֹ וְהַעַל אֹתָם הֹר הָהָר: וְהַפְשֵׁט
אֶת־אַהֲרֹן אֶת־בְּגָדָיו וְהִלְבַּשְׁתָּם אֶת־אֶלְעָזָר בְּנוֹ וְאַהֲרֹן יֵאָסֵף
כו וּמֵת שָׁם: וַיַּעַשׂ מֹשֶׁה כַּאֲשֶׁר צִוָּה יְהֹוָה וַיַּעֲלוּ אֶל־הֹר הָהָר
כז לְעֵינֵי כָּל־הָעֵדָה: וַיַּפְשֵׁט מֹשֶׁה אֶת־אַהֲרֹן אֶת־בְּגָדָיו וַיַּלְבֵּשׁ
כח אֹתָם אֶת־אֶלְעָזָר בְּנוֹ וַיָּמָת אַהֲרֹן שָׁם בְּרֹאשׁ הָהָר וַיֵּרֶד
כט מֹשֶׁה וְאֶלְעָזָר מִן־הָהָר: וַיִּרְאוּ כָּל־הָעֵדָה כִּי גָוַע אַהֲרֹן וַיִּבְכּוּ

CLASSIC COMMENTATORS

Why did God emphasize the details of removing Aharon's clothes and placing them on Elazar?

IBN EZRA

Aharon will die as soon as he removes the High Priest's vestments.

אבן עזרא

וטעם ואהרן יאסף – כי בעת שתפשיט בגדיו, מיד ימות.

RABBI YOSEF BEKHOR SHOR

It was a consolation to Aharon to witness his son Elazar being installed as the next High Priest prior to his own death.

ר' יוסף בכור שור

והלבשתם את אלעזר בנו – שיראה בנו כהן גדול בימיו ואחר כך יאסף אל אבותיו.

RABBI OVADYA SFORNO

After removing the clothes particular to the High Priest, Aharon remained dressed in the four garments of a common priest. He was therefore clothed in the way he presented himself to enter the Holy of Holies, and looked like God's angels do when they appear to man.

ר' עובדיה ספורנו

ובכן נשאר אהרן בד' בגדי כהן הדיוט, "לבוש הבדים", כמו שהיה ענינו בהכנס לפני ולפנים, וכענין הראות מלאכי אלהים לעבדיו.

QUESTIONS FOR THOUGHT

- In what way are the explanations of Ibn Ezra and Bekhor Shor exact opposites?
- What idea does Sforno introduce here which is dramatically different from the other two?
- Imagining that you were planning a ceremony for a rabbi who was retiring. Which of the above comments would you use as an inspiration for the ceremony, and what elements would you include in the ceremony as a result?

BEMIDBAR | CHAPTER 21 — ḤUKAT | 192

> **21:1–3** When the Canaanites living in Arad hear that Benei Yisrael are nearby, they attack and take some captives. Benei Yisrael vow that if God helps them in counterattacking, they will make those Canaanite cities חרם, completely dedicated to God. Benei Yisrael counterattack, and God helps them. They name the place Ḥorma, commemorating the חרם that they declared.

21 1 the whole House of Israel wept for Aharon for thirty days. When the Canaanite king of Arad, dwelling in the Negev, heard that the Israelites were coming by the way of Atarim, 2 he attacked the Israelites and took captives. And the Israelites vowed to the Lord: "If 3 You give this people over into our hands, we will utterly destroy their towns." The Lord listened to Israel's plea and gave over the Canaanites. They completely destroyed them and their cities; and so the place was named Ḥorma.

QUESTIONS FOR THOUGHT

- Ramban offers two explanations. According to the first one, the place was called Ḥorma only after it was captured in the period after Yehoshua. Why is this such a radical suggestion?
- Ramban's second explanation suggests that the place was named Ḥorma twice, once here and again in Judges. How does he explain the need to name it twice?
- Are you familiar with other places in the Torah where the same place is given the same name on two different occasions?

TEXTUAL SKILLS

1. This is only the second time in nearly forty years that *Benei Yisrael* were attacked on the road. What was the first, and in what ways are they different?
2. This short passage contains three verses. In some way, the third verse is the opposite of the first. The middle verse is where the transformation takes place. Notice the content of the middle verse.
3. This is the second time that we hear of a place called Ḥorma. The first is in 14:45. Are they connected?

WISDOM OF THE HEART

Rashi comments that the Canaanites decided to attack *Benei Yisrael* when they heard that Aharon had died and that as a result the cloud of glory, which normally accompanied and protected *Benei Yisrael*, was gone. Rav Yisrael of Rizhin explains that when two people love each other and embrace, they generate a cloud of glory. Aharon was one of the key architects of the special relationship between God and *Benei Yisrael*, and his work in the *Mishkan* was primarily geared to help maintain that relationship. When his soul departed, the cloud – representing God's deep bond to *Benei Yisrael* – temporarily left as well.

What do you think it means that there is a special protective cloud enveloping two people who are deeply in love?

במדבר | פרק כא

א אֶת־אַהֲרֹ֖ן שְׁלֹשִׁ֣ים י֑וֹם כֹּ֖ל בֵּ֥ית יִשְׂרָאֵֽל׃ וַיִּשְׁמַ֡ע הַכְּנַעֲנִ֤י מֶֽלֶךְ־עֲרָד֙ יֹשֵׁ֣ב הַנֶּ֔גֶב כִּ֚י בָּ֣א יִשְׂרָאֵ֔ל דֶּ֖רֶךְ הָאֲתָרִ֑ים וַיִּלָּ֨חֶם֙ בְּיִשְׂרָאֵ֔ל וַיִּ֥שְׁבְּ ׀ מִמֶּ֖נּוּ שֶֽׁבִי׃ ב וַיִּדַּ֨ר יִשְׂרָאֵ֥ל נֶ֛דֶר לַֽיהֹוָ֖ה וַיֹּאמַ֑ר אִם־נָתֹ֨ן תִּתֵּ֜ן אֶת־הָעָ֤ם הַזֶּה֙ בְּיָדִ֔י וְהַחֲרַמְתִּ֖י אֶת־עָרֵיהֶֽם׃ ג וַיִּשְׁמַ֨ע יְהֹוָ֜ה בְּק֣וֹל יִשְׂרָאֵ֗ל וַיִּתֵּן֙ אֶת־הַֽכְּנַעֲנִ֔י וַיַּחֲרֵ֥ם אֶתְהֶ֖ם וְאֶת־עָרֵיהֶ֑ם וַיִּקְרָ֥א שֵׁם־הַמָּק֖וֹם חָרְמָֽה׃

CLASSIC COMMENTATORS

The Torah tells us that *Benei Yisrael* named the place Ḥorma as a result of their actions, but in the book of Judges (1:17) we are told about a city called Tzefat that Yehuda and Shimon captured and which *they* called Ḥorma. Do these texts relate to the same event and place, or do they describe altogether different sites and circumstances?

RAMBAN

It seems to me that the king of Arad ruled in the south.... When the Canaanite king heard that Israel was approaching, he came "by the Atarim route" to the Plains of Moav to engage them there.... The text next reports that the Lord heeded Israel's prayer for assistance; they vowed and immediately fulfilled it in Moshe's time by destroying the enemy...and devoting all of the captured plunder to the treasury of the Lord's house. The text also informs us here what Israel later did when they entered the land of Canaan, namely that they razed these cities following the death of Yehoshua, which was also a fulfillment of their vow, and they also named the place Ḥorma, a detail which is recounted in the book of Judges.... It was only then that they completed fulfilling the vow that they made now, even though the Torah describes it here to finish its discussion of the encounter with the king of Arad. It is also possible to suggest an alternative, that Israel defeated this king and his nation now and immediately named it Ḥorma. Later, when they crossed the Jordan, Yehoshua slew the king of Arad who reigned at that time. Thus, when the tribe of Yehuda conquered those towns, they too destroyed them and named the ruins "Ḥorma" in fulfillment of the vow undertaken by their ancestors.... Therefore, everything that is described here happened at once – in the time of Moshe – except for this detail: "They completely destroyed…their cities" (21:3). That took place somewhat later, when Israel moved into the area.

רמב״ן

והנכון בעיני: כי זה מלך ערד הוא יושב בנגב ... ושמע מרחוק בבוא בני ישראל, ובא דרך האתרים אל ערבות מואב וילחם עמהם שם ... וספר הכתוב כי שמע ה' תפלתם ונדרו נדר לה' ושלמו אותו, כי הרגו אתהם בימי משה ונתנו כל שללם לאוצר בית ה'. והשלים עוד בכאן לספר כי החרימו ישראל גם את עריהם אחרי בואם בארץ כנען ואחרי מות יהושע, לקיים את נדרם אשר נדרו, ויקראו שם הערים חרמה, והוא שנאמר בספר שופטים (א׳:י״ז) ... ושם נשלם הנדר הזה, אבל השלים הכתוב להזכיר הענין בכאן ... גם נכון הוא לומר שהחרימו ישראל עתה בימי משה את המלך הזה ואת עמו לפי חרב, וקראו שם מקום המלחמה חרמה, ואחרי עברם את הירדן המית יהושע גם את מלך ערד אשר מלך אחרי כן ... ובני יהודה בבואם בעריהם החרימו אותם גם כן, וקראו שם הערים חרמה כי השלימו את נדרם אשר נדרו אבותם ... והנה כל הנזכר בכאן היה בבת אחת זולתי שהזכיר: "ואת עריהם" (כ״א:ג'), שהיה לעתיד בבואם בעריהם.

21:4–9 *As Benei Yisrael detour around Edom, lengthening their route into the land, they lose patience with wilderness life. God sends serpents that bite them, and many Israelites die. When the people come to Moshe to confess that they were sinful, Moshe turns to God, who instructs him to make a bronze serpent and display it high up so that anyone who has been bitten can look at it and live. Moshe does this, and those who gaze at the bronze serpent are saved.*

4 They set out from Mount Hor by the way to the Reed Sea, going around the land of
5 Edom. But the people became restive along the way. The people spoke out against God and Moshe: "Why did you bring us up from Egypt to die in the desert? There is
6 no bread, there is no water; we detest this miserable food!" The Lord sent venomous
7 snakes among the people; they bit the people, and many Israelites died. The people came to Moshe and said, "We sinned when we spoke against the Lord and you. Pray
8 to the Lord to take the snakes away from us." Moshe prayed for the people. The Lord then said to Moshe, "Fashion a snake and place it on a pole. Anyone who is bitten shall
9 look at that and live." Moshe fashioned a bronze snake and placed it on a pole. When

QUESTIONS FOR THOUGHT

- In what way is Rashbam's explanation different from the other two?
- In your opinion, which of the commentaries offers the best explanation of why it was specifically a serpent that Moshe was supposed to make? Why do you think that explanation is best?
- How do you think each of the explanations could be meaningful today?

TEXTUAL SKILLS

1. Notice the play between the word for serpent, the word for bronze, and the word for bite.
2. In 11:1–2 there is a similar story about people getting burned for something they were saying and Moshe getting involved. In what ways are the two stories very different?

WISDOM OF THE HEART

As the people lose patience with the long route they need to take, going far out of the way to circle around Edom instead of passing through it, God responds by sending serpents which kill many people. After God instructs Moshe to make a serpent and mount it on a high pole to be visible, Moshe does so, and makes the serpent (נחש) out of bronze (נחשת). This linguistic connection is understood by Ramban to be more than just a play on words; it points to a mysterious quality and suggests that נחש and נחשת are somehow related. Perhaps the Torah's message is that the way past the dragon is sometimes in confronting the dragon itself. Instead of running from our fears we are better served by facing them.

What fears do you have that you know you can get past with just a little extra help?

ד וַיִּסְעוּ מֵהֹר הָהָר דֶּרֶךְ יַם־סוּף לִסְבֹב אֶת־אֶרֶץ אֱדוֹם וַתִּקְצַר
ה נֶפֶשׁ־הָעָם בַּדָּרֶךְ: וַיְדַבֵּר הָעָם בֵּאלֹהִים וּבְמֹשֶׁה לָמָה הֶעֱלִיתֻנוּ
מִמִּצְרַיִם לָמוּת בַּמִּדְבָּר כִּי אֵין לֶחֶם וְאֵין מַיִם וְנַפְשֵׁנוּ קָצָה
ו בַּלֶּחֶם הַקְּלֹקֵל: וַיְשַׁלַּח יהוה בָּעָם אֵת הַנְּחָשִׁים הַשְּׂרָפִים
ז וַיְנַשְּׁכוּ אֶת־הָעָם וַיָּמָת עַם־רָב מִיִּשְׂרָאֵל: וַיָּבֹא הָעָם אֶל־
מֹשֶׁה וַיֹּאמְרוּ חָטָאנוּ כִּי־דִבַּרְנוּ בַיהוה וָבָךְ הִתְפַּלֵּל אֶל־
יהוה וְיָסֵר מֵעָלֵינוּ אֶת־הַנָּחָשׁ וַיִּתְפַּלֵּל מֹשֶׁה בְּעַד הָעָם:
ח וַיֹּאמֶר יהוה אֶל־מֹשֶׁה עֲשֵׂה לְךָ שָׂרָף וְשִׂים אֹתוֹ עַל־נֵס
ט וְהָיָה כָּל־הַנָּשׁוּךְ וְרָאָה אֹתוֹ וָחָי: וַיַּעַשׂ מֹשֶׁה נְחַשׁ נְחֹשֶׁת
וַיְשִׂמֵהוּ עַל־הַנֵּס וְהָיָה אִם־נָשַׁךְ הַנָּחָשׁ אֶת־אִישׁ וְהִבִּיט אֶל־

CLASSIC COMMENTATORS

Why did God ask Moshe to make a serpent? Couldn't God have simply ended the plague?

RASHBAM
רשב״ם
שיסתכל לשמים למעלה.

Benei Yisrael were meant to look skyward and beyond.

AKEDAT YITZHAK
עקדת יצחק
דן אותם ה' יתברך על פי דרכם. אמר: כיון שאין חפצכם לחיות כי אם על המנהג הטבעי, אף אני אעשה זאת לכם, שאניח הנחשים השרפים אשר במדבר על טבעם ולא אחסום פיהם מהזיק לכם, כמו שעשיתי עד הנה. וכן עשה. ... שידעו ויכירו שאי אפשר להם לחיות בארץ ההיא רק דרך נס. ולזה הודו במה שחטאו עליו ראשונה.

God here punished Israel according to the way they had behaved. Said the Almighty to the nation: you have made it clear that you wish to lead an all-natural existence, and so that is what I shall grant you. In your direction, I hereby release snakes and serpents, common denizens of the wilderness. Furthermore, I will in no way prevent these reptiles from biting you as I have done until now. And that is exactly what God did…Israel thereby learned that there was no way they could possibly survive in the wilderness without God's miraculous providence. This acknowledgement is what Israel admitted when they confessed their sin to Moshe.

RABBI SAMSON RAPHAEL HIRSCH
ר' שמשון רפאל הירש
כל הנשוך הוטל עליו רק לשים מעיניו בדמות הנחש למען ידע ויבין ... כי הסכנות מצויות תמיד ובכל יום ובכל שעה, והקב״ה שומרו ומצילו.

When any individual was bitten, all he had to do was glance at the image of the serpent to know and understand that he is was constantly surrounded by threats and dangers from which, the Holy One, blessed be He, protects and saves him

BEMIDBAR | CHAPTER 21 HUKAT | 196

21:10–20 *As Benei Yisrael continue their roundabout route to the Promised Land, they pass around the land of Moav. Several mysterious things happen on that journey, including a battle about which we know nothing and an event involving a well of water. The incident with the water inspires Benei Yisrael to burst out in song.*

10 anyone was bitten by a snake, he would look at the bronze snake and live. The Israelites
11 moved on and camped at Ovot. Then they moved on from Ovot, and camped at Iyei
12 HaAvarim in the wilderness bordering Moav to the east. From there they moved on
13 and camped at the Zered Stream. From there they moved on and camped beyond the Arnon, in the wilderness that extends from the border of the Amorites, for the Arnon
14 marks the border of Moav, between Moav and the Amorites. That is why the Book of
15 the Wars of the LORD records: "Vahev in Sufa and the wadis, Arnon and the wadi slopes
16 that lead to the settlement of Ar and lie along the border of Moav." And from there to Be'er, the well where the LORD said to Moshe, "Gather the people, and I will give them

---

ABARBANEL

אברבנאל

The site of this narrative was called Be'er, and it was so named because the Holy One, blessed be He, provided water for Israel even though the nation had not expressly asked for it. Thus the verse states, "Gather the people, and I will give them water," meaning: I am presenting water to Israel without them lodging such a request.... And once Israel saw how readily and willingly the Almighty gave them water, with no hint of chastisement, the nation felt compelled to sing a song of thanks to God, and to praise His great name.

המקום הזה "בארה" נקרא כן לפי ששם הקדוש ברוך הוא מעצמו, מבלי שישאלו ממנו ישראל מים, אמר אל משה: "אסוף את העם ואתנה להם מים" רוצה לומר: מבלי שאלתם ובקשתם ... והנה ישראל בראותם שהקדוש ברוך הוא היה נותן להם מים ברצון פשוט, לא מכוח תרעומת, נתנו לפניו שירה רבה, ברכות והודאות לשמו הגדול.

QUESTIONS FOR THOUGHT

- Rashi thinks that this is the same incident as the one described earlier. What problems does Rashi feel that he needs to answer?
- What problems does Rashi's explanation raise that may have caused most of the other commentaries to separate between this incident and an earlier one in which God gets angry with Moshe?
- According to Abarbanel, this incident is dramatically different from every other incident we know about in the wilderness. In what way is it different?
- Which of the commentaries understands that this well did not involve obvious divine intervention? If there was no obvious direct divine intervention, why did *Benei Yisrael* erupt in song?
- Why do you think that the other commentaries did not feel a need to answer the questions which bothered Rashi?
- When things happen to you, whether good or bad, how do you know if God was involved or not? For which of those do you choose to credit (or blame) God?

במדבר | פרק כא | חקת

יא נְחַשׁ הַנְּחֹשֶׁת וָחָי: וַיִּסְעוּ בְּנֵי יִשְׂרָאֵל וַיַּחֲנוּ בְּאֹבֹת: וַיִּסְעוּ ששי
מֵאֹבֹת וַיַּחֲנוּ בְּעִיֵּי הָעֲבָרִים בַּמִּדְבָּר אֲשֶׁר עַל־פְּנֵי מוֹאָב
יב מִמִּזְרַח הַשָּׁמֶשׁ: מִשָּׁם נָסָעוּ וַיַּחֲנוּ בְּנַחַל זָרֶד: מִשָּׁם נָסָעוּ
יג וַיַּחֲנוּ מֵעֵבֶר אַרְנוֹן אֲשֶׁר בַּמִּדְבָּר הַיֹּצֵא מִגְּבֻל הָאֱמֹרִי כִּי
אַרְנוֹן גְּבוּל מוֹאָב בֵּין מוֹאָב וּבֵין הָאֱמֹרִי: עַל־כֵּן יֵאָמַר בְּסֵפֶר
יד מִלְחֲמֹת יְהוָה אֶת־וָהֵב בְּסוּפָה וְאֶת־הַנְּחָלִים אַרְנוֹן: וְאֶשֶׁד
טו הַנְּחָלִים אֲשֶׁר נָטָה לְשֶׁבֶת עָר וְנִשְׁעַן לִגְבוּל מוֹאָב: וּמִשָּׁם
טז בְּאֵרָה הִוא הַבְּאֵר אֲשֶׁר אָמַר יְהוָה לְמֹשֶׁה אֱסֹף אֶת־הָעָם

CLASSIC COMMENTATORS

The Torah refers to an incident involving a well after which *Benei Yisrael* sang. Is that the same incident as when God got angry with Moshe, or was it something different?

רש"י
אז ישיר ישראל – ולמה לא נזכר משה בשירה זו? לפי שלקה על ידי הבאר. וכיוון שלא נזכר שמו של משה, לא נזכר שמו של הקדוש ברוך הוא.

RASHI
Why is Moshe not mentioned explicitly in this song? Because it was the source of his downfall. And since the name of Moshe was excluded from this passage, the Holy One, blessed be He, is not mentioned either.

אבן עזרא
וזאת הבאר גם היא היתה פלא, ואיננה הבאר הנקרא "באר מרים" לפי דעתי, רק היה המקום שציוה משה וחפרוהו שרי ישראל במשענותם, ומיד נבקעו מים.

IBN EZRA
This well was also a miraculous source of water, and in my opinion was not the same spring known as "Miriam's Well." Rather, this water emerged after Moshe commanded that a well be dug in a particular place. The Israelite leaders excavated at this spot with their staffs, and water immediately flowed out.

ר' יוסף אבן כספי
זה המעשה והאמירה היא עתה, ולא היה בזה פלא כמו הצור והסלע, רק שציוה משה לגדולי ישראל שיכרו שם באר וימצאו שם מים ברצון האל, ולכן השיר לישראל.

RABBI YOSEF IBN KASPI
The episode and the discussion of it which are presented here do not represent any sort of wonder akin to the earlier incidents concerning the stone and rock. Moshe simply instructed the "nobles of the people" to bore into the ground, where they would reveal water according to God's will. This explains why Israel sang here.

¹⁷ ¹⁸ water." Then the Israelites sang this song: "Spring up, well – sing to her – that the nobles of the people carved out with their scepter and their staffs." They went from the desert ¹⁹ ²⁰ to Matana, from Matana to Naḥaliel, from Naḥaliel to Bamot, and from Bamot to the valley in the fields of Moav, to the top of Pisga, overlooking the wasteland.

The Torah usually separates between incidents by putting in spaces. Sometimes it is a space that leaves the rest of the line open (called a petuḥa), and sometimes it is a space in the middle of a line where there is writing on either side of the space (called a setuma). Between the incident of the serpents (vv.1–9) and the continuation of the travels of *Benei Yisrael* on their way to the Promised Land (vv. 10–16) there is no space. If you look at the story of the snakes, it starts by describing that *Benei Yisrael* were on their way but got tired of the traveling and lashed out at Moshe and God, which sparked God to respond. Apparently, after God's response, the Torah wants us to relate to this a nothing more than speedbump on their journey, as it continues without a pause to describe the continuation of their trip, as if nothing could stop them now. In our own lives, things don't usually go exactly as planned. There are glitches, unforeseen delays, and last-minute problems that always seem to derail even our most careful planning. That's OK. It's important to learn how to roll with those problems, take them as they come, and not let them sidetrack us from our real goals.

WISDOM OF THE HEART

The Torah relates that *Benei Yisrael* traveled from Ovot to a place identified as Iyei HaAvarim (עִיֵּי הָעֲבָרִים). The word HaAvarim means passageways, but there is a debate about what Iyei means. Rashi and Rashbam understand that it means a destroyed place, like the second city that *Benei Yisrael* captured when they entered the land, Ai, עַי. The name of this place would thus mean: The passageway of destruction. Bekhor Shor and R. Hirsch, however, understand that the ע of עִיֵּי is interchangeable with the letter א, so that עִיֵּי would actually be אִיֵּי, meaning islands. That would describe the place as the islands of the passageway. If we consider that they could both be correct, we end up with an intriguing idea. Whenever we leave one phase of our lives and go on to another, we go through a passage, and we need to give up something of ourselves – childhood toys and clothes, childish dreams, unrealistic expectations, old ways of doing things. Every passage, every moving forward, involves sacrifice, a destruction of a piece of who we once were that we are not taking with us. At the same time, when moving through passageways of life, it is sometimes reassuring to have islands of safety, like rocks in a stream we are trying to cross. They allow us to feel safe enough to leave behind what we need to and take the next step forward.

Think of a transition you've been through in which you needed to leave something behind. Can you imagine your next transition?

יז וָאֶתְּנָה לָהֶם מָיִם: אָז יָשִׁיר יִשְׂרָאֵל אֶת־הַשִּׁירָה
יח הַזֹּאת עֲלִי בְאֵר עֱנוּ־לָהּ: בְּאֵר חֲפָרוּהָ שָׂרִים כָּרוּהָ נְדִיבֵי
יט הָעָם בִּמְחֹקֵק בְּמִשְׁעֲנֹתָם וּמִמִּדְבָּר מַתָּנָה: וּמִמַּתָּנָה נַחֲלִיאֵל
כ וּמִנַּחֲלִיאֵל בָּמוֹת: וּמִבָּמוֹת הַגַּיְא אֲשֶׁר בִּשְׂדֵה מוֹאָב רֹאשׁ הַפִּסְגָּה וְנִשְׁקָפָה עַל־פְּנֵי הַיְשִׁימֹן:

TEXTUAL SKILLS

1. Edom, whom *Benei Yisrael* dealt with earlier, is descended from Esav. How is the nation of Moav related to *Benei Yisrael*?

2. There is a book mentioned in this passage that we apparently don't have. What is the name of that book?

QUICK BITES

Commenting on verse 14, which speaks of the aftermath of a battle, the Talmud offers a suggestion to read Vahev and Sufa not as places but poetic ways of saying: Love [*ohev*], and: In the end [*sofa*]. The Talmud explains that this describes two Torah scholars, or even a father and son, learning intensely – they can often disagree, turning the learning into a battle. But when they finish their study, when they've clarified the Torah, they walk away loving each other even more, appreciating what that battle helped them achieve.

The Gaon of Vilna understands that the song sung at the well (v. 18) is a metaphor. The well, dug by the nobles, is the well of Torah, carved by Moshe and Aharon and all the sages who followed. They are the ones who legislated (מחוקק), with their staffs. The power to do so came from their humility, transforming themselves into a wilderness (מדבר). When people are humble like that, then the Torah comes to them as a gift (מתנה).

This is the second time in the Torah that we have a song that starts with the words אז ישיר. When we compare them carefully we realize that they are quite different. The first is led by Moshe while this seems to be the result of a grassroots movement sprung forth by the people; the first is in response to a miracle that the Torah described in great detail while this one is mysterious, leaving us guessing what really took place. *Benei Yisrael* seemed to have learned an important lesson. We don't need to wait for someone else to tell us when or how to be thankful to God. Sometimes we see things that no one else does, or we understand things in ways that others don't – we have the right, and maybe even the responsibility, to understand that God plays an important role in our lives, and that we can and should be thankful.

> **21:21–30** Benei Yisrael send a message to Siḥon, king of the Amorites, asking for permission to pass through his land. Siḥon refuses, challenging Benei Yisrael in battle. Benei Yisrael defeat Siḥon and take of his lands, which include lands he had earlier captured from Amon and Moav.

21,22 Then the Israelites sent messengers to Siḥon, king of the Amorites: "Let us pass through your land. We will not turn aside into any field or vineyard, nor will we drink water from any well. We will walk on the king's highway until we have passed through your 23 territory." But Siḥon would not allow the Israelites to pass through his territory. He gathered all his people and went out to confront the Israelites in the wilderness. When 24 he arrived at Yahatz, he launched an attack on the Israelites. The Israelites struck him down with their swords and took possession of his land from the Arnon to the Yabok, 25 as far as the Amonites, for the border of the Amonites was strong. The Israelites took all these cities, and they settled in all the cities of the Amorites, in Ḥeshbon and all its 26 surrounding settlements. Ḥeshbon was the city of Siḥon, king of the Amorites, who had fought against the former king of Moav and had taken all his land from him as 27 far as the Arnon. That is why the ballad singers sing: "Come to Ḥeshbon, build and 28 refound the town of Siḥon. For fire had gone forth from Ḥeshbon, a flame from the 29 town of Siḥon. It consumed Ar of Moav the masters of Arnon's high shrines. Woe for you, Moav! You are destroyed, men of Kemosh! He made his sons fugitives, his daugh- 30 ters fugitives, to Siḥon the Amorite king. Yet we – we threw them wholly down, from

TEXTUAL SKILLS

1. What significant event in Genesis took place at the Yabok Stream mentioned here?
2. Is the poem described in verses 27–31 describing this current battle or some previous one?
3. Compare verse 21 with 20:14.

WISDOM OF THE HEART

The Sages placed a great emphasis on placing fences around the Torah and its laws to protect it from being violated. It is not always easy to understand these, and they might sometimes seem excessive – until we cross those fences and realize just how important they are, like guardrails on the edge of a cliff. R. Yonatan Eybeschutz points out that the city of Ḥeshbon was a Moabite border city that was taken over by Siḥon. Had the Moabites understood the importance of protecting their borders they would have invested more in doing so, but because they didn't, they lost the city.

Many people put up virtual protective fences around themselves. It is often important to respect those boundaries, so that others do not feel threatened. When do those protections become harmful to those who erect them? How do we help people learn to drop those defenses?

במדבר | פרק כא | חקת

כא וַיִּשְׁלַח יִשְׂרָאֵל מַלְאָכִים אֶל־סִיחֹן מֶלֶךְ־הָאֱמֹרִי לֵאמֹר: *שביעי /רביעי/*
כב אֶעְבְּרָה בְאַרְצֶךָ לֹא נִטֶּה בְּשָׂדֶה וּבְכֶרֶם לֹא נִשְׁתֶּה מֵי בְאֵר בְּדֶרֶךְ הַמֶּלֶךְ נֵלֵךְ עַד אֲשֶׁר־נַעֲבֹר גְּבֻלֶךָ:
כג וְלֹא־נָתַן סִיחֹן אֶת־יִשְׂרָאֵל עֲבֹר בִּגְבֻלוֹ וַיֶּאֱסֹף סִיחֹן אֶת־כָּל־עַמּוֹ וַיֵּצֵא לִקְרַאת יִשְׂרָאֵל הַמִּדְבָּרָה וַיָּבֹא יָהְצָה וַיִּלָּחֶם בְּיִשְׂרָאֵל:
כד וַיַּכֵּהוּ יִשְׂרָאֵל לְפִי־חָרֶב וַיִּירַשׁ אֶת־אַרְצוֹ מֵאַרְנֹן עַד־יַבֹּק עַד־בְּנֵי עַמּוֹן כִּי עַז גְּבוּל בְּנֵי עַמּוֹן:
כה וַיִּקַּח יִשְׂרָאֵל אֵת כָּל־הֶעָרִים הָאֵלֶּה וַיֵּשֶׁב יִשְׂרָאֵל בְּכָל־עָרֵי הָאֱמֹרִי בְּחֶשְׁבּוֹן וּבְכָל־בְּנֹתֶיהָ:
כו כִּי חֶשְׁבּוֹן עִיר סִיחֹן מֶלֶךְ הָאֱמֹרִי הִוא וְהוּא נִלְחַם בְּמֶלֶךְ מוֹאָב הָרִאשׁוֹן וַיִּקַּח אֶת־כָּל־אַרְצוֹ מִיָּדוֹ עַד־אַרְנֹן:
כז עַל־כֵּן יֹאמְרוּ הַמֹּשְׁלִים בֹּאוּ חֶשְׁבּוֹן תִּבָּנֶה וְתִכּוֹנֵן עִיר סִיחוֹן:
כח כִּי־אֵשׁ יָצְאָה מֵחֶשְׁבּוֹן לֶהָבָה מִקִּרְיַת סִיחֹן אָכְלָה עָר מוֹאָב בַּעֲלֵי בָּמוֹת אַרְנֹן:
כט אוֹי־לְךָ מוֹאָב אָבַדְתָּ עַם־כְּמוֹשׁ נָתַן בָּנָיו פְּלֵיטִם וּבְנֹתָיו בַּשְּׁבִית לְמֶלֶךְ אֱמֹרִי סִיחוֹן:
ל וַנִּירָם אָבַד חֶשְׁבּוֹן עַד־דִּיבֹן וַנַּשִּׁים עַד־נֹפַח

CLASSIC COMMENTATORS

Were *Benei Yisrael* supposed to ask permission from Siḥon?

RASHI — רש״י

Even though God had not commanded Israel to try a peaceful approach with Amorites, nevertheless, the nation tried to avoid fighting Siḥon.

אף על פי שלא נצטוו לפתוח להם בשלום בקשו שלום.

RAMBAN — רמב״ן

Israel was commanded to try a peaceful approach with all the nations they encountered except for Amon and Moav.

בכל האומות נצטוו לפתוח להם לשלום חוץ מעמון ומואב.

QUESTIONS FOR THOUGHT

- What practical difference is there between the opinions of Rashi and Ramban?
- Which of the above positions would be easier to defend in a public discussion about Israel and the ethics of war?

> **21:31–22:1** *Following the defeat of Siḥon, Moshe sends spies to check out the Amorite area of Yazer. As Benei Yisrael conquer it, Og, the fearsome king of Bashan, attacks Benei Yisrael. God reassures Moshe, and Benei Yisrael defeat Og as well and take his land. From there they camp in the plains of Moav.*

31 Ḥeshbon to Divon, laid waste as far as Nofaḥ, as far as Meideva." So Israel settled in the
32 land of the Amorites. And Moshe sent spies to Yazer. And Israel captured its surround-
33 ing settlements and dispossessed the Amorites who were there. Then they turned and journeyed along the road toward Bashan. Og, king of Bashan, with all his people came
34 out to Edrei to engage them in battle. But the LORD said to Moshe: "Do not be afraid of him, for I have given him into your hand, with all his people and his land. Do to him
35 what you did to Siḥon, king of the Amorites, who lived in Ḥeshbon." So they struck him down, together with his sons and all his people until there were no survivors, and
22 1 they took possession of his land. The Israelites moved on and encamped in the plains of Moav across the Jordan from Yeriḥo.

QUESTIONS FOR THOUGHT

- How would you describe the main difference between Rashi's approach and the other two approaches?
- Which of the commentaries suggests that Moshe had more reason to fear Og than he did other kings he faced?
- In the previous passage we saw that Ramban believes that, with two exceptions, *Benei Yisrael* were always to pursue the path of peace over the path of war. Is Ramban here consistent with that position? Explain.

TEXTUAL SKILLS

1. Compare verse 32 with verse 21. How do you explain the difference?
2. Notice God's message in verse 34. Why do you think that there was no similar message before the earlier battle with Siḥon?

WISDOM OF THE HEART

According to a midrashic tradition, Og was the anonymous messenger who came to tell Avram that Lot had been captured. That same tradition provides a motive for Og – he wanted Avram to get killed in battle so that he could marry Sarai. Based on that tradition, Rashi comments here that Moshe was afraid of Og because he had the merit of instigating Avram to save Lot. One could ask why that is a credit to Og. After all, wasn't that all just a sinister ploy to get rid of Avram? R. Moshe Feinstein learns from this that when someone does something positive, even if the intentions were less than noble, some merit is nonetheless generated. This demonstrates the power of a good deed, even when done without intention, and even when done with negative intention.

Which do you think is more meaningful – a positive done with bad intentions or a negative action in which the intentions were good? Can you think of examples of each?

אֲשֶׁ֖ר עַד־מֵֽידְבָֽא׃ וַיֵּ֨שֶׁב֙ יִשְׂרָאֵ֔ל בְּאֶ֖רֶץ הָאֱמֹרִֽי׃ וַיִּשְׁלַ֤ח מֹשֶׁה֙ לְרַגֵּ֣ל אֶת־יַעְזֵ֔ר וַֽיִּלְכְּד֖וּ בְּנֹתֶ֑יהָ וַיּ֖וֹרֶשׁ אֶת־הָאֱמֹרִ֥י אֲשֶׁר־שָֽׁם׃ וַיִּפְנוּ֙ וַֽיַּעֲל֔וּ דֶּ֖רֶךְ הַבָּשָׁ֑ן וַיֵּצֵ֣א עוֹג֩ מֶֽלֶךְ־הַבָּשָׁ֨ן לִקְרָאתָ֜ם ה֧וּא וְכׇל־עַמּ֛וֹ לַמִּלְחָמָ֖ה אֶדְרֶֽעִי׃ וַיֹּ֨אמֶר יְהֹוָ֤ה אֶל־מֹשֶׁה֙ אַל־תִּירָ֣א אֹת֔וֹ כִּ֣י בְיָדְךָ֞ נָתַ֧תִּי אֹת֛וֹ וְאֶת־כׇּל־עַמּ֖וֹ וְאֶת־אַרְצ֑וֹ וְעָשִׂ֣יתָ לּ֔וֹ כַּאֲשֶׁ֣ר עָשִׂ֗יתָ לְסִיחֹן֙ מֶ֣לֶךְ הָֽאֱמֹרִ֔י אֲשֶׁ֥ר יוֹשֵׁ֖ב בְּחֶשְׁבּֽוֹן׃ וַיַּכּ֨וּ אֹת֤וֹ וְאֶת־בָּנָיו֙ וְאֶת־כׇּל־עַמּ֔וֹ עַד־בִּלְתִּ֥י הִשְׁאִֽיר־ל֖וֹ שָׂרִ֑יד וַיִּֽירְשׁ֖וּ אֶת־אַרְצֽוֹ׃ וַיִּסְע֖וּ בְּנֵ֣י יִשְׂרָאֵ֑ל וַֽיַּחֲנוּ֙ בְּעַֽרְב֣וֹת מוֹאָ֔ב מֵעֵ֖בֶר לְיַרְדֵּ֥ן יְרֵחֽוֹ׃

CLASSIC COMMENTATORS

Why would Moshe have been afraid of Og?

RASHI

Moshe worried that perhaps the merit of Avraham would help the king to prevail. Earlier, when "a fugitive came…to Avram the Hebrew" (Gen. 14:13), that was referring to Og. He is referred to there as a fugitive because he alone had escaped from among the Refaim, who had been defeated by Kedorlaomer and his allies at Ashterot Karnayim.

רש״י

שהיה משה ירא שמא תעמוד לו זכותו של אברהם, שנאמר: "ויבא הפליט" (בראשית י״ד:י״ג), הוא עוג שפלט מן הרפאים שהכו כדרלעומר וחבריו בעשתרת קרנים.

RAMBAN

Moshe had not considered conquering the lands of Siḥon and Og on behalf of Israel.… However, Siḥon challenged the nation in the wilderness and fought Israel against their will.… Og, on the other hand, assembled his army at the city of Edrei, situated on his border. At that point the Israelites could have turned aside and avoided the conflict, as they did with Esav's people. However, God assured Moshe that he need not fear Og and commanded him to battle Og, saying "I have given him into your hand."

רמב״ן

לא היה בדעתו של משה להוריש עתה לישראל ארץ סיחון ועוג … והנה סיחון יצא לקראת ישראל המדברה וילחם בם על כורחם … אבל עוג אסף כל חילו אדרעי, והיא עיר בקצה גבולו. והיה ישראל יכולים לנטות מעליו כאשר נטו מעל עשו, והשם אמר לו: אל תירא אותו ולך אצלו והתגר בו מלחמה, כי בידך נתתי אותו.

ABARBANEL

Moshe and the nation of Israel trembled in fear when they learned that Og was amassing for war against them. Since this challenge came after their defeat of the Amorites, Israel imagined that Og was not only fearless and undeterred by their victory, but that he was seeking revenge for the overthrow of Siḥon.

אברבנאל

משה וכל ישראל פחד קראם ורעדה, בחשבם שבהיות עוג יוצא לקראתם אחרי נצחון מלך האמורי, לא היה אלא מפני שאמיץ לבו בגיבורים וחם לבו בקרבו לנקום את נקמת סיחון.

MORE QUICK BITES

- **21:2** In this short incident there are three sets of words which are doubled. 1) אם נתן נתן (2, וישב ממנו שבי, and 3) וידר ישראל נדר. The first set describes the actions of the Canaanites, who took captives; the second describes *Benei Yisrael*'s response, taking a vow; the third describes what *Benei Yisrael* hope that God will do, that is, to "give" the Canaanites into their hands. The incident closes with a final language triple around the word חרם – it is the climax of the story, in which *Benei Yisrael* follow through on their promise to dedicate everything from the battle to God, who helped them win.

- **21:5** The complaint about bread and water seems absurd – didn't God provide for their daily sustenance? Rabbeinu Bahya suggests that they were distressed by being reliant on God – they wanted to be self-sufficient.

- **21:34** At first glance it does not seem like the destruction of Siḥon and Og was part of the original plan. After all, if Amon or Moav would have allowed *Benei Yisrael* to pass through then there would never have been a battle with Siḥon and Og. Looking ahead, however, it becomes clear that the destruction of these two kings had a profound effect – all the other nations in the area, including the Canaanites, began to fear *Benei Yisrael*. That fear would make the conquest of the land of Israel easier.

EXPLORING HASHKAFA
Do Mitzvot Make Sense?

"Why should I do this? It sounds ridiculous!"

Ever since there were mitzvot there was the question of whether we should try to understand them or not. Some argue that the very process of trying to find meaning is illegitimate – who are we, as puny humans with limited intellect, that we should think that we can possibly understand God's infinite thoughts? On the other end of the spectrum are those who argue that the mitzvot don't represent the totality of God's thoughts, only those which are meaningful to humans, so that the whole point of the mitzvot is to understand them and that we would be missing out on God's message to us if we did not try to understand them.

Between those two extremes there are many questions. For example, are the mitzvot an expression of God's wisdom or of His kindness and compassion? You may be familiar with all sorts of statements from the Talmud that lean one way or the other, and this is an important question. If the mitzvot are an expression of God's wisdom, it may be difficult to learn from them, but if they are an expression of His compassion, then we can definitely learn those values. When people say about some behavior that, "it doesn't feel right," even though they can't prove that it is forbidden, they are reflecting the sense that the mitzvot point them in a certain direction and that this behavior seems to violate that general direction. It is this sense of the spirit of the mitzvot which likely prompted much of the legislation of the Rabbis – there was a sense that Shabbat needed to "feel" a certain way, or that *kashrut* or interpersonal mitzvot were meant to convey a certain value, and they added legislation to promote and preserve those values. That is what is called כל דתיקון רבנן כעין דאורייתא תיקון, meaning that whenever the Rabbis legislated they were following the spirit of the Torah's laws.

There is the possibility that all of the above are correct. The Torah uses multiple words to describe God's commands – תורה, מצוות, עדות, חוקים, משפטים – and there are many different explanations as to what each means. Regardless of what the specifics of each one are, it does seem that there are different types of commands. Perhaps some are an expression of God's infinite wisdom, some are designed to make us better people, some are designed to teach us values, and some are meant to help us identify with our nation and its history. With that idea, it seems like we can try to learn from the mitzvot and try to understand what they are trying to accomplish. That being said, when there are things that we don't understand or which seem to us to be absurd, perhaps we could all use a dose of humility. Maybe we cannot understand the depth of God's thought. And maybe, we are not yet ready to understand

פרשת בלק
PARASHAT BALAK

> "Dark times lie ahead of us and there will be a time when
> we must choose between what is easy and what is right."
> J. K. Rowling, *Harry Potter and the Goblet of Fire*

From ancient Egyptian pottery fragments to recently discovered Hebrew "curse" tablets dating back nearly three thousand years, invoking divine power to curse one's enemies was a common practice in the time of Tanakh. Balak, king of Moav, sought out the most powerful prophet of his time to curse *Benei Yisrael*, whom he regarded as a mortal enemy. Little did he know that the power to curse or bless rests only in the hands of God.

PARASHAT BALAK

> **22:2–6** *Having earlier rebuffed Benei Yisrael and heard reports of the defeat of the two mighty kings, Siḥon and Og, at the hands of Benei Yisrael, Balak king of Moav is gripped by fear now that Benei Yisrael has camped on his northern border. He sends messengers to hire the well-known sorcerer, Bilam, to curse Benei Yisrael, so that he can chase them away.*

22 **2** And Balak son of Tzipor had seen all that the Israelites had done to the Amorites. The Moabites were in deep dread of the people because they were so numerous. Fearful of **4** the Israelites, the Moabites said to the elders of Midyan, "This horde will now lick up everything around us, as an ox licks up grass in the field." Balak son of Tzipor was king **5** of Moav at that time. He sent messengers to summon Bilam son of Beor who was at Petor near the River in his native land: "A people has come out of Egypt, and now they **6** cover the face of the land – and they have settled down alongside me. Please, come now and curse this people for me, for they are stronger than I. Perhaps then I will be able to defeat them and drive them from the land, for I know that whomsoever you

TEXTUAL SKILLS

1. What similarities can you find between verse 3 and Exodus 1:9–12? In what way does verse 6 here present a motive which is exactly the opposite of the one in Exodus?
2. The Rabbis in the Talmud and Midrash often compare and contrast Bilam and Avraham. What line in verse 6 reminds you of a similar line used to describe Avraham? In what way are they different?
3. In what way is Balak's fear a fulfillment of the Song at the Sea (Ex. 15:1–19)?
4. Balak describes *Benei Yisrael* as a people who left Egypt. When you think about this in the context of Numbers, why is this an unusual description?

WISDOM OF THE HEART

Why should we have been concerned if Bilam uttered a curse? Does he have a power to curse that is independent of God's will? Some sages – like Ramban and Ralbag – believe that there are forces in the universe which can be manipulated by those who know how to access them and which can bring harm to those who are being cursed. Others, like Naftali Tzvi Yehuda Berlin (Netziv), think that while there are no "black magic" powers, the power of the evil eye is built into the natural world, so that if Bilam saw the people he could use those natural forces. Still others, like Ibn Kaspi, believe that the real damage was psychological. It's not that there are dark forces, rather, there are people who believe that those forces exist. If they were to hear that a powerful sorcerer cursed them, it would cause them to despair and lose hope.

What would you do differently in your life if you believed that there were mysterious forces which could be manipulated to affect people and their fate?

פרשת בלק

כב ‏וַיַּרְא בָּלָק בֶּן־צִפּוֹר אֵת כָּל־אֲשֶׁר־עָשָׂה יִשְׂרָאֵל לָאֱמֹרִי: וַיָּגָר יט
מוֹאָב מִפְּנֵי הָעָם מְאֹד כִּי רַב־הוּא וַיָּקָץ מוֹאָב מִפְּנֵי בְּנֵי יִשְׂרָאֵל:
וַיֹּאמֶר מוֹאָב אֶל־זִקְנֵי מִדְיָן עַתָּה יְלַחֲכוּ הַקָּהָל אֶת־כָּל־ ד
סְבִיבֹתֵינוּ כִּלְחֹךְ הַשּׁוֹר אֵת יֶרֶק הַשָּׂדֶה וּבָלָק בֶּן־צִפּוֹר מֶלֶךְ
לְמוֹאָב בָּעֵת הַהִוא: וַיִּשְׁלַח מַלְאָכִים אֶל־בִּלְעָם בֶּן־בְּעוֹר ה
פְּתוֹרָה אֲשֶׁר עַל־הַנָּהָר אֶרֶץ בְּנֵי־עַמּוֹ לִקְרֹא־לוֹ לֵאמֹר הִנֵּה
עַם יָצָא מִמִּצְרַיִם הִנֵּה כִסָּה אֶת־עֵין הָאָרֶץ וְהוּא יֹשֵׁב מִמֻּלִי:
וְעַתָּה לְכָה־נָּא אָרָה־לִּי אֶת־הָעָם הַזֶּה כִּי־עָצוּם הוּא מִמֶּנִּי ו
אוּלַי אוּכַל נַכֶּה־בּוֹ וַאֲגָרְשֶׁנּוּ מִן־הָאָרֶץ כִּי יָדַעְתִּי אֵת אֲשֶׁר־

CLASSIC COMMENTATORS

Balak sends a message to "Bilam son of Beor who was at Petor near the River in his native land." That is a complicated description. What does the detail tell us, and in whose "native land" was Bilam?

RASHI — רש"י

This refers to Balak's native land, where the king grew up. And Bilam used to prophesy and say to him: Some day you will become king.

ארץ בני עמו – של בלק. משם היה, וזה היה מתנבא ואומר לו: עתיד אתה למלוך.

RABBI YOSEF BEKHOR SHOR — ר' יוסף בכור שור

The native land was Bilam's own country.

ארץ בני עמו – של בלעם.

RABBI SAMSON RAPHAEL HIRSCH — ר' שמשון רפאל הירש

Balak sent messengers to Aram, which was in the district of the Euphrates River. For that was where the forefather of this terrifying and wondrous nation had been born.

שלח בלק שלוחים לארם שבמחוז הפרת, למולדת אבותיו של עם מטיל-אימה פועל-נפלאות זה.

QUESTIONS FOR THOUGHT

- According to each of the above commentaries, to whose "native land" did Balak send messengers?
- For each of the commentaries, why is this information significant?
- Looking at the text, there is another nation mentioned here, Midyan. Is Midyan connected to Balak or to Bilam, and in what way are they connected?

22:7–14 *When the representatives of Moav and Midyan present their request to Bilam, he asks them to wait overnight before he can respond so that he can get direction from God. After Bilam tells God what he is being asked to do, God tells him not to go, since the nation that they want to curse is actually blessed. Bilam relays God's response to the messengers, who report back to Balak.*

7 bless is blessed and whomsoever you curse is cursed." So the elders of Moav and Midyan went, carrying with them payment for divination. They came to Bilam and repeated 8 Balak's words to him. "Spend the night here," he said, "and I will give you your reply the 9 Lord speaks to me." So the princes of Moav stayed the night with Bilam. God came to 10 Bilam and said, "Who are these men with you?" And Bilam replied to God, "Balak son 11 of Tzipor, king of Moav, has sent me a message: 'A people has come out of Egypt and covers the face of the land. Now come and curse them for me. Perhaps I will be able to 12 fight against them and drive them away.'" "Do not go with them," said God to Bilam. 13 "Do not curse this people, for they are blessed." Then Bilam arose in the morning and said to Balak's princes, "Go back to your land, because the Lord has refused to let me 14 go with you." The princes of Moav rose and went to Balak and said, "Bilam refuses to

QUESTIONS FOR THOUGHT

- In what way are the suggestions of Rashi and Ibn Ezra similar?
- According to both Rashi and Ibn Ezra, sending the wizarding tools was a way to convince Bilam to accept the job. Which of these two commentators explains why they were concerned with what Bilam would say? Which of them understands that the messengers had a high regard for Bilam's professionalism?
- Bekhor Shor cites a dramatically different approach than the other two. What forced him into making this claim? What is the greatest difficulty with his explanation?

WISDOM OF THE HEART

There are two great mistakes that we as people make in understanding our abilities. One is arrogance, overestimating our abilities. This leads to unnecessary and unhealthy competition, as people seek to take on positions for which they are not qualified. It also causes people to stagnate, since if they do not recognize their weaknesses they can never improve them. The other great mistake is underestimating our abilities. It prevents us from accomplishing what we truly can and generates low self-esteem, which is so damaging. This is true of groups as well. As a nation, it is easy for the chosen people to fall into the trap of arrogance, thinking that we are innately better than others. That can hold us back from improving ourselves. But it is just as easy to think that we are small and unworthy, which can lead to hopelessness and despair. God reminds us frequently in the Torah that we are blessed.

Which do you think holds you back more – arrogance or low self-esteem?
How can being aware of it help you move forward?

ז תֵּבָרֵךְ מְבֹרָךְ וַאֲשֶׁר תָּאֹר יוּאָר: וַיֵּלְכוּ זִקְנֵי מוֹאָב וְזִקְנֵי מִדְיָן וּקְסָמִים בְּיָדָם וַיָּבֹאוּ אֶל־בִּלְעָם וַיְדַבְּרוּ אֵלָיו דִּבְרֵי בָלָק:
ח וַיֹּאמֶר אֲלֵיהֶם לִינוּ פֹה הַלַּיְלָה וַהֲשִׁבֹתִי אֶתְכֶם דָּבָר כַּאֲשֶׁר יְדַבֵּר יְהוָה אֵלָי וַיֵּשְׁבוּ שָׂרֵי־מוֹאָב עִם־בִּלְעָם: ט וַיָּבֹא אֱלֹהִים אֶל־בִּלְעָם וַיֹּאמֶר מִי הָאֲנָשִׁים הָאֵלֶּה עִמָּךְ: י וַיֹּאמֶר בִּלְעָם אֶל־הָאֱלֹהִים בָּלָק בֶּן־צִפֹּר מֶלֶךְ מוֹאָב שָׁלַח אֵלָי: יא הִנֵּה הָעָם הַיֹּצֵא מִמִּצְרַיִם וַיְכַס אֶת־עֵין הָאָרֶץ עַתָּה לְכָה קָבָה־לִּי אֹתוֹ אוּלַי אוּכַל לְהִלָּחֶם בּוֹ וְגֵרַשְׁתִּיו: יב וַיֹּאמֶר אֱלֹהִים אֶל־בִּלְעָם לֹא תֵלֵךְ עִמָּהֶם לֹא תָאֹר אֶת־הָעָם כִּי בָרוּךְ הוּא: יג וַיָּקָם בִּלְעָם בַּבֹּקֶר וַיֹּאמֶר אֶל־שָׂרֵי בָלָק לְכוּ אֶל־אַרְצְכֶם כִּי מֵאֵן יְהוָה לְתִתִּי לַהֲלֹךְ עִמָּכֶם: יד וַיָּקוּמוּ שָׂרֵי מוֹאָב וַיָּבֹאוּ אֶל־בָּלָק

CLASSIC COMMENTATORS

The Torah says that the representatives of Moav and Midyan went to Bilam bringing קסמים, literally, "tools used for wizardry." Why would they need to bring wizarding tools to the greatest sorcerer in the region?

RASHI
רש"י
כל מיני קסמים, שלא יאמר: אין כלי תשמישי עמי.

The messengers carried with them all sorts of instruments for performing divination, lest Bilam protest that he lacked the proper tools to do what they wanted.

IBN EZRA
אבן עזרא
כמשמעו, וספר הכתוב ששלח אל קוסם קוסמים כמוהו.

Indeed, this should be taken literally. The text teaches that Balak sent sorcerers like the wizard Bilam to him.

RABBI YOSEF BEKHOR SHOR
ר' יוסף בכור שור
יש מפרשים שכר קסמים בידם. וראיתי כתוב בתרגום ירושלמי: ואגרתא דקסמיא', והיינו שכר הקסמים.

Some commentators claim that Balak sent the payment for divination to Bilam. Similarly, I have seen that Targum Yerushalmi renders this as: with the wizardry payment in their hands.

22:15–20 *Undeterred by Bilam's refusal, Balak sends another delegation – larger and more impressive than the first, promising Bilam great glory and inviting Bilam to name his price. Bilam's initial response is that no amount of money will sway his decision, as he cannot defy God's will. Nonetheless, Bilam is willing to ask God again. When he does, God tells him that he may go, but that he is bound to do as God says.*

15 go with us." Balak then sent other princes, yet more numerous and eminent than the
16 first. They came to Bilam and said to him, "This is what Balak son of Tzipor says: 'Do
17 not let anything prevent you from coming to me, for I will do you great honor, and
18 whatever else you ask of me. Please – come and curse this people for me.'" Bilam replied
   to Balak's servants, "Even if Balak were to give me his palace full of silver and gold, I
19 could not do anything, small or great, to transgress the word of the Lord my God. But
   now, you too remain here tonight so that I may know what else the Lord may tell me."
20 God came to Bilam that night and said to him, "If the men have come to summon you,

QUESTIONS FOR THOUGHT

- Find one support in the text for the position of R. Se'adya Gaon.
- Find one refutation in the text to the position of R. Se'adya Gaon.
- Which of the above two opinions do you think fits best in the text of the Torah? Why do you think that?
- Can you think of a different reason that God might have given two seemingly opposite responses to Bilam's question?

TEXTUAL SKILLS

1. Who is not included in the second delegation sent to Bilam but was in the first?
2. What phrase in verse 18 would we not expect to be coming out of Bilam's mouth?

WISDOM OF THE HEART

God initially told Bilam not to go with Balak's messengers, but then seemingly changed His mind. Even stranger is that when Bilam does go, God is angry with him. The Gaon of Vilna explains that that there are two different Hebrew words, עִם and אֶת, both of which we translate as "with," but which actually have very different meanings. One kind of "going with" (אֶת) can be compared to multiple people traveling on the same airplane. Even though they start and finish their trips in the same airports and are traveling with each other, they share very little outside of that. The other "going with" (עִם) can be compared to two players on a team. When they step onto the court or field, they share common goal and work together to accomplish them. God told Bilam not to join Balak's team, but did allow him to go on the trip with them, since God's plan was to have Bilam bless *Benei Yisrael*, while their goal was to have him curse them. Bilam, however, wanted to join their team (he went עִם Balak's emissaries), and that sparked God's displeasure with him.

Do you sometimes join a group, not because you really want to be with them but because you think that you can gain something from being with them? How do you feel when others do that to you?

טו וַיֹּאמְרוּ מֵאֵן בִּלְעָם הֲלֹךְ עִמָּנוּ: וַיֹּסֶף עוֹד בָּלָק שְׁלֹחַ שָׂרִים
טז רַבִּים וְנִכְבָּדִים מֵאֵלֶּה: וַיָּבֹאוּ אֶל־בִּלְעָם וַיֹּאמְרוּ לוֹ כֹּה אָמַר
יז בָּלָק בֶּן־צִפּוֹר אַל־נָא תִמָּנַע מֵהֲלֹךְ אֵלָי: כִּי־כַבֵּד אֲכַבֶּדְךָ
מְאֹד וְכֹל אֲשֶׁר־תֹּאמַר אֵלַי אֶעֱשֶׂה וּלְכָה־נָּא קָבָה־לִּי אֵת
יח הָעָם הַזֶּה: וַיַּעַן בִּלְעָם וַיֹּאמֶר אֶל־עַבְדֵי בָלָק אִם־יִתֶּן־לִי בָלָק
מְלֹא בֵיתוֹ כֶּסֶף וְזָהָב לֹא אוּכַל לַעֲבֹר אֶת־פִּי יְהֹוָה אֱלֹהָי
יט לַעֲשׂוֹת קְטַנָּה אוֹ גְדוֹלָה: וְעַתָּה שְׁבוּ נָא בָזֶה גַּם־אַתֶּם הַלָּיְלָה
כ וְאֵדְעָה מַה־יֹּסֵף יְהֹוָה דַּבֵּר עִמִּי: וַיָּבֹא אֱלֹהִים ׀ אֶל־בִּלְעָם
לַיְלָה וַיֹּאמֶר לוֹ אִם־לִקְרֹא לְךָ בָּאוּ הָאֲנָשִׁים קוּם לֵךְ אִתָּם

CLASSIC COMMENTATORS

Why did God initially deny permission for Bilam to go and then reverse that decision?

RAV SE'ADYA GAON

The reader might protest: How could God first forbid Bilam to leave with the messengers, but then say to him, "You may get up and go with them"? The explanation is that the Almighty did not want Bilam to accede to the first group of messengers, but waited for a more illustrious delegation to escort him to Balak.

ר' סעדיה גאון

אם יטעון טוען ויאמר, אחר שאמר השם: לא תלך עמהם, איך אמר: קום לך אתם? יש להשיב: כי השם לא רצה שילך עם הראשונים, עד שיבואו שרים נכבדים מהם.

RAMBAN

Said God to Bilam: I have already explained to you that Israel is a blessed nation and that you are powerless to curse them. And yet now a second delegation has arrived. If their task is merely to accompany you to their king, and if they agree to the previously stated condition that you cannot curse Israel, then "you may get up and go with them; but do only what I tell you to do." Meaning: even if I instruct you to *bless* Israel you must do so, without fear of Balak's repercussions. This, then, is the sense of the term *im* at the start of the verse: *If* the men have come [only] to summon you, you may go. Furthermore, it had been God's wish all along that Bilam leave with the messengers after informing them that he would not curse Israel, and stressing to them that he was bound to obey the will of God. For it was the wish of the Almighty that Israel should be blessed by this prophet of the nations.

רמב"ן

כבר הודעתיך כי העם ברוך הוא ולא תוכל לקללם, ועתה חזרו לפניך בלבד באו, כלומר שיתרצו בלכתך עמהם על מנת שלא לקלל את העם כאשר הודעתם מתחלה, קום לך אתם ואך את הדבר אשר אדבר אליך אותו תעשה, שאף אם אצוה אותך לברך שתברכם, ולא תירא מבלק. וזה טעם: אם. וכן היה החפץ לשם הנכבד מתחלה שילך עמהם אחרי הודיעו אותם שלא יקללם, וישתנהג בענינם כאשר יצוה, כי הרצון לפניו יתברך שיברך את ישראל מפי נביא לגוים.

BEMIDBAR | CHAPTER 22 — BALAK | 214

> **22:21–27** *In the morning, Bilam goes with the delegation from Moav. God is angry that Bilam goes, and sends a terrifying angel which appears to Bilam's donkey. Frightened, the donkey veers off the path into the field, and Bilam strikes her. As the donkey turns onto a narrow path the angel again blocks her, and as she squeezes against a wall Bilam's leg gets squeezed as well. He hits her again. The third time the angel appears there is no place for the donkey to move, so she sits, and gets beaten by Bilam with a stick.*

21 you may get up and go with them; but do only what I tell you to do." So Bilam rose in
22 the morning, saddled his donkey, and went along with the princes of Moav. God was furious at his going, and an angel of the Lord stood in the road to oppose him as he
23 was riding on his donkey, his two servants with him. The donkey saw the angel of the Lord standing in the road, drawn sword in hand, and she swerved from the road into
24 a field. And Bilam beat the donkey to urge her back onto the road. Then the angel of the Lord was standing in a narrow path between vineyards with a wall on either side.
25 When the donkey saw the angel of the Lord, she pressed against the wall, crushing
26 Bilam's foot against it. He beat her once again. And the angel of the Lord went ahead
27 and stood in a narrow place where there was no room at all to turn right or left. When the donkey saw the angel of the Lord, she lay down under Bilam. Bilam was furious

---

QUESTIONS FOR THOUGHT

- Regarding what do the above commentaries agree?
- Which of the above commentaries inserts a cynical tone into someone's words?
- Inserting punctuation or a tone of voice can be a very powerful tool for interpreting a written text. Can you think of how it could be used improperly?
- Reading Bilam's words, do you think that Bilam believed that he could "trick" God and be able to curse *Benei Yisrael*?

TEXTUAL SKILLS

1. Bilam saddles his donkey and goes on a journey with two young boys assisting him. Of what similar scene from Genesis does this remind you?

2. The phrase חרבו שלופה בידו appears four times in Tanakh. Twice here, once in Joshua 5:13, and once in I Chronicles 21:16. What do they all have in common?

WISDOM OF THE HEART

There is a long-standing tradition to view Bilam as fundamentally evil. After all, in the end he offered a suggestion which brought great damage to *Benei Yisrael*, and he is related to later in Tanakh as one who conspired against *Benei Yisrael*. Yet when we look at the text of the Torah by itself, it is not clear at all that he started out evil. Look at what Bilam says – he cannot agree to go to Balak if God does not give him permission, and at every step along the way he reiterates to Balak that he is powerless to harm the people that God has blessed. Perhaps the Torah is trying to highlight that there is a fine line between good and evil, and that it is up to us to ensure that the qualities we desire are nurtured and developed properly.

Have you ever been exposed to someone who used their capabilities for good and then used those same capabilities for bad, or vice versa?

כא וַיֹּ֣אמֶר אֶת־הַדָּבָ֥ר אֲשֶׁר־אֲדַבֵּ֖ר אֵלֶ֣יךָ אֹת֣וֹ תַעֲשֶׂ֑ה וַיָּ֥קָם בִּלְעָ֖ם *שלישי*
כב בַּבֹּ֔קֶר וַֽיַּחֲבֹ֖שׁ אֶת־אֲתֹנ֑וֹ וַיֵּ֖לֶךְ עִם־שָׂרֵ֥י מוֹאָֽב: וַיִּֽחַר־אַ֣ף אֱלֹהִים֮ כִּֽי־הוֹלֵ֣ךְ הוּא֒ וַיִּתְיַצֵּ֞ב מַלְאַ֧ךְ יְהֹוָ֛ה בַּדֶּ֖רֶךְ לְשָׂטָ֣ן ל֑וֹ וְה֣וּא רֹכֵ֣ב
כג עַל־אֲתֹנ֔וֹ וּשְׁנֵ֥י נְעָרָ֖יו עִמּֽוֹ: וַתֵּ֣רֶא הָאָתוֹן֩ אֶת־מַלְאַ֨ךְ יְהֹוָ֜ה נִצָּ֣ב בַּדֶּ֗רֶךְ וְחַרְבּ֤וֹ שְׁלוּפָה֙ בְּיָד֔וֹ וַתֵּ֤ט הָֽאָתוֹן֙ מִן־הַדֶּ֔רֶךְ וַתֵּ֖לֶךְ
כד בַּשָּׂדֶ֑ה וַיַּ֤ךְ בִּלְעָם֙ אֶת־הָ֣אָת֔וֹן לְהַטֹּתָ֖הּ הַדָּֽרֶךְ: וַֽיַּעֲמֹד֙ מַלְאַ֣ךְ
כה יְהֹוָ֔ה בְּמִשְׁע֖וֹל הַכְּרָמִ֑ים גָּדֵ֥ר מִזֶּ֖ה וְגָדֵ֥ר מִזֶּֽה: וַתֵּ֨רֶא הָאָת֜וֹן אֶת־מַלְאַ֣ךְ יְהֹוָ֗ה וַתִּלָּחֵץ֙ אֶל־הַקִּ֔יר וַתִּלְחַ֛ץ אֶת־רֶ֥גֶל בִּלְעָ֖ם
כו אֶל־הַקִּ֑יר וַיֹּ֖סֶף לְהַכֹּתָֽהּ: וַיּ֥וֹסֶף מַלְאַךְ־יְהֹוָ֖ה עֲב֑וֹר וַֽיַּעֲמֹד֙
כז בְּמָק֣וֹם צָ֔ר אֲשֶׁ֛ר אֵֽין־דֶּ֥רֶךְ לִנְט֖וֹת יָמִ֥ין וּשְׂמֹֽאול: וַתֵּ֤רֶא הָֽאָתוֹן֙ אֶת־מַלְאַ֣ךְ יְהֹוָ֔ה וַתִּרְבַּ֖ץ תַּ֣חַת בִּלְעָ֑ם וַיִּֽחַר־אַ֣ף בִּלְעָ֔ם וַיַּ֥ךְ

CLASSIC COMMENTATORS

If God told Bilam that he could go with the delegates from Moav, why did God get angry when he actually went?

RABBI YOSEF BEKHOR SHOR

Even though God granted Bilam permission to go with Balak's messengers, the sorcerer's actions betrayed his evil motives. For if he had truly planned on fulfilling God's command, he would have said to this delegation: Since I have no intention of cursing Israel and will never honor Balak's requests, why should I bother leaving home? Does it make sense to go to his land just to argue with him? The fact that Bilam set out on the journey proves that he hoped to curse Israel even without the Almighty's approval.

RABBI YOSEF IBN KASPI

A person's words commonly hold conflicting meanings – their tone of voice reveals whether their statement is meant to be taken at face value or sarcastically. There are many such cases throughout the Bible. For example, consider the verse which states, "Who was it that said, 'Should Sha'ul reign over us?'" (I Sam. 11:12).... In the present instance as well, even though God had said to Bilam, "get up and go with them," it should have been clear to the prophet that God uttered these words out of anger and unwillingness to let Bilam go.

ר' יוסף בכור שור

אף על פי שנתן לו רשות לילך, מחשבתו הרעה נכרת מתוך מעשיו, שאם היה דעתו לעשות מצות המקום, היה לו לומר: מאחר שלא אקלל ולא אעשה מה שהוא מבקש, למה אלך, וכי אלך להתקוטט עמו בארצו? אלא ודאי מה שהיה הולך, דעתו היה לקללם שלא ברשות המקום.

ר' יוסף אבן כספי

הדבור האחד יש לו הוראות מתנגדות, מצד הערת המדבר אם ברצוי אם בהפך, ורבים כן בכל המקרא כמו שכתוב על דרך משל מי האומר שאול ימלוך עלינו (שמואל א י"א:י"ב) ... לכן אף על פי שאמר השם לבלעם: קום לך אתם, היתה צורת הדבור בצאתו מפיו דרך כעס והעדר הרצוי.

28 and beat the donkey with his stick. Then the LORD opened the donkey's mouth and – "What have I done to you," she said to Bilam, "that you have struck me these three
29 times?" "You are playing games with me," said Bilam to the donkey. "If only I had a
30 sword in my hand, I would kill you here and now." But the donkey said to Bilam, "Am I not your donkey on whom you have always ridden to this day? Have I been in the
31 habit of doing this to you?" "No," he replied. Then the LORD uncovered Bilam's eyes, and he saw the angel of the LORD standing in the road, drawn sword in hand. He bowed
32 and prostrated himself facedown. The angel of the LORD said to him, "Why have you beaten your donkey these three times? It was I who came out here to oppose you,
33 because your way is perverse to me. The donkey saw me and turned away from me these three times. If she had not turned away from me, I would certainly have killed you by
34 now and let her live." Bilam said to the angel of the LORD, "I have sinned, for I did not

---

ר' עובדיה ספורנו

ויפתח ה' את פי האתון: נתן בה כח לדבר כענין ה' שפתי תפתח. וכל זה היה כדי שיתעורר בלעם לשוב בתשובה בזכרו כי מה' מענה לשון גם לבלתי מוכן.

RABBI OVADYA SFORNO

God granted the donkey the ability to talk, similar to the verse which states, "O LORD, open my lips, and my mouth will declare Your praise" (Ps. 51:17). God orchestrated this incident to convince Bilam to repent by showing him that God grants His creatures the power of speech, even when the individual is unprepared to speak.

QUESTIONS FOR THOUGHT

- Which commentaries do not believe that there was a miracle at all?
- What challenge from the text do those commentaries need to deal with?
- According to those who say it was a miracle, why do they think that God deemed it necessary?
- What challenge (not from the text) would you present to both of those commentators?
- Ramban's comment reminds us of Exodus 4:11. Why might you learn from that?

WISDOM OF THE HEART

There are those who suggest that Bilam's power was his ability to look deeply into a person and tap into that insight while connecting to mystical powers in the universe. R. Menahem Recanati, a thirteenth-century mystic, suggested that just as we can destroy people by capitalizing on and highlighting their weaknesses, so too can we build people up by identifying and championing their strengths. In simple terms, a nasty look or a scowl can ruin someone's day, but a smile can make the loneliest person feel welcomed and loved.

**Imagine someone sitting in a corner at some event.
Is she aloof and arrogant, or just shy?
How can you find out?**

אֶת־הָאָת֖וֹן בַּמַּקֵּֽל: וַיִּפְתַּ֤ח יְהֹוָה֙ אֶת־פִּ֣י הָאָת֔וֹן וַתֹּ֥אמֶר לְבִלְעָ֖ם כח
מֶה־עָשִׂ֣יתִי לְךָ֔ כִּ֣י הִכִּיתָ֔נִי זֶ֖ה שָׁלֹ֥שׁ רְגָלִֽים: וַיֹּ֨אמֶר בִּלְעָ֜ם כט
לָאָת֗וֹן כִּ֤י הִתְעַלַּ֙לְתְּ֙ בִּ֔י ל֥וּ יֶשׁ־חֶ֙רֶב֙ בְּיָדִ֔י כִּ֥י עַתָּ֖ה הֲרַגְתִּֽיךְ:
וַתֹּ֨אמֶר הָאָת֜וֹן אֶל־בִּלְעָ֗ם הֲלוֹא֩ אָנֹכִ֨י אֲתֹֽנְךָ֜ אֲשֶׁר־רָכַ֣בְתָּ ל
עָלַ֗י מֵעֽוֹדְךָ֙ עַד־הַיּ֣וֹם הַזֶּ֔ה הַֽהַסְכֵּ֣ן הִסְכַּ֔נְתִּי לַעֲשׂ֥וֹת לְךָ֖ כֹּ֑ה
וַיֹּ֖אמֶר לֹֽא: וַיְגַ֣ל יְהֹוָה֮ אֶת־עֵינֵ֣י בִלְעָם֒ וַיַּ֞רְא אֶת־מַלְאַ֤ךְ יְהֹוָה֙ לא
נִצָּ֣ב בַּדֶּ֔רֶךְ וְחַרְבּ֥וֹ שְׁלֻפָ֖ה בְּיָד֑וֹ וַיִּקֹּ֥ד וַיִּשְׁתַּ֖חוּ לְאַפָּֽיו: וַיֹּ֤אמֶר לב
אֵלָיו֙ מַלְאַ֣ךְ יְהֹוָ֔ה עַל־מָ֗ה הִכִּ֙יתָ֙ אֶת־אֲתֹ֣נְךָ֔ זֶ֖ה שָׁל֣וֹשׁ רְגָלִ֑ים
הִנֵּ֤ה אָנֹכִי֙ יָצָ֣אתִי לְשָׂטָ֔ן כִּֽי־יָרַ֥ט הַדֶּ֖רֶךְ לְנֶגְדִּֽי: וַתִּרְאַ֙נִי֙ הָֽאָת֔וֹן לג
וַתֵּ֣ט לְפָנַ֔י זֶ֖ה שָׁלֹ֣שׁ רְגָלִ֑ים אוּלַי֙ נָטְתָ֣ה מִפָּנַ֔י כִּ֥י עַתָּ֛ה גַּם־אֹתְכָ֥ה
הָרַ֖גְתִּי וְאוֹתָ֥הּ הֶחֱיֵֽיתִי: וַיֹּ֨אמֶר בִּלְעָ֜ם אֶל־מַלְאַ֤ךְ יְהֹוָה֙ חָטָ֔אתִי לד
כִּ֚י לֹ֣א יָדַ֔עְתִּי כִּ֥י אַתָּ֛ה נִצָּ֥ב לִקְרָאתִ֖י בַּדָּ֑רֶךְ וְעַתָּ֛ה אִם־רַ֥ע

CLASSIC COMMENTATORS

Did the donkey actually speak and, if so, why was this extraordinary miracle necessary?

RAV SE'ADYA GAON

ר' סעדיה גאון

It was the angel who addressed Bilam, but because he was positioned next to the donkey, it seemed as though the animal itself was talking.

המלאך דבר בסמוך לאתון, ודימה בלעם כי היא דברה.

RABBI YOSEF IBN KASPI

ר' יוסף אבן כספי

This entire episode took place within a prophetic vision. In reality the donkey never spoke a word.

היה כל זה במראה הנבואה ולא דברה האתון כלל.

RAMBAN

רמב"ן

God performed this miracle in order to show Bilam that it is He who gives man the power of speech, and that He can cause even the mute to speak. Conversely, God can silence people who wish to talk.

וטעם הנס הזה, להראות לבלעם מי שם פה לאדם או מי ישום אילם, להודיעו כי השם פותח פי הנאלמים, וכל שכן שיאלם ברצונו פי המדברים.

22:35–40 *The angel directs Bilam to continue his journey, reminding him that Bilam will only be able to say what God tells him to. When Bilam arrives in Moav he is greeted by Balak, who reprimands him for not coming sooner. Bilam notes that he did come, but that he is limited by what God places into his mouth. Together they go to Kiryat Ḥutzot, where Balak offers sacrifices and sends something to Bilam and his entourage.*

know that you were standing against me in the road. Now, if you consider it wrong, I will go back." The angel of the Lord said to Bilam, "Go with the men, but say nothing except what I tell you." So Bilam continued on with Balak's princes. When Balak heard that Bilam was coming, he went out to meet him at the city of Moav, at the Arnon border on the edge of his territory. Balak said to Bilam, "Did I not send to summon you? Why did you not come to me? Am I really not able to offer you any honor?" Bilam replied to Balak, "Well, I have come to you now. But can I speak any words I choose? I can only say the word God puts into my mouth." Then Bilam went with Balak and they came to

QUESTIONS FOR THOUGHT

- In what way are the comments of Sforno and the Gaon of Vilna exactly the opposite of R. Hirsch's explanation?
- Which of the explanations links the gift sent to Bilam with the sacrifices Balak brings?
- Which commentaries connect Balak's actions with what Bilam had just said to Balak?
- Honored guests usually have meals together with their hosts. Which commentaries could be understood as explaining why Bilam is not eating with Balak?

TEXTUAL SKILLS

1. Notice the differences between Bilam's description of his limitation (v. 35) and the way this was expressed by God (v. 20) or the angel (v. 35). Can you explain the reason for the change?

2. What similarity and difference do you see between Bilam's limitation and Lavan's limitation when speaking with Yaakov (Gen. 31:24–30)?

WISDOM OF THE HEART

Bilam's donkey plays a central role in the story. It is she who sees the angel, she who bears the brunt of Bilam's ignorance, and she who demonstrates to Bilam that there is no power independent of God – only those who are authorized to see can actually see. You would think that this donkey would have become a biblical heroine, and yet she is not. In fact, after this scene she disappears from the story. She is not even present when Bilam goes home. We never really understand the big picture. Sometimes people are put into this world for purposes that we cannot even imagine, and then they are gone. On a human level it is incomprehensible. And yet, perhaps we can consider that it is not their disappearance which should occupy our thoughts, but the fact that they were here at all. What might have been the purpose of their being brought into our lives? What could we learn from them?

Can you imagine your own existence as serving a purpose other than your own life? Would that be comforting for you or frustrating?

לה בְּעֵינֶ֖יךָ אָשֽׁוּבָה לִּֽי: וַיֹּ֨אמֶר מַלְאַ֤ךְ יְהֹוָה֙ אֶל־בִּלְעָ֔ם לֵ֖ךְ עִם־הָ֣אֲנָשִׁ֑ים וְאֶ֗פֶס אֶת־הַדָּבָ֛ר אֲשֶׁר־אֲדַבֵּ֥ר אֵלֶ֖יךָ אֹת֣וֹ תְדַבֵּ֑ר וַיֵּ֥לֶךְ
לו בִּלְעָ֖ם עִם־שָׂרֵ֥י בָלָֽק: וַיִּשְׁמַ֥ע בָּלָ֖ק כִּ֣י בָ֣א בִלְעָ֑ם וַיֵּצֵ֨א לִקְרָאת֜וֹ
לז אֶל־עִ֣יר מוֹאָ֗ב אֲשֶׁר֙ עַל־גְּב֣וּל אַרְנֹ֔ן אֲשֶׁ֖ר בִּקְצֵ֥ה הַגְּבֽוּל: וַיֹּ֨אמֶר בָּלָ֜ק אֶל־בִּלְעָ֗ם הֲלֹא֩ שָׁלֹ֨חַ שָׁלַ֤חְתִּי אֵלֶ֨יךָ֙ לִקְרֹא־לָ֔ךְ לָ֥מָּה
לח לֹא־הָלַ֖כְתָּ אֵלָ֑י הַֽאֻמְנָ֔ם לֹ֥א אוּכַ֖ל כַּבְּדֶֽךָ: וַיֹּ֨אמֶר בִּלְעָ֜ם אֶל־בָּלָ֗ק הִֽנֵּה־בָ֨אתִי֙ אֵלֶ֔יךָ עַתָּ֕ה הֲיָכֹ֥ל אוּכַ֖ל דַּבֵּ֣ר מְא֑וּמָה הַדָּבָ֗ר
לט אֲשֶׁ֨ר יָשִׂ֧ים אֱלֹהִ֛ים בְּפִ֖י אֹת֥וֹ אֲדַבֵּֽר: וַיֵּ֥לֶךְ בִּלְעָ֖ם עִם־בָּלָ֑ק
מ וַיָּבֹ֖אוּ קִרְיַ֥ת חֻצֽוֹת: וַיִּזְבַּ֥ח בָּלָ֖ק בָּקָ֣ר וָצֹ֑אן וַיְשַׁלַּ֣ח לְבִלְעָ֔ם

רביעי
/ששי/

CLASSIC COMMENTATORS

Balak offers sacrifices and sends something to Bilam and his entourage. Why is any of this relevant?

RABBI OVADYA SFORNO

In addition to the meal he served him, Balak sent Bilam a gift to honor him.

THE GAON OF VILNA

All of this was meant to honor Bilam. Balak first sent these items to Bilam, and then he offered the sacrifices on the altar.

RABBI SAMSON RAPHAEL HIRSCH

Curiously the text does not report that Balak laid out a feast for Bilam.... Apparently, the king was displeased with the prophet's introductory statement.

HAAMEK DAVAR

Balak understood that although Bilam would have a look at the people of Israel, he had been cautioned against cursing the nation. As such, Balak considered ways to change Bilam's mind, and nothing makes a man more compliant than being wined and dined.

ר׳ עובדה ספורנו

מנחת כבוד מלבד ארוחתו.

הגאון מווילנא

כולם לכבודו של בלעם ותחילה שלח אותם לבלעם ואחר כך הקריב הקרבנות על המזבח.

ר׳ שמשון רפאל הירש

לא נאמר "ויעש משתה"; הוא לא הזמינם לסעודה.... נראה שדברי בלעם לא מצאו חן בעיני בלק.

העמק דבר

באשר בלק התבונן ההכרח שבלעם יתן עינו על ישראל, אלא שהוא מוזהר על זה, ביקש עצות להעבירהו על אזהרתו, ואין עצה כאכילה ושתיה.

BEMIDBAR | CHAPTER 23 — BALAK

> **22:41–23:6** *Balak takes Bilam to Bamot Baal, where he sees the edge of the camp of Benei Yisrael. At Bilam's request Balak builds seven altars and prepares a bull and a ram for each, and together they offer the sacrifices. Bilam instructs Balak to stay with the sacrifices as he goes to get guidance from God about what to say.*

40 Kiryat Ḥutzot. Balak sacrificed oxen and sheep and sent them to Bilam and the princes
41 who were with him. In the morning Balak took Bilam up to Bamot Baal, where he could
23 1 see part of the people. Bilam said to Balak, "Build me seven altars here and prepare for
2 me seven bulls and seven rams." Balak did as Bilam said, and Balak and Bilam offered a
3 bull and a ram on each altar. Then Bilam said to Balak, "Stand by your offerings and I will go; perhaps the Lord will come to meet me. Whatever He shows me, I will tell
4 you." And he went off alone. God met Bilam, who said to Him, "I have prepared seven
5 altars; on each altar I have offered a bull and a ram." And the Lord put a word in Bilam's mouth, "Go back to Balak and say this."

QUESTIONS FOR THOUGHT

- In what way is the comment of Ibn Kaspi dramatically different from the other three?
- One of the commentaries understands that the number seven has mystical meaning, while another understands that it serves as a metaphor. Which commentaries express those positions? On what do they both agree?
- Which commentary tries to offer a rational explanation which fits the context of this story?
- These commentaries raise a basic question of whether Bilam has a deep understanding of God or if he is simply someone with whom God chose to communicate? A related question is whether Bilam's intentions were deeply evil (that is, he recognizes God and chooses to actively defy Him) or simply misguided? What do you think?
- Do you think that the Torah is interested in the character of Bilam, or is he simply part of a bigger story with a message that does not focus on him?

TEXTUAL SKILLS

1. What unusual word describes the interaction between God and Bilam in both verses 23:3 and 23:4?

2. What unusual thing does Bilam ask Balak to do in 23:3 (which 23:6 indicates that Balak actually does)?

WISDOM OF THE HEART

One of the recurring words throughout the story of Bilam's prophecy is the root ק-ר-ה, as in a happenstance. When God appears to Bilam the Torah describes it as ויקר. By contrast, the opening of Leviticus begins with God calling, ויקרא, to Moshe. That one little א makes all the difference between a prophet like Moshe and one like Bilam. While the text seems to suggest that God's revelations to these two key figures were very different in nature, R. Avraham of Sokhotchov suggests that it wasn't God's word which was different; rather, it was the prophets themselves who were different. God called to both in the same way. Moshe stepped into the prophecy to become who he was, but Bilam did not rise to the occasion and did not see prophecy as an invitation to be elevated.

Do you think that all people are given an equal chance to live meaningful and noble lives?

במדבר | פרק כג

מא וְלַשָּׂרִים אֲשֶׁר אִתּֽוֹ: וַיְהִי בַבֹּקֶר וַיִּקַּח בָּלָק אֶת־בִּלְעָם וַיַּעֲלֵהוּ
כג א בָּמוֹת בָּעַל וַיַּרְא מִשָּׁם קְצֵה הָעָם: וַיֹּאמֶר בִּלְעָם אֶל־בָּלָק
בְּנֵה־לִי בָזֶה שִׁבְעָה מִזְבְּחֹת וְהָכֵן לִי בָּזֶה שִׁבְעָה פָרִים וְשִׁבְעָה
ב אֵילִֽים: וַיַּעַשׂ בָּלָק כַּאֲשֶׁר דִּבֶּר בִּלְעָם וַיַּעַל בָּלָק וּבִלְעָם פָּר
ג וָאַיִל בַּמִּזְבֵּֽחַ: וַיֹּאמֶר בִּלְעָם לְבָלָק הִתְיַצֵּב עַל־עֹלָתֶךָ וְאֵלְכָה
אוּלַי יִקָּרֵה יְהֹוָה לִקְרָאתִי וּדְבַר מַה־יַּרְאֵנִי וְהִגַּדְתִּי לָךְ וַיֵּלֶךְ
ד שֶֽׁפִי: וַיִּקָּר אֱלֹהִים אֶל־בִּלְעָם וַיֹּאמֶר אֵלָיו אֶת־שִׁבְעַת
ה הַֽמִּזְבְּחֹת עָרַכְתִּי וָאַעַל פָּר וָאַיִל בַּמִּזְבֵּֽחַ: וַיָּשֶׂם יְהֹוָה דָּבָר בְּפִי
ו בִלְעָם וַיֹּאמֶר שׁוּב אֶל־בָּלָק וְכֹה תְדַבֵּֽר: וַיָּשָׁב אֵלָיו וְהִנֵּה נִצָּב

CLASSIC COMMENTATORS

Balak had earlier built a single altar upon which he brought two sacrifices, while Bilam asks Balak to build seven altars (which he repeats twice more afterward). What is the significance of the seven altars?

IBN EZRA
אבן עזרא

The Torah contains deep secrets that are accessible only to a select few. The number seven holds one of these mysteries; the seventh day of the week is holy, as is the seventh month [Tishrei], and the seventh year in the Sabbatical cycle is significant. Seven lambs are sacrificed as burnt offerings on the festivals, and there are seven sprinklings of sacrificial blood on Yom Kippur. God also instructed Iyov, "Now take seven bulls and seven rams" (Job 42:8).

יש סודות עמוקים לא יבינום כי אם מתי מספר. ושביעי בימים, ובחדשים, ובשנים, ושבעה כבשי עולה, ושבע הזאות, גם השם אמר לאיוב: קחו לכם שבעה פרים (איוב מ״ב:ח׳).

RABBI YOSEF IBN KASPI
ר׳ יוסף אבן כספי

We have no need to explore this further. Rather, Bilam did what he did based on his practices.

אין לנו לחפור בכאן דבר, אבל בלעם ידע מה עשה לפי מנהגו ומלאכתו.

RABBI SAMSON RAPHAEL HIRSCH
ר׳ שמשון רפאל הירש

The number seven is significant in that all seven altars were constructed to honor the one invisible God.

המספר שבע מורה שהמזבחות נבנו לשם האל האחד הבלתי־נראה.

HAAMEK DAVAR
העמק דבר

Bilam built seven altars to correspond to the seven nations that Israel was about to vanquish.

נגד שבעה אומות שישראל באים לכלותם.

23:7–12 *Bilam's first oration, written in poetic form, describes his inability to curse Benei Yisrael in light of the fact that God has blessed them. Balak is displeased, as he brought Bilam to curse them, but Bilam explains that he is bound to say only that which God places into his mouth.*

6 He went back to him, and found him standing by his offering together with all the
7 princes of Moav. And Bilam took up his oracle and said: "Balak brought me from Aram, the king of Moav from the eastern hills. 'Go: curse Yaakov for me; go: denounce Israel.'
8 How can I curse whom God has not cursed? How can I denounce whom the LORD has
9 not denounced? From the tops of crags I see him; from the hills I gaze down: a people
10 that dwells alone; not reckoning itself among nations. Who can number the dust of Yaakov, count even a fourth of Israel? Let me die the death of the upright, and let my
11 end be like his." And Balak said to Bilam, "What have you done to me? I brought you
12 to curse my enemies, and you have blessed them." He answered, "Am I not obliged to

QUESTIONS FOR THOUGHT

- The three different opinions above could be described using these adjectives: a) resistant, b) obedient, and c) active. Match these three adjectives with the commentaries.
- Can you imagine a fourth opinion which is not expressed above? How would you describe that?
- What difference does it make if Bilam is resistant, obedient, or active? What does that change about our understanding of the story?
- Does a blessing or curse uttered by a person have any effect?

TEXTUAL SKILLS

1. Notice how verses 7 and 8 are linked.
2. Compare verse 12 with 22:38. Find the one minor difference between them. Can you explain the reason for that difference?

WISDOM OF THE HEART

Bilam describes *Benei Yisrael* as a nation which dwells alone. Throughout its many of years of exile that was true, and although this reality was sometimes forced upon *Benei Yisrael*, it was also a mark of pride. When the rest of world was wallowing in idolatry, Israel stood alone. When most of the nations had sunk into immorality, Israel rose above. Part of the nature of *Benei Yisrael* was to be countercultural – just because everyone else was doing something didn't make it right. Nevertheless, the ultimate goal of *Benei Yisrael* is to be a beacon for the rest of humanity. Standing alone is not the goal; it is the means to maintain a clear vision of what is good and right – not for the purpose of being able to brag about being superior but so that there could be a voice of religious, ethical, and moral clarity from which the rest of the world could learn. This is why God chooses Avraham, a choice which represents the ultimate goal for the people who are to be a kingdom of priests representing God and Godly values to the rest of humanity.

Do you see integration of the Jewish people into the rest of the world as the greatest threat to Jewish survival or the greatest achievement of Jewish existence?

עַל־עֹלָת֔וֹ ה֖וּא וְכָל־שָׂרֵ֣י מוֹאָֽב׃ וַיִּשָּׂ֥א מְשָׁל֖וֹ וַיֹּאמַ֑ר מִן־אֲ֠רָ֠ם יַנְחֵ֨נִי בָלָ֤ק מֶֽלֶךְ־מוֹאָב֙ מֵֽהַרְרֵי־קֶ֔דֶם לְכָה֙ אָֽרָה־לִּ֣י יַעֲקֹ֔ב וּלְכָ֖ה זֹעֲמָ֥ה יִשְׂרָאֵֽל׃ מָ֣ה אֶקֹּ֔ב לֹ֥א קַבֹּ֖ה אֵ֑ל וּמָ֣ה אֶזְעֹ֔ם לֹ֥א זָעַ֖ם יְהוָֽה׃ כִּֽי־מֵרֹ֤אשׁ צֻרִים֙ אֶרְאֶ֔נּוּ וּמִגְּבָע֖וֹת אֲשׁוּרֶ֑נּוּ הֶן־עָם֙ לְבָדָ֣ד יִשְׁכֹּ֔ן וּבַגּוֹיִ֖ם לֹ֥א יִתְחַשָּֽׁב׃ מִ֤י מָנָה֙ עֲפַ֣ר יַעֲקֹ֔ב וּמִסְפָּ֖ר אֶת־רֹ֣בַע יִשְׂרָאֵ֑ל תָּמֹ֤ת נַפְשִׁי֙ מ֣וֹת יְשָׁרִ֔ים וּתְהִ֥י אַחֲרִיתִ֖י כָּמֹֽהוּ׃ וַיֹּ֤אמֶר בָּלָק֙ אֶל־בִּלְעָ֔ם מֶ֥ה עָשִׂ֖יתָ לִ֑י לָקֹ֤ב אֹיְבַי֙ לְקַחְתִּ֔יךָ וְהִנֵּ֖ה בֵּרַ֥כְתָּ בָרֵֽךְ׃ וַיַּ֖עַן וַיֹּאמַ֑ר הֲלֹ֗א אֵת֩ אֲשֶׁ֨ר יָשִׂ֤ים יְהוָה֙ בְּפִ֔י אֹת֥וֹ אֶשְׁמֹ֖ר

CLASSIC COMMENTATORS

God "put a word in Bilam's mouth" (23:5). What is Bilam's role in the blessings he gives to *Benei Yisrael*?

RASHI

Once Bilam heard that he had no permission to curse Israel he thought: Why should I return to Balak only to distress him? Thus the Holy One, blessed be He, figuratively put into Bilam's mouth a bridle and a hook, like one affixes around an animal's snout to lead it wherever one wants.

רש״י

כשהיה שומע שאינו נרשה לקלל אמר: מה אני חוזר אצל בלק לצערו? ונתן לו הקב״ה רסן וחכה בפיו כאדם הפוקס בהמה בחכה להוליכה אל אשר ירצה.

RAMBAM

The second degree of prophecy occurs when an individual finds himself possessed by a new power that compels him to speak. He then opens his mouth to speak of wisdom, to sing praises, to caution people, or to speak of Godly matters.... This is what we mean when we say that a person's speech was guided by divine inspiration. That faculty allowed David to compose the book of Psalms, and for Shlomo to write Proverbs, Ecclesiastes, and Song of Songs.... Recognize that Bilam was also a member of that company during his good moments, as the verse states, "And the Lord put a word in Bilam's mouth." That is tantamount to the Torah stating: Bilam spoke while imbued with the spirit of God.

רמב״ם

והמדרגה השניה (מהנבואה) הוא שימצא האדם כאילו ענין אחד חל עליו וכח אחר התחדש וישימהו לדבר, וידבר בחכמות או בתשבחות, או בדברי אזהרה או בעניינים אלוקיים ... וזהו אשר יאמר עליו שהוא מדבר ברוח הקודש, ובזה המין מרוח הקודש חיבר דוד תהלים וחיבר שלמה משלי וקהלת ושיר השירים... ודע שבלעם גם כן מזאת הכת היה, בעת שהיה טוב, וזה העניין רוצה באמרו "וישם ה' דבר בפי בלעם" כאילו הוא אומר שברוח ה' ידבר.

RAMBAN

What does the text connote when it states, "And the Lord *put* a word in Bilam's mouth"? God taught Bilam which words to review in his mouth so that he would not forget them, and so that he would repeat exactly what God wished him to say. We find a similar usage of the verb in the verse, "So now write down this song and teach it to the Israelites. Place it in their mouths" (Deut. 31:19).

רמב״ן

טעם "וישם" הלימוד, שלימדו הדברים שיגרוס אותם בפיו ולא ישכח ולא יפיל מהם דבר, כטעם: ולמדה את בני ישראל שימה בפיהם (דברים ל״א:י״ט).

> **23:13–26** Balak tries a second time to get Bilam to curse Benei Yisrael, taking him to a place where he could see only part of the nation. He takes him to the field of Tzofim (literally, "the lookout point"), where Bilam again asks for seven altars with seven bulls and rams to be offered as sacrifices. God again comes to Bilam and tells him what to say. This second oration begins by affirming that God does not change His mind and that His blessing of Benei Yisrael cannot be undone. It concludes with a proclamation that Benei Yisrael is mighty because God is with them, and that they are immune to sorcery.

13 speak strictly the words the Lord puts in my mouth?" Then Balak said to him, "Come with me to another place where you will see them. You will see only part of them; you
14 will not see them all. Curse them for me from there." He took him to the field of Tzofim, to the top of Pisga. He built seven altars and on each altar offered a bull and
15 a ram. Then Bilam said to Balak, "Stand here beside your offering, while I seek a
16 meeting there." The Lord met Bilam and put a word in his mouth. "Go back to Balak,"
17 He said, "and tell him this." He came to him and found him standing by his offering
18 together with the princes of Moav. Balak asked him, "What did the Lord say?" So he
19 took up his oracle and said: "Stand up, Balak, listen; pay attention, son of Tzipor. Not man is God, to lie; no mortal, to change His mind. Would He speak and not fulfill,
20 would He promise and not keep? I received an order to bless. He has blessed; I cannot

---

העמק דבר

לא הביט און ביעקב - ה"און" שישנו "ביעקב" אינו בעצם מושרש בלב יעקב, כמשמעות לשון 'הבטה' כמו שכתבתי ... שהוא הסתכלות בתוך ופנים הדבר. וזהו דבר הכתוב: הקב"ה "לא הביט" שה"און" מושרש בלב "יעקב", אלא כמו שאדם רוצה לעשות 'און' על ידי רוח שטות שהיא טבע התאוה וכדומה.

HAAMEK DAVAR

Any wrong within the masses of Yaakov does not represent a fundamental characteristic of the people. As I have explained, the verb *habata* ["looking"] connotes a deep investigation into the nature of an object. Thus, here the verse means that the Holy One, blessed be He, has not seen within Yaakov a deep-seated desire to do wrong. Rather, any wrongdoing on their part is the result is like the sudden, silly impulses or desires that sometimes drive people.

QUESTIONS FOR THOUGHT

- Both Rashi and *Haamek Davar* understand that the one who is not "seeing" is God and that what God does not see is what *Benei Yisrael* do wrong. However, on what do they disagree?
- In what way does Rashi's explanation seem to be contradicted by many of the stories in Numbers? How do you think Rashi might respond?
- Ramban understands that the one doing the "seeing" is *Benei Yisrael* and that און refers to untruths. What untruths do *Benei Yisrael* not "see," and how is the first half of this verse connected to the second half?
- According to R. Reggio, who is doing the "seeing" and what is he not seeing?
- *Haamek Davar* provides a penetrating insight into our misdeeds. What deep conviction does he express?
- Which of the above commentaries do you think fits the verse best? Which fits best into the overall context of Bilam's message in this oration?

יג לַדֶּבֶר: וַיֹּאמֶר אֵלָיו בָּלָק לְךָ־נָּא אִתִּי אֶל־מָקוֹם אַחֵר אֲשֶׁר חמישי
תִּרְאֶנּוּ מִשָּׁם אֶפֶס קָצֵהוּ תִרְאֶה וְכֻלּוֹ לֹא תִרְאֶה וְקָבְנוֹ־לִי
יד מִשָּׁם: וַיִּקָּחֵהוּ שְׂדֵה צֹפִים אֶל־רֹאשׁ הַפִּסְגָּה וַיִּבֶן שִׁבְעָה
טו מִזְבְּחֹת וַיַּעַל פָּר וָאַיִל בַּמִּזְבֵּחַ: וַיֹּאמֶר אֶל־בָּלָק הִתְיַצֵּב כֹּה
טז עַל־עֹלָתֶךָ וְאָנֹכִי אִקָּרֶה כֹּה: וַיִּקָּר יהוה אֶל־בִּלְעָם וַיָּשֶׂם דָּבָר
יז בְּפִיו וַיֹּאמֶר שׁוּב אֶל־בָּלָק וְכֹה תְדַבֵּר: וַיָּבֹא אֵלָיו וְהִנּוֹ נִצָּב
עַל־עֹלָתוֹ וְשָׂרֵי מוֹאָב אִתּוֹ וַיֹּאמֶר לוֹ בָּלָק מַה־דִּבֶּר יהוה:
יח וַיִּשָּׂא מְשָׁלוֹ וַיֹּאמַר קוּם בָּלָק וּשֲׁמָע הַאֲזִינָה עָדַי בְּנוֹ צִפֹּר:
יט לֹא אִישׁ אֵל וִיכַזֵּב וּבֶן־אָדָם וְיִתְנֶחָם הַהוּא אָמַר וְלֹא יַעֲשֶׂה
כ וְדִבֶּר וְלֹא יְקִימֶנָּה: הִנֵּה בָרֵךְ לָקָחְתִּי וּבֵרֵךְ וְלֹא אֲשִׁיבֶנָּה:

CLASSIC COMMENTATORS

Like much poetry, Bilam's orations are often difficult to understand. Verse 21 is filled with ambiguous statements. What are אָוֶן and עָמָל? Who did not see them, and why is that important?

RASHI

The Holy One, blessed be He, does not take real notice of the wrongs committed by the Israelites. Even when they violate His commandments, He does not examine their behavior meticulously to detect their disobedience.

רש״י

לא הביט - הקב״ה, און שביעקב - כשהן עוברים על דבריו אינו מדקדק אחריהם, להתבונן באוניות שלהן ובעמלן שהן עוברין על דתו.

RAMBAN

The One who the nation trusts is not false; the One upon whom they rely will not disappoint. Rather, all of their blessings and assurances will endure forever.

רמב״ן

לא הביט אדם ביעקב ולא ראה איש בישראל און ודבר כזב, אין בטחונם שקר, ואין תוחלתם נכזבת, אבל כל ברכותיהם ובטחונם יתקיימו לעולם.

RABBI ISAAC SAMUEL REGGIO

The one who glimpses is the prophet who sees the future as if it were today. Such an individual views no wrong, or sorrow, or pain in Yaakov. Similarly, one who is privy to the visions of God sees no toil, or exhaustion, or punishment in Israel. In other words, there are no decrees of suffering or torment for the people, only good things and success.

ר׳ יצחק שמואל רג׳יו

המביט, והוא הנביא הרואה העתיד כמוני היום, לא יביט שום און ושבר וצער ביעקב, וכן הרואה במראות אלהים לא יראה עמל ויגיעה ופורענות בישראל, כלומר לא נגזר להם צרה ויגון אלא טובות והצלחות.

21 revoke it. He has glimpsed no wrong in Yaakov, He has seen no sin in Israel. The Lord
22 their God is with them, in them the King's horn blasts sounds. God, who freed them
23 from Egypt, is like the oryx's proud horn for them. There is no divination over Yaakov, no spell against Israel can hold. It will now be said of Yaakov, of Israel, 'See what God
24 has done.' A people – see – rises like a lioness, lifts itself up like a lion. It will not lie down
25 until it eats its meat and drinks the blood of the slain." Balak said to Bilam, "Do not curse
26 or bless them." But Bilam answered, "Did I not tell you, 'I must do whatever the Lord

---

QUICK BITES

Bilam's second blessing opens with the declaration that God is not like a man – people make decisions and change their minds, but God does not change His mind. The problem, of course, is that Tanakh is filled with descriptions of God regretting things He had done, using exactly the same word – נחם – that Bilam does. For example, Genesis 6:6–8 describes God as regretting having created people, Exodus 32:14 describes God taking back His threat to destroy *Benei Yisrael*, and the prophets (Jonah 4:2) identify God as taking back decisions to destroy. In fact, one foundation of prayer is that we ask God to change His mind. The Gaon of Vilna suggests that unlike people, who change their minds on a whim, or because of an error in judgment, or even because their initial decision was made hastily and without much thought, God will change His decisions only when there is a compelling reason, such as human repentance.

Repeatedly, Bilam instructs Balak to build a set of seven altars, then they bring two sets of sacrifices, and then Bilam tells Balak to stand next to them while he seeks God's words. The image of standing next to the sacrifice is not found anywhere else in the Torah and is quite telling. It reminds us that the Hebrew word for sacrifice, קרבן, comes from the root ק-ר-ב, which means to come close. The root suggests movement, that the sacrifice is intended to cause us to move closer to God. This is the opposite of pagan concepts of sacrifice, which suggest that they are intended to be a human attempt to move God and impel Him to do our bidding.

Bilam's second oration opens with the pronouncement that God is not like man; He won't take back the blessing He initially gave. Midrash Rabba suggests that Bilam is not referring to the initially blessing that he gave, but to the covenant that God made with Avraham, Yitzḥak, and Yaakov. Throughout the generations there have been those who proclaimed that the covenant was broken, that *Benei Yisrael* used to be the Chosen People but no longer were. Those claims, however, did not understand the nature of covenant, especially as expressed by Bilam. Covenant is eternal. The difference between a covenant and a contract is that when someone breaks a contract the other party is freed from obligation. In a covenant, when one side doesn't live up to their obligations the other side has to work even harder to make sure that the covenant is maintained. God's covenant with *Benei Yisrael* is eternal.

במדבר | פרק כג

כא לֹא־הִבִּיט אָ֫וֶן בְּיַעֲקֹב וְלֹא־רָאָה עָמָל בְּיִשְׂרָאֵל יהוה אֱלֹהָיו
כב עִמּוֹ וּתְרוּעַת מֶלֶךְ בּוֹ: אֵל מוֹצִיאָם מִמִּצְרָיִם כְּתוֹעֲפֹת רְאֵם
כג לוֹ: כִּי לֹא־נַחַשׁ בְּיַעֲקֹב וְלֹא־קֶסֶם בְּיִשְׂרָאֵל כָּעֵת יֵאָמֵר לְיַעֲקֹב
כד וּלְיִשְׂרָאֵל מַה־פָּעַל אֵל: הֶן־עָם כְּלָבִיא יָקוּם וְכַאֲרִי יִתְנַשָּׂא
כה לֹא יִשְׁכַּב עַד־יֹאכַל טֶרֶף וְדַם־חֲלָלִים יִשְׁתֶּה: וַיֹּאמֶר בָּלָק
כו אֶל־בִּלְעָם גַּם־קֹב לֹא תִקֳּבֶנּוּ גַּם־בָּרֵךְ לֹא תְבָרֲכֶנּוּ: וַיַּעַן בִּלְעָם
וַיֹּאמֶר אֶל־בָּלָק הֲלֹא דִּבַּרְתִּי אֵלֶיךָ לֵאמֹר כֹּל אֲשֶׁר־יְדַבֵּר

TEXTUAL SKILLS

1. Compare verse 24 with Genesis 49:9 and 49:27.
2. In what ways are the messages of verses 9 and 23 similar? What does verse 23 add?
3. Notice that Bilam's first oration describes *Benei Yisrael* as passive and peaceful while his second oration describes them as active and dangerous. Why do you think God does that?
4. Notice that in both of Bilam's first two orations there is a verse which begins with the words הן עם.
5. In what way is verse 26 similar to, and different from, verse 12?

WISDOM OF THE HEART

When Bilam is unable to curse *Benei Yisrael*, Balak suggests that they go to another place, from which Bilam will be able to see only part of the people. The Rebbe of Kotzk points out that it is easy to judge someone negatively when we look at them selectively, highlighting only the things we dislike or which annoy us. It is an easy trap to fall into, and we can get caught up in a frenzy of negativity when we obsess about the one thing which bothers us. This is perhaps what Yehoshua ben Peraḥya (Avot 1:6) was warning about when he advised that when we judge, we should look at the entirety of the person (כל האדם), to be able to judge them favorably, to give them the benefit of the doubt. The same thing applies when we look at groups of people. If we look only at one slice of the group, the slice we don't like, it is easy to generalize. We are apt to make unfounded sweeping statements and paint the entire group as bad. Honesty, however, demands that that we look at the entirety of the group to determine whether they are good or bad, worthy or unworthy.

Who do you think suffers more damage – the person being judged unfairly or the one who is judging others unfairly?

> **23:27–24:2** Balak tries a third time to get Bilam to curse Benei Yisrael. He takes him to yet a different place, the top of Peor, where Bilam again instructs him to build seven altars and bring the same set of offerings on each. Bilam sees Benei Yisrael and is inspired to offer a full, unrestrained blessing.

27 says'?" Then Balak said to Bilam, "Come now and I will take you to another place. Perhaps
28 God will deem it right to let you curse them for me there." So Balak took Bilam to the top
29 of Peor, overlooking the wasteland. Bilam said to Balak, "Build me seven altars here and
30 prepare for me seven bulls and seven rams." Balak did as Bilam had said, and offered a bull
24 1 and a ram on each altar. When Bilam saw that it pleased the Lord to bless the Israelites, he did not go as at other times to seek omens. Instead, he turned toward the wilderness.
2 And Bilam raised his eyes and saw Israel encamped there tribe by tribe, and God's spirit

---

- Which of the commentaries understands that Bilam thought that God might actually agree to allow him to curse *Benei Yisrael*?
- For what purpose do you think God included the details of what Bilam was thinking in this story?

TEXTUAL SKILLS

1. The first place that Balak took Bilam was Bamot Baal; the third place, here, was the top of Peor. What do these two names have in common?
2. Bilam hits his donkey three times, after which the donkey speaks. Balak tries three times to get Bilam to curse *Benei Yisrael*, after which Bilam offers an unrestrained blessing. What connection do you see between these occurrences?

WISDOM OF THE HEART

In the preparation for the third blessing there are three core elements which are different than in the previous attempts. First, Bilam recognizes that God wants to bless *Benei Yisrael* and doesn't even try to curse them. Second, Bilam "raises his eyes" and sees that the people are camped organized by tribes. The third is that God's spirit descends upon him, unlike in the previous times, when God placed words in his mouth. Let's translate these into human terms. The first step he takes is an honest assessment of reality. Without that, there can be no moving forward in any growth process. The second step, which is a natural outgrowth of the first, is that he is able to see what was there all along but which others could not see. This is the same language that the Torah uses, for example, to describe Avraham seeing Mount Moria on the third day, and Moshe seeing the burning bush. It is only after we are truly honest with ourselves that we are prepared to see things as they really are, and not as we wish them to be. That work that Bilam did enables the third step to happen: God's spirit descending upon him. That third step is different – it is the only one which is not in our hands to do.

Do you sometimes see that there are steps you can take that will help you move forward, but you still can't imagine how that will truly solve the situation you are stuck in?

כז יהוה אֹתוֹ אֶעֱשֶׂה: וַיֹּאמֶר בָּלָק אֶל־בִּלְעָם לְכָה־נָּא אֶקָּחֲךָ ששי
אֶל־מָקוֹם אַחֵר אוּלַי יִישַׁר בְּעֵינֵי הָאֱלֹהִים וְקַבֹּתוֹ לִי מִשָּׁם: /שביעי/
כח וַיִּקַּח בָּלָק אֶת־בִּלְעָם רֹאשׁ הַפְּעוֹר הַנִּשְׁקָף עַל־פְּנֵי הַיְשִׁימֹן:
כט וַיֹּאמֶר בִּלְעָם אֶל־בָּלָק בְּנֵה־לִי בָזֶה שִׁבְעָה מִזְבְּחֹת וְהָכֵן לִי
ל בָּזֶה שִׁבְעָה פָרִים וְשִׁבְעָה אֵילִים: וַיַּעַשׂ בָּלָק כַּאֲשֶׁר אָמַר בִּלְעָם
כד א וַיַּעַל פָּר וָאַיִל בַּמִּזְבֵּחַ: וַיַּרְא בִּלְעָם כִּי טוֹב בְּעֵינֵי יהוה לְבָרֵךְ
אֶת־יִשְׂרָאֵל וְלֹא־הָלַךְ כְּפַעַם־בְּפַעַם לִקְרַאת נְחָשִׁים וַיָּשֶׁת
ב אֶל־הַמִּדְבָּר פָּנָיו: וַיִּשָּׂא בִלְעָם אֶת־עֵינָיו וַיַּרְא אֶת־יִשְׂרָאֵל

CLASSIC COMMENTATORS

Bilam had earlier (23:23) stated that there was no נחש in Israel; here the Torah states that he did not go to seek נחשים (which here does not mean snakes). What is it that Bilam does not try this time?

רש"י **RASHI**

לנחש אולי יקרה לקראתו כרצונו. To divine (*lenaḥesh*) whether the Lord would meet with him and do as he wished.

רשב"ם **RASHBAM**

לנסות ממקום למקום אולי יוכל לקללם. He would not move from place to place looking for a suitable place to curse Israel.

רמב"ן **RAMBAN**

כי בפעמים הראשונים היה מנחש ורוצה לקלל אותם בנחש, והיה השם בא אליו בדרך מקרה, לא בכונתו לנבואה ולא ממעלתו שהגיע אליה, ועתה כאשר נאמר לו: כי לא נחש ביעקב ולא קסם בישראל (במדבר כ"ג:כ"ג) להרע או להיטיב להם, הניח את הנחשים ולא הלך כפעם בפעם לקראתם.
In the first two rounds, Bilam attempted to use his divination techniques (*nihush*) to curse the Israelites. During those efforts God appeared to Bilam by chance, for the sorcerer had not been trying to exercise his prophetic powers. Nor had Bilam attained any elevated status. However, now that Bilam had learned that "there is no divination over Yaakov, no spell against Israel" (23:23), either for good or for ill, Bilam put his sorcery aside, and no longer sought "to seek omens" (24:2).

QUESTIONS FOR THOUGHT

- The above commentaries offer three different interpretations for the word לנחש: a) to try sorcery, b) to guess, c) to make an attempt. Match those three definitions with the commentaries.
- Which of the commentaries seems to believe that sorcery works, just that God blocked Bilam?

24:3–9 Instead of declaring that Benei Yisrael are not and cannot be cursed, Bilam's third oration describes many of their positive attributes. This includes his famous observation מה טבו אהליך יעקב משכנותיך ישראל, as well as blessings reminiscent of those given by God to Avraham and by Yaakov to Yehuda.

3 came upon him. He took up his oracle and said: "The word of Bilam, son of Beor; the
4 word of the man whose eye is opened. The word of one who hears God's speech, who sees
5 a vision of Shaddai, who falls, but with eyes unveiled. How good are your tents, Yaakov,
6 your homes, O Israel. Like palm groves stretching forth, like gardens by the river, like aloes
7 the LORD planted, like cedars by the waters. Water will drip from his branches; his seed
has abundant water; his king will be higher than Agag, his kingdom exalted.
8 God, who freed him from Egypt, is the oryx's proud horn to him. He will devour enemy
9 nations, break their bones, pierce them with arrows. Like a lion he crouches, lies down,
like a lioness; who dares to rouse him? Blessing on all who bless you, on those who curse

---

- In what way are the opinions of Rashi and Abarbanel similar?
- In what way is the opinion of Sforno dramatically different from all the others?
- In the context of what Bilam is trying to convey in this third blessing, which of the above opinions do you think makes the most sense? Why?

TEXTUAL SKILLS

1. Notice the similarities and differences between the following sets of verses: 24:8 and 23:22; 24:9 and 23:24..
2. Which part of this third blessing sounds like something God said to Avraham?
3. In what way is the first half of this blessing (vv. 5–7) dramatically different from the second half (vv. 7–9)?
4. Notice that the root א-ה-ל appears in both verses 5 and 6, but means very different things.

WISDOM OF THE HEART

Balak hires Bilam to curse *Benei Yisrael*. On Bilam's first attempt, he can say barely more than that they cannot be cursed. On the second attempt he confirms that he could not take back what he said the first time, and adds a small positive comment. The third attempt is different – it speaks only in the positive. God takes Bilam through a slow process in which he must shed his own preconceptions and then replace those with completely new ideas. This fundamental process is similar to that of personal therapy and of *teshuva* ("repentance"), in which recognizing the error or problem is the first step toward fixing it.

Why do some people find it difficult to acknowledge that they've made a mistake? Would you rather trust someone who owns up to their mistakes and learns from them or someone who is absolutely convinced that they never make mistakes?

שֹׁכֵ֣ן לִשְׁבָטָ֔יו וַתְּהִ֥י עָלָ֖יו ר֣וּחַ אֱלֹהִֽים: וַיִּשָּׂ֥א מְשָׁל֖וֹ וַיֹּאמַ֑ר נְאֻ֤ם
בִּלְעָם֙ בְּנ֣וֹ בְעֹ֔ר וּנְאֻ֥ם הַגֶּ֖בֶר שְׁתֻ֥ם הָעָֽיִן: נְאֻ֕ם שֹׁמֵ֖עַ אִמְרֵי־אֵ֑ל
אֲשֶׁ֨ר מַחֲזֵ֤ה שַׁדַּי֙ יֶֽחֱזֶ֔ה נֹפֵ֖ל וּגְל֥וּי עֵינָֽיִם: מַה־טֹּ֥בוּ אֹהָלֶ֖יךָ יַעֲקֹ֑ב
מִשְׁכְּנֹתֶ֖יךָ יִשְׂרָאֵֽל: כִּנְחָלִ֣ים נִטָּ֔יוּ כְּגַנֹּ֖ת עֲלֵ֣י נָהָ֑ר כַּאֲהָלִים֙ נָטַ֣ע
יְהֹוָ֔ה כַּאֲרָזִ֖ים עֲלֵי־מָֽיִם: יִזַּל־מַ֙יִם֙ מִדָּ֣לְיָ֔ו וְזַרְע֖וֹ בְּמַ֣יִם רַבִּ֑ים
וְיָרֹ֤ם מֵֽאֲגַג֙ מַלְכּ֔וֹ וְתִנַּשֵּׂ֖א מַלְכֻתֽוֹ: אֵ֚ל מוֹצִיא֣וֹ מִמִּצְרַ֔יִם
כְּתוֹעֲפֹ֥ת רְאֵ֖ם ל֑וֹ יֹאכַ֞ל גּוֹיִ֣ם צָרָ֗יו וְעַצְמֹתֵיהֶ֛ם יְגָרֵ֖ם וְחִצָּ֥יו
יִמְחָֽץ: כָּרַ֨ע שָׁכַ֧ב כַּאֲרִ֛י וּכְלָבִ֖יא מִ֣י יְקִימֶ֑נּוּ מְבָרֲכֶ֣יךָ בָר֔וּךְ

CLASSIC COMMENTATORS

The רְאֵם (in v. 8) is an oryx, a large and powerful deer with long, straight horns. As Bilam mentions that God took *Benei Yisrael* out of Egypt, he describes someone having oryx-like horns. Who is Bilam describing as having those horns?

RASHI
רש"י
"God, who freed them from Egypt" with His strength loftiness, I "will devour the nation" which are His rivals.

אל המוציאם ממצרים בתוקף ורום שלו, יאכל את הגוים שהם צריו

IBN EZRA
אבן עזרא
"God, who freed" Israel from Egypt empowered the nation to be as strong as the horns of the oryx.

האל המוציאו ממצרים שם לו כוח כתועפות ראם.

ABARBANEL
אברבנאל
Even though the Egyptians wielded the strength of the oryx's horns, when God blasted the trumpet that anointed Him as King over Israel, the nation quit the country with a mighty hand.

עם היות שתועפות ראם יש לו למצרים, כי בהיות תרועת המלך ה' לישראל – יצאו ממצרים ביד חזקה.

RABBI OVADYA SFORNO
ר' עובדיה ספורנו
The people of Israel do not ravage and devour their prey like a lion does. Instead, they drive their enemies away like an oryx butts with its horns. For it was God's intention to expel the Canaanite nations from the land to make room for the Israelites, without having to kill the inhabitants.

כתועפות ראם לו, לעם ישראל שאינו טורף ואוכל כארי, אבל דוחה בקרניו כמו הראם, כי היתה הכוונה לגרש האומות ולהכניס את ישראל לארץ בלתי הריגת האומות.

QUESTIONS FOR THOUGHT

- There are three different opinions regarding who has oryx-like horns: God, Egypt, and Israel. Match those opinions with the above commentaries.

BEMIDBAR | CHAPTER 24 — BALAK | 232

10 you, curse." Balak was furious with Bilam. He struck his hands together. Balak said to
Bilam, "I summoned you to curse my enemies. Instead you have blessed them these three
11 times over. Now get away from here and go home. I said that I would honor you, but the
12 LORD has denied you all honor." Bilam replied to Balak, "Did I not tell the messengers
13 whom you sent to me, 'Even if Balak were to give me his palace full of silver and gold, I
could not do anything to transgress the word of the LORD, doing either good or bad of
14 my own accord. What the LORD says is what I must say.' So now that I am going back to
my people, let me advise you what this people will do to your people in days to come."

RABBI YOSEF BEKHOR SHOR | ר' יוסף בכור שור

אתן לך עצה שלא תתגרה עמהם, שאין לך לירא מהם
כלום, כי לא יזיקוך ולא לעמך כל ימיך,
כי את אשר יעשה העם הזה לעמך – באחרית הימים
יהיה, ולא עתה.

Said Bilam to Balak: if you take my advice, you will not start up with the Israelites, for you and your nation have nothing to fear from them at the moment. When Israel eventually turns against your people, that will be in the days to come, and not now.

QUESTIONS FOR THOUGHT

- Both Rashbam and Bekhor Shor understand that the word עצה actually does mean advice. The problem is that the advice seems to be absent from the text. How does each fill in the missing advice? How does each explain why the advice is missing from the text?
- What punctuation would those two commentaries put after the words לכה איעצך?
- R. Yosef Kara disagrees with the other two precisely because it means adding external information into the text which is not there. How does he define the word עצה?
- Which of the above commentaries do you think reads more smoothly in the text? Why do you think that?

TEXTUAL SKILLS

1. What word appears three times in verse 11? What does it mean in this context?
2. In verse 13, Bilam describes his limitation regarding what he was able to do. Notice the similarity and differences between this verse and 22:18.

WISDOM OF THE HEART

Bilam reiterates what he said initially to Balak – that no money in the world could enable him to curse *Benei Yisrael* if God would not agree. When we look at the world it often appears that wealth brings power, and that unbridled wealth brings limitless power. That usually generates two kinds of responses. The first is to seek wealth, so as to attain power. That pursuit leads to intense competition, power plays, and all sorts of nasty behavior as people elbow their way to the top and get there by stepping on others. The alternative response is a sense of futility, hopeless, powerlessness, and sometimes even despair. Bilam's perspective teaches us that there is a third path. We can strive to do what we can, accepting our limitations but continually pushing to make things better. We counteract the despair by understanding that ultimately God will ensure that those who abuse their power will be humbled and that the oppressed will be redeemed.

Can you find places in the daily prayers and in Hallel that address the hope that God will bring justice to the world, bringing down the arrogant and raising up the downtrodden?

וְאֹרְרֶיךָ אָרוּר: וַיִּחַר־אַף בָּלָק אֶל־בִּלְעָם וַיִּסְפֹּק אֶת־כַּפָּיו וַיֹּאמֶר בָּלָק אֶל־בִּלְעָם לָקֹב אֹיְבַי קְרָאתִיךָ וְהִנֵּה בֵּרַכְתָּ בָרֵךְ זֶה שָׁלֹשׁ פְּעָמִים: וְעַתָּה בְּרַח־לְךָ אֶל־מְקוֹמֶךָ אָמַרְתִּי כַּבֵּד אֲכַבֶּדְךָ וְהִנֵּה מְנָעֲךָ יְהוָה מִכָּבוֹד: וַיֹּאמֶר בִּלְעָם אֶל־בָּלָק הֲלֹא גַּם אֶל־מַלְאָכֶיךָ אֲשֶׁר־שָׁלַחְתָּ אֵלַי דִּבַּרְתִּי לֵאמֹר: אִם־יִתֶּן־לִי בָלָק מְלֹא בֵיתוֹ כֶּסֶף וְזָהָב לֹא אוּכַל לַעֲבֹר אֶת־פִּי יְהוָה לַעֲשׂוֹת טוֹבָה אוֹ רָעָה מִלִּבִּי אֲשֶׁר־יְדַבֵּר יְהוָה אֹתוֹ אֲדַבֵּר: וְעַתָּה הִנְנִי הוֹלֵךְ לְעַמִּי לְכָה אִיעָצְךָ אֲשֶׁר יַעֲשֶׂה הָעָם

שביעי

CLASSIC COMMENTATORS

Bilam opens this final set of orations by suggesting that he is advising (עצה) Balak. What advice is he offering Balak and how does that connect with the rest of the verse?

ר' יוסף קרא

אינו מקרא קצר כי איעצך לשון גילוי אוזן הוא. שכל דבר שנאמר בלשון לחשב נופל בו לשון עיצה, ודיבר הכתוב בהווה, לשון בני אדם כשאדם רוצה למסור סוד מכוסה לחביריו דבר שאינו רוצה שידעו בו רבים, הוא אומר לו לכה איעצך אף על פי שאינו עיצה.

RABBI YOSEF KARA

This does not represent a word of advice, since the verb איעצך connotes some sort of disclosure. When one thinks of revealing to a confidant a secret he wishes to keep private from others, he says, "come let me tell you something confidential – איעצך"; the matter has nothing to do with counseling.

רשב"ם

עצה להכשילם, לפי שידעתי אשר יעשה העם הזה לעמך באחרית הימים, אבל עתה בקרוב בחייך לא תירא מהם. וזו היא העצה: הן הנה היו לבני ישראל בדבר בלעם וגו' (במדבר ל"א:ט"ז). וכאן סתם משה את העצה, לפי שבלחש אמרה בלעם לבלק, ולא נודעה העצה עד שפרשה משה בשעת הצורך.

RASHBAM

Allow me to advise you as to the best way to bring about Israel's downfall, for I know "what this people will do to your people in the days to come." However, you, in the near future of your lifetime, need not fear Israel. The suggestion that Bilam offered Balak is later referenced in the verse, "These were the very ones who, on Bilam's advice, induced the Israelites to betray the Lord during the Peor affair, so that a plague struck down the Lord's community" (31:16). However, when Moshe wrote the present text, he did not elaborate on this advice. Since the sorcerer had whispered the matter into the king's ear, the actual scheme did not become known until Moshe revealed it at a later, relevant time.

24:15–25 *Bilam issues a final set of unsolicited orations about what will happen later in history between Benei Yisrael and other nations, after which he and Balak part ways.*

15 He took up his oracle, saying: "The word of Bilam son of Beor, the word of a man whose
16 eye is opened. The word of one who hears God's speech, and has knowledge from the
17 Most High, who sees a vision of Shaddai, who falls, but with eyes unveiled. I see him, but not now; I gaze upon him, though not near: A star will shoot forth from Yaakov; a scepter will arise from Israel, and smash the brow of Moav, and devastate all children of
18 Shet. Edom will become a possession, Se'ir the possession of its foes. But Israel will act
19
20 valiantly. From Yaakov will come forth a ruler and empty the city of survivors." He looked at Amalek; he took up his oracle and said: "Amalek is first among nations, but its end will
21 be death forever." He looked at the Kenites; he took up his oracle and said: "Invincible
22 your dwelling, your nest set in the rock. Yet Kayin is destined for burning, when Assyria
23 seizes you captive." And he took up his oracle and said, "Alas! Who will live when God
24 does this? Ships from the coast of Kitim will afflict Assyria, afflict Ever; they too will per-
25 ish for all time." Then Bilam rose and returned home, and Balak also set off upon his way.

HAAMEK DAVAR

According to Rashi, this entire passage is about the reign of King David.... However, I find such an interpretation difficult, for how does the clause, "and devastate all children of Shet" fit into that analysis? After all, King David challenged only those peoples who lived in proximity to the land of Israel.... Ramban, on the other hand, sees these verses as referring exclusively to the Messiah, which is also incorrect. For I fail to see why that figure would "smash the brow of Moav" – what state of Moav will exist in that period?...Instead, I agree with Rambam's explanation in *Hilkhot Melakhim* (11:1), that our text refers to both David's rule and to messianic times. Thus the clause, "I see him, but not now" relates to David, whereas "I gaze upon him, though not near" is an allusion to the Messiah.

העמק דבר

רש״י מפרש כל המקרא על דוד המלך ... ואי אפשר לומר כן, דאם כן היאך יתפרש "וקרקר כל בני שת", והלא דוד המלך לא נגע אלא באומות סביבות ארץ ישראל ... והרמב״ן פירש הכל על המשיח. וגם זה אינו נכון, דאם כן היאך שייך לומר "ומחץ פאתי מואב", ואיזו אומת מואב תהיה בימי המשיח ... אלא העיקר כמו שכתב הרמב״ם הלכות מלכים (י״א:א׳) שזה המקרא קאי גם על דוד גם על המשיח. ופירוש אראנו ולא עתה — על דוד, אשורנו ולא קרוב — על המשיח.

QUESTIONS FOR THOUGHT

- What phrase from verse 14 is at the core of the debate between the commentaries?
- *Haamek Davar* explains the double language in verse 17. How do you think the others would explain the repetition?
- In the commentaries of Ramban and *Haamek Davar*, why do you think that the only reference in the Torah to the messianic era would come in a message delivered by a non-Jewish prophet to a non-Jewish king?

WISDOM OF THE HEART

Bilam offers advice based on seeing into the future. Yogi Berra famously said that if you don't know where you are going you are probably not going to get there. The vision of the messianic era shared by Jews offers the world a path for us to bring it closer to being a reality.

טו הֶזֶּה לְעַמְּךָ בְּאַחֲרִית הַיָּמִים: וַיִּשָּׂא מְשָׁלוֹ וַיֹּאמַר נְאֻם בִּלְעָם
טז בְּנוֹ בְעֹר וּנְאֻם הַגֶּבֶר שְׁתֻם הָעָיִן: נְאֻם שֹׁמֵעַ אִמְרֵי־אֵל וְיֹדֵעַ
יז דַּעַת עֶלְיוֹן מַחֲזֵה שַׁדַּי יֶחֱזֶה נֹפֵל וּגְלוּי עֵינָיִם: אֶרְאֶנּוּ וְלֹא
עַתָּה אֲשׁוּרֶנּוּ וְלֹא קָרוֹב דָּרַךְ כּוֹכָב מִיַּעֲקֹב וְקָם שֵׁבֶט מִיִּשְׂרָאֵל
יח וּמָחַץ פַּאֲתֵי מוֹאָב וְקַרְקַר כָּל־בְּנֵי־שֵׁת: וְהָיָה אֱדוֹם יְרֵשָׁה
יט וְהָיָה יְרֵשָׁה שֵׂעִיר אֹיְבָיו וְיִשְׂרָאֵל עֹשֶׂה חָיִל: וְיֵרְדְּ מִיַּעֲקֹב
כ וְהֶאֱבִיד שָׂרִיד מֵעִיר: וַיַּרְא אֶת־עֲמָלֵק וַיִּשָּׂא מְשָׁלוֹ וַיֹּאמַר
כא רֵאשִׁית גּוֹיִם עֲמָלֵק וְאַחֲרִיתוֹ עֲדֵי אֹבֵד: וַיַּרְא אֶת־הַקֵּינִי וַיִּשָּׂא
כב מְשָׁלוֹ וַיֹּאמַר אֵיתָן מוֹשָׁבֶךָ וְשִׂים בַּסֶּלַע קִנֶּךָ: כִּי אִם־יִהְיֶה
כג לְבָעֵר קָיִן עַד־מָה אַשּׁוּר תִּשְׁבֶּךָּ: וַיִּשָּׂא מְשָׁלוֹ וַיֹּאמַר אוֹי מִי
כד יִחְיֶה מִשֻּׂמוֹ אֵל: וְצִים מִיַּד כִּתִּים וְעִנּוּ אַשּׁוּר וְעִנּוּ־עֵבֶר וְגַם־
כה הוּא עֲדֵי אֹבֵד: וַיָּקָם בִּלְעָם וַיֵּלֶךְ וַיָּשָׁב לִמְקֹמוֹ וְגַם־בָּלָק הָלַךְ
לְדַרְכּוֹ:

CLASSIC COMMENTATORS

When Bilam refers to things that will happen later in history, what period is he talking about?

RASHI
רש״י

שבט – מלך רודה ומושל.
ומחץ פאתי מואב – זה דוד.

A scepter will arise: A ruling king will dominate.
And smash the brow of Moav: This refers to David.

RAMBAN
רמב״ן

דרך כוכב מיעקב – בעבור כי המשיח יקבץ נדחי ישראל מקצה הארץ, ימשילנו לכוכב הדורך ברקיע מקצה השמים ... ויקום ממנו שבט מושל, ומחץ פאתי מואב וקרקר כל בני שת, בן אדם שהוא אבי כל האומות. והזכיר: פאתי מואב – להודיע לבלק כי עמו לא יפול ביד ישראל עתה, אבל באחרית הימים לא ינצל מואב מיד השבט המושל בו.

"A star will shoot forth from Yaakov" refers to the Messiah. That figure will gather all of Israel's scattered members from their exile around the world. Bilam compares that leader to a star shooting across the heavens from one end of the sky to the other..."a scepter will arise from Israel, and smash the brow of Moav, and devastate all children of Shet." Shet was the son of Adam, who was the patriarch of all the earth's nations. Bilam mentions "the brow of Moav" to convey to Balak that his nation would not now succumb to Israel's forces, but that in the end of days, they will be unable to escape the scepter of Israel's sovereign.

25 1 Israel was dwelling at Shitim. And the men began to consort with Moabite women,
2 who invited the people to join the sacrifices to their god; the men ate, and then they
3 worshipped the women's god. Israel allied itself with Baal Peor, and the LORD was
4 filled with fury against Israel. "Take all the people's leaders," said the LORD to Moshe,
"and have them impaled before the LORD in broad daylight, so that the LORD's fury
5 with Israel may be allayed." Moshe said to Israel's judges, "Each of you kill those of
6 your men who have allied themselves with Baal Peor." At that moment, an Israelite
man brought a Midianite woman to his friends before the eyes of Moshe and the
entire Israelite community, who were weeping at the entrance to the Tent of Meeting.
7 When Pinḥas son of Elazar son of Aharon the priest saw this, he rose from the midst of
8 the community, took a spear in his hand, went after the Israelite man into the tent, and
stabbed both of them, the Israelite man and the woman, through the stomach – and
9 the plague among the Israelites ended. Those who had died by the plague numbered
twenty-four thousand.

HO'IL MOSHE
הואיל משה

The people saw that the judges were not heeding their call to action and were turning a blind eye to the offenders, because the offenders were many and respected.

והמה בוכים - כי ראו שלא שמעו השופטים לקולם ונשאו פנים לחוטאים כי רבים ונכבדים היו.

QUESTIONS FOR THOUGHT

- According to each commentary, who was crying?
- According to each commentary, who was expected to do something, but seemed powerless?
- History is filled with leaders who freeze at a critical moment. How can leaders recover their leadership after critical failures?

TEXTUAL SKILLS

1. This is the second time in this *parasha* that we hear about Peor. Where is the first?
2. The word קבה appears twice in this section. What does it mean here? Notice the play on a different form of the word which appears eight times earlier in this *parasha*.

WISDOM OF THE HEART

As part of the Torah's description of Pinḥas's zealotry we are told that he "took a spear in his hand." R. Meir Druck suggests that the Torah is emphasizing that the spear was not in his hand earlier, as Pinḥas was not a warrior. His action was not a reflection of his natural behavior; rather, it was a dramatic departure from the way he would normally have behaved. Perhaps this is the reason he was rewarded; he overcame his nature to do what he believed with every fiber in his body needed to be done.

Think about things that you would never imagine doing, if only because of who you are as a person. What could possibly motivate you to overcome those barriers?

במדבר | פרק כה

כה א וַיֵּשֶׁב יִשְׂרָאֵל בַּשִּׁטִּים וַיָּחֶל הָעָם לִזְנוֹת אֶל־בְּנוֹת מוֹאָב:
ב וַתִּקְרֶאןָ לָעָם לְזִבְחֵי אֱלֹהֵיהֶן וַיֹּאכַל הָעָם וַיִּשְׁתַּחֲווּ לֵאלֹהֵיהֶן:
ג וַיִּצָּמֶד יִשְׂרָאֵל לְבַעַל פְּעוֹר וַיִּחַר־אַף יְהֹוָה בְּיִשְׂרָאֵל: ד וַיֹּאמֶר יְהֹוָה אֶל־מֹשֶׁה קַח אֶת־כָּל־רָאשֵׁי הָעָם וְהוֹקַע אוֹתָם לַיהֹוָה נֶגֶד הַשָּׁמֶשׁ וְיָשֹׁב חֲרוֹן אַף־יְהֹוָה מִיִּשְׂרָאֵל: ה וַיֹּאמֶר מֹשֶׁה אֶל־שֹׁפְטֵי יִשְׂרָאֵל הִרְגוּ אִישׁ אֲנָשָׁיו הַנִּצְמָדִים לְבַעַל פְּעוֹר: ו וְהִנֵּה אִישׁ מִבְּנֵי יִשְׂרָאֵל בָּא וַיַּקְרֵב אֶל־אֶחָיו אֶת־הַמִּדְיָנִית לְעֵינֵי מֹשֶׁה וּלְעֵינֵי כָּל־עֲדַת בְּנֵי־יִשְׂרָאֵל וְהֵמָּה בֹכִים פֶּתַח אֹהֶל מוֹעֵד:

מפטיר ז וַיַּרְא פִּינְחָס בֶּן־אֶלְעָזָר בֶּן־אַהֲרֹן הַכֹּהֵן וַיָּקָם מִתּוֹךְ הָעֵדָה וַיִּקַּח רֹמַח בְּיָדוֹ: ח וַיָּבֹא אַחַר אִישׁ־יִשְׂרָאֵל אֶל־הַקֻּבָּה וַיִּדְקֹר אֶת־שְׁנֵיהֶם אֵת אִישׁ יִשְׂרָאֵל וְאֶת־הָאִשָּׁה אֶל־קֳבָתָהּ וַתֵּעָצַר הַמַּגֵּפָה מֵעַל בְּנֵי יִשְׂרָאֵל: ט וַיִּהְיוּ הַמֵּתִים בַּמַּגֵּפָה אַרְבָּעָה וְעֶשְׂרִים אָלֶף:

CLASSIC COMMENTATORS

Moshe, Aharon, and a crowd are crying while the man parades his Midianite consort. Who is crying, and why?

RASHI

Zimri presented Kozbi to Moshe and asked him: Tell me, Moshe, is she permitted or forbidden to me? And if you forbid her to me, you will then have to explain who allowed you to marry the daughter of Yitro!... Moshe suddenly forgot the law regarding this matter, which caused the public to break down and weep, saying: "The same Moshe who stood up to 600,000 people in the sin of the golden calf is now incapacitated!"

RABBI SAMSON RAPHAEL HIRSCH

The weeping community of Israel was the assembly of judges Moshe had appointed. What they were witnessing so distressed them that it broke their hearts. These men therefore lacked any fortitude to take initiative for what had to be done.

רש"י

בא לפני משה, אמר לו: משה, זו אסורה או מותרת? ואם תאמר זו אסורה, בת יתרו מי התירה לך... והמה בוכים - נתעלמה ממנו הלכה, געו כולם בבכייה. בעגל עמד משה כנגד ששים רבוא ... וכאן רפו ידיו.

ר' שמשון רפאל הירש

עדת בני ישראל - היא אסיפת הדיינים שנקראו על ידי משה. והמה בכים - המראה שראו כל כך כאב להם, עד ששבר את לבם ולא יכלו לאמץ כוח או לאזור את מתניהם לפעול כאיש.

MORE QUICK BITES

- **23:10** *Benei Yisrael* are often compared to the dust of the earth. Rav David Lifshitz, the Rebbe of Suvalk, who taught at Yeshiva University for many years, observed that dust has a unique quality. People step on it all the time, but it nevertheless continues to provide fertile soil to provide sustenance to all.

- **24:3** Bilam describes himself as *shetum ha'ayin*. Onkelos understands this as meaning that he had very keen sight, while Rashi interprets it as having an eye which was closed up. There are different kinds of vision. A person with a single, very sharp eye can see very well, but lacks depth perception. People with two bad eyes can see depth but may perceive it as blurry and unfocused. And then there is vision in which we see beyond the surface, like when we can read someone's emotions or understand the significance of events beyond the immediate.

EXPLORING HASHKAFA
The Power of Magic

In the entire story of Bilam it sounds as though forces in the world exist that can be accessed and "tapped into" by people with special capabilities, like some kind of black magic. Other stories in Tanakh echo similar ideas, especially the story (I Sam. ch. 28) in which Sha'ul asks a woman who engages in necromancy (בעלת אוב) to raise Shmuel from the dead, which she apparently does. Does Judaism believe that these things are possible?

It is not only in Tanakh that we find stories like these. The Talmud is filled with stories about miracle workers, astrology, demons, the evil eye, and more – and many of those traditions have been kept alive by various sub-groups within Judaism throughout the ages. It is not uncommon to find people engaging in superstitious traditions and practices, and in some circles, even rabbinic figures using amulets, incantations, and exorcism to ensure wealth, health, a good marriage, righteous children, success in business…and so much more.

Despite the popularity of some of these ideas, some of the greatest luminaries – led by Rambam – have decried them all as foolishness. He regards them all, including the stories told in Tanakh and the Talmud, as nothing more than ancient versions of shysters, tricksters, masters of deception, misdirection, and sleight of hand, or perhaps as allegories meant to teach us a lesson.

It is fascinating that the Torah forbids these practices. For those who believe that they actually work, that prohibition means that God acknowledges that these forces exist, as He likely created them, but that we are forbidden from trying to circumvent God's dominion in the world or our direct relationship with Him by engaging with these alternate forces. For Rambam and his rationalist followers, believing that these things work is simple stupidity, and to paraphrase Rav Soloveitchik, the Torah forbids stupidity!

פרשת פינחס
PARASHAT PINḤAS

> "A leader takes people where they want to go.
> A great leader takes people where
> they don't want to go, but ought to be."
> Rosalynn Carter

After many delays, the march to the Promised Land finally resumes. The people need to be counted so that an army can be organized and so that decisions can be made about apportioning the land to the various tribes and families. The resumption of the journey is bittersweet – the dream of the people will be fulfilled, but Moshe's dream of entering the land will not. Faithful to his people, Moshe insists that an appropriate leader be appointed to replace him. Yehoshua represents the next generation, the generation of fighters who will conquer the land.

PARASHAT PINḤAS

25 ¹⁰₁₁ The LORD spoke to Moshe: "Pinḥas son of Elazar son of Aharon the priest has allayed My rage against the Israelites. Because he was passionate on My behalf among you, I ¹² did not destroy the Israelites in My own passion. Therefore, say this: I grant him My ¹³ covenant of peace. For him and for his descendants, it shall be a covenant of everlasting priesthood, because he was passionate for his God and made atonement on the part of ¹⁴ the Israelites." The name of the slain Israelite man who was killed with the Midianite ¹⁵ woman was Zimri son of Salu, leader of the ancestral House of Shimon. The name of the Midianite woman who was killed was Kozbi, daughter of Tzur the tribal leader of a Midianite ancestral house. ^{16,17,18} And the LORD spoke to Moshe: "Attack the Midianites and defeat them, for they attacked you by the deception they practiced against you in the Peor affair, and in the affair of their sister Kozbi, daughter of a Midianite leader, who was killed on the

---

העמק דבר

בשכר שהניח כעסו וחמתו של הקב״ה ברכו במדת השלום - שלא יקפיד ולא ירגיז. ובשביל כי טבע המעשה שעשה פינחס להרוג נפש בידו היה נותן להשאיר בלב הרגש עז גם אחר כך, אבל באשר היה לשם שמים משום הכי באה הברכה שיהא תמיד בנחת ובמדת השלום.

HAAMEK DAVAR

As a reward for assuaging the anger and the wrath of the Holy One, blessed be He, God blessed Pinḥas by assuring him that he would not become testy or angry. The act that Pinḥas perpetrated – that is, the killing of Zimri with his own hands – risked turning him into a vicious individual even after the event. However, since Pinḥas acted purely for the sanctification of God's name, the Almighty promised him that he would remain a calm person with a peaceful personality.

QUESTIONS FOR THOUGHT

- How would each of the commentaries answer each of the three questions posed?
- According to two of the above commentaries, God is responding to some fear that Pinḥas had, but they disagree about what his fear was. What does each one say he was afraid of?
- Which of the commentaries understands that God is not responding to a fear but simply offering a reward?
- After Avram kills the four kings, God tells him not to fear (Gen. 15:1). Look at the comments of Rashi and Radak there. Which of those could explain God's promise to Pinḥas?

WISDOM OF THE HEART

Facing a disastrous situation and leaders who seemed frozen, Pinḥas fights his peacemaker nature and rises to the occasion, taking a strong moral and religious stand. In response, God promises him a covenant of peace, understood by some to be a promise that he will never again be put into a situation where violence will be necessary. One might have thought that his act of zealotry – which certainly brings him fame – would define him or change him in some way. Pinḥas resists that, knowing that his path of peace is the one he must stick to.

If you had the choice between fame or a quiet life pursuing your true ambition, which would you choose?

פרשת פינחס

וַיְדַבֵּר יְהֹוָה אֶל־מֹשֶׁה לֵּאמֹר: פִּינְחָס בֶּן־אֶלְעָזָר בֶּן־אַהֲרֹן הַכֹּהֵן הֵשִׁיב אֶת־חֲמָתִי מֵעַל בְּנֵי־יִשְׂרָאֵל בְּקַנְאוֹ אֶת־קִנְאָתִי בְּתוֹכָם וְלֹא־כִלִּיתִי אֶת־בְּנֵי־יִשְׂרָאֵל בְּקִנְאָתִי: לָכֵן אֱמֹר הִנְנִי נֹתֵן לוֹ אֶת־בְּרִיתִי שָׁלוֹם: וְהָיְתָה לּוֹ וּלְזַרְעוֹ אַחֲרָיו בְּרִית כְּהֻנַּת עוֹלָם תַּחַת אֲשֶׁר קִנֵּא לֵאלֹהָיו וַיְכַפֵּר עַל־בְּנֵי יִשְׂרָאֵל: וְשֵׁם אִישׁ יִשְׂרָאֵל הַמֻּכֶּה אֲשֶׁר הֻכָּה אֶת־הַמִּדְיָנִית זִמְרִי בֶּן־סָלוּא נְשִׂיא בֵית־אָב לַשִּׁמְעֹנִי: וְשֵׁם הָאִשָּׁה הַמֻּכָּה הַמִּדְיָנִית כָּזְבִּי בַת־צוּר רֹאשׁ אֻמּוֹת בֵּית־אָב בְּמִדְיָן הוּא: וַיְדַבֵּר יְהֹוָה אֶל־מֹשֶׁה לֵּאמֹר: צָרוֹר אֶת־הַמִּדְיָנִים וְהִכִּיתֶם אוֹתָם: כִּי צֹרְרִים הֵם לָכֶם בְּנִכְלֵיהֶם אֲשֶׁר־נִכְּלוּ לָכֶם עַל־דְּבַר פְּעוֹר וְעַל־דְּבַר כָּזְבִּי בַת־נְשִׂיא מִדְיָן אֲחֹתָם הַמֻּכָּה בְיוֹם־

CLASSIC COMMENTATORS

God grants Pinḥas a covenant of peace. What is it, why does Pinḥas need it, and why is it an appropriate reward for what Pinḥas did?

IBN EZRA

אבן עזרא

God promised that Pinḥas need not fear retribution from Zimri's brothers, despite the fact that Zimri was a tribal prince of his father's house.

שלא יגור מאחי זמרי, כי הוא נשיא בית אב.

RABBI OVADYA SFORNO

ר' עובדיה ספורנו

Pinḥas's new covenant of peace protected him from the angel of death…God's pledge was fulfilled by the fact that Pinḥas lived an exceedingly long time, outliving his entire generation. Indeed, Pinḥas officiated in the *Mishkan* at Shilo during the incident of the concubine at Giva. That episode most certainly took place after the death of Yehoshua and the elders who governed after Yehoshua's death, and even more so if he was still alive during the rule of Yiftaḥ, whose letter to the king of Amon describes that it took place three hundred years after Israel's encounter with Moav in the wilderness (Judges 11:26).

שלום – ממלאך המות... וזה אמנם נתקיים בפינחס שהאריך ימים הרבה מאד מכל שאר אנשי דורו, עד שהיה הוא משמש במשכן שילה בזמן פלגש בגבעה, שהיה בלי ספק אחרי מות יהושע ושאר הזקנים אשר האריכו ימים אחרי יהושע (שופטים ב':ז'), וכל שכן אם היה בזמן יפתח שכתב שכתב למלך בני עמון "בשבת בני ישראל בחשבון ובבנותיה וכו' שלש מאות שנה" (שופטים י"א:כ"ו).

BEMIDBAR | CHAPTER 26

PINHAS | 244

26:1–11 Following the plague, God instructs Moshe and Elazar, now the High Priest, to take a census of Benei Yisrael similar to the one done by Moshe and Aharon nearly forty years earlier. They begin with the tribe of Reuven.

26 1 day of the plague in the Peor affair." After the plague – the LORD said to Moshe and 2 Elazar son of Aharon the priest: "Take a census of the entire Israelite community, from twenty years of age and upward, by their ancestral houses: everyone in Israel 3 capable of active service." Moshe and Elazar the priest spoke to them in the plains 4 of Moav by the Jordan opposite Yeriho: "Take a census of those twenty years of age and upward just as the LORD commanded Moshe and the Israelites who came out of 5 Egypt." Reuven was Yisrael's firstborn. Reuven's descendants: of Hanokh, the clan of 6 Hanokh; of Palu, the clan of Palu; of Hetzron, the clan of Hetzron; of Karmi, the clan 7 of Karmi. These are the Reubenite clans. Their tally was 43,730. Palu's descendants: 8 Eliav. Eliav's descendants: Nemuel, Datan, and Aviram. These were the same Datan 9 and Aviram, elect of the community, who rebelled against Moshe and Aharon in the 10 company of Korah, when they rebelled against the LORD. The earth opened its mouth and swallowed them, along with Korah, when the company died and fire consumed 11 the two hundred fifty men; and they became a sign. But the sons of Korah did not die.

IBN EZRA

We know that Korah's sons did not die, since the prophet Shmuel, his sons, and his grandsons, served as singers in the Temple (as I Chr. 6:18–23 attests). And these men are identified as "Korahites," for example in the verse, "To the lead singer – a psalm of the sons of Korah" (Ps. 49:1).... The sons of Korah are listed here in conjunction with the descendants of Reuven, because both the adult and minor sons of Datan and Aviram did perish in their fathers' rebellion. We learn from here that the villainy of Datan and Aviram was greater than that of Korah himself.

אבן עזרא

והעד: שמואל ובניו ובני בניו המשוררים (דברי הימים א' ו':י"ח-כ"ג), והן הנקראין הקרחים (דברי הימים ב' כ':י"ט), לבני קרח מזמור (תהלים מ"ט:א')... והזכיר הכתוב: ובני קרח עם בני ראובן, בעבור כי בני דתן ואבירם גדולים וקטנים מתו. והנה רעת דתן ואבירם קשה מרעת קרח.

QUESTIONS FOR THOUGHT

- In what way is Rashi's opinion very different from that of the other two commentaries?
- What evidence does Ibn Ezra bring which seems to challenge Rashi's opinion?
- Why does Ibn Ezra feel a need in his last line to contrast the evil of Korah with that of Datan and Aviram?

WISDOM OF THE HEART

The Torah goes out of its way to remind us that while Korah died in his rebellion, Korah's sons did not. In fact, we later find that they are guardians of the *Beit Hamikdash* and authors of some psalms. Our parents may influence us, but our destiny is ultimately determined by our own decisions.

How do we demonstrate respect for our parents even as we choose paths which are different from theirs?

כו א הַמַּגֵּפָה עַל־דְּבַר־פְּעוֹר: וַיְהִי אַחֲרֵי הַמַּגֵּפָה
וַיֹּאמֶר יְהוָה אֶל־מֹשֶׁה וְאֶל אֶלְעָזָר בֶּן־אַהֲרֹן הַכֹּהֵן לֵאמֹר:
ב שְׂאוּ אֶת־רֹאשׁ ׀ כָּל־עֲדַת בְּנֵי־יִשְׂרָאֵל מִבֶּן עֶשְׂרִים שָׁנָה
וָמַעְלָה לְבֵית אֲבֹתָם כָּל־יֹצֵא צָבָא בְּיִשְׂרָאֵל: וַיְדַבֵּר מֹשֶׁה
וְאֶלְעָזָר הַכֹּהֵן אֹתָם בְּעַרְבֹת מוֹאָב עַל־יַרְדֵּן יְרֵחוֹ לֵאמֹר:
ד מִבֶּן עֶשְׂרִים שָׁנָה וָמָעְלָה כַּאֲשֶׁר צִוָּה יְהוָה אֶת־מֹשֶׁה וּבְנֵי
ה יִשְׂרָאֵל הַיֹּצְאִים מֵאֶרֶץ מִצְרָיִם: רְאוּבֵן בְּכוֹר יִשְׂרָאֵל בְּנֵי   שני
ו רְאוּבֵן חֲנוֹךְ מִשְׁפַּחַת הַחֲנֹכִי לְפַלּוּא מִשְׁפַּחַת הַפַּלֻּאִי: לְחֶצְרֹן
ז מִשְׁפַּחַת הַחֶצְרוֹנִי לְכַרְמִי מִשְׁפַּחַת הַכַּרְמִי: אֵלֶּה מִשְׁפְּחֹת
הָרֻאוּבֵנִי וַיִּהְיוּ פְקֻדֵיהֶם שְׁלֹשָׁה וְאַרְבָּעִים אֶלֶף וּשְׁבַע מֵאוֹת
ח וּשְׁלֹשִׁים: וּבְנֵי פַלּוּא אֱלִיאָב: וּבְנֵי אֱלִיאָב נְמוּאֵל וְדָתָן
ט וַאֲבִירָם הוּא־דָתָן וַאֲבִירָם קְרוּאֵי הָעֵדָה אֲשֶׁר הִצּוּ עַל־ קְרִאֵי
מֹשֶׁה וְעַל־אַהֲרֹן בַּעֲדַת־קֹרַח בְּהַצֹּתָם עַל־יְהוָה: וַתִּפְתַּח
י הָאָרֶץ אֶת־פִּיהָ וַתִּבְלַע אֹתָם וְאֶת־קֹרַח בְּמוֹת הָעֵדָה בַּאֲכֹל
יא הָאֵשׁ אֵת חֲמִשִּׁים וּמָאתַיִם אִישׁ וַיִּהְיוּ לְנֵס: וּבְנֵי־קֹרַח לֹא־

CLASSIC COMMENTATORS

In counting Reuven, the Torah recalls those members of Reuven's tribe who died in the Koraḥ rebellion. In the process, the Torah mentions that Koraḥ's sons did not die. Why did they not die, and why does the Torah bother to include this?

רש״י | **RASHI**

הם היו בעצה תחלה, ובשעת המחלוקת הירהרו תשובה בלבם, לפיכך נתבצר להם מקום גבוה בגיהנם וישבו שם.

Initially, Koraḥ's sons plotted the rebellion with him. However, during the actual confrontation with Moshe they decided in their hearts to withdraw and repent. As such, a special elevation within the depths of hell was set aside for them and they resided there.

ר' יוסף בכור שור | **RABBI YOSEF BEKHOR SHOR**

בניו כבר היו מוחלקין ממנו, ולא נצטרפו עמו במחלוקת, ולא מתו.

Koraḥ's sons had already distanced themselves from their father, so they did not join in his revolt, and were therefore not killed.

26:12–27 *The counting continues with the tribes who camp with Reuven (Shimon and Gad), followed by Yehuda and the tribes who camp with it (Yissakhar and Zevulun).*

12 Shimon's descendants by their clans: of Nemuel, the clan of Nemuel; of Yamin, the
13 clan of Yamin; of Yakhin, the clan of Yakhin; of Zeraḥ, the clan of Zeraḥ; of Sha'ul, the
14 clan of Sha'ul. These are the Simeonite clans: 22,200. Gad's descendants by their clans:
15 of Tzefon, the clan of Tzefon; of Ḥagi, the clan of Ḥagi; of Shuni, the clan of Shuni;
16 of Ozni, the clan of Ozni; of Eri, the clan of Eri; of Arod, the clan of Arod; of Areli,
17
18 the clan of Areli. These are the Gadite clans. Their tally was 40,500. Among Yehuda's
19
20 sons were Er and Onan; Er and Onan died in the land of Canaan. Yehuda's descendants by their clans: of Shela, the clan of Shela; of Peretz, the clan of Peretz; of Zeraḥ,
21 the clan of Zeraḥ. Peretz's descendants: of Ḥetzron, the clan of Ḥetzron; of Ḥamul,
22 the clan of Ḥamul. These are the clans of Yehuda. Their tally was 76,500. Yissakhar's
23
24 descendants by their clans: of Tola, the clan of Tola; of Puva, the clan of Puva; of
25 Yashuv, the clan of Yashuv; of Shimron, the clan of Shimron. These are the clans of
26 Yissakhar. Their tally was 64,300. Zevulun's descendants by their clans: of Sered, the
27 clan of Sered; of Elon, the clan of Elon; of Yaḥle'el, the clan of Yaḥle'el. These are the

---

WISDOM OF THE HEART

One of the families of Gad is identified as being from Ozni, a name not mentioned in any previous census. Rashi suggests that this family was previously known as Etzbon. Noticing that Etzbon sounds like the Hebrew word for finger while Ozni is like the word for ear, the Rebbe of Ishbitz suggests that in Egypt they plugged their ears with their fingers so that they not hear impure ideas, but now that they are entering the holy land they open their ears to its sanctity.

From your experience, how do you think the things we hear impact us?

QUICK BITE

Why do we need to be told about Er and Onan? They died even before the family went down to Egypt? If we remember the story in Genesis, they were married to Tamar. Their deaths began the process through which Yehuda got together with Tamar, bringing Peretz and Zeraḥ into the world. These would become the two main families in Yehuda, including the family from which all future kings would come. Even though they died as a result of their sins, the Torah wants us to remember them as the ones who were the catalysts for the emergence of royalty in *Am Yisrael*.

במדבר | פרק כו

יב מַתּוּ: בְּנֵי שִׁמְעוֹן לְמִשְׁפְּחֹתָם לִנְמוּאֵל מִשְׁפַּחַת
יג הַנְּמוּאֵלִי לְיָמִין מִשְׁפַּחַת הַיָּמִינִי לְיָכִין מִשְׁפַּחַת הַיָּכִינִי: לְזֶרַח
יד מִשְׁפַּחַת הַזַּרְחִי לְשָׁאוּל מִשְׁפַּחַת הַשָּׁאוּלִי: אֵלֶּה מִשְׁפְּחֹת
טו הַשִּׁמְעֹנִי שְׁנַיִם וְעֶשְׂרִים אֶלֶף וּמָאתָיִם: בְּנֵי גָד
לְמִשְׁפְּחֹתָם לִצְפוֹן מִשְׁפַּחַת הַצְּפוֹנִי לְחַגִּי מִשְׁפַּחַת הַחַגִּי
טז לְשׁוּנִי מִשְׁפַּחַת הַשּׁוּנִי: לְאָזְנִי מִשְׁפַּחַת הָאָזְנִי לְעֵרִי מִשְׁפַּחַת
יז הָעֵרִי: לַאֲרוֹד מִשְׁפַּחַת הָאֲרוֹדִי לְאַרְאֵלִי מִשְׁפַּחַת הָאַרְאֵלִי:
יח אֵלֶּה מִשְׁפְּחֹת בְּנֵי־גָד לִפְקֻדֵיהֶם אַרְבָּעִים אֶלֶף וַחֲמֵשׁ
יט מֵאוֹת: בְּנֵי יְהוּדָה עֵר וְאוֹנָן וַיָּמָת עֵר וְאוֹנָן בְּאֶרֶץ
כ כְּנָעַן: וַיִּהְיוּ בְנֵי־יְהוּדָה לְמִשְׁפְּחֹתָם לְשֵׁלָה מִשְׁפַּחַת הַשֵּׁלָנִי
כא לְפֶרֶץ מִשְׁפַּחַת הַפַּרְצִי לְזֶרַח מִשְׁפַּחַת הַזַּרְחִי: וַיִּהְיוּ בְנֵי־
פֶרֶץ לְחֶצְרֹן מִשְׁפַּחַת הַחֶצְרֹנִי לְחָמוּל מִשְׁפַּחַת הֶחָמוּלִי:
כב אֵלֶּה מִשְׁפְּחֹת יְהוּדָה לִפְקֻדֵיהֶם שִׁשָּׁה וְשִׁבְעִים אֶלֶף וַחֲמֵשׁ
כג מֵאוֹת: בְּנֵי יִשָּׂשכָר לְמִשְׁפְּחֹתָם תּוֹלָע מִשְׁפַּחַת
כד הַתּוֹלָעִי לְפֻוָּה מִשְׁפַּחַת הַפּוּנִי: לְיָשׁוּב מִשְׁפַּחַת הַיָּשֻׁבִי לְשִׁמְרֹן
כה מִשְׁפַּחַת הַשִּׁמְרֹנִי: אֵלֶּה מִשְׁפְּחֹת יִשָּׂשכָר לִפְקֻדֵיהֶם אַרְבָּעָה
כו וְשִׁשִּׁים אֶלֶף וּשְׁלֹשׁ מֵאוֹת: בְּנֵי זְבוּלֻן לְמִשְׁפְּחֹתָם
לְסֶרֶד מִשְׁפַּחַת הַסַּרְדִּי לְאֵלוֹן מִשְׁפַּחַת הָאֵלֹנִי לְיַחְלְאֵל
כז מִשְׁפַּחַת הַיַּחְלְאֵלִי: אֵלֶּה מִשְׁפְּחֹת הַזְּבוּלֹנִי לִפְקֻדֵיהֶם שִׁשִּׁים

TEXTUAL SKILLS

1. Compare the size of Shimon with its size in the first counting. Can you explain the dramatic change?

2. What information does the Torah include in this passage which seems out of place?

26:28–41 *The camp of Yosef (Menashe-Efrayim) and Binyamin, all descendants of Raḥel, is the third to be counted.*

28 Zebulunite clans. Their tally was 60,500. Yosef's descendants by their clans: Menashe and
29 Efrayim – Menashe's descendants: of Makhir, the clan of Makhir. Makhir had a son
30 Gilad. Of Gilad, the clan of Gilad. These are Gilad's descendants: of I'ezer, the clan of
31 I'ezer; of Ḥelek, the clan of Ḥelek; of Asriel, the clan of Asriel; of Shekhem, the clan
32/33 of Shekhem; of Shemida, the clan of Shemida; and of Ḥefer, the clan of Ḥefer. But
Tzelofḥad son of Ḥefer had no sons, only daughters. The names of Tzelofḥad's daugh-
34 ters were Maḥla, Noa, Ḥogla, Milka, and Tirtza. These are the clans of Menashe. Their
35 tally was 52,700. These are Efrayim's descendants by their clans: of Shutelaḥ, the clan of
36 Shutelaḥ; of Bekher, the clan of Bekher; of Taḥan, the clan of Taḥan. These are Shutelaḥ's
37 descendants: of Eran, the clan of Eran. These are the clans of Efrayim. Their tally was
38 32,500. All these are Yosef's descendants by their clans. Binyamin's descendants by their
clans: of Bela, the clan of Bela; of Ashbel, the clan of Ashbel; of Aḥiram, the clan of
39/40 Aḥiram; of Shefufam, the clan of Shefufam; of Ḥufam, the clan of Ḥufam. Bela's descen-
41 dants were Ard and Naaman: the clan of Ard; of Naaman, the clan of Naaman. These

---

TEXTUAL SKILLS

1. While the tribes on average remained the same size over the course of forty years, Efrayim increased by more than half. Can you find an explanation?
2. If you consider Efrayim and Menashe to be one tribe, Yosef, it turns out that Yosef and one other are the largest tribes, by far. Which is the other one?
3. There is one family highlighted in Menashe, who, like Reuven and Yehuda in their camps, was the leader of his camp. Which family is that, and what is special about them?

QUICK BITE

The Torah tells us here about the children of Makhir, the son of Menashe. The end of Genesis (50:23) tells us that the children of Makhir were raised on Yosef's lap. Yosef's great-grandchildren were third generation born and raised in Egyptian royalty. Yosef took great care to ensure that they would remember their heritage, and that despite their current privileged status, they would eventually be enslaved but brought by God to their ancestral homeland. It is here that we see Yosef's long-term vision come to fruition and his investment paying off.

כח אֶ֖לֶף וַחֲמֵ֣שׁ מֵא֑וֹת׃ בְּנֵ֥י יוֹסֵ֖ף לְמִשְׁפְּחֹתָ֑ם מְנַשֶּׁ֖ה
כט וְאֶפְרָֽיִם׃ בְּנֵ֣י מְנַשֶּׁ֗ה לְמָכִיר֙ מִשְׁפַּ֣חַת הַמָּכִירִ֔י וּמָכִ֖יר הוֹלִ֣יד
ל אֶת־גִּלְעָ֑ד לְגִלְעָ֕ד מִשְׁפַּ֖חַת הַגִּלְעָדִֽי׃ אֵ֚לֶּה בְּנֵ֣י גִלְעָ֔ד אִיעֶ֕זֶר
לא מִשְׁפַּ֖חַת הָאִֽיעֶזְרִ֑י לְחֵ֕לֶק מִשְׁפַּ֖חַת הַֽחֶלְקִֽי׃ וְאַ֨שְׂרִיאֵ֔ל מִשְׁפַּ֖חַת
לב הָֽאַשְׂרִֽאֵלִ֑י וְשֶׁ֕כֶם מִשְׁפַּ֖חַת הַשִּׁכְמִֽי׃ וּשְׁמִידָ֕ע מִשְׁפַּ֖חַת
לג הַשְּׁמִידָעִ֑י וְחֵ֕פֶר מִשְׁפַּ֖חַת הַֽחֶפְרִֽי׃ וּצְלָפְחָ֣ד בֶּן־חֵ֗פֶר לֹא־הָ֥יוּ
ל֛וֹ בָּנִ֖ים כִּ֣י אִם־בָּנ֑וֹת וְשֵׁם֙ בְּנ֣וֹת צְלָפְחָ֔ד מַחְלָ֣ה וְנֹעָ֔ה חָגְלָ֥ה
לד מִלְכָּ֖ה וְתִרְצָֽה׃ אֵ֖לֶּה מִשְׁפְּחֹ֣ת מְנַשֶּׁ֑ה וּפְקֻ֣דֵיהֶ֔ם שְׁנַ֥יִם וַחֲמִשִּׁ֖ים
לה אֶ֖לֶף וּשְׁבַ֥ע מֵאֽוֹת׃ אֵ֣לֶּה בְנֵֽי־אֶפְרַ֘יִם֮ לְמִשְׁפְּחֹתָם֒
לְשׁוּתֶ֗לַח מִשְׁפַּ֙חַת֙ הַשֻּׁ֣תַלְחִ֔י לְבֶ֕כֶר מִשְׁפַּ֖חַת הַבַּכְרִ֑י לְתַ֕חַן
לו מִשְׁפַּ֖חַת הַֽתַּחֲנִֽי׃ וְאֵ֖לֶּה בְּנֵ֣י שׁוּתָ֑לַח לְעֵרָ֕ן מִשְׁפַּ֖חַת הָעֵרָנִֽי׃
לז אֵ֣לֶּה מִשְׁפְּחֹ֤ת בְּנֵֽי־אֶפְרַ֙יִם֙ לִפְקֻ֣דֵיהֶ֔ם שְׁנַ֧יִם וּשְׁלֹשִׁ֛ים אֶ֖לֶף
וַחֲמֵ֣שׁ מֵא֑וֹת אֵ֥לֶּה בְנֵי־יוֹסֵ֖ף לְמִשְׁפְּחֹתָֽם׃ בְּנֵ֣י בִנְיָמִן֮
לח לְמִשְׁפְּחֹתָם֒ לְבֶ֗לַע מִשְׁפַּ֙חַת֙ הַבַּלְעִ֔י לְאַשְׁבֵּ֕ל מִשְׁפַּ֖חַת הָֽאַשְׁבֵּלִ֑י
לט לַֽאֲחִירָ֕ם מִשְׁפַּ֖חַת הָאֲחִֽירָמִֽי׃ לִשְׁפוּפָ֕ם מִשְׁפַּ֖חַת הַשּׁוּפָמִ֑י
מ לְחוּפָ֕ם מִשְׁפַּ֖חַת הַחוּפָמִֽי׃ וַיִּהְי֥וּ בְנֵי־בֶ֖לַע אַ֣רְדְּ וְנַעֲמָ֑ן מִשְׁפַּ֙חַת֙
מא הָֽאַרְדִּ֔י לְנַֽעֲמָ֕ן מִשְׁפַּ֖חַת הַֽנַּעֲמִֽי׃ אֵ֥לֶּה בְנֵֽי־בִנְיָמִ֖ן לְמִשְׁפְּחֹתָ֑ם

WISDOM OF THE HEART

Genesis (46:21) mentions ten sons of Binyamin, yet only five are listed here. According to a midrash, five had strayed so far from Avraham's path that they never left Egypt. It is interesting that when Binyamin is born his mother names him Ben Oni, son of my suffering, while his father calls him Binyamin, son of my strength. Perhaps those who saw themselves as defined by suffering ultimately succumbed to it in Egypt, but those who defined themselves as strong used that fortitude to pull through.

42 are the clans of Binyamin. Their tally was 45,600. These are Dan's descendants by their
43 clans: of Shuham, the clan of Shuham. These are the clans of Dan; all the Shuhamite
44 clans according to their tally were 64,400. Asher's descendants by their clans: of Yimna,
45 the clan of Yimna; of Yishvi, the clan of Yishvi; of Beria, the clan of Beria. Of Beria's
46 descendants: of Ḥever, the clan of Ḥever; of Malkiel, the clan of Malkiel. The name
47 of Asher's daughter was Seraḥ. These are the clans of Asher; their tally was 53,400.
48 Naftali's descendants by their clans: of Yaḥze'el, the clan of Yaḥtze'el; of Guni, the clan
49 of Guni; of Yetzer, the clan of Yetzer; of Shilem, the clan of Shilem. These are all the
50
51 clans of Naftali. Their tally was 45,400. The total number of those Israelite men was 601,730.
52 The LORD spoke to Moshe: "The land shall be apportioned to them for inheritance
53
54 by the tally of their names. To those who are many, give a large inheritance; to those who are few, a small inheritance. Let each be given its inheritance in keeping with its
55 number. The land must be apportioned by lot. By the names of their ancestral tribes
56 they shall inherit. Whether large or small, each tribe will inherit by means of the lot."

RAMBAN רמב״ן

לשבטים נתחלקה, שנים עשר חלקים שווים עשו ממנה ונטל כל שבט החלק שיצא לו הגורל עליו.

The land of Israel was divided among the tribes; it was split into twelve regions of equal size. A lottery determined which tribe inherited which area.

QUESTIONS FOR THOUGHT

- In what way does verse 54 seem to contradict verses 55–56? Which of those seems to be the foundation for Rashi's opinion and which is the basis for Ramban's?
- Aside from the size of the portions of land, what other considerations do you think need to be taken into account when dividing up the land?

TEXTUAL SKILLS

1. Who stands out in the counting of Asher?
2. What two words stand out in verses 54 and 56, and which two highlight the conflict between those two verses?

WISDOM OF THE HEART

We know that the different parts of the Promised Land had different capacities – some were good for wheat, others for grapes, others for grazing, and so on. R. Yeshaya Halevi Horowitz, in his *Shenei Luḥot Habrit*, suggests that each portion of land also had a different kind of spiritual potential. The lottery for dividing the land was designed to match the spiritual potential of the land with the capacity of the tribe to bring that potential into reality.

People experience spirituality differently from each other. What kinds of experiences give you a spiritual feeling?

במדבר | פרק כו

מב וּפְקֻדֵיהֶ֕ם חֲמִשָּׁ֧ה וְאַרְבָּעִ֛ים אֶ֖לֶף וְשֵׁ֥שׁ מֵאֽוֹת׃ אֵ֣לֶּה בְנֵי־דָן֙ לְמִשְׁפְּחֹתָ֔ם לְשׁוּחָם֙ מִשְׁפַּ֣חַת הַשּׁוּחָמִ֔י אֵ֥לֶּה מִשְׁפְּחֹ֖ת דָּ֥ן לְמִשְׁפְּחֹתָֽם׃
מג כָּל־מִשְׁפְּחֹ֥ת הַשּׁוּחָמִ֖י לִפְקֻדֵיהֶ֑ם אַרְבָּעָ֧ה וְשִׁשִּׁ֛ים אֶ֖לֶף וְאַרְבַּ֥ע מֵאֽוֹת׃
מד בְּנֵ֣י אָשֵׁר֮ לְמִשְׁפְּחֹתָם֒ לְיִמְנָ֗ה מִשְׁפַּ֙חַת֙ הַיִּמְנָ֔ה לְיִשְׁוִ֕י מִשְׁפַּ֖חַת הַיִּשְׁוִ֑י לִבְרִיעָ֕ה מִשְׁפַּ֖חַת הַבְּרִיעִֽי׃
מה לִבְנֵ֣י בְרִיעָ֔ה לְחֶ֕בֶר מִשְׁפַּ֖חַת הַחֶבְרִ֑י לְמַ֨לְכִּיאֵ֔ל מִשְׁפַּ֖חַת הַמַּלְכִּיאֵלִֽי׃
מו וְשֵׁ֥ם בַּת־אָשֵׁ֖ר שָֽׂרַח׃
מז אֵ֛לֶּה מִשְׁפְּחֹ֥ת בְּנֵי־אָשֵׁ֖ר לִפְקֻדֵיהֶ֑ם שְׁלֹשָׁ֧ה וַחֲמִשִּׁ֛ים אֶ֖לֶף וְאַרְבַּ֥ע מֵאֽוֹת׃
מח בְּנֵ֤י נַפְתָּלִי֙ לְמִשְׁפְּחֹתָ֔ם לְיַ֨חְצְאֵ֔ל מִשְׁפַּ֖חַת הַיַּחְצְאֵלִ֑י לְגוּנִ֕י מִשְׁפַּ֖חַת הַגּוּנִֽי׃
מט לְיֵ֕צֶר מִשְׁפַּ֖חַת הַיִּצְרִ֑י לְשִׁלֵּ֕ם מִשְׁפַּ֖חַת הַשִּׁלֵּמִֽי׃
נ אֵ֛לֶּה מִשְׁפְּחֹ֥ת נַפְתָּלִ֖י לְמִשְׁפְּחֹתָ֑ם וּפְקֻ֣דֵיהֶ֔ם חֲמִשָּׁ֧ה וְאַרְבָּעִ֛ים אֶ֖לֶף וְאַרְבַּ֥ע מֵאֽוֹת׃
נא אֵ֗לֶּה פְּקוּדֵי֙ בְּנֵ֣י יִשְׂרָאֵ֔ל שֵׁשׁ־מֵא֥וֹת אֶ֖לֶף וָאָ֑לֶף שְׁבַ֥ע מֵא֖וֹת וּשְׁלֹשִֽׁים׃

שלישי

נב וַיְדַבֵּ֥ר יְהֹוָ֖ה אֶל־מֹשֶׁ֥ה לֵּאמֹֽר׃
נג לָאֵ֗לֶּה תֵּחָלֵ֥ק הָאָ֛רֶץ בְּנַחֲלָ֖ה בְּמִסְפַּ֥ר שֵׁמֽוֹת׃
נד לָרַ֗ב תַּרְבֶּה֙ נַחֲלָת֔וֹ וְלַמְעַ֕ט תַּמְעִ֖יט נַחֲלָת֑וֹ אִ֚ישׁ לְפִ֣י פְקֻדָ֔יו יֻתַּ֖ן נַחֲלָתֽוֹ׃
נה אַךְ־בְּגוֹרָ֕ל יֵחָלֵ֖ק אֶת־הָאָ֑רֶץ לִשְׁמ֥וֹת מַטּוֹת־אֲבֹתָ֖ם יִנְחָֽלוּ׃
נו עַל־פִּי֙ הַגּוֹרָ֔ל תֵּחָלֵ֖ק נַחֲלָת֑וֹ בֵּ֥ין

CLASSIC COMMENTATORS

How was it decided who would get which portion of land and what size?

RASHI

A tribe with a large population was granted a commensurate area of land. Now even though this meant that the tribal territories were necessarily of different sizes – since the bigger tribes received more land than the smaller tribes – still, a lottery was employed to divide the land.

רש״י

לשבט שהיה מרובה באוכלוסין נתנו חלק רב, ואף על פי שלא היו החלקים שווים, שהרי הכל לפי ריבוי השבט חלקו החלקים.

BEMIDBAR | CHAPTER 26

> **26:57–65** *Parallel to the counting of Benei Yisrael by families is the counting of Levi by families, even though Levi gets no portion in the land.*

57 These are the numbers of the Levites by their clans: of Gershon, the clan of Gershon;
58 of Kehat, the clan of Kehat; of Merari, the clan of Merari. These are the Levite clans: the clan of Livna, the clan of Ḥevron, the clan of Maḥli, the clan of Mushi, and the clan of
59 Koraḥ. Kehat had a son Amram. The name of Amram's wife was Yokheved daughter of Levi; she had been born to Levi in Egypt. She bore to Amram Aharon, Moshe, and their
60 sister Miriam. To Aharon were born Nadav, Avihu, Elazar, and Itamar. Nadav and Avihu
61
62 died when they offered unauthorized fire before the Lord. Their number was 23,000, this including every male one month of age and upward. They were not numbered along with the Israelites because no land inheritance was given to them in the Israelites'
63 midst. This was the census that Moshe and Elazar the priest took of the Israelites on the
64 plains of Moav by the Jordan opposite Yeriḥo. It contained not one man who had been counted by Moshe and Aharon the priest when they took the census of the Israelites
65 in the Sinai Desert. For the Lord had said of those, "They shall die in the wilderness." Not one of them was left now except for Kalev son of Yefuneh and Yehoshua son of

---

QUESTIONS FOR THOUGHT

- What two different answers does Ramban offer to his question?
- Can you find support within this chapter for either of those two answers?

TEXTUAL SKILLS

1. As with four of the other tribes, there appears to be extra information in the counting of Levi. What is it?
2. Earlier, verses 52–56 seem to be a concluding section for the counting. Why is there a need for a second concluding section in verses 64–65?
3. In the earlier counting (ch. 1), Levi was also not counted together with *Benei Yisrael*. What reason was offered there for their exclusion, and in what way did that reason change in this counting?

WISDOM OF THE HEART

Since the land was divided by the male family heads, it makes sense that the people named in this census are males. There are four exceptions. One is the daughters of Tzelofḥad, who end up receiving their father's portion in the land. A second is Seraḥ, daughter of Asher, who is also listed among those who went down to Egypt. The third is Yokheved, the matriarch of the leadership of the exodus, the leadership which includes the fourth, Miriam. The Torah wants to make sure that we understand that even though women are often not at the center of the story, their contributions should not be hidden.

במדבר | פרק כו

נז וְאֵ֛לֶּה פְקוּדֵ֥י הַלֵּוִ֖י לְמִשְׁפְּחֹתָ֑ם לְגֵרְשׁ֗וֹן רַ֣ב לִמְעָֽט׃
מִשְׁפַּ֤חַת הַגֵּֽרְשֻׁנִּ֙י לִקְהָ֔ת מִשְׁפַּ֥חַת הַקְּהָתִ֖י לִמְרָרִ֑י מִשְׁפַּ֖חַת
נח הַמְּרָרִֽי׃ אֵ֣לֶּה ׀ מִשְׁפְּחֹ֣ת לֵוִ֗י מִשְׁפַּ֨חַת הַלִּבְנִ֜י מִשְׁפַּ֤חַת הַֽחֶבְרֹנִי֙
מִשְׁפַּ֣חַת הַמַּחְלִ֔י מִשְׁפַּ֖חַת הַמּוּשִׁ֑י מִשְׁפַּ֖חַת הַקָּרְחִ֑י וּקְהָ֖ת
נט הוֹלִ֥ד אֶת־עַמְרָֽם׃ וְשֵׁ֣ם ׀ אֵ֣שֶׁת עַמְרָ֗ם יוֹכֶ֙בֶד֙ בַּת־לֵוִ֔י אֲשֶׁ֨ר
יָלְדָ֥ה אֹתָ֛הּ לְלֵוִ֖י בְּמִצְרָ֑יִם וַתֵּ֣לֶד לְעַמְרָ֗ם אֶֽת־אַהֲרֹן֙ וְאֶת־
ס מֹשֶׁ֔ה וְאֵ֖ת מִרְיָ֥ם אֲחֹתָֽם׃ וַיִּוָּלֵ֣ד לְאַהֲרֹ֔ן אֶת־נָדָ֖ב וְאֶת־אֲבִיה֑וּא
סא אֶת־אֶלְעָזָ֖ר וְאֶת־אִֽיתָמָֽר׃ וַיָּ֥מָת נָדָ֖ב וַאֲבִיה֑וּא בְּהַקְרִיבָ֥ם
סב אֵשׁ־זָרָ֖ה לִפְנֵ֥י יְהוָֽה׃ וַיִּהְי֣וּ פְקֻדֵיהֶ֗ם שְׁלֹשָׁ֤ה וְעֶשְׂרִים֙ אֶ֔לֶף
כָּל־זָכָ֖ר מִבֶּן־חֹ֣דֶשׁ וָמָ֑עְלָה כִּ֣י ׀ לֹ֣א הָתְפָּקְד֗וּ בְּתוֹךְ֙ בְּנֵ֣י יִשְׂרָאֵ֔ל
סג כִּ֠י לֹא־נִתַּ֤ן לָהֶם֙ נַחֲלָ֔ה בְּת֖וֹךְ בְּנֵ֣י יִשְׂרָאֵֽל׃ אֵ֚לֶּה פְּקוּדֵ֣י מֹשֶׁ֔ה
וְאֶלְעָזָ֖ר הַכֹּהֵ֑ן אֲשֶׁ֨ר פָּֽקְד֜וּ אֶת־בְּנֵ֤י יִשְׂרָאֵל֙ בְּעַֽרְבֹ֣ת מוֹאָ֔ב עַ֖ל
סד יַרְדֵּ֥ן יְרֵחֽוֹ׃ וּבְאֵ֙לֶּה֙ לֹא־הָ֣יָה אִ֔ישׁ מִפְּקוּדֵ֣י מֹשֶׁ֔ה וְאַהֲרֹ֖ן הַכֹּהֵ֑ן
סה אֲשֶׁ֥ר פָּקְד֛וּ אֶת־בְּנֵ֥י יִשְׂרָאֵ֖ל בְּמִדְבַּ֣ר סִינָֽי׃ כִּֽי־אָמַ֤ר יְהוָה֙ לָהֶ֔ם
מ֥וֹת יָמֻ֖תוּ בַּמִּדְבָּ֑ר וְלֹא־נוֹתַ֤ר מֵהֶם֙ אִ֔ישׁ כִּ֚י אִם־כָּלֵ֣ב בֶּן־יְפֻנֶּ֔ה

CLASSIC COMMENTATORS

If the counting here is for dividing up the land, why is Levi counted at all?

רמב״ן

לא ידעתי למה ימנה בני לוי ומה תועלת עתה במנינם. אולי לאלה נתנו הערים לשבת ומגרשיהם לבהמתם לא לנולדים אחרי כן, או שנעשה לכבוד להם מאת י״י, שלא יהא לגיון של מלך פחות, שלא ישגיחו עליו למנותו כשאר העם.

RAMBAN

I do not know why the tribe of Levi was counted, or what purpose was served by their census. Perhaps this group was tabulated for the sake of establishing the Levite cities and the accompanying pastureland for their cattle, so that only the current Levites were allotted these places, and not those who were born later. Alternately, the Levites were now tabulated for the sake of being honored by God, so that the "King's Legion" would not be treated less respectfully than the other tribes, ignoring them when everybody else was being counted.

27 1 Nun. Then the daughters of Tzelofḥad son of Ḥefer son of Gilad son of Makhir son of Menashe, of the clans of Menashe son of Yosef, came forward; the daughters' names 2 were Maḥla, Noa, Ḥogla, Milka, and Tirtza. And they stood before Moshe, Elazar the priest, the princes, and all the community at the entrance to the Tent of Meeting, and 3 said, "Our father died in the wilderness. He was not among the company of those who gathered together against the Lord in the company of Koraḥ; he died in his own sin, 4 and had no sons. Why should our father's name be lost to his family only because he 5 had no son? Give us a portion of land along with our father's brothers." Moshe brought their case before the Lord. 6/7 And the Lord said to Moshe: "What Tzelofḥad's daughters say is right. You must certainly give them a heritable portion of land along with their father's kin. Transfer their 8 father's portion to them. Speak to the Israelites; tell them: If a man dies and has no son, 9 you shall transfer his property to his daughters. If he does not have a daughter, you shall 10 give his property to his brothers. If he has no brothers, you shall give his property to his 11 father's brothers. If his father had no brothers, give his property to the closest relative in his clan, and that person shall inherit it." This shall be a decree of law for the Israelites, as the Lord commanded Moshe.

RAMBAN
רמב״ן
שאינו במתי המגפות, אבל מת במדבר על מטתו.

The daughters claimed that Tzelofḥad was not among the people killed in one of the plagues. Rather, he died in the wilderness, at home in his bed.

RALBAG
רלב״ג
רוצה לומר שחטאו היה סיבה שמת בלא בנים, כי כל עונש ראוי שייוחס אל חטא.

Tzelofḥad's daughters explained that the punishment for their father's sin was that he died without sons. For every retribution must be traced back to its cause.

QUESTIONS FOR THOUGHT

- What do the explanations of Bekhor Shor and Ramban have in common? What is the primary difference between them?
- Tzelofḥad's daughters mention specifically that he was not part of Koraḥ's rebellion. Does that strengthen or weaken the explanations of Bekhor Shor and Ramban?
- Look at the *taamei hamikra* (the *trop*) on verse 3. Does it support or challenge Ralbag's explanation?

WISDOM OF THE HEART

The story of Tzelofḥad's daughters is a story about humility – their humility in their polite request of Moshe, and Moshe's humility in bringing their case to God and acknowledging his own limitations.

במדבר | פרק כז

כז א וִיהוֹשֻׁעַ בִּן־נְוּן: וַתִּקְרַבְנָה בְּנוֹת צְלָפְחָד בֶּן־חֵפֶר בֶּן־גִּלְעָד בֶּן־מָכִיר בֶּן־מְנַשֶּׁה לְמִשְׁפְּחֹת מְנַשֶּׁה בֶן־יוֹסֵף וְאֵלֶּה ב שְׁמוֹת בְּנֹתָיו מַחְלָה נֹעָה וְחָגְלָה וּמִלְכָּה וְתִרְצָה: וַתַּעֲמֹדְנָה לִפְנֵי מֹשֶׁה וְלִפְנֵי אֶלְעָזָר הַכֹּהֵן וְלִפְנֵי הַנְּשִׂיאִם וְכָל־הָעֵדָה ג פֶּתַח אְֹהֶל־מוֹעֵד לֵאמֹר: אָבִינוּ מֵת בַּמִּדְבָּר וְהוּא לֹא־הָיָה בְּתוֹךְ הָעֵדָה הַנּוֹעָדִים עַל־יְהוָה בַּעֲדַת־קֹרַח כִּי־בְחֶטְאוֹ מֵת ד וּבָנִים לֹא־הָיוּ לוֹ: לָמָּה יִגָּרַע שֵׁם־אָבִינוּ מִתּוֹךְ מִשְׁפַּחְתּוֹ כִּי אֵין לוֹ בֵּן תְּנָה־לָּנוּ אֲחֻזָּה בְּתוֹךְ אֲחֵי אָבִינוּ: ה וַיַּקְרֵב מֹשֶׁה אֶת־מִשְׁפָּטָן לִפְנֵי יְהוָה:

רביעי ו וַיֹּאמֶר יְהוָה אֶל־מֹשֶׁה לֵּאמֹר: ז כֵּן בְּנוֹת צְלָפְחָד דֹּבְרֹת נָתֹן תִּתֵּן לָהֶם אֲחֻזַּת נַחֲלָה בְּתוֹךְ אֲחֵי אֲבִיהֶם וְהַעֲבַרְתָּ אֶת־נַחֲלַת אֲבִיהֶן לָהֶן: ח וְאֶל־בְּנֵי יִשְׂרָאֵל תְּדַבֵּר לֵאמֹר אִישׁ כִּי־יָמוּת וּבֵן אֵין לוֹ וְהַעֲבַרְתֶּם אֶת־נַחֲלָתוֹ לְבִתּוֹ: ט וְאִם־אֵין לוֹ בַּת וּנְתַתֶּם אֶת־נַחֲלָתוֹ לְאֶחָיו: י וְאִם־אֵין לוֹ אַחִים וּנְתַתֶּם אֶת־נַחֲלָתוֹ לַאֲחֵי אָבִיו: יא וְאִם־אֵין אַחִים לְאָבִיו וּנְתַתֶּם אֶת־נַחֲלָתוֹ לִשְׁאֵרוֹ הַקָּרֹב אֵלָיו מִמִּשְׁפַּחְתּוֹ וְיָרַשׁ אֹתָהּ וְהָיְתָה לִבְנֵי יִשְׂרָאֵל לְחֻקַּת מִשְׁפָּט כַּאֲשֶׁר צִוָּה יְהוָה אֶת־מֹשֶׁה:

CLASSIC COMMENTATORS

Why do Tzelofḥad's daughters have to mention that he died as a result of his own sin?

RABBI YOSEF BEKHOR SHOR — ר' יוסף בכור שור

According to Tzelofḥad's daughters, no other people died as a result of their father's transgression; he was not the cause of any compatriots' deaths like the spies were…and as happened during the Koraḥ revolt. Such instigators deserved no share in the land, because of their effect on other Israelites. However, Tzelofḥad's sin led solely to his own death.

כלומר: לא מתו אחרים בחטאו, לא גרם לאחרים שימותו כמו שעשו מרגלים... וכעדת קרח... ודין הוא שלא יחלקו בארץ. אבל אבינו לא מת אלא הוא לבדו.

12 The Lord said to Moshe, "Ascend this mountain of Avarim, and gaze upon the land
13 that I have given to the Israelites. After you have seen it, you too will be gathered to
14 your people, like Aharon your brother, because when the community rebelled in the Wilderness of Tzin, you disobeyed Me, failing to affirm My sanctity in their eyes through
15 the water." These were the waters of Merivat Kadesh in the Wilderness of Tzin. Moshe
16 spoke to the Lord: "Let the Lord, God of the spirit of all flesh, appoint a man over
17 the community who will go out before them and come in before them, who will lead them out and bring them home. Let not the Lord's community be like sheep without

רמב״ן

ואיננה מצוה שיצוונו הקב״ה לעשות כן עתה, שאם כן יהיה מתחייב לעלות שם מיד, אבל טעמו תעלה אל הר העברים וראית את הארץ, כי בעבור שציוהו לאלה תחלק הארץ (לעיל כ״ו:נ״ג) הודיעו כי לא על ידך תחלק, כי אתה תעלה לראש הר העברים טרם שיסעו ישראל מארץ מואב ותמות בו ולא יגיעך מן הארץ לבד הראיה.

RAMBAN

The Holy One, blessed be He, was not actually commanding Moshe to look out at the land, for if He was, the prophet would have been obligated to immediately climb the mountain. Rather, this is what God meant when He said to Moshe, "Ascend this mountain of Avarim, and gaze upon the land": Since He had just instructed Moshe to divide up the land, He now informed him that he would not be the individual to carry out that mission. Instead, Moshe is to ascend the mountain of Avarim, where he will die before Israel breaks camp from the land of Moav. The only enjoyment of the land that he will derive will be seeing it.

QUESTIONS FOR THOUGHT

- Rashi offers two explanations for why Moshe is reminded now that he is not going into the land. What do both of those explanations have in common?
- At first glance it seems like Ramban is saying the same thing as Rashi, but a careful reading reveals that his understanding is very different. What is the main difference between Rashi's approach and Ramban's?
- R. Hirsch takes a completely different approach to understanding why Moshe isn't entering the land, and why that is mentioned precisely here. What is his opinion and what makes it so radical?

WISDOM OF THE HEART

When God tells Moshe to prepare for his death, Moshe's first response is to ask God to find a suitable replacement for himself. Leadership expert Jim Collins identifies this as one of the five most important qualities of a great leader: he understands that leadership is not about himself but about the people and the institution that he leads, and that great leaders always make sure that there is someone who can take the reins. Rabbi Jonathan Sacks portrays this even more starkly. It's not just that Moshe is occupied with the question of who will succeed him, but this is his primary concern when he hears about his own imminent death.

There is a natural instinct of self-protection for people in positions of power to try to preserve their influence. In the process of protecting their position they eliminate rivals and promote only those who are loyal to them. What qualities or understandings do they need in order to be able to overcome those tendencies?

יב וַיֹּאמֶר יְהוָה אֶל־מֹשֶׁה עֲלֵה אֶל־הַר הָעֲבָרִים הַזֶּה וּרְאֵה
אֶת־הָאָרֶץ אֲשֶׁר נָתַתִּי לִבְנֵי יִשְׂרָאֵל: וְרָאִיתָה אֹתָהּ וְנֶאֱסַפְתָּ
יג אֶל־עַמֶּיךָ גַּם־אָתָּה כַּאֲשֶׁר נֶאֱסַף אַהֲרֹן אָחִיךָ: כַּאֲשֶׁר מְרִיתֶם
יד פִּי בְּמִדְבַּר־צִן בִּמְרִיבַת הָעֵדָה לְהַקְדִּישֵׁנִי בַמַּיִם לְעֵינֵיהֶם הֵם
טו מֵי־מְרִיבַת קָדֵשׁ מִדְבַּר־צִן: וַיְדַבֵּר מֹשֶׁה אֶל־יְהוָה כד
טז לֵאמֹר: יִפְקֹד יְהוָה אֱלֹהֵי הָרוּחֹת לְכָל־בָּשָׂר אִישׁ עַל־הָעֵדָה:
יז אֲשֶׁר־יֵצֵא לִפְנֵיהֶם וַאֲשֶׁר יָבֹא לִפְנֵיהֶם וַאֲשֶׁר יוֹצִיאֵם וַאֲשֶׁר

CLASSIC COMMENTATORS

Why does God tell Moshe now to look at the land from a distance, reminding him that he will not be entering the land?

RASHI

רש״י

Why is the preparation for Moshe's death mentioned at this point? Since the Holy One, blessed be He, instructed the prophet, "you must certainly give them a heritable portion" (27:7), Moshe reasoned to himself: God has commanded me to apportion the land among the Israelites; perhaps His decree that I shall not enter the land has been nullified. But the Holy One, blessed be He, said to him: No, My decision remains in place. Another interpretation: Once Moshe entered the territory given to Reuven and Gad [on the eastern side of the Jordan River], he rejoiced and thought: It seems to me that the vow against me has been retracted.

למה נסמכה לכאן? כיוון שאמר הקב״ה: נתן תתן להם, אמר: אותי ציוה המקום להנחיל שמא הותרה הגזירה ואכנס לארץ? אמר לו הקב״ה: גזרתי במקומה עומדת. דבר אחר: כיון שנכנס משה לנחלת בני גד ובני ראובן שמח ואמר כמדומה שהותר לי נדרי.

RABBI SAMSON RAPHAEL HIRSCH

ר׳ שמשון רפאל הירש

Since the instructions for the division of the land were now completed, it made sense to add that Moshe himself would not be entering the land. Moshe's task was confined to leading the nation to the land of the Torah and to preparing the people for settling their home where they would fulfill the commandments. Moshe was to die at the border of the land to which he had brought the Israelites; he would not be going into it. All he could do was to look at the nation's destination. Of course, this restriction was nothing new to Moshe; God had issued the decree of his future, back at the incident at Kadesh. However, the fact is now recalled to remind Moshe that his mission on earth had reached its conclusion. As such, he had the chance to do whatever last things he wished to do before his demise.

נסתיים סדר חלוקת הארץ. לזה נוסף הביאור שמשה בעצמו לא יכנס אל הארץ. תפקידו של משה מוגבל בהולכת העם אל ארץ התורה והכנתו הגמורה להתנחלות בה ולשמירת פקודתו בתוכה. הוא ימות בראותו את הארץ שאליה, אבל לא אל תוכה, יוליך את העם. זה לא היה דבר חדש למשה. הגזרה הזאת נודעה לו כבר מימי המאורע בקדש. אבל כאן בא הדיבור להזכיר למשה, כי הגיע אל תכלית הליכתו עלי אדמות, כדי שיבצע עוד כל מה שבלבו לעשות בטרם לכתו.

BEMIDBAR | CHAPTER 27 — PINḤAS | 258

18 a shepherd." The LORD said to Moshe, "Take Yehoshua son of Nun, a man infused with
19 My spirit, and lay your hand upon him. Have him stand before Elazar the priest and the
20 entire community, and in their sight, give him this charge. Give over to him some of your
21 majesty, so that the entire Israelite community will obey him. Let him stand before Elazar
the priest, who shall seek the decision of the Urim before the LORD on his behalf. By
this word they will go out and by this word they will return, he and all Israel, the entire
22 community." Moshe did as the LORD commanded him. He took Yehoshua and had him
23 stand before Elazar the priest and the entire community. And he laid his hands upon him
and commissioned him, as the LORD had spoken through Moshe.

ר׳ יצחק רג׳יו

רוח מלכות וממשלה הצריכה להיות בלב הנגיד היא הנקראת כאן "הוד"... והנה אין זה ביד האדם להאציל מרוחו על זולתו, אבל ה׳ מבטיח שאם יסמוך משה את ידיו עליו ויעמידהו לפני העדה ויצווהו לעיניהם, אזי יתן ה׳ עליו מהוד משה.

RABBI ISAAC SAMUEL REGGIO

The term הוד refers to regal bearing and prestige, which are prerequisites for effective governance.... Now generally speaking, an individual has no power to transfer aspects of his own personality to somebody else. However, in this instance, the Almighty promised Moshe that if he placed his hands on Yehoshua's head and presented him to the congregation, God would imbue his apprentice with Moshe's spirit.

QUESTIONS FOR THOUGHT

- Which two of the commentaries understand that Moshe is to give something practical to Yehoshua?
- Which of the commentaries understand that what Moshe is to give to Yehoshua is mostly psychological?
- Whose opinion is R. Reggio rejecting? Based on what does he reject it?
- Of all the things God tells Moshe to do in confirming Yehoshua as the new leader, Moshe does them all except for placing his glory on him. How do you think each of the above commentaries would explain why he didn't do it?
- What do you think will be the greatest challenge for Yehoshua as the new leader? What advice would you offer to someone facing a similar situation?

WISDOM OF THE HEART

According to one midrash, when Moshe learned that Tzelofḥad's daughters would receive their father's portion, he wanted to pass on his leadership to his son. God's response, appointing Yehoshua, taught Moshe an important lesson – some things are not passed down through inheritance but must be earned, through hard work and the right qualities.

Are there times that you think it would be appropriate for a position to be passed from parent to child? What might those be? When would it not be appropriate?

QUICK BITE

The opening mishna in *Pirkei Avot*, describing the chain of transmission, begins with Moshe handing the Torah over to Yehoshua. Rav Leibele Eiger explains that this transmission is not just a passing on of knowledge but an infusion of the very essence of the teacher into the student, as the Torah describes God instructing Moshe to fill Yehoshua with some of his own majesty. That kind of transfer requires intense work over an extended period of time, on the part of both the giver and the receiver.

יח יְבִיאֵ֑ם וְלֹ֤א תִֽהְיֶה֙ עֲדַ֣ת יְהֹוָ֔ה כַּצֹּ֕אן אֲשֶׁ֥ר אֵין־לָהֶ֖ם רֹעֶֽה: וַיֹּ֨אמֶר יְהֹוָ֜ה אֶל־מֹשֶׁ֗ה קַח־לְךָ֙ אֶת־יְהוֹשֻׁ֣עַ בִּן־נ֔וּן אִ֖ישׁ אֲשֶׁר־ר֣וּחַ
יט בּ֑וֹ וְסָמַכְתָּ֥ אֶת־יָדְךָ֖ עָלָֽיו: וְהַֽעֲמַדְתָּ֣ אֹת֔וֹ לִפְנֵ֖י אֶלְעָזָ֣ר הַכֹּהֵ֑ן
כ וְלִפְנֵ֖י כָּל־הָֽעֵדָ֑ה וְצִוִּיתָ֥ה אֹת֖וֹ לְעֵֽינֵיהֶֽם: וְנָתַתָּ֥ה מֵהֽוֹדְךָ֖ עָלָ֑יו
כא לְמַ֣עַן יִשְׁמְע֔וּ כָּל־עֲדַ֖ת בְּנֵ֥י יִשְׂרָאֵֽל: וְלִפְנֵ֨י אֶלְעָזָ֤ר הַכֹּהֵן֙ יַֽעֲמֹ֔ד וְשָׁ֥אַל ל֛וֹ בְּמִשְׁפַּ֥ט הָֽאוּרִ֖ים לִפְנֵ֣י יְהֹוָ֑ה עַל־פִּ֨יו יֵֽצְא֜וּ וְעַל־פִּ֣יו
כב יָבֹ֗אוּ ה֛וּא וְכָל־בְּנֵֽי־יִשְׂרָאֵ֥ל אִתּ֖וֹ וְכָל־הָֽעֵדָֽה: וַיַּ֣עַשׂ מֹשֶׁ֔ה כַּֽאֲשֶׁ֛ר צִוָּ֥ה יְהֹוָ֖ה אֹת֑וֹ וַיִּקַּ֣ח אֶת־יְהוֹשֻׁ֗עַ וַיַּֽעֲמִדֵ֨הוּ֙ לִפְנֵי֙ אֶלְעָזָ֣ר
כג הַכֹּהֵ֔ן וְלִפְנֵ֖י כָּל־הָֽעֵדָֽה: וַיִּסְמֹ֧ךְ אֶת־יָדָ֛יו עָלָ֖יו וַיְצַוֵּ֑הוּ כַּֽאֲשֶׁ֛ר דִּבֶּ֥ר יְהֹוָ֖ה בְּיַד־מֹשֶֽׁה:

CLASSIC COMMENTATORS

God tells Moshe to place some of his "glory" (**הוד**) on Yehoshua. What exactly does that mean?

רש"י
זה קירון עור פנים.

RASHI
This refers to the rays emanating from Moshe's face [as described in Exodus 34:35].

אבן עזרא
לחלוק לו כבוד לעיני ישראל. למען ישמעו – כי הם כבר האמינו בך, וכאשר יראו כי אתה כבדתו, כך יכבדוהו, כי ילכו אחרי מעשיך.

IBN EZRA
Moshe was instructed to honor Yehoshua in full sight of the people of Israel. Since Moshe had long ago earned the trust of the Israelites, once they saw that the prophet respected Yehoshua, they too would be convinced to obey him. The nation would naturally follow Moshe's lead.

רלב"ג
רוצה לומר מיופי תכונותיך ועניניך בהנהגה.

RALBAG
Moshe was to teach Yehoshua the values underlying his character as well as his style of leadership.

ר' עובדיה ספורנו
תן לו איזה שררה בחייך שיתחילו לנהוג בו כבוד.

RABBI OVADYA SFORNO
God told Moshe to grant Yehoshua some measure of authority while he was still alive. In that way, the people would learn to respect Yehoshua too.

> **28:1–15** *Every day, every Shabbat, and every special day of the year is marked by offerings in the Mishkan.*

28 ¹ ² The Lord spoke to Moshe: "Command the Israelites; say to them: Take care to present My offering of foodstuffs – fire offerings of pleasing aroma to Me – at its appointed ³ times. Say to them: This is the fire offering you must present to the Lord: two year- ⁴ ling lambs without blemish as a regular burnt offering each day. Offer one lamb in the ⁵ morning and the second in the afternoon, with a tenth of an ephah of fine flour as a grain ⁶ offering mixed with a quarter of a hin of beaten oil. This is the regular burnt offering ⁷ instituted at Mount Sinai, as a pleasing aroma, a fire offering to the Lord. Its libation shall be a quarter of a hin for each lamb, to be poured out in the Sanctuary as a libation ⁸ of fermented drink to the Lord. Offer the other lamb in the afternoon together with a grain offering and libation as in the morning; a fire offering, a pleasing aroma to the Lord.

⁹ On the Sabbath day: two yearling lambs without blemish and two-tenths of a measure ¹⁰ of fine flour as a grain offering, mixed with oil, and its libation. This is the burnt offering for every Sabbath, to be brought in addition to the regular daily burnt offering and ¹¹ its libation. On your New Moons you shall present a burnt offering to the Lord: two ¹² young bulls, one ram, and seven yearling lambs, all without blemish. There shall be a grain offering of three-tenths of a measure of fine flour mixed with oil for each bull, a ¹³ grain offering of two-tenths of fine flour mixed with oil for each ram, and a grain offering of one-tenth of fine flour mixed with oil for each lamb. This shall be a burnt offering of ¹⁴ pleasing aroma, a fire offering to the Lord. Their libations shall be half a hin of wine for a bull, a third of a hin of wine for a ram, and a quarter of a hin of wine for a lamb. This ¹⁵ is the monthly burnt offering for each New Moon of the year. One male goat shall be brought as a purification offering to the Lord, in addition to the regular burnt offering

---

TEXTUAL SKILLS

1. The section of the daily offerings is nearly identical to Exodus 29:38–46. Find the differences!
2. What name is given in verse 10 to the daily offerings?
3. Look throughout the next two chapters. Which days are identified as מקרא קודש?

WISDOM OF THE HEART

According to R. Shimon ben Pazi, the verse describing the two daily offerings captures the very heart of the Torah. We encounter its essence not in the pomp and ceremony or in splashy displays, but in the simply daily work that never ceases, the commitment to never miss.

חמישי

כח א וַיְדַבֵּר יהוה אֶל־מֹשֶׁה לֵּאמֹר: צַו אֶת־בְּנֵי יִשְׂרָאֵל וְאָמַרְתָּ
אֲלֵהֶם אֶת־קָרְבָּנִי לַחְמִי לְאִשַּׁי רֵיחַ נִיחֹחִי תִּשְׁמְרוּ לְהַקְרִיב
לִי בְּמוֹעֲדוֹ: וְאָמַרְתָּ לָהֶם זֶה הָאִשֶּׁה אֲשֶׁר תַּקְרִיבוּ לַיהוה
כְּבָשִׂים בְּנֵי־שָׁנָה תְמִימִם שְׁנַיִם לַיּוֹם עֹלָה תָמִיד: אֶת־הַכֶּבֶשׂ
אֶחָד תַּעֲשֶׂה בַבֹּקֶר וְאֵת הַכֶּבֶשׂ הַשֵּׁנִי תַּעֲשֶׂה בֵּין הָעַרְבָּיִם:
וַעֲשִׂירִית הָאֵיפָה סֹלֶת לְמִנְחָה בְּלוּלָה בְּשֶׁמֶן כָּתִית רְבִיעִת
הַהִין: עֹלַת תָּמִיד הָעֲשֻׂיָה בְּהַר סִינַי לְרֵיחַ נִיחֹחַ אִשֶּׁה לַיהוה:
וְנִסְכּוֹ רְבִיעִת הַהִין לַכֶּבֶשׂ הָאֶחָד בַּקֹּדֶשׁ הַסֵּךְ נֶסֶךְ שֵׁכָר
לַיהוה: וְאֵת הַכֶּבֶשׂ הַשֵּׁנִי תַּעֲשֶׂה בֵּין הָעַרְבָּיִם כְּמִנְחַת הַבֹּקֶר
וּכְנִסְכּוֹ תַּעֲשֶׂה אִשֵּׁה רֵיחַ נִיחֹחַ לַיהוה:
ט וּבְיוֹם הַשַּׁבָּת שְׁנֵי־כְבָשִׂים בְּנֵי־שָׁנָה תְּמִימִם וּשְׁנֵי עֶשְׂרֹנִים
סֹלֶת מִנְחָה בְּלוּלָה בַשֶּׁמֶן וְנִסְכּוֹ: עֹלַת שַׁבַּת בְּשַׁבַּתּוֹ עַל־עֹלַת
הַתָּמִיד וְנִסְכָּהּ:
יא וּבְרָאשֵׁי חָדְשֵׁיכֶם תַּקְרִיבוּ עֹלָה לַיהוה פָּרִים בְּנֵי־בָקָר שְׁנַיִם
וְאַיִל אֶחָד כְּבָשִׂים בְּנֵי־שָׁנָה שִׁבְעָה תְּמִימִם: וּשְׁלֹשָׁה עֶשְׂרֹנִים
סֹלֶת מִנְחָה בְּלוּלָה בַשֶּׁמֶן לַפָּר הָאֶחָד וּשְׁנֵי עֶשְׂרֹנִים סֹלֶת
מִנְחָה בְּלוּלָה בַשֶּׁמֶן לָאַיִל הָאֶחָד: וְעִשָּׂרֹן עִשָּׂרוֹן סֹלֶת מִנְחָה
בְּלוּלָה בַשֶּׁמֶן לַכֶּבֶשׂ הָאֶחָד עֹלָה רֵיחַ נִיחֹחַ אִשֶּׁה לַיהוה:
יד וְנִסְכֵּיהֶם חֲצִי הַהִין יִהְיֶה לַפָּר וּשְׁלִישִׁת הַהִין לָאַיִל וּרְבִיעִת
הַהִין לַכֶּבֶשׂ יָיִן זֹאת עֹלַת חֹדֶשׁ בְּחָדְשׁוֹ לְחָדְשֵׁי הַשָּׁנָה:
טו וּשְׂעִיר עִזִּים אֶחָד לְחַטָּאת לַיהוה עַל־עֹלַת הַתָּמִיד יֵעָשֶׂה

28:16–31 *Pesaḥ is on the fourteenth day of the first month. It is followed by a seven-day holiday. The day of first produce is when the first offerings from the new wheat crop are brought.*

16 and its libation. On the fourteenth day of the first month, a Passover sacrifice shall be
17 brought to the Lord. And the fifteenth day of this month will be a festival. For seven
18 days unleavened bread shall be eaten. The first day shall be a sacred assembly; you shall
19 perform no laborious work. You shall offer a burnt fire offering to the Lord: two young
20 bulls, one ram, and seven yearling lambs, all unblemished. Their grain offering shall be
fine flour mixed with oil: three-tenths of a measure for each bull, two-tenths for the ram,
21
22 and one-tenth for each of the seven lambs, together with one male goat as a purifica-
23 tion offering to make your atonement. These you shall offer in addition to the morning
24 burnt offering, the regular daily offering. In the same way you shall offer daily for seven
days the foodstuffs of a fire offering, a pleasing aroma to the Lord. It shall be offered in
25 addition to the regular burnt offering and its libation. The seventh day shall be for you
26 a sacred assembly; you shall perform no laborious work. The day of first produce, when
you bring an offering of new grain to the Lord on your Festival of Weeks, shall be a
27 sacred assembly for you. On it you shall perform no laborious work. You shall present
a burnt offering as a pleasing aroma to the Lord: two young bulls, one ram, and seven
28 yearling lambs. Their grain offering shall be fine flour mixed with oil: three-tenths of a
29 measure for each bull, two-tenths for the one ram, and one-tenth for each of the seven
30
31 lambs. Offer one male goat to atone for you. These you shall offer in addition to the
regular burnt offering, its grain offering and libations. They shall be without blemish.

TEXTUAL SKILLS

1. Is Pesaḥ the name of the day or of the offering brought on that day?

2. Which word in verse 26 is unusual?

WISDOM OF THE HEART

The Torah identifies the offering of Shavuot as two bulls and one ram, but in Leviticus it is one bull and two rams. Rav Schwab, based on a conversation in the Talmud, suggest that there are two different aspects to Shavuot. One relates to the end of the period of the Omer, while the other is the holiday celebrating the giving of the Torah.

במדבר | פרק כח

טז וְנִסְכּֽוֹ: וּבַחֹ֣דֶשׁ הָרִאשׁ֗וֹן בְּאַרְבָּעָ֨ה עָשָׂ֥ר י֛וֹם לַחֹ֖דֶשׁ ששי
יז פֶּ֣סַח לַיהוָֹ֑ה: וּבַחֲמִשָּׁ֨ה עָשָׂ֥ר י֛וֹם לַחֹ֥דֶשׁ הַזֶּ֖ה חָ֑ג שִׁבְעַ֣ת יָמִ֔ים
יח מַצּ֖וֹת יֵֽאָכֵֽל: בַּיּ֣וֹם הָֽרִאשׁ֔וֹן מִקְרָא־קֹ֑דֶשׁ כָּל־מְלֶ֥אכֶת עֲבֹדָ֖ה
יט לֹ֥א תַעֲשֽׂוּ: וְהִקְרַבְתֶּ֨ם אִשֶּׁ֤ה עֹלָה֙ לַֽיהוָ֔ה פָּרִ֧ים בְּנֵי־בָקָ֛ר שְׁנַ֖יִם
כ וְאַ֣יִל אֶחָ֑ד וְשִׁבְעָ֧ה כְבָשִׂ֛ים בְּנֵ֥י שָׁנָ֖ה תְּמִימִ֣ם יִֽהְי֣וּ לָכֶֽם: וּמִ֨נְחָתָ֔ם
סֹ֖לֶת בְּלוּלָ֣ה בַשָּׁ֑מֶן שְׁלֹשָׁ֨ה עֶשְׂרֹנִ֜ים לַפָּ֗ר וּשְׁנֵ֧י עֶשְׂרֹנִ֛ים לָאַ֖יִל
כא תַּעֲשֽׂוּ: עִשָּׂר֤וֹן עִשָּׂרוֹן֙ תַּעֲשֶׂ֔ה לַכֶּ֖בֶשׂ הָאֶחָ֑ד לְשִׁבְעַ֖ת הַכְּבָשִֽׂים:
כב וּשְׂעִ֥יר חַטָּ֖את אֶחָ֑ד לְכַפֵּ֖ר עֲלֵיכֶֽם: מִלְּבַד֙ עֹלַ֣ת הַבֹּ֔קֶר אֲשֶׁ֖ר
כג-כד לְעֹלַ֣ת הַתָּמִ֑יד תַּעֲשׂ֖וּ אֶת־אֵֽלֶּה: כָּאֵ֜לֶּה תַּעֲשׂ֤וּ לַיּוֹם֙ שִׁבְעַ֣ת
יָמִ֔ים לֶ֛חֶם אִשֵּׁ֥ה רֵֽיחַ־נִיחֹ֖חַ לַיהוָ֑ה עַל־עוֹלַ֧ת הַתָּמִ֛יד יֵעָשֶׂ֖ה
כה וְנִסְכּֽוֹ: וּבַיּוֹם֙ הַשְּׁבִיעִ֔י מִקְרָא־קֹ֖דֶשׁ יִהְיֶ֣ה לָכֶ֑ם כָּל־מְלֶ֥אכֶת
כו עֲבֹדָ֖ה לֹ֥א תַעֲשֽׂוּ: וּבְי֣וֹם הַבִּכּוּרִ֗ים בְּהַקְרִ֨יבְכֶ֜ם מִנְחָ֤ה כה
חֲדָשָׁה֙ לַֽיהוָ֔ה בְּשָׁבֻעֹ֣תֵיכֶ֑ם מִקְרָא־קֹ֨דֶשׁ֙ יִהְיֶ֣ה לָכֶ֔ם כָּל־מְלֶ֥אכֶת
כז עֲבֹדָ֖ה לֹ֥א תַעֲשֽׂוּ: וְהִקְרַבְתֶּ֨ם עוֹלָ֜ה לְרֵ֤יחַ נִיחֹ֨חַ֙ לַֽיהוָ֔ה פָּרִ֧ים
כח בְּנֵי־בָקָ֛ר שְׁנַ֖יִם אַ֣יִל אֶחָ֑ד שִׁבְעָ֥ה כְבָשִׂ֖ים בְּנֵ֥י שָׁנָֽה: וּמִ֨נְחָתָ֔ם
סֹ֖לֶת בְּלוּלָ֣ה בַשָּׁ֑מֶן שְׁלֹשָׁ֤ה עֶשְׂרֹנִים֙ לַפָּ֣ר הָֽאֶחָ֔ד שְׁנֵי֙ עֶשְׂרֹנִ֔ים
כט לָאַ֖יִל הָֽאֶחָֽד: עִשָּׂר֣וֹן עִשָּׂר֔וֹן לַכֶּ֖בֶשׂ הָאֶחָ֑ד לְשִׁבְעַ֖ת הַכְּבָשִֽׂים:
ל-לא שְׂעִ֥יר עִזִּ֖ים אֶחָ֑ד לְכַפֵּ֖ר עֲלֵיכֶֽם: מִלְּבַ֛ד עֹלַ֥ת הַתָּמִ֖יד וּמִנְחָת֑וֹ
תַּעֲשׂ֕וּ תְּמִימִ֥ם יִֽהְיוּ־לָכֶ֖ם וְנִסְכֵּיהֶֽם:

29:1–11 *The offerings on the first two holidays of the seventh month are quite different from those of the previous holidays.*

29 1 The first day of the seventh month shall be a sacred assembly for you; you shall perform 2 no laborious work on it. It shall be for you a day of the horn's sounding. You shall present a burnt offering as a pleasing aroma to the LORD: one young bull, one ram, and seven 3 yearling lambs, all without blemish. Their grain offering shall be fine flour mixed with 4 oil, three-tenths of a measure for the bull, two-tenths for the ram, and one-tenth for each 5 of the seven lambs; and there shall be one male goat as a purification offering to atone 6 for you. This will be in addition to the monthly burnt offering with its grain offering, and the regular burnt offering with its grain offering and libations as prescribed. It shall 7 be a pleasing aroma, a fire offering to the LORD. The tenth day of this seventh month shall be a sacred assembly for you; you shall afflict yourselves on it and perform no work 8 at all. You shall present a burnt offering to the LORD for a pleasing aroma: one young 9 bull, one ram, and seven yearling lambs, all without blemish. Their grain offering shall be fine flour mixed with oil, three-tenths of a measure for the bull, two-tenths for the 10/11 single ram, and one-tenth for each of the seven sheep. There shall be one male goat as a purification offering, in addition to the special purification offering of atonement and

---

We know Yom Kippur as a day of enormous awe. The Torah here almost skips that, emphasizing instead that it is a holiday – one more holiday, with its own unique holiday offerings. Here we see that Yom Kippur is a day of celebration, not just of fasting and tears

WISDOM OF THE HEART

Despite the variations in sacrifices between the different holidays, including the New Moon, all are accompanied by a goat as a חטאת offering. The one exception is Shabbat, on which there is no חטאת. Some explain that on Shabbat we overlook our sins, while others explain that the sanctity of Shabbat erases all sin. Either way, on Shabbat there is no חטאת offering and no mention of sin. Rav Soloveitchik explains that this is why the Shabbat prayers describe Shabbat as God's gift to Israel, given with love and favor – because sin is not even part of the discussion on Shabbat.

Even the closest friends have arguments and misunderstandings. Imagine that you set aside a time – perhaps one hour a day, one day a week, one week per month during which you banished any negative thoughts about your friends. How do you think that would affect your friendships?

במדבר | פרק כט

א וּבַחֹ֙דֶשׁ֙ הַשְּׁבִיעִ֔י בְּאֶחָ֖ד לַחֹ֑דֶשׁ מִֽקְרָא־קֹ֙דֶשׁ֙ יִהְיֶ֣ה לָכֶ֔ם כָּל־
ב מְלֶ֥אכֶת עֲבֹדָ֖ה לֹ֣א תַעֲשׂ֑וּ י֥וֹם תְּרוּעָ֖ה יִהְיֶ֥ה לָכֶֽם: וַעֲשִׂיתֶ֨ם
עֹלָ֜ה לְרֵ֤יחַ נִיחֹ֙חַ֙ לַֽיהוָ֔ה פַּ֧ר בֶּן־בָּקָ֛ר אֶחָ֖ד אַ֣יִל אֶחָ֑ד כְּבָשִׂ֧ים
ג בְּנֵֽי־שָׁנָ֛ה שִׁבְעָ֖ה תְּמִימִֽם: וּמִנְחָתָ֔ם סֹ֖לֶת בְּלוּלָ֣ה בַשָּׁ֑מֶן שְׁלֹשָׁ֤ה
ד עֶשְׂרֹנִים֙ לַפָּ֔ר שְׁנֵ֥י עֶשְׂרֹנִ֖ים לָאָֽיִל: וְעִשָּׂר֣וֹן אֶחָ֔ד לַכֶּ֖בֶשׂ הָאֶחָ֑ד
ה לְשִׁבְעַ֖ת הַכְּבָשִֽׂים: וּשְׂעִיר־עִזִּ֥ים אֶחָ֖ד חַטָּ֑את לְכַפֵּ֖ר עֲלֵיכֶֽם:
ו מִלְּבַ֞ד עֹלַ֤ת הַחֹ֙דֶשׁ֙ וּמִנְחָתָ֔הּ וְעֹלַ֧ת הַתָּמִ֛יד וּמִנְחָתָ֖הּ וְנִסְכֵּיהֶ֑ם
כְּמִשְׁפָּטָ֖ם לְרֵ֣יחַ נִיחֹ֑חַ אִשֶּׁ֖ה לַֽיהוָֽה: וּבֶֽעָשׂוֹר֩ לַחֹ֨דֶשׁ
ז הַשְּׁבִיעִ֜י הַזֶּ֗ה מִֽקְרָא־קֹ֙דֶשׁ֙ יִהְיֶ֣ה לָכֶ֔ם וְעִנִּיתֶ֖ם אֶת־נַפְשֹׁתֵיכֶ֑ם
ח כָּל־מְלָאכָ֖ה לֹ֣א תַעֲשֽׂוּ: וְהִקְרַבְתֶּ֨ם עֹלָ֤ה לַֽיהוָה֙ רֵ֣יחַ נִיחֹ֔חַ פַּ֧ר
בֶּן־בָּקָ֛ר אֶחָ֖ד אַ֣יִל אֶחָ֑ד כְּבָשִׂ֧ים בְּנֵֽי־שָׁנָ֛ה שִׁבְעָ֖ה תְּמִימִ֣ם יִהְי֥וּ
ט לָכֶֽם: וּמִנְחָתָ֔ם סֹ֖לֶת בְּלוּלָ֣ה בַשָּׁ֑מֶן שְׁלֹשָׁ֤ה עֶשְׂרֹנִים֙ לַפָּ֔ר שְׁנֵי֙
י עֶשְׂרֹנִ֔ים לָאַ֖יִל הָאֶחָֽד: עִשָּׂרוֹן֙ עִשָּׂר֔וֹן לַכֶּ֖בֶשׂ הָאֶחָ֑ד לְשִׁבְעַ֖ת
יא הַכְּבָשִֽׂים: שְׂעִיר־עִזִּ֥ים אֶחָ֖ד חַטָּ֑את מִלְּבַ֞ד חַטַּ֤את הַכִּפֻּרִים֙

TEXTUAL SKILLS

1. The Torah describes three different categories of offerings for the first day of the seventh month. What are they?
2. On all the other days identified as מקרא קודש, the Torah writes the restriction כל מלאכת עבודה לא תעשו (see 28:18, 28:26, 29:1, and 29:12). On the tenth day of the seventh month, the Torah describes the restriction differently. What is different about that one? Can you explain the reason for the difference?

QUICK BITES

The first day of Tishrei, known today as Rosh Hashana, is identified in the Torah as יום תרועה, a day of short shofar blasts. It is not called a day of תקיעה, long shofar blasts, or a day of the shofar. R. Yaakov Yitzḥak Horowitz, better known as the Seer of Lublin, suggested a Hasidic reading, that the word תרועה is related to the idea of רעות, friendship. The function of Rosh Hashana is to help all of Benei Yisrael bind to each other in friendship.

> **29:12–30:1** *This unusual seven-day holiday has an eighth day as an add-on. The offerings brought seem related to the holiday of the first month and the one which follows, but at the same time are dramatically different. The eighth, "add-on," day stands out in a completely different way.*

12 the regular burnt offering with its grain offering and libations. The fifteenth day of the seventh month shall be a sacred assembly for you; you shall perform no laborious work
13 on it; you shall celebrate a festival to the Lord for seven days. And you shall present a burnt offering, a fire offering, for a pleasing aroma to the Lord: thirteen young bulls,
14 two rams, and fourteen yearling lambs, all without blemish. Their grain offering shall be fine flour mixed with oil: three-tenths of a measure for each of the thirteen bulls,
15 two-tenths for each of the two rams, and one-tenth for each of the fourteen lambs.
16 There shall be one male goat as a purification offering, in addition to the regular burnt
17 offering with its grain offering and libation. On the second day: twelve young bulls, two
18 rams, and fourteen yearling lambs, all without blemish. The grain offering and libations
19 for the bulls, rams, and sheep shall be as prescribed for their number. There shall be one male goat as a purification offering, in addition to the regular burnt offering with
20 its grain offering and libations. On the third day: eleven bulls, two rams, and fourteen
21 yearling lambs, all without blemish. The grain offering and libations for the bulls, rams,
22 and lambs shall be as prescribed for their number. There shall be one male goat as a purification offering, in addition to the regular burnt offering with its grain offering
23 and libation. On the fourth day: ten bulls, two rams, and fourteen yearling lambs, all

---

WISDOM OF THE HEART

The offerings of Sukkot are dramatically different from all the other holidays. First, there are fourteen sheep brought daily, whereas the other pilgrimage festivals have seven. Second, the number of bulls brought changes from day to day, beginning with thirteen on the first day and decreasing to seven on the seventh day, whereas all the others have only two. This requires the Torah to describe each day separately, which is not done for any of the other holidays, and became the model for Beit Shammai's suggestion that the number of Ḥanukka candles decrease with each passing day. Rav Yoel Bin Nun suggests that Sukkot is the grand finale of a number of the cycles of the year. It is the last of the three pilgrimage festivals, it concludes the holidays of Tishrei, and it is the end of the harvest year but just after the beginning of a different cycle. Perhaps that is why the Torah describes this holiday as the one with the greatest joy – it is like the closing of a symphony, during which all the pieces of the orchestra join in a rousing crescendo.

בְּעֹלַת הַתָּמִיד וּמִנְחָתָהּ וְנִסְכֵּיהֶם: וּבַחֲמִשָּׁה עָשָׂר שביעי
יוֹם לַחֹדֶשׁ הַשְּׁבִיעִי מִקְרָא־קֹדֶשׁ יִהְיֶה לָכֶם כָּל־מְלֶאכֶת עֲבֹדָה
לֹא תַעֲשׂוּ וְחַגֹּתֶם חַג לַיהוה שִׁבְעַת יָמִים: וְהִקְרַבְתֶּם עֹלָה
אִשֵּׁה רֵיחַ נִיחֹחַ לַיהוה פָּרִים בְּנֵי־בָקָר שְׁלֹשָׁה עָשָׂר אֵילִם
שְׁנַיִם כְּבָשִׂים בְּנֵי־שָׁנָה אַרְבָּעָה עָשָׂר תְּמִימִם יִהְיוּ: וּמִנְחָתָם
סֹלֶת בְּלוּלָה בַשֶּׁמֶן שְׁלֹשָׁה עֶשְׂרֹנִים לַפָּר הָאֶחָד לִשְׁלֹשָׁה עָשָׂר
פָּרִים שְׁנֵי עֶשְׂרֹנִים לָאַיִל הָאֶחָד לִשְׁנֵי הָאֵילִם: וְעִשָּׂרוֹן עִשָּׂרוֹן
לַכֶּבֶשׂ הָאֶחָד לְאַרְבָּעָה עָשָׂר כְּבָשִׂים: וּשְׂעִיר־עִזִּים אֶחָד
חַטָּאת מִלְּבַד עֹלַת הַתָּמִיד מִנְחָתָהּ וְנִסְכָּהּ: וּבַיּוֹם
הַשֵּׁנִי פָּרִים בְּנֵי־בָקָר שְׁנֵים עָשָׂר אֵילִם שְׁנָיִם כְּבָשִׂים בְּנֵי־
שָׁנָה אַרְבָּעָה עָשָׂר תְּמִימִם: וּמִנְחָתָם וְנִסְכֵּיהֶם לַפָּרִים לָאֵילִם
וְלַכְּבָשִׂים בְּמִסְפָּרָם כַּמִּשְׁפָּט: וּשְׂעִיר־עִזִּים אֶחָד חַטָּאת
מִלְּבַד עֹלַת הַתָּמִיד וּמִנְחָתָהּ וְנִסְכֵּיהֶם: וּבַיּוֹם
הַשְּׁלִישִׁי פָּרִים עַשְׁתֵּי־עָשָׂר אֵילִם שְׁנָיִם כְּבָשִׂים בְּנֵי־שָׁנָה
אַרְבָּעָה עָשָׂר תְּמִימִם: וּמִנְחָתָם וְנִסְכֵּיהֶם לַפָּרִים לָאֵילִם
וְלַכְּבָשִׂים בְּמִסְפָּרָם כַּמִּשְׁפָּט: וּשְׂעִיר חַטָּאת אֶחָד מִלְּבַד
עֹלַת הַתָּמִיד וּמִנְחָתָהּ וְנִסְכָּהּ: וּבַיּוֹם הָרְבִיעִי פָּרִים
עֲשָׂרָה אֵילִם שְׁנָיִם כְּבָשִׂים בְּנֵי־שָׁנָה אַרְבָּעָה עָשָׂר תְּמִימִם:

יב
יג
יד
טו
טז
יז
יח
יט
כ
כא
כב
כג

TEXTUAL SKILLS

1. Notice the pattern of the offerings in the first seven days of this holiday.
2. Look at the last word of each of the seven paragraphs describing the offerings of the seven days.
3. One day of both seven-day holidays must fall on Shabbat, yet the Torah makes no reference to what should happen when it does. Based on what the Torah does say about the offerings, would you conclude that the Shabbat offerings are replaced by the holiday ones or added to them?

24 without blemish. The grain offering and libations for the bulls, rams, and sheep shall
25 be as prescribed for their number. And there shall be one male goat as a purification offering, in addition to the regular burnt offering with its grain offering and libation.
26 On the fifth day: nine bulls, two rams, and fourteen yearling lambs, all without blemish.
27 The grain offering and libations for the bulls, rams, and lambs shall be as prescribed for
28 their number. And there shall be one male goat as a purification offering, in addition
29 to the regular burnt offering with its grain offering and libation. On the sixth day: eight
30 bulls, two rams, and fourteen yearling lambs, all without blemish. The grain offering
31 and libations for the bulls, rams, and lambs shall be as prescribed for their number. And there shall be one male goat as a purification offering, in addition to the regular burnt
32 offering with its grain offering and libations. On the seventh day: seven bulls, two rams,
33 and fourteen yearling lambs, all without blemish. The grain offering and libation for
34 the bulls, rams, and lambs shall be as prescribed for their number. And there shall be one male goat as a purification offering, in addition to the regular burnt offering with
35 its grain offering and libation. On the eighth day you shall hold an assembly; you shall
36 perform no laborious work on it. You shall present a burnt offering, a fire offering, for a pleasing aroma to the LORD: one bull, one ram, and seven yearling lambs, all without
37 blemish. The grain offering and libations for the bull, ram, and lambs shall be as pre-
38 scribed for their number. And there shall be one male goat as a purification offering,
39 in addition to the regular burnt offering with its grain offering and libation. These you shall offer to the LORD on your festivals, in addition to your vows and freewill offerings:
30 1 your burnt offerings, grain offerings, libations, and peace offerings." And Moshe told the Israelites all that the LORD had commanded him.

כד מִנְחָתָם וְנִסְכֵּיהֶם לַפָּר לָאֵילִם וְלַכְּבָשִׂים בְּמִסְפָּרָם כַּמִּשְׁפָּט:
כה וּשְׂעִיר־עִזִּים אֶחָד חַטָּאת מִלְּבַד עֹלַת הַתָּמִיד מִנְחָתָהּ וְנִסְכָּהּ:
כו וּבַיּוֹם הַחֲמִישִׁי פָּרִים תִּשְׁעָה אֵילִם שְׁנָיִם כְּבָשִׂים בְּנֵי־שָׁנָה אַרְבָּעָה עָשָׂר תְּמִימִם:
כז וּמִנְחָתָם וְנִסְכֵּיהֶם
כח לַפָּרִים לָאֵילִם וְלַכְּבָשִׂים בְּמִסְפָּרָם כַּמִּשְׁפָּט: וּשְׂעִיר חַטָּאת אֶחָד מִלְּבַד עֹלַת הַתָּמִיד וּמִנְחָתָהּ וְנִסְכָּהּ:
כט וּבַיּוֹם הַשִּׁשִּׁי פָּרִים שְׁמֹנָה אֵילִם שְׁנָיִם כְּבָשִׂים בְּנֵי־שָׁנָה אַרְבָּעָה עָשָׂר תְּמִימִם:
ל וּמִנְחָתָם וְנִסְכֵּיהֶם לַפָּרִים לָאֵילִם וְלַכְּבָשִׂים בְּמִסְפָּרָם כַּמִּשְׁפָּט:
לא וּשְׂעִיר חַטָּאת אֶחָד מִלְּבַד עֹלַת הַתָּמִיד מִנְחָתָהּ וּנְסָכֶיהָ:
לב וּבַיּוֹם הַשְּׁבִיעִי פָּרִים שִׁבְעָה אֵילִם שְׁנָיִם כְּבָשִׂים בְּנֵי־שָׁנָה אַרְבָּעָה עָשָׂר תְּמִימִם:
לג וּמִנְחָתָם וְנִסְכֵּהֶם
לד לַפָּרִים לָאֵילִם וְלַכְּבָשִׂים בְּמִסְפָּרָם כְּמִשְׁפָּטָם: וּשְׂעִיר חַטָּאת אֶחָד מִלְּבַד עֹלַת הַתָּמִיד מִנְחָתָהּ וְנִסְכָּהּ:

מפטיר
לה בַּיּוֹם הַשְּׁמִינִי עֲצֶרֶת תִּהְיֶה לָכֶם כָּל־מְלֶאכֶת עֲבֹדָה לֹא תַעֲשׂוּ:
לו וְהִקְרַבְתֶּם עֹלָה אִשֵּׁה רֵיחַ נִיחֹחַ לַיהוָה פַּר אֶחָד אַיִל אֶחָד כְּבָשִׂים בְּנֵי־שָׁנָה שִׁבְעָה תְּמִימִם:
לז מִנְחָתָם וְנִסְכֵּיהֶם לַפָּר לָאַיִל וְלַכְּבָשִׂים בְּמִסְפָּרָם כַּמִּשְׁפָּט:
לח וּשְׂעִיר חַטָּאת אֶחָד מִלְּבַד עֹלַת הַתָּמִיד וּמִנְחָתָהּ וְנִסְכָּהּ:
לט אֵלֶּה תַּעֲשׂוּ לַיהוָה בְּמוֹעֲדֵיכֶם לְבַד מִנִּדְרֵיכֶם וְנִדְבֹתֵיכֶם לְעֹלֹתֵיכֶם וּלְמִנְחֹתֵיכֶם וּלְנִסְכֵּיכֶם וּלְשַׁלְמֵיכֶם:

ל א וַיֹּאמֶר מֹשֶׁה אֶל־בְּנֵי יִשְׂרָאֵל כְּכֹל אֲשֶׁר־צִוָּה יְהוָה אֶת־מֹשֶׁה:

DAY	DAILY (תמיד) OFFERING	SPECIAL, ADDITIONAL (מוסף) OFFERINGS
Seventh month Day 16	2 lambs (1 morning, 1 afternoon)	12 young bulls 2 rams 14 lambs 1 goat – חטאת
Seventh month Day 17	2 lambs (1 morning, 1 afternoon)	11 young bulls 2 rams 14 lambs 1 goat – חטאת
Seventh month Day 18	2 lambs (1 morning, 1 afternoon)	10 young bulls 2 rams 14 lambs 1 goat – חטאת
Seventh month Day 19	2 lambs (1 morning, 1 afternoon)	9 young bulls 2 rams 14 lambs 1 goat – חטאת
Seventh month Day 20	2 lambs (1 morning, 1 afternoon)	8 young bulls 2 rams 14 lambs 1 goat – חטאת
Seventh month Day 21	2 lambs (1 morning, 1 afternoon)	7 young bulls 2 rams 14 lambs 1 goat – חטאת
Seventh month Day 22	2 lambs (1 morning, 1 afternoon)	1 young bull 1 ram 7 lambs 1 goat – חטאת

TEXTUAL SKILLS

1. What patterns can you detect in these offerings?
2. What days stand out as unusual breaks in the patterns?
3. Notice in the text that many of the days have a brief description. Which have names?
4. Notice in the above chart which month of the year stands out regarding the special days and offerings.

THE DAILY (תמיד) AND SPECIAL (מוסף) OFFERINGS:

DAY	DAILY (תמיד) OFFERING	SPECIAL, ADDITIONAL (מוסף) OFFERINGS
Daily	2 lambs (1 morning, 1 afternoon)	
Shabbat	2 lambs (1 morning, 1 afternoon)	2 lambs
First day of every month (New Moon)	2 lambs (1 morning, 1 afternoon)	2 young bulls 1 ram 7 lambs 1 goat – **חטאת**
First month Days 15–21	2 lambs (1 morning, 1 afternoon)	2 young bulls 1 ram 7 lambs 1 goat – **חטאת**
No date given (The day of the first produce)	2 lambs (1 morning, 1 afternoon)	2 young bulls 1 ram 7 lambs 1 goat – **חטאת**
Seventh month Day 1	2 lambs (1 morning, 1 afternoon)	1 young bull 1 ram 7 lambs 1 goat – **חטאת** (The above are in addition to the other special offering brought on the first day of every month)
Seventh month Day 10	2 lambs (1 morning, 1 afternoon)	1 young bull 1 ram 7 lambs 1 goat – **חטאת** (Additional goat as a special **חטאת** for *Yom Hakippurim* as described in Lev. ch. 16)
Seventh month Day 15	2 lambs (1 morning, 1 afternoon)	13 young bulls 2 rams 14 lambs 1 goat – **חטאת**

EXPLORING HASHKAFA
Love and Zealotry

Pinḥas kills two people in an act of zealotry, and this *parasha* opens with his reward. Is the Torah trying to encourage people to act like Pinḥas?

Ḥazon Ish suggested that when the overwhelming majority of the community observed the Torah and the violators, who flaunted their sins in the face of the community, were the rare minority, zealotry may have been favored in order to discourage those violations. In our era, however, when large swaths of the community are not observant and were not raised with any kind of sensitivity to mitzvot, the correct approach is to embrace those who lack knowledge and to lovingly draw them closer to their roots.

Other twentieth-century thinkers took a different approach. Rav Kook, in what was then called Palestine, and Rav Soloveitchik, in the US, each independently wrote essays making very similar arguments. Zealotry, they argued, was encouraged by the Torah, but only for a person who could be absolutely certain that their motives were pure and that there was not even a tinge of personal anger involved. They learned this from the Talmud's account of the addition of the nineteenth blessing in the *Amida*, which asks God to deal with Jews who were undermining the Jewish community. The Talmud records that although there was one man, Shimon Hapekuli, who authored the original eighteen blessings, they could not find anyone to author the nineteenth until they identified Shmuel Hakatan.

Why was it so difficult to find an author? Were the other Sages incapable of composing a single paragraph?

Apparently, the challenge was to find someone who could ask God to foil those who undermine the community but who also felt no personal animosity toward those evildoers. None of the Rabbis felt that they were pure enough at heart. Shmuel Hakatan, however, with his intense humility and respect for all, was the only one who could be trusted to compose such a prayer.

These two great twentieth-century sages taught that only someone filled with humility and love for every person can truly claim to be zealous for God and for God alone.

פרשת מטות
PARASHAT MATTOT

"Among the things you give and still keep
are your word, a smile, and a grateful heart."
Zig Ziglar

Words are powerful. They can create ideas and they can destroy people. They can help and hurt. And they can obligate. This *parasha* opens and closes with words that obligate. The Rebbe of Ishbitz notes that these words of commitment precede the review of the travels of *Benei Yisrael* through the wilderness, as if to say, "God, if I make it through this, then I promise…"

PARASHAT MATTOT

30 ² Moshe spoke to the tribal heads of the Israelites: "This is what the Lord has commanded: ³ When a man makes a vow to the Lord or takes an oath binding himself to an ⁴ obligation, he must not break his word; whatever he speaks, that he must fulfill. When a woman makes a vow to the Lord or takes an oath binding herself to an obligation while ⁵ still a girl in her father's house, and her father hears of her vow or self-imposed obligation ⁶ and remains silent, then all her vows and self-imposed obligations stand. But if her father restrains her on the day he hears her, none of her vows or self-imposed obligations shall ⁷ stand. The Lord will forgo them for her, because her father has restrained her. If she ⁸ marries, having made vows or verbally bound herself, and her husband hears of it and on the day he does so keeps silent, then her vow or any pledge by which she has bound ⁹ herself shall stand. But if, on the day that her husband hears of it, he restrains her, he can annul her vow or the pledge by which she has bound herself, and the Lord will

---

RAMBAN

According to our Rabbis, there is a specific allusion hidden in the fact that Moshe "spoke to the tribal heads of the Israelites" regarding the matter of vows. Experts in these laws hold the power and the ability to release individuals from their personal vows. Now, nowhere does the Torah explicitly discuss the existence of such a mechanism; rather, it represents a law which God transmitted to Moshe at Mount Sinai and which has but the slightest reference in the text. As our Sages state: The phenomenon of releasing somebody from his or her vow "floats in the air" and has virtually no support from the Torah. It derives only from the fact that the verse states, "he must not break [*yaḥel*] his word" (30:3), instead of, "he must not violate his word." The wording of the verse indicates that the individual is cautioned not to desecrate his own words. One way to protect from that desecration is to appear before the court which can find a way to release him from the vow, so that acting contrary to the vow would not constitute a desecration of his word.

רמב״ן

וטעם וידבר משה אל ראשי המטות ... וירמוז עוד למדרש רבותינו, כי לראשי המטות יד ושם בנדרים יותר משאר העם, שיחיד מומחה מתיר בנדר. והנה היתר הנדרים לא נתפרש בתורה, אבל הוא הלכה למשה מסיני ותלאו הכתוב בחוט השערה, כמו שאמרו: "היתר נדרים פורחין באויר ואין להם על מה שיסמכו" אלא שרמז לו הכתוב: "לא יחל דברו" – כלומר שלא אמר: "לא יעבור על דברו" – אבל ציוה שלא יחלל דברו, שלא יעשה בנדר חילול, כי בבואו לבית דין וימצאו לו פתח וניחם עליו והם ימחלו לו, איננו מחלל אותו.

QUESTIONS FOR THOUGHT

- Ramban offers two possible hints from the Torah for the idea of התרת נדרים. Which of those do you find more convincing? Why?
- *Haketav Vehakabbala* comments on the same word that Ramban does. In what way is this suggestion different from Ramban's?

WISDOM OF THE HEART

Noting that the laws of vows were addressed to the tribal leaders, Rabbi Eliezer Fishof comments that leaders often make promises to their people, and the Torah teaches that they need to model making promises only when they can keep them and intend to do so.

פרשת מטות

ל

וַיְדַבֵּ֤ר מֹשֶׁה֙ אֶל־רָאשֵׁ֣י הַמַּטּ֔וֹת לִבְנֵ֥י יִשְׂרָאֵ֖ל לֵאמֹ֑ר זֶ֣ה הַדָּבָ֔ר כו
אֲשֶׁ֖ר צִוָּ֥ה יְהוָֽה׃ אִישׁ֩ כִּֽי־יִדֹּ֨ר נֶ֜דֶר לַֽיהוָ֗ה אֽוֹ־הִשָּׁ֤בַע שְׁבֻעָה֙
לֶאְסֹ֤ר אִסָּר֙ עַל־נַפְשׁ֔וֹ לֹ֥א יַחֵ֖ל דְּבָר֑וֹ כְּכָל־הַיֹּצֵ֥א מִפִּ֖יו יַעֲשֶֽׂה׃
וְאִשָּׁ֕ה כִּֽי־תִדֹּ֥ר נֶ֖דֶר לַֽיהוָ֑ה וְאָסְרָ֥ה אִסָּ֛ר בְּבֵ֥ית אָבִ֖יהָ בִּנְעֻרֶֽיהָ׃
וְשָׁמַ֨ע אָבִ֜יהָ אֶת־נִדְרָ֗הּ וֶֽאֱסָרָהּ֙ אֲשֶׁ֣ר אָֽסְרָ֣ה עַל־נַפְשָׁ֔הּ וְהֶחֱרִ֥ישׁ
לָ֖הּ אָבִ֑יהָ וְקָ֨מוּ֙ כָּל־נְדָרֶ֔יהָ וְכָל־אִסָּ֛ר אֲשֶׁר־אָסְרָ֥ה עַל־נַפְשָׁ֖הּ
יָקֽוּם׃ וְאִם־הֵנִ֨יא אָבִ֤יהָ אֹתָהּ֙ בְּי֣וֹם שָׁמְע֔וֹ כָּל־נְדָרֶ֛יהָ וֶאֱסָרֶ֖יהָ
אֲשֶׁר־אָסְרָ֥ה עַל־נַפְשָׁ֖הּ לֹ֣א יָק֑וּם וַיהוָה֙ יִֽסְלַח־לָ֔הּ כִּי־הֵנִ֥יא
אָבִ֖יהָ אֹתָֽהּ׃ וְאִם־הָי֤וֹ תִֽהְיֶה֙ לְאִ֔ישׁ וּנְדָרֶ֖יהָ עָלֶ֑יהָ א֚וֹ מִבְטָ֣א
שְׂפָתֶ֔יהָ אֲשֶׁ֥ר אָסְרָ֖ה עַל־נַפְשָֽׁהּ׃ וְשָׁמַ֤ע אִישָׁהּ֙ בְּי֣וֹם שָׁמְע֔וֹ
וְהֶחֱרִ֖ישׁ לָ֑הּ וְקָ֣מוּ נְדָרֶ֗יהָ וֶֽאֱסָרֶ֛הָ אֲשֶׁר־אָסְרָ֥ה עַל־נַפְשָׁ֖הּ יָקֻֽמוּ׃
וְ֠אִם בְּי֨וֹם שְׁמֹ֣עַ אִישָׁהּ֮ יָנִ֣יא אוֹתָהּ֒ וְהֵפֵ֗ר אֶת־נִדְרָהּ֙ אֲשֶׁ֣ר עָלֶ֔יהָ
וְאֵת֙ מִבְטָ֣א שְׂפָתֶ֔יהָ אֲשֶׁ֥ר אָסְרָ֖ה עַל־נַפְשָׁ֑הּ וַיהוָ֖ה יִֽסְלַֽח־לָֽהּ׃

CLASSIC COMMENTATORS

The Torah here discusses a father or husband annulling the vows of his daughter or wife, respectively. Such annulment of vows is called הפרת נדרים. There is a different concept, called התרת נדרים, in which a religious leader or a *beit din* can release a person from a vow. What might be the source for this idea?

HAKETAV VEHAKABBALA

The vocalization of the verb *lo yaḥel* ("he must not break") in the active voice is significant, since the *yod* appears with a *pataḥ*, not a *tzerei*. Had the term been in the passive form *lo yeiḥel* ("it cannot be broken") it would mean that it is never possible for an individual to break his word. This teaches that although the person who made the vow is by himself forbidden to undo the vow, if he enlists the assistance of others, he might be able to break it, for example if the court or the expert releases him from the vow.

הכתב והקבלה

היו"ד פתוחה, ולא אמר יחל ביו"ד צרויה... דאם כן – היה משמעותו דלא משכחת ליה כלל לחלל נדרו... לכן אמר קרא בלשון פועל, להורות שהוא מצד עצמותו אין לו רשות לחלל, אבל להיות נפעל ע"י אחרים רשאי לחלל, והיינו בהתרת אחרים.

BEMIDBAR | CHAPTER 30 — MATTOT

10 forgo them for her. The vow of a widow or a divorcée – whatever she binds herself by –
11 stands. If, while in her husband's house, a woman makes a vow or takes an oath binding
12 herself to an obligation and her husband hears and keeps silent, and does not restrain
13 her, then all her vows and the obligations by which she binds herself shall stand. But if her husband annuls them on the day when he hears them, then the words she spoke as a vow or the obligation by which she bound herself will not stand. Her husband has
14 annulled them, and the Lord will forgo them for her. Every vow or binding by oath
15 may be upheld by her husband or else annulled by her husband. But if her husband keeps silent from that day to the next, then he has upheld all her vows and the obligations by which she has bound herself. He has upheld them by remaining silent on the day when
16 he heard them. If he nullifies them some time after he has heard of them, he shall bear her
17 guilt." These are the decrees that the Lord issued to Moshe, between a husband and his wife and between a father and his daughter while she is a girl in her father's home.

RAMBAN

רמב״ן

ובאה הפרשה הזאת בכאן, מפני שהזכיר נדרי גבוה (במדבר כ״ט:ל״ט) "לבד מנדריכם ונדבותיכם לעולותיכם ולמנחותיכם ולנסכיכם ולשלמיכם", אמר עוד: מלבד אלה הנדרים הנזכרים יש עוד נדרי הדיוט, וככל היוצא מפיו של אדם חייב לקיים ולעשות כל אשר אסר על נפשו, ובכולן לא יחל דברו.

The laws regarding vows are placed here in the Torah following a declaration in the previous chapter: "These you shall offer to the Lord on your festivals, in addition to your vows and freewill offerings: your burnt offerings, grain offerings, libations, and peace offerings" (29:39). Thus our text now continues: Alongside the vows regarding holy matters there exists another category, of secular vows. For those as well, an individual is required to honor the statements that come out of his mouth; he must observe every restriction he has placed upon himself. Therefore, a person must take care to never break his vow.

QUESTIONS FOR THOUGHT

- Which of the two commentaries connects this passage to what was described just before in the Torah and which suggests that the Torah states this here in anticipation of what is going to happen later?
- What support does Ibn Ezra bring from the language of the Torah?
- According to each of the commentaries, are the vows discussed those that a person makes to God or those that a person makes to another person? How would the phrase לא יחל דברו (v. 3) take on a different meaning depending on whether it was a vow to God or a vow to another person?

WISDOM OF THE HEART

The law of annulment of vows is dependent on the father or husband objecting to the vow on the same day that he hears it. If he remains silent, then the vow stands. People often think that their job as a friend is to support whatever their friend does, to have their back. A true friend, however, is someone who really cares and knows that they need to push back when they see that their friend is truly wrong or going down a bad path.

Can you think of a time when you would have been better off if a good friend had been really honest with you? Do you think a good friend might become resentful if you could have given them a different perspective but you refrained from doing so?

י וְנֵ֥דֶר אַלְמָנָ֖ה וּגְרוּשָׁ֑ה כֹּ֛ל אֲשֶׁר־אָסְרָ֥ה עַל־נַפְשָׁ֖הּ יָק֥וּם עָלֶֽיהָ׃
יא וְאִם־בֵּ֥ית אִישָׁ֖הּ נָדָ֑רָה אוֹ־אָסְרָ֥ה אִסָּ֛ר עַל־נַפְשָׁ֖הּ בִּשְׁבֻעָֽה׃
יב וְשָׁמַ֤ע אִישָׁהּ֙ וְהֶחֱרִ֣שׁ לָ֔הּ לֹ֥א הֵנִ֖יא אֹתָ֑הּ וְקָ֙מוּ֙ כָּל־נְדָרֶ֔יהָ
וְכָל־אִסָּ֛ר אֲשֶׁר־אָסְרָ֥ה עַל־נַפְשָׁ֖הּ יָק֑וּם וְאִם־הָפֵ֙ר יָפֵ֥ר אֹתָ֣ם ׀
יג אִישָׁהּ֮ בְּי֣וֹם שָׁמְעוֹ֒ כָּל־מוֹצָ֨א שְׂפָתֶ֧יהָ לִנְדָרֶ֛יהָ וּלְאִסַּ֥ר נַפְשָׁ֖הּ
לֹ֣א יָק֑וּם אִישָׁ֣הּ הֲפֵרָ֔ם וַיהֹוָ֖ה יִֽסְלַֽח־לָֽהּ׃
יד כָּל־נֵ֛דֶר וְכָל־שְׁבֻעַ֥ת אִסָּ֖ר לְעַנֹּ֣ת נָ֑פֶשׁ אִישָׁ֥הּ יְקִימֶ֖נּוּ וְאִישָׁ֥הּ יְפֵרֶֽנּוּ׃ וְאִם־הַחֲרֵשׁ֩
יַחֲרִ֨ישׁ לָ֥הּ אִישָׁהּ֮ מִיּ֣וֹם אֶל־יוֹם֒ וְהֵקִים֙ אֶת־כָּל־נְדָרֶ֔יהָ א֥וֹ
אֶת־כָּל־אֱסָרֶ֖יהָ אֲשֶׁ֣ר עָלֶ֑יהָ הֵקִ֣ים אֹתָ֔ם כִּי־הֶחֱרִ֥שׁ לָ֖הּ בְּי֥וֹם
טו שָׁמְעֽוֹ׃ וְאִם־הָפֵ֥ר יָפֵ֛ר אֹתָ֖ם אַחֲרֵ֣י שָׁמְע֑וֹ וְנָשָׂ֖א אֶת־עֲוֺנָֽהּ׃ אֵ֣לֶּה
טז הַֽחֻקִּ֗ים אֲשֶׁ֨ר צִוָּ֤ה יְהֹוָה֙ אֶת־מֹשֶׁ֔ה בֵּ֥ין אִ֖ישׁ לְאִשְׁתּ֑וֹ בֵּֽין־אָ֣ב
לְבִתּ֔וֹ בִּנְעֻרֶ֖יהָ בֵּ֥ית אָבִֽיהָ׃

TEXTUAL SKILLS

1. The first part of this chapter discusses a married woman, as does this second half. Can you find the differences between them?

2. To what does the Torah compare the husband's inaction about his wife's vow (that is, his decision not to annul it)?

CLASSIC COMMENTATORS

Why does the section about annulling vows appear here?

IBN EZRA / אבן עזרא

The text relates that the people of Gad approached Moshe, Elazar, and the leaders of the congregation and presented their request. In response, "Moshe gave instructions concerning them to Elazar the priest, Yehoshua son of Nun, and the family heads of the Israelite tribes" (32:28), referring to the tribal leaders who have already been mentioned. Now, since Moshe demanded to the tribes of Gad and Reuven that they "do what you have promised" (32:24), we also read, in the present passage, "Moshe spoke to the tribal heads of the Israelites" (30:2). This section on vows includes as well the statement, "whatever he speaks, that he must fulfill" (30:3).

הכתוב אמר, שבאו בני גד אל משה ואל אלעזר ואל נשיאי העדה ודברו דבריהם ואחרי כן כתוב (במדבר ל׳:ב׳:כ״ח) "ויצו להם משה את אלעזר הכהן ואת יהושע בן נון ואת ראשי אבות המטות" – הם נשיאי העדה הנזכרים. ובעבור שאמר משה לבני גד ולבני ראובן (ל׳:ב׳:כ״ד) "והיוצא מפיכם תעשו" על כן כתוב (ל׳:ב׳) "וידבר משה אל ראשי המטות..." ושם כתוב (ל׳:ג׳) "ככל היוצא מפיו יעשה".

BEMIDBAR | CHAPTER 31   MATTOT | 278

31 1,2 The Lord spoke to Moshe: "Take revenge for the Israelites against the Midianites; after that you will be gathered in to your people." Moshe spoke to the people: "Equip men from among you for active service, to go out against Midyan, to execute the Lord's 3 vengeance against Midyan. For this service, call up one thousand from each of Israel's 4,5 tribes." And so, of the thousands of Israel, one thousand men were selected from each 6 tribe, twelve thousand in all, all armed for battle. Moshe sent them, a thousand from each tribe, into service, together with Pinḥas son of Elazar the priest, who was in

---

TZEROR HAMOR   צרור המור

Israel is commanded to not battle the Moabites, for the sake of Ruth the Moabite and Naama the Amonite, who were destined to emerge from that nation.

ולא מאת המואבים בשביל רות המואביה ונעמה העמונית שעתידה לצאת מהם.

KELI YAKAR   כלי יקר

Why does God not order Moshe to take revenge against the Moabites? Does the earlier verse not state, "Israel was dwelling at Shitim. And the men began to consort with Moabite women" (25:1)? Furthermore, why does the text say that the Israelites *began* to consort with these women? It was the Israelite men who started up with the Moabite women, by going to worship their gods and enticing the women.... Because the Torah recognizes that the one who initiates a sin is primarily at fault, it does not blame Moav for this debacle. The opposite may be said about Midyan: that nation sent their daughters to sleep with the Israelite men. Proof for this can be seen with Zimri – would this man have had the audacity to solicit the daughter of a king? No, it must have been she who approached him.

ולא צוה לצרור המואבים לפי שנאמר (במדבר כ"ה:א') ויחל העם לזנות אל בנות מואב. מהו ויחל אלא כך פירושו שישראל היו המתחילין ותובעים את בנות מואב והלכו להם לאהליהם ותובעים את הנשים ומפתים אותם ... על כן לא נתחייבו מואב כי המתחיל בקלקלה הוא העיקר ובו תלוי החטא. אבל במדינים היה הדבר בהפך, שאדרבה המדינים הפקירו את בנותיהם שתבעו את ישראל לזנות, והסברא נותנת כי איך מלאו לבו של זמרי לתבוע את בת מלך אלא ודאי שהיא תבעתו.

QUESTIONS FOR THOUGHT

- Three of the commentaries try to clear the Moabite women of guilt. Which of those understands that the Moabite women had a justified reason for seducing the men of *Benei Yisrael*?
- Regarding what do Abarbanel and *Keli Yakar* agree? Which of those two explains why men from *Benei Yisrael* who were being seduced by women from Midyan ended up worshipping Baal Peor, a Moabite god?
- What challenge would you present to the author of *Tzeror Hamor*?
- Why do you think that God wants specifically Moshe to be in charge of the vengeance against Midyan? Why could that not be part of the battles Yehoshua would fight after Moshe's death?

TEXTUAL SKILLS

1. Look carefully at verses 1 and 3. Whose vengeance is this?
2. Why do you think that, of all people, Pinḥas was chosen to accompany the army which would fight Midyan?
3. The phrase אלף למטה אלף למטה ("one thousand per tribe, one thousand per tribe"), is reminiscent of the language at the beginning of chapter 13. What do you think might be the connection between these two incidents?

במדבר | פרק לא | מטות

לא א וַיְדַבֵּר יְהוָה אֶל־מֹשֶׁה לֵּאמֹר: נְקֹם נִקְמַת בְּנֵי יִשְׂרָאֵל מֵאֵת כז שני
ב הַמִּדְיָנִים אַחַר תֵּאָסֵף אֶל־עַמֶּיךָ: וַיְדַבֵּר מֹשֶׁה אֶל־הָעָם
ג לֵאמֹר הֵחָלְצוּ מֵאִתְּכֶם אֲנָשִׁים לַצָּבָא וְיִהְיוּ עַל־מִדְיָן לָתֵת
ד נִקְמַת־יְהוָה בְּמִדְיָן: אֶלֶף לַמַּטֶּה אֶלֶף לַמַּטֶּה לְכֹל מַטּוֹת
ה יִשְׂרָאֵל תִּשְׁלְחוּ לַצָּבָא: וַיִּמָּסְרוּ מֵאַלְפֵי יִשְׂרָאֵל אֶלֶף לַמַּטֶּה
ו שְׁנֵים־עָשָׂר אֶלֶף חֲלוּצֵי צָבָא: וַיִּשְׁלַח אֹתָם מֹשֶׁה אֶלֶף לַמַּטֶּה
לַצָּבָא אֹתָם וְאֶת־פִּינְחָס בֶּן־אֶלְעָזָר הַכֹּהֵן לַצָּבָא וּכְלֵי הַקֹּדֶשׁ

CLASSIC COMMENTATORS

In the incident with Baal Peor (Num. 25:1–9), there were two nations whose daughters were involved, Moav and Midyan. Why does God instruct them to exact vengeance only on Midyan but not on Moav?

רש״י / RASHI

ולא מאת המואבים, שהמואבים נכנסו לדבר מחמת יראה שהיו יראים מהם שהיו ישראל שוללים אותם, ... אבל מדינים נתעברו על ריב לא להם.

Why does God not demand vengeance against the Moabites? This is explained by the fact that the Moabites instigated their conflict with Israel out of fear that they would be plundered by the Israelites.... The Midianites, on the other hand, entered into a conflict that had nothing to do with them.

אברבנאל / ABARBANEL

הרעה הזאת ממדין יצאה ולא ממואב ובלק כאשר שמע שבלעם אמר כי שלום ואמת יהיה בימיו הלך לדרכו אך בלעם בשובו לארצו עבר בארץ מדין ושם יעץ את המדינים שלא יוכלו להסית את ישראל ולהורידם מקדושתם ומאהבת השם אותם כי אם באמצעות הנשים שהנה תהיינה סבה למפלתם כי אלהי ישראל שונא זמה הוא והמדינים נתרצו בזה לעשותו ולכך נתעכב שם בלעם לסדר הדבר ולדעת מה יהיה בהם. ובעבור שבעל פעור היה בגבול מואב הפקידו המדיני' את בנותיהם לזנות שם עם ישראל ותתנכרנה כאלו היו מואביות שהיו באות אל המחנה למכור להם מזונות ושאר הדברים כי המואבים השלימו עם ישראל לא המדינים וחשבו ישראל בתחלה שהיו מואביות ...

The villainy of that incident was perpetrated by Midyan and not by Moav. For when Balak heard Bilam's pronouncement that only peace and truth would prevail over Israel, he went on his way. However, Bilam passed through the land of Midyan on his way home. While he was there he advised the Midianite leaders that the only way they could entrap Israel and knock them off their holy perch where they were beloved by God would be to dispatch women who would entice them into licentiousness. That represented a promising strategy because the God of Israel loathes licentiousness and those who practice it. The Midianites approved of this idea and put it into action, while Bilam remained on hand to arrange matters and to observe the outcome. Now, since the place of Baal Peor is situated on the border of Moav, the Midianites sent their women to prostitute themselves among the Israelites while dressed as Moabites. Under that disguise the Midianite women gained access to the Israelite camp by pretending to be local merchants arriving to sell food and other items to the Israelites, as the Moabites had made peace with Israel whereas the Midianites had not. Hence at first, the Israelites believed that the visiting women were in fact Moabites.

7 charge of the sacred utensils and the trumpets for sounding the blast. And they did battle against Midyan as the Lord had commanded Moshe, and killed every male.
8 And, among the slain, they killed the kings of Midyan: Evi, Rekem, Tzur, Ḥur, and Reva – all five kings of Midyan. At the sword's edge they also killed Bilam son of Beor.
9 The Israelites took captive the Midianite women and children, and took as booty all
10 their cattle, flocks, and wealth. They burned all the towns where they lived and their
11 encampments. They gathered all the spoil and plunder, people and animals, and they
12 brought the captives and the plunder and spoil to Moshe, Elazar the priest, and the Israelite community, at the camp on the plains of Moav by the Jordan across from

---

אבן עזרא

יש אומרים: אחר ששב אל מקומו, בא אל מדין, כאשר שמע דבר המגפה שהיה ישראל בעצתו, לקחת ממון מזקני מדין.

IBN EZRA

According to some commentators Bilam returned to Midyan after he had gone home. Once he heard that the Israelites had been stricken with a plague as a result of his counsel, he came to the Midianite elders to collect his fee.

ר' יוסף אבן כספי

אין לנו בזה רק מה שעינינו רואות, והוא כי נמצא במדין, אם כי לא נדע סבת המצאו שם, כי לא פורש בתורה ומי ינבא, ואם לא זכר מציאותו לא ידענוהו.

RABBI YOSEF IBN KASPI

We can only really know what the text tells us, which is that Bilam was found in Midyan. The text does not explain what he was doing there, and no prophet has explained this. Had the Torah not mentioned his presence we would not know anything about it.

QUESTIONS FOR THOUGHT

- In what way is Ibn Kaspi's explanation very different from the other two?
- What is the strength of the explanation of *Ho'il Moshe*? What is its weakness?
- Which of these commentaries portrays Bilam in the worst light?
- One approach which is common among some midrashim and commentaries is that they seem to take every opportunity to portray the "good" people as always good, even when the text seems to say otherwise, and the "bad" people as always bad, even though the text doesn't necessarily support that. What do you think might be motivating those commentators? Which do you think presents a more meaningful picture – characters who are either completely black or completely white, or characters who have a mixture of black and white?

WISDOM OF THE HEART

When reading *Parashat Balak* it's hard to find fault in Bilam. He receives a job offer to curse *Benei Yisrael* from the king of Moav and insists on consulting with God before accepting. When God refuses, so does Bilam, and he repeatedly proclaims God's message that he is powerless to do anything on his own, that he is bound to God's words. Moreover, at the end he freely issues an unrestricted blessing. Here, however, we find Bilam squarely with the Midianite kings (not his own people), as *Benei Yisrael* avenge the Midianite plot against them. People can be complex. Sometimes they show one aspect of themselves and hide others from us, and sometimes other circumstances bring out different aspects of who they are.

וַחֲצֹצְר֥וֹת הַתְּרוּעָ֖ה בְּיָד֑וֹ: וַֽיִּצְבְּאוּ֙ עַל־מִדְיָ֔ן כַּאֲשֶׁ֛ר צִוָּ֥ה יְהוָ֖ה אֶת־מֹשֶׁ֑ה וַיַּֽהַרְג֖וּ כָּל־זָכָֽר: וְאֶת־מַלְכֵ֨י מִדְיָ֜ן הָרְג֣וּ עַל־חַלְלֵיהֶ֗ם אֶת־אֱוִ֤י וְאֶת־רֶ֨קֶם֙ וְאֶת־צ֣וּר וְאֶת־ח֔וּר וְאֶת־רֶ֖בַע חֲמֵ֣שֶׁת מַלְכֵ֣י מִדְיָ֑ן וְאֵת֙ בִּלְעָ֣ם בֶּן־בְּע֔וֹר הָרְג֖וּ בֶּחָֽרֶב: וַיִּשְׁבּ֧וּ בְנֵֽי־יִשְׂרָאֵ֛ל אֶת־נְשֵׁ֥י מִדְיָ֖ן וְאֶת־טַפָּ֑ם וְאֵ֨ת כָּל־בְּהֶמְתָּ֧ם וְאֶת־כָּל־מִקְנֵהֶ֛ם וְאֶת־כָּל־חֵילָ֖ם בָּזָֽזוּ: וְאֵ֤ת כָּל־עָרֵיהֶם֙ בְּמ֣וֹשְׁבֹתָ֔ם וְאֵ֖ת כָּל־טִֽירֹתָ֑ם שָׂרְפ֖וּ בָּאֵֽשׁ: וַיִּקְחוּ֙ אֶת־כָּל־הַשָּׁלָ֔ל וְאֵ֖ת כָּל־הַמַּלְק֑וֹחַ בָּאָדָ֖ם וּבַבְּהֵמָֽה: וַיָּבִ֡אוּ אֶל־מֹשֶׁה֩ וְאֶל־אֶלְעָזָ֨ר הַכֹּהֵ֜ן וְאֶל־עֲדַ֣ת בְּנֵֽי־יִשְׂרָאֵ֗ל אֶת־הַשְּׁבִ֧י וְאֶת־הַמַּלְק֛וֹחַ וְאֶת־הַשָּׁלָ֖ל אֶל־הַֽמַּחֲנֶ֑ה אֶל־עַרְבֹ֣ת מוֹאָ֔ב אֲשֶׁ֖ר עַל־יַרְדֵּֽן

CLASSIC COMMENTATORS

Bilam is not from Midyan. What was he doing there during the battle with *Benei Yisrael*, the battle in which he lost his life?

HO'IL MOSHE

An earlier report reveals that "Bilam rose and returned home" (24:25). And yet, after a short period, he somehow manages to come all the way back from Petor, on the Euphrates River, to the land of Midyan, which seems quite impossible. I have therefore come to the conclusion that the "home" referred to in *Parashat Balak* is not actually Petor, but Kiryat Ḥutzot, where Balak first hosted Bilam after he arrived from Petor [as described in 22:39]. Bilam then set out with Balak from Kiryat Ḥutzot to Bamot Baal [in 22:41], then to the field of Tzofim, and from there they moved to the top of Peor [in 23:28]. However, when Bilam realized that he would be unable to curse Israel, he returned to Kiryat Ḥutzot. From there he planned on eventually leaving for his homeland. Meanwhile, Balak took his leave from Bilam and went back to his town of Ar of Moav [21:28], which was his capital city. Thus when Balak tells Bilam, "Now get away from here and go home" (24:11), he is sending the sorcerer back to Kiryat Ḥutzot [and not to Petor].

הואיל משה

ולמעלה (כ״ד:כ״ה) הוא אומר שבלעם שב למקומו, ובזמן מועט כזה חזר מפתור אשר על נהר פרת עד ארץ מדין! זהו דבר שאין הדעת סובלתו; על כן הואלתי לפרש שמקומו האמור בפרשת בלק אינו פתור רק קרית חוצות שבה הושיבהו בלק בבואו לו מפתור, ומקרית חוצות עלה עם בלק לבמות בעל, ואח״כ אל שדה צופים, ואח״כ אל ראש הפעור, ובראותו כי לא הצליח לקלל את ישראל חזר לקרית חוצות לשוב לארצו בימים הבאים, וגם בלק הלך לדרכו לבוא לעיר מואב שהיא עיר ממלכתו, וכן "ברח לך אל מקומך" (כ״ד:י״א) נפרש שמדבר על קרית חוצות.

31:13–20 *When Moshe sees what the soldiers brought back from the battle he is enraged at the leadership. The Midianite women were the source of Benei Yisrael's troubles in the incident with Baal Peor; how could it be that the leaders now willingly bring them into the camp? He commands that the spoils and the camp both be purified.*

13 Yeriḥo. Moshe, Elazar the priest, and all the community princes went to meet them
14 outside the camp. And Moshe grew furious with the commanders of the forces, the
15 officers of thousands and of hundreds, now returned from the service of war. "Have
16 you left all the women alive?" Moshe demanded. "These were the very ones who, on Bilam's advice, induced the Israelites to betray the LORD during the Peor affair, so that
17 a plague struck down the LORD's community. Now, therefore, kill every male child
18 and kill every woman who has had relations with a man. All the young girls who have
19 not had relations with any man – them you may spare alive. You must stay outside the camp for seven days. Every one among you or your captives who has killed a person
20 or touched a corpse must purify himself or herself on the third and seventh days. You must also purify every garment, as well as every article of leather, goats' hair, or wood."

QUESTIONS FOR THOUGHT

- Both R. Hirsch and *Haamek Davar* suggest technical answers to the question. What is the difference between their answers?
- In what way is Ralbag's explanation similar to that of R. Hirsch? In what way is it very different?
- Ibn Ezra suggests that the laws were different in this case than they would be under usual circumstances. What idea does he suggest, and how can that be applicable today in our lives?

TEXTUAL SKILLS

1. There is a common notion, originating in midrash and echoed by many commentaries, that the Midianite women who seduced *Benei Yisrael* both sexually and religiously did so on the advice of Bilam. Find the verse in this passage which could be the source for that idea.

2. The word תתחטאו appears in both verse 19 and verse 20. What is the root of that word?

WISDOM OF THE HEART

Moshe is angry with the military leaders, who showed mercy at an inappropriate time. Imagine a surgeon who hesitates to make a cut because she doesn't want to hurt her patient, or a parent who doesn't push others aside to rescue his child who is running into traffic to retrieve a ball. The real challenge is to develop the judgment to know when being compassionate demands that we act in ways which seem cruel.

What are the dangers in performing "unmerciful" acts in the name of justified compassion?

יג וַיֵּצְא֗וּ מֹשֶׁ֜ה וְאֶלְעָזָ֤ר הַכֹּהֵן֙ וְכָל־נְשִׂיאֵ֣י הָעֵדָ֔ה שלישי /שני/
לִקְרָאתָ֑ם אֶל־מִח֖וּץ לַֽמַּחֲנֶֽה: יד וַיִּקְצֹ֣ף מֹשֶׁ֔ה עַ֖ל פְּקוּדֵ֣י הֶחָ֑יִל
שָׂרֵ֤י הָאֲלָפִים֙ וְשָׂרֵ֣י הַמֵּא֔וֹת הַבָּאִ֖ים מִצְּבָ֥א הַמִּלְחָמָֽה: טו וַיֹּ֥אמֶר
אֲלֵיהֶ֖ם מֹשֶׁ֑ה הַֽחִיִּיתֶ֖ם כָּל־נְקֵבָֽה: טז הֵ֣ן הֵ֜נָּה הָי֨וּ לִבְנֵ֤י יִשְׂרָאֵל֙
בִּדְבַ֣ר בִּלְעָ֔ם לִמְסָר־מַ֥עַל בַּיהֹוָ֖ה עַל־דְּבַר־פְּע֑וֹר וַתְּהִ֥י הַמַּגֵּפָ֖ה
בַּעֲדַ֥ת יְהֹוָֽה: יז וְעַתָּ֕ה הִרְג֥וּ כָל־זָכָ֖ר בַּטָּ֑ף וְכָל־אִשָּׁ֗ה יֹדַ֥עַת אִ֛ישׁ
לְמִשְׁכַּ֥ב זָכָ֖ר הֲרֹֽגוּ: יח וְכֹל֙ הַטַּ֣ף בַּנָּשִׁ֔ים אֲשֶׁ֥ר לֹא־יָדְע֖וּ מִשְׁכַּ֣ב
זָכָ֑ר הַחֲי֖וּ לָכֶֽם: יט וְאַתֶּ֗ם חֲנ֛וּ מִח֥וּץ לַֽמַּחֲנֶ֖ה שִׁבְעַ֣ת יָמִ֑ים כֹּל֩ הֹרֵ֨ג
נֶ֜פֶשׁ וְכֹ֣ל ׀ נֹגֵ֣עַ בֶּֽחָלָ֗ל תִּֽתְחַטְּא֞וּ בַּיּ֤וֹם הַשְּׁלִישִׁי֙ וּבַיּ֣וֹם הַשְּׁבִיעִ֔י
אַתֶּ֖ם וּשְׁבִיכֶֽם: כ וְכָל־בֶּ֧גֶד וְכָל־כְּלִי־ע֛וֹר וְכָל־מַעֲשֵׂ֥ה עִזִּ֖ים וְכָל־

CLASSIC COMMENTATORS

Moshe tells the soldiers that both they and their captives need to be purified. The problem is that the captives are not yet part of *Benei Yisrael*, so ostensibly the laws of purity would not apply to them. Why then would the captives need to be purified?

IBN EZRA

The captives had to be purified due to the fact that the Divine Presence dwelled in Israel's midst.

אבן עזרא

בעבור הכבוד השוכן בתוכם.

RALBAG

Since the captives were incorporated into the nation of Israel, the law was established that they too became impure after contact with dead Midianites, just as the Israelites did.

רלב״ג

לפי שהשבי נכנס בכלל ישראל עשה דינם להטמא בהרוגי מדין כדין ישראל.

RABBI SAMSON RAPHAEL HIRSCH

The captive women were subject to impurity only once they converted to Israel's faith and law system. This was a process that was immediately available for most of these women.

ר' שמשון רפאל הירש

השבויות היו ראויות לקבל טומאה רק לאחר שנתגיירו, פעולה שניתן היה לעשותה באופן מידי בהרבה מהן.

HAAMEK DAVAR

It is true that during the slaughter of the Midianite army the women were gentiles and hence did not become impure. Furthermore, now that they converted they were no longer in contact with any corpses. Still, these women undoubtedly touched the swords that had been used in the battle, and that was tantamount to touching a dead body.

העמק דבר

אף על גב שבשעת הרג רב היו גוים ולא נטמאו, ועתה שנתגיירו שוב אין כאן מת וחלל, מכל מקום ודאי נוגעים בחרב שהוא כחלל.

21 Elazar the priest said to the soldiers returning from war, "This is the Law's decree that
22 the Lord commanded Moshe: Gold, silver, bronze, iron, tin, and lead – anything that
23 can withstand fire – you shall pass through the fire and it will be purified, though it
must also be purified with the water of lustration. Anything that cannot withstand fire,
24 you must immerse in water. You shall wash your clothes on the seventh day and you

---

הואיל משה

לזקני העם היה מבאר משה הדברים יותר ממה שהיה כותב בספר, כי בפרשת חקת לא כתב מאומה על כלי מתכות שצריכים לבוא באש כדי לטהרם, וגם לא הגיד לנו שם שצריך להעביר במים דבר שלא יבוא באש, רק שצריך להזות עליו, וכאן שבאה הלכה למעשה, בא אלעזר הכהן הגדול שעליו להשגיח על טהרת העם למען לא יטמאו המקדש, וביאר להם תוכן הענין.

HO'IL MOSHE

Moshe explained to the nation's elders far more than what is printed in the text. For *Parashat Ḥukat* says nothing about purifying metal utensils by passing them through fire. Nor does that text explain that objects which are flammable should be put in water instead. That earlier passage only describes the sprinkling of water. However, since the present text deals with the practical application of the law, Elazar the High Priest now teaches the nation the particulars of these processes. It was his responsibility to ensure that the people remained pure and did not impurify the Tabernacle.

QUESTIONS FOR THOUGHT

- In what ways is Rashi's explanation different from the others?
- In what way are the explanations of Ibn Ezra and Sforno similar? In what way are they different?
- In what way are the explanations of *Tur* and *Ho'il Moshe* similar? In what ways are they different?
- The Rabbis were very concerned about people trying to "show Moshe up" by teaching or deciding halakha while he was present. For example, they invoked this principle to explain the deaths of Nadav and Avihu (Lev. 10) and were concerned about it in the story regarding Pinḥas. Here too, the commentaries above were clearly concerned about it. Why do you think that it is such a concern? Can you imagine situations in which a great scholar would want a student to decide halakha even in the presence of the teacher?

TEXTUAL SKILLS

1. The phrase זאת חקת התורה also appears at the beginning of chapter 19. What do these two passages have in common?

2. What is missing before verse 21?

WISDOM OF THE HEART

Ramban points out that the obligation to purge (make kosher) the utensils captured in battle is first introduced regarding the battle with Midyan, even though there was a prior battle with Siḥon and Og. This, he explains, is because the Talmud rules that it was permissible to eat non-kosher food during battle, but Ramban understands that the leniency applies only to battles related to the conquest of the land of Israel. Since the battle for Siḥon and Og qualifies, there was no need to purify the vessels. The battle for Midyan, however, does not qualify, so there was a need to purge the plundered vessels. The Torah was prepared to sacrifice even some of its own laws for the conquest of the land of Israel.

We often find that we need to sacrifice some of our values to uphold others which are more important. How do we decide which of our values are more important than others? Where is the point beyond which if we continue to sacrifice we will no longer be bending, but will be breaking?

כא כְּלִי־עֵץ תִּתְחַטָּאוּ: וַיֹּאמֶר אֶלְעָזָר הַכֹּהֵן אֶל־אַנְשֵׁי
הַצָּבָא הַבָּאִים לַמִּלְחָמָה זֹאת חֻקַּת הַתּוֹרָה אֲשֶׁר־צִוָּה יְהֹוָה
כב אֶת־מֹשֶׁה: אַךְ אֶת־הַזָּהָב וְאֶת־הַכָּסֶף אֶת־הַנְּחֹשֶׁת אֶת־הַבַּרְזֶל
כג אֶת־הַבְּדִיל וְאֶת־הָעֹפָרֶת: כָּל־דָּבָר אֲשֶׁר־יָבֹא בָאֵשׁ תַּעֲבִירוּ
בָאֵשׁ וְטָהֵר אַךְ בְּמֵי נִדָּה יִתְחַטָּא וְכֹל אֲשֶׁר לֹא־יָבֹא בָּאֵשׁ
כד תַּעֲבִירוּ בַמָּיִם: וְכִבַּסְתֶּם בִּגְדֵיכֶם בַּיּוֹם הַשְּׁבִיעִי וּטְהַרְתֶּם

CLASSIC COMMENTATORS

It is highly unusual for Elazar to be instructing *Benei Yisrael* in mitzvot. That is usually Moshe's job.

RASHI

Moshe's anger led him to err, and he forgot the laws of purifying gentile utensils. [This explains why Elazar had to transmit this teaching in Moshe's stead.] We find a similar phenomenon on the eighth day of the Tabernacle's inauguration, regarding which the verse states about Moshe, "He was furious with Elazar and Itamar" (Lev. 10:16). In addition, because Moshe got angry, he made a mistake [which Aharon then corrected]. And again, when Moshe lost his temper and declared, "Listen now, rebels! Shall we produce water for you from this rock?" (20:11), it was because he got angry that he erred [and struck the stone instead of speaking to it].

IBN EZRA

The ritual of the red cow had been entrusted to Elazar (19:3). As such, although Moshe gave the people the general instruction to purify themselves, it was Elazar who explained to the nation what to do.

TUR

Moshe taught the laws of purification to the officers of the thousands and of the hundreds, but Elazar spoke directly to the soldiers regarding the utensils. It was the soldiers who plundered the household vessels from the Midianite homes, whereas the officers merely took illustrious clothing for themselves.

RABBI OVADYA SFORNO

Elazar told the nation: The instruction that Moshe gave to purify yourselves on the third and seventh days is what is known as "the Law's decree." It is the ritual of the red cow that is required upon contact with a human corpse.

רש״י

ויאמר אלעזר הכהן וגומר – לפי שבא משה לכלל כעס בא לכלל טעות, שנתעלמה ממנו הילכות גיעולי גוים. וכן אתה מוצא בשביעי למילואים, שנאמר: ויקצוף משה על אלעזר ועל איתמר (ויקרא י׳:ט״ז) – בא לכלל כעס בא לכלל טעות. וכן: בשמעו נא המורים, ויך את הסלע (במדבר כ׳:י׳-י״א) – על ידי כעס טעה.

אבן עזרא

כי חוקת תורה לאלעזר הפרה נתנה (במדבר י״ט:ג׳), ומשה אמר להם כלל: תתחטאו (במדבר ל״א:י״ט-כ׳), ואלעזר פירש להם.

טור

ויאמר אלעזר הכהן אל אנשי הצבא – משה אמר פרשת טהרה אל שרי האלפים והמאות אבל אלעזר שאמר דין טהרת הכלים אמר אל אנשי הצבא ששללו ובזזו מכלי התשמיש הנמצאים בבתים אבל שרי האלפים לא לקחו אלא בגדים חשובים.

ר׳ עובדיה ספורנו

מה שאמר לכם משה שתתחטאו שלישי ושביעי (פסוק י״ט) הוא דין "חקת התורה" של פרה אדומה לטהר מטומאת מת.

> **31:25–54** *God instructs Moshe to split the spoils of the war between those who fought and the rest of the camp. From the half which goes to the fighters there is a 0.2% tax given to Elazar; from the half which goes to the rest of the nation there is a 2% tax given to the Levites. When the commanders realize that not a single soldier was killed in battle, they donate to the Mishkan a wealth of golden jewelry which they plundered.*

will then be pure, and may enter the camp." The Lord said to Moshe: "Together with Elazar the priest and the family heads of the community, you must make an inventory of the plunder that was taken, people and animals, giving half to the soldiers who went into battle and half to the rest of the community. Levy a tribute to the Lord. From the soldiers who took part in the battle, take one part of every five hundred, be it of people, oxen, donkeys, or flocks. Take this from their half and give it to Elazar the priest as an upraised gift to the Lord. From the Israelites' half, take one out of every fifty, be it of people, cattle, donkeys, or flock – all the animals – and give them to the Levites who carry out the duties of the Lord's Tabernacle." Moshe and Elazar the priest did as the Lord commanded Moshe. The plunder, aside from the spoil the troops had taken, was 675,000 sheep, 72,000 oxen, 61,000 donkeys, and 32,000 women who had not had relations with a man. The half share of those who had served in battle was 337,500 sheep, of which the Lord's tribute was 675. The cattle were 36,000, of which the Lord's

---

WISDOM OF THE HEART

The Torah goes to great lengths to describes the fair distribution of the spoils of war. Human history has witnessed countless times, during war or other periods of chaos, that people throw rules aside, and behave in a cutthroat, dog-eat-dog manner. The Torah emphasizes that during these times we need to be extra careful to ensure fairness, kindness, and justice. Some of the Jewish people's greatest heroes were those who acted with kindness and compassion during the most difficult times.

How would you want to conduct yourself during times of scarce resources – selfishly or selflessly?

QUICK BITE

Rav Yisrael of Rizhin points out that the soldiers who fought got proportionally much more and paid only one-tenth of the taxes than the people who were in the camp, highlighting the gratitude necessary toward those who go to the front lines.

כה וְאַחַר תָּבֹאוּ אֶל־הַֽמַּחֲנֶֽה׃ כו וַיֹּ֧אמֶר יְהֹוָ֛ה אֶל־מֹשֶׁ֖ה רביעי
לֵּאמֹֽר׃ שָׂ֗א אֵ֣ת רֹ֤אשׁ מַלְק֙וֹחַ֙ הַשְּׁבִ֔י בָּאָדָ֖ם וּבַבְּהֵמָ֑ה אַתָּה֙
וְאֶלְעָזָ֣ר הַכֹּהֵ֔ן וְרָאשֵׁ֖י אֲב֥וֹת הָעֵדָֽה׃ כז וְחָצִ֙יתָ֙ אֶת־הַמַּלְק֔וֹחַ
בֵּ֚ין תֹּפְשֵׂ֣י הַמִּלְחָמָ֔ה הַיֹּצְאִ֖ים לַצָּבָ֑א וּבֵ֖ין כָּל־הָעֵדָֽה׃ כח וַהֲרֵמֹתָ֨
מֶ֜כֶס לַֽיהֹוָ֗ה מֵאֵ֞ת אַנְשֵׁ֤י הַמִּלְחָמָה֙ הַיֹּצְאִ֣ים לַצָּבָ֔א אֶחָ֣ד נֶ֔פֶשׁ
מֵחֲמֵ֖שׁ הַמֵּא֑וֹת מִן־הָֽאָדָם֙ וּמִן־הַבָּקָ֔ר וּמִן־הַחֲמֹרִ֖ים וּמִן־
הַצֹּֽאן׃ כט מִמַּחֲצִיתָ֖ם תִּקָּ֑חוּ וְנָתַתָּ֛ה לְאֶלְעָזָ֥ר הַכֹּהֵ֖ן תְּרוּמַ֥ת
יְהֹוָֽה׃ ל וּמִמַּחֲצִ֨ת בְּנֵֽי־יִשְׂרָאֵ֜ל תִּקַּ֣ח ׀ אֶחָ֣ד ׀ אָחֻ֣ז מִן־הַחֲמִשִּׁ֗ים
מִן־הָאָדָ֧ם מִן־הַבָּקָ֛ר מִן־הַחֲמֹרִ֥ים וּמִן־הַצֹּ֖אן מִכָּל־הַבְּהֵמָ֑ה
וְנָתַתָּ֤ה אֹתָם֙ לַלְוִיִּ֔ם שֹׁמְרֵ֕י מִשְׁמֶ֖רֶת מִשְׁכַּ֥ן יְהֹוָֽה׃ לא וַיַּ֣עַשׂ מֹשֶׁ֔ה
וְאֶלְעָזָ֖ר הַכֹּהֵ֑ן כַּאֲשֶׁ֛ר צִוָּ֥ה יְהֹוָ֖ה אֶת־מֹשֶֽׁה׃ לב וַיְהִי֙ הַמַּלְק֔וֹחַ יֶ֣תֶר
הַבָּ֔ז אֲשֶׁ֥ר בָּזְז֖וּ עַ֣ם הַצָּבָ֑א צֹ֗אן שֵׁשׁ־מֵא֥וֹת אֶ֛לֶף וְשִׁבְעִ֥ים אֶ֖לֶף
וַחֲמֵֽשֶׁת־אֲלָפִֽים׃ לג וּבָקָ֕ר שְׁנַ֥יִם וְשִׁבְעִ֖ים אָֽלֶף׃ לד וַחֲמֹרִ֕ים אֶחָ֥ד
וְשִׁשִּׁ֖ים אָֽלֶף׃ לה וְנֶ֣פֶשׁ אָדָ֔ם מִן־הַ֨נָּשִׁ֔ים אֲשֶׁ֥ר לֹֽא־יָדְע֖וּ מִשְׁכַּ֣ב
זָכָ֑ר כָּל־נֶ֕פֶשׁ שְׁנַ֥יִם וּשְׁלֹשִׁ֖ים אָֽלֶף׃ לו וַתְּהִי֙ הַֽמֶּחֱצָ֔ה חֵ֕לֶק הַיֹּצְאִ֖ים
בַּצָּבָ֑א מִסְפַּ֣ר הַצֹּ֗אן שְׁלֹשׁ־מֵא֥וֹת אֶ֛לֶף וּשְׁלֹשִׁ֥ים אֶ֖לֶף וְשִׁבְעַ֥ת
אֲלָפִ֖ים וַחֲמֵ֥שׁ מֵאֽוֹת׃ לז וַיְהִ֛י הַמֶּ֥כֶס לַֽיהֹוָ֖ה מִן־הַצֹּ֑אן שֵׁ֥שׁ מֵא֖וֹת
חָמֵ֥שׁ וְשִׁבְעִֽים׃ לח וְהַ֨בָּקָ֔ר שִׁשָּׁ֥ה וּשְׁלֹשִׁ֖ים אָ֑לֶף וּמִכְסָ֖ם לַֽיהֹוָ֥ה

TEXTUAL SKILLS

1. The word אחז means "percent" in modern Hebrew. It appears twice here, but nowhere else in Tanakh in a similar context. What do you think it means?

2. The tax which was levied included people who were taken captive. In fact, the word אדם, describing them, appears seven times in this passage. What do you think the High Priest and the Levites did with those captives?

39 tribute was 72. The donkeys were 30,500, of which the Lord's tribute was 61. There were
40
41 16,000 people, of which the Lord's tribute was 32 persons. Moshe gave the tribute, an upraised gift for the Lord, to Elazar the priest, as the Lord had commanded Moshe.
42 The half share that Moshe took for the Israelites from those who had served in battle as
43
44 the community's half consisted of 337,500 sheep, 36,000 heads of cattle, 30,500 donkeys,
45
46 and 16,000 people. Moshe took from the Israelites' half one out of every 50 humans and
47 animals. These he gave to the Levites who keep the charge of the Lord's Tabernacle, as
48 the Lord had commanded Moshe. The commanders over the thousands of the warriors
49 – officers over thousands and officers over hundreds – approached Moshe and said to him, "Your servants have counted the warriors in our charge; not one of us is missing.
50 And so we make an offering to the Lord of the gold articles each man found – anklets, bracelets, signet rings, earrings, and pendants – to make our atonement before the
51 Lord." Moshe and Elazar the priest took all the gold from them, all the crafted objects.
52 All the gold for the upraised gift presented to the Lord by the officers of thousands
53 and the officers of hundreds was worth 16,750 shekel. Yet the men of the army each kept
54 plunder for themselves. Moshe and Elazar the priest took the gold from the officers of thousands and of hundreds, and brought it to the Tent of Meeting as a remembrance for the Israelites before the Lord.

לט שְׁנַ֖יִם וְשִׁבְעִֽים: וַחֲמֹרִ֕ים שְׁלֹשִׁ֥ים אֶ֖לֶף וַחֲמֵ֣שׁ מֵא֑וֹת וּמִכְסָ֣ם
מ לַֽיהוָ֔ה אֶחָ֖ד וְשִׁשִּֽׁים: וְנֶ֣פֶשׁ אָדָ֔ם שִׁשָּׁ֥ה עָשָׂ֖ר אָ֑לֶף וּמִכְסָם֙
מא לַֽיהוָ֔ה שְׁנַ֥יִם וּשְׁלֹשִׁ֖ים נָֽפֶשׁ: וַיִּתֵּ֣ן מֹשֶׁ֗ה אֶת־מֶ֙כֶס֙ תְּרוּמַ֣ת יְהוָ֔ה
מב לְאֶלְעָזָ֖ר הַכֹּהֵ֑ן כַּאֲשֶׁ֛ר צִוָּ֥ה יְהוָ֖ה אֶת־מֹשֶֽׁה: וּמִֽמַּחֲצִ֖ית בְּנֵ֣י   חמישי
מג יִשְׂרָאֵ֑ל אֲשֶׁר֙ חָצָ֣ה מֹשֶׁ֔ה מִן־הָאֲנָשִׁ֖ים הַצֹּבְאִֽים: וַתְּהִ֛י מֶחֱצַ֥ת
הָעֵדָ֖ה מִן־הַצֹּ֑אן שְׁלֹשׁ־מֵא֣וֹת אֶ֗לֶף וּשְׁלֹשִׁ֥ים אֶ֛לֶף שִׁבְעַ֥ת
מד אֲלָפִ֖ים וַחֲמֵ֥שׁ מֵאֽוֹת: וּבָקָ֕ר שִׁשָּׁ֥ה וּשְׁלֹשִׁ֖ים אָֽלֶף: וַחֲמֹרִ֕ים
מה
מו שְׁלֹשִׁ֥ים אֶ֖לֶף וַחֲמֵ֥שׁ מֵאֽוֹת: וְנֶ֣פֶשׁ אָדָ֔ם שִׁשָּׁ֥ה עָשָׂ֖ר אָֽלֶף: וַיִּקַּ֨ח
מֹשֶׁ֜ה מִמַּחֲצִ֣ת בְּנֵֽי־יִשְׂרָאֵ֗ל אֶת־הָֽאָחֻז֙ אֶחָ֣ד מִן־הַחֲמִשִּׁ֔ים מִן־
הָאָדָ֖ם וּמִן־הַבְּהֵמָ֑ה וַיִּתֵּ֨ן אֹתָ֜ם לַלְוִיִּ֗ם שֹֽׁמְרֵי֙ מִשְׁמֶ֙רֶת֙ מִשְׁכַּ֣ן
מח יְהוָ֔ה כַּאֲשֶׁ֛ר צִוָּ֥ה יְהוָ֖ה אֶת־מֹשֶֽׁה: וַֽיִּקְרְבוּ֙ אֶל־מֹשֶׁ֔ה הַפְּקֻדִ֕ים
מט אֲשֶׁ֖ר לְאַלְפֵ֣י הַצָּבָ֑א שָׂרֵ֥י הָאֲלָפִ֖ים וְשָׂרֵ֥י הַמֵּאֽוֹת: וַיֹּֽאמְרוּ֙ אֶל־
מֹשֶׁ֔ה עֲבָדֶ֣יךָ נָֽשְׂא֗וּ אֶת־רֹ֛אשׁ אַנְשֵׁ֥י הַמִּלְחָמָ֖ה אֲשֶׁ֣ר בְּיָדֵ֑נוּ
נ וְלֹא־נִפְקַ֥ד מִמֶּ֖נּוּ אִֽישׁ: וַנַּקְרֵ֞ב אֶת־קָרְבַּ֣ן יְהוָ֗ה אִישׁ֩ אֲשֶׁ֨ר מָצָ֤א
כְלִֽי־זָהָב֙ אֶצְעָדָ֣ה וְצָמִ֔יד טַבַּ֖עַת עָגִ֣יל וְכוּמָ֑ז לְכַפֵּ֥ר עַל־נַפְשֹׁתֵ֖ינוּ
נא לִפְנֵ֥י יְהוָֽה: וַיִּקַּ֨ח מֹשֶׁ֜ה וְאֶלְעָזָ֤ר הַכֹּהֵן֙ אֶת־הַזָּהָ֔ב מֵֽאִתָּ֑ם כֹּ֖ל
נב כְּלִ֥י מַעֲשֶֽׂה: וַיְהִ֣י ׀ כָּל־זְהַ֣ב הַתְּרוּמָ֗ה אֲשֶׁ֤ר הֵרִ֙ימוּ֙ לַֽיהוָ֔ה שִׁשָּׁ֨ה
עָשָׂ֥ר אֶ֛לֶף שְׁבַע־מֵא֥וֹת וַחֲמִשִּׁ֖ים שָׁ֑קֶל מֵאֵת֙ שָׂרֵ֣י הָאֲלָפִ֔ים
נג וּמֵאֵ֖ת שָׂרֵ֥י הַמֵּאֽוֹת: אַנְשֵׁי֙ הַצָּבָ֔א בָּזְז֖וּ אִ֥ישׁ לֽוֹ: וַיִּקַּ֨ח מֹשֶׁ֜ה
נד וְאֶלְעָזָ֤ר הַכֹּהֵן֙ אֶת־הַזָּהָ֔ב מֵאֵ֛ת שָׂרֵ֥י הָאֲלָפִ֖ים וְהַמֵּא֑וֹת וַיָּבִ֤אוּ
אֹתוֹ֙ אֶל־אֹ֣הֶל מוֹעֵ֔ד זִכָּר֥וֹן לִבְנֵֽי־יִשְׂרָאֵ֖ל לִפְנֵ֥י יְהוָֽה:

BEMIDBAR | CHAPTER 32

> **32:1–5** *Following the earlier defeat of Siḥon and Og (Num. 21:21–35), Benei Yisrael now unexpectedly control a significant amount of land. This territory is on the eastern side of the Jordan River and is not part of the land initially intended for them to settle. Two tribes, Reuven and Gad, approach the leadership of the nation – Moshe, Elazar, and the heads of the other tribes – pointing out that they have a great abundance of sheep and the eastern lands are excellent for grazing sheep.*

32 1 The people of Reuven and Gad had much cattle – in this they were very rich. And
    2 seeing the lands of Yazer and Gilad they noticed that this was cattle country. So the people of Gad and Reuven came to Moshe, Elazar the priest, and the princes of the
    3 community and said: "Atarot, Divon, Yazer, Nimra, Ḥeshbon, Elaleh, Sevam, Nevo,
    4 and Beon, the land that the Lord struck down before the community of Israel, is good
    5 cattle country, and your servants keep cattle." They said, "If we have found favor with you, let this land be given to your servants as our possession. Do not make us cross the

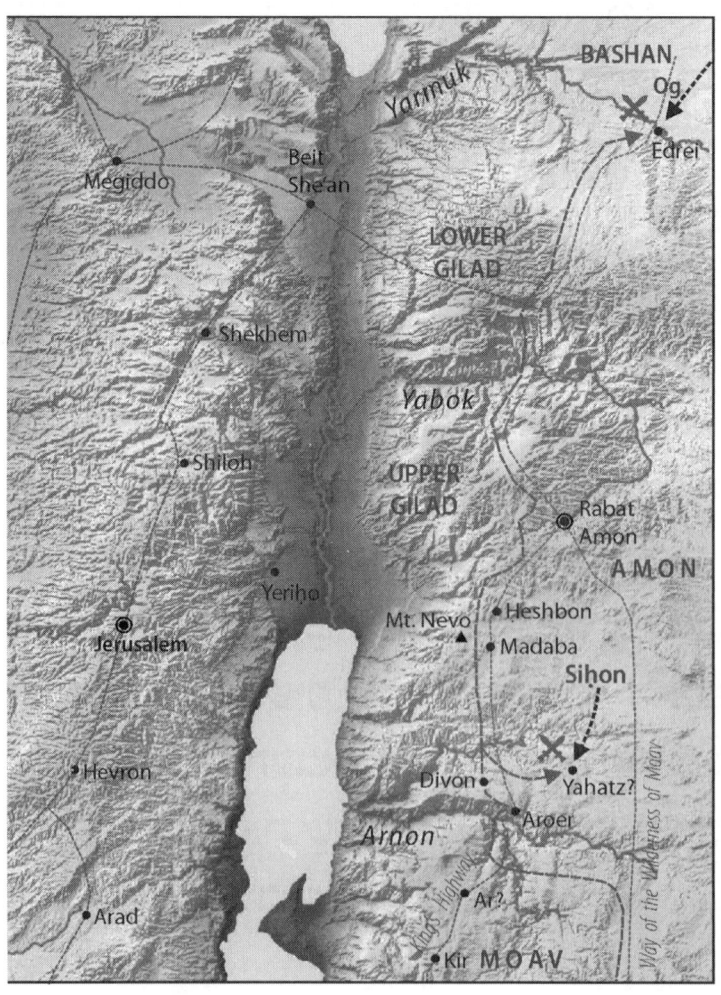

The land of Siḥon and Og on the eastern side of the Jordan River

במדבר | פרק לב

לב א וּמִקְנֶה ׀ רַב הָיָה לִבְנֵי רְאוּבֵן וְלִבְנֵי־גָד עָצוּם מְאֹד וַיִּרְאוּ אֶת־אֶרֶץ יַעְזֵר וְאֶת־אֶרֶץ גִּלְעָד וְהִנֵּה הַמָּקוֹם מְקוֹם מִקְנֶה: ב וַיָּבֹאוּ בְנֵי־גָד וּבְנֵי רְאוּבֵן וַיֹּאמְרוּ אֶל־מֹשֶׁה וְאֶל־אֶלְעָזָר הַכֹּהֵן וְאֶל־נְשִׂיאֵי הָעֵדָה לֵאמֹר: ג עֲטָרוֹת וְדִיבֹן וְיַעְזֵר וְנִמְרָה וְחֶשְׁבּוֹן וְאֶלְעָלֵה וּשְׂבָם וּנְבוֹ וּבְעֹן: ד הָאָרֶץ אֲשֶׁר הִכָּה יהוה לִפְנֵי עֲדַת יִשְׂרָאֵל אֶרֶץ מִקְנֶה הִוא וְלַעֲבָדֶיךָ מִקְנֶה: ה וַיֹּאמְרוּ אִם־מָצָאנוּ חֵן בְּעֵינֶיךָ יֻתַּן אֶת־הָאָרֶץ הַזֹּאת לַעֲבָדֶיךָ לַאֲחֻזָּה

TEXTUAL SKILLS

1. What do Reuven and Gad *not* say, which you would have expected them to?
2. What word appears four times in these four verses and seems to be its theme word?
3. Look back at chapter 2. What was the relationship between Reuven and Gad?

WISDOM OF THE HEART

There are two different descriptions offered to describe the flocks of Reuven and Gad – מקנה רב and עצום מאד. These might refer to two different aspects, one relating to the quantity of what they had and the other referring to what that quantity accomplished. Some people who are blessed with abundant wealth understand that their blessing is an opportunity to do good things. Others, however, see their wealth as a source of power, and they look to wield that power and gain more. As the Mishna (Avot 3:7) warns, it is important to recognize that any gifts God gives us – financial or otherwise – are given to us for a reason. Ultimately, God will want to know if we used the gifts for His purposes or our own.

What kinds of gifts, other than financial, do you see people having? What kinds of gifts do you think God has bestowed on you? How do you think that you can use them to help make some part of the world a little better?

QUICK BITE

The quest of Reuven and Gad to settle east of the Jordan River is driven by their cattle, and their material wealth. That same motive encouraged Lot (Gen. 13:10–11) and Esav (Gen. 36:6–7) to settle outside of the land of God's promise. It is amazing that someone growing up in Avraham's or Yitzḥak's home, or even in the wilderness under God's protective canopy, could choose to prioritize financial gain. Our environment is important, but even more significant is who we are.

> **32:6–15** *When Reuven and Gad finally ask for the land east of the Jordan, Moshe erupts in a fierce speech, accusing them of nothing less than being a second iteration of the spies who discouraged Benei Yisrael from entering the land and causing a forty-year disaster.*

6 Jordan." But Moshe asked the Gadites and Reubenites, "Are your brothers to go to war
7 while you stay here? Why would you discourage the Israelites from crossing into the
8 land the Lord has given them? That is what your fathers did when I sent them from
9 Kadesh Barnea to see the land. They went as far as the Eshkol Ravine and saw the land, but they discouraged the Israelites from entering the land the Lord had given them,
10/11 and on that day the Lord's rage burned, and He swore: None of the men twenty years of age or above who left Egypt will see the land that I swore to give Avraham, Yitzḥak,
12 and Yaakov, because they did not follow Me wholeheartedly – none except Kalev son of Yefuneh the Kenizzite and Yehoshua son of Nun, because they wholeheartedly fol-
13 lowed the Lord. The Lord was incensed at Israel, and He made them wander in the wilderness for forty years until the whole generation that had done evil in the Lord's
14 sight was gone. And here you are, a brood of sinners, taking your fathers' places and
15 bringing yet more of the Lord's burning rage down upon Israel. If you turn back from following Him, He will once again leave them in the wilderness, and you will destroy

---

QUESTIONS FOR THOUGHT

- One of the commentaries suggests that Moshe is saying that it would be unfair for them to stay behind while the rest of the nation has to go fight. The other says that the very idea of staying behind would discourage *Benei Yisrael* from wanting to fight. Match the commentaries with these two opinions.
- Most commentaries agree with the one who thinks that this means that it would be unfair for them not to fight. What in the continuation of Moshe's speech prompted the other one to advance a very different idea?
- What do you think are the implications in Moshe's argument for contemporary Jewish life?

TEXTUAL SKILLS

1. Moshe makes two distinct arguments in this speech. What are they?
2. Moshe's reaction to the request of these two tribes is the longest and fiercest speech he has given until now. Look carefully at their request and identify what he found so distressing.
3. Reuven and Gad had been speaking since verse 2. Why does verse 5 need to open with another introduction of ויאמרו ("they spoke")?

WISDOM OF THE HEART

The opening line of Moshe's tirade against Reuven and Gad resonates for anyone with a sense that all of *Am Yisrael* is in the same boat, with responsibilities to the individuals and the nation as a whole. No one can simply decide that they are exempt from the obligation to protect the nation and help it accomplish its mission.

מטות | פרק לב

ז אֶל־תַּעֲבְרוּ אֶת־הַיַּרְדֵּן: וַיֹּאמֶר מֹשֶׁה לִבְנֵי־גָד וְלִבְנֵי רְאוּבֵן
הַאַחֵיכֶם יָבֹאוּ לַמִּלְחָמָה וְאַתֶּם תֵּשְׁבוּ פֹה: וְלָמָּה תְנִיאוּן אֶת־
ח לֵב בְּנֵי יִשְׂרָאֵל מֵעֲבֹר אֶל־הָאָרֶץ אֲשֶׁר־נָתַן לָהֶם יְהוָה: כֹּה
עָשׂוּ אֲבֹתֵיכֶם בְּשָׁלְחִי אֹתָם מִקָּדֵשׁ בַּרְנֵעַ לִרְאוֹת אֶת־הָאָרֶץ:
ט וַיַּעֲלוּ עַד־נַחַל אֶשְׁכּוֹל וַיִּרְאוּ אֶת־הָאָרֶץ וַיָּנִיאוּ אֶת־לֵב בְּנֵי
י יִשְׂרָאֵל לְבִלְתִּי־בֹא אֶל־הָאָרֶץ אֲשֶׁר־נָתַן לָהֶם יְהוָה: וַיִּחַר־אַף
יא יְהוָה בַּיּוֹם הַהוּא וַיִּשָּׁבַע לֵאמֹר: אִם־יִרְאוּ הָאֲנָשִׁים הָעֹלִים
מִמִּצְרַיִם מִבֶּן עֶשְׂרִים שָׁנָה וָמַעְלָה אֵת הָאֲדָמָה אֲשֶׁר נִשְׁבַּעְתִּי
יב לְאַבְרָהָם לְיִצְחָק וּלְיַעֲקֹב כִּי לֹא־מִלְאוּ אַחֲרָי: בִּלְתִּי כָּלֵב בֶּן־
יג יְפֻנֶּה הַקְּנִזִּי וִיהוֹשֻׁעַ בִּן־נוּן כִּי מִלְאוּ אַחֲרֵי יְהוָה: וַיִּחַר־אַף
יְהוָה בְּיִשְׂרָאֵל וַיְנִעֵם בַּמִּדְבָּר אַרְבָּעִים שָׁנָה עַד־תֹּם כָּל־הַדּוֹר
יד הָעֹשֶׂה הָרַע בְּעֵינֵי יְהוָה: וְהִנֵּה קַמְתֶּם תַּחַת אֲבֹתֵיכֶם תַּרְבּוּת
טו אֲנָשִׁים חַטָּאִים לִסְפּוֹת עוֹד עַל חֲרוֹן אַף־יְהוָה אֶל־יִשְׂרָאֵל: כִּי
תְשׁוּבֻן מֵאַחֲרָיו וְיָסַף עוֹד לְהַנִּיחוֹ בַּמִּדְבָּר וְשִׁחַתֶּם לְכָל־הָעָם:

CLASSIC COMMENTATORS

Moshe opens by asking the challenging question: "Are your brothers to go to war while you stay here?" The commentaries debate what Moshe's intention is.

RABBI OVADYA SFORNO   ר' עובדיה ספורנו

Said Moshe to these two tribes: Do you really imagine that your brothers will agree to go and conquer the land of Canaan while you stay here in a region that has already been captured?

האמנם תחשבו שאחיכם ירצו לבוא להלחם כדי לכבוש ואתם תשבו פה במה שכבר נכבש.

HAAMEK DAVAR   העמק דבר

Said Moshe to these two tribes: You are committing a terrible injustice against the rest of the nation. Why should you settle down in an area that that entire people fought to obtain, while the rest of Israel continues to endanger themselves in battle?

זו עוולה נגד ישראל, שתהא לכם ארץ שכבר נכבשה על ידי כולם, והמה יסכנו עצמם למלחמה.

16 this entire people." Then they set forward and said to him, "Let us build sheep pens
17 here for our livestock and towns for our children. But we will arm ourselves and go ahead of the Israelites until we have seen them safely to their place. Meanwhile, our children will remain in the fortified towns, protected from the inhabitants of the land.
18 We will not return to our homes until every one of the Israelites has taken possession
19 of his inheritance. We, however, will not take possession with them on the far side of the Jordan, for our inheritance will be on the east side of the Jordan."
20 Moshe replied to them, "If you do this – if you arm yourselves for battle before the Lord,
21 and each of your armed men crosses the Jordan before the Lord until He has driven out
22 His enemies before Him, and the land has been subdued before the Lord – then you may return and be clear before the Lord and before Israel, and this land will be yours
23 as a possession before the Lord. But if you do not do this, you will have sinned against
24 the Lord, and know that your sin will find you. Build towns for your children and

---

HAAMEK DAVAR

העמק דבר

In their response, Gad and Reuven dispel Moshe's initial complaint about how unfair it would be for the entire nation to cross the river to fight while they sit safely in their new homes. This is why the two tribes offer to march ahead of the others into battle. Furthermore, they also address Moshe's second concern, that their preference for the eastern bank will be interpreted by everybody else as a sign of fear and lack of faith in God. The complete opposite is true, they say; by abandoning their children in fortified cities and leading the army against the Canaanites, they will show how much trust they have that God will protect their families.

הוסרה הטענה הראשונה של משה, איך ימצאו לב שבני ישראל יבואו למלחמה והם ישבו, הרי אנו הולכים חושים למלחמה. וגם הטענה השניה ש(בני") יאמרו שאין ידאים ואין אנחנו סומכים על השגחתו ית"ש, אדרבה בשעה שנלך חושים וישב טפנו בערי המבצר, הרי אין אנו יראים לעזוב את הבנים וסומכים אנחנו על השגחתו יתברך עליהם.

QUESTIONS FOR THOUGHT

- What did each of the above commentaries understand to be Moshe's concern?
- Both commentaries agree that Moshe was concerned about a faith issue, but they disagree as to what that issue was. What positions do they each take on that question? Which of those acts of faith would the Torah seem more likely to support? Why do you say that?
- *Ho'il Moshe* (not cited above) points out that, based on Joshua 4:14, about 40,000 soldiers from Reuven and Gad (and half of Menashe) led the battle, less than half of the available soldiers based on the census in Numbers, chapter 26. He suggests that they left behind enough soldiers to defend their wives, children, and sheep. Which of the two opinions above does he challenge?

WISDOM OF THE HEART

Moshe tells the two tribes that when they fulfill their commitments they will be "clean" in the eyes of God and Israel. It is not enough to know that one is doing the right thing; it is important to make sure that there is not even an appearance of wrongdoing.

Why do you think it is important that people not suspect us of doing something wrong?

| במדבר | פרק לב

טז וַיִּגְּשׁוּ אֵלָיו וַיֹּאמְרוּ גִּדְרֹת צֹאן נִבְנֶה לְמִקְנֵנוּ הֲזֶה:
פֹּה וְעָרִים לְטַפֵּנוּ: יז וַאֲנַחְנוּ נֵחָלֵץ חֻשִׁים לִפְנֵי בְּנֵי יִשְׂרָאֵל עַד
אֲשֶׁר אִם־הֲבִיאֹנֻם אֶל־מְקוֹמָם וְיָשַׁב טַפֵּנוּ בְּעָרֵי הַמִּבְצָר
מִפְּנֵי יֹשְׁבֵי הָאָרֶץ: יח לֹא נָשׁוּב אֶל־בָּתֵּינוּ עַד הִתְנַחֵל בְּנֵי יִשְׂרָאֵל
אִישׁ נַחֲלָתוֹ: יט כִּי לֹא נִנְחַל אִתָּם מֵעֵבֶר לַיַּרְדֵּן וָהָלְאָה כִּי בָאָה
נַחֲלָתֵנוּ אֵלֵינוּ מֵעֵבֶר הַיַּרְדֵּן מִזְרָחָה:
כ וַיֹּאמֶר אֲלֵיהֶם מֹשֶׁה אִם־תַּעֲשׂוּן אֶת־הַדָּבָר הַזֶּה אִם־תֵּחָלְצוּ   שביעי /רביעי/
לִפְנֵי יְהוָה לַמִּלְחָמָה: כא וְעָבַר לָכֶם כָּל־חָלוּץ אֶת־הַיַּרְדֵּן לִפְנֵי
יְהוָה עַד הוֹרִישׁוֹ אֶת־אֹיְבָיו מִפָּנָיו: כב וְנִכְבְּשָׁה הָאָרֶץ לִפְנֵי
יְהוָה וְאַחַר תָּשֻׁבוּ וִהְיִיתֶם נְקִיִּם מֵיְהוָה וּמִיִּשְׂרָאֵל וְהָיְתָה
הָאָרֶץ הַזֹּאת לָכֶם לַאֲחֻזָּה לִפְנֵי יְהוָה: כג וְאִם־לֹא תַעֲשׂוּן כֵּן הִנֵּה
חֲטָאתֶם לַיהוָה וּדְעוּ חַטַּאתְכֶם אֲשֶׁר תִּמְצָא אֶתְכֶם: כד בְּנוּ־לָכֶם

TEXTUAL SKILLS

1. Compare Reuven and Gad's offer in verse 16 with Moshe's response in verse 24. What subtle changes can you detect that Moshe made?

2. Aside from the differences between verses 16 and 24, as Moshe reiterates their offer he makes some seemingly small but potentially very important changes. Find two of them.

CLASSIC COMMENTATORS

How do these two tribes understand Moshe's concerns, and how does their offer address these issues?

RALBAG

The tribes of Gad and Reuven agreed not to arouse fear in the hearts of the nation. They will quickly build pens for their flocks, and fortified cities to protect their children from the neighboring peoples. And to prevent the rest of Israel from being dissuaded to go into the land they volunteer to lead the charge against the Canaanite states without any hesitation. This will demonstrate their complete trust that God Almighty will crush the land's inhabitants on their behalf.

רלב״ג

והנה ענו בני גד ובני ראובן כי הם יקחו עצה שלא יניאו בזה לב העם; וזה, שהם יבנו במהירות גדרות צאן למקניהם וערים לטפיהם, וישב טפם בערי המבצר מפני יושבי הארץ, ובעבור שלא יניאו לב העם יחלצו במהירות לצבא, בזולת שום עצלה, לבאר שהם בוטחים בה׳ יתעלה שינצחו הגוים אשר שם.

32:25–32 *As the two tribes appear to reach an agreement with Moshe, Moshe gathers the leaders of the next generation – Yehoshua, Elazar the High Priest, and the heads of the other tribes – and charges them with the task of upholding the deal.*

25 pens for your flocks, but do what you have promised." The people of Gad and Reuven
26 replied to Moshe, "Your servants will do just as my lord charges us. Our children, wives,
27 livestock, and all our animals will remain here in the towns of Gilad, but your servants, all equipped for war, will cross over to do battle before the Lord, as my lord has said."
28 Moshe gave instructions concerning them to Elazar the priest, Yehoshua son of Nun,
29 and the family heads of the Israelite tribes. Moshe said to them, "If the men of Gad and Reuven cross the Jordan with you, each equipped for battle before the Lord, and the land is subdued before you, then you shall give them the land of Gilad as a possession.
30 But if they do not cross with you, equipped for war, then they must have their pos-
31 session with you in the land of Canaan." The Gadites and the Reubenites answered,
32 "What the Lord has spoken to your servants, we will do. We will cross into the land of Canaan equipped for war before the Lord, and we shall then have our hereditary land

QUESTIONS FOR THOUGHT

- Which of the commentaries understands the response of Reuven and Gad, which claim that Moshe misunderstood their intentions in requesting their portion on the eastern bank of the Jordan?
- Read the sequel to this story in Joshua, chapter 22. Whose opinion does that seem to support?

TEXTUAL SKILLS

1. In verses 25–27, what did the two tribes change from their earlier request (vv. 16–19)?
2. When Moshe presents the deal to the leaders of the next generation (Yehoshua, Elazar, and the heads of the tribes), what does he add that had not been agreed upon earlier?
3. What do the two tribes add in verse 31 which was absent from the entire discussion up until this point?

WISDOM OF THE HEART

Chapter 32 deals with Reuven and Gad's request to settle on the eastern bank of the Jordan River. According to the Netziv this wasn't a choice of good versus bad; rather, it was a question of priorities. Reuven and Gad thought that it was more important to take care of their families and their livelihoods; Moshe did not deny that value but believed that the national need outweighed the personal one. Many decisions in our lives are not between good and bad. That is what makes them so difficult, as they force us to place one of the things we value above others.

When we choose one value over others, we sometimes justify the decision to ourselves by overly minimizing the value we did not place on top. How do you think you can affirm your values even when they are not your primary ones?

במדבר | פרק לב

כה עָרִים לְטַפֵּנוּ וּגְדֵרֹת לְצֹנַאֲכֶם וְהַיֹּצֵא מִפִּיכֶם תַּעֲשֽׂוּ: וַיֹּאמֶר
בְּנֵי־גָד וּבְנֵי רְאוּבֵן אֶל־מֹשֶׁה לֵאמֹר עֲבָדֶיךָ יַעֲשׂוּ כַּאֲשֶׁר אֲדֹנִי
כו מְצַוֶּה: טַפֵּנוּ נָשֵׁינוּ מִקְנֵנוּ וְכָל־בְּהֶמְתֵּנוּ יִהְיוּ־שָׁם בְּעָרֵי הַגִּלְעָד:
כז וַעֲבָדֶיךָ יַעַבְרוּ כָּל־חֲלוּץ צָבָא לִפְנֵי יְהֹוָה לַמִּלְחָמָה כַּאֲשֶׁר
כח אֲדֹנִי דֹּבֵר: וַיְצַו לָהֶם מֹשֶׁה אֵת אֶלְעָזָר הַכֹּהֵן וְאֵת יְהוֹשֻׁעַ
כט בִּן־נוּן וְאֶת־רָאשֵׁי אֲבוֹת הַמַּטּוֹת לִבְנֵי יִשְׂרָאֵל: וַיֹּאמֶר מֹשֶׁה
אֲלֵהֶם אִם־יַעַבְרוּ בְנֵי־גָד וּבְנֵי־רְאוּבֵן ׀ אִתְּכֶם אֶת־הַיַּרְדֵּן כָּל־
חָלוּץ לַמִּלְחָמָה לִפְנֵי יְהֹוָה וְנִכְבְּשָׁה הָאָרֶץ לִפְנֵיכֶם וּנְתַתֶּם
ל לָהֶם אֶת־אֶרֶץ הַגִּלְעָד לַאֲחֻזָּה: וְאִם־לֹא יַעַבְרוּ חֲלוּצִים אִתְּכֶם
לא וְנֹאחֲזוּ בְתֹכְכֶם בְּאֶרֶץ כְּנָעַן: וַיַּעֲנוּ בְנֵי־גָד וּבְנֵי רְאוּבֵן לֵאמֹר
לב אֵת אֲשֶׁר דִּבֶּר יְהֹוָה אֶל־עֲבָדֶיךָ כֵּן נַעֲשֶׂה: נַחְנוּ נַעֲבֹר חֲלוּצִים
לִפְנֵי יְהֹוָה אֶרֶץ כְּנָעַן וְאִתָּנוּ אֲחֻזַּת נַחֲלָתֵנוּ מֵעֵבֶר לַיַּרְדֵּן:

CLASSIC COMMENTATORS

Moshe had suspected that the two tribes were abandoning their national responsibility, and in response they amended their request. Was Moshe right in his suspicion?

ABARBANEL

Now behold, the tribes of Gad and Reuven were terrified at Moshe's reaction to their request. And hence they argued, that with all due respect to the prophet's great Torah wisdom, he had thoroughly misconstrued their intentions. For when they said, "Do not make us cross the Jordan" (32:5), that in no way signaled their reluctance to enter the land to fight alongside the other tribes. Rather, what they meant was that they would prefer not to cross the river in order to inherit land on the western side of that border.

MALBIM

The two tribes now admit that Moshe's assessment of their request was correct, which is why they do not repeat their initial comment, "Do not make us cross the Jordan." At this point they promise that in fact they will lead the marching infantry in Israel's war against the Canaanites. Still, that effort will be delayed somewhat until Gad and Reuven can manage to build pens for their flocks and fortified cities for their children.

אברבנאל

והנה בני גד ובני ראובן, פחד קראם ורעדה מדברי משה רבנו, ורצו לאמר שחוץ ממעלת תורתו לא הבין כונתם, כי הם באומרם "אל תעבירנו את הירדן", לא כיוונו שלא ילכו שמה עם אחיהם, אלא לעניין הירושה אמרו כן, שלא יעבירם שם להתנחל בארץ.

מלבי״ם

הנה הודו, כי צדקו דברי משה וחדלו עוד מבקשה השנייה שביקשו: אל תעבירנו את הירדן, כי הבטיחו שיעברו חלוצים לפני בני ישראל למלחמה, רק שלפי זה צריך להתעכב עד שיבנו גדרות צאן וערי מבצר.

33 across the Jordan." So Moshe gave to them – the people of Gad and Reuven, and half the tribe of Menashe son of Yosef – the kingdom of Siḥon, king of the Amorites, and the kingdom of Og, king of Bashan, the land along with its towns and the territory of
34 the surrounding towns. The Gadites rebuilt Divon, Atarot, Aroer, Atrot Shofan, Yazer,
35
36 Yogbeha, Beit Nimra, and Beit Haran, as fortified towns and enclosures for flocks. The
37
38 Reubenites built Ḥeshbon, Elaleh, Kiryatayim, Nevo and Baal Meon – the names of
39 which were changed – and Sivma. They named the cities that they built up. The descendants of Makhir son of Menashe went to Gilad and captured it, driving out the Amorites
40 who were there. So Moshe gave Gilad to Makhir son of Menashe, and he settled there.
41 Yair son of Menashe went and captured their villages, naming them Hamlets of Yair.
42 Novaḥ went and captured Kenat and its surrounding villages, renaming it Novaḥ after himself.

HAAMEK DAVAR

העמק דבר

יש להתבונן עוד שהרבה משה רבינו חלקת חצי שבט מנשה הרבה לפי ערך שני שבטים אלו וגם לא התנה עמם תנאי בני גד ובני ראובן ... ונראה דבשביל שראה משה רבינו דבעבר הירדן כח התורה מעט ... על כן השתדל להשתיל בקרבם גדולי תורה שיאירו מחשכי הארץ באור כח שלהם.

Why does Moshe grant to part of the tribe of Menashe as much land as he did to the two tribes of Reuven and Gad? Furthermore, why did he not set a similar condition with Menashe as he demanded of the others? It seems that Moshe realized that the level of Torah observance would be lower on the eastern side of the river. In order to counter that tendency, Moshe planted within the midst of Reuven and Gad a group of Torah scholars from the tribe of Menashe who would illuminate the land with the powerful light of their learning.

QUESTIONS FOR THOUGHT

- What do the explanations of Ralbag and *Haamek Davar* have in common? In what way are they different?
- Which of the above thinks that there was absolutely no difference between Reuven and Gad on the one hand, and half of Menashe on the other?
- In what way are the explanations of Ramban and Ralbag similar? What is the main difference between them?

TEXTUAL SKILLS

1. What did Reuven and Menashe do with their cities that Gad did not do?

2. Aside from conquering their land, what did Menashe do that the other two tribes did not?

WISDOM OF THE HEART

The entire chapter records the request of Reuven and Gad to settle on the eastern bank of the Jordan, and the intense negotiations they have with Moshe about it. When Moshe gives them the land, we find that half of Menashe is added on. *Tzeror Hamor* suggests that Moshe assigned half of Menashe to live with Reuven and Gad because he was afraid that the tribes would stray from God's path, while he trusted that half of Menashe would help to keep them in line and have a positive influence on them. Sometimes, the effort to help those who seem far away involves personal sacrifice, even sacrifices that take a toll on one's own spiritual quest.

במדבר | פרק לב

לג וַיִּתֵּ֣ן לָהֶ֣ם ׀ מֹשֶׁ֡ה לִבְנֵי־גָד֩ וְלִבְנֵ֨י רְאוּבֵ֜ן וְלַחֲצִ֣י ׀ שֵׁ֣בֶט ׀ מְנַשֶּׁ֣ה בֶן־יוֹסֵ֗ף אֶת־מַמְלֶ֙כֶת֙ סִיחֹן֙ מֶ֣לֶךְ הָֽאֱמֹרִ֔י וְאֶת־מַמְלֶ֔כֶת ע֖וֹג מֶ֣לֶךְ הַבָּשָׁ֑ן הָאָ֗רֶץ לְעָרֶ֙יהָ֙ בִּגְבֻלֹ֔ת עָרֵ֥י הָאָ֖רֶץ סָבִֽיב: לד וַיִּבְנ֣וּ בְנֵי־גָ֔ד אֶת־דִּיבֹ֖ן וְאֶת־עֲטָרֹ֑ת וְאֵ֖ת עֲרֹעֵֽר: לה וְאֶת־עַטְרֹ֤ת שׁוֹפָן֙ וְאֶת־יַעְזֵ֣ר וְיָגְבֳּהָ֔ה: לו וְאֶת־בֵּ֥ית נִמְרָ֖ה וְאֶת־בֵּ֣ית הָרָ֑ן עָרֵ֥י מִבְצָ֖ר וְגִדְרֹ֥ת צֹֽאן: לז וּבְנֵ֣י רְאוּבֵ֣ן בָּנ֔וּ אֶת־חֶשְׁבּ֖וֹן וְאֶת־אֶלְעָלֵ֑א וְאֵ֖ת קִרְיָתָֽיִם: לח וְאֶת־נְב֞וֹ וְאֶת־בַּ֧עַל מְע֛וֹן מֽוּסַבֹּ֥ת שֵׁ֖ם וְאֶת־שִׂבְמָ֑ה וַיִּקְרְא֣וּ בְשֵׁמֹ֔ת אֶת־שְׁמ֖וֹת הֶעָרִ֥ים אֲשֶׁ֥ר בָּנֽוּ: לט וַיֵּ֨לְכ֜וּ בְּנֵ֨י מָכִ֧יר בֶּן־מְנַשֶּׁ֛ה גִּלְעָ֖דָה וַֽיִּלְכְּדֻ֑הָ וַיּ֖וֹרֶשׁ אֶת־הָאֱמֹרִ֥י אֲשֶׁר־בָּֽהּ: מ וַיִּתֵּ֤ן מֹשֶׁה֙ אֶת־הַגִּלְעָ֔ד לְמָכִ֖יר בֶּן־מְנַשֶּׁ֑ה וַיֵּ֖שֶׁב בָּֽהּ: מא וְיָאִ֤יר בֶּן־מְנַשֶּׁה֙ הָלַ֔ךְ וַיִּלְכֹּ֖ד אֶת־חַוֺּתֵיהֶ֑ם וַיִּקְרָ֥א אֶתְהֶ֖ן חַוֺּ֥ת יָאִֽיר: מב וְנֹ֣בַח הָלַ֔ךְ וַיִּלְכֹּ֥ד אֶת־קְנָ֖ת וְאֶת־בְּנֹתֶ֑יהָ וַיִּקְרָ֧א לָ֦ה נֹ֖בַח בִּשְׁמֽוֹ:

מפטיר

CLASSIC COMMENTATORS

How did half of the tribe of Menashe get added to this deal?

IBN EZRA / **אבן עזרא**

The people of Menashe have not been mentioned until this point since those wishing to stay in the east represented only half the tribe.

ולא הזכיר עד עתה חצי שבט מנשה, בעבור היותו חצי השבט.

RAMBAN / **רמב״ן**

The tribe of Menashe was not initially part of the delegation asking to settle on the east side of the river. However, once the region was surveyed for apportionment to Reuven and Gad, it became clear that it was actually a larger territory than was appropriate for them, so Moshe sought others who could share it with them. Some families of Menashe were interested, possibly because they were also shepherds, so Moshe gave them their portion of the pastureland there.

מתחלה לא באו לפניו שבט מנשה, אבל כאשר חלק הארץ לשני השבטים ראה שהיא ארץ גדולה יותר מן הראוי להם וביקש מי שירצה להתנחל עמהם, והיו אנשים משבט מנשה שרצו בה, אולי אנשי מקנה היו, ונתן להם חלקם.

RALBAG / **רלב״ג**

God revealed to Moshe that it was not appropriate for the entire region east of the Jordan River to be given just to the tribes of Gad and Reuven. Therefore, Moshe distributed part of the area to half the tribe of Menashe as well.

מפני שנתבאר למשה מפי הגבורה שאין ראוי שתגיע כל הארץ אשר מעבר הירדן מזרחה לבני גד ולבני ראובן, שם בזאת הנחלה גם כן חצי שבט מנשה.

MORE QUICK BITES

- **31:16** One could read verse 16 as suggesting that God's anger with Midyan was not only because they caused *Benei Yisrael* to sin but also because they created a situation in which God needed to punish *Benei Yisrael*. In a well-known quote Golda Meir said that the Jewish people may one day be able to forgive their enemies for killing their children, but they will never be able to forgive them for making them kill their enemy's children.

- **31:23** R. Tzvi Hirsch, the Rebbe of Nadvorno, in his *Tzemaḥ Hashem Letzvi*, interprets verse 23 to mean that the Torah, which was given to *Benei Yisrael* through fire at Sinai, must pass through *Benei Yisrael* with their fire, passion, and energy.

- **32:25** Rabbi David Horowitz argues that the decision of the tribe of Reuven to settle on the eastern bank of the Jordan River is another expression of the hastiness and rash decision-making of the tribe's progenitor and namesake displayed in Genesis, for which he was criticized by Yaakov (Gen. 49:3–4). As the opening mishna in Avot suggests, don't rush into decisions. Be deliberate. Do your research. And then be confident.

EXPLORING HASHKAFA
Benefiting from Bad

The interaction between *Benei Yisrael* and the booty from Midyan raises interesting questions about benefiting from tainted sources. To be sure, the Torah forbids deriving any kind of benefit from objects which were worshipped in idolatrous rites and even objects used in idol worship, and later the Rabbis forbid a slew of practices which they call *darkei ha'emori* (the path of the Amorites), because their origins were pagan. Over the course of time complex issues have arisen. What about art that was used to inspire idolatrous worship? What about items which were used in a type of worship that the Torah forbids for Jews but not for non-Jews?

The questions get more nuanced when we consider areas like literature and music. Rabbi Aharon Lichtenstein would regularly quote from non-Jewish religious literature, as he appreciated its authentic and deep expression of religious yearning. Many Sephardic halakhic authorities ruled that it was not only permissible, but a positive act to include music from other religions, even into the synagogue service, as "music cannot become impure" and using it for divine worship elevates and sanctifies it. The reality is that this has been happening for many years, whether we are conscious of it or not. It is not an accident that Sephardic liturgical music sounds Arabic and classic Ashkenazic *nusaḥ* sounds much like music used in medieval churches.

The range of responses to these kinds of issues is expressed not only in terms like "forbidden" or "permitted," but also in terms such as "desirable" and "inappropriate." Consider, for example, music composed by the antisemite Richard Wagner, which was taboo in Israel until Daniel Barenboim led the Israeli Philharmonic in a hotly debated 2001 concert. Or how about beautiful and inspirational religious literature and music composed by Jewish individuals who used their positions of fame or authority to abuse others? Do their other actions render what they created tainted and unusable? If their works are to be shunned, is there a statute of limitations – like perhaps excluding them only in their lifetimes – or should their works be banned forever to dissuade others from thinking that their misdeeds can be swept away?

For many of these questions there are not, and will never be, clear answers. Perhaps the lack of clarity, which will stir debate and discussion, is what will keep the questions and the values they wrestle with alive and present in our minds – and in that there is true and lasting value.

פרשת מסעי
PARASHAT MASEI

> "The journey is long but the goal is in each step."
> Sri Sri Ravi Shankar

This entire book has been a journey, following *Benei Yisrael* through a forty-year process. That journey is not just about getting to the destination; the space in between the beginning and the conclusion isn't just a means to an end. The journey itself is significant; each stop along the way has been another opportunity to learn and grow.

PARASHAT MASEI

> **33:1–49** *The journey, beginning with the exodus from Egypt and lasting until Benei Yisrael camp in the plains of Moav facing Yeriḥo, had forty stations, which are enumerated. Some of those stations were mentioned earlier in the Torah, including incidents which made them stand out, but others are listed here for the first time.*

33 1 These were the journeys of the Israelites when they left Egypt by their divisions under 2 the leadership of Moshe and Aharon. Moshe recorded the places of their setting out on every journey at the LORD's command. These are their journeys, by the places from 3 which they set out. They set out from Ramesses on the fifteenth day of the first month. On the day after the Passover the Israelites went out defiantly, before all the Egyptians' 4 eyes, while the Egyptians were burying their firstborns, whom the LORD had struck 5 down, every one. The LORD had executed judgments even against their gods. The 6 Israelites set out from Ramesses and camped at Sukkot. They set out from Sukkot and 7 camped at Etam on the edge of the wilderness. They set out from Etam and turned 8 back to Pi Haḥirot, which faces Baal Tzefon, and camped before Migdol. They set out from Pi Haḥirot and passed through the sea into the wilderness – and they made

---

RABBI OVADYA SFORNO

ר׳ עובדיה ספורנו

God wanted the journeys of Israel to be recorded to show Israel's devotion to Him. For the nation willingly followed God throughout the desolate wilderness, demonstrating that they were worthy of entering the land.

רצה האל יתברך שיכתבו מסעי ישראל להודיע זכותם 'בלכתם אחריו במדבר בארץ לא זרועה', באופן שהיו ראויים להכנס לארץ.

QUESTIONS FOR THOUGHT

- Both Rashi and Sforno agree that the detail is presented to teach about *ḥesed*. According to each commentator, who do they think did what kind of *ḥesed*, and for whom?
- After reading through the list of travels, what do both of these explanations leave unexplained?

TEXTUAL SKILLS

1. Notice which incidents the Torah describes as part of the list of travels. Which significant incidents are missing that you might have expected the Torah to mention?
2. Find where the camping stops switch from the ones which took place during the time of the book of Exodus to the ones which took place during the time of the book of Numbers.
3. Notice that there is a phrase which appears twice in verse 2, and that the second time it is reversed.
4. Look at the list of places listed here and compare them to the places where the Torah earlier mentioned where they camped (see Ex. ch. 12–19 and Num. 10:11–22:1). Which places are mentioned here that were never mentioned earlier?
5. There is one place which is mentioned earlier (Num. 11:3) which does not appear in this list!

פרשת מסעי

לג א אֵ֚לֶּה מַסְעֵ֣י בְנֵֽי־יִשְׂרָאֵ֔ל אֲשֶׁ֥ר יָצְא֛וּ מֵאֶ֥רֶץ מִצְרַ֖יִם לְצִבְאֹתָ֑ם בְּיַד־מֹשֶׁ֥ה וְאַהֲרֹֽן: ב וַיִּכְתֹּ֨ב מֹשֶׁ֜ה אֶת־מוֹצָאֵיהֶ֛ם לְמַסְעֵיהֶ֖ם עַל־פִּ֣י יְהוָ֑ה וְאֵ֥לֶּה מַסְעֵיהֶ֖ם לְמוֹצָאֵיהֶֽם: ג וַיִּסְע֤וּ מֵֽרַעְמְסֵס֙ בַּחֹ֣דֶשׁ הָרִאשׁ֔וֹן בַּחֲמִשָּׁ֥ה עָשָׂ֛ר י֖וֹם לַחֹ֣דֶשׁ הָרִאשׁ֑וֹן מִֽמָּחֳרַ֣ת הַפֶּ֗סַח יָצְא֤וּ בְנֵֽי־יִשְׂרָאֵל֙ בְּיָ֣ד רָמָ֔ה לְעֵינֵ֖י כָּל־מִצְרָֽיִם: ד וּמִצְרַ֣יִם מְקַבְּרִ֗ים אֵת֩ אֲשֶׁ֨ר הִכָּ֧ה יְהוָ֛ה בָּהֶ֖ם כָּל־בְּכ֑וֹר וּבֵאלֹ֣הֵיהֶ֔ם עָשָׂ֥ה יְהוָ֖ה שְׁפָטִֽים: ה וַיִּסְע֥וּ בְנֵֽי־יִשְׂרָאֵ֖ל מֵֽרַעְמְסֵ֑ס וַֽיַּחֲנ֖וּ בְּסֻכֹּֽת: ו וַיִּסְע֖וּ מִסֻּכֹּ֑ת וַיַּחֲנ֣וּ בְאֵתָ֔ם אֲשֶׁ֖ר בִּקְצֵ֥ה הַמִּדְבָּֽר: ז וַיִּסְעוּ֙ מֵֽאֵתָ֔ם וַיָּ֨שָׁב֙ עַל־פִּ֣י הַֽחִירֹ֔ת אֲשֶׁ֥ר עַל־פְּנֵ֖י בַּ֣עַל צְפ֑וֹן וַֽיַּחֲנ֖וּ לִפְנֵ֥י מִגְדֹּֽל: ח וַיִּסְעוּ֙ מִפְּנֵ֣י הַֽחִירֹ֔ת וַיַּעַבְר֥וּ בְתוֹךְ־הַיָּ֖ם הַמִּדְבָּ֑רָה וַיֵּ֨לְכ֜וּ דֶּ֣רֶךְ שְׁלֹ֤שֶׁת יָמִים֙ בְּמִדְבַּ֣ר אֵתָ֔ם וַֽיַּחֲנ֖וּ בְּמָרָֽה:

CLASSIC COMMENTATORS

Why does the Torah need to provide a detailed description of all the travels of *Benei Yisrael*?

רש"י

להודיעך חסדיו של מקום שאף על פי שגזר עליהם לטלטלם ולהניעם במדבר, לא תאמר שיהיו נעים ומטולטלים ממסע למסע כל ארבעים שנה ולא היתה להם מנוחה, שהרי אין כאן אלא ארבעים ושתים מסעות. צא מהן ארבע עשרה שכולם היו בשנה ראשונה קודם גזירה ... ועוד צא מהן שמונה מסעות שהיו לאחר מיתת אהרן מהר ההר עד ערבות מואב בשנת הארבעים, נמצא שכל שלשים ושמונה לא נסעו אלא עשרים מסעות.

RASHI

This lengthy description teaches us about the kindness of the Almighty. For even though God had decreed that Israel would wander in the wilderness for forty years, He did not force them to endure constant movement, taking one journey after another with no respite whatsoever. That this was not the case is evident from the number of journeys identified in the following passage. According to these verses, Israel embarked on forty-two travels, fourteen of which occurred during the first year of the nation's liberation, before the punishment against them was declared.... Additionally, we can subtract from the total another eight journeys that took place after Aharon's death. These were trips Israel made from Mount Hor [mentioned in v. 38] to the plains of Moav (v. 48) which took place in the fortieth year. That means that in the thirty-eight years in the wilderness there were only twenty trips.

9   a three-day journey through the Wilderness of Etam and camped at Mara. They set
    out from Mara and came to Eilim. At Eilim there were twelve springs and seventy
10 date palms, and they encamped there. They set out from Eilim and camped by the
11 Sea of Reeds. They set out from the Sea of Reeds and camped in the Wilderness of
12,13 Sin. They set out from the wilderness of Sin and camped at Dofka. They set out from
14 Dofka and camped at Alush. They set out from Alush and camped at Refidim, where
15 there was no water for the people to drink. They set out from Refidim and camped
16 in the Sinai Desert. They set out from the Sinai Desert and camped at Kivrot HaTaava.
17,18 They set out from Kivrot HaTaava and camped at Ḥatzerot. They set out from Ḥatzerot
19,20 and camped at Ritma. They set out from Ritma and camped at Rimon Peretz. They set
21 out from Rimon Peretz and camped at Livna. They set out from Livna and camped
22,23 at Risa. They set out from Risa and camped at Kehelata. They set out from Kehelata
24 and camped at Mount Shefer. They set out from Mount Shefer and camped at Ḥarada.
25,26 They set out from Ḥarada and camped at Mak'helot. They set out from Mak'helot and
27,28 camped at Taḥat. They set out from Taḥat and camped at Teraḥ. They set out from Teraḥ
29,30 and camped at Mitka. They set out from Mitka and camped at Ḥashmona. They set
31 out from Ḥashmona and camped at Moserot. They set out from Moserot and camped
32,33 at Benei Yaakan. They set out from Benei Yaakan and camped at Ḥor HaGidgad. They
34 set out from Ḥor HaGidgad and camped at Yotvata. They set out from Yotvata and
35,36 camped at Avrona. They set out from Avrona and camped at Etzyon Gever. They set
37 out from Etzyon Gever and camped in the Wilderness of Tzin, that is, Kadesh. They
38 set out from Kadesh and camped at Mount Hor, at the edge of the land of Edom. And
    Aharon the priest ascended Mount Hor at the Lord's command, and he died there in
39 the fortieth year, on the first day of the fifth month after the Israelites left Egypt. Aharon

---

WISDOM OF THE HEART

Many understand *Benei Yisrael*'s journey as not just a list of places in which they camped, but as a representation of the stages of growth and development as they mature from a divided people who left Egypt and were afraid to enter the promised land to a nation that was united and confident and prepared for their destiny. The Maggid of Kozhnitz points out that the forty-two stops of the journey of *Benei Yisrael* parallel the twenty-one days and twenty-one nights of the three weeks between the Seventeenth of Tamuz and the Ninth of Av, during which we always read *Parashat Masei*. Like *Benei Yisrael*'s journey, every day and night of this period is an opportunity to undo some of the destruction. As Rav Kook has famously noted, if the Temple was destroyed through baseless hatred, then it will be rebuilt through baseless love.

Do you think that people hate for no reason at all?

ט וַיִּסְעוּ מִמָּרָה וַיָּבֹאוּ אֵילִמָה וּבְאֵילִם שְׁתֵּים עֶשְׂרֵה עֵינֹת מַיִם
י וְשִׁבְעִים תְּמָרִים וַיַּחֲנוּ־שָׁם: וַיִּסְעוּ מֵאֵילִם וַיַּחֲנוּ עַל־יַם־סוּף:
יא וַיִּסְעוּ מִיַּם־סוּף וַיַּחֲנוּ בְּמִדְבַּר־סִין: וַיִּסְעוּ מִמִּדְבַּר־סִין וַיַּחֲנוּ
יג בְּדָפְקָה: וַיִּסְעוּ מִדָּפְקָה וַיַּחֲנוּ בְּאָלוּשׁ: וַיִּסְעוּ מֵאָלוּשׁ וַיַּחֲנוּ
יד בִּרְפִידִם וְלֹא־הָיָה שָׁם מַיִם לָעָם לִשְׁתּוֹת: וַיִּסְעוּ מֵרְפִידִם
טז וַיַּחֲנוּ בְּמִדְבַּר סִינָי: וַיִּסְעוּ מִמִּדְבַּר סִינָי וַיַּחֲנוּ בְּקִבְרֹת הַתַּאֲוָה:
יז וַיִּסְעוּ מִקִּבְרֹת הַתַּאֲוָה וַיַּחֲנוּ בַּחֲצֵרֹת: וַיִּסְעוּ מֵחֲצֵרֹת וַיַּחֲנוּ
יט בְּרִתְמָה: וַיִּסְעוּ מֵרִתְמָה וַיַּחֲנוּ בְּרִמֹּן פָּרֶץ: וַיִּסְעוּ מֵרִמֹּן פָּרֶץ
כא וַיַּחֲנוּ בְּלִבְנָה: וַיִּסְעוּ מִלִּבְנָה וַיַּחֲנוּ בְּרִסָּה: וַיִּסְעוּ מֵרִסָּה וַיַּחֲנוּ
כג בִּקְהֵלָתָה: וַיִּסְעוּ מִקְּהֵלָתָה וַיַּחֲנוּ בְּהַר־שָׁפֶר: וַיִּסְעוּ מֵהַר־
כה שָׁפֶר וַיַּחֲנוּ בַּחֲרָדָה: וַיִּסְעוּ מֵחֲרָדָה וַיַּחֲנוּ בְּמַקְהֵלֹת: וַיִּסְעוּ
כו מִמַּקְהֵלֹת וַיַּחֲנוּ בְּתָחַת: וַיִּסְעוּ מִתָּחַת וַיַּחֲנוּ בְּתָרַח: וַיִּסְעוּ
כט מִתָּרַח וַיַּחֲנוּ בְּמִתְקָה: וַיִּסְעוּ מִמִּתְקָה וַיַּחֲנוּ בְּחַשְׁמֹנָה: וַיִּסְעוּ
לא מֵחַשְׁמֹנָה וַיַּחֲנוּ בְּמֹסֵרוֹת: וַיִּסְעוּ מִמֹּסֵרוֹת וַיַּחֲנוּ בִּבְנֵי יַעֲקָן:
לב וַיִּסְעוּ מִבְּנֵי יַעֲקָן וַיַּחֲנוּ בְּחֹר הַגִּדְגָּד: וַיִּסְעוּ מֵחֹר הַגִּדְגָּד וַיַּחֲנוּ
לה בְּיָטְבָתָה: וַיִּסְעוּ מִיָּטְבָתָה וַיַּחֲנוּ בְּעַבְרֹנָה: וַיִּסְעוּ מֵעַבְרֹנָה
לו וַיַּחֲנוּ בְּעֶצְיֹן גָּבֶר: וַיִּסְעוּ מֵעֶצְיֹן גָּבֶר וַיַּחֲנוּ בְמִדְבַּר־צִן הִוא
לז קָדֵשׁ: וַיִּסְעוּ מִקָּדֵשׁ וַיַּחֲנוּ בְּהֹר הָהָר בִּקְצֵה אֶרֶץ אֱדוֹם:
לח וַיַּעַל אַהֲרֹן הַכֹּהֵן אֶל־הֹר הָהָר עַל־פִּי יְהוָה וַיָּמָת שָׁם בִּשְׁנַת
הָאַרְבָּעִים לְצֵאת בְּנֵי־יִשְׂרָאֵל מֵאֶרֶץ מִצְרַיִם בַּחֹדֶשׁ הַחֲמִישִׁי
לט בְּאֶחָד לַחֹדֶשׁ: וְאַהֲרֹן בֶּן־שָׁלֹשׁ וְעֶשְׂרִים וּמְאַת שָׁנָה בְּמֹתוֹ

40 was one hundred and twenty-three years old when he died on Mount Hor. And the Canaanite king of Arad, who lived in the Negev in the land of Canaan, heard that the
41,42 Israelites were coming. They set out from Mount Hor and camped at Tzalmona. They
43 set out from Tzalmona and camped at Punon. They set out from Punon and camped at
44 Ovot. They set out from Ovot and camped at Iyei HaAvarim in the territory of Moav.
45,46 They set out from Iyim and camped at Divon Gad. They set out from Divon Gad and
47 camped at Almon Divlatayma. They set out from Almon Divlatayma and camped in
48 the Mountains of Avarim, before Nevo. They set out from the Mountains of Avarim and
49 camped in the plains of Moav by the Jordan across from Yeriḥo. And they camped by the

---

QUICK BITES

Of all the forty-two stops the Torah describes *Benei Yisrael* making in the wilderness, only three of them have events associated with them and they do not include any of the major events – not the miracles of the manna or the quail, not the giving of the Torah or the sin of the golden calf, not the place from which the spies were sent or where the sin of Baal Peor happened. The first is Eilim, where we are told that there were twelve springs of water and seventy palm trees; the second is Refidim, where *Benei Yisrael* did not have water; the third is Mount Hor, where Aharon dies. It is hard to understand why these are the only three places that the Torah pauses to remind us of the events which took place there, but perhaps they are connected. All three revolve around water. At Eilim, God provides water for them soon after crossing the Sea of Reeds, and both Refidim and Aharon's death are related to complaints about the lack of water – Aharon died before entering the land as a consequence in his role with the incident of hitting the rock at the waters of Meriva. In fact, all three deal with legitimate complaints – in both Refidim and the waters of Meriva the Torah confirms that they lacked water.

Perhaps the Torah is trying to point out that in any journey there are likely to be problems, legitimate ones, and it is appropriate to point them out to the people in charge. The true test of leadership is the ability to distinguish between legitimate complaints and improper ones, and perhaps even more importantly, to respond appropriately to the problems which inevitably arise.

מ	בְּהֹר הָהָר: וַיִּשְׁמַע הַכְּנַעֲנִי מֶלֶךְ־עֲרָד וְהוּא־יֹשֵׁב
מא	בַּנֶּגֶב בְּאֶרֶץ כְּנָעַן בְּבֹא בְּנֵי יִשְׂרָאֵל: וַיִּסְעוּ מֵהֹר הָהָר וַיַּחֲנוּ
מב מג	בְּצַלְמֹנָה: וַיִּסְעוּ מִצַּלְמֹנָה וַיַּחֲנוּ בְּפוּנֹן: וַיִּסְעוּ מִפּוּנֹן וַיַּחֲנוּ
מד	בְּאֹבֹת: וַיִּסְעוּ מֵאֹבֹת וַיַּחֲנוּ בְּעִיֵּי הָעֲבָרִים בִּגְבוּל מוֹאָב:
מה	וַיִּסְעוּ מֵעִיִּים וַיַּחֲנוּ בְּדִיבֹן גָּד: וַיִּסְעוּ מִדִּיבֹן גָּד וַיַּחֲנוּ בְּעַלְמֹן
מז	דִּבְלָתָיְמָה: וַיִּסְעוּ מֵעַלְמֹן דִּבְלָתָיְמָה וַיַּחֲנוּ בְּהָרֵי הָעֲבָרִים לִפְנֵי
מח	נְבוֹ: וַיִּסְעוּ מֵהָרֵי הָעֲבָרִים וַיַּחֲנוּ בְּעַרְבֹת מוֹאָב עַל יַרְדֵּן יְרֵחוֹ:
מט	וַיַּחֲנוּ עַל־הַיַּרְדֵּן מִבֵּית הַיְשִׁמֹת עַד אָבֵל הַשִּׁטִּים בְּעַרְבֹת

QUICK BITES

This *parasha* opens by outlining the forty-two stations where *Benei Yisrael* camped and later mentions the forty-two cities which were allotted to the Levites in Israel. At first glance there does not seem to be any connection between them. Perhaps the Levite cities, in which the Levites lived but did not have the permanence of ownership, were to serve as a reminder to *Benei Yisrael* that they, too, once lived without permanence. Like the Levites, who were dependent on *Benei Yisrael* for their food, *Benei Yisrael* in the wilderness were completely dependent on God. The Levites and their cities remind *Benei Yisrael* that even though they are the masters of their land, they should not slide into the arrogance of their own comfort and success.

According to *Or HaḤayyim*, the place called Ḥatzerot (vv. 17–18), which literally means "courtyard," represents God's courtyard, the *beit midrash* (see Ps. 92:14, 116:19, and 135:2). R. Aharon Lichtenstein noted that if one views the world as worthless, then running to the *beit midrash* is a way to seek refuge from worthlessness. For those who view the world as beautiful, however, the *beit midrash* becomes the place to turn that beauty into sanctity.

BEMIDBAR | CHAPTER 33 — MASEI

> **33:50–56** *God emphasizes two essential responsibilities that Benei Yisrael have when they enter the land. First, it is essential that they cleanse the land of the idolatry which pervades it. Second, they must banish the people who worship those idols, lest their idolatrous culture filter its way into the culture of Benei Yisrael.*

50 Jordan from Beit HaYeshimot to Avel HaShitim in the plains of Moav. And the Lord
51 spoke to Moshe on the plains of Moav by the Jordan across from Yeriḥo: "Speak to the
52 Israelites. Say: When you cross the Jordan into the land of Canaan, you shall drive out all the inhabitants of the land before you. You shall destroy all their carved images and
53 all their molten idols and demolish all their high shrines. You shall take possession of
54 the land and settle there, for I have given you the land to possess. You shall divide up the land by lot among your clans: to a large clan give a large inheritance, and to a small one a small inheritance. Whatever falls to them by lot will be theirs. According to your
55 ancestral tribes you shall inherit. But if you do not drive the inhabitants out of the land before you, then those you allow to remain will be barbs in your eyes and thorns in your
56 sides. They will harass you in the land where you settle. Then, what I intended to do to them, I will do instead to you."

ר׳ עובדיה ספורנו / RABBI OVADYA SFORNO

כאשר תבערו יושבי הארץ, אז תזכו להוריש את הארץ לבניכם, שאם לא תבערו אותם, אף על פי שאתם תכבשו את הארץ, לא תזכו להורישה לבניכם.

If you expunge the natives from the land, your children will inherit it. But if you do not remove the Canaanites, you will be unable to bequeath the land to your descendants even if you conquer it.

QUESTIONS FOR THOUGHT

- How do Rashi and Ramban each understand what **והורשתם** means?
- With whom does Sforno agree regarding the definition of **והורשתם**?
- In what way is Sforno's understanding of the mitzva different from both Rashi's and Ramban's?
- Which of the above commentaries seems to fit the text of the Torah best?

TEXTUAL SKILLS

1. Why is it important for the Torah to describe where this instruction took place?

2. Notice the similarity between verses 54 and 26:54–55.

WISDOM OF THE HEART

Homer's *The Iliad* is a story of going out, of honor and conquest, as Odysseus and his entourage set out for Troy to avenge the abduction of Helen. By contrast, *The Odyssey* is a story of return after the battle. Every great adventure needs a return home, the completion of a cycle. It provides closure, a sense of mission accomplished, a way to compare the before and the after. We know this from literature, from music, and from life. At the end of a long journey that began with Yaakov's descent to Egypt, his descendants, now a nation, are returning home.

Why do we find closure so satisfying?

במדבר | פרק לג | מסעי

מוֹאָ֑ב: וַיְדַבֵּ֧ר יְהוָ֛ה אֶל־מֹשֶׁ֖ה בְּעַֽרְבֹ֣ת מוֹאָ֑ב עַל־ יַרְדֵּ֥ן יְרֵח֖וֹ לֵאמֹֽר: דַּבֵּר֙ אֶל־בְּנֵ֣י יִשְׂרָאֵ֔ל וְאָמַרְתָּ֖ אֲלֵהֶ֑ם כִּ֥י אַתֶּ֛ם עֹֽבְרִ֥ים אֶת־הַיַּרְדֵּ֖ן אֶל־אֶ֥רֶץ כְּנָֽעַן: וְה֨וֹרַשְׁתֶּ֜ם אֶת־כָּל־יֹשְׁבֵ֤י הָאָ֙רֶץ֙ מִפְּנֵיכֶ֔ם וְאִ֨בַּדְתֶּ֔ם אֵ֖ת כָּל־מַשְׂכִּיֹּתָ֑ם וְאֵ֨ת כָּל־צַלְמֵ֤י מַסֵּֽכֹתָם֙ תְּאַבֵּ֔דוּ וְאֵ֥ת כָּל־בָּמוֹתָ֖ם תַּשְׁמִֽידוּ: וְהֽוֹרַשְׁתֶּ֥ם אֶת־ הָאָ֖רֶץ וִֽישַׁבְתֶּם־בָּ֑הּ כִּ֥י לָכֶ֛ם נָתַ֥תִּי אֶת־הָאָ֖רֶץ לָרֶ֥שֶׁת אֹתָֽהּ: וְהִתְנַֽחַלְתֶּם֩ אֶת־הָאָ֨רֶץ בְּגוֹרָ֜ל לְמִשְׁפְּחֹֽתֵיכֶ֗ם לָרַ֞ב תַּרְבּ֤וּ אֶת־ נַֽחֲלָתוֹ֙ וְלַמְעַט֙ תַּמְעִ֣יט אֶת־נַֽחֲלָת֔וֹ אֶל֩ אֲשֶׁר־יֵ֨צֵא ל֥וֹ שָׁ֛מָּה הַגּוֹרָ֖ל ל֣וֹ יִֽהְיֶ֑ה לְמַטּ֥וֹת אֲבֹֽתֵיכֶ֖ם תִּתְנֶחָֽלוּ: וְאִם־לֹ֨א תוֹרִ֜ישׁוּ אֶת־יֹשְׁבֵ֣י הָאָרֶץ֮ מִפְּנֵיכֶם֒ וְהָיָה֙ אֲשֶׁ֣ר תּוֹתִ֣ירוּ מֵהֶ֔ם לְשִׂכִּ֖ים בְּעֵֽינֵיכֶ֑ם וְלִצְנִינִ֖ם בְּצִדֵּיכֶ֑ם וְצָֽרְר֣וּ אֶתְכֶ֔ם עַל־הָאָ֕רֶץ אֲשֶׁ֥ר אַתֶּ֖ם יֹֽשְׁבִ֥ים בָּֽהּ: וְהָיָ֗ה כַּֽאֲשֶׁ֥ר דִּמִּ֛יתִי לַֽעֲשׂ֥וֹת לָהֶ֖ם אֶֽעֱשֶׂ֥ה לָכֶֽם:

שלישי /חמישי/

נ
נא
נב
נג
נד
נה
נו

CLASSIC COMMENTATORS

The Torah describes one of the responsibilities of *Benei Yisrael* using the word וְהוֹרַשְׁתֶּם, which appears four times in this short passage. It is unclear what the word actually means and what the mitzva here is.

RASHI

You shall drive out [*vehorashtem*]: You shall chase away. You shall take possession of [*vehorashtem*] the land: You shall evacuate the inhabitants from the land, and then "you shall settle there." For if you expel the Canaanites you will be able to endure in the land, but if you fail to, you will not last long [for the people living there will drive you out].

רש"י

והורשתם: וגירשתם. והורשתם אותה מיושביה, ואז "וישבתם בה", תוכלו להתקיים בה, ואם לאו - לא תוכלו להתקיים בה.

RAMBAN

I believe that this represents a positive commandment for Israel to settle the land and inherit it, for it has been given to them. The nation must not despise God's portion.

רמב"ן

על דעתי, זו מצות עשה היא, יצוה אותם שישבו בארץ ויירשו אותה כי הוא נתנה להם, ולא ימאסו בנחלת ה'.

BEMIDBAR | CHAPTER 34 — MASEI

34 ¹ The Lord said to Moshe: ² "Command the Israelites. Say to them: As you enter the land of Canaan – this is the land that will become your possession, the land of Canaan with ³ its borders: Your southern sector shall extend from the Wilderness of Tzin alongside ⁴ Edom; your southern border to the east begins at the end of the Dead Sea. The border shall then turn south of Scorpion Ascent and cross toward Tzin. Its outer limit shall be ⁵ south of Kadesh Barne'a, extending to Ḥatzar Adar and continuing toward Atzmon. The ⁶ border shall then turn from Atzmon to the Ravine of Egypt and end at the sea. Your western border will be the Great Sea and its coast; this shall be your western border. ⁷ This shall be your northern border: from the Great Sea, mark a line to Mount Hor. ⁸ From Mount Hor mark a line to Levo Ḥamat. The outer limit of the border shall be ⁹ at Tzedad; the border shall then extend to Zifron, and its outer limit shall be Ḥatzar ¹⁰ Einan. This shall be your northern border. Mark your eastern border from Ḥatzar Einan ¹¹ to Shefam. The border will run down from Shefam to Rivla on the east side of Ayin. It ¹² will then continue down to reach the eastern slope of the Sea of Galilee. From there the border will run down along the Jordan, ending at the Dead Sea. This is to be your ¹³ land with its borders on all sides." Moshe commanded the Israelites: "This is the land of which you take possession by lot, which the Lord has commanded to give to the ¹⁴ nine and a half tribes – for the tribe of Reuven by its ancestral houses, and the tribe of Gad by its ancestral houses, and half the tribe of Menashe have taken their possession. ¹⁵ The two and a half tribes have taken their possession across the Jordan from Yeriḥo to the east as the sun rises."

WISDOM OF THE HEART

The princes of the tribes were responsible for identifying the areas that would best serve the tribal members. R. Menachem Mendel Schneerson, the Rebbe of Lubavitch, suggests that the greatness of the prince was neither his wealth nor his Torah scholarship, but his limitless dedication to his people.

Do you think that leaders should be treated as royalty or as those who serve the public good?

QUICK BITE

Rabbi Shimon bar Yoḥai observes that every time the Torah issues a command (using the word צו, at the root of the word mitzva), it also implies that the Torah feels it necessary to add an extra push, since obligations demand something of us, including financial commitment. The one exception, he continues, is in 34:2, where God commands the boundaries of the land. R. Shaul Yedidya of Modzhitz learns from here that since there was no need for an extra push to encourage people to live in the land, it obviously does not involve a financial commitment, despite how it appears on the surface.

במדבר | פרק לד | מסעי

לד א וַיְדַבֵּ֥ר יְהֹוָ֖ה אֶל־מֹשֶׁ֥ה לֵּאמֹֽר: ב צַ֞ו אֶת־בְּנֵ֤י יִשְׂרָאֵל֙ וְאָמַרְתָּ֣ אֲלֵהֶ֔ם כִּֽי־אַתֶּ֥ם בָּאִ֖ים אֶל־הָאָ֣רֶץ כְּנָ֑עַן זֹ֣את הָאָ֗רֶץ אֲשֶׁ֨ר תִּפֹּ֤ל לָכֶם֙ בְּנַֽחֲלָ֔ה אֶ֥רֶץ כְּנַ֖עַן לִגְבֻלֹתֶֽיהָ: ג וְהָיָ֨ה לָכֶ֤ם פְּאַת־נֶ֨גֶב֙ מִמִּדְבַּר־צִ֔ן עַל־יְדֵ֖י אֱד֑וֹם וְהָיָ֤ה לָכֶם֙ גְּב֣וּל נֶ֔גֶב מִקְצֵ֥ה יָם־הַמֶּ֖לַח קֵֽדְמָה: ד וְנָסַ֣ב לָכֶם֩ הַגְּב֨וּל מִנֶּ֜גֶב לְמַעֲלֵ֤ה עַקְרַבִּים֙ וְעָ֣בַר צִ֔נָה וְהָיוּ֙ תּֽוֹצְאֹתָ֔יו מִנֶּ֖גֶב לְקָדֵ֣שׁ בַּרְנֵ֑עַ וְיָצָ֥א חֲצַר־אַדָּ֖ר וְעָבַ֥ר עַצְמֹֽנָה: ה וְנָסַ֧ב הַגְּב֛וּל מֵעַצְמ֖וֹן נַ֣חְלָה מִצְרָ֑יִם וְהָי֥וּ תוֹצְאֹתָ֖יו הַיָּֽמָּה: ו וּגְב֣וּל יָ֔ם וְהָיָ֥ה לָכֶ֛ם הַיָּ֥ם הַגָּד֖וֹל וּגְב֑וּל זֶה־יִּֽהְיֶ֥ה לָכֶ֖ם גְּב֥וּל יָֽם: ז וְזֶה־יִּֽהְיֶ֥ה לָכֶ֖ם גְּב֣וּל צָפ֑וֹן מִן־הַיָּם֙ הַגָּדֹ֔ל תְּתָא֥וּ לָכֶ֖ם הֹ֥ר הָהָֽר: ח מֵהֹ֣ר הָהָ֔ר תְּתָא֖וּ לְבֹ֣א חֲמָ֑ת וְהָי֛וּ תּוֹצְאֹ֥ת הַגְּבֻ֖ל צְדָֽדָה: ט וְיָצָ֤א הַגְּבֻל֙ זִפְרֹ֔נָה וְהָי֥וּ תוֹצְאֹתָ֖יו חֲצַ֣ר עֵינָ֑ן זֶה־יִּֽהְיֶ֥ה לָכֶ֖ם גְּב֥וּל צָפֽוֹן: י וְהִתְאַוִּיתֶ֥ם לָכֶ֖ם לִגְב֣וּל קֵ֑דְמָה מֵחֲצַ֥ר עֵינָ֖ן שְׁפָֽמָה: יא וְיָרַ֨ד הַגְּבֻ֧ל מִשְּׁפָ֛ם הָרִבְלָ֖ה מִקֶּ֣דֶם לָעָ֑יִן וְיָרַ֣ד הַגְּב֔וּל וּמָחָ֛ה עַל־כֶּ֥תֶף יָם־כִּנֶּ֖רֶת קֵֽדְמָה: יב וְיָרַ֤ד הַגְּבוּל֙ הַיַּרְדֵּ֔נָה וְהָי֥וּ תוֹצְאֹתָ֖יו יָ֣ם הַמֶּ֑לַח זֹאת֩ תִּֽהְיֶ֨ה לָכֶ֥ם הָאָ֛רֶץ לִגְבֻלֹתֶ֖יהָ סָבִֽיב: יג וַיְצַ֣ו מֹשֶׁ֔ה אֶת־בְּנֵ֥י יִשְׂרָאֵ֖ל לֵאמֹ֑ר זֹ֣את הָאָ֗רֶץ אֲשֶׁ֨ר תִּתְנַחֲל֤וּ אֹתָהּ֙ בְּגוֹרָ֔ל אֲשֶׁר֙ צִוָּ֣ה יְהֹוָ֔ה לָתֵ֛ת לְתִשְׁעַ֥ת הַמַּטּ֖וֹת וַחֲצִ֥י הַמַּטֶּֽה: יד כִּ֣י לָקְח֞וּ מַטֵּ֨ה בְנֵ֤י הָראוּבֵנִי֙ לְבֵ֣ית אֲבֹתָ֔ם וּמַטֵּ֥ה בְנֵי־הַגָּדִ֖י לְבֵ֣ית אֲבֹתָ֑ם וַחֲצִי֙ מַטֵּ֣ה מְנַשֶּׁ֔ה לָקְח֖וּ נַחֲלָתָֽם: טו שְׁנֵ֥י הַמַּטּ֖וֹת וַחֲצִ֣י הַמַּטֶּ֑ה לָקְח֣וּ נַחֲלָתָ֗ם מֵעֵ֛בֶר לְיַרְדֵּ֥ן יְרֵח֖וֹ קֵ֥דְמָה מִזְרָֽחָה:

16 And the Lord spoke to Moshe: "These are the names of the men who shall apportion
17
18 the land to you for possession: Elazar the priest and Yehoshua son of Nun. And you
19 shall also take one leader from each tribe to apportion the land. These are the names of
20 the men: for the tribe of Yehuda, Kalev son of Yefuneh; for the tribe of the Simeonites,
21 Shmuel son of Amihud; for the tribe of Binyamin, Elidad son of Kislon; for the tribe of
22
23 the Danites, a leader, Buki son of Yogli. For the descendants of Yosef: for the tribe of the
24 Manassites a leader, Ḥaniel son of Efod; for the tribe of the Efraimites a leader, Kemuel
25 son of Shiftan. For the tribe of the Zebulunites a leader, Elitzafan son of Parnakh. For
26
27 the tribe of the Issacharites a leader, Paltiel son of Azan. For the tribe of the Asherites
28 a leader, Aḥihud son of Shelomi. For the tribe of the Naftalites a leader, Pedahel son of
29 Amihud." These were the ones whom the Lord commanded to apportion the possession for the Israelites in the land of Canaan.

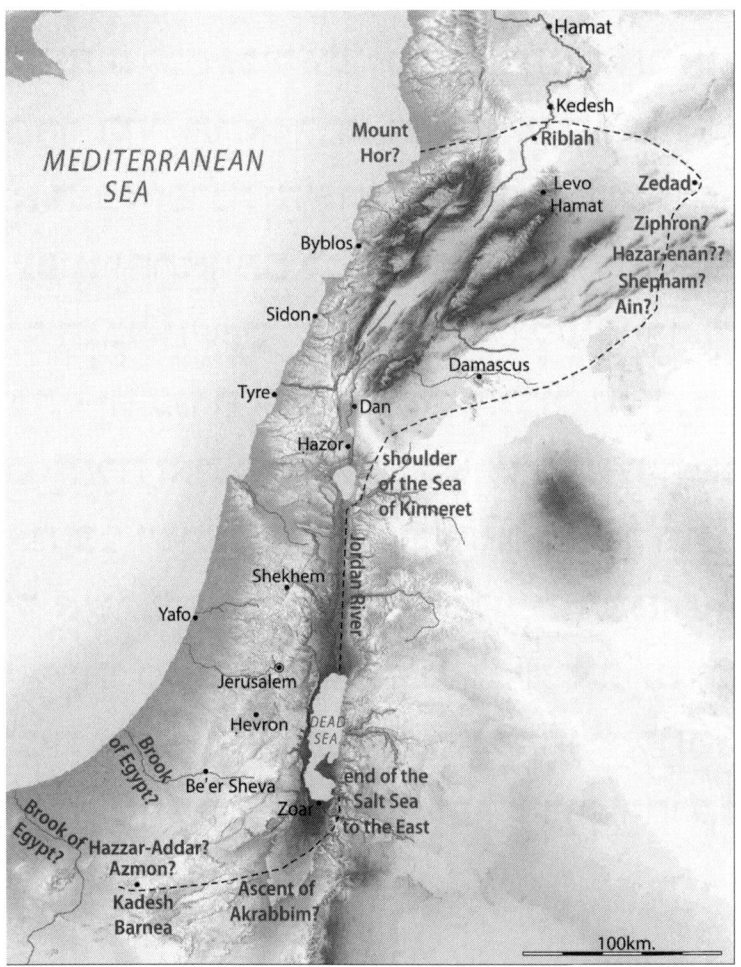

The boundaries of the land to be divided amongst the nine and a half tribes

במדבר | פרק לד

טז וַיְדַבֵּ֥ר יְהֹוָ֖ה אֶל־מֹשֶׁ֥ה לֵּאמֹֽר׃ אֵ֚לֶּה שְׁמ֣וֹת הָֽאֲנָשִׁ֔ים אֲשֶׁר־ <small>רביעי /ששי/</small>
יז יִנְחֲל֥וּ לָכֶ֖ם אֶת־הָאָ֑רֶץ אֶלְעָזָר֙ הַכֹּהֵ֔ן וִיהוֹשֻׁ֖עַ בִּן־נֽוּן׃ וְנָשִׂ֥יא
יח אֶחָ֛ד נָשִׂ֥יא אֶחָ֖ד מִמַּטֶּ֑ה תִּקְח֖וּ לִנְחֹ֥ל אֶת־הָאָֽרֶץ׃ וְאֵ֖לֶּה שְׁמ֣וֹת
יט הָֽאֲנָשִׁ֑ים לְמַטֵּ֣ה יְהוּדָ֔ה כָּלֵ֖ב בֶּן־יְפֻנֶּֽה׃ וּלְמַטֵּה֙ בְּנֵ֣י שִׁמְע֔וֹן
כ שְׁמוּאֵ֖ל בֶּן־עַמִּיהֽוּד׃ לְמַטֵּ֣ה בִנְיָמִ֔ן אֱלִידָ֖ד בֶּן־כִּסְלֽוֹן׃ וּלְמַטֵּ֥ה
כא בְנֵי־דָ֖ן נָשִׂ֑יא בֻּקִּ֖י בֶּן־יׇגְלִֽי׃ לִבְנֵ֣י יוֹסֵ֔ף לְמַטֵּ֥ה בְנֵֽי־מְנַשֶּׁ֖ה נָשִׂ֑יא
כב חַנִּיאֵ֖ל בֶּן־אֵפֹֽד׃ וּלְמַטֵּ֥ה בְנֵֽי־אֶפְרַ֖יִם נָשִׂ֑יא קְמוּאֵ֖ל בֶּן־שִׁפְטָֽן׃
כג וּלְמַטֵּ֥ה בְנֵֽי־זְבוּלֻ֖ן נָשִׂ֑יא אֱלִיצָפָ֖ן בֶּן־פַּרְנָֽךְ׃ וּלְמַטֵּ֥ה בְנֵֽי־יִשָּׂשכָ֖ר
כד נָשִׂ֑יא פַּלְטִיאֵ֖ל בֶּן־עַזָּֽן׃ וּלְמַטֵּ֥ה בְנֵֽי־אָשֵׁ֖ר נָשִׂ֑יא אֲחִיה֖וּד בֶּן־
כה שְׁלֹמִֽי׃ וּלְמַטֵּ֥ה בְנֵֽי־נַפְתָּלִ֖י נָשִׂ֑יא פְּדַהְאֵ֖ל בֶּן־עַמִּיהֽוּד׃ אֵ֕לֶּה
כט אֲשֶׁ֖ר צִוָּ֣ה יְהֹוָ֑ה לְנַחֵ֛ל אֶת־בְּנֵֽי־יִשְׂרָאֵ֖ל בְּאֶ֥רֶץ כְּנָֽעַן׃

QUICK BITE

Not all of the tribes are represented here. Reuven and Gad are absent, as they received their portions from Moshe on the other side of the Jordan. Perhaps even more interesting is that the order of the tribes seems to be strange. A look at a map reveals what may be the secret – they seem to be listed from south to north based on their portions in the land. Yehuda and Shimon in the south, Binyamin and Dan above them, Efrayim and Menashe a bit higher up, Yissakhar and Zevulun in the Galil, and Asher and Naftali in the far northern regions. What makes this even more interesting is that while we know this, based on the division of the land in the book of Joshua, in Moshe's time this was not known!

BEMIDBAR | CHAPTER 35 MASEI | 316

> **35:1–8** *The Levites do not get their own portion of the land, but they will be given forty-two cities distributed throughout the land, in which they are to live. In addition, the six cities of refuge will also be set aside as Levite cities.*

35 1 The LORD spoke to Moshe in the plains of Moav by the Jordan across from Yeriḥo: 2 "Command the Israelites to grant the Levites towns to live in, among the inheritance they will possess. 3 Grant them also pasturelands around the towns. The towns shall be theirs to live in, and the pasturelands shall be for their cattle, all that they own, and all their animals. 4 The pasturelands of the towns that you shall give to the Levites shall extend from the town wall outward for a thousand cubits in all directions; 5 you shall measure out from the town, two thousand cubits on the east side, two thousand cubits on the south side, two thousand cubits on the west side, and two thousand cubits on the north side, with the town in the middle, and this shall belong to them as pastureland for their towns. 6 Six of the towns that you give to the Levites shall be towns of refuge, which you will designate as places to which a manslayer may flee. In addition to these, you shall give them forty-two more towns. 7 Thus the total number of towns you shall give to the Levites shall be forty-eight, 8 along with their pastureland. As for the towns that you give from the possession of the Israelites, take more from the larger tribes and fewer from the smaller so that each grants towns to the Levites in proportion to its own inheritance."

QUESTIONS FOR THOUGHT

- How does Rashi resolve the contradiction between the two different dimensions described in the Torah?
- What values regarding planning cities does Rashi reveal in his understanding?
- Notice that the Torah describes the one thousand cubits and the two thousand cubits completely differently. Based on this difference, can you suggest a different answer to the problem?

TEXTUAL SKILLS

1. This is the second time in this *parasha* where the Torah specifies the location where God spoke to Moshe (the first is in 33:50). What do these two instances have in common, and why does the Torah specify the place for these two instructions?

2. What language in verse 8 describing where the Levites will live parallels the language describing the land given to the tribes (see 33:54)?

WISDOM OF THE HEART

The cities of refuge for accidental killers are also cities that were given to the Levites. What is the connection between them? Traditionally, the Levites are the educators – they are the ones held most responsible for teaching Torah to the nation. Care for human life is a primary goal of education; carelessness in this area suggests that something in the educational process is not working. The Levites need to see the product of their efforts and intensify those efforts to build a healthy and sensitive society.

How much do you think education impacts on people's nature?

במדבר | פרק לה

חמישי

א וַיְדַבֵּ֧ר יְהֹוָ֛ה אֶל־מֹשֶׁ֖ה בְּעַֽרְבֹ֣ת מוֹאָ֑ב עַל־יַרְדֵּ֥ן יְרֵח֖וֹ לֵאמֹֽר:

ב צַו֮ אֶת־בְּנֵ֣י יִשְׂרָאֵל֒ וְנָתְנ֣וּ לַלְוִיִּ֗ם מִֽנַּחֲלַ֛ת אֲחֻזָּתָ֖ם עָרִ֣ים לָשָׁ֑בֶת וּמִגְרָ֗שׁ לֶֽעָרִים֙ סְבִיבֹ֣תֵיהֶ֔ם תִּתְּנ֖וּ לַלְוִיִּֽם:

ג וְהָי֧וּ הֶֽעָרִ֛ים לָהֶ֖ם לָשָׁ֑בֶת וּמִגְרְשֵׁיהֶ֗ם יִֽהְי֤וּ לִבְהֶמְתָּם֙ וְלִרְכֻשָׁ֔ם וּלְכֹ֖ל חַיָּתָֽם:

ד וּמִגְרְשֵׁי֙ הֶֽעָרִ֔ים אֲשֶׁ֥ר תִּתְּנ֖וּ לַלְוִיִּ֑ם מִקִּ֤יר הָעִיר֙ וָח֔וּצָה אֶ֥לֶף אַמָּ֖ה סָבִֽיב:

ה וּמַדֹּתֶ֞ם מִח֣וּץ לָעִ֗יר אֶת־פְּאַת־קֵ֣דְמָה אַלְפַּ֣יִם בָּאַמָּ֡ה וְאֶת־פְּאַת־נֶ֩גֶב֩ אַלְפַּ֨יִם בָּאַמָּ֜ה וְאֶת־פְּאַת־יָ֣ם ׀ אַלְפַּ֣יִם בָּאַמָּ֗ה וְאֵ֨ת פְּאַ֥ת צָפ֛וֹן אַלְפַּ֥יִם בָּאַמָּ֖ה וְהָעִ֣יר בַּתָּ֑וֶךְ זֶ֚ה יִֽהְיֶ֣ה לָהֶ֔ם מִגְרְשֵׁ֖י הֶעָרִֽים:

ו וְאֵ֣ת הֶֽעָרִ֗ים אֲשֶׁ֤ר תִּתְּנוּ֙ לַלְוִיִּ֔ם אֵ֚ת שֵׁשׁ־עָרֵ֣י הַמִּקְלָ֔ט אֲשֶׁ֣ר תִּתְּנ֔וּ לָנֻ֥ס שָׁ֖מָּה הָֽרֹצֵ֑חַ וַעֲלֵיהֶ֣ם תִּתְּנ֔וּ אַרְבָּעִ֥ים וּשְׁתַּ֖יִם עִֽיר:

ז כָּל־הֶעָרִ֗ים אֲשֶׁ֤ר תִּתְּנוּ֙ לַלְוִיִּ֔ם אַרְבָּעִ֥ים וּשְׁמֹנֶ֖ה עִ֑יר אֶתְהֶ֖ן וְאֶת־מִגְרְשֵׁיהֶֽן:

ח וְהֶֽעָרִ֗ים אֲשֶׁ֤ר תִּתְּנוּ֙ מֵאֲחֻזַּ֣ת בְּנֵֽי־יִשְׂרָאֵ֔ל מֵאֵ֤ת הָרַב֙ תַּרְבּ֔וּ וּמֵאֵ֥ת הַמְעַ֖ט תַּמְעִ֑יטוּ אִ֗ישׁ כְּפִ֤י נַחֲלָתוֹ֙ אֲשֶׁ֣ר יִנְחָ֔לוּ יִתֵּ֥ן מֵעָרָ֖יו לַלְוִיִּֽם:

CLASSIC COMMENTATORS

The Torah emphasizes that there needs to be unbuilt space surrounding the Levite cities, but mentions it twice, each time with a different dimension. This caused complex debates amongst the commentaries.

RASHI

This refers to a strip of land outside the city and surrounding it that serves to beautify the environment. The Levites are not permitted to build houses there, nor may they plant vineyards or sow seeds in these areas. How do we reconcile the requirement here of "a thousand cubits in all directions" with the next verse, which states, "you shall measure out from the town two thousand cubits"? The Levite cities were granted two thousand cubits on each side: the inner one thousand cubits were set aside for pastureland, while the outer one thousand could be used for fields and vineyards.

רש"י

ריוח מקום חלק חוץ לעיר סביב להיות לעיר לנוי, ואין רשאין לבנות בו בית ולא ליטע כרם ולא לזרוע זריעה. אלף אמה סביב (ל"ה:ד') - ואחריו הוא אומר: אלפים אמה (ל"ה:ה'), הא כיצד? אלפים הוא נותן להם סביב, ומהם אלף פנימיים למגרש והחיצונים לשדות וכרמים.

BEMIDBAR | CHAPTER 35   **MASEI | 318**

> **35:9–15** *There are to be six cities of refuge, three on the eastern side of the Jordan and three on the western side. If someone kills another person accidentally, he can run to these cities for protection from relatives of the victim who are seeking vengeance. That protection is to be extended until the accused can be tried in court.*

9,10 The LORD spoke to Moshe: "Speak to the Israelites. Tell them: When you cross the 11 Jordan into the land of Canaan, select towns to be your refuge cities, to which a person 12 who kills another unintentionally may flee. The cities shall be a refuge for you from avengers, so that no person who has killed another may die without standing trial before 13,14 the community. The towns that you designate shall be six cities of refuge for you; you shall designate three towns across the Jordan and three in the land of Canaan as cities 15 of refuge. These six towns shall be a place of refuge for Israelites, migrants, and temporary residents alike, so that anyone who kills a person unintentionally may flee there.

QUESTIONS FOR THOUGHT

- There is a difference between explaining the reason for the institution of the city of refuge and figuring out what message we can learn from it. Which of the above commentaries fit into each of the two different approaches?
- Two of the commentaries explain how the city of refuge can help the accidental killer, but they disagree greatly on how it helps. What are the two different ways in which it can help, and which commentary makes which claim?
- Which of the above commentaries could easily be applicable to situations in your life, even assuming that you will never kill anyone even by accident?

WISDOM OF THE HEART

In many cultures the motive of vengeance drives families and clans to endless battle for generations. One nasty or selfish act spawns an equal or greater response; the need to get even or to win overtakes rationality or logic and generates endless cycles of violence and retribution. The Torah is very much aware of how powerful the impulse for vengeance is and puts a lid on it. If the initial act was unintentional, then the perpetrator must be given the opportunity to save himself from bloodthirsty relatives. Breaking the cycle of violence and knee-jerk impulsivity is essential if we are to build a society of different people who live and flourish together.

How can we learn to build a separation between the feeling of needing to avenge and acting on that feeling? Do you think that people can learn to transform the desire for vengeance into a positive force?

QUICK BITE

Rav Chaim Kanievsky notes that the word רוצח, meaning murderer, is used seventeen times here, referring mostly to someone who killed accidentally. He points out that in the rest of Tanakh, there are seventeen murders which are committed intentionally.

במדבר | פרק לה

ששי
/שביעי/

י וַיְדַבֵּר יהוה אֶל־מֹשֶׁה לֵּאמֹר: דַּבֵּר אֶל־בְּנֵי יִשְׂרָאֵל וְאָמַרְתָּ אֲלֵהֶם
יא כִּי אַתֶּם עֹבְרִים אֶת־הַיַּרְדֵּן אַרְצָה כְּנָעַן: וְהִקְרִיתֶם לָכֶם עָרִים
עָרֵי מִקְלָט תִּהְיֶינָה לָכֶם וְנָס שָׁמָּה רֹצֵחַ מַכֵּה־נֶפֶשׁ בִּשְׁגָגָה:
יב וְהָיוּ לָכֶם הֶעָרִים לְמִקְלָט מִגֹּאֵל וְלֹא יָמוּת הָרֹצֵחַ עַד־עָמְדוֹ
יג לִפְנֵי הָעֵדָה לַמִּשְׁפָּט: וְהֶעָרִים אֲשֶׁר תִּתֵּנוּ שֵׁשׁ־עָרֵי מִקְלָט
יד תִּהְיֶינָה לָכֶם: אֵת ׀ שְׁלֹשׁ הֶעָרִים תִּתְּנוּ מֵעֵבֶר לַיַּרְדֵּן וְאֵת שְׁלֹשׁ
טו הֶעָרִים תִּתְּנוּ בְּאֶרֶץ כְּנָעַן עָרֵי מִקְלָט תִּהְיֶינָה: לִבְנֵי יִשְׂרָאֵל
וְלַגֵּר וְלַתּוֹשָׁב בְּתוֹכָם תִּהְיֶינָה שֵׁשׁ־הֶעָרִים הָאֵלֶּה לְמִקְלָט

CLASSIC COMMENTATORS

What is the reason for the institution of the cities of refuge?

RAMBAM

The one responsible for the manslaughter flees to the city of refuge to allow the blood relative's rage to cool off. This will happen if the perpetrator is out of sight.

SEFER HAḤINUKH

Murder is an extremely severe matter and leads to the destruction of the world.... It therefore makes sense that when an individual kills another, he should suffer the anguish of exile which is almost equivalent to execution. For when one is forced to live in a city of refuge, he is separated from his loved ones and his homeland, and is made to live his whole life among strangers. This must be done even if the person killed accidentally, for it was his actions which caused the loss of human life.

RABBEINU BAḤYA

A person who kills another inadvertently may flee to a city of refuge. He is not given capital punishment, because he did not murder intentionally. Now this law demonstrates that the heart is the core of a man's personality, and is responsible for all of his good deeds and his sins. Thus, if an individual's heart had no wish to murder somebody and his behavior shows that, he cannot be killed for his actions, but is exiled. Fulfillment of commandments is judged in the same way; if a person fulfills a mitzva but without the intention of fulfilling God's word, he will not be rewarded for the result.

רמב״ם

אמנם היות רוצח בשגגה גולה הוא להשקיט נפש גואל הדם עד שלא יראה מי שבאה התקלה הזאת על ידו.

ספר החינוך

משורשי המצווה הזאת, לפי שעניין הרציחה חמור עד מאוד שבה השחתת העולם... ולכן ראוי למי שהרג אפילו שוגג - מכיוון שבאה תקלה גדולה כזו על ידו - שיצטער עליה צער גלות ששקול כמעט כצער מיתה, שנפרד האדם מאוהביו ומארץ מולדתו ושוכן כל ימיו עם זרים.

רבינו בחיי

ונס שמה רוצח מכה נפש, אבל אינו חייב מיתה, כיון שלא הרגו במזיד. והדין הזה יורה שהלב עיקר האדם ועיקר כל המצוות וכל העבירות, ועל כן הוא נענש בגלות ולא במיתה, לפי שלא היה לבו בהסכמת הרציחה ואין בתנועתו והלב בכוונתו, וכיון שלא הסכימו שניהם בכך - גולה ואינו נהרג. וכן לעניין המצוה הכל תלוי בלב, שאם עשה מצוה ולא נתכוון בה בלבו לעשותה לשם שמים - אין לך שכר.

16 If a person strikes another with an iron object, however, and he dies, that person is a
17 murderer; the murderer must be put to death. If he strikes him with a hand held stone that could cause death and he dies, that person is a murderer; the murderer must be put
18 to death. Likewise, if he strikes him with a wooden tool that could cause death and he
19 dies, that person is a murderer; the murderer must be put to death. The blood avenger
20 shall put the murderer to death; whenever he meets him, he may put him to death. So too if one person pushes another in hate, or throws something at him with prior intent,
21 he shall be put to death. If in enmity someone strikes a person with his hand and he dies, the one who struck the blow is a murderer and shall be put to death. The blood
22 avenger shall put the murderer to death whenever they meet. If, however, one person pushes another suddenly, without enmity, or throws an object at him unintentionally,
23 or drops a fatal stone on him without seeing him and he dies – they were not enemies,
24 he intended him no harm – then the community must judge between the killer and
25 the blood avenger in accordance with these laws. And the community must protect the manslayer from the avenger of blood and return him to the refuge city to which he fled. There he shall live until the death of the High Priest anointed with the sacred oil.

RABBI OVADYA SFORNO / ר׳ עובדיה ספורנו

בהיות מיני השגגות בלתי שוות כי מהם קרובות לאונס ומהן קרובות אל המזיד, נתן לגלות זמן בלתי שוה בכל השוגגים. כי מהם שתהיה שגגתו מעט קודם מיתת הכהן, ומהן שימות הרוצח בגלות קודם שימות הכהן. וזה במשפט האל יתברך היודע ועד, שיענוש את השוגג כפי מדרגת שגגתו, כאמרו והאלהים אנה לידו.

The category of unintentional acts comprises a variety of behaviors, since some deeds are almost completely accidental, while others stem from negligence. Correspondingly, the lengths of exile also vary for inadvertent killers: some individuals spend just a short time in the city of refuge before the death of the High Priest, while other people will end up dying in exile before that personality passes away. All of this is orchestrated by the Almighty who knows all: He punishes the inadvertent killer according to the degree of his misdeed.

QUESTIONS FOR THOUGHT

- Three different positions are represented above. One suggests that the death of the High Priest reminds the avenging family that accidents sometimes happen, a second suggests that the death of the High Priest reminds the avenging family that ultimate judgment is in God's hands, and the third presents the death of the High Priest as a period of general amnesty. Match these positions with the commentaries above.
- Can you think of other reasons that the killer would go free with the death of the High Priest?

WISDOM OF THE HEART

Th institution of the cities of refuge represents not only an obligation for the accidental killer to flee, but the obligation of the broader community to make sure that justice is taken out of the hands of individual vigilantes and put squarely in the hands of the impartial communal leadership.

טז לָנוּס שָׁמָּה כָּל־מַכֵּה־נֶפֶשׁ בִּשְׁגָגָה: וְאִם־בִּכְלִי בַרְזֶל ׀ הִכָּהוּ
יז וַיָּמֹת רֹצֵחַ הוּא מוֹת יוּמַת הָרֹצֵחַ: וְאִם בְּאֶבֶן יָד אֲשֶׁר־יָמוּת בָּהּ
יח הִכָּהוּ וַיָּמֹת רֹצֵחַ הוּא מוֹת יוּמַת הָרֹצֵחַ: אוֹ בִּכְלִי עֵץ־יָד אֲשֶׁר־
יט יָמוּת בּוֹ הִכָּהוּ וַיָּמֹת רֹצֵחַ הוּא מוֹת יוּמַת הָרֹצֵחַ: גֹּאֵל הַדָּם הוּא
כ יָמִית אֶת־הָרֹצֵחַ בְּפִגְעוֹ־בוֹ הוּא יְמִיתֶנּוּ: וְאִם־בְּשִׂנְאָה יֶהְדֳּפֶנּוּ
כא אוֹ־הִשְׁלִיךְ עָלָיו בִּצְדִיָּה וַיָּמֹת: אוֹ בְאֵיבָה הִכָּהוּ בְיָדוֹ וַיָּמֹת
מוֹת־יוּמַת הַמַּכֶּה רֹצֵחַ הוּא גֹּאֵל הַדָּם יָמִית אֶת־הָרֹצֵחַ בְּפִגְעוֹ־
כב בוֹ: וְאִם־בְּפֶתַע בְּלֹא־אֵיבָה הֲדָפוֹ אוֹ־הִשְׁלִיךְ עָלָיו כָּל־כְּלִי
כג בְּלֹא צְדִיָּה: אוֹ בְכָל־אֶבֶן אֲשֶׁר־יָמוּת בָּהּ בְּלֹא רְאוֹת וַיַּפֵּל
כד עָלָיו וַיָּמֹת וְהוּא לֹא־אוֹיֵב לוֹ וְלֹא מְבַקֵּשׁ רָעָתוֹ: וְשָׁפְטוּ הָעֵדָה
כה בֵּין הַמַּכֶּה וּבֵין גֹּאֵל הַדָּם עַל הַמִּשְׁפָּטִים הָאֵלֶּה: וְהִצִּילוּ
הָעֵדָה אֶת־הָרֹצֵחַ מִיַּד גֹּאֵל הַדָּם וְהֵשִׁיבוּ אֹתוֹ הָעֵדָה אֶל־
עִיר מִקְלָטוֹ אֲשֶׁר־נָס שָׁמָּה וְיָשַׁב בָּהּ עַד־מוֹת הַכֹּהֵן הַגָּדֹל

CLASSIC COMMENTATORS

Why does the death of the High Priest signal the end of the stay in the city of refuge?

RASHBAM — רשב״ם

The killer may be released only when the highest judge in the land passes away.

לפי פשוטו, כל ימי השופט הגדול.

RAMBAM — רמב״ם

The Torah links the release of the killer to the death of the High Priest, a figure who is the most respected and beloved individual within the nation of Israel, as that will bring consolation to the blood relative of the victim. For it is completely natural for people who are in pain to feel comforted when they realize that accidents sometimes happen, even to the greatest of people.

ותלה חזרתו במות האיש אשר הוא הנכבד בבני אדם והאהוב לכל ישראל; שבזה תנוח דעת הגואל אשר נהרג קרובו, שזה עניין טבעי לאדם, כל מי שתקראהו צרה – כשתבוא גם כן לזולתו כיוצא בה או גדולה ממנה, ימצא נחמה בזה על מקרהו.

26 But if the manslayer ever goes outside the limits of the city of refuge to which he fled
27 and the blood avenger finds him outside the limits of his city of refuge and kills him,
28 the avenger is not liable for murder; the manslayer must stay in his city of refuge until the High Priest dies. After the death of the High Priest the manslayer may return to his
29 own hereditary land. These shall be a decree of law for you throughout your generations,
30 wherever you should live. If anyone kills a human being, the murderer shall be put to death on the evidence of eyewitnesses. No one shall be put to death on the testimony of
31 one witness alone. You may not accept a ransom for the life of a murderer found guilty
32 of a capital crime; he must be put to death. Nor may you accept a ransom for someone who has fled to his city of refuge, to allow him to return and live on his land before the
33 priest dies. You shall not pollute the land in which you live; blood pollutes the land. And the land can have no atonement for the blood that is shed in it – except through
34 the blood of the one who shed it. Do not defile the land in which you live, and in the midst of which I dwell – for I the Lord dwell in the midst of Israel."

ר' יוסף בכור שור
על מי שהוציאו בית דין לדונו וראו שיש עליו לנוס, ורוצה לתת כופר שלא ינוס.

RABBI YOSEF BEKHOR SHOR
If a court has determined that an accidental killer must be exiled to a city of refuge, he may not pay money to avoid having to go there.

רמב"ן
ולא היה הצורך לומר שלא ניקח כפר שלא ינוס שם כלל, כי כל הורג נפש בשגגה מתחילה יפחד מגואל הדם, שלא ימיתהו בחם לבבו.

RAMBAN
The Torah need not warn us not to accept payment to spare a killer from exile. For anybody who causes the death of another will *want* to go there to escape death at the hands of his victim's relatives!

QUESTIONS FOR THOUGHT

- What are the three different possibilities raised by the first three commentaries?
- Whose position does Ramban reject?
- How would each of the commentaries explain the word לנוס in verse 32? Which of these fits the word best?
- Which of the above best fits the context of this verse?
- Which do you think represents a greater corruption – someone trying to pay their way out of punishment for an intentional crime or someone trying to pay their way out of punishment for a crime they committed without malice?

TEXTUAL SKILLS

1. What are the two different words used to describe the idea that the land will be defiled or corrupted by a killer "paying his way" out of his punishment?
2. Notice how the root כ-פ-ר is used in verses 31–33. What two meanings does the word have in this context? Are those meanings related?
3. Based on verse 34, complete the following sentence: "God dwells in…"

כו אֲשֶׁר־מָשַׁח אֹתוֹ בְּשֶׁמֶן הַקֹּדֶשׁ: וְאִם־יָצֹא יֵצֵא הָרֹצֵחַ אֶת־
כז גְּבוּל עִיר מִקְלָטוֹ אֲשֶׁר יָנוּס שָׁמָּה: וּמָצָא אֹתוֹ גֹּאֵל הַדָּם
מִחוּץ לִגְבוּל עִיר מִקְלָטוֹ וְרָצַח גֹּאֵל הַדָּם אֶת־הָרֹצֵחַ אֵין לוֹ
כח דָּם: כִּי בְעִיר מִקְלָטוֹ יֵשֵׁב עַד־מוֹת הַכֹּהֵן הַגָּדֹל וְאַחֲרֵי־מוֹת
כט הַכֹּהֵן הַגָּדֹל יָשׁוּב הָרֹצֵחַ אֶל־אֶרֶץ אֲחֻזָּתוֹ: וְהָיוּ אֵלֶּה לָכֶם
ל לְחֻקַּת מִשְׁפָּט לְדֹרֹתֵיכֶם בְּכֹל מוֹשְׁבֹתֵיכֶם: כָּל־מַכֵּה־נֶפֶשׁ
לְפִי עֵדִים יִרְצַח אֶת־הָרֹצֵחַ וְעֵד אֶחָד לֹא־יַעֲנֶה בְנֶפֶשׁ לָמוּת:
לא וְלֹא־תִקְחוּ כֹפֶר לְנֶפֶשׁ רֹצֵחַ אֲשֶׁר־הוּא רָשָׁע לָמוּת כִּי־מוֹת
לב יוּמָת: וְלֹא־תִקְחוּ כֹפֶר לָנוּס אֶל־עִיר מִקְלָטוֹ לָשׁוּב לָשֶׁבֶת
לג בָּאָרֶץ עַד־מוֹת הַכֹּהֵן: וְלֹא־תַחֲנִיפוּ אֶת־הָאָרֶץ אֲשֶׁר אַתֶּם
בָּהּ כִּי הַדָּם הוּא יַחֲנִיף אֶת־הָאָרֶץ וְלָאָרֶץ לֹא־יְכֻפַּר לַדָּם
לד אֲשֶׁר שֻׁפַּךְ־בָּהּ כִּי־אִם בְּדַם שֹׁפְכוֹ: וְלֹא תְטַמֵּא אֶת־הָאָרֶץ
אֲשֶׁר אַתֶּם יֹשְׁבִים בָּהּ אֲשֶׁר אֲנִי שֹׁכֵן בְּתוֹכָהּ כִּי אֲנִי יְהוָה שֹׁכֵן
בְּתוֹךְ בְּנֵי יִשְׂרָאֵל:

CLASSIC COMMENTATORS

In the context of the prohibition against accepting bribery related to punishment, verse 32 stands out as ambiguous. From whom are we to not accept the bribe, and what consequence is the killer trying to avoid with that bribe?

SIFREI / ספרי

The verse states, "Nor may you accept a ransom for someone who has fled to his city of refuge." This applies even to somebody who has killed intentionally – he may not pay money for the right to live in the city of refuge and thereby save his life. Thus the verse should be understood as: Nor may you accept a ransom so that someone may flee to his city of refuge.

"ולא תקחו כפר לנוס אל עיר מקלט" – הרי שהרג את הנפש במזיד, שומע אני, אם יתן ממון יגלה? תלמוד לומר: "ולא תקחו כפר לנוס אל עיר מקלטו".

RASHI / רש״י

If an individual has killed somebody accidentally and has escaped to a city of refuge, he cannot get himself released from exile by paying money "to allow him to return and live on his land." Rather, he must wait until the death of the High Priest in order to leave.

למי שנס אל עיר מקלט שהרג בשוגג אינו נפטר מגלות בממון ליתן כפר לשבת בארץ בטרם ימות הכהן.

36:1–5 *The leaders of the family of Gilad, from the tribe of Menashe, present Moshe with a problem. If the daughters of Tzelofḥad receive their father's portion and then marry men from a different tribe, when they die their land will be inherited by their children. As those children will be members of their father's tribe, Menashe's portion will be diminished. Moshe confirms that their observation indeed poses a problem.*

36 1 The heads of the ancestral houses of the descendants of Gilad son of Makhir son of Menashe, one of the families of Yosef's sons, came forward and spoke before Moshe and 2 the leaders, the heads of the ancestral houses of the Israelites. "The Lord," they said, "commanded my lord to give the land as an inheritance to the Israelites by lot. But my lord was also commanded by the Lord to give the inheritance of our brother Tzelofḥad 3 to his daughters. If they marry men from another Israelite tribe, their share will be taken away from our ancestral inheritance and given to the tribe into which they marry. It 4 will be taken away from the allotted portion of our inheritance. When the Israelites observe the Jubilee, their inheritance will be added to that of the tribe into which they married; their inheritance will be taken away from the inheritance of our forefathers' 5 tribe." Then Moshe, at the Lord's word, commanded the Israelites: "What the tribe

---

QUESTIONS FOR THOUGHT

- Ralbag claims that the question is based on a misreading of the text. What creative reading does he offer to suggest that?
- According to Abarbanel, how did the leaders of Menashe understand what Moshe was doing in the previous few chapters? How does that help him explain why their request comes now?
- *Tzeror Hamor* explains that the leaders of Menashe initially did not have concerns, but that those concerns emerged over time. Why would it have taken time for them to be aware of the problem?
- What challenges would you present to each of the above commentaries?

TEXTUAL SKILLS

1. What word can you identify as a key word in this passage, appearing ten times?
2. Notice that these leaders are concerned that their portion will be diminished, יגרע. That was the same word used by Tzelofḥad's daughters in their initial request for land (27:4). What do you think might be the intention of that linkage?

WISDOM OF THE HEART

The request made by the leaders of Gilad is introduced by the word ויקרבו, just like the daughters of Tzelofḥad (see 27:1). Their approach was similar – an attempt to come close. Not to confront, but to draw closer. When we approach with respect, we are more likely to achieve our goals then when we attack.

במדבר | פרק לו

שביעי

לו א וַיִּקְרְב֞וּ רָאשֵׁ֣י הָאָב֗וֹת לְמִשְׁפַּ֤חַת בְּנֵֽי־גִלְעָד֙ בֶּן־מָכִ֣יר בֶּן־מְנַשֶּׁ֔ה מִֽמִּשְׁפְּחֹ֖ת בְּנֵ֣י יוֹסֵ֑ף וַֽיְדַבְּר֞וּ לִפְנֵ֤י מֹשֶׁה֙ וְלִפְנֵ֣י הַנְּשִׂאִ֔ים רָאשֵׁ֥י אָב֖וֹת לִבְנֵ֥י יִשְׂרָאֵֽל׃ ב וַיֹּאמְר֗וּ אֶת־אֲדֹנִי֙ צִוָּ֣ה יְהֹוָ֔ה לָתֵ֨ת אֶת־הָאָ֧רֶץ בְּנַחֲלָ֛ה בְּגוֹרָ֖ל לִבְנֵ֣י יִשְׂרָאֵ֑ל וַֽאדֹנִי֙ צֻוָּ֣ה בַֽיהֹוָ֔ה לָתֵ֗ת אֶֽת־נַחֲלַ֛ת צְלָפְחָ֥ד אָחִ֖ינוּ לִבְנֹתָֽיו׃ ג וְ֠הָי֠וּ לְאֶחָ֞ד מִבְּנֵ֨י שִׁבְטֵ֥י בְנֵֽי־יִשְׂרָאֵל֮ לְנָשִׁים֒ וְנִגְרְעָ֤ה נַחֲלָתָן֙ מִנַּחֲלַ֣ת אֲבֹתֵ֔ינוּ וְנוֹסַ֕ף עַ֚ל נַחֲלַ֣ת הַמַּטֶּ֔ה אֲשֶׁ֥ר תִּהְיֶ֖ינָה לָהֶ֑ם וּמִגֹּרַ֥ל נַחֲלָתֵ֖נוּ יִגָּרֵֽעַ׃ ד וְאִם־יִהְיֶ֣ה הַיֹּבֵל֮ לִבְנֵ֣י יִשְׂרָאֵל֒ וְנֽוֹסְפָה֙ נַחֲלָתָ֔ן עַ֚ל נַחֲלַ֣ת הַמַּטֶּ֔ה אֲשֶׁ֥ר תִּהְיֶ֖ינָה לָהֶ֑ם וּמִנַּחֲלַת֙ מַטֵּ֣ה אֲבֹתֵ֔ינוּ יִגָּרַ֖ע נַחֲלָתָֽן׃ ה וַיְצַ֤ו מֹשֶׁה֙ אֶת־בְּנֵ֣י יִשְׂרָאֵ֔ל עַל־פִּ֥י יְהֹוָ֖ה לֵאמֹ֑ר כֵּ֛ן מַטֵּ֥ה בְנֵֽי־יוֹסֵ֖ף

CLASSIC COMMENTATORS

Why did this problem arise now? Wouldn't it have made more sense for them to raise the question with Moshe immediately after he gave Tzelofḥad's daughters their father's portion in the land?

RALBAG

The text now reports what had previously been raised by the descendants of Gilad, son of Makhir, son of Menashe regarding God's instruction to grant land to the daughters of Tzelofḥad.

ABARBANEL

The heads of the ancestral houses of the tribe of Yosef saw that Moshe was issuing instructions prior to his death like a man does at the end of his life regarding his bequests. This prompted the men to approach the prophet with their concern about whether Tzelofḥad's daughters should be allowed to marry into other tribes or not. This explains why this discussion appears at this point in the text.

TZEROR HAMOR

Tzelofḥad's daughters loved the land of Israel, and as a reward for that they were courted by men from various tribes who wanted to marry them. When the heads of the families in Menashe saw how sought after these women were, they worried that they would intermarry with men from other tribes. After all, these ancestral leaders wanted to betroth the daughters of Tzelofḥad to their own sons!

רלב״ג

הנה אחר זה זכר שכבר קרבו ראשי האבות למשפחת בני גלעד בן מכיר בן מנשה על דבר הנחלה שגזר ה' יתעלה שתנתן לבנות צלפחד.

אברבנאל

ולפי שראו ראשי האבות למטה יוסף שמשה רבנו היה מצוה מחמת מיתה בעניני חלוקת הארץ ונחלתה כאדם ביום מותו באו לפניו על ענין בנות צלפחד אם ינשאו לאנשי שבט אחר אם לא ולזה נכתב הספור הזה אחרי הדבור הזה.

צרור המור

לפי שבנות צלפחד חבבו הארץ, זכו בשכר זה שכל השבטים היו רצים אחריהם, וכולם היו רוצים וחפצים להזדווג להם, באופן שכשראו זה ראשי האבות של מנשה, נתיראו שיזדווגו לשבט אחר, והם היו רוצים להשיאן לבניהם.

6 of Yosef's descendants say is right. This is the word that the LORD has commanded to Tzelofḥad's daughters: They may marry whomever they wish as long as they marry
7 within a clan of their father's tribe, so that the Israelites' inheritance does not pass from one tribe to another. Thus the Israelites will each stay attached to the inheritance of
8 their ancestral tribes. Every daughter among the Israelite tribes who inherits land must marry a member of her father's tribe, so that the Israelites may possess the inheritance of
9 their ancestors. No inheritance may pass from one tribe to another; each Israelite tribe
10 shall remain attached to its own inheritance." Tzelofḥad's daughters did as the LORD
11 commanded Moshe. Maḥla, Tirtza, Ḥogla, Milka, and Noa, Tzelofḥad's daughters, were
12 each married to men who were their cousins. They thus married into the families of Menashe son of Yosef, and their inheritance remained within the tribe of their father's
13 clan. All these are the commandments and laws that the LORD gave through Moshe to the Israelites on the plains of Moav, by the Jordan, across from Yeriḥo.

ר' שמשון רפאל הירש

מצוות הנפתחות ב"זה הדבר", נוהגות בדרך כלל רק לשעה; וכבר הערנו בפסוק ב' שהגבלת הנישואין האמורה כאן, בנוגע לבנות היורשות נחלה, נהגה רק באותו הדור שנטל חלק בכיבוש הארץ.

RABBI SAMSON RAPHAEL HIRSCH

When the Torah introduces a law with the phrase "This is the word" (36:6), that generally implies that the rule is a temporary measure. I have already explained that the marriage restrictions laid down in this passage regarding women who are slated to inherit land applied only to that generation, which received portions of the land following Israel's conquest.

העמק דבר

בנות צלפחד הותרו להעביר נחלה ... והא דכתיב כאן "אך למשפחת וגו'" אינו אלא עצה ... ונתבאר לעיל שמפני חשיבותן הרשה המקום להעביר נחלה ... אך בעצה שלא יהיו נראות כחשובות מכל בנות שבטן, על כן יתנהגו כמו כולן, שאסורות להעביר נחלה באותו הדור.

HAAMEK DAVAR

The daughters of Tzelofḥad were technically permitted to transfer land from one tribe to another.... The statement that seems to demand that these women marry within their tribe was only a suggestion.... However, due to their public exposure, God wanted to avoid the appearance of special licensing for them, and so recommended that they abide by the same rules as everyone else.

QUESTIONS FOR THOUGHT

- Both Ramban and *Haamek Davar* limit the prohibition even further. Regarding what two things do they disagree?
- R. Hirsch fundamentally agrees with Ramban. What does Ramban offer that R. Hirsch does not, and what does R. Hirsch offer that Ramban does not?
- What important legislative idea can we learn from Ramban's explanation?
- What important ethical value can we learn from the explanation of *Haamek Davar*?

א ‎דְּבָרִים: זֶה הַדָּבָר אֲשֶׁר־צִוָּה יְהֹוָה לִבְנוֹת צְלׇפְחָד לֵאמֹר לַטּוֹב
בְּעֵינֵיהֶם תִּהְיֶינָה לְנָשִׁים אַךְ לְמִשְׁפַּחַת מַטֵּה אֲבִיהֶם תִּהְיֶינָה
ב ‎לְנָשִׁים: וְלֹא־תִסֹּב נַחֲלָה לִבְנֵי יִשְׂרָאֵל מִמַּטֶּה אֶל־מַטֶּה כִּי
ח ‎אִישׁ בְּנַחֲלַת מַטֵּה אֲבֹתָיו יִדְבְּקוּ בְּנֵי יִשְׂרָאֵל: וְכׇל־בַּת יֹרֶשֶׁת
נַחֲלָה מִמַּטּוֹת בְּנֵי יִשְׂרָאֵל לְאֶחָד מִמִּשְׁפַּחַת מַטֵּה אָבִיהָ תִּהְיֶה
ט ‎לְאִשָּׁה לְמַעַן יִירְשׁוּ בְּנֵי יִשְׂרָאֵל אִישׁ נַחֲלַת אֲבֹתָיו: וְלֹא־תִסֹּב
נַחֲלָה מִמַּטֶּה לְמַטֶּה אַחֵר כִּי־אִישׁ בְּנַחֲלָתוֹ יִדְבְּקוּ מַטּוֹת בְּנֵי
י ‎יִשְׂרָאֵל: כַּאֲשֶׁר צִוָּה יְהֹוָה אֶת־מֹשֶׁה כֵּן עָשׂוּ בְּנוֹת צְלׇפְחָד:
יא ‎וַתִּהְיֶינָה מַחְלָה תִרְצָה וְחׇגְלָה וּמִלְכָּה וְנֹעָה בְּנוֹת צְלׇפְחָד לִבְנֵי   מפטיר
יב ‎דֹדֵיהֶן לְנָשִׁים: מִמִּשְׁפְּחֹת בְּנֵי־מְנַשֶּׁה בֶן־יוֹסֵף הָיוּ לְנָשִׁים וַתְּהִי
יג ‎נַחֲלָתָן עַל־מַטֵּה מִשְׁפַּחַת אֲבִיהֶן: אֵלֶּה הַמִּצְוֺת וְהַמִּשְׁפָּטִים
אֲשֶׁר צִוָּה יְהֹוָה בְּיַד־מֹשֶׁה אֶל־בְּנֵי יִשְׂרָאֵל בְּעַרְבֹת מוֹאָב עַל
יַרְדֵּן יְרֵחוֹ:

CLASSIC COMMENTATORS

The requirement that women who inherit land are limited to marrying men from their own tribe seems a little extreme, so much so that the Talmud (Taanit 30b) says that it was suspended in the era of the judges.

RAMBAN

רמב״ן

לא חשש הכתוב אלא לתקן העת ההיא, כי אם היו בישראל נשים נשואות לשבט אחר והן יורשות נחלה היום, או שתירשנה מיום זה ואילך ... על כרחנו תסוב נחלתן ממטה אל מטה, ומי יוכל לתקן ... כי לא רצתה התורה לצוות שלא יירשו אותן הבן והבעל, שלא ראתה לעקור משפט הירושה. וכן לא יחוש הכתוב למקרים העתידים לבא, כי הבנות שאינן יורשות נחלה יכולות להנשא לכל השבטים, ואפשר שתהיינה יורשות נחלה בזמן הבא, כי ימותו אחיהן בחיי האב ותעבור נחלת אביהן או קרוביהן להן.

The Torah only tried to correct the situation of Tzelofḥad's daughters, who were unmarried at the time. There might have been women who were already married to men from different tribes and who stood to receive portions of land now or at some later time, and there is no way to prevent that from happening…. The Torah did not wish to command that their husbands or sons could not inherit land from their wives or mothers who were from a different tribe, as that would have meant repealing the laws of inheritance. Similarly, the Torah was not concerned about all future marriages between tribes. Women who do not have land inheritance coming to them may marry anyone, even if it means that they may eventually inherit land which will get passed on to their husbands or sons.

MORE QUICK BITES

- **33:54** Rav Zalman Sorotzkin notices that 33:54 begins with the plural word תרבו but closes with the singular word תמעיט. He suggests that when we share good news, such as receiving extra territory, the news should be made public. But when we reveal bad news, like a diminishing of one's portion, it should be more private. As the saying goes, success has many fathers but failure is an orphan.

EXPLORING HASHKAFA
The Journey and the Destination

It happens often. We set out to achieve something but somehow never get to finish it. Sometimes it can be a competition; only one of us makes it to the end. Sometimes it can be a personal goal that we set too high. The generation that left Egypt never made it to their promised land. Are we all nothing but failures?

Judaism sets some very high goals. Our role models sometimes seem so far away from us that we could never even aspire to be like them. Perhaps there is a value not only in achieving goals, but even in aspiring to them. The goals that we set establish our values, our ultimate priorities. That, in itself, is very significant. But even more, every step we take toward those goals moves us forward on our life's journey, regardless of whether we actually achieve our destination.

The Mishna in *Pirkei Avot* says, לא עליך המלאכה לגמור ולא אתה בן חורין להבטל ממנה. The job is not ours alone to complete, but the fact that we can't complete it alone doesn't mean that we can refrain from doing our part. Every mitzva that we do brings us closer to redemption, and even if it takes a thousand generations, each generation and every individual can move the needle just a little.

What we need to do is redefine success. Life is not a zero-sum game like Monopoly in which there is only one winner and winner-takes-all. Success is about doing the best that we can – and perhaps even a drop more – and moving ourselves and others further along in our paths. That shift in mindset suggests that we are not failures at all just because we don't "make it."

Benei Yisrael take a forty-year journey through the wilderness with forty-two stops. With two notable exceptions, none who started that journey finished, but *Benei Yisrael* as a whole did eventually make it to their destination. In his *Orot Hateshuva*, Rav Avraham Yitzḥak Hakohen Kook points out that perfection is an impossibility for humans, but that striving for perfection is a very noble human pursuit. The journey itself, and every stopping point and stepping stone along the way, is of supreme importance in leading a meaningful Jewish life.

ספר במדבר עם רש"י
SEFER BEMIDBAR WITH RASHI

פרק א

א וַיְדַבֵּ֨ר יְהוָ֧ה אֶל־מֹשֶׁ֛ה בְּמִדְבַּ֥ר סִינַ֖י בְּאֹ֣הֶל מוֹעֵ֑ד בְּאֶחָד֩ לַחֹ֨דֶשׁ
ב הַשֵּׁנִ֜י בַּשָּׁנָ֣ה הַשֵּׁנִ֗ית לְצֵאתָ֛ם מֵאֶ֥רֶץ מִצְרַ֖יִם לֵאמֹֽר: שְׂא֗וּ
אֶת־רֹאשׁ֙ כָּל־עֲדַ֣ת בְּנֵֽי־יִשְׂרָאֵ֔ל לְמִשְׁפְּחֹתָ֖ם לְבֵ֣ית אֲבֹתָ֑ם
ג בְּמִסְפַּ֣ר שֵׁמ֔וֹת כָּל־זָכָ֖ר לְגֻלְגְּלֹתָֽם: מִבֶּ֨ן עֶשְׂרִ֤ים שָׁנָה֙ וָמַ֔עְלָה
כָּל־יֹצֵ֥א צָבָ֖א בְּיִשְׂרָאֵ֑ל תִּפְקְד֥וּ אֹתָ֛ם לְצִבְאֹתָ֖ם אַתָּ֥ה וְאַהֲרֹֽן:
ד וְאִתְּכֶ֣ם יִהְי֔וּ אִ֥ישׁ אִ֖ישׁ לַמַּטֶּ֑ה אִ֛ישׁ רֹ֥אשׁ לְבֵית־אֲבֹתָ֖יו הֽוּא:
ה וְאֵ֨לֶּה֙ שְׁמ֣וֹת הָֽאֲנָשִׁ֔ים אֲשֶׁ֥ר יַֽעַמְד֖וּ אִתְּכֶ֑ם לִרְאוּבֵ֕ן אֱלִיצ֖וּר בֶּן־
ו שְׁדֵיאֽוּר: לְשִׁמְע֕וֹן שְׁלֻֽמִיאֵ֖ל בֶּן־צוּרִֽישַׁדָּֽי: לִֽיהוּדָ֕ה נַחְשׁ֖וֹן בֶּן־
ז עַמִּֽינָדָֽב: לְיִ֨שָּׂשכָ֔ר נְתַנְאֵ֖ל בֶּן־צוּעָֽר: לִזְבוּלֻ֕ן אֱלִיאָ֖ב בֶּן־חֵלֹֽן:
ח לִבְנֵ֣י יוֹסֵ֔ף לְאֶפְרַ֕יִם אֱלִישָׁמָ֖ע בֶּן־עַמִּיה֑וּד לִמְנַשֶּׁ֕ה גַּמְלִיאֵ֖ל בֶּן־
י פְּדָהצֽוּר: לְבִ֨נְיָמִ֔ן אֲבִידָ֖ן בֶּן־גִּדְעֹנִֽי: לְדָ֕ן אֲחִיעֶ֖זֶר בֶּן־עַמִּֽישַׁדָּֽי:
יא לְאָשֵׁ֕ר פַּגְעִיאֵ֖ל בֶּן־עָכְרָֽן: לְגָ֕ד אֶלְיָסָ֖ף בֶּן־דְּעוּאֵֽל: לְנַפְתָּלִ֕י
יב אֲחִירַ֖ע בֶּן־עֵינָֽן: אֵ֚לֶּה קְרִיאֵ֣י הָעֵדָ֔ה נְשִׂיאֵ֖י מַטּ֣וֹת אֲבוֹתָ֑ם
יג רָאשֵׁ֥י אַלְפֵ֖י יִשְׂרָאֵ֥ל הֵֽם: וַיִּקַּ֥ח מֹשֶׁ֖ה וְאַהֲרֹ֑ן אֵ֚ת הָאֲנָשִׁ֣ים הָאֵ֔לֶּה
יד אֲשֶׁ֥ר נִקְּב֖וּ בְּשֵׁמֹֽת: וְאֵ֨ת כָּל־הָעֵדָ֜ה הִקְהִ֗ילוּ בְּאֶחָד֙ לַחֹ֣דֶשׁ

א) בְּמִדְבַּר סִינַי בְּאֶחָד לַחֹדֶשׁ. מִתּוֹךְ חִבָּתָן לְפָנָיו מוֹנֶה אוֹתָם כָּל שָׁעָה. כְּשֶׁיָּצְאוּ מִמִּצְרַיִם מְנָאָן (שמות יב, לז), וּכְשֶׁנָּפְלוּ בָּעֵגֶל מְנָאָן לֵידַע הַנּוֹתָרִים. וּכְשֶׁבָּא לְהַשְׁרוֹת שְׁכִינָתוֹ עֲלֵיהֶם מְנָאָם. בְּאֶחָד בְּנִיסָן הוּקַם הַמִּשְׁכָּן וּבְאֶחָד בְּאִיָּר מְנָאָם:

ב) לְמִשְׁפְּחֹתָם. דַּע מִנְיַן כָּל שֵׁבֶט וָשֵׁבֶט: לְבֵית אֲבֹתָם. מִי שֶׁאָבִיו מִשֵּׁבֶט אֶחָד וְאִמּוֹ מִשֵּׁבֶט אַחֵר יָקוּם עַל שֵׁבֶט אָבִיו: לְגֻלְגְּלֹתָם. עַל יְדֵי שְׁקָלִים, בֶּקַע לַגֻּלְגֹּלֶת:

ג) כָּל יֹצֵא צָבָא. מַגִּיד שֶׁאֵין יוֹצֵא בַּצָּבָא פָּחוֹת מִבֶּן עֶשְׂרִים:

ד) וְאִתְּכֶם יִהְיוּ. כְּשֶׁתִּפְקְדוּ אוֹתָם יִהְיוּ עִמָּכֶם נְשִׂיא כָל שֵׁבֶט וָשֵׁבֶט:

טז) אֵלֶּה קְרוּאֵי הָעֵדָה. הַנִּקְרָאִים לְכָל דְּבַר חֲשִׁיבוּת שֶׁבָּעֵדָה:

יז) אֵת הָאֲנָשִׁים הָאֵלֶּה. אֶת שְׁנֵים עָשָׂר נְשִׂיאִים הַלָּלוּ: אֲשֶׁר נִקְּבוּ. לוֹ כָאן בְּשֵׁמוֹת:

יח) וַיִּתְיַלְדוּ עַל מִשְׁפְּחֹתָם. הֵבִיאוּ סִפְרֵי יִחוּסֵיהֶם וְעֵדֵי חֶזְקַת לֵדָתָם, כָּל אֶחָד וְאֶחָד לְהִתְיַחֵס עַל הַשֵּׁבֶט:

יט הַשֵּׁנִי וַיִּתְיַלְד֤וּ עַל־מִשְׁפְּחֹתָם֙ לְבֵ֣ית אֲבֹתָ֔ם בְּמִסְפַּ֣ר שֵׁמ֔וֹת מִבֶּ֨ן עֶשְׂרִ֥ים שָׁנָ֛ה וָמַ֖עְלָה לְגֻלְגְּלֹתָֽם: כַּאֲשֶׁ֛ר צִוָּ֥ה יְהֹוָ֖ה אֶת־מֹשֶׁ֑ה

כ וַֽיִּפְקְדֵ֖ם בְּמִדְבַּ֥ר סִינָֽי: ‏ שני ‏ וַיִּהְי֤וּ בְנֵֽי־רְאוּבֵן֙ בְּכֹ֣ר יִשְׂרָאֵ֔ל תּוֹלְדֹתָ֥ם לְמִשְׁפְּחֹתָ֖ם לְבֵ֣ית אֲבֹתָ֑ם בְּמִסְפַּ֤ר שֵׁמוֹת֙ לְגֻלְגְּלֹתָ֔ם

כא כָּל־זָכָ֗ר מִבֶּ֨ן עֶשְׂרִ֤ים שָׁנָה֙ וָמַ֔עְלָה כֹּ֖ל יֹצֵ֥א צָבָֽא: פְּקֻדֵיהֶ֖ם לְמַטֵּ֣ה רְאוּבֵ֑ן שִׁשָּׁ֧ה וְאַרְבָּעִ֛ים אֶ֖לֶף וַחֲמֵ֥שׁ מֵאֽוֹת:

כב לִבְנֵ֣י שִׁמְע֔וֹן תּוֹלְדֹתָ֥ם לְמִשְׁפְּחֹתָ֖ם לְבֵ֣ית אֲבֹתָ֑ם פְּקֻדָ֗יו בְּמִסְפַּ֤ר שֵׁמוֹת֙ לְגֻלְגְּלֹתָ֔ם כָּל־זָכָ֗ר מִבֶּ֨ן עֶשְׂרִ֤ים שָׁנָה֙ וָמַ֔עְלָה כֹּ֖ל יֹצֵ֥א

כג צָבָֽא: פְּקֻדֵיהֶ֖ם לְמַטֵּ֣ה שִׁמְע֑וֹן תִּשְׁעָ֧ה וַחֲמִשִּׁ֛ים אֶ֖לֶף וּשְׁלֹ֥שׁ מֵאֽוֹת:

כד לִבְנֵ֣י גָ֔ד תּוֹלְדֹתָ֥ם לְמִשְׁפְּחֹתָ֖ם לְבֵ֣ית אֲבֹתָ֑ם בְּמִסְפַּ֣ר שֵׁמ֗וֹת

כה מִבֶּ֨ן עֶשְׂרִ֤ים שָׁנָה֙ וָמַ֔עְלָה כֹּ֖ל יֹצֵ֥א צָבָֽא: פְּקֻדֵיהֶ֖ם לְמַטֵּ֣ה גָ֑ד חֲמִשָּׁ֤ה וְאַרְבָּעִים֙ אֶ֔לֶף וְשֵׁ֥שׁ מֵא֖וֹת וַחֲמִשִּֽׁים:

כו לִבְנֵ֣י יְהוּדָ֔ה תּוֹלְדֹתָ֥ם לְמִשְׁפְּחֹתָ֖ם לְבֵ֣ית אֲבֹתָ֑ם בְּמִסְפַּ֣ר שֵׁמֹ֗ת

כז מִבֶּ֨ן עֶשְׂרִ֤ים שָׁנָה֙ וָמַ֔עְלָה כֹּ֖ל יֹצֵ֣א צָבָֽא: פְּקֻדֵיהֶ֖ם לְמַטֵּ֣ה יְהוּדָ֑ה אַרְבָּעָ֧ה וְשִׁבְעִ֛ים אֶ֖לֶף וְשֵׁ֥שׁ מֵאֽוֹת:

כח לִבְנֵ֣י יִשָּׂשכָ֔ר תּוֹלְדֹתָ֥ם לְמִשְׁפְּחֹתָ֖ם לְבֵ֣ית אֲבֹתָ֑ם בְּמִסְפַּ֣ר

כט שֵׁמֹ֗ת מִבֶּ֨ן עֶשְׂרִ֤ים שָׁנָה֙ וָמַ֔עְלָה כֹּ֖ל יֹצֵ֥א צָבָֽא: פְּקֻדֵיהֶ֖ם לְמַטֵּ֣ה יִשָּׂשכָ֑ר אַרְבָּעָ֧ה וַחֲמִשִּׁ֛ים אֶ֖לֶף וְאַרְבַּ֥ע מֵאֽוֹת:

ל לִבְנֵ֣י זְבוּלֻ֔ן תּוֹלְדֹתָ֥ם לְמִשְׁפְּחֹתָ֖ם לְבֵ֣ית אֲבֹתָ֑ם בְּמִסְפַּ֣ר שֵׁמֹ֗ת

לא מִבֶּ֨ן עֶשְׂרִ֤ים שָׁנָה֙ וָמַ֔עְלָה כֹּ֖ל יֹצֵ֥א צָבָֽא: פְּקֻדֵיהֶ֖ם לְמַטֵּ֣ה זְבוּלֻ֑ן שִׁבְעָ֧ה וַחֲמִשִּׁ֛ים אֶ֖לֶף וְאַרְבַּ֥ע מֵאֽוֹת:

לב לִבְנֵי יוֹסֵף לִבְנֵי אֶפְרַיִם תּוֹלְדֹתָם לְמִשְׁפְּחֹתָם לְבֵית אֲבֹתָם
לג בְּמִסְפַּר שֵׁמֹת מִבֶּן עֶשְׂרִים שָׁנָה וָמַעְלָה כֹּל יֹצֵא צָבָא: פְּקֻדֵיהֶם לְמַטֵּה אֶפְרָיִם אַרְבָּעִים אֶלֶף וַחֲמֵשׁ מֵאוֹת:
לד לִבְנֵי מְנַשֶּׁה תּוֹלְדֹתָם לְמִשְׁפְּחֹתָם לְבֵית אֲבֹתָם בְּמִסְפַּר שֵׁמוֹת
לה מִבֶּן עֶשְׂרִים שָׁנָה וָמַעְלָה כֹּל יֹצֵא צָבָא: פְּקֻדֵיהֶם לְמַטֵּה מְנַשֶּׁה שְׁנַיִם וּשְׁלֹשִׁים אֶלֶף וּמָאתָיִם:
לו לִבְנֵי בִנְיָמִן תּוֹלְדֹתָם לְמִשְׁפְּחֹתָם לְבֵית אֲבֹתָם בְּמִסְפַּר שֵׁמֹת
לז מִבֶּן עֶשְׂרִים שָׁנָה וָמַעְלָה כֹּל יֹצֵא צָבָא: פְּקֻדֵיהֶם לְמַטֵּה בִנְיָמִן חֲמִשָּׁה וּשְׁלֹשִׁים אֶלֶף וְאַרְבַּע מֵאוֹת:
לח לִבְנֵי דָן תּוֹלְדֹתָם לְמִשְׁפְּחֹתָם לְבֵית אֲבֹתָם בְּמִסְפַּר שֵׁמֹת
לט מִבֶּן עֶשְׂרִים שָׁנָה וָמַעְלָה כֹּל יֹצֵא צָבָא: פְּקֻדֵיהֶם לְמַטֵּה דָן שְׁנַיִם וְשִׁשִּׁים אֶלֶף וּשְׁבַע מֵאוֹת:
מ לִבְנֵי אָשֵׁר תּוֹלְדֹתָם לְמִשְׁפְּחֹתָם לְבֵית אֲבֹתָם בְּמִסְפַּר שֵׁמֹת
מא מִבֶּן עֶשְׂרִים שָׁנָה וָמַעְלָה כֹּל יֹצֵא צָבָא: פְּקֻדֵיהֶם לְמַטֵּה אָשֵׁר אֶחָד וְאַרְבָּעִים אֶלֶף וַחֲמֵשׁ מֵאוֹת:
מב בְּנֵי נַפְתָּלִי תּוֹלְדֹתָם לְמִשְׁפְּחֹתָם לְבֵית אֲבֹתָם בְּמִסְפַּר שֵׁמֹת
מג מִבֶּן עֶשְׂרִים שָׁנָה וָמַעְלָה כֹּל יֹצֵא צָבָא: פְּקֻדֵיהֶם לְמַטֵּה נַפְתָּלִי שְׁלֹשָׁה וַחֲמִשִּׁים אֶלֶף וְאַרְבַּע מֵאוֹת:
מד אֵלֶּה הַפְּקֻדִים אֲשֶׁר פָּקַד מֹשֶׁה וְאַהֲרֹן וּנְשִׂיאֵי יִשְׂרָאֵל שְׁנֵים
מה עָשָׂר אִישׁ אִישׁ־אֶחָד לְבֵית־אֲבֹתָיו הָיוּ: וַיִּהְיוּ כָּל־פְּקוּדֵי בְנֵי־יִשְׂרָאֵל לְבֵית אֲבֹתָם מִבֶּן עֶשְׂרִים שָׁנָה וָמַעְלָה כָּל־יֹצֵא צָבָא
מו בְּיִשְׂרָאֵל: וַיִּהְיוּ כָּל־הַפְּקֻדִים שֵׁשׁ־מֵאוֹת אֶלֶף וּשְׁלֹשֶׁת אֲלָפִים

מז וַחֲמֵשׁ מֵאוֹת וַחֲמִשִּׁים: וְהַלְוִיִּם לְמַטֵּה אֲבֹתָם לֹא הָתְפָּקְדוּ בְּתוֹכָם:

מח מט וַיְדַבֵּר יְהוָה אֶל־מֹשֶׁה לֵּאמֹר: אַךְ אֶת־מַטֵּה לֵוִי לֹא תִפְקֹד וְאֶת־רֹאשָׁם לֹא תִשָּׂא בְּתוֹךְ בְּנֵי יִשְׂרָאֵל: נ וְאַתָּה הַפְקֵד אֶת־הַלְוִיִּם עַל־מִשְׁכַּן הָעֵדֻת וְעַל כָּל־כֵּלָיו וְעַל כָּל־אֲשֶׁר־לוֹ הֵמָּה יִשְׂאוּ אֶת־הַמִּשְׁכָּן וְאֶת־כָּל־כֵּלָיו וְהֵם יְשָׁרְתֻהוּ וְסָבִיב לַמִּשְׁכָּן יַחֲנוּ: נא וּבִנְסֹעַ הַמִּשְׁכָּן יוֹרִידוּ אֹתוֹ הַלְוִיִּם וּבַחֲנֹת הַמִּשְׁכָּן יָקִימוּ אֹתוֹ הַלְוִיִּם וְהַזָּר הַקָּרֵב יוּמָת: נב וְחָנוּ בְּנֵי יִשְׂרָאֵל אִישׁ עַל־מַחֲנֵהוּ וְאִישׁ עַל־דִּגְלוֹ לְצִבְאֹתָם: נג וְהַלְוִיִּם יַחֲנוּ סָבִיב לְמִשְׁכַּן הָעֵדֻת וְלֹא־יִהְיֶה קֶצֶף עַל־עֲדַת בְּנֵי יִשְׂרָאֵל וְשָׁמְרוּ הַלְוִיִּם אֶת־מִשְׁמֶרֶת מִשְׁכַּן הָעֵדוּת: נד וַיַּעֲשׂוּ בְּנֵי יִשְׂרָאֵל כְּכֹל אֲשֶׁר צִוָּה יְהוָה אֶת־מֹשֶׁה כֵּן עָשׂוּ:

ב א וַיְדַבֵּר יְהוָה אֶל־מֹשֶׁה וְאֶל־אַהֲרֹן לֵאמֹר: ב אִישׁ עַל־דִּגְלוֹ בְאֹתֹת לְבֵית אֲבֹתָם יַחֲנוּ בְּנֵי יִשְׂרָאֵל מִנֶּגֶד סָבִיב לְאֹהֶל־מוֹעֵד יַחֲנוּ:

שלישי

מט] **אַךְ אֶת מַטֵּה לֵוִי לֹא תִפְקֹד.** כְּדַאי הוּא לִגְיוֹן שֶׁל מֶלֶךְ לִהְיוֹת נִמְנֶה לְבַדּוֹ. דָּבָר אַחֵר, צָפָה הַקָּדוֹשׁ בָּרוּךְ הוּא שֶׁעֲתִידָה לַעֲמֹד גְּזֵרָה עַל כָּל הַנִּמְנִין מִבֶּן עֶשְׂרִים שָׁנָה וָמַעְלָה שֶׁיָּמוּתוּ בַּמִּדְבָּר, אָמַר: אַל יִהְיוּ אֵלּוּ בַּכְּלָל, לְפִי שֶׁהֵם שֶׁלִּי, שֶׁלֹּא טָעוּ בָּעֵגֶל:

נ] **וְאַתָּה הַפְקֵד אֶת הַלְוִיִּם.** כְּתַרְגּוּמוֹ "מַנִּי", לְשׁוֹן מִנּוּי שְׂרָרָה עַל דָּבָר שֶׁהוּא מְמֻנֶּה עָלָיו, כְּמוֹ "וַיַּפְקֵד הַמֶּלֶךְ פְּקִידִים" (אסתר ב, ג):

נא] **יוֹרִידוּ אֹתוֹ.** כְּתַרְגּוּמוֹ: "יְפָרְקוּן", כְּשֶׁבָּאִין לִסַּע בַּמִּדְבָּר מִמַּסָּע לְמַסָּע הָיוּ מְפָרְקִין אוֹתוֹ מֵהֲקָמָתוֹ, וְנוֹשְׂאִין אוֹתוֹ עַד מְקוֹם אֲשֶׁר יִשְׁכֹּן שָׁם הֶעָנָן, וְיַחֲנוּ

שָׁם, וּמְקִימִין אוֹתוֹ: **וְהַזָּר הַקָּרֵב.** לַעֲבוֹדָתָם זוֹ: **יוּמָת.** בִּידֵי שָׁמַיִם:

נב] **וְאִישׁ עַל דִּגְלוֹ.** כְּמוֹ שֶׁהַדְּגָלִים סְדוּרִים בַּסֵּפֶר הַזֶּה, שְׁלֹשָׁה שְׁבָטִים לְכָל דֶּגֶל:

נג] **וְלֹא יִהְיֶה קֶצֶף.** אִם תַּעֲשׂוּ כְּמִצְוָתִי לֹא יִהְיֶה קֶצֶף, וְאִם לָאו, שֶׁיִּכָּנְסוּ זָרִים בַּעֲבוֹדָתָם זוֹ, יִהְיֶה קֶצֶף, כְּמוֹ שֶׁמָּצִינוּ בְּמַעֲשֵׂה קֹרַח: "כִּי יָצָא הַקֶּצֶף" וְגוֹ' (להלן יז, יא):

פרק ב

ב] **בְּאֹתֹת.** כָּל דֶּגֶל יִהְיֶה לוֹ אוֹת, מַפָּה צְבוּעָה תְּלוּיָה בוֹ, צִבְעוֹ שֶׁל זֶה לֹא כְּצִבְעוֹ שֶׁל זֶה, צֶבַע כָּל אֶחָד כְּגוֹן אַבְנוֹ הַקְּבוּעָה בַּחֹשֶׁן, וּמִתּוֹךְ כָּךְ

וְהַחֹנִים֙ קֵ֣דְמָה מִזְרָ֔חָה דֶּ֛גֶל מַחֲנֵ֥ה יְהוּדָ֖ה לְצִבְאֹתָ֑ם וְנָשִׂיא֙ לִבְנֵ֣י ג
יְהוּדָ֔ה נַחְשׁ֖וֹן בֶּן־עַמִּינָדָֽב: וּצְבָא֖וֹ וּפְקֻדֵיהֶ֑ם אַרְבָּעָ֧ה וְשִׁבְעִ֛ים ד
אֶ֖לֶף וְשֵׁ֥שׁ מֵאֽוֹת: וְהַחֹנִ֥ים עָלָ֖יו מַטֵּ֣ה יִשָּׂשכָ֑ר וְנָשִׂיא֙ לִבְנֵ֣י ה
יִשָּׂשכָ֔ר נְתַנְאֵ֖ל בֶּן־צוּעָֽר: וּצְבָא֖וֹ וּפְקֻדָ֑יו אַרְבָּעָ֧ה וַחֲמִשִּׁ֛ים ו
אֶ֖לֶף וְאַרְבַּ֥ע מֵאֽוֹת: מַטֵּ֖ה זְבוּלֻ֑ן וְנָשִׂיא֙ לִבְנֵ֣י זְבוּלֻ֔ן אֱלִיאָ֖ב ז
בֶּן־חֵלֹֽן: וּצְבָא֖וֹ וּפְקֻדָ֑יו שִׁבְעָ֧ה וַחֲמִשִּׁ֛ים אֶ֖לֶף וְאַרְבַּ֥ע מֵאֽוֹת: ח
כָּֽל־הַפְּקֻדִ֞ים לְמַחֲנֵ֣ה יְהוּדָ֗ה מְאַ֨ת אֶ֜לֶף וּשְׁמֹנִ֥ים אֶ֛לֶף וְשֵֽׁשֶׁת־ ט
אֲלָפִ֥ים וְאַרְבַּע־מֵא֖וֹת לְצִבְאֹתָ֑ם רִֽאשֹׁנָ֖ה יִסָּֽעוּ: דֶּ֣גֶל י
מַחֲנֵ֧ה רְאוּבֵ֛ן תֵּימָ֖נָה לְצִבְאֹתָ֑ם וְנָשִׂיא֙ לִבְנֵ֣י רְאוּבֵ֔ן אֱלִיצ֖וּר בֶּן־
שְׁדֵיאֽוּר: וּצְבָא֖וֹ וּפְקֻדָ֑יו שִׁשָּׁ֧ה וְאַרְבָּעִ֛ים אֶ֖לֶף וַחֲמֵ֥שׁ מֵאֽוֹת: יא
וְהַחוֹנִ֥ם עָלָ֖יו מַטֵּ֣ה שִׁמְע֑וֹן וְנָשִׂיא֙ לִבְנֵ֣י שִׁמְע֔וֹן שְׁלֻמִיאֵ֖ל בֶּן־ יב
צוּרִֽישַׁדָּֽי: וּצְבָא֖וֹ וּפְקֻדֵיהֶ֑ם תִּשְׁעָ֧ה וַחֲמִשִּׁ֛ים אֶ֖לֶף וּשְׁלֹ֥שׁ מֵאֽוֹת: יג
וּמַטֵּ֖ה גָּ֑ד וְנָשִׂיא֙ לִבְנֵ֣י גָ֔ד אֶלְיָסָ֖ף בֶּן־רְעוּאֵֽל: וּצְבָא֖וֹ וּפְקֻדֵיהֶ֑ם יד
חֲמִשָּׁ֧ה וְאַרְבָּעִ֛ים אֶ֖לֶף וְשֵׁ֥שׁ מֵא֖וֹת וַחֲמִשִּֽׁים: כָּל־הַפְּקֻדִ֞ים טו
לְמַחֲנֵ֣ה רְאוּבֵ֗ן מְאַ֨ת אֶ֜לֶף וְאֶחָ֨ד וַחֲמִשִּׁ֥ים אֶ֛לֶף וְאַרְבַּע־מֵא֖וֹת טז

יַכִּיר כָּל אֶחָד אֶת דִּגְלוֹ. דָּבָר אַחֵר, "בְּאֹתֹת לְבֵית אֲבֹתָם", בְּאוֹת שֶׁמָּסַר לָהֶם יַעֲקֹב אֲבִיהֶם כְּשֶׁנְּשָׂאוּהוּ מִמִּצְרַיִם, שֶׁנֶּאֱמַר: "וַיַּעֲשׂוּ בָנָיו לוֹ כֵּן כַּאֲשֶׁר צִוָּם" (בראשית נ, יב) – יְהוּדָה וְיִשָּׂשכָר וּזְבוּלֻן יִשָּׂאוּהוּ מִן הַמִּזְרָח, וּרְאוּבֵן וְשִׁמְעוֹן וְגָד מִן הַדָּרוֹם וְכוּ', כִּדְאִיתָא בְּתַנְחוּמָא בְּפָרָשָׁה זוֹ (יב). מִנֶּגֶד. מֵרָחוֹק מִיל, כְּמוֹ שֶׁנֶּאֱמַר בִּיהוֹשֻׁעַ: "אַךְ רָחוֹק יִהְיֶה בֵּינֵיכֶם

וּבֵינָו כְּאַלְפַּיִם אַמָּה" (יהושע ג, ד), שֶׁיּוּכְלוּ לָבֹא בְּשַׁבָּת. מֹשֶׁה וְאַהֲרֹן וּבָנָיו וְהַלְוִיִּם חוֹנִים בְּסָמוּךְ לוֹ:

ג) קֵדְמָה. לִפְנֵי הַקָּרוּי 'קֶדֶם', וְאֵיזֶה? זֶה רוּחַ מִזְרָחִית, וְהַמַּעֲרָב קָרוּי אָחוֹר:

י) רִאשׁוֹנָה יִסָּעוּ. כְּשֶׁרוֹאִין הֶעָנָן מִסְתַּלֵּק, תּוֹקְעִין הַכֹּהֲנִים בַּחֲצוֹצְרוֹת וְנוֹסֵעַ מַחֲנֵה יְהוּדָה תְּחִלָּה; וּכְשֶׁהוֹלְכִין – הוֹלְכִין כְּדֶרֶךְ חֲנִיָּתָן, הַלְוִיִּם וְהָעֲגָלוֹת

| יז | וַחֲמִשִּׁים לְצִבְאֹתָם וּשְׁנַיִם יִסָּעוּ: וְנָסַע אֹהֶל־מוֹעֵד
מַחֲנֵה הַלְוִיִּם בְּתוֹךְ הַמַּחֲנֹת כַּאֲשֶׁר יַחֲנוּ כֵּן יִסָּעוּ אִישׁ עַל־
| יח | יָדוֹ לְדִגְלֵיהֶם: דֶּגֶל מַחֲנֵה אֶפְרַיִם לְצִבְאֹתָם יָמָּה
| יט | וְנָשִׂיא לִבְנֵי אֶפְרַיִם אֱלִישָׁמָע בֶּן־עַמִּיהוּד: וּצְבָאוֹ וּפְקֻדֵיהֶם
| כ | אַרְבָּעִים אֶלֶף וַחֲמֵשׁ מֵאוֹת: וְעָלָיו מַטֵּה מְנַשֶּׁה וְנָשִׂיא לִבְנֵי
| כא | מְנַשֶּׁה גַּמְלִיאֵל בֶּן־פְּדָהצוּר: וּצְבָאוֹ וּפְקֻדֵיהֶם שְׁנַיִם וּשְׁלֹשִׁים
| כב | אֶלֶף וּמָאתָיִם: וּמַטֵּה בִּנְיָמִן וְנָשִׂיא לִבְנֵי בִנְיָמִן אֲבִידָן בֶּן־
| כג | גִּדְעֹנִי: וּצְבָאוֹ וּפְקֻדֵיהֶם חֲמִשָּׁה וּשְׁלֹשִׁים אֶלֶף וְאַרְבַּע מֵאוֹת:
| כד | כָּל־הַפְּקֻדִים לְמַחֲנֵה אֶפְרַיִם מְאַת אֶלֶף וּשְׁמֹנַת־אֲלָפִים
| כה | וּמֵאָה לְצִבְאֹתָם וּשְׁלֹשִׁים יִסָּעוּ: דֶּגֶל מַחֲנֵה דָן
| כו | צָפֹנָה לְצִבְאֹתָם וְנָשִׂיא לִבְנֵי דָן אֲחִיעֶזֶר בֶּן־עַמִּישַׁדָּי: וּצְבָאוֹ
| כז | וּפְקֻדֵיהֶם שְׁנַיִם וְשִׁשִּׁים אֶלֶף וּשְׁבַע מֵאוֹת: וְהַחֹנִים עָלָיו מַטֵּה
| כח | אָשֵׁר וְנָשִׂיא לִבְנֵי אָשֵׁר פַּגְעִיאֵל בֶּן־עָכְרָן: וּצְבָאוֹ וּפְקֻדֵיהֶם
| כט | אֶחָד וְאַרְבָּעִים אֶלֶף וַחֲמֵשׁ מֵאוֹת: וּמַטֵּה נַפְתָּלִי וְנָשִׂיא לִבְנֵי
| ל | נַפְתָּלִי אֲחִירַע בֶּן־עֵינָן: וּצְבָאוֹ וּפְקֻדֵיהֶם שְׁלֹשָׁה וַחֲמִשִּׁים אֶלֶף
| לא | וְאַרְבַּע מֵאוֹת: כָּל־הַפְּקֻדִים לְמַחֲנֵה דָן מְאַת אֶלֶף וְשִׁבְעָה
וַחֲמִשִּׁים אֶלֶף וְשֵׁשׁ מֵאוֹת לָאַחֲרֹנָה יִסְעוּ לְדִגְלֵיהֶם:

בָּאֶמְצַע, דֶּגֶל יְהוּדָה בַּמִּזְרָח, וְשֶׁל רְאוּבֵן בַּדָּרוֹם, וְשֶׁל אֶפְרַיִם בַּמַּעֲרָב, וְשֶׁל דָּן בַּצָּפוֹן:

יז וְנָסַע אֹהֶל מוֹעֵד. לְאַחַר שְׁנֵי דְגָלִים הַלָּלוּ: כַּאֲשֶׁר יַחֲנוּ כֵּן יִסָּעוּ. כְּמוֹ שֶׁפֵּרַשְׁתִּי, הֲלִיכָתָן כַּחֲנִיָּתָן, כָּל דֶּגֶל

מְהַלֵּךְ לָרוּחַ הַקָּבוּעַ לוֹ: עַל יָדוֹ. עַל מְקוֹמוֹ, וְאֵין לְשׁוֹן "יָד" זָז מִמַּשְׁמָעוֹ, רוּחַ שֶׁל צִדּוֹ קָרוּי "עַל יָדוֹ", הַסְּמוּכָה לוֹ לְכָל הוֹשָׁטַת יָדוֹ, אינשו"ן אישי"א בְּלַעַז:

כ וְעָלָיו. כְּתַרְגּוּמוֹ: "וְדִסְמִיכִין עֲלוֹהִי":

פרק ג

לב אֵלֶּה פְּקוּדֵי בְנֵי־יִשְׂרָאֵל לְבֵית אֲבֹתָם כָּל־פְּקוּדֵי הַמַּחֲנֹת לְצִבְאֹתָם שֵׁשׁ־מֵאוֹת אֶלֶף וּשְׁלֹשֶׁת אֲלָפִים וַחֲמֵשׁ מֵאוֹת וַחֲמִשִּׁים:
לג וְהַלְוִיִּם לֹא הָתְפָּקְדוּ בְּתוֹךְ בְּנֵי יִשְׂרָאֵל כַּאֲשֶׁר צִוָּה יהוה אֶת־מֹשֶׁה:
לד וַיַּעֲשׂוּ בְּנֵי יִשְׂרָאֵל כְּכֹל אֲשֶׁר־צִוָּה יהוה אֶת־מֹשֶׁה כֵּן־חָנוּ לְדִגְלֵיהֶם וְכֵן נָסָעוּ אִישׁ לְמִשְׁפְּחֹתָיו עַל־בֵּית אֲבֹתָיו:

פרק ג

רביעי
א וְאֵלֶּה תּוֹלְדֹת אַהֲרֹן וּמֹשֶׁה בְּיוֹם דִּבֶּר יהוה אֶת־מֹשֶׁה בְּהַר סִינָי:
ב וְאֵלֶּה שְׁמוֹת בְּנֵי־אַהֲרֹן הַבְּכוֹר ׀ נָדָב וַאֲבִיהוּא אֶלְעָזָר וְאִיתָמָר:
ג אֵלֶּה שְׁמוֹת בְּנֵי אַהֲרֹן הַכֹּהֲנִים הַמְּשֻׁחִים אֲשֶׁר־מִלֵּא יָדָם לְכַהֵן:
ד וַיָּמָת נָדָב וַאֲבִיהוּא לִפְנֵי יהוה בְּהַקְרִבָם אֵשׁ זָרָה לִפְנֵי יהוה בְּמִדְבַּר סִינַי וּבָנִים לֹא־הָיוּ לָהֶם וַיְכַהֵן אֶלְעָזָר וְאִיתָמָר עַל־פְּנֵי אַהֲרֹן אֲבִיהֶם:
ה וַיְדַבֵּר יהוה אֶל־מֹשֶׁה לֵּאמֹר: הַקְרֵב אֶת־מַטֵּה לֵוִי וְהַעֲמַדְתָּ אֹתוֹ לִפְנֵי אַהֲרֹן הַכֹּהֵן וְשֵׁרְתוּ אֹתוֹ:
ז וְשָׁמְרוּ אֶת־מִשְׁמַרְתּוֹ וְאֶת־מִשְׁמֶרֶת כָּל־הָעֵדָה לִפְנֵי אֹהֶל מוֹעֵד לַעֲבֹד אֶת־עֲבֹדַת הַמִּשְׁכָּן:
ח וְשָׁמְרוּ אֶת־כָּל־כְּלֵי אֹהֶל מוֹעֵד וְאֶת־מִשְׁמֶרֶת בְּנֵי

פרק ג

א וְאֵלֶּה תּוֹלְדֹת אַהֲרֹן וּמֹשֶׁה. וְאֵינוֹ מַזְכִּיר אֶלָּא בְּנֵי אַהֲרֹן, וְנִקְרְאוּ תּוֹלְדוֹת מֹשֶׁה, לְפִי שֶׁלִּמְּדָן תּוֹרָה. מְלַמֵּד שֶׁכָּל הַמְלַמֵּד אֶת בֶּן חֲבֵרוֹ תּוֹרָה מַעֲלֶה עָלָיו הַכָּתוּב כְּאִלּוּ יְלָדוֹ: בְּיוֹם דִּבֶּר ה' אֶת מֹשֶׁה. נַעֲשׂוּ אֵלּוּ הַתּוֹלָדוֹת שֶׁלּוֹ, שֶׁלִּמְּדָן מַה שֶּׁלָּמַד מִפִּי הַגְּבוּרָה.

ד עַל פְּנֵי אַהֲרֹן. בְּחַיָּיו:

ו וְשֵׁרְתוּ אֹתוֹ. וּמַהוּ הַשֵּׁרוּת? "וְשָׁמְרוּ אֶת מִשְׁמַרְתּוֹ". לְפִי שֶׁשְּׁמִירַת הַמִּקְדָּשׁ עָלָיו שֶׁלֹּא יִקְרַב זָר, כְּמוֹ שֶׁנֶּאֱמַר: "אַתָּה וּבָנֶיךָ וּבֵית אָבִיךָ אִתָּךְ תִּשְׂאוּ אֶת עֲוֹן הַמִּקְדָּשׁ" (להלן יח, א), וְהַלְוִיִּם הַלָּלוּ מְסַיְּעִין אוֹתָם, זוֹ הִיא הַשֵּׁרוּת:

ז וְשָׁמְרוּ אֶת מִשְׁמַרְתּוֹ. כָּל מִנּוּי שֶׁהָאָדָם מְמֻנֶּה עָלָיו וּמֻטָּל עָלָיו לַעֲשׂוֹתוֹ קָרוּי 'מִשְׁמֶרֶת' בְּכָל הַמִּקְרָא וּבִלְשׁוֹן מִשְׁנָה, כְּמוֹ שֶׁאָמְרוּ בַּבִּגְדִין וְתֵדַע: "וַהֲלֹא אֵין מִשְׁמַרְתִּי וּמִשְׁמַרְתְּךָ שָׁוָה", וְכֵן מִשְׁמְרוֹת כְּהֻנָּה וּלְוִיָּה:

ח וְאֶת מִשְׁמֶרֶת בְּנֵי יִשְׂרָאֵל. שֶׁכֻּלָּן הָיוּ זְקוּקִין

במדבר | פרק ג

ט יִשְׂרָאֵ֔ל לַעֲבֹ֖ד אֶת־עֲבֹדַ֣ת הַמִּשְׁכָּֽן: וְנָתַתָּה֙ אֶת־הַלְוִיִּ֔ם לְאַהֲרֹ֖ן
י וּלְבָנָ֑יו נְתוּנִ֨ם נְתוּנִ֥ם הֵ֛מָּה ל֖וֹ מֵאֵ֥ת בְּנֵ֥י יִשְׂרָאֵֽל: וְאֶת־אַהֲרֹ֤ן
וְאֶת־בָּנָיו֙ תִּפְקֹ֔ד וְשָׁמְר֖וּ אֶת־כְּהֻנָּתָ֑ם וְהַזָּ֥ר הַקָּרֵ֖ב יוּמָֽת:
יא וַיְדַבֵּ֥ר יְהוָ֖ה אֶל־מֹשֶׁ֥ה לֵּאמֹֽר: וַאֲנִ֞י הִנֵּ֧ה לָקַ֣חְתִּי אֶת־הַלְוִיִּ֗ם
מִתּוֹךְ֙ בְּנֵ֣י יִשְׂרָאֵ֔ל תַּ֧חַת כָּל־בְּכ֛וֹר פֶּ֥טֶר רֶ֖חֶם מִבְּנֵ֣י יִשְׂרָאֵ֑ל
יג וְהָ֥יוּ לִ֖י הַלְוִיִּֽם: כִּ֣י לִי֮ כָּל־בְּכוֹר֒ בְּיוֹם֩ הַכֹּתִ֨י כָל־בְּכוֹר֙ בְּאֶ֣רֶץ
מִצְרַ֗יִם הִקְדַּ֨שְׁתִּי לִ֤י כָל־בְּכוֹר֙ בְּיִשְׂרָאֵ֔ל מֵאָדָ֖ם עַד־בְּהֵמָ֑ה
לִ֥י יִהְי֖וּ אֲנִ֥י יְהוָֽה:
יד וַיְדַבֵּ֤ר יְהוָה֙ אֶל־מֹשֶׁ֔ה בְּמִדְבַּ֥ר סִינַ֖י לֵאמֹֽר: פְּקֹד֙ אֶת־בְּנֵ֣י לֵוִ֔י חמישי
לְבֵ֥ית אֲבֹתָ֖ם לְמִשְׁפְּחֹתָ֑ם כָּל־זָכָ֛ר מִבֶּן־חֹ֥דֶשׁ וָמַ֖עְלָה תִּפְקְדֵֽם:
טז וַיִּפְקֹ֥ד אֹתָ֛ם מֹשֶׁ֖ה עַל־פִּ֣י יְהוָ֑ה כַּאֲשֶׁ֖ר צֻוָּֽה: וַיִּֽהְיוּ־אֵ֥לֶּה בְנֵי־

לְעָרְכֵי הַמִּקְדָּשׁ, חֶלְקָם שֶׁהַלְוִיִּם בָּאִים תַּחְתֵּיהֶם בִּשְׁלִיחוּתָם, לְפִיכָךְ לוֹקְחִים מֵהֶם הַמַּעֲשְׂרוֹת בִּשְׂכָרָן, שֶׁנֶּאֱמַר: "כִּי שָׂכָר הוּא לָכֶם חֵלֶף עֲבֹדַתְכֶם" (להלן יח, לא):

י **נְתוּנִם הֵמָּה לוֹ.** לַעֲבוֹדָה: **מֵאֵת בְּנֵי יִשְׂרָאֵל.** כְּמוֹ "מִתּוֹךְ בְּנֵי יִשְׂרָאֵל", כְּלוֹמַר מִשְּׁאָר כָּל הָעֵדָה נִבְדְּלוּ לְכָךְ בִּגְזֵרַת הַמָּקוֹם וְהוּא נְתָנָם לוֹ, שֶׁנֶּאֱמַר: "וָאֶתְּנָה אֶת הַלְוִיִם נְתֻנִים" וְגוֹ' (להלן ח, יט):

י **וְאֶת אַהֲרֹן וְאֶת בָּנָיו תִּפְקֹד.** לְשׁוֹן פְּקִידוּת, וְאֵינוֹ לְשׁוֹן מִנְיָן: **וְשָׁמְרוּ אֶת כְּהֻנָּתָם.** קַבָּלַת דָּמִים וּזְרִיקָה וְהַקְטָרָה וַעֲבוֹדוֹת הַמְּסוּרוֹת לַכֹּהֲנִים:

יב **וַאֲנִי הִנֵּה לָקַחְתִּי.** וַאֲנִי מֵהֵיכָן זָכִיתִי בָּהֶן "מִתּוֹךְ בְּנֵי יִשְׂרָאֵל", שֶׁיִּהְיוּ יִשְׂרָאֵל שׂוֹכְרִין אוֹתָן לְשֵׁרוּת שֶׁלִּי? עַל יְדֵי הַבְּכוֹרוֹת זָכִיתִי בָּהֶם וּלְקַחְתִּים תְּמוּרָתָם. לְפִי שֶׁהָיְתָה הָעֲבוֹדָה בַּבְּכוֹרוֹת, וּכְשֶׁחָטְאוּ בָּעֵגֶל נִפְסְלוּ, וְהַלְוִיִּם שֶׁלֹּא עָבְדוּ עֲבוֹדָה זָרָה נִבְחֲרוּ תַחְתֵּיהֶם:

טו **מִבֶּן חֹדֶשׁ וָמַעְלָה.** מִשֶּׁיָּצָא מִכְּלַל נְפָלִים הוּא נִמְנֶה לִקָּרֵא שׁוֹמֵר מִשְׁמֶרֶת הַקֹּדֶשׁ. אָמַר רַבִּי יְהוּדָה בְּרַבִּי שָׁלוֹם: לִמּוּד הוּא אוֹתוֹ הַשֵּׁבֶט לִהְיוֹת נִמְנֶה מִן הַבֶּטֶן, שֶׁנֶּאֱמַר: "אֲשֶׁר יָלְדָה אֹתָהּ לְלֵוִי בְּמִצְרָיִם" (להלן כו, נט), עִם כְּנִיסָתָהּ בְּפֶתַח מִצְרַיִם יָלְדָה אוֹתָהּ וְנִמְנֵית בְּשִׁבְעִים נָפֶשׁ, שֶׁכְּשֶׁאַתָּה מוֹנֶה חֶשְׁבּוֹנָם לֹא תִמְצָאֵם אֶלָּא שִׁבְעִים חָסֵר אַחַת, וְהִיא הִשְׁלִימָה אֶת הַמִּנְיָן:

טז **עַל פִּי ה'.** אָמַר מֹשֶׁה לִפְנֵי הַקָּדוֹשׁ בָּרוּךְ הוּא: הֵיאַךְ אֲנִי נִכְנָס לְתוֹךְ אָהֳלֵיהֶם לָדַעַת מִנְיַן יוֹנְקֵיהֶם? אָמַר לוֹ הַקָּדוֹשׁ בָּרוּךְ הוּא: עֲשֵׂה אַתָּה שֶׁלְּךָ וַאֲנִי אֶעֱשֶׂה שֶׁלִּי. הָלַךְ מֹשֶׁה וְעָמַד עַל פֶּתַח הָאֹהֶל, וְהַשְּׁכִינָה מַקְדֶּמֶת לְפָנָיו, וּבַת קוֹל יוֹצֵאת מִן הָאֹהֶל וְאוֹמֶרֶת: כָּךְ וְכָךְ תִּינוֹקוֹת יֵשׁ בְּאֹהֶל זֶה, לְכָךְ נֶאֱמַר: "עַל פִּי ה'":

לֵוִ֔י בִּשְׁמֹתָ֑ם גֵּרְשׁ֕וֹן וּקְהָ֖ת וּמְרָרִֽי: וְאֵ֛לֶּה שְׁמ֥וֹת בְּֽנֵי־גֵרְשׁ֖וֹן יח
לְמִשְׁפְּחֹתָ֑ם לִבְנִ֖י וְשִׁמְעִֽי: וּבְנֵ֥י קְהָ֖ת לְמִשְׁפְּחֹתָ֑ם עַמְרָ֣ם וְיִצְהָ֔ר יט
חֶבְר֖וֹן וְעֻזִּיאֵֽל: וּבְנֵ֥י מְרָרִ֖י לְמִשְׁפְּחֹתָ֑ם מַחְלִ֖י וּמוּשִׁ֑י אֵ֥לֶּה הֵ֛ם כ
מִשְׁפְּחֹ֥ת הַלֵּוִ֖י לְבֵ֥ית אֲבֹתָֽם: לְגֵ֣רְשׁ֔וֹן מִשְׁפַּ֨חַת֙ הַלִּבְנִ֔י וּמִשְׁפַּ֖חַת כא
הַשִּׁמְעִ֑י אֵ֣לֶּה הֵ֔ם מִשְׁפְּחֹ֖ת הַגֵּרְשֻׁנִּֽי: פְּקֻדֵיהֶם֙ בְּמִסְפַּ֣ר כָּל־זָכָ֔ר כב
מִבֶּן־חֹ֖דֶשׁ וָמָ֑עְלָה פְּקֻ֣דֵיהֶ֔ם שִׁבְעַ֥ת אֲלָפִ֖ים וַחֲמֵ֥שׁ מֵאֽוֹת:
מִשְׁפְּחֹ֖ת הַגֵּרְשֻׁנִּ֑י אַחֲרֵ֧י הַמִּשְׁכָּ֛ן יַחֲנ֖וּ יָֽמָּה: וּנְשִׂ֥יא בֵֽית־אָ֖ב כג
לַגֵּרְשֻׁנִּ֑י אֶלְיָסָ֖ף בֶּן־לָאֵֽל: וּמִשְׁמֶ֤רֶת בְּנֵֽי־גֵרְשׁוֹן֙ בְּאֹ֣הֶל מוֹעֵ֔ד כה
הַמִּשְׁכָּ֖ן וְהָאֹ֑הֶל מִכְסֵ֕הוּ וּמָסַ֕ךְ פֶּ֖תַח אֹ֥הֶל מוֹעֵֽד: וְקַלְעֵ֣י כו
הֶֽחָצֵ֗ר וְאֶת־מָסַךְ֙ פֶּ֣תַח הֶֽחָצֵ֔ר אֲשֶׁ֧ר עַל־הַמִּשְׁכָּ֛ן וְעַל־הַמִּזְבֵּ֖חַ
סָבִ֑יב וְאֵת֙ מֵֽיתָרָ֔יו לְכֹ֖ל עֲבֹדָתֽוֹ: וּלְקֵהָ֕ת מִשְׁפַּ֨חַת֙ כז
הַֽעַמְרָמִ֔י וּמִשְׁפַּ֨חַת֙ הַיִּצְהָרִ֔י וּמִשְׁפַּ֖חַת הַֽחֶבְרֹנִ֑י וּמִשְׁפַּ֖חַת
הָֽעָזִּֽיאֵלִ֑י אֵ֣לֶּה הֵ֔ם מִשְׁפְּחֹ֖ת הַקְּהָתִֽי: בְּמִסְפַּר֙ כָּל־זָכָ֔ר מִבֶּן־ כח
חֹ֖דֶשׁ וָמָ֑עְלָה שְׁמֹנַ֤ת אֲלָפִים֙ וְשֵׁ֣שׁ מֵא֔וֹת שֹׁמְרֵ֖י מִשְׁמֶ֥רֶת
הַקֹּֽדֶשׁ: מִשְׁפְּחֹ֥ת בְּנֵֽי־קְהָ֖ת יַחֲנ֑וּ עַ֛ל יֶ֥רֶךְ הַמִּשְׁכָּ֖ן תֵּימָֽנָה: וּנְשִׂ֤יא כט
בֵֽית־אָב֙ לְמִשְׁפְּחֹ֣ת הַקְּהָתִ֔י אֶלִיצָפָ֖ן בֶּן־עֻזִּיאֵֽל: וּמִשְׁמַרְתָּ֗ם לא
הָאָרֹ֤ן וְהַשֻּׁלְחָן֙ וְהַמְּנֹרָ֣ה וְהַֽמִּזְבְּחֹ֔ת וּכְלֵ֣י הַקֹּ֔דֶשׁ אֲשֶׁ֥ר יְשָׁרְת֖וּ

כא **לְגֵרְשׁוֹן מִשְׁפַּחַת הַלִּבְנִי.** כְּלוֹמַר, לְגֵרְשׁוֹן הָיוּ הַפְּקוּדִים מִשְׁפַּחַת הַלִּבְנִי וּמִשְׁפַּחַת הַשִּׁמְעִי, פְּקוּדֵיהֶם כָּךְ וְכָךְ.

כה **הַמִּשְׁכָּן.** יְרִיעוֹת הַתַּחְתּוֹנוֹת. **וְהָאֹהֶל.** יְרִיעוֹת עִזִּים הָעֲשׂוּיוֹת לְגַג. **מִכְסֵהוּ.** עוֹרוֹת אֵילִים וּתְחָשִׁים. **וּמָסַךְ פֶּתַח.** הוּא הַוִּילוֹן:

כו **וְאֵת מֵיתָרָיו.** שֶׁל מִשְׁכָּן וְהָאֹהֶל, וְלֹא שֶׁל חָצֵר:

כט **מִשְׁפַּחַת בְּנֵי קְהָת יַחֲנוּ... תֵּימָנָה.** וּסְמוּכִין לָהֶם דֶּגֶל רְאוּבֵן הַחוֹנִים תֵּימָנָה, אוֹי לָרָשָׁע וְאוֹי לִשְׁכֵנוֹ, לְכָךְ לָקוּ מֵהֶם דָּתָן וַאֲבִירָם וּמָאתַיִם וַחֲמִשִּׁים אִישׁ עִם קֹרַח וַעֲדָתוֹ, שֶׁנִּמְשְׁכוּ עִמָּהֶם בְּמַחֲלָקְתָּם:

לא **וְהַמָּסָךְ.** הִיא הַפָּרֹכֶת, שֶׁאַף הִיא קְרוּיָה "פָּרֹכֶת הַמָּסָךְ" (להלן ד, ה):

לב בָּהֶם וְהַמָּסָךְ וְכֹל עֲבֹדָתוֹ: וּנְשִׂיא נְשִׂיאֵי הַלֵּוִי אֶלְעָזָר בֶּן־אַהֲרֹן
לג הַכֹּהֵן פְּקֻדַּת שֹׁמְרֵי מִשְׁמֶרֶת הַקֹּדֶשׁ: לִמְרָרִי מִשְׁפַּחַת הַמַּחְלִי
לד וּמִשְׁפַּחַת הַמּוּשִׁי אֵלֶּה הֵם מִשְׁפְּחֹת מְרָרִי: וּפְקֻדֵיהֶם בְּמִסְפַּר
לה כָּל־זָכָר מִבֶּן־חֹדֶשׁ וָמָעְלָה שֵׁשֶׁת אֲלָפִים וּמָאתָיִם: וּנְשִׂיא
בֵית־אָב לְמִשְׁפְּחֹת מְרָרִי צוּרִיאֵל בֶּן־אֲבִיחָיִל עַל יֶרֶךְ הַמִּשְׁכָּן
לו יַחֲנוּ צָפֹנָה: וּפְקֻדַּת מִשְׁמֶרֶת בְּנֵי מְרָרִי קַרְשֵׁי הַמִּשְׁכָּן וּבְרִיחָיו
לז וְעַמֻּדָיו וַאֲדָנָיו וְכָל־כֵּלָיו וְכֹל עֲבֹדָתוֹ: וְעַמֻּדֵי הֶחָצֵר סָבִיב
וְאַדְנֵיהֶם וִיתֵדֹתָם וּמֵיתְרֵיהֶם: וְהַחֹנִים לִפְנֵי הַמִּשְׁכָּן קֵדְמָה
לח לִפְנֵי אֹהֶל־מוֹעֵד ׀ מִזְרָחָה מֹשֶׁה ׀ וְאַהֲרֹן וּבָנָיו שֹׁמְרִים מִשְׁמֶרֶת
הַמִּקְדָּשׁ לְמִשְׁמֶרֶת בְּנֵי יִשְׂרָאֵל וְהַזָּר הַקָּרֵב יוּמָת: כָּל־פְּקוּדֵי
לט הַלְוִיִּם אֲשֶׁר פָּקַד מֹשֶׁה וְאַהֲרֹן עַל־פִּי יְהוָה לְמִשְׁפְּחֹתָם כָּל־
מ זָכָר מִבֶּן־חֹדֶשׁ וָמַעְלָה שְׁנַיִם וְעֶשְׂרִים אָלֶף: ששי וַיֹּאמֶר
יְהוָה אֶל־מֹשֶׁה פְּקֹד כָּל־בְּכֹר זָכָר לִבְנֵי יִשְׂרָאֵל מִבֶּן־חֹדֶשׁ
מא וָמָעְלָה וְשָׂא אֵת מִסְפַּר שְׁמֹתָם: וְלָקַחְתָּ אֶת־הַלְוִיִּם לִי אֲנִי
יְהוָה תַּחַת כָּל־בְּכֹר בִּבְנֵי יִשְׂרָאֵל וְאֵת בֶּהֱמַת הַלְוִיִּם תַּחַת

לב | וּנְשִׂיא נְשִׂיאֵי הַלֵּוִי. מְמֻנֶּה עַל כֻּלָּם, וְעַל מָה הָיָה נְשִׂיאוּתוֹ? "פְּקֻדַּת שֹׁמְרֵי מִשְׁמֶרֶת", עַל יָדוֹ הָיָה פְּקֻדַּת כֻּלָּם:

לח | מֹשֶׁה וְאַהֲרֹן וּבָנָיו. וּסְמוּכִין לָהֶם דֶּגֶל מַחֲנֵה יְהוּדָה וְהַחוֹנִים עָלָיו יִשָּׂשכָר וּזְבוּלֻן, טוֹב לַצַּדִּיק טוֹב לִשְׁכֵנוֹ, לְפִי שֶׁהָיוּ שְׁכֵנָיו שֶׁל מֹשֶׁה שֶׁהָיָה עוֹסֵק בַּתּוֹרָה, נַעֲשׂוּ גְּדוֹלִים בַּתּוֹרָה, שֶׁנֶּאֱמַר: "יְהוּדָה מְחֹקְקִי" (תהלים ס, ט), "וּמִבְּנֵי יִשָּׂשכָר יוֹדְעֵי בִינָה וְגוֹ'" (דברי הימים א' יב, לג) מָאתַיִם רָאשֵׁי סַנְהֶדְרָאוֹת, "וּמִזְּבוּלֻן מֹשְׁכִים בְּשֵׁבֶט סֹפֵר" (שופטים ה, יד):

לט | אֲשֶׁר פָּקַד מֹשֶׁה וְאַהֲרֹן. נָקוּד עַל וְאַהֲרֹן,

לוֹמַר שֶׁלֹּא הָיָה בְּמִנְיַן הַלְוִיִּם: שְׁנַיִם וְעֶשְׂרִים אָלֶף. וּבִפְרָטָן אַתָּה מוֹצֵא שְׁלֹשׁ מֵאוֹת יְתֵרִים: בְּנֵי גֵרְשׁוֹן שִׁבְעַת אֲלָפִים וַחֲמֵשׁ מֵאוֹת, בְּנֵי קְהָת שְׁמֹנַת אֲלָפִים וְשֵׁשׁ מֵאוֹת, בְּנֵי מְרָרִי שֵׁשֶׁת אֲלָפִים וּמָאתַיִם! וְלָמָּה לֹא כְלָלָן עִם הַשְּׁאָר וְיִפְדּוּ אֶת הַבְּכוֹרוֹת, וְלֹא יִהְיוּ זְקוּקִים הַשְּׁלֹשִׁים וְשִׁבְעִים וּמָאתַיִם בְּכוֹרוֹת הָעוֹדְפִים עַל הַמִּנְיָן לְפִדְיוֹן? אָמְרוּ רַבּוֹתֵינוּ בְּמַסֶּכֶת בְּכוֹרוֹת (דף ה ע"א): אוֹתָן שְׁלֹשׁ מֵאוֹת לְוִיִּם בְּכוֹרוֹת הָיוּ, וְדַיִּם שֶׁיַּפְקִיעוּ עַצְמָם מִן הַפִּדְיוֹן:

מ | פְּקֹד כָּל בְּכֹר זָכָר וְגוֹ' מִבֶּן חֹדֶשׁ וָמַעְלָה. מִשֶּׁיָּצָא מִכְּלַל סְפֵק נְפָלִים:

פרק ג | במדבר

מב כָּל־בְּכוֹר בְּבֶהֱמַת בְּנֵי יִשְׂרָאֵל: וַיִּפְקֹד מֹשֶׁה כַּאֲשֶׁר צִוָּה יְהוָה
מג אֹתוֹ אֶת־כָּל־בְּכוֹר בִּבְנֵי יִשְׂרָאֵל: וַיְהִי כָל־בְּכוֹר זָכָר בְּמִסְפַּר שֵׁמֹת מִבֶּן־חֹדֶשׁ וָמַעְלָה לִפְקֻדֵיהֶם שְׁנַיִם וְעֶשְׂרִים אֶלֶף שְׁלֹשָׁה וְשִׁבְעִים וּמָאתָיִם:
מד וַיְדַבֵּר יְהוָה אֶל־מֹשֶׁה לֵּאמֹר: קַח אֶת־הַלְוִיִּם תַּחַת כָּל־בְּכוֹר
מה בִּבְנֵי יִשְׂרָאֵל וְאֶת־בֶּהֱמַת הַלְוִיִּם תַּחַת בְּהֶמְתָּם וְהָיוּ־לִי הַלְוִיִּם
מו אֲנִי יְהוָה: וְאֵת פְּדוּיֵי הַשְּׁלֹשָׁה וְהַשִּׁבְעִים וְהַמָּאתָיִם הָעֹדְפִים
מז עַל־הַלְוִיִּם מִבְּכוֹר בְּנֵי יִשְׂרָאֵל: וְלָקַחְתָּ חֲמֵשֶׁת שְׁקָלִים לַגֻּלְגֹּלֶת בְּשֶׁקֶל הַקֹּדֶשׁ תִּקָּח עֶשְׂרִים גֵּרָה הַשָּׁקֶל: וְנָתַתָּה
מח הַכֶּסֶף לְאַהֲרֹן וּלְבָנָיו פְּדוּיֵי הָעֹדְפִים בָּהֶם: וַיִּקַּח מֹשֶׁה אֵת
מט כֶּסֶף הַפִּדְיוֹם מֵאֵת הָעֹדְפִים עַל פְּדוּיֵי הַלְוִיִּם: מֵאֵת בְּכוֹר בְּנֵי
נ יִשְׂרָאֵל לָקַח אֶת־הַכָּסֶף חֲמִשָּׁה וְשִׁשִּׁים וּשְׁלֹשׁ מֵאוֹת וָאֶלֶף
נא בְּשֶׁקֶל הַקֹּדֶשׁ: וַיִּתֵּן מֹשֶׁה אֶת־כֶּסֶף הַפְּדֻיִם לְאַהֲרֹן וּלְבָנָיו עַל־פִּי יְהוָה כַּאֲשֶׁר צִוָּה יְהוָה אֶת־מֹשֶׁה:

מה | **וְאֶת בֶּהֱמַת הַלְוִיִּם וְגו'.** לֹא פָדוּ בֶּהֱמוֹת הַלְוִיִּם אֶת בְּכוֹרֵי בְּהֵמָה טְהוֹרָה שֶׁל יִשְׂרָאֵל, אֶלָּא אֶת פִּטְרֵי חֲמוֹרֵיהֶם, וְשֶׂה אֶחָד שֶׁל בֶּן לֵוִי פָּטַר כַּמָּה פִּטְרֵי חֲמוֹרִים שֶׁל יִשְׂרָאֵל. תֵּדַע, שֶׁהֲרֵי מָנָה הָעוֹדְפִים בָּאָדָם וְלֹא מָנָה הָעוֹדְפִים בַּבְּהֵמָה:

מו-מז | **וְאֵת פְּדוּיֵי הַשְּׁלֹשָׁה וְגו'.** וְאֵת הַבְּכוֹרוֹת הַצְּרִיכִין לְהִפָּדוֹת בָּהֶם, אֵלּוּ שְׁלֹשָׁה וְשִׁבְעִים וּמָאתַיִם הָעוֹדְפִים בָּהֶם יְתֵרִים עַל הַלְוִיִּם, מֵהֶם תִּקַּח חֲמֵשֶׁת שְׁקָלִים לַגֻּלְגֹּלֶת. כָּךְ הָיְתָה מְכִירָתוֹ שֶׁל יוֹסֵף, עֶשְׂרִים כֶּסֶף, שֶׁהָיָה בְּכוֹרָהּ שֶׁל רָחֵל:

מט | **הָעֹדְפִים עַל פְּדוּיֵי הַלְוִיִּם.** עַל אוֹתָן שֶׁפָּדוּ הַלְוִיִּם בְּגוּפָן:

נ | חֲמִשָּׁה וְשִׁשִּׁים וּשְׁלֹשׁ מֵאוֹת וָאֶלֶף. כָּךְ סְכוּם הַחֶשְׁבּוֹן: חֲמֵשֶׁת שְׁקָלִים לַגֻּלְגֹּלֶת, לְמָאתַיִם בְּכוֹרוֹת – אֶלֶף שֶׁקֶל, לְשִׁבְעִים בְּכוֹרוֹת – שְׁלֹשׁ מֵאוֹת וַחֲמִשִּׁים שֶׁקֶל, לִשְׁלֹשָׁה בְּכוֹרוֹת – חֲמִשָּׁה עָשָׂר שֶׁקֶל. אָמַר: כֵּיצַד אֶעֱשֶׂה? בְּכוֹר שֶׁאוֹמַר לוֹ: תֵּן חֲמֵשֶׁת שְׁקָלִים! יֹאמַר לִי: אֲנִי מִפְּדוּיֵי הַלְוִיִּם. מֶה עָשָׂה? הֵבִיא שְׁנַיִם וְעֶשְׂרִים אֶלֶף פְּתָקִין וְכָתַב עֲלֵיהֶן בֶּן לֵוִי, וּמָאתַיִם וְשִׁבְעִים וּשְׁלֹשָׁה פְּתָקִין כָּתַב עֲלֵיהֶן חֲמֵשֶׁת שְׁקָלִים. בְּלָלָן וּנְתָנָן בְּקַלְפִּי. אָמַר לָהֶם: בֹּאוּ וּטְלוּ פִתְקֵיכֶם לְפִי הַגּוֹרָל:

במדבר | פרק ד

שביעי

א וַיְדַבֵּ֣ר יְהֹוָ֔ה אֶל־מֹשֶׁ֥ה וְאֶֽל־אַהֲרֹ֖ן לֵאמֹֽר: ב נָשֹׂ֗א אֶת־רֹאשׁ֙ בְּנֵ֣י קְהָ֔ת מִתּ֖וֹךְ בְּנֵ֣י לֵוִ֑י לְמִשְׁפְּחֹתָ֖ם לְבֵ֥ית אֲבֹתָֽם: ג מִבֶּ֨ן שְׁלֹשִׁ֤ים שָׁנָה֙ וָמַ֔עְלָה וְעַ֖ד בֶּן־חֲמִשִּׁ֣ים שָׁנָ֑ה כָּל־בָּא֙ לַצָּבָ֔א לַעֲשׂ֥וֹת מְלָאכָ֖ה בְּאֹ֥הֶל מוֹעֵֽד: ד זֹ֛את עֲבֹדַ֥ת בְּנֵי־קְהָ֖ת בְּאֹ֣הֶל מוֹעֵ֑ד קֹ֖דֶשׁ הַקֳּדָשִֽׁים: ה וּבָ֨א אַהֲרֹ֤ן וּבָנָיו֙ בִּנְסֹ֣עַ הַֽמַּחֲנֶ֔ה וְהוֹרִ֕דוּ אֵ֖ת פָּרֹ֣כֶת הַמָּסָ֑ךְ וְכִ֨סּוּ־בָ֔הּ אֵ֖ת אֲרֹ֥ן הָעֵדֻֽת: ו וְנָתְנ֣וּ עָלָ֗יו כְּסוּי֙ ע֣וֹר תַּ֔חַשׁ וּפָרְשׂ֧וּ בֶֽגֶד־כְּלִ֛יל תְּכֵ֖לֶת מִלְמָ֑עְלָה וְשָׂמ֖וּ בַּדָּֽיו: ז וְעַ֣ל | שֻׁלְחַ֣ן הַפָּנִ֗ים יִפְרְשׂוּ֙ בֶּ֣גֶד תְּכֵ֔לֶת וְנָתְנ֣וּ עָ֠לָ֠יו אֶת־הַקְּעָרֹ֤ת וְאֶת־הַכַּפֹּת֙ וְאֶת־הַמְּנַקִּיֹּ֔ת וְאֵ֖ת קְשׂ֣וֹת הַנָּ֑סֶךְ וְלֶ֥חֶם הַתָּמִ֖יד עָלָ֥יו יִהְיֶֽה: ח וּפָרְשׂ֣וּ עֲלֵיהֶ֗ם בֶּ֚גֶד תּוֹלַ֣עַת שָׁנִ֔י וְכִסּ֣וּ אֹת֔וֹ בְּמִכְסֵ֖ה ע֣וֹר תָּ֑חַשׁ וְשָׂמ֖וּ אֶת־בַּדָּֽיו: ט וְלָקְח֣וּ | בֶּ֣גֶד תְּכֵ֗לֶת וְכִסּ֞וּ אֶת־מְנֹרַ֤ת הַמָּאוֹר֙ וְאֶת־נֵ֣רֹתֶ֔יהָ וְאֶת־מַלְקָחֶ֖יהָ וְאֶת־מַחְתֹּתֶ֑יהָ וְאֵת֙ כָּל־כְּלֵ֣י שַׁמְנָ֔הּ אֲשֶׁ֥ר יְשָׁרְתוּ־לָ֖הּ בָּהֶֽם: י וְנָתְנ֤וּ אֹתָהּ֙ וְאֶת־כָּל־כֵּלֶ֔יהָ אֶל־מִכְסֵ֖ה ע֣וֹר תָּ֑חַשׁ וְנָתְנ֖וּ עַל־הַמּֽוֹט: יא וְעַ֣ל | מִזְבַּ֣ח הַזָּהָ֗ב

פרק ד

ב) **נָשֹׂא אֶת רֹאשׁ וְגוֹ'.** מְנֵה מֵהֶם אֶת הָרְאוּיִין לַעֲבוֹדַת מַשָּׂא, וְהֵם מִבֶּן שְׁלֹשִׁים וְעַד בֶּן חֲמִשִּׁים שָׁנָה, וְהַפָּחוֹת מִשְּׁלֹשִׁים לֹא נִתְמַלֵּא כֹחוֹ, מִכָּאן אָמְרוּ: "בֶּן שְׁלֹשִׁים לַכֹּחַ" (אבות ה, כא), וְהַיּוֹתֵר עַל בֶּן חֲמִשִּׁים כֹּחוֹ מַכְחִישׁ מֵעַתָּה:

ד) **קֹדֶשׁ הַקֳּדָשִׁים.** הַמְקֻדָּשׁ שֶׁבְּכֻלָּן, הָאָרוֹן וְהַשֻּׁלְחָן וְהַמְּנוֹרָה וְהַמִּזְבְּחוֹת וְהַפָּרֹכֶת וּכְלֵי שָׁרֵת:

ה) **וּבָא אַהֲרֹן וּבָנָיו וְגוֹ'.** יַכְנִיסוּ כָּל כְּלִי וּכְלִי לְנַרְתִּיקוֹ הַמְפֹרָשׁ לוֹ בְּפָרָשָׁה זוֹ, וְלֹא יִצְטָרְכוּ הַלְוִיִּם

בְּנֵי קְהָת אֶלָּא לָשֵׂאת: **בִּנְסֹעַ הַמַּחֲנֶה.** כְּשֶׁהֶעָנָן מִסְתַּלֵּק, הֵן יוֹדְעִין שֶׁיִּסְּעוּ:

ז) **קְעָרֹת וְכַפֹּת וּקְשׂוֹת וּמְנַקִּיֹּת.** כְּבָר פֵּרַשְׁתִּים בִּמְלֶאכֶת הַמִּשְׁכָּן (שמות כה, כט): **הַנָּסֶךְ.** הַכִּסּוּי, לְשׁוֹן מָסָךְ, כְּדִכְתִיב: "אֲשֶׁר יֻסַּךְ בָּהֵן" (שם):

ט) **מַלְקָחֶיהָ.** כְּמִין צְבָת שֶׁמּוֹשֵׁךְ בָּהּ אֶת הַפְּתִילָה לְכָל צַד שֶׁיִּרְצֶה: **מַחְתֹּתֶיהָ.** כְּמִין כַּף קְטַנָּה וְשׁוּלֶיהָ פְּשׁוּטִין וְלֹא סְגַלְגַּלִּים וְאֵין לָהּ מְחִצָּה לְפָנֶיהָ אֶלָּא מִצִּדֶּיהָ, וְחוֹתֶה בָּהּ אֶת דֶּשֶׁן הַנֵּרוֹת כְּשֶׁמֵּטִיבָן: **נֵרֹתֶיהָ.** לוע"ז בְּלַעַז, שֶׁנּוֹתְנִים בָּהֶן הַשֶּׁמֶן וְהַפְּתִילוֹת:

י) **אֶל מִכְסֵה עוֹר תַּחַשׁ.** כְּמִין מַרְצוּף:

יִפְרְשׂוּ בֶּגֶד תְּכֵלֶת וְכִסּוּ אֹתוֹ בְּמִכְסֵה עוֹר תָּחַשׁ וְשָׂמוּ אֶת־
בַּדָּיו: וְלָקְחוּ אֶת־כָּל־כְּלֵי הַשָּׁרֵת אֲשֶׁר יְשָׁרְתוּ־בָם בַּקֹּדֶשׁ
וְנָתְנוּ אֶל־בֶּגֶד תְּכֵלֶת וְכִסּוּ אוֹתָם בְּמִכְסֵה עוֹר תָּחַשׁ וְנָתְנוּ
עַל־הַמּוֹט: וְדִשְּׁנוּ אֶת־הַמִּזְבֵּחַ וּפָרְשׂוּ עָלָיו בֶּגֶד אַרְגָּמָן: וְנָתְנוּ
עָלָיו אֶת־כָּל־כֵּלָיו אֲשֶׁר יְשָׁרְתוּ עָלָיו בָּהֶם אֶת־הַמַּחְתֹּת אֶת־
הַמִּזְלָגֹת וְאֶת־הַיָּעִים וְאֶת־הַמִּזְרָקֹת כֹּל כְּלֵי הַמִּזְבֵּחַ וּפָרְשׂוּ
עָלָיו כְּסוּי עוֹר תַּחַשׁ וְשָׂמוּ בַדָּיו: וְכִלָּה אַהֲרֹן־וּבָנָיו לְכַסֹּת
אֶת־הַקֹּדֶשׁ וְאֶת־כָּל־כְּלֵי הַקֹּדֶשׁ בִּנְסֹעַ הַמַּחֲנֶה וְאַחֲרֵי־כֵן
יָבֹאוּ בְנֵי־קְהָת לָשֵׂאת וְלֹא־יִגְּעוּ אֶל־הַקֹּדֶשׁ וָמֵתוּ אֵלֶּה מַשָּׂא
בְנֵי־קְהָת בְּאֹהֶל מוֹעֵד: וּפְקֻדַּת אֶלְעָזָר ׀ בֶּן־אַהֲרֹן הַכֹּהֵן שֶׁמֶן
הַמָּאוֹר וּקְטֹרֶת הַסַּמִּים וּמִנְחַת הַתָּמִיד וְשֶׁמֶן הַמִּשְׁחָה פְּקֻדַּת
כָּל־הַמִּשְׁכָּן וְכָל־אֲשֶׁר־בּוֹ בְּקֹדֶשׁ וּבְכֵלָיו:

יב) אֶת כָּל כְּלֵי הַשָּׁרֵת אֲשֶׁר יְשָׁרְתוּ בָם בַּקֹּדֶשׁ. בְּתוֹךְ הַמִּשְׁכָּן שֶׁהוּא קֹדֶשׁ, וְהֵן כְּלֵי הַקְּטֹרֶת שֶׁמְּשָׁרְתִין בָּהֶם בַּמִּזְבֵּחַ הַפְּנִימִי:

יג) וְדִשְּׁנוּ אֶת הַמִּזְבֵּחַ. מִזְבַּח הַנְּחֹשֶׁת. וְדִשְּׁנוּ. יִטְּלוּ אֶת הַדֶּשֶׁן מֵעָלָיו: וּפָרְשׂוּ עָלָיו בֶּגֶד אַרְגָּמָן. וְאֵשׁ שֶׁיָּרְדָה מִן הַשָּׁמַיִם רְבוּצָה תַּחַת הַבֶּגֶד כַּאֲרִי בִּשְׁעַת הַמַּסָּעוֹת, וְאֵינָהּ שׂוֹרַפְתּוֹ, שֶׁהָיוּ כוֹפִין עָלֶיהָ פְּסַכְתֵּר שֶׁל נְחֹשֶׁת:

יד) מַחְתֹּת. שֶׁבָּהֶן חוֹתִין גֶּחָלִים לִתְרוּמַת הַדֶּשֶׁן. עֲשׂוּיָה כְּמִין מַחֲבַת שֶׁאֵין לָהּ אֶלָּא שׁוּלַיִם מִלְּמַטָּה וּמְלַפָּנֶיהָ שׁוֹאֶבֶת אֶת הַגֶּחָלִים: מִזְלָגֹת. עֲגוּדוֹת שֶׁל נְחֹשֶׁת שֶׁבָּהֶן מַכִּין בָּאֵבָרִים שֶׁעַל הַמִּזְבֵּחַ לְהַפְּכָן כְּדֵי שֶׁיִּתְעַכְּלוּ יָפֶה וּמַהֵר: יָעִים. הֵם מַגְרֵפוֹת, וּבְלַעַ"

ז וודי"ל, וְהֵן שֶׁל נְחֹשֶׁת, וּבָהֶן מְכַבְּדִין אֶת הַדֶּשֶׁן מֵעַל הַמִּזְבֵּחַ:

טו) לְכַסֹּת אֶת הַקֹּדֶשׁ. הָאָרוֹן וְהַמִּזְבֵּחַ: וְאֶת כָּל כְּלֵי הַקֹּדֶשׁ. הַמְּנוֹרָה וּכְלֵי שָׁרֵת: וָמֵתוּ. שֶׁאִם יִגְּעוּ חַיָּבִין מִיתָה בִּידֵי שָׁמַיִם:

טז) וּפְקֻדַּת אֶלְעָזָר. שֶׁהוּא מְמֻנֶּה עֲלֵיהֶם לָשֵׂאת אוֹתָם, שֶׁמֶן וּקְטֹרֶת וְשֶׁמֶן הַמִּשְׁחָה וּמִנְחַת הַתָּמִיד, עָלָיו מֻטָּל לָצַוּוֹת וּלְזָרֵז וּלְהַקְרִיב בְּעֵת חֲנָיָתָן: פְּקֻדַּת כָּל הַמִּשְׁכָּן. וְעוֹד הָיָה מְמֻנֶּה עַל מַשָּׂא בְּנֵי קְהָת, לְצַוּוֹת אִישׁ אִישׁ עַל עֲבוֹדָתוֹ וְעַל מַשָּׂאוֹ, וְהוּא הַמִּשְׁכָּן וְכָל אֲשֶׁר בּוֹ, כָּל הַסְּדוּרִים לְמַעְלָה בְּפָרָשָׁה זוֹ. אֲבָל מַשָּׂא בְּנֵי גֵרְשׁוֹן וּמְרָרִי, שֶׁאֵינָן מִקָּדְשֵׁי הַקָּדָשִׁים, עַל פִּי אִיתָמָר הָיָה, כְּמוֹ שֶׁכָּתוּב בְּפָרָשַׁת "נָשֹׂא" (להלן ד, כח; לג):

במדבר | פרק ד | נשא

יח וַיְדַבֵּ֥ר יְהֹוָ֖ה אֶל־מֹשֶׁ֥ה וְאֶֽל־אַהֲרֹ֖ן לֵאמֹֽר: אַל־תַּכְרִ֕יתוּ אֶת־ שֵׁ֖בֶט מִשְׁפְּחֹ֣ת הַקְּהָתִ֑י מִתּ֖וֹךְ הַלְוִיִּֽם: וְזֹ֣את ׀ עֲשׂ֣וּ לָהֶ֗ם וְחָיוּ֙ וְלֹ֣א יָמֻ֔תוּ בְּגִשְׁתָּ֖ם אֶת־קֹ֣דֶשׁ הַקֳּדָשִׁ֑ים אַהֲרֹ֤ן וּבָנָיו֙ יָבֹ֔אוּ וְשָׂמ֣וּ אוֹתָ֔ם אִ֥ישׁ אִ֖ישׁ עַל־עֲבֹדָת֖וֹ וְאֶל־מַשָּׂאֽוֹ: וְלֹא־יָבֹ֧אוּ לִרְא֛וֹת כְּבַלַּ֥ע אֶת־הַקֹּ֖דֶשׁ וָמֵֽתוּ:

כב וַיְדַבֵּ֥ר יְהֹוָ֖ה אֶל־מֹשֶׁ֥ה לֵּאמֹֽר: נָשֹׂ֗א אֶת־רֹ֛אשׁ בְּנֵ֥י גֵרְשׁ֖וֹן גַּם־ **נשא** הֵ֑ם לְבֵ֥ית אֲבֹתָ֖ם לְמִשְׁפְּחֹתָֽם: מִבֶּן֩ שְׁלֹשִׁ֨ים שָׁנָ֜ה וָמַ֗עְלָה עַ֛ד בֶּן־חֲמִשִּׁ֥ים שָׁנָ֖ה תִּפְקֹ֣ד אוֹתָ֑ם כָּל־הַבָּא֙ לִצְבֹ֣א צָבָ֔א לַעֲבֹ֥ד עֲבֹדָ֖ה בְּאֹ֥הֶל מוֹעֵֽד: זֹ֣את עֲבֹדַ֔ת מִשְׁפְּחֹ֖ת הַגֵּרְשֻׁנִּ֑י לַעֲבֹ֖ד וּלְמַשָּֽׂא: וְנָ֨שְׂא֜וּ אֶת־יְרִיעֹ֤ת הַמִּשְׁכָּן֙ וְאֶת־אֹ֣הֶל מוֹעֵ֔ד מִכְסֵ֕הוּ וּמִכְסֵ֛ה הַתַּ֥חַשׁ אֲשֶׁר־עָלָ֖יו מִלְמָ֑עְלָה וְאֶ֨ת־מָסַ֔ךְ פֶּ֖תַח אֹ֥הֶל מוֹעֵֽד: וְאֵת֩ קַלְעֵ֨י הֶחָצֵ֜ר וְאֶת־מָסַ֣ךְ ׀ פֶּ֣תַח ׀ שַׁ֣עַר הֶחָצֵ֗ר אֲשֶׁ֨ר עַל־הַמִּשְׁכָּ֤ן וְעַל־הַמִּזְבֵּ֨חַ֙ סָבִ֔יב וְאֵת֙ מֵ֣יתְרֵיהֶ֔ם וְאֶֽת־ כָּל־כְּלֵ֖י עֲבֹדָתָ֑ם וְאֵ֨ת כָּל־אֲשֶׁ֧ר יֵעָשֶׂ֛ה לָהֶ֖ם וְעָבָֽדוּ: עַל־פִּי֩ אַהֲרֹ֨ן וּבָנָ֜יו תִּהְיֶ֗ה כָּל־עֲבֹדַת֙ בְּנֵ֣י הַגֵּרְשֻׁנִּ֔י לְכָל־מַשָּׂאָ֖ם וּלְכֹ֣ל עֲבֹדָתָ֑ם וּפְקַדְתֶּ֤ם עֲלֵהֶם֙ בְּמִשְׁמֶ֔רֶת אֵ֖ת כָּל־מַשָּׂאָֽם: זֹ֣את

יח) **אל תכריתו.** אל תגרמו להם שימותו:

כ) **ולא יבואו לראות כבלע את הקדש.** לתוך נרתיק שלו, כמו שפרשתי למעלה בפרשה זו (פסוק ה), ופרשו עליו בגד פלוני וכסו אותו במכסה פלוני, ובלוע שלו הוא כסויו:

כב) **נשא את ראש בני גרשון גם הם.** כמו שצויתיך על בני קהת, לראות כמה יש שהגיעו לכלל עבודה:

כה) **את יריעות המשכן.** עשר תחתונות: **ואת אהל מועד.** יריעות עזים העשויות לאהל עליו: **מכסהו.** עורות אילים מאדמים: **מסך פתח.** וילון המזרחי:

כו) **אשר על המשכן.** כלומר: הקלעים והמסך של חצר, הסוככים ומגנים על המשכן ועל מזבח הנחשת סביב: **ואת כל אשר יעשה להם.** כתרגומו: "וית כל די יתמסר להון", לבני גרשון:

כז) **על פי אהרן ובניו.** ואי זה מהבנים ממונה עליהם? "בְּיַד אִיתָמָר בֶּן אַהֲרֹן הַכֹּהֵן" (להלן פסוק כח):

עֲבֹדַת מִשְׁפְּחֹת בְּנֵי הַגֵּרְשֻׁנִּי בְּאֹהֶל מוֹעֵד וּמִשְׁמַרְתָּם בְּיַד
אִיתָמָר בֶּן־אַהֲרֹן הַכֹּהֵן: בְּנֵי מְרָרִי לְמִשְׁפְּחֹתָם
לְבֵית־אֲבֹתָם תִּפְקֹד אֹתָם: מִבֶּן שְׁלֹשִׁים שָׁנָה וָמַעְלָה וְעַד
בֶּן־חֲמִשִּׁים שָׁנָה תִּפְקְדֵם כָּל־הַבָּא לַצָּבָא לַעֲבֹד אֶת־עֲבֹדַת
אֹהֶל מוֹעֵד: וְזֹאת מִשְׁמֶרֶת מַשָּׂאָם לְכָל־עֲבֹדָתָם בְּאֹהֶל
מוֹעֵד קַרְשֵׁי הַמִּשְׁכָּן וּבְרִיחָיו וְעַמּוּדָיו וַאֲדָנָיו: וְעַמּוּדֵי הֶחָצֵר
סָבִיב וְאַדְנֵיהֶם וִיתֵדֹתָם וּמֵיתְרֵיהֶם לְכָל־כְּלֵיהֶם וּלְכֹל עֲבֹדָתָם
וּבְשֵׁמֹת תִּפְקְדוּ אֶת־כְּלֵי מִשְׁמֶרֶת מַשָּׂאָם: זֹאת עֲבֹדַת
מִשְׁפְּחֹת בְּנֵי מְרָרִי לְכָל־עֲבֹדָתָם בְּאֹהֶל מוֹעֵד בְּיַד אִיתָמָר
בֶּן־אַהֲרֹן הַכֹּהֵן: וַיִּפְקֹד מֹשֶׁה וְאַהֲרֹן וּנְשִׂיאֵי הָעֵדָה אֶת־בְּנֵי
הַקְּהָתִי לְמִשְׁפְּחֹתָם וּלְבֵית אֲבֹתָם: מִבֶּן שְׁלֹשִׁים שָׁנָה וָמַעְלָה
וְעַד בֶּן־חֲמִשִּׁים שָׁנָה כָּל־הַבָּא לַצָּבָא לַעֲבֹדָה בְּאֹהֶל מוֹעֵד:
וַיִּהְיוּ פְקֻדֵיהֶם לְמִשְׁפְּחֹתָם אַלְפַּיִם שְׁבַע מֵאוֹת וַחֲמִשִּׁים: אֵלֶּה
פְקוּדֵי מִשְׁפְּחֹת הַקְּהָתִי כָּל־הָעֹבֵד בְּאֹהֶל מוֹעֵד אֲשֶׁר פָּקַד
מֹשֶׁה וְאַהֲרֹן עַל־פִּי יהוה בְּיַד־מֹשֶׁה: וּפְקוּדֵי בְּנֵי
גֵרְשׁוֹן לְמִשְׁפְּחוֹתָם וּלְבֵית אֲבֹתָם: מִבֶּן שְׁלֹשִׁים שָׁנָה וָמַעְלָה
וְעַד בֶּן־חֲמִשִּׁים שָׁנָה כָּל־הַבָּא לַצָּבָא לַעֲבֹדָה בְּאֹהֶל מוֹעֵד:
וַיִּהְיוּ פְקֻדֵיהֶם לְמִשְׁפְּחֹתָם לְבֵית אֲבֹתָם אַלְפַּיִם וְשֵׁשׁ מֵאוֹת

לב | וִיתֵדֹתָם וּמֵיתְרֵיהֶם. שֶׁל עַמּוּדִים, שֶׁהֲרֵי יְתֵדוֹת וּמֵיתְרֵי הַקְּלָעִים בְּמַשָּׂא בְּנֵי גֵרְשׁוֹן הָיוּ, וִיתֵדוֹת וּמֵיתָרִים הָיוּ לַיְרִיעוֹת וְלַקְּלָעִים מִלְּמַטָּה שֶׁלֹּא תַּגְבִּיהֵם הָרוּחַ, וִיתֵדוֹת וּמֵיתָרִים הָיוּ לָעַמּוּדִים סָבִיב לִתְלוֹת בָּהֶם הַקְּלָעִים בִּשְׂפָתָם הָעֶלְיוֹנָה בִּכְלוֹנְסוֹת וְקֻנְטֵיסִין, כְּמוֹ שֶׁשְּׁנוּיָה בִּמְלֶאכֶת הַמִּשְׁכָּן

(ברייתא דמלאכת המשכן פרק ה):

במדבר | פרק ה

מא וּשְׁלֹשִׁים: אֵ֚לֶּה פְּקוּדֵי֙ מִשְׁפְּחֹ֣ת בְּנֵ֣י גֵרְשׁ֔וֹן כָּל־הָעֹבֵ֖ד בְּאֹ֣הֶל
מב מוֹעֵ֑ד אֲשֶׁ֨ר פָּקַ֥ד מֹשֶׁ֛ה וְאַהֲרֹ֖ן עַל־פִּ֥י יְהוָֹֽה: וּפְקוּדֵ֕י מִשְׁפְּחֹ֖ת
מג בְּנֵ֣י מְרָרִ֑י לְמִשְׁפְּחֹתָ֖ם לְבֵ֣ית אֲבֹתָֽם: מִבֶּ֨ן שְׁלֹשִׁ֤ים שָׁנָה֙ וָמַ֔עְלָה
וְעַ֖ד בֶּן־חֲמִשִּׁ֣ים שָׁנָ֑ה כָּל־הַבָּא֙ לַצָּבָ֔א לַעֲבֹדָ֖ה בְּאֹ֥הֶל מוֹעֵֽד:
מד וַיִּֽהְי֥וּ פְקֻדֵיהֶ֖ם לְמִשְׁפְּחֹתָ֑ם שְׁלֹ֥שֶׁת אֲלָפִ֖ים וּמָאתָֽיִם: אֵ֣לֶּה
מה פְקוּדֵי֙ מִשְׁפְּחֹ֣ת בְּנֵ֣י מְרָרִ֔י אֲשֶׁ֨ר פָּקַ֥ד מֹשֶׁ֛ה וְאַהֲרֹ֖ן עַל־פִּ֥י
מו יְהוָֹ֖ה בְּיַד־מֹשֶֽׁה: כָּל־הַפְּקֻדִ֡ים אֲשֶׁר֩ פָּקַ֨ד מֹשֶׁ֤ה וְאַהֲרֹן֙ וּנְשִׂיאֵ֣י
יִשְׂרָאֵ֔ל אֶת־הַֽלְוִיִּ֑ם לְמִשְׁפְּחֹתָ֖ם וּלְבֵ֣ית אֲבֹתָֽם: מִבֶּ֨ן שְׁלֹשִׁ֤ים
מז שָׁנָה֙ וָמַ֔עְלָה וְעַ֖ד בֶּן־חֲמִשִּׁ֣ים שָׁנָ֑ה כָּל־הַבָּ֗א לַעֲבֹ֤ד עֲבֹדַ֤ת
עֲבֹדָה֙ וַעֲבֹדַ֣ת מַשָּׂ֔א בְּאֹ֖הֶל מוֹעֵֽד: וַיִּֽהְי֖וּ פְקֻדֵיהֶ֑ם שְׁמֹנַ֣ת
מח אֲלָפִ֔ים וַחֲמֵ֥שׁ מֵא֖וֹת וּשְׁמֹנִֽים: עַל־פִּ֨י יְהוָֹ֜ה פָּקַ֤ד אוֹתָם֙ בְּיַד־
מט מֹשֶׁ֔ה אִ֥ישׁ אִ֛ישׁ עַל־עֲבֹדָת֖וֹ וְעַל־מַשָּׂא֑וֹ וּפְקֻדָ֕יו אֲשֶׁר־צִוָּ֥ה
יְהוָֹ֖ה אֶת־מֹשֶֽׁה:

שלישי
ה א וַיְדַבֵּ֥ר יְהוָֹ֖ה אֶל־מֹשֶׁ֥ה לֵּאמֹֽר: צַ֚ו אֶת־בְּנֵ֣י יִשְׂרָאֵ֔ל וִֽישַׁלְּחוּ֙ מִן־
ב
ג הַֽמַּחֲנֶ֔ה כָּל־צָר֖וּעַ וְכָל־זָ֑ב וְכֹ֖ל טָמֵ֥א לָנָֽפֶשׁ: מִזָּכָ֤ר עַד־נְקֵבָה֙

מז] **עבדת עבדה.** הוּא הַשִּׁיר בִּמְצִלְתַּיִם וְכִנּוֹרוֹת, שֶׁהִיא עֲבוֹדָה לַעֲבוֹדָה אַחֶרֶת. **ועבדת משא.** כְּמַשְׁמָעוֹ:

מט] **ופקדיו אשר צוה ה' את משה.** וְאוֹתָן הַפְּקוּדִים הָיוּ בַּמַּעְלָה מִבֶּן שְׁלֹשִׁים שָׁנָה וְעַד בֶּן חֲמִשִּׁים:

פרק ה

ב] **צו את בני ישראל וגו'.** פָּרָשָׁה זוֹ נֶאֶמְרָה בַּיּוֹם שֶׁהוּקַם הַמִּשְׁכָּן, וּשְׁמוֹנֶה פָּרָשִׁיּוֹת נֶאֶמְרוּ בּוֹ בַּיּוֹם, כִּדְאִיתָא בְּמַסֶּכֶת גִּטִּין בְּפֶרֶק הַנִּזָּקִין (דף ס ע"א). **וישלחו מן המחנה.** שָׁלֹשׁ מַחֲנוֹת הָיוּ שָׁם בִּשְׁעַת חֲנִיָּתָן: תּוֹךְ הַקְּלָעִים הִיא מַחֲנֵה שְׁכִינָה, חֲנִיַּת

הַלְוִיִּם סָבִיב כְּמוֹ שֶׁמְּפוֹרָשׁ בְּפָרָשַׁת בְּמִדְבַּר סִינַי (לעיל א, נ) הִיא מַחֲנֵה לְוִיָּה, וּמִשָּׁם וְעַד סוֹף מַחֲנֵה הַדְּגָלִים לְכָל אַרְבַּע הָרוּחוֹת הִיא מַחֲנֵה יִשְׂרָאֵל. הַצָּרוּעַ נִשְׁתַּלַּח חוּץ לְכֻלָּן, הַזָּב מֻתָּר בְּמַחֲנֵה יִשְׂרָאֵל וּמְשֻׁלָּח מִן הַשְּׁתַּיִם, וְטָמֵא לָנֶפֶשׁ מֻתָּר אַף בְּשֶׁל לְוִיָּה וְאֵינוֹ מְשֻׁלָּח אֶלָּא מִשֶּׁל שְׁכִינָה. וְכָל זֶה דָּרְשׁוּ רַבּוֹתֵינוּ מִן הַמִּקְרָאוֹת בְּמַסֶּכֶת פְּסָחִים (דף סז ע"א): **טמא לנפש.** לְטָמֵי נַפְשָׁא דֶּאֱנָשָׁא, חוֹמֵר אֲנִי שֶׁהוּא לְשׁוֹן עַצְמוֹת אָדָם בִּלְשׁוֹן אֲרַמִּי. וְהַרְבֵּה יֵשׁ בִּבְרֵאשִׁית רַבָּה: "אַדְרִיָּנוּס שְׁחִיק טְמַיָּא", שְׁחִיק עֲצָמוֹת:

תְּשַׁלְּח֖וּ אֶל־מִח֣וּץ לַֽמַּחֲנֶ֑ה תְּשַׁלְּח֔וּם וְלֹ֤א יְטַמְּאוּ֙ אֶת־מַ֣חֲנֵיהֶ֔ם אֲשֶׁ֥ר אֲנִ֖י שֹׁכֵ֥ן בְּתוֹכָֽם: וַיַּֽעֲשׂוּ־כֵן֙ בְּנֵ֣י יִשְׂרָאֵ֔ל וַיְשַׁלְּח֣וּ אוֹתָ֔ם אֶל־מִח֖וּץ לַֽמַּחֲנֶ֑ה כַּאֲשֶׁ֨ר דִּבֶּ֤ר יְהֹוָה֙ אֶל־מֹשֶׁ֔ה כֵּ֥ן עָשׂ֖וּ בְּנֵ֥י יִשְׂרָאֵֽל:

ה וַיְדַבֵּ֥ר יְהֹוָ֖ה אֶל־מֹשֶׁ֥ה לֵּאמֹֽר: דַּבֵּר֮ אֶל־בְּנֵ֣י יִשְׂרָאֵל֒ אִ֣ישׁ אֽוֹ־אִשָּׁ֗ה כִּ֤י יַעֲשׂוּ֙ מִכָּל־חַטֹּ֣את הָֽאָדָ֔ם לִמְעֹ֥ל מַ֖עַל בַּֽיהֹוָ֑ה וְאָֽשְׁמָ֖ה הַנֶּ֥פֶשׁ הַהִֽוא: ז וְהִתְוַדּ֗וּ אֶת־חַטָּאתָם֮ אֲשֶׁ֣ר עָשׂוּ֒ וְהֵשִׁ֤יב אֶת־אֲשָׁמוֹ֙ בְּרֹאשׁ֔וֹ וַחֲמִֽישִׁת֖וֹ יֹסֵ֣ף עָלָ֑יו וְנָתַ֕ן לַאֲשֶׁ֖ר אָשַׁ֥ם לֽוֹ: ח וְאִם־אֵ֨ין לָאִ֜ישׁ גֹּאֵ֗ל לְהָשִׁ֤יב הָאָשָׁם֙ אֵלָ֔יו הָאָשָׁ֛ם הַמּוּשָׁ֥ב לַיהֹוָ֖ה לַכֹּהֵ֑ן מִלְּבַ֗ד אֵ֚יל הַכִּפֻּרִ֔ים אֲשֶׁ֥ר יְכַפֶּר־בּ֖וֹ עָלָֽיו: ט וְכָל־תְּרוּמָ֞ה לְכָל־קָדְשֵׁ֧י בְנֵי־יִשְׂרָאֵ֛ל אֲשֶׁר־יַקְרִ֥יבוּ לַכֹּהֵ֖ן ל֥וֹ יִהְיֶֽה: י וְאִ֥ישׁ אֶת־קֳדָשָׁ֖יו ל֣וֹ יִֽהְי֑וּ אִ֛ישׁ אֲשֶׁר־יִתֵּ֥ן לַכֹּהֵ֖ן ל֥וֹ יִהְיֶֽה:

ו לִמְעֹל מַעַל בַּה׳. הֲרֵי חָזַר וְכָתַב כָּאן פָּרָשַׁת גּוֹזֵל וְנִשְׁבַּע עַל שֶׁקֶר, הִיא הָאֲמוּרָה בְּפָרָשַׁת וַיִּקְרָא: "וּמָעֲלָה מַעַל בַּה׳ וְכִחֵשׁ בַּעֲמִיתוֹ" וְגוֹ׳ (ויקרא ה, כא). וְנִשְׁנֵית כָּאן בִּשְׁבִיל שְׁנֵי דְבָרִים שֶׁנִּתְחַדְּשׁוּ בָּהּ: הָאֶחָד — שֶׁכָּתַב "וְהִתְוַדּוּ" (להלן פסוק ז), לִמֵּד שֶׁאֵינוֹ חַיָּב חֹמֶשׁ וְאָשָׁם עַל פִּי עֵדִים עַד שֶׁיּוֹדֶה בַּדָּבָר; וְהַשֵּׁנִי — שֶׁפֵּרַשׁ עַל גֵּזֶל הַגֵּר שֶׁהוּא נָתוּן לַכֹּהֲנִים:

ז אֶת אֲשָׁמוֹ בְּרֹאשׁוֹ. הוּא הַקֶּרֶן שֶׁנִּשְׁבַּע עָלָיו: לַאֲשֶׁר אָשַׁם לוֹ. לְמִי שֶׁנִּתְחַיֵּב לוֹ:

ח וְאִם אֵין לָאִישׁ גֹּאֵל. שֶׁמֵּת הַתּוֹבֵעַ שֶׁהִשְׁבִּיעוֹ וְאֵין לוֹ יוֹרְשִׁים: לְהָשִׁיב הָאָשָׁם אֵלָיו. כְּשֶׁנִּמְלַךְ זֶה לְהִתְוַדּוֹת עַל עֲוֹנוֹ. וְאָמְרוּ רַבּוֹתֵינוּ: וְכִי יֵשׁ לְךָ אָדָם בְּיִשְׂרָאֵל שֶׁאֵין לוֹ גּוֹאֲלִים, אוֹ בֵן אוֹ בַת אוֹ אָח אוֹ שְׁאָר בָּשָׂר הַקָּרוֹב מִמִּשְׁפַּחַת אָבִיו לְמַעְלָה עַד יַעֲקֹב? אֶלָּא זֶה הַגֵּר שֶׁמֵּת וְאֵין לוֹ יוֹרְשִׁים: הָאָשָׁם הַמּוּשָׁב. זֶה הַקֶּרֶן וְהַחֹמֶשׁ: לַה׳ לַכֹּהֵן. קְנָאוֹ הַשֵּׁם

וּנְתָנוֹ לַכֹּהֵן שֶׁבְּאוֹתוֹ מִשְׁמָר: מִלְּבַד אֵיל הַכִּפֻּרִים. הָאָמוּר בְּ"וַיִּקְרָא" (ה, כה), שֶׁהוּא צָרִיךְ לְהָבִיא:

ט וְכָל תְּרוּמָה וְגוֹ׳. אָמַר רַבִּי יִשְׁמָעֵאל, וְכִי תְרוּמָה מַקְרִיבִין לַכֹּהֵן? וַהֲלֹא הוּא הַמְחַזֵּר אַחֲרֶיהָ לְבֵית הַגֳּרָנוֹת, וּמַה תַּלְמוּד לוֹמַר: "אֲשֶׁר יַקְרִיבוּ לַכֹּהֵן"? אֵלּוּ הַבִּכּוּרִים, שֶׁנֶּאֱמַר בָּהֶם: "תָּבִיא בֵּית ה׳ אֱלֹהֶיךָ" (שמות כג, יט), וְאֵינִי יוֹדֵעַ מַה יֵּעָשֶׂה בָּהֶם, תַּלְמוּד לוֹמַר: "לַכֹּהֵן לוֹ יִהְיֶה", בָּא הַכָּתוּב וְלִמֵּד עַל הַבִּכּוּרִים שֶׁיִּהְיוּ נִתָּנִין לַכֹּהֵן:

י וְאִישׁ אֶת קֳדָשָׁיו לוֹ יִהְיוּ. לְפִי שֶׁנֶּאֶמְרוּ מַתְּנוֹת כְּהֻנָּה וּלְוִיָּה, יָכוֹל יָבוֹאוּ וְיִטְּלוּם בְּזְרוֹעַ? תַּלְמוּד לוֹמַר: "וְאִישׁ אֶת קֳדָשָׁיו לוֹ יִהְיוּ", מַגִּיד שֶׁטּוֹבַת הֲנָאָתָן לַבְּעָלִים. וְעוֹד מִדְרָשִׁים הַרְבֵּה דָּרְשׁוּ בוֹ בְּסִפְרֵי (י). וּמִדְרַשׁ אַגָּדָה: "וְאִישׁ אֶת קֳדָשָׁיו לוֹ יִהְיוּ", מִי שֶׁמְּעַכֵּב מַעַשְׂרוֹתָיו וְאֵינוֹ נוֹתְנָן, לוֹ יִהְיוּ הַמַּעַשְׂרוֹת, סוֹף שֶׁאֵין שָׂדֵהוּ עוֹשָׂה אֶלָּא אֶחָד

יב וַיְדַבֵּ֥ר יְהוָ֖ה אֶל־מֹשֶׁ֥ה לֵּאמֹֽר: דַּבֵּר֙ אֶל־בְּנֵ֣י יִשְׂרָאֵ֔ל וְאָמַרְתָּ֖ ה רביעי
יג אֲלֵהֶ֑ם אִ֣ישׁ אִ֗ישׁ כִּֽי־תִשְׂטֶ֤ה אִשְׁתּוֹ֙ וּמָעֲלָ֥ה ב֖וֹ מָֽעַל: וְשָׁכַ֨ב
אִ֣ישׁ אֹתָ֗הּ שִׁכְבַת־זֶ֨רַע֙ וְנֶעְלַם֙ מֵעֵינֵ֣י אִישָׁ֔הּ וְנִסְתְּרָ֖ה וְהִ֣יא
יד נִטְמָ֑אָה וְעֵד֙ אֵ֣ין בָּ֔הּ וְהִ֖וא לֹ֥א נִתְפָּֽשָׂה: וְעָבַ֨ר עָלָ֤יו רֽוּחַ־קִנְאָה֙
וְקִנֵּ֣א אֶת־אִשְׁתּ֔וֹ וְהִ֖וא נִטְמָ֑אָה אוֹ־עָבַ֨ר עָלָ֤יו רֽוּחַ־קִנְאָה֙ וְקִנֵּ֣א
טו אֶת־אִשְׁתּ֔וֹ וְהִ֖יא לֹ֥א נִטְמָֽאָה: וְהֵבִ֨יא הָאִ֣ישׁ אֶת־אִשְׁתּוֹ֮ אֶל־
הַכֹּהֵן֒ וְהֵבִ֤יא אֶת־קָרְבָּנָהּ֙ עָלֶ֔יהָ עֲשִׂירִ֥ת הָאֵיפָ֖ה קֶ֣מַח שְׂעֹרִ֑ים
לֹֽא־יִצֹ֨ק עָלָ֜יו שֶׁ֗מֶן וְלֹֽא־יִתֵּ֤ן עָלָיו֙ לְבֹנָ֔ה כִּֽי־מִנְחַ֤ת קְנָאֹת֙ ה֔וּא
טז מִנְחַ֥ת זִכָּר֖וֹן מַזְכֶּ֥רֶת עָוֹֽן: וְהִקְרִ֥יב אֹתָ֖הּ הַכֹּהֵ֑ן וְהֶֽעֱמִדָ֖הּ לִפְנֵ֥י
יז יְהוָֽה: וְלָקַ֧ח הַכֹּהֵ֛ן מַ֥יִם קְדֹשִׁ֖ים בִּכְלִי־חָ֑רֶשׂ וּמִן־הֶֽעָפָ֗ר אֲשֶׁ֤ר
יח יִהְיֶה֙ בְּקַרְקַ֣ע הַמִּשְׁכָּ֔ן יִקַּ֥ח הַכֹּהֵ֖ן וְנָתַ֥ן אֶל־הַמָּֽיִם: וְהֶעֱמִ֨יד

מַעֲשֶׂ֣רָה שֶׁהָיְתָ֣ה לְמוּדָ֣ה לַעֲשׂוֹת. "אִישׁ אֲשֶׁר יִתֵּן
לַכֹּהֵן" מַתְּנוֹת הָרְאוּיוֹת לוֹ, "לוֹ יִהְיֶה" מָמוֹן הַרְבֵּה:

יב | אִישׁ אִישׁ כִּי תִשְׂטֶה אִשְׁתּוֹ. מַה כָּתוּב לְמַעְלָה
מִן הָעִנְיָן? "וְאִישׁ אֶת קֳדָשָׁיו לוֹ יִהְיוּ" (לעיל פסוק י),
אִם אַתָּה מְעַכֵּב מַתְּנוֹת הַכֹּהֵן, חַיֶּיךָ שֶׁתִּצְטָרֵךְ לָבֹא
אֶצְלוֹ לְהָבִיא לוֹ אֶת הַסּוֹטָה: כִּי תִשְׂטֶה. תָּנוּ מַדְרְכֵי
צְנִיעוּת וְתֹאחַד בְּעֵינָיו, כְּמוֹ: "שָׂטֵה מֵעָלָיו וַעֲבוֹר" (משלי
ד, טו), "אַל יֵשְׂטְ אֶל דְּרָכֶיהָ לִבֶּךָ" (שם ז, כה): וּמָעֲלָה בוֹ
מָעַל. וּמַהוּ הַמַּעַל? "וְשָׁכַב אִישׁ אֹתָהּ":

יג | וְנֶעְלַם מֵעֵינֵי אִישָׁהּ. פְּרָט אִם הָיָה רוֹאֶה וּמַעֲמִים,
אֵין הַמַּיִם בּוֹדְקִין אוֹתָהּ: וְנִסְתָּרָה. שִׁעוּר שֶׁתִּתְרָאֶה
לְטֻמְאַת בִּיאָה: וְעֵד אֵין בָּהּ. הָא אִם יֵשׁ בָּהּ אֲפִלּוּ
עֵד אֶחָד שֶׁאָמַר "נִטְמֵאת", לֹא הָיְתָה שׁוֹתָה: וְעֵד
אֵין בָּהּ. בַּטֻּמְאָה, אֲבָל יֵשׁ עֵדִים לַסְּתִירָה: נִתְפָּשָׂה.
נֶאֱנְסָה, כְּמוֹ: "וּתְפָשָׂהּ וְשָׁכַב עִמָּהּ" (דברים כב, כח):

יד | וְעָבַר עָלָיו. קֹדֶם לַסְּתִירָה: רוּחַ קִנְאָה וְקִנֵּא.
פֵּרְשׁוּ רַבּוֹתֵינוּ לְשׁוֹן הַתְרָאָה, שֶׁמַּתְרֶה בָּהּ: 'אַל
תִּסָּתְרִי עִם אִישׁ פְּלוֹנִי': וְהִיא נִטְמָאָה אוֹ עָבַר עָלָיו

וְגוֹ'. כְּלוֹמַר, הוּא הִתְרָה בָּהּ וְעָבְרָה עַל הַתְרָאָתוֹ,
וְאֵין יָדוּעַ אִם נִטְמְאָה אִם לָאו:

טו | קֶמַח. שֶׁלֹּא יְהֵא מְסֹלֶת: שְׂעֹרִים. וְלֹא חִטִּים,
הִיא עָשְׂתָה מַעֲשֵׂה בְהֵמָה וְקָרְבָּנָהּ מַאֲכַל בְּהֵמָה:
לֹא יִצֹק עָלָיו שֶׁמֶן. שֶׁלֹּא יְהֵא קָרְבָּנָהּ מְהֻדָּר, שֶׁהַשֶּׁמֶן
קָרוּי 'אוֹר', וְהִיא עָשְׂתָה בַּחֹשֶׁךְ: וְלֹא יִתֵּן עָלָיו לְבֹנָה.
שֶׁהָאִמָּהוֹת נִקְרָאוֹת לְבוֹנָה, שֶׁנֶּאֱמַר: "אֶל גִּבְעַת
הַלְּבוֹנָה" (שיר השירים ד, ו), וְהִיא פֵּרְשָׁה מִדַּרְכֵיהֶן: כִּי
מִנְחַת קְנָאֹת הוּא. הַקֶּמַח הַזֶּה, 'קֶמַח' לְשׁוֹן זָכָר:
מִנְחַת קְנָאֹת. מְעוֹרֶרֶת עָלֶיהָ שְׁתֵּי קְנָאוֹת, קִנְאַת
הַמָּקוֹם וְקִנְאַת הַבַּעַל:

יז | מַיִם קְדֹשִׁים. שֶׁקִּדְּשׁוֹ בַּכִּיּוֹר. לְפִי שֶׁנַּעֲשָׂה הַכִּיּוֹר
מִנְּחֹשֶׁת מַרְאוֹת הַצּוֹבְאוֹת, וְזוֹ פֵּרְשָׁה מִדַּרְכֵיהֶן,
שֶׁהָיוּ נִבְעָלוֹת לְבַעֲלֵיהֶן בְּמִצְרַיִם תַּחַת הַתַּפּוּחַ וְזוֹ
קִלְקְלָה לְאַחֵר, תִּבָּדֵק בּוֹ: בִּכְלִי חָרֶשׂ. הִיא הִשְׁקַת
אֶת הַנּוֹאֵף יַיִן מְשֻׁבָּח בְּכוֹסוֹת מְשֻׁבָּחִים, לְפִיכָךְ
תִּשְׁתֶּה מַיִם הַמָּרִים בִּמְקֵדָה בְּזוּיָה שֶׁל חָרֶשׂ:

יח | וְהֶעֱמִיד הַכֹּהֵן וְגוֹ'. וַהֲלֹא כְּבָר נֶאֱמַר: "וְהֶעֱמִדָהּ

הַכֹּהֵן אֶת־הָאִשָּׁה לִפְנֵי יהוה וּפָרַע אֶת־רֹאשׁ הָאִשָּׁה וְנָתַן עַל־כַּפֶּיהָ אֵת מִנְחַת הַזִּכָּרוֹן מִנְחַת קְנָאֹת הִוא וּבְיַד הַכֹּהֵן יִהְיוּ מֵי הַמָּרִים הַמְאָרְרִים: וְהִשְׁבִּיעַ אֹתָהּ הַכֹּהֵן וְאָמַר אֶל־הָאִשָּׁה אִם־לֹא שָׁכַב אִישׁ אֹתָךְ וְאִם־לֹא שָׂטִית טֻמְאָה תַּחַת אִישֵׁךְ הִנָּקִי מִמֵּי הַמָּרִים הַמְאָרְרִים הָאֵלֶּה: וְאַתְּ כִּי שָׂטִית תַּחַת אִישֵׁךְ וְכִי נִטְמֵאת וַיִּתֵּן אִישׁ בָּךְ אֶת־שְׁכָבְתּוֹ מִבַּלְעֲדֵי אִישֵׁךְ: וְהִשְׁבִּיעַ הַכֹּהֵן אֶת־הָאִשָּׁה בִּשְׁבֻעַת הָאָלָה וְאָמַר הַכֹּהֵן לָאִשָּׁה יִתֵּן יהוה אוֹתָךְ לְאָלָה וְלִשְׁבֻעָה בְּתוֹךְ עַמֵּךְ בְּתֵת יהוה אֶת־יְרֵכֵךְ נֹפֶלֶת וְאֶת־בִּטְנֵךְ צָבָה: וּבָאוּ הַמַּיִם הַמְאָרְרִים הָאֵלֶּה בְּמֵעַיִךְ לַצְבּוֹת בֶּטֶן וְלַנְפִּל יָרֵךְ וְאָמְרָה הָאִשָּׁה אָמֵן

יט

כ

כא

כב

לִפְנֵי ה׳ (לעיל פסוק טז). חֶלָּא מַשְׁמִיעִין הָיוּ אוֹתָהּ מִמְּקוֹמָהּ לְמָקוֹם, כְּדֵי לְיַגְּעָהּ וְתִטָּרֵף דַּעְתָּהּ וְתוֹדֶה. **וּפָרַע.** סוֹתֵר אֶת קְלִיעַת שְׂעָרָהּ כְּדֵי לְבַזּוֹתָהּ, מִכָּאן לִבְנוֹת יִשְׂרָאֵל שֶׁגִּלּוּי הָרֹאשׁ גְּנַאי לָהֶן. **לִפְנֵי ה׳.** בְּשַׁעַר נִיקָנוֹר, הוּא שַׁעַר הָעֲזָרָה הַמִּזְרָחִי, דֶּרֶךְ כָּל הַנִּכְנָסִים: **וְנָתַן עַל כַּפֶּיהָ.** לְיַגְּעָהּ, אוּלַי תִּטָּרֵף דַּעְתָּהּ וְתוֹדֶה, וְלֹא יִמָּחֶה שֵׁם הַמְיֻחָד עַל הַמַּיִם הַמָּרִים. **עַל שֵׁם סוֹפָן,** שֶׁהֵם מָרִים לָהּ. **הַמְאָרְרִים.** הַמְחַסְּרִים אוֹתָהּ מִן הָעוֹלָם, לְשׁוֹן ״סַלּוֹן מַמְאִיר״ (יחזקאל כח, כד). וְלֹא יִתָּכֵן לְפָרֵשׁ מַיִם אֲרוּרִים שֶׁהֲרֵי קְדוֹשִׁים הֵן, וְלֹא ״אֲרוּרִים״ כָּתַב הַכָּתוּב אֶלָּא ״מְאָרְרִים״ אֶת אֲחֵרִים. וְאַף אוּנְקְלוֹס לֹא תִרְגֵּם ״לִיטַיָּא״ אֶלָּא ״מְלַטְּטַיָּא״, שֶׁמַּרְאוֹת קְלָלָה בְּגוּפָהּ שֶׁל זוֹ:

יט **וְהִשְׁבִּיעַ וְגוֹ׳.** וּמַה הִיא הַשְּׁבוּעָה? ״אִם לֹא שָׁכַב הִנָּקִי״, הָא אִם שָׁכַב – חִנָּקִי, שֶׁמִּכְּלַל לָאו אַתָּה שׁוֹמֵעַ הֵן, אֶלָּא שֶׁמִּצְוָה לִפְתֹּחַ בְּדִינֵי נְפָשׁוֹת תְּחִלָּה לִזְכוּת:

כ **וְאַתְּ כִּי שָׂטִית.** ״כִּי״ מְשַׁמֵּשׁ בִּלְשׁוֹן ״אִם״:

כא **בִּשְׁבֻעַת הָאָלָה.** שְׁבוּעָה שֶׁל קְלָלָה: **יִתֵּן ה׳ אוֹתָךְ לְאָלָה וְגוֹ׳.** שֶׁיִּהְיוּ הַכֹּל מְקַלְּלִין בִּיךְ: יְכוּלַךְ כְּדֶרֶךְ שֶׁבָּא לִפְלוֹנִית. **וְלִשְׁבֻעָה.** שֶׁיִּהְיוּ הַכֹּל נִשְׁבָּעִין בִּיךְ, אִם לֹא יְאָרַע לִי כְּדֶרֶךְ שֶׁאֵרַע לִפְלוֹנִית, וְכֵן הוּא אוֹמֵר: ״וְהִנַּחְתֶּם שִׁמְכֶם לִשְׁבוּעָה לִבְחִירַי״ (ישעיהו סה, טו), שֶׁהַצַּדִּיקִים נִשְׁבָּעִים בְּפֻרְעֲנוּתָן שֶׁל רְשָׁעִים. וְכֵן לְעִנְיַן הַבְּרָכָה: ״וְנִבְרְכוּ וְגוֹ׳״ (בראשית יב, ג), ״בְּךָ יְבָרֵךְ יִשְׂרָאֵל לֵאמֹר״ (שם מח, כ): **אֶת יְרֵכֵךְ.** בַּקְּלָלָה הִקְדִּים יָרֵךְ לַבֶּטֶן, לְפִי שֶׁבָּהּ הִתְחִילָה בָּעֲבֵרָה תְּחִלָּה: **צָבָה.** כְּתַרְגּוּמוֹ, נְפוּחָה:

כב **לַצְבּוֹת בֶּטֶן.** כְּמוֹ לְהַצְבּוֹת בֶּטֶן, זֶהוּ שִׁמּוּשׁ פַּתָּח שֶׁהַלָּמֶ״ד נְקוּדָה בּוֹ. וְכֵן ״לַנְחֹתָם הַדֶּרֶךְ״ (שמות יג, כא), ״לַלַּחְתְּכֶם בַּדֶּרֶךְ אֲשֶׁר תֵּלְכוּ בָהּ״ (דברים א, לג), וְכֵן ״וְלַנְפִּל יָרֵךְ״, לְהַפִּיל יָרֵךְ, שֶׁהַמַּיִם מַעְמִּיסִים אֶת הַבֶּטֶן וּמַפִּילִים אֶת הַיָּרֵךְ: **לַצְבּוֹת בֶּטֶן וְלַנְפִּל יָרֵךְ.** בִּטְנוֹ וִירֵכוֹ שֶׁל בּוֹעֵל, אוֹ אֵינוֹ אֶלָּא שֶׁל נֶעֱלֶבֶת? כְּשֶׁהוּא אוֹמֵר: ״אֶת יְרֵכֵךְ נֹפֶלֶת וְאֶת בִּטְנֵךְ צָבָה״ (לעיל פסוק כא), הֲרֵי שֶׁל נֶעֱלֶבֶת אָמוּר: **אָמֵן אָמֵן.** קַבָּלַת שְׁבוּעָה, אָמֵן אִם שָׁכַב, אָמֵן אִם יִשְׁכַּב, אָמֵן אִם מֵאִישׁ זֶה, אָמֵן אִם מֵאִישׁ אַחֵר, אָמֵן עַל הָאָלָה אָמֵן עַל הַשְּׁבוּעָה:

כג אָמֵֽן׃ וְכָתַ֨ב אֶת־הָאָלֹ֤ת הָאֵ֙לֶּה֙ הַכֹּהֵ֔ן בַּסֵּ֑פֶר וּמָחָ֖ה אֶל־מֵ֥י
כד הַמָּרִֽים׃ וְהִשְׁקָה֙ אֶת־הָ֣אִשָּׁ֔ה אֶת־מֵ֥י הַמָּרִ֖ים הַמְאָֽרֲרִ֑ים וּבָ֨אוּ
בָ֜הּ הַמַּ֥יִם הַֽמְאָרֲרִ֖ים לְמָרִֽים׃ וְלָקַ֤ח הַכֹּהֵן֙ מִיַּ֣ד הָֽאִשָּׁ֔ה אֵ֖ת
כה מִנְחַ֣ת הַקְּנָאֹ֑ת וְהֵנִ֤יף אֶת־הַמִּנְחָה֙ לִפְנֵ֣י יְהֹוָ֔ה וְהִקְרִ֥יב אֹתָ֖הּ
אֶל־הַמִּזְבֵּֽחַ׃ וְקָמַ֨ץ הַכֹּהֵ֤ן מִן־הַמִּנְחָה֙ אֶת־אַזְכָּ֣רָתָ֔הּ וְהִקְטִ֖יר
כו הַמִּזְבֵּ֑חָה וְאַחַ֛ר יַשְׁקֶ֥ה אֶת־הָאִשָּׁ֖ה אֶת־הַמָּֽיִם׃ וְהִשְׁקָ֣הּ אֶת־
כז הַמַּ֗יִם וְהָיְתָ֣ה אִֽם־נִטְמְאָה֮ וַתִּמְעֹ֣ל מַ֣עַל בְּאִישָׁהּ֒ וּבָ֨אוּ בָ֜הּ
הַמַּ֤יִם הַֽמְאָֽרֲרִים֙ לְמָרִ֔ים וְצָבְתָ֣ה בִטְנָ֔הּ וְנָפְלָ֖ה יְרֵכָ֑הּ וְהָיְתָ֧ה
כח הָאִשָּׁ֛ה לְאָלָ֖ה בְּקֶ֥רֶב עַמָּֽהּ׃ וְאִם־לֹ֤א נִטְמְאָה֙ הָֽאִשָּׁ֔ה וּטְהֹרָ֖ה
כט הִ֑וא וְנִקְּתָ֖ה וְנִזְרְעָ֥ה זָֽרַע׃ זֹ֥את תּוֹרַ֖ת הַקְּנָאֹ֑ת אֲשֶׁ֨ר תִּשְׂטֶ֥ה
ל אִשָּׁ֛ה תַּ֥חַת אִישָׁ֖הּ וְנִטְמָֽאָה׃ א֣וֹ אִ֗ישׁ אֲשֶׁ֨ר תַּעֲבֹ֥ר עָלָ֛יו ר֥וּחַ
קִנְאָ֖ה וְקִנֵּ֣א אֶת־אִשְׁתּ֑וֹ וְהֶעֱמִ֤יד אֶת־הָֽאִשָּׁה֙ לִפְנֵ֣י יְהֹוָ֔ה וְעָ֤שָׂה

כד | וְהִשְׁקָה אֶת הָאִשָּׁה. אֵין זֶה סֵדֶר הַמַּעֲשֶׂה, שֶׁהֲרֵי בַּתְּחִלָּה מַקְרִיב מִנְחָתָהּ; אֶלָּא הַכָּתוּב מְבַשֶּׂרְךָ שֶׁכְּשֶׁיַּשְׁקֶנָּה יָבֹאוּ בָהּ לְמָרִים. לְפִי שֶׁנֶּאֱמַר בֶּטֶן וְיָרֵךְ, מִנַּיִן לִשְׁאָר כָּל הַגּוּף? תַּלְמוּד לוֹמַר: "וּבָאוּ בָהּ", בְּכֻלָּהּ. אִם כֵּן מַה תַּלְמוּד לוֹמַר בֶּטֶן וְיָרֵךְ? לְפִי שֶׁהֵן הִתְחִילוּ בַּעֲבֵרָה תְּחִלָּה, לְפִיכָךְ הִתְחִיל מֵהֶם הַפֻּרְעָנוּת: לְמָרִים. לִהְיוֹת לָהּ רָעִים וּמָרִים:

כה | וְהֵנִיף. מוֹלִיךְ וּמֵבִיא מַעֲלֶה וּמוֹרִיד, וְאַף הִיא מְנִיפָה עִמּוֹ, שֶׁיָּדָהּ לְמַעְלָה מִיָּדוֹ שֶׁל כֹּהֵן: וְהִקְרִיב אֹתָהּ. זוֹ הִיא הַגָּשָׁתָהּ בְּקֶרֶן דְּרוֹמִית מַעֲרָבִית שֶׁל מִזְבֵּחַ קֹדֶם קְמִיצָה, כִּשְׁאָר מְנָחוֹת:

כו | אַזְכָּרָתָהּ. הוּא הַקֹּמֶץ, שֶׁעַל יְדֵי הַקְטָרָתוֹ הַמִּנְחָה בָּאָה לְזִכָּרוֹן לַגָּבוֹהַּ:

כז | וְהִשְׁקָהּ אֶת הַמַּיִם. לְרַבּוֹת שֶׁאִם אָמְרָה "אֵינִי

שׁוֹתָה" לְאַחַר שֶׁנִּמְחֲקָה הַמְּגִלָּה, מְעַרְעֲרִין אוֹתָהּ וּמַשְׁקִין אוֹתָהּ בְּעַל כָּרְחָהּ, אֶלָּא אִם כֵּן אָמְרָה "טְמֵאָה אֲנִי": וְצָבְתָה בִטְנָהּ וְגוֹ'. אַף עַל פִּי שֶׁבַּקְּלָלָה הִזְכִּיר יָרֵךְ תְּחִלָּה, הַמַּיִם אֵינָן בּוֹדְקִין אֶלָּא כְּדֶרֶךְ כְּנִיסָתָן בָּהּ: וְהָיְתָה הָאִשָּׁה לְאָלָה. כְּמוֹ שֶׁפֵּרַשְׁתִּי, שֶׁיְּהוּ הַכֹּל חַלִּין בָּהּ: בְּקֶרֶב עַמָּהּ. הֶפְרֵשׁ יֵשׁ בֵּין אָדָם הַמִּתְנַוֵּל בְּמָקוֹם שֶׁנִּכָּר לְאָדָם הַמִּתְנַוֵּל בְּמָקוֹם שֶׁאֵינוֹ נִכָּר:

כח | וְאִם לֹא נִטְמְאָה הָאִשָּׁה. בִּסְתִירָה זוֹ: וּטְהֹרָה הִוא. מִמָּקוֹם אַחֵר: וְנִקְּתָה. מִמַּיִם הַמְאָרֲרִים, וְלֹא עוֹד אֶלָּא וְנִזְרְעָה זָרַע, אִם הָיְתָה יוֹלֶדֶת בְּצַעַר תֵּלֵד בְּרֶוַח, אִם הָיְתָה יוֹלֶדֶת שְׁחוֹרִים יוֹלֶדֶת לְבָנִים:

ל | אוֹ אִישׁ. כְּמוֹ "אוֹ נוֹדַע" (שמות כא, לו), כְּלוֹמַר, אִם אִישׁ קַנַּאי הוּא, לְכָךְ "וְהֶעֱמִיד אֶת הָאִשָּׁה":

לָהּ הַכֹּהֵן אֵת כָּל־הַתּוֹרָה הַזֹּאת: וְנִקָּה הָאִישׁ מֵעָוֺן וְהָאִשָּׁה לא
הַהִוא תִּשָּׂא אֶת־עֲוֺנָהּ:

וַיְדַבֵּר יְהוָה אֶל־מֹשֶׁה לֵּאמֹר: דַּבֵּר אֶל־בְּנֵי יִשְׂרָאֵל וְאָמַרְתָּ ו א ב
אֲלֵהֶם אִישׁ אוֹ־אִשָּׁה כִּי יַפְלִא לִנְדֹּר נֶדֶר נָזִיר לְהַזִּיר לַיהוָה:
מִיַּיִן וְשֵׁכָר יַזִּיר חֹמֶץ יַיִן וְחֹמֶץ שֵׁכָר לֹא יִשְׁתֶּה וְכָל־מִשְׁרַת ג
עֲנָבִים לֹא יִשְׁתֶּה וַעֲנָבִים לַחִים וִיבֵשִׁים לֹא יֹאכֵל: כָּל יְמֵי ד
נִזְרוֹ מִכֹּל אֲשֶׁר יֵעָשֶׂה מִגֶּפֶן הַיַּיִן מֵחַרְצַנִּים וְעַד־זָג לֹא יֹאכֵל:
כָּל־יְמֵי נֶדֶר נִזְרוֹ תַּעַר לֹא־יַעֲבֹר עַל־רֹאשׁוֹ עַד־מְלֹאת הַיָּמִם ה
אֲשֶׁר־יַזִּיר לַיהוָה קָדֹשׁ יִהְיֶה גַּדֵּל פֶּרַע שְׂעַר רֹאשׁוֹ: כָּל־יְמֵי ו
הַזִּירוֹ לַיהוָה עַל־נֶפֶשׁ מֵת לֹא יָבֹא: לְאָבִיו וּלְאִמּוֹ לְאָחִיו ז
וּלְאַחֹתוֹ לֹא־יִטַּמָּא לָהֶם בְּמֹתָם כִּי נֵזֶר אֱלֹהָיו עַל־רֹאשׁוֹ: כָּל ח
יְמֵי נִזְרוֹ קָדֹשׁ הוּא לַיהוָה: וְכִי־יָמוּת מֵת עָלָיו בְּפֶתַע פִּתְאֹם ט
וְטִמֵּא רֹאשׁ נִזְרוֹ וְגִלַּח רֹאשׁוֹ בְּיוֹם טָהֳרָתוֹ בַּיּוֹם הַשְּׁבִיעִי

לא | וְנִקָּה הָאִישׁ מֵעָוֺן. חָס כִּדְקוּק הַמַּיִם, אַל יִדְאַג לוֹמַר 'חַבְתִּי בְּמִיתָתָהּ', נָקִי הוּא מִן הָעֹנֶשׁ. דָּבָר אַחֵר, מִשֶּׁיַּשְׁקֶנָּה תְּהֵא אֶצְלוֹ בְּהֶתֵּר וְנִקָּה מֵעָוֺן, שֶׁהַסּוֹטָה אֲסוּרָה לְבַעְלָהּ:

פרק ו

ב | כִּי יַפְלִא. "יְפָרֵשׁ". לָמָּה נִסְמְכָה פָּרָשַׁת נָזִיר לְפָרָשַׁת סוֹטָה? לוֹמַר לְךָ שֶׁכָּל הָרוֹאֶה סוֹטָה בְּקִלְקוּלָהּ יַזִּיר עַצְמוֹ מִן הַיַּיִן שֶׁהוּא מֵבִיא לִידֵי נִאוּף: נֶדֶר נָזִיר. אֵין נְזִירָה בְּכָל מָקוֹם אֶלָּא פְּרִישָׁה, אַף כָּאן שֶׁפֵּרַשׁ מִן הַיַּיִן: לְהַזִּיר לַה'. לְהַבְדִּיל עַצְמוֹ מִן הַיַּיִן לְשֵׁם שָׁמַיִם:

ג | מִיַּיִן וְשֵׁכָר. כְּתַרְגּוּמוֹ: "מֵחֲמַר חֲדַת וְעַתִּיק", שֶׁהַיַּיִן מְשַׁכֵּר כְּשֶׁהוּא יָשָׁן: וְכָל־מִשְׁרַת. לְשׁוֹן צְבִיעָה בְּמַיִם וּבְכָל מַשְׁקֶה, וּבִלְשׁוֹן מִשְׁנָה יֵשׁ הַרְבֵּה: "אֵין

שׁוֹרִין דְּיוֹ וְסַמְמָנִים" (שבת יז ע״א), "נָזִיר שֶׁשָּׁרָה פִּתּוֹ בְּיַיִן" (נזיר לז ע״א):

ד | חַרְצַנִּים. הֵם הַגַּרְעִינִין: זָג. הֵם קְלִפּוֹת שֶׁמִּבַּחוּץ, שֶׁהַחַרְצַנִּים בְּתוֹכָן כְּעִנְבָּל בַּזּוֹג:

ה | קָדֹשׁ יִהְיֶה. הַשֵּׂעָר שֶׁלּוֹ, לְגַדֵּל הַפֶּרַע שֶׁל שְׂעַר רֹאשׁוֹ: פֶּרַע שֵׂעָר. נָקוּד פַּתָּח לְפִי שֶׁהוּא דָבוּק לִ"שְׂעַר לֹאשׁוֹ", פֶּרַע שֶׁל שֵׂעָר. וּפֵרוּשׁוֹ שֶׁל "פֶּרַע" גִּדּוּל שֶׁל שֵׂעָר, וְכֵן "אֶת לֹאשׁוֹ לֹא יִפְרָע" (ויקרא כא). וְאֵין קָרוּי פֶּרַע פָּחוֹת מִשְּׁלֹשִׁים יוֹם:

ח | כָּל יְמֵי נִזְרוֹ קָדֹשׁ הוּא. זוֹ קְדֻשַּׁת הַגּוּף מִלְּהִטַּמֵּא לְמֵתִים:

ט | פֶּתַע. זֶה אֹנֶס. פִּתְאֹם. זֶה שׁוֹגֵג. וְיֵשׁ אוֹמְרִים: "פֶּתַע פִּתְאֹם" דָּבָר אֶחָד הוּא, מִקְרֶה שֶׁל פִּתְאֹם: וְכִי יָמוּת מֵת עָלָיו. בָּאֹהֶל שֶׁהוּא בּוֹ: בְּיוֹם טָהֳרָתוֹ.

במדבר | פרק ו

י יְגַלְּחֶנּוּ: וּבַיּוֹם הַשְּׁמִינִי יָבִא שְׁתֵּי תֹרִים אוֹ שְׁנֵי בְנֵי יוֹנָה אֶל־
יא הַכֹּהֵן אֶל־פֶּתַח אֹהֶל מוֹעֵד: וְעָשָׂה הַכֹּהֵן אֶחָד לְחַטָּאת וְאֶחָד
לְעֹלָה וְכִפֶּר עָלָיו מֵאֲשֶׁר חָטָא עַל־הַנָּפֶשׁ וְקִדַּשׁ אֶת־רֹאשׁוֹ
יב בַּיּוֹם הַהוּא: וְהִזִּיר לַיהוָה אֶת־יְמֵי נִזְרוֹ וְהֵבִיא כֶּבֶשׂ בֶּן־שְׁנָתוֹ
יג לְאָשָׁם וְהַיָּמִים הָרִאשֹׁנִים יִפְּלוּ כִּי טָמֵא נִזְרוֹ: וְזֹאת תּוֹרַת
הַנָּזִיר בְּיוֹם מְלֹאת יְמֵי נִזְרוֹ יָבִיא אֹתוֹ אֶל־פֶּתַח אֹהֶל מוֹעֵד:
יד וְהִקְרִיב אֶת־קָרְבָּנוֹ לַיהוָה כֶּבֶשׂ בֶּן־שְׁנָתוֹ תָמִים אֶחָד לְעֹלָה
וְכַבְשָׂה אַחַת בַּת־שְׁנָתָהּ תְּמִימָה לְחַטָּאת וְאַיִל־אֶחָד תָּמִים
טו לִשְׁלָמִים: וְסַל מַצּוֹת סֹלֶת חַלֹּת בְּלוּלֹת בַּשֶּׁמֶן וּרְקִיקֵי מַצּוֹת
טז מְשֻׁחִים בַּשָּׁמֶן וּמִנְחָתָם וְנִסְכֵּיהֶם: וְהִקְרִיב הַכֹּהֵן לִפְנֵי יְהוָה
יז וְעָשָׂה אֶת־חַטָּאתוֹ וְאֶת־עֹלָתוֹ: וְאֶת־הָאַיִל יַעֲשֶׂה זֶבַח שְׁלָמִים
לַיהוָה עַל סַל הַמַּצּוֹת וְעָשָׂה הַכֹּהֵן אֶת־מִנְחָתוֹ וְאֶת־נִסְכּוֹ:

בַּיּוֹם הַזֶּה. אוֹ אֵינוֹ אֶלָּא בַּשְּׁמִינִי שֶׁהוּא טָהוֹר לְגַמְרֵי? תַּלְמוּד לוֹמַר: "בַּיּוֹם הַשְּׁבִיעִי". אִי שְׁבִיעִי, יָכוֹל אֲפִלּוּ לֹא הֵבִיא? תַּלְמוּד לוֹמַר: "בְּיוֹם טָהֳרָתוֹ":

י) וּבַיּוֹם הַשְּׁמִינִי יָבִא שְׁתֵּי תֹרִים. לְהוֹצִיא אֶת הַשְּׁבִיעִי. אוֹ אֵינוֹ אֶלָּא לְהוֹצִיא אֶת הַתְּשִׁיעִי? קָבַע זְמַן לַקְּרֵבִין וְקָבַע זְמַן לַמַּקְרִיבִין, מַה קְּרֵבִין הֻכְשַׁר שְׁמִינִי וּמִשְּׁמִינִי וָהָלְאָה, אַף מַקְרִיבִין שְׁמִינִי וּמִשְּׁמִינִי וָהָלְאָה:

יא) מֵאֲשֶׁר חָטָא עַל הַנָּפֶשׁ. שֶׁלֹּא נִזְהַר מִטֻּמְאַת הַמֵּת. רַבִּי אֶלְעָזָר הַקַּפָּר אוֹמֵר: שֶׁצִּעֵר עַצְמוֹ מִן הַיַּיִן: וְקִדַּשׁ אֶת רֹאשׁוֹ. לַחֲזוֹר וּלְהַתְחִיל מִנְיַן נְזִירוּתוֹ:

יב) וְהִזִּיר לַה' אֶת יְמֵי נִזְרוֹ. יַחֲזֹר וְיִמְנֶה נְזִירוּתוֹ

כְּבַתְּחִלָּה: וְהַיָּמִים הָרִאשֹׁנִים יִפְּלוּ. לֹא יַעֲלוּ מִן הַמִּנְיָן:

יג) יָבִיא אֹתוֹ. יָבִיא אֶת עַצְמוֹ, וְזֶה אֶחָד מִשְּׁלֹשָׁה אֶתִּים שֶׁהָיָה רַבִּי יִשְׁמָעֵאל דּוֹרֵשׁ כֵּן. כַּיּוֹצֵא בּוֹ: "וְהִשִּׂיאוּ אוֹתָם עֲוֹן אַשְׁמָה" (ויקרא כב, טז), אֶת עַצְמָם; כַּיּוֹצֵא בּוֹ: "וַיִּקְבֹּר אֹתוֹ בַגַּי" (דברים לד, ו), הוּא קָבַר אֶת עַצְמוֹ:

טו) וּמִנְחָתָם וְנִסְכֵּיהֶם. שֶׁל עוֹלָה וּשְׁלָמִים, לְפִי שֶׁהָיוּ בִּכְלָל וְיָצְאוּ לִדּוֹן בְּדָבָר שֶׁיִּטְּעֶנּוּ לֶחֶם, הֶחֱזִירָן לִכְלָלָן שֶׁיִּטְּעֲנוּ נְסָכִים כְּדִין עוֹלָה וּשְׁלָמִים: חַלֹּת בְּלוּלֹת וּרְקִיקֵי מַצּוֹת. עֶשֶׂר מִכָּל מִין:

יז) זֶבַח שְׁלָמִים לַה' עַל סַל הַמַּצּוֹת. יִשְׁחַט אֶת הַשְּׁלָמִים עַל מְנָת לְקַדֵּשׁ אֶת הַלֶּחֶם: אֶת מִנְחָתוֹ וְאֶת נִסְכּוֹ. שֶׁל אַיִל:

יח וְגִלַּח הַנָּזִיר פֶּתַח אֹהֶל מוֹעֵד אֶת־רֹאשׁ נִזְרוֹ וְלָקַח אֶת־שְׂעַר
רֹאשׁ נִזְרוֹ וְנָתַן עַל־הָאֵשׁ אֲשֶׁר־תַּחַת זֶבַח הַשְּׁלָמִים: יט וְלָקַח
הַכֹּהֵן אֶת־הַזְּרֹעַ בְּשֵׁלָה מִן־הָאַיִל וְחַלַּת מַצָּה אַחַת מִן־הַסַּל
וּרְקִיק מַצָּה אֶחָד וְנָתַן עַל־כַּפֵּי הַנָּזִיר אַחַר הִתְגַּלְּחוֹ אֶת־נִזְרוֹ:
כ וְהֵנִיף אוֹתָם הַכֹּהֵן ׀ תְּנוּפָה לִפְנֵי יְהֹוָה קֹדֶשׁ הוּא לַכֹּהֵן עַל חֲזֵה
הַתְּנוּפָה וְעַל שׁוֹק הַתְּרוּמָה וְאַחַר יִשְׁתֶּה הַנָּזִיר יָיִן: כא זֹאת תּוֹרַת
הַנָּזִיר אֲשֶׁר יִדֹּר קָרְבָּנוֹ לַיהֹוָה עַל־נִזְרוֹ מִלְּבַד אֲשֶׁר־תַּשִּׂיג יָדוֹ
כְּפִי נִדְרוֹ אֲשֶׁר יִדֹּר כֵּן יַעֲשֶׂה עַל תּוֹרַת נִזְרוֹ:

ו כב וַיְדַבֵּר יְהֹוָה אֶל־מֹשֶׁה לֵּאמֹר: כג דַּבֵּר אֶל־אַהֲרֹן וְאֶל־בָּנָיו לֵאמֹר
כֹּה תְבָרֲכוּ אֶת־בְּנֵי יִשְׂרָאֵל אָמוֹר לָהֶם: כד יְבָרֶכְךָ יְהֹוָה
וְיִשְׁמְרֶךָ: כה יָאֵר יְהֹוָה ׀ פָּנָיו אֵלֶיךָ וִיחֻנֶּךָּ: כו יִשָּׂא

יח **וְגִלַּח הַנָּזִיר פֶּתַח אֹהֶל מוֹעֵד.** יָכוֹל יְגַלַּח
בָּעֲזָרָה? הֲרֵי זֶה דֶּרֶךְ בִּזָּיוֹן! אֶלָּא "וְגִלַּח הַנָּזִיר"
לְאַחַר שְׁחִיטַת הַשְּׁלָמִים שֶׁכָּתוּב בָּהֶן: "וּשְׁחָטוֹ פֶּתַח
אֹהֶל מוֹעֵד" (ויקרא ג, ב): **אֲשֶׁר תַּחַת זֶבַח הַשְּׁלָמִים.**
תַּחַת הַדּוּד שֶׁהוּא מְבַשְּׁלָן בּוֹ, לְפִי שֶׁשַּׁלְמֵי נָזִיר הָיוּ
מִתְבַּשְּׁלִין בָּעֲזָרָה, שֶׁצָּרִיךְ לִטֹּל הַכֹּהֵן הַזְּרוֹעַ אַחַר
שֶׁנִּתְבַּשְּׁלָה וּלְהָנִיף לִפְנֵי ה':

יט **הַזְּרֹעַ בְּשֵׁלָה.** לְאַחַר שֶׁנִּתְבַּשְּׁלָה:

כ **קֹדֶשׁ הוּא לַכֹּהֵן.** הַחַלָּה וְהָרָקִיק וְהַזְּרוֹעַ תְּרוּמָה
הֵן לַכֹּהֵן. **עַל חֲזֵה הַתְּנוּפָה.** מִלְּבַד חֲזֶה וָשׁוֹק
הָרְאוּיִים לוֹ מִכָּל שְׁלָמִים, מוּסָף עַל שַׁלְמֵי נָזִיר
הַזְּרוֹעַ הַזֶּה. לְפִי שֶׁהָיוּ שַׁלְמֵי נָזִיר בִּכְלָל וְיָצְאוּ לִדּוֹן
בַּדָּבָר הֶחָדָשׁ לְהַפְרָשַׁת זְרוֹעַ, הֻצְרַךְ לְהַחֲזִירָן לִכְלָלָן
לִדּוֹן אַף בְּחָזֶה וָשׁוֹק:

כא **מִלְּבַד אֲשֶׁר תַּשִּׂיג יָדוֹ.** שֶׁאִם אָמַר: "הֲרֵינִי
נָזִיר עַל מְנָת לְגַלֵּחַ עַל מֵאָה עוֹלוֹת וְעַל מֵאָה
שְׁלָמִים" – "כְּפִי נִדְרוֹ אֲשֶׁר יִדֹּר כֵּן יַעֲשֶׂה" מוּסָף

"עַל תּוֹרַת נִזְרוֹ", עַל תּוֹרַת הַנָּזִיר מוֹסִיף וְלֹא יְחַסֵּר,
שֶׁאִם אָמַר: "הֲרֵינִי נָזִיר חָמֵשׁ נְזִירוּת עַל מְנָת לְגַלֵּחַ
עַל שֶׁלֹּשׁ בְּהֵמוֹת הַלָּלוּ", אֵין אֲנִי קוֹרֵא בּוֹ "כַּאֲשֶׁר
יִדֹּר כֵּן יַעֲשֶׂה":

כג **אָמוֹר לָהֶם.** כְּמוֹ 'זָכוֹר', 'שָׁמוֹר', בְּלַעַ"ז דיסנ"ט.
אָמוֹר לָהֶם. שֶׁיִּהְיוּ כֻּלָּם שׁוֹמְעִים: **אָמוֹר.** מָלֵא, לֹא
תְבָרְכֵם בְּחִפָּזוֹן וּבְהָלוּת אֶלָּא בְּכַוָּנָה וּבְלֵב שָׁלֵם:

כד **יְבָרֶכְךָ.** שֶׁיִּתְבָּרְכוּ נְכָסֶיךָ: **וְיִשְׁמְרֶךָ.** שֶׁלֹּא יָבוֹאוּ
עָלֶיךָ שׁוֹדְדִים לִטֹּל מָמוֹנְךָ, שֶׁהַנּוֹתֵן מַתָּנָה לְעַבְדּוֹ
אֵינוֹ יָכוֹל לְשָׁמְרוֹ מִכָּל אָדָם, וְכֵיוָן שֶׁבָּאִים לִסְטִים
עָלָיו וְנוֹטְלִין אוֹתָהּ מִמֶּנּוּ, מַה הֲנָאָה יֵשׁ לוֹ בְּמַתָּנָה
זוֹ? אֲבָל הַקָּדוֹשׁ בָּרוּךְ הוּא, הוּא הַנּוֹתֵן הוּא הַשּׁוֹמֵר.
וְהַרְבֵּה מִדְרָשִׁים דָּרְשׁוּ בּוֹ בְּסִפְרֵי (מ):

כה **יָאֵר ה' פָּנָיו אֵלֶיךָ.** יַרְאֶה לְךָ פָּנִים שׂוֹחֲקוֹת,
פָּנִים צְהֻבּוֹת: **וִיחֻנֶּךָּ.** יִתֵּן לְךָ חֵן:

כו **יִשָּׂא ה' פָּנָיו אֵלֶיךָ.** יִכְבֹּשׁ כַּעֲסוֹ:

במדבר | פרק ז | נשא

כז יְהוָה ׀ פָּנָיו אֵלֶיךָ וְיָשֵׂם לְךָ שָׁלוֹם: וְשָׂמוּ אֶת־שְׁמִי
עַל־בְּנֵי יִשְׂרָאֵל וַאֲנִי אֲבָרְכֵם:

ז א וַיְהִי בְּיוֹם כַּלּוֹת חמישי
מֹשֶׁה לְהָקִים אֶת־הַמִּשְׁכָּן וַיִּמְשַׁח אֹתוֹ וַיְקַדֵּשׁ אֹתוֹ וְאֶת־
כָּל־כֵּלָיו וְאֶת־הַמִּזְבֵּחַ וְאֶת־כָּל־כֵּלָיו וַיִּמְשָׁחֵם וַיְקַדֵּשׁ אֹתָם:
ב וַיַּקְרִיבוּ נְשִׂיאֵי יִשְׂרָאֵל רָאשֵׁי בֵּית אֲבֹתָם הֵם נְשִׂיאֵי הַמַּטֹּת
הֵם הָעֹמְדִים עַל־הַפְּקֻדִים: וַיָּבִיאוּ אֶת־קָרְבָּנָם לִפְנֵי יְהוָה
ג שֵׁשׁ־עֶגְלֹת צָב וּשְׁנֵי־עָשָׂר בָּקָר עֲגָלָה עַל־שְׁנֵי הַנְּשִׂאִים וְשׁוֹר
לְאֶחָד וַיַּקְרִיבוּ אוֹתָם לִפְנֵי הַמִּשְׁכָּן: וַיֹּאמֶר יְהוָה אֶל־מֹשֶׁה
ד ה לֵּאמֹר: קַח מֵאִתָּם וְהָיוּ לַעֲבֹד אֶת־עֲבֹדַת אֹהֶל מוֹעֵד וְנָתַתָּה
ו אוֹתָם אֶל־הַלְוִיִּם אִישׁ כְּפִי עֲבֹדָתוֹ: וַיִּקַּח מֹשֶׁה אֶת־הָעֲגָלֹת

כז] וְשָׂמוּ אֶת שְׁמִי. יְבָרְכוּם בַּשֵׁם הַמְפֹרָשׁ: וַאֲנִי
אֲבָרְכֵם. לְיִשְׂרָאֵל, וְאַסְכִּים עִם הַכֹּהֲנִים. דָּבָר אַחֵר,
"וַאֲנִי אֲבָרְכֵם" לַכֹּהֲנִים:

פרק ז
א] וַיְהִי בְּיוֹם כַּלּוֹת מֹשֶׁה. "כַּלַּת" כְּתִיב, יוֹם הֲקָמַת
הַמִּשְׁכָּן הָיוּ יִשְׂרָאֵל כְּכַלָּה הַנִּכְנֶסֶת לַחֻפָּה: כַּלּוֹת
מֹשֶׁה. בְּצַלְאֵל וְאָהֳלִיאָב וְכָל חֲכַם לֵב עָשׂוּ אֶת
הַמִּשְׁכָּן, וּתְלָאוֹ הַכָּתוּב בְּמֹשֶׁה, לְפִי שֶׁמָּסַר נַפְשׁוֹ
עָלָיו לִרְאוֹת תַּבְנִית כָּל דָּבָר וְדָבָר כְּמוֹ שֶׁהֶרְאָהוּ
בָּהָר, לְהוֹרוֹת לְעוֹשֵׂי הַמְּלָאכָה, וְלֹא טָעָה בְּתַבְנִית
אַחַת. וְכֵן מָצִינוּ בְּדָוִד, לְפִי שֶׁמָּסַר נַפְשׁוֹ עַל בִּנְיַן בֵּית
הַמִּקְדָּשׁ, שֶׁנֶּאֱמַר: "זְכוֹר ה' לְדָוִד אֵת כָּל עֻנּוֹתוֹ אֲשֶׁר
נִשְׁבַּע לַה'" וְגוֹ' (תהלים קלב, א-ב), לְפִיכָךְ נִקְרָא עַל שְׁמוֹ,
שֶׁנֶּאֱמַר: "רְאֵה בֵיתְךָ דָּוִד" (מלכים א' יב, טז): בְּיוֹם כַּלּוֹת
מֹשֶׁה לְהָקִים. וְלֹא נֶאֱמַר 'בְּיוֹם הָקִים', מְלַמֵּד שֶׁכָּל
שִׁבְעַת יְמֵי הַמִּלּוּאִים הָיָה מֹשֶׁה מַעֲמִידוֹ וּמְפָרְקוֹ,
וּבְאוֹתוֹ הַיּוֹם הֶעֱמִידוֹ וְלֹא פֵּרְקוֹ, לְכָךְ נֶאֱמַר: "בְּיוֹם
כַּלּוֹת מֹשֶׁה לְהָקִים", אוֹתוֹ הַיּוֹם כָּלוּ הֲקָמוֹתָיו,

וְלֶחֶם חֹדֶשׁ נִיסָן הָיָה. בַּשֵּׁנִי – נִשְׂרְפָה הַפָּרָה,
בַּשְּׁלִישִׁי – הֻזָּה הַזָּאָה רִאשׁוֹנָה, וּבַשְּׁבִיעִי – גִּלְּחוּ:

ב] הֵם נְשִׂיאֵי הַמַּטֹּת. שֶׁהָיוּ שׁוֹטְרִים עֲלֵיהֶם
בְּמִצְרַיִם וְהָיוּ מֻכִּים עֲלֵיהֶם, שֶׁנֶּאֱמַר: "וַיֻּכּוּ שֹׁטְרֵי
בְּנֵי יִשְׂרָאֵל" וְגוֹ' (שמות ה, יד): הֵם הָעֹמְדִים עַל הַפְּקֻדִים.
שֶׁעָמְדוּ עִם מֹשֶׁה וְאַהֲרֹן כְּשֶׁמָּנוּ אֶת יִשְׂרָאֵל,
שֶׁנֶּאֱמַר: "וְאִתְּכֶם יִהְיוּ" וְגוֹ' (לעיל א, ד):

ג] שֵׁשׁ עֶגְלֹת צָב. אֵין "צָב" אֶלָּא מְחֻפִּים, וְכֵן:
"בַּצַּבִּים וּבַפְּרָדִים" (ישעיה סו, כ), עֲגָלוֹת מְכֻסּוֹת קְרוּיוֹת
'צַבִּים': וַיַּקְרִיבוּ אוֹתָם לִפְנֵי הַמִּשְׁכָּן. שֶׁלֹּא קִבֵּל
מֹשֶׁה מִיָּדָם עַד שֶׁנֶּאֱמַר לוֹ מִפִּי הַמָּקוֹם. אָמַר
רַבִּי נָתָן: מָה רָאוּ הַנְּשִׂיאִים לְהִתְנַדֵּב כָּאן בַּתְּחִלָּה
וּבִמְלֶאכֶת הַמִּשְׁכָּן לֹא הִתְנַדְּבוּ תְּחִלָּה? אֶלָּא כָּךְ
אָמְרוּ הַנְּשִׂיאִים: יִתְנַדְּבוּ צִבּוּר מַה שֶּׁיִּתְנַדְּבוּ וּמַה
שֶּׁמְּחַסְּרִין אָנוּ מַשְׁלִימִין, כֵּיוָן שֶׁרָאוּ שֶׁהִשְׁלִימוּ צִבּוּר
אֶת הַכֹּל, שֶׁנֶּאֱמַר: "וְהַמְּלָאכָה הָיְתָה דַיָּם" (שמות לו, ז),
אָמְרוּ: מֵעַתָּה מַה לָּנוּ לַעֲשׂוֹת? הֵבִיאוּ אֶת הָאַבְנֵי הַשֹּׁהַם
וְהַמִּלּוּאִים לָאֵפוֹד וְלַחֹשֶׁן (עי' לה, כז), לְכָךְ הִתְנַדְּבוּ
כָּאן תְּחִלָּה:

ז וְאֵת הַבָּקָר וַיִּתֵּן אוֹתָם אֶל־הַלְוִיִּם: אֵת ׀ שְׁתֵּי הָעֲגָלוֹת וְאֵת
ח אַרְבַּעַת הַבָּקָר נָתַן לִבְנֵי גֵרְשׁוֹן כְּפִי עֲבֹדָתָם: וְאֵת ׀ אַרְבַּע
הָעֲגָלֹת וְאֵת שְׁמֹנַת הַבָּקָר נָתַן לִבְנֵי מְרָרִי כְּפִי עֲבֹדָתָם בְּיַד
ט אִיתָמָר בֶּן־אַהֲרֹן הַכֹּהֵן: וְלִבְנֵי קְהָת לֹא נָתָן כִּי־עֲבֹדַת הַקֹּדֶשׁ
י עֲלֵהֶם בַּכָּתֵף יִשָּׂאוּ: וַיַּקְרִיבוּ הַנְּשִׂאִים אֵת חֲנֻכַּת הַמִּזְבֵּחַ בְּיוֹם
הִמָּשַׁח אֹתוֹ וַיַּקְרִיבוּ הַנְּשִׂיאִם אֶת־קָרְבָּנָם לִפְנֵי הַמִּזְבֵּחַ: וַיֹּאמֶר
יא יהוה אֶל־מֹשֶׁה נָשִׂיא אֶחָד לַיּוֹם נָשִׂיא אֶחָד לַיּוֹם יַקְרִיבוּ
יב אֶת־קָרְבָּנָם לַחֲנֻכַּת הַמִּזְבֵּחַ: וַיְהִי הַמַּקְרִיב בַּיּוֹם
הָרִאשׁוֹן אֶת־קָרְבָּנוֹ נַחְשׁוֹן בֶּן־עַמִּינָדָב לְמַטֵּה יְהוּדָה: וְקָרְבָּנוֹ
יג קַעֲרַת־כֶּסֶף אַחַת שְׁלֹשִׁים וּמֵאָה מִשְׁקָלָהּ מִזְרָק אֶחָד כֶּסֶף
שִׁבְעִים שֶׁקֶל בְּשֶׁקֶל הַקֹּדֶשׁ שְׁנֵיהֶם ׀ מְלֵאִים סֹלֶת בְּלוּלָה
בַשֶּׁמֶן לְמִנְחָה: כַּף אַחַת עֲשָׂרָה זָהָב מְלֵאָה קְטֹרֶת: פַּר אֶחָד
יד
טו בֶּן־בָּקָר אַיִל אֶחָד כֶּבֶשׂ־אֶחָד בֶּן־שְׁנָתוֹ לְעֹלָה: שְׂעִיר־עִזִּים
טז

ז | כְּפִי עֲבֹדָתָם. שֶׁהָיָה מַשָּׂא בְּנֵי גֵרְשׁוֹן קַל מִשֶּׁל מְרָרִי שֶׁהָיוּ נוֹשְׂאִים הַקְּרָשִׁים וְהָעַמּוּדִים וְהָאֲדָנִים:

ט | כִּי עֲבֹדַת הַקֹּדֶשׁ עֲלֵהֶם. מַשָּׂא דְּבַר הַקְּדֻשָּׁה, הָאָרוֹן וְהַשֻּׁלְחָן וְגוֹ' (לעיל ג, לא), לְפִיכָךְ "בַּכָּתֵף יִשָּׂאוּ":

י | וַיַּקְרִיבוּ הַנְּשִׂאִים אֵת חֲנֻכַּת הַמִּזְבֵּחַ. לְאַחַר שֶׁהִתְנַדְּבוּ הָעֲגָלוֹת וְהַבָּקָר לָשֵׂאת הַמִּשְׁכָּן, נְשָׂאָם לִבָּם לְהִתְנַדֵּב קָרְבָּנוֹת הַמִּזְבֵּחַ לְחַנְּכוֹ. וַיַּקְרִיבוּ הַנְּשִׂיאִם אֶת קָרְבָּנָם לִפְנֵי הַמִּזְבֵּחַ. כִּי לֹא קִבֵּל מֹשֶׁה מִיָּדָם עַד שֶׁנֶּאֱמַר לוֹ מִפִּי הַגְּבוּרָה:

יא | יַקְרִיבוּ אֶת קָרְבָּנָם לַחֲנֻכַּת הַמִּזְבֵּחַ. וַעֲדַיִן לֹא הָיָה יוֹדֵעַ מֹשֶׁה הֵיאַךְ יַקְרִיבוּ, אִם כְּסֵדֶר תּוֹלְדוֹתָם אִם כְּסֵדֶר הַמַּסָּעוֹת, עַד שֶׁנֶּאֱמַר לוֹ מִפִּי הַקָּדוֹשׁ בָּרוּךְ הוּא: יַקְרִיבוּ לַמַּסָּעוֹת אִישׁ יוֹמוֹ:

יב | בַּיּוֹם הָרִאשׁוֹן. אוֹתוֹ הַיּוֹם נָטַל עֶשֶׂר עֲטָרוֹת, רִאשׁוֹן לַמַּעֲשֶׂה בְּרֵאשִׁית, רִאשׁוֹן לַנְּשִׂיאִים וְכוּ', כִּדְאִיתָא בְּסֵדֶר עוֹלָם (פרק ז): לְמַטֵּה יְהוּדָה. יִחֲסוֹ הַכָּתוּב עַל שִׁבְטוֹ, וְלֹא שֶׁגָּבָה מִשִּׁבְטוֹ וְהִקְרִיב. אוֹ אֵינוֹ אוֹמֵר "לְמַטֵּה יְהוּדָה" אֶלָּא שֶׁגָּבָה מִשִּׁבְטוֹ וְהֵבִיא? תַּלְמוּד לוֹמַר: "זֶה קָרְבַּן נַחְשׁוֹן" (להלן פסוק יז), מִשֶּׁלּוֹ הֵבִיא:

יג | שְׁנֵיהֶם מְלֵאִים סֹלֶת. לְמִנְחַת נְדָבָה:

יד | עֲשָׂרָה זָהָב. כְּתַרְגּוּמוֹ, מִשְׁקַל עֶשֶׂר שִׁקְלֵי הַקֹּדֶשׁ הָיָה בָהּ: מְלֵאָה קְטֹרֶת. לֹא מָצִינוּ קְטֹרֶת לְיָחִיד וְלֹא עַל מִזְבֵּחַ הַחִיצוֹן אֶלָּא זוֹ בִּלְבַד, וְהוֹרָאַת שָׁעָה הָיְתָה:

טו | פַּר אֶחָד. מְיֻחָד שֶׁבְּעֶדְרוֹ:

טז | שְׂעִיר עִזִּים אֶחָד לְחַטָּאת. לְכַפֵּר עַל קֶבֶר הַתְּהוֹם, טֻמְאַת סָפֵק:

במדבר | פרק ז

יז אֶחָד לְחַטָּאת: וּלְזֶבַח הַשְּׁלָמִים בָּקָר שְׁנַיִם אֵילִם חֲמִשָּׁה
עַתּוּדִים חֲמִשָּׁה כְּבָשִׂים בְּנֵי־שָׁנָה חֲמִשָּׁה זֶה קָרְבַּן נַחְשׁוֹן
בֶּן־עַמִּינָדָב:

יח בַּיּוֹם הַשֵּׁנִי הִקְרִיב נְתַנְאֵל בֶּן־צוּעָר נְשִׂיא יִשָּׂשכָר: הִקְרִב
אֶת־קָרְבָּנוֹ קַעֲרַת־כֶּסֶף אַחַת שְׁלֹשִׁים וּמֵאָה מִשְׁקָלָהּ מִזְרָק
אֶחָד כֶּסֶף שִׁבְעִים שֶׁקֶל בְּשֶׁקֶל הַקֹּדֶשׁ שְׁנֵיהֶם ׀ מְלֵאִים סֹלֶת
כ בְּלוּלָה בַשֶּׁמֶן לְמִנְחָה: כַּף אַחַת עֲשָׂרָה זָהָב מְלֵאָה קְטֹרֶת:
כא פַּר אֶחָד בֶּן־בָּקָר אַיִל אֶחָד כֶּבֶשׂ־אֶחָד בֶּן־שְׁנָתוֹ לְעֹלָה:
כב שְׂעִיר־עִזִּים אֶחָד לְחַטָּאת: וּלְזֶבַח הַשְּׁלָמִים בָּקָר שְׁנַיִם אֵילִם
כג

יח-יט **הִקְרִיב נְתַנְאֵל בֶּן צוּעָר, הִקְרִב אֶת קָרְבָּנוֹ.** מַה תַּלְמוּד לוֹמַר "הִקְרִיב" בְּשִׁבְטוֹ שֶׁל יִשָּׂשׂכָר מַה שֶּׁלֹּא נֶאֱמַר בְּכָל הַשְּׁבָטִים? לְפִי שֶׁבָּא רְאוּבֵן וְעִרְעֵר וְאָמַר: דַּיִּי שֶׁקְּדָמַנִי יְהוּדָה אָחִי, אַקְרִיב אֲנִי אַחֲרָיו. אָמַר לוֹ מֹשֶׁה: מִפִּי הַגְּבוּרָה נֶאֱמַר לִי שֶׁיַּקְרִיבוּ כְּסֵדֶר מַסָּעָן לְדִגְלֵיהֶם. לְכָךְ אָמַר: "הַקְרֵב אֶת קָרְבָּנוֹ" וְהוּא חָסֵר יוּ"ד, שֶׁהוּא מַשְׁמַע 'הַקְרֵב' לְשׁוֹן צִוּוּי, שֶׁמִּפִּי הַגְּבוּרָה מְצֻוֶּה 'הַקְרֵב'. וּמַהוּ "הִקְרִיב הִקְרִב" שְׁנֵי פְעָמִים? שֶׁבִּשְׁבִיל שְׁנֵי דְבָרִים זָכָה לְהַקְרִיב שֵׁנִי לַשְּׁבָטִים: אַחַת - שֶׁהָיוּ יוֹדְעִים בַּתּוֹרָה, שֶׁנֶּאֱמַר: "וּמִבְּנֵי יִשָּׂשׂכָר יוֹדְעֵי בִינָה לָעִתִּים" (דברי הימים א' יב, לג). וְאַחַת - שֶׁהֵם נָתְנוּ עֵצָה לַנְּשִׂיאִים לְהִתְנַדֵּב קָרְבָּנוֹת הַלָּלוּ. וּבִיסוֹדוֹ שֶׁל רַבִּי מֹשֶׁה הַדַּרְשָׁן מָצָאתִי: אָמַר רַבִּי פִּנְחָס בֶּן יָאִיר: נְתַנְאֵל בֶּן צוּעָר הַשִּׂיאָן עֵצָה זוֹ. **קַעֲרַת כֶּסֶף.** מִנְיַן אוֹתִיּוֹתָיו בְּגִימַטְרִיָּא תתק"ל, כְּנֶגֶד שְׁנוֹתָיו שֶׁל אָדָם הָרִאשׁוֹן. **שְׁלֹשִׁים וּמֵאָה מִשְׁקָלָהּ.** עַל שֵׁם שֶׁכְּשֶׁהֶעֱמִיד תּוֹלָדוֹת לְקִיּוּם הָעוֹלָם בֶּן מֵאָה וּשְׁלֹשִׁים שָׁנָה הָיָה, שֶׁנֶּאֱמַר: "וַיְחִי אָדָם שְׁלֹשִׁים וּמְאַת שָׁנָה וַיּוֹלֶד בִּדְמוּתוֹ" וְגוֹ' (בראשית ה, ג). **מִזְרָק אֶחָד כֶּסֶף.** בְּגִימַטְרִיָּא תק"כ, עַל שֵׁם נֹחַ שֶׁהֶעֱמִיד תּוֹלָדוֹת בֶּן ת"ק שָׁנָה, וְעַל שֵׁם ק' עֶשְׂרִים שָׁנָה שֶׁנִּגְזְרָה

גְּזֵרַת הַמַּבּוּל קֹדֶם תּוֹלְדוֹתָיו, כְּמוֹ שֶׁפֵּרַשְׁתִּי אֵצֶל "וְהָיוּ יָמָיו מֵאָה וְעֶשְׂרִים שָׁנָה" (שם ג). לְפִיכָךְ נֶאֱמַר: "מִזְרָק אֶחָד כֶּסֶף" וְלֹא נֶאֱמַר 'מִזְרָק כֶּסֶף אֶחָד' כְּמוֹ שֶׁנֶּאֱמַר בַּקְּעָרָה, לוֹמַר שֶׁאַף אוֹתִיּוֹת שֶׁל 'אֶחָד' מִצְטָרְפוֹת לַמִּנְיָן: **שִׁבְעִים שֶׁקֶל.** כְּנֶגֶד שִׁבְעִים אֻמּוֹת שֶׁיָּצְאוּ מִבָּנָיו:

כ **כַּף אַחַת.** כְּנֶגֶד הַתּוֹרָה שֶׁנִּתְּנָה מִיָּדוֹ שֶׁל הַקָּדוֹשׁ בָּרוּךְ הוּא: **עֲשָׂרָה זָהָב.** כְּנֶגֶד עֲשֶׂרֶת הַדִּבְּרוֹת: **מְלֵאָה קְטֹרֶת.** גִּימַטְרִיָּא שֶׁל קְטֹרֶת תרי"ג מִצְווֹת, וּבִלְבַד שֶׁתַּחֲלִיף קוּ"ף בְּדָלֶ"ת עַל יְדֵי א"ת ב"ש ג"ר ד"ק:

כא **פַּר אֶחָד.** כְּנֶגֶד אַבְרָהָם, שֶׁנֶּאֱמַר בּוֹ: "וַיִּקַּח בֶּן בָּקָר" (שם יח, ז): **אַיִל אֶחָד.** כְּנֶגֶד יִצְחָק: "וַיִּקַּח אֶת הָאַיִל" וְגוֹ' (שם כב, יג): **כֶּבֶשׂ אֶחָד.** כְּנֶגֶד יַעֲקֹב: "וְהַכְּשָׂבִים הִפְרִיד יַעֲקֹב" (שם ל, מ):

כב **שְׂעִיר עִזִּים.** לְכַפֵּר עַל מְכִירַת יוֹסֵף, שֶׁנֶּאֱמַר בּוֹ: "וַיִּשְׁחֲטוּ שְׂעִיר עִזִּים" (שם לז, לא):

כג **וּלְזֶבַח הַשְּׁלָמִים בָּקָר שְׁנַיִם.** כְּנֶגֶד מֹשֶׁה וְאַהֲרֹן שֶׁנָּתְנוּ שָׁלוֹם בֵּין יִשְׂרָאֵל לַאֲבִיהֶם שֶׁבַּשָּׁמַיִם: **אֵילִם עַתּוּדִים כְּבָשִׂים.** שְׁלֹשָׁה מִינִים, כְּנֶגֶד כֹּהֲנִים וּלְוִיִּים וְיִשְׂרְאֵלִים, וּכְנֶגֶד תּוֹרָה נְבִיאִים וּכְתוּבִים. שָׁלֹשׁ

חֲמִשָּׁ֤ה עַתֻּדִים֙ חֲמִשָּׁ֔ה כְּבָשִׂ֥ים בְּנֵֽי־שָׁנָ֖ה חֲמִשָּׁ֑ה זֶ֛ה קָרְבַּ֥ן נְתַנְאֵ֖ל בֶּן־צוּעָֽר׃

כה בַּיּוֹם֙ הַשְּׁלִישִׁ֔י נָשִׂ֖יא לִבְנֵ֣י זְבוּלֻ֑ן אֱלִיאָ֖ב בֶּן־חֵלֹֽן׃ קָרְבָּנ֞וֹ קַֽעֲרַת־כֶּ֣סֶף אַחַ֗ת שְׁלֹשִׁ֣ים וּמֵאָה֮ מִשְׁקָלָהּ֒ מִזְרָ֤ק אֶחָד֙ כֶּ֔סֶף שִׁבְעִ֥ים שֶׁ֖קֶל בְּשֶׁ֣קֶל הַקֹּ֑דֶשׁ שְׁנֵיהֶ֣ם ׀ מְלֵאִ֗ים סֹ֛לֶת בְּלוּלָ֥ה בַשֶּׁ֖מֶן לְמִנְחָֽה׃ כו כַּ֥ף אַחַ֛ת עֲשָׂרָ֥ה זָהָ֖ב מְלֵאָ֥ה קְטֹֽרֶת׃ פַּ֣ר אֶחָ֞ד בֶּן־ כז בָּקָ֗ר אַ֧יִל אֶחָ֛ד כֶּֽבֶשׂ־אֶחָ֥ד בֶּן־שְׁנָת֖וֹ לְעֹלָֽה׃ שְׂעִיר־עִזִּ֥ים כח אֶחָ֖ד לְחַטָּֽאת׃ וּלְזֶ֣בַח הַשְּׁלָמִים֮ בָּקָ֣ר שְׁנַ֒יִם֒ אֵילִ֤ם חֲמִשָּׁה֙ כט עַתֻּדִ֣ים חֲמִשָּׁ֔ה כְּבָשִׂ֥ים בְּנֵי־שָׁנָ֖ה חֲמִשָּׁ֑ה זֶ֛ה קָרְבַּ֥ן אֱלִיאָ֖ב בֶּן־חֵלֹֽן׃

ל בַּיּוֹם֙ הָרְבִיעִ֔י נָשִׂ֖יא לִבְנֵ֣י רְאוּבֵ֑ן אֱלִיצ֖וּר בֶּן־שְׁדֵיאֽוּר׃ קָרְבָּנ֞וֹ לא קַֽעֲרַת־כֶּ֣סֶף אַחַ֗ת שְׁלֹשִׁ֣ים וּמֵאָה֮ מִשְׁקָלָהּ֒ מִזְרָ֤ק אֶחָד֙ כֶּ֔סֶף שִׁבְעִ֥ים שֶׁ֖קֶל בְּשֶׁ֣קֶל הַקֹּ֑דֶשׁ שְׁנֵיהֶ֣ם ׀ מְלֵאִ֗ים סֹ֛לֶת בְּלוּלָ֥ה בַשֶּׁ֖מֶן לְמִנְחָֽה׃ לב כַּ֥ף אַחַ֛ת עֲשָׂרָ֥ה זָהָ֖ב מְלֵאָ֥ה קְטֹֽרֶת׃ פַּ֣ר אֶחָ֞ד לג בֶּן־בָּקָ֗ר אַ֧יִל אֶחָ֛ד כֶּֽבֶשׂ־אֶחָ֥ד בֶּן־שְׁנָת֖וֹ לְעֹלָֽה׃ שְׂעִיר־עִזִּ֥ים לד אֶחָ֖ד לְחַטָּֽאת׃ וּלְזֶ֣בַח הַשְּׁלָמִים֮ בָּקָ֣ר שְׁנַ֒יִם֒ אֵילִ֤ם חֲמִשָּׁה֙ לה עַתֻּדִ֣ים חֲמִשָּׁ֔ה כְּבָשִׂ֥ים בְּנֵי־שָׁנָ֖ה חֲמִשָּׁ֑ה זֶ֛ה קָרְבַּ֥ן אֱלִיצ֖וּר בֶּן־שְׁדֵיאֽוּר׃

חֲמִשִׁיּוֹת, כְּנֶגֶד חֲמִשָּׁה חוּמְשִׁין, וַחֲמֶשֶׁת הַדִּבְּרוֹת הַכְּתוּבִין עַל לוּחַ אֶחָד, וַחֲמִשָּׁה הַכְּתוּבִין עַל הַשֵּׁנִי. עַד כָּאן מִיסוֹדוֹ שֶׁל רַבִּי מֹשֶׁה הַדַּרְשָׁן:

כד **בַּיּוֹם הַשְּׁלִישִׁי נָשִׂיא וְגוֹ'.** בַּיּוֹם הַשְּׁלִישִׁי הָיָה הַנָּשִׂיא הַמַּקְרִיב לִבְנֵי זְבוּלֻן, וְכֵן כֻּלָּם. אֲבָל בִּנְתַנְאֵל

שֶׁנֶּאֱמַר בּוֹ: "הַקְרֵב נְתַנְאֵל" (לְעֵיל פָּסוּק יח) נוֹפֵל מַחֲרָיו הַלָּשׁוֹן לוֹמַר: "נָשִׂיא יִשָּׂשכָר", לְפִי שֶׁכְּבָר הִזְכִּיר שְׁמוֹ וְהַקְרָבָתוֹ, וּבִשְׁאָר שֶׁלֹּא נֶאֱמַר בָּהֶן 'הַקְרֵב', נוֹפֵל עֲלֵיהֶן לָשׁוֹן זֶה: "נָשִׂיא לִבְנֵי פְּלוֹנִי", אוֹתוֹ הַיּוֹם הָיָה הַנָּשִׂיא הַמַּקְרִיב לְשֵׁבֶט פְּלוֹנִי:

| לו | בַּיּוֹם֙ הַֽחֲמִישִׁ֔י נָשִׂ֖יא לִבְנֵ֣י שִׁמְע֑וֹן שְׁלֻֽמִיאֵ֖ל בֶּן־צוּרִֽישַׁדָּֽי:
| לז | קָרְבָּנ֞וֹ קַֽעֲרַת־כֶּ֣סֶף אַחַ֗ת שְׁלֹשִׁ֣ים וּמֵאָה֮ מִשְׁקָלָהּ֒ מִזְרָ֤ק אֶחָד֙ כֶּ֔סֶף שִׁבְעִ֥ים שֶׁ֖קֶל בְּשֶׁ֣קֶל הַקֹּ֑דֶשׁ שְׁנֵיהֶ֣ם ׀ מְלֵאִ֗ים סֹ֛לֶת בְּלוּלָ֥ה בַשֶּׁ֖מֶן לְמִנְחָֽה:
| לח | כַּ֥ף אַחַ֛ת עֲשָׂרָ֥ה זָהָ֖ב מְלֵאָ֥ה קְטֹֽרֶת: פַּ֣ר אֶחָ֞ד בֶּן־בָּקָ֗ר אַ֧יִל אֶחָ֛ד כֶּֽבֶשׂ־אֶחָ֥ד בֶּן־שְׁנָת֖וֹ לְעֹלָֽה:
| מ | שְׂעִיר־עִזִּ֥ים אֶחָ֖ד לְחַטָּֽאת:
| מא | וּלְזֶ֣בַח הַשְּׁלָמִים֮ בָּקָ֣ר שְׁנַ֒יִם֒ אֵילִ֤ם חֲמִשָּׁה֙ עַתֻּדִ֣ים חֲמִשָּׁ֔ה כְּבָשִׂ֥ים בְּנֵֽי־שָׁנָ֖ה חֲמִשָּׁ֑ה זֶ֛ה קָרְבַּ֥ן שְׁלֻֽמִיאֵ֖ל בֶּן־צוּרִֽישַׁדָּֽי:

ששי
| מב | בַּיּוֹם֙ הַשִּׁשִּׁ֔י נָשִׂ֖יא לִבְנֵ֣י גָ֑ד אֶלְיָסָ֖ף בֶּן־דְּעוּאֵֽל:
| מג | קָרְבָּנ֞וֹ קַֽעֲרַת־כֶּ֣סֶף אַחַ֗ת שְׁלֹשִׁ֣ים וּמֵאָה֮ מִשְׁקָלָהּ֒ מִזְרָ֤ק אֶחָד֙ כֶּ֔סֶף שִׁבְעִ֥ים שֶׁ֖קֶל בְּשֶׁ֣קֶל הַקֹּ֑דֶשׁ שְׁנֵיהֶ֣ם ׀ מְלֵאִ֗ים סֹ֛לֶת בְּלוּלָ֥ה בַשֶּׁ֖מֶן לְמִנְחָֽה:
| מד מה | כַּ֥ף אַחַ֛ת עֲשָׂרָ֥ה זָהָ֖ב מְלֵאָ֥ה קְטֹֽרֶת: פַּ֣ר אֶחָ֞ד בֶּן־בָּקָ֗ר אַ֧יִל אֶחָ֛ד כֶּֽבֶשׂ־אֶחָ֥ד בֶּן־שְׁנָת֖וֹ לְעֹלָֽה:
| מו | שְׂעִיר־עִזִּ֥ים אֶחָ֖ד לְחַטָּֽאת:
| מז | וּלְזֶ֣בַח הַשְּׁלָמִים֮ בָּקָ֣ר שְׁנַ֒יִם֒ אֵילִ֤ם חֲמִשָּׁה֙ עַתֻּדִ֣ים חֲמִשָּׁ֔ה כְּבָשִׂ֥ים בְּנֵֽי־שָׁנָ֖ה חֲמִשָּׁ֑ה זֶ֛ה קָרְבַּ֥ן אֶלְיָסָ֖ף בֶּן־דְּעוּאֵֽל:

| מח מט | בַּיּוֹם֙ הַשְּׁבִיעִ֔י נָשִׂ֖יא לִבְנֵ֣י אֶפְרָ֑יִם אֱלִֽישָׁמָ֖ע בֶּן־עַמִּיהֽוּד: קָרְבָּנ֞וֹ קַֽעֲרַת־כֶּ֣סֶף אַחַ֗ת שְׁלֹשִׁ֣ים וּמֵאָה֮ מִשְׁקָלָהּ֒ מִזְרָ֤ק אֶחָד֙ כֶּ֔סֶף שִׁבְעִ֥ים שֶׁ֖קֶל בְּשֶׁ֣קֶל הַקֹּ֑דֶשׁ שְׁנֵיהֶ֣ם ׀ מְלֵאִ֗ים סֹ֛לֶת בְּלוּלָ֥ה בַשֶּׁ֖מֶן לְמִנְחָֽה:

ז

| נא | כַּ֥ף אַחַ֛ת עֲשָׂרָ֥ה זָהָ֖ב מְלֵאָ֥ה קְטֹֽרֶת: פַּ֣ר אֶחָ֞ד בֶּן־בָּקָ֗ר אַ֧יִל אֶחָ֛ד כֶּֽבֶשׂ־אֶחָ֥ד בֶּן־שְׁנָת֖וֹ לְעֹלָֽה:
| נב | שְׂעִיר־עִזִּ֥ים
| נג | אֶחָ֖ד לְחַטָּֽאת: וּלְזֶ֣בַח הַשְּׁלָמִים֮ בָּקָ֣ר שְׁנַ֒יִם֒ אֵילִ֤ם חֲמִשָּׁה֙

עַתֻּדִים חֲמִשָּׁה כְּבָשִׂים בְּנֵי־שָׁנָה חֲמִשָּׁה זֶה קָרְבַּן אֱלִישָׁמָע בֶּן־עַמִּיהוּד:

נג בַּיּוֹם הַשְּׁמִינִי נָשִׂיא לִבְנֵי מְנַשֶּׁה גַּמְלִיאֵל בֶּן־פְּדָהצוּר: קָרְבָּנוֹ קַעֲרַת־כֶּסֶף אַחַת שְׁלֹשִׁים וּמֵאָה מִשְׁקָלָהּ מִזְרָק אֶחָד כֶּסֶף שִׁבְעִים שֶׁקֶל בְּשֶׁקֶל הַקֹּדֶשׁ שְׁנֵיהֶם ׀ מְלֵאִים סֹלֶת בְּלוּלָה בַשֶּׁמֶן לְמִנְחָה: נז כַּף אַחַת עֲשָׂרָה זָהָב מְלֵאָה קְטֹרֶת: נח פַּר אֶחָד בֶּן־בָּקָר אַיִל אֶחָד כֶּבֶשׂ־אֶחָד בֶּן־שְׁנָתוֹ לְעֹלָה: שְׂעִיר־עִזִּים אֶחָד לְחַטָּאת: נט וּלְזֶבַח הַשְּׁלָמִים בָּקָר שְׁנַיִם אֵילִם חֲמִשָּׁה עַתֻּדִים חֲמִשָּׁה כְּבָשִׂים בְּנֵי־שָׁנָה חֲמִשָּׁה זֶה קָרְבַּן גַּמְלִיאֵל בֶּן־פְּדָהצוּר:

ס בַּיּוֹם הַתְּשִׁיעִי נָשִׂיא לִבְנֵי בִנְיָמִן אֲבִידָן בֶּן־גִּדְעֹנִי: קָרְבָּנוֹ קַעֲרַת־כֶּסֶף אַחַת שְׁלֹשִׁים וּמֵאָה מִשְׁקָלָהּ מִזְרָק אֶחָד כֶּסֶף שִׁבְעִים שֶׁקֶל בְּשֶׁקֶל הַקֹּדֶשׁ שְׁנֵיהֶם ׀ מְלֵאִים סֹלֶת בְּלוּלָה בַשֶּׁמֶן לְמִנְחָה: סג כַּף אַחַת עֲשָׂרָה זָהָב מְלֵאָה קְטֹרֶת: סד פַּר אֶחָד בֶּן־בָּקָר אַיִל אֶחָד כֶּבֶשׂ־אֶחָד בֶּן־שְׁנָתוֹ לְעֹלָה: שְׂעִיר־עִזִּים אֶחָד לְחַטָּאת: סה וּלְזֶבַח הַשְּׁלָמִים בָּקָר שְׁנַיִם אֵילִם חֲמִשָּׁה עַתֻּדִים חֲמִשָּׁה כְּבָשִׂים בְּנֵי־שָׁנָה חֲמִשָּׁה זֶה קָרְבַּן אֲבִידָן בֶּן־גִּדְעֹנִי:

סו בַּיּוֹם הָעֲשִׂירִי נָשִׂיא לִבְנֵי דָן אֲחִיעֶזֶר בֶּן־עַמִּישַׁדָּי: קָרְבָּנוֹ קַעֲרַת־כֶּסֶף אַחַת שְׁלֹשִׁים וּמֵאָה מִשְׁקָלָהּ מִזְרָק אֶחָד כֶּסֶף שִׁבְעִים שֶׁקֶל בְּשֶׁקֶל הַקֹּדֶשׁ שְׁנֵיהֶם ׀ מְלֵאִים סֹלֶת בְּלוּלָה

סח בַּשֶּׁמֶן לְמִנְחָה: כַּף אַחַת עֲשָׂרָה זָהָב מְלֵאָה קְטֹרֶת: פַּר אֶחָד
סט בֶּן־בָּקָר אַיִל אֶחָד כֶּבֶשׂ־אֶחָד בֶּן־שְׁנָתוֹ לְעֹלָה: שְׂעִיר־עִזִּים
ע אֶחָד לְחַטָּאת: וּלְזֶבַח הַשְּׁלָמִים בָּקָר שְׁנַיִם אֵילִם חֲמִשָּׁה
עא עַתֻּדִים חֲמִשָּׁה כְּבָשִׂים בְּנֵי־שָׁנָה חֲמִשָּׁה זֶה קָרְבַּן אֲחִיעֶזֶר בֶּן־עַמִּישַׁדָּי:

עב בְּיוֹם עַשְׁתֵּי עָשָׂר יוֹם נָשִׂיא לִבְנֵי אָשֵׁר פַּגְעִיאֵל בֶּן־עָכְרָן: שביעי
עג קָרְבָּנוֹ קַעֲרַת־כֶּסֶף אַחַת שְׁלֹשִׁים וּמֵאָה מִשְׁקָלָהּ מִזְרָק אֶחָד כֶּסֶף שִׁבְעִים שֶׁקֶל בְּשֶׁקֶל הַקֹּדֶשׁ שְׁנֵיהֶם ׀ מְלֵאִים סֹלֶת בְּלוּלָה
עד בַשֶּׁמֶן לְמִנְחָה: כַּף אַחַת עֲשָׂרָה זָהָב מְלֵאָה קְטֹרֶת: פַּר אֶחָד
עה בֶּן־בָּקָר אַיִל אֶחָד כֶּבֶשׂ־אֶחָד בֶּן־שְׁנָתוֹ לְעֹלָה: שְׂעִיר־עִזִּים
עו אֶחָד לְחַטָּאת: וּלְזֶבַח הַשְּׁלָמִים בָּקָר שְׁנַיִם אֵילִם חֲמִשָּׁה
עז עַתֻּדִים חֲמִשָּׁה כְּבָשִׂים בְּנֵי־שָׁנָה חֲמִשָּׁה זֶה קָרְבַּן פַּגְעִיאֵל בֶּן־עָכְרָן:

עח בְּיוֹם שְׁנֵים עָשָׂר יוֹם נָשִׂיא לִבְנֵי נַפְתָּלִי אֲחִירַע בֶּן־עֵינָן: קָרְבָּנוֹ
עט קַעֲרַת־כֶּסֶף אַחַת שְׁלֹשִׁים וּמֵאָה מִשְׁקָלָהּ מִזְרָק אֶחָד כֶּסֶף שִׁבְעִים שֶׁקֶל בְּשֶׁקֶל הַקֹּדֶשׁ שְׁנֵיהֶם ׀ מְלֵאִים סֹלֶת בְּלוּלָה
פ בַשֶּׁמֶן לְמִנְחָה: כַּף אַחַת עֲשָׂרָה זָהָב מְלֵאָה קְטֹרֶת: פַּר אֶחָד
פא בֶּן־בָּקָר אַיִל אֶחָד כֶּבֶשׂ־אֶחָד בֶּן־שְׁנָתוֹ לְעֹלָה: שְׂעִיר־עִזִּים
פב אֶחָד לְחַטָּאת: וּלְזֶבַח הַשְּׁלָמִים בָּקָר שְׁנַיִם אֵילִם חֲמִשָּׁה
פג עַתֻּדִים חֲמִשָּׁה כְּבָשִׂים בְּנֵי־שָׁנָה חֲמִשָּׁה זֶה קָרְבַּן אֲחִירַע בֶּן־עֵינָן:

פד זֹאת ׀ חֲנֻכַּ֣ת הַמִּזְבֵּ֗חַ בְּיוֹם֙ הִמָּשַׁ֣ח אֹת֔וֹ מֵאֵ֖ת נְשִׂיאֵ֣י יִשְׂרָאֵ֑ל קַעֲרֹ֨ת כֶּ֜סֶף שְׁתֵּ֣ים עֶשְׂרֵ֗ה מִֽזְרְקֵי־כֶ֨סֶף֙ שְׁנֵ֣ים עָשָׂ֔ר כַּפּ֥וֹת זָהָ֖ב שְׁתֵּ֥ים עֶשְׂרֵֽה:
פה שְׁלֹשִׁ֣ים וּמֵאָ֗ה הַקְּעָרָ֤ה הָֽאַחַת֙ כֶּ֔סֶף וְשִׁבְעִ֖ים הַמִּזְרָ֣ק הָאֶחָ֑ד כֹּ֚ל כֶּ֣סֶף הַכֵּלִ֔ים אַלְפַּ֥יִם וְאַרְבַּע־מֵא֖וֹת בְּשֶׁ֥קֶל הַקֹּֽדֶשׁ:
פו כַּפּ֨וֹת זָהָ֤ב שְׁתֵּים־עֶשְׂרֵה֙ מְלֵאֹ֣ת קְטֹ֔רֶת עֲשָׂרָ֧ה עֲשָׂרָ֛ה הַכַּ֖ף בְּשֶׁ֣קֶל הַקֹּ֑דֶשׁ כָּל־זְהַ֥ב הַכַּפּ֖וֹת עֶשְׂרִ֥ים וּמֵאָֽה:

מפטיר

פז כָּל־הַבָּקָ֨ר לָעֹלָ֜ה שְׁנֵ֧ים עָשָׂ֣ר פָּרִ֗ים אֵילִ֤ם שְׁנֵים־עָשָׂר֙ כְּבָשִׂ֧ים בְּנֵֽי־שָׁנָ֛ה שְׁנֵ֥ים עָשָׂ֖ר וּמִנְחָתָ֑ם וּשְׂעִירֵ֥י עִזִּ֛ים שְׁנֵ֥ים עָשָׂ֖ר לְחַטָּֽאת:
פח וְכֹ֞ל בְּקַ֣ר ׀ זֶ֣בַח הַשְּׁלָמִ֗ים עֶשְׂרִ֣ים וְאַרְבָּעָה֙ פָּרִ֔ים אֵילִ֤ם שִׁשִּׁים֙ עַתֻּדִ֣ים שִׁשִּׁ֔ים כְּבָשִׂ֥ים בְּנֵי־שָׁנָ֖ה שִׁשִּׁ֑ים זֹ֚את חֲנֻכַּ֣ת הַמִּזְבֵּ֔חַ אַחֲרֵ֖י הִמָּשַׁ֥ח אֹתֽוֹ:
פט וּבְבֹ֨א מֹשֶׁ֜ה אֶל־אֹ֣הֶל מוֹעֵד֮ לְדַבֵּ֣ר אִתּוֹ֒ וַיִּשְׁמַ֨ע אֶת־הַקּ֜וֹל מִדַּבֵּ֣ר אֵלָ֗יו מֵעַ֤ל הַכַּפֹּ֨רֶת֙ אֲשֶׁר֙ עַל־אֲרֹ֣ן הָעֵדֻ֔ת מִבֵּ֖ין שְׁנֵ֣י הַכְּרֻבִ֑ים וַיְדַבֵּ֖ר אֵלָֽיו:

פד בְּיוֹם הִמָּשַׁח אֹתוֹ. בּוֹ בַּיּוֹם שֶׁנִּמְשַׁח הִקְרִיב, וּמָה אֲנִי מְקַיֵּם "אַחֲרֵי הִמָּשַׁח" (להלן פסוק פח)? שֶׁנִּמְשַׁח תְּחִלָּה וְאַחַר כָּךְ הִקְרִיב. אוֹ: "אַחֲרֵי הִמָּשַׁח" לְאַחַר זְמַן, וְלֹא בָּא לְלַמֵּד "בְּיוֹם הִמָּשַׁח" אֶלָּא לוֹמַר שֶׁנִּמְשַׁח בַּיּוֹם? כְּשֶׁהוּא אוֹמֵר: "בְּיוֹם מָשְׁחוֹ אֹתָם" (ויקרא ז, לו), לָמַדְנוּ שֶׁנִּמְשַׁח בַּיּוֹם, וּמַה תַּלְמוּד לוֹמַר: "בְּיוֹם הִמָּשַׁח אֹתוֹ"? בַּיּוֹם שֶׁנִּמְשַׁח הִקְרִיב. קַעֲרֹת כֶּסֶף שְׁתֵּים עֶשְׂרֵה. הֵם הֵם שֶׁהִתְנַדְּבוּ, וְלֹא אֵרַע בָּהֶם פְּסוּל:

פה שְׁלֹשִׁים וּמֵאָה הַקְּעָרָה הָאַחַת וְגוֹ'. מַה תַּלְמוּד לוֹמַר? לְפִי שֶׁנֶּאֱמַר: "שְׁלֹשִׁים וּמֵאָה מִשְׁקָלָהּ", וְלֹא פֵּרֵשׁ בְּאֵי זֶה שֶׁקֶל, לְכָךְ חָזַר וּשְׁנָאָהּ כָּאן וְכָלַל בְּכֻלָּן "כָּל כֶּסֶף הַכֵּלִים... בְּשֶׁקֶל הַקֹּדֶשׁ": כָּל כֶּסֶף הַכֵּלִים וְגוֹ'. לִמֶּדְךָ שֶׁהָיוּ כְּלֵי הַמִּקְדָּשׁ מְכֻוָּנִים בְּמִשְׁקָלָן,

שׁוֹקְלָן אֶחָד אֶחָד וְשׁוֹקְלָן כֻּלָּן כְּאֶחָד, לֹא רִבָּה וְלֹא מִעֵט:

פו כַּפּוֹת זָהָב שְׁתֵּים עֶשְׂרֵה. לָמָּה נֶאֱמַר? לְפִי שֶׁנֶּאֱמַר: "כַּף אַחַת עֲשָׂרָה זָהָב", הִיא שֶׁל זָהָב וּמִשְׁקָלָהּ עֲשָׂרָה שְׁקָלִים שֶׁל כֶּסֶף, אוֹ אֵינוֹ אֶלָּא כַּף אַחַת שֶׁל כֶּסֶף וּמִשְׁקָלָהּ עֲשָׂרָה שִׁקְלֵי זָהָב – וְשִׁקְלֵי זָהָב אֵין מִשְׁקָלָם שָׁוֶה לְשֶׁל כֶּסֶף? תַּלְמוּד לוֹמַר: "כַּפּוֹת זָהָב", שֶׁל זָהָב הָיוּ:

פט וּבְבֹא מֹשֶׁה. שְׁנֵי כְּתוּבִים הַמַּכְחִישִׁים זֶה אֶת זֶה, בָּא שְׁלִישִׁי וְהִכְרִיעַ בֵּינֵיהֶם. כָּתוּב אֶחָד אוֹמֵר: "וַיְדַבֵּר ה' אֵלָיו מֵאֹהֶל מוֹעֵד" (ויקרא א, א), וְהוּא חוּץ לַפָּרֹכֶת, וְכָתוּב אֶחָד אוֹמֵר: "וְדִבַּרְתִּי אִתְּךָ מֵעַל הַכַּפֹּרֶת" (שמות כה, כב), בָּא זֶה וְהִכְרִיעַ בֵּינֵיהֶם: מֹשֶׁה בָּא אֶל אֹהֶל מוֹעֵד, וְשָׁם שׁוֹמֵעַ אֶת הַקּוֹל הַבָּא

במדבר | פרק ח

א וַיְדַבֵּ֥ר יְהֹוָ֖ה אֶל־מֹשֶׁ֥ה לֵּאמֹֽר: דַּבֵּר֙ אֶֽל־אַהֲרֹ֔ן וְאָמַרְתָּ֖ אֵלָ֑יו בְּהַעֲלֹֽתְךָ֙ אֶת־הַנֵּרֹ֔ת אֶל־מוּל֙ פְּנֵ֣י הַמְּנוֹרָ֔ה יָאִ֖ירוּ שִׁבְעַ֥ת הַנֵּרֽוֹת: ג וַיַּ֤עַשׂ כֵּן֙ אַהֲרֹ֔ן אֶל־מוּל֙ פְּנֵ֣י הַמְּנוֹרָ֔ה הֶעֱלָ֖ה נֵרֹתֶ֑יהָ כַּאֲשֶׁ֛ר צִוָּ֥ה יְהֹוָ֖ה אֶת־מֹשֶֽׁה: ד וְזֶ֨ה מַעֲשֵׂ֤ה הַמְּנֹרָה֙ מִקְשָׁ֣ה זָהָ֔ב עַד־יְרֵכָ֥הּ עַד־פִּרְחָ֖הּ מִקְשָׁ֣ה הִ֑וא כַּמַּרְאֶ֗ה אֲשֶׁ֨ר הֶרְאָ֤ה יְהֹוָה֙ אֶת־מֹשֶׁ֔ה כֵּ֥ן עָשָׂ֖ה אֶת־הַמְּנֹרָֽה:

ה וַיְדַבֵּ֥ר יְהֹוָ֖ה אֶל־מֹשֶׁ֥ה לֵּאמֹֽר: ו קַ֚ח אֶת־הַלְוִיִּ֔ם מִתּ֖וֹךְ בְּנֵ֣י יִשְׂרָאֵ֑ל וְטִהַרְתָּ֖ אֹתָֽם: ז וְכֹֽה־תַעֲשֶׂ֤ה לָהֶם֙ לְטַֽהֲרָ֔ם הַזֵּ֥ה עֲלֵיהֶ֖ם מֵ֥י

מֵעַל הַכַּפֹּרֶת מִבֵּין שְׁנֵי הַכְּרֻבִים, הַקּוֹל יוֹצֵא מִן הַשָּׁמַיִם לְבֵין שְׁנֵי הַכְּרוּבִים, וּמִשָּׁם יוֹצֵא לְאֹהֶל מוֹעֵד. **מִדַּבֵּר.** כְּמוֹ 'מִתְדַּבֵּר', כְּבוֹדוֹ שֶׁל מַעְלָה לוֹמַר כֵּן, מְדַבֵּר בֵּינוֹ לְבֵין עַצְמוֹ, וּמֹשֶׁה שׁוֹמֵעַ מֵאֵלָיו: **וַיְדַבֵּר אֵלָיו.** לְמַעֵט אֶת אַהֲרֹן מִן הַדִּבְּרוֹת: **וַיִּשְׁמַע אֶת הַקּוֹל.** יָכוֹל קוֹל נָמוּךְ? תַּלְמוּד לוֹמַר: "אֶת הַקּוֹל", הוּא הַקּוֹל שֶׁנִּדְבַּר עִמּוֹ בְּסִינַי, וּכְשֶׁמַּגִּיעַ לַפֶּתַח הָיָה נִפְסָק וְלֹא הָיָה יוֹצֵא חוּץ לָאֹהֶל:

פרק ח

ב **בְּהַעֲלֹתְךָ.** לָמָּה נִסְמְכָה פָּרָשַׁת הַמְּנוֹרָה לְפָרָשַׁת הַנְּשִׂיאִים? לְפִי שֶׁכְּשֶׁרָאָה אַהֲרֹן חֲנֻכַּת הַנְּשִׂיאִים חָלְשָׁה דַעְתּוֹ, שֶׁלֹּא הָיָה עִמָּהֶם בַּחֲנֻכָּה לֹא הוּא וְלֹא שִׁבְטוֹ, אָמַר לוֹ הַקָּדוֹשׁ בָּרוּךְ הוּא: חַיֶּיךָ, שֶׁלְּךָ גְּדוֹלָה מִשֶּׁלָּהֶם, שֶׁאַתָּה מַדְלִיק וּמֵטִיב אֶת הַנֵּרוֹת. **בְּהַעֲלֹתְךָ.** עַל שֵׁם שֶׁהַלַּהַב עוֹלֶה כָּתוּב בְּהַדְלָקָתָן לְשׁוֹן עֲלִיָּה, שֶׁצָּרִיךְ לְהַדְלִיק עַד שֶׁתְּהֵא שַׁלְהֶבֶת עוֹלָה מֵאֵלֶיהָ. וְעוֹד דָּרְשׁוּ רַבּוֹתֵינוּ מִכָּאן שֶׁמַּעֲלָה הָיְתָה לִפְנֵי הַמְּנוֹרָה שֶׁעָלֶיהָ הַכֹּהֵן עוֹמֵד וּמֵטִיב: **אֶל מוּל פְּנֵי הַמְּנוֹרָה.** אֶל מוּל נֵר הָאֶמְצָעִי, שֶׁאֵינוֹ בַּקָּנִים אֶלָּא בְּגוּף שֶׁל מְנוֹרָה: **יָאִירוּ שִׁבְעַת הַנֵּרוֹת.** שִׁשָּׁה שֶׁעַל שֵׁשֶׁת הַקָּנִים, שְׁלֹשָׁה הַמִּזְרָחִיִּים פּוֹנִים לְמוּל הָאֶמְצָעִי הַפְּתִילוֹת שֶׁבָּהֶן, וְכֵן שְׁלֹשָׁה הַמַּעֲרָבִיִּים רָאשֵׁי הַפְּתִילוֹת לְמוּל הָאֶמְצָעִי. וְלָמָּה? כְּדֵי שֶׁלֹּא יֹאמְרוּ: לְאוֹרָה הוּא צָרִיךְ:

ג **וַיַּעַשׂ כֵּן אַהֲרֹן.** לְהַגִּיד שִׁבְחוֹ שֶׁל אַהֲרֹן שֶׁלֹּא שִׁנָּה:

ד **וְזֶה מַעֲשֵׂה הַמְּנֹרָה.** שֶׁהֶרְאָהוּ הַקָּדוֹשׁ בָּרוּךְ הוּא בָּאֶצְבַּע לְפִי שֶׁנִּתְקַשָּׁה בָּהּ, לְכָךְ נֶאֱמַר: "זֶה": **מִקְשָׁה.** בטדי"ץ בְּלַעַז, לְשׁוֹן: "דָּא לְדָא נָקְשָׁן" (דניאל ה, ו). עֲשֶׁשֶׁת שֶׁל כִּכַּר זָהָב הָיְתָה, וּמַקִּישׁ בְּקֻרְנָס וְחוֹתֵךְ בְּכַשִּׁיל לְפַשֵּׁט אֵיבָרֶיהָ כְּתִקּוּנָן, וְלֹא נַעֲשֵׂית אֵיבָרִים אֵיבָרִים עַל יְדֵי חִבּוּר. **יְרֵכָהּ.** הִיא הַשִּׁדָּה שֶׁעַל הָרַגְלַיִם, חָלוּל, כְּדֶרֶךְ מְנוֹרוֹת כֶּסֶף שֶׁלִּפְנֵי הַשָּׂרִים: **עַד יְרֵכָהּ עַד פִּרְחָהּ.** כְּלוֹמַר גּוּפָהּ שֶׁל מְנוֹרָה כֻּלָּהּ וְכָל הַתָּלוּי בָּהּ: **עַד יְרֵכָהּ.** שֶׁהוּא אֵיבָר גָּדוֹל. **עַד פִּרְחָהּ.** שֶׁהוּא מַעֲשֶׂה דַּק שֶׁבָּהּ, הַכֹּל "מִקְשָׁה". וְדֶרֶךְ 'עַד' לְשַׁמֵּשׁ בַּלָּשׁוֹן זֶה, כְּמוֹ: "מִגָּדִישׁ וְעַד קָמָה וְעַד כֶּרֶם זָיִת" (שופטים טו, ה): **כַּמַּרְאֶה אֲשֶׁר הֶרְאָה וְגוֹ'.** כְּתַבְנִית אֲשֶׁר הֶרְאָהוּ בָּהָר, כְּמוֹ שֶׁנֶּאֱמַר: "וּרְאֵה וַעֲשֵׂה כְּתַבְנִיתָם וְגוֹ'" (שמות כה, מ): **כֵּן עָשָׂה אֶת הַמְּנֹרָה.** מִי שֶׁעֲשָׂאָהּ. וּמִדְרַשׁ אַגָּדָה: עַל יְדֵי הַקָּדוֹשׁ בָּרוּךְ הוּא נַעֲשֵׂית מֵאֵלֶיהָ:

ו **קַח אֶת הַלְוִיִּם.** קָחֵם בִּדְבָרִים: 'אַשְׁרֵיכֶם שֶׁתִּזְכּוּ לִהְיוֹת שַׁמָּשִׁים לַמָּקוֹם':

ז **הַזֵּה עֲלֵיהֶם מֵי חַטָּאת.** שֶׁל אֵפֶר הַפָּרָה, מִפְּנֵי טְמֵאֵי מֵתִים שֶׁבָּהֶם: **וְהֶעֱבִירוּ תַעַר.** מָצָאתִי בְּדִבְרֵי רַבִּי מֹשֶׁה הַדַּרְשָׁן, לְפִי שֶׁנִּתְּנוּ כַּפָּרָה עַל הַבְּכוֹרוֹת שֶׁעָבְדוּ עֲבוֹדָה זָרָה, וְהִיא קְרוּיָה 'זִבְחֵי מֵתִים'

פרק ח | במדבר

חַטָּאת וְהֶעֱבִ֤ירוּ תַ֨עַר֙ עַל־כָּל־בְּשָׂרָ֔ם וְכִבְּס֥וּ בִגְדֵיהֶ֖ם וְהִטֶּהָֽרוּ׃
ח וְלָֽקְחוּ֙ פַּ֣ר בֶּן־בָּקָ֔ר וּמִנְחָת֔וֹ סֹ֖לֶת בְּלוּלָ֣ה בַשָּׁ֑מֶן וּפַר־שֵׁנִ֥י בֶן־
ט בָּקָ֖ר תִּקַּ֥ח לְחַטָּֽאת׃ וְהִקְרַבְתָּ֙ אֶת־הַלְוִיִּ֔ם לִפְנֵ֖י אֹ֣הֶל מוֹעֵ֑ד
י וְהִ֨קְהַלְתָּ֔ אֶֽת־כָּל־עֲדַ֖ת בְּנֵ֥י יִשְׂרָאֵֽל׃ וְהִקְרַבְתָּ֥ אֶת־הַלְוִיִּ֖ם לִפְנֵ֣י
יא יְהוָ֑ה וְסָמְכ֧וּ בְנֵי־יִשְׂרָאֵ֛ל אֶת־יְדֵיהֶ֖ם עַל־הַלְוִיִּֽם׃ וְהֵנִיף֩ אַהֲרֹ֨ן
אֶת־הַלְוִיִּ֤ם תְּנוּפָה֙ לִפְנֵ֣י יְהוָ֔ה מֵאֵ֖ת בְּנֵ֣י יִשְׂרָאֵ֑ל וְהָי֕וּ לַעֲבֹ֖ד
יב אֶת־עֲבֹדַ֥ת יְהוָֽה׃ וְהַלְוִיִּם֙ יִסְמְכ֣וּ אֶת־יְדֵיהֶ֔ם עַ֖ל רֹ֣אשׁ הַפָּרִ֑ים
וַ֠עֲשֵׂה אֶת־הָאֶחָ֨ד חַטָּ֜את וְאֶת־הָאֶחָ֤ד עֹלָה֙ לַֽיהוָ֔ה לְכַפֵּ֖ר עַל־
יג הַלְוִיִּֽם׃ וְהַֽעֲמַדְתָּ֙ אֶת־הַלְוִיִּ֔ם לִפְנֵ֥י אַהֲרֹ֖ן וְלִפְנֵ֣י בָנָ֑יו וְהֵנַפְתָּ֥
יד אֹתָ֛ם תְּנוּפָ֖ה לַֽיהוָֽה׃ וְהִבְדַּלְתָּ֙ אֶת־הַלְוִיִּ֔ם מִתּ֖וֹךְ בְּנֵ֣י יִשְׂרָאֵ֑ל
טו וְהָ֥יוּ לִ֖י הַלְוִיִּֽם׃ וְאַחֲרֵי־כֵן֙ יָבֹ֣אוּ הַלְוִיִּ֔ם לַעֲבֹ֖ד אֶת־אֹ֣הֶל מוֹעֵ֑ד
וְטִֽהַרְתָּ֣ אֹתָ֔ם וְהֵנַפְתָּ֥ אֹתָ֖ם תְּנוּפָֽה׃ כִּי֩ נְתֻנִ֨ים נְתֻנִ֥ים הֵ֨מָּה֙
טז לִ֣י מִתּ֣וֹךְ בְּנֵ֣י יִשְׂרָאֵ֔ל תַּ֣חַת פִּטְרַ֥ת כָּל־רֶ֛חֶם בְּכ֥וֹר כֹּ֖ל מִבְּנֵ֣י
יז יִשְׂרָאֵ֑ל לָקַ֥חְתִּי אֹתָ֖ם לִֽי׃ כִּ֣י לִ֣י כָל־בְּכוֹר֮ בִּבְנֵ֣י יִשְׂרָאֵל֒ בָּאָדָ֖ם

שני

(תהלים קו, כח), וְהַמַּדְוֶה קָרוּי 'מֵת' (להלן יב, יב), הַחֲזָקִים תְּחִלַּת כִּמְעַדְעִים:

ח וְלָקְחוּ פַּר בֶּן בָּקָר. וְהוּא עוֹלָה, כְּמוֹ שֶׁכָּתוּב: "וַעֲשֵׂה אֶת הָאֶחָד... עוֹלָה" (להלן פסוק יב), וְהוּא קָרְבַּן צִבּוּר עֲבוּר עֲבוֹדָה זָרָה (להלן טו, כד). וּפַר שֵׁנִי. מַה תַּלְמוּד לוֹמַר "שֵׁנִי"? לוֹמַר לָךְ, מָה עוֹלָה לֹא נֶאֱכֶלֶת אַף חַטָּאת לֹא נֶאֱכֶלֶת, וּבְזוֹ יֵשׁ סֶמֶךְ לַדְּבָרִים בְּתוֹרַת כֹּהֲנִים (חובה פרק ג, ד). וְאוֹמֵר אֲנִי שֶׁהוֹרָאַת שָׁעָה הָיְתָה, שֶׁשָּׂעִיר הָיָה לָהֶם לְהָבִיא לְחַטַּאת עֲבוֹדָה זָרָה עִם פַּר הָעוֹלָה:

ט וְהִקְהַלְתָּ אֶת כָּל עֲדַת. לְפִי שֶׁהַלְוִיִּם נְתוּנִים קָרְבַּן כַּפָּרָה תַּחְתֵּיהֶם, יָבוֹאוּ וְיַעַמְדוּ עַל קָרְבָּנָם וְיִסְמְכוּ אֶת יְדֵיהֶם עֲלֵיהֶם:

יא וְהֵנִיף אַהֲרֹן אֶת הַלְוִיִּם תְּנוּפָה. כְּדֶרֶךְ שֶׁאֲשַׁם מְצֹרָע טָעוּן תְּנוּפָה חַי (ויקרא יד, יב). שָׁלֹשׁ תְּנוּפוֹת נֶאֶמְרוּ בְּפָרָשָׁה זוֹ: הָרִאשׁוֹנָה לִבְנֵי קְהָת, לְכָךְ נֶאֱמַר בָּם: "וְהָיוּ לַעֲבֹד אֶת עֲבֹדַת ה'", לְפִי שֶׁעֲבוֹדַת קֹדֶשׁ הַקֳּדָשִׁים עֲלֵיהֶם, "הָאָרוֹן וְהַשֻּׁלְחָן" וְגוֹ' (לעיל ג, לא). הַשְּׁנִיָּה לִבְנֵי גֵרְשׁוֹן, לְכָךְ נֶאֱמַר בָּם: "תְּנוּפָה לַה'" (להלן פסוק יג), שֶׁאַף עֲלֵיהֶם הָיְתָה עֲבוֹדַת הַקֹּדֶשׁ: יְרִיעוֹת וּקְרָסִים הַנִּרְאִים בְּבֵית קֹדֶשׁ הַקֳּדָשִׁים. וְהַשְּׁלִישִׁית לִבְנֵי מְרָרִי (להלן פסוק טו):

טז נְתֻנִים נְתֻנִים. נְתוּנִים לְמַשָּׂא, נְתוּנִים לְשִׁיר: פִּטְרַת. פְּתִיחַת:

יז כִּי לִי כָל בְּכוֹר. שֶׁלִּי הָיוּ הַבְּכוֹרוֹת בְּקַו הַדִּין, שֶׁהֲגִנֹּתִי עֲלֵיהֶם בֵּין בְּכוֹרֵי מִצְרַיִם וְלָקַחְתִּי אוֹתָם

במדבר | פרק ח

וּבַבְּהֵמָה בְּיוֹם הַכֹּתִי כָל־בְּכוֹר בְּאֶרֶץ מִצְרַיִם הִקְדַּשְׁתִּי אֹתָם
יט לִי: וָאֶקַּח אֶת־הַלְוִיִּם תַּחַת כָּל־בְּכוֹר בִּבְנֵי יִשְׂרָאֵל: וָאֶתְּנָה
אֶת־הַלְוִיִּם נְתֻנִים ׀ לְאַהֲרֹן וּלְבָנָיו מִתּוֹךְ בְּנֵי יִשְׂרָאֵל לַעֲבֹד
אֶת־עֲבֹדַת בְּנֵי־יִשְׂרָאֵל בְּאֹהֶל מוֹעֵד וּלְכַפֵּר עַל־בְּנֵי יִשְׂרָאֵל
וְלֹא יִהְיֶה בִּבְנֵי יִשְׂרָאֵל נֶגֶף בְּגֶשֶׁת בְּנֵי־יִשְׂרָאֵל אֶל־הַקֹּדֶשׁ:
כ וַיַּעַשׂ מֹשֶׁה וְאַהֲרֹן וְכָל־עֲדַת בְּנֵי־יִשְׂרָאֵל לַלְוִיִּם כְּכֹל אֲשֶׁר־צִוָּה
כא יְהוָה אֶת־מֹשֶׁה לַלְוִיִּם כֵּן־עָשׂוּ לָהֶם בְּנֵי יִשְׂרָאֵל: וַיִּתְחַטְּאוּ
הַלְוִיִּם וַיְכַבְּסוּ בִּגְדֵיהֶם וַיָּנֶף אַהֲרֹן אֹתָם תְּנוּפָה לִפְנֵי יְהוָה
כב וַיְכַפֵּר עֲלֵיהֶם אַהֲרֹן לְטַהֲרָם: וְאַחֲרֵי־כֵן בָּאוּ הַלְוִיִּם לַעֲבֹד אֶת־
עֲבֹדָתָם בְּאֹהֶל מוֹעֵד לִפְנֵי אַהֲרֹן וְלִפְנֵי בָנָיו כַּאֲשֶׁר צִוָּה יְהוָה
כג אֶת־מֹשֶׁה עַל־הַלְוִיִּם כֵּן עָשׂוּ לָהֶם: וַיְדַבֵּר יְהוָה
כד אֶל־מֹשֶׁה לֵּאמֹר: זֹאת אֲשֶׁר לַלְוִיִּם מִבֶּן חָמֵשׁ וְעֶשְׂרִים שָׁנָה
כה וָמַעְלָה יָבוֹא לִצְבֹא צָבָא בַּעֲבֹדַת אֹהֶל מוֹעֵד: וּמִבֶּן חֲמִשִּׁים
כו שָׁנָה יָשׁוּב מִצְּבָא הָעֲבֹדָה וְלֹא יַעֲבֹד עוֹד: וְשֵׁרֵת אֶת־אֶחָיו

לִי, עַד שֶׁטָּעוּ בָּעֵגֶל, וְעַכְשָׁיו: "וָאֶקַּח אֶת הַלְוִיִּם" וְגוֹ' (להלן פסוק יח).

יט] **וָאֶתְּנָה וְגוֹ'.** חֲמִשָּׁה פְּעָמִים נֶאֱמַר "בְּנֵי יִשְׂרָאֵל" בְּמִקְרָא זֶה, לְהוֹדִיעַ חִבָּתָן שֶׁנִּכְפְּלוּ אַזְכְּרוֹתֵיהֶן בְּמִקְרָא אֶחָד כְּמִנְיַן חֲמִשָּׁה חֻמְּשֵׁי תוֹרָה, כָּךְ רָאִיתִי בִּבְרֵאשִׁית רַבָּה (ג, ה): **וְלֹא יִהְיֶה בִבְנֵי יִשְׂרָאֵל נֶגֶף.** שֶׁלֹּא יִצְטָרְכוּ לָגֶשֶׁת אֶל הַקֹּדֶשׁ, שֶׁאִם יִגְּשׁוּ יִהְיֶה נֶגֶף:

כ] **וַיַּעַשׂ מֹשֶׁה וְאַהֲרֹן וְכָל עֲדַת וְגוֹ'.** מֹשֶׁה הֶעֱמִידָן, וְאַהֲרֹן הֱנִיפָן, וְיִשְׂרָאֵל סָמְכוּ אֶת יְדֵיהֶם:

כב] **כַּאֲשֶׁר צִוָּה ה' וְגוֹ' כֵּן עָשׂוּ.** לְהַגִּיד שֶׁבַח הָעוֹשִׂין וְהַנַּעֲשֶׂה בָּהֶן, שֶׁאֶחָד מֵהֶם לֹא עִכֵּב:

כד] **זֹאת אֲשֶׁר לַלְוִיִּם.** שָׁנִים פּוֹסְלִים בָּהֶם, וְאֵין הַמּוּמִין פּוֹסְלִין בָּהֶם: **מִבֶּן חָמֵשׁ וְעֶשְׂרִים.** וּבְמָקוֹם אַחֵר אוֹמֵר: "מִבֶּן שְׁלֹשִׁים שָׁנָה" (לעיל ד, ג), הָא כֵּיצַד? מִבֶּן עֶשְׂרִים וְחָמֵשׁ בָּא לִלְמֹד הִלְכוֹת עֲבוֹדָה וְלוֹמֵד חָמֵשׁ שָׁנִים, וּבֶן שְׁלֹשִׁים עוֹבֵד. מִכָּאן לְתַלְמִיד שֶׁלֹּא רָאָה סִימָן יָפֶה בְּמִשְׁנָתוֹ בְּחָמֵשׁ שָׁנִים, שׁוּב אֵינוֹ רוֹאֶה:

כה] **וְלֹא יַעֲבֹד עוֹד.** עֲבוֹדַת מַשָּׂא בַּכָּתֵף, אֲבָל חוֹזֵר הוּא לִנְעִילַת שְׁעָרִים וְלָשִׁיר וְלִטְעֹן עֲגָלוֹת, וְזֶהוּ: "וְשֵׁרֵת אֶת אֶחָיו" (להלן פסוק כו), "עִם אֲחוֹהִי", כְּתַרְגּוּמוֹ:

כו] **לִשְׁמֹר מִשְׁמֶרֶת.** לַחֲנוֹת סָבִיב לָאֹהֶל וּלְהָקִים וּלְהוֹרִיד בִּשְׁעַת הַמַּסָּעוֹת:

בְּאֹהֶל מוֹעֵד לִשְׁמֹר מִשְׁמֶרֶת וַעֲבֹדָה לֹא יַעֲבֹד כָּכָה תַּעֲשֶׂה לַלְוִיִּם בְּמִשְׁמְרֹתָם:

שלישי

ט א וַיְדַבֵּר יְהוָה אֶל־מֹשֶׁה בְמִדְבַּר־סִינַי בַּשָּׁנָה הַשֵּׁנִית לְצֵאתָם מֵאֶרֶץ מִצְרַיִם בַּחֹדֶשׁ הָרִאשׁוֹן לֵאמֹר: ב וְיַעֲשׂוּ בְנֵי־יִשְׂרָאֵל אֶת־הַפָּסַח בְּמוֹעֲדוֹ: ג בְּאַרְבָּעָה עָשָׂר־יוֹם בַּחֹדֶשׁ הַזֶּה בֵּין הָעַרְבַּיִם תַּעֲשׂוּ אֹתוֹ בְּמוֹעֲדוֹ כְּכָל־חֻקֹּתָיו וּכְכָל־מִשְׁפָּטָיו תַּעֲשׂוּ אֹתוֹ: ד וַיְדַבֵּר מֹשֶׁה אֶל־בְּנֵי יִשְׂרָאֵל לַעֲשֹׂת הַפָּסַח: ה וַיַּעֲשׂוּ אֶת־הַפֶּסַח בָּרִאשׁוֹן בְּאַרְבָּעָה עָשָׂר יוֹם לַחֹדֶשׁ בֵּין הָעַרְבַּיִם בְּמִדְבַּר סִינָי כְּכֹל אֲשֶׁר צִוָּה יְהוָה אֶת־מֹשֶׁה כֵּן עָשׂוּ בְּנֵי יִשְׂרָאֵל: ו וַיְהִי אֲנָשִׁים אֲשֶׁר הָיוּ טְמֵאִים לְנֶפֶשׁ אָדָם וְלֹא־יָכְלוּ לַעֲשֹׂת־הַפֶּסַח בַּיּוֹם הַהוּא וַיִּקְרְבוּ לִפְנֵי מֹשֶׁה וְלִפְנֵי אַהֲרֹן בַּיּוֹם הַהוּא: ז וַיֹּאמְרוּ הָאֲנָשִׁים הָהֵמָּה אֵלָיו אֲנַחְנוּ טְמֵאִים לְנֶפֶשׁ אָדָם

פרק ט

א] **בַּחֹדֶשׁ הָרִאשׁוֹן.** פָּרָשָׁה שֶׁבְּרֹאשׁ הַסֵּפֶר לֹא נֶאֶמְרָה עַד אִיָּר, לָמַדְתָּ שֶׁאֵין סֵדֶר מֻקְדָּם וּמְאֻחָר בַּתּוֹרָה. וְלָמָּה לֹא פָּתַח בְּזוֹ? מִפְּנֵי שֶׁהוּא גְּנוּתָן שֶׁל יִשְׂרָאֵל, שֶׁכָּל אַרְבָּעִים שָׁנָה שֶׁהָיוּ יִשְׂרָאֵל בַּמִּדְבָּר לֹא הִקְרִיבוּ אֶלָּא פֶּסַח זֶה בִּלְבַד:

ב] **בְּמוֹעֲדוֹ.** אַף בְּשַׁבָּת, אַף בְּטֻמְאָה:

ג] **כְּכָל חֻקֹּתָיו.** אֵלּוּ מִצְוֹת שֶׁבְּגוּפוֹ: "שֶׂה תָמִים זָכָר בֶּן שָׁנָה": **וּכְכָל מִשְׁפָּטָיו.** אֵלּוּ מִצְוֹת שֶׁעַל גּוּפוֹ מִמָּקוֹם אַחֵר: לְשִׁבְעַת יָמִים לַמַּצָּה וּלְבִעוּר חָמֵץ:

ד] **וַיְדַבֵּר מֹשֶׁה וְגוֹ'.** מַה תַּלְמוּד לוֹמַר? וַהֲלֹא כְּבָר נֶאֱמַר: "וַיְדַבֵּר מֹשֶׁה אֶת מֹעֲדֵי ה'" (ויקרא כג, מד)? אֶלָּא

כְּשֶׁשָּׁמַע פָּרָשַׁת מוֹעֲדִים מִסִּינַי אֲמָרָהּ לָהֶם, וְחָזַר וְהִזְהִירָם בִּשְׁעַת מַעֲשֶׂה:

ו] **לִפְנֵי מֹשֶׁה וְלִפְנֵי אַהֲרֹן.** כְּשֶׁשְּׁנֵיהֶם יוֹשְׁבִין בְּבֵית הַמִּדְרָשׁ בָּאוּ וּשְׁאָלוּם. וְלֹא יִתָּכֵן לוֹמַר זֶה אַחַר זֶה, שֶׁאִם מֹשֶׁה לֹא הָיָה יוֹדֵעַ, אַהֲרֹן מִנַּיִן לוֹ?:

ז] **לָמָּה נִגָּרַע.** אָמַר לָהֶם: אֵין קָדָשִׁים קְרֵבִים בְּטֻמְאָה. אָמְרוּ לוֹ: יִזָּרֵק הַדָּם עָלֵינוּ בְּכֹהֲנִים טְהוֹרִים וְיֵאָכֵל הַבָּשָׂר לִטְהוֹרִים, אָמַר לָהֶם: "עִמְדוּ וְאֶשְׁמְעָה" (להלן פסוק ח), כְּתַלְמִיד הַמֻּבְטָח לִשְׁמֹעַ מִפִּי רַבּוֹ. אַשְׁרֵי יְלוּד אִשָּׁה שֶׁכָּךְ מֻבְטָח, שֶׁכָּל זְמַן שֶׁהָיָה רוֹצֶה הָיָה מְדַבֵּר עִם הַשְּׁכִינָה. וּרְאוּיָה הָיְתָה פָּרָשָׁה זוֹ לְהֵאָמֵר עַל יְדֵי מֹשֶׁה כִּשְׁאָר כָּל הַתּוֹרָה כֻּלָּהּ, אֶלָּא שֶׁזָּכוּ אֵלּוּ שֶׁתֵּאָמֵר עַל יְדֵיהֶן, שֶׁמְּגַלְגְּלִין זְכוּת עַל יְדֵי זַכַּאי:

לָ֚מָּה נִגָּרַ֔ע לְבִלְתִּ֨י הַקְרִ֜ב אֶת־קָרְבַּ֤ן יְהוָה֙ בְּמֹ֣עֲד֔וֹ בְּת֖וֹךְ בְּנֵ֥י יִשְׂרָאֵֽל: וַיֹּ֥אמֶר אֲלֵהֶ֖ם מֹשֶׁ֑ה עִמְד֣וּ וְאֶשְׁמְעָ֔ה מַה־יְצַוֶּ֥ה יְהוָ֖ה לָכֶֽם:

ט וַיְדַבֵּ֥ר יְהוָ֖ה אֶל־מֹשֶׁ֥ה לֵּאמֹֽר: דַּבֵּ֛ר אֶל־בְּנֵ֥י יִשְׂרָאֵ֖ל לֵאמֹ֑ר אִ֣ישׁ אִ֣ישׁ כִּי־יִהְיֶֽה־טָמֵ֣א ׀ לָנֶ֡פֶשׁ אוֹ֩ בְדֶ֨רֶךְ רְחֹקָ֜ה֗ לָכֶ֗ם א֖וֹ לְדֹרֹ֣תֵיכֶ֑ם וְעָ֥שָׂה פֶ֖סַח לַיהוָֽה: בַּחֹ֨דֶשׁ הַשֵּׁנִ֜י בְּאַרְבָּעָ֨ה עָשָׂ֥ר

יא יוֹם בֵּ֧ין הָעַרְבַּ֛יִם יַעֲשׂ֥וּ אֹת֖וֹ עַל־מַצּ֥וֹת וּמְרֹרִ֖ים יֹאכְלֻֽהוּ: לֹֽא־

יב יַשְׁאִ֤ירוּ מִמֶּ֙נּוּ֙ עַד־בֹּ֔קֶר וְעֶ֖צֶם לֹ֣א יִשְׁבְּרוּ־ב֑וֹ כְּכָל־חֻקַּ֥ת הַפֶּ֖סַח

יג יַעֲשׂ֥וּ אֹתֽוֹ: וְהָאִישׁ֩ אֲשֶׁר־ה֨וּא טָה֜וֹר וּבְדֶ֣רֶךְ לֹא־הָיָ֗ה וְחָדַל֙ לַעֲשׂ֣וֹת הַפֶּ֔סַח וְנִכְרְתָ֛ה הַנֶּ֥פֶשׁ הַהִ֖וא מֵֽעַמֶּ֑יהָ כִּ֣י ׀ קָרְבַּ֣ן יְהוָ֗ה

יד לֹ֤א הִקְרִיב֙ בְּמֹ֣עֲד֔וֹ חֶטְא֥וֹ יִשָּׂ֖א הָאִ֥ישׁ הַהֽוּא: וְכִֽי־יָג֨וּר אִתְּכֶ֜ם גֵּ֗ר וְעָ֣שָׂה פֶ֙סַח֙ לַֽיהוָ֔ה כְּחֻקַּ֥ת הַפֶּ֖סַח וּכְמִשְׁפָּט֑וֹ כֵּ֣ן יַעֲשֶׂ֑ה חֻקָּ֤ה

טו אַחַת֙ יִהְיֶ֣ה לָכֶ֔ם וְלַגֵּ֖ר וּלְאֶזְרַ֥ח הָאָֽרֶץ: רביעי וּבְיוֹם֙ הָקִ֣ים אֶת־הַמִּשְׁכָּ֗ן כִּסָּ֤ה הֶֽעָנָן֙ אֶת־הַמִּשְׁכָּ֔ן לְאֹ֖הֶל הָעֵדֻ֑ת וּבָעֶ֗רֶב יִהְיֶ֧ה

טז עַל־הַמִּשְׁכָּ֛ן כְּמַרְאֵה־אֵ֖שׁ עַד־בֹּֽקֶר: כֵּ֚ן יִהְיֶ֣ה תָמִ֔יד הֶעָנָ֖ן יְכַסֶּ֑נּוּ

יז וּמַרְאֵה־אֵ֖שׁ לָֽיְלָה: וּלְפִ֞י הֵעָל֤וֹת הֶֽעָנָן֙ מֵעַ֣ל הָאֹ֔הֶל וְאַ֣חֲרֵי־

י **אוֹ בְדֶרֶךְ רְחֹקָה.** נָקוּד עָלָיו, לוֹמַר לֹא שֶׁרְחוֹקָה וַדַּאי, אֶלָּא שֶׁהָיָה חוּץ לְאַסְקוּפַּת הָעֲזָרָה כָּל זְמַן שְׁחִיטָה. **פֶּסַח שֵׁנִי** – מַצָּה וְחָמֵץ עִמּוֹ בַּבַּיִת, וְאֵין שָׁם יוֹם טוֹב, וְאֵין חָמֵץ אָסוּר אֶלָּא עִמּוֹ בַּאֲכִילָתוֹ:

יד **וְכִי יָגוּר אִתְּכֶם גֵּר וְעָשָׂה פֶסַח.** יָכוֹל כָּל הַמִּתְגַּיֵּר יַעֲשֶׂה פֶסַח מִיָּד? תַּלְמוּד לוֹמַר: "חֻקָּה אַחַת וְגוֹ'", אֶלָּא כָּךְ מַשְׁמָעוֹ: "וְכִי יָגוּר אִתְּכֶם גֵּר" וּבָא עֵת לַעֲשׂוֹת פֶּסַח עִם חֲבֵרָיו, כַּחֻקָּה וְכַמִּשְׁפָּט יַעֲשֶׂה:

טו **הַמִּשְׁכָּן לְאֹהֶל הָעֵדֻת.** הַמִּשְׁכָּן הֶעָשׂוּי לִהְיוֹת אֹהֶל לְלוּחוֹת הָעֵדוּת: **יִהְיֶה עַל הַמִּשְׁכָּן.** כְּמוֹ 'הֱוֵה עַל הַמִּשְׁכָּן', וְכֵן לְשׁוֹן כָּל הַפָּרָשָׁה:

יז **הֵעָלוֹת הֶעָנָן.** כְּתַרְגּוּמוֹ: "אִסְתַּלְּקוּת", וְכֵן: "וְנַעֲלָה הֶעָנָן" (להלן פסוק כא). וְלֹא יִתָּכֵן לִכְתֹּב: 'וּלְפִי עֲלוֹת הֶעָנָן וְעָלָה הֶעָנָן', שֶׁאֵין זֶה לְשׁוֹן סִלּוּק אֶלָּא צִמּוּחַ וַעֲלִיָּה, כְּמוֹ: "הִנֵּה עָב קְטַנָּה כְּכַף אִישׁ עֹלָה מִיָּם" (מלכים א' יח, מד):

כֵּן יִסְעוּ בְּנֵי יִשְׂרָאֵל וּבִמְקוֹם אֲשֶׁר יִשְׁכָּן־שָׁם הֶעָנָן שָׁם יַחֲנוּ
בְנֵי יִשְׂרָאֵל: עַל־פִּי יְהֹוָה יִסְעוּ בְּנֵי יִשְׂרָאֵל וְעַל־פִּי יְהֹוָה יַחֲנוּ יח
כָּל־יְמֵי אֲשֶׁר יִשְׁכֹּן הֶעָנָן עַל־הַמִּשְׁכָּן יַחֲנוּ: וּבְהַאֲרִיךְ הֶעָנָן יט
עַל־הַמִּשְׁכָּן יָמִים רַבִּים וְשָׁמְרוּ בְנֵי־יִשְׂרָאֵל אֶת־מִשְׁמֶרֶת יְהֹוָה
וְלֹא יִסָּעוּ: וְיֵשׁ אֲשֶׁר יִהְיֶה הֶעָנָן יָמִים מִסְפָּר עַל־הַמִּשְׁכָּן עַל־ כ
פִּי יְהֹוָה יַחֲנוּ וְעַל־פִּי יְהֹוָה יִסָּעוּ: וְיֵשׁ אֲשֶׁר־יִהְיֶה הֶעָנָן מֵעֶרֶב כא
עַד־בֹּקֶר וְנַעֲלָה הֶעָנָן בַּבֹּקֶר וְנָסָעוּ אוֹ יוֹמָם וָלַיְלָה וְנַעֲלָה הֶעָנָן
וְנָסָעוּ: אוֹ־יֹמַיִם אוֹ־חֹדֶשׁ אוֹ־יָמִים בְּהַאֲרִיךְ הֶעָנָן עַל־הַמִּשְׁכָּן כב
לִשְׁכֹּן עָלָיו יַחֲנוּ בְנֵי־יִשְׂרָאֵל וְלֹא יִסָּעוּ וּבְהֵעָלֹתוֹ יִסָּעוּ: עַל־פִּי כג
יְהֹוָה יַחֲנוּ וְעַל־פִּי יְהֹוָה יִסָּעוּ אֶת־מִשְׁמֶרֶת יְהֹוָה שָׁמָרוּ עַל־פִּי
יְהֹוָה בְּיַד־מֹשֶׁה:

וַיְדַבֵּר יְהֹוָה אֶל־מֹשֶׁה לֵּאמֹר: עֲשֵׂה לְךָ שְׁתֵּי חֲצוֹצְרֹת כֶּסֶף א י
מִקְשָׁה תַּעֲשֶׂה אֹתָם וְהָיוּ לְךָ לְמִקְרָא הָעֵדָה וּלְמַסַּע אֶת־
הַמַּחֲנוֹת: וְתָקְעוּ בָּהֵן וְנוֹעֲדוּ אֵלֶיךָ כָּל־הָעֵדָה אֶל־פֶּתַח אֹהֶל ג

יח עַל פִּי ה' יִסְעוּ. שָׁנִינוּ בִּמְלֶאכֶת הַמִּשְׁכָּן (ברייתא דמלאכת המשכן פי"ג): כֵּיוָן שֶׁהָיוּ יִשְׂרָאֵל נוֹסְעִים, הָיָה עַמּוּד הֶעָנָן מִתְקַפֵּל וְנִמְשָׁךְ עַל גַּבֵּי בְּנֵי יְהוּדָה כְּמִין קוֹרָה, תָּקְעוּ וְהֵרִיעוּ וְתָקְעוּ, וְלֹא הָיָה מְהַלֵּךְ עַד שֶׁמֹּשֶׁה אוֹמֵר: "קוּמָה ה'" (להלן י, לה), וְנָסַע דֶּגֶל מַחֲנֵה יְהוּדָה. זוֹ בְּסִפְרֵי (פד): וְעַל פִּי ה' יַחֲנוּ. כֵּיוָן שֶׁהָיוּ יִשְׂרָאֵל חוֹנִים, עַמּוּד הֶעָנָן מִתַּמֵּר וְעוֹלֶה וְנִמְשָׁךְ עַל גַּבֵּי בְנֵי יְהוּדָה כְּמִין סֻכָּה, וְלֹא הָיָה נִפְרָשׂ עַד שֶׁמֹּשֶׁה אוֹמֵר: "שׁוּבָה ה' רִבְבוֹת אַלְפֵי יִשְׂרָאֵל" (להלן לו). הֱוֵי אוֹמֵר: עַל פִּי ה' וּבְיַד מֹשֶׁה (ראה להלן פסוק כג):

כ וְיֵשׁ. כְּלוֹמַר, וּפְעָמִים: יָמִים מִסְפָּר. יָמִים מוּעָטִים:

כב אוֹ יָמִים. שָׁנָה, כְּמוֹ: "יָמִים תִּהְיֶה גְאֻלָּתוֹ" (ויקרא כה, כט):

פרק י

ב לְמִקְרָא הָעֵדָה. כְּשֶׁתִּרְצֶה לְדַבֵּר עִם הַסַּנְהֶדְרִין וּשְׁאָר הָעָם וְתִקְרָאֵם לֶאֱסֹף אֵלֶיךָ, תִּקְרָאֵם עַל יְדֵי חֲצוֹצְרוֹת: וּלְמַסַּע אֶת הַמַּחֲנוֹת. בִּשְׁעַת סִלּוּק מַסָּעוֹת תִּתְקְעוּ בָּהֶם לְסִימָן. נִמְצֵאתָ אַתָּה אוֹמֵר, עַל פִּי שְׁלֹשָׁה הָיוּ נוֹסְעִים: עַל פִּי הַקָּדוֹשׁ בָּרוּךְ הוּא וְעַל פִּי מֹשֶׁה וְעַל פִּי חֲצוֹצְרוֹת: מִקְשָׁה. מִן הָעֶשֶׁת תַּעֲשֶׂה בְּהַקָּשַׁת הַקֻּרְנָס:

ג וְתָקְעוּ בָּהֵן. בִּשְׁתֵּיהֶן, וְהוּא סִימָן לְמִקְרָא הָעֵדָה,

ד מוֹעֵֽד: וְאִם־בְּאַחַ֥ת יִתְקָ֑עוּ וְנוֹעֲד֤וּ אֵלֶ֙יךָ֙ הַנְּשִׂיאִ֔ים רָאשֵׁ֖י אַלְפֵ֥י
ה יִשְׂרָאֵֽל: וּתְקַעְתֶּ֖ם תְּרוּעָ֑ה וְנָֽסְעוּ֙ הַֽמַּחֲנ֔וֹת הַחֹנִ֖ים קֵֽדְמָה:
ו וּתְקַעְתֶּ֤ם תְּרוּעָה֙ שֵׁנִ֔ית וְנָֽסְעוּ֙ הַֽמַּחֲנ֔וֹת הַחֹנִ֖ים תֵּימָ֑נָה תְּרוּעָ֥ה
ז יִתְקְע֖וּ לְמַסְעֵיהֶֽם: וּבְהַקְהִ֖יל אֶת־הַקָּהָ֑ל תִּתְקְע֖וּ וְלֹ֥א תָרִֽיעוּ:
ח וּבְנֵ֤י אַהֲרֹן֙ הַכֹּ֣הֲנִ֔ים יִתְקְע֖וּ בַּחֲצֹֽצְר֑וֹת וְהָי֥וּ לָכֶ֛ם לְחֻקַּ֥ת עוֹלָ֖ם
ט לְדֹרֹתֵיכֶֽם: וְכִֽי־תָבֹ֨אוּ מִלְחָמָ֜ה בְּאַרְצְכֶ֗ם עַל־הַצַּר֙ הַצֹּרֵ֣ר אֶתְכֶ֔ם
וַהֲרֵעֹתֶ֖ם בַּחֲצֹֽצְרֹ֑ת וְנִזְכַּרְתֶּ֗ם לִפְנֵי֙ יהוה אֱלֹ֣הֵיכֶ֔ם וְנוֹשַׁעְתֶּ֖ם
י מֵאֹיְבֵיכֶֽם: וּבְי֨וֹם שִׂמְחַתְכֶ֥ם וּֽבְמוֹעֲדֵיכֶם֮ וּבְרָאשֵׁ֣י חׇדְשֵׁכֶם֒
וּתְקַעְתֶּ֣ם בַּחֲצֹֽצְרֹ֗ת עַ֚ל עֹלֹ֣תֵיכֶ֔ם וְעַ֖ל זִבְחֵ֣י שַׁלְמֵיכֶ֑ם וְהָי֨וּ לָכֶ֤ם
לְזִכָּרוֹן֙ לִפְנֵ֣י אֱלֹֽהֵיכֶ֔ם אֲנִ֖י יהוה אֱלֹהֵיכֶֽם:
יא וַיְהִ֞י בַּשָּׁנָ֧ה הַשֵּׁנִ֛ית בַּחֹ֥דֶשׁ הַשֵּׁנִ֖י בְּעֶשְׂרִ֣ים בַּחֹ֑דֶשׁ נַעֲלָה֙ הֶֽעָנָ֔ן

חמישי

שֶׁנֶּאֱמַר: "וְנוֹעֲדוּ אֵלֶיךָ כָּל הָעֵדָה אֶל פֶּתַח אֹהֶל מוֹעֵד":

ד | וְאִם בְּאַחַת יִתְקָעוּ. הוּא סִימָן לְמִקְרָא הַנְּשִׂיאִים, שֶׁנֶּאֱמַר: "וְנוֹעֲדוּ אֵלֶיךָ הַנְּשִׂיאִים", וְאַף הֵן יְעִידָתָן אֶל פֶּתַח אֹהֶל מוֹעֵד, וּמִגְּזֵרָה שָׁוָה הוּא בָּא בְּסִפְרֵי (עג):

ה | וּתְקַעְתֶּם תְּרוּעָה. סִימָן מַסַּע הַמַּחֲנוֹת. תְּקִיעָה תְּרוּעָה וּתְקִיעָה, כָּךְ הוּא נִדְרָשׁ בְּסִפְרֵי מִן הַמִּקְרָאוֹת הַיְתֵרִים (סס):

ז | וּבְהַקְהִיל אֶת הַקָּהָל וְגו׳. לְפִי שֶׁהוּא אוֹמֵר: "וְהָיוּ לְךָ לְמִקְרָא הָעֵדָה וּלְמַסַּע אֶת הַמַּחֲנוֹת" (לעיל פסוק ב), מַה מִּקְרָא הָעֵדָה תּוֹקֵעַ בִּשְׁנֵי כֹהֲנִים וּבִשְׁתֵּיהֶן, שֶׁנֶּאֱמַר: "וְתָקְעוּ בָהֵן" וְגו׳ (לעיל פסוק ג), אַף מַסַּע הַמַּחֲנוֹת בִּשְׁתֵּיהֶן. יָכוֹל מַה מַּסַּע הַמַּחֲנוֹת תּוֹקֵעַ וּמֵרִיעַ וְתוֹקֵעַ, אַף מִקְרָא הָעֵדָה תּוֹקֵעַ וּמֵרִיעַ וְתוֹקֵעַ, וּמֵעַתָּה אֵין חִלּוּק בֵּין מִקְרָא הָעֵדָה

לְמַסַּע אֶת הַמַּחֲנוֹת? תַּלְמוּד לוֹמַר: "וּבְהַקְהִיל אֶת הַקָּהָל" וְגו׳, לוֹמַר שֶׁאֵין תְּרוּעָה לְמִקְרָא הָעֵדָה, וְהוּא הַדִּין לַנְּשִׂיאִים. הֲרֵי סִימָן לִשְׁלָשְׁתָּם: מִקְרָא הָעֵדָה בִּשְׁתַּיִם, וְשֶׁל נְשִׂיאִים בְּאַחַת, וְזוֹ וָזוֹ אֵין בָּהֶם תְּרוּעָה, וּמַסַּע הַמַּחֲנוֹת בִּשְׁתַּיִם עַל יְדֵי תְּרוּעָה וּתְקִיעָה:

ח | וּבְנֵי אַהֲרֹן יִתְקְעוּ. בַּמִּקְרָאוֹת וּבַמַּסָּעוֹת הַלָּלוּ:

י | עַל עֹלֹתֵיכֶם. בְּקׇרְבַּן צִבּוּר הַכָּתוּב מְדַבֵּר: אֲנִי ה׳ אֱלֹהֵיכֶם. מִכָּאן לְמָדְנוּ מַלְכֻיּוֹת עִם זִכְרוֹנוֹת וְשׁוֹפְרוֹת, שֶׁנֶּאֱמַר: "וּתְקַעְתֶּם" – הֲרֵי שׁוֹפְרוֹת, "לְזִכָּרוֹן" – הֲרֵי זִכְרוֹנוֹת, "אֲנִי ה׳ אֱלֹהֵיכֶם" – זוֹ מַלְכֻיּוֹת וְכוּ׳:

יא | בַּחֹדֶשׁ הַשֵּׁנִי. נִמְצֵאתָ אַתָּה אוֹמֵר, שְׁנֵים עָשָׂר חֹדֶשׁ חָסֵר עֲשָׂרָה יָמִים עָשׂוּ בְחוֹרֵב, שֶׁהֲרֵי בְּרֹאשׁ חֹדֶשׁ סִיוָן חָנוּ שָׁם (שמות יט, א) וְלֹא נָסְעוּ עַד עֶשְׂרִים בְּאִיָּר לַשָּׁנָה הַבָּאָה:

מֵעַל מִשְׁכַּן הָעֵדֻת: וַיִּסְעוּ בְנֵי־יִשְׂרָאֵל לְמַסְעֵיהֶם מִמִּדְבַּר
סִינָי וַיִּשְׁכֹּן הֶעָנָן בְּמִדְבַּר פָּארָן: וַיִּסְעוּ בָּרִאשֹׁנָה עַל־פִּי יהוה
בְּיַד־מֹשֶׁה: וַיִּסַּע דֶּגֶל מַחֲנֵה בְנֵי־יְהוּדָה בָּרִאשֹׁנָה לְצִבְאֹתָם
וְעַל־צְבָאוֹ נַחְשׁוֹן בֶּן־עַמִּינָדָב: וְעַל־צְבָא מַטֵּה בְּנֵי יִשָּׂשכָר
נְתַנְאֵל בֶּן־צוּעָר: וְעַל־צְבָא מַטֵּה בְּנֵי זְבוּלֻן אֱלִיאָב בֶּן־חֵלֹן:
וְהוּרַד הַמִּשְׁכָּן וְנָסְעוּ בְנֵי־גֵרְשׁוֹן וּבְנֵי מְרָרִי נֹשְׂאֵי הַמִּשְׁכָּן:
וְנָסַע דֶּגֶל מַחֲנֵה רְאוּבֵן לְצִבְאֹתָם וְעַל־צְבָאוֹ אֱלִיצוּר בֶּן־
שְׁדֵיאוּר: וְעַל־צְבָא מַטֵּה בְּנֵי שִׁמְעוֹן שְׁלֻמִיאֵל בֶּן־צוּרִישַׁדָּי:
וְעַל־צְבָא מַטֵּה בְנֵי־גָד אֶלְיָסָף בֶּן־דְּעוּאֵל: וְנָסְעוּ הַקְּהָתִים
נֹשְׂאֵי הַמִּקְדָּשׁ וְהֵקִימוּ אֶת־הַמִּשְׁכָּן עַד־בֹּאָם: וְנָסַע דֶּגֶל מַחֲנֵה
בְנֵי־אֶפְרַיִם לְצִבְאֹתָם וְעַל־צְבָאוֹ אֱלִישָׁמָע בֶּן־עַמִּיהוּד: וְעַל־
צְבָא מַטֵּה בְּנֵי מְנַשֶּׁה גַּמְלִיאֵל בֶּן־פְּדָהצוּר: וְעַל־צְבָא מַטֵּה
בְּנֵי בִנְיָמִן אֲבִידָן בֶּן־גִּדְעוֹנִי: וְנָסַע דֶּגֶל מַחֲנֵה בְנֵי־דָן מְאַסֵּף

יב
יג
יד
טו
טז
יז
יח
יט
כ
כא
כב
כג
כד
כה

יב׀ לְמַסְעֵיהֶם. כַּמִּשְׁפָּט הַמְפֹרָשׁ לְמַסַּע דִּגְלֵיהֶם מִי רִאשׁוֹן וּמִי אַחֲרוֹן. בְּמִדְבַּר פָּארָן. קִבְרוֹת הַתַּאֲוָה בְּמִדְבַּר פָּארָן הָיָה, וְשָׁם חָנוּ מִמַּסָּע זֶה:

יז׀ וְהוּרַד הַמִּשְׁכָּן. כֵּיוָן שֶׁנּוֹסֵעַ דֶּגֶל יְהוּדָה, נִכְנְסוּ אַהֲרֹן וּבָנָיו וּפֵרְקוּ אֶת הַפָּרֹכֶת וְכִסּוּ בָהּ אֶת הָאָרוֹן, שֶׁנֶּאֱמַר: "וּבָא אַהֲרֹן וּבָנָיו בִּנְסֹעַ הַמַּחֲנֶה" (לעיל ד, ה), וּבְנֵי גֵרְשׁוֹן וּבְנֵי מְרָרִי פוֹרְקִין הַמִּשְׁכָּן וְטוֹעֲנִין אוֹתוֹ בָּעֲגָלוֹת, וְהָאָרוֹן וּכְלֵי הַקֹּדֶשׁ שֶׁל מַטָּה בְּנֵי קְהָת עוֹמְדִים מְכֻסִּין וּנְתוּנִין עַל הַמּוֹטוֹת, עַד שֶׁנָּסַע דֶּגֶל מַחֲנֵה רְאוּבֵן, וְאַחַר כָּךְ "וְנָסְעוּ הַקְּהָתִים" (להלן פסוק כא):

כא׀ נֹשְׂאֵי הַמִּקְדָּשׁ. נוֹשְׂאֵי דְבָרִים הַמְקֻדָּשִׁים: וְהֵקִימוּ אֶת הַמִּשְׁכָּן. בְּנֵי גֵרְשׁוֹן וּבְנֵי מְרָרִי, שֶׁהָיוּ קוֹדְמִים לָהֶם מַסַּע שְׁנֵי דְגָלִים, הָיוּ מְקִימִין אֶת

הַמִּשְׁכָּן כְּשֶׁהָיָה הֶעָנָן שׁוֹכֵן, וְסִימָן הַחֲנָיָה נִרְאָה בְּדֶגֶל מַחֲנֵה יְהוּדָה וְהֵם חוֹנִים, וַעֲדַיִן בְּנֵי קְהָת בָּאִים מֵאַחֲרֵיהֶם עִם שְׁנֵי דְגָלִים הָאַחֲרוֹנִים, הָיוּ בְּנֵי גֵרְשׁוֹן וּבְנֵי מְרָרִי מְקִימִין אֶת הַמִּשְׁכָּן, וּכְשֶׁבָּאִים בְּנֵי קְהָת מוֹצְאִים אוֹתוֹ עַל מְכוֹנוֹ, וּמַכְנִיסִין בּוֹ הָאָרוֹן וְהַשֻּׁלְחָן וְהַמְּנוֹרָה וְהַמִּזְבְּחוֹת. וְזֶהוּ מַשְׁמָעוּת הַמִּקְרָא: "וְהֵקִימוּ מְקִימֵי הַמִּשְׁכָּן אוֹתוֹ, עַד" – טֶרֶם "בֹּאָם" שֶׁל בְּנֵי קְהָת:

כה׀ מְאַסֵּף לְכָל הַמַּחֲנֹת. תַּלְמוּד יְרוּשַׁלְמִי (עירובין ה, א), לְפִי שֶׁהָיָה שִׁבְטוֹ שֶׁל דָּן מְרֻבֶּה בְּאֻכְלוּסִין הָיָה נוֹסֵעַ בָּאַחֲרוֹנָה, וְכָל מִי שֶׁהָיָה מְאַבֵּד דָּבָר הָיָה מַחֲזִירוֹ לוֹ. אַתְיָא כְּמַאן דַּאֲמַר כְּנֻסִּיָּה הָיוּ מְהַלְּכִין, וּמַפִּיק לֵיהּ מִן "כַּאֲשֶׁר יַחֲנוּ כֵּן יִסָּעוּ" (לעיל ב, יז). וְאִית דְּאָמְרֵי: כְּקוֹרָה הָיוּ מְהַלְּכִין, וּמַפִּיק לֵיהּ מִן "מְאַסֵּף לְכָל הַמַּחֲנֹת":

במדבר | פרק י

לְכָל־הַמַּחֲנֹת לְצִבְאֹתָם וְעַל־צְבָאוֹ אֲחִיעֶזֶר בֶּן־עַמִּישַׁדָּי:
כו וְעַל־צְבָא מַטֵּה בְּנֵי אָשֵׁר פַּגְעִיאֵל בֶּן־עָכְרָן: וְעַל־צְבָא מַטֵּה
כח בְּנֵי נַפְתָּלִי אֲחִירַע בֶּן־עֵינָן: אֵלֶּה מַסְעֵי בְנֵי־יִשְׂרָאֵל לְצִבְאֹתָם
כט וַיִּסָּעוּ: וַיֹּאמֶר מֹשֶׁה לְחֹבָב בֶּן־רְעוּאֵל הַמִּדְיָנִי חֹתֵן
מֹשֶׁה נֹסְעִים ׀ אֲנַחְנוּ אֶל־הַמָּקוֹם אֲשֶׁר אָמַר יְהֹוָה אֹתוֹ אֶתֵּן
לָכֶם לְכָה אִתָּנוּ וְהֵטַבְנוּ לָךְ כִּי־יְהֹוָה דִּבֶּר־טוֹב עַל־יִשְׂרָאֵל:
ל וַיֹּאמֶר אֵלָיו לֹא אֵלֵךְ כִּי אִם־אֶל־אַרְצִי וְאֶל־מוֹלַדְתִּי אֵלֵךְ:
לא וַיֹּאמֶר אַל־נָא תַּעֲזֹב אֹתָנוּ כִּי ׀ עַל־כֵּן יָדַעְתָּ חֲנֹתֵנוּ בַּמִּדְבָּר
לב וְהָיִיתָ לָּנוּ לְעֵינָיִם: וְהָיָה כִּי־תֵלֵךְ עִמָּנוּ וְהָיָה ׀ הַטּוֹב הַהוּא
לג אֲשֶׁר יֵיטִיב יְהֹוָה עִמָּנוּ וְהֵטַבְנוּ לָךְ: וַיִּסְעוּ מֵהַר יְהֹוָה דֶּרֶךְ
שְׁלֹשֶׁת יָמִים וַאֲרוֹן בְּרִית־יְהֹוָה נֹסֵעַ לִפְנֵיהֶם דֶּרֶךְ שְׁלֹשֶׁת

כח] **אלה מסעי.** זה סדר מסעיהם: **ויסעו.** ביום ההוא נסעו:

כט] **חבב.** הוא יתרו, שנאמר: "מבני חבב חתן משה" (שופטים ד, יא), ומה תלמוד לומר: "ותבאנה אל רעואל אביהן" (שמות ב, יח)? מלמד שהתינוקות קורין לאבי אביהן 'אבא'. ושמות הרבה היו לו: יתרו – על שם שייתר פרשה אחת בתורה, חובב – על שחיבב את התורה וכו': **נסעים אנחנו אל המקום.** מיד עד שלשה ימים אנו נכנסין לארץ, שבמסע זה הראשון נסעו על מנת להכנס לארץ ישראל, אלא שחטאו במתאוננים. ומפני מה שתף משה עצמו עמהם? שעדיין לא נגזרה עליו גזרה וכסבור שהוא נכנס:

ל] **אל ארצי ואל מולדתי.** אם בשביל נכסי, אם בשביל משפחתי:

לא] **אל נא תעזב.** אין 'נא' אלא לשון בקשה, שלא יאמרו לא נתגייר יתרו מחבה, סבור היה שיש

לגרים חלק בארץ, עכשיו שראה שאין להם חלק הניחם והלך לו: **כי על כן ידעת חנתנו במדבר.** כי נאה לך לעשות זאת, על אשר ידעת חנותנו במדבר וראית נסים וגבורות שנעשו לנו: **כי על כן ידעת.** כמו: 'על אשר ידעת', כמו: "כי על כן לא נתתיה לשלה בני" (בראשית לח, כו), "כי על כן באו" (לעיל יט, ח), "כי על כן ראיתי פניך" (שם לג, י): **והיית לנו לעינים.** לשון עבר, כתרגומו. דבר אחר לשון עתיד, כל דבר ודבר שיתעלם מעינינו תהיה מאיר עינינו. דבר אחר, שתהא חביב עלינו כגלגל עינינו, שנאמר: "ואהבתם את הגר" (דברים י, יט):

לב] **והיה הטוב ההוא וגו'.** מה טובה היטיבו לו? אמרו, כשהיו ישראל מחלקין את הארץ היה דשנה של יריחו חמש מאות אמה על חמש מאות אמה, והניחוהו מלחלק. אמרו, מי שיבנה בית המקדש בחלקו הוא יטלנו, ובין כך ובין כך נתנוהו לבני יתרו ליונדב בן רכב:

לג] **דרך שלשת ימים.** מהלך שלשת ימים הלכו

פרק יא | במדבר | בהעלתך

יָמִים לָתוּר לָהֶם מְנוּחָה: וַעֲנַן יהוה עֲלֵיהֶם יוֹמָם בְּנָסְעָם מִן־ לד
הַמַּחֲנֶה: ס   וַיְהִי בִּנְסֹעַ הָאָרֹן וַיֹּאמֶר מֹשֶׁה קוּמָה ׀ לה ששי
יהוה וְיָפֻצוּ אֹיְבֶיךָ וְיָנֻסוּ מְשַׂנְאֶיךָ מִפָּנֶיךָ: וּבְנֻחֹה יֹאמַר שׁוּבָה לו
יהוה רִבְבוֹת אַלְפֵי יִשְׂרָאֵל: ס
וַיְהִי הָעָם כְּמִתְאֹנְנִים רַע בְּאָזְנֵי יהוה וַיִּשְׁמַע יהוה וַיִּחַר אַפּוֹ א יא
וַתִּבְעַר־בָּם אֵשׁ יהוה וַתֹּאכַל בִּקְצֵה הַמַּחֲנֶה: וַיִּצְעַק הָעָם ב
אֶל־מֹשֶׁה וַיִּתְפַּלֵּל מֹשֶׁה אֶל־יהוה וַתִּשְׁקַע הָאֵשׁ: וַיִּקְרָא שֵׁם־ ג

בְּיוֹם אֶחָד, שֶׁהָיָה הַקָּדוֹשׁ בָּרוּךְ הוּא חָפֵץ לְהַכְנִיסָם לָאָרֶץ מִיָּד: **וַאֲרוֹן בְּרִית ה' נֹסֵעַ לִפְנֵיהֶם דֶּרֶךְ שְׁלֹשֶׁת יָמִים.** זֶה הָאָרוֹן הַיּוֹצֵא עִמָּהֶם לַמִּלְחָמָה וּבוֹ שִׁבְרֵי לוּחוֹת מֻנָּחִים, וּמַקְדִּים לִפְנֵיהֶם דֶּרֶךְ שְׁלֹשֶׁת יָמִים לְתַקֵּן לָהֶם מְקוֹם חֲנִיָּה:

לד **וַעֲנַן ה' עֲלֵיהֶם יוֹמָם.** שִׁבְעָה עֲנָנִים כְּתוּבִים בְּמַסְעֵיהֶם, אַרְבָּעָה מֵאַרְבַּע רוּחוֹת, וְאֶחָד לְמַעְלָה וְאֶחָד לְמַטָּה, וְאֶחָד לִפְנֵיהֶם, מַנְמִיךְ אֶת הַגָּבוֹהַּ וּמַגְבִּיהַּ אֶת הַנָּמוּךְ וְהוֹרֵג נְחָשִׁים וְעַקְרַבִּים:

לה **וַיְהִי בִּנְסֹעַ הָאָרֹן.** עָשָׂה לוֹ סִימָנִיּוֹת מִלְּפָנָיו וּמִלְּאַחֲרָיו לוֹמַר שֶׁאֵין זֶה מְקוֹמוֹ, וְלָמָּה נִכְתַּב כָּאן? כְּדֵי לְהַפְסִיק בֵּין פֻּרְעָנוּת לְפֻרְעָנוּת וְכוּ', כִּדְאִיתָא בְּ"כָל כִּתְבֵי הַקֹּדֶשׁ" (שבת קטז ע"א - קטז ע"ב). **קוּמָה ה'.** לְפִי שֶׁהָיָה מַקְדִּים לִפְנֵיהֶם מַהֲלַךְ שְׁלֹשֶׁת יָמִים, הָיָה מֹשֶׁה אוֹמֵר: עֲמֹד וְהַמְתֵּן לָנוּ וְאַל תִּתְרַחֵק יוֹתֵר. בְּמִדְרַשׁ תַּנְחוּמָא בַּוַּיְהֵל (ה). **וְיָפֻצוּ אֹיְבֶיךָ.** הַמְכֻנָּסִין: **וְיָנֻסוּ מְשַׂנְאֶיךָ.** אֵלּוּ הָרוֹדְפִים: **מְשַׂנְאֶיךָ.** אֵלּוּ שׂוֹנְאֵי יִשְׂרָאֵל, שֶׁכָּל הַשּׂוֹנֵא אֶת יִשְׂרָאֵל שׂוֹנֵא אֶת מִי שֶׁאָמַר וְהָיָה הָעוֹלָם, שֶׁנֶּאֱמַר: "וּמְשַׂנְאֶיךָ נָשְׂאוּ רֹאשׁ" (תהלים פג, ג), וּמִי הֵם? "עַל עַמְּךָ יַעֲרִימוּ סוֹד" (שם ד):

לו **שׁוּבָה ה'.** מְנַחֵם תִּרְגְּמוֹ לְשׁוֹן מַרְגּוֹעַ, וְכֵן: "בְּשׁוּבָה וָנַחַת תִּוָּשֵׁעוּן" (ישעיה ל, טו): **רִבְבוֹת אַלְפֵי יִשְׂרָאֵל.** מַגִּיד שֶׁאֵין הַשְּׁכִינָה שׁוֹרָה בְּיִשְׂרָאֵל פְּחוּתִים מִשְּׁנֵי אֲלָפִים וּשְׁתֵּי רְבָבוֹת:

פרק יא

א **וַיְהִי הָעָם כְּמִתְאֹנְנִים.** אֵין "הָעָם" אֶלָּא רְשָׁעִים, וְכֵן הוּא אוֹמֵר: "מָה אֶעֱשֶׂה לָעָם הַזֶּה" (שמות יז, ד) וְאוֹמֵר: "הָעָם הַזֶּה הָרָע" (ירמיה יג, י), וּכְשֶׁהֵם כְּשֵׁרִים קְרוּאִים "עַמִּי", שֶׁנֶּאֱמַר: "שַׁלַּח עַמִּי" (שמות ח, טז), "עַמִּי מֶה עָשִׂיתִי לְךָ" (מיכה ו, ג): **כְּמִתְאֹנְנִים.** אֵין "מִתְאוֹנְנִים" אֶלָּא לְשׁוֹן עֲלִילָה, מְבַקְשִׁים עֲלִילָה הֵיאַךְ לִפְרֹשׁ מֵאַחֲרֵי הַמָּקוֹם, וְכֵן הוּא אוֹמֵר בְּשִׁמְשׁוֹן: "כִּי תֹאֲנָה הוּא מְבַקֵּשׁ" (שופטים יד, ד): **רַע בְּאָזְנֵי ה'.** תֹּאֲנָה שֶׁהָיְתָה רָעָה בְּאָזְנֵי ה', שֶׁמִּתְכַּוְּנִים שֶׁתָּבוֹא בְּאָזְנָיו וְיַקְנִיט. אָמְרוּ: אוֹי לָנוּ, כַּמָּה לָבַטְנוּ בַּדֶּרֶךְ הַזֶּה, שְׁלֹשָׁה יָמִים שֶׁלֹּא נַחְנוּ מֵעִנּוּי הַדֶּרֶךְ: **וַיִּחַר אַפּוֹ.** אֲנִי הָיִיתִי מִתְכַּוֵּן לְטוֹבַתְכֶם שֶׁתִּכָּנְסוּ לָאָרֶץ מִיָּד: **בִּקְצֵה הַמַּחֲנֶה.** בַּמֻּקְצִין שֶׁבָּהֶם לְשִׁפְלוּת, אֵלּוּ עֵרֶב רַב. רַבִּי שִׁמְעוֹן בֶּן מְנַסְיָא אוֹמֵר: בַּקְּצִינִים שֶׁבָּהֶם וּבַגְּדוֹלִים:

ב **וַיִּצְעַק הָעָם אֶל מֹשֶׁה.** מָשָׁל לְמֶלֶךְ בָּשָׂר וָדָם שֶׁכָּעַס עַל בְּנוֹ, וְהָלַךְ הַבֵּן אֵצֶל אוֹהֲבוֹ שֶׁל אָבִיו וְאָמַר לוֹ: צֵא וּבַקֵּשׁ עָלַי מֵאַבָּא: **וַתִּשְׁקַע הָאֵשׁ.** שָׁקְעָה בִּמְקוֹמָהּ בָּאָרֶץ, שֶׁאִלּוּ חָזְרָה לְאַחַת הָרוּחוֹת הָיְתָה מְקַפֶּלֶת וְהוֹלֶכֶת כָּל אוֹתָהּ הָרוּחַ:

במדבר | פרק יא | בהעלתך

ד הַמָּקוֹם הַהוּא תַּבְעֵרָה כִּי־בָעֲרָה בָם אֵשׁ יהוה: וְהָאסַפְסֻף
אֲשֶׁר בְּקִרְבּוֹ הִתְאַוּוּ תַּאֲוָה וַיָּשֻׁבוּ וַיִּבְכּוּ גַּם בְּנֵי יִשְׂרָאֵל וַיֹּאמְרוּ
ה מִי יַאֲכִלֵנוּ בָּשָׂר: זָכַרְנוּ אֶת־הַדָּגָה אֲשֶׁר־נֹאכַל בְּמִצְרַיִם חִנָּם
אֵת הַקִּשֻּׁאִים וְאֵת הָאֲבַטִּחִים וְאֶת־הֶחָצִיר וְאֶת־הַבְּצָלִים
ו וְאֶת־הַשּׁוּמִים: וְעַתָּה נַפְשֵׁנוּ יְבֵשָׁה אֵין כֹּל בִּלְתִּי אֶל־הַמָּן
ז עֵינֵינוּ: וְהַמָּן כִּזְרַע־גַּד הוּא וְעֵינוֹ כְּעֵין הַבְּדֹלַח: שָׁטוּ הָעָם
וְלָקְטוּ וְטָחֲנוּ בָרֵחַיִם אוֹ דָכוּ בַּמְּדֹכָה וּבִשְּׁלוּ בַּפָּרוּר וְעָשׂוּ
ט אֹתוֹ עֻגוֹת וְהָיָה טַעְמוֹ כְּטַעַם לְשַׁד הַשָּׁמֶן: וּבְרֶדֶת הַטַּל עַל־

ד) **וְהָאסַפְסֻף.** אֵלּוּ עֵרֶב רַב שֶׁנֶּאֶסְפוּ עֲלֵיהֶם בְּצֵאתָם מִמִּצְרַיִם. **וַיָּשֻׁבוּ.** גַּם בְּנֵי יִשְׂרָאֵל וַיִּבְכּוּ עִמָּהֶם: **מִי יַאֲכִלֵנוּ בָּשָׂר.** וְכִי לֹא הָיָה לָהֶם בָּשָׂר? וַהֲלֹא כְבָר נֶאֱמַר: "וְגַם עֵרֶב רַב עָלָה אִתָּם וְצֹאן וּבָקָר" וְגוֹ' (שמות יב, לח), וְאִם תֹּאמַר אֲכָלוּם, וַהֲלֹא בִּכְנִיסָתָם לָאָרֶץ נֶאֱמַר: "וּמִקְנֶה רַב הָיָה לִבְנֵי רְאוּבֵן" וְגוֹ' (להלן לב, א)? אֶלָּא שֶׁמְּבַקְּשִׁים עֲלִילָה:

ה) **אֲשֶׁר נֹאכַל בְּמִצְרַיִם חִנָּם.** אִם תֹּאמַר שֶׁמִּצְרִיִּים נוֹתְנִים לָהֶם דָּגִים חִנָּם, וַהֲלֹא כְבָר נֶאֱמַר: "וְתֶבֶן לֹא יִנָּתֵן לָכֶם" (שמות ה, יח), אִם תֶּבֶן לֹא הָיוּ נוֹתְנִים לָהֶם חִנָּם, דָּגִים הָיוּ נוֹתְנִים לָהֶם חִנָּם?! וּמַהוּ אוֹמֵר: "חִנָּם"? חִנָּם מִן הַמִּצְוֹת. **אֵת הַקִּשֻּׁאִים.** אָמַר רַבִּי שִׁמְעוֹן: מִפְּנֵי מָה הַמָּן מִשְׁתַּנֶּה לְכָל דָּבָר חוּץ מֵאֵלּוּ? מִפְּנֵי שֶׁהֵן קָשִׁים לַמֵּנִיקוֹת, אוֹמְרִים לְאִשָּׁה: אַל תֹּאכְלִי שׁוּם וּבָצָל, מִפְּנֵי הַתִּינוֹק. מָשָׁל לְמֶלֶךְ כו' [בָּשָׂר וָדָם שֶׁמָּסַר בְּנוֹ לְפֵדָגוֹג, וְהָיָה יוֹשֵׁב וּמַפְקִידוֹ וְאוֹמֵר לוֹ, הִזָּהֵר שֶׁלֹּא יֹאכַל מַאֲכָל רַע וְלֹא יִשְׁתֶּה מַשְׁקֶה רַע. וּבְכָל כָּךְ הָיָה הַבֵּן הַהוּא מִתְרַעֵם עַל אָבִיו לוֹמַר, לֹא מִפְּנֵי שֶׁאוֹהֲבֵנִי, אֶלָּא מִפְּנֵי שֶׁאִי אֶפְשָׁר לוֹ שֶׁאוֹכַל], כִּדְאִיתָא בְּסִפְרֵי (פט): **הַקִּשֻּׁאִים.** הֵם קוקומבר״ש בְּלַעַז: **אֲבַטִּחִים.** בודיק״ש: **הֶחָצִיר.** כְּרֵשִׁין, פוריל״ש, וְתַרְגּוּמוֹ: "יָת בּוּצִינַיָּא" וכו':

ו) **אֶל הַמָּן עֵינֵינוּ.** מָן בַּשַּׁחַר, מָן בָּעֶרֶב:

ז) **וְהַמָּן כִּזְרַע־גַּד.** מִי שֶׁאָמַר זֶה לֹא אָמַר זֶה. יִשְׂרָאֵל אוֹמְרִים: "בִּלְתִּי אֶל הַמָּן עֵינֵינוּ", וְהַקָּדוֹשׁ בָּרוּךְ הוּא הִכְתִּיב בַּתּוֹרָה: "וְהַמָּן כִּזְרַע גַּד" וְגוֹ', כְּלוֹמַר, רְאוּ בָּאֵי עוֹלָם עַל מַה מִּתְלוֹנְנִים בָּנַי, וְהַמָּן כָּךְ וְכָךְ הוּא חָשׁוּב. **כִּזְרַע גַּד.** עָגֹל כְּגִדָּא, זֶרַע קוליינדר״ו: **בְּדֹלַח.** שֵׁם אֶבֶן טוֹבָה, קריסט״ל:

ח) **שָׁטוּ.** אֵין "שַׁיִט" אֶלָּא לְשׁוֹן טִיּוּל, איישבני״ר, בְּלֹא עָמָל: **וְטָחֲנוּ בָרֵחַיִם וְגוֹ'.** לֹא יָרַד בָּרֵחַיִם וְלֹא בַּקְּדֵרָה וְלֹא בַּמְּדֹכָה, אֶלָּא מִשְׁתַּנֶּה הָיָה טַעְמוֹ לְנִטְחָנִין וְלַנִּדּוֹכִין וְלַמְבֻשָּׁלִין: **בַּפָּרוּר.** קְדֵרָה: **לְשַׁד הַשָּׁמֶן.** לֶחְלוּחַ שֶׁל שֶׁמֶן, כָּךְ פֵּרוּשׁוֹ דֻּגְמָא. וְדוֹמֶה לוֹ: "נֶהְפַּךְ לְשַׁדִּי בְּחַרְבֹנֵי קַיִץ" (תהלים לב, ד), "וְהַלָּמֶ״ד" יְסוֹד, נֶהְפַּךְ לֵחְלוּחִי בְּחַרְבוֹנֵי קַיִץ. וְרַבּוֹתֵינוּ פֵּרְשׁוּהוּ לְשׁוֹן שָׁדַיִם, אַךְ אֵין עִנְיַן שָׁדַיִם אֵצֶל שָׁמֶן. וְאִי אֶפְשָׁר לוֹמַר "לְשַׁד הַשָּׁמֶן" לְשׁוֹן "וַיִּשְׁמַן יְשֻׁרוּן" (דברים לב, טו), שֶׁאִם כֵּן הָיָה הַמֶּ״ם נָקוּד קָמָץ קָטָן (צֵירִי) וְטַעְמוֹ לְמַטָּה תַּחַת הַמֶּ״ם, עַכְשָׁיו שֶׁהַמֶּ״ם נָקוּד פַּתָּח קָטָן (סֶגּוֹל) וְהַטַּעַם תַּחַת הַשִּׁי״ן, לְשׁוֹן שֶׁמֶן הוּא, וְהַשִּׁי״ן הַנְּקוּדָה בְּקָמָץ גָּדוֹל וְאֵינָהּ נְקוּדָה בְּפַתָּח קָטָן מִפְּנֵי שֶׁהוּא סוֹף פָּסוּק. דָּבָר אַחֵר, "לְשַׁד" לְשׁוֹן עֲטַרִיקוֹן לַיַ״ש שֶׁמֶ״ן דְּבַ״שׁ, כַּעֲסָה הַנִּלּוֹשָׁה בְּשֶׁמֶן וּקְטוּפָה בִּדְבַשׁ. וְתַרְגּוּם שֶׁל אֻנְקְלוֹס דִּמְתַרְגֵּם: "דְּלִישׁ בְּמִשְׁחָא" נוֹטֶה לְפִתְרוֹנוֹ שֶׁל דֻּגְמָא, שֶׁהָעִסָּה הַנִּלּוֹשָׁה בְּשֶׁמֶן לַחְלוּחִית שֶׁמֶן יֵשׁ בָּהּ:

פרק יא | במדבר

הַמַּחֲנֶה לָיְלָה יֵרֵד הַמָּן עָלָיו: וַיִּשְׁמַע מֹשֶׁה אֶת־הָעָם בֹּכֶה
לְמִשְׁפְּחֹתָיו אִישׁ לְפֶתַח אָהֳלוֹ וַיִּחַר־אַף יְהוָה מְאֹד וּבְעֵינֵי
מֹשֶׁה רָע: וַיֹּאמֶר מֹשֶׁה אֶל־יְהוָה לָמָה הֲרֵעֹתָ לְעַבְדֶּךָ וְלָמָּה
לֹא־מָצָתִי חֵן בְּעֵינֶיךָ לָשׂוּם אֶת־מַשָּׂא כָּל־הָעָם הַזֶּה עָלָי:
הֶאָנֹכִי הָרִיתִי אֵת כָּל־הָעָם הַזֶּה אִם־אָנֹכִי יְלִדְתִּיהוּ כִּי־תֹאמַר
אֵלַי שָׂאֵהוּ בְחֵיקֶךָ כַּאֲשֶׁר יִשָּׂא הָאֹמֵן אֶת־הַיֹּנֵק עַל הָאֲדָמָה
אֲשֶׁר נִשְׁבַּעְתָּ לַאֲבֹתָיו: מֵאַיִן לִי בָּשָׂר לָתֵת לְכָל־הָעָם הַזֶּה
כִּי־יִבְכּוּ עָלַי לֵאמֹר תְּנָה־לָּנוּ בָשָׂר וְנֹאכֵלָה: לֹא־אוּכַל אָנֹכִי
לְבַדִּי לָשֵׂאת אֶת־כָּל־הָעָם הַזֶּה כִּי כָבֵד מִמֶּנִּי: וְאִם־כָּכָה ׀
אַתְּ־עֹשֶׂה לִּי הָרְגֵנִי נָא הָרֹג אִם־מָצָאתִי חֵן בְּעֵינֶיךָ וְאַל־אֶרְאֶה
בְּרָעָתִי:

וַיֹּאמֶר יְהוָה אֶל־מֹשֶׁה אֶסְפָה־לִּי שִׁבְעִים אִישׁ מִזִּקְנֵי יִשְׂרָאֵל
אֲשֶׁר יָדַעְתָּ כִּי־הֵם זִקְנֵי הָעָם וְשֹׁטְרָיו וְלָקַחְתָּ אֹתָם אֶל־אֹהֶל

י בֹּכֶה לְמִשְׁפְּחֹתָיו. מִשְׁפָּחוֹת מִשְׁפָּחוֹת נֶאֱסָפִים וּבוֹכִים, לְפַרְסֵם תַּרְעֻמְתָּן בְּגָלוּי. וְרַבּוֹתֵינוּ אָמְרוּ: "לְמִשְׁפְּחֹתָיו", עַל עִסְקֵי מִשְׁפָּחוֹת, עַל עֲרָיוֹת הַנֶּאֱסָרוֹת לָהֶם:

יב כִּי תֹאמַר אֵלַי. שֶׁאַתָּה אוֹמֵר אֵלַי: שָׂאֵהוּ בְחֵיקֶךָ, וְהֵיכָן אָמַר לוֹ כֵן? "לֵךְ נְחֵה אֶת הָעָם" (שמות לב, לד), וְאוֹמֵר: "וַיְצַוֵּם אֶל בְּנֵי יִשְׂרָאֵל" (שם ו, יג), עַל מְנָת שֶׁיִּהְיוּ סוֹקְלִים אֶתְכֶם וּמְחָרְפִין אֶתְכֶם: עַל הָאֲדָמָה אֲשֶׁר נִשְׁבַּעְתָּ לַאֲבֹתָיו. אַתָּה אוֹמֵר לִי לְשֵׂאתָם פְּחַיִּי:

טו וְאִם כָּכָה אַתְּ עֹשֶׂה לִּי. תָּשַׁשׁ כֹּחוֹ שֶׁל מֹשֶׁה כִּנְקֵבָה כְּשֶׁהֶרְאָהוּ הַקָּדוֹשׁ בָּרוּךְ הוּא הַפֻּרְעָנוּת שֶׁהוּא עָתִיד לְהָבִיא עֲלֵיהֶם עַל זֹאת, אָמַר לְפָנָיו: אִם כֵּן, הָרְגֵנִי תְּחִלָּה. וְאַל אֶרְאֶה בְּרָעָתִי. 'בְּרָעָתָם'

הָיָה לוֹ לִכְתֹּב, אֶלָּא שֶׁכִּנָּה הַכָּתוּב, וְזֶה אֶחָד מִתִּקּוּנֵי סוֹפְרִים בַּתּוֹרָה לְכִנּוּי וּלְתִקּוּן לָשׁוֹן:

טז אֶסְפָה לִּי. הֲרֵי תְּשׁוּבָה לִתְלוּנָתְךָ שֶׁאָמַרְתָּ: "לֹא אוּכַל אָנֹכִי לְבַדִּי" (לעיל פסוק יד). וְהַזְּקֵנִים הָרִאשׁוֹנִים הֵיכָן הָיוּ? וַהֲלֹא אַף בְּמִצְרַיִם יָשְׁבוּ עִמָּהֶם, שֶׁנֶּאֱמַר: "לֵךְ וְאָסַפְתָּ אֶת זִקְנֵי יִשְׂרָאֵל" (שמות ג, טז), אֶלָּא בְּאֵשׁ תַּבְעֵרָה מֵתוּ. וּרְאוּיִים הָיוּ לְכָךְ מִסִּינַי, דִּכְתִיב: "וַיֶּחֱזוּ אֶת הָאֱלֹהִים" (שמות כד, יא), שֶׁנָּהֲגוּ קַלּוּת רֹאשׁ כְּנוֹשֵׁךְ פִּתּוֹ וּמְדַבֵּר בִּפְנֵי הַמֶּלֶךְ, וְזֶהוּ: "וַיֹּאכְלוּ וַיִּשְׁתּוּ" (שם), וְלֹא רָצָה הַקָּדוֹשׁ בָּרוּךְ הוּא לִתֵּן אֲבֵלוּת בְּמַתַּן תּוֹרָה, וּפָרַע לָהֶם כָּאן: אֲשֶׁר יָדַעְתָּ כִּי הֵם וְגוֹ'. אוֹתָן שֶׁאַתָּה מַכִּיר שֶׁנִּתְמַנּוּ עֲלֵיהֶם שׁוֹטְרִים בְּמִצְרַיִם בַּעֲבוֹדַת פֶּרֶךְ, וְהָיוּ מְרַחֲמִים עֲלֵיהֶם וּמֻכִּים עַל יָדָם, שֶׁנֶּאֱמַר: "וַיֻּכּוּ שֹׁטְרֵי בְּנֵי יִשְׂרָאֵל" (שמות ה, יד), עַתָּה יִתְמַנּוּ בִּגְדֻלָּתָן, כְּדֶרֶךְ שֶׁנִּצְטַעֲרוּ בְּצָרָתָן:

במדבר | פרק יא

יז מוֹעֵד וְהִתְיַצְּבוּ שָׁם עִמָּךְ: וְיָרַדְתִּי וְדִבַּרְתִּי עִמְּךָ שָׁם וְאָצַלְתִּי מִן־הָרוּחַ אֲשֶׁר עָלֶיךָ וְשַׂמְתִּי עֲלֵיהֶם וְנָשְׂאוּ אִתְּךָ בְּמַשָּׂא הָעָם וְלֹא־תִשָּׂא אַתָּה לְבַדֶּךָ: יח וְאֶל־הָעָם תֹּאמַר הִתְקַדְּשׁוּ לְמָחָר וַאֲכַלְתֶּם בָּשָׂר כִּי בְּכִיתֶם בְּאָזְנֵי יְהוָה לֵאמֹר מִי יַאֲכִלֵנוּ בָּשָׂר כִּי־טוֹב לָנוּ בְּמִצְרָיִם וְנָתַן יְהוָה לָכֶם בָּשָׂר וַאֲכַלְתֶּם: יט לֹא יוֹם אֶחָד תֹּאכְלוּן וְלֹא יוֹמָיִם וְלֹא ׀ חֲמִשָּׁה יָמִים וְלֹא עֲשָׂרָה יָמִים וְלֹא עֶשְׂרִים יוֹם: כ עַד ׀ חֹדֶשׁ יָמִים עַד אֲשֶׁר־יֵצֵא מֵאַפְּכֶם וְהָיָה לָכֶם לְזָרָא יַעַן כִּי־מְאַסְתֶּם אֶת־יְהוָה אֲשֶׁר בְּקִרְבְּכֶם וַתִּבְכּוּ לְפָנָיו לֵאמֹר לָמָּה זֶּה יָצָאנוּ מִמִּצְרָיִם: כא וַיֹּאמֶר מֹשֶׁה שֵׁשׁ־מֵאוֹת אֶלֶף רַגְלִי הָעָם אֲשֶׁר אָנֹכִי בְּקִרְבּוֹ וְאַתָּה אָמַרְתָּ בָּשָׂר אֶתֵּן לָהֶם וְאָכְלוּ חֹדֶשׁ יָמִים: כב הֲצֹאן וּבָקָר יִשָּׁחֵט לָהֶם וּמָצָא לָהֶם אִם אֶת־כָּל־דְּגֵי הַיָּם יֵאָסֵף לָהֶם וּמָצָא לָהֶם:

וּלְקַחְתָּ אֹתָם. קָחֵם בִּדְבָרִים, אַשְׁרֵיכֶם שֶׁנִּתְמַנִּיתֶם פַּרְנָסִים עַל בָּנָיו שֶׁל מָקוֹם: וְהִתְיַצְּבוּ שָׁם עִמָּךְ. כְּדֵי שֶׁיִּרְאוּ יִשְׂרָאֵל וְיִנְהֲגוּ בָּהֶם גְּדֻלָּה וְכָבוֹד, וְיֹאמְרוּ: חֲבִיבִין אֵלּוּ שֶׁנִּכְנְסוּ עִם מֹשֶׁה לִשְׁמֹעַ דִּבּוּר מִפִּי הַקָּדוֹשׁ בָּרוּךְ הוּא:

יז] וְיָרַדְתִּי. זוֹ אַחַת מֵעֶשֶׂר יְרִידוֹת הַכְּתוּבוֹת בַּתּוֹרָה. וְדִבַּרְתִּי עִמְּךָ. וְלֹא עִמָּהֶם: וְאָצַלְתִּי. כְּתַרְגּוּמוֹ "וַאֲרַבֵּי", כְּמוֹ: "וְאֶל אֲצִילֵי בְּנֵי יִשְׂרָאֵל" (שמות כד, יא): וְשַׂמְתִּי עֲלֵיהֶם. לְמָה מֹשֶׁה דּוֹמֶה בְּאוֹתָהּ שָׁעָה? לְנֵר שֶׁמֻּנָּח עַל גַּבֵּי מְנוֹרָה, וְהַכֹּל מַדְלִיקִין הֵימֶנּוּ וְאֵין חֶסְרוֹנוֹ חָסֵר כְּלוּם: וְנָשְׂאוּ אִתָּךְ. הַתְנֵה עִמָּהֶם, עַל מְנָת שֶׁיְּקַבְּלוּ עֲלֵיהֶם טֹרַח בָּנַי, שֶׁהֵם טַרְחָנִים וְסַרְבָנִים: וְלֹא תִשָּׂא אַתָּה לְבַדֶּךָ. הֲרֵי תְּשׁוּבָה לְמָה שֶּׁאָמַרְתָּ "לֹא אוּכַל אָנֹכִי לְבַדִּי" (לעיל פסוק יד):

יח] הִתְקַדְּשׁוּ. הַזְמִינוּ עַצְמְכֶם לְפֻרְעָנוּת, וְכֵן הוּא אוֹמֵר: "וְהַקְדִּשֵׁם לְיוֹם הֲרֵגָה" (ירמיה יב, ג):

כ] עַד חֹדֶשׁ יָמִים. זוֹ בַּכְּשֵׁרִים שֶׁמִּתְמַצִּין עַל מִטּוֹתֵיהֶן וְאַחַר כָּךְ נִשְׁמָתָן יוֹצְאָה; וּבָרְשָׁעִים הוּא אוֹמֵר "הַבָּשָׂר עוֹדֶנּוּ בֵּין שִׁנֵּיהֶם" (להלן פסוק לג), כָּךְ הִיא שְׁנוּיָה בְּסִפְרֵי (עג): חֲבָל בַּמְּכִילְתָּא (ויסע פי"ד) שְׁנוּיָה חִלּוּף: הָרְשָׁעִים אוֹכְלִין וּמִצְטַעֲרִין שְׁלֹשִׁים יוֹם, וְהַכְּשֵׁרִים – "הַבָּשָׂר עוֹדֶנּוּ בֵּין שִׁנֵּיהֶם": עַד אֲשֶׁר יֵצֵא מֵאַפְּכֶם. כְּתַרְגּוּמוֹ: "דְּתִקּוּצוּן בֵּיהּ", יְהֵא דּוֹמֶה לָכֶם כְּאִלּוּ אֲכַלְתֶּם מִמֶּנּוּ יוֹתֵר מִדַּאי עַד שֶׁיּוֹצֵא וְנִגְעַל לַחוּץ דֶּרֶךְ הָחֹטֶם: וְהָיָה לָכֶם לְזָרָא. שֶׁתִּהְיוּ מְרַחֲקִין אוֹתוֹ יוֹתֵר מִמַּה שֶּׁקֵּרַבְתֶּם. וּבְדִבְרֵי רַבִּי מֹשֶׁה הַדַּרְשָׁן רָאִיתִי, שֶׁיֵּשׁ לָשׁוֹן שֶׁקּוֹרִין לַחֶרֶב "זָרָא": אֶת ה' אֲשֶׁר בְּקִרְבְּכֶם. אִם לֹא שֶׁנָּטַעְתִּי שְׁכִינָתִי בֵּינֵיכֶם, לֹא גָּסָה לְבַבְכֶם לִכָּנֵס לְכָל הַדְּבָרִים הַלָּלוּ:

כא] שֵׁשׁ מֵאוֹת אֶלֶף רַגְלִי. לֹא חָשׁ לִמְנוֹת אֶת הַפְּרָט, שְׁלֹשֶׁת אֲלָפִים הַיְתֵרִים (לעיל א, מו). וְרַבִּי מֹשֶׁה הַדַּרְשָׁן פֵּרֵשׁ, שֶׁלֹּא בָּכוּ אֶלָּא אוֹתָן שֶׁיָּצְאוּ מִמִּצְרָיִם:

כב-כג] הֲצֹאן וּבָקָר יִשָּׁחֵט. זֶה אֶחָד מֵאַרְבָּעָה דְּבָרִים שֶׁהָיָה רַבִּי עֲקִיבָא דּוֹרֵשׁ וְאֵין רַבִּי שִׁמְעוֹן דּוֹרֵשׁ

פרק יא | במדבר

כג וַיֹּאמֶר יהוה אֶל־מֹשֶׁה הֲיַד יהוה תִּקְצָר עַתָּה תִרְאֶה הֲיִקְרְךָ
דְבָרִי אִם־לֹא: וַיֵּצֵא מֹשֶׁה וַיְדַבֵּר אֶל־הָעָם אֵת דִּבְרֵי יהוה
כד וַיֶּאֱסֹף שִׁבְעִים אִישׁ מִזִּקְנֵי הָעָם וַיַּעֲמֵד אֹתָם סְבִיבֹת הָאֹהֶל:
וַיֵּרֶד יהוה ׀ בֶּעָנָן וַיְדַבֵּר אֵלָיו וַיָּאצֶל מִן־הָרוּחַ אֲשֶׁר עָלָיו וַיִּתֵּן
כה עַל־שִׁבְעִים אִישׁ הַזְּקֵנִים וַיְהִי כְּנוֹחַ עֲלֵיהֶם הָרוּחַ וַיִּתְנַבְּאוּ
וְלֹא יָסָפוּ: וַיִּשָּׁאֲרוּ שְׁנֵי־אֲנָשִׁים ׀ בַּמַּחֲנֶה שֵׁם הָאֶחָד ׀ אֶלְדָּד
כו וְשֵׁם הַשֵּׁנִי מֵידָד וַתָּנַח עֲלֵיהֶם הָרוּחַ וְהֵמָּה בַּכְּתֻבִים וְלֹא

כְּמוֹתָם. רַבִּי עֲקִיבָא חוֹמֵר: "שָׂם מֵאוֹת אֶלֶף רַגְלִי, וְעוֹף כַּקָּשֶׁה, דָּגִים וַחֲגָבִים בַּקָּשֶׁה. אָמַר לוֹ: חַס
וְעַתָּה עָמַדְתָּ בָּשָׂר אֶתֵּן לָהֶם וְאָכְלוּ חֹדֶשׁ יָמִים, כֵּן יֹאמְרוּ שֶׁקְּעָרָה יָדִי. אָמַר לְפָנָיו: הֲרֵינִי הוֹלֵךְ
הַצֹּאן וּבָקָר" וְגוֹ', הַכֹּל כְּמַשְׁמָעוֹ, מִי מַסְפִּיק לָהֶם? וּמְפַיְּסָן. אָמַר לוֹ: "עַתָּה תִרְאֶה הֲיִקְרְךָ דְבָרִי",
כָּעִנְיָן שֶׁנֶּאֱמַר: "וּמָצָא כְּדֵי גְאֻלָּתוֹ" (ויקרא כה, כו). שֶׁלֹּא יִשְׁמְעוּ לָךְ. הָלַךְ מֹשֶׁה לְפַיְּסָן, אָמַר לָהֶם:
וְאֵיזוֹ קָשָׁה, זוֹ אוֹ "שִׁמְעוּ נָא הַמֹּרִים" (להלן כ, י)? "הֲיַד ה' תִּקְצָר", "הֵן הִכָּה צוּר וַיָּזוּבוּ מַיִם וְגוֹ' הֲגַם
אֶלָּא לְפִי שֶׁלֹּא אָמַר בָּרַבִּים, חָשַׂךְ לוֹ הַכָּתוּב לֶחֶם יוּכַל תֵּת" (תהלים עח, כ). אָמְרוּ: פְּשָׁרָה הִיא זוֹ,
וְלֹא נִפְרַע מִמֶּנּוּ, וְזוֹ שֶׁל מְרִיבָה הָיְתָה בַּגָּלוּי, אֵין בּוֹ כֹּחַ לְמַלְּאוֹת שְׁאֵלָתֵנוּ, וְזֶהוּ שֶׁנֶּאֱמַר: "וַיֵּצֵא
לְפִיכָךְ לֹא חָשַׂךְ לוֹ הַכָּתוּב. רַבִּי שִׁמְעוֹן חוֹמֵר: מֹשֶׁה וַיְדַבֵּר אֶל הָעָם" (להלן פסוק כד), כֵּיוָן שֶׁלֹּא שָׁמְעוּ
חַס וְשָׁלוֹם, לֹא עָלְתָה עַל דַּעְתּוֹ שֶׁל אוֹתוֹ צַדִּיק לוֹ, "וַיֶּאֱסֹף שִׁבְעִים אִישׁ וְגוֹ'" (שם):
כָּךְ! מִי שֶׁכָּתוּב בּוֹ: "בְּכָל בֵּיתִי נֶאֱמָן הוּא" (להלן

יב, ז) יֹאמַר: 'אֵין הַמָּקוֹם מַסְפִּיק לָנוּ'?! אֶלָּא, כָּךְ וְלֹא יָסָפוּ. לֹא נִתְנַבְּאוּ אֶלָּא אוֹתוֹ הַיּוֹם לְבַדּוֹ,
אָמַר: "שֵׂם מֵאוֹת אֶלֶף רַגְלִי וְגוֹ', וְעַתָּה עָמַדְתָּ כָּךְ מֻפְלָא בִּסְפָרֵי (כה), וְאוּנְקְלוֹס תִּרְגֵּם: "וְלָא
בָּשָׂר אֶתֵּן" לְחֹדֶשׁ יָמִים, וְאַחַר כָּךְ תַּהֲרֹג אֻמָּה פָּסְקִין, שֶׁלֹּא פָּסְקָה נְבוּאָה מֵהֶם:
גְּדוֹלָה כָּזוֹ, "הֲצֹאן וּבָקָר יִשָּׁחֵט לָהֶם" כְּדֵי שֶׁיֵּהָרְגוּ
וּתְהֵא אֲכִילָה זוֹ מַסְפַּקְתָּן עַד עוֹלָם? וְכִי שִׁבְחֲךָ וַיִּשָּׁאֲרוּ שְׁנֵי אֲנָשִׁים. מֵאוֹתָן שֶׁנִּבְחֲרוּ, אָמְרוּ: אֵין
הוּא זֶה? אוֹמְרִים לוֹ לַחֲמוֹר: טֹל כֹּד שֶׁל שְׂעוֹרִים אָנוּ כְּדַאי לִגְדֻלָּה זוֹ. וְהֵמָּה בַּכְּתֻבִים. בַּמְּבֹרָרִים
וַחֲתֹךְ רֹאשְׁךָ? הֱשִׁיבוֹ הַקָּדוֹשׁ בָּרוּךְ הוּא: וְאִם שֶׁבָּהֶם לַסַּנְהֶדְרִין. וְנִכְתְּבוּ כֻלָּם נְקוּבִים בְּשֵׁמוֹת וְעַל
לֹא אֶתֵּן, יֹאמְרוּ שֶׁקְּצָרָה יָדִי, הֲטוֹב בְּעֵינֶיךָ שֶׁיַּד יְדֵי גּוֹרָל, לְפִי שֶׁהִתְחַשְּׁבוּ עוֹלֶה לִשְׁנֵים עָשָׂר שְׁבָטִים
ה' תִּקְצָר בְּעֵינֵיהֶם? יֹאבְדוּ הֵם וּמֵאָה כַּיּוֹצֵא בָהֶם שִׁשָּׁה שִׁשָּׁה לְכָל שֵׁבֶט וָשֵׁבֶט, חוּץ מִשְּׁנֵי שְׁבָטִים שֶׁאֵין
וְאַל תְּהִי יָדִי קְצָרָה לִפְנֵיהֶם אֲפִלּוּ שָׁעָה אֶחָת, מַגִּיעַ אֲלֵיהֶם אֶלָּא חֲמִשָּׁה חֲמִשָּׁה. אָמַר מֹשֶׁה: אֵין
"עַתָּה תִרְאֶה הֲיִקְרְךָ דְבָרִי". רַבָּן גַּמְלִיאֵל בְּנוֹ שֶׁל שֵׁבֶט שׁוֹמֵעַ לִי לִפְתֹּחַ לוֹ שְׁבָטוֹ זָקֵן חָסֵר. מֶה עָשָׂה?
רַבִּי יְהוּדָה הַנָּשִׂיא אוֹמֵר: מִי שֶׁאֶפְשָׁר לַעֲמֹד עַל נָטַל שִׁבְעִים וּשְׁנַיִם פִּתְקִין וְכָתַב עַל שִׁבְעִים
הַטֹּפֵל, מֵאַחַר שֶׁאֵינָן מְבַקְשִׁים אֶלָּא עֲלִילָה לֹא וְעַל שְׁנַיִם חָלָק, וּבָרַר מִכָּל שֵׁבֶט וָשֵׁבֶט שִׁשָּׁה, וְהָיוּ
תַסְפִּיק לָהֶם, סוֹפָן לָדוּן אַחֲרֶיךָ, אִם אַתָּה נוֹתֵן שִׁבְעִים וּשְׁנָיִם. אָמַר לָהֶם: טְלוּ פִתְקֵיכֶם מִתּוֹךְ
לָהֶם בְּשַׂר בְּהֵמָה גַּסָּה, יֹאמְרוּ: דַּקָּה בִּקַּשְׁנוּ, וְאִם קַלְפִּי. מִי שֶׁעָלָה בְּיָדוֹ "זָקֵן", נִתְקַדֵּשׁ; מִי שֶׁעָלָה בְּיָדוֹ
אַתָּה נוֹתֵן לָהֶם דַּקָּה, יֹאמְרוּ: גַּסָּה בִּקַּשְׁנוּ, חַיָּה חָלָק, אָמַר לוֹ: הַמָּקוֹם לֹא חָפֵץ בָּךְ:

במדבר | פרק יא

כז יָצְא֣וּ הָאֹ֔הֱלָה וַיִּֽתְנַבְּא֖וּ בַּֽמַּחֲנֶֽה: וַיָּ֣רׇץ הַנַּ֔עַר וַיַּגֵּ֥ד לְמֹשֶׁ֖ה
כח וַיֹּאמַ֑ר אֶלְדָּ֣ד וּמֵידָ֔ד מִֽתְנַבְּאִ֖ים בַּֽמַּחֲנֶֽה: וַיַּ֜עַן יְהוֹשֻׁ֣עַ בִּן־נ֗וּן
כט מְשָׁרֵ֥ת מֹשֶׁ֛ה מִבְּחֻרָ֖יו וַיֹּאמַ֑ר אֲדֹנִ֥י מֹשֶׁ֖ה כְּלָאֵֽם: וַיֹּ֧אמֶר ל֣וֹ
מֹשֶׁ֗ה הַֽמְקַנֵּ֥א אַתָּ֖ה לִ֑י וּמִ֨י יִתֵּ֜ן כׇּל־עַ֤ם יְהוָה֙ נְבִיאִ֔ים כִּי־יִתֵּ֧ן
ל יְהוָ֛ה אֶת־רוּח֖וֹ עֲלֵיהֶֽם: וַיֵּאָסֵ֥ף מֹשֶׁ֖ה אֶל־הַֽמַּחֲנֶ֑ה ה֖וּא וְזִקְנֵ֥י שביעי
לא יִשְׂרָאֵֽל: וְר֜וּחַ נָסַ֣ע ׀ מֵאֵ֣ת יְהוָ֗ה וַיָּ֣גׇז שַׂלְוִים֮ מִן־הַיָּם֒ וַיִּטֹּ֨שׁ
עַל־הַֽמַּחֲנֶ֜ה כְּדֶ֧רֶךְ י֣וֹם כֹּ֗ה וּכְדֶ֤רֶךְ יוֹם֙ כֹּ֔ה סְבִיב֖וֹת הַֽמַּחֲנֶ֑ה
לב וּכְאַמָּתַ֖יִם עַל־פְּנֵ֥י הָאָֽרֶץ: וַיָּ֣קׇם הָעָ֡ם כׇּל־הַיּוֹם֩ הַה֨וּא וְכׇל־
הַלַּ֜יְלָה וְכֹ֣ל ׀ י֣וֹם הַֽמׇּחֳרָ֗ת וַיַּֽאַסְפוּ֙ אֶת־הַשְּׂלָ֔ו הַמַּמְעִ֕יט אָסַ֖ף
לג עֲשָׂרָ֣ה חֳמָרִ֑ים וַיִּשְׁטְח֤וּ לָהֶם֙ שָׁט֔וֹחַ סְבִיב֖וֹת הַֽמַּחֲנֶֽה: הַבָּשָׂ֗ר
עוֹדֶ֨נּוּ֙ בֵּ֣ין שִׁנֵּיהֶ֔ם טֶ֖רֶם יִכָּרֵ֑ת וְאַ֤ף יְהוָה֙ חָרָ֣ה בָעָ֔ם וַיַּ֤ךְ יְהוָה֙
לד בָּעָ֔ם מַכָּ֖ה רַבָּ֥ה מְאֹֽד: וַיִּקְרָ֛א אֶת־שֵֽׁם־הַמָּק֥וֹם הַה֖וּא קִבְר֥וֹת

כז) וַיָּרׇץ הַנַּעַר. יֵשׁ אוֹמְרִים: גֵּרְשֹׁם בֶּן מֹשֶׁה הָיָה:

כח) כְּלָאֵם. הַטֵּל עֲלֵיהֶם צׇרְכֵי צִבּוּר וְהֵם כָּלִים מֵאֲלֵיהֶם. דָּבָר אַחֵר, תְּנֵם אֶל בֵּית הַכֶּלֶא, לְפִי שֶׁהָיוּ מִתְנַבְּאִים: מֹשֶׁה מֵת וִיהוֹשֻׁעַ מַכְנִיס אֶת יִשְׂרָאֵל לָאָרֶץ:

כט) הַמְקַנֵּא אַתָּה לִי. "הַקֹנְאָתִי אַתְּ מְקַנֵּא". לִי. כְּמוֹ בִּשְׁבִילִי. כׇּל לְשׁוֹן קִנְאָה, אָדָם הַנּוֹתֵן לֵב עַל הַדָּבָר אוֹ לִנְקֹם אוֹ לַעֲזֹר, אנפר"נמנ"ט בְּלַעַ"ז, אוֹחֵז בְּעָבֳּיוֹ שֶׁל מַשָּׂא:

ל) וַיֵּאָסֵף מֹשֶׁה. מִפֶּתַח אֹהֶל מוֹעֵד: אֶל הַמַּחֲנֶה. נִכְנְסוּ אִישׁ לְאָהֳלוֹ: וַיֵּאָסֵף. לְשׁוֹן כְּנִיסָה אֶל הַבַּיִת, כְּמוֹ: "וַאֲסַפְתּוֹ אֶל תּוֹךְ בֵּיתֶךָ" (דברים כב, ב), "וְאֵין אִישׁ מְאַסֵּף אוֹתָם הַבַּיְתָה" (שופטים יט, יח), "וַעֲבַד לֹא יֵדַע מִי יֵאַסְפֵם" (תהלים לט, ז). מְלַמֵּד שֶׁלֹּא

הֵבִיא עֲלֵיהֶם פֻּרְעָנוּת עַד שֶׁנִּכְנְסוּ הַצַּדִּיקִים אִישׁ לְאָהֳלוֹ:

לא) וַיָּגׇז. וַיַּפְרִיחַ, וְכֵן: "כִּי גָז חִישׁ" (תהלים צ, י), "וְכֵן גָּזוּ וְעָבָר" (נחום א, יב): וַיִּטֹּשׁ. וַיִּפְשֹׁט, כְּמוֹ: "וְהִנֵּה נְטֻשִׁים עַל פְּנֵי כׇל הָאָרֶץ" (שמואל א' ל, טז), "וּנְטַשְׁתִּיךָ הַמִּדְבָּרָה" (יחזקאל כט, ה): וּכְאַמָּתַיִם. פּוֹרְחוֹת בְּגֹבַהּ עַד שֶׁהֵן כְּנֶגֶד לִבּוֹ שֶׁל אָדָם, כְּדֵי שֶׁלֹּא יְהֵא טֹרַח בַּאֲסִיפָתָן לֹא לְהַגְבִּיהַּ וְלֹא לִשְׁחוֹת:

לב) הַמַּמְעִיט. מִי שֶׁאוֹסֵף פָּחוֹת מִכֻּלָּם, הָעֲצֵלִים וְהַחִגְּרִים, "אָסַף עֲשָׂרָה חֳמָרִים": וַיִּשְׁטְחוּ. עָשׂוּ אוֹתָן מַשְׁטִיחִין מַשְׁטִיחִין:

לג) טֶרֶם יִכָּרֵת. כְּתַרְגּוּמוֹ: "עַד לָא פְסַק". דָּבָר אַחֵר, אֵינוֹ מַסְפִּיק לְפָסְקוֹ בְּשִׁנָּיו עַד שֶׁנִּשְׁמָתוֹ יוֹצְאָה:

הַתַּאֲוָה כִּי־שָׁם קָבְרוּ אֶת־הָעָם הַמִּתְאַוִּים: מִקִּבְרוֹת הַתַּאֲוָה
נָסְעוּ הָעָם חֲצֵרוֹת וַיִּהְיוּ בַּחֲצֵרוֹת:

יב א וַתְּדַבֵּר מִרְיָם וְאַהֲרֹן בְּמֹשֶׁה עַל־אֹדוֹת הָאִשָּׁה הַכֻּשִׁית אֲשֶׁר
ב לָקָח כִּי־אִשָּׁה כֻשִׁית לָקָח: וַיֹּאמְרוּ הֲרַק אַךְ־בְּמֹשֶׁה דִּבֶּר יְהֹוָה
ג הֲלֹא גַּם־בָּנוּ דִבֵּר וַיִּשְׁמַע יְהֹוָה: וְהָאִישׁ מֹשֶׁה עָנָו מְאֹד מִכֹּל
ד הָאָדָם אֲשֶׁר עַל־פְּנֵי הָאֲדָמָה: וַיֹּאמֶר יְהֹוָה פִּתְאֹם
אֶל־מֹשֶׁה וְאֶל־אַהֲרֹן וְאֶל־מִרְיָם צְאוּ שְׁלָשְׁתְּכֶם אֶל־אֹהֶל
ה מוֹעֵד וַיֵּצְאוּ שְׁלָשְׁתָּם: וַיֵּרֶד יְהֹוָה בְּעַמּוּד עָנָן וַיַּעֲמֹד פֶּתַח

פרק יב

א **וַתְּדַבֵּר.** אֵין דִּבּוּר בְּכָל מָקוֹם אֶלָּא לְשׁוֹן קָשָׁה,
וְכֵן הוּא אוֹמֵר: "דִּבֶּר הָאִישׁ אֲדֹנֵי הָאָרֶץ אִתָּנוּ
קָשׁוֹת" (בראשית מב, ל). וְאֵין אֲמִירָה בְּכָל מָקוֹם אֶלָּא
לְשׁוֹן תַּחֲנוּנִים, וְכֵן הוּא אוֹמֵר: "וַיֹּאמֶר אַל נָא
אַחַי תָּרֵעוּ" (בראשית יט, ז), "וַיֹּאמֶר שִׁמְעוּ נָא דְבָרָי"
(להלן פסוק ו), כָּל "נָא" לְשׁוֹן בַּקָּשָׁה: **וַתְּדַבֵּר מִרְיָם
וְאַהֲרֹן.** הִיא פָּתְחָה בַּדִּבּוּר תְּחִלָּה, לְפִיכָךְ הִקְדִּימָהּ
הַכָּתוּב. וּמִנַּיִן הָיְתָה יוֹדַעַת מִרְיָם שֶׁפֵּרֵשׁ מֹשֶׁה מִן
הָאִשָּׁה? רַבִּי נָתָן אוֹמֵר: מִרְיָם הָיְתָה בְּצַד צִפּוֹרָה
בְּשָׁעָה שֶׁנֶּאֱמַר לְמֹשֶׁה: "אֶלְדָּד וּמֵידָד מִתְנַבְּאִים
בַּמַּחֲנֶה" (לעיל יא, כז), כֵּיוָן שֶׁשָּׁמְעָה צִפּוֹרָה אָמְרָה:
אוֹי לִנְשׁוֹתֵיהֶן שֶׁל אֵלּוּ אִם הֵם נִזְקָקִים לִנְבוּאָה,
שֶׁיִּהְיוּ פּוֹרְשִׁין מִנְּשׁוֹתֵיהֶן כְּדֶרֶךְ שֶׁפֵּרַשׁ בַּעְלִי מִמֶּנִּי.
וּמִשָּׁם יָדְעָה מִרְיָם וְהִגִּידָה לְאַהֲרֹן. וּמָה מִרְיָם שֶׁלֹּא
נִתְכַּוְּנָה לִגְנוּתוֹ, כָּךְ נֶעֶנְשָׁה, קַל וָחֹמֶר לַמְסַפֵּר
בִּגְנוּתוֹ שֶׁל חֲבֵרוֹ: **הָאִשָּׁה הַכֻּשִׁית.** מַגִּיד שֶׁהַכֹּל
מוֹדִים בְּיָפְיָהּ, כְּשֵׁם שֶׁהַכֹּל מוֹדִים בְּשַׁחֲרוּרִיתוֹ שֶׁל
כּוּשִׁי. **כֻּשִׁית.** בְּגִימַטְרִיָּא "יְפַת מַרְאֶה": **עַל אֹדוֹת
הָאִשָּׁה.** עַל אוֹדוֹת גֵּרוּשֶׁיהָ. **כִּי אִשָּׁה כֻשִׁית לָקָח.**
מַה תַּלְמוּד לוֹמַר? אֶלָּא יֵשׁ לְךָ אִשָּׁה נָאָה בְּיָפְיָהּ
וְאֵינָהּ נָאָה בְּמַעֲשֶׂיהָ, בְּמַעֲשֶׂיהָ וְלֹא בְיָפְיָהּ, אֲבָל זֹאת
נָאָה בַּכֹּל: **הָאִשָּׁה הַכֻּשִׁית.** עַל שֵׁם נוֹיָהּ נִקְרֵאת
'כּוּשִׁית', כְּאָדָם הַקּוֹרֵא אֶת בְּנוֹ נָאֶה 'כּוּשִׁי' כְּדֵי

שֶׁלֹּא תִשְׁלֹט בּוֹ עַיִן רָעָה: **כִּי אִשָּׁה כֻשִׁית לָקָח.**
וְעַתָּה גֵּרְשָׁהּ:

ב **הֲרַק אַךְ בְּמֹשֶׁה.** עִמּוֹ לְבַדּוֹ "דִּבֶּר ה'": **הֲלֹא גַּם
בָּנוּ דִבֵּר.** וְלֹא פֵרַשְׁנוּ מִדֶּרֶךְ אֶרֶץ:

ג **עָנָו.** שָׁפָל וְסַבְלָן:

ד **פִּתְאֹם.** נִגְלָה עֲלֵיהֶם פִּתְאֹם וְהֵם טְמֵאִים בְּדֶרֶךְ
אֶרֶץ, וְהָיוּ צוֹעֲקִים: מַיִם מַיִם, לְהוֹדִיעָם שֶׁיָּפֶה עָשָׂה
מֹשֶׁה שֶׁפֵּרַשׁ מִן הָאִשָּׁה, מֵאַחַר שֶׁנִּגְלֵית עָלָיו שְׁכִינָה
תָּדִיר, וְאֵין עֵת קְבוּעָה לַדִּבּוּר: **צְאוּ שְׁלָשְׁתְּכֶם.** מַגִּיד
שֶׁשְּׁלָשְׁתָּן נִקְרְאוּ בְּדִבּוּר אֶחָד, מַה שֶּׁאִי אֶפְשָׁר לַפֶּה
לוֹמַר וְלָאֹזֶן לִשְׁמֹעַ:

ה **בְּעַמּוּד עָנָן.** יָצָא יְחִידִי, שֶׁלֹּא כְמִדַּת בָּשָׂר וָדָם,
מֶלֶךְ בָּשָׂר וָדָם כְּשֶׁיּוֹצֵא לַמִּלְחָמָה יוֹצֵא בְּאֻכְלוּסִין
וּכְשֶׁיּוֹצֵא לְשָׁלוֹם יוֹצֵא בְּמֻעָטִין, וּמִדַּת הַקָּדוֹשׁ
בָּרוּךְ הוּא יוֹצֵא לַמִּלְחָמָה יְחִידִי, שֶׁנֶּאֱמַר: "ה'
אִישׁ מִלְחָמָה" (שמות טו, ג), וְיוֹצֵא לְשָׁלוֹם בְּאֻכְלוּסִין,
שֶׁנֶּאֱמַר: "רֶכֶב אֱלֹהִים רִבֹּתַיִם אַלְפֵי שִׁנְאָן" (תהלים
סח, יח): **וַיִּקְרָא אַהֲרֹן וּמִרְיָם.** שֶׁיִּהְיוּ נִמְשָׁכִין וְיוֹצְאִין
מִן הֶחָצֵר לִקְרַאת הַדִּבּוּר: **וַיֵּצְאוּ שְׁנֵיהֶם.** וּמִפְּנֵי
מָה מְשָׁכָן וְהִפְרִידָן מִמֹּשֶׁה, לְפִי שֶׁאוֹמְרִים מִקְצָת
שִׁבְחוֹ שֶׁל אָדָם בְּפָנָיו וְכֻלּוֹ שֶׁלֹּא בְּפָנָיו. וְכֵן מָצִינוּ
בְנֹחַ, שֶׁלֹּא בְּפָנָיו נֶאֱמַר: "אִישׁ צַדִּיק תָּמִים" (בראשית

במדבר | פרק יב | בהעלתך

א הָאֹהֶל וַיִּקְרָא אַהֲרֹן וּמִרְיָם וַיֵּצְאוּ שְׁנֵיהֶם: וַיֹּאמֶר שִׁמְעוּ־נָא
דְבָרָי אִם־יִהְיֶה נְבִיאֲכֶם יְהוָה בַּמַּרְאָה אֵלָיו אֶתְוַדָּע בַּחֲלוֹם
ב אֲדַבֶּר־בּוֹ: לֹא־כֵן עַבְדִּי מֹשֶׁה בְּכָל־בֵּיתִי נֶאֱמָן הוּא: פֶּה אֶל־
פֶּה אֲדַבֶּר־בּוֹ וּמַרְאֶה וְלֹא בְחִידֹת וּתְמֻנַת יְהוָה יַבִּיט וּמַדּוּעַ
ג לֹא יְרֵאתֶם לְדַבֵּר בְּעַבְדִּי בְמֹשֶׁה: וַיִּחַר־אַף יְהוָה בָּם וַיֵּלַךְ:
ד וְהֶעָנָן סָר מֵעַל הָאֹהֶל וְהִנֵּה מִרְיָם מְצֹרַעַת כַּשָּׁלֶג וַיִּפֶן אַהֲרֹן
ה אֶל־מִרְיָם וְהִנֵּה מְצֹרָעַת: וַיֹּאמֶר אַהֲרֹן אֶל־מֹשֶׁה בִּי אֲדֹנִי אַל־
ו נָא תָשֵׁת עָלֵינוּ חַטָּאת אֲשֶׁר נוֹאַלְנוּ וַאֲשֶׁר חָטָאנוּ: אַל־נָא

ז, ט), וּבְפָנָיו נֶאֱמַר: "כִּי אֹתְךָ רָאִיתִי צַדִּיק לְפָנַי" (בראשית ז, א). דָּבָר אַחֵר, שֶׁלֹּא יִשְׁמַע בִּנְזִיפָתוֹ שֶׁל אַהֲרֹן:

ו **שִׁמְעוּ נָא דְבָרָי.** אֵין "נָא" אֶלָּא לְשׁוֹן בַּקָּשָׁה. **אִם יִהְיֶה נְבִיאֲכֶם.** אִם יִהְיוּ לָכֶם נְבִיאִים, ה' **בַּמַּרְאָה אֵלָיו אֶתְוַדָּע.** שְׁכִינַת שְׁמִי אֵין נִגְלֵית עָלָיו בְּאַסְפַּקְלַרְיָה הַמְּאִירָה, אֶלָּא בַּחֲלוֹם וְחִזָּיוֹן:

ח **פֶּה אֶל פֶּה.** אָמַרְתִּי לוֹ לִפְרֹשׁ מִן הָאִשָּׁה. וְהֵיכָן אָמַרְתִּי לוֹ? בְּסִינַי: "לֵךְ אֱמֹר לָהֶם שׁוּבוּ לָכֶם לְאָהֳלֵיכֶם וְאַתָּה פֹּה עֲמֹד עִמָּדִי" (דברים ה, כו-כז). **וּמַרְאֶה וְלֹא בְחִידֹת.** "מַרְאֶה" זֶה מַרְאֶה דִבּוּר, שֶׁאֲנִי מְפָרֵשׁ לוֹ דִּבּוּרִי בְּמַרְאִית פָּנִים שֶׁבּוֹ, וְאֵינִי סוֹתְמוֹ לוֹ בְּחִידוֹת, כָּעִנְיָן שֶׁנֶּאֱמַר לִיחֶזְקֵאל: "חוּד חִידָה וְגוֹ'" (יחזקאל יז, ב). יָכוֹל מַרְאֵה שְׁכִינָה? תַּלְמוּד לוֹמַר: "לֹא תוּכַל לִרְאֹת אֶת פָּנָי" (שמות לג, כ): **וּתְמֻנַת ה' יַבִּיט.** זֶה מַרְאֵה אֲחוֹרַיִם, כָּעִנְיָן שֶׁנֶּאֱמַר: "וְרָאִיתָ אֶת אֲחֹרָי" (שמות לג, כג): **בְּעַבְדִּי בְמֹשֶׁה.** אֵינוֹ אוֹמֵר 'בְּעַבְדִּי מֹשֶׁה', אֶלָּא "בְּעַבְדִּי בְמֹשֶׁה", בְּעַבְדִּי אַף עַל פִּי שֶׁאֵינוֹ מֹשֶׁה, בְּמֹשֶׁה אֲפִלּוּ אֵינוֹ עַבְדִּי, כְּדַאי הֱיִיתֶם לִירֹא מִפָּנַי, וְכָל שֶׁכֵּן שֶׁהוּא עַבְדִּי, וְעֶבֶד מֶלֶךְ - מֶלֶךְ, וְהָיָה לָכֶם לוֹמַר: אֵין הַמֶּלֶךְ אוֹהֲבוֹ חִנָּם. וְאִם תֹּאמְרוּ: אֵינוֹ מַכִּיר בְּמַעֲשָׂיו - זוֹ קָשָׁה מִן הָרִאשׁוֹנָה:

ט **וַיִּחַר אַף ה' בָּם וַיֵּלַךְ.** מֵאַחַר שֶׁהוֹדִיעָם סִרְחוֹנָם

גָּזַר עֲלֵיהֶם נִדּוּי, קַל וָחֹמֶר לְבָשָׂר וָדָם, שֶׁלֹּא יִכְעַס עַל חֲבֵרוֹ עַד שֶׁיּוֹדִיעֶנּוּ סִרְחוֹנוֹ:

י **וְהֶעָנָן סָר.** וְאַחַר כָּךְ "וְהִנֵּה מִרְיָם מְצֹרַעַת כַּשָּׁלֶג", מָשָׁל לְמֶלֶךְ שֶׁאָמַר לַפֵּדָגוֹג: רְדֵה אֶת בְּנִי, אֲבָל לֹא תִּרְדֶּנּוּ עַד שֶׁאֵלֵךְ מֵאֶצְלְךָ, שֶׁרַחֲמַי עָלָיו:

יא **נוֹאַלְנוּ.** כְּתַרְגּוּמוֹ, לְשׁוֹן אֱוִיל:

יב **אַל נָא תְהִי.** אֲחוֹתֵנוּ זוֹ: **כַּמֵּת.** שֶׁהַמְצֹרָע חָשׁוּב כַּמֵּת, מַה מֵּת מְטַמֵּא בְּבִיאָה אַף מְצֹרָע מְטַמֵּא בְּבִיאָה: **אֲשֶׁר בְּצֵאתוֹ מֵרֶחֶם אִמּוֹ.** 'אִמֵּנוּ' הָיָה לוֹ לוֹמַר, אֶלָּא שֶׁכִּנָּה הַכָּתוּב. וְכֵן 'חֲצִי בְשָׂרֵנוּ' הָיָה לוֹ לוֹמַר, אֶלָּא שֶׁכִּנָּה הַכָּתוּב. מֵאַחַר שֶׁיָּצְאָה מֵרֶחֶם אִמֵּנוּ, הָיָה לָנוּ כְּאִלּוּ נֶאֱכַל חֲצִי בְשָׂרֵנוּ, כָּעִנְיָן שֶׁנֶּאֱמַר: "כִּי אָחִינוּ בְשָׂרֵנוּ הוּא" (בראשית לז, כו). וּלְפִי מַשְׁמָעוֹ, אַף הוּא נִרְאֶה כֵן, אֵין רָאוּי לְאָח לְהַנִּיחַ אֶת אֲחוֹתוֹ לִהְיוֹת כַּמֵּת. **אֲשֶׁר בְּצֵאתוֹ.** מֵאַחַר שֶׁיָּצָא זֶה מֵרֶחֶם אִמּוֹ שֶׁל זֶה שֶׁיֵּשׁ כֹּחַ בְּיָדוֹ לַעֲזֹר וְאֵינוֹ עוֹזְרוֹ, הֲרֵי נֶאֱכַל חֲצִי בְשָׂרוֹ, שֶׁאָחִיו בְּשָׂרוֹ הוּא. דָּבָר אַחֵר, "אַל נָא תְהִי כַּמֵּת" - אִם אֵינְךָ רוֹפְאָהּ בִּתְפִלָּה, מִי מַסְגִּירָהּ אוֹ מִי מְטַהֲרָהּ? אֲנִי אִי אֶפְשָׁר לִרְאוֹתָהּ, שֶׁאֲנִי קָרוֹב וְאֵין קָרוֹב רוֹאֶה אֶת הַנְּגָעִים, וְכֹהֵן אַחֵר אֵין בָּעוֹלָם. וְזֶהוּ "אֲשֶׁר בְּצֵאתוֹ מֵרֶחֶם אִמּוֹ":

תְּהִי כַּמֵּת אֲשֶׁר בְּצֵאתוֹ מֵרֶחֶם אִמּוֹ וַיֵּאָכֵל חֲצִי בְשָׂרוֹ: וַיִּצְעַק יג
מֹשֶׁה אֶל־יהוה לֵאמֹר אֵל נָא רְפָא נָא לָהּ:

מפטיר וַיֹּאמֶר יהוה אֶל־מֹשֶׁה וְאָבִיהָ יָרֹק יָרַק בְּפָנֶיהָ הֲלֹא תִכָּלֵם יד
שִׁבְעַת יָמִים תִּסָּגֵר שִׁבְעַת יָמִים מִחוּץ לַמַּחֲנֶה וְאַחַר תֵּאָסֵף:
וַתִּסָּגֵר מִרְיָם מִחוּץ לַמַּחֲנֶה שִׁבְעַת יָמִים וְהָעָם לֹא נָסַע טו
עַד־הֵאָסֵף מִרְיָם: וְאַחַר נָסְעוּ הָעָם מֵחֲצֵרוֹת וַיַּחֲנוּ בְּמִדְבַּר טז
פָּארָן:

שלח יב וַיְדַבֵּר יהוה אֶל־מֹשֶׁה לֵאמֹר: שְׁלַח־לְךָ אֲנָשִׁים וְיָתֻרוּ אֶת־ א יג
אֶרֶץ כְּנַעַן אֲשֶׁר־אֲנִי נֹתֵן לִבְנֵי יִשְׂרָאֵל אִישׁ אֶחָד אִישׁ אֶחָד
לְמַטֵּה אֲבֹתָיו תִּשְׁלָחוּ כֹּל נָשִׂיא בָהֶם: וַיִּשְׁלַח אֹתָם מֹשֶׁה ג

יג. **אֵל נָא רְפָא נָא לָהּ.** בָּא הַכָּתוּב לְלַמֶּדְךָ דֶּרֶךְ
אֶרֶץ, שֶׁהַשּׁוֹאֵל דָּבָר מֵחֲבֵרוֹ צָרִיךְ לוֹמַר שְׁנַיִם אוֹ
שְׁלֹשָׁה דִּבְרֵי תַחֲנוּנִים, וְאַחַר כָּךְ יְבַקֵּשׁ שְׁאֵלוֹתָיו
לֵאמֹר. מַה תַּלְמוּד לוֹמַר? אָמַר לוֹ: הֲשִׁיבֵנִי אִם
אַתָּה מְרַפֵּא אוֹתָהּ אִם לָאו, עַד שֶׁהֱשִׁיבוֹ: "וְאָבִיהָ
יָרֹק יָרַק" וְגוֹ'. רַבִּי אֶלְעָזָר בֶּן עֲזַרְיָה אוֹמֵר:
בְּאַרְבָּעָה מְקוֹמוֹת בִּקֵּשׁ מֹשֶׁה מִלִּפְנֵי הַקָּדוֹשׁ בָּרוּךְ
הוּא לַהֲשִׁיבוֹ אִם יַעֲשֶׂה שְׁאֵלוֹתָיו אִם לָאו. כַּיּוֹצֵא
בוֹ: "וַיְדַבֵּר מֹשֶׁה לִפְנֵי ה' לֵאמֹר" וְגוֹ' (שמות ו, יב), מַה
תַּלְמוּד לוֹמַר: "לֵאמֹר"? הֲשִׁיבֵנִי אִם גּוֹאֲלָם אַתָּה
אִם לָאו, עַד שֶׁהֱשִׁיבוֹ: "עַתָּה תִרְאֶה" וְגוֹ' (שם פסוק א).
כַּיּוֹצֵא בוֹ: "וַיְדַבֵּר מֹשֶׁה אֶל ה' לֵאמֹר יִפְקֹד ה' אֱלֹהֵי
הָרוּחֹת לְכָל בָּשָׂר" (להלן כז, טו-טז), הֱשִׁיבוֹ: "קַח לְךָ"
(שם פסוק יח). כַּיּוֹצֵא בוֹ: "וָאֶתְחַנַּן אֶל ה' בָּעֵת הַהִוא
לֵאמֹר" (דברים ג, כג), הֱשִׁיבוֹ: "רַב לָךְ" (שם פסוק כו): **רְפָא
נָא לָהּ.** מִפְּנֵי מָה לֹא הֶאֱרִיךְ מֹשֶׁה בִּתְפִלָּה? שֶׁלֹּא
יִהְיוּ יִשְׂרָאֵל אוֹמְרִים, אֲחוֹתוֹ עוֹמֶדֶת בְּצָרָה וְהוּא
עוֹמֵד וּמַרְבֶּה בִּתְפִלָּה:

יד. **וְאָבִיהָ יָרֹק יָרַק בְּפָנֶיהָ.** וְאִם אָבִיהָ הֶרְאָה לָהּ
פָּנִים זוֹעֲפוֹת, "הֲלֹא תִכָּלֵם שִׁבְעַת יָמִים", קַל וָחֹמֶר
לַשְּׁכִינָה אַרְבָּעָה עָשָׂר יוֹם, אֶלָּא דַּיּוֹ לַבָּא מִן הַדִּין

לִהְיוֹת כַּנִּדּוֹן, לְפִיכָךְ אַף בִּנְזִיפָתִי "תִּסָּגֵר שִׁבְעַת
יָמִים": **וְאַחַר תֵּאָסֵף.** אוֹמֵר אֲנִי, כָּל הָאֲסִיפוֹת
הָאֲמוּרוֹת בַּמְצֹרָעִים, עַל שֵׁם שֶׁהוּא מְשֻׁלָּח מִחוּץ
לַמַּחֲנֶה, וּכְשֶׁהוּא נִרְפָּא נֶאֱסָף אֶל הַמַּחֲנֶה, לְכָךְ
כָּתוּב בּוֹ אֲסִיפָה, לְשׁוֹן הַכְנָסָה:

טו. **וְהָעָם לֹא נָסַע.** זֶה הַכָּבוֹד חָלַק לָהּ הַמָּקוֹם
בִּשְׁבִיל שָׁעָה אַחַת שֶׁנִּתְעַכְּבָה לְמֹשֶׁה כְּשֶׁהִשְׁלִיכוֹ
לַיְאוֹר, שֶׁנֶּאֱמַר: "וַתֵּתַצַּב אֲחֹתוֹ מֵרָחֹק" וְגוֹ' (שמות ב, ד):

פרק יג

ב. **שְׁלַח לְךָ אֲנָשִׁים.** לָמָּה נִסְמְכָה פָּרָשַׁת מְרַגְּלִים
לְפָרָשַׁת מִרְיָם? לְפִי שֶׁלָּקְתָה עַל עִסְקֵי דִבָּה שֶׁדִּבְּרָה
בְּאָחִיהָ, וּרְשָׁעִים הַלָּלוּ רָאוּ וְלֹא לָקְחוּ מוּסָר: **שְׁלַח
לְךָ.** לְדַעְתְּךָ, אֲנִי אֵינִי מְצַוֶּה לְךָ, אִם תִּרְצֶה שְׁלַח.
לְפִי שֶׁבָּאוּ יִשְׂרָאֵל וְאָמְרוּ: "נִשְׁלְחָה אֲנָשִׁים לְפָנֵינוּ"
(דברים א, כב), כְּמָה שֶׁנֶּאֱמַר: "וַתִּקְרְבוּן אֵלַי כֻּלְּכֶם" וְגוֹ'
(שם), וּמֹשֶׁה נִמְלַךְ בַּשְּׁכִינָה, אָמַר: אֲנִי אָמַרְתִּי לָהֶם
שֶׁהִיא טוֹבָה, שֶׁנֶּאֱמַר: "אַעֲלֶה אֶתְכֶם מֵעֳנִי מִצְרַיִם"
וְגוֹ' (שמות ג, יז), חַיֵּיהֶם שֶׁאֲנִי נוֹתֵן לָהֶם מָקוֹם לִטְעוֹת
בְּדִבְרֵי הַמְרַגְּלִים, לְמַעַן לֹא יִירָשׁוּהָ:

ג. **עַל פִּי ה'.** בִּרְשׁוּתוֹ, שֶׁלֹּא עִכֵּב עַל יָדוֹ: **כֻּלָּם**

ממדבר פארן על־פי יהוה כלם אנשים ראשי בני־ישראל
המה: ואלה שמותם למטה ראובן שמוע בן־זכור: למטה
שמעון שפט בן־חורי: למטה יהודה כלב בן־יפנה: למטה
יששכר יגאל בן־יוסף: למטה אפרים הושע בן־נון: למטה
בנימן פלטי בן־רפוא: למטה זבולן גדיאל בן־סודי: למטה
יוסף למטה מנשה גדי בן־סוסי: למטה דן עמיאל בן־גמלי:
למטה אשר סתור בן־מיכאל: למטה נפתלי נחבי בן־ופסי:
למטה גד גאואל בן־מכי: אלה שמות האנשים אשר־שלח
משה לתור את־הארץ ויקרא משה להושע בן־נון יהושע:
וישלח אתם משה לתור את־ארץ כנען ויאמר אלהם עלו
זה בנגב ועליתם את־ההר: וראיתם את־הארץ מה־הוא
ואת־העם הישב עליה החזק הוא הרפה המעט הוא אם־רב:
ומה הארץ אשר־הוא ישב בה הטובה הוא אם־רעה ומה
הערים אשר־הוא יושב בהנה הבמחנים אם במבצרים: ומה
הארץ השמנה הוא אם־רזה היש־בה עץ אם־אין והתחזקתם

ה
ו
ז
ח
ט
י
יא
יב
יג
יד
טו
טז
יז
יח
יט
כ

אנשים. כל 'אנשים' שבמקרא לשון חשיבות, ואותה שעה כשרים היו:

טז) **ויקרא משה להושע וגו'.** נתפלל עליו: יה יושיעך מעצת מרגלים:

יז) **עלו זה בנגב.** הוא היה הפסלת של ארץ ישראל, שכן דרך התגרים, מראים את הפסלת תחלה ואחר כך מראים את השבח:

יח) **את הארץ מה הוא.** יש ארץ מגדלת גבורים ויש ארץ מגדלת חלשים, יש מגדלת אכלוסין ויש

ממעטת אכלוסין: **החזק הוא הרפה.** סימן מסר להם, אם בפרזים יושבין – חזקים הם, שסומכין על גבורתם, ואם בערים בצורות הם יושבין – חלשים הם:

יט) **הבמחנים.** תרגומו: "הבפצחין", כרכין פתיחין ופתיחין מאין חומה: **הטובה הוא.** במעינות ותהומות טובים ובריאים:

כ) **היש בה עץ.** אם יש בהם אדם כשר שיגן עליהם בזכותו: **בכורי ענבים.** ימים שהענבים מתבשלין בבכור:

שני כא וּלְקַחְתֶּם מִפְּרִי הָאָרֶץ וְהַיָּמִים יְמֵי בִּכּוּרֵי עֲנָבִים: וַיַּעֲלוּ וַיָּתֻרוּ
כב אֶת־הָאָרֶץ מִמִּדְבַּר־צִן עַד־רְחֹב לְבֹא חֲמָת: וַיַּעֲלוּ בַנֶּגֶב וַיָּבֹא
עַד־חֶבְרוֹן וְשָׁם אֲחִימַן שֵׁשַׁי וְתַלְמַי יְלִידֵי הָעֲנָק וְחֶבְרוֹן שֶׁבַע
כג שָׁנִים נִבְנְתָה לִפְנֵי צֹעַן מִצְרָיִם: וַיָּבֹאוּ עַד־נַחַל אֶשְׁכֹּל וַיִּכְרְתוּ
מִשָּׁם זְמוֹרָה וְאֶשְׁכּוֹל עֲנָבִים אֶחָד וַיִּשָּׂאֻהוּ בַמּוֹט בִּשְׁנָיִם וּמִן־
כד הָרִמֹּנִים וּמִן־הַתְּאֵנִים: לַמָּקוֹם הַהוּא קָרָא נַחַל אֶשְׁכּוֹל עַל
כה אֹדוֹת הָאֶשְׁכּוֹל אֲשֶׁר־כָּרְתוּ מִשָּׁם בְּנֵי יִשְׂרָאֵל: וַיָּשֻׁבוּ מִתּוּר
כו הָאָרֶץ מִקֵּץ אַרְבָּעִים יוֹם: וַיֵּלְכוּ וַיָּבֹאוּ אֶל־מֹשֶׁה וְאֶל־אַהֲרֹן

כא | **מִמִּדְבַּר צִן עַד רְחֹב לְבֹא חֲמָת.** הָלְכוּ בִּגְבוּלֶיהָ בָּאֹרֶךְ וּבָרֹחַב כְּמִין "גַּאם", הָלְכוּ רוּחַ גְּבוּל דְּרוֹמִית מִמִּקְצוֹעַ מִזְרָח עַד מִקְצוֹעַ מַעֲרָב, כְּמוֹ שֶׁצִּוָּה מֹשֶׁה: "עֲלוּ זֶה בַּנֶּגֶב" (לעיל פסוק יז) דֶּרֶךְ גְּבוּל דְּרוֹמִית מִזְרָחִית, עַד הַיָּם, שֶׁהַיָּם הוּא גְּבוּל מַעֲרָבִי, וּמִשָּׁם חָזְרוּ וְהָלְכוּ כָּל גְּבוּל מַעֲרָבִי עַל שְׂפַת הַיָּם עַד לְבֹא חֲמָת, שֶׁהוּא אֵצֶל הֹר הָהָר בְּמִקְצוֹעַ מַעֲרָבִית צְפוֹנִית, כְּמוֹ שֶׁמְּפֹרָשׁ בִּגְבוּלוֹת הָאָרֶץ בְּפָרָשַׁת אֵלֶּה מַסְעֵי (להלן לד, ז):

כב | **וַיָּבֹא עַד חֶבְרוֹן.** כָּלֵב לְבַדּוֹ הָלַךְ שָׁם, וְנִשְׁתַּטֵּחַ עַל קִבְרֵי אָבוֹת שֶׁלֹּא יְהֵא נִסָּת לַחֲבֵרָיו לִהְיוֹת בַּעֲצָתָם, וְכֵן הוּא אוֹמֵר: "וְלוֹ אֶתֵּן אֶת הָאָרֶץ אֲשֶׁר דָּרַךְ בָּהּ" (דברים א, לו), וּכְתִיב: "וַיִּתְּנוּ לְכָלֵב אֶת חֶבְרוֹן" (שופטים א, כ): **שֶׁבַע שָׁנִים נִבְנְתָה.** אֶפְשָׁר שֶׁבָּנָה חָם אֶת חֶבְרוֹן לִכְנַעַן בְּנוֹ הַקָּטָן קֹדֶם שֶׁיִּבְנֶה אֶת צֹעַן לְמִצְרַיִם בְּנוֹ הַגָּדוֹל? אֶלָּא שֶׁהָיְתָה מְבֻנָּה בְּכָל טוּב עַל אֶחָד מִשִּׁבְעָה בְּצֹעַן, וּבָא לְהוֹדִיעֲךָ שִׁבְחָהּ שֶׁל אֶרֶץ יִשְׂרָאֵל, שֶׁאֵין לְךָ טְרָשִׁין בְּאֶרֶץ יִשְׂרָאֵל יוֹתֵר מֵחֶבְרוֹן, לְפִיכָךְ הִקְצוּהָ לִקְבֹּר בָּהּ מֵתִים, וְאֵין לְךָ מְעֻלָּה בְּכָל הָאֲרָצוֹת כְּמִצְרַיִם, שֶׁנֶּאֱמַר: "כְּגַן ה' כְּאֶרֶץ מִצְרַיִם" (בראשית יג, י), וְצֹעַן הִיא הַמְּעֻלָּה שֶׁבְּאֶרֶץ מִצְרַיִם, שֶׁשָּׁם מוֹשַׁב הַמְּלָכִים, שֶׁנֶּאֱמַר: "כִּי הָיוּ בְצֹעַן שָׂרָיו" (ישעיה ל, ד), וְהָיְתָה חֶבְרוֹן טוֹבָה מִמֶּנָּה שִׁבְעָה חֲלָקִים:

כג | **זְמוֹרָה.** שׂוֹכַת גֶּפֶן, וְאֶשְׁכּוֹל שֶׁל עֲנָבִים תָּלוּי בָּהּ: **וַיִּשָּׂאֻהוּ בַמּוֹט בִּשְׁנָיִם.** מִמַּשְׁמַע שֶׁנֶּאֱמַר: "וַיִּשָּׂאֻהוּ בַמּוֹט", אֵינִי יוֹדֵעַ שֶׁהוּא בִּשְׁנַיִם? מַה תַּלְמוּד לוֹמַר "בִּשְׁנָיִם"? בִּשְׁנֵי מוֹטוֹת. הָא כֵּיצַד? שְׁמוֹנָה נָטְלוּ אֶשְׁכּוֹל, אֶחָד נָטַל תְּאֵנָה וְאֶחָד רִמּוֹן, יְהוֹשֻׁעַ וְכָלֵב לֹא נָטְלוּ כְּלוּם, לְפִי שֶׁכָּל עַצְמָם לְהוֹצִיא דִּבָּה נִתְכַּוְּנוּ: כְּשֵׁם שֶׁפִּרְיָהּ מְשֻׁנֶּה כָּךְ עַמָּהּ מְשֻׁנֶּה. וְאִם חָפֵץ אַתָּה לֵידַע כַּמָּה מַשָּׂאוֹי אֶחָד מֵהֶם, צֵא וּלְמַד מֵאֲבָנִים שֶׁהֵקִימוּ בַּגִּלְגָּל, הֲרִימוּ לָהֶם אִישׁ אֶבֶן אַחַת מִן הַיַּרְדֵּן וֶהֱקִימוּהָ בַגִּלְגָּל, וּשְׁקָלוּם רַבּוֹתֵינוּ מִשְׁקַל כָּל אַחַת אַרְבָּעִים סְאָה, וּגְמִירֵי, טוֹעַן דְּמַדְלֵי אֱנָשׁ עַל כַּתְפֵּיהּ אֵינוֹ מַלֵּא שְׁלִישׁ מַשָּׂאוֹי בְּמַשָּׂאוֹי שֶׁמַּסִּיעִין אוֹתוֹ לְהָרִים:

כה | **וַיָּשֻׁבוּ מִתּוּר הָאָרֶץ מִקֵּץ אַרְבָּעִים יוֹם.** וַהֲלֹא אַרְבַּע מֵאוֹת פַּרְסָה עַל אַרְבַּע מֵאוֹת פַּרְסָה הִיא, וּמַהֲלַךְ אָדָם בֵּינוֹנִי עֲשָׂרָה פַּרְסָאוֹת לַיּוֹם, הֲרֵי מַהֲלַךְ אַרְבָּעִים יוֹם מִן הַמִּזְרָח לַמַּעֲרָב, וְהֵם הָלְכוּ אָרְכָּהּ וְרָחְבָּהּ! אֶלָּא שֶׁגָּלוּי לִפְנֵי הַקָּדוֹשׁ בָּרוּךְ הוּא שֶׁיִּגְזֹר עֲלֵיהֶם יוֹם לַשָּׁנָה, קִצֵּר לִפְנֵיהֶם אֶת הַדֶּרֶךְ:

כו | **וַיֵּלְכוּ וַיָּבֹאוּ.** מַהוּ "וַיֵּלְכוּ"? לְהַקִּישׁ הֲלִיכָתָן לְבִיאָתָן, מַה בִּיאָתָן בְּעֵצָה רָעָה, אַף הֲלִיכָתָן בְּעֵצָה רָעָה: **וַיָּשִׁיבוּ אוֹתָם דָּבָר.** אֶת מֹשֶׁה וְאֶת אַהֲרֹן:

וְאֶל־כָּל־עֲדַת בְּנֵֽי־יִשְׂרָאֵ֛ל אֶל־מִדְבַּ֥ר פָּארָ֖ן קָדֵ֑שָׁה וַיָּשִׁ֣יבוּ
כז אוֹתָ֤ם דָּבָר֙ וְאֶת־כָּל־הָ֣עֵדָ֔ה וַיַּרְא֖וּם אֶת־פְּרִ֥י הָאָֽרֶץ: וַיְסַפְּרוּ־לוֹ֙
וַיֹּ֣אמְר֔וּ בָּ֕אנוּ אֶל־הָאָ֖רֶץ אֲשֶׁ֣ר שְׁלַחְתָּ֑נוּ וְ֠גַ֠ם זָבַ֨ת חָלָ֥ב וּדְבַ֛שׁ
כח הִ֖וא וְזֶה־פִּרְיָֽהּ: אֶ֚פֶס כִּֽי־עַ֣ז הָעָ֔ם הַיֹּשֵׁ֖ב בָּאָ֑רֶץ וְהֶֽעָרִ֗ים בְּצֻר֤וֹת
כט גְּדֹלֹת֙ מְאֹ֔ד וְגַם־יְלִדֵ֥י הָעֲנָ֖ק רָאִ֥ינוּ שָֽׁם: עֲמָלֵ֥ק יוֹשֵׁ֖ב בְּאֶ֣רֶץ
הַנֶּ֑גֶב וְ֠הַֽחִתִּ֠י וְהַיְבוּסִ֤י וְהָֽאֱמֹרִי֙ יוֹשֵׁ֣ב בָּהָ֔ר וְהַֽכְּנַעֲנִי֙ יֹשֵׁ֣ב עַל־
ל הַיָּ֔ם וְעַ֖ל יַ֥ד הַיַּרְדֵּֽן: וַיַּ֧הַס כָּלֵ֛ב אֶת־הָעָ֖ם אֶל־מֹשֶׁ֑ה וַיֹּ֗אמֶר
לא עָלֹ֤ה נַעֲלֶה֙ וְיָרַ֣שְׁנוּ אֹתָ֔הּ כִּֽי־יָכ֥וֹל נוּכַ֖ל לָֽהּ: וְהָ֨אֲנָשִׁ֜ים אֲשֶׁר־
עָל֤וּ עִמּוֹ֙ אָֽמְר֔וּ לֹ֥א נוּכַ֖ל לַעֲל֣וֹת אֶל־הָעָ֑ם כִּֽי־חָזָ֥ק ה֖וּא מִמֶּֽנּוּ:
לב וַיֹּצִ֜יאוּ דִּבַּ֤ת הָאָ֙רֶץ֙ אֲשֶׁ֣ר תָּר֣וּ אֹתָ֔הּ אֶל־בְּנֵ֥י יִשְׂרָאֵ֖ל לֵאמֹ֑ר
הָאָ֡רֶץ אֲשֶׁר֩ עָבַ֨רְנוּ בָ֜הּ לָת֣וּר אֹתָ֗הּ אֶ֣רֶץ אֹכֶ֤לֶת יוֹשְׁבֶ֙יהָ֙ הִ֔וא
לג וְכָל־הָעָ֛ם אֲשֶׁר־רָאִ֥ינוּ בְתוֹכָ֖הּ אַנְשֵׁ֥י מִדּֽוֹת: וְשָׁ֣ם רָאִ֗ינוּ אֶת־
הַנְּפִילִ֛ים בְּנֵ֥י עֲנָ֖ק מִן־הַנְּפִלִ֑ים וַנְּהִ֤י בְעֵינֵ֙ינוּ֙ כַּֽחֲגָבִ֔ים וְכֵ֥ן הָיִ֖ינוּ

כז זָבַת חָלָב וּדְבַשׁ. כָּל דְּבַר שֶׁקֶר שֶׁאֵין אוֹמְרִים בּוֹ קְצָת אֱמֶת בִּתְחִלָּתוֹ, אֵין מִתְקַיֵּם בְּסוֹפוֹ:

כח בְּצֻרוֹת. לְשׁוֹן חֹזֶק, וְתַרְגּוּמוֹ: "כְּרִיכָן", לְשׁוֹן בִּירָנִיּוֹת עֲגוֹלוֹת, וּבִלְשׁוֹן אֲרַמִּי חֲרָרָה 'כְּרִיךְ' – עָגֹל:

כט עֲמָלֵק יוֹשֵׁב וְגוֹ'. לְפִי שֶׁנִּכְווּ בַּעֲמָלֵק כְּבָר, הִזְכִּירוּהוּ מְרַגְּלִים כְּדֵי לְיָרְאָם: וְעַל יַד הַיַּרְדֵּן. יַד כְּמַשְׁמָעוֹ, אֵצֶל הַיַּרְדֵּן, וְלֹא תּוּכְלוּ לַעֲבֹר:

ל וַיַּהַס כָּלֵב. הִשְׁתִּיק אֶת כֻּלָּם. אֶל מֹשֶׁה. לִשְׁמֹעַ מַה שֶּׁיְּדַבֵּר בְּמֹשֶׁה, צָוַח וְאָמַר: וְכִי זוֹ בִּלְבַד עָשָׂה לָנוּ בֶּן עַמְרָם? הַשּׁוֹמֵעַ הָיָה סָבוּר שֶׁבָּא לְסַפֵּר בִּגְנוּתוֹ, וּמִתּוֹךְ שֶׁהָיָה בְּלִבָּם עַל מֹשֶׁה בִּשְׁבִיל דִּבְרֵי הַמְרַגְּלִים שָׁתְקוּ כֻּלָּם לִשְׁמֹעַ גְּנוּתוֹ, אָמַר: וַהֲלֹא קָרַע לָנוּ אֶת הַיָּם, וְהוֹרִיד לָנוּ אֶת הַמָּן, וְהֵגִיז לָנוּ אֶת הַשְּׂלָו. עָלֹה נַעֲלֶה. אֲפִלּוּ בַּשָּׁמַיִם, וְהוּא אוֹמֵר: עֲשׂוּ סֻלָּמוֹת וַעֲלוּ שָׁם! נַצְלִיחַ בְּכָל דְּבָרָיו: וַיַּהַס. לְשׁוֹן

שְׁתִיקָה, וְכֵן: "הַס כָּל בָּשָׂר" (זכריה ב, יז), "הַס כִּי לֹא לְהַזְכִּיר" (עמוס ו, י), כֵּן דֶּרֶךְ בְּנֵי אָדָם, הָרוֹצֶה לְשַׁתֵּק אֲגֻדַּת אֲנָשִׁים אוֹמֵר שִׁ"ט:

לא חָזָק הוּא מִמֶּנּוּ. כִּבְיָכוֹל כְּלַפֵּי מַעְלָה אָמְרוּ:

לב אֹכֶלֶת יוֹשְׁבֶיהָ. בְּכָל מָקוֹם שֶׁעָבַרְנוּ מְצָאנוּם קוֹבְרֵי מֵתִים, וְהַקָּדוֹשׁ בָּרוּךְ הוּא עָשָׂה לְטוֹבָה כְּדֵי לְטָרְדָם בְּאֶבְלָם וְלֹא יִתְּנוּ לֵב לְאֵלּוּ: אַנְשֵׁי מִדּוֹת. גְּדוֹלִים וּגְבוֹהִים וְצָרִיךְ לָתֵת לָהֶם מִדָּה, כְּגוֹן גָּלְיָת: "גָּבְהוֹ שֵׁשׁ אַמּוֹת וָזָרֶת" (שמואל ב' י"ז, ד), וְכֵן: "אִישׁ מָדוֹן" (שמואל ב' כ"א, כ), "אִישׁ מִדָּה" (דברי הימים א' י"א, כג):

לג הַנְּפִילִים. עֲנָקִים, מִבְּנֵי שַׁמְחֲזַאי וַעֲזָאֵל שֶׁנָּפְלוּ מִן הַשָּׁמַיִם בִּימֵי דּוֹר אֱנוֹשׁ: וְכֵן הָיִינוּ בְעֵינֵיהֶם. שָׁמַעְנוּ אוֹמְרִים זֶה לָזֶה: נְמָלִים יֵשׁ בַּכְּרָמִים כַּאֲנָשִׁים: עֲנָק. שֶׁמַּעֲנִיקִים חַמָּה בְּקוֹמָתָן:

בְּעֵינֵיהֶֽם: וַתִּשָּׂא֙ כָּל־הָ֣עֵדָ֔ה וַֽיִּתְּנ֖וּ אֶת־קוֹלָ֑ם וַיִּבְכּ֥וּ הָעָ֖ם בַּלַּ֥יְלָה
הַהֽוּא: וַיִּלֹּ֨נוּ֙ עַל־מֹשֶׁ֣ה וְעַֽל־אַהֲרֹ֔ן כֹּ֖ל בְּנֵ֣י יִשְׂרָאֵ֑ל וַיֹּאמְר֨וּ
אֲלֵהֶ֜ם כָּל־הָעֵדָ֗ה לוּ־מַ֙תְנוּ֙ בְּאֶ֣רֶץ מִצְרַ֔יִם א֛וֹ בַּמִּדְבָּ֥ר הַזֶּ֖ה לוּ־
מָֽתְנוּ: וְלָמָ֣ה יְ֠הֹוָה מֵבִ֨יא אֹתָ֜נוּ אֶל־הָאָ֤רֶץ הַזֹּאת֙ לִנְפֹּ֣ל בַּחֶ֔רֶב
נָשֵׁ֥ינוּ וְטַפֵּ֖נוּ יִהְי֣וּ לָבַ֑ז הֲל֧וֹא ט֦וֹב לָ֖נוּ שׁ֥וּב מִצְרָֽיְמָה: וַיֹּאמְר֖וּ
אִ֣ישׁ אֶל־אָחִ֑יו נִתְּנָ֥ה רֹ֖אשׁ וְנָשׁ֥וּבָה מִצְרָֽיְמָה: וַיִּפֹּ֥ל מֹשֶׁ֛ה
וְאַהֲרֹ֖ן עַל־פְּנֵיהֶ֑ם לִפְנֵ֕י כָּל־קְהַ֥ל עֲדַ֖ת בְּנֵ֥י יִשְׂרָאֵֽל: וִיהוֹשֻׁ֣עַ
בִּן־נ֗וּן וְכָלֵב֙ בֶּן־יְפֻנֶּ֔ה מִן־הַתָּרִ֖ים אֶת־הָאָ֑רֶץ קָרְע֖וּ בִּגְדֵיהֶֽם:
וַיֹּ֣אמְר֔וּ אֶל־כָּל־עֲדַ֥ת בְּנֵֽי־יִשְׂרָאֵ֖ל לֵאמֹ֑ר הָאָ֗רֶץ אֲשֶׁ֨ר עָבַ֤רְנוּ
בָהּ֙ לָת֣וּר אֹתָ֔הּ טוֹבָ֥ה הָאָ֖רֶץ מְאֹ֥ד מְאֹֽד: אִם־חָפֵ֥ץ בָּ֙נוּ֙ יְהֹוָ֔ה
וְהֵבִ֤יא אֹתָ֙נוּ֙ אֶל־הָאָ֣רֶץ הַזֹּ֔את וּנְתָנָ֖הּ לָ֑נוּ אֶ֕רֶץ אֲשֶׁר־הִ֛וא
זָבַ֥ת חָלָ֖ב וּדְבָֽשׁ: אַ֣ךְ בַּֽיהֹוָה֮ אַל־תִּמְרֹ֒דוּ֒ וְאַתֶּ֗ם אַל־תִּֽירְאוּ֙
אֶת־עַ֣ם הָאָ֔רֶץ כִּ֥י לַחְמֵ֖נוּ הֵ֑ם סָ֣ר צִלָּ֧ם מֵעֲלֵיהֶ֛ם וַיהֹוָ֥ה אִתָּ֖נוּ
אַל־תִּירָאֻֽם: וַיֹּֽאמְרוּ֙ כָּל־הָ֣עֵדָ֔ה לִרְגּ֥וֹם אֹתָ֖ם בָּאֲבָנִ֑ים וּכְב֣וֹד
יְהֹוָ֗ה נִרְאָה֙ בְּאֹ֣הֶל מוֹעֵ֔ד אֶֽל־כָּל־בְּנֵ֖י יִשְׂרָאֵֽל:

וַיֹּ֤אמֶר יְהֹוָה֙ אֶל־מֹשֶׁ֔ה עַד־אָ֥נָה יְנַאֲצֻ֖נִי הָעָ֣ם הַזֶּ֑ה וְעַד־אָ֙נָה֙
לֹא־יַאֲמִ֣ינוּ בִ֔י בְּכֹל֙ הָֽאֹת֔וֹת אֲשֶׁ֥ר עָשִׂ֖יתִי בְּקִרְבּֽוֹ: אַכֶּ֥נּוּ בַדֶּ֖בֶר

פרק יד

ב׀ לוּ מַתְנוּ. הַלְוַאי וּמַתְנוּ:

ד׀ נִתְּנָה רֹאשׁ. כְּתַרְגּוּמוֹ: ״נְמַנֵּי רֵישָׁא״, נָשִׂים עָלֵינוּ
מֶלֶךְ. וְרַבּוֹתֵינוּ פֵּרְשׁוּ, לְשׁוֹן עֲבוֹדָה זָרָה:

ט׀ אַל תִּמְרֹדוּ. וְשׁוּב ״וְאַתֶּם אַל תִּירְאוּ״: כִּי לַחְמֵנוּ
הֵם. נֹאכְלֵם כַּלֶּחֶם: סָר צִלָּם. מָגִנָּם וְחָזְקָם, כְּשֵׁרִים
שֶׁבָּהֶם מֵתוּ, אִיּוֹב שֶׁהָיָה מֵגֵן עֲלֵיהֶם. דָּבָר אַחֵר, צִלּוֹ
שֶׁל הַמָּקוֹם סָר מֵעֲלֵיהֶם:

י׀ לִרְגּוֹם אֹתָם. אֶת יְהוֹשֻׁעַ וְכָלֵב: וּכְבוֹד ה׳. הֶעָנָן
יָרַד שָׁם:

יא׀ עַד אָנָה. עַד הֵיכָן: יְנַאֲצֻנִי. יַרְגִּיזוּנִי: בְּכֹל
הָאֹתוֹת. בִּשְׁבִיל כָּל הַנִּסִּים שֶׁעָשִׂיתִי לָהֶם הָיָה
לָהֶם לְהַאֲמִין שֶׁהַיְכֹלֶת בְּיָדִי לְקַיֵּם הַבְטָחָתִי:

יב׀ וְאוֹרִשֶׁנּוּ. כְּתַרְגּוּמוֹ, ״תֵּרְכִין״, וְכֵן תֹּאמַר: מָה
אֶעֱשֶׂה לִשְׁבוּעַת אָבוֹת? ״וְאֶעֱשֶׂה אֹתְךָ לְגוֹי גָּדוֹל״,
שֶׁאַתָּה מִזַּרְעָם:

במדבר | פרק יד

יג וְאוֹרִשֶׁנּוּ וְאֶעֱשֶׂה אֹתְךָ לְגוֹי־גָּדוֹל וְעָצוּם מִמֶּנּוּ: וַיֹּאמֶר מֹשֶׁה אֶל־יהוה וְשָׁמְעוּ מִצְרַיִם כִּי־הֶעֱלִיתָ בְכֹחֲךָ אֶת־הָעָם הַזֶּה מִקִּרְבּוֹ:

יד וְאָמְרוּ אֶל־יוֹשֵׁב הָאָרֶץ הַזֹּאת שָׁמְעוּ כִּי־אַתָּה יהוה בְּקֶרֶב הָעָם הַזֶּה אֲשֶׁר־עַיִן בְּעַיִן נִרְאָה ׀ אַתָּה יהוה וַעֲנָנְךָ עֹמֵד עֲלֵהֶם וּבְעַמֻּד עָנָן אַתָּה הֹלֵךְ לִפְנֵיהֶם יוֹמָם וּבְעַמּוּד אֵשׁ לָיְלָה:

טו וְהֵמַתָּה אֶת־הָעָם הַזֶּה כְּאִישׁ אֶחָד וְאָמְרוּ הַגּוֹיִם אֲשֶׁר־שָׁמְעוּ אֶת־שִׁמְעֲךָ לֵאמֹר:

טז מִבִּלְתִּי יְכֹלֶת יהוה לְהָבִיא אֶת־הָעָם הַזֶּה אֶל־הָאָרֶץ אֲשֶׁר־נִשְׁבַּע לָהֶם וַיִּשְׁחָטֵם בַּמִּדְבָּר:

יז וְעַתָּה יִגְדַּל־נָא כֹּחַ אֲדֹנָי כַּאֲשֶׁר דִּבַּרְתָּ לֵאמֹר: יהוה אֶרֶךְ אַפַּיִם וְרַב־חֶסֶד נֹשֵׂא עָוֺן וָפָשַׁע וְנַקֵּה לֹא יְנַקֶּה פֹּקֵד עֲוֺן אָבוֹת עַל־בָּנִים עַל־שִׁלֵּשִׁים וְעַל־רִבֵּעִים:

יט סְלַח־נָא לַעֲוֺן הָעָם הַזֶּה כְּגֹדֶל חַסְדֶּךָ וְכַאֲשֶׁר נָשָׂאתָה לָעָם הַזֶּה מִמִּצְרַיִם וְעַד־הֵנָּה:

יג-יד | **וְשָׁמְעוּ מִצְרַיִם. וְשָׁמְעוּ אֶת אֲשֶׁר תַּהַרְגֵם: כִּי הֶעֱלִיתָ.** "כִּי" מְשַׁמֵּשׁ בִּלְשׁוֹן "אֲשֶׁר". וְהֵם רָאוּ אֶת אֲשֶׁר הֶעֱלִיתָ בְּכֹחֲךָ הַגָּדוֹל אוֹתָם מִקִּרְבָּם, וּכְשֶׁיִּשְׁמְעוּ שֶׁאַתָּה הוֹרְגָם, לֹא יֹאמְרוּ שֶׁחָטְאוּ לְךָ, אֶלָּא יֹאמְרוּ שֶׁכְּנֶגְדָּם יָכֹלְתָּ לְהִלָּחֵם אֲבָל כְּנֶגֶד יוֹשְׁבֵי הָאָרֶץ לֹא יָכֹלְתָּ לְהִלָּחֵם, וְזוֹ הִיא: **וְאָמְרוּ אֶל יוֹשֵׁב הָאָרֶץ הַזֹּאת.** כְּמוֹ "עַל יוֹשֵׁב הָאָרֶץ הַזֹּאת". וּמָה יֹאמְרוּ עֲלֵיהֶם? מַה שֶּׁאָמוּר בְּסוֹף הָעִנְיָן: "מִבִּלְתִּי יְכֹלֶת ה'" בִּשְׁבִיל שֶׁ"שָׁמְעוּ כִּי אַתָּה ה'" (להלן פסוק טז), שׁוֹכֵן בְּקִרְבָּם וְעַיִן בְּעַיִן אַתָּה נִרְאָה לָהֶם, וְהַכֹּל בְּדֶרֶךְ חִבָּה, וְלֹא הִכִּירוּ בְךָ שֶׁנִּתְּקָה אַהֲבָתְךָ מֵהֶם עַד הֵנָּה:

טו | **וְהֵמַתָּה אֶת הָעָם הַזֶּה כְּאִישׁ אֶחָד.** פִּתְאֹם, וּמִתּוֹךְ כָּךְ: "וְאָמְרוּ הַגּוֹיִם אֲשֶׁר שָׁמְעוּ אֶת שִׁמְעֲךָ" וְגוֹ':

טז | **מִבִּלְתִּי יְכֹלֶת ה' וְגוֹ'.** לְפִי שֶׁיּוֹשְׁבֵי הָאָרֶץ חֲזָקִים וְגִבּוֹרִים, וְאֵינוֹ דּוֹמֶה פַּרְעֹה לִשְׁלֹשִׁים וְאֶחָד מְלָכִים, זֹאת יֹאמְרוּ עַל יוֹשְׁבֵי הָאָרֶץ הַזֹּאת: "מִבִּלְתִּי יְכֹלֶת", מִתּוֹךְ שֶׁלֹּא הָיָה יָכֹלֶת בְּיָדוֹ לַהֲבִיאָם, שְׁחָטָם: **יְכֹלֶת.** שֵׁם דָּבָר הוּא:

יז-יח | **כַּאֲשֶׁר דִּבַּרְתָּ לֵאמֹר.** וּמַהוּ הַדִּבּוּר? **ה' אֶרֶךְ אַפַּיִם.** לַצַּדִּיקִים וְלָרְשָׁעִים. כְּשֶׁעָלָה מֹשֶׁה לַמָּרוֹם מְצָאוֹ לְהַקָּדוֹשׁ בָּרוּךְ הוּא שֶׁהָיָה יוֹשֵׁב וְכוֹתֵב: "ה' אֶרֶךְ אַפַּיִם", אָמַר לוֹ: לַצַּדִּיקִים? אָמַר לוֹ הַקָּדוֹשׁ בָּרוּךְ הוּא: אַף לָרְשָׁעִים. אָמַר לוֹ: רְשָׁעִים יֹאבֵדוּ. אָמַר לוֹ הַקָּדוֹשׁ בָּרוּךְ הוּא: חַיֶּיךָ שֶׁתִּצְטָרֵךְ לַדָּבָר. כְּשֶׁחָטְאוּ יִשְׂרָאֵל בָּעֵגֶל וּבַמְרַגְּלִים הִתְפַּלֵּל מֹשֶׁה לְפָנָיו בְּ"אֶרֶךְ אַפַּיִם", אָמַר לוֹ הַקָּדוֹשׁ בָּרוּךְ הוּא: וַהֲלֹא אָמַרְתָּ לִי לַצַּדִּיקִים! אָמַר לוֹ: וַהֲלֹא אַתָּה אָמַרְתָּ לִי אַף לָרְשָׁעִים: יִגְדַּל נָא כֹּחַ אֲדֹנָי. לַעֲשׂוֹת דִּבּוּרְךָ: **וְנַקֵּה לֹא יְנַקֶּה. לַפְּשָׁעִים: וְנַקֵּה.** לַשָּׁבִים: לְשָׁבִים:

שלח | 386 פרק יד | במדבר

כא וַיֹּ֣אמֶר יְהוָ֔ה סָלַ֖חְתִּי כִּדְבָרֶֽךָ: וְאוּלָ֖ם חַי־אָ֑נִי וְיִמָּלֵ֥א כְבוֹד־יְהוָ֖ה
כב אֶת־כָּל־הָאָֽרֶץ: כִּ֣י כָל־הָאֲנָשִׁ֗ים הָרֹאִ֤ים אֶת־כְּבֹדִי֙ וְאֶת־אֹ֣תֹתַ֔י
אֲשֶׁר־עָשִׂ֥יתִי בְמִצְרַ֖יִם וּבַמִּדְבָּ֑ר וַיְנַסּ֣וּ אֹתִ֗י זֶ֚ה עֶ֣שֶׂר פְּעָמִ֔ים וְלֹ֥א
כג שָׁמְע֖וּ בְּקוֹלִֽי: אִם־יִרְאוּ֙ אֶת־הָאָ֔רֶץ אֲשֶׁ֥ר נִשְׁבַּ֖עְתִּי לַאֲבֹתָ֑ם
כד וְכָל־מְנַאֲצַ֖י לֹ֥א יִרְאֽוּהָ: וְעַבְדִּ֣י כָלֵ֗ב עֵ֣קֶב הָֽיְתָ֞ה ר֤וּחַ אַחֶ֙רֶת֙
עִמּ֔וֹ וַיְמַלֵּ֖א אַחֲרָ֑י וַהֲבִֽיאֹתִ֗יו אֶל־הָאָ֙רֶץ֙ אֲשֶׁר־בָּ֣א שָׁ֔מָּה וְזַרְע֖וֹ
כה יוֹרִשֶֽׁנָּה: וְהָעֲמָלֵקִ֥י וְהַֽכְּנַעֲנִ֖י יוֹשֵׁ֣ב בָּעֵ֑מֶק מָחָ֗ר פְּנ֨וּ וּסְע֥וּ לָכֶ֛ם
הַמִּדְבָּ֖ר דֶּ֥רֶךְ יַם־סֽוּף:

רביעי כו וַיְדַבֵּ֣ר יְהוָ֔ה אֶל־מֹשֶׁ֥ה וְאֶֽל־אַהֲרֹ֖ן לֵאמֹֽר: עַד־מָתַ֗י לָעֵדָ֤ה
הָֽרָעָה֙ הַזֹּ֔את אֲשֶׁ֛ר הֵ֥מָּה מַלִּינִ֖ים עָלָ֑י אֶת־תְּלֻנּ֞וֹת בְּנֵ֣י יִשְׂרָאֵ֗ל
כח אֲשֶׁ֨ר הֵ֧מָּה מַלִּינִ֛ים עָלַ֖י שָׁמָֽעְתִּי: אֱמֹ֣ר אֲלֵהֶ֔ם חַי־אָ֙נִי֙ נְאֻם־

כא **כדברך.** בשביל מה שאמרת, פן יאמרו: "מבלתי יכלת ה'" (לעיל פסוק טז):

כא-כג **ואולם.** כמו 'אבל', זאת אעשה להם: **חי אני.** לשון שבועה, כשם שאני חי וכבודי ימלא את כל הארץ, כך אקיים להם, "כי כל האנשים הרואים וגו' אם יראו את הארץ"; הרי זה מקרא מסורס: חי אני כי כל האנשים אם יראו את הארץ, וכבודי ימלא את כל הארץ, שלא יתחלל שמי במגפה הזאת לאמר: "מבלתי יכלת ה' להביאם", שלא אמיתם פתאם כאיש אחד, אלא באחור ארבעים שנה מעט מעט:

כב **וינסו.** כמשמעו. **זה עשר פעמים.** שנים בים ושנים במן ושנים בשלו וכו', כדאיתא במסכת ערכין (דף טו ע"א - טו ע"ב):

כג **אם יראו.** לא יראו:

כד **רוח אחרת.** שתי רוחות, אחת בפה ואחת בלב. למרגלים אמר: 'אני עמכם בעצה', ובלבו היה לומר האמת, ועל ידי כן היה בו כח להשתיקם,

כמו שנאמר: "ויהס כלב" (לעיל יג, ל), שהיו סבורים שיאמר כמותם. זהו שנאמר בספר יהושע: "ואשב אותו דבר כאשר עם לבבי" (יהושע יד, ז), ולא כאשר עם פי: **וימלא אחרי.** וימלא את לבו אחרי, וזה מקרא קצר: **אשר בא שמה.** חברון תנתן לו: **יורשנה.** כתרגומו: "יתרכנה", יורישו את הענקים ואת העם אשר בה, ואין לתרגמו 'ירתנה' אלא במקום 'יירשנה':

כה **והעמלקי וגו'.** אם תלכו שם יהרגו אתכם, מאחר שאיני עמכם: **מחר פנו.** לאחוריכם, "וסעו לכם" וגו':

כו **לעדה הרעה וגו'.** אלו המרגלים, מכאן לעדה שהיא עשרה: **אשר המה מלינים.** את ישראל "עלי": **את תלנות בני ישראל אשר המה.** המרגלים, "מלינים" חוזר "עלי, שמעתי":

כח **חי אני.** לשון שבועה, אם לא כן אעשה - כביכול חיני אני: **כאשר דברתם.** שבקשתם ממני: "או במדבר הזה לו מתנו" (לעיל פסוק ב):

במדבר | פרק יד

כט יְהוָה אִם־לֹא כַּאֲשֶׁר דִּבַּרְתֶּם בְּאָזְנָי כֵּן אֶעֱשֶׂה לָכֶם: בַּמִּדְבָּר
הַזֶּה יִפְּלוּ פִגְרֵיכֶם וְכָל־פְּקֻדֵיכֶם לְכָל־מִסְפַּרְכֶם מִבֶּן עֶשְׂרִים
שָׁנָה וָמָעְלָה אֲשֶׁר הֲלִינֹתֶם עָלָי:
ל אִם־אַתֶּם תָּבֹאוּ אֶל־הָאָרֶץ אֲשֶׁר נָשָׂאתִי אֶת־יָדִי לְשַׁכֵּן אֶתְכֶם בָּהּ כִּי אִם־כָּלֵב בֶּן־יְפֻנֶּה
לא וִיהוֹשֻׁעַ בִּן־נוּן: וְטַפְּכֶם אֲשֶׁר אֲמַרְתֶּם לָבַז יִהְיֶה וְהֵבֵיאתִי
אֹתָם וְיָדְעוּ אֶת־הָאָרֶץ אֲשֶׁר מְאַסְתֶּם בָּהּ:
לב וּפִגְרֵיכֶם אַתֶּם יִפְּלוּ בַּמִּדְבָּר הַזֶּה:
לג וּבְנֵיכֶם יִהְיוּ רֹעִים בַּמִּדְבָּר אַרְבָּעִים שָׁנָה וְנָשְׂאוּ אֶת־זְנוּתֵיכֶם עַד־תֹּם פִּגְרֵיכֶם בַּמִּדְבָּר:
לד בְּמִסְפַּר הַיָּמִים אֲשֶׁר־תַּרְתֶּם אֶת־הָאָרֶץ אַרְבָּעִים יוֹם יוֹם לַשָּׁנָה יוֹם לַשָּׁנָה
תִּשְׂאוּ אֶת־עֲוֹנֹתֵיכֶם אַרְבָּעִים שָׁנָה וִידַעְתֶּם אֶת־תְּנוּאָתִי: אֲנִי
לה יְהוָה דִּבַּרְתִּי אִם־לֹא ׀ זֹאת אֶעֱשֶׂה לְכָל־הָעֵדָה הָרָעָה הַזֹּאת
לו הַנּוֹעָדִים עָלָי בַּמִּדְבָּר הַזֶּה יִתַּמּוּ וְשָׁם יָמֻתוּ: וְהָאֲנָשִׁים אֲשֶׁר־

כט] **וְכָל־פְּקֻדֵיכֶם לְכָל־מִסְפַּרְכֶם.** כָּל הַנִּמְנֶה לְכָל מִסְפָּר שֶׁאַתֶּם נִמְנִים בּוֹ, כְּגוֹן לָצֵאת וְלָבֹא לַצָּבָא וְלָתֵת שְׁקָלִים, כָּל הַמְּנוּיִים לְכָל אוֹתָן מִסְפָּרוֹת יָמוּתוּ, וְאֵלּוּ הֵן: "מִבֶּן עֶשְׂרִים שָׁנָה וְגוֹ'" — לְהוֹצִיא שִׁבְטוֹ שֶׁל לֵוִי שֶׁאֵין פְּקוּדֵיהֶם מִבֶּן עֶשְׂרִים:

לב] **וּפִגְרֵיכֶם אַתֶּם.** כְּתַרְגּוּמוֹ, לְפִי שֶׁדִּבֵּר עַל הַבָּנִים לְהַכְנִיסָם לָאָרֶץ וּבִקֵּשׁ לוֹמַר: "וְאַתֶּם תָּמוּתוּ", נוֹפֵל לָשׁוֹן זֶה כָּאן לוֹמַר "אַתֶּם":

לג] **אַרְבָּעִים שָׁנָה.** לֹא מֵת אֶחָד מֵהֶם פָּחוּת מִבֶּן שִׁשִּׁים, לְכָךְ נִגְזַר אַרְבָּעִים, כְּדֵי שֶׁיִּהְיוּ אוֹתָן שֶׁל בְּנֵי עֶשְׂרִים מַגִּיעִין לִכְלָל שִׁשִּׁים. וְשָׁנָה רִאשׁוֹנָה הָיְתָה בַּכְּלָל, וְאַף עַל פִּי שֶׁקָּדְמָה לִשְׁלוּחַ הַמְּרַגְּלִים, לְפִי שֶׁמִּשֶּׁעָשׂוּ אֶת הָעֵגֶל עָלְתָה גְּזֵרָה זוֹ בְּמַחֲשָׁבָה, אֶלָּא שֶׁהִמְתִּין לָהֶם עַד שֶׁתִּתְמַלֵּא סְאָתָם, וְזֶהוּ שֶׁנֶּאֱמַר: "וּבְיוֹם פָּקְדִי", בַּמְּרַגְּלִים, "וּפָקַדְתִּי עֲלֵהֶם חַטָּאתָם" (שמות לב, לד). וְאַף כָּאן נֶאֱמַר: "תִּשְׂאוּ אֶת עֲוֹנֹתֵיכֶם",

שְׁתֵּי עֲוֹנוֹת, שֶׁל עֵגֶל וְשֶׁל תְּלוּנָה, וְחִשֵּׁב לָהֶם בְּמִנְיַן חַיֵּיהֶם מִקְצָת שָׁנָה כְּכֻלָּה, וּכְשֶׁנִּכְנְסוּ לִשְׁנַת שִׁשִּׁים מֵתוּ אוֹתָם שֶׁל בְּנֵי עֶשְׂרִים: **וְנָשְׂאוּ אֶת זְנוּתֵיכֶם.** כְּתַרְגּוּמוֹ, יִסְבְּלוּ אֶת חַטָּאתְכֶם:

לד] **אֶת תְּנוּאָתִי.** שֶׁהֲנִיאוֹתֶם אֶת לְבַבְכֶם מֵאַחֲרָי. "תְּנוּאָה" לְשׁוֹן הֲסָרָה, כְּמוֹ: "כִּי הֵנִיא אָבִיהָ אֹתָהּ" (להלן ל, ו):

לו] **וַיִּשֻׁבוּ וַיַּלִּינוּ עָלָיו.** וּכְשֶׁשָּׁבוּ מִתּוּר הָאָרֶץ הִרְעִימוּ עָלָיו אֶת כָּל הָעֵדָה בְּהוֹצָאַת דִּבָּה, אוֹתָן הָאֲנָשִׁים "וַיָּמֻתוּ" (להלן פסוק לו). כָּל הוֹצָאַת דִּבָּה לְשׁוֹן חִנּוּךְ דְּבָרִים, שֶׁמַּלְקִיחִים לְשׁוֹנָם לְאָדָם לְדַבֵּר בּוֹ, כְּמוֹ: "דּוֹבֵב שִׂפְתֵי יְשֵׁנִים" (שיר השירים ז, י), וְיֶשְׁנָה לְטוֹבָה וְיֶשְׁנָה לְרָעָה, לְכָךְ נֶאֱמַר כָּאן: "מוֹצִאֵי דִבַּת הָאָרֶץ רָעָה" (להלן פסוק לז), שֶׁיֵּשׁ דִּבָּה שֶׁהִיא טוֹבָה. **דִּבָּה.** פרלדי"ץ בְּלַעַ"ז:

וַיֵּלְכוּ שָׁלַח מֹשֶׁה לָתוּר אֶת־הָאָרֶץ וַיָּשֻׁבוּ וילינו עָלָיו אֶת־כָּל־הָעֵדָה
לְהוֹצִיא דִבָּה עַל־הָאָרֶץ: וַיָּמֻתוּ הָאֲנָשִׁים מוֹצִאֵי דִבַּת־הָאָרֶץ לז
רָעָה בַּמַּגֵּפָה לִפְנֵי יְהוָה: וִיהוֹשֻׁעַ בִּן־נוּן וְכָלֵב בֶּן־יְפֻנֶּה חָיוּ לח
מִן־הָאֲנָשִׁים הָהֵם הַהֹלְכִים לָתוּר אֶת־הָאָרֶץ: וַיְדַבֵּר מֹשֶׁה לט
אֶת־הַדְּבָרִים הָאֵלֶּה אֶל־כָּל־בְּנֵי יִשְׂרָאֵל וַיִּתְאַבְּלוּ הָעָם מְאֹד:
וַיַּשְׁכִּמוּ בַבֹּקֶר וַיַּעֲלוּ אֶל־רֹאשׁ־הָהָר לֵאמֹר הִנֶּנּוּ וְעָלִינוּ אֶל־ מ
הַמָּקוֹם אֲשֶׁר־אָמַר יְהוָה כִּי חָטָאנוּ: וַיֹּאמֶר מֹשֶׁה לָמָּה זֶּה מא
אַתֶּם עֹבְרִים אֶת־פִּי יְהוָה וְהִוא לֹא תִצְלָח: אַל־תַּעֲלוּ כִּי אֵין מב
יְהוָה בְּקִרְבְּכֶם וְלֹא תִּנָּגְפוּ לִפְנֵי אֹיְבֵיכֶם: כִּי הָעֲמָלֵקִי וְהַכְּנַעֲנִי מג
שָׁם לִפְנֵיכֶם וּנְפַלְתֶּם בֶּחָרֶב כִּי־עַל־כֵּן שַׁבְתֶּם מֵאַחֲרֵי יְהוָה
וְלֹא־יִהְיֶה יְהוָה עִמָּכֶם: וַיַּעְפִּלוּ לַעֲלוֹת אֶל־רֹאשׁ הָהָר וַאֲרוֹן מד
בְּרִית־יְהוָה וּמֹשֶׁה לֹא־מָשׁוּ מִקֶּרֶב הַמַּחֲנֶה: וַיֵּרֶד הָעֲמָלֵקִי מה
וְהַכְּנַעֲנִי הַיֹּשֵׁב בָּהָר הַהוּא וַיַּכּוּם וַיַּכְּתוּם עַד־הַחָרְמָה:

לו] **בַּמַּגֵּפָה לִפְנֵי ה׳.** בְּאוֹתָהּ מִיתָה הַהֲגוּנָה לָהֶם, מִדָּה כְּנֶגֶד מִדָּה. הֵם חָטְאוּ בַּלָּשׁוֹן, וְנִשְׁתַּרְבֵּב לְשׁוֹנָם עַד טַבּוּרָם, וְתוֹלָעִים יוֹצְאִים מִלְּשׁוֹנָם וּבָאִין לְתוֹךְ טַבּוּרָם, לְכָךְ נֶאֱמַר: "בַּמַּגֵּפָה" וְלֹא "בְּמַגֵּפָה", וְזֶהוּ "לִפְנֵי ה׳", בְּאוֹתָהּ הָרְאוּיָה לָהֶם עַל פִּי מִדּוֹתָיו שֶׁל הַקָּדוֹשׁ בָּרוּךְ הוּא שֶׁהוּא מוֹדֵד מִדָּה כְּנֶגֶד מִדָּה:

לח] **וִיהוֹשֻׁעַ וְכָלֵב חָיוּ וְגוֹ׳.** מַה תַּלְמוּד לוֹמַר: "חָיוּ מִן הָאֲנָשִׁים הָהֵם"? אֶלָּא מְלַמֵּד שֶׁנָּטְלוּ חֶלְקָם שֶׁל מְרַגְּלִים בָּאָרֶץ וְקָמוּ תַּחְתֵּיהֶם לַחַיִּים:

מ] **אֶל רֹאשׁ הָהָר.** הִיא הַדֶּרֶךְ הָעוֹלָה לָאָרֶץ יִשְׂרָאֵל. **הִנֶּנּוּ וְעָלִינוּ אֶל הַמָּקוֹם.** לָאָרֶץ יִשְׂרָאֵל, אֲשֶׁר אָמַר ה׳. לָתֵת לָנוּ, שָׁם נַעֲלֶה. **כִּי חָטָאנוּ.** עַל אֲשֶׁר אָמַרְנוּ: "הֲלוֹא טוֹב לָנוּ שׁוּב מִצְרַיְמָה" (לְעֵיל פסוק ג):

מא] **וְהִוא לֹא תִצְלָח.** זוֹ שֶׁאַתֶּם עוֹשִׂים לֹא תִצְלָח:

מג] **כִּי עַל כֵּן שַׁבְתֶּם.** כְּלוֹמַר, כִּי זֹאת תָּבֹא לָכֶם עַל אֲשֶׁר שַׁבְתֶּם וְגוֹ׳:

מד] **וַיַּעְפִּלוּ.** לְשׁוֹן חֹזֶק, וְכֵן: "הִנֵּה עֻפְּלָה" (חבקוק ב, ד), אינגרי"ש בְּלַעַ"ז, לְשׁוֹן עַזּוּת, וְכֵן: "עֹפֶל בַּת צִיּוֹן" (מיכה ד, ח), "עֹפֶל וָבַחַן" (ישעיה לב, יד). וּמִדְרַשׁ תַּנְחוּמָא מְפָרְשׁוֹ לְשׁוֹן אֹפֶל, הָלְכוּ חֲשֵׁכִים שֶׁלֹּא בִּרְשׁוּת:

מה] **וַיַּכְּתוּם.** כְּמוֹ: "וָאֶכֹּת אוֹתוֹ טָחוֹן" (דברים ט, כא), מַכָּה אַחַר מַכָּה. **עַד הַחָרְמָה.** שֵׁם הַמָּקוֹם נִקְרָא עַל שֵׁם הַמְאֹרָע:

במדבר | פרק טו | שלח

א וַיְדַבֵּ֥ר יְהוָ֖ה אֶל־מֹשֶׁ֥ה לֵּאמֹֽר: ב דַּבֵּר֙ אֶל־בְּנֵ֣י יִשְׂרָאֵ֔ל וְאָמַרְתָּ֖ אֲלֵהֶ֑ם כִּ֣י תָבֹ֗אוּ אֶל־אֶ֙רֶץ֙ מוֹשְׁבֹ֣תֵיכֶ֔ם אֲשֶׁ֥ר אֲנִ֖י נֹתֵ֥ן לָכֶֽם: ג וַעֲשִׂיתֶ֨ם אִשֶּׁ֤ה לַֽיהוָה֙ עֹלָ֣ה אוֹ־זֶ֔בַח לְפַלֵּא־נֶ֖דֶר א֣וֹ בִנְדָבָ֑ה א֚וֹ בְּמֹ֣עֲדֵיכֶ֔ם לַעֲשׂ֞וֹת רֵ֤יחַ נִיחֹ֙חַ֙ לַֽיהוָ֔ה מִן־הַבָּקָ֖ר א֥וֹ מִן־הַצֹּֽאן: ד וְהִקְרִ֛יב הַמַּקְרִ֥יב קָרְבָּנ֖וֹ לַֽיהוָ֑ה מִנְחָה֙ סֹ֣לֶת עִשָּׂר֔וֹן בָּל֕וּל בִּרְבִעִ֥ית הַהִ֖ין שָֽׁמֶן: ה וְיַ֤יִן לַנֶּ֙סֶךְ֙ רְבִיעִ֣ית הַהִ֔ין תַּעֲשֶׂ֥ה עַל־הָעֹלָ֖ה א֣וֹ לַזָּ֑בַח לַכֶּ֖בֶשׂ הָאֶחָֽד: ו א֤וֹ לָאַ֙יִל֙ תַּעֲשֶׂ֣ה מִנְחָ֔ה סֹ֖לֶת שְׁנֵ֣י עֶשְׂרֹנִ֑ים בְּלוּלָ֥ה בַשֶּׁ֖מֶן שְׁלִשִׁ֥ית הַהִֽין: ז וְיַ֥יִן לַנֶּ֖סֶךְ שְׁלִשִׁ֣ית הַהִ֑ין תַּקְרִ֥יב רֵֽיחַ־נִיחֹ֖חַ לַיהוָֽה: ח וְכִֽי־תַעֲשֶׂ֥ה בֶן־בָּקָ֖ר עֹלָ֣ה אוֹ־זָ֑בַח לְפַלֵּא־נֶ֥דֶר אֽוֹ־שְׁלָמִ֖ים לַֽיהוָֽה: ט וְהִקְרִ֤יב עַל־בֶּן־הַבָּקָר֙ מִנְחָ֔ה סֹ֖לֶת שְׁלֹשָׁ֣ה עֶשְׂרֹנִ֑ים בָּל֥וּל בַּשֶּׁ֖מֶן חֲצִ֥י הַהִֽין: י וְיַ֛יִן תַּקְרִ֥יב לַנֶּ֖סֶךְ חֲצִ֣י הַהִ֑ין אִשֵּׁ֛ה רֵֽיחַ־נִיחֹ֖חַ לַיהוָֽה: יא כָּ֣כָה יֵעָשֶׂ֗ה לַשּׁוֹר֙ הָֽאֶחָ֔ד א֖וֹ לָאַ֣יִל הָאֶחָ֑ד אֽוֹ־לַשֶּׂ֥ה בַכְּבָשִׂ֖ים א֥וֹ בָעִזִּֽים: יב כַּמִּסְפָּ֖ר אֲשֶׁ֣ר תַּעֲשׂ֑וּ כָּ֛כָה תַּעֲשׂ֥וּ לָאֶחָ֖ד כְּמִסְפָּרָֽם: יג כָּל־הָאֶזְרָ֥ח יַעֲשֶׂה־כָּ֖כָה

חמישי

פרק טו
ב) **כי תבאו.** בִּשֵּׂר לָהֶם שֶׁיִּכָּנְסוּ לָאָרֶץ:

ג) **ועשיתם אשה.** אֵין זֶה צִוּוּי, אֶלָּא כְּשֶׁתָּבוֹאוּ שָׁם וְתַעֲלֶה עַל לְבַבְכֶם לַעֲשׂוֹת אִשֶּׁה לַה': **ריח ניחח.** נַחַת רוּחַ לְפָנַי: **לפלא נדר או בנדבה.** אוֹ שֶׁתַּעֲשׂוּ הָאִשֶּׁה בִּשְׁבִיל חוֹבַת מוֹעֲדֵיכֶם, שֶׁחִיַּבְתִּי אֶתְכֶם לַעֲשׂוֹת בַּמּוֹעֵד:

ד) **והקריב המקריב.** תַּקְרִיבוּ נְסָכִים וּמִנְחָה לְכָל בְּהֵמָה, הַמִּנְחָה כָּלִיל וְהַשֶּׁמֶן נִבְלָל בְּתוֹכָהּ, וְהַיַּיִן לַסְּפָלִים, כְּמוֹ שֶׁשָּׁנִינוּ בְּמַסֶּכֶת סֻכָּה (דף מח ע"ב):

ה) **לכבש האחד.** עַל כָּל הָאָמוּר לְמַעְלָה הוּא מוּסָב, עַל הַמִּנְחָה וְעַל הַשֶּׁמֶן וְעַל הַיַּיִן:

ו) **או לאיל.** וְאִם אַיִל הוּא. וְרַבּוֹתֵינוּ דָּרְשׁוּ: "אוֹ" לְרַבּוֹת אֶת הַפַּלְגָּס לְנִסְכֵּי אַיִל:

י) **אשה ריח.** אֵינוֹ מוּסָב עַל הַמִּנְחָה וְהַשֶּׁמֶן, אֶלָּא עַל הַיַּיִן הַיַּיִן אִשֶּׁה, שֶׁאֵינוֹ נִתָּן עַל הָאֵשׁ:

יא) **או לשה.** בֵּין שֶׁהוּא בַכְּבָשִׂים בֵּין שֶׁהוּא בָעִזִּים. "כֶּבֶשׂ" וָ"שֶׂה" קְרוּיִים בְּתוֹךְ שְׁנָתָם, "אַיִל" בֶּן שְׁלֹשָׁה עָשָׂר חֹדֶשׁ וְיוֹם אֶחָד:

יב) **כמספר אשר תעשו.** כְּמִסְפַּר הַבְּהֵמוֹת אֲשֶׁר תַּקְרִיבוּ לְקָרְבָּן, כָּכָה תַּעֲשׂוּ נְסָכִים לְכָל אֶחָד מֵהֶם, כְּמִסְפָּרָם שֶׁל בְּהֵמוֹת מִסְפָּרָם שֶׁל נְסָכִים:

אֶת־אֵלֶּה לְהַקְרִיב אִשֵּׁה רֵיחַ־נִיחֹחַ לַיהוה: וְכִי־יָגוּר אִתְּכֶם
גֵּר אוֹ אֲשֶׁר־בְּתוֹכְכֶם לְדֹרֹתֵיכֶם וְעָשָׂה אִשֵּׁה רֵיחַ־נִיחֹחַ לַיהוה
כַּאֲשֶׁר תַּעֲשׂוּ כֵּן יַעֲשֶׂה: הַקָּהָל חֻקָּה אַחַת לָכֶם וְלַגֵּר הַגָּר
חֻקַּת עוֹלָם לְדֹרֹתֵיכֶם כָּכֶם כַּגֵּר יִהְיֶה לִפְנֵי יהוה: תּוֹרָה אַחַת
וּמִשְׁפָּט אֶחָד יִהְיֶה לָכֶם וְלַגֵּר הַגָּר אִתְּכֶם:

ששי וַיְדַבֵּר יהוה אֶל־מֹשֶׁה לֵּאמֹר: דַּבֵּר אֶל־בְּנֵי יִשְׂרָאֵל וְאָמַרְתָּ
אֲלֵהֶם בְּבֹאֲכֶם אֶל־הָאָרֶץ אֲשֶׁר אֲנִי מֵבִיא אֶתְכֶם שָׁמָּה: וְהָיָה
בַּאֲכָלְכֶם מִלֶּחֶם הָאָרֶץ תָּרִימוּ תְרוּמָה לַיהוה: רֵאשִׁית עֲרִסֹתֵכֶם
חַלָּה תָּרִימוּ תְרוּמָה כִּתְרוּמַת גֹּרֶן כֵּן תָּרִימוּ אֹתָהּ: מֵרֵאשִׁית
עֲרִסֹתֵיכֶם תִּתְּנוּ לַיהוה תְּרוּמָה לְדֹרֹתֵיכֶם: וְכִי
תִשְׁגּוּ וְלֹא תַעֲשׂוּ אֵת כָּל־הַמִּצְוֹת הָאֵלֶּה אֲשֶׁר־דִּבֶּר יהוה

טו **כָּכֶם כַּגֵּר.** כְּמוֹתְכֶם כֵּן גֵּר, וְכֵן דֶּרֶךְ לָשׁוֹן עִבְרִית: "כְּגַן ה' כְּאֶרֶץ מִצְרַיִם" (בראשית יג, י) כֵּן אֶרֶץ מִצְרַיִם, "כָּמוֹנִי כָמוֹךָ כְּעַמִּי כְעַמֶּךָ" (מלכים א' כב, ד):

יח **בְּבֹאֲכֶם אֶל הָאָרֶץ.** מְשֻׁנָּה בִּיאָה זוֹ מִכָּל בִּיאוֹת שֶׁבַּתּוֹרָה, שֶׁבְּכֻלָּן נֶאֱמַר: "כִּי תָבֹא" "כִּי תָבֹאוּ", לְפִיכָךְ כֻּלָּן לְמֵדוֹת זוֹ מִזּוֹ, וְכֵיוָן שֶׁפָּרַט לְךָ הַכָּתוּב בְּאַחַת מֵהֶן שֶׁאֵינָהּ אֶלָּא לְאַחַר יְרֻשָּׁה וִישִׁיבָה, אַף כֻּלָּן כֵּן. אֲבָל זוֹ נֶאֱמַר בָּהּ: "בְּבֹאֲכֶם", מִשֶּׁנִּכְנְסוּ בָהּ וְאָכְלוּ מִלַּחְמָהּ נִתְחַיְּבוּ בַחַלָּה:

כ **רֵאשִׁית עֲרִסֹתֵכֶם.** כְּשֶׁתָּלוּשׁוּ כְּדֵי עֲרִיסוֹתֵיכֶם שֶׁאַתֶּם רְגִילִין לָלוּשׁ בַּמִּדְבָּר, וְכַמָּה הִיא? "וַיָּמֹדּוּ בָעֹמֶר" (שמות טז, יח), "עֹמֶר לַגֻּלְגֹּלֶת" (שם פסוק טז) תָּרִימוּ מֵרֵאשִׁיתָהּ, כְּלוֹמַר, קֹדֶם שֶׁתֹּאכְלוּ מִמֶּנָּה, רֵאשִׁית חֶלְקָהּ חַלָּה אַחַת מִמֶּנָּה "תָּרִימוּ תְרוּמָה לַשֵּׁם ה'". חַלָּה. טוֹרְטִי"ל בְּלַעַז: **כִּתְרוּמַת גֹּרֶן.** שֶׁלֹּא נֶאֱמַר בָּהּ שִׁעוּר, וְלֹא כִּתְרוּמַת מַעֲשֵׂר שֶׁנֶּאֱמַר בָּהּ שִׁעוּר.

אֲבָל חֲכָמִים נָתְנוּ שִׁעוּר, לְבַעַל הַבַּיִת אֶחָד מֵעֶשְׂרִים וְאַרְבָּעָה, וְלַנַּחְתּוֹם אֶחָד מֵאַרְבָּעִים וּשְׁמוֹנָה:

כא **מֵרֵאשִׁית עֲרִסֹתֵיכֶם.** לָמָּה נֶאֱמַר? לְפִי שֶׁנֶּאֱמַר: "רֵאשִׁית עֲרִסֹתֵכֶם" (לעיל פסוק כ), שׁוֹמֵעַ אֲנִי רִאשׁוֹנָה שֶׁבָּעִסּוֹת? תַּלְמוּד לוֹמַר: "מֵרֵאשִׁית", מִקְצָתָהּ וְלֹא כֻלָּהּ. תִּתְּנוּ לָהּ תְּרוּמָה. לְפִי שֶׁלֹּא שָׁמַעְנוּ שִׁעוּר לַחַלָּה נֶאֱמַר: "תִּתְּנוּ", שֶׁיְּהֵא בָהּ כְּדֵי נְתִינָה:

כב **וְכִי תִשְׁגּוּ וְלֹא תַעֲשׂוּ.** עֲבוֹדָה זָרָה הָיְתָה בִּכְלָל כָּל הַמִּצְוֹת שֶׁהַצִּבּוּר מְבִיאִין עָלֶיהָ פַּר, וַהֲרֵי הַכָּתוּב מוֹצִיאָהּ כָּאן מִכְּלָלָהּ לָדוּן בְּפַר לְעוֹלָה וְשָׂעִיר לְחַטָּאת. **וְכִי תִשְׁגּוּ וְגוֹ'.** בַּעֲבוֹדָה זָרָה הַכָּתוּב מְדַבֵּר, אוֹ אֵינוֹ אֶלָּא בְּאַחַת מִכָּל הַמִּצְוֹת? תַּלְמוּד לוֹמַר: "אֵת כָּל הַמִּצְוֹת הָאֵלֶּה", מִצְוָה אַחַת שֶׁהִיא כְּכָל הַמִּצְוֹת. מָה הָעוֹבֵר עַל כָּל הַמִּצְוֹת פּוֹרֵק עֹל וּמֵפֵר בְּרִית וּמְגַלֶּה פָנִים, אַף מִצְוָה זוֹ פּוֹרֵק בָּהּ עֹל וּמֵפֵר בְּרִית וּמְגַלֶּה פָנִים, וְאֵיזוֹ? זוֹ עֲבוֹדָה

כג אֶל־מֹשֶׁה: אֵת כָּל־אֲשֶׁר צִוָּה יהוה אֲלֵיכֶם בְּיַד־מֹשֶׁה מִן־הַיּוֹם
כד אֲשֶׁר צִוָּה יהוה וָהָלְאָה לְדֹרֹתֵיכֶם: וְהָיָה אִם מֵעֵינֵי הָעֵדָה נֶעֶשְׂתָה לִשְׁגָגָה וְעָשׂוּ כָל־הָעֵדָה פַּר בֶּן־בָּקָר אֶחָד לְעֹלָה לְרֵיחַ נִיחֹחַ לַיהוה וּמִנְחָתוֹ וְנִסְכּוֹ כַּמִּשְׁפָּט וּשְׂעִיר־עִזִּים אֶחָד
כה לְחַטָּת: וְכִפֶּר הַכֹּהֵן עַל־כָּל־עֲדַת בְּנֵי יִשְׂרָאֵל וְנִסְלַח לָהֶם כִּי־שְׁגָגָה הִוא וְהֵם הֵבִיאוּ אֶת־קָרְבָּנָם אִשֶּׁה לַיהוה וְחַטָּאתָם
כו לִפְנֵי יהוה עַל־שִׁגְגָתָם: וְנִסְלַח לְכָל־עֲדַת בְּנֵי יִשְׂרָאֵל וְלַגֵּר הַגָּר בְּתוֹכָם כִּי לְכָל־הָעָם בִּשְׁגָגָה:
כז וְאִם־נֶפֶשׁ אַחַת שביעי תֶּחֱטָא בִשְׁגָגָה וְהִקְרִיבָה עֵז בַּת־שְׁנָתָהּ לְחַטָּאת: וְכִפֶּר הַכֹּהֵן
כח עַל־הַנֶּפֶשׁ הַשֹּׁגֶגֶת בְּחֶטְאָה בִשְׁגָגָה לִפְנֵי יהוה לְכַפֵּר עָלָיו
כט וְנִסְלַח לוֹ: הָאֶזְרָח בִּבְנֵי יִשְׂרָאֵל וְלַגֵּר הַגָּר בְּתוֹכָם תּוֹרָה אַחַת
ל יִהְיֶה לָכֶם לָעֹשֶׂה בִּשְׁגָגָה: וְהַנֶּפֶשׁ אֲשֶׁר־תַּעֲשֶׂה ׀ בְּיָד רָמָה מִן־הָאֶזְרָח וּמִן־הַגֵּר אֶת־יהוה הוּא מְגַדֵּף וְנִכְרְתָה הַנֶּפֶשׁ הַהִוא

זֶה: **אֲשֶׁר דִּבֶּר ה' אֶל מֹשֶׁה.** "אָנֹכִי" וְ"לֹא יִהְיֶה לְךָ" מִפִּי הַגְּבוּרָה שְׁמַעֲנוּם. "אַחַת דִּבֶּר אֱלֹהִים שְׁתַּיִם זוּ שָׁמָעְתִּי" (תהלים סב, יב):

כג אֵת כָּל אֲשֶׁר צִוָּה וְגוֹ'. מַגִּיד שֶׁכָּל הַמּוֹדֶה בַעֲבוֹדָה זָרָה כְּכוֹפֵר בְּכָל הַתּוֹרָה כֻּלָּהּ וּבְכָל מַה שֶּׁנִּתְנַבְּאוּ הַנְּבִיאִים, שֶׁנֶּאֱמַר: "מִן הַיּוֹם אֲשֶׁר צִוָּה ה' וָהָלְאָה":

כד אִם מֵעֵינֵי הָעֵדָה נֶעֶשְׂתָה לִשְׁגָגָה. אִם מֵעֵינֵי הָעֵדָה נֶעֶשְׂתָה עֲבֵרָה זוֹ עַל יְדֵי שׁוֹגֵג, כְּגוֹן שֶׁשָּׁגְגוּ וְהוֹרוּ עַל אַחַת מִן הָעֲבוֹדוֹת שֶׁהִיא מֻתֶּרֶת לַעֲבֹד עֲבוֹדָה זָרָה בְּכָךְ: **לְחַטָּת.** חָסֵר הָ"א, שֶׁאֵינוֹ כִּשְׁאָר חַטָּאוֹת, שֶׁכָּל חַטָּאוֹת שֶׁבַּתּוֹרָה הַבָּאוֹת עִם עוֹלָה הַחַטָּאת קוֹדֶמֶת לָעוֹלָה, שֶׁנֶּאֱמַר: "וְאֵת הַשֵּׁנִי יַעֲשֶׂה עֹלָה" (ויקרא ה, י), וְזוֹ עוֹלָה קוֹדֶמֶת לְחַטָּאת:

כה הֵבִיאוּ אֶת קָרְבָּנָם אִשֶּׁה לַה'. זֶה הָאָמוּר בַּפָּרָשָׁה, הוּא פַר הָעוֹלָה, שֶׁנֶּאֱמַר: "אִשֶּׁה לַה'": **וְחַטָּאתָם.** זֶה הַשָּׂעִיר:

כז תֶּחֱטָא בִשְׁגָגָה. בַּעֲבוֹדָה זָרָה: **עֵז בַּת שְׁנָתָהּ.** שְׁאָר עֲבֵרוֹת יָחִיד מֵבִיא כִּשְׂבָּה אוֹ שְׂעִירָה, וּבְזוֹ קָבַע לָהּ שְׂעִירָה:

ל בְּיָד רָמָה. בְּמֵזִיד: **מְגַדֵּף.** מְחָרֵף, כְּמוֹ: "וְהָיְתָה חֶרְפָּה וּגְדוּפָה" (יחזקאל ה, טו), "אֲשֶׁר גִּדְּפוּ נַעֲרֵי מֶלֶךְ אַשּׁוּר" (ישעיה לז, ו). וְעוֹד דָּרְשׁוּ רַבּוֹתֵינוּ, מִכָּאן לַמְבָרֵךְ אֶת הַשֵּׁם שֶׁהוּא בְּכָרֵת:

שלח | 392

מִקֶּ֥רֶב עַמָּֽהּ: כִּ֤י דְבַר־יהוה֙ בָּזָ֔ה וְאֶת־מִצְוָת֖וֹ הֵפַ֑ר הִכָּרֵ֧ת לא
תִכָּרֵ֛ת הַנֶּ֥פֶשׁ הַהִ֖וא עֲוֺנָ֥ה בָֽהּ:
וַיִּהְי֥וּ בְנֵֽי־יִשְׂרָאֵ֖ל בַּמִּדְבָּ֑ר וַֽיִּמְצְא֗וּ אִ֛ישׁ מְקֹשֵׁ֥שׁ עֵצִ֖ים בְּי֥וֹם לב
הַשַּׁבָּֽת: וַיַּקְרִ֣יבוּ אֹת֔וֹ הַמֹּצְאִ֥ים אֹת֖וֹ מְקֹשֵׁ֣שׁ עֵצִ֑ים אֶל־מֹשֶׁה֙ לג
וְאֶֽל־אַהֲרֹ֔ן וְאֶ֖ל כָּל־הָֽעֵדָֽה: וַיַּנִּ֥יחוּ אֹת֖וֹ בַּמִּשְׁמָ֑ר כִּ֚י לֹ֣א פֹרַ֔שׁ לד
מַה־יֵּֽעָשֶׂ֖ה לֽוֹ: וַיֹּ֤אמֶר יהוה֙ אֶל־מֹשֶׁ֔ה מ֥וֹת יוּמַ֖ת לה
הָאִ֑ישׁ רָג֨וֹם אֹת֤וֹ בָֽאֲבָנִים֙ כָּל־הָ֣עֵדָ֔ה מִח֖וּץ לַֽמַּחֲנֶֽה: וַיֹּצִ֨יאוּ לו
אֹת֜וֹ כָּל־הָעֵדָ֗ה אֶל־מִחוּץ֙ לַֽמַּחֲנֶ֔ה וַיִּרְגְּמ֥וּ אֹת֛וֹ בָּֽאֲבָנִ֖ים וַיָּמֹ֑ת
כַּאֲשֶׁ֛ר צִוָּ֥ה יהוה֖ אֶת־מֹשֶֽׁה:

מפטיר וַיֹּ֥אמֶר יהוה אֶל־מֹשֶׁ֥ה לֵּאמֹֽר: דַּבֵּ֞ר אֶל־בְּנֵ֤י יִשְׂרָאֵל֙ וְאָמַרְתָּ֣ לז־לח
אֲלֵהֶ֔ם וְעָשׂ֨וּ לָהֶ֥ם צִיצִ֛ת עַל־כַּנְפֵ֥י בִגְדֵיהֶ֖ם לְדֹרֹתָ֑ם וְנָ֥תְנ֛וּ
עַל־צִיצִ֥ת הַכָּנָ֖ף פְּתִ֥יל תְּכֵֽלֶת: וְהָיָ֣ה לָכֶם֮ לְצִיצִת֒ וּרְאִיתֶ֣ם לט
אֹת֗וֹ וּזְכַרְתֶּם֙ אֶת־כָּל־מִצְוֺ֣ת יהוה֔ וַעֲשִׂיתֶ֖ם אֹתָ֑ם וְלֹ֣א תָתֻ֜רוּ

לא] **דְּבַר ה׳.** אַזְהָרַת עֲבוֹדָה זָרָה מִפִּי הַגְּבוּרָה, וְהַשְּׁאָר מִפִּי מֹשֶׁה. **עֲוֺנָה בָהּ.** בִּזְמַן שֶׁעֲוֺנָה בָהּ, שֶׁלֹּא עָשָׂה תְשׁוּבָה:

לב] **וַיִּהְיוּ בְנֵי יִשְׂרָאֵל בַּמִּדְבָּר וַיִּמְצְאוּ.** בִּגְנוּתָן שֶׁל יִשְׂרָאֵל דִּבֶּר הַכָּתוּב, שֶׁלֹּא שָׁמְרוּ אֶלָּא שַׁבָּת רִאשׁוֹנָה, וּבַשְּׁנִיָּה בָּא זֶה וְחִלְּלָהּ:

לג] **הַמֹּצְאִים אֹתוֹ מְקֹשֵׁשׁ.** שֶׁהִתְרוּ בוֹ, וְלֹא הִנִּיחַ מִלְּקוֹשֵׁשׁ אַף מִשֶּׁמְּצָאוּהוּ וְהִתְרוּ בוֹ:

לד] **כִּי לֹא פֹרַשׁ מַה יֵּעָשֶׂה לוֹ.** לֹא הָיוּ יוֹדְעִים בְּאֵיזוֹ מִיתָה יָמוּת, אֲבָל יוֹדְעִים הָיוּ שֶׁהַמְחַלֵּל שַׁבָּת בְּמִיתָה:

לה] **רָגוֹם.** עָשׂה, פיישנ״ט בְּלַעַז, וְכֵן: "הָלוֹךְ" חלנ״ט, וְכֵן: "זָכוֹר" (שמות כ, ח) וְ"שָׁמוֹר" (דברים ה, יב):

לו] **וַיֹּצִיאוּ אֹתוֹ.** מִכָּאן שֶׁבֵּית הַסְּקִילָה חוּץ וְרָחוֹק מִבֵּית דִּין:

לח] **וְעָשׂוּ לָהֶם צִיצִת.** עַל שֵׁם הַפְּתִילִים הַתְּלוּיִים בָּהּ, כְּמוֹ: "וַיִּקָּחֵנִי בְּצִיצִת רֹאשִׁי" (יחזקאל ח, ג). דָּבָר אַחֵר, "צִיצִת" עַל שֵׁם "וּרְאִיתֶם אֹתוֹ", כְּמוֹ "מֵצִיץ מִן הַחֲרַכִּים" (שיר השירים ב, ט): **תְּכֵלֶת.** צֶבַע יָרֹק שֶׁל חִלָּזוֹן:

לט] **וּזְכַרְתֶּם אֶת כָּל מִצְוֺת ה׳.** שֶׁמִּנְיַן גִּימַטְרִיָּא שֶׁל צִיצִית שֵׁשׁ מֵאוֹת, וּשְׁמוֹנָה חוּטִים וַחֲמִשָּׁה קְשָׁרִים הֲרֵי תַּרְיַ״ג: **וְלֹא תָתוּרוּ אַחֲרֵי לְבַבְכֶם.** כְּמוֹ "מִתּוּר הָאָרֶץ" (לעיל יג, כה), הַלֵּב וְהָעֵינַיִם הֵם מְרַגְּלִים לַגּוּף, מְסַרְסְרִים לוֹ אֶת הָעֲבֵרוֹת, הָעַיִן רוֹאָה וְהַלֵּב חוֹמֵד וְהַגּוּף עוֹשֶׂה אֶת הָעֲבֵרוֹת:

אַחֲרֵי לְבַבְכֶם וְאַחֲרֵי עֵינֵיכֶם אֲשֶׁר־אַתֶּם זֹנִים אַחֲרֵיהֶם: לְמַעַן תִּזְכְּרוּ וַעֲשִׂיתֶם אֶת־כָּל־מִצְוֹתָי וִהְיִיתֶם קְדֹשִׁים לֵאלֹהֵיכֶם: אֲנִי יְהֹוָה אֱלֹהֵיכֶם אֲשֶׁר הוֹצֵאתִי אֶתְכֶם מֵאֶרֶץ מִצְרַיִם לִהְיוֹת לָכֶם לֵאלֹהִים אֲנִי יְהֹוָה אֱלֹהֵיכֶם:

טז קרח וַיִּקַּח קֹרַח בֶּן־יִצְהָר בֶּן־קְהָת בֶּן־לֵוִי וְדָתָן וַאֲבִירָם בְּנֵי אֱלִיאָב וְאוֹן בֶּן־פֶּלֶת בְּנֵי רְאוּבֵן: וַיָּקֻמוּ לִפְנֵי מֹשֶׁה וַאֲנָשִׁים מִבְּנֵי־יִשְׂרָאֵל חֲמִשִּׁים וּמָאתָיִם נְשִׂיאֵי עֵדָה קְרִאֵי מוֹעֵד אַנְשֵׁי־שֵׁם:

מא | **אֲנִי ה'.** נֶאֱמָן לְשַׁלֵּם שָׂכָר. **אֱלֹהֵיכֶם.** נֶאֱמָן לִפָּרַע. **אֲשֶׁר הוֹצֵאתִי אֶתְכֶם.** עַל מְנָת כֵּן פָּדִיתִי אֶתְכֶם שֶׁתְּקַבְּלוּ עֲלֵיכֶם גְּזֵרוֹתַי. **אֲנִי ה' אֱלֹהֵיכֶם.** עוֹד לָמָּה נֶאֱמַר? כְּדֵי שֶׁלֹּא יֹאמְרוּ יִשְׂרָאֵל: מִפְּנֵי מָה אָמַר הַמָּקוֹם, לֹא שֶׁנַּעֲשֶׂה וְנִטּוֹל שָׂכָר? אָנוּ לֹא עוֹשִׂים וְלֹא נוֹטְלִים שָׂכָר! עַל כָּרְחֲכֶם אֲנִי מַלְכְּכֶם, וְכֵן הוּא אוֹמֵר: "אִם לֹא בְּיָד חֲזָקָה... אֶמְלוֹךְ עֲלֵיכֶם" (יחזקאל כ, לג). דָּבָר אַחֵר, לָמָּה נֶאֱמַר יְצִיאַת מִצְרַיִם? אֲנִי הוּא שֶׁהִבְחַנְתִּי בְּמִצְרַיִם בֵּין טִפָּה שֶׁל בְּכוֹר לְשֶׁאֵינָהּ שֶׁל בְּכוֹר, אֲנִי הוּא עָתִיד לְהַבְחִין וּלְהִפָּרַע מִן הַתּוֹלֶה קָלָא אִילָן בְּבִגְדּוֹ וְאוֹמֵר: תְּכֵלֶת הִיא.

וּמִיסוֹדוֹ שֶׁל רַבִּי מֹשֶׁה הַדַּרְשָׁן הֶעְתַּקְתִּי: לָמָּה נִסְמְכָה פָּרָשַׁת מְקוֹשֵׁשׁ לְפָרָשַׁת עֲבוֹדָה זָרָה? לוֹמַר שֶׁהַמְחַלֵּל אֶת הַשַּׁבָּת כְּעוֹבֵד עֲבוֹדָה זָרָה, שֶׁאַף הִיא שְׁקוּלָה כְּכָל הַמִּצְוֹת. וְכֵן הוּא אוֹמֵר בְּעֶזְרָא: "וְעַל הַר סִינַי יָרַדְתָּ... וַתִּתֵּן לְעַמְּךָ תּוֹרָה וּמִצְוֹת וְאֶת שַׁבַּת קָדְשְׁךָ הוֹדַעְתָּ לָהֶם" (נחמיה ט, יג-יד). וְאַף פָּרָשַׁת צִיצִית לְכָךְ נִסְמְכָה לְכָאן, לְפִי שֶׁאַף הִיא שְׁקוּלָה כְּנֶגֶד כָּל הַמִּצְוֹת, שֶׁנֶּאֱמַר: "וַעֲשִׂיתֶם אֶת כָּל מִצְוֹתַי". **עַל כַּנְפֵי בִגְדֵיהֶם.** כְּנֶגֶד "וָאֶשָּׂא אֶתְכֶם עַל כַּנְפֵי נְשָׁרִים" (שמות יט, ד). עַל אַרְבַּע כְּנָפוֹת, וְלֹא בַּעֲלַת שָׁלֹשׁ וְלֹא בַּעֲלַת חָמֵשׁ, כְּנֶגֶד אַרְבַּע לְשׁוֹנוֹת שֶׁל גְּאֻלָּה שֶׁנֶּאֶמְרוּ בְּמִצְרַיִם: "וְהוֹצֵאתִי", "וְהִצַּלְתִּי", "וְגָאַלְתִּי", "וְלָקַחְתִּי" (שמות ו, ו-ז). **פְּתִיל תְּכֵלֶת.** עַל שֵׁם שִׁכּוּל בְּכוֹרוֹת, תַּרְגּוּמוֹ שֶׁל שִׁכּוּל: 'תְּכָלָא'. וּמַכָּתָם הָיְתָה בַּלַּיְלָה, וְכֵן צֶבַע הַתְּכֵלֶת דּוֹמֶה לָרָקִיעַ הַמַּשְׁחִיר לְעֵת עֶרֶב. וּשְׁמוֹנָה חוּטִים שֶׁבָּהּ, כְּנֶגֶד שְׁמוֹנָה יָמִים שֶׁשָּׁהוּ יִשְׂרָאֵל מִשֶּׁיָּצְאוּ מִמִּצְרַיִם עַד שֶׁאָמְרוּ שִׁירָה עַל הַיָּם:

פרק טז

א | **וַיִּקַּח קֹרַח.** פָּרָשָׁה זוֹ יָפֶה נִדְרֶשֶׁת בְּמִדְרַשׁ רַבִּי תַּנְחוּמָא. **וַיִּקַּח קֹרַח.** לָקַח אֶת עַצְמוֹ לְצַד אֶחָד לִהְיוֹת נֶחֱלָק מִתּוֹךְ הָעֵדָה לְעוֹרֵר עַל הַכְּהֻנָּה, וְזֶהוּ שֶׁתִּרְגֵּם אוּנְקְלוֹס: "וְאִתְפְּלֵג", נֶחֱלַק מִשְּׁאָר הָעֵדָה לְהַחֲזִיק בְּמַחֲלֹקֶת. וְכֵן: "מַה יִּקָּחֲךָ לִבֶּךָ" (איוב טו, יב), לוֹקֵחַ אוֹתְךָ לְהַפְלִיגְךָ מִשְּׁאָר בְּנֵי אָדָם. דָּבָר אַחֵר, "וַיִּקַּח קֹרַח", מָשַׁךְ רָאשֵׁי סַנְהֶדְרָאוֹת שֶׁבָּהֶם בִּדְבָרִים, כְּמוֹ שֶׁנֶּאֱמַר: "קַח אֶת אַהֲרֹן" (ויקרא ח, ב), "קְחוּ עִמָּכֶם דְּבָרִים" (הושע יד, ג). **בֶּן־יִצְהָר בֶּן־קְהָת בֶּן־לֵוִי.** וְלֹא הִזְכִּיר "בֶּן יַעֲקֹב", שֶׁבִּקֵּשׁ רַחֲמִים עַל עַצְמוֹ שֶׁלֹּא יִזָּכֵר שְׁמוֹ עַל מַחְלָקְתָּם, שֶׁנֶּאֱמַר: "בִּקְהָלָם אַל תֵּחַד כְּבֹדִי" (בראשית מט, ו). וְהֵיכָן נִזְכַּר שְׁמוֹ עַל קֹרַח? בְּהִתְיַחֲסָם עַל הַדּוּכָן בְּדִבְרֵי הַיָּמִים, שֶׁנֶּאֱמַר: "בֶּן אֶבְיָסָף בֶּן קֹרַח בֶּן יִצְהָר בֶּן קְהָת בֶּן לֵוִי בֶּן יִשְׂרָאֵל" (דברי הימים א' ו, כב-כג). **וְדָתָן וַאֲבִירָם.** בִּשְׁבִיל שֶׁהָיָה שֵׁבֶט רְאוּבֵן שָׁרוּי בַּחֲנִיָּתָם תֵּימָנָה, שָׁכֵן לִקְהָת וּבָנָיו הַחוֹנִים תֵּימָנָה, נִשְׁתַּתְּפוּ עִם קֹרַח בְּמַחְלָקְתּוֹ, אוֹי לָרָשָׁע אוֹי לִשְׁכֵנוֹ. וּמָה רָאָה קֹרַח לַחֲלֹק עִם מֹשֶׁה? נִתְקַנֵּא עַל נְשִׂיאוּתוֹ שֶׁל אֱלִיצָפָן בֶּן עֻזִּיאֵל, שֶׁמִּנָּהוּ מֹשֶׁה נָשִׂיא עַל בְּנֵי קְהָת עַל פִּי הַדִּבּוּר. אָמַר קֹרַח: אַחֵי אַבָּא אַרְבָּעָה הָיוּ, שֶׁנֶּאֱמַר: "וּבְנֵי קְהָת" וְגוֹ' (שמות ו, יח), עַמְרָם הַבְּכוֹר נָטְלוּ שְׁנֵי בָנָיו גְּדֻלָּה, אֶחָד מֶלֶךְ וְאֶחָד כֹּהֵן גָּדוֹל, מִי רָאוּי לִטֹּל אֶת הַשְּׁנִיָּה? לֹא אֲנִי, שֶׁאֲנִי בֶּן יִצְהָר שֶׁהוּא שֵׁנִי לְעַמְרָם? וְהוּא

ג וַיִּקָּהֲל֞וּ עַל־מֹשֶׁ֣ה וְעַֽל־אַהֲרֹ֗ן וַיֹּאמְר֣וּ אֲלֵהֶם֮ רַב־לָכֶם֒ כִּ֤י כָל־הָֽעֵדָה֙ כֻּלָּ֣ם קְדֹשִׁ֔ים וּבְתוֹכָ֖ם יְהוָ֑ה וּמַדּ֥וּעַ תִּֽתְנַשְּׂא֖וּ עַל־קְהַ֥ל יְהוָֽה׃
ד וַיִּשְׁמַ֣ע מֹשֶׁ֔ה וַיִּפֹּ֖ל עַל־פָּנָֽיו׃ וַיְדַבֵּ֨ר אֶל־קֹ֜רַח וְאֶֽל־
ה כָּל־עֲדָתוֹ֮ לֵאמֹר֒ בֹּ֠קֶר וְיֹדַ֨ע יְהוָ֧ה אֶת־אֲשֶׁר־ל֛וֹ וְאֶת־הַקָּד֖וֹשׁ וְהִקְרִ֣יב אֵלָ֑יו וְאֵ֛ת אֲשֶׁ֥ר יִבְחַר־בּ֖וֹ יַקְרִ֥יב אֵלָֽיו׃
ו זֹ֖את עֲשׂ֑וּ קְחוּ־לָכֶ֣ם מַחְתּ֔וֹת קֹ֖רַח וְכָל־עֲדָתֽוֹ׃ וּתְנ֣וּ בָהֵ֣ן ׀ אֵ֗שׁ וְשִׂימוּ֩
ז עֲלֵיהֶ֨ן קְטֹ֜רֶת לִפְנֵ֤י יְהוָה֙ מָחָ֔ר וְהָיָ֗ה הָאִ֛ישׁ אֲשֶׁר־יִבְחַ֥ר

מָנָה נָשִׂיא אֶת בֶּן אָחִיו הַקָּטָן מִכֻּלָּם! הֲרֵינִי חוֹלֵק עָלָיו וּמְבַטֵּל אֶת דְּבָרָיו. מֶה עָשָׂה? עָמַד וְכִנֵּס מָאתַיִם וַחֲמִשִּׁים רָאשֵׁי סַנְהֶדְרָאוֹת, רֻבָּן מִשֵּׁבֶט רְאוּבֵן שְׁכֵנָיו, וְהֵם אֱלִיצוּר בֶּן שְׁדֵיאוּר וַחֲבֵרָיו וְכַיּוֹצֵא בּוֹ, שֶׁנֶּאֱמַר: "נְשִׂיאֵי עֵדָה קְרִאֵי מוֹעֵד" (להלן פסוק ב), וּלְהַלָּן הוּא אוֹמֵר: "אֵלֶּה קְרוּאֵי הָעֵדָה" (לעיל א, טז), וְהִלְבִּישָׁן טַלִּיתוֹת שֶׁכֻּלָּן תְּכֵלֶת, בָּאוּ וְעָמְדוּ לִפְנֵי מֹשֶׁה, אָמְרוּ לוֹ: טַלִּית שֶׁכֻּלָּהּ שֶׁל תְּכֵלֶת חַיֶּבֶת בְּצִיצִית אוֹ פְּטוּרָה? אָמַר לָהֶם: חַיֶּבֶת. הִתְחִילוּ לִשְׂחֹק עָלָיו: אֶפְשָׁר טַלִּית שֶׁל מִין אַחֵר, חוּט אֶחָד שֶׁל תְּכֵלֶת פּוֹטְרָהּ, זוֹ שֶׁכֻּלָּהּ תְּכֵלֶת לֹא תִּפְטֹר אֶת עַצְמָהּ?!: בְּנֵי רְאוּבֵן. דָּתָן וַאֲבִירָם וְאוֹן בֶּן פֶּלֶת:

ג רַב לָכֶם. הַרְבֵּה יוֹתֵר מִדַּאי לְקַחְתֶּם לְעַצְמְכֶם גְּדֻלָּה: כֻּלָּם קְדֹשִׁים. כֻּלָּם שָׁמְעוּ דְבָרִים בְּסִינַי מִפִּי הַגְּבוּרָה: וּמַדּוּעַ תִּתְנַשְּׂאוּ. אִם לָקַחְתָּ אַתָּה מַלְכוּת, לֹא הָיָה לְךָ לִבְרֹר לְךָ אָחִיךָ כְּהֻנָּה, לֹא אַתֶּם לְבַדְּכֶם שְׁמַעְתֶּם בְּסִינַי: "אָנֹכִי ה' אֱלֹהֶיךָ", כָּל הָעֵדָה שָׁמָעוּ:

ד וַיִּפֹּל עַל פָּנָיו. מִפְּנֵי הַמַּחֲלֹקֶת, שֶׁכְּבָר זֶה בְּיָדָם סִרְחוֹן רְבִיעִי. [חָטְאוּ בָּעֵגֶל, "וַיְחַל מֹשֶׁה" (שמות לב, יא), בַּמִּתְאוֹנְנִים, "וַיִּתְפַּלֵּל מֹשֶׁה" (לעיל יא, ב), בַּמְּרַגְּלִים, "וַיֹּאמֶר מֹשֶׁה אֶל ה'" (לעיל יד, יג), וְשָׁמְעוּ מִמִּצְרַיִם בְּמַחְלָקְתּוֹ שֶׁל קֹרַח נִתְרַשְּׁלוּ יָדָיו. מָשָׁל לְבֶן מֶלֶךְ שֶׁסָּרַח עַל אָבִיו, וּפִיֵּס עָלָיו אוֹהֲבוֹ פַּעַם וּשְׁתַּיִם וְשָׁלֹשׁ, כְּשֶׁסָּרַח רְבִיעִית נִתְרַשְּׁלוּ יְדֵי הָאוֹהֵב הַהוּא, אָמַר: עַד מָתַי אַטְרִיחַ עַל הַמֶּלֶךְ? שֶׁמָּא לֹא יְקַבֵּל עוֹד מִמֶּנִּי:

ה בֹּקֶר וְיֹדַע וְגוֹ'. עַתָּה עֵת שִׁכְרוּת הוּא לָנוּ וְלֹא נָכוֹן לְהֵרָאוֹת לְפָנָיו. וְהוּא הָיָה מִתְכַּוֵּן לְדַחוֹתָם, שֶׁמָּא יַחְזְרוּ בָּהֶם: בֹּקֶר וְיֹדַע ה' אֶת אֲשֶׁר לוֹ. לַעֲבוֹדַת לְוִיָּה: וְאֶת הַקָּדוֹשׁ. לִכְהֻנָּה: וְהִקְרִיב. אוֹתָם "אֵלָיו":

ו-ז [תּוֹסֶפֶת מֵאִגֶּרֶת רַבֵּנוּ שְׁמַעְיָה: זֹאת עֲשׂוּ קְחוּ לָכֶם מַחְתּוֹת. מָה רָאָה לוֹמַר לָהֶם כָּךְ? אָמַר לָהֶם: בְּדַרְכֵי הַגּוֹיִם יֵשׁ נִמּוּסִים הַרְבֵּה וּכְמָרִים הַרְבֵּה, וְאֵין כֻּלָּם מִתְקַבְּצִין בְּבַיִת אֶחָד. אָנוּ אֵין לָנוּ אֶלָּא ה' אֶחָד, אָרוֹן אֶחָד וְתוֹרָה אַחַת וּמִזְבֵּחַ אֶחָד וְכֹהֵן גָּדוֹל אֶחָד, וְאַתֶּם חֲמִשִּׁים וּמָאתַיִם אִישׁ מְבַקְּשִׁים כְּהֻנָּה גְּדוֹלָה? אַף אֲנִי רוֹצֶה בְּכָךְ. הֵא לָכֶם תַּשְׁמִישׁ חָבִיב מִכֹּל, הִיא הַקְּטֹרֶת הַחֲבִיבָה מִכָּל הַקָּרְבָּנוֹת, וְסַם הַמָּוֶת נָתוּן בְּתוֹכוֹ שֶׁבּוֹ נִשְׂרְפוּ נָדָב וַאֲבִיהוּא, לְפִיכָךְ הִתְרָה בָּהֶם: "וְהָיָה הָאִישׁ אֲשֶׁר יִבְחַר ה' הוּא הַקָּדוֹשׁ" (להלן פסוק ז), כְּבָר הוּא בִּקְדֻשָּׁתוֹ, וְכִי אֵין אָנוּ יוֹדְעִים שֶׁמִּי שֶׁיִּבְחַר הוּא הַקָּדוֹשׁ? אֶלָּא אָמַר לָהֶם מֹשֶׁה: הֲרֵינִי אוֹמֵר לָכֶם, שֶׁלֹּא תִתְחַיְּבוּ, מִי שֶׁיִּבְחַר בּוֹ יֵצֵא חַי וְכֻלְּכֶם אוֹבְדִים: רַב לָכֶם בְּנֵי לֵוִי. דָּבָר גָּדוֹל אָמַרְתִּי לָכֶם, וְלֹא טִפְּשִׁים הָיוּ שֶׁכָּךְ הִתְרָה בָּהֶם וְקִבְּלוּ עֲלֵיהֶם לְקָרֵב, אֶלָּא הֵם חָטְאוּ עַל נַפְשׁוֹתָם, שֶׁנֶּאֱמַר: "אֵת מַחְתּוֹת הַחַטָּאִים הָאֵלֶּה בְּנַפְשֹׁתָם" (להלן יז, ג): וְקֹרַח שֶׁפִּקֵּחַ הָיָה, מָה רָאָה לִשְׁטוּת זוֹ? עֵינוֹ הִטְעַתּוֹ, רָאָה שַׁלְשֶׁלֶת גְּדוֹלָה יוֹצְאָה מִמֶּנּוּ – שְׁמוּאֵל שֶׁשָּׁקוּל כְּנֶגֶד מֹשֶׁה וְאַהֲרֹן, אָמַר: בִּשְׁבִילוֹ אֲנִי נִמְלָט, וְעֶשְׂרִים וְאַרְבָּעָה מִשְׁמָרוֹת עוֹמְדוֹת לִבְנֵי בָנָיו כֻּלָּם מִתְנַבְּאִים בְּרוּחַ הַקֹּדֶשׁ, שֶׁנֶּאֱמַר: "כָּל אֵלֶּה בָנִים לְהֵימָן" (דברי הימים א' כה,

ח יהוה הוא הַקָּדוֹשׁ רַב־לָכֶם בְּנֵי לֵוִי: וַיֹּאמֶר מֹשֶׁה אֶל־קֹרַח
ט שִׁמְעוּ־נָא בְּנֵי לֵוִי: הַמְעַט מִכֶּם כִּי־הִבְדִּיל אֱלֹהֵי יִשְׂרָאֵל
אֶתְכֶם מֵעֲדַת יִשְׂרָאֵל לְהַקְרִיב אֶתְכֶם אֵלָיו לַעֲבֹד אֶת־עֲבֹדַת
י מִשְׁכַּן יהוה וְלַעֲמֹד לִפְנֵי הָעֵדָה לְשָׁרְתָם: וַיַּקְרֵב אֹתְךָ וְאֶת־
כָּל־אַחֶיךָ בְנֵי־לֵוִי אִתָּךְ וּבִקַּשְׁתֶּם גַּם־כְּהֻנָּה: לָכֵן אַתָּה וְכָל־
יא עֲדָתְךָ הַנֹּעָדִים עַל־יהוה וְאַהֲרֹן מַה־הוּא כִּי תַלִּינוּ [תַלּוֹנוּ] עָלָיו:
יב וַיִּשְׁלַח מֹשֶׁה לִקְרֹא לְדָתָן וְלַאֲבִירָם בְּנֵי אֱלִיאָב וַיֹּאמְרוּ לֹא
יג נַעֲלֶה: הַמְעַט כִּי הֶעֱלִיתָנוּ מֵאֶרֶץ זָבַת חָלָב וּדְבַשׁ לַהֲמִיתֵנוּ
יד בַּמִּדְבָּר כִּי־תִשְׂתָּרֵר עָלֵינוּ גַּם־הִשְׂתָּרֵר: אַף לֹא אֶל־אֶרֶץ שני
זָבַת חָלָב וּדְבַשׁ הֲבִיאֹתָנוּ וַתִּתֶּן־לָנוּ נַחֲלַת שָׂדֶה וָכָרֶם הַעֵינֵי

ח. אָמַר. חָפְשׁוּ אֶפְשָׁר כָּל הָעֵדָה הַזֹּאת עֲתִידָה לַעֲמֹד מִמֶּנִּי וַחֲנִי לְחַד? לְכָךְ נִשְׁתַּתֵּף לָהֶם לְחוֹתָה חֲזָקָה, שֶׁיִּשְׁמַע מִפִּי מֹשֶׁה שֶׁכֻּלָּם אוֹבְדִים וְאֶחָד נִמְלָט – "אֲשֶׁר יִבְחַר ה' הוּא הַקָּדוֹשׁ", טָעָה וְתָלָה בְּעַצְמוֹ. וְלֹא דָּחָה יָפֶה, לְפִי שֶׁבָּנָיו עָשׂוּ תְּשׁוּבָה, וּמֹשֶׁה הָיָה רוֹאֶה. תַּנְחוּמָא (ה'). מַחְתּוֹת. כֵּלִים שֶׁחוֹתִין בָּהֶם גֶּחָלִים וְיֵשׁ לָהֶם בֵּית יָד: רַב לָכֶם. דָּבָר גָּדוֹל נְטַלְתֶּם בְּעַצְמְכֶם, לַחֲלֹק עַל הַקָּדוֹשׁ בָּרוּךְ הוּא:

ח. וַיֹּאמֶר מֹשֶׁה אֶל קֹרַח שִׁמְעוּ נָא בְּנֵי לֵוִי. הִתְחִיל לְדַבֵּר עִמּוֹ דְּבָרִים רַכִּים, כֵּיוָן שֶׁרָאָהוּ קְשֵׁה עֹרֶף, אָמַר: עַד שֶׁלֹּא יִשְׁתַּתְּפוּ שְׁאָר הַשְּׁבָטִים וְיֹאבְדוּ עִמּוֹ אֲדַבֵּר גַּם אֶל כֻּלָּם. הִתְחִיל לוֹמַר לָהֶם: "שִׁמְעוּ נָא בְּנֵי לֵוִי":

ט. וְלַעֲמֹד לִפְנֵי הָעֵדָה. לָשִׁיר עַל הַדּוּכָן:

י. וַיַּקְרֵב אֹתְךָ. לְאוֹתוֹ שֵׁרוּת שֶׁהִרְחִיק מִמֶּנּוּ שְׁאָר עֲדַת יִשְׂרָאֵל:

יא. לָכֵן. בִּשְׁבִיל כָּךְ, "אַתָּה וְכָל עֲדָתְךָ הַנֹּעָדִים" אִתָּךְ, "עַל ה'", כִּי בִּשְׁלִיחוּתוֹ עָשִׂיתִי לָתֵת כְּהֻנָּה לְאַהֲרֹן, וְלֹא לָנוּ הוּא הַמַּחֲלֹקֶת הַזֶּה:

יב. וַיִּשְׁלַח מֹשֶׁה וְגוֹ'. מִכָּאן שֶׁאֵין מַחֲזִיקִין בְּמַחֲלֹקֶת, שֶׁהָיָה מֹשֶׁה מְחַזֵּר אַחֲרֵיהֶם לְהַשְׁלִימָם בְּדִבְרֵי שָׁלוֹם: לֹא נַעֲלֶה. פִּיהֶם הִכְשִׁילָם, שֶׁאֵין לָהֶם אֶלָּא יְרִידָה:

יד. וַתִּתֶּן לָנוּ. הַדָּבָר מוּסָב עַל 'לֹא' הָאָמוּר לְמַעְלָה, כְּלוֹמַר: לֹא הֲבִיאֹתָנוּ וְלֹא נָתַתָּ לָנוּ נַחֲלַת שָׂדֶה וָכָרֶם. אָמַרְתָּ לָנוּ: מַעֲלֶה אֶתְכֶם מֵעֳנִי מִצְרַיִם אֶל אֶרֶץ טוֹבָה וְגוֹ' (שמות ג, ח), מִשָּׁם הוֹצֵאתָנוּ, וְלֹא אֶל אֶרֶץ זָבַת חָלָב וּדְבַשׁ הֲבִיאֹתָנוּ, אֶלָּא גָּזַרְתָּ עָלֵינוּ לַהֲמִיתֵנוּ בַּמִּדְבָּר, שֶׁאָמַרְתָּ לָנוּ: "בַּמִּדְבָּר הַזֶּה יִפְּלוּ פִגְרֵיכֶם" (לעיל יד, כט): הַעֵינֵי הָאֲנָשִׁים הָהֵם תְּנַקֵּר וְגוֹ'. אֲפִלּוּ אַתָּה שׁוֹלֵחַ לְנַקֵּר אֶת עֵינֵינוּ אִם לֹא נַעֲלֶה אֵלֶיךָ, לֹא נַעֲלֶה: הָאֲנָשִׁים הָהֵם. כְּאָדָם הַתּוֹלֶה קִלְלָתוֹ בַּחֲבֵרוֹ:

הָאֲנָשִׁ֧ים הָהֵ֛ם תְּנַקֵּ֖ר לֹ֣א נַעֲלֶֽה: וַיִּ֤חַר לְמֹשֶׁה֙ מְאֹ֔ד וַיֹּ֙אמֶר֙ אֶל־יְהֹוָ֔ה אַל־תֵּ֖פֶן אֶל־מִנְחָתָ֑ם לֹ֠א חֲמ֨וֹר אֶחָ֤ד מֵהֶם֙ נָשָׂ֔אתִי וְלֹ֥א הֲרֵעֹ֖תִי אֶת־אַחַ֥ד מֵהֶֽם: וַיֹּ֤אמֶר מֹשֶׁה֙ אֶל־קֹ֔רַח אַתָּה֙ וְכׇל־עֲדָ֣תְךָ֔ הֱי֖וּ לִפְנֵ֣י יְהֹוָ֑ה אַתָּ֥ה וָהֵ֛ם וְאַהֲרֹ֖ן מָחָֽר: וּקְח֣וּ ׀ אִ֣ישׁ מַחְתָּת֗וֹ וּנְתַתֶּ֤ם עֲלֵיהֶם֙ קְטֹ֔רֶת וְהִקְרַבְתֶּ֞ם לִפְנֵ֤י יְהֹוָה֙ אִ֣ישׁ מַחְתָּת֔וֹ חֲמִשִּׁ֥ים וּמָאתַ֖יִם מַחְתֹּ֑ת וְאַתָּ֥ה וְאַהֲרֹ֖ן אִ֥ישׁ מַחְתָּתֽוֹ: וַיִּקְח֞וּ אִ֣ישׁ מַחְתָּת֗וֹ וַיִּתְּנ֤וּ עֲלֵיהֶם֙ אֵ֔שׁ וַיָּשִׂ֥ימוּ עֲלֵיהֶ֖ם קְטֹ֑רֶת וַֽיַּעַמְד֗וּ פֶּ֛תַח אֹ֥הֶל מוֹעֵ֖ד וּמֹשֶׁ֥ה וְאַהֲרֹֽן: וַיַּקְהֵ֤ל עֲלֵיהֶם֙ קֹ֔רַח אֶת־כׇּל־הָעֵדָ֔ה אֶל־פֶּ֖תַח אֹ֣הֶל מוֹעֵ֑ד וַיֵּרָ֥א כְבוֹד־יְהֹוָ֖ה אֶל־כׇּל־הָעֵדָֽה: וַיְדַבֵּ֣ר יְהֹוָ֔ה אֶל־מֹשֶׁ֥ה וְאֶֽל־אַהֲרֹ֖ן לֵאמֹֽר: הִבָּ֣דְל֔וּ מִתּ֖וֹךְ הָעֵדָ֣ה הַזֹּ֑את וַאֲכַלֶּ֥ה אֹתָ֖ם כְּרָֽגַע: וַיִּפְּל֣וּ עַל־פְּנֵיהֶ֔ם וַיֹּ֣אמְר֔וּ אֵ֕ל אֱלֹהֵ֥י הָרוּחֹ֖ת לְכׇל־בָּשָׂ֑ר הָאִ֤ישׁ אֶחָד֙ יֶחֱטָ֔א וְעַ֥ל כׇּל־הָעֵדָ֖ה תִּקְצֹֽף: וַיְדַבֵּ֥ר יְהֹוָ֖ה אֶל־מֹשֶׁ֥ה

טו **אל תפן אל מנחתם.** לפי פשוטו, הקטורת שהם מקריבין לפניך מחר אל תפן אליהם. ומדרש אומר: יודע אני שיש להם חלק בתמידי צבור, אף חלקם לא יקבל לפניך לרצון, תניחנו האש ולא תאכלנו. **לא חמור אחד מהם נשאתי.** לא חמורו של אחד מהם נטלתי, אפלו כשהלכתי ממדין למצרים והרכבתי את אשתי ואת בני על החמור, והיה לי לטול אותו החמור משלהם, לא נטלתי אלא משלי. "שחרית", לשון ארמי, כך נקראת אתגריא של מלך 'שחור':

וָהֵם. עֲדָתְךָ:

טז **וְהִקְרַבְתֶּם... אִישׁ מַחְתָּתוֹ. הַחֲמִשִּׁים וּמָאתַיִם אִישׁ שֶׁבָּכֶם**:

יט **וַיַּקְהֵל עֲלֵיהֶם קֹרַח.** בְּדִבְרֵי לַעֲגוּת. כָּל הַלַּיְלָה הַהוּא הָלַךְ אֵצֶל הַשְּׁבָטִים וּפִתָּה אוֹתָם: כִּסְבוּרִין אַתֶּם שֶׁעָלַי לְבַדִּי אֲנִי מַקְפִּיד? אֵינִי מַקְפִּיד אֶלָּא בִּשְׁבִיל כֻּלְּכֶם, אֵלּוּ בָּאִין וְנוֹטְלִין כָּל הַגְּדֻלּוֹת, לוֹ הַמַּלְכוּת וּלְאָחִיו הַכְּהֻנָּה! עַד שֶׁנִּתְפַּתּוּ כֻלָּם: **וַיֵּרָא כְבוֹד ה'.** בָּא בְּעַמּוּד עָנָן:

כב **אֵל אֱלֹהֵי הָרוּחֹת.** יוֹדֵעַ מַחְשָׁבוֹת. אֵין מִדָּתְךָ כְמִדַּת בָּשָׂר וָדָם, מֶלֶךְ בָּשָׂר וָדָם שֶׁסָּרְחָה עָלָיו מִקְצָת מְדִינָה אֵינוֹ יוֹדֵעַ מִי הַחוֹטֵא, לְפִיכָךְ כְּשֶׁהוּא כּוֹעֵס נִפְרָע מִכֻּלָּם. אֲבָל אַתָּה, לְפָנֶיךָ גְּלוּיוֹת כָּל הַמַּחֲשָׁבוֹת וְיוֹדֵעַ אַתָּה מִי הַחוֹטֵא: **הָאִישׁ אֶחָד.** הוּא הַחוֹטֵא וְאַתָּה "עַל כָּל הָעֵדָה תִּקְצֹף"? אָמַר הַקָּדוֹשׁ בָּרוּךְ הוּא: יָפֶה אֲמַרְתֶּם, אֲנִי יוֹדֵעַ וּמוֹדִיעַ מִי חָטָא וּמִי לֹא חָטָא:

כד לֵאמֹר: דַּבֵּר אֶל־הָעֵדָה לֵאמֹר הֵעָלוּ מִסָּבִיב לְמִשְׁכַּן־קֹרַח
כה דָּתָן וַאֲבִירָם: וַיָּקָם מֹשֶׁה וַיֵּלֶךְ אֶל־דָּתָן וַאֲבִירָם וַיֵּלְכוּ אַחֲרָיו
זִקְנֵי יִשְׂרָאֵל: וַיְדַבֵּר אֶל־הָעֵדָה לֵאמֹר סוּרוּ נָא מֵעַל אָהֳלֵי
הָאֲנָשִׁים הָרְשָׁעִים הָאֵלֶּה וְאַל־תִּגְּעוּ בְּכָל־אֲשֶׁר לָהֶם פֶּן־
כז תִּסָּפוּ בְּכָל־חַטֹּאתָם: וַיֵּעָלוּ מֵעַל מִשְׁכַּן־קֹרַח דָּתָן וַאֲבִירָם
מִסָּבִיב וְדָתָן וַאֲבִירָם יָצְאוּ נִצָּבִים פֶּתַח אָהֳלֵיהֶם וּנְשֵׁיהֶם
כח וּבְנֵיהֶם וְטַפָּם: וַיֹּאמֶר מֹשֶׁה בְּזֹאת תֵּדְעוּן כִּי־יהוה שְׁלָחַנִי
כט לַעֲשׂוֹת אֵת כָּל־הַמַּעֲשִׂים הָאֵלֶּה כִּי־לֹא מִלִּבִּי: אִם־כְּמוֹת כָּל־
הָאָדָם יְמֻתוּן אֵלֶּה וּפְקֻדַּת כָּל־הָאָדָם יִפָּקֵד עֲלֵיהֶם לֹא יהוה
ל שְׁלָחָנִי: וְאִם־בְּרִיאָה יִבְרָא יהוה וּפָצְתָה הָאֲדָמָה אֶת־פִּיהָ
וּבָלְעָה אֹתָם וְאֶת־כָּל־אֲשֶׁר לָהֶם וְיָרְדוּ חַיִּים שְׁאֹלָה וִידַעְתֶּם
לא כִּי נִאֲצוּ הָאֲנָשִׁים הָאֵלֶּה אֶת־יהוה: וַיְהִי כְּכַלֹּתוֹ לְדַבֵּר אֵת
לב כָּל־הַדְּבָרִים הָאֵלֶּה וַתִּבָּקַע הָאֲדָמָה אֲשֶׁר תַּחְתֵּיהֶם: וַתִּפְתַּח
הָאָרֶץ אֶת־פִּיהָ וַתִּבְלַע אֹתָם וְאֶת־בָּתֵּיהֶם וְאֵת כָּל־הָאָדָם
לג אֲשֶׁר לְקֹרַח וְאֵת כָּל־הָרְכוּשׁ: וַיֵּרְדוּ הֵם וְכָל־אֲשֶׁר לָהֶם חַיִּים

כד | הֵעָלוּ וְגוֹ'. כְּתַרְגּוּמוֹ, "הִסְתַּלָּקוּ" מִסְּבִיבוֹת מִשְׁכַּן קֹרַח:

כה | וַיָּקָם מֹשֶׁה. כְּסָבוּר שֶׁיִּשְּׂאוּ לוֹ פָּנִים וְלֹא עָשׂוּ:

כו | יָצְאוּ נִצָּבִים. בְּקוֹמָה זְקוּפָה לְחָרֵף וּלְגַדֵּף, כְּמוֹ "וַיִּתְיַצֵּב אַרְבָּעִים יוֹם" (שמואל א' י"ז, ט"ז): וּנְשֵׁיהֶם וּבְנֵיהֶם וְטַפָּם. בֹּא וּרְאֵה כַּמָּה קָשָׁה הַמַּחֲלֹקֶת, שֶׁהֲרֵי בֵּית דִּין שֶׁל מַטָּה אֵין עוֹנְשִׁין אֶלָּא עַד שֶׁיָּבִיא שְׁתֵּי שְׂעָרוֹת, וּבֵית דִּין שֶׁל מַעְלָה עַד עֶשְׂרִים שָׁנָה, וְכָאן אָבְדוּ אַף יוֹנְקֵי שָׁדַיִם:

כח | לַעֲשׂוֹת אֵת כָּל הַמַּעֲשִׂים הָאֵלֶּה. שֶׁעָשִׂיתִי עַל פִּי הַדִּבּוּר, לָתֵת לְאַהֲרֹן כְּהֻנָּה גְּדוֹלָה, וּבָנָיו סְגָנֵי כְהֻנָּה, וֶאֱלִיצָפָן נְשִׂיא הַקְּהָתִי:

כט | לֹא ה' שְׁלָחָנִי. אֶלָּא אֲנִי עָשִׂיתִי הַכֹּל מִדַּעְתִּי, וּבַדִּין הוּא חוֹלֵק עָלַי:

ל | וְאִם בְּרִיאָה. חֲדָשָׁה: יִבְרָא ה'. לְהָמִית אוֹתָם בְּמִיתָה שֶׁלֹּא מֵת בָּהּ אָדָם עַד הֵנָּה, וּמַה הִיא הַבְּרִיאָה? "וּפָצְתָה הָאֲדָמָה אֶת פִּיהָ" וְתִבְלָעֵם, אָז "וִידַעְתֶּם כִּי נִאֲצוּ" הֵם, וַאֲנִי מִפִּי הַגְּבוּרָה אָמַרְתִּי. וְרַבּוֹתֵינוּ פֵּרְשׁוּ: "אִם בְּרִיאָה" – פֶּה לָאָרֶץ מִשֵּׁשֶׁת יְמֵי בְרֵאשִׁית, מוּטָב, וְאִם לָאו – "יִבְרָא ה'":

פרק יז | במדבר

לד שָׁאֹלָה וַתְּכַס עֲלֵיהֶם הָאָרֶץ וַיֹּאבְדוּ מִתּוֹךְ הַקָּהָל: וְכָל־יִשְׂרָאֵל
לה אֲשֶׁר סְבִיבֹתֵיהֶם נָסוּ לְקֹלָם כִּי אָמְרוּ פֶּן־תִּבְלָעֵנוּ הָאָרֶץ: וְאֵשׁ
יָצְאָה מֵאֵת יְהוָה וַתֹּאכַל אֵת הַחֲמִשִּׁים וּמָאתַיִם אִישׁ מַקְרִיבֵי
הַקְּטֹרֶת: וַיְדַבֵּר יְהוָה אֶל־מֹשֶׁה לֵּאמֹר: אֱמֹר א יז
אֶל־אֶלְעָזָר בֶּן־אַהֲרֹן הַכֹּהֵן וְיָרֵם אֶת־הַמַּחְתֹּת מִבֵּין הַשְּׂרֵפָה
ג וְאֶת־הָאֵשׁ זְרֵה־הָלְאָה כִּי קָדֵשׁוּ: אֵת מַחְתּוֹת הַחַטָּאִים הָאֵלֶּה
בְּנַפְשֹׁתָם וְעָשׂוּ אֹתָם רִקֻּעֵי פַחִים צִפּוּי לַמִּזְבֵּחַ כִּי־הִקְרִיבֻם
ד לִפְנֵי־יְהוָה וַיִּקְדָּשׁוּ וְיִהְיוּ לְאוֹת לִבְנֵי יִשְׂרָאֵל: וַיִּקַּח אֶלְעָזָר
הַכֹּהֵן אֵת מַחְתּוֹת הַנְּחֹשֶׁת אֲשֶׁר הִקְרִיבוּ הַשְּׂרֻפִים וַיְרַקְּעוּם
ה צִפּוּי לַמִּזְבֵּחַ: זִכָּרוֹן לִבְנֵי יִשְׂרָאֵל לְמַעַן אֲשֶׁר לֹא־יִקְרַב אִישׁ
זָר אֲשֶׁר לֹא מִזֶּרַע אַהֲרֹן הוּא לְהַקְטִיר קְטֹרֶת לִפְנֵי יְהוָה וְלֹא־
יִהְיֶה כְקֹרַח וְכַעֲדָתוֹ כַּאֲשֶׁר דִּבֶּר יְהוָה בְּיַד־מֹשֶׁה לוֹ:
ו וַיִּלֹּנוּ כָּל־עֲדַת בְּנֵי־יִשְׂרָאֵל מִמָּחֳרָת עַל־מֹשֶׁה וְעַל־אַהֲרֹן
ז לֵאמֹר אַתֶּם הֲמִתֶּם אֶת־עַם יְהוָה: וַיְהִי בְּהִקָּהֵל הָעֵדָה
עַל־מֹשֶׁה וְעַל־אַהֲרֹן וַיִּפְנוּ אֶל־אֹהֶל מוֹעֵד וְהִנֵּה כִסָּהוּ

לד| נָסוּ לְקֹלָם. בִּשְׁבִיל הַקּוֹל הַיּוֹצֵא עַל בְּלִיעָתָן:

פרק יז

ב| וְאֶת הָאֵשׁ. שֶׁבְּתוֹךְ הַמַּחְתּוֹת: זְרֵה הָלְאָה. לָאָרֶץ מֵעַל הַמַּחְתּוֹת: כִּי קָדֵשׁוּ. הַמַּחְתּוֹת, וַאֲסוּרִין בַּהֲנָאָה, שֶׁהֲרֵי עֲשָׂאוּם כְּלֵי שָׁרֵת:

ג| הַחַטָּאִים הָאֵלֶּה בְּנַפְשֹׁתָם. שֶׁנַּעֲשׂוּ פּוֹשְׁעִים בְּנַפְשׁוֹתָם, שֶׁנֶּחְלְקוּ עַל הַקָּדוֹשׁ בָּרוּךְ הוּא: רִקֻּעֵי. רְדוּדִין: פַּחִים. טַסִּים מְרֻדָּדִין, טינביד"ש בְּלַעַז: צִפּוּי לַמִּזְבֵּחַ. לְמִזְבַּח הַנְּחֹשֶׁת: וְיִהְיוּ לְאוֹת. לְזִכָּרוֹן, שֶׁיֹּאמְרוּ: אֵלּוּ הָיוּ מֵאוֹתָן שֶׁנֶּחְלְקוּ עַל הַכְּהֻנָּה וְנִשְׂרְפוּ:

ד| וַיְרַקְּעוּם. אינטי"בידי"ט בְּלַעַז:

ה| וְלֹא יִהְיֶה כְקֹרַח. כְּדֵי שֶׁלֹּא יִהְיֶה כְקֹרַח: כַּאֲשֶׁר דִּבֶּר ה' בְּיַד מֹשֶׁה לוֹ. כְּמוֹ "עָלָיו", עַל אַהֲרֹן דִּבֶּר אֶל מֹשֶׁה שֶׁיִּהְיֶה הוּא וּבָנָיו כֹּהֲנִים, לְפִיכָךְ "לֹא יִקְרַב אִישׁ זָר אֲשֶׁר לֹא מִזֶּרַע אַהֲרֹן" וְגוֹ'. וְכֵן כָּל "לִי" וְ"לוֹ" וְ"לָהֶם" הַסְּמוּכִים אֵצֶל דִּבּוּר, פִּתְרוֹנָם כְּמוֹ "עַל". וּמִדְרָשׁוֹ, עַל קֹרַח. וּמַהוּ "בְּיַד מֹשֶׁה" וְלֹא כָתַב "אֶל מֹשֶׁה"? רֶמֶז לַחוֹלְקִים עַל הַכְּהֻנָּה שֶׁלּוֹקִין בְּצָרַעַת כְּמוֹ שֶׁלָּקָה מֹשֶׁה בְּיָדוֹ, שֶׁנֶּאֱמַר: "וַיּוֹצִאָהּ וְהִנֵּה יָדוֹ מְצֹרַעַת כַּשָּׁלֶג" (שמות ד, ו), וְעַל כֵּן לָקָה עֻזִּיָּה בְּצָרַעַת (דברי הימים ב' כו, טז-כ):

במדבר | פרק יז

ח הֶעָנָ֔ן וְנִרְאָ֖ה כְּב֥וֹד יְהוָֽה: וַיָּבֹ֤א מֹשֶׁה֙ וְאַֽהֲרֹ֔ן אֶל־פְּנֵ֖י אֹ֥הֶל
ט מוֹעֵֽד: וַיְדַבֵּ֥ר יְהוָ֖ה אֶל־מֹשֶׁ֥ה לֵּאמֹֽר: הֵרֹ֗מּוּ מִתּוֹךְ֙ רביעי
י הָֽעֵדָ֣ה הַזֹּ֔את וַֽאֲכַלֶּ֥ה אֹתָ֖ם כְּרָ֑גַע וַֽיִּפְּל֖וּ עַל־פְּנֵיהֶֽם: וַיֹּ֨אמֶר
יא מֹשֶׁ֜ה אֶֽל־אַֽהֲרֹ֗ן קַ֣ח אֶת־הַ֠מַּחְתָּ֠ה וְתֶן־עָלֶ֨יהָ אֵ֜שׁ מֵעַ֤ל הַמִּזְבֵּ֨חַ֙
וְשִׂ֣ים קְטֹ֔רֶת וְהוֹלֵ֧ךְ מְהֵרָ֛ה אֶל־הָֽעֵדָ֖ה וְכַפֵּ֣ר עֲלֵיהֶ֑ם כִּֽי־יָצָ֥א
הַקֶּ֛צֶף מִלִּפְנֵ֥י יְהוָ֖ה הֵחֵ֥ל הַנָּֽגֶף: וַיִּקַּ֨ח אַֽהֲרֹ֜ן כַּֽאֲשֶׁ֣ר ׀ דִּבֶּ֣ר
יב מֹשֶׁ֗ה וַיָּ֨רָץ֙ אֶל־תּ֣וֹךְ הַקָּהָ֔ל וְהִנֵּ֛ה הֵחֵ֥ל הַנֶּ֖גֶף בָּעָ֑ם וַיִּתֵּן֙ אֶת־
יג הַקְּטֹ֔רֶת וַיְכַפֵּ֖ר עַל־הָעָֽם: וַיַּֽעֲמֹ֥ד בֵּֽין־הַמֵּתִ֖ים וּבֵ֣ין הַֽחַיִּ֑ים
יד וַתֵּֽעָצַ֖ר הַמַּגֵּפָֽה: וַיִּֽהְי֗וּ הַמֵּתִים֙ בַּמַּגֵּפָ֔ה אַרְבָּעָ֥ה עָשָׂ֛ר אֶ֖לֶף וּשְׁבַ֣ע
טו מֵא֑וֹת מִלְּבַ֥ד הַמֵּתִ֖ים עַל־דְּבַר־קֹֽרַח: וַיָּ֤שָׁב אַֽהֲרֹן֙ אֶל־מֹשֶׁ֔ה
אֶל־פֶּ֖תַח אֹ֣הֶל מוֹעֵ֑ד וְהַמַּגֵּפָ֖ה נֶֽעֱצָֽרָה:

טז וַיְדַבֵּ֥ר יְהוָ֖ה אֶל־מֹשֶׁ֥ה לֵּאמֹֽר: דַּבֵּ֣ר ׀ אֶל־בְּנֵ֣י יִשְׂרָאֵ֗ל וְקַ֣ח חמישי
מֵֽאִתָּ֡ם מַטֶּ֣ה מַטֶּה֩ לְבֵ֨ית אָ֜ב מֵאֵ֤ת כָּל־נְשִֽׂיאֵהֶם֙ לְבֵ֣ית אֲבֹתָ֔ם
יז שְׁנֵ֥ים עָשָׂ֖ר מַטּ֑וֹת אִ֣ישׁ אֶת־שְׁמ֔וֹ תִּכְתֹּ֖ב עַל־מַטֵּֽהוּ: וְאֵת֙ שֵׁ֣ם
יח אַֽהֲרֹ֔ן תִּכְתֹּ֖ב עַל־מַטֵּ֣ה לֵוִ֑י כִּ֚י מַטֶּ֣ה אֶחָ֔ד לְרֹ֖אשׁ בֵּ֥ית אֲבוֹתָֽם:

יא | וְכַפֵּר עֲלֵיהֶם. רָז זֶה מָסַר לוֹ מַלְאַךְ הַמָּוֶת כְּשֶׁעָלָה לָרָקִיעַ, שֶׁהַקְּטֹרֶת עוֹצֶרֶת הַמַּגֵּפָה, כִּדְאִיתָא בְּמַסֶּכֶת שַׁבָּת (דף פט ע״א):

יג | וַיַּעֲמֹד בֵּין הַמֵּתִים וְגוֹ׳. אָחַז אֶת הַמַּלְאָךְ וְהֶעֱמִידוֹ עַל כָּרְחוֹ. אָמַר לוֹ הַמַּלְאָךְ: הַנַּח לִי לַעֲשׂוֹת שְׁלִיחוּתִי. אָמַר לוֹ: מֹשֶׁה צִוַּנִי לְעַכֵּב עַל יָדְךָ. אָמַר לוֹ: אֲנִי שְׁלוּחוֹ שֶׁל מָקוֹם וְאַתָּה שְׁלוּחוֹ שֶׁל מֹשֶׁה. אָמַר לוֹ: אֵין מֹשֶׁה אוֹמֵר כְּלוּם מִלִּבּוֹ אֶלָּא מִפִּי הַגְּבוּרָה, אִם אֵין אַתָּה מַאֲמִין, הֲרֵי הַקָּדוֹשׁ בָּרוּךְ הוּא וּמֹשֶׁה אֶל פֶּתַח אֹהֶל מוֹעֵד, בֹּא

עִמִּי וּשְׁאַל. וְזֶהוּ שֶׁנֶּאֱמַר: ״וַיָּשָׁב אַהֲרֹן אֶל מֹשֶׁה״ (להלן פסוק טו). דָּבָר אַחֵר, לָמָּה בַּקְּטֹרֶת? לְפִי שֶׁהָיוּ יִשְׂרָאֵל מְלִיזִים וּמְרַנְּנִים אַחַר הַקְּטֹרֶת לוֹמַר: סַם הַמָּוֶת הוּא, עַל יָדוֹ מֵתוּ נָדָב וַאֲבִיהוּא, עַל יָדוֹ נִשְׂרְפוּ חֲמִשִּׁים וּמָאתַיִם אִישׁ. אָמַר הַקָּדוֹשׁ בָּרוּךְ הוּא: תִּרְאוּ שֶׁעוֹצֵר מַגֵּפָה הוּא, וְהַחֵטְא הוּא הַמֵּמִית:

יח | כִּי מַטֶּה אֶחָד. אַף עַל פִּי שֶׁחִלַּקְתִּים לִשְׁתֵּי מִשְׁפָּחוֹת, מִשְׁפַּחַת כְּהֻנָּה לְבַד וּלְוִיָּה לְבַד, מִכָּל מָקוֹם שֵׁבֶט אֶחָד הוּא:

וְהִנַּחְתָּם בְּאֹהֶל מוֹעֵד לִפְנֵי הָעֵדוּת אֲשֶׁר אִוָּעֵד לָכֶם שָׁמָּה: וְהָיָה הָאִישׁ אֲשֶׁר אֶבְחַר־בּוֹ מַטֵּהוּ יִפְרָח וַהֲשִׁכֹּתִי מֵעָלַי אֶת־תְּלֻנּוֹת בְּנֵי יִשְׂרָאֵל אֲשֶׁר הֵם מַלִּינִם עֲלֵיכֶם: וַיְדַבֵּר מֹשֶׁה אֶל־בְּנֵי יִשְׂרָאֵל וַיִּתְּנוּ אֵלָיו ׀ כָּל־נְשִׂיאֵיהֶם מַטֶּה לְנָשִׂיא אֶחָד מַטֶּה לְנָשִׂיא אֶחָד לְבֵית אֲבֹתָם שְׁנֵים עָשָׂר מַטּוֹת וּמַטֵּה אַהֲרֹן בְּתוֹךְ מַטּוֹתָם: וַיַּנַּח מֹשֶׁה אֶת־הַמַּטֹּת לִפְנֵי יהוה בְּאֹהֶל הָעֵדֻת: וַיְהִי מִמָּחֳרָת וַיָּבֹא מֹשֶׁה אֶל־אֹהֶל הָעֵדוּת וְהִנֵּה פָּרַח מַטֵּה־אַהֲרֹן לְבֵית לֵוִי וַיֹּצֵא פֶרַח וַיָּצֵץ צִיץ וַיִּגְמֹל שְׁקֵדִים: וַיֹּצֵא מֹשֶׁה אֶת־כָּל־הַמַּטֹּת מִלִּפְנֵי יהוה אֶל־כָּל־בְּנֵי יִשְׂרָאֵל וַיִּרְאוּ וַיִּקְחוּ אִישׁ מַטֵּהוּ:

ששי וַיֹּאמֶר יהוה אֶל־מֹשֶׁה הָשֵׁב אֶת־מַטֵּה אַהֲרֹן לִפְנֵי הָעֵדוּת לְמִשְׁמֶרֶת לְאוֹת לִבְנֵי־מֶרִי וּתְכַל תְּלוּנֹּתָם מֵעָלַי וְלֹא יָמֻתוּ: וַיַּעַשׂ מֹשֶׁה כַּאֲשֶׁר צִוָּה יהוה אֹתוֹ כֵּן עָשָׂה: וַיֹּאמְרוּ בְּנֵי יִשְׂרָאֵל אֶל־מֹשֶׁה לֵאמֹר הֵן גָּוַעְנוּ אָבַדְנוּ כֻּלָּנוּ אָבַדְנוּ: כֹּל הַקָּרֵב ׀ הַקָּרֵב אֶל־מִשְׁכַּן יהוה יָמוּת הַאִם תַּמְנוּ:

כ׳ וַהֲשִׁכֹּתִי. כְּמוֹ: "וַיִּשְׁכּוּ הַמַּיִם" (בראשית ח, א), "וַחֲמַת הַמֶּלֶךְ שָׁכָכָה" (אסתר ז, י):

כא׳ בְּתוֹךְ מַטּוֹתָם. הִנִּיחוֹ בָּאֶמְצַע, שֶׁלֹּא יֹאמְרוּ: מִפְּנֵי שֶׁהִנִּיחוֹ בְּצַד שְׁכִינָה פָּרַח:

כג׳ וַיֹּצֵא פֶרַח. כְּמַשְׁמָעוֹ: **צִיץ.** הוּא חֲנָטַת הַפְּרִי כְּשֶׁהַפֶּרַח נוֹפֵל: **וַיִּגְמֹל שְׁקֵדִים.** כְּשֶׁהֻכַּר הַפְּרִי הֻכַּר שֶׁהֵן שְׁקֵדִים, לְשׁוֹן: "וַיִּגְדַּל הַיֶּלֶד וַיִּגָּמַל" (בראשית כא, ח), וְלָשׁוֹן זֶה מָצוּי בִּפְרִי הָאִילָן, כְּמוֹ: "וּבֹסֶר גֹּמֵל יִהְיֶה נִצָּה" (ישעיה יח, ה). וְלָמָּה שְׁקֵדִים? הוּא הַפְּרִי הַמְמַהֵר לְהַפְרִיחַ מִכָּל הַפֵּרוֹת, אַף הַמְעוֹרֵר עַל הַכְּהֻנָּה פֻּרְעָנוּתוֹ מְמַהֶרֶת לָבוֹא, כְּמוֹ שֶׁמָּצִינוּ בְּעֻזִּיָּהוּ:

כה׳ וּתְכַל תְּלוּנֹּתָם. כְּמוֹ "וּתְכַלֶּה תְּלוּנֹּתָם", לְשׁוֹן שֵׁם מִפְעַל יָחִיד לִנְקֵבָה, כְּמוֹ מורמוּרדי״ן בְּלַעַז: **לְמִשְׁמֶרֶת לְאוֹת.** לְזִכָּרוֹן שֶׁבָּחַרְתִּי בְּאַהֲרֹן לְכֹהֵן, וְלֹא יִלּוֹנוּ עוֹד עַל הַכְּהֻנָּה:

כח׳ כֹּל הַקָּרֵב הַקָּרֵב וְגוֹ׳. אֵין אָנוּ יְכוֹלִין לִהְיוֹת זְהִירִין בְּכָךְ, כֻּלָּנוּ רַשָּׁאִין לְהִכָּנֵס לַחֲצַר אֹהֶל מוֹעֵד, וְאֶחָד שֶׁיַּקְרִיב עַצְמוֹ יוֹתֵר מֵחֲבֵרָיו וְיִכָּנֵס לְתוֹךְ אֹהֶל מוֹעֵד יָמוּת: **הַאִם תַּמְנוּ לִגְוֹעַ.** שֶׁמָּא הֻפְקַרְנוּ לְמִיתָה?!

"וְהַזְּרוֹעַ זָרְחָה בְמִזְרָחוֹ" (דברי הימים ב׳ כו, יט), וְתַרְגּוּמוֹ: "וְכַפִּית שְׁגִדִין", כְּמִין אֶשְׁכּוֹל שְׁקֵדִים יַחַד כְּפוּתִים זֶה עַל זֶה:

במדבר | פרק יח

א וַיֹּאמֶר יהוה אֶל־אַהֲרֹן אַתָּה וּבָנֶיךָ וּבֵית־אָבִיךָ אִתָּךְ תִּשְׂאוּ אֶת־עֲוֺן הַמִּקְדָּשׁ וְאַתָּה וּבָנֶיךָ אִתָּךְ תִּשְׂאוּ אֶת־עֲוֺן כְּהֻנַּתְכֶם: ב וְגַם אֶת־אַחֶיךָ מַטֵּה לֵוִי שֵׁבֶט אָבִיךָ הַקְרֵב אִתָּךְ וְיִלָּווּ עָלֶיךָ וִישָׁרְתוּךָ וְאַתָּה וּבָנֶיךָ אִתָּךְ לִפְנֵי אֹהֶל הָעֵדֻת: ג וְשָׁמְרוּ מִשְׁמַרְתְּךָ וּמִשְׁמֶרֶת כָּל־הָאֹהֶל אַךְ אֶל־כְּלֵי הַקֹּדֶשׁ וְאֶל־הַמִּזְבֵּחַ לֹא יִקְרָבוּ וְלֹא־יָמֻתוּ גַם־הֵם גַּם־אַתֶּם: ד וְנִלְווּ עָלֶיךָ וְשָׁמְרוּ אֶת־מִשְׁמֶרֶת אֹהֶל מוֹעֵד לְכֹל עֲבֹדַת הָאֹהֶל וְזָר לֹא־יִקְרַב אֲלֵיכֶם: ה וּשְׁמַרְתֶּם אֵת מִשְׁמֶרֶת הַקֹּדֶשׁ וְאֵת מִשְׁמֶרֶת הַמִּזְבֵּחַ וְלֹא־יִהְיֶה עוֹד קֶצֶף עַל־בְּנֵי יִשְׂרָאֵל: ו וַאֲנִי הִנֵּה לָקַחְתִּי אֶת־אֲחֵיכֶם הַלְוִיִּם מִתּוֹךְ בְּנֵי יִשְׂרָאֵל לָכֶם מַתָּנָה נְתֻנִים לַיהוה לַעֲבֹד אֶת־עֲבֹדַת אֹהֶל מוֹעֵד: ז וְאַתָּה וּבָנֶיךָ אִתְּךָ תִּשְׁמְרוּ אֶת־כְּהֻנַּתְכֶם לְכָל־דְּבַר הַמִּזְבֵּחַ וּלְמִבֵּית לַפָּרֹכֶת וַעֲבַדְתֶּם עֲבֹדַת מַתָּנָה אֶתֵּן אֶת־כְּהֻנַּתְכֶם וְהַזָּר הַקָּרֵב יוּמָת:

פרק יח

א] **וַיֹּאמֶר ה' אֶל אַהֲרֹן.** לְמֹשֶׁה אָמַר שֶׁיֹּאמַר לְאַהֲרֹן, לְהַזְהִירוֹ עַל תַּקָּנַת יִשְׂרָאֵל שֶׁלֹּא יִכָּנְסוּ לַמִּקְדָּשׁ: **אַתָּה וּבָנֶיךָ וּבֵית אָבִיךָ.** הֵם בְּנֵי קְהָת אֲבִי עַמְרָם: **תִּשְׂאוּ אֶת עֲוֺן הַמִּקְדָּשׁ.** עֲלֵיכֶם אֲנִי מַטִּיל עֹנֶשׁ הַזָּרִים שֶׁיֶּחֶטְאוּ בְּעִסְקֵי הַדְּבָרִים הַמְקֻדָּשִׁים הַמְּסוּרִים לָכֶם, הוּא הָאֹהֶל וְהָאָרוֹן וְהַשֻּׁלְחָן וּכְלֵי הַקֹּדֶשׁ, אַתֶּם תֵּשְׁבוּ וְתַזְהִירוּ עַל כָּל זָר הַבָּא לִגַּע: **וְאַתָּה וּבָנֶיךָ.** הַכֹּהֲנִים: **תִּשְׂאוּ אֶת עֲוֺן כְּהֻנַּתְכֶם.** שֶׁאֵינָהּ מְסוּרָה לַלְוִיִּם, וְתַזְהִירוּ הַלְוִיִּם הַשּׁוֹגְגִים שֶׁלֹּא יִגְּעוּ אֲלֵיכֶם בַּעֲבוֹדַתְכֶם:

ב] **וְגַם אֶת אַחֶיךָ.** בְּנֵי גֵרְשׁוֹן וּבְנֵי מְרָרִי: **וְיִלָּווּ.** וְיִתְחַבְּרוּ אֲלֵיכֶם, לְהַזְהִיר גַּם אֵת הַזָּרִים מִלִּקְרַב אֲלֵיהֶם: **וִישָׁרְתוּךָ.** בִּשְׁמִירַת הַשְּׁעָרִים וּלְמַנּוֹת מֵהֶם גִּזְבָּרִין וַאֲמַרְכָּלִין:

ד] **וְזָר לֹא יִקְרַב אֲלֵיכֶם.** אֶתְכֶם אֲנִי מַזְהִיר עַל כָּךְ:

ה] **וְלֹא יִהְיֶה עוֹד קֶצֶף.** כְּמוֹ שֶׁהָיָה כְּבָר, שֶׁנֶּאֱמַר: "כִּי יָצָא הַקֶּצֶף" (לעיל יז, יא):

ו] **לָכֶם מַתָּנָה נְתֻנִים.** יָכוֹל לַעֲבוֹדַתְכֶם שֶׁל הֶדְיוֹט? תַּלְמוּד לוֹמַר: "לַה'", כְּמוֹ שֶׁמְּפֹרָשׁ לְמַעְלָה, לִשְׁמֹר מִשְׁמֶרֶת גִּזְבָּרִין וַאֲמַרְכָּלִין:

ז] **עֲבֹדַת מַתָּנָה.** בְּמַתָּנָה נְתַתִּיהָ לָכֶם:

ח וַיְדַבֵּר יְהוָה אֶל־אַהֲרֹן וַאֲנִי הִנֵּה נָתַתִּי לְךָ אֶת־מִשְׁמֶרֶת תְּרוּמֹתָי לְכָל־קָדְשֵׁי בְנֵי־יִשְׂרָאֵל לְךָ נְתַתִּים לְמָשְׁחָה וּלְבָנֶיךָ לְחָק־עוֹלָם: ט זֶה־יִהְיֶה לְךָ מִקֹּדֶשׁ הַקֳּדָשִׁים מִן־הָאֵשׁ כָּל־קָרְבָּנָם לְכָל־מִנְחָתָם וּלְכָל־חַטָּאתָם וּלְכָל־אֲשָׁמָם אֲשֶׁר יָשִׁיבוּ לִי קֹדֶשׁ קָדָשִׁים לְךָ הוּא וּלְבָנֶיךָ: י בְּקֹדֶשׁ הַקֳּדָשִׁים תֹּאכֲלֶנּוּ כָּל־זָכָר יֹאכַל אֹתוֹ קֹדֶשׁ יִהְיֶה־לָּךְ: יא וְזֶה־לְּךָ תְּרוּמַת מַתָּנָם לְכָל־תְּנוּפֹת בְּנֵי יִשְׂרָאֵל לְךָ נְתַתִּים וּלְבָנֶיךָ וְלִבְנֹתֶיךָ אִתְּךָ לְחָק־עוֹלָם כָּל־טָהוֹר בְּבֵיתְךָ יֹאכַל אֹתוֹ: יב כֹּל חֵלֶב יִצְהָר וְכָל־חֵלֶב תִּירוֹשׁ וְדָגָן רֵאשִׁיתָם אֲשֶׁר־יִתְּנוּ לַיהוָה לְךָ נְתַתִּים: יג בִּכּוּרֵי כָּל־אֲשֶׁר בְּאַרְצָם אֲשֶׁר־יָבִיאוּ לַיהוָה לְךָ יִהְיֶה כָּל־טָהוֹר בְּבֵיתְךָ יֹאכֲלֶנּוּ: יד כָּל־חֵרֶם בְּיִשְׂרָאֵל לְךָ יִהְיֶה: טו כָּל־פֶּטֶר רֶחֶם לְכָל־בָּשָׂר אֲשֶׁר־יַקְרִיבוּ לַיהוָה בָּאָדָם וּבַבְּהֵמָה יִהְיֶה־לָּךְ אַךְ פָּדֹה תִפְדֶּה אֵת בְּכוֹר הָאָדָם וְאֵת בְּכוֹר־הַבְּהֵמָה הַטְּמֵאָה תִּפְדֶּה: טז וּפְדוּיָו מִבֶּן־חֹדֶשׁ תִּפְדֶּה בְּעֶרְכְּךָ כֶּסֶף חֲמֵשֶׁת שְׁקָלִים בְּשֶׁקֶל הַקֹּדֶשׁ עֶשְׂרִים גֵּרָה הוּא: יז אַךְ בְּכוֹר־שׁוֹר אוֹ־בְכוֹר כֶּשֶׂב

ח וַאֲנִי הִנֵּה נָתַתִּי לְךָ. בְּשִׂמְחָה. לְשׁוֹן שִׂמְחָה הוּא זֶה, כְּמוֹ: "הִנֵּה הוּא יֹצֵא לִקְרָאתֶךָ וְרָאֲךָ וְשָׂמַח בְּלִבּוֹ" (שמות ד, יד). מָשָׁל לְמֶלֶךְ שֶׁנָּתַן שָׂדֶה לְאוֹהֲבוֹ וְלֹא כָתַב וְלֹא חָתַם וְלֹא הֶעֱלָה בְּעַרְכָּאִין. בָּא אֶחָד וְעִרְעֵר עַל הַשָּׂדֶה, אָמַר לוֹ הַמֶּלֶךְ: כָּל מִי שֶׁיִּרְצֶה יָבֹא וִיעַרְעֵר לְנֶגְדְּךָ, הֲרֵינִי כוֹתֵב וְחוֹתֵם לְךָ וּמַעֲלֶה בְּעַרְכָּאִין. אַף כָּאן, לְפִי שֶׁבָּא קֹרַח וְעִרְעֵר כְּנֶגֶד אַהֲרֹן עַל הַכְּהֻנָּה, בָּא הַכָּתוּב וְנָתַן לוֹ עֶשְׂרִים וְאַרְבַּע מַתְּנוֹת כְּהֻנָּה בִּבְרִית מֶלַח עוֹלָם, וּלְכָךְ נִסְמְכָה פָּרָשָׁה זוֹ לְכָאן: מִשְׁמֶרֶת תְּרוּמֹתָי. שֶׁאַתָּה צָרִיךְ לְשָׁמְרָן בְּטָהֳרָה: לְמָשְׁחָה. לִגְדֻלָּה:

ט מִן הָאֵשׁ. לְאַחַר הַקְטָרַת הָאִשִּׁים: כָּל קָרְבָּנָם. כְּגוֹן זִבְחֵי שַׁלְמֵי צִבּוּר: מִנְחָתָם חַטָּאתָם וַאֲשָׁמָם. כְּמַשְׁמָעוֹ: אֲשֶׁר יָשִׁיבוּ לִי. זֶה גֶּזֶל הַגֵּר:

י בְּקֹדֶשׁ הַקֳּדָשִׁים תֹּאכֲלֶנּוּ וְגוֹ'. לִמֵּד עַל קָדְשֵׁי קָדָשִׁים שֶׁאֵין נֶאֱכָלִין אֶלָּא בָּעֲזָרָה וְלִזִכְרֵי כְהֻנָּה:

יא תְּרוּמַת מַתָּנָם. הַמּוּרָם מִן הַתּוֹדָה וּמֵהַשְּׁלָמִים וּמֵאֵיל נָזִיר: לְכָל תְּנוּפֹת. שֶׁהֲרֵי אֵלּוּ טְעוּנִין תְּנוּפָה: כָּל טָהוֹר. וְלֹא טְמֵאִים. דָּבָר אַחֵר, "כָּל טָהוֹר" לְרַבּוֹת אִשְׁתּוֹ:

יב רֵאשִׁיתָם. הִיא תְּרוּמָה גְּדוֹלָה:

אֽוֹ־בְכ֨וֹר עֵ֜ז לֹ֣א תִפְדֶּה֮ קֹ֣דֶשׁ הֵם֒ אֶת־דָּמָ֗ם תִּזְרֹ֤ק עַל־הַמִּזְבֵּ֙חַ֙ וְאֶת־חֶלְבָּ֣ם תַּקְטִ֔יר אִשֶּׁ֛ה לְרֵ֥יחַ נִיחֹ֖חַ לַיהוָֽה: וּבְשָׂרָ֖ם יִֽהְיֶה־
יח לָּ֑ךְ כַּחֲזֵ֧ה הַתְּנוּפָ֛ה וּכְשׁ֥וֹק הַיָּמִ֖ין לְךָ֥ יִֽהְיֶֽה: כֹּ֣ל ׀ תְּרוּמֹ֣ת
יט הַקֳּדָשִׁ֗ים אֲשֶׁ֨ר יָרִ֤ימוּ בְנֵֽי־יִשְׂרָאֵל֙ לַֽיהוָ֔ה נָתַ֧תִּי לְךָ֛ וּלְבָנֶ֥יךָ וְלִבְנֹתֶ֖יךָ אִתְּךָ֑ לְחָק־עוֹלָ֑ם בְּרִית֩ מֶ֨לַח עוֹלָ֥ם הִוא֙ לִפְנֵ֣י יְהוָ֔ה
כ לְךָ֖ וּלְזַרְעֲךָ֥ אִתָּֽךְ: וַיֹּ֨אמֶר יְהוָ֜ה אֶֽל־אַהֲרֹ֗ן בְּאַרְצָם֙ לֹ֣א תִנְחָ֔ל וְחֵ֕לֶק לֹא־יִהְיֶ֥ה לְךָ֖ בְּתוֹכָ֑ם אֲנִ֤י חֶלְקְךָ֙ וְנַחֲלָ֣תְךָ֔ בְּת֖וֹךְ בְּנֵ֥י
כא יִשְׂרָאֵֽל: וְלִבְנֵ֣י לֵוִ֔י הִנֵּ֥ה נָתַ֖תִּי כָּל־מַֽעֲשֵׂ֣ר בְּיִשְׂרָאֵ֑ל שביעי
לְנַחֲלָ֑ה חֵ֤לֶף עֲבֹֽדָתָם֙ אֲשֶׁר־הֵ֣ם עֹֽבְדִ֔ים אֶת־עֲבֹדַ֖ת אֹ֥הֶל
כב מוֹעֵֽד: וְלֹא־יִקְרְב֥וּ ע֛וֹד בְּנֵ֥י יִשְׂרָאֵ֖ל אֶל־אֹ֣הֶל מוֹעֵ֑ד לָשֵׂ֥את
כג חֵ֖טְא לָמֽוּת: וְעָבַ֨ד הַלֵּוִ֜י ה֗וּא אֶת־עֲבֹדַת֙ אֹ֣הֶל מוֹעֵ֔ד וְהֵ֖ם יִשְׂא֣וּ עֲוֺנָ֑ם חֻקַּ֤ת עוֹלָם֙ לְדֹרֹ֣תֵיכֶ֔ם וּבְתוֹךְ֙ בְּנֵ֣י יִשְׂרָאֵ֔ל לֹ֥א יִנְחֲל֖וּ
כד נַחֲלָֽה: כִּ֞י אֶת־מַעְשַׂ֣ר בְּנֵֽי־יִשְׂרָאֵ֗ל אֲשֶׁ֨ר יָרִ֤ימוּ לַֽיהוָה֙ תְּרוּמָ֔ה נָתַ֥תִּי לַלְוִיִּ֖ם לְנַחֲלָ֑ה עַל־כֵּן֙ אָמַ֣רְתִּי לָהֶ֔ם בְּתוֹךְ֙ בְּנֵ֣י יִשְׂרָאֵ֔ל לֹ֥א יִנְחֲל֖וּ נַחֲלָֽה:

יח] כַּחֲזֵה הַתְּנוּפָה וּכְשׁוֹק הַיָּמִין. שֶׁל שְׁלָמִים, שֶׁנֶּאֱכָלִים לַכֹּהֲנִים וְלִנְשֵׁיהֶם לִבְנֵיהֶם וְלְעַבְדֵיהֶם לִשְׁנֵי יָמִים וְלַיְלָה אֶחָד, אַף הַבְּכוֹר נֶאֱכָל לִשְׁנֵי יָמִים וְלַיְלָה אֶחָד. בָּא רַבִּי עֲקִיבָא וְלָמַד: הוֹסִיף לְךָ הַכָּתוּב הֲוָיָה אַחֶרֶת, שֶׁלֹּא תֹאמַר, כַּחֲזֶה וָשׁוֹק שֶׁל תּוֹדָה שֶׁאֵינוֹ נֶאֱכָל אֶלָּא לְיוֹם וָלַיְלָה.

יט] כֹּל תְּרוּמֹת הַקֳּדָשִׁים. מֵחִבָּתָהּ שֶׁל פָּרָשָׁה זוֹ, כְּלָלָהּ בַּתְּחִלָּה וּכְלָלָהּ בַּסּוֹף וּפָרַט בָּאֶמְצַע: בְּרִית מֶלַח עוֹלָם. כָּרַת בְּרִית עִם אַהֲרֹן בְּדָבָר הַבָּרִיא וּמַתְקַיֵּם וּמַבְרִיא אֶת אֲחֵרִים: בְּרִית מֶלַח. כַּבְּרִית הַכְּרוּתָה לַמֶּלַח, שֶׁאֵינוֹ מַסְרִיחַ לְעוֹלָם:

כ] וְחֵלֶק לֹא יִהְיֶה לְךָ בְּתוֹכָם. אַף בַּבִּזָּה:

כג] וְהֵם. הַלְוִיִּם, "יִשְׂאוּ עֲוֺנָם" שֶׁל יִשְׂרָאֵל, שֶׁעֲלֵיהֶם לְהַזְהִיר הַזָּרִים מִגֶּשֶׁת אֲלֵיהֶם:

כד] אֲשֶׁר יָרִימוּ לַה' תְּרוּמָה. הַכָּתוּב קְרָאוֹ 'תְּרוּמָה' עַד שֶׁיַּפְרִישׁ מִמֶּנּוּ תְּרוּמַת מַעֲשֵׂר:

פרק יח

יז וַיְדַבֵּר יהוה אֶל־מֹשֶׁה לֵּאמֹר: וְאֶל־הַלְוִיִּם תְּדַבֵּר וְאָמַרְתָּ אֲלֵהֶם כִּי־תִקְחוּ מֵאֵת בְּנֵי־יִשְׂרָאֵל אֶת־הַמַּעֲשֵׂר אֲשֶׁר נָתַתִּי לָכֶם מֵאִתָּם בְּנַחֲלַתְכֶם וַהֲרֵמֹתֶם מִמֶּנּוּ תְּרוּמַת יהוה מַעֲשֵׂר מִן־הַמַּעֲשֵׂר: **כז** וְנֶחְשַׁב לָכֶם תְּרוּמַתְכֶם כַּדָּגָן מִן־הַגֹּרֶן וְכַמְלֵאָה מִן־הַיָּקֶב: **כח** כֵּן תָּרִימוּ גַם־אַתֶּם תְּרוּמַת יהוה מִכֹּל מַעְשְׂרֹתֵיכֶם אֲשֶׁר תִּקְחוּ מֵאֵת בְּנֵי יִשְׂרָאֵל וּנְתַתֶּם מִמֶּנּוּ אֶת־תְּרוּמַת יהוה לְאַהֲרֹן הַכֹּהֵן: **כט** מִכֹּל מַתְּנֹתֵיכֶם תָּרִימוּ אֵת כָּל־תְּרוּמַת יהוה מִכָּל־חֶלְבּוֹ אֶת־מִקְדְּשׁוֹ מִמֶּנּוּ:

מפטיר

וְאָמַרְתָּ אֲלֵהֶם בַּהֲרִימְכֶם אֶת־חֶלְבּוֹ מִמֶּנּוּ וְנֶחְשַׁב לַלְוִיִּם כִּתְבוּאַת גֹּרֶן וְכִתְבוּאַת יָקֶב: **לא** וַאֲכַלְתֶּם אֹתוֹ בְּכָל־מָקוֹם אַתֶּם וּבֵיתְכֶם כִּי־שָׂכָר הוּא לָכֶם חֵלֶף עֲבֹדַתְכֶם בְּאֹהֶל מוֹעֵד: **לב** וְלֹא־תִשְׂאוּ עָלָיו חֵטְא בַּהֲרִימְכֶם אֶת־חֶלְבּוֹ מִמֶּנּוּ וְאֶת־קָדְשֵׁי בְנֵי־יִשְׂרָאֵל לֹא תְחַלְּלוּ וְלֹא תָמוּתוּ:

כז וְנֶחְשַׁב לָכֶם תְּרוּמַתְכֶם כַּדָּגָן מִן הַגֹּרֶן. תְּרוּמַת מַעֲשֵׂר שֶׁלָּכֶם אֲסוּרָה לְזָרִים וְלִטְמֵאִים, וְחַיָּבִין עָלֶיהָ מִיתָה וְחֹמֶשׁ, כִּתְרוּמָה גְדוֹלָה שֶׁנִּקְרֵאת רֵאשִׁית דָּגָן מִן הַגֹּרֶן: וְכַמְלֵאָה מִן הַיָּקֶב. כִּתְרוּמַת תִּירוֹשׁ וְיִצְהָר הַנִּטֶּלֶת מִן הַיְקָבִים: מְלֵאָה. לְשׁוֹן בִּשּׁוּל תְּבוּאָה שֶׁנִּתְמַלְּאָה: יֶקֶב. הוּא הַבּוֹר שֶׁלִּפְנֵי הַגַּת שֶׁהַיַּיִן יוֹרֵד לְתוֹכוֹ. וְכָל לְשׁוֹן 'יֶקֶב' חֲפִירַת קַרְקַע הוּא, וְכֵן: "יִקְבֵי הַמֶּלֶךְ" (זכריה יד, י), הוּא יָם אוֹקְיָנוֹס, חֲפִירָה שֶׁחָפַר מַלְכּוֹ שֶׁל עוֹלָם:

כח כֵּן תָּרִימוּ גַם אַתֶּם. כְּמוֹ שֶׁיִּשְׂרָאֵל מְרִימִים מִגָּרְנָם וּמִיִּקְבֵיהֶם תָּרִימוּ אַתֶּם מִמַּעֲשֵׂר שֶׁלָּכֶם, כִּי הוּא נַחֲלַתְכֶם:

כט מִכֹּל מַתְּנֹתֵיכֶם תָּרִימוּ אֵת כָּל תְּרוּמַת ה'. בִּתְרוּמָה גְדוֹלָה הַכָּתוּב מְדַבֵּר, שֶׁאִם הִקְדִּים לֵוִי אֶת הַכֹּהֵן בַּכְּרִי וְקִבֵּל מַעְשְׂרוֹתָיו קֹדֶם שֶׁיִּטֹּל כֹּהֵן

תְּרוּמָה גְדוֹלָה מִן הַכְּרִי, צָרִיךְ לְהַפְרִישׁ הַלֵּוִי מִן הַמַּעֲשֵׂר תְּחִלָּה אֶחָד מֵחֲמִשִּׁים לִתְרוּמָה גְדוֹלָה, וְיַחֲזֹר וְיַפְרִישׁ תְּרוּמַת מַעֲשֵׂר:

ל בַּהֲרִימְכֶם אֶת חֶלְבּוֹ מִמֶּנּוּ. לְאַחַר שֶׁתָּרִימוּ תְּרוּמַת מַעֲשֵׂר מִמֶּנּוּ, "וְנֶחְשַׁב" הַמּוֹתָר "לַלְוִיִּם" חֻלִּין גְּמוּרִין, "כִּתְבוּאַת גֹּרֶן" לְיִשְׂרָאֵל. שֶׁלֹּא תֹּאמַר: הוֹאִיל וּקְרָאוֹ הַכָּתוּב 'תְּרוּמָה', שֶׁנֶּאֱמַר: "כִּי אֶת מַעֲשַׂר בְּנֵי יִשְׂרָאֵל אֲשֶׁר יָרִימוּ לַה' תְּרוּמָה" (לעיל פסוק כד), יָכוֹל יְהֵא כֻּלּוֹ אָסוּר? תַּלְמוּד לוֹמַר: "וְנֶחְשַׁב לַלְוִיִּם כִּתְבוּאַת גֹּרֶן", מַה שֶׁל יִשְׂרָאֵל חֻלִּין, אַף שֶׁל לֵוִי חֻלִּין:

לא בְּכָל מָקוֹם. אֲפִלּוּ בְּבֵית הַקְּבָרוֹת:

לב וְלֹא תִשְׂאוּ עָלָיו חֵטְא וְגוֹ'. הָא אִם לֹא תָרִימוּ, תִּשְׂאוּ חֵטְא: וְלֹא תָמוּתוּ. הָא אִם תְּחַלְּלוּ, תָּמוּתוּ:

במדבר | פרק יט

פרק יט

א וַיְדַבֵּר יְהוָה אֶל־מֹשֶׁה וְאֶל־אַהֲרֹן לֵאמֹר: ב זֹאת חֻקַּת הַתּוֹרָה אֲשֶׁר־צִוָּה יְהוָה לֵאמֹר דַּבֵּר ׀ אֶל־בְּנֵי יִשְׂרָאֵל וְיִקְחוּ אֵלֶיךָ פָרָה אֲדֻמָּה תְּמִימָה אֲשֶׁר אֵין־בָּהּ מוּם אֲשֶׁר לֹא־עָלָה עָלֶיהָ עֹל: ג וּנְתַתֶּם אֹתָהּ אֶל־אֶלְעָזָר הַכֹּהֵן וְהוֹצִיא אֹתָהּ אֶל־מִחוּץ לַמַּחֲנֶה וְשָׁחַט אֹתָהּ לְפָנָיו: ד וְלָקַח אֶלְעָזָר הַכֹּהֵן מִדָּמָהּ בְּאֶצְבָּעוֹ וְהִזָּה אֶל־נֹכַח פְּנֵי אֹהֶל־מוֹעֵד מִדָּמָהּ שֶׁבַע פְּעָמִים: ה וְשָׂרַף אֶת־הַפָּרָה לְעֵינָיו אֶת־עֹרָהּ וְאֶת־בְּשָׂרָהּ וְאֶת־דָּמָהּ עַל־פִּרְשָׁהּ יִשְׂרֹף: ו וְלָקַח הַכֹּהֵן עֵץ אֶרֶז וְאֵזוֹב וּשְׁנִי תוֹלָעַת וְהִשְׁלִיךְ אֶל־תּוֹךְ שְׂרֵפַת הַפָּרָה: ז וְכִבֶּס בְּגָדָיו הַכֹּהֵן וְרָחַץ בְּשָׂרוֹ בַּמַּיִם וְאַחַר יָבוֹא אֶל־הַמַּחֲנֶה וְטָמֵא הַכֹּהֵן עַד־הָעָרֶב: ח וְהַשֹּׂרֵף אֹתָהּ יְכַבֵּס בְּגָדָיו בַּמַּיִם וְרָחַץ בְּשָׂרוֹ בַּמָּיִם וְטָמֵא עַד־הָעָרֶב: ט וְאָסַף ׀ אִישׁ טָהוֹר אֵת אֵפֶר הַפָּרָה וְהִנִּיחַ מִחוּץ

פרק יט

ב) **זאת חקת התורה.** לְפִי שֶׁהַשָּׂטָן וְאֻמּוֹת הָעוֹלָם מוֹנִין אֶת יִשְׂרָאֵל, לוֹמַר: מָה הַמִּצְוָה הַזֹּאת וּמַה טַּעַם יֵשׁ בָּהּ? לְפִיכָךְ כָּתַב בָּהּ 'חֻקָּה' – גְּזֵרָה הִיא מִלְּפָנַי, אֵין לְךָ רְשׁוּת לְהַרְהֵר אַחֲרֶיהָ. **ויקחו אליך.** לְעוֹלָם הִיא נִקְרֵאת עַל שִׁמְךָ, פָּרָה שֶׁעָשָׂה מֹשֶׁה בַּמִּדְבָּר. **אדמה תמימה.** שֶׁתְּהֵא תְּמִימָה בְּאַדְמִימוּת, שֶׁאִם הָיוּ בָּהּ שְׁתֵּי שְׂעָרוֹת שְׁחוֹרוֹת פְּסוּלָה:

ג) **אלעזר.** מִצְוָתָהּ בַּסְּגָן: **אל מחוץ למחנה.** חוּץ לְשָׁלֹשׁ מַחֲנוֹת: **ושחט אתה לפניו.** זָר שׁוֹחֵט וְאֶלְעָזָר רוֹאֶה:

ד) **אל נכח פני אהל מועד.** עוֹמֵד בְּמִזְרָחוֹ שֶׁל יְרוּשָׁלַיִם וּמִתְכַּוֵּן וְרוֹאֶה פִּתְחוֹ שֶׁל הֵיכָל בִּשְׁעַת הַזָּאַת הַדָּם:

ז) **אל המחנה.** לְמַחֲנֵה שְׁכִינָה, שֶׁאֵין טָמֵא מְשֻׁלָּח חוּץ לִשְׁתֵּי מַחֲנוֹת אֶלָּא זָב וּבַעַל קֶרִי וּמְצֹרָע: **וטמא הכהן עד הערב.** סַרְסֵהוּ וְדָרְשֵׁהוּ: וְטָמֵא עַד הָעֶרֶב וְאַחַר יָבֹא אֶל הַמַּחֲנֶה:

ט) **והניח מחוץ למחנה.** לִשְׁלֹשָׁה חֲלָקִים מְחַלְּקָהּ: אֶחָד נָתַן בְּהַר הַמִּשְׁחָה, וְאֶחָד מִתְחַלֵּק לְכָל הַמִּשְׁמָרוֹת, וְאֶחָד נָתַן בַּחֵיל. זֶה שֶׁל מִשְׁמָרוֹת הָיָה חוּץ לָעֲזָרָה, לִטֹּל מִמֶּנּוּ בְּנֵי הָעֲיָרוֹת וְכָל הַצְּרִיכִין לִטַּהֵר. וְזֶה שֶׁבְּהַר הַמִּשְׁחָה כֹּהֲנִים גְּדוֹלִים לְפָרוֹת אֲחֵרוֹת מְקַדְּשִׁין הֵימֶנָּה. וְזֶה שֶׁבַּחֵיל נָתוּן לְמִשְׁמֶרֶת מִגְּזֵרַת הַכָּתוּב, שֶׁנֶּאֱמַר: "וְהָיְתָה לַעֲדַת בְּנֵי יִשְׂרָאֵל לְמִשְׁמֶרֶת": **למי נדה.** לְמֵי הַזָּיָה, כְּמוֹ: "יַדּוּ אֶבֶן בִּי" (איכה ג, נג), "לְיַדּוֹת אֶת קַרְנוֹת הַגּוֹיִם" (זכריה ב), לְשׁוֹן זְרִיקָה: **חטאת הוא.** לְשׁוֹן חִטּוּי כִּפְשׁוּטוֹ, וּלְפִי הֲלָכוֹתָיו קְרָאָהּ הַכָּתוּב 'חַטָּאת', לוֹמַר שֶׁהִיא כְּקָדָשִׁים לֵאָסֵר בַּהֲנָאָה:

לַמַּחֲנֶה בְּמָקוֹם טָהוֹר וְהָיְתָה לַעֲדַת בְּנֵי־יִשְׂרָאֵל לְמִשְׁמֶרֶת לְמֵי נִדָּה חַטָּאת הִוא: וְכִבֶּס הָאֹסֵף אֶת־אֵפֶר הַפָּרָה אֶת־בְּגָדָיו וְטָמֵא עַד־הָעָרֶב וְהָיְתָה לִבְנֵי יִשְׂרָאֵל וְלַגֵּר הַגָּר בְּתוֹכָם לְחֻקַּת עוֹלָם: הַנֹּגֵעַ בְּמֵת לְכָל־נֶפֶשׁ אָדָם וְטָמֵא שִׁבְעַת יָמִים: הוּא יִתְחַטָּא־בוֹ בַּיּוֹם הַשְּׁלִישִׁי וּבַיּוֹם הַשְּׁבִיעִי יִטְהָר וְאִם־לֹא יִתְחַטָּא בַּיּוֹם הַשְּׁלִישִׁי וּבַיּוֹם הַשְּׁבִיעִי לֹא יִטְהָר: כָּל־הַנֹּגֵעַ בְּמֵת בְּנֶפֶשׁ הָאָדָם אֲשֶׁר־יָמוּת וְלֹא יִתְחַטָּא אֶת־מִשְׁכַּן יְהוה טִמֵּא וְנִכְרְתָה הַנֶּפֶשׁ הַהִוא מִיִּשְׂרָאֵל כִּי מֵי נִדָּה לֹא־זֹרַק עָלָיו טָמֵא יִהְיֶה עוֹד טֻמְאָתוֹ בוֹ: זֹאת הַתּוֹרָה אָדָם כִּי־יָמוּת בְּאֹהֶל כָּל־הַבָּא אֶל־הָאֹהֶל וְכָל־אֲשֶׁר בָּאֹהֶל יִטְמָא שִׁבְעַת יָמִים: וְכֹל כְּלִי פָתוּחַ אֲשֶׁר אֵין־צָמִיד פָּתִיל עָלָיו טָמֵא הוּא: וְכֹל אֲשֶׁר־יִגַּע עַל־פְּנֵי הַשָּׂדֶה בַּחֲלַל־חֶרֶב אוֹ בְמֵת אוֹ־בְעֶצֶם אָדָם אוֹ בְקָבֶר יִטְמָא שִׁבְעַת יָמִים: וְלָקְחוּ לַטָּמֵא מֵעֲפַר שְׂרֵפַת הַחַטָּאת וְנָתַן עָלָיו מַיִם חַיִּים אֶל־כֶּלִי: וְלָקַח אֵזוֹב וְטָבַל בַּמַּיִם אִישׁ טָהוֹר וְהִזָּה עַל־הָאֹהֶל וְעַל־כָּל־הַכֵּלִים

יב' **הוא יתחטא בו.** בְּאֵפֶר הַפָּרָה:

יג' **במת בנפש.** וְאֵיזֶה מֵת? שֶׁל "נֶפֶשׁ הָאָדָם", לְהוֹצִיא נֶפֶשׁ בְּהֵמָה שֶׁאֵין טֻמְאָתָהּ צְרִיכָה הַזָּאָה. דָּבָר אַחֵר, "בְּנֶפֶשׁ" זוֹ רְבִיעִית דָּם: **אֶת מִשְׁכַּן ה' טִמֵּא.** אִם נִכְנַס לָעֲזָרָה, אֲפִלּוּ בִּטְבִילָה, בְּלֹא הַזָּאַת שְׁלִישִׁי וּשְׁבִיעִי: **עוֹד טֻמְאָתוֹ בוֹ.** אַף עַל פִּי שֶׁטָּבַל:

יד' **כל הבא אל האהל.** בְּעוֹד שֶׁהַמֵּת בְּתוֹכוֹ:

טו' **וכל כלי פתוח.** בִּכְלִי חֶרֶס הַכָּתוּב מְדַבֵּר, שֶׁאֵין מְקַבֵּל טֻמְאָה מִגַּבּוֹ אֶלָּא מִתּוֹכוֹ, לְפִיכָךְ אִם אֵין מְגוּפַת צְמִידָתוֹ פְּתוּלָה עָלָיו יָפֶה בְּחִבּוּר "טָמֵא הוּא", הָא אִם יֵשׁ צָמִיד פָּתִיל עָלָיו – טָהוֹר. "פָּתִיל" לְשׁוֹן מְחֻבָּר בִּלְשׁוֹן עַרְבִי, וְכֵן: "נַפְתּוּלֵי אֱלֹהִים נִפְתַּלְתִּי" (בראשית ל, ח), נִתְחַבַּרְתִּי עִם אֲחוֹתִי:

טז' **על פני השדה.** רַבּוֹתֵינוּ דָּרְשׁוּ לְרַבּוֹת גּוֹלֵל וְדוֹפֵק. וּפְשׁוּטוֹ: "עַל פְּנֵי הַשָּׂדֶה", שֶׁאֵין שָׁם אֹהֶל, מְטַמֵּא הַמֵּת שָׁם בְּנָגְעוֹ:

במדבר | פרק יט

וְעַל־הַנְּפָשׁוֹת אֲשֶׁר הָיוּ־שָׁם וְעַל־הַנֹּגֵעַ בַּעֶצֶם אוֹ בֶחָלָל אוֹ
בַמֵּת אוֹ בַקָּבֶר: וְהִזָּה הַטָּהֹר עַל־הַטָּמֵא בַּיּוֹם הַשְּׁלִישִׁי וּבַיּוֹם
הַשְּׁבִיעִי וְחִטְּאוֹ בַּיּוֹם הַשְּׁבִיעִי וְכִבֶּס בְּגָדָיו וְרָחַץ בַּמַּיִם וְטָהֵר
בָּעָרֶב: וְאִישׁ אֲשֶׁר־יִטְמָא וְלֹא יִתְחַטָּא וְנִכְרְתָה הַנֶּפֶשׁ הַהִוא
מִתּוֹךְ הַקָּהָל כִּי אֶת־מִקְדַּשׁ יהוה טִמֵּא מֵי נִדָּה לֹא־זֹרַק עָלָיו
טָמֵא הוּא: וְהָיְתָה לָהֶם לְחֻקַּת עוֹלָם וּמַזֵּה מֵי־הַנִּדָּה יְכַבֵּס
בְּגָדָיו וְהַנֹּגֵעַ בְּמֵי הַנִּדָּה יִטְמָא עַד־הָעָרֶב: וְכֹל אֲשֶׁר־יִגַּע־בּוֹ
הַטָּמֵא יִטְמָא וְהַנֶּפֶשׁ הַנֹּגַעַת תִּטְמָא עַד־הָעָרֶב:

יט | **וְחִטְּאוֹ בַּיּוֹם הַשְּׁבִיעִי.** הוּא גְּמַר טַהֲרָתוֹ:

כ | **וְאִישׁ אֲשֶׁר יִטְמָא וְגוֹ'.** אִם נֶאֱמַר 'מִקְדָּשׁ' לָמָּה נֶאֱמַר 'מִשְׁכָּן' (לעיל פסוק יג)? כּוּ' כִּדְאִיתָא בִּשְׁבוּעוֹת (דף טז ע"ב):

כא | **וּמַזֵּה מֵי הַנִּדָּה.** רַבּוֹתֵינוּ אָמְרוּ שֶׁהַמַּזֶּה טָהוֹר, וְזֶה בָּא לְלַמֵּד שֶׁהַנּוֹשֵׂא מֵי חַטָּאת טָמֵא טֻמְאָה חֲמוּרָה לְטַמֵּא בְּגָדִים שֶׁעָלָיו, מַה שֶּׁאֵין כֵּן בַּנּוֹגֵעַ. וְזֶה שֶׁהוֹצִיאוֹ בִּלְשׁוֹן 'מַזֶּה', לוֹמַר לְךָ שֶׁאֵינָן מְטַמְּאִין עַד שֶׁיְּהֵא בָּהֶן שִׁעוּר הַזָּאָה: **וְהַנֹּגֵעַ... יִטְמָא.** וְאֵין טָעוּן כִּבּוּס בְּגָדִים:

כב | **וְכֹל אֲשֶׁר יִגַּע בּוֹ הַטָּמֵא.** הַזֶּה שֶׁנִּטְמָא בַּמֵּת, "יִטְמָא": **וְהַנֶּפֶשׁ הַנֹּגַעַת.** בּוֹ בַּטָּמֵא מֵת: **תִּטְמָא עַד הָעָרֶב.** כָּאן לָמַדְנוּ שֶׁהַמֵּת אֲבִי אֲבוֹת הַטֻּמְאָה, וְהַנּוֹגֵעַ בּוֹ אַב הַטֻּמְאָה וּמְטַמֵּא אָדָם. זֶהוּ פֵּרוּשָׁהּ לְפִי מַשְׁמָעָהּ וְהִלְכוֹתֶיהָ:

וּמִדְרַשׁ אַגָּדָה הֶעְתַּקְתִּי מִיסוֹדוֹ שֶׁל רַבִּי מֹשֶׁה הַדַּרְשָׁן. וְזֶהוּ:

ב | **וְיִקְחוּ אֵלֶיךָ.** מִשֶּׁלָּהֶם. כְּשֵׁם שֶׁהֵם פֵּרְקוּ נִזְמֵי הַזָּהָב לָעֵגֶל מִשֶּׁלָּהֶם, כָּךְ יָבִיאוּ זוֹ לְכַפָּרָה מִשֶּׁלָּהֶם: **פָּרָה אֲדֻמָּה.** מָשָׁל לְבֶן שִׁפְחָה שֶׁטִּנֵּף פַּלְטִין שֶׁל מֶלֶךְ, אָמְרוּ: תָּבֹא אִמּוֹ וּתְקַנַּח הַצּוֹאָה, כָּךְ תָּבֹא פָּרָה

וּתְכַפֵּר עַל הָעֵגֶל: **אֲדֻמָּה.** עַל שֵׁם: "אִם יַאְדִּימוּ כַתּוֹלָע" (ישעיה א, יח), שֶׁהַחֵטְא קָרוּי אָדָם: **תְּמִימָה.** עַל שֵׁם יִשְׂרָאֵל שֶׁהָיוּ תְּמִימִים וְנַעֲשׂוּ בּוֹ בַּעֲלֵי מוּמִין, תָּבֹא זוֹ וּתְכַפֵּר עֲלֵיהֶם וְיַחְזְרוּ לִתְמִימוּתָם: **לֹא עָלָה עָלֶיהָ עֹל.** כְּשֵׁם שֶׁפָּרְקוּ מֵעֲלֵיהֶם עֹל שָׁמַיִם:

ג | **אֶל אֶלְעָזָר הַכֹּהֵן.** כְּשֵׁם שֶׁנִּקְהֲלוּ עַל אַהֲרֹן, שֶׁהוּא כֹּהֵן, לַעֲשׂוֹת הָעֵגֶל. וּלְפִי שֶׁאַהֲרֹן עָשָׂה אֶת הָעֵגֶל לֹא נַעֲשֵׂית עֲבוֹדָה זוֹ עַל יָדוֹ, שֶׁאֵין קָטֵגוֹר נַעֲשֶׂה סָנֵגוֹר:

ד | **וְשָׂרַף אֶת הַפָּרָה.** כְּשֵׁם שֶׁנִּשְׂרַף הָעֵגֶל:

ו | **עֵץ אֶרֶז וְאֵזוֹב וּשְׁנִי תוֹלָעַת.** שְׁלֹשָׁה מִינִין הַלָּלוּ כְּנֶגֶד שְׁלֹשֶׁת אַלְפֵי אִישׁ שֶׁנָּפְלוּ בָּעֵגֶל. וְאֶרֶז הוּא הַגָּבוֹהַּ מִכָּל הָאִילָנוֹת, וְאֵזוֹב נָמוּךְ מִכֻּלָּם, סִימָן שֶׁהַגָּבוֹהַּ שֶׁנִּתְגָּאָה וְחָטָא יַשְׁפִּיל אֶת עַצְמוֹ כָּאֵזוֹב וְתוֹלַעַת וְיִתְכַּפֵּר לוֹ:

ט | **לְמִשְׁמֶרֶת.** כְּמוֹ שֶׁפֶּשַׁע הָעֵגֶל שָׁמוּר לְדוֹרוֹת לְפֻרְעָנוּת, וְאֵין לְךָ פְּקֻדָּה שֶׁאֵין בָּהּ מִפְּקֻדַּת הָעֵגֶל, שֶׁנֶּאֱמַר: "וּבְיוֹם פָּקְדִי וּפָקַדְתִּי" וְגוֹ' (שמות לב, לד). וּכְשֵׁם שֶׁהָעֵגֶל מְטַמֵּא כָּל הָעוֹסְקִין בּוֹ, כָּךְ פָּרָה מְטַמְּאָה כָּל הָעוֹסְקִין בָּהּ, וּכְשֵׁם שֶׁנִּטְהֲרוּ בְּאֶפְרוֹ, שֶׁנֶּאֱמַר: "וַיִּזֶר עַל פְּנֵי הַמַּיִם" וְגוֹ' (שמות לב, כ), כָּךְ: "וְלָקְחוּ לַטָּמֵא מֵעֲפַר שְׂרֵפַת הַחַטָּאת" וְגוֹ' (להלן פסוק יז):

פרק כ

א וַיָּבֹאוּ בְנֵי־יִשְׂרָאֵל כָּל־הָעֵדָה מִדְבַּר־צִן בַּחֹדֶשׁ הָרִאשׁוֹן וַיֵּשֶׁב
ב הָעָם בְּקָדֵשׁ וַתָּמָת שָׁם מִרְיָם וַתִּקָּבֵר שָׁם: וְלֹא־הָיָה מַיִם לָעֵדָה
ג וַיִּקָּהֲלוּ עַל־מֹשֶׁה וְעַל־אַהֲרֹן: וַיָּרֶב הָעָם עִם־מֹשֶׁה וַיֹּאמְרוּ
ד לֵאמֹר וְלוּ גָוַעְנוּ בִּגְוַע אַחֵינוּ לִפְנֵי יהוה: וְלָמָה הֲבֵאתֶם אֶת־
ה קְהַל יהוה אֶל־הַמִּדְבָּר הַזֶּה לָמוּת שָׁם אֲנַחְנוּ וּבְעִירֵנוּ: וְלָמָה
הֶעֱלִיתֻנוּ מִמִּצְרַיִם לְהָבִיא אֹתָנוּ אֶל־הַמָּקוֹם הָרָע הַזֶּה לֹא ׀
ו מְקוֹם זֶרַע וּתְאֵנָה וְגֶפֶן וְרִמּוֹן וּמַיִם אַיִן לִשְׁתּוֹת: וַיָּבֹא מֹשֶׁה
וְאַהֲרֹן מִפְּנֵי הַקָּהָל אֶל־פֶּתַח אֹהֶל מוֹעֵד וַיִּפְּלוּ עַל־פְּנֵיהֶם
וַיֵּרָא כְבוֹד־יהוה אֲלֵיהֶם:

שלישי / שני /

ז וַיְדַבֵּר יהוה אֶל־מֹשֶׁה לֵּאמֹר: קַח אֶת־הַמַּטֶּה וְהַקְהֵל אֶת־
ח הָעֵדָה אַתָּה וְאַהֲרֹן אָחִיךָ וְדִבַּרְתֶּם אֶל־הַסֶּלַע לְעֵינֵיהֶם וְנָתַן
מֵימָיו וְהוֹצֵאתָ לָהֶם מַיִם מִן־הַסֶּלַע וְהִשְׁקִיתָ אֶת־הָעֵדָה
ט וְאֶת־בְּעִירָם: וַיִּקַּח מֹשֶׁה אֶת־הַמַּטֶּה מִלִּפְנֵי יהוה כַּאֲשֶׁר
י צִוָּהוּ: וַיַּקְהִלוּ מֹשֶׁה וְאַהֲרֹן אֶת־הַקָּהָל אֶל־פְּנֵי הַסָּלַע וַיֹּאמֶר

פרק כ

א | **כָּל הָעֵדָה.** עֵדָה הַשְּׁלֵמָה, שֶׁכְּבָר מֵתוּ מֵתֵי מִדְבָּר וְאֵלּוּ פָּרְשׁוּ לְחַיִּים. **וַתָּמָת שָׁם מִרְיָם.** לָמָּה נִסְמְכָה מִיתַת מִרְיָם לְפָרָשַׁת פָּרָה אֲדֻמָּה? לוֹמַר לְךָ, מַה קָּרְבָּנוֹת מְכַפְּרִין, אַף מִיתַת צַדִּיקִים מְכַפֶּרֶת. **וַתָּמָת שָׁם מִרְיָם.** אַף הִיא בִּנְשִׁיקָה מֵתָה, וּמִפְּנֵי מָה לֹא נֶאֱמַר בָּהּ: "עַל פִּי ה'"? שֶׁאֵינוֹ דֶּרֶךְ כָּבוֹד שֶׁל מַעְלָה. וּבְאַהֲרֹן נֶאֱמַר: "עַל פִּי ה'" בְּחֻלָּה מַסְעֵי (להלן לג, לח).

ב | **וְלֹא הָיָה מַיִם לָעֵדָה.** מִכָּאן שֶׁכָּל אַרְבָּעִים שָׁנָה הָיָה לָהֶם הַבְּאֵר בִּזְכוּת מִרְיָם:

ג | **וְלוּ גָוַעְנוּ.** הַלְוַאי שֶׁגָּוַעְנוּ. **בִּגְוַע אַחֵינוּ.** בְּמִיתַת אַחֵינוּ בַּדֶּבֶר, לָמַד שֶׁמִּיתַת צָמָא מְגֻנָּה מִמֶּנָּה. **בִּגְוַע.**

שֵׁם דָּבָר הוּא, כְּמוֹ: 'בִּמְיתַת אַחֵינוּ'. וְלֹא יִתָּכֵן לְפָרְשׁוֹ כְּשֶׁמֵּתוּ אַחֵינוּ, שֶׁאִם כֵּן הָיָה לוֹ לְהִנָּקֵד 'בִּגְוֹעַ':

ח | **וְאֶת בְּעִירָם.** מִכָּאן שֶׁחָס הַקָּדוֹשׁ בָּרוּךְ הוּא עַל מָמוֹנָם שֶׁל יִשְׂרָאֵל:

י | **וַיַּקְהִלוּ וְגוֹ'.** זֶה אֶחָד מִן הַמְּקוֹמוֹת שֶׁהֶחֱזִיק מְעַט אֶת הַמְּרֻבֶּה. **הֲמִן הַסֶּלַע הַזֶּה נוֹצִיא.** לְפִי שֶׁלֹּא הָיוּ מַכִּירִין אוֹתוֹ, לְפִי שֶׁהָלַךְ הַסֶּלַע וְיָשַׁב לוֹ בֵּין הַסְּלָעִים כְּשֶׁנִּסְתַּלֵּק הַבְּאֵר, וְהָיוּ יִשְׂרָאֵל אוֹמְרִים לָהֶם: מַה לָּכֶם, מֵאֵיזֶה סֶּלַע תּוֹצִיאוּ לָנוּ מַיִם? לְכָךְ אָמַר לָהֶם: "הַמֹּרִים", סָרְבָנִים, לְשׁוֹן יְוָנִי שׁוֹטִים, מוֹרִים אֶת מוֹרֵיהֶם, "הֲמִן הַסֶּלַע הַזֶּה" שֶׁלֹּא נִצְטַוִּינוּ עָלָיו, "נוֹצִיא לָכֶם מַיִם"?

לָהֶ֔ם שִׁמְעוּ־נָ֖א הַמֹּרִ֑ים הֲמִן־הַסֶּ֣לַע הַזֶּ֔ה נוֹצִ֥יא לָכֶ֖ם מָֽיִם:
יא וַיָּ֨רֶם מֹשֶׁ֜ה אֶת־יָד֗וֹ וַיַּ֧ךְ אֶת־הַסֶּ֛לַע בְּמַטֵּ֖הוּ פַּעֲמָ֑יִם וַיֵּצְאוּ֙ מַ֣יִם רַבִּ֔ים וַתֵּ֥שְׁתְּ הָעֵדָ֖ה וּבְעִירָֽם:
יב וַיֹּ֣אמֶר יְהֹוָה֮ אֶל־מֹשֶׁ֣ה וְאֶֽל־אַהֲרֹן֒ יַ֚עַן לֹא־הֶאֱמַנְתֶּ֣ם בִּ֔י לְהַ֨קְדִּישֵׁ֔נִי לְעֵינֵ֖י בְּנֵ֣י יִשְׂרָאֵ֑ל לָכֵ֗ן לֹ֤א תָבִ֙יאוּ֙ אֶת־הַקָּהָ֣ל הַזֶּ֔ה אֶל־הָאָ֖רֶץ אֲשֶׁר־נָתַ֥תִּי לָהֶֽם:
יג הֵ֚מָּה מֵ֣י מְרִיבָ֔ה אֲשֶׁר־רָב֥וּ בְנֵֽי־יִשְׂרָאֵ֖ל אֶת־יְהֹוָ֑ה וַיִּקָּדֵ֖שׁ בָּֽם:
יד וַיִּשְׁלַ֨ח מֹשֶׁ֧ה מַלְאָכִ֛ים מִקָּדֵ֖שׁ אֶל־מֶ֣לֶךְ אֱד֑וֹם כֹּ֤ה אָמַר֙ אָחִ֣יךָ יִשְׂרָאֵ֔ל אַתָּ֣ה יָדַ֔עְתָּ אֵ֥ת כׇּל־הַתְּלָאָ֖ה אֲשֶׁ֥ר מְצָאָֽתְנוּ: וַיֵּרְד֤וּ אֲבֹתֵ֙ינוּ֙ מִצְרַ֔יְמָה וַנֵּ֥שֶׁב בְּמִצְרַ֖יִם יָמִ֣ים רַבִּ֑ים
טו וַיָּרֵ֥עוּ לָ֛נוּ מִצְרַ֖יִם וְלַאֲבֹתֵֽינוּ: וַנִּצְעַ֤ק אֶל־יְהֹוָה֙ וַיִּשְׁמַ֣ע קֹלֵ֔נוּ
טז

רביעי

יא) פַּעֲמָיִם. לְפִי שֶׁבָּרִאשׁוֹנָה לֹא הוֹצִיא אֶלָּא טִפִּין, לְפִי שֶׁלֹּא צִוָּה הַמָּקוֹם לְהַכּוֹת, אֶלָּא "וְדִבַּרְתֶּם אֶל הַסֶּלַע", וְהֵמָּה דִּבְּרוּ אֶל סֶלַע אַחֵר וְלֹא הוֹצִיא, אָמְרוּ: שֶׁמָּא צָרִיךְ לְהַכּוֹת כְּבָרִאשׁוֹנָה, שֶׁנֶּאֱמַר: "וְהִכִּיתָ בַצּוּר" (שמות יז, ו), וְנִזְדַּמֵּן לָהֶם אוֹתוֹ סֶלַע וְהִכָּהוּ:

יב) לְהַקְדִּישֵׁנִי. שֶׁאִלּוּ דִּבַּרְתֶּם אֶל הַסֶּלַע וְהוֹצִיא, הָיִיתִי מְקֻדָּשׁ לְעֵינֵי הָעֵדָה, וְאוֹמְרִים: מַה סֶּלַע זֶה, שֶׁאֵינוֹ מְדַבֵּר וְאֵינוֹ שׁוֹמֵעַ וְאֵינוֹ צָרִיךְ לְפַרְנָסָה, מְקַיֵּם דִּבּוּרוֹ שֶׁל מָקוֹם, קַל וָחֹמֶר אָנוּ: לָכֵן לֹא תָבִיאוּ. בִּשְׁבוּעָה, נִשְׁבַּע בִּקְפִיצָה, שֶׁלֹּא יַרְבּוּ בִּתְפִלָּה עַל כָּךְ: יַעַן לֹא הֶאֱמַנְתֶּם בִּי. גִּלָּה הַכָּתוּב שֶׁאִלּוּלֵי חֵטְא זֶה בִּלְבַד הָיוּ נִכְנָסִין לָאָרֶץ, כְּדֵי שֶׁלֹּא יֹאמְרוּ עֲלֵיהֶם: כַּעֲוֹן שְׁאָר דּוֹר הַמִּדְבָּר שֶׁנִּגְזַר עֲלֵיהֶם שֶׁלֹּא יִכָּנְסוּ לָאָרֶץ, כָּךְ הָיָה עֲוֹן מֹשֶׁה וְאַהֲרֹן. וַהֲלֹא "הֲשִׁמְעוּ נָא הַמֹּרִים" קָשָׁה מִזּוֹ? אֶלָּא לְפִי שֶׁבַּסֵּתֶר חִסֵּךְ עָלָיו הַכָּתוּב, וְכָאן שֶׁבְּמַעֲמַד כָּל יִשְׂרָאֵל לֹא חִסֵּךְ עָלָיו הַכָּתוּב, מִפְּנֵי קִדּוּשׁ הַשֵּׁם:

יג) הֵמָּה מֵי מְרִיבָה. הֵם הַנִּזְכָּרִים בְּמָקוֹם אַחֵר, אֶת אֵלּוּ רָאוּ אִצְטַגְנִינֵי פַרְעֹה שֶׁמּוֹשִׁיעָן שֶׁל יִשְׂרָאֵל לוֹקֶה בַּמַּיִם, לְכָךְ גָּזְרוּ: "כָּל הַבֵּן הַיִּלּוֹד הַיְאֹרָה תַּשְׁלִיכֻהוּ" (שמות א, כב): וַיִּקָּדֵשׁ בָּם. שֶׁמֵּתוּ מֹשֶׁה וְאַהֲרֹן עַל יָדָם, שֶׁכְּשֶׁהַקָּדוֹשׁ בָּרוּךְ הוּא עוֹשֶׂה דִין בִּמְקֻדָּשָׁיו הוּא יָראוּי וּמִתְקַדֵּשׁ עַל הַבְּרִיּוֹת, וְכֵן הוּא אוֹמֵר: "נוֹרָא אֱלֹהִים מִמִּקְדָּשֶׁיךָ" (תהלים סח, לו), וְכֵן הוּא אוֹמֵר: "בִּקְרֹבַי אֶקָּדֵשׁ" (ויקרא י, ג):

יד) אָחִיךָ יִשְׂרָאֵל. מָה רָאָה לְהַזְכִּיר כָּאן אַחֲוָה? אֶלָּא אָמַר לוֹ: אַחִים אֲנַחְנוּ בְּנֵי אַבְרָהָם, שֶׁנֶּאֱמַר לוֹ: "כִּי גֵר יִהְיֶה זַרְעֲךָ" (בראשית טו, יג), וְעַל שְׁנֵינוּ הָיָה אוֹתוֹ הַחוֹב לְפָרְעוֹ: אַתָּה יָדַעְתָּ אֵת כָּל הַתְּלָאָה. לְפִיכָךְ פֵּרַשׁ אֲבִיכֶם מֵעַל אָבִינוּ, שֶׁנֶּאֱמַר: "וַיֵּלֶךְ אֶל אֶרֶץ מִפְּנֵי יַעֲקֹב אָחִיו" (שם לו, ו), מִפְּנֵי הַשְּׁטָר חוֹב הַמֻּטָּל עֲלֵיהֶם, וְהִטִּילוֹ עַל יַעֲקֹב:

טו) וַיָּרֵעוּ לָנוּ. סָבַלְנוּ צָרוֹת רַבּוֹת: וְלַאֲבֹתֵינוּ. מִכָּאן שֶׁהָאָבוֹת מִצְטַעֲרִים בַּקֶּבֶר כְּשֶׁפֻּרְעָנוּת בָּאָה עַל יִשְׂרָאֵל:

טז) וַיִּשְׁמַע קֹלֵנוּ. בַּבְּרָכָה שֶׁבֵּרְכָנוּ אָבִינוּ: "הַקֹּל קוֹל יַעֲקֹב" (בראשית כז, כב), שֶׁאָנוּ צוֹעֲקִים וְנַעֲנִים: מַלְאָךְ.

פרק כ | במדבר | חקת | 410

וַיִּשְׁלַח מַלְאָךְ וַיֹּצִאֵנוּ מִמִּצְרָיִם וְהִנֵּה אֲנַחְנוּ בְקָדֵשׁ עִיר קְצֵה
גְבוּלֶךָ: נַעְבְּרָה־נָּא בְאַרְצֶךָ לֹא נַעֲבֹר בְּשָׂדֶה וּבְכֶרֶם וְלֹא יז
נִשְׁתֶּה מֵי בְאֵר דֶּרֶךְ הַמֶּלֶךְ נֵלֵךְ לֹא נִטֶּה יָמִין וּשְׂמֹאול עַד
אֲשֶׁר־נַעֲבֹר גְּבֻלֶךָ: וַיֹּאמֶר אֵלָיו אֱדוֹם לֹא תַעֲבֹר בִּי פֶּן־בַּחֶרֶב יח
אֵצֵא לִקְרָאתֶךָ: וַיֹּאמְרוּ אֵלָיו בְּנֵי־יִשְׂרָאֵל בַּמְסִלָּה נַעֲלֶה וְאִם־ יט
מֵימֶיךָ נִשְׁתֶּה אֲנִי וּמִקְנַי וְנָתַתִּי מִכְרָם רַק אֵין־דָּבָר בְּרַגְלַי
אֶעֱבֹרָה: וַיֹּאמֶר לֹא תַעֲבֹר וַיֵּצֵא אֱדוֹם לִקְרָאתוֹ בְּעַם כָּבֵד כ
וּבְיָד חֲזָקָה: וַיְמָאֵן ׀ אֱדוֹם נְתֹן אֶת־יִשְׂרָאֵל עֲבֹר בִּגְבֻלוֹ וַיֵּט כא
יִשְׂרָאֵל מֵעָלָיו:

וַיִּסְעוּ מִקָּדֵשׁ וַיָּבֹאוּ בְנֵי־יִשְׂרָאֵל כָּל־הָעֵדָה הֹר הָהָר: וַיֹּאמֶר כב
יְהוָה אֶל־מֹשֶׁה וְאֶל־אַהֲרֹן בְּהֹר הָהָר עַל־גְּבוּל אֶרֶץ־אֱדוֹם כג
לֵאמֹר: יֵאָסֵף אַהֲרֹן אֶל־עַמָּיו כִּי לֹא יָבֹא אֶל־הָאָרֶץ אֲשֶׁר כד

חמישי
/שלישי/

זֶה מֹשֶׁה, מִכָּאן שֶׁהַנְּבִיאִים קְרוּיִין מַלְאָכִים, וְאוֹמֵר: "וַיִּהְיוּ מַלְעִבִים בְּמַלְאֲכֵי הָאֱלֹהִים" (דברי הימים ב׳ לו, טז).

יז נַעְבְּרָה נָּא בְאַרְצֶךָ. אֵין לְךָ לַעֲבֹר עַל הַיְרֻשָּׁה שֶׁל אֶרֶץ יִשְׂרָאֵל, כְּשֵׁם שֶׁלֹּא פָרַעְתָּ הַחוֹב, עֲשֵׂה לָנוּ עֵזֶר מְעַט לַעֲבֹר דֶּרֶךְ אַרְצְךָ: וְלֹא נִשְׁתֶּה מֵי בְאֵר. 'מֵי בוֹרוֹת' הָיָה צָרִיךְ לוֹמַר, אֶלָּא כָּךְ אָמַר מֹשֶׁה: אַף עַל פִּי שֶׁיֵּשׁ בְּיָדֵנוּ מָן לֶאֱכֹל וּבְאֵר לִשְׁתּוֹת, לֹא נִשְׁתֶּה מִמֶּנּוּ, אֶלָּא נִקְנֶה מִכֶּם אֹכֶל וּמַיִם לַהֲנָאַתְכֶם, מִכָּאן לְאַכְסְנַאי שֶׁאַף עַל פִּי שֶׁיֵּשׁ בְּיָדוֹ לֶאֱכֹל יִקְנֶה מִן הַחֶנְוָנִי, כְּדֵי לַהֲנוֹת אֶת אַכְסַנְיוֹ: דֶּרֶךְ הַמֶּלֶךְ נֵלֵךְ וְגוֹ'. אָנוּ חוֹסְמִים אֶת בְּהֶמְתֵּנוּ וְלֹא יִטּוּ לְכָאן וּלְכָאן לֶאֱכֹל:

יח פֶּן בַּחֶרֶב אֵצֵא לִקְרָאתֶךָ. אַתֶּם מִתְגָּאִים בַּקּוֹל שֶׁהוֹרִישְׁכֶם אֲבִיכֶם, וְאוֹמְרִים: "וַנִּצְעַק אֶל ה' וַיִּשְׁמַע

קֹלֵנוּ" (לעיל פסוק טז), וַאֲנִי אֵצֵא עֲלֵיכֶם בַּמֶּה שֶׁהוֹרִישַׁנִי אָבִי: "וְעַל חַרְבְּךָ תִחְיֶה" (בראשית כז, מ):

יט רַק אֵין דָּבָר. אֵין שׁוּם דָּבָר מַזִּיקְךָ:

כ וּבְיָד חֲזָקָה. בְּהַבְטָחַת זְקֵנֵנוּ: "וְהַיָּדַיִם יְדֵי עֵשָׂו" (בראשית כז, כב):

כב כָּל הָעֵדָה. כֻּלָּם שְׁלֵמִים וְעוֹמְדִים לְהִכָּנֵס לָאָרֶץ, שֶׁלֹּא הָיָה בָהֶן אֶחָד מֵאוֹתָם שֶׁנִּגְזְרָה גְזֵרָה עֲלֵיהֶם, שֶׁכְּבָר כָּלוּ מֵתֵי מִדְבָּר, וְאֵלּוּ מֵאוֹתָן שֶׁכָּתוּב בָּהֶן: "חַיִּים כֻּלְּכֶם הַיּוֹם" (דברים ד, ד): הֹר הָהָר. הַר עַל גַּבֵּי הַר, כְּתַפּוּחַ קָטָן עַל גַּבֵּי תַפּוּחַ גָּדוֹל, וְאַף עַל פִּי שֶׁהֶעָנָן הוֹלֵךְ לִפְנֵיהֶם וּמַשְׁוֶה אֶת הֶהָרִים, שְׁלֹשָׁה נִשְׁאֲרוּ בָהֶן: הַר סִינַי לַתּוֹרָה, הֹר הָהָר לִקְבוּרַת אַהֲרֹן, וְהַר נְבוֹ לִקְבוּרַת מֹשֶׁה:

כג עַל גְּבוּל אֶרֶץ אֱדוֹם. מַגִּיד שֶׁמִּפְּנֵי שֶׁנִּתְחַבְּרוּ

במדבר | פרק כא | חקת | 411

כה נָתַ֣תִּי לִבְנֵֽי־יִשְׂרָאֵ֑ל עַ֛ל אֲשֶׁר־מְרִיתֶ֥ם אֶת־פִּ֖י לְמֵ֥י מְרִיבָֽה: קַ֚ח
כו אֶֽת־אַהֲרֹ֔ן וְאֶת־אֶלְעָזָ֖ר בְּנ֑וֹ וְהַ֥עַל אֹתָ֖ם הֹ֥ר הָהָֽר: וְהַפְשֵׁ֤ט
אֶֽת־אַהֲרֹן֙ אֶת־בְּגָדָ֔יו וְהִלְבַּשְׁתָּ֖ם אֶת־אֶלְעָזָ֣ר בְּנ֑וֹ וְאַהֲרֹ֥ן יֵאָסֵ֖ף
כז וּמֵ֥ת שָֽׁם: וַיַּ֣עַשׂ מֹשֶׁ֔ה כַּאֲשֶׁ֖ר צִוָּ֣ה יְהוָ֑ה וַֽיַּעֲלוּ֙ אֶל־הֹ֣ר הָהָ֔ר
כח לְעֵינֵ֖י כָּל־הָעֵדָֽה: וַיַּפְשֵׁט֩ מֹשֶׁ֨ה אֶֽת־אַהֲרֹ֜ן אֶת־בְּגָדָ֗יו וַיַּלְבֵּ֤שׁ
אֹתָם֙ אֶת־אֶלְעָזָ֣ר בְּנ֔וֹ וַיָּ֧מָת אַהֲרֹ֛ן שָׁ֖ם בְּרֹ֣אשׁ הָהָ֑ר וַיֵּ֧רֶד מֹשֶׁ֛ה
כט וְאֶלְעָזָ֖ר מִן־הָהָֽר: וַיִּרְאוּ֙ כָּל־הָ֣עֵדָ֔ה כִּ֥י גָוַ֖ע אַהֲרֹ֑ן וַיִּבְכּ֤וּ אֶת־
כא א אַהֲרֹן֙ שְׁלֹשִׁ֣ים י֔וֹם כֹּ֖ל בֵּ֥ית יִשְׂרָאֵֽל: וַיִּשְׁמַ֞ע הַכְּנַעֲנִ֤י
מֶֽלֶךְ־עֲרָד֙ יֹשֵׁ֣ב הַנֶּ֔גֶב כִּ֚י בָּ֣א יִשְׂרָאֵ֔ל דֶּ֖רֶךְ הָאֲתָרִ֑ים וַיִּלָּ֙חֶם֙

כאן להתקרב לעשות הרשע נפרע מעשיהם וחסרו הצדיק הזה:

כה] **קח את אהרן.** בדברים של נחומים, אמר לו: אשריך שתראה כתרך נתון לבנך, מה שאין אני זכאי לכך:

כו] **את בגדיו.** בגדי כהנה גדולה הלבישהו והפשיטם מעליו לתתם על בנו בפניו. אמר לו: הכנס למערה, ונכנס. ראה מטה מצעת ונר דלוק. אמר לו: עלה למטה, ועלה. פשט ידיך, ופשט. קמץ פיך, וקמץ. עצם עיניך, ועצם. מיד חמד משה לאותה מיתה. וזהו שנאמר לו: "כַּאֲשֶׁר מֵת אַהֲרֹן אָחִיךָ" (דברים לב, נ) מיתה שנתאוית לה:

כז] **ויעש משה.** אף על פי שהדבר קשה לו, לא עכב:

כט] **ויראו כל העדה וגו'.** כשראוהו משה ואלעזר יורדים ואהרן לא ירד, אמרו: היכן הוא אהרן? אמר להם: מת. אמרו: אפשר מי שעמד כנגד המלאך ועצר את המגפה (במדבר יז, יג) ישלוט בו מלאך המות?! מיד בקש משה רחמים והראוהו מלאכי השרת להם מטל במטה, ראו והאמינו: כל

בית ישראל. האנשים והנשים, לפי שהיה אהרן רודף שלום ומטיל אהבה בין בעלי מריבה ובין איש לאשתו: **כי גוע.** אומר אני שהמתרגם 'דְּכָא מִית' טועה הוא, אלא אם כן מתרגם 'וַיִּרְאוּ' — 'וְאִתְחֲזִיאוּ', שלא אמרו רבותינו זכרונם לברכה 'כי' זה משמש בלשון 'דְּהָא', אלא על מדרש שנסתלקו ענני כבוד, וכדאמר רבי אבהו: אל תקרי 'וַיִּרְאוּ' אלא 'וַיֵּרָאוּ', ועל לשון זה נופל לשון 'דְּהָא', לפי שהיא נתינת טעם למה שלמעלה הימנו: למה 'וַיֵּרָאוּ'? לפי שהרי מת אהרן. אבל על תרגום: "וַחֲזוֹ כָּל כְּנִשְׁתָּא" אין לשון 'דְּהָא' נופל, אלא לשון 'אֲשֶׁר', שהוא מגזרת שמוש 'חִי', 'שָׁמְעוּ', 'הֵס' משמש בלשון 'אֲשֶׁר', כמו: "וְהֵס מַדּוּעַ לֹא תָקְעוּ רוּחִי" (איוב כו, ד), וְהַרְבֵּה מְפֻלָּשִׁים מִזֶּה הַלָּשׁוֹן: "הֵס חָרוּצִים יָמָיו" (תהלים לט, ה):

פרק כא

א] **וישמע הכנעני.** שמע שמת אהרן ונסתלקו ענני כבוד כו', כדאיתא בראש השנה (דף ג ע"א). ועמלק מעולם רצועת מרדות לישראל, מזמן בכל עת לפרענות: **יֹשֵׁב הַנֶּגֶב.** זה עמלק, שנאמר: "עֲמָלֵק יוֹשֵׁב בְּאֶרֶץ הַנֶּגֶב" (לעיל יג, כט), ושנה את לשונו לדבר

חקת | פרק כא | במדבר

בְּיִשְׂרָאֵל וַיֵּשֶׁב מִמֶּנּוּ שֶׁבִי: וַיִּדַּר יִשְׂרָאֵל נֶדֶר לַיהוָה וַיֹּאמַר ב
אִם־נָתֹן תִּתֵּן אֶת־הָעָם הַזֶּה בְּיָדִי וְהַחֲרַמְתִּי אֶת־עָרֵיהֶם:
וַיִּשְׁמַע יְהוָה בְּקוֹל יִשְׂרָאֵל וַיִּתֵּן אֶת־הַכְּנַעֲנִי וַיַּחֲרֵם אֶתְהֶם ג
וְאֶת־עָרֵיהֶם וַיִּקְרָא שֵׁם־הַמָּקוֹם חָרְמָה:
וַיִּסְעוּ מֵהֹר הָהָר דֶּרֶךְ יַם־סוּף לִסְבֹב אֶת־אֶרֶץ אֱדוֹם וַתִּקְצַר ד
נֶפֶשׁ־הָעָם בַּדָּרֶךְ: וַיְדַבֵּר הָעָם בֵּאלֹהִים וּבְמֹשֶׁה לָמָה הֶעֱלִיתֻנוּ ה
מִמִּצְרַיִם לָמוּת בַּמִּדְבָּר כִּי אֵין לֶחֶם וְאֵין מַיִם וְנַפְשֵׁנוּ קָצָה
בַּלֶּחֶם הַקְּלֹקֵל: וַיְשַׁלַּח יְהוָה בָּעָם אֵת הַנְּחָשִׁים הַשְּׂרָפִים ו

בִּלְשׁוֹן כְּנַעַן, כְּדֵי שֶׁיִּהְיוּ יִשְׂרָאֵל מִתְפַּלְלִים לְהַקָּדוֹשׁ בָּרוּךְ הוּא לָתֵת כְּנַעֲנִים בְּיָדָם, וְהֵם אֵינָם כְּנַעֲנִים. רָאוּ יִשְׂרָאֵל לְבוּשֵׁיהֶם כִּלְבוּשֵׁי עֲמָלֵקִים וּלְשׁוֹנָם לְשׁוֹן כְּנַעַן, אָמְרוּ: נִתְפַּלֵּל סְתָם, שֶׁנֶּאֱמַר: "אִם נָתֹן תִּתֵּן אֶת הָעָם הַזֶּה בְּיָדִי" (להלן פסוק כג). **דֶּרֶךְ הָאֲתָרִים**. דֶּרֶךְ הַנֶּגֶב שֶׁהָלְכוּ בָהּ מְרַגְּלִים, שֶׁנֶּאֱמַר: "וַיַּעֲלוּ בַנֶּגֶב" (לעיל יג, כב). דָּבָר אַחֵר, "דֶּרֶךְ הָאֲתָרִים", דֶּרֶךְ הַתַּיָּר הַגָּדוֹל הַנּוֹסֵעַ לִפְנֵיהֶם, שֶׁנֶּאֱמַר: "דֶּרֶךְ שְׁלֹשֶׁת יָמִים לָתוּר לָהֶם מְנוּחָה" (לעיל י, לג). **וַיֵּשֶׁב מִמֶּנּוּ שֶׁבִי**. אֵינָהּ אֶלָּא שִׁפְחָה אַחַת:

ב **וְהַחֲרַמְתִּי**. אַקְדִּישׁ שְׁלָלָם לַגָּבוֹהַּ:

ג **וַיַּחֲרֵם אֶתְהֶם**. בַּהֲרִיגָה. **וְאֶת עָרֵיהֶם**. חֶרְמֵי גָּבוֹהַּ:

ד **דֶּרֶךְ יַם סוּף**. כֵּיוָן שֶׁמֵּת אַהֲרֹן וּבָאת עֲלֵיהֶם מִלְחָמָה זוֹ, חָזְרוּ לַאֲחוֹרֵיהֶם דֶּרֶךְ יַם סוּף, הוּא הַדֶּרֶךְ שֶׁחָזְרוּ לָהֶם כְּשֶׁנִּגְזְרָה עֲלֵיהֶם גְּזֵרַת מְרַגְּלִים, שֶׁנֶּאֱמַר: "וּסְעוּ הַמִּדְבָּרָה דֶּרֶךְ יַם סוּף" (דברים א, מ). וְכָאן חָזְרוּ לַאֲחוֹרֵיהֶם שֶׁבַע מַסָּעוֹת, שֶׁנֶּאֱמַר: "וּבְנֵי יִשְׂרָאֵל נָסְעוּ מִבְּאֵרֹת בְּנֵי יַעֲקָן מוֹסֵרָה שָׁם מֵת אַהֲרֹן" (שם י, ו). וְכִי בְּמוֹסֵרָה מֵת? וַהֲלֹא בְּהֹר הָהָר מֵת! אֶלָּא שָׁם חָזְרוּ וְהִתְאַבְּלוּ עָלָיו וְהִסְפִּידוּהוּ כְּאִלּוּ הוּא בִּפְנֵיהֶם. וְצֵא וּבְדֹק בַּמַּסָּעוֹת וְתִמְצָאֵם שֶׁבַע מַסָּעוֹת מִן מוֹסֵרָה עַד הֹר הָהָר. **לִסְבֹב אֶת אֶרֶץ אֱדוֹם**. שֶׁלֹּא נְתָנָם לַעֲבֹר בְּאַרְצוֹ. **וַתִּקְצַר נֶפֶשׁ הָעָם**

בַּדָּרֶךְ. בְּטֹרַח הַדֶּרֶךְ שֶׁהֻקְשָׁה לָהֶם, אָמְרוּ: עַכְשָׁיו הָיִינוּ קְרוֹבִים לִכָּנֵס לָאָרֶץ וְאָנוּ חוֹזְרִים לַאֲחוֹרֵינוּ, כָּךְ חָזְרוּ אֲבוֹתֵינוּ וְנִשְׁתַּהוּ שְׁלֹשִׁים וּשְׁמוֹנֶה שָׁנָה עַד הַיּוֹם, לְפִיכָךְ קָצְרָה נַפְשָׁם בְּעִנּוּיֵי הַדֶּרֶךְ. וּבִלְשׁוֹן לַעַ"ז אנק"רוטולי"ר. וְלֹא יִתָּכֵן לוֹמַר "וַתִּקְצַר נֶפֶשׁ הָעָם בַּדָּרֶךְ" בִּהְיוֹתָם בַּדֶּרֶךְ, וְלֹא פֵּרֵשׁ בּוֹ בַּמֶּה קָצְרָה, שֶׁכָּל מָקוֹם שֶׁתִּמְצָא קִצּוּר נֶפֶשׁ בַּמִּקְרָא מְפֹרָשׁ שָׁם בַּמֶּה קָצְרָה, כְּגוֹן: "וַתִּקְצַר נַפְשִׁי בָּהֶם" (זכריה יא, ח), וּכְגוֹן: "וַתִּקְצַר נַפְשׁוֹ בַּעֲמַל יִשְׂרָאֵל" (שופטים י, טז). וְכָל דָּבָר הַקָּשֶׁה עַל אָדָם נוֹפֵל בּוֹ לְשׁוֹן קִצּוּר נֶפֶשׁ, כְּאָדָם שֶׁהַטֹּרַח בָּא עָלָיו וְאֵין דַּעְתּוֹ רְחָבָה לְקַבֵּל אוֹתוֹ הַדָּבָר, וְאֵין לוֹ מָקוֹם בְּתוֹךְ לִבּוֹ לָגוּר שָׁם אוֹתוֹ הַצַּעַר, וּבַדָּבָר הַמַּטְרִיחַ נוֹפֵל לְשׁוֹן גֹּדֶל, שֶׁגָּדוֹל הוּא וְכָבֵד עַל הָאָדָם, כְּגוֹן: "וְגַם נַפְשָׁם בָּחֲלָה בִי" (זכריה שם), גָּדְלָה עָלַי, "וְיִגְאֶה כַּשַּׁחַל תְּצוּדֵנִי" (איוב י, טז). כְּלָלוֹ שֶׁל פֵּרוּשׁ, כָּל לְשׁוֹן קִצּוּר נֶפֶשׁ בְּדָבָר, לְשׁוֹן "שֶׁאֵין יָכוֹל לְסָבְלוֹ" הוּא, שֶׁאֵין הַדַּעַת סוֹבַלְתּוֹ:

ה **בֵּאלֹהִים וּבְמֹשֶׁה**. הִשְׁווּ עֶבֶד לְקוֹנוֹ: **לָמָה הֶעֱלִיתֻנוּ**. שְׁנֵיהֶם שָׁוִים: **וְנַפְשֵׁנוּ קָצָה**. אַף זֶה לְשׁוֹן קִצּוּר נֶפֶשׁ וּמִאוּס: **בַּלֶּחֶם הַקְּלֹקֵל**. לְפִי שֶׁהַמָּן נִבְלָע בָּאֵיבָרִים קְרָאוּהוּ "קְלֹקֵל", אָמְרוּ: עָתִיד הַמָּן הַזֶּה שֶׁיִּתְפַּח בְּמֵעֵינוּ, כְּלוּם יֵשׁ יְלוּד אִשָּׁה שֶׁמַּכְנִיס וְאֵינוֹ מוֹצִיא?

ו **אֵת הַנְּחָשִׁים הַשְּׂרָפִים**. שֶׁשּׂוֹרְפִים אֶת הָאָדָם

במדבר | פרק כא | חקת

ז וַיְנַשְּׁכוּ אֶת־הָעָם וַיָּמָת עַם־רָב מִיִּשְׂרָאֵל: וַיָּבֹא הָעָם אֶל־מֹשֶׁה וַיֹּאמְרוּ חָטָאנוּ כִּי־דִבַּרְנוּ בַיהוָה וָבָךְ הִתְפַּלֵּל אֶל־יְהוָה וְיָסֵר מֵעָלֵינוּ אֶת־הַנָּחָשׁ וַיִּתְפַּלֵּל מֹשֶׁה בְּעַד הָעָם: ח וַיֹּאמֶר יְהוָה אֶל־מֹשֶׁה עֲשֵׂה לְךָ שָׂרָף וְשִׂים אֹתוֹ עַל־נֵס וְהָיָה כָּל־הַנָּשׁוּךְ וְרָאָה אֹתוֹ וָחָי: ט וַיַּעַשׂ מֹשֶׁה נְחַשׁ נְחֹשֶׁת וַיְשִׂמֵהוּ עַל־הַנֵּס וְהָיָה אִם־נָשַׁךְ הַנָּחָשׁ אֶת־אִישׁ וְהִבִּיט אֶל־נְחַשׁ הַנְּחֹשֶׁת וָחָי: ששי י וַיִּסְעוּ בְּנֵי יִשְׂרָאֵל וַיַּחֲנוּ בְּאֹבֹת: וַיִּסְעוּ מֵאֹבֹת וַיַּחֲנוּ בְּעִיֵּי הָעֲבָרִים יא בַּמִּדְבָּר אֲשֶׁר עַל־פְּנֵי מוֹאָב מִמִּזְרַח הַשָּׁמֶשׁ: מִשָּׁם נָסָעוּ יב וַיַּחֲנוּ בְּנַחַל זָרֶד: מִשָּׁם נָסָעוּ וַיַּחֲנוּ מֵעֵבֶר אַרְנוֹן אֲשֶׁר בַּמִּדְבָּר יג הַיֹּצֵא מִגְּבֻל הָאֱמֹרִי כִּי אַרְנוֹן גְּבוּל מוֹאָב בֵּין מוֹאָב וּבֵין

בְּחֵרֶם שְׁפִיפוֹן. **וַיְנַשְּׁכוּ אֶת־הָעָם.** יָבֹא נָחָשׁ שֶׁלָּקָה עַל הוֹצָאַת דִּבָּה וְיִפָּרַע מִמּוֹצִיאֵי דִּבָּה, יָבֹא נָחָשׁ שֶׁכָּל הַמִּינִין נִטְעָמִין לוֹ טַעַם אֶחָד וְיִפָּרַע מִכְּפוּיֵי טוֹבָה שֶׁדָּבָר אֶחָד מִשְׁתַּנֶּה לָהֶם לְכַמָּה טְעָמִים:

ז] **וַיִּתְפַּלֵּל מֹשֶׁה.** מִכָּאן לְמִי שֶׁמְּבַקְשִׁים מִמֶּנּוּ מְחִילָה שֶׁלֹּא יְהֵא אַכְזָרִי מִלִּמְחוֹל:

ח] **עַל נֵס.** עַל כְּלוֹנָס שֶׁקּוֹרִין פירק״א בְּלַעַ"ז, וְכֵן: "וְכַנֵּס עַל הַגִּבְעָה" (ישעיה ל, יז), "אָרִים נִסִּי" (שם מט, כב), "שְׂאוּ נֵס" (שם יג, ב), וּלְפִי שֶׁהוּא גָּבוֹהַּ לְאוֹת וְלִרְאָיָה קוֹרְאוֹ "נֵס": **כָּל הַנָּשׁוּךְ.** אֲפִלּוּ כֶּלֶב אוֹ חֲמוֹר נוֹשֵׁךְ הָיָה נִזּוֹק וּמִתְנַוְּנֶה וְהוֹלֵךְ, אֶלָּא שֶׁנְּשִׁיכַת הַנָּחָשׁ מְמַהֶרֶת לְהָמִית, לְכָךְ נֶאֱמַר כָּאן: "וְרָאָה אֹתוֹ" רְאִיָּה בְּעָלְמָא, וּבִנְשִׁיכַת הַנָּחָשׁ נֶאֱמַר: "וְהִבִּיט", "וְהָיָה אִם נָשַׁךְ הַנָּחָשׁ אֶת אִישׁ וְהִבִּיט" וְגוֹ' (להלן פסוק ט), שֶׁלֹּא הָיָה מְמַהֵר נְשׁוּךְ הַנָּחָשׁ לְהִתְרַפְּאוֹת אֶלָּא אִם כֵּן מַבִּיט בּוֹ בְּכַוָּנָה. וְאָמְרוּ רַבּוֹתֵינוּ: וְכִי נָחָשׁ מֵמִית אוֹ מְחַיֶּה? אֶלָּא בִּזְמַן שֶׁהָיוּ יִשְׂרָאֵל מִסְתַּכְּלִין כְּלַפֵּי מַעְלָה וּמְשַׁעְבְּדִין אֶת לִבָּם לַאֲבִיהֶם שֶׁבַּשָּׁמַיִם הָיוּ מִתְרַפְּאִים, וְאִם לָאו הָיוּ נִמּוֹקִים:

ט] **נְחַשׁ נְחֹשֶׁת.** לֹא נֶאֱמַר לוֹ לַעֲשׂוֹתוֹ שֶׁל נְחֹשֶׁת, אֶלָּא אָמַר מֹשֶׁה: הַקָּדוֹשׁ בָּרוּךְ הוּא קוֹרְאוֹ נָחָשׁ וַאֲנִי אֶעֱשֶׂנּוּ שֶׁל נְחֹשֶׁת, לָשׁוֹן נוֹפֵל עַל לָשׁוֹן:

יא] **בְּעִיֵּי הָעֲבָרִים.** לֹא יָדַעְתִּי לָמָּה נִקְרָא שְׁמָם עִיִּים, וְעִי״ לְשׁוֹן חָרְבָּה הוּא, דָּבָר הַטָּאוּט בְּמַטְאֲטֵא, וְהָעַיִ״ן בּוֹ יְסוֹד לְבַדָּהּ, וְהוּא מִלְּשׁוֹן "יָעִים" (לעיל ד, יד), "וְיָעָה בָרָד" (ישעיה כח, יז): **הָעֲבָרִים.** דֶּרֶךְ מַעֲבַר הָעוֹבְרִים שָׁם אֶת הַר נְבוֹ אֶל אֶרֶץ כְּנַעַן, שֶׁהוּא מַפְסִיק בֵּין אֶרֶץ מוֹאָב לְאֶרֶץ אֱמוֹרִי: **עַל פְּנֵי מוֹאָב מִמִּזְרַח הַשָּׁמֶשׁ.** בְּמִזְרָחָהּ שֶׁל אֶרֶץ מוֹאָב:

יג] **מִגְּבֻל הָאֱמֹרִי.** תְּחוּם סוֹף מֶצֶר שֶׁלָּהֶם, וְכֵן "גְּבוּל מוֹאָב", לְשׁוֹן קָצֶה וָסוֹף: **מֵעֵבֶר אַרְנוֹן.** הִקִּיפוּ אֶרֶץ מוֹאָב כָּל דְּרוֹמָהּ וּמִזְרָחָהּ, עַד שֶׁבָּאוּ מֵעֵבֶר הַשֵּׁנִי לְאַרְנוֹן בְּתוֹךְ אֶרֶץ הָאֱמוֹרִי, בִּצְפוֹנָהּ שֶׁל אֶרֶץ מוֹאָב: **הַיֹּצֵא מִגְּבֻל הָאֱמֹרִי.** רְצוּעָה יוֹצְאָה מִגְּבוּל הָאֱמוֹרִי וְהִיא שֶׁל אֱמוֹרִיִּים, וְנִכְנֶסֶת לִגְבוּל מוֹאָב עַד אַרְנוֹן שֶׁהוּא גְּבוּל מוֹאָב, וְשָׁם חָנוּ יִשְׂרָאֵל וְלֹא בָּאוּ לִגְבוּל מוֹאָב, "כִּי אַרְנוֹן גְּבוּל מוֹאָב", וְהֵם לֹא נָתְנוּ לָהֶם רְשׁוּת לַעֲבֹר בְּאַרְצָם. וְאַף עַל פִּי שֶׁלֹּא פֵּרְשָׁהּ מֹשֶׁה, פֵּרְשָׁהּ יִפְתָּח, כְּמוֹ שֶׁאָמַר יִפְתָּח: "וְגַם אֶל מֶלֶךְ מוֹאָב שָׁלַח וְלֹא אָבָה" (שופטים יא, יז), וּמֹשֶׁה רְמָזָהּ:

פרק כא | במדבר

יד הָאֱמֹרִי: עַל־כֵּן֙ יֵֽאָמַ֔ר בְּסֵ֖פֶר מִלְחֲמֹ֣ת יְהוָ֑ה אֶת־וָהֵ֣ב בְּסוּפָ֔ה
טו וְאֶת־הַנְּחָלִ֖ים אַרְנֽוֹן: וְאֶ֙שֶׁד֙ הַנְּחָלִ֔ים אֲשֶׁ֥ר נָטָ֖ה לְשֶׁ֣בֶת עָ֑ר
טז וְנִשְׁעַ֖ן לִגְב֥וּל מוֹאָֽב: וּמִשָּׁ֖ם בְּאֵ֑רָה הִ֣וא הַבְּאֵ֗ר אֲשֶׁ֙ר אָמַ֤ר יְהוָה֙
לְמֹשֶׁ֔ה אֱסֹף֙ אֶת־הָעָ֔ם וְאֶתְּנָ֥ה לָהֶ֖ם מָֽיִם: אָ֚ז יָשִׁ֣יר
יז יִשְׂרָאֵ֔ל אֶת־הַשִּׁירָ֖ה הַזֹּ֑את עֲלִ֥י בְאֵ֖ר עֱנוּ־לָֽהּ: בְּאֵ֞ר חֲפָר֣וּהָ
יח שָׂרִ֗ים כָּר֙וּהָ֙ נְדִיבֵ֣י הָעָ֔ם בִּמְחֹקֵ֖ק בְּמִשְׁעֲנֹתָ֑ם וּמִמִּדְבָּ֖ר מַתָּנָֽה:
יט וּמִמַּתָּנָ֖ה נַחֲלִיאֵ֑ל וּמִנַּחֲלִיאֵ֖ל בָּמֽוֹת: וּמִבָּמ֗וֹת הַגַּיְא֙ אֲשֶׁר֙
בִּשְׂדֵ֣ה מוֹאָ֔ב רֹ֖אשׁ הַפִּסְגָּ֑ה וְנִשְׁקָ֖פָה עַל־פְּנֵ֥י הַיְשִׁימֹֽן:

"כַּאֲשֶׁ֣ר עָ֤שׂוּ לִי֙ בְּנֵ֣י עֵשָׂ֔ו הַיֹּשְׁבִים֙ בְּשֵׂעִ֔יר וְהַמּ֣וֹאָבִ֔ים הַיֹּשְׁבִ֖ים בְּעָ֑ר" (דברים ב, כט), מָה אֵלּוּ לֹא נְתָנוּם לַעֲבֹד בְּתוֹךְ אַרְצָם אֶלָּא הִקִּיפוּם סָבִיב, אַף מוֹאָב כֵּן.

יד-טו עַל כֵּן. עַל חֲנָיָה זוֹ וְנִסִּים שֶׁנַּעֲשׂוּ בָּהּ "יֵאָמַר בְּסֵפֶר מִלְחֲמֹת ה'", כְּשֶׁמְּסַפְּרִים נִסִּים שֶׁנַּעֲשׂוּ לַאֲבוֹתֵינוּ, יְסַפְּרוּ: "אֶת וָהֵב וְגוֹ'": **אֶת וָהֵב.** כְּמוֹ 'אֶת יָהֵב', כְּמוֹ שֶׁיֵּאָמֵר מִן 'יָעַד' 'וָעֵד', כֵּן יֵאָמֵר מִן יָהַב 'וָהֵב', וְהַוָי"ו יְסוֹד הוּא, כְּלוֹמַר אֶת אֲשֶׁר יָהַב לָהֶם וְהִרְבָּה נִסִּים בְּיַם סוּף: **וְאֶת הַנְּחָלִים אַרְנוֹן.** כְּשֵׁם שֶׁמְּסַפְּרִים בְּנִסֵּי יַם סוּף, כָּךְ יֵשׁ לְסַפֵּר בְּנִסֵּי נַחֲלֵי אַרְנוֹן, שֶׁאַף כָּאן נַעֲשׂוּ נִסִּים גְּדוֹלִים, וּמָה הֵם הַנִּסִּים? **וְאֶשֶׁד הַנְּחָלִים.** תַּרְגּוּם שֶׁל שֶׁפֶךְ – 'אֶשֶׁד', שֶׁפֶךְ הַנְּחָלִים, שֶׁנִּשְׁפַּךְ שָׁם דַּם אֱמוֹרִיִּים שֶׁהָיוּ נֶחְבָּאִים שָׁם, לְפִי שֶׁהָיוּ הֶהָרִים גְּבוֹהִים וְהַנַּחַל עָמֹק וְקָצָר וְהֶהָרִים סְמוּכִים זֶה לָזֶה, אָדָם עוֹמֵד עַל הָהָר מִזֶּה וּמְדַבֵּר עִם חֲבֵרוֹ בָּהָר מִזֶּה, וְהַדֶּרֶךְ עוֹבֵר בְּתוֹךְ הַנַּחַל, אָמְרוּ אֱמוֹרִיִּים: כְּשֶׁיִּכָּנְסוּ יִשְׂרָאֵל לְתוֹךְ הַנַּחַל לַעֲבֹר, נֵצֵא מִן הַמְּעָרוֹת שֶׁבֶּהָרִים שֶׁלְּמַעְלָה מֵהֶם וְנַהַרְגֵם בְּחִצִּים וְאַבְנֵי בַּלִּיסְטְרָאוֹת, וְהָיוּ אוֹתָן הַנְּקָעִים בָּהָר שֶׁל צַד מוֹאָב, וּבָהָר שֶׁל צַד אֱמוֹרִיִּים הָיוּ כְּנֶגֶד אוֹתָן נְקָעִים כְּמִין קְרָנוֹת וְשָׁדַיִם בּוֹלְטִין לַחוּץ, כֵּיוָן שֶׁבָּאוּ יִשְׂרָאֵל לַעֲבֹר, נִזְדַּעֲזֵעַ הָהָר שֶׁל אֶרֶץ יִשְׂרָאֵל כְּשִׁפְחָה הַיּוֹצֵאת לְהַקְבִּיל פְּנֵי גְבִרְתָּהּ, וְנִתְקָרֵב לְצַד הַר שֶׁל מוֹאָב, וְנִכְנְסוּ אוֹתָן הַשָּׁדַיִם

לְתוֹךְ אוֹתָן נְקָעִים וַהֲרָגוּם, וְזֶהוּ: "אֲשֶׁר נָטָה לְשֶׁבֶת עָר", שֶׁהָהָר נָטָה מִמְּקוֹמוֹ וְנִתְקָרֵב לְצַד מוֹאָב וְנִדְבַּק בּוֹ, וְזֶהוּ: "וְנִשְׁעַן לִגְבוּל מוֹאָב":

טז וּמִשָּׁם בְּאֵרָה. מִשָּׁם בָּא הָאֶשֶׁד אֶל הַבְּאֵר. כֵּיצַד? אָמַר הַקָּדוֹשׁ בָּרוּךְ הוּא, מִי מוֹדִיעַ לְבָנַי הַנִּסִּים הַלָּלוּ? הַמָּשָׁל אוֹמֵר: נָתַתָּ פַּת לְתִינוֹק, הוֹדַע לְאִמּוֹ. לְאַחַר שֶׁעָבְרוּ חָזְרוּ הֶהָרִים לִמְקוֹמָם, וְהַבְּאֵר יָרְדָה לְתוֹךְ הַנַּחַל וְהֶעֶלְתָה מִשָּׁם דַּם הַהֲרוּגִים וּזְרוֹעוֹת וְאֵיבָרִים וּמוֹלִיכָתָן סָבִיב הַמַּחֲנֶה, וְיִשְׂרָאֵל רָאוּ וְאָמְרוּ שִׁירָה:

יז עֲלִי בְאֵר. מִתּוֹךְ הַנַּחַל, וְהַעֲלִי מַה שֶּׁאַתְּ מַעֲלָה. וּמִנַּיִן שֶׁהַבְּאֵר הוֹדִיעָה לָהֶם? שֶׁנֶּאֱמַר: "וּמִשָּׁם בְּאֵרָה", וְכִי מִשָּׁם הָיְתָה? וַהֲלֹא מִתְּחִלַּת אַרְבָּעִים שָׁנָה הָיְתָה עִמָּהֶם! אֶלָּא שֶׁיָּרְדָה לְפַרְסֵם אֶת הַנִּסִּים. וְכֵן "אָז יָשִׁיר", הַשִּׁירָה הַזֹּאת נֶאֶמְרָה בְּסוֹף אַרְבָּעִים, וְהַבְּאֵר נִתְּנָה לָהֶם מִתְּחִלַּת אַרְבָּעִים, מַה רָאָה לִכָּתֵב כָּאן? אֶלָּא הָעִנְיָן הַזֶּה נִדְרַשׁ לְמַעְלָה הֵימֶנּוּ:

יח-כ בְּאֵר חֲפָרוּהָ. זֹאת הִיא הַבְּאֵר אֲשֶׁר "חֲפָרוּהָ שָׂרִים", מֹשֶׁה וְאַהֲרֹן: **בְּמִשְׁעֲנֹתָם.** בַּמַּטֶּה: **וּמִמִּדְבָּר.** נִתְּנָה לָהֶם: **וּמִמַּתָּנָה נַחֲלִיאֵל.** כְּתַרְגּוּמוֹ: **וּמִבָּמוֹת הַגַּיְא אֲשֶׁר בִּשְׂדֵה מוֹאָב.** כִּי שָׁם מֵת מֹשֶׁה וְשָׁם בָּטְלָה הַבְּאֵר. דָּבָר אַחֵר, "בְּאֵר חֲפָרוּהָ שָׂרִים", כָּל נָשִׂיא וְנָשִׂיא כְּשֶׁהָיוּ חוֹנִים נוֹטֵל מַקְלוֹ וּמוֹשֵׁךְ אֵצֶל דִּגְלוֹ

במדבר | פרק כא

כא וַיִּשְׁלַ֤ח יִשְׂרָאֵל֙ מַלְאָכִ֔ים אֶל־סִיחֹ֥ן מֶֽלֶךְ־הָאֱמֹרִ֖י לֵאמֹֽר: *שביעי /רביעי/*
כב אֶעְבְּרָ֣ה בְאַרְצֶ֗ךָ לֹ֤א נִטֶּה֙ בְּשָׂדֶ֣ה וּבְכֶ֔רֶם לֹ֥א נִשְׁתֶּ֖ה מֵ֣י בְאֵ֑ר בְּדֶ֤רֶךְ הַמֶּ֨לֶךְ֙ נֵלֵ֔ךְ עַ֥ד אֲשֶֽׁר־נַעֲבֹ֖ר גְּבֻלֶֽךָ:
כג וְלֹא־נָתַ֨ן סִיחֹ֣ן אֶת־יִשְׂרָאֵל֮ עֲבֹ֣ר בִּגְבֻלוֹ֒ וַיֶּאֱסֹ֨ף סִיחֹ֜ן אֶת־כָּל־עַמּ֗וֹ וַיֵּצֵ֞א לִקְרַ֤את יִשְׂרָאֵל֙ הַמִּדְבָּ֔רָה וַיָּבֹ֖א יָ֑הְצָה וַיִּלָּ֖חֶם בְּיִשְׂרָאֵֽל:
כד וַיַּכֵּ֥הוּ יִשְׂרָאֵ֖ל לְפִי־חָ֑רֶב וַיִּירַ֨שׁ אֶת־אַרְצ֜וֹ מֵֽאַרְנֹ֗ן עַד־יַבֹּק֙ עַד־בְּנֵ֣י עַמּ֔וֹן כִּ֣י עַ֔ז גְּב֖וּל בְּנֵ֥י עַמּֽוֹן:
כה וַיִּקַּח֙ יִשְׂרָאֵ֔ל אֵ֥ת כָּל־הֶעָרִ֖ים הָאֵ֑לֶּה וַיֵּ֤שֶׁב יִשְׂרָאֵל֙ בְּכָל־עָרֵ֣י הָֽאֱמֹרִ֔י בְּחֶשְׁבּ֖וֹן וּבְכָל־בְּנֹתֶֽיהָ:
כו כִּ֣י חֶשְׁבּ֔וֹן עִ֗יר סִיחֹ֛ן מֶ֥לֶךְ הָאֱמֹרִ֖י הִ֑וא וְה֣וּא נִלְחַ֗ם בְּמֶ֤לֶךְ מוֹאָב֙ הָרִאשׁ֔וֹן

פרק כא | במדבר

כז וַיִּקַּח אֶת־כָּל־אַרְצ֛וֹ מִיָּד֖וֹ עַד־אַרְנֹ֑ן: עַל־כֵּ֛ן יֹאמְר֥וּ הַמֹּשְׁלִ֖ים
כח בֹּ֣אוּ חֶשְׁבּ֑וֹן תִּבָּנֶ֥ה וְתִכּוֹנֵ֖ן עִ֥יר סִיחֽוֹן: כִּי־אֵשׁ֙ יָצְאָ֣ה מֵחֶשְׁבּ֔וֹן
כט לֶהָבָ֖ה מִקִּרְיַ֣ת סִיחֹ֑ן אָֽכְלָה֙ עָ֣ר מוֹאָ֔ב בַּעֲלֵ֖י בָּמ֥וֹת אַרְנֹֽן: אֽוֹי־
לְךָ֣ מוֹאָ֔ב אָבַ֖דְתָּ עַם־כְּמ֑וֹשׁ נָתַ֨ן בָּנָ֤יו פְּלֵיטִם֙ וּבְנֹתָ֣יו בַּשְּׁבִ֔ית
ל לְמֶ֥לֶךְ אֱמֹרִ֖י סִיחֽוֹן: וַנִּירָ֛ם אָבַ֥ד חֶשְׁבּ֖וֹן עַד־דִּיבֹ֑ן וַנַּשִּׁ֣ים עַד־
לא נֹ֔פַח אֲשֶׁ֖ר עַד־מֵֽידְבָֽא: וַיֵּ֙שֶׁב֙ יִשְׂרָאֵ֔ל בְּאֶ֖רֶץ הָאֱמֹרִֽי: וַיִּשְׁלַ֤ח
לג מֹשֶׁה֙ לְרַגֵּ֣ל אֶת־יַעְזֵ֔ר וַֽיִּלְכְּד֖וּ בְּנֹתֶ֑יהָ *וַיּ֕וֹרֶשׁ* אֶת־הָאֱמֹרִ֥י אֲשֶׁר־
שָֽׁם: וַיִּפְנוּ֙ וַֽיַּעֲל֔וּ דֶּ֖רֶךְ הַבָּשָׁ֑ן וַיֵּצֵ֣א ע֣וֹג מֶֽלֶךְ־הַבָּשָׁ֡ן לִקְרָאתָם֩
לד ה֨וּא וְכָל־עַמּ֧וֹ לַמִּלְחָמָ֛ה אֶדְרֶֽעִי: וַיֹּ֨אמֶר יְהוָ֤ה אֶל־מֹשֶׁה֙ אַל־
תִּירָ֣א אֹת֔וֹ כִּ֣י בְיָדְךָ֞ נָתַ֧תִּי אֹת֛וֹ וְאֶת־כָּל־עַמּ֖וֹ וְאֶת־אַרְצ֑וֹ וְעָשִׂ֣יתָ
לּ֔וֹ כַּאֲשֶׁ֣ר עָשִׂ֗יתָ לְסִיחֹן֙ מֶ֣לֶךְ הָֽאֱמֹרִ֔י אֲשֶׁ֥ר יוֹשֵׁ֖ב בְּחֶשְׁבּֽוֹן:

מפטיר

שֶׁנֶּאֱמַר: "אַל תָּצַר אֶת מוֹאָב" (דברים ב, ט), וְחֶשְׁבּוֹן
מִשֶּׁל מוֹאָב הָיְתָה, כָּתַב לָנוּ שֶׁסִּיחוֹן לְקָחָהּ מֵהֶם
וְעַל יָדוֹ טָהֲרָה לְיִשְׂרָאֵל. מִיָּדוֹ. מֵרְשׁוּתוֹ:

כז עַל כֵּן. עַל אוֹתָהּ מִלְחָמָה שֶׁנִּלְחַם סִיחוֹן בְּמוֹאָב:
יֹאמְרוּ הַמֹּשְׁלִים. בִּלְעָם, שֶׁנֶּאֱמַר בּוֹ: "וַיִּשָּׂא מְשָׁלוֹ"
(להלן כג, ז): הַמֹּשְׁלִים. בִּלְעָם וּבְעוֹר, וְהֵם אָמְרוּ: "בֹּאוּ
חֶשְׁבּוֹן", שֶׁלֹּא הָיָה סִיחוֹן יָכוֹל לְכָבְשָׁהּ וְהָלַךְ וְשָׂכַר
אֶת בִּלְעָם לְקַלְּלוֹ, וְזֶהוּ שֶׁאָמַר לוֹ בָּלָק: "כִּי יָדַעְתִּי
אֵת אֲשֶׁר תְּבָרֵךְ מְבֹרָךְ וְגוֹ'" (להלן כב, ו): תִּבָּנֶה וְתִכּוֹנֵן.
חֶשְׁבּוֹן בְּשֵׁם סִיחוֹן לִהְיוֹת עִירוֹ:

כח כִּי אֵשׁ יָצְאָה מֵחֶשְׁבּוֹן. מִשֶּׁכְּבָשָׁהּ סִיחוֹן: אָֽכְלָה
עָר מוֹאָב. שֵׁם אוֹתָהּ הַמְּדִינָה קָרוּי 'עָר' בִּלְשׁוֹן
עִבְרִי וּ'לְחָיַת' בִּלְשׁוֹן אֲרַמִּי: עָר מוֹאָב. עָר שֶׁל
מוֹאָב:

כט אוֹי לְךָ מוֹאָב. שֶׁקִּלְלוּ אֶת מוֹאָב שֶׁיִּמָּסְרוּ בְּיָדוֹ:
כְּמוֹשׁ. שֵׁם אֱלֹהֵי מוֹאָב (שופטים יא, כד): נָתַן. הַנּוֹתֵן

אֶת בָּנָיו שֶׁל מוֹאָב: פְּלֵיטִם. נָסִים וּפְלֵטִים מֵחֶרֶב,
וְאֶת בְּנוֹתָיו בַּשְּׁבִית וְגוֹ':

ל וַנִּירָם אָבַד. מַלְכוּת שֶׁלָּהֶם: אָבַד חֶשְׁבּוֹן עַד דִּיבֹן.
מַלְכוּת וְעֹל שֶׁהָיָה לְמוֹאָב בְּחֶשְׁבּוֹן אָבַד מִשָּׁם, וְכֵן
'עַד דִּיבוֹן', תַּרְגּוּם שֶׁל 'סָר' – 'עַד', כְּלוֹמַר סָר נִיר
מִדִּיבוֹן. 'נִיר' לְשׁוֹן מַלְכוּת וְעֹל מֶמְשֶׁלֶת אִישׁ, כְּמוֹ:
"לְמַעַן הֱיוֹת נִיר לְדָוִיד עַבְדִּי" (מלכים א יא, לו): וַנַּשִּׁים.
שִׁי"ן דְּגוּשָׁה, לְשׁוֹן שְׁמָמָה. כָּךְ יֹאמְרוּ הַמֹּשְׁלִים:
"וַנַּשִּׁים" אוֹתָם "עַד נֹפַח", הֲשִׁמּוֹנוּם עַד נֹפַח:

לב וַיִּשְׁלַח מֹשֶׁה לְרַגֵּל אֶת יַעְזֵר וְגוֹ'. הַמְרַגְּלִים
לְכָדוּהָ, אָמְרוּ: לֹא נַעֲשֶׂה כָּרִאשׁוֹנִים, בְּטוּחִים אָנוּ
בְּכֹחַ תְּפִלָּתוֹ שֶׁל מֹשֶׁה לְהִלָּחֵם:

לד אַל תִּירָא אֹתוֹ. שֶׁהָיָה מֹשֶׁה יָרֵא לְהִלָּחֵם, שֶׁמָּא
תַּעֲמֹד לוֹ זְכוּתוֹ שֶׁל אַבְרָהָם, שֶׁנֶּאֱמַר: "וַיָּבֹא הַפָּלִיט"
(בראשית יד, יג), הוּא עוֹג שֶׁפָּלַט מִן הָרְפָאִים שֶׁהִכּוּ
כְּדָרְלָעֹמֶר וַחֲבֵרָיו בְּעַשְׁתְּרוֹת קַרְנַיִם, שֶׁנֶּאֱמַר: "רַק
עוֹג מֶלֶךְ הַבָּשָׁן נִשְׁאַר מִיֶּתֶר הָרְפָאִים" (דברים ג, יא):

לה וַיַּהַרְגוּ אֹתוֹ וְאֶת־בָּנָיו וְאֶת־כָּל־עַמּוֹ עַד־בִּלְתִּי הִשְׁאִיר־לוֹ שָׂרִיד
כב א וַיִּירְשׁוּ אֶת־אַרְצוֹ: וַיִּסְעוּ בְּנֵי יִשְׂרָאֵל וַיַּחֲנוּ בְּעַרְבוֹת מוֹאָב
ב מֵעֵבֶר לְיַרְדֵּן יְרֵחוֹ: וַיַּרְא בָּלָק בֶּן־צִפּוֹר אֵת כָּל־
ג אֲשֶׁר־עָשָׂה יִשְׂרָאֵל לָאֱמֹרִי: וַיָּגָר מוֹאָב מִפְּנֵי הָעָם מְאֹד כִּי
ד רַב־הוּא וַיָּקָץ מוֹאָב מִפְּנֵי בְּנֵי יִשְׂרָאֵל: וַיֹּאמֶר מוֹאָב אֶל־זִקְנֵי
מִדְיָן עַתָּה יְלַחֲכוּ הַקָּהָל אֶת־כָּל־סְבִיבֹתֵינוּ כִּלְחֹךְ הַשּׁוֹר אֵת
ה יֶרֶק הַשָּׂדֶה וּבָלָק בֶּן־צִפּוֹר מֶלֶךְ לְמוֹאָב בָּעֵת הַהִוא: וַיִּשְׁלַח
מַלְאָכִים אֶל־בִּלְעָם בֶּן־בְּעֹר פְּתוֹרָה אֲשֶׁר עַל־הַנָּהָר אֶרֶץ
בְּנֵי־עַמּוֹ לִקְרֹא־לוֹ לֵאמֹר הִנֵּה עַם יָצָא מִמִּצְרַיִם הִנֵּה כִסָּה

יט בלק

פרק כב

לה וַיַּהַרְגוּ אֹתוֹ. מֹשֶׁה הֲרָגוֹ, כְּדִאִיתָא בִּבְרָכוֹת בַּ"הָרוֹאֶה" (דף נד ע"ב): עָקַר טוּרָא בַּר תְּלָתָא פַּרְסֵי וְכוּ':

פרק כב

ב] וַיַּרְא בָּלָק בֶּן־צִפּוֹר אֵת כָּל־אֲשֶׁר־עָשָׂה יִשְׂרָאֵל לָאֱמֹרִי. אָמַר: אֵלּוּ שְׁנֵי מְלָכִים שֶׁהָיִינוּ בְּטוּחִים עֲלֵיהֶם לֹא עָמְדוּ בִּפְנֵיהֶם, אָנוּ עַל אַחַת כַּמָּה וְכַמָּה, לְפִיכָךְ: "וַיָּגָר מוֹאָב":

ג] וַיָּגָר. לְשׁוֹן מוֹרָא, כְּמוֹ: "גּוּרוּ לָכֶם" (איוב יט, כט): וַיָּקָץ מוֹאָב. קָצוּ בְּחַיֵּיהֶם:

ד] אֶל־זִקְנֵי מִדְיָן. וַהֲלֹא מֵעוֹלָם הָיוּ שׂוֹנְאִים זֶה אֶת זֶה, שֶׁנֶּאֱמַר: "הַמַּכֶּה אֶת מִדְיָן בִּשְׂדֵה מוֹאָב" (בראשית לו, לה), שֶׁבָּאוּ מִדְיָן עַל מוֹאָב לַמִּלְחָמָה! אֶלָּא מִיִּרְאָתָן שֶׁל יִשְׂרָאֵל עָשׂוּ שָׁלוֹם בֵּינֵיהֶם. וּמָה רָאָה מוֹאָב לִטֹּל עֵצָה מִמִּדְיָן? כֵּיוָן שֶׁרָאוּ אֶת יִשְׂרָאֵל נוֹצְחִים שֶׁלֹּא כְּמִנְהַג הָעוֹלָם, אָמְרוּ: מַנְהִיגָם שֶׁל אֵלּוּ בְּמִדְיָן נִתְגַּדֵּל, נִשְׁאַל מֵהֶם מַה מִּדָּתוֹ. אָמְרוּ לָהֶם: אֵין כֹּחוֹ אֶלָּא בְּפִיו. אָמְרוּ: אַף אָנוּ נָבוֹא עֲלֵיהֶם בְּאָדָם שֶׁכֹּחוֹ בְּפִיו: כִּלְחֹךְ הַשּׁוֹר. כָּל מַה שֶּׁהַשּׁוֹר

מְלַחֵךְ אֵין בּוֹ בְרָכָה: בָּעֵת הַהִוא. לֹא הָיָה רָאוּי לְמַלְכוּת, מִנְּסִיכֵי מִדְיָן הָיָה, וְכֵיוָן שֶׁמֵּת סִיחוֹן מִנּוּהוּ עֲלֵיהֶם לְצֹרֶךְ שָׁעָה:

ה] פְּתוֹרָה. כַּשֻּׁלְחָנִי הַזֶּה שֶׁהַכֹּל מְרִיצִין לוֹ מָעוֹת, כָּךְ כָּל הַמְּלָכִים מְרִיצִין לוֹ אִגְּרוֹתֵיהֶן. וּלְפִי פְשׁוּטוֹ שֶׁל מִקְרָא כָּךְ שֵׁם הַמָּקוֹם: אֶרֶץ בְּנֵי־עַמּוֹ. שֶׁל בָּלָק, מִשָּׁם הָיָה, וְזֶה הָיָה מִתְנַבֵּא וְאוֹמֵר לוֹ: עָתִיד אַתָּה לִמְלֹךְ. וְאִם תֹּאמַר: מִפְּנֵי מָה הִשְׁרָה הַקָּדוֹשׁ בָּרוּךְ הוּא שְׁכִינָתוֹ עַל גּוֹי רָשָׁע? כְּדֵי שֶׁלֹּא יְהֵא פִּתְחוֹן פֶּה לָאֻמּוֹת לוֹמַר: אִלּוּ הָיוּ לָנוּ נְבִיאִים חָזַרְנוּ לְמוּטָב. הֶעֱמִיד לָהֶם נְבִיאִים, וְהֵם פָּרְצוּ גֶדֶר הָעוֹלָם, שֶׁבַּתְּחִלָּה הָיוּ גְדוּרִים בַּעֲרָיוֹת, וְזֶה נָתַן לָהֶם עֵצָה לְהַפְקִיר עַצְמָן לִזְנוּת: לִקְרֹא־לוֹ. הַקְּרִיאָה הָיְתָה שֶׁלּוֹ וַהֲנָאָתוֹ, שֶׁהָיָה פּוֹסֵק לוֹ מָמוֹן הַרְבֵּה: עַם יָצָא מִמִּצְרָיִם. וְאִם תֹּאמַר: מַה מַּזִּיקְךָ? הִנֵּה כִסָּה אֶת־עֵין הָאָרֶץ. סִיחוֹן וְעוֹג שֶׁהָיוּ שׁוֹמְרִים אוֹתָנוּ, עָמְדוּ עֲלֵיהֶם וַהֲרָגוּם: וְהוּא יֹשֵׁב מִמֻּלִי. חָסֵר כְּתִיב, קְרוֹבִים הֵם לְהַכְרִיתֵנִי, כְּמוֹ: "כִּי אֲמִילַם" (תהלים קיח, י):

אֶת־עֵין הָאָרֶץ וְהוּא יֹשֵׁב מִמֻּלִי: וְעַתָּה לְכָה־נָּא אָרָה־לִּי אֶת־ ו
הָעָם הַזֶּה כִּי־עָצוּם הוּא מִמֶּנִּי אוּלַי אוּכַל נַכֶּה־בּוֹ וַאֲגָרְשֶׁנּוּ
מִן־הָאָרֶץ כִּי יָדַעְתִּי אֵת אֲשֶׁר־תְּבָרֵךְ מְבֹרָךְ וַאֲשֶׁר תָּאֹר יוּאָר:
וַיֵּלְכוּ זִקְנֵי מוֹאָב וְזִקְנֵי מִדְיָן וּקְסָמִים בְּיָדָם וַיָּבֹאוּ אֶל־בִּלְעָם ז
וַיְדַבְּרוּ אֵלָיו דִּבְרֵי בָלָק: וַיֹּאמֶר אֲלֵיהֶם לִינוּ פֹה הַלַּיְלָה ח
וַהֲשִׁבֹתִי אֶתְכֶם דָּבָר כַּאֲשֶׁר יְדַבֵּר יְהוָה אֵלָי וַיֵּשְׁבוּ שָׂרֵי־מוֹאָב
עִם־בִּלְעָם: וַיָּבֹא אֱלֹהִים אֶל־בִּלְעָם וַיֹּאמֶר מִי הָאֲנָשִׁים הָאֵלֶּה ט
עִמָּךְ: וַיֹּאמֶר בִּלְעָם אֶל־הָאֱלֹהִים בָּלָק בֶּן־צִפֹּר מֶלֶךְ מוֹאָב י
שָׁלַח אֵלָי: הִנֵּה הָעָם הַיֹּצֵא מִמִּצְרַיִם וַיְכַס אֶת־עֵין הָאָרֶץ יא
עַתָּה לְכָה קָבָה־לִּי אֹתוֹ אוּלַי אוּכַל לְהִלָּחֶם בּוֹ וְגֵרַשְׁתִּיו:
וַיֹּאמֶר אֱלֹהִים אֶל־בִּלְעָם לֹא תֵלֵךְ עִמָּהֶם לֹא תָאֹר אֶת־הָעָם יב

ו נכה בו. חָנִי וְעַמִּי נַכֶּה בָּהֶם. דָּבָר אַחֵר, לְשׁוֹן
מִשְׁנָה הוּא: "מְנֻכֶּה לוֹ מִן הַדָּמִים" (חולין קלב ע"א),
לַחְסֵר מֵהֶם מְעַט: כי ידעתי וגו'. עַל יְדֵי מִלְחֶמֶת
סִיחוֹן שֶׁעֲזַרְתּוֹ לְהַכּוֹת אֶת מוֹאָב:

ז וקסמים בידם. כָּל מִינֵי קְסָמִים, שֶׁלֹּא יֹאמַר: אֵין
כְּלֵי תַשְׁמִישִׁי עִמִּי. דָּבָר אַחֵר, קֶסֶם זֶה נָטְלוּ בְּיָדָם
זִקְנֵי מִדְיָן, אָמְרוּ: אִם יָבֹא עִמָּנוּ בַּפַּעַם הַזֹּאת יֵשׁ
בּוֹ מַמָּשׁ, וְאִם יִדְחֵנוּ אֵין בּוֹ תּוֹעֶלֶת. לְפִיכָךְ כְּשֶׁאָמַר
לָהֶם: "לִינוּ פֹה הַלַּיְלָה" (להלן פסוק ח) אָמְרוּ: אֵין בּוֹ
תִּקְוָה, הִנִּיחוּהוּ וְהָלְכוּ לָהֶם, שֶׁנֶּאֱמַר: "וַיֵּשְׁבוּ שָׂרֵי
מוֹאָב עִם בִּלְעָם" (שם), אֲבָל זִקְנֵי מִדְיָן הָלְכוּ לָהֶם:

ח לינו פה הלילה. אֵין רוּחַ הַקֹּדֶשׁ שׁוֹרָה עָלָיו
אֶלָּא בַּלַּיְלָה, וְכֵן לְכָל נְבִיאֵי אֻמּוֹת הָעוֹלָם, וְכֵן
לָבָן בַּחֲלוֹם הַלַּיְלָה, שֶׁנֶּאֱמַר: "וַיָּבֹא אֱלֹהִים אֶל
לָבָן הָאֲרַמִּי בַּחֲלוֹם הַלָּיְלָה" (בראשית לא, כד), כְּאָדָם
הַהוֹלֵךְ אֵצֶל פִּילַגְשׁוֹ בְּהֶחְבֵּא: כאשר ידבר ה' אלי.
אִם יַמְלִיכֵנִי לָלֶכֶת עִם בְּנֵי אָדָם כְּמוֹתְכֶם אֵלֵךְ

עִמָּכֶם, שֶׁמָּא אֵין כְּבוֹדוֹ לְתִתִּי לַהֲלֹךְ אֶלָּא עִם שָׂרִים
גְּדוֹלִים: וישבו. לְשׁוֹן עַכָּבָה:

ט מי האנשים האלה עמך. לְהַטְעוֹתוֹ בָּא, אָמַר:
פְּעָמִים שֶׁאֵין הַכֹּל גָּלוּי לְפָנָיו, אֵין דַּעְתּוֹ שָׁוָה עָלָיו,
אַף אֲנִי אֶרְאֶה עֵת שֶׁאוּכַל לְקַלֵּל וְלֹא יָבִין:

י בלק בן צפור מלך מואב. אַף עַל פִּי שֶׁאֵינִי חָשׁוּב
בְּעֵינֶךָ, חָשׁוּב אֲנִי בְּעֵינֵי הַמְּלָכִים:

יא קבה לי. זוֹ קָשָׁה מֵ"אָרָה לִּי", שֶׁהוּא נוֹקֵב
וּמְפָרֵשׁ: וגרשתיו. מִן הָעוֹלָם, וּבָלָק לֹא אָמַר אֶלָּא
"וַאֲגָרְשֶׁנּוּ מִן הָאָרֶץ" (לעיל פסוק ו), אֵינִי מְבַקֵּשׁ אֶלָּא
לְהַסִּיעָם מֵעָלַי, וּבִלְעָם הָיָה שׂוֹנְאָם יוֹתֵר מִבָּלָק:

יב לא תלך עמהם. אָמַר לוֹ: אִם כֵּן אֲקַלְּלֵם
בִּמְקוֹמִי. אָמַר לוֹ: "לֹא תָאֹר אֶת הָעָם". אָמַר לוֹ:
אִם כֵּן אֲבָרְכֵם. אָמַר לוֹ: אֵינָם צְרִיכִים לְבִרְכָתְךָ,
"כִּי בָרוּךְ הוּא". מָשָׁל אוֹמְרִים לַצִּרְעָה: לֹא מִדֻּבְשֵׁךְ
וְלֹא מֵעֻקְצֵךְ:

במדבר | פרק כב

יג וַיָּקָם בִּלְעָם בַּבֹּקֶר וַיֹּאמֶר אֶל־שָׂרֵי בָלָק לְכוּ שני
כִּי בֵּרוּךְ הוּא: /חמישי/
אֶל־אַרְצְכֶם כִּי מֵאֵן יְהֹוָה לְתִתִּי לַהֲלֹךְ עִמָּכֶם: וַיָּקוּמוּ שָׂרֵי יד
מוֹאָב וַיָּבֹאוּ אֶל־בָּלָק וַיֹּאמְרוּ מֵאֵן בִּלְעָם הֲלֹךְ עִמָּנוּ: וַיֹּסֶף טו
עוֹד בָּלָק שְׁלֹחַ שָׂרִים רַבִּים וְנִכְבָּדִים מֵאֵלֶּה: וַיָּבֹאוּ אֶל־בִּלְעָם טז
וַיֹּאמְרוּ לוֹ כֹּה אָמַר בָּלָק בֶּן־צִפּוֹר אַל־נָא תִמָּנַע מֵהֲלֹךְ אֵלָי:
כִּי־כַבֵּד אֲכַבֶּדְךָ מְאֹד וְכֹל אֲשֶׁר־תֹּאמַר אֵלַי אֶעֱשֶׂה וּלְכָה־נָּא יז
קָבָה־לִּי אֵת הָעָם הַזֶּה: וַיַּעַן בִּלְעָם וַיֹּאמֶר אֶל־עַבְדֵי בָלָק יח
אִם־יִתֶּן־לִי בָלָק מְלֹא בֵיתוֹ כֶּסֶף וְזָהָב לֹא אוּכַל לַעֲבֹר אֶת־פִּי
יְהֹוָה אֱלֹהָי לַעֲשׂוֹת קְטַנָּה אוֹ גְדוֹלָה: וְעַתָּה שְׁבוּ נָא בָזֶה יט
גַּם־אַתֶּם הַלָּיְלָה וְאֵדְעָה מַה־יֹּסֵף יְהֹוָה דַּבֵּר עִמִּי: וַיָּבֹא כ
אֱלֹהִים ׀ אֶל־בִּלְעָם לַיְלָה וַיֹּאמֶר לוֹ אִם־לִקְרֹא לְךָ בָּאוּ
הָאֲנָשִׁים קוּם לֵךְ אִתָּם וְאַךְ אֶת־הַדָּבָר אֲשֶׁר־אֲדַבֵּר אֵלֶיךָ
אֹתוֹ תַעֲשֶׂה: וַיָּקָם בִּלְעָם בַּבֹּקֶר וַיַּחֲבֹשׁ אֶת־אֲתֹנוֹ וַיֵּלֶךְ עִם־ כא שלישי

יג| לַהֲלֹךְ עִמָּכֶם. שֶׁלֹּא עִם שָׂרִים גְּדוֹלִים מִכֶּם,
לָמַדְנוּ שֶׁרוּחוֹ גְּבוֹהָה, וְלֹא רָצָה לְגַלּוֹת שֶׁהוּא בִּרְשׁוּתוֹ
שֶׁל מָקוֹם אֶלָּא בִּלְשׁוֹן גַּסּוּת, לְפִיכָךְ "וַיֹּסֶף עוֹד
בָּלָק" (להלן פסוק טו):

יז| כִּי כַבֵּד אֲכַבֶּדְךָ מְאֹד. יוֹתֵר מִמַּה שֶּׁהָיִיתָ נוֹטֵל
לְשֶׁעָבַר אֲנִי נוֹתֵן לָךְ:

יח| מְלֹא בֵיתוֹ כֶּסֶף וְזָהָב. לָמַדְנוּ שֶׁנַּפְשׁוֹ רְחָבָה
וּמְחַמֵּד מָמוֹן אֲחֵרִים. אָמַר: רָאוּי לוֹ לִתֶּן לִי כָּל
כֶּסֶף וְזָהָב שֶׁלּוֹ, שֶׁהֲרֵי צָרִיךְ לִשְׂכֹּר חֲיָלוֹת רַבּוֹת,
סָפֵק נוֹצֵחַ סָפֵק אֵינוֹ נוֹצֵחַ, וַאֲנִי וַדַּאי נוֹצֵחַ: לֹא
אוּכַל לַעֲבֹר. עַל כָּרְחוֹ גִּלָּה שֶׁהוּא בִּרְשׁוּת אֲחֵרִים,
וְנִתְנַבֵּא כָּאן שֶׁאֵינוֹ יָכוֹל לְבַטֵּל הַבְּרָכוֹת שֶׁנִּתְבָּרְכוּ
הָאָבוֹת מִפִּי הַשְּׁכִינָה:

יט| גַּם אַתֶּם. פִּיו הִכְשִׁילוֹ, "גַּם אַתֶּם" סוֹפְכֶם לֵילֵךְ
בְּפַחֵי נֶפֶשׁ כָּרִאשׁוֹנִים: מַה יֹּסֵף. לֹא יְשַׁנֶּה דְּבָרָיו
מִבְּרָכָה לִקְלָלָה, הַלְוַאי שֶׁלֹּא יוֹסִיף לְבָרֵךְ. כָּאן
נִתְנַבֵּא שֶׁעָתִיד לְהוֹסִיף לָהֶם בְּרָכוֹת עַל יָדוֹ:

כ| אִם לִקְרֹא לְךָ. אִם הַקְּרִיאָה שֶׁלְּךָ וְסָבוּר אַתָּה
לִטֹּל עָלֶיהָ שָׂכָר, "קוּם לֵךְ אִתָּם": וְאַךְ. עַל כָּרְחֲךָ
"אֶת הַדָּבָר אֲשֶׁר אֲדַבֵּר אֵלֶיךָ אוֹתוֹ תַעֲשֶׂה", וְאַף עַל
פִּי כֵן "וַיֵּלֶךְ בִּלְעָם", אָמַר: שֶׁמָּא אֲפַתֶּנּוּ וְיִתְרַצֶּה:

כא| וַיַּחֲבֹשׁ אֶת אֲתֹנוֹ. מִכָּאן שֶׁהַשִּׂנְאָה מְקַלְקֶלֶת
אֶת הַשּׁוּרָה, שֶׁחָבַשׁ הוּא בְּעַצְמוֹ. אָמַר הַקָּדוֹשׁ בָּרוּךְ
הוּא: רָשָׁע, כְּבָר קְדָמְךָ אַבְרָהָם אֲבִיהֶם, שֶׁנֶּאֱמַר:
"וַיַּשְׁכֵּם אַבְרָהָם בַּבֹּקֶר וַיַּחֲבֹשׁ אֶת חֲמֹרוֹ" (בראשית כב,
ג): עִם שָׂרֵי מוֹאָב. לִבּוֹ כְּלִבָּם שָׁוֶה:

שָׂרֵי מוֹאָב: וַיִּחַר־אַף אֱלֹהִים כִּי־הוֹלֵךְ הוּא וַיִּתְיַצֵּב מַלְאַךְ כב
יְהוָה בַּדֶּרֶךְ לְשָׂטָן לוֹ וְהוּא רֹכֵב עַל־אֲתֹנוֹ וּשְׁנֵי נְעָרָיו עִמּוֹ:
וַתֵּרֶא הָאָתוֹן אֶת־מַלְאַךְ יְהוָה נִצָּב בַּדֶּרֶךְ וְחַרְבּוֹ שְׁלוּפָה בְּיָדוֹ כג
וַתֵּט הָאָתוֹן מִן־הַדֶּרֶךְ וַתֵּלֶךְ בַּשָּׂדֶה וַיַּךְ בִּלְעָם אֶת־הָאָתוֹן
לְהַטֹּתָהּ הַדָּרֶךְ: וַיַּעֲמֹד מַלְאַךְ יְהוָה בְּמִשְׁעוֹל הַכְּרָמִים גָּדֵר כד
מִזֶּה וְגָדֵר מִזֶּה: וַתֵּרֶא הָאָתוֹן אֶת־מַלְאַךְ יְהוָה וַתִּלָּחֵץ אֶל־ כה
הַקִּיר וַתִּלְחַץ אֶת־רֶגֶל בִּלְעָם אֶל־הַקִּיר וַיֹּסֶף לְהַכֹּתָהּ: וַיּוֹסֶף כו
מַלְאַךְ־יְהוָה עֲבוֹר וַיַּעֲמֹד בְּמָקוֹם צָר אֲשֶׁר אֵין־דֶּרֶךְ לִנְטוֹת
יָמִין וּשְׂמֹאול: וַתֵּרֶא הָאָתוֹן אֶת־מַלְאַךְ יְהוָה וַתִּרְבַּץ תַּחַת כז
בִּלְעָם וַיִּחַר־אַף בִּלְעָם וַיַּךְ אֶת־הָאָתוֹן בַּמַּקֵּל: וַיִּפְתַּח יְהוָה כח
אֶת־פִּי הָאָתוֹן וַתֹּאמֶר לְבִלְעָם מֶה־עָשִׂיתִי לְךָ כִּי הִכִּיתַנִי זֶה
שָׁלֹשׁ רְגָלִים: וַיֹּאמֶר בִּלְעָם לָאָתוֹן כִּי הִתְעַלַּלְתְּ בִּי לוּ יֶשׁ־חֶרֶב כט

כב) **כִּי הוֹלֵךְ הוּא.** רָאָה שֶׁהַדָּבָר רַע בְּעֵינֵי הַמָּקוֹם וְנִתְאַוָּה לֵילֵךְ: **לְשָׂטָן לוֹ.** מַלְאָךְ שֶׁל רַחֲמִים הָיָה, וְהָיָה רוֹצֶה לְמָנְעוֹ מִלַּחֲטוֹא שֶׁלֹּא יֶחֱטָא וְיֹאבַד: **וּשְׁנֵי נְעָרָיו עִמּוֹ.** מִכָּאן לְאָדָם חָשׁוּב הַיּוֹצֵא לַדֶּרֶךְ יוֹלִיךְ עִמּוֹ שְׁנֵי אֲנָשִׁים לְשַׁמְּשׁוֹ, וְחוֹזְרִים וּמְשַׁמְּשִׁים זֶה אֶת זֶה:

כג) **וַתֵּרֶא הָאָתוֹן.** וְהוּא לֹא רָאָה, שֶׁנָּתַן הַקָּדוֹשׁ בָּרוּךְ הוּא רְשׁוּת לַבְּהֵמָה לִרְאוֹת יוֹתֵר מִן הָאָדָם, שֶׁמִּתּוֹךְ שֶׁיֵּשׁ בּוֹ דַעַת תִּטָּרֵף דַּעְתּוֹ כְּשֶׁיִּרְאֶה מַזִּיקִין: **וְחַרְבּוֹ שְׁלוּפָה בְּיָדוֹ.** אָמַר: רָשָׁע זֶה הִנִּיחַ כְּלֵי אֻמָּנוּתוֹ, שֶׁכְּלֵי זֵיְנָן שֶׁל אֻמּוֹת הָעוֹלָם בַּחֶרֶב, וְהוּא בָּא עֲלֵיהֶם בְּפִיו שֶׁהוּא אֻמָּנוּת שֶׁלָּהֶם, אַף אֲנִי אֶתְפֹּשׂ אֶת שֶׁלּוֹ וְאָבֹא עָלָיו בְּאֻמָּנוּתוֹ, וְכֵן הָיָה סוֹפוֹ: "וְאֶת בִּלְעָם בֶּן בְּעוֹר הָרְגוּ בֶּחָרֶב" (להלן לא, ח):

כד) **בְּמִשְׁעוֹל.** כְּתַרְגּוּמוֹ: "בִּשְׁבִיל", וְכֵן: "אִם יִשְׂפֹּק עֲפַר שֹׁמְרוֹן לִשְׁעָלִים" (מלכים א' כ, י), עֲפַר הַנִּדְבָּק בְּכַפּוֹת הָרַגְלַיִם בַּהֲלוּכָן. וְכֵן: "מִי מָדַד בְּשָׁעֳלוֹ מַיִם" (ישעיה מ, יב), בְּרַגְלָיו וּבַהֲלוּכוֹ: **גָּדֵר מִזֶּה וְגָדֵר מִזֶּה.** סְתָם "גָּדֵר" שֶׁל אֲבָנִים הוּא:

כה) **וַתִּלָּחֵץ.** הִיא עַצְמָהּ: **וַתִּלְחַץ.** אֶת אֲחֵרִים, אֶת רֶגֶל בִּלְעָם:

כו) **וַיּוֹסֶף מַלְאַךְ ה' עֲבוֹר.** לַעֲבֹר עוֹד לְפָנָיו לַהֲלֹךְ לִהְיוֹת לְפָנָיו בְּמָקוֹם אַחֵר, כְּמוֹ: "וְהוּא עָבַר לִפְנֵיהֶם" (בראשית לג, ג). וּמִדְרַשׁ אַגָּדָה יֵשׁ בְּתַנְחוּמָא, מָה רָאָה לַעֲמֹד בִּשְׁלֹשָׁה מְקוֹמוֹת? סִימָנֵי אָבוֹת הֶרְאָהוּ:

כח) **זֶה שָׁלֹשׁ רְגָלִים.** רְמָזָה לוֹ, אַתָּה מְבַקֵּשׁ לַעֲקֹר אֻמָּה הַחוֹגֶגֶת שָׁלֹשׁ רְגָלִים בַּשָּׁנָה:

כט) **הִתְעַלַּלְתְּ.** כְּתַרְגּוּמוֹ, לְשׁוֹן גְּנַאי וּבִזָּיוֹן: **לוּ יֶשׁ חֶרֶב בְּיָדִי.** גְּנוּת גְּדוֹלָה הָיָה לוֹ דָּבָר זֶה בְּעֵינֵי הַשָּׂרִים, זֶה הוֹלֵךְ לַהֲרֹג אֻמָּה שְׁלֵמָה בְּפִיו, וְלָאָתוֹן זוֹ צָרִיךְ לִכְלֵי זַיִן:

לְ בְיָדִ֔י כִּ֥י עַתָּ֖ה הֲרַגְתִּֽיךְ: וַתֹּ֨אמֶר הָאָת֜וֹן אֶל־בִּלְעָ֗ם הֲלוֹא֩ אָנֹכִ֨י
אֲתֹֽנְךָ֜ אֲשֶׁר־רָכַ֣בְתָּ עָלַ֗י מֵעֽוֹדְךָ֙ עַד־הַיּ֣וֹם הַזֶּ֔ה הַֽהַסְכֵּ֣ן הִסְכַּ֔נְתִּי
לא לַעֲשׂ֥וֹת לְךָ֖ כֹּ֑ה וַיֹּ֖אמֶר לֹֽא: וַיְגַ֣ל יְהוָה֮ אֶת־עֵינֵ֣י בִלְעָם֒ וַיַּ֞רְא
אֶת־מַלְאַ֤ךְ יְהוָה֙ נִצָּ֣ב בַּדֶּ֔רֶךְ וְחַרְבּ֥וֹ שְׁלֻפָ֖ה בְּיָד֑וֹ וַיִּקֹּ֥ד וַיִּשְׁתַּ֖חוּ
לב לְאַפָּֽיו: וַיֹּ֣אמֶר אֵלָיו֮ מַלְאַ֣ךְ יְהוָה֒ עַל־מָ֗ה הִכִּ֙יתָ֙ אֶת־אֲתֹ֣נְךָ֔ זֶ֖ה
שָׁל֣וֹשׁ רְגָלִ֑ים הִנֵּ֤ה אָנֹכִי֙ יָצָ֣אתִי לְשָׂטָ֔ן כִּֽי־יָרַ֥ט הַדֶּ֖רֶךְ לְנֶגְדִּֽי:
לג וַתִּרְאַ֣נִי הָֽאָת֔וֹן וַתֵּ֣ט לְפָנַ֔י זֶ֖ה שָׁלֹ֣שׁ רְגָלִ֑ים אוּלַי֙ נָטְתָ֣ה מִפָּנַ֔י
כִּ֥י עַתָּ֛ה גַּם־אֹתְכָ֥ה הָרַ֖גְתִּי וְאוֹתָ֥הּ הֶחֱיֵֽיתִי: וַיֹּ֨אמֶר בִּלְעָ֜ם אֶל־
לד מַלְאַ֤ךְ יְהוָה֙ חָטָ֔אתִי כִּ֚י לֹ֣א יָדַ֔עְתִּי כִּ֥י אַתָּ֛ה נִצָּ֥ב לִקְרָאתִ֖י בַּדָּ֑רֶךְ
לה וְעַתָּ֛ה אִם־רַ֥ע בְּעֵינֶ֖יךָ אָשׁ֥וּבָה לִּֽי: וַיֹּאמֶר֩ מַלְאַ֨ךְ יְהוָ֜ה אֶל־
בִּלְעָ֗ם לֵ֚ךְ עִם־הָ֣אֲנָשִׁ֔ים וְאֶ֗פֶס אֶת־הַדָּבָ֛ר אֲשֶׁר־אֲדַבֵּ֥ר אֵלֶ֖יךָ

לו] **הַהַסְכֵּן הִסְכַּנְתִּי.** כְּתַרְגּוּמוֹ, וְכֵן: "הֲלַאֵל יִסְכָּן
גָּבֶר" (איוב כב, ב). וְרַבּוֹתֵינוּ דָּרְשׁוּ מִקְרָא זֶה בַּתַּלְמוּד,
אָמְרוּ לֵיהּ: מַאי טַעֲמָא לָא רְכַבְתְּ אַסּוּסְיָא? אָמַר
לְהוֹן: בִּרְטִיבָא שַׁדַּאי לֵיהּ כוּ', כִּדְאִיתָא בְּמַסֶּכֶת
עֲבוֹדָה זָרָה (דף ד ע"ב):

לב] **כִּי יָרַט הַדֶּרֶךְ לְנֶגְדִּי.** רַבּוֹתֵינוּ חַכְמֵי הַמִּשְׁנָה
דְּרָשׁוּהוּ נוֹטָרִיקוֹן: יָרְאָה, רָאֲתָה, נָטְתָה, בִּשְׁבִיל
שֶׁהַדֶּרֶךְ לְנֶגְדִּי, כְּלוֹמַר לְקִנְחָתִי וּלְהַקְנִיטֵנִי. וּלְפִי
מַשְׁמָעוֹ, כִּי חָרַד הַדֶּרֶךְ לְנֶגְדִּי, לְשׁוֹן רֶטֶט, כִּי לְחָיֵית
בַּעַל הַדֶּרֶךְ שֶׁחָרַד וּמִהֵר הַדֶּרֶךְ שֶׁהוּא לְעֻמָּתָם
וּלְהַמְרוֹתָם, וּמִקְרָא קָצָר הוּא, כְּמוֹ: "וַתְּכַל דָּוִד"
(שמואל ב' יג, לט) שֶׁרוֹצֶה לוֹמַר: וַתְּכַל נֶפֶשׁ דָּוִד. לְשׁוֹן
אַחֵר, "יָרַט" לְשׁוֹן רָצוֹן, וְכֵן: "וְעַל יְדֵי רְשָׁעִים יַרְטֵנִי"
(איוב טז, יא), מְפַיֵּס וּמְנַחֵם אוֹתִי עַל יְדֵי רְשָׁעִים, שֶׁאֵינָן
אֶלָּא מַקְנִיטִים:

לג] **אוּלַי נָטְתָה.** כְּמוֹ לוּלֵא, פְּעָמִים שֶׁ"אוּלַי" מְשַׁמֵּשׁ
בִּלְשׁוֹן לוּלֵא. **הֲרֵי זֶה מִקְרָא**
מְסֹרָס, וְהוּא כְּמוֹ: "גַּם הֲרַגְתִּי אוֹתְךָ". כְּלוֹמַר, לֹא

הָעַכָּבָה בִּלְבַד קִלְקַלְתָּ עַל יָדִי, כִּי גַּם הַהֲרִיגָה.
וְאוֹתָהּ הֶחֱיֵיתִי. וְעַתָּה מִפְּנֵי שֶׁדִּבְּרָה וְהוֹכִיחַתְךָ, וְלֹא
יָכֹלְתָּ לַעֲמֹד בְּתוֹכַחְתָּהּ, כְּמוֹ שֶׁכָּתוּב: "וַיֹּאמֶר לֹא"
(לעיל פסוק ל) – הֲרַגְתִּיהָ, שֶׁלֹּא יֹאמְרוּ: זוֹ הִיא שֶׁסִּלְּקָה
אֶת בִּלְעָם בְּתוֹכַחְתָּהּ וְלֹא יָכֹל לְהָשִׁיב, שֶׁחָס הַמָּקוֹם
עַל כְּבוֹד הַבְּרִיּוֹת. וְכֵן: "וְאֶת הַבְּהֵמָה תַּהֲרֹגוּ" (ויקרא כ,
טו), וְכֵן: "וְהָרַגְתָּ אֶת הָאִשָּׁה וְאֶת הַבְּהֵמָה" (שם פסוק טז):

לד] **כִּי לֹא יָדַעְתִּי.** גַּם זֶה גְּנוּתוֹ, וְעַל כָּרְחוֹ הוֹדָה,
שֶׁהוּא הָיָה מִשְׁתַּבֵּחַ שֶׁיּוֹדֵעַ דַּעַת עֶלְיוֹן, וּפִיו הֵעִיד:
"לֹא יָדַעְתִּי": **אִם רַע בְּעֵינֶיךָ אָשׁוּבָה לִּי.** לְהַתְרִיס
נֶגֶד הַמָּקוֹם הִיא תְּשׁוּבָה זוֹ, אָמַר לוֹ: הוּא בְּעַצְמוֹ
צִוַּנִי לָלֶכֶת, וְאַתָּה מַלְאָךְ מְבַטֵּל אֶת דְּבָרָיו, לָמוּד
הוּא בְּכָךְ שֶׁאוֹמֵר דָּבָר וּמַלְאָךְ מַחֲזִירוֹ, אָמַר
לְאַבְרָהָם: "קַח נָא אֶת בִּנְךָ" וְגוֹ' (בראשית כב, ב), וְעַל
יְדֵי מַלְאָךְ בִּטֵּל אֶת דְּבָרוֹ, אַף אֲנִי אִם רַע בְּעֵינֶיךָ
צָרִיךְ אֲנִי לָשׁוּב:

לה] **לֵךְ עִם הָאֲנָשִׁים.** בְּדֶרֶךְ שֶׁאָדָם רוֹצֶה לֵילֵךְ בָּהּ
מוֹלִיכִין אוֹתוֹ: **לֵךְ עִם הָאֲנָשִׁים.** כִּי חֶלְקְךָ עִמָּהֶם

פרק כג | במדבר

לו אִתּוֹ תְּדַבֵּר וַיֵּלֶךְ בִּלְעָם עִם־שָׂרֵי בָלָק: וַיִּשְׁמַע בָּלָק כִּי־בָא
בִלְעָם וַיֵּצֵא לִקְרָאתוֹ אֶל־עִיר מוֹאָב אֲשֶׁר עַל־גְּבוּל אַרְנֹן
לז אֲשֶׁר בִּקְצֵה הַגְּבוּל: וַיֹּאמֶר בָּלָק אֶל־בִּלְעָם הֲלֹא שָׁלֹחַ שָׁלַחְתִּי
אֵלֶיךָ לִקְרֹא־לָךְ לָמָּה לֹא־הָלַכְתָּ אֵלָי הַאֻמְנָם לֹא אוּכַל כַּבְּדֶךָ:
לח וַיֹּאמֶר בִּלְעָם אֶל־בָּלָק הִנֵּה־בָאתִי אֵלֶיךָ עַתָּה הֲיָכֹל אוּכַל
רביעי / ששי / דַּבֵּר מְאוּמָה הַדָּבָר אֲשֶׁר יָשִׂים אֱלֹהִים בְּפִי אֹתוֹ אֲדַבֵּר: וַיֵּלֶךְ
לט בִּלְעָם עִם־בָּלָק וַיָּבֹאוּ קִרְיַת חֻצוֹת: וַיִּזְבַּח בָּלָק בָּקָר וָצֹאן
מ וַיְשַׁלַּח לְבִלְעָם וְלַשָּׂרִים אֲשֶׁר אִתּוֹ: וַיְהִי בַבֹּקֶר וַיִּקַּח בָּלָק
מא אֶת־בִּלְעָם וַיַּעֲלֵהוּ בָּמוֹת בָּעַל וַיַּרְא מִשָּׁם קְצֵה הָעָם: וַיֹּאמֶר
כג א בִּלְעָם אֶל־בָּלָק בְּנֵה־לִי בָזֶה שִׁבְעָה מִזְבְּחֹת וְהָכֵן לִי בָּזֶה
שִׁבְעָה פָרִים וְשִׁבְעָה אֵילִים: וַיַּעַשׂ בָּלָק כַּאֲשֶׁר דִּבֶּר בִּלְעָם
ב וַיַּעַל בָּלָק וּבִלְעָם פָּר וָאַיִל בַּמִּזְבֵּחַ: וַיֹּאמֶר בִּלְעָם לְבָלָק הִתְיַצֵּב
ג עַל־עֹלָתֶךָ וְאֵלְכָה אוּלַי יִקָּרֵה יהוה לִקְרָאתִי וּדְבַר מַה־יַּרְאֵנִי
ד וְהִגַּדְתִּי לָךְ וַיֵּלֶךְ שֶׁפִי: וַיִּקָּר אֱלֹהִים אֶל־בִּלְעָם וַיֹּאמֶר אֵלָיו

וְסוֹפְךָ לַחֲסַר מִן הָעוֹלָם. וְאֶפֶס. עַל כָּרְחֲךָ, "אֵת הַדָּבָר אֲשֶׁר אֲדַבֵּר" וְגוֹ'. עִם שָׂרֵי בָלָק. שָׂמֵחַ לְקַלְּלָם כְּמוֹתָם:

לו | וַיִּשְׁמַע בָּלָק. שָׁלַח שְׁלוּחִים לְבַשְּׂרוֹ: אֶל עִיר מוֹאָב. אֶל מֶטְרוֹפּוֹלִין שֶׁלוֹ, עִיר הַחֲשׁוּבָה שֶׁלוֹ, לוֹמַר: רְאֵה מָה אֵלוּ מְבַקְשִׁים לַעֲקֹר:

לז | הַאֻמְנָם לֹא אוּכַל כַּבְּדֶךָ. נִתְנַבֵּא שֶׁסּוֹפוֹ לָצֵאת מֵעִמּוֹ בְּקָלוֹן:

לט | קִרְיַת חֻצוֹת. עִיר מְלֵאָה שְׁוָקִים אֲנָשִׁים נָשִׁים וָטַף בְּחוּצוֹתֶיהָ, לוֹמַר: רְאֵה וְרַחֵם שֶׁלֹּא יֵעָקְרוּ אֵלּוּ:

מ | בָּקָר וָצֹאן. דָּבָר מוּעָט, בָּקָר אֶחָד וְצֹאן אֶחָד בִּלְבָד:

מא | בָּמוֹת בָּעַל. כְּתַרְגּוּמוֹ: "לְרָמַת דַּחֲלָתֵיהּ", שֵׁם עֲבוֹדָה זָרָה:

פרק כג

ג | אוּלַי יִקָּרֵה ה' לִקְרָאתִי. אֵינוֹ רָגִיל לְדַבֵּר עִמִּי בַּיּוֹם: וַיֵּלֶךְ שֶׁפִי. כְּתַרְגּוּמוֹ: "יְחִידִי", לְשׁוֹן שֹׁפִי וָשֶׁקֶט, שֶׁאֵין עִמּוֹ אֶלָּא שְׁתִיקָה:

ד | וַיִּקָּר. לְשׁוֹן עֲרַאי, לְשׁוֹן גְּנַאי, לְשׁוֹן טֻמְאַת קֶרִי, כְּלוֹמַר בְּקֹשִׁי וּבְבִזָּיוֹן, וְלֹא הָיָה נִגְלֶה עָלָיו בַּיּוֹם אֶלָּא בִּשְׁבִיל לְהַרְאוֹת חִבָּתָן שֶׁל יִשְׂרָאֵל: אֶת שִׁבְעַת

במדבר | פרק כג | בלק

ה אֶת־שִׁבְעַת הַמִּזְבְּחֹת עָרַכְתִּי וָאַעַל פָּר וָאַיִל בַּמִּזְבֵּחַ: וַיָּשֶׂם
ו יְהוָה דָּבָר בְּפִי בִלְעָם וַיֹּאמֶר שׁוּב אֶל־בָּלָק וְכֹה תְדַבֵּר: וַיָּשָׁב
ז אֵלָיו וְהִנֵּה נִצָּב עַל־עֹלָתוֹ הוּא וְכָל־שָׂרֵי מוֹאָב: וַיִּשָּׂא מְשָׁלוֹ
וַיֹּאמַר מִן־אֲרָם יַנְחֵנִי בָלָק מֶלֶךְ־מוֹאָב מֵהַרְרֵי־קֶדֶם לְכָה
ח אָרָה־לִּי יַעֲקֹב וּלְכָה זֹעֲמָה יִשְׂרָאֵל: מָה אֶקֹּב לֹא קַבֹּה אֵל
ט וּמָה אֶזְעֹם לֹא זָעַם יְהוָה: כִּי־מֵרֹאשׁ צֻרִים אֶרְאֶנּוּ וּמִגְּבָעוֹת
אֲשׁוּרֶנּוּ הֶן־עָם לְבָדָד יִשְׁכֹּן וּבַגּוֹיִם לֹא יִתְחַשָּׁב: מִי מָנָה עֲפַר
י יַעֲקֹב וּמִסְפָּר אֶת־רֹבַע יִשְׂרָאֵל תָּמֹת נַפְשִׁי מוֹת יְשָׁרִים וּתְהִי

הַמִּזְבְּחֹת. 'שִׁבְעָה מִזְבְּחֹת עָרַכְתִּי' אֵין כְּתִיב כָּאן אֶלָּא "אֶת שִׁבְעַת הַמִּזְבְּחֹת", אָמַר לְפָנָיו: אֲבוֹתֵיהֶם שֶׁל אֵלּוּ בָּנוּ לְפָנֶיךָ שִׁבְעָה מִזְבְּחוֹת, וַאֲנִי עָרַכְתִּי כְּנֶגֶד כֻּלָּם. אַבְרָהָם בָּנָה אַרְבָּעָה: "וַיִּבֶן שָׁם מִזְבֵּחַ לַה' הַנִּרְאֶה אֵלָיו" (בראשית יב, ז), "וַיַּעְתֵּק מִשָּׁם הָהָרָה" וְגוֹ' (שם פסוק ח), "וַיֹּאהַל אַבְרָם" וְגוֹ' (שם יג, יח), וְאֶחָד בְּהַר הַמּוֹרִיָּה (שם כב, ט). וְיִצְחָק בָּנָה אֶחָד, "וַיִּבֶן שָׁם מִזְבֵּחַ" וְגוֹ' (שם כו, כה). וְיַעֲקֹב בָּנָה שְׁנַיִם: אֶחָד בִּשְׁכֶם (שם לג, כ) וְאֶחָד בְּבֵית אֵל (שם לה, ז): וָאַעַל פָּר וָאַיִל בַּמִּזְבֵּחַ. וְאַבְרָהָם לֹא הֶעֱלָה אֶלָּא אַיִל אֶחָד:

ז אָרָה לִּי יַעֲקֹב וּלְכָה זֹעֲמָה יִשְׂרָאֵל. בִּשְׁנֵי שְׁמוֹתֵיהֶם אָמַר לוֹ לְקַלְּלָם, שֶׁמָּא אֶחָד מֵהֶם אֵינוֹ מֻבְהָק:

ח מָה אֶקֹּב לֹא קַבֹּה אֵל. כְּשֶׁהָיוּ רְאוּיִים לְהִתְקַלֵּל לֹא נִתְקַלְּלוּ, כְּשֶׁהִזְכִּיר אֲבִיהֶם אֶת עֲווֹנָם: "כִּי בְאַפָּם הָרְגוּ אִישׁ" (בראשית מט, ו), לֹא קִלֵּל אֶלָּא אַפָּם, שֶׁנֶּאֱמַר: "אָרוּר אַפָּם" (שם פסוק ז). כְּשֶׁנִּכְנַס אֲבִיהֶם בְּמִרְמָה אֵצֶל אָבִיו הָיָה רָאוּי לְהִתְקַלֵּל, מַה נֶּאֱמַר שָׁם – "גַּם בָּרוּךְ יִהְיֶה" (שם כז, לג). בַּמְבָרְכִים נֶאֱמַר: "אֵלֶּה יַעַמְדוּ לְבָרֵךְ אֶת הָעָם" (דברים כז, יב). בַּמְקַלְלִים לֹא נֶאֱמַר: 'אֵלֶּה יַעַמְדוּ לְקַלֵּל אֶת הָעָם', אֶלָּא "וְאֵלֶּה יַעַמְדוּ עַל הַקְּלָלָה" (שם פסוק יג), לֹא רָצָה לְהַזְכִּיר עֲלֵיהֶם שֵׁם קְלָלָה. לֹא זָעַם ה'. אֲנִי אֵין כֹּחִי אֶלָּא

שֶׁאֲנִי יוֹדֵעַ לְכַוֵּן הַשָּׁעָה שֶׁהַקָּדוֹשׁ בָּרוּךְ הוּא כּוֹעֵס בָּהּ, וְהוּא לֹא כָעַס כָּל הַיָּמִים הַלָּלוּ שֶׁבָּאתִי אֵלֶיךָ. וְזֶהוּ שֶׁנֶּאֱמַר: "עַמִּי זְכָר נָא מַה יָּעַץ" וְגוֹ' וּמֶה עָנָה אֹתוֹ בִּלְעָם וְגוֹ' לְמַעַן דַּעַת צִדְקוֹת ה'" (מיכה ו, ה):

ט כִּי מֵרֹאשׁ צֻרִים אֶרְאֶנּוּ. אֲנִי מִסְתַּכֵּל בְּרֵאשִׁיתָם וּבִתְחִלַּת שָׁרְשֵׁיהֶם, וַאֲנִי רוֹאֶה אוֹתָם מְיֻסָּדִים וַחֲזָקִים כַּצּוּרִים וּגְבָעוֹת הַלָּלוּ, עַל יְדֵי אָבוֹת וְאִמָּהוֹת: הֶן עָם לְבָדָד יִשְׁכֹּן. הוּא אֲשֶׁר זָכוּ לוֹ אֲבוֹתָיו לִשְׁכֹּן בָּדָד, כְּתַרְגּוּמוֹ. וּבַגּוֹיִם לֹא יִתְחַשָּׁב. כְּתַרְגּוּמוֹ, לֹא יִהְיוּ נַעֲשִׂין כָּלָה עִם שְׁאָר הָאֻמּוֹת, שֶׁנֶּאֱמַר: "כִּי אֶעֱשֶׂה כָלָה בְּכָל הַגּוֹיִם" וְגוֹ' (ירמיה ל, יא), אֵינָן נִמְנִין עִם הַשְּׁאָר. דָּבָר אַחֵר, כְּשֶׁהֵן שְׂמֵחִין אֵין אֻמָּה שְׂמֵחָה עִמָּהֶם, שֶׁנֶּאֱמַר: "ה' בָּדָד יַנְחֶנּוּ" (דברים לב, יב). וּכְשֶׁהָאֻמּוֹת בְּטוֹבָה הֵם אוֹכְלִין עִם כָּל אֶחָד וְאֶחָד וְאֵין עוֹלֶה לָהֶם מִן הַחֶשְׁבּוֹן, וְזֶהוּ "וּבַגּוֹיִם לֹא יִתְחַשָּׁב":

י מִי מָנָה עֲפַר יַעֲקֹב וְגוֹ'. כְּתַרְגּוּמוֹ: 'דַּעְדְּקַיָּא דְּבֵית יַעֲקֹב כוּ' מֵאַרְבַּע מַשִּׁירְיָתָא' מֵאַרְבָּעָה דְּגָלִים. דָּבָר אַחֵר, "עֲפַר יַעֲקֹב", אֵין חֶשְׁבּוֹן בַּמִּצְווֹת שֶׁהֵם מְקַיְּמִין בֶּעָפָר: "לֹא תַחֲרשׁ בְּשׁוֹר וּבַחֲמֹר" (דברים כב, י), "לֹא תִזְרַע כִּלְאָיִם" (ויקרא יט, יט), אֵפֶר פָּרָה (לעיל יט, ט), וַעֲפַר סוֹטָה (לעיל ה, יז), וְכַיּוֹצֵא בָהֶם: וּמִסְפָּר אֶת רֹבַע יִשְׂרָאֵל. רְבִיעוֹתֵיהֶן, זֶרַע הַיּוֹצֵא מִן הַתַּשְׁמִישׁ שֶׁלָּהֶם: תָּמֹת נַפְשִׁי מוֹת יְשָׁרִים. שֶׁבָּהֶם:

אַחֲרִיתִי כָּמֹהוּ: וַיֹּאמֶר בָּלָק אֶל־בִּלְעָם מֶה עָשִׂיתָ לִי לָקֹב
יא
אֹיְבַי לְקַחְתִּיךָ וְהִנֵּה בֵּרַכְתָּ בָרֵךְ: וַיַּעַן וַיֹּאמַר הֲלֹא אֵת אֲשֶׁר
יב
יָשִׂים יהוה בְּפִי אֹתוֹ אֶשְׁמֹר לְדַבֵּר: וַיֹּאמֶר אֵלָיו בָּלָק לך־נָא
יג
אִתִּי אֶל־מָקוֹם אַחֵר אֲשֶׁר תִּרְאֶנּוּ מִשָּׁם אֶפֶס קָצֵהוּ תִרְאֶה
וְכֻלּוֹ לֹא תִרְאֶה וְקָבְנוֹ־לִי מִשָּׁם: וַיִּקָּחֵהוּ שְׂדֵה צֹפִים אֶל־רֹאשׁ
יד
הַפִּסְגָּה וַיִּבֶן שִׁבְעָה מִזְבְּחֹת וַיַּעַל פָּר וָאַיִל בַּמִּזְבֵּחַ: וַיֹּאמֶר
טו
אֶל־בָּלָק הִתְיַצֵּב כֹּה עַל־עֹלָתֶךָ וְאָנֹכִי אִקָּרֶה כֹּה: וַיִּקָּר יהוה
טז
אֶל־בִּלְעָם וַיָּשֶׂם דָּבָר בְּפִיו וַיֹּאמֶר שׁוּב אֶל־בָּלָק וְכֹה תְדַבֵּר:
וַיָּבֹא אֵלָיו וְהִנּוֹ נִצָּב עַל־עֹלָתוֹ וְשָׂרֵי מוֹאָב אִתּוֹ וַיֹּאמֶר לוֹ
יז
בָּלָק מַה־דִּבֶּר יהוה: וַיִּשָּׂא מְשָׁלוֹ וַיֹּאמַר קוּם בָּלָק וּשֲׁמָע
יח
הַאֲזִינָה עָדַי בְּנוֹ צִפֹּר: לֹא אִישׁ אֵל וִיכַזֵּב וּבֶן־אָדָם וְיִתְנֶחָם
יט
הַהוּא אָמַר וְלֹא יַעֲשֶׂה וְדִבֶּר וְלֹא יְקִימֶנָּה: הִנֵּה בָרֵךְ לָקָחְתִּי
כ

יג) **וְקָבְנוֹ לִי.** לְשׁוֹן צִוּוּי, קַלְּלֵהוּ לִי:

יד) **שְׂדֵה צֹפִים.** מָקוֹם גָּבוֹהַּ הָיָה, שֶׁשָּׁם הַצּוֹפֶה עוֹמֵד לִשְׁמֹר אִם יָבוֹא חַיִל עַל הָעִיר: **רֹאשׁ הַפִּסְגָּה.** בִּלְעָם לֹא הָיָה קוֹסֵם כְּבָלָק, רָאָה בָלָק שֶׁעֲתִידָה פִּרְצָה לְהִפָּרֵץ בְּיִשְׂרָאֵל מִשָּׁם, שֶׁשָּׁם מֵת מֹשֶׁה, כִּסָּבוּר שֶׁשָּׁם תָּחוּל עֲלֵיהֶם הַקְּלָלָה וְזוֹ הִיא הַפִּרְצָה שֶׁאֲנִי רוֹאֶה:

טו) **אִקָּרֶה כֹּה.** מֵאֵת הַקָּדוֹשׁ בָּרוּךְ הוּא, 'אִקָּרֶה' לְשׁוֹן מִתְפַּעֵל:

טז) **וַיָּשֶׂם דָּבָר בְּפִיו.** וּמַה הִיא הַשִּׂימָה הַזֹּאת, וּמַה חָסֵר הַמִּקְרָא בְּאָמְרוֹ: "שׁוּב אֶל בָּלָק וְכֹה תְדַבֵּר"? אֶלָּא כְּשֶׁהָיָה שׁוֹמֵעַ שֶׁאֵינוֹ נִרְשֶׁה לְקַלֵּל, אָמַר: מָה אֲנִי חוֹזֵר אֵצֶל בָּלָק לְצַעֲרוֹ, וְנָתַן לוֹ הַקָּדוֹשׁ בָּרוּךְ הוּא לֶסֶן וְחַכָּה בְּפִיו כְּאָדָם הַפּוֹקֵס בְּהֵמָה בְּחַכָּה לְהוֹלִיכָהּ אֶל אֲשֶׁר יִרְצֶה, אָמַר לוֹ: עַל כָּרְחֲךָ תָּשׁוּב אֶל בָּלָק:

יז) **וְשָׂרֵי מוֹאָב אִתּוֹ.** וּלְמַעְלָה הוּא אוֹמֵר: "וְכָל שָׂרֵי מוֹאָב" (לעיל פסוק ז), כֵּיוָן שֶׁרָאוּ שֶׁאֵין בּוֹ תִּקְוָה הָלְכוּ לָהֶם מִקְצָתָם, וְלֹא נִשְׁאֲרוּ אֶלָּא מִקְצָתָם: **מַה דִּבֶּר ה'.** לְשׁוֹן צְחוֹק הוּא זֶה, כְּלוֹמַר אֵינְךָ בִּרְשׁוּתְךָ:

יח) **קוּם בָּלָק.** כֵּיוָן שֶׁרָאָהוּ מְצַחֵק בּוֹ, נִתְכַּוֵּן לְצַעֲרוֹ: עֲמֹד עַל רַגְלֶיךָ, אֵינְךָ רַשַּׁאי לֵישֵׁב וַאֲנִי שָׁלוּחַ אֵלֶיךָ בִּשְׁלִיחוּתוֹ שֶׁל מָקוֹם: **בְּנוֹ צִפֹּר.** לְשׁוֹן מִקְרָא הוּא כֵן, כְּמוֹ, "חַיְתוֹ יַעַר" (תהלים נ, י), "וְחַיְתוֹ אֶרֶץ" (בראשית א, כד), "לְמַעְיְנוֹ מָיִם" (תהלים קיד, ח):

יט) **לֹא אִישׁ אֵל וְגוֹ'.** כְּבָר נִשְׁבַּע לָהֶם לַהֲבִיאָם וּלְהוֹרִישָׁם אֶרֶץ שִׁבְעָה עֲמָמִים, וְאַתָּה סָבוּר לַהֲמִיתָם בַּמִּדְבָּר?: **הַהוּא אָמַר וְגוֹ'.** בִּלְשׁוֹן תְּמִיָּה, וְתַרְגּוּמוֹ: "תָּיְבִין וּמִתְמַלְּכִין", חוֹזְרִים וְנִמְלָכִים לַחֲזֹר בָּהֶם:

כ) **הִנֵּה בָרֵךְ לָקָחְתִּי.** אַתָּה שׁוֹאֲלֵנִי: "מַה דִּבֶּר ה'" (לעיל פסוק יז), קִבַּלְתִּי מִמֶּנּוּ לְבָרֵךְ אוֹתָם: וּבֵרֵךְ וְלֹא

במדבר | פרק כג

כא וּבֵרֵךְ וְלֹא אֲשִׁיבֶנָּה: לֹא־הִבִּיט אָוֶן בְּיַעֲקֹב וְלֹא־רָאָה עָמָל
כב בְּיִשְׂרָאֵל יְהוָה אֱלֹהָיו עִמּוֹ וּתְרוּעַת מֶלֶךְ בּוֹ: אֵל מוֹצִיאָם
כג מִמִּצְרָיִם כְּתוֹעֲפֹת רְאֵם לוֹ: כִּי לֹא־נַחַשׁ בְּיַעֲקֹב וְלֹא־קֶסֶם
כד בְּיִשְׂרָאֵל כָּעֵת יֵאָמֵר לְיַעֲקֹב וּלְיִשְׂרָאֵל מַה־פָּעַל אֵל: הֶן־עָם
כְּלָבִיא יָקוּם וְכַאֲרִי יִתְנַשָּׂא לֹא יִשְׁכַּב עַד־יֹאכַל טֶרֶף וְדַם־

אֲשִׁיבֶנָּה. הוּא בֵּרֵךְ אוֹתָם, וַאֲנִי לֹא אָשִׁיב אֶת בִּרְכָתוֹ: **וּבֵרֵךְ.** כְּמוֹ "וּבֵרַךְ" וְכֵן הוּא גִּזְרַת רֵי"שׁ, כְּמוֹ: "חוֹיֵב חַיֵּךְ" (תהלים עד, יח) כְּמוֹ "חִיֵּךְ", וְכֵן: "וּבֹלֵעַ בֵּרַךְ" (סס י, ג), הַמְהַלֵּל וּמְבָרֵךְ אֶת הַגּוֹזֵל וְאוֹמֵר לוֹ: אַל תִּדְאַג כִּי לֹא תֵּעָנֵשׁ, שָׁלוֹם יִהְיֶה לְךָ, מַרְגִּיז הוּא לְהַקָּדוֹשׁ בָּרוּךְ הוּא. וְאֵין לוֹמַר "בֵּרַךְ" שֵׁם דָּבָר, שֶׁאִם כֵּן הָיָה נָקוּד בְּפַתָּח קָטָן (סגול) וְטַעֲמוֹ לְמַעְלָה, אֲבָל לְפִי שֶׁהוּא לְשׁוֹן פָּעַל, הוּא נָקוּד קָמָץ קָטָן (צירי) וְטַעֲמוֹ לְמַטָּה:

כא לֹא הִבִּיט אָוֶן וְגוֹ׳. כְּתַרְגּוּמוֹ. דָּבָר אַחֵר, אַחֲרֵי פְּשׁוּטוֹ הוּא נִדְרָשׁ מִדְרָשׁ נָאֶה: "לֹא הִבִּיט" הַקָּדוֹשׁ בָּרוּךְ הוּא אָוֶן שֶׁבְּיַעֲקֹב, כְּשֶׁהֵן עוֹבְרִין עַל דְּבָרָיו, אֵינוֹ מְדַקְדֵּק אַחֲרֵיהֶם לְהִתְבּוֹנֵן בְּאוֹנִיּוֹת שֶׁלָּהֶם וּבַעֲמָלָן שֶׁהֵן עוֹבְרִין עַל דָּתוֹ: **עָמָל.** לְשׁוֹן עֲבֵרָה, כְּמוֹ: "הָרָה עָמָל" (תהלים ז, טו), "כִּי אַתָּה עָמָל וָכַעַס תַּבִּיט" (תהלים י, יד), לְפִי שֶׁהָעֲבֵרָה הִיא עָמָל לִפְנֵי הַמָּקוֹם: **ה׳ אֱלֹהָיו עִמּוֹ.** אֲפִלּוּ מַכְעִיסִין וּמַמְרִים לְפָנָיו אֵינוֹ זָז מִתּוֹכָן: **וּתְרוּעַת מֶלֶךְ בּוֹ.** לְשׁוֹן חִבָּה וְרֵעוּת, כְּמוֹ: "רֵעֶה דָוִד" (שמואל ב טו, לז), "אוֹהֵב דָּוִד", "וַיִּתְּנָהּ לְמֵרֵעֵהוּ" (שופטים טו, ו). וְכֵן תִּרְגֵּם אוֹנְקְלוֹס "וּשְׁכִינַת מַלְכְּהוֹן בֵּינֵיהוֹן":

כב אֵל מוֹצִיאָם מִמִּצְרָיִם. אַתָּה אָמַרְתָּ: "הִנֵּה עַם יָצָא מִמִּצְרָיִם" (לעיל כב, ה), לֹא יָצָא מֵעַצְמוֹ אֶלָּא הָאֱלֹהִים הוֹצִיאָם: **כְּתוֹעֲפֹת רְאֵם לוֹ.** כְּתֹקֶף רוּם וְגֹבַהּ שֶׁלּוֹ, וְכֵן: "וְכֶסֶף תּוֹעָפוֹת" (איוב כב, כה), לְשׁוֹן מָעוֹן הֵמָּה. וְאוֹמֵר אֲנִי שֶׁהוּא לְשׁוֹן: "וְעוֹף יְעוֹפֵף" (בראשית א, כ), הַמְעוֹפֵף בְּרוּם וָגֹבַהּ, וְתֹקֶף רַב הוּא זֶה.

כג כִּי לֹא נַחַשׁ בְּיַעֲקֹב. כִּי רְאוּיִים הֵם לִבְרָכָה, שֶׁאֵין בָּהֶם מְנַחֲשִׁים וְקוֹסְמִים: **כָּעֵת יֵאָמֵר לְיַעֲקֹב וְגוֹ׳.** עוֹד עָתִיד לִהְיוֹת עֵת כָּעֵת הַזֹּאת אֲשֶׁר תִּגָּלֶה חִבָּתָן לְעֵין כֹּל, שֶׁהֵן יוֹשְׁבִין לְפָנָיו וְלוֹמְדִים תּוֹרָה מִפִּיו וּמְחִצָּתָן לִפְנִים מִמַּלְאֲכֵי הַשָּׁרֵת, וְהֵם יִשְׁאֲלוּ לָהֶם: "מַה פָּעַל אֵל", וְזֶהוּ שֶׁנֶּאֱמַר: "וְהָיוּ עֵינֶיךָ רֹאוֹת אֶת מוֹרֶיךָ" (ישעיה ל, כ). דָּבָר אַחֵר, "יֵאָמֵר לְיַעֲקֹב" אֵינוֹ לְשׁוֹן עָתִיד אֶלָּא לְשׁוֹן הֹוֶה, אֵינָן צְרִיכִין לִמְנַחֵשׁ וְקוֹסֵם, כִּי בְּכָל עֵת שֶׁצָּרִיךְ לְהֵאָמֵר לְיַעֲקֹב וּלְיִשְׂרָאֵל מַה פָּעַל הַקָּדוֹשׁ בָּרוּךְ הוּא וּמַה גְּזֵרוֹתָיו בַּמָּרוֹם, אֵינָן מְנַחֲשִׁים וְקוֹסְמִים, אֶלָּא נֶאֱמַר לָהֶם עַל פִּי נְבִיאֵיהֶם מַה הִיא גְּזֵרַת הַמָּקוֹם, אוֹ אוּרִים וְתֻמִּים מַגִּידִים לָהֶם. וְאוֹנְקְלוֹס לֹא תִרְגֵּם כֵּן:

כד הֶן עָם כְּלָבִיא יָקוּם וְגוֹ׳. כְּשֶׁהֵן עוֹמְדִין מִשְּׁנָתָם שַׁחֲרִית הֵן מִתְגַּבְּרִים כְּלָבִיא וְכַאֲרִי לַחֲטוֹף אֶת הַמִּצְוֹת, לִלְבֹּשׁ טַלִּית, לִקְרוֹא אֶת שְׁמַע וּלְהָנִיחַ תְּפִלִּין: **לֹא יִשְׁכַּב.** בַּלַּיְלָה עַל מִטָּתוֹ עַד שֶׁהוּא אוֹכֵל וּמְחַבֵּל כָּל מַזִּיק הַבָּא לְטָרְפוֹ. כֵּיצַד? קוֹרֵא אֶת שְׁמַע עַל מִטָּתוֹ וּמַפְקִיד רוּחוֹ בְּיַד הַמָּקוֹם. בָּא מַחֲנֶה וְגַיִס לְהַזִּיקָם, הַקָּדוֹשׁ בָּרוּךְ הוּא שׁוֹמְרָם וְנִלְחָם מִלְחֲמוֹתֵיהֶם וּמַפִּילָם חֲלָלִים. דָּבָר אַחֵר, "הֶן עָם כְּלָבִיא יָקוּם וְגוֹ׳", כְּתַרְגּוּמוֹ: **וְדַם חֲלָלִים** יִשְׁתֶּה. נִתְנַבֵּא שֶׁאֵין מֹשֶׁה מֵת עַד שֶׁיַּפִּיל מַלְכֵי מִדְיָן חֲלָלִים וְיֵהָרֵג הוּא עִמָּהֶם, שֶׁנֶּאֱמַר: "וְאֶת בִּלְעָם בֶּן בְּעוֹר הַקּוֹסֵם הָרְגוּ בְנֵי יִשְׂרָאֵל בַּחֶרֶב אֶל חַלְלֵיהֶם" (יהושע יג, כב):

"וְתוּעֲפַת רְאֵם" עֲפִיפַת גֹּבַהּ. דָּבָר אַחֵר, "תּוֹעֲפַת רְאֵם", תֹּקֶף רְאֵמִים, וְאָמְרוּ רַבּוֹתֵינוּ: אֵלּוּ הַשֵּׁדִים:

פרק כד | במדבר | בלק

חֲלָלִ֖ים יִשְׁתֶּֽה: וַיֹּ֤אמֶר בָּלָק֙ אֶל־בִּלְעָ֔ם גַּם־קֹ֖ב לֹ֣א תִקֳּבֶ֑נּוּ
גַּם־בָּרֵ֖ךְ לֹ֥א תְבָרְכֶֽנּוּ: וַיַּ֣עַן בִּלְעָ֔ם וַיֹּ֖אמֶר אֶל־בָּלָ֑ק הֲלֹ֗א דִּבַּ֤רְתִּי
אֵלֶ֙יךָ֙ לֵאמֹ֔ר כֹּ֛ל אֲשֶׁר־יְדַבֵּ֥ר יְהוָ֖ה אֹת֥וֹ אֶֽעֱשֶֽׂה: וַיֹּ֤אמֶר בָּלָק֙
אֶל־בִּלְעָ֔ם לְכָה־נָּא֙ אֶקָּ֣חֲךָ֔ אֶל־מָק֖וֹם אַחֵ֑ר אוּלַ֙י יִישַׁ֤ר בְּעֵינֵי֙
הָאֱלֹהִ֔ים וְקַבֹּ֥תוֹ לִ֖י מִשָּֽׁם: וַיִּקַּ֥ח בָּלָ֖ק אֶת־בִּלְעָ֑ם רֹ֣אשׁ הַפְּע֔וֹר
הַנִּשְׁקָ֖ף עַל־פְּנֵ֥י הַיְשִׁימֹֽן: וַיֹּ֤אמֶר בִּלְעָם֙ אֶל־בָּלָ֔ק בְּנֵה־לִ֥י בָזֶ֖ה
שִׁבְעָ֣ה מִזְבְּחֹ֑ת וְהָכֵ֥ן לִי֙ בָּזֶ֔ה שִׁבְעָ֥ה פָרִ֖ים וְשִׁבְעָ֥ה אֵילִֽם: וַיַּ֣עַשׂ
בָּלָ֔ק כַּאֲשֶׁ֖ר אָמַ֣ר בִּלְעָ֑ם וַיַּ֛עַל פָּ֥ר וָאַ֖יִל בַּמִּזְבֵּֽחַ: וַיַּ֣רְא בִּלְעָ֗ם
כִּ֣י ט֞וֹב בְּעֵינֵ֤י יְהוָה֙ לְבָרֵ֣ךְ אֶת־יִשְׂרָאֵ֔ל וְלֹא־הָלַ֥ךְ כְּפַֽעַם־בְּפַ֖עַם
לִקְרַ֣את נְחָשִׁ֑ים וַיָּ֥שֶׁת אֶל־הַמִּדְבָּ֖ר פָּנָֽיו: וַיִּשָּׂ֨א בִלְעָ֜ם אֶת־
עֵינָ֗יו וַיַּרְא֙ אֶת־יִשְׂרָאֵ֔ל שֹׁכֵ֖ן לִשְׁבָטָ֑יו וַתְּהִ֥י עָלָ֖יו ר֥וּחַ אֱלֹהִֽים:
וַיִּשָּׂ֥א מְשָׁל֖וֹ וַיֹּאמַ֑ר נְאֻ֤ם בִּלְעָם֙ בְּנ֣וֹ בְעֹ֔ר וּנְאֻ֥ם הַגֶּ֖בֶר שְׁתֻ֥ם

ששי
/שביעי/

כה
כו
כז

כח
כט
ל

פרק כד
א

ב

ג

כה| **גַּם קֹב לֹא תִקֳּבֶנּוּ.** "גַּם" רִאשׁוֹן מוּסָף עַל "גַּם"
הַשֵּׁנִי וְ"גַּם" שֵׁנִי עַל "גַּם" רִאשׁוֹן, וְכֵן: "גַּם לִי גַּם לָךְ
לֹא יִהְיֶה" (מלכים א ג, כו), וְכֵן: "גַּם בָּחוּר גַּם בְּתוּלָה"
(דברים לב, כה):

כז| **וְקַבֹּתוֹ לִי.** אֵין זֶה לְשׁוֹן צִוּוּי כְּמוֹ "וְקָבְנוֹ" (לעיל
פסוק יג), אֶלָּא לְשׁוֹן עָתִיד, אוּלַי יִישַׁר בְּעֵינָיו וְתִקֳּבֶנּוּ
לִי מִשָּׁם. מלדיר"ש לוי בְּלַעַז:

כח| **רֹאשׁ הַפְּעוֹר.** קוֹסֵם גָּדוֹל הָיָה בָּלָק, וְרָאָה שֶׁהֵן
עֲתִידִין לִלְקוֹת עַל יְדֵי פְּעוֹר, וְלֹא הָיָה יוֹדֵעַ בַּמָּה.
אָמַר: שֶׁמָּא הַקְּלָלָה תָּחוּל עֲלֵיהֶם מִשָּׁם. וְכֵן כָּל
הַחוֹזִים בַּכּוֹכָבִים רוֹאִים וְאֵין יוֹדְעִין מָה רוֹאִים:

פרק כד

א| **וַיַּרְא בִּלְעָם כִּי טוֹב וְגוֹ'.** אָמַר: אֵינִי צָרִיךְ לִבְדֹּק
עוֹד בְּהַקָּדוֹשׁ בָּרוּךְ הוּא, כִּי לֹא יַחְפֹּץ לְקַלְּלָם:

וְלֹא הָלַךְ כְּפַעַם בְּפַעַם. כַּאֲשֶׁר עָשָׂה שְׁתֵּי פְעָמִים:
לִקְרַאת נְחָשִׁים. לְנַחֵשׁ אוּלַי יִקָּרֶה ה' לִקְרָאתוֹ
כִּרְצוֹנוֹ. אָמַר: רוֹצֶה וְלֹא רוֹצֶה לְקַלְּלָם, אַזְכִּיר
עֲוֹנוֹתֵיהֶם, וְהַקְּלָלָה עַל הַזְכָּרַת עֲוֹנוֹתֵיהֶם תָּחוּל:
וַיָּשֶׁת אֶל הַמִּדְבָּר פָּנָיו. כְּתַרְגּוּמוֹ:

ב| **וַיִּשָּׂא בִלְעָם אֶת עֵינָיו.** בִּקֵּשׁ לְהַכְנִיס בָּהֶם
עַיִן רָעָה. וַהֲרֵי יֵשׁ לְךָ שָׁלֹשׁ מִדּוֹתָיו: עַיִן רָעָה,
וְרוּחַ גְּבוֹהָה וְנֶפֶשׁ רְחָבָה דְּחוּקָה לְמַעְלָה: **שֹׁכֵן
לִשְׁבָטָיו.** רָאָה כָּל שֵׁבֶט וָשֵׁבֶט שׁוֹכֵן לְעַצְמוֹ וְאֵינָן
מְעֹרָבִין. רָאָה שֶׁאֵין פִּתְחֵיהֶם מְכֻוָּנִין זֶה כְּנֶגֶד זֶה,
שֶׁלֹּא יָצִיץ יַיִן לְתוֹךְ אֹהֶל חֲבֵרוֹ: **וַתְּהִי עָלָיו רוּחַ אֱלֹהִים.**
עָלָה בְּלִבּוֹ שֶׁלֹּא יְקַלְּלֵם:

ג| **בְּנוֹ בְעֹר.** כְּמוֹ: "לְמַעְיְנוֹ מָיִם" (תהלים קיד, ח). וּמִדְרַשׁ
אַגָּדָה, שְׁנֵיהֶם הָיוּ גְּדוֹלִים מֵאֲבוֹתֵיהֶם. בָּלָק "בְּנוֹ

במדבר | פרק כד

ד הָעָיִן: נְאֻם שֹׁמֵעַ אִמְרֵי־אֵל אֲשֶׁר מַחֲזֵה שַׁדַּי יֶחֱזֶה נֹפֵל וּגְלוּי
ה עֵינָיִם: מַה־טֹּבוּ אֹהָלֶיךָ יַעֲקֹב מִשְׁכְּנֹתֶיךָ יִשְׂרָאֵל: כִּנְחָלִים
נִטָּיוּ כְּגַנֹּת עֲלֵי נָהָר כַּאֲהָלִים נָטַע יְהוָה כַּאֲרָזִים עֲלֵי־מָיִם:
ז יִזַּל־מַיִם מִדָּלְיָו וְזַרְעוֹ בְּמַיִם רַבִּים וְיָרֹם מֵאֲגַג מַלְכּוֹ וְתִנַּשֵּׂא
ח מַלְכֻתוֹ: אֵל מוֹצִיאוֹ מִמִּצְרַיִם כְּתוֹעֲפֹת רְאֵם לוֹ יֹאכַל גּוֹיִם

עָפָר" (לעיל כג, יח), חָבִיו בְּנוֹ הָיָה בַּמַּלְכוּת, וּבִלְעָם
גָּדוֹל מֵחָבִיו בִּנְבִיאוּת, מְנֵה בֶן פְּרָס הָיָה: שְׁתֻם
הָעָיִן. עֵינוֹ נְקוּרָה וּמוֹצֵאת לַחוּץ וְחוֹר שֶׁלָּהּ נִרְאָה
פָּתוּחַ. וּלְשׁוֹן מִשְׁנָה הוּא: "כְּדֵי שֶׁיִּשְׁתֹּם וְיִסְתֹּם
וְיִגֹּב" (עבודה זרה סט ע"ב). וְרַבּוֹתֵינוּ אָמְרוּ: לְפִי שֶׁאָמַר
"וּמִסְפָּר אֶת רֹבַע יִשְׂרָאֵל" (לעיל כג, י) שֶׁהַקָּדוֹשׁ בָּרוּךְ
הוּא יוֹשֵׁב וּמוֹנֶה רְבִיעוֹתֵיהֶן שֶׁל יִשְׂרָאֵל מָתַי תָּבוֹא
טִפָּה שֶׁנּוֹלַד הַצַּדִּיק מִמֶּנָּה, אָמַר בְּלִבּוֹ, מִי שֶׁהוּא
קָדוֹשׁ וּמְשָׁרְתָיו קְדוֹשִׁים יִסְתַּכֵּל בַּדְּבָרִים הַלָּלוּ,
וְעַל דָּבָר זֶה נִסְמֵית עֵינוֹ שֶׁל בִּלְעָם. וְיֵשׁ מְפָרְשִׁים
"שְׁתֻם הָעָיִן" פְּתוּחַ הָעַיִן, כְּמוֹ שֶׁתִּרְגֵּם אוּנְקְלוֹס,
וְעַל שֶׁאָמַר "שְׁתֻם הָעָיִן" וְלֹא אָמַר "שְׁתֻם הָעֵינַיִם"
לָמַדְנוּ שֶׁסּוּמָא בְּאַחַת מֵעֵינָיו הָיָה:

ד נֹפֵל וּגְלוּי עֵינָיִם. פְּשׁוּטוֹ כְּתַרְגּוּמוֹ, שֶׁאֵין נִרְאֶה
עָלָיו אֶלָּא בַּלַּיְלָה כְּשֶׁהוּא שׁוֹכֵב. וּמִדְרָשׁוֹ, כְּשֶׁהָיָה
נִגְלֶה עָלָיו לֹא הָיָה בּוֹ כֹּחַ לַעֲמֹד עַל רַגְלָיו וְנוֹפֵל
עַל פָּנָיו, לְפִי שֶׁהָיָה עָרֵל, וּמָאוּס לִהְיוֹת נִגְלֶה עָלָיו
בְּקוֹמָה זְקוּפָה לְפָנָיו:

ה מַה טֹּבוּ אֹהָלֶיךָ. עַל שֶׁרָאָה פִּתְחֵיהֶם שֶׁאֵינָן
מְכֻוָּנִין זֶה מוּל זֶה. מִשְׁכְּנֹתֶיךָ. חֲנִיּוֹתֶיךָ, כְּתַרְגּוּמוֹ.
דָּבָר אַחֵר, "מַה טֹּבוּ אֹהָלֶיךָ", מַה טֹּבוּ אֹהֶל שִׁילֹה
וּבֵית עוֹלָמִים בְּיִשּׁוּבָן, שֶׁמַּקְרִיבִין בָּהֶן קָרְבָּנוֹת
לְכַפֵּר עֲלֵיכֶם. מִשְׁכְּנֹתֶיךָ. אַף כְּשֶׁהֵן חֲרֵבִין, לְפִי
שֶׁהֵן מַשְׁכּוֹן עֲלֵיהֶן וְחֻרְבָּנָן כַּפָּרָה עַל הַנְּפָשׁוֹת,
שֶׁנֶּאֱמַר: "כִּלָּה ה' אֶת חֲמָתוֹ" (איכה ד, יא), וּבַמָּה כִלָּה?
"וַיַּצֶּת אֵשׁ בְּצִיּוֹן":

ו כִּנְחָלִים נִטָּיוּ. שֶׁנִּמְשְׁכוּ וְנִמְתְּחוּ לִנְטוֹת לְמֵרָחוֹק.
אָמְרוּ רַבּוֹתֵינוּ: מִבִּרְכוֹתָיו שֶׁל אוֹתוֹ רָשָׁע אָנוּ לְמֵדִים
מַה הָיָה בְּלִבּוֹ לְקַלְּלָם כְּשֶׁאָמַר לַהֲשִׁיתוֹ אֶל הַמִּדְבָּר

פָּנָיו, וּכְשֶׁהָפַךְ הַמָּקוֹם אֶת פִּיו בֵּרְכָם מֵעֵין חוֹתַם
קְלָלוֹת שֶׁבִּקֵּשׁ לוֹמַר כו', כִּדְאִיתָא בְּ"חֵלֶק" (סנהדרין קה
ע"ב): כַּאֲהָלִים. כְּתַרְגּוּמוֹ, לְשׁוֹן "מֹר וַאֲהָלוֹת" (תהלים
מה, ט): נָטַע ה'. בְּגַן עֵדֶן. לָשׁוֹן אַחֵר, "כַּאֲהָלִים נָטַע
ה'", כַּשָּׁמַיִם הַמְּתוּחִין כְּאֹהֶל, שֶׁנֶּאֱמַר: "וַיִּמְתָּחֵם
כָּאֹהֶל לָשָׁבֶת" (ישעיה מ, כב): נָטַע ה'. לְשׁוֹן נְטִיעָה מָצִינוּ
בְּאֹהָלִים, שֶׁנֶּאֱמַר: "וְיִטַּע אָהֳלֵי אַפַּדְנוֹ" (דניאל יא, מה):

ז מִדָּלְיָו. מִבְּאֵרוֹתָיו, וּפֵרוּשׁוֹ כְּתַרְגּוּמוֹ. וְזַרְעוֹ בְּמַיִם
רַבִּים. לְשׁוֹן הַצְלָחָה הוּא זֶה, כְּזֶרַע הַזָּרוּעַ עַל פְּנֵי
הַמַּיִם: וְיָרֹם מֵאֲגַג מַלְכּוֹ. מֶלֶךְ רִאשׁוֹן שֶׁלָּהֶם יִכְבֹּשׁ
אֶת אֲגַג מֶלֶךְ עֲמָלֵק: וְתִנַּשֵּׂא מַלְכֻתוֹ. שֶׁל יַעֲקֹב
יוֹתֵר וְיוֹתֵר, שֶׁיָּבֹא אַחֲרָיו דָּוִד וּשְׁלֹמֹה:

ח אֵל מוֹצִיאוֹ מִמִּצְרָיִם. מִי גוֹרֵם לָהֶם הַגְּדֻלָּה
הַזֹּאת? אֵל הַמּוֹצִיאָם מִמִּצְרַיִם, בְּתָקְפּוֹ וְרוּמוֹ שֶׁלּוֹ
"יֹאכַל" אֶת הַגּוֹיִם שֶׁהֵם "צָרָיו", וְעַצְמֹתֵיהֶם שֶׁל
עָרִים: יְגָרֵם. מְנַחֵם פֵּתֵר בּוֹ לְשׁוֹן שְׁבִירָה, וְכֵן: "לֹא
גָרְמוּ לַבֹּקֶר" (צפניה ג, ג). וְכֵן: "וְאֶת חֲרָשֶׂיהָ תְּגָרֵמִי"
(יחזקאל כג, לד). וַאֲנִי אוֹמֵר, לְשׁוֹן עֶצֶם הוּא, שֶׁמְּגָרֵר
הַבָּשָׂר בְּשִׁנָּיו מִסָּבִיב וְהַמֹּחַ שֶׁבִּפְנִים, וּמַעֲמִיד הָעֶצֶם
עַל עַרְמִימוּתוֹ: וְחִצָּיו יִמְחָץ. אוּנְקְלוֹס תִּרְגֵּם "חִצָּיו"
שֶׁל עָרִים, חֶלְקָה שֶׁלָּהֶם, כְּמוֹ: "בַּעֲלֵי חִצִּים" (בראשית
מט, כג), מָרֵי פַלְגוּתָא - לְשׁוֹן חֶלְקָה וַחֲצִי. וְכֵן
"יִמְחָץ" לְשׁוֹן "וּמָחֲצָה וְחָלְפָה רַקָּתוֹ" (שופטים ה, כו),
שֶׁיְּשַׁסֵּעַ אֶת אַרְצָם. וְיֵשׁ לְפָתֵּר לְשׁוֹן חִצִּים מַמָּשׁ,
"חִצָּיו" שֶׁל הַקָּדוֹשׁ בָּרוּךְ הוּא יִמְחַץ בְּדָמָם שֶׁל
עָרִים, יִטְבֹּל וְיִצְטַבַּע בְּדָמָם, כְּמוֹ: "לְמַעַן תִּמְחַץ
רַגְלְךָ בְּדָם" (תהלים סח, כד). וְאֵינוֹ זָז מִלְּשׁוֹן מַכָּה, כְּמוֹ
"מָחַצְתִּי" (דברים לב, לט), שֶׁהַטּוֹבֵעַ בְּדָם נִרְאֶה כְּאִלּוּ
מָחוּץ וְנָגוּעַ:

ט צָרָיו וְעַצְמֹתֵיהֶם יְגָרֵם וְחִצָּיו יִמְחָץ: כָּרַע שָׁכַב כַּאֲרִי וּכְלָבִיא
י מִי יְקִימֶנּוּ מְבָרֲכֶיךָ בָרוּךְ וְאֹרְרֶיךָ אָרוּר: וַיִּחַר־אַף בָּלָק אֶל־
בִּלְעָם וַיִּסְפֹּק אֶת־כַּפָּיו וַיֹּאמֶר בָּלָק אֶל־בִּלְעָם לָקֹב אֹיְבַי
יא קְרָאתִיךָ וְהִנֵּה בֵּרַכְתָּ בָרֵךְ זֶה שָׁלֹשׁ פְּעָמִים: וְעַתָּה בְּרַח־לְךָ
אֶל־מְקוֹמֶךָ אָמַרְתִּי כַּבֵּד אֲכַבֶּדְךָ וְהִנֵּה מְנָעֲךָ יְהוָה מִכָּבוֹד:
יב וַיֹּאמֶר בִּלְעָם אֶל־בָּלָק הֲלֹא גַּם אֶל־מַלְאָכֶיךָ אֲשֶׁר־שָׁלַחְתָּ
יג אֵלַי דִּבַּרְתִּי לֵאמֹר: אִם־יִתֶּן־לִי בָלָק מְלֹא בֵיתוֹ כֶּסֶף וְזָהָב
לֹא אוּכַל לַעֲבֹר אֶת־פִּי יְהוָה לַעֲשׂוֹת טוֹבָה אוֹ רָעָה מִלִּבִּי
אֲשֶׁר־יְדַבֵּר יְהוָה אֹתוֹ אֲדַבֵּר: וְעַתָּה הִנְנִי הוֹלֵךְ לְעַמִּי לְכָה שביעי
יד אִיעָצְךָ אֲשֶׁר יַעֲשֶׂה הָעָם הַזֶּה לְעַמְּךָ בְּאַחֲרִית הַיָּמִים: וַיִּשָּׂא
טו מְשָׁלוֹ וַיֹּאמַר נְאֻם בִּלְעָם בְּנוֹ בְעֹר וּנְאֻם הַגֶּבֶר שְׁתֻם הָעָיִן:
טז נְאֻם שֹׁמֵעַ אִמְרֵי־אֵל וְיֹדֵעַ דַּעַת עֶלְיוֹן מַחֲזֵה שַׁדַּי יֶחֱזֶה נֹפֵל
יז וּגְלוּי עֵינָיִם: אֶרְאֶנּוּ וְלֹא עַתָּה אֲשׁוּרֶנּוּ וְלֹא קָרוֹב דָּרַךְ כּוֹכָב

ט **כָּרַע שָׁכַב כַּאֲרִי.** כְּתַרְגּוּמוֹ, יִתְיַשְּׁבוּ בְאַרְצָם בְּכֹחַ וּבִגְבוּרָה:

י **וַיִּסְפֹּק.** הִכָּה זוֹ עַל זוֹ:

יג **לַעֲבֹר אֶת פִּי ה'.** כָּאן לֹא נֶאֱמַר 'אֱלֹהַי', כְּמוֹ שֶׁאָמַר בָּרִאשׁוֹנָה, לְפִי שֶׁיָּדַע שֶׁנִּבְאַשׁ בְּהַקָּדוֹשׁ בָּרוּךְ הוּא וְנִטְרַד:

יד **הוֹלֵךְ לְעַמִּי.** מֵעַתָּה הֲרֵינִי כִּשְׁאָר עַמִּי, שֶׁנִּסְתַּלֵּק הַקָּדוֹשׁ בָּרוּךְ הוּא מֵעָלָיו: **לְכָה אִיעָצְךָ.** מַה לְּךָ לַעֲשׂוֹת, וּמַה הִיא הָעֵצָה? אֱלֹהֵיהֶם שֶׁל אֵלּוּ שׂוֹנֵא זִמָּה הוּא כו', כִּדְאִיתָא בְּ'חֵלֶק' (סנהדרין קו ע"א). תֵּדַע שֶׁבִּלְעָם הִשִּׂיא עֵצָה זוֹ לְהַכְשִׁילָם בְּזִמָּה, שֶׁהֲרֵי נֶאֱמַר: "הֵן הֵנָּה הָיוּ לִבְנֵי יִשְׂרָאֵל בִּדְבַר בִּלְעָם" (להלן לא, טז): **אֲשֶׁר יַעֲשֶׂה הָעָם הַזֶּה לְעַמְּךָ.** מִקְרָא קָצָר הוּא זֶה, אִיעָצְךָ לְהַכְשִׁילָם, וְאוֹמַר לְךָ מַה שֶּׁהֵן עֲתִידִין לְהָרַע

לְמוֹאָב בְּאַחֲרִית הַיָּמִים: "וּמָחַץ פַּאֲתֵי מוֹאָב" (להלן פסוק יז). הַתַּרְגּוּם מְפָרֵשׁ קֶצֶר הָעִבְרִי:

טו **וְיֹדֵעַ דַּעַת עֶלְיוֹן.** לְכַוֵּן הַשָּׁעָה שֶׁכּוֹעֵס בָּהּ:

יז **אֶרְאֶנּוּ.** רוֹאֶה אֲנִי שִׁבְחוֹ שֶׁל יַעֲקֹב וּגְדֻלָּתוֹ, אַךְ לֹא עַתָּה הוּא אֶלָּא לְאַחַר זְמַן: **דָּרַךְ כּוֹכָב מִיַּעֲקֹב.** כְּתַרְגּוּמוֹ, לְשׁוֹן "דָּרַךְ קַשְׁתּוֹ" (איכה ב, ד), שֶׁהַכּוֹכָב עוֹבֵר כַּחֵץ, וּבְלַעַ"ז דיש"טנט, כְּלוֹמַר יָקוּם מַזָּל. **וְקָם שֵׁבֶט.** מֶלֶךְ רוֹדֶה וּמוֹשֵׁל: **וּמָחַץ פַּאֲתֵי מוֹאָב.** זֶה דָּוִד, שֶׁנֶּאֱמַר בּוֹ: "הַשְׁכֵּב אוֹתָם אַרְצָה וַיְמַדֵּד שְׁנֵי חֲבָלִים לְהָמִית" (שמואל ב' ח, ב) וְגוֹ': **וְקַרְקַר.** לְשׁוֹן קוֹרֵה, כְּמוֹ: "אֲנִי קַרְתִּי" (ישעיה לז, כה), "מַקֶּבֶת בּוֹר נֻקַּרְתֶּם" (ישעיה נא, א), "יִקְּרוּהָ עֹרְבֵי נַחַל" (משלי ל, יז), טור"יר בְּלַעַ"ז: **כָּל בְּנֵי שֵׁת.** כָּל הָאֻמּוֹת, שֶׁכֻּלָּם יָצְאוּ מִן שֵׁת בְּנוֹ שֶׁל אָדָם הָרִאשׁוֹן:

במדבר | פרק כד

מִיַּעֲקֹב וְהֶאֱבִיד שָׂרִיד מֵעִיר: וַיַּרְא אֶת־עֲמָלֵק וַיִּשָּׂא מְשָׁלוֹ וַיֹּאמַר רֵאשִׁית גּוֹיִם עֲמָלֵק וְאַחֲרִיתוֹ עֲדֵי אֹבֵד: וַיַּרְא אֶת־הַקֵּינִי וַיִּשָּׂא מְשָׁלוֹ וַיֹּאמַר אֵיתָן מוֹשָׁבֶךָ וְשִׂים בַּסֶּלַע קִנֶּךָ: כִּי אִם־יִהְיֶה לְבָעֵר קָיִן עַד־מָה אַשּׁוּר תִּשְׁבֶּךָ: וַיִּשָּׂא מְשָׁלוֹ וַיֹּאמַר אוֹי מִי יִחְיֶה מִשֻּׂמוֹ אֵל: וְצִים מִיַּד כִּתִּים וְעִנּוּ אַשּׁוּר וְעִנּוּ־עֵבֶר וְגַם־הוּא עֲדֵי אֹבֵד: וַיָּקָם בִּלְעָם וַיֵּלֶךְ וַיָּשָׁב לִמְקֹמוֹ וְגַם־בָּלָק הָלַךְ לְדַרְכּוֹ:

יח) **וְהָיָה יְרֵשָׁה שֵׂעִיר אֹיְבָיו.** לְאוֹיְבָיו יִשְׂרָאֵל:

יט) **וְיֵרְדְּ מִיַּעֲקֹב.** וְעוֹד יִהְיֶה מוֹשֵׁל אַחֵר מִיַּעֲקֹב. **וְהֶאֱבִיד שָׂרִיד מֵעִיר.** הַחֲשׁוּבָה שֶׁל אֱדוֹם, הִיא רוֹמִי. וְעַל מֶלֶךְ הַמָּשִׁיחַ אוֹמֵר כֵּן, שֶׁנֶּאֱמַר בּוֹ: "וְיֵרְדְּ מִיָּם עַד יָם" (תהלים עב, ח), "וְלֹא יִהְיֶה שָׂרִיד לְבֵית עֵשָׂו" (עובדיה א, יח):

כ) **וַיַּרְא אֶת עֲמָלֵק.** נִסְתַּכֵּל בְּפֻרְעָנוּתוֹ שֶׁל עֲמָלֵק. **רֵאשִׁית גּוֹיִם עֲמָלֵק.** הוּא קִדֵּם אֶת כֻּלָּם לְהִלָּחֵם בְּיִשְׂרָאֵל, וְכָךְ תִּרְגֵּם אוּנְקְלוֹס, "וְאַחֲרִיתוֹ" לֶאֱבֹד בְּיָדָם, שֶׁנֶּאֱמַר: "תִּמְחֶה אֶת זֵכֶר עֲמָלֵק" (דברים כה, יט):

כא) **וַיַּרְא אֶת הַקֵּינִי.** לְפִי שֶׁהָיָה קֵינִי תָּקוּעַ אֵצֶל עֲמָלֵק, כָּעִנְיָן שֶׁנֶּאֱמַר: "וַיֹּאמֶר שָׁאוּל אֶל הַקֵּינִי וְגוֹ'" (שמואל א' טו, ו), הִזְכִּירוֹ אַחַר עֲמָלֵק. נִסְתַּכֵּל בְּגַדְלֻתָּם שֶׁל בְּנֵי יִתְרוֹ שֶׁנֶּאֱמַר בָּהֶם: "תִּרְעָתִים שִׁמְעָתִים שׂוּכָתִים" (דברי הימים א' ב, נה). **אֵיתָן מוֹשָׁבֶךָ.** תָּמֵהַּ אֲנִי מֵהֵיכָן זָכִיתָ לְכָךְ, הֲלֹא אַתָּה עִמִּי הָיִיתָ בַּעֲצַת "הָבָה נִתְחַכְּמָה לוֹ" (שמות א, י), וְעַתָּה נִתְיַשַּׁבְתָּ בְּאֵיתָן וּמָעוֹז שֶׁל יִשְׂרָאֵל:

כב) **כִּי אִם יִהְיֶה לְבָעֵר קַיִן וְגוֹ'.** אַשְׁרֶיךָ שֶׁנִּתְקַעְתָּ לְתֹקֶף זֶה, שֶׁאֵינְךָ נִטְרָד עוֹד מִן הָעוֹלָם, כִּי אַף אִם אַתָּה עָתִיד לִגְלוֹת עִם עֲשֶׂרֶת הַשְּׁבָטִים וְתִהְיֶה לְבָעֵר מִמָּקוֹם שֶׁנִּתְיַשַּׁבְתָּ שָׁם, מַה בְּכָךְ? **עַד מָה אַשּׁוּר תִּשְׁבֶּךָ.** עַד הֵיכָן הוּא מַגְלֶה אוֹתְךָ, שֶׁמָּא לַחְלַח וְחָבוֹר, אֵין זֶה טֵרוּד מִן הָעוֹלָם, אֶלָּא טִלְטוּל מִמָּקוֹם לְמָקוֹם, וְתָשׁוּב עִם שְׁאָר הַגָּלֻיּוֹת:

כג-כד) **וַיִּשָּׂא מְשָׁלוֹ וְגוֹ'.** כֵּיוָן שֶׁהִזְכִּיר אֶת שְׁבִית אַשּׁוּר, אָמַר. **אוֹי מִי יִחְיֶה מִשֻּׂמוֹ אֵל.** מִי יָכוֹל לְהַחֲיוֹת אֶת עַצְמוֹ מִשּׂוּמוֹ אֶת אֵלֶּה, שֶׁלֹּא יָשִׂים עָלָיו הַגּוֹזֵר אֶת אֵלֶּה, שֶׁיַּעֲמֹד סַנְחֵרִיב וִיבַלְבֵּל אֶת כָּל הָאֻמּוֹת, וְעוֹד יָבוֹאוּ "צִים מִיַּד כִּתִּים" וְיַעַבְדוּ כִתִּים שֶׁהֵן רוֹמִיִּים בִּסְפִינוֹת גְּדוֹלוֹת עַל אַשּׁוּר: **וְעִנּוּ עֵבֶר.** וְעִנּוּ אוֹתָם שֶׁבְּעֵבֶר הַנָּהָר: **וְגַם הוּא עֲדֵי אֹבֵד.** וְכֵן פֵּרַשׁ דָּנִיֵּאל: "עַד דִּי קְטִילַת חֵיוְתָא וְהוּבַד גִּשְׁמַהּ" (דניאל ז, יא). **וְצִים.** סְפִינוֹת גְּדוֹלוֹת, כְּדִכְתִיב: "וְצִי אַדִּיר" (ישעיה לג, כא), תַּרְגּוּמוֹ "וּבוּרְנֵי רַבְּתָא":

בלק | פרק כה | במדבר

א וַיֵּשֶׁב יִשְׂרָאֵל בַּשִּׁטִּים וַיָּחֶל הָעָם לִזְנוֹת אֶל־בְּנוֹת מוֹאָב: ב וַתִּקְרֶאןָ לָעָם לְזִבְחֵי אֱלֹהֵיהֶן וַיֹּאכַל הָעָם וַיִּשְׁתַּחֲוּוּ לֵאלֹהֵיהֶן: ג וַיִּצָּמֶד יִשְׂרָאֵל לְבַעַל פְּעוֹר וַיִּחַר־אַף יהוה בְּיִשְׂרָאֵל: ד וַיֹּאמֶר יהוה אֶל־מֹשֶׁה קַח אֶת־כָּל־רָאשֵׁי הָעָם וְהוֹקַע אוֹתָם לַיהוה נֶגֶד הַשָּׁמֶשׁ וְיָשֹׁב חֲרוֹן אַף־יהוה מִיִּשְׂרָאֵל: ה וַיֹּאמֶר מֹשֶׁה אֶל־שֹׁפְטֵי יִשְׂרָאֵל הִרְגוּ אִישׁ אֲנָשָׁיו הַנִּצְמָדִים לְבַעַל פְּעוֹר: ו וְהִנֵּה אִישׁ מִבְּנֵי יִשְׂרָאֵל בָּא וַיַּקְרֵב אֶל־אֶחָיו אֶת־הַמִּדְיָנִית לְעֵינֵי מֹשֶׁה וּלְעֵינֵי כָּל־עֲדַת בְּנֵי־יִשְׂרָאֵל וְהֵמָּה בֹכִים פֶּתַח אֹהֶל מוֹעֵד:

מפטיר ז וַיַּרְא פִּינְחָס בֶּן־אֶלְעָזָר בֶּן־אַהֲרֹן הַכֹּהֵן וַיָּקָם מִתּוֹךְ הָעֵדָה וַיִּקַּח רֹמַח בְּיָדוֹ: ח וַיָּבֹא אַחַר אִישׁ־יִשְׂרָאֵל אֶל־הַקֻּבָּה

פרק כה

א **בַּשִּׁטִּים.** כָּךְ שְׁמָהּ: **לִזְנוֹת אֶל בְּנוֹת מוֹאָב.** עַל יְדֵי עֲצַת בִּלְעָם, כִּדְאִיתָא בְּ"חֵלֶק" (סנהדרין קו ע"א):

ב **וַיִּשְׁתַּחֲווּ לֵאלֹהֵיהֶן.** כְּשֶׁתָּקַף יִצְרוֹ עָלָיו וְאוֹמֵר לָהּ: הִשָּׁמְעִי לִי! וְהִיא מוֹצִיאָה לוֹ דְּמוּת פְּעוֹר מֵחֵיקָהּ וְאוֹמֶרֶת לוֹ הִשְׁתַּחֲוֵה לָזֶה:

ג **פְּעוֹר.** עַל שֵׁם שֶׁפּוֹעֲרִין לְפָנָיו פִּי הַטַּבַּעַת וּמוֹצִיאִין רְעִי, וְזוֹ הִיא עֲבוֹדָתוֹ: **וַיִּחַר אַף ה' בְּיִשְׂרָאֵל.** שָׁלַח בָּם מַגֵּפָה:

ד **קַח אֶת כָּל רָאשֵׁי הָעָם.** לִשְׁפֹּט אֶת הָעוֹבְדִים לִפְעוֹר: **וְהוֹקַע אוֹתָם.** אֶת הָעוֹבְדִים. **וְהוֹקַע.** הִיא תְּלִיָּה, כְּמוֹ שֶׁמָּצִינוּ בִּבְנֵי שָׁאוּל: "וְהוֹקַעֲנוּם לַה'" (שמואל ב' כא, ו), וְשָׁם תְּלִיָּה מְפֹרֶשֶׁת, עֲבוֹדָה זָרָה בִּסְקִילָה, וְכָל הַנִּסְקָלִין נִתְלִין: **נֶגֶד הַשֶּׁמֶשׁ.** לְעֵין כֹּל. וּמִדְרַשׁ אַגָּדָה: הַשֶּׁמֶשׁ מוֹדִיעַ אֶת הַחוֹטְאִים, הֶעָנָן נִקְפָּל מִכְּנֶגְדּוֹ וְהַחַמָּה זוֹרַחַת עָלָיו:

ה **הִרְגוּ אִישׁ אֲנָשָׁיו.** כָּל אֶחָד וְאֶחָד מִדַּיָּנֵי יִשְׂרָאֵל הָיָה הוֹרֵג שְׁנַיִם, וְדַיָּנֵי יִשְׂרָאֵל רִבּוֹא וּשְׁמוֹנַת אֲלָפִים, כִּדְאִיתָא בְּסַנְהֶדְרִין (דף יח ע"א):

ו **וְהִנֵּה אִישׁ וְגוֹ'.** נִתְקַבְּצוּ שִׁבְטוֹ שֶׁל שִׁמְעוֹן אֵצֶל זִמְרִי שֶׁהָיָה נָשִׂיא שֶׁלָּהֶם, אָמְרוּ לוֹ: אָנוּ נִדּוֹנִין בְּמִיתָה וְאַתָּה יוֹשֵׁב? וְכוּ', כִּדְאִיתָא בְּ"אֵלּוּ הֵן הַנִּשְׂרָפִין" (סנהדרין פב ע"א): **אֶת הַמִּדְיָנִית.** כָּזְבִּי בַת צוּר: **לְעֵינֵי מֹשֶׁה.** אָמַר לוֹ: מֹשֶׁה, זוֹ אֲסוּרָה אוֹ מֻתֶּרֶת? אִם תֹּאמַר אֲסוּרָה, בַּת יִתְרוֹ מִי הִתִּירָהּ לְךָ? וְכוּ', כִּדְאִיתָא הָתָם: **וְהֵמָּה בֹכִים.** נִתְעַלְּמָה מִמֶּנּוּ הֲלָכָה, גָּעוּ כֻּלָּם בִּבְכִיָּה. בָּעֵגֶל עָמַד מֹשֶׁה כְּנֶגֶד שִׁשִּׁים רִבּוֹא, שֶׁנֶּאֱמַר: "וַיִּטְחַן עַד אֲשֶׁר דָּק" וְגוֹ' (שמות לב, כ), וְכָאן רָפוּ יָדָיו? אֶלָּא כְּדֵי שֶׁיָּבֹא פִּינְחָס וְיִטֹּל אֶת הָרָאוּי לוֹ:

ז **וַיַּרְא פִּינְחָס.** רָאָה מַעֲשֶׂה וְנִזְכַּר הֲלָכָה. אָמַר לוֹ לְמֹשֶׁה: מְקֻבְּלַנִי מִמְּךָ, הַבּוֹעֵל אֲרַמִּית קַנָּאִין פּוֹגְעִין בּוֹ. אָמַר לוֹ: קַרְיָנָא דְּאִגַּרְתָּא אִיהוּ לֶהֱוֵי פַּרְוַנְקָא. מִיָּד — "וַיִּקַּח רֹמַח בְּיָדוֹ" וְגוֹ':

ח **אֶל הַקֻּבָּה.** אֶל הָאֹהֶל: **אֶל קֳבָתָהּ.** כְּמוֹ: "וְהַלְּחָיַיִם וְהַקֵּבָה" (דברים יח, ג), כִּוֵּן בְּתוֹךְ זַכְרוּת שֶׁל זִמְרִי וְנַקְבוּת שֶׁלָּהּ, וְרָאוּ כֻּלָּם שֶׁלֹּא לְחִנָּם הֲרָגָם, וְהַרְבֵּה נִסִּים נַעֲשׂוּ לוֹ וְכוּ', כִּדְאִיתָא הָתָם (סנהדרין פב ע"ב):

במדבר | פרק כה | פינחס

וַיִּדְקֹ֤ר אֶת־שְׁנֵיהֶם֙ אֵ֣ת אִ֣ישׁ יִשְׂרָאֵ֔ל וְאֶת־הָאִשָּׁ֖ה אֶל־קֳבָתָ֑הּ
וַתֵּֽעָצַר֙ הַמַּגֵּפָ֔ה מֵעַ֖ל בְּנֵ֥י יִשְׂרָאֵֽל: וַיִּהְי֕וּ הַמֵּתִ֖ים בַּמַּגֵּפָ֑ה אַרְבָּעָ֥ה
וְעֶשְׂרִ֖ים אָֽלֶף:

כב **פינחס**

וַיְדַבֵּ֥ר יְהֹוָ֖ה אֶל־מֹשֶׁ֥ה לֵּאמֹֽר: פִּֽינְחָ֨ס בֶּן־אֶלְעָזָ֜ר בֶּן־אַהֲרֹ֣ן
הַכֹּהֵ֗ן הֵשִׁ֤יב אֶת־חֲמָתִי֙ מֵעַ֣ל בְּנֵֽי־יִשְׂרָאֵ֔ל בְּקַנְא֥וֹ אֶת־קִנְאָתִ֖י
בְּתוֹכָ֑ם וְלֹא־כִלִּ֥יתִי אֶת־בְּנֵֽי־יִשְׂרָאֵ֖ל בְּקִנְאָתִֽי: לָכֵ֖ן אֱמֹ֑ר הִנְנִ֨י
נֹתֵ֥ן ל֛וֹ אֶת־בְּרִיתִ֖י שָׁלֽוֹם: וְהָ֤יְתָה לּוֹ֙ וּלְזַרְע֣וֹ אַחֲרָ֔יו בְּרִ֥ית כְּהֻנַּ֖ת
עוֹלָ֑ם תַּ֗חַת אֲשֶׁ֤ר קִנֵּא֙ לֵֽאלֹהָ֔יו וַיְכַפֵּ֖ר עַל־בְּנֵ֥י יִשְׂרָאֵֽל: וְשֵׁם֩
אִ֨ישׁ יִשְׂרָאֵ֜ל הַמֻּכֶּ֗ה אֲשֶׁ֤ר הֻכָּה֙ אֶת־הַמִּדְיָנִ֔ית זִמְרִ֖י בֶּן־סָל֑וּא
נְשִׂ֥יא בֵֽית־אָ֖ב לַשִּׁמְעֹנִֽי: וְשֵׁ֨ם הָֽאִשָּׁ֧ה הַמֻּכָּ֛ה הַמִּדְיָנִ֖ית כָּזְבִּ֣י
בַת־צ֑וּר רֹ֣אשׁ אֻמּ֥וֹת בֵּֽית־אָ֛ב בְּמִדְיָ֖ן הֽוּא:

יא| **פִּינְחָס בֶּן אֶלְעָזָר בֶּן אַהֲרֹן הַכֹּהֵן.** לְפִי שֶׁהָיוּ הַשְּׁבָטִים מְבַזִּים אוֹתוֹ, הַרְאִיתֶם בֶּן פּוּטִי זֶה שֶׁפִּטֵּם אֲבִי אִמּוֹ עֲגָלִים לַעֲבוֹדָה זָרָה וְהָרַג נְשִׂיא שֵׁבֶט מִיִּשְׂרָאֵל, לְפִיכָךְ בָּא הַכָּתוּב וְיִחֲסוֹ אַחַר אַהֲרֹן: **בְּקַנְאוֹ אֶת קִנְאָתִי.** בְּנָקְמוֹ אֶת נִקְמָתִי, בְּקָצְפּוֹ אֶת הַקֶּצֶף שֶׁהָיָה לִי לִקְצֹף. כָּל לְשׁוֹן 'קִנְאָה' הוּא הַמִּתְחָרֶה לִנְקֹם נִקְמַת דָּבָר, אנפרינמנ"ט בְּלַעַ"ז:

יב| **אֶת בְּרִיתִי שָׁלוֹם.** שֶׁתְּהֵא לוֹ לִבְרִית שָׁלוֹם, כְּאָדָם הַמַּחֲזִיק טוֹבָה וְחָנוֹת לְמִי שֶׁעוֹשֶׂה עִמּוֹ טוֹבָה, אַף כָּאן פֵּרַשׁ לוֹ הַקָּדוֹשׁ בָּרוּךְ הוּא שְׁלוֹמוֹתָיו:

יג| **וְהָיְתָה לּוֹ.** בְּרִיתִי זֹאת. **בְּרִית כְּהֻנַּת עוֹלָם.** שֶׁאַף עַל פִּי שֶׁכְּבָר נִתְּנָה כְּהֻנָּה לְזַרְעוֹ שֶׁל אַהֲרֹן, לֹא נִתְּנָה אֶלָּא לְאַהֲרֹן וּלְבָנָיו שֶׁנִּמְשְׁחוּ עִמּוֹ וּלְתוֹלְדוֹתֵיהֶם שֶׁיּוֹלִידוּ אַחַר הַמְשָׁחָתָן, אֲבָל פִּינְחָס שֶׁנּוֹלַד קֹדֶם לָכֵן וְלֹא נִמְשַׁח, לֹא בָא בִכְלַל כְּהֻנָּה עַד כָּאן. וְכֵן שָׁנִינוּ בִּזְבָחִים: לֹא נִתְכַּהֵן פִּינְחָס עַד שֶׁהֲרָגוֹ לְזִמְרִי (זבחים קא ע"ב): **לֵאלֹהָיו.** בִּשְׁבִיל אֱלֹהָיו, כְּמוֹ

"הַמְקַנֵּא אַתָּה לִי" (לעיל יא, כט), "קִנֵּאתִי לְצִיּוֹן" (זכריה ח, ג), בִּשְׁבִיל צִיּוֹן:

יד| **וְשֵׁם אִישׁ יִשְׂרָאֵל וְגוֹ'.** בְּמָקוֹם שֶׁיִּחֵס אֶת הַצַּדִּיק לְשֶׁבַח, יִחֵס אֶת הָרָשָׁע לִגְנַאי: **נְשִׂיא בֵית אָב לַשִּׁמְעֹנִי.** לְאֶחָד מֵחֲמֵשֶׁת בָּתֵּי אָבוֹת שֶׁהָיוּ לְשֵׁבֶט שִׁמְעוֹן. דָּבָר אַחֵר, לְהוֹדִיעַ שִׁבְחוֹ שֶׁל פִּינְחָס, שֶׁאַף עַל פִּי שֶׁזֶּה הָיָה נָשִׂיא, לֹא מָנַע אֶת עַצְמוֹ מִלְּקַנֵּא לְחִלּוּל הַשֵּׁם, לְכָךְ הוֹדִיעֲךָ הַכָּתוּב מִי הוּא הַמֻּכֶּה:

טו| **וְשֵׁם הָאִשָּׁה הַמֻּכָּה וְגוֹ'.** לְהוֹדִיעֲךָ שִׂנְאָתָן שֶׁל מִדְיָנִים, שֶׁהִפְקִירוּ בַּת מֶלֶךְ לִזְנוּת כְּדֵי לְהַחֲטִיא אֶת יִשְׂרָאֵל: **רֹאשׁ אֻמּוֹת.** אֶחָד מֵחֲמֵשֶׁת מַלְכֵי מִדְיָן: "אֶת אֱוִי וְאֶת רֶקֶם וְאֶת צוּר וְגוֹ'" (להלן לא, ח), וְהוּא הָיָה חָשׁוּב מִכֻּלָּם, שֶׁנֶּאֱמַר: "רָאשֵׁי אֻמּוֹת", וּלְפִי שֶׁנָּהַג בִּזָּיוֹן בְּעַצְמוֹ לְהַפְקִיר בִּתּוֹ מְנָאוֹ שְׁלִישִׁי: **בֵּית אָב.** חֲמִשָּׁה בָתֵּי אָבוֹת הָיוּ לְמִדְיָן: "עֵיפָה וָעֵפֶר וַחֲנוֹךְ וַאֲבִידָע וְאֶלְדָּעָה" (בראשית כה, ד), וְזֶה הָיָה מֶלֶךְ לְאֶחָד מֵהֶם:

פרק כו | במדבר

וַיְדַבֵּ֥ר יְהֹוָ֖ה אֶל־מֹשֶׁ֥ה לֵּאמֹֽר: צָר֖וֹר אֶת־הַמִּדְיָנִ֑ים וְהִכִּיתֶ֖ם אוֹתָֽם: כִּי־צֹרְרִ֥ים הֵם֙ לָכֶ֔ם בְּנִכְלֵיהֶ֛ם אֲשֶׁר־נִכְּל֥וּ לָכֶ֖ם עַל־דְּבַר־פְּע֑וֹר וְעַל־דְּבַ֞ר כָּזְבִּ֣י בַת־נְשִׂ֣יא מִדְיָ֗ן אֲחֹתָ֛ם הַמֻּכָּ֥ה בְיוֹם־הַמַּגֵּפָ֖ה עַל־דְּבַר־פְּעֽוֹר: וַיְהִ֖י אַחֲרֵ֥י הַמַּגֵּפָ֑ה

פרק כו

וַיֹּ֤אמֶר יְהֹוָה֙ אֶל־מֹשֶׁ֔ה וְאֶ֧ל אֶלְעָזָ֛ר בֶּן־אַהֲרֹ֥ן הַכֹּהֵ֖ן לֵאמֹֽר: שְׂא֞וּ אֶת־רֹ֣אשׁ ׀ כָּל־עֲדַ֣ת בְּנֵי־יִשְׂרָאֵ֗ל מִבֶּ֨ן עֶשְׂרִ֥ים שָׁנָ֛ה וָמַ֖עְלָה לְבֵ֣ית אֲבֹתָ֑ם כָּל־יֹצֵ֥א צָבָ֖א בְּיִשְׂרָאֵֽל: וַיְדַבֵּ֨ר מֹשֶׁ֜ה וְאֶלְעָזָ֧ר הַכֹּהֵ֛ן אֹתָ֖ם בְּעַֽרְבֹ֣ת מוֹאָ֑ב עַל־יַרְדֵּ֥ן יְרֵח֖וֹ לֵאמֹֽר: מִבֶּ֛ן עֶשְׂרִ֥ים שָׁנָ֖ה וָמָ֑עְלָה כַּאֲשֶׁר֩ צִוָּ֨ה יְהֹוָ֤ה אֶת־מֹשֶׁה֙ וּבְנֵ֣י יִשְׂרָאֵ֔ל הַיֹּצְאִ֖ים מֵאֶ֥רֶץ מִצְרָֽיִם: רְאוּבֵ֖ן בְּכ֣וֹר יִשְׂרָאֵ֑ל בְּנֵ֣י רְאוּבֵ֗ן חֲנוֹךְ֙ מִשְׁפַּ֣חַת הַחֲנֹכִ֔י לְפַלּ֕וּא מִשְׁפַּ֖חַת הַפַּלֻּאִֽי: לְחֶצְרֹ֕ן מִשְׁפַּ֖חַת

יז צָרוֹר. כְּמוֹ: "זָכוֹר", "שָׁמוֹר", לְשׁוֹן הֹוֶה, עֲלֵיכֶם לְאַיֵּב אוֹתָם:

יח כִּי צֹרְרִים הֵם לָכֶם וְגוֹ' עַל דְּבַר פְּעוֹר. שֶׁהִפְקִירוּ בְּנוֹתֵיהֶם לִזְנוּת כְּדֵי לְהַטְעוֹתְכֶם אַחַר פְּעוֹר. וְאֶת מוֹאָב לֹא צִוָּה לְהַשְׁמִיד, מִפְּנֵי רוּת שֶׁהָיְתָה עֲתִידָה לָצֵאת מֵהֶם, כִּדְאַמְרִינַן בְּבָבָא קַמָּא (דף לח ע"ב):

פרק כו

א וַיְהִי אַחֲרֵי הַמַּגֵּפָה וְגוֹ'. מָשָׁל לְרוֹעֶה שֶׁנִּכְנְסוּ זְאֵבִים לְתוֹךְ עֶדְרוֹ וְהָרְגוּ בָּהֶן, וְהוּא מוֹנֶה אוֹתָן לֵידַע מִנְיַן הַנּוֹתָרוֹת. דָּבָר אַחֵר, כְּשֶׁיָּצְאוּ מִמִּצְרַיִם וְנִמְסְרוּ לְמֹשֶׁה, נִמְסְרוּ לוֹ בְּמִנְיָן, עַכְשָׁיו שֶׁקָּרַב לָמוּת וּלְהַחֲזִיר צֹאנוֹ, מַחֲזִירָם בְּמִנְיָן:

ב לְבֵית אֲבֹתָם. עַל שֵׁבֶט הָאָב יִתְיַחֲסוּ וְלֹא אַחַר הָאֵם:

ג וַיְדַבֵּר מֹשֶׁה וְאֶלְעָזָר הַכֹּהֵן אֹתָם. דִּבְּרוּ עִמָּם עַל זֹאת, שֶׁצִּוָּה הַמָּקוֹם לִמְנוֹתָם: לֵאמֹר. אָמְרוּ לָהֶם צְרִיכִים אַתֶּם לְהִמָּנוֹת:

ד מִבֶּן עֶשְׂרִים שָׁנָה וָמַעְלָה כַּאֲשֶׁר צִוָּה וְגוֹ'. שֶׁיְּהֵא מִנְיָנָם מִבֶּן עֶשְׂרִים שָׁנָה וָמַעְלָה, שֶׁנֶּאֱמַר: "כָּל הָעֹבֵר עַל הַפְּקֻדִים" וְגוֹ' (שמות ל, יג):

ה מִשְׁפַּחַת הַחֲנֹכִי. לְפִי שֶׁהָיוּ הָאֻמּוֹת מְבַזִּין אוֹתָם וְאוֹמְרִים, מָה אֵלּוּ מִתְיַחֲסִין עַל שִׁבְטֵיהֶם? סְבוּרִין הֵם שֶׁלֹּא שָׁלְטוּ הַמִּצְרִים בְּאִמּוֹתֵיהֶם? אִם בְּגוּפָם הָיוּ מוֹשְׁלִים קַל וָחֹמֶר בִּנְשׁוֹתֵיהֶם! לְפִיכָךְ הִטִּיל הַקָּדוֹשׁ בָּרוּךְ הוּא שְׁמוֹ עֲלֵיהֶם, הַ"ה מִצַּד זֶה וְיוּ"ד מִצַּד זֶה, לוֹמַר, מֵעִיד אֲנִי עֲלֵיהֶם שֶׁהֵם בְּנֵי אֲבוֹתֵיהֶם. וְזֶה הוּא שֶׁמְּפֹרָשׁ עַל יְדֵי דָוִד: "שִׁבְטֵי יָהּ עֵדוּת לְיִשְׂרָאֵל" (תהלים קכב, ד), הַשֵּׁם הַזֶּה מֵעִיד עֲלֵיהֶם לְשִׁבְטֵיהֶם. לְפִיכָךְ בְּכֻלָּם כְּתִיב: "הַחֲנֹכִי", "הַפַּלֻּאִי", אֲבָל בְּ"יִמְנָה" (להלן פסוק מד) לֹא הֻצְרַךְ לוֹמַר "מִשְׁפַּחַת הַיִּמְנִי", לְפִי שֶׁהַשֵּׁם קָבוּעַ בּוֹ, יוּ"ד בָּרֹאשׁ וְהֵ"א בַּסּוֹף:

במדבר | פרק כו

ז הַחֶצְרוֹנִ֕י לְכַרְמִ֕י מִשְׁפַּ֖חַת הַכַּרְמִ֑י: אֵ֖לֶּה מִשְׁפְּחֹ֣ת הָרֽאוּבֵנִ֑י
וַיִּהְי֣וּ פְקֻדֵיהֶ֗ם שְׁלֹשָׁ֤ה וְאַרְבָּעִים֙ אֶ֔לֶף וּשְׁבַ֥ע מֵא֖וֹת וּשְׁלֹשִֽׁים:
ח וּבְנֵ֥י פַלּ֖וּא אֱלִיאָֽב: וּבְנֵ֣י אֱלִיאָ֔ב נְמוּאֵ֖ל וְדָתָ֣ן וַאֲבִירָ֑ם הֽוּא־
ט דָתָ֨ן וַאֲבִירָ֜ם קרואי קְרִיאֵ֣י הָעֵדָ֗ה אֲשֶׁ֨ר הִצּ֤וּ עַל־מֹשֶׁה֙ וְעַֽל־אַהֲרֹ֔ן
בַּעֲדַת־קֹ֖רַח בְּהַצֹּתָ֥ם עַל־יהוֽה: וַתִּפְתַּ֨ח הָאָ֜רֶץ אֶת־פִּ֗יהָ
י וַתִּבְלַ֥ע אֹתָ֛ם וְאֶת־קֹ֖רַח בְּמ֣וֹת הָעֵדָ֑ה בַּאֲכֹ֣ל הָאֵ֗שׁ אֵ֣ת חֲמִשִּׁ֤ים
יא וּמָאתַ֨יִם֙ אִ֔ישׁ וַיִּהְי֖וּ לְנֵֽס: וּבְנֵי־קֹ֖רַח לֹא־מֵֽתוּ: בְּנֵ֣י
שִׁמְעוֹן֙ לְמִשְׁפְּחֹתָ֔ם לִנְמוּאֵ֕ל מִשְׁפַּ֖חַת הַנְּמוּאֵלִ֑י לְיָמִ֕ין מִשְׁפַּ֖חַת
יג הַיָּמִינִ֑י לְיָכִ֕ין מִשְׁפַּ֖חַת הַיָּכִינִֽי: לְזֶ֕רַח מִשְׁפַּ֖חַת הַזַּרְחִ֑י לְשָׁא֕וּל
יד מִשְׁפַּ֖חַת הַשָּׁאוּלִֽי: אֵ֖לֶּה מִשְׁפְּחֹ֣ת הַשִּׁמְעֹנִ֑י שְׁנַ֧יִם וְעֶשְׂרִ֛ים אֶ֖לֶף
טו וּמָאתָֽיִם: בְּנֵ֣י גָד֙ לְמִשְׁפְּחֹתָ֔ם לִצְפ֕וֹן מִשְׁפַּ֖חַת הַצְּפוֹנִ֑י
טז לְחַגִּ֕י מִשְׁפַּ֖חַת הַֽחַגִּ֑י לְשׁוּנִ֕י מִשְׁפַּ֖חַת הַשּׁוּנִֽי: לְאָזְנִ֕י מִשְׁפַּ֖חַת

ט | אֲשֶׁר הִצּוּ. אֶת יִשְׂרָאֵל "עַל מֹשֶׁה": בְּהַצֹּתָם. אֶת
הָעָם "עַל ה'": הִצּוּ. הֱשִׁיאוּם אֶת יִשְׂרָאֵל לָרִיב "עַל
מֹשֶׁה", לְשׁוֹן הִפְעִילוּ:

י | וַיִּהְיוּ לְנֵס. לְאוֹת וּלְזִכָּרוֹן, לְמַעַן אֲשֶׁר לֹא יִקְרַב
אִישׁ זָר לַחֲלֹק עוֹד עַל הַכְּהֻנָּה:

יא | וּבְנֵי קֹרַח לֹא מֵתוּ. הֵם הָיוּ בָּעֵצָה תְּחִלָּה, וּבִשְׁעַת
הַמַּחְלֹקֶת הִרְהֲרוּ תְּשׁוּבָה בְּלִבָּם, לְפִיכָךְ נִתְבַּצֵּר
לָהֶם מָקוֹם גָּבוֹהַּ בַּגֵּיהִנֹּם וְיָשְׁבוּ שָׁם:

יג | לְזֶרַח. הוּא צֹחַר (שמות ו, טו), לְשׁוֹן צֹהַר, אֲבָל
מִשְׁפַּחַת אֹהַד בְּטֵלָה. וְכֵן חָמֵשׁ מִשֵּׁבֶט בִּנְיָמִין, שֶׁהֲרֵי
בַּעֲשָׂרָה בָּנִים יָרַד לְמִצְרַיִם (בראשית מו, כא), וְכָאן לֹא מָנָה
אֶלָּא חֲמִשָּׁה, וְכֵן אֵצֶל גָּד, הֲרֵי שֶׁבַע מִשְׁפָּחוֹת.
וּמָצָאתִי בְּתַלְמוּד יְרוּשַׁלְמִי (סוטה ח, ג) שֶׁכְּשֶׁמֵּת אַהֲרֹן
נִסְתַּלְּקוּ עַנְנֵי כָּבוֹד וּבָאוּ הַכְּנַעֲנִים לְהִלָּחֵם בְּיִשְׂרָאֵל,
וְנָתְנוּ לֵב לַחֲזֹר לְמִצְרַיִם, וְחָזְרוּ לַאֲחוֹרֵיהֶם שְׁמוֹנָה

מַסָּעוֹת מֵהֹר הָהָר לְמוֹסֵרָה, שֶׁנֶּאֱמַר: "וּבְנֵי יִשְׂרָאֵל
נָסְעוּ מִבְּאֵרֹת בְּנֵי יַעֲקָן מוֹסֵרָה, שָׁם מֵת אַהֲרֹן"
(דברים י, ו), וַהֲלֹא בְּהֹר הָהָר מֵת, וּמִמּוֹסֵרָה עַד הֹר
הָהָר שְׁמוֹנֶה מַסָּעוֹת יֵשׁ לְמַפְרֵעַ? אֶלָּא שֶׁחָזְרוּ
לַאֲחוֹרֵיהֶם, וְרָדְפוּ בְּנֵי לֵוִי אַחֲרֵיהֶם לְהַחֲזִירָם,
וְהָרְגוּ מֵהֶם שֶׁבַע מִשְׁפָּחוֹת, וּמִבְּנֵי לֵוִי נָפְלוּ אַרְבַּע
מִשְׁפָּחוֹת: מִשְׁפַּחַת שִׁמְעִי וְעָזִיאֵלִי, וּמִבְּנֵי יִצְהָר לֹא
נִמְנוּ כָּאן אֶלָּא מִשְׁפַּחַת הַקָּרְחִי, וְהָרְבִיעִית לֹא
יָדַעְתִּי מַה הִיא. וְדִבְרֵי תַּנְחוּמָא דְּלָא שְׁמִיתָה בַּמַּגֵּפָה
בִּדְבַר בִּלְעָם (מדרש תנחומא ה) אֲבָל לְפִי הַחֶסְרוֹן שֶׁחָסֵר
מִשֵּׁבֶט שִׁמְעוֹן בְּמִנְיָן זֶה מִמִּנְיָן הָרִאשׁוֹן שֶׁבַּמִּדְבָּר
סִינַי, נִרְאֶה שֶׁכָּל עֶשְׂרִים וְאַרְבָּעָה אֶלֶף נָפְלוּ מִשִּׁבְטוֹ
שֶׁל שִׁמְעוֹן:

טז | לְאָזְנִי. אוֹמֵר אֲנִי שֶׁזּוֹ מִשְׁפַּחַת אֶצְבּוֹן, וְאֵינִי יוֹדֵעַ
לָמָּה לֹא נִקְרֵאת מִשְׁפַּחְתּוֹ עַל שְׁמוֹ:

יז הָאזְנִי לְעֵרִי מִשְׁפַּחַת הָעֵרִי: לַאֲרוֹד מִשְׁפַּחַת הָאֲרוֹדִי לְאַרְאֵלִי
יח מִשְׁפַּחַת הָאַרְאֵלִי: אֵלֶּה מִשְׁפְּחֹת בְּנֵי־גָד לִפְקֻדֵיהֶם אַרְבָּעִים
יט אֶלֶף וַחֲמֵשׁ מֵאוֹת: בְּנֵי יְהוּדָה עֵר וְאוֹנָן וַיָּמָת
כ עֵר וְאוֹנָן בְּאֶרֶץ כְּנָעַן: וַיִּהְיוּ בְנֵי־יְהוּדָה לְמִשְׁפְּחֹתָם לְשֵׁלָה
מִשְׁפַּחַת הַשֵּׁלָנִי לְפֶרֶץ מִשְׁפַּחַת הַפַּרְצִי לְזֶרַח מִשְׁפַּחַת הַזַּרְחִי:
כא וַיִּהְיוּ בְנֵי־פֶרֶץ לְחֶצְרֹן מִשְׁפַּחַת הַחֶצְרֹנִי לְחָמוּל מִשְׁפַּחַת
כב הֶחָמוּלִי: אֵלֶּה מִשְׁפְּחֹת יְהוּדָה לִפְקֻדֵיהֶם שִׁשָּׁה וְשִׁבְעִים
כג אֶלֶף וַחֲמֵשׁ מֵאוֹת: בְּנֵי יִשָּׂשכָר לְמִשְׁפְּחֹתָם תּוֹלָע
כד מִשְׁפַּחַת הַתּוֹלָעִי לְפֻוָה מִשְׁפַּחַת הַפּוּנִי: לְיָשׁוּב מִשְׁפַּחַת הַיָּשֻׁבִי
כה לְשִׁמְרֹן מִשְׁפַּחַת הַשִּׁמְרֹנִי: אֵלֶּה מִשְׁפְּחֹת יִשָּׂשכָר לִפְקֻדֵיהֶם
אַרְבָּעָה וְשִׁשִּׁים אֶלֶף וּשְׁלֹשׁ מֵאוֹת: בְּנֵי זְבוּלֻן
כו לְמִשְׁפְּחֹתָם לְסֶרֶד מִשְׁפַּחַת הַסַּרְדִּי לְאֵלוֹן מִשְׁפַּחַת הָאֵלֹנִי
כז לְיַחְלְאֵל מִשְׁפַּחַת הַיַּחְלְאֵלִי: אֵלֶּה מִשְׁפְּחֹת הַזְּבוּלֹנִי לִפְקֻדֵיהֶם
כח שִׁשִּׁים אֶלֶף וַחֲמֵשׁ מֵאוֹת: בְּנֵי יוֹסֵף לְמִשְׁפְּחֹתָם
כט מְנַשֶּׁה וְאֶפְרָיִם: בְּנֵי מְנַשֶּׁה לְמָכִיר מִשְׁפַּחַת הַמָּכִירִי וּמָכִיר

כד **לישוב.** הוא יוב האמור ביורדי מצרים, כי כל המשפחות נקראו על שם יורדי מצרים, והנולדין משם והלאה לא נקראו המשפחות על שמם, חוץ ממשפחות אפרים ומנשה שנולדו כלם במצרים, וארד ונעמן בני בלע בן בנימין. ומצאתי ביסודו של רבי משה הדרשן, שירדה אמן למצרים כשהיתה מעוברת מהם, לכך נחלקו למשפחות, כחצרון וחמול שהיו בני פרץ ליהודה, וחבר ומלכיאל שהיו בני בריעה של אשר. ואם אגדה היא הרי טוב, ואם לאו אומר אני שהיו לבלע בני בנים הרבה, ומשנים הללו ארד ונעמן יצאה מכל אחד משפחה רבה, ונקראו תולדות שאר הבנים על שם בלע, ותולדות השנים הללו נקראו על שמם. וכן אני אומר בבני מכיר שנחלקו לשתי משפחות, אחת נקראת על שמו ואחת נקראת על שם גלעד בנו. חמש משפחות חסרו מבניו של בנימין, כאן נתקיימה מקצת נבואת אמו שקראתו "בן אוני" (בראשית לה, יח), בן אנינתי, ובפילגש בגבעה נתקיימה כלה. זו מצאתי ביסודו של רבי משה הדרשן:

ל	הוֹלִ֣יד אֶת־גִּלְעָ֑ד לְגִלְעָ֕ד מִשְׁפַּ֖חַת הַגִּלְעָדִֽי׃ אֵ֖לֶּה בְּנֵ֥י גִלְעָ֑ד
לא	אִיעֶ֕זֶר מִשְׁפַּ֖חַת הָאִֽיעֶזְרִ֑י לְחֵ֕לֶק מִשְׁפַּ֖חַת הַֽחֶלְקִֽי׃ וְאַ֨שְׂרִיאֵ֔ל
לב	מִשְׁפַּ֖חַת הָֽאַשְׂרִֽאֵלִ֑י וְשֶׁ֕כֶם מִשְׁפַּ֖חַת הַשִּׁכְמִֽי׃ וּשְׁמִידָ֕ע מִשְׁפַּ֖חַת
לג	הַשְּׁמִידָעִ֑י וְחֵ֖פֶר מִשְׁפַּ֣חַת הַֽחֶפְרִֽי׃ וּצְלָפְחָ֣ד בֶּן־חֵ֗פֶר לֹא־הָ֥יוּ ל֛וֹ בָּנִ֖ים כִּ֣י אִם־בָּנ֑וֹת וְשֵׁם֙ בְּנ֣וֹת צְלָפְחָ֔ד מַחְלָ֣ה וְנֹעָ֔ה חָגְלָ֖ה
לד	מִלְכָּ֥ה וְתִרְצָֽה׃ אֵ֖לֶּה מִשְׁפְּח֣וֹת מְנַשֶּׁ֑ה וּפְקֻ֣דֵיהֶ֔ם שְׁנַ֧יִם וַחֲמִשִּׁ֛ים
לה	אֶ֖לֶף וּשְׁבַ֥ע מֵאֽוֹת׃ אֵ֣לֶּה בְנֵי־אֶפְרַ֘יִם֮ לְמִשְׁפְּחֹתָם֒ לְשׁוּתֶ֗לַח מִשְׁפַּ֙חַת֙ הַשֻּׁ֣תַלְחִ֔י לְבֶ֕כֶר מִשְׁפַּ֖חַת הַבַּכְרִ֑י לְתַ֕חַן
לו	מִשְׁפַּ֖חַת הַֽתַּחֲנִֽי׃ וְאֵ֖לֶּה בְּנֵ֣י שׁוּתָ֑לַח לְעֵרָ֕ן מִשְׁפַּ֖חַת הָעֵרָנִֽי׃
לז	אֵ֣לֶּה מִשְׁפְּחֹ֤ת בְּנֵי־אֶפְרַ֙יִם֙ לִפְקֻ֣דֵיהֶ֔ם שְׁנַ֥יִם וּשְׁלֹשִׁ֖ים אֶ֑לֶף וַחֲמֵ֣שׁ מֵא֑וֹת אֵ֥לֶּה בְנֵי־יוֹסֵ֖ף לְמִשְׁפְּחֹתָֽם׃
לח	בְּנֵ֣י בִנְיָמִן֮ לְמִשְׁפְּחֹתָם֒ לְבֶ֗לַע מִשְׁפַּ֙חַת֙ הַבַּלְעִ֔י לְאַשְׁבֵּ֕ל מִשְׁפַּ֖חַת
לט	הָֽאַשְׁבֵּלִ֑י לַֽאֲחִירָ֕ם מִשְׁפַּ֖חַת הָאֲחִירָמִֽי׃ לִשְׁפוּפָ֕ם מִשְׁפַּ֖חַת הַשּׁוּפָמִ֑י לְחוּפָ֕ם מִשְׁפַּ֖חַת הַחוּפָמִֽי׃
מ	וַיִּהְי֥וּ בְנֵי־בֶ֖לַע אַ֣רְדְּ
מא	וְנַעֲמָ֑ן מִשְׁפַּ֙חַת֙ הָֽאַרְדִּ֔י לְנַ֣עֲמָ֔ן מִשְׁפַּ֖חַת הַֽנַּעֲמִֽי׃ אֵ֥לֶּה בְנֵֽי־בִנְיָמִ֖ן לְמִשְׁפְּחֹתָ֑ם וּפְקֻ֣דֵיהֶ֔ם חֲמִשָּׁ֧ה וְאַרְבָּעִ֛ים אֶ֖לֶף וְשֵׁ֥שׁ

לו׀ וְאֵלֶּה בְּנֵי שׁוּתֶלַח וְגוֹ׳. שְׁאָר בְּנֵי שׁוּתֶלַח נִקְרְאוּ תוֹלְדוֹתֵיהֶם עַל שֵׁם שׁוּתֶלַח, וּמֵעֵרָן יָצְאָה מִשְׁפָּחָה רַבָּה וְנִקְרֵאת עַל שְׁמוֹ, וְנֶחְשְׁבוּ בְנֵי שׁוּתֶלַח לִשְׁתֵּי מִשְׁפָּחוֹת. צֵא וַחֲשֹׁב, וְתִמְצָא בְּפָרָשָׁה זוֹ חֲמִשִּׁים וְשֶׁבַע מִשְׁפָּחוֹת וּמִבְּנֵי לֵוִי שְׁמוֹנֶה, הֲרֵי שִׁשִּׁים וְחָמֵשׁ, וְזֶהוּ שֶׁנֶּאֱמַר: "כִּי אַתֶּם הַמְעַט" וְגוֹ׳ (דברים ז, ז), הֵ"א מְעַט, חָמֵשׁ אַתֶּם חֲסֵרִים מִמִּשְׁפְּחוֹת כָּל הָעַמִּים שֶׁהֵן שִׁבְעִים. אַף זֶה הֵבַנְתִּי מִיסוֹדוֹ שֶׁל

רַבִּי מֹשֶׁה הַדַּרְשָׁן, אַךְ הֻצְרַכְתִּי לִפְחֹת וּלְהוֹסִיף בִּדְבָרָיו:

לח׀ לַאֲחִירָם. הוּא אֲחִי שֶׁיָּרַד לְמִצְרַיִם (בראשית מו, כא), וּלְפִי שֶׁנִּקְרָא עַל שֵׁם יוֹסֵף שֶׁהָיָה אָחִיו וְרָם מִמֶּנּוּ נִקְרָא אֲחִירָם:

לט׀ לִשְׁפוּפָם. הוּא מֻפִּים (בראשית שם), עַל שֵׁם שֶׁהָיָה יוֹסֵף שָׁפוּף בֵּין הָאֻמּוֹת:

מב אֵלֶּה בְנֵי־דָן לְמִשְׁפְּחֹתָם לְשׁוּחָם מֵאוֹת:
מג מִשְׁפַּחַת הַשּׁוּחָמִי אֵלֶּה מִשְׁפְּחֹת דָּן לְמִשְׁפְּחֹתָם: כׇּל־מִשְׁפְּחֹת הַשּׁוּחָמִי לִפְקֻדֵיהֶם אַרְבָּעָה וְשִׁשִּׁים אֶלֶף וְאַרְבַּע מֵאוֹת:
מד בְּנֵי אָשֵׁר לְמִשְׁפְּחֹתָם לְיִמְנָה מִשְׁפַּחַת הַיִּמְנָה לְיִשְׁוִי מִשְׁפַּחַת הַיִּשְׁוִי לִבְרִיעָה מִשְׁפַּחַת הַבְּרִיעִי:
מה לִבְנֵי בְרִיעָה לְחֶבֶר מִשְׁפַּחַת הַחֶבְרִי לְמַלְכִּיאֵל מִשְׁפַּחַת הַמַּלְכִּיאֵלִי:
מו וְשֵׁם בַּת־אָשֵׁר שָׂרַח: אֵלֶּה מִשְׁפְּחֹת בְּנֵי־אָשֵׁר לִפְקֻדֵיהֶם שְׁלֹשָׁה וַחֲמִשִּׁים אֶלֶף וְאַרְבַּע מֵאוֹת:
מח בְּנֵי נַפְתָּלִי לְמִשְׁפְּחֹתָם לְיַחְצְאֵל מִשְׁפַּחַת הַיַּחְצְאֵלִי לְגוּנִי מִשְׁפַּחַת הַגּוּנִי:
מט לְיֵצֶר מִשְׁפַּחַת הַיִּצְרִי לְשִׁלֵּם מִשְׁפַּחַת הַשִּׁלֵּמִי: אֵלֶּה מִשְׁפְּחֹת נַפְתָּלִי לְמִשְׁפְּחֹתָם וּפְקֻדֵיהֶם חֲמִשָּׁה וְאַרְבָּעִים אֶלֶף וְאַרְבַּע מֵאוֹת:
נא אֵלֶּה פְּקוּדֵי בְּנֵי יִשְׂרָאֵל שֵׁשׁ־מֵאוֹת אֶלֶף וָאָלֶף שְׁבַע מֵאוֹת וּשְׁלֹשִׁים:

שלישי נב וַיְדַבֵּר יְהֹוָה אֶל־מֹשֶׁה לֵּאמֹר:
נג לָאֵלֶּה תֵּחָלֵק הָאָרֶץ בְּנַחֲלָה בְּמִסְפַּר שֵׁמוֹת:
נד לָרַב תַּרְבֶּה נַחֲלָתוֹ וְלַמְעַט תַּמְעִיט נַחֲלָתוֹ

מב) **לְשׁוּחָם.** הוּא חֻשִׁים (ס״ס כ״ג):

מו) **וְשֵׁם בַּת אָשֵׁר שָׂרַח.** לְפִי שֶׁהָיְתָה קַיֶּמֶת בַּחַיִּים מְנָאָהּ כָּאן:

נג) **לָאֵלֶּה תֵּחָלֵק הָאָרֶץ.** וְלֹא לְפָחוּתִים מִבֶּן עֶשְׂרִים, אַף עַל פִּי שֶׁבָּאוּ לִכְלַל עֶשְׂרִים בְּטֶרֶם חִלּוּק הָאָרֶץ, שֶׁהֲרֵי שֶׁבַע שָׁנִים כָּבְשׁוּ וְשֶׁבַע חִלְּקוּ, לֹא נָטְלוּ חֵלֶק בָּאָרֶץ אֶלָּא אֵלּוּ שֵׁשׁ מֵאוֹת אֶלֶף וָאֶלֶף, וְאִם הָיוּ לְאֶחָד מֵהֶם שִׁשָּׁה בָנִים, לֹא נָטְלוּ אֶלָּא חֵלֶק אֲבִיהֶם לְבַדּוֹ:

נד) **לָרַב תַּרְבֶּה נַחֲלָתוֹ.** לְשֵׁבֶט שֶׁהָיָה מְרֻבֶּה

בְּאוּכְלוּסִין נָתְנוּ חֵלֶק רַב. וְאַף עַל פִּי שֶׁלֹּא הָיוּ הַחֲלָקִים שָׁוִים, שֶׁהֲרֵי הַכֹּל לְפִי רִבּוּי הַשֵּׁבֶט חִלְּקוּ הַחֲלָקִים, לֹא עָשׂוּ אֶלָּא עַל יְדֵי גּוֹרָל, וְהַגּוֹרָל הָיָה עַל פִּי רוּחַ הַקֹּדֶשׁ, כְּמוֹ שֶׁמְּפֹרָשׁ בְּבָבָא בַּתְרָא (דף קכב ע״א): אֶלְעָזָר הַכֹּהֵן הָיָה מְלֻבָּשׁ בְּאוּרִים וְתֻמִּים וְאוֹמֵר בְּרוּחַ הַקֹּדֶשׁ: אִם שֵׁבֶט פְּלוֹנִי עוֹלֶה, תְּחוּם פְּלוֹנִי עוֹלֶה עִמּוֹ: וְהַשְּׁבָטִים הָיוּ כְתוּבִים בִּשְׁנֵים עָשָׂר פְּתָקִין וּשְׁנֵים עָשָׂר גְּבוּלִין בִּשְׁנֵים עָשָׂר פְּתָקִין, וּבְלָלוּם בַּקַּלְפִּי, וְהַנָּשִׂיא מַכְנִיס יָדוֹ לְתוֹכָהּ וְנוֹטֵל שְׁנֵי פְתָקִין. עוֹלֶה בְּיָדוֹ פֶּתֶק שֶׁל שֵׁם שִׁבְטוֹ וּפֶתֶק שֶׁל גְּבוּל הַמְפֹרָשׁ לוֹ, וְהַגּוֹרָל עַצְמוֹ הָיָה צוֹוֵחַ וְאוֹמֵר: אֲנִי

במדבר | פרק כו | פינחס

נה אִ֣ישׁ לְפִ֥י פְקֻדָ֖יו יֻתַּ֥ן נַחֲלָתֽוֹ׃ אַךְ־בְּגוֹרָ֕ל יֵחָלֵ֖ק אֶת־הָאָ֑רֶץ
נו לִשְׁמ֥וֹת מַטּוֹת־אֲבֹתָ֖ם יִנְחָֽלוּ׃ עַל־פִּי֙ הַגּוֹרָ֔ל תֵּחָלֵ֖ק נַחֲלָת֑וֹ בֵּ֥ין
רַ֖ב לִמְעָֽט׃
נז וְאֵ֨לֶּה פְקוּדֵ֤י הַלֵּוִי֙ לְמִשְׁפְּחֹתָ֔ם לְגֵרְשׁ֕וֹן
מִשְׁפַּ֨חַת֙ הַגֵּ֣רְשֻׁנִּ֔י לִקְהָ֕ת מִשְׁפַּ֖חַת הַקְּהָתִ֑י לִמְרָרִ֕י מִשְׁפַּ֖חַת
נח הַמְּרָרִֽי׃ אֵ֣לֶּה ׀ מִשְׁפְּחֹ֣ת לֵוִ֗י מִשְׁפַּ֨חַת הַלִּבְנִ֜י מִשְׁפַּ֤חַת הַֽחֶבְרֹנִי֙
מִשְׁפַּ֣חַת הַמַּחְלִ֔י מִשְׁפַּ֖חַת הַמּוּשִׁ֑י מִשְׁפַּ֖חַת הַקָּרְחִ֑י וּקְהָ֖ת
נט הוֹלִ֥ד אֶת־עַמְרָֽם׃ וְשֵׁ֣ם ׀ אֵ֣שֶׁת עַמְרָ֗ם יוֹכֶ֨בֶד֙ בַּת־לֵוִ֔י אֲשֶׁ֨ר יָלְדָ֤ה
אֹתָהּ֙ לְלֵוִ֔י בְּמִצְרָ֑יִם וַתֵּ֣לֶד לְעַמְרָ֗ם אֶֽת־אַהֲרֹן֙ וְאֶת־מֹשֶׁ֔ה וְאֵ֖ת
ס מִרְיָ֥ם אֲחֹתָֽם׃ וַיִּוָּלֵ֣ד לְאַהֲרֹ֔ן אֶת־נָדָ֖ב וְאֶת־אֲבִיה֑וּא אֶת־אֶלְעָזָ֖ר
סא וְאֶת־אִיתָמָֽר׃ וַיָּ֥מָת נָדָ֖ב וַאֲבִיה֑וּא בְּהַקְרִיבָ֥ם אֵשׁ־זָרָ֖ה לִפְנֵ֥י
סב יהוה׃ וַיִּהְי֣וּ פְקֻדֵיהֶ֗ם שְׁלֹשָׁ֤ה וְעֶשְׂרִים֙ אֶ֔לֶף כׇּל־זָכָ֖ר מִבֶּן־חֹ֣דֶשׁ
וָמָ֑עְלָה כִּ֣י ׀ לֹ֣א הָתְפָּקְד֗וּ בְּתוֹךְ֙ בְּנֵ֣י יִשְׂרָאֵ֔ל כִּ֠י לֹא־נִתַּ֤ן לָהֶם֙

הַגּוֹרָל עָלִיתִי לִגְבוּל לְשֵׁבֶט פְּלוֹנִי, שֶׁנֶּאֱמַר: "עַל פִּי הַגּוֹרָל". וְלֹא נִתְחַלְּקָה הָאָרֶץ בְּמִדָּה, לְפִי שֶׁיֵּשׁ גְּבוּל מְשֻׁבָּח מֵחֲבֵרוֹ, אֶלָּא בְּשׁוּמָא: בֵּית כּוֹר רָע כְּנֶגֶד בֵּית סְאָה טוֹב, הַכֹּל לְפִי הַדָּמִים:

נה) **לִשְׁמוֹת מַטּוֹת אֲבוֹתָם.** אֵלּוּ יוֹצְאֵי מִצְרַיִם. שִׁנָּה הַכָּתוּב נַחֲלָה זוֹ מִכָּל הַנְּחָלוֹת שֶׁבַּתּוֹרָה, שֶׁכָּל הַנְּחָלוֹת, הַחַיִּים יוֹרְשִׁים אֶת הַמֵּתִים, וְכָאן מֵתִים יוֹרְשִׁים אֶת הַחַיִּים. כֵּיצַד? שְׁנֵי אַחִים מִיּוֹצְאֵי מִצְרַיִם שֶׁהָיוּ לָהֶם בָּנִים בְּבָאֵי הָאָרֶץ, לָזֶה אֶחָד וְלָזֶה שְׁלֹשָׁה, הָאֶחָד נָטַל חֵלֶק אֶחָד, וְהַשְּׁלֹשָׁה נָטְלוּ שְׁלֹשָׁה, שֶׁנֶּאֱמַר: "לָאֵלֶּה תֵּחָלֵק הָאָרֶץ", חָזְרָה נַחֲלָתָן אֵצֶל אֲבִי אֲבִיהֶן וְחוֹלְקִין הַכֹּל בְּשָׁוֶה, וְזֶהוּ שֶׁנֶּאֱמַר: "לִשְׁמוֹת מַטּוֹת אֲבוֹתָם יִנְחָלוּ", שֶׁאַחַר שֶׁנָּטְלוּ הַבָּנִים חִלְּקוּם לְפִי הָאָבוֹת שֶׁיָּצְאוּ מִמִּצְרַיִם. וְאִלּוּ מִתְּחִלָּה חִלְּקוּהוּ לְמִנְיַן יוֹצְאֵי מִצְרַיִם, לֹא הָיוּ נוֹטְלִין אֵלּוּ הָאַרְבָּעָה אֶלָּא שְׁנֵי חֲלָקִים, עַכְשָׁו נָטְלוּ אַרְבָּעָה חֲלָקִים:

נו) **עַל פִּי הַגּוֹרָל.** הַגּוֹרָל הָיָה מְדַבֵּר כְּמוֹ שֶׁפֵּרַשְׁתִּי לְמַעְלָה, מַגִּיד שֶׁנִּתְחַלְּקָה בְּרוּחַ הַקֹּדֶשׁ, וְכֵן הוּא אוֹמֵר: "וַיִּתְּנוּ לְכָלֵב אֶת חֶבְרוֹן [כַּאֲשֶׁר דִּבֶּר מֹשֶׁה]" (שופטים א, כ), וְאוֹמֵר: "עַל פִּי ה' נָתְנוּ לוֹ אֶת הָעִיר אֲשֶׁר שָׁאָל" (יהושע יט, נ): **מַטּוֹת אֲבוֹתָם.** יָצְאוּ גֵּרִים וַעֲבָדִים:

נח) **אֵלֶּה מִשְׁפְּחוֹת לֵוִי.** חָסֵר כָּאן מִשְׁפְּחוֹת הַשִּׁמְעִי וְהָעׇזִּיאֵלִי וּקְצָת מִן הַיִּצְהָרִי:

נט) **אֲשֶׁר יָלְדָה אֹתָהּ לְלֵוִי בְּמִצְרָיִם.** אִשְׁתּוֹ יְלָדַתָּה בְּמִצְרַיִם וְאֵין הוֹרָתָהּ בְּמִצְרַיִם, כְּשֶׁנִּכְנְסוּ לְתוֹךְ הַחוֹמָה יְלָדַתָּה, וְהִיא הַשְּׁלִימָה מִנְיַן שִׁבְעִים, שֶׁהֲרֵי בְּפְרָטָן אִי אַתָּה מוֹצֵא אֶלָּא שִׁשִּׁים וָתֵשַׁע:

סב) **כִּי לֹא הָתְפָּקְדוּ בְּתוֹךְ בְּנֵי יִשְׂרָאֵל.** לִהְיוֹת נִמְנִין בְּנֵי עֶשְׂרִים שָׁנָה, מַה טַּעַם? "כִּי לֹא נִתַּן לָהֶם נַחֲלָה", וְהַנִּמְנִין מִבֶּן עֶשְׂרִים שָׁנָה הָיוּ בְּנֵי נַחֲלָה, שֶׁנֶּאֱמַר: "אִישׁ לְפִי פְקֻדָיו יֻתַּן נַחֲלָתוֹ" (לעיל פסוק נד):

פינחס | פרק כז | במדבר

סג נַחֲלָה בְּתוֹךְ בְּנֵי יִשְׂרָאֵל: אֵלֶּה פְּקוּדֵי מֹשֶׁה וְאֶלְעָזָר הַכֹּהֵן אֲשֶׁר פָּקְדוּ אֶת־בְּנֵי יִשְׂרָאֵל בְּעַרְבֹת מוֹאָב עַל יַרְדֵּן יְרֵחוֹ:
סד וּבְאֵלֶּה לֹא־הָיָה אִישׁ מִפְּקוּדֵי מֹשֶׁה וְאַהֲרֹן הַכֹּהֵן אֲשֶׁר פָּקְדוּ אֶת־בְּנֵי יִשְׂרָאֵל בְּמִדְבַּר סִינָי:
סה כִּי־אָמַר יהוה לָהֶם מוֹת יָמֻתוּ בַּמִּדְבָּר וְלֹא־נוֹתַר מֵהֶם אִישׁ כִּי אִם־כָּלֵב בֶּן־יְפֻנֶּה וִיהוֹשֻׁעַ בִּן־נוּן:

פרק כז

א וַתִּקְרַבְנָה בְּנוֹת צְלָפְחָד בֶּן־חֵפֶר בֶּן־גִּלְעָד בֶּן־מָכִיר בֶּן־מְנַשֶּׁה לְמִשְׁפְּחֹת מְנַשֶּׁה בֶן־יוֹסֵף וְאֵלֶּה שְׁמוֹת בְּנֹתָיו מַחְלָה נֹעָה וְחָגְלָה וּמִלְכָּה וְתִרְצָה:
ב וַתַּעֲמֹדְנָה לִפְנֵי מֹשֶׁה וְלִפְנֵי אֶלְעָזָר הַכֹּהֵן וְלִפְנֵי הַנְּשִׂיאִם וְכָל־הָעֵדָה פֶּתַח אֹהֶל־מוֹעֵד לֵאמֹר:
ג אָבִינוּ מֵת בַּמִּדְבָּר וְהוּא לֹא־הָיָה בְּתוֹךְ הָעֵדָה הַנּוֹעָדִים עַל־יהוה בַּעֲדַת־קֹרַח כִּי־בְחֶטְאוֹ מֵת וּבָנִים

סד **וּבְאֵלֶּה לֹא הָיָה אִישׁ וְגוֹ'.** אֲבָל עַל הַנָּשִׁים לֹא נִגְזְרָה גְּזֵרַת הַמְרַגְּלִים, לְפִי שֶׁהֵן הָיוּ מְחַבְּבוֹת אֶת הָאָרֶץ, הָאֲנָשִׁים אוֹמְרִים: "נִתְּנָה רֹאשׁ וְנָשׁוּבָה מִצְרָיְמָה" (לעיל יד, ד), וְהַנָּשִׁים אוֹמְרוֹת: "תְּנָה לָּנוּ אֲחֻזָּה" (להלן כז, ד), לְכָךְ נִסְמְכָה פָּרָשַׁת בְּנוֹת צְלָפְחָד לְכָאן:

הַנִּזְכָּרִים עִמּוֹ לְרָעָה הָיוּ: **מַחְלָה נֹעָה וְגוֹ'.** וּלְהַלָּן (לו, יא) הוּא אוֹמֵר: "וַתִּהְיֶינָה מַחְלָה תִרְצָה", מַגִּיד שֶׁכֻּלָּן שְׁקוּלוֹת זוֹ כָזוֹ, לְפִיכָךְ שִׁנָּה אֶת סִדְרָן:

פרק כז

א **לְמִשְׁפְּחֹת מְנַשֶּׁה בֶן־יוֹסֵף.** לָמָּה נֶאֱמַר? וַהֲלֹא כְּבָר נֶאֱמַר: "בֶּן מְנַשֶּׁה", אֶלָּא לוֹמַר לְךָ, יוֹסֵף חִבֵּב אֶת הָאָרֶץ, שֶׁנֶּאֱמַר: "וְהַעֲלִתֶם אֶת עַצְמֹתַי וְגוֹ'" (בראשית נ, כה), וּבְנוֹתָיו חִבְּבוּ אֶת הָאָרֶץ, שֶׁנֶּאֱמַר: "תְּנָה לָּנוּ אֲחֻזָּה" (להלן פסוק ד). וּלְלַמֶּדְךָ שֶׁהָיוּ כֻּלָּם צַדִּיקִים, שֶׁכָּל מִי שֶׁמַּעֲשָׂיו וּמַעֲשֵׂה אֲבוֹתָיו סְתוּמִים וּפֵרַט לְךָ הַכָּתוּב בְּאֶחָד מֵהֶם לְיַחֲסוֹ לְשֶׁבַח, הֲרֵי זֶה צַדִּיק בֶּן צַדִּיק, וְאִם יִחֲסוֹ לִגְנַאי, כְּגוֹן: "בָּא יִשְׁמָעֵאל בֶּן נְתַנְיָה בֶּן אֱלִישָׁמָע" (מלכים ב׳ כה, כה), בְּיָדוּעַ שֶׁכָּל

ב **לִפְנֵי מֹשֶׁה וְלִפְנֵי אֶלְעָזָר.** מַגִּיד שֶׁלֹּא עָמְדוּ לִפְנֵיהֶם אֶלָּא בִּשְׁנַת הָאַרְבָּעִים אַחַר שֶׁמֵּת אַהֲרֹן לִפְנֵי מֹשֶׁה. וְאַחַר כָּךְ "לִפְנֵי אֶלְעָזָר", אֶפְשָׁר אִם מֹשֶׁה לֹא יָדַע אֶלְעָזָר יוֹדֵעַ? אֶלָּא סָרֵס הַמִּקְרָא וְדָרְשֵׁהוּ, דִּבְרֵי רַבִּי יֹאשִׁיָּה. אַבָּא חָנָן מִשּׁוּם רַבִּי אֶלְעָזָר אוֹמֵר: בְּבֵית הַמִּדְרָשׁ הָיוּ יוֹשְׁבִים, וְעָמְדוּ לִפְנֵי כֻּלָּם:

ג **וְהוּא לֹא הָיָה וְגוֹ'.** לְפִי שֶׁהָיוּ בָּאוֹת לוֹמַר "בְּחֶטְאוֹ מֵת", נִזְקְקוּ לוֹמַר: לֹא בְּחֵטְא מִתְלוֹנְנִים וְלֹא בַּעֲדַת קֹרַח שֶׁהִצָּה עַל הַקָּדוֹשׁ בָּרוּךְ הוּא, אֶלָּא בְּחֶטְאוֹ לְבַדּוֹ מֵת וְלֹא הֶחֱטִיא אֶת אֲחֵרִים עִמּוֹ. רַבִּי עֲקִיבָא אוֹמֵר: מְקוֹשֵׁשׁ עֵצִים הָיָה; וְרַבִּי שִׁמְעוֹן אוֹמֵר: מִן הַמַּעְפִּילִים הָיָה:

במדבר | פרק כז

ד לֹא־הָיוּ לוֹ: לָמָּה יִגָּרַע שֵׁם־אָבִינוּ מִתּוֹךְ מִשְׁפַּחְתּוֹ כִּי אֵין לוֹ בֵּן
ה תְּנָה־לָּנוּ אֲחֻזָּה בְּתוֹךְ אֲחֵי אָבִינוּ: וַיַּקְרֵב מֹשֶׁה אֶת־מִשְׁפָּטָן
לִפְנֵי יהוה:

רביעי ו וַיֹּאמֶר יהוה אֶל־מֹשֶׁה לֵּאמֹר: כֵּן בְּנוֹת צְלָפְחָד דֹּבְרֹת נָתֹן
תִּתֵּן לָהֶם אֲחֻזַּת נַחֲלָה בְּתוֹךְ אֲחֵי אֲבִיהֶם וְהַעֲבַרְתָּ אֶת־נַחֲלַת
ז אֲבִיהֶן לָהֶן: וְאֶל־בְּנֵי יִשְׂרָאֵל תְּדַבֵּר לֵאמֹר אִישׁ כִּי־יָמוּת וּבֵן
ח אֵין לוֹ וְהַעֲבַרְתֶּם אֶת־נַחֲלָתוֹ לְבִתּוֹ: וְאִם־אֵין לוֹ בַּת וּנְתַתֶּם
ט אֶת־נַחֲלָתוֹ לְאֶחָיו: וְאִם־אֵין לוֹ אַחִים וּנְתַתֶּם אֶת־נַחֲלָתוֹ
י לַאֲחֵי אָבִיו: וְאִם־אֵין אַחִים לְאָבִיו וּנְתַתֶּם אֶת־נַחֲלָתוֹ לִשְׁאֵרוֹ
הַקָּרֹב אֵלָיו מִמִּשְׁפַּחְתּוֹ וְיָרַשׁ אֹתָהּ וְהָיְתָה לִבְנֵי יִשְׂרָאֵל לְחֻקַּת
מִשְׁפָּט כַּאֲשֶׁר צִוָּה יהוה אֶת־מֹשֶׁה:

יא וַיֹּאמֶר יהוה אֶל־מֹשֶׁה עֲלֵה אֶל־הַר הָעֲבָרִים הַזֶּה וּרְאֵה

ד| **לָמָּה יִגָּרַע שֵׁם־אָבִינוּ.** אָנוּ בִּמְקוֹם בֵּן עוֹמְדוֹת, וְאִם אֵין הַנְּקֵבוֹת חֲשׁוּבוֹת זֶרַע תִּתְיַבֵּם אִמֵּנוּ לְיָבָם: **כִּי אֵין לוֹ בֵּן.** הָא אִם הָיָה לוֹ בֵן לֹא הָיוּ תּוֹבְעוֹת כְּלוּם, מַגִּיד שֶׁחַכְמָנִיּוֹת הָיוּ:

ה| **וַיַּקְרֵב מֹשֶׁה אֶת מִשְׁפָּטָן.** נִתְעַלְּמָה הֲלָכָה מִמֶּנּוּ. וְכָאן נִפְרַע עַל שֶׁנָּטַל עֲטָרָה לוֹמַר: "וְהַדָּבָר אֲשֶׁר יִקְשֶׁה מִכֶּם תַּקְרִבוּן אֵלָי" (דברים א, יז). דָּבָר אַחֵר, רְאוּיָה הָיְתָה פָּרָשָׁה זוֹ לְהִכָּתֵב עַל יְדֵי מֹשֶׁה, אֶלָּא שֶׁזָּכוּ בְּנוֹת צְלָפְחָד וְנִכְתְּבָה עַל יָדָן:

ו| **כֵּן בְּנוֹת צְלָפְחָד דֹּבְרֹת.** כְּתַרְגּוּמוֹ: "יָאוּת". כָּךְ כְּתוּבָה פָּרָשָׁה זוֹ לְפָנַי בַּמָּרוֹם, מַגִּיד שֶׁרָאֲתָה עֵינָן מַה שֶּׁלֹּא רָאֲתָה עֵינוֹ שֶׁל מֹשֶׁה: **כֵּן בְּנוֹת צְלָפְחָד דֹּבְרֹת.** יָפֶה תָּבְעוּ, אַשְׁרֵי אָדָם שֶׁהַקָּדוֹשׁ בָּרוּךְ הוּא מוֹדֶה לִדְבָרָיו: **נָתֹן תִּתֵּן.** שְׁנֵי חֲלָקִים, חֵלֶק אֲבִיהֶן שֶׁהָיָה מִיּוֹצְאֵי מִצְרַיִם, וְחֶלְקוֹ עִם אֶחָיו בְּנִכְסֵי חֵפֶר: **וְהַעֲבַרְתָּ.** לְשׁוֹן עֶבְרָה הוּא, בְּמִי שֶׁאֵינוֹ מַנִּיחַ בֵּן

לְיָרְשׁוֹ. דָּבָר אַחֵר, עַל שֵׁם שֶׁהַבַּת מַעֲבֶרֶת נַחֲלָה מִשֵּׁבֶט לְשֵׁבֶט, שֶׁבְּנָהּ וּבַעְלָהּ יוֹרְשִׁין אוֹתָהּ, שֶׁלֹּא תִסֹּב נַחֲלָה (להלן לו, ז) לֹא נִצְטַוָּה אֶלָּא לְאוֹתוֹ הַדּוֹר בִּלְבַד, וְכֵן, "וְהַעֲבַרְתֶּם אֶת נַחֲלָתוֹ לְבִתּוֹ" (להלן פסוק ח), בְּכֻלָּן הוּא אוֹמֵר: "וּנְתַתֶּם" (להלן פסוקים ט-י), וּבַבַּת הוּא אוֹמֵר: "וְהַעֲבַרְתֶּם":

יא| **לִשְׁאֵרוֹ הַקָּרֹב אֵלָיו מִמִּשְׁפַּחְתּוֹ.** וְאֵין מִשְׁפָּחָה קְרוּיָה אֶלָּא מִשְׁפַּחַת הָאָב:

יב| **עֲלֵה אֶל הַר הָעֲבָרִים.** לָמָּה נִסְמְכָה לְכָאן? כֵּיוָן שֶׁאָמַר הַקָּדוֹשׁ בָּרוּךְ הוּא: "נָתֹן תִּתֵּן לָהֶם" (לעיל פסוק ז), אָמַר, אוֹתִי צִוָּה הַמָּקוֹם לְהַנְחִיל, שֶׁמָּא הִתִּירָה גְּזֵרָה וְאֶכָּנֵס לָאָרֶץ, אָמַר לוֹ הַקָּדוֹשׁ בָּרוּךְ הוּא: גְּזֵרָתִי בִּמְקוֹמָהּ עוֹמֶדֶת. דָּבָר אַחֵר, כֵּיוָן שֶׁנִּכְנַס מֹשֶׁה לְנַחֲלַת בְּנֵי גָד וּבְנֵי רְאוּבֵן, שָׂמַח וְאָמַר: כִּמְדֻמֶּה שֶׁהֻתַּר לִי נִדְרִי. מָשָׁל לְמֶלֶךְ שֶׁגָּזַר עַל בְּנוֹ שֶׁלֹּא יִכָּנֵס לְפֶתַח פַּלְטֵרִין שֶׁלּוֹ, נִכְנַס לַשַּׁעַר וְהוּא

פרק כז | במדבר

יג אֶת־הָאָרֶץ אֲשֶׁר נָתַתִּי לִבְנֵי יִשְׂרָאֵל: וְרָאִיתָה אֹתָהּ וְנֶאֱסַפְתָּ
יד אֶל־עַמֶּיךָ גַּם־אָתָּה כַּאֲשֶׁר נֶאֱסַף אַהֲרֹן אָחִיךָ: כַּאֲשֶׁר מְרִיתֶם
פִּי בְּמִדְבַּר־צִן בִּמְרִיבַת הָעֵדָה לְהַקְדִּישֵׁנִי בַמַּיִם לְעֵינֵיהֶם הֵם
כד מֵי־מְרִיבַת קָדֵשׁ מִדְבַּר־צִן: וַיְדַבֵּר מֹשֶׁה אֶל־יהוה
טו לֵאמֹר: יִפְקֹד יהוה אֱלֹהֵי הָרוּחֹת לְכָל־בָּשָׂר אִישׁ עַל־הָעֵדָה:
טז אֲשֶׁר־יֵצֵא לִפְנֵיהֶם וַאֲשֶׁר יָבֹא לִפְנֵיהֶם וַאֲשֶׁר יוֹצִיאֵם וַאֲשֶׁר
יז יְבִיאֵם וְלֹא תִהְיֶה עֲדַת יהוה כַּצֹּאן אֲשֶׁר אֵין־לָהֶם רֹעֶה: וַיֹּאמֶר
יח יהוה אֶל־מֹשֶׁה קַח־לְךָ אֶת־יְהוֹשֻׁעַ בִּן־נוּן אִישׁ אֲשֶׁר־רוּחַ

אַחֲרָיו, לְחֶצֶר וְהוּא אַחֲרָיו, לַטְּרַקְלִין וְהוּא אַחֲרָיו, כֵּיוָן שֶׁבָּא לְהִכָּנֵס לְקִיטוֹן אָמַר לוֹ: בְּנִי, מִכָּאן וְאֵילָךְ אַתָּה אָסוּר לִכָּנֵס:

יד. כַּאֲשֶׁר נֶאֱסַף אַהֲרֹן אָחִיךָ. מִכָּאן שֶׁנִּתְאַוָּה מֹשֶׁה לְמִיתָתוֹ שֶׁל אַהֲרֹן. דָּבָר אַחֵר, אֵין אַתָּה טוֹב מִמֶּנּוּ. "עַל אֲשֶׁר לֹא קִדַּשְׁתֶּם" (דברים לב, נא), הָא חָס קִדַּשְׁתֶּם אוֹתִי עֲדַיִן לֹא הִגִּיעַ זְמַנְכֶם לְהִפָּטֵר מִן הָעוֹלָם. בְּכָל מָקוֹם שֶׁכָּתַב מִיתָתָם כָּתַב סֻרְחָנָם, לְפִי שֶׁנִּגְזְרָה גְזֵרָה עַל דּוֹר הַמִּדְבָּר לָמוּת בַּמִּדְבָּר בַּעֲוֹן שֶׁלֹּא הֶאֱמִינוּ, לְכָךְ בִּקֵּשׁ מֹשֶׁה שֶׁיִּכָּתֵב סֻרְחָנוֹ, שֶׁלֹּא יֹאמְרוּ: אַף הוּא מִן הַמַּמְרִים הָיָה. מָשָׁל לִשְׁתֵּי נָשִׁים שֶׁלּוֹקוֹת בְּבֵית דִּין, אַחַת קִלְקְלָה וְאַחַת אָכְלָה פַּגֵּי שְׁבִיעִית וְכוּ׳. [אָמְרָה לָהֶן אוֹתָהּ שֶׁאָכְלָה פַּגֵּי שְׁבִיעִית: בְּבַקָּשָׁה מִכֶּם, הוֹדִיעוּ עַל מָה הִיא לוֹקָה, שֶׁלֹּא יֹאמְרוּ עַל מַה שֶּׁזּוֹ לוֹקָה זוֹ לוֹקָה. הֵבִיאוּ פַּגֵּי שְׁבִיעִית וְתָלוּ בְּצַוָּארָהּ, וְהָיוּ מַכְרִיזִין לְפָנֶיהָ וְאוֹמְרִים: עַל עִסְקֵי שְׁבִיעִית הִיא לוֹקָה] (יומא פו ע"ב). אַף כָּאן בְּכָל מָקוֹם שֶׁהִזְכִּיר מִיתָתָן הִזְכִּיר סֻרְחָנָם, לְהוֹדִיעַ שֶׁלֹּא הָיְתָה בָּהֶם אֶלָּא זוֹ בִּלְבַד:

יד. הֵם מֵי מְרִיבַת קָדֵשׁ. הֵם לְבַדָּם, אֵין בָּהֶם עָוֹן אַחֵר. דָּבָר אַחֵר, הֵם שֶׁהָמְרוּ בְּמָרָה, הֵם הָיוּ שֶׁהָמְרוּ בְּיַם סוּף, הֵם עַצְמָם שֶׁהָמְרוּ בְּמִדְבַּר צִן:

טו. וַיְדַבֵּר מֹשֶׁה אֶל ה' וְגוֹ'. לְהוֹדִיעַ שִׁבְחָן שֶׁל צַדִּיקִים, שֶׁכְּשֶׁנִּפְטָרִים מִן הָעוֹלָם מַנִּיחִין צָרְכָּן

וְעוֹסְקִין בְּצָרְכֵי צִבּוּר: לֵאמֹר. אָמַר לוֹ: הֲשִׁיבֵנִי אִם אַתָּה מְמַנֶּה לָהֶם פַּרְנָס אִם לָאו:

טז. יִפְקֹד ה'. כֵּיוָן שֶׁשָּׁמַע מֹשֶׁה שֶׁאָמַר לוֹ הַמָּקוֹם תֵּן נַחֲלַת צְלָפְחָד לִבְנוֹתָיו, אָמַר: הִגִּיעַ שָׁעָה שֶׁאֶתְבַּע צְרָכַי שֶׁיִּירְשׁוּ בָנַי אֶת גְּדֻלָּתִי. אָמַר לוֹ הַקָּדוֹשׁ בָּרוּךְ הוּא: לֹא כָךְ עָלְתָה בְּמַחֲשָׁבָה לְפָנַי, כְּדַאי הוּא יְהוֹשֻׁעַ לִטֹּל שְׂכַר שִׁמּוּשׁוֹ, שֶׁלֹּא מָשׁ מִתּוֹךְ הָאֹהֶל. וְזֶהוּ שֶׁאָמַר שְׁלֹמֹה: "נֹצֵר תְּאֵנָה יֹאכַל פִּרְיָהּ" (משלי כז):

אֱלֹהֵי הָרוּחֹת. לָמָּה נֶאֱמַר? אָמַר לְפָנָיו: רִבּוֹנוֹ שֶׁל עוֹלָם, גָּלוּי לְפָנֶיךָ דַּעְתּוֹ שֶׁל כָּל אֶחָד וְאֶחָד וְאֵינָן דּוֹמִין זֶה לָזֶה, מַנֵּה עֲלֵיהֶם מַנְהִיג שֶׁיְּהֵא סוֹבֵל כָּל אֶחָד וְאֶחָד לְפִי דַּעְתּוֹ:

יז. אֲשֶׁר יֵצֵא לִפְנֵיהֶם. לֹא כְּדֶרֶךְ מַלְכֵי הָאֻמּוֹת שֶׁיּוֹשְׁבִים בְּבָתֵּיהֶם וּמְשַׁלְּחִין אֶת חֵילוֹתֵיהֶם לַמִּלְחָמָה, אֶלָּא כְּמוֹ שֶׁעָשִׂיתִי אֲנִי, שֶׁנִּלְחַמְתִּי בְּסִיחוֹן וְעוֹג, שֶׁנֶּאֱמַר: "אַל תִּירָא אֹתוֹ" (במדבר כא, לד), וּכְדֶרֶךְ שֶׁעָשָׂה יְהוֹשֻׁעַ, שֶׁנֶּאֱמַר: "וַיֵּלֶךְ יְהוֹשֻׁעַ אֵלָיו וַיֹּאמֶר לוֹ הֲלָנוּ אַתָּה" (יהושע ה, יג) וְגוֹ', וְכֵן בְּדָוִד הוּא אוֹמֵר: "כִּי הוּא יוֹצֵא וָבָא לִפְנֵיהֶם" (שמואל א' יח, טז), יוֹצֵא בָּרֹאשׁ וְנִכְנָס בָּרֹאשׁ: וַאֲשֶׁר יוֹצִיאֵם. בִּזְכֻיּוֹתָיו: וַאֲשֶׁר יְבִיאֵם. בִּזְכֻיּוֹתָיו. דָּבָר אַחֵר, וַאֲשֶׁר יְבִיאֵם, שֶׁלֹּא תַּעֲשֶׂה לוֹ כְּדֶרֶךְ שֶׁאַתָּה עוֹשֶׂה לִי, שֶׁאֵינִי מַכְנִיסָן לָאָרֶץ:

יח. קַח לְךָ. קָחֶנּוּ בִּדְבָרִים, אַשְׁרֶיךָ שֶׁזָּכִיתָ לְהַנְהִיג בָּנָיו שֶׁל מָקוֹם: לְךָ. אֶת שֶׁבָּדוּק לְךָ, אֶת זֶה אַתָּה

במדבר | פרק כח

יט בּוֹ וְסָמַכְתָּ אֶת־יָדְךָ עָלָיו: וְהַעֲמַדְתָּ אֹתוֹ לִפְנֵי אֶלְעָזָר הַכֹּהֵן
כ וְלִפְנֵי כָּל־הָעֵדָה וְצִוִּיתָה אֹתוֹ לְעֵינֵיהֶם: וְנָתַתָּה מֵהוֹדְךָ עָלָיו
כא לְמַעַן יִשְׁמְעוּ כָּל־עֲדַת בְּנֵי יִשְׂרָאֵל: וְלִפְנֵי אֶלְעָזָר הַכֹּהֵן יַעֲמֹד
וְשָׁאַל לוֹ בְּמִשְׁפַּט הָאוּרִים לִפְנֵי יְהוָה עַל־פִּיו יֵצְאוּ וְעַל־פִּיו
כב יָבֹאוּ הוּא וְכָל־בְּנֵי־יִשְׂרָאֵל אִתּוֹ וְכָל־הָעֵדָה: וַיַּעַשׂ מֹשֶׁה
כַּאֲשֶׁר צִוָּה יְהוָה אֹתוֹ וַיִּקַּח אֶת־יְהוֹשֻׁעַ וַיַּעֲמִדֵהוּ לִפְנֵי אֶלְעָזָר
כג הַכֹּהֵן וְלִפְנֵי כָּל־הָעֵדָה: וַיִּסְמֹךְ אֶת־יָדָיו עָלָיו וַיְצַוֵּהוּ כַּאֲשֶׁר
דִּבֶּר יְהוָה בְּיַד־מֹשֶׁה:

כח א וַיְדַבֵּר יְהוָה אֶל־מֹשֶׁה לֵּאמֹר: צַו אֶת־בְּנֵי יִשְׂרָאֵל וְאָמַרְתָּ
אֲלֵהֶם אֶת־קָרְבָּנִי לַחְמִי לְאִשַּׁי רֵיחַ נִיחֹחִי תִּשְׁמְרוּ לְהַקְרִיב

חמישי

מַכִּיר: אֲשֶׁר רוּחַ בּוֹ. כַּאֲשֶׁר שָׁאַלְתָּ, שֶׁיּוּכַל לַהֲלֹךְ כְּנֶגֶד רוּחוֹ שֶׁל כָּל אֶחָד וְאֶחָד: **וְסָמַכְתָּ אֶת יָדְךָ עָלָיו.** תֵּן לוֹ מְתֻרְגְּמָן שֶׁיִּדְרֹשׁ בְּחַיֶּיךָ, שֶׁלֹּא יֹאמְרוּ עָלָיו: לֹא הָיָה לוֹ לְהָרִים רֹאשׁ בִּימֵי מֹשֶׁה:

יט] וְצִוִּיתָה אֹתוֹ. עַל יִשְׂרָאֵל. דַּע שֶׁטַּרְחָנִין הֵם, סַרְבָנִים הֵם, עַל מְנָת שֶׁתְּקַבֵּל עָלֶיךָ:

כ] וְנָתַתָּה מֵהוֹדְךָ עָלָיו. זֶה קֵרוּן עוֹר פָּנִים: **מֵהוֹדְךָ.** וְלֹא כָּל הוֹדְךָ, נִמְצֵינוּ לְמֵדִין, פְּנֵי מֹשֶׁה כַּחַמָּה, פְּנֵי יְהוֹשֻׁעַ כַּלְּבָנָה: **לְמַעַן יִשְׁמְעוּ כָּל עֲדַת בְּנֵי יִשְׂרָאֵל.** שֶׁיִּהְיוּ נוֹהֲגִין בּוֹ כָּבוֹד וְיִרְאָה כְּדֶרֶךְ שֶׁנּוֹהֲגִין בְּךָ:

כא] וְלִפְנֵי אֶלְעָזָר הַכֹּהֵן יַעֲמֹד. הֲרֵי שְׁאֵלָתְךָ שֶׁשָּׁאַלְתָּ, שֶׁאֵין הַכָּבוֹד הַזֶּה זָז מִבֵּית אָבִיךָ, שֶׁאַף יְהוֹשֻׁעַ יְהֵא צָרִיךְ לְאֶלְעָזָר: **וְשָׁאַל לוֹ.** כְּשֶׁיִּצְטָרֵךְ לָצֵאת לַמִּלְחָמָה: **עַל פִּיו.** שֶׁל אֶלְעָזָר: **וְכָל הָעֵדָה.** סַנְהֶדְרִין:

כב] וַיִּקַּח אֶת יְהוֹשֻׁעַ. לְקָחוֹ בִּדְבָרִים, וְהוֹדִיעוֹ מַתַּן שְׂכַר פַּרְנְסֵי יִשְׂרָאֵל לָעוֹלָם הַבָּא:

כג] וַיִּסְמֹךְ אֶת יָדָיו. בְּעַיִן יָפָה, יוֹתֵר וְיוֹתֵר מִמַּה שֶּׁנִּצְטַוָּה, שֶׁהַקָּדוֹשׁ בָּרוּךְ הוּא אָמַר לוֹ: "וְסָמַכְתָּ אֶת יָדְךָ" (לעיל פסוק יח) וְהוּא עָשָׂה בִּשְׁתֵּי יָדָיו, וַעֲשָׂאוֹ כִּכְלִי מָלֵא וְגָדוּשׁ וּמִלְּאוֹ חָכְמָתוֹ בְּעַיִן יָפָה: **כַּאֲשֶׁר דִּבֶּר ה'.** אַף לְעִנְיַן הַהוֹד, נָתַן מֵהוֹדוֹ עָלָיו:

פרק כח

ב] צַו אֶת בְּנֵי יִשְׂרָאֵל. מָה אָמוּר לְמַעְלָה? "יִפְקֹד ה'" (לעיל כז, טז), אָמַר לוֹ הַקָּדוֹשׁ בָּרוּךְ הוּא: עַד שֶׁאַתָּה מְצַוֵּנִי עַל בָּנַי, צַוֵּה אֶת בָּנַי עָלַי, מָשָׁל לְבַת מֶלֶךְ שֶׁהָיְתָה נִפְטֶרֶת מִן הָעוֹלָם וְהָיְתָה מְפַקֶּדֶת לְבַעְלָהּ עַל בָּנֶיהָ וְכוּ' [אָמְרָה לוֹ: בְּבַקָּשָׁה מִמְּךָ הִזָּהֵר לִי בְּבָנַי. אָמַר לָהּ: עַד שֶׁאַתְּ מְפַקְּדַתְנִי עַל בָּנַי פַּקְּדִי אֶת בָּנַי עָלַי, שֶׁלֹּא יִמְרְדוּ בִי וְשֶׁלֹּא יִנְהֲגוּ בִי מִנְהַג בִּזָּיוֹן], כִּדְאִיתָא בְּסִפְרֵי (קמב): **קָרְבָּנִי.** זֶה הַדָּם: **לַחְמִי.** אֵלּוּ אֵמוּרִין, וְכֵן הוּא אוֹמֵר: "וְהִקְטִירָם הַכֹּהֵן הַמִּזְבֵּחָה לֶחֶם אִשֶּׁה" (ויקרא ג, טז): **לְאִשַּׁי.** הַנְּתָנִין לְאִשַּׁי מִזְבְּחִי: **תִּשְׁמְרוּ.** שֶׁיִּהְיוּ כֹּהֲנִים וּלְוִיִּם וְיִשְׂרְאֵלִים עוֹמְדִין עַל גַּבָּיו, מִכָּאן לָמְדוּ וְתִקְּנוּ מַעֲמָדוֹת: **בְּמוֹעֲדוֹ.** בְּכָל יוֹם הוּא מוֹעֵד הַתְּמִידִים:

פרק כח | במדבר

ג לִי בְּמוֹעֲדֽוֹ: וְאָמַרְתָּ֣ לָהֶ֔ם זֶ֚ה הָֽאִשֶּׁ֔ה אֲשֶׁ֥ר תַּקְרִ֖יבוּ לַֽיהֹוָ֑ה
ד כְּבָשִׂ֨ים בְּנֵֽי־שָׁנָ֧ה תְמִימִ֛ם שְׁנַ֥יִם לַיּ֖וֹם עֹלָ֥ה תָמִֽיד: אֶת־הַכֶּ֥בֶשׂ
אֶחָ֖ד תַּֽעֲשֶׂ֣ה בַבֹּ֑קֶר וְאֵת֙ הַכֶּ֣בֶשׂ הַשֵּׁנִ֔י תַּֽעֲשֶׂ֖ה בֵּ֥ין הָֽעַרְבָּֽיִם:
ה וַֽעֲשִׂירִ֧ית הָֽאֵיפָ֛ה סֹ֖לֶת לְמִנְחָ֑ה בְּלוּלָ֛ה בְּשֶׁ֥מֶן כָּתִ֖ית רְבִיעִ֥ת
ו הַהִֽין: עֹלַ֖ת תָּמִ֑יד הָֽעֲשֻׂיָה֙ בְּהַ֣ר סִינַ֔י לְרֵ֣יחַ נִיחֹ֔חַ אִשֶּׁ֖ה לַֽיהֹוָֽה:
ז וְנִסְכּוֹ֙ רְבִיעִ֣ת הַהִ֔ין לַכֶּ֖בֶשׂ הָאֶחָ֑ד בַּקֹּ֗דֶשׁ הַסֵּ֛ךְ נֶ֥סֶךְ שֵׁכָ֖ר
ח לַֽיהֹוָֽה: וְאֵת֙ הַכֶּ֣בֶשׂ הַשֵּׁנִ֔י תַּֽעֲשֶׂ֖ה בֵּ֣ין הָֽעַרְבָּ֑יִם כְּמִנְחַ֨ת הַבֹּ֤קֶר
וּכְנִסְכּוֹ֙ תַּֽעֲשֶׂ֔ה אִשֵּׁ֛ה רֵ֥יחַ נִיחֹ֖חַ לַֽיהֹוָֽה:
ט וּבְיוֹם֙ הַשַּׁבָּ֔ת שְׁנֵֽי־כְבָשִׂ֥ים בְּנֵֽי־שָׁנָ֖ה תְּמִימִ֑ם וּשְׁנֵ֣י עֶשְׂרֹנִ֗ים
י סֹ֛לֶת מִנְחָ֖ה בְּלוּלָ֣ה בַשֶּׁ֣מֶן וְנִסְכּֽוֹ: עֹלַ֥ת שַׁבַּ֖ת בְּשַׁבַּתּ֑וֹ עַל־עֹלַ֥ת
הַתָּמִ֖יד וְנִסְכָּֽהּ:
יא וּבְרָאשֵׁי֙ חָדְשֵׁיכֶ֔ם תַּקְרִ֥יבוּ עֹלָ֖ה לַֽיהֹוָ֑ה פָּרִ֨ים בְּנֵֽי־בָקָ֤ר שְׁנַ֙יִם֙
יב וְאַ֣יִל אֶחָ֔ד כְּבָשִׂ֧ים בְּנֵֽי־שָׁנָ֛ה שִׁבְעָ֖ה תְּמִימִֽם: וּשְׁלֹשָׁ֣ה עֶשְׂרֹנִ֗ים

ג| וְאָמַרְתָּ לָהֶם. אַזְהָרָה לְבֵית דִּין: שְׁנַיִם לַיּוֹם. כִּפְשׁוּטוֹ. וְעִקָּרוֹ בָּא לְלַמֵּד שֶׁיִּהְיוּ נִשְׁחָטִין כְּנֶגֶד הַיּוֹם, תָּמִיד שֶׁל שַׁחַר בַּמַּעֲרָב וְשֶׁל בֵּין הָעַרְבַּיִם בְּמִזְרָחָן שֶׁל טַבָּעוֹת:

ד| אֶת הַכֶּבֶשׂ אֶחָד. אַף עַל פִּי שֶׁכְּבָר נֶאֱמַר בְּפָרָשַׁת וְאַתָּה תְּצַוֶּה: "וְזֶה אֲשֶׁר תַּעֲשֶׂה" וְגוֹ' (שמות כט, לח-לט), הִיא הָיְתָה אַזְהָרָה לִימֵי הַמִּלּוּאִים, וְכָאן צִוָּה לְדוֹרוֹת:

ה| סֹלֶת לְמִנְחָה. מִנְחַת נְסָכִים:

ו| הָעֲשֻׂיָה בְּהַר סִינַי. כְּאוֹתָן שֶׁנַּעֲשׂוּ בִּימֵי הַמִּלּוּאִים. דָּבָר אַחֵר, "הָעֲשֻׂיָה בְּהַר סִינַי", מַקִּישׁ עוֹלַת תָּמִיד לְעוֹלַת הַר סִינַי, אוֹתָהּ שֶׁקָּרְבָה לִפְנֵי מַתַּן תּוֹרָה שֶׁכָּתוּב בָּהּ: "וַיָּשֶׂם בָּאַגָּנֹת" (שמות כד, ו), מְלַמֵּד שֶׁטְּעוּנָה כֶּלִי:

ז| וְנִסְכּוֹ. יַיִן: בַּקֹּדֶשׁ הַסֵּךְ. עַל הַמִּזְבֵּחַ יִתְנַסְּכוּ: נֶסֶךְ שֵׁכָר. יַיִן הַמְשַׁכֵּר, פְּרָט לְיַיִן מִגִּתּוֹ:

ח| רֵיחַ נִיחֹחַ. נַחַת רוּחַ לְפָנַי שֶׁאָמַרְתִּי וְנַעֲשָׂה רְצוֹנִי:

י| עֹלַת שַׁבָּת בְּשַׁבַּתּוֹ. וְלֹא עוֹלַת שַׁבָּת בְּשַׁבָּת אַחֶרֶת, הֲרֵי שֶׁלֹּא הִקְרִיב בְּשַׁבָּת זוֹ, שׁוֹמֵעַ אֲנִי יַקְרִיב שְׁתַּיִם לַשַּׁבָּת הַבָּאָה? תַּלְמוּד לוֹמַר: "בְּשַׁבַּתּוֹ", מַגִּיד שֶׁאִם עָבַר יוֹמוֹ בָּטֵל קָרְבָּנוֹ: עַל עֹלַת הַתָּמִיד. אֵלּוּ מוּסָפִין, לְבַד אוֹתָן שְׁנֵי כְּבָשִׂים שֶׁל עוֹלַת הַתָּמִיד. וּמַגִּיד שֶׁאֵין קְרֵבִין אֶלָּא בֵּין שְׁנֵי הַתְּמִידִין, וְכֵן בְּכָל הַמּוּסָפִין נֶאֱמַר: "עַל עוֹלַת הַתָּמִיד" לְתַלְמוּד זֶה:

יב| וּשְׁלֹשָׁה עֶשְׂרֹנִים. כְּמִשְׁפַּט נִסְכֵּי פָר, שֶׁכֵּן הֵן קְצוּבִין בְּפָרָשַׁת נְסָכִים (לעיל טו, ח-י):

סֹ֣לֶת מִנְחָ֔ה בְּלוּלָ֖ה בַשֶּׁ֑מֶן לַפָּ֣ר הָאֶחָ֗ד וּשְׁנֵ֧י עֶשְׂרֹנִ֛ים סֹ֥לֶת
יג מִנְחָ֖ה בְּלוּלָ֣ה בַשֶּׁ֑מֶן לָאַ֖יִל הָאֶחָֽד: וְעִשָּׂרֹ֣ן עִשָּׂר֗וֹן סֹ֤לֶת מִנְחָה֙
בְּלוּלָ֣ה בַשֶּׁ֔מֶן לַכֶּ֖בֶשׂ הָאֶחָ֑ד עֹלָה֙ רֵ֣יחַ נִיחֹ֔חַ אִשֶּׁ֖ה לַיהוָֽה:
יד וְנִסְכֵּיהֶ֗ם חֲצִ֣י הַהִין֩ יִהְיֶ֨ה לַפָּ֜ר וּשְׁלִישִׁ֧ת הַהִ֣ין לָאַ֗יִל וּרְבִיעִ֧ת
הַהִ֛ין לַכֶּ֖בֶשׂ יָ֑יִן זֹ֣את עֹלַ֥ת חֹ֙דֶשׁ֙ בְּחָדְשׁ֔וֹ לְחָדְשֵׁ֖י הַשָּׁנָֽה:
טו וּשְׂעִ֨יר עִזִּ֥ים אֶחָ֛ד לְחַטָּ֖את לַיהוָ֑ה עַל־עֹלַ֧ת הַתָּמִ֛יד יֵעָשֶׂ֖ה
וְנִסְכּֽוֹ: ששי טז וּבַחֹ֣דֶשׁ הָרִאשׁ֔וֹן בְּאַרְבָּעָ֥ה עָשָׂ֛ר י֖וֹם לַחֹ֑דֶשׁ
פֶּ֖סַח לַיהוָֽה: יז וּבַחֲמִשָּׁ֨ה עָשָׂ֥ר י֛וֹם לַחֹ֥דֶשׁ הַזֶּ֖ה חָ֑ג שִׁבְעַ֣ת יָמִ֔ים
מַצּ֖וֹת יֵאָכֵֽל: יח בַּיּ֣וֹם הָרִאשׁ֔וֹן מִקְרָא־קֹ֑דֶשׁ כָּל־מְלֶ֥אכֶת עֲבֹדָ֖ה
לֹ֥א תַעֲשֽׂוּ: יט וְהִקְרַבְתֶּ֨ם אִשֶּׁ֤ה עֹלָה֙ לַֽיהוָ֔ה פָּרִ֧ים בְּנֵי־בָקָ֛ר שְׁנַ֖יִם
וְאַ֣יִל אֶחָ֑ד וְשִׁבְעָ֧ה כְבָשִׂ֛ים בְּנֵ֥י שָׁנָ֖ה תְּמִימִ֣ם יִהְי֣וּ לָכֶֽם: כ וּמִ֨נְחָתָ֔ם
סֹ֖לֶת בְּלוּלָ֣ה בַשָּׁ֑מֶן שְׁלֹשָׁ֤ה עֶשְׂרֹנִים֙ לַפָּ֔ר וּשְׁנֵ֥י עֶשְׂרֹנִ֖ים לָאַ֥יִל
כא תַּעֲשֽׂוּ: עִשָּׂר֤וֹן עִשָּׂרוֹן֙ תַּעֲשֶׂ֔ה לַכֶּ֖בֶשׂ הָאֶחָ֑ד לְשִׁבְעַ֖ת הַכְּבָשִֽׂים:
כב וּשְׂעִ֥יר חַטָּ֖את אֶחָ֑ד לְכַפֵּ֖ר עֲלֵיכֶֽם: כג מִלְּבַד֙ עֹלַ֣ת הַבֹּ֔קֶר אֲשֶׁ֖ר

יד זֹאת עֹלַת חֹדֶשׁ בְּחָדְשׁוֹ. שֶׁאִם עָבַר יוֹמוֹ בָּטֵל
קָרְבָּנוֹ וְשׁוּב אֵין לוֹ תַּשְׁלוּמִין:

טו וּשְׂעִיר עִזִּים וְגוֹ'. כָּל שְׂעִירֵי הַמּוּסָפִין בָּאִין
לְכַפֵּר עַל טֻמְאַת מִקְדָּשׁ וְקָדָשָׁיו, הַכֹּל כְּמוֹ שֶׁמְפֹרָשׁ
בְּמַסֶּכֶת שְׁבוּעוֹת (דף ב ע"א-ע"ב). וְנִשְׁתַּנָּה שְׂעִיר רֹאשׁ
חֹדֶשׁ שֶׁנֶּאֱמַר בּוֹ: "לַה'", לְלַמֶּדְךָ שֶׁמְּכַפֵּר עַל שֶׁאֵין
בּוֹ יְדִיעָה לֹא בַּתְּחִלָּה וְלֹא בַּסּוֹף, שֶׁאֵין מַכִּיר בַּחֵטְא
אֶלָּא הַקָּדוֹשׁ בָּרוּךְ הוּא בִּלְבַד, וּשְׁאָר הַשְּׂעִירִין
לְמֵדִין מִמֶּנּוּ. וּמִדְרָשׁוֹ בָּאַגָּדָה: אָמַר הַקָּדוֹשׁ בָּרוּךְ
הוּא: הָבִיאוּ כַפָּרָה עָלַי עַל שֶׁמִּעַטְתִּי אֶת הַיָּרֵחַ:

עַל עֹלַת הַתָּמִיד יֵעָשֶׂה. כָּל הַקָּרְבָּן הַזֶּה. וְנִסְכּוֹ.
אֵין 'וְנִסְכּוֹ' מוּסָב עַל הַשָּׂעִיר, שֶׁאֵין נְסָכִים לַחַטָּאת:

יח כָּל מְלֶאכֶת עֲבֹדָה. אֲפִלּוּ מְלָאכָה הַצְּרִיכָה
לָכֶם, כְּגוֹן דָּבָר הָאָבֵד הַמֻּתָּר בְּחֻלּוֹ שֶׁל מוֹעֵד,
אֲסוּרָה בְּיוֹם טוֹב:

יט פָּרִים. כְּנֶגֶד אַבְרָהָם, שֶׁנֶּאֱמַר: "וְאֶל הַבָּקָר רָץ
אַבְרָהָם" (בראשית יח, ז). אֵילִים. כְּנֶגֶד אֵילוֹ שֶׁל יִצְחָק
(שם כב, יג). כְּבָשִׂים. כְּנֶגֶד יַעֲקֹב, שֶׁנֶּאֱמַר: "וְהַכְּשָׂבִים
הִפְרִיד יַעֲקֹב" (שם ל, מ). בִּיסוֹדוֹ שֶׁל רַבִּי מֹשֶׁה הַדַּרְשָׁן
רָאִיתִי זֹאת:

לְעֹלַ֤ת הַתָּמִיד֙ תֵּֽעָשֶׂ֔ה וְנִסְכּֽוֹ׃ כָּאֵ֜לֶּה תַּעֲשׂ֤וּ לַיּוֹם֙ שִׁבְעַ֣ת יָמִ֔ים לֶ֛חֶם אִשֵּׁ֥ה רֵֽיחַ־נִיחֹ֖חַ לַיהוָ֑ה עַל־עוֹלַ֧ת הַתָּמִ֛יד יֵעָשֶׂ֖ה וְנִסְכּֽוֹ׃ וּבַיּוֹם֙ הַשְּׁבִיעִ֔י מִֽקְרָא־קֹ֖דֶשׁ יִהְיֶ֣ה לָכֶ֑ם כָּל־מְלֶ֥אכֶת עֲבֹדָ֖ה לֹ֥א תַעֲשֽׂוּ׃ וּבְי֣וֹם הַבִּכּוּרִ֗ים בְּהַקְרִֽיבְכֶ֞ם מִנְחָ֤ה חֲדָשָׁה֙ לַֽיהוָ֔ה בְּשָׁבֻעֹ֖תֵיכֶ֑ם מִֽקְרָא־קֹ֙דֶשׁ֙ יִהְיֶ֣ה לָכֶ֔ם כָּל־מְלֶ֥אכֶת עֲבֹדָ֖ה לֹ֥א תַעֲשֽׂוּ׃ וְהִקְרַבְתֶּ֨ם עוֹלָ֜ה לְרֵ֤יחַ נִיחֹ֙חַ֙ לַֽיהוָ֔ה פָּרִ֧ים בְּנֵֽי־בָקָ֛ר שְׁנַ֖יִם אַ֣יִל אֶחָ֑ד שִׁבְעָ֥ה כְבָשִׂ֖ים בְּנֵ֥י שָׁנָֽה׃ וּמִ֨נְחָתָ֔ם סֹ֖לֶת בְּלוּלָ֣ה בַשָּׁ֑מֶן שְׁלֹשָׁ֤ה עֶשְׂרֹנִים֙ לַפָּ֣ר הָֽאֶחָ֔ד שְׁנֵי֙ עֶשְׂרֹנִ֔ים לָאַ֖יִל הָאֶחָֽד׃ עִשָּׂר֣וֹן עִשָּׂר֔וֹן לַכֶּ֖בֶשׂ הָאֶחָ֑ד לְשִׁבְעַ֖ת הַכְּבָשִֽׂים׃ שְׂעִ֥יר עִזִּ֛ים אֶחָ֖ד לְכַפֵּ֥ר עֲלֵיכֶֽם׃ מִלְּבַ֞ד עֹלַ֧ת הַתָּמִ֛יד וּמִנְחָת֖וֹ תַּעֲשׂ֑וּ תְּמִימִ֥ם יִֽהְיוּ־לָכֶ֖ם וְנִסְכֵּיהֶֽם׃

וּבַחֹ֤דֶשׁ הַשְּׁבִיעִי֙ בְּאֶחָ֣ד לַחֹ֔דֶשׁ מִֽקְרָא־קֹ֖דֶשׁ יִהְיֶ֣ה לָכֶ֑ם כָּל־מְלֶ֥אכֶת עֲבֹדָ֖ה לֹ֣א תַעֲשׂ֑וּ י֥וֹם תְּרוּעָ֖ה יִהְיֶ֥ה לָכֶֽם׃ וַעֲשִׂיתֶ֨ם עֹלָ֜ה לְרֵ֤יחַ נִיחֹ֙חַ֙ לַֽיהוָ֔ה פַּ֧ר בֶּן־בָּקָ֛ר אֶחָ֖ד אַ֣יִל אֶחָ֑ד כְּבָשִׂ֧ים בְּנֵי־שָׁנָ֛ה שִׁבְעָ֖ה תְּמִימִֽם׃ וּמִ֨נְחָתָ֔ם סֹ֖לֶת בְּלוּלָ֣ה בַשָּׁ֑מֶן שְׁלֹשָׁ֣ה עֶשְׂרֹנִ֗ים לַפָּ֛ר שְׁנֵ֥י עֶשְׂרֹנִ֖ים לָאָֽיִל׃ וְעִשָּׂר֣וֹן אֶחָ֔ד לַכֶּ֖בֶשׂ הָאֶחָ֑ד לְשִׁבְעַ֖ת הַכְּבָשִֽׂים׃ וּשְׂעִיר־עִזִּ֥ים אֶחָ֛ד חַטָּ֖את לְכַפֵּ֥ר עֲלֵיכֶֽם׃ מִלְּבַד֩ עֹלַ֨ת הַחֹ֜דֶשׁ וּמִנְחָתָ֗הּ וְעֹלַ֤ת הַתָּמִיד֙ וּמִנְחָתָ֔הּ וְנִסְכֵּיהֶ֖ם

כד **כָּאֵלֶּה תַּעֲשׂוּ לַיּוֹם.** שֶׁלֹּא יִהְיוּ פּוֹחֲתִין וְהוֹלְכִין כְּפָרֵי הֶחָג:

כו **וּבְיוֹם הַבִּכּוּרִים.** חַג הַשָּׁבוּעוֹת קָרוּי "בִּכּוּרֵי קְצִיר חִטִּים" (שמות לד, כב), עַל שֵׁם שְׁתֵּי הַלֶּחֶם שֶׁהֵם רִאשׁוֹנִים לְמִנְחַת חִטִּים הַבָּאָה מִן הֶחָדָשׁ:

לא **תְּמִימִם יִהְיוּ לָכֶם וְנִסְכֵּיהֶם.** אַף הַנְּסָכִים יִהְיוּ תְּמִימִים, לָמְדוּ רַבּוֹתֵינוּ מִכָּאן שֶׁהַיַּיִן שֶׁהֶעֱלָה קְמָחִין פָּסוּל לִנְסָכִים:

פרק כט

ו **מִלְּבַד עֹלַת הַחֹדֶשׁ.** מוּסְפֵי רֹאשׁ חֹדֶשׁ שֶׁהוּא בְּיוֹם רֹאשׁ הַשָּׁנָה:

ז כְּמִשְׁפָּטָם לְרֵיחַ נִיחֹחַ אִשֶּׁה לַיהוָה: וּבֶעָשׂוֹר לַחֹדֶשׁ הַשְּׁבִיעִי הַזֶּה מִקְרָא־קֹדֶשׁ יִהְיֶה לָכֶם וְעִנִּיתֶם אֶת־נַפְשֹׁתֵיכֶם
ח כָּל־מְלָאכָה לֹא תַעֲשׂוּ: וְהִקְרַבְתֶּם עֹלָה לַיהוָה רֵיחַ נִיחֹחַ פַּר בֶּן־בָּקָר אֶחָד אַיִל אֶחָד כְּבָשִׂים בְּנֵי־שָׁנָה שִׁבְעָה תְּמִימִם יִהְיוּ
ט לָכֶם: וּמִנְחָתָם סֹלֶת בְּלוּלָה בַשָּׁמֶן שְׁלֹשָׁה עֶשְׂרֹנִים לַפָּר שְׁנֵי עֶשְׂרֹנִים לָאַיִל הָאֶחָד:
י עֶשְׂרֹנִים לָאַיִל הָאֶחָד: עִשָּׂרוֹן עִשָּׂרוֹן לַכֶּבֶשׂ הָאֶחָד לְשִׁבְעַת
יא הַכְּבָשִׂים: שְׂעִיר־עִזִּים אֶחָד חַטָּאת מִלְּבַד חַטַּאת הַכִּפֻּרִים
יב וְעֹלַת הַתָּמִיד וּמִנְחָתָהּ וְנִסְכֵּיהֶם: שביעי וּבַחֲמִשָּׁה עָשָׂר יוֹם לַחֹדֶשׁ הַשְּׁבִיעִי מִקְרָא־קֹדֶשׁ יִהְיֶה לָכֶם כָּל־מְלֶאכֶת עֲבֹדָה
יג לֹא תַעֲשׂוּ וְחַגֹּתֶם חַג לַיהוָה שִׁבְעַת יָמִים: וְהִקְרַבְתֶּם עֹלָה אִשֵּׁה רֵיחַ נִיחֹחַ לַיהוָה פָּרִים בְּנֵי־בָקָר שְׁלֹשָׁה עָשָׂר אֵילִם
יד שְׁנַיִם כְּבָשִׂים בְּנֵי־שָׁנָה אַרְבָּעָה עָשָׂר תְּמִימִם יִהְיוּ: וּמִנְחָתָם סֹלֶת בְּלוּלָה בַשֶּׁמֶן שְׁלֹשָׁה עֶשְׂרֹנִים לַפָּר הָאֶחָד לִשְׁלֹשָׁה עָשָׂר
טו פָּרִים שְׁנֵי עֶשְׂרֹנִים לָאַיִל הָאֶחָד לִשְׁנֵי הָאֵילִם: וְעִשָּׂרוֹן עִשָּׂרוֹן
טז לַכֶּבֶשׂ הָאֶחָד לְאַרְבָּעָה עָשָׂר כְּבָשִׂים: וּשְׂעִיר־עִזִּים אֶחָד חַטָּאת מִלְּבַד עֹלַת הַתָּמִיד מִנְחָתָהּ וְנִסְכָּהּ: וּבַיּוֹם
יז הַשֵּׁנִי פָּרִים בְּנֵי־בָקָר שְׁנֵים עָשָׂר אֵילִם שְׁנָיִם כְּבָשִׂים בְּנֵי־שָׁנָה

יא | **מִלְּבַד חַטַּאת הַכִּפֻּרִים.** שָׂעִיר הַנַּעֲשֶׂה בִּפְנִים הָאָמוּר בְּ"אַחֲרֵי מוֹת" (ויקרא טז, ט, טו), שֶׁגַּם הוּא חַטָּאת: **וְעֹלַת הַתָּמִיד. וּמִלְבַד עוֹלַת הַתָּמִיד** תַּעֲשׂוּ עוֹלוֹת הַלָּלוּ: **וְנִסְכֵּיהֶם.** מוּסָב עַל הַמּוּסָפִין הַכְּתוּבִין וְעַל "תַּעֲשׂוּ", וְהוּא לְשׁוֹן צִוּוּי, מִלְּבַד עוֹלַת הַתָּמִיד וּמִנְחָתָהּ תַּעֲשׂוּ אֶת אֵלֶּה וְנִסְכֵּיהֶם. וְכֵן כָּל "וְנִסְכֵּיהֶם" הָאֲמוּרִים בְּכָל הַמּוֹעֲדוֹת, חוּץ מִשֶּׁל קָרְבְּנוֹת הֶחָג, שֶׁכָּל "וְנִסְכָּה", "וְנִסְכֵּיהֶם", "וּנְסָכֶיהָ" שֶׁבָּהֶם מוּסָפִים עַל הַתָּמִיד הֵן, וְאֵינָן לְשׁוֹן צִוּוּי, שֶׁהֲרֵי נִסְכֵּיהֶם שֶׁל מוּסָפִין כְּתוּבִין לְעַצְמָן בְּכָל יוֹם וָיוֹם:

פינחס | 446 פרק כט | במדבר

יח אַרְבָּעָה עָשָׂר תְּמִימִם: וּמִנְחָתָם וְנִסְכֵּיהֶם לַפָּרִים לָאֵילִם
יט וְלַכְּבָשִׂים בְּמִסְפָּרָם כַּמִּשְׁפָּט: וּשְׂעִיר־עִזִּים אֶחָד חַטָּאת
כ מִלְּבַד עֹלַת הַתָּמִיד וּמִנְחָתָהּ וְנִסְכֵּיהֶם: וּבַיּוֹם
הַשְּׁלִישִׁי פָּרִים עַשְׁתֵּי־עָשָׂר אֵילִם שְׁנָיִם כְּבָשִׂים בְּנֵי־שָׁנָה
כא אַרְבָּעָה עָשָׂר תְּמִימִם: וּמִנְחָתָם וְנִסְכֵּיהֶם לַפָּרִים לָאֵילִם
כב וְלַכְּבָשִׂים בְּמִסְפָּרָם כַּמִּשְׁפָּט: וּשְׂעִיר חַטָּאת אֶחָד מִלְּבַד
כג עֹלַת הַתָּמִיד וּמִנְחָתָהּ וְנִסְכָּהּ: וּבַיּוֹם הָרְבִיעִי פָּרִים
עֲשָׂרָה אֵילִם שְׁנָיִם כְּבָשִׂים בְּנֵי־שָׁנָה אַרְבָּעָה עָשָׂר תְּמִימִם:
כד מִנְחָתָם וְנִסְכֵּיהֶם לַפָּרִים לָאֵילִם וְלַכְּבָשִׂים בְּמִסְפָּרָם כַּמִּשְׁפָּט:
כה וּשְׂעִיר־עִזִּים אֶחָד חַטָּאת מִלְּבַד עֹלַת הַתָּמִיד מִנְחָתָהּ
כו וְנִסְכָּהּ: וּבַיּוֹם הַחֲמִישִׁי פָּרִים תִּשְׁעָה אֵילִם שְׁנָיִם
כז כְּבָשִׂים בְּנֵי־שָׁנָה אַרְבָּעָה עָשָׂר תְּמִימִם: וּמִנְחָתָם וְנִסְכֵּיהֶם
כח לַפָּרִים לָאֵילִם וְלַכְּבָשִׂים בְּמִסְפָּרָם כַּמִּשְׁפָּט: וּשְׂעִיר חַטָּאת
כט אֶחָד מִלְּבַד עֹלַת הַתָּמִיד וּמִנְחָתָהּ וְנִסְכָּהּ: וּבַיּוֹם
הַשִּׁשִּׁי פָּרִים שְׁמֹנָה אֵילִם שְׁנָיִם כְּבָשִׂים בְּנֵי־שָׁנָה אַרְבָּעָה עָשָׂר
ל תְּמִימִם: וּמִנְחָתָם וְנִסְכֵּיהֶם לַפָּרִים לָאֵילִם וְלַכְּבָשִׂים בְּמִסְפָּרָם
לא כַּמִּשְׁפָּט: וּשְׂעִיר חַטָּאת אֶחָד מִלְּבַד עֹלַת הַתָּמִיד מִנְחָתָהּ
לב וּנְסָכֶיהָ: וּבַיּוֹם הַשְּׁבִיעִי פָּרִים שִׁבְעָה אֵילִם שְׁנָיִם

יח | וּמִנְחָתָם וְנִסְכֵּיהֶם לַפָּרִים. פָּרֵי הֶחָג שִׁבְעִים הֵם, כְּנֶגֶד שִׁבְעִים אֻמּוֹת, שֶׁמִּתְמַעֲטִים וְהוֹלְכִים, סִימָן כְּלָיָה הוּא לָהֶם, וּבִימֵי הַמִּקְדָּשׁ הָיוּ מְגִנִּים עֲלֵיהֶם מִן הַיִּסּוּרִין, וְהַכְּבָשִׂים כְּנֶגֶד יִשְׂרָאֵל שֶׁנִּקְרְאוּ: "שֶׂה פְזוּרָה" (ירמיה נ, יז), וְהֵם קְבוּעִים, וּמִנְיָנָם תִּשְׁעִים וּשְׁמוֹנָה, לְכַלּוֹת מֵהֶם תִּשְׁעִים וּשְׁמוֹנָה קְלָלוֹת שֶׁבְּמִשְׁנֵה תּוֹרָה. בַּשֵּׁנִי נֶאֱמַר: "וְנִסְכֵּיהֶם" (להלן פסוק יט) עַל שְׁנֵי תְמִידֵי הַיּוֹם, וְלֹא שִׁנָּה הַלָּשׁוֹן אֶלָּא לִדְרֹשׁ, כְּמוֹ שֶׁאָמְרוּ רַבּוֹתֵינוּ זִכְרוֹנָם לִבְרָכָה: בַּשֵּׁנִי "וְנִסְכֵּיהֶם", בַּשִּׁשִּׁי "וּנְסָכֶיהָ" (להלן פסוק לא), בַּשְּׁבִיעִי "כְּמִשְׁפָּטָם" (להלן פסוק לג), מ"ם יו"ד מ"ם, הֲרֵי כָּאן 'מַיִם', רֶמֶז לְנִסּוּךְ הַמַּיִם מִן הַתּוֹרָה בֶּחָג:

במדבר | פרק ל | מטות

לג כְּבָשִׂים בְּנֵי־שָׁנָה אַרְבָּעָה עָשָׂר תְּמִימִם: וּמִנְחָתָם וְנִסְכֵּיהֶם
לד לַפָּרִים לָאֵילִם וְלַכְּבָשִׂים בְּמִסְפָּרָם כַּמִּשְׁפָּט: וּשְׂעִיר חַטָּאת
לה אֶחָד מִלְּבַד עֹלַת הַתָּמִיד מִנְחָתָהּ וְנִסְכָּהּ:

מפטיר

בַּיּוֹם הַשְּׁמִינִי עֲצֶרֶת תִּהְיֶה לָכֶם כָּל־מְלֶאכֶת עֲבֹדָה לֹא תַעֲשׂוּ:
לו וְהִקְרַבְתֶּם עֹלָה אִשֵּׁה רֵיחַ נִיחֹחַ לַיהוה פַּר אֶחָד אַיִל אֶחָד
לז כְּבָשִׂים בְּנֵי־שָׁנָה שִׁבְעָה תְּמִימִם: מִנְחָתָם וְנִסְכֵּיהֶם לַפָּר לָאַיִל
לח וְלַכְּבָשִׂים בְּמִסְפָּרָם כַּמִּשְׁפָּט: וּשְׂעִיר חַטָּאת אֶחָד מִלְּבַד
לט עֹלַת הַתָּמִיד וּמִנְחָתָהּ וְנִסְכָּהּ: אֵלֶּה תַּעֲשׂוּ לַיהוה בְּמוֹעֲדֵיכֶם
לְבַד מִנִּדְרֵיכֶם וְנִדְבֹתֵיכֶם לְעֹלֹתֵיכֶם וּלְמִנְחֹתֵיכֶם וּלְנִסְכֵּיכֶם
ל א וּלְשַׁלְמֵיכֶם: וַיֹּאמֶר מֹשֶׁה אֶל־בְּנֵי יִשְׂרָאֵל כְּכֹל אֲשֶׁר־צִוָּה
יהוה אֶת־מֹשֶׁה:

כו מטות
ב וַיְדַבֵּר מֹשֶׁה אֶל־רָאשֵׁי הַמַּטּוֹת לִבְנֵי יִשְׂרָאֵל לֵאמֹר זֶה הַדָּבָר

לה) **עֲצֶרֶת תִּהְיֶה לָכֶם.** עֲצוּרִים בַּעֲשִׂיַּת מְלָאכָה. דָּבָר אַחֵר, "עֲצֶרֶת", עִצְרוּ מִלָּצֵאת, מְלַמֵּד שֶׁטָּעוּן לִינָה. וּמִדְרָשׁוֹ בָּאַגָּדָה: לְפִי שֶׁכָּל יְמוֹת הָרֶגֶל הִקְרִיבוּ כְּנֶגֶד שִׁבְעִים אֻמּוֹת, וּבָאִין לָלֶכֶת, אָמַר לָהֶם הַמָּקוֹם: בְּבַקָּשָׁה מִכֶּם עֲשׂוּ לִי סְעוּדָה קְטַנָּה, כְּדֵי שֶׁאֵהָנֶה מִכֶּם:

לו) **פַּר אֶחָד אַיִל אֶחָד.** אֵלּוּ כְּנֶגֶד יִשְׂרָאֵל, הִתְעַכְּבוּ לִי מְעַט עוֹד, וּלְשׁוֹן חִבָּה הוּא זֶה, כְּבָנִים הַנִּפְטָרִים מֵאֲבִיהֶם וְהוּא אוֹמֵר לָהֶם: קָשָׁה עָלַי פְּרֵדַתְכֶם, עַכְּבוּ עוֹד יוֹם אֶחָד. מָשָׁל לְמֶלֶךְ שֶׁעָשָׂה סְעוּדָה וְכוּ', כִּדְאִיתָא בְּמַסֶּכֶת סֻכָּה (דף נה ע"ב) [מָשָׁל לְמֶלֶךְ בָּשָׂר וָדָם שֶׁאָמַר לַעֲבָדָיו: עֲשׂוּ לִי סְעוּדָה גְּדוֹלָה. לְיוֹם אַחֲרוֹן אָמַר לְאוֹהֲבוֹ: עֲשֵׂה לִי סְעוּדָה קְטַנָּה, כְּדֵי שֶׁאֵהָנֶה מִמְּךָ]. וּבְמִדְרַשׁ רַבִּי תַּנְחוּמָא (ח) לִמְּדָה תּוֹרָה דֶּרֶךְ אֶרֶץ, שֶׁמִּי שֶׁיֵּשׁ לוֹ אַכְסְנַאי, יוֹם רִאשׁוֹן יַאֲכִילֶנּוּ פְּטוּמוֹת, יַאֲכִילֶנּוּ דָּגִים, לְמָחָר יַאֲכִילֶנּוּ בְּשַׂר בְּהֵמָה, לְמָחָר מַאֲכִילוֹ קְטָנִיּוֹת, לְמָחָר מַאֲכִילוֹ יָרָק, פּוֹחֵת וְהוֹלֵךְ כִּפְרִי הֶחָג:

לט) **אֵלֶּה תַּעֲשׂוּ לַה' בְּמוֹעֲדֵיכֶם.** דָּבָר הַקָּצוּב לְחוֹבָה: **לְבַד מִנִּדְרֵיכֶם.** אִם בָּאתֶם לִדֹּר קָרְבָּנוֹת בָּרֶגֶל, מִצְוָה הִיא בְּיֶדְכֶם, אוֹ נְדָרִים אוֹ נְדָבוֹת שֶׁנְּדַרְתֶּם כָּל הַשָּׁנָה הַקְרִיבוּם בָּרֶגֶל, שֶׁמָּא יִקְשֶׁה לוֹ לַחֲזֹר וְלַעֲלוֹת לִירוּשָׁלַיִם וּלְהַקְרִיב נְדָרָיו, וְנִמְצָא עוֹבֵר בְּבַל תְּאַחֵר:

פרק ל
א) **וַיֹּאמֶר מֹשֶׁה אֶל בְּנֵי יִשְׂרָאֵל.** לְהַפְסִיק הָעִנְיָן, דִּבְרֵי רַבִּי יִשְׁמָעֵאל. לְפִי שֶׁעַד כָּאן דְּבָרָיו שֶׁל מָקוֹם וּפָרָשַׁת נְדָרִים מַתְחֶלֶת בְּדִבּוּרוֹ שֶׁל מֹשֶׁה, הֻצְרַךְ לְהַפְסִיק תְּחִלָּה וְלוֹמַר שֶׁחָזַר מֹשֶׁה וְאָמַר פָּרָשָׁה זוֹ לְיִשְׂרָאֵל, שֶׁאִם לֹא כֵן יֵשׁ בְּמַשְׁמָע שֶׁלֹּא אָמַר לָהֶם זוֹ, אֶלָּא בְּפָרָשַׁת נְדָרִים הִתְחִיל דְּבָרָיו:

ב) **רָאשֵׁי הַמַּטּוֹת.** חָלַק כָּבוֹד לַנְּשִׂיאִים לְלַמְּדָם

אֲשֶׁר־צִוָּה יְהוָה: אִישׁ כִּי־יִדֹּר נֶדֶר לַיהוָה אוֹ־הִשָּׁבַע שְׁבֻעָה ג
לֶאְסֹר אִסָּר עַל־נַפְשׁוֹ לֹא יַחֵל דְּבָרוֹ כְּכָל־הַיֹּצֵא מִפִּיו יַעֲשֶׂה:
וְאִשָּׁה כִּי־תִדֹּר נֶדֶר לַיהוָה וְאָסְרָה אִסָּר בְּבֵית אָבִיהָ בִּנְעֻרֶיהָ: ד
וְשָׁמַע אָבִיהָ אֶת־נִדְרָהּ וֶאֱסָרָהּ אֲשֶׁר אָסְרָה עַל־נַפְשָׁהּ וְהֶחֱרִישׁ ה
לָהּ אָבִיהָ וְקָמוּ כָּל־נְדָרֶיהָ וְכָל־אִסָּר אֲשֶׁר־אָסְרָה עַל־נַפְשָׁהּ
יָקוּם: וְאִם־הֵנִיא אָבִיהָ אֹתָהּ בְּיוֹם שָׁמְעוֹ כָּל־נְדָרֶיהָ וֶאֱסָרֶיהָ ו
אֲשֶׁר־אָסְרָה עַל־נַפְשָׁהּ לֹא יָקוּם וַיהוָה יִסְלַח־לָהּ כִּי־הֵנִיא
אָבִיהָ אֹתָהּ: וְאִם־הָיוֹ תִהְיֶה לְאִישׁ וּנְדָרֶיהָ עָלֶיהָ אוֹ מִבְטָא ז

תְּחִלָּה, וְאַחַר כָּךְ לְכָל בְּנֵי יִשְׂרָאֵל. וּמִנַּיִן שֶׁאַף שְׁאָר הַדִּבְּרוֹת כֵּן? תַּלְמוּד לוֹמַר: "וַיָּשֻׁבוּ אֵלָיו אַהֲרֹן וְכָל הַנְּשִׂאִים בָּעֵדָה וַיְדַבֵּר מֹשֶׁה אֲלֵהֶם, וְאַחֲרֵי כֵן נִגְּשׁוּ כָל בְּנֵי יִשְׂרָאֵל" (שמות לד, לא-לב). וּמָה רָאָה לְאָמְרָהּ כָּאן? לְמַד שֶׁהֲפָרַת נְדָרִים בְּיָחִיד מֻמְחֶה, וְאִם אֵין יָחִיד מֻמְחֶה מֵפֵר בִּשְׁלֹשָׁה הֶדְיוֹטוֹת. אוֹ יָכוֹל שֶׁלֹּא אָמַר מֹשֶׁה פָּרָשָׁה זוֹ אֶלָּא לַנְּשִׂיאִים בִּלְבַד? נֶאֱמַר כָּאן: "זֶה הַדָּבָר", וְנֶאֱמַר בִּשְׁחוּטֵי חוּץ: "זֶה הַדָּבָר" (ויקרא יז, ב). מַה לְּהַלָּן נֶאֶמְרָה לְאַהֲרֹן וּלְבָנָיו וּלְכָל בְּנֵי יִשְׂרָאֵל, שֶׁנֶּאֱמַר: "דַּבֵּר אֶל אַהֲרֹן וְגוֹ'" (שם), אַף זוֹ נֶאֶמְרָה לְכֻלָּן: זֶה הַדָּבָר. מֹשֶׁה נִתְנַבֵּא בְּ"כֹה אָמַר ה' כַּחֲצֹת הַלַּיְלָה" (שמות יא, ד) וְהַנְּבִיאִים נִתְנַבְּאוּ בְּ"כֹה אָמַר ה'", מוּסָף עֲלֵיהֶם מֹשֶׁה, שֶׁנִּתְנַבֵּא בִּלְשׁוֹן "זֶה הַדָּבָר". דָּבָר אַחֵר, "זֶה הַדָּבָר" מִעוּט הוּא, לוֹמַר שֶׁהוּא מִתְחַכֵּם בִּלְשׁוֹן הַתּוֹרָה וּבַעַל בִּלְשׁוֹן הֲפָרָה, כִּלְשׁוֹן הַכָּתוּב כָּאן, וְאִם חִלְּפוּ מֵפֵר אֵין מוּפָר:

ג נֶדֶר. הָאוֹמֵר: הֲרֵי עָלַי קוֹנָם שֶׁלֹּא אֹכַל אוֹ שֶׁלֹּא אֶעֱשֶׂה דָּבָר פְּלוֹנִי. יָכוֹל אֲפִלּוּ נִשְׁבַּע שֶׁיֹּאכַל נְבֵלוֹת אֲנִי קוֹרֵא עָלָיו: "כְּכָל הַיֹּצֵא מִפִּיו יַעֲשֶׂה"? תַּלְמוּד לוֹמַר: "לֶאְסֹר אִסָּר", לֶאֱסֹר אֶת הַמֻּתָּר וְלֹא לְהַתִּיר אֶת הָאָסוּר: לֹא יַחֵל דְּבָרוֹ. כְּמוֹ: לֹא יְחַלֵּל דְּבָרוֹ, לֹא יַעֲשֶׂה דְּבָרָיו חֻלִּין:

ד בְּבֵית אָבִיהָ. בִּרְשׁוּת אָבִיהָ, וַאֲפִלּוּ אֵינָהּ בְּבֵיתוֹ: בִּנְעֻרֶיהָ. וְלֹא קְטַנָּה וְלֹא בּוֹגֶרֶת, שֶׁהַקְּטַנָּה אֵין

נִדְרָהּ נֶדֶר, וְהַבּוֹגֶרֶת אֵינָהּ בִּרְשׁוּתוֹ שֶׁל אָבִיהָ לְהָפֵר נְדָרֶיהָ. וְאֵי זוֹ הִיא קְטַנָּה? אָמְרוּ רַבּוֹתֵינוּ: בַּת אַחַת עֶשְׂרֵה שָׁנָה וְיוֹם אֶחָד נְדָרֶיהָ נִבְדָּקִין, אִם יָדְעָה לְשֵׁם מִי נָדְרָה וּלְשֵׁם מִי הִקְדִּישָׁה, נִדְרָהּ נֶדֶר. בַּת שְׁתֵּים עֶשְׂרֵה שָׁנָה וְיוֹם אֶחָד אֵינָהּ צְרִיכָה לִבָּדֵק:

ו וְאִם הֵנִיא אָבִיהָ אֹתָהּ. אִם מָנַע אוֹתָהּ מִן הַנֶּדֶר, כְּלוֹמַר שֶׁהֵפֵר לָהּ. הֲנָאָה זוֹ אֵינִי יוֹדֵעַ מַה הִיא, כְּשֶׁהוּא אוֹמֵר: "וְאִם בְּיוֹם שְׁמֹעַ אִישָׁהּ יָנִיא אוֹתָהּ וְהֵפֵר" (להלן פסוק ט), הֱוֵי אוֹמֵר הֲנָאָה זוֹ הֲפָרָה. וּפְשׁוּטוֹ, לְשׁוֹן מְנִיעָה וַהֲסָרָה, וְכֵן: "וְלָמָּה תְנִיאוּן" (להלן לב, ז), וְכֵן: "שֶׁמֶן רֹאשׁ אַל יָנִי רֹאשִׁי" (תהלים קמא, ה), וְכֵן: "וִידַעְתֶּם אֶת תְּנוּאָתִי" (לעיל יד, לד), אֶת אֲשֶׁר סַרְתֶּם מֵעָלָי: וַה' יִסְלַח לָהּ. בַּמֶּה הַכָּתוּב מְדַבֵּר? בְּאִשָּׁה שֶׁנָּדְרָה בְנָזִיר וְשָׁמַע בַּעְלָהּ וְהֵפֵר לָהּ וְהִיא לֹא יָדְעָה, וְעוֹבֶרֶת עַל נִדְרָהּ וְשׁוֹתָה יַיִן וּמִטַּמְּאָה לְמֵתִים, זוֹ הִיא שֶׁצְּרִיכָה סְלִיחָה וְאַף עַל פִּי שֶׁהוּא מוּפָר. וְאִם הַמּוּפָרִין צְרִיכִין סְלִיחָה, קַל וָחֹמֶר לְשֶׁאֵינָן מוּפָרִין:

ז וְאִם הָיוֹ תִהְיֶה לְאִישׁ. זוֹ אֲרוּסָה, אוֹ אֵינוֹ אֶלָּא נְשׂוּאָה? כְּשֶׁהוּא אוֹמֵר: "וְאִם בֵּית אִישָׁהּ נָדָרָה" (להלן פסוק יא), הֲרֵי נְשׂוּאָה אָמוּר, וְכָאן בַּאֲרוּסָה, וּבָא לַחֲלֹק בָּהּ, שֶׁאָבִיהָ וּבַעְלָהּ מְפִירִין נְדָרֶיהָ. הֵפֵר הָאָב וְלֹא הֵפֵר הַבַּעַל, אוֹ הֵפֵר הַבַּעַל וְלֹא הֵפֵר הָאָב, הֲרֵי זֶה אֵינוֹ מוּפָר, וְאֵין צָרִיךְ לוֹמַר אִם קִיֵּם אֶחָד

במדבר | פרק ל | מטות

ח שְׂפָתֶ֔יהָ אֲשֶׁ֥ר אָסְרָ֖ה עַל־נַפְשָֽׁהּ: וְשָׁמַ֨ע אִישָׁ֜הּ בְּי֣וֹם שָׁמְע֗וֹ וְהֶחֱרִ֖ישׁ לָ֑הּ וְקָ֣מוּ נְדָרֶ֔יהָ וֶֽאֱסָרֶ֛הָ אֲשֶׁר־אָסְרָ֥ה עַל־נַפְשָׁ֖הּ
ט יָקֻֽמוּ: וְ֠אִם בְּי֨וֹם שְׁמֹ֣עַ אִישָׁהּ֮ יָנִ֣יא אוֹתָהּ֒ וְהֵפֵ֗ר אֶת־נִדְרָהּ֙ אֲשֶׁ֣ר עָלֶ֔יהָ וְאֵת֙ מִבְטָ֣א שְׂפָתֶ֔יהָ אֲשֶׁ֥ר אָסְרָ֖ה עַל־נַפְשָׁ֑הּ וַיהֹוָ֖ה
י יִֽסְלַח־לָֽהּ: וְנֵ֥דֶר אַלְמָנָ֖ה וּגְרוּשָׁ֑ה כֹּ֛ל אֲשֶׁר־אָסְרָ֥ה עַל־נַפְשָׁ֖הּ
יא יָק֥וּם עָלֶֽיהָ: וְאִם־בֵּ֥ית אִישָׁ֖הּ נָדָ֑רָה אֽוֹ־אָסְרָ֥ה אִסָּ֛ר עַל־נַפְשָׁ֖הּ
יב בִּשְׁבֻעָֽה: וְשָׁמַ֤ע אִישָׁהּ֙ וְהֶחֱרִ֣שׁ לָ֔הּ לֹ֥א הֵנִ֖יא אֹתָ֑הּ וְקָ֙מוּ֙ כָּל־
יג נְדָרֶ֔יהָ וְכָל־אִסָּ֛ר אֲשֶׁר־אָסְרָ֥ה עַל־נַפְשָׁ֖הּ יָקֽוּם: וְאִם־הָפֵר֩ יָפֵ֨ר אֹתָ֥ם ׀ אִישָׁהּ֮ בְּי֣וֹם שָׁמְעוֹ֒ כָּל־מוֹצָ֨א שְׂפָתֶ֧יהָ לִנְדָרֶ֛יהָ וּלְאִסַּ֥ר
יד נַפְשָׁ֖הּ לֹ֣א יָק֑וּם אִישָׁ֣הּ הֲפֵרָ֔ם וַיהֹוָ֖ה יִֽסְלַח־לָֽהּ: כָּל־נֵ֛דֶר וְכָל־
טו שְׁבֻעַ֥ת אִסָּ֖ר לְעַנֹּ֣ת נָ֑פֶשׁ אִישָׁ֥הּ יְקִימֶ֖נּוּ וְאִישָׁ֥הּ יְפֵרֶֽנּוּ: וְאִם־הַחֲרֵשׁ֩ יַחֲרִ֨ישׁ לָ֥הּ אִישָׁהּ֮ מִיּ֣וֹם אֶל־יוֹם֒ וְהֵקִים֙ אֶת־כָּל־נְדָרֶ֔יהָ א֥וֹ אֶת־כָּל־אֱסָרֶ֖יהָ אֲשֶׁ֣ר עָלֶ֑יהָ הֵקִ֣ים אֹתָ֔ם כִּי־הֶחֱרִ֥שׁ לָ֖הּ
טז בְּי֥וֹם שָׁמְעֽוֹ: וְאִם־הָפֵ֥ר יָפֵ֛ר אֹתָ֖ם אַחֲרֵ֣י שָׁמְע֑וֹ וְנָשָׂ֖א אֶת־עֲוֺנָֽהּ:

מֵהֶם: וּנְדָרֶ֫יהָ עָלֶיהָ. שֶׁנָּדְרָה בְּבֵית אָבִיהָ וְלֹא שָׁמַע בָּהֶן אָבִיהָ, וְלֹא הוּפְרוּ וְלֹא הוּקְמוּ:

ח] וְשָׁמַע אִישָׁהּ וְגוֹ׳. הֲרֵי לְךָ שֶׁאִם קִיֵּם הַבַּעַל שֶׁהוּא קַיָּם:

ט] וְהֵפֵר אֶת נִדְרָהּ אֲשֶׁר עָלֶיהָ. יָכוֹל אֲפִלּוּ לֹא הֵפֵר הָאָב? תַּלְמוּד לוֹמַר: ״בִּנְעֻרֶיהָ בֵּית אָבִיהָ״ (להלן פסוק יז), כָּל שֶׁבִּנְעוּרֶיהָ בִּרְשׁוּת אָבִיהָ הִיא:

י] אֲשֶׁר אָסְרָה עַל נַפְשָׁהּ יָקוּם עָלֶיהָ. לְפִי שֶׁאֵינָהּ לֹא בִּרְשׁוּת אָב וְלֹא בִּרְשׁוּת בַּעַל, וּבָאַלְמָנָה מִן הַנִּשּׂוּאִין הַכָּתוּב מְדַבֵּר, אֲבָל אַלְמָנָה מִן הָאֵרוּסִין, מֵת הַבַּעַל, נִתְרוֹקְנָה וְחָזְרָה לִרְשׁוּת אָב:

יא] וְאִם בֵּית אִישָׁהּ נָדָרָה. בִּנְשׂוּאָה הַכָּתוּב מְדַבֵּר:

יד] כָּל נֵדֶר וְכָל שְׁבֻעַת אִסָּר וְגוֹ׳. לְפִי שֶׁאָמַר שֶׁהַבַּעַל מֵפֵר, יָכוֹל כָּל נְדָרִים בְּמַשְׁמַע? תַּלְמוּד לוֹמַר: ״לְעַנֹּת נָפֶשׁ״, אֵינוֹ מֵפֵר אֶלָּא נִדְרֵי עִנּוּי נֶפֶשׁ בִּלְבַד, וְהֵם מְפֹרָשִׁים בְּמַסֶּכֶת נְדָרִים (דף עט ע״א וחולך):

טו] מִיּוֹם אֶל יוֹם. שֶׁלֹּא תֹּאמַר מֵעֵת לְעֵת, לְכָךְ נֶאֱמַר: ״מִיּוֹם אֶל יוֹם״, לְלַמֶּדְךָ שֶׁאֵין מֵפֵר אֶלָּא עַד שֶׁתֶּחְשַׁךְ:

טז] אַחֲרֵי שָׁמְעוֹ. אַחֲרֵי שֶׁשָּׁמַע וְקִיֵּם, שֶׁאָמַר: חָפֵצִי בּוֹ, וְחָזַר וְהֵפֵר לָהּ, אֲפִלּוּ בּוֹ בַיּוֹם: וְנָשָׂא אֶת עֲוֺנָהּ.

פרק לא | במדבר

יז אֵ֣לֶּה הַֽחֻקִּ֗ים אֲשֶׁ֨ר צִוָּ֤ה יְהוָה֙ אֶת־מֹשֶׁ֔ה בֵּ֥ין אִ֖ישׁ לְאִשְׁתּ֑וֹ בֵּֽין־אָ֣ב לְבִתּ֔וֹ בִּנְעֻרֶ֖יהָ בֵּ֥ית אָבִֽיהָ׃

שני א וַיְדַבֵּ֥ר יְהוָ֖ה אֶל־מֹשֶׁ֥ה לֵּאמֹֽר׃ ב נְקֹ֗ם נִקְמַת֙ בְּנֵ֣י יִשְׂרָאֵ֔ל מֵאֵ֖ת הַמִּדְיָנִ֑ים אַחַ֖ר תֵּאָסֵ֥ף אֶל־עַמֶּֽיךָ׃ ג וַיְדַבֵּ֤ר מֹשֶׁה֙ אֶל־הָעָ֣ם לֵאמֹ֔ר הֵחָלְצ֧וּ מֵאִתְּכֶ֛ם אֲנָשִׁ֖ים לַצָּבָ֑א וְיִהְיוּ֙ עַל־מִדְיָ֔ן לָתֵ֥ת נִקְמַת־יְהוָ֖ה בְּמִדְיָֽן׃ ד אֶ֚לֶף לַמַּטֶּ֔ה אֶ֖לֶף לַמַּטֶּ֑ה לְכֹל֙ מַטּ֣וֹת יִשְׂרָאֵ֔ל תִּשְׁלְח֖וּ לַצָּבָֽא׃ ה וַיִּמָּֽסְרוּ֙ מֵאַלְפֵ֣י יִשְׂרָאֵ֔ל אֶ֖לֶף לַמַּטֶּ֑ה שְׁנֵים־עָשָׂ֥ר אֶ֖לֶף חֲלוּצֵ֥י צָבָֽא׃ ו וַיִּשְׁלַ֨ח אֹתָ֥ם מֹשֶׁ֛ה אֶ֥לֶף לַמַּטֶּ֖ה לַצָּבָ֑א אֹ֠תָם וְאֶת־פִּ֨ינְחָ֜ס בֶּן־אֶלְעָזָ֤ר הַכֹּהֵן֙ לַצָּבָ֔א וּכְלֵ֥י הַקֹּ֛דֶשׁ וַחֲצֹצְר֥וֹת הַתְּרוּעָ֖ה בְּיָדֽוֹ׃ ז וַֽיִּצְבְּאוּ֙ עַל־מִדְיָ֔ן כַּאֲשֶׁ֛ר צִוָּ֥ה יְהוָ֖ה אֶת־מֹשֶׁ֑ה

הוּא מְכַנֵּס תְּחִלָּתוֹ. לָמַדְנוּ מִכָּאן שֶׁהַגּוֹרֵם תַּקָּלָה לַחֲבֵרוֹ הוּא נִכְנָס תְּחִלָּתוֹ לְכָל עֹנָשִׁין:

פרק לא

ב **מֵאֵת הַמִּדְיָנִים.** וְלֹא מֵאֵת הַמּוֹאָבִים, שֶׁהַמּוֹאָבִים נִכְנְסוּ לַדָּבָר מֵחֲמַת יִרְאָה, שֶׁהָיוּ יְרֵאִים מֵהֶם שֶׁיִּהְיוּ שׁוֹלְלִים אוֹתָם, שֶׁלֹּא נֶאֱמַר אֶלָּא "אַל תִּתְגָּר בָּם מִלְחָמָה" (דברים ב, ט), אֲבָל מִדְיָנִים נִתְעַבְּרוּ עַל רִיב לֹא לָהֶם. דָּבָר אַחֵר, מִפְּנֵי שְׁתֵּי פְּרֵידוֹת טוֹבוֹת שֶׁיֵּשׁ לִי לְהוֹצִיא מֵהֶם, רוּת הַמּוֹאֲבִיָּה וְנַעֲמָה הָעַמּוֹנִית:

ג **וַיְדַבֵּר מֹשֶׁה וְגוֹ'.** אַף עַל פִּי שֶׁשָּׁמַע שֶׁמִּיתָתוֹ תְּלוּיָה בַּדָּבָר, עָשָׂה בְּשִׂמְחָה וְלֹא אֵחַר: **הֵחָלְצוּ.** כְּתַרְגּוּמוֹ, לְשׁוֹן חֲלוּצֵי צָבָא, מְזֻיָּנִים: **אֲנָשִׁים.** צַדִּיקִים, וְכֵן: "בְּחַר לָנוּ אֲנָשִׁים" (שמות יז, ט), וְכֵן: "אֲנָשִׁים חֲכָמִים וּנְבוֹנִים" (דברים א, יג). **נִקְמַת ה'.** שֶׁהָעוֹמֵד כְּנֶגֶד יִשְׂרָאֵל כְּאִלּוּ עוֹמֵד כְּנֶגֶד הַקָּדוֹשׁ בָּרוּךְ הוּא:

ד **לְכֹל מַטּוֹת יִשְׂרָאֵל.** לְרַבּוֹת שֵׁבֶט לֵוִי:

ה **וַיִּמָּסְרוּ.** לְהוֹדִיעֲךָ שִׁבְחָן שֶׁל רוֹעֵי יִשְׂרָאֵל, כַּמָּה הֵם חֲבִיבִים עַל יִשְׂרָאֵל. עַד שֶׁלֹּא שָׁמְעוּ בְּמִיתָתוֹ, מַה הוּא אוֹמֵר? "עוֹד מְעַט וּסְקָלֻנִי" (שמות יז, ד),

וּמִשֶּׁשָּׁמְעוּ שֶׁמִּיתַת מֹשֶׁה תְּלוּיָה בְּנִקְמַת מִדְיָן, לֹא רָצוּ לָלֶכֶת עַד שֶׁנִּמְסְרוּ עַל כָּרְחָן:

ו **אֹתָם וְאֶת־פִּינְחָס.** מַגִּיד שֶׁהָיָה פִּינְחָס שָׁקוּל כְּנֶגֶד כֻּלָּם. וּמִפְּנֵי מָה הָלַךְ פִּינְחָס וְלֹא הָלַךְ אֶלְעָזָר? אָמַר הַקָּדוֹשׁ בָּרוּךְ הוּא: מִי שֶׁהִתְחִיל בַּמִּצְוָה, שֶׁהָרַג כָּזְבִּי בַת צוּר, יִגְמֹר. דָּבָר אַחֵר, שֶׁהָלַךְ לִנְקֹם נִקְמַת יוֹסֵף אֲבִי אִמּוֹ, שֶׁנֶּאֱמַר: "וְהַמְּדָנִים מָכְרוּ אֹתוֹ" (בראשית לז, לו). וּמִנַּיִן שֶׁהָיְתָה אִמּוֹ שֶׁל פִּינְחָס מִשֶּׁל יוֹסֵף? שֶׁנֶּאֱמַר: "מִבְּנוֹת פּוּטִיאֵל" (שמות ו, כה), מִזֶּרַע יִתְרוֹ שֶׁפִּטֵּם עֲגָלִים לַעֲבוֹדָה זָרָה, וּמִזֶּרַע יוֹסֵף שֶׁפִּטְפֵּט בְּיִצְרוֹ. דָּבָר אַחֵר, שֶׁהָיָה מְשׁוּחַ מִלְחָמָה: **וּכְלֵי הַקֹּדֶשׁ.** זֶה הָאָרוֹן וְהַצִּיץ, שֶׁהָיָה בִּלְעָם עִמָּהֶם וּמַפְרִיחַ מַלְכֵי מִדְיָן בִּכְשָׁפִים, וְהוּא עַצְמוֹ פּוֹרֵחַ עִמָּהֶם, הֶרְאָה לָהֶם אֶת הַצִּיץ שֶׁהַשֵּׁם חָקוּק בּוֹ, וְהֵם נוֹפְלִים, לְכָךְ נֶאֱמַר: "עַל חַלְלֵיהֶם" (להלן פסוק ח) בְּמַלְכֵי מִדְיָן, שֶׁנּוֹפְלִים עַל הַחֲלָלִים מִן הָאֲוִיר. וְכֵן בְּבִלְעָם כְּתִיב: "אֶל חַלְלֵיהֶם" בְּסֵפֶר יְהוֹשֻׁעַ (יג, כב): **בְּיָדוֹ.** בִּרְשׁוּתוֹ. וְכֵן: "וַיִּקַּח אֶת כָּל אַרְצוֹ מִיָּדוֹ" (במדבר כא, כו):

במדבר | פרק לא

ח וַיַּהַרְגוּ כָּל־זָכָר: וְאֶת־מַלְכֵי מִדְיָן הָרְגוּ עַל־חַלְלֵיהֶם אֶת־אֱוִי וְאֶת־רֶקֶם וְאֶת־צוּר וְאֶת־חוּר וְאֶת־רֶבַע חֲמֵשֶׁת מַלְכֵי מִדְיָן
וְאֵת בִּלְעָם בֶּן־בְּעוֹר הָרְגוּ בֶּחָרֶב: ט וַיִּשְׁבּוּ בְנֵי־יִשְׂרָאֵל אֶת־נְשֵׁי מִדְיָן וְאֶת־טַפָּם וְאֵת כָּל־בְּהֶמְתָּם וְאֶת־כָּל־מִקְנֵהֶם וְאֶת־
כָּל־חֵילָם בָּזָזוּ: י וְאֵת כָּל־עָרֵיהֶם בְּמוֹשְׁבֹתָם וְאֵת כָּל־טִירֹתָם שָׂרְפוּ בָּאֵשׁ: יא וַיִּקְחוּ אֶת־כָּל־הַשָּׁלָל וְאֵת כָּל־הַמַּלְקוֹחַ בָּאָדָם
וּבַבְּהֵמָה: יב וַיָּבִאוּ אֶל־מֹשֶׁה וְאֶל־אֶלְעָזָר הַכֹּהֵן וְאֶל־עֲדַת בְּנֵי־יִשְׂרָאֵל אֶת־הַשְּׁבִי וְאֶת־הַמַּלְקוֹחַ וְאֶת־הַשָּׁלָל אֶל־הַמַּחֲנֶה
אֶל־עַרְבֹת מוֹאָב אֲשֶׁר עַל־יַרְדֵּן יְרֵחוֹ: יג וַיֵּצְאוּ מֹשֶׁה וְאֶלְעָזָר הַכֹּהֵן וְכָל־נְשִׂיאֵי הָעֵדָה לִקְרָאתָם אֶל־מִחוּץ
לַמַּחֲנֶה: יד וַיִּקְצֹף מֹשֶׁה עַל פְּקוּדֵי הֶחָיִל שָׂרֵי הָאֲלָפִים וְשָׂרֵי

שלישי
/שני/

ח **חֲמֵשֶׁת מַלְכֵי מִדְיָן.** וְכִי אֵינִי רוֹאֶה שֶׁחֲמִשָּׁה מָנָה הַכָּתוּב? לָמָּה הֻזְקַק לוֹמַר 'חֲמֵשֶׁת'? אֶלָּא לְלַמֶּדְךָ שֶׁשָּׁווּ כֻּלָּם בְּעֵצָה וְהִשְׁווּ כֻּלָּם בַּפֻּרְעָנוּת. בִּלְעָם הָלַךְ שָׁם לִטֹּל שְׂכַר עֶשְׂרִים וְאַרְבָּעָה אֶלֶף שֶׁהִפִּיל מִיִּשְׂרָאֵל בַּעֲצָתוֹ, וְיָצָא מִמִּדְיָן לִקְרַאת יִשְׂרָאֵל וּמַשִּׁיאָן עֵצָה רָעָה, אָמַר לָהֶם: אִם כְּשֶׁהֱיִיתֶם שִׁשִּׁים רִבּוֹא לֹא יְכָלְתֶּם לָהֶם, עַתָּה בִּשְׁנֵים עָשָׂר אֶלֶף אַתֶּם בָּאִים לְהִלָּחֵם? נָתְנוּ לוֹ שְׂכָרוֹ מְשֻׁלָּם וְלֹא קִפְּחוּהוּ: **בֶּחָרֶב.** הוּא בָּא עַל יִשְׂרָאֵל וְהֶחֱלִיף אֻמָּנוּתוֹ בְּאֻמָּנוּתָם, שֶׁאֵין נוֹשְׁעִים אֶלָּא בְּפִיהֶם עַל יְדֵי תְּפִלָּה וּבַקָּשָׁה, וּבָא הוּא וְתָפַשׂ אֻמָּנוּתָם לְקַלְּלָם בְּפִיו, אַף הֵם בָּאוּ עָלָיו וְהֶחֱלִיפוּ אֻמָּנוּתָם בְּאֻמָּנוּת הָאֻמּוֹת שֶׁבָּאִין בַּחֶרֶב, שֶׁנֶּאֱמַר: "וְעַל חַרְבְּךָ תִחְיֶה" (בראשית כז, מ):

י **טִירֹתָם.** מְקוֹם פַּלְטְרִין שֶׁלָּהֶם, שֶׁהוּא לְשׁוֹן מוֹשַׁב כְּמָרִים יוֹדְעֵי חֻקֵּיהֶם. דָּבָר אַחֵר, לְשׁוֹן מוֹשַׁב שָׂרֵיהֶם, כְּמוֹ שֶׁמְּתַרְגֵּם "סַרְנֵי פְלִשְׁתִּים" (יהושע יג, ג) – "טוּרְנֵי פְלִשְׁתָּאֵי":

יא **וַיִּקְחוּ אֶת כָּל הַשָּׁלָל וְגוֹ'.** מַגִּיד שֶׁהָיוּ כְּשֵׁרִים וְצַדִּיקִים, וְלֹא נֶחְשְׁדוּ עַל הַגֶּזֶל לִשְׁלוֹחַ יָד בַּבִּזָּה שֶׁלֹּא בִּרְשׁוּת, שֶׁנֶּאֱמַר: "אֶת כָּל הַשָּׁלָל וְגוֹ'", וַעֲלֵיהֶם מְפֹרָשׁ בַּקַּבָּלָה: "שִׁנַּיִךְ כְּעֵדֶר הָרְחֵלִים וְגוֹ'" (שיר השירים ד, ב), אַף אַנְשֵׁי הַמִּלְחָמָה שֶׁבָּךְ כֻּלָּם צַדִּיקִים: **שָׁלָל.** הֵן מִטַּלְטְלִין שֶׁל מַלְבּוּשׁ וְתַכְשִׁיטִין: **בַּז.** הוּא בִּזַּת מִטַּלְטְלִין שֶׁאֵינָם תַּכְשִׁיטִין: **מַלְקוֹחַ.** אָדָם וּבְהֵמָה. וּבִמְקוֹם שֶׁכָּתוּב 'שְׁבִי' אֵצֶל 'מַלְקוֹחַ', 'שְׁבִי' בָּאָדָם וּ'מַלְקוֹחַ' בַּבְּהֵמָה:

יג **וַיֵּצְאוּ מֹשֶׁה וְאֶלְעָזָר הַכֹּהֵן.** לְפִי שֶׁרָאוּ אֶת נַעֲרֵי יִשְׂרָאֵל יוֹצְאִים לַחֲטֹף מִן הַבִּזָּה:

יד **וַיִּקְצֹף מֹשֶׁה עַל פְּקוּדֵי הֶחָיִל.** מְמֻנִּים עַל הַחַיִל, לְלַמֶּדְךָ שֶׁכָּל סִרְחוֹן הַדּוֹר תָּלוּי בַּגְּדוֹלִים שֶׁיֵּשׁ כֹּחַ בְּיָדָם לִמְחוֹת:

הַמֵּאוֹת הַבָּאִים מִצְּבָא הַמִּלְחָמָה: וַיֹּאמֶר אֲלֵיהֶם מֹשֶׁה
הַחִיִּיתֶם כָּל־נְקֵבָה: הֵן הֵנָּה הָיוּ לִבְנֵי יִשְׂרָאֵל בִּדְבַר בִּלְעָם
לִמְסָר־מַעַל בַּיהוה עַל־דְּבַר־פְּעוֹר וַתְּהִי הַמַּגֵּפָה בַּעֲדַת יהוה:
וְעַתָּה הִרְגוּ כָל־זָכָר בַּטָּף וְכָל־אִשָּׁה יֹדַעַת אִישׁ לְמִשְׁכַּב זָכָר
הֲרֹגוּ: וְכֹל הַטַּף בַּנָּשִׁים אֲשֶׁר לֹא־יָדְעוּ מִשְׁכַּב זָכָר הַחֲיוּ
לָכֶם: וְאַתֶּם חֲנוּ מִחוּץ לַמַּחֲנֶה שִׁבְעַת יָמִים כֹּל הֹרֵג נֶפֶשׁ
וְכֹל ׀ נֹגֵעַ בֶּחָלָל תִּתְחַטְּאוּ בַּיּוֹם הַשְּׁלִישִׁי וּבַיּוֹם הַשְּׁבִיעִי אַתֶּם
וּשְׁבִיכֶם: וְכָל־בֶּגֶד וְכָל־כְּלִי־עוֹר וְכָל־מַעֲשֵׂה עִזִּים וְכָל־כְּלִי־עֵץ
תִּתְחַטָּאוּ: וַיֹּאמֶר אֶלְעָזָר הַכֹּהֵן אֶל־אַנְשֵׁי הַצָּבָא
הַבָּאִים לַמִּלְחָמָה זֹאת חֻקַּת הַתּוֹרָה אֲשֶׁר־צִוָּה יהוה אֶת־

טו
טז
יז
יח
יט
כ
כא

מטות | 453

כב מֹשֶׁה: אַ֥ךְ אֶת־הַזָּהָ֖ב וְאֶת־הַכָּ֑סֶף אֶֽת־הַנְּחֹ֖שֶׁת אֶת־הַבַּרְזֶֽל
כג אֶת־הַבְּדִ֖יל וְאֶת־הָעֹפָֽרֶת: כָּל־דָּבָ֞ר אֲשֶׁר־יָבֹ֣א בָאֵ֗שׁ תַּעֲבִ֤ירוּ
בָאֵשׁ֙ וְטָהֵ֔ר אַ֕ךְ בְּמֵ֥י נִדָּ֖ה יִתְחַטָּ֑א וְכֹ֨ל אֲשֶׁ֧ר לֹֽא־יָבֹ֛א בָּאֵ֖שׁ
כד תַּעֲבִ֥ירוּ בַמָּֽיִם: וְכִבַּסְתֶּ֧ם בִּגְדֵיכֶ֛ם בַּיּ֥וֹם הַשְּׁבִיעִ֖י וּטְהַרְתֶּ֑ם
כה וְאַחַ֖ר תָּבֹ֥אוּ אֶל־הַֽמַּחֲנֶֽה: וַיֹּ֥אמֶר יְהֹוָ֖ה אֶל־מֹשֶׁ֥ה כו רביעי
כו לֵּאמֹֽר: שָׂ֗א אֵ֣ת רֹ֤אשׁ מַלְק֙וֹחַ֙ הַשְּׁבִ֔י בָּאָדָ֖ם וּבַבְּהֵמָ֑ה אַתָּה֙
כז וְאֶלְעָזָ֣ר הַכֹּהֵ֔ן וְרָאשֵׁ֖י אֲב֣וֹת הָעֵדָֽה: וְחָצִ֙יתָ֙ אֶת־הַמַּלְק֔וֹחַ
בֵּ֚ין תֹּפְשֵׂ֣י הַמִּלְחָמָ֔ה הַיֹּצְאִ֖ים לַצָּבָ֑א וּבֵ֖ין כָּל־הָעֵדָֽה: וַהֲרֵמֹתָ֨
כח מֶ֜כֶס לַֽיהוָ֗ה מֵאֵ֞ת אַנְשֵׁ֤י הַמִּלְחָמָה֙ הַיֹּצְאִ֣ים לַצָּבָ֔א אֶחָ֣ד נֶ֔פֶשׁ
מֵחֲמֵ֖שׁ הַמֵּא֑וֹת מִן־הָאָדָם֙ וּמִן־הַבָּקָ֔ר וּמִן־הַחֲמֹרִ֖ים וּמִן־
כט הַצֹּֽאן: מִמַּֽחֲצִיתָ֖ם תִּקָּ֑חוּ וְנָתַתָּ֛ה לְאֶלְעָזָ֥ר הַכֹּהֵ֖ן תְּרוּמַ֥ת
ל יְהוָֽה: וּמִמַּחֲצִ֨ת בְּנֵֽי־יִשְׂרָאֵ֜ל תִּקָּ֣ח ׀ אֶחָ֣ד ׀ אָחֻ֣ז מִן־הַחֲמִשִּׁ֗ים
מִן־הָאָדָ֧ם מִן־הַבָּקָ֛ר מִן־הַחֲמֹרִ֖ים וּמִן־הַצֹּ֑אן מִכָּל־הַבְּהֵמָ֑ה

נַח הַמַּרְגִּישׁ' — "וַיַּךְ אֶת הַסֶּלַע" (לעיל כ, יא), עַל יְדֵי
הַכַּעַס טָעָה: אֲשֶׁר צִוָּה ה' וְגוֹ'. תָּלָה הַהוֹרָאָה בְּרַבּוֹ:

כב) אַךְ אֶת הַזָּהָב וְגוֹ'. אַךְ עַל פִּי שֶׁלֹּא הִזְהִיר לָכֶם
מֹשֶׁה אֶלָּא עַל הִלְכוֹת טֻמְאָה, עוֹד יֵשׁ לְהַזְהִיר
לָכֶם עַל הִלְכוֹת גִּעוּל, וְ'אַךְ' לְשׁוֹן מִעוּט, כְּלוֹמַר,
מְמֻעָטִין אַתֶּם מִלְּהִשְׁתַּמֵּשׁ בַּכֵּלִים, אֲפִלּוּ לְאַחַר
טַהֲרָתָן מִטֻּמְאַת הַמֵּת, עַד שֶׁיִּטָּהֲרוּ מִבְּלִיעַת אִסּוּר
נְבֵלוֹת. וְרַבּוֹתֵינוּ אָמְרוּ: "אַךְ אֶת הַזָּהָב", לוֹמַר,
שֶׁצָּרִיךְ לְהַעֲבִיר חֲלֻדָּה שֶׁלּוֹ קֹדֶם שֶׁיַּגְעִילֶנּוּ, וְזֶהוּ
לְשׁוֹן 'אַךְ', שֶׁלֹּא יְהֵא שָׁם חֲלֻדָּה, אַךְ הַמַּתֶּכֶת יִהְיֶה
כְּמוֹת שֶׁהוּא:

כג) כָּל דָּבָר אֲשֶׁר יָבֹא בָאֵשׁ. לְבַשֵּׁל בּוֹ כְּלוּם: תַּעֲבִירוּ
בָאֵשׁ. כְּדַרְכּוֹ תַּשְׁמִישׁוֹ הַגְעָלָתוֹ, מִי שֶׁתַּשְׁמִישׁוֹ עַל יְדֵי
חַמִּין יַגְעִילֶנּוּ בְּחַמִּין, וּמִי שֶׁתַּשְׁמִישׁוֹ עַל יְדֵי צָלִי,

כְּגוֹן הַשִּׁפּוּד וְהָאַסְכְּלָה, יְלַבְּנֶנּוּ בָּאוּר: אַךְ בְּמֵי נִדָּה
יִתְחַטָּא. לְפִי פְּשׁוּטוֹ, חִטּוּי זֶה לְטַהֲרוֹ מִטֻּמְאַת
מֵת, אָמַר לָהֶם: צְרִיכִין הַכֵּלִים גִּעוּל לְטַהֲרָם מִן
הָאִסּוּר, וְחִטּוּי לְטַהֲרָן מִן הַטֻּמְאָה. וְרַבּוֹתֵינוּ דָּרְשׁוּ
מִכָּאן שֶׁאַף לְהַכְשִׁירָן מִן הָאִסּוּר הִטְעִין טְבִילָה
לִכְלֵי מַתָּכוֹת, וּ"מֵי נִדָּה" הַכְּתוּבִין כָּאן דָּרְשׁוּ: מַיִם
הָרְאוּיִין לִטְבֹּל בָּהֶם נִדָּה, וְכַמָּה הֵם? אַרְבָּעִים
סְאָה:

כד) אֶל הַמַּחֲנֶה. לְמַחֲנֵה שְׁכִינָה, שֶׁאֵין טְמֵא מֵת
טָעוּן שִׁלּוּחַ מִמַּחֲנֵה לְוִיָּה וּמִמַּחֲנֵה יִשְׂרָאֵל:

כו) שָׂא אֵת רֹאשׁ. קַח אֶת חֶשְׁבּוֹן:

כז) וְחָצִיתָ אֶת הַמַּלְקוֹחַ בֵּין תֹּפְשֵׂי הַמִּלְחָמָה וְגוֹ'.
חֶצְיוֹ לְאֵלּוּ וְחֶצְיוֹ לְאֵלּוּ:

לא וְנָתַתָּ֣ה אֹתָ֔ם לַלְוִיִּ֕ם שֹׁמְרֵ֖י מִשְׁמֶ֣רֶת מִשְׁכַּ֣ן יְהוָ֑ה: וַיַּ֣עַשׂ מֹשֶׁ֗ה
לב וְאֶלְעָזָ֣ר הַכֹּהֵ֔ן כַּאֲשֶׁ֛ר צִוָּ֥ה יְהוָ֖ה אֶת־מֹשֶֽׁה: וַיְהִי֙ הַמַּלְק֔וֹחַ יֶ֣תֶר
הַבָּ֔ז אֲשֶׁ֥ר בָּזְז֖וּ עַ֣ם הַצָּבָ֑א צֹ֗אן שֵׁשׁ־מֵא֥וֹת אֶ֛לֶף וְשִׁבְעִ֥ים אֶ֖לֶף
לג וַחֲמֵ֥שֶׁת אֲלָפִֽים: וּבָקָ֕ר שְׁנַ֥יִם וְשִׁבְעִ֖ים אָֽלֶף: וַחֲמֹרִ֕ים אֶחָ֥ד
לה וְשִׁשִּׁ֖ים אָֽלֶף: וְנֶ֣פֶשׁ אָדָ֔ם מִן־הַ֨נָּשִׁ֔ים אֲשֶׁ֥ר לֹֽא־יָדְע֖וּ מִשְׁכַּ֣ב
לו זָכָ֑ר כָּל־נֶ֕פֶשׁ שְׁנַ֥יִם וּשְׁלֹשִׁ֖ים אָֽלֶף: וַתְּהִי֙ הַֽמֶּחֱצָ֔ה חֵ֕לֶק הַיֹּצְאִ֖ים
בַּצָּבָ֑א מִסְפַּ֣ר הַצֹּ֗אן שְׁלֹשׁ־מֵא֥וֹת אֶ֛לֶף וּשְׁלֹשִׁ֥ים אֶ֖לֶף וְשִׁבְעַ֥ת
לז אֲלָפִ֖ים וַחֲמֵ֥שׁ מֵאֽוֹת: וַיְהִ֛י הַמֶּ֥כֶס לַֽיהוָ֖ה מִן־הַצֹּ֑אן שֵׁ֥שׁ מֵא֖וֹת
לח חָמֵ֥שׁ וְשִׁבְעִֽים: וְהַ֨בָּקָ֔ר שִׁשָּׁ֥ה וּשְׁלֹשִׁ֖ים אָ֑לֶף וּמִכְסָ֖ם לַיהוָ֥ה
לט שְׁנַ֥יִם וְשִׁבְעִֽים: וַחֲמֹרִ֕ים שְׁלֹשִׁ֥ים אֶ֖לֶף וַחֲמֵ֣שׁ מֵא֑וֹת וּמִכְסָ֥ם
מ לַיהוָ֖ה אֶחָ֥ד וְשִׁשִּֽׁים: וְנֶ֣פֶשׁ אָדָ֔ם שִׁשָּׁ֥ה עָשָׂ֖ר אָ֑לֶף וּמִכְסָם֙
מא לַֽיהוָ֔ה שְׁנַ֥יִם וּשְׁלֹשִׁ֖ים נָֽפֶשׁ: וַיִּתֵּ֣ן מֹשֶׁ֗ה אֶת־מֶ֨כֶס֙ תְּרוּמַ֣ת יְהוָ֔ה

חמישי

לְאֶלְעָזָ֖ר הַכֹּהֵ֑ן כַּאֲשֶׁ֛ר צִוָּ֥ה יְהוָ֖ה אֶת־מֹשֶֽׁה: וּמִֽמַּחֲצִ֖ית בְּנֵ֣י
מב יִשְׂרָאֵ֑ל אֲשֶׁר֙ חָצָ֣ה מֹשֶׁ֔ה מִן־הָאֲנָשִׁ֖ים הַצֹּבְאִֽים: וַתְּהִ֛י מֶחֱצַ֥ת
מג הָעֵדָ֖ה מִן־הַצֹּ֑אן שְׁלֹשׁ־מֵא֥וֹת אֶ֛לֶף וּשְׁלֹשִׁ֥ים אֶ֖לֶף שִׁבְעַ֥ת
מד אֲלָפִ֖ים וַחֲמֵ֥שׁ מֵאֽוֹת: וּבָקָ֕ר שִׁשָּׁ֥ה וּשְׁלֹשִׁ֖ים אָֽלֶף: וַחֲמֹרִ֕ים
מה שְׁלֹשִׁ֥ים אֶ֖לֶף וַחֲמֵ֥שׁ מֵאֽוֹת: וְנֶ֣פֶשׁ אָדָ֔ם שִׁשָּׁ֥ה עָשָׂ֖ר אָֽלֶף: וַיִּקַּ֨ח
מו מֹשֶׁ֜ה מִמַּחֲצִ֣ת בְּנֵֽי־יִשְׂרָאֵ֗ל אֶת־הָֽאָחֻז֙ אֶחָ֣ד מִן־הַחֲמִשִּׁ֔ים מִן־

לב׀ וַיְהִי הַמַּלְקוֹחַ יֶתֶר הַבָּז. לְפִי שֶׁלֹּא נִצְטַוּוּ לְהָרִים מֶכֶס מִן הַמִּטַּלְטְלִין חֵלֶק מִן הַמַּלְקוֹחַ, כָּתַב אֶת הַלָּשׁוֹן הַזֶּה: "וַיְהִי הַמַּלְקוֹחַ" שֶׁבָּא לִכְלַל חֲלֻקָּה וְלִכְלַל מֶכֶס, שֶׁהָיָה עוֹדֵף עַל בַּז הַמִּטַּלְטְלִין "אֲשֶׁר בָּזְזוּ עַם הַצָּבָא" חִיֵּם לוֹ וְלֹא בָא לִכְלַל חֲלֻקָּה, מִסְפַּר הַצֹּאן וְגוֹ':

מב׀ וּמִמַּחֲצִית בְּנֵי יִשְׂרָאֵל אֲשֶׁר חָצָה מֹשֶׁה. לָעֵדָה, וְהוֹצִיאָהּ לָהֶם "מִן הָאֲנָשִׁים הַצֹּבְאִים":

מג-מו׀ וַתְּהִי מֶחֱצַת הָעֵדָה. כָּךְ וְכָךְ, "וַיִּקַּח מֹשֶׁה" וְגוֹ':

מח׀ הַפְּקֻדִים. הַמְמֻנִּים:

הָאָדָ֖ם וּמִן־הַבְּהֵמָ֑ה וַיִּתֵּ֨ן אֹתָ֜ם לַלְוִיִּ֗ם שֹֽׁמְרֵי֙ מִשְׁמֶ֣רֶת מִשְׁכַּ֣ן
יְהוָ֔ה כַּאֲשֶׁ֛ר צִוָּ֥ה יְהוָ֖ה אֶת־מֹשֶֽׁה: וַֽיִּקְרְבוּ֙ אֶל־מֹשֶׁ֔ה הַפְּקֻדִ֕ים
אֲשֶׁ֖ר לְאַלְפֵ֣י הַצָּבָ֑א שָׂרֵ֤י הָאֲלָפִים֙ וְשָׂרֵ֣י הַמֵּא֔וֹת: וַיֹּֽאמְרוּ֙ אֶל־
מֹשֶׁ֔ה עֲבָדֶ֣יךָ נָֽשְׂא֗וּ אֶת־רֹ֛אשׁ אַנְשֵׁ֥י הַמִּלְחָמָ֖ה אֲשֶׁ֣ר בְּיָדֵ֑נוּ
וְלֹא־נִפְקַ֥ד מִמֶּ֖נּוּ אִֽישׁ: וַנַּקְרֵ֞ב אֶת־קָרְבַּ֣ן יְהוָ֗ה אִישׁ֩ אֲשֶׁ֨ר מָצָ֤א
כְלִי־זָהָב֙ אֶצְעָדָ֣ה וְצָמִ֔יד טַבַּ֖עַת עָגִ֣יל וְכוּמָ֑ז לְכַפֵּ֥ר עַל־נַפְשֹׁתֵ֖ינוּ
לִפְנֵ֥י יְהוָֽה: וַיִּקַּ֨ח מֹשֶׁ֜ה וְאֶלְעָזָ֤ר הַכֹּהֵן֙ אֶת־הַזָּהָ֖ב מֵֽאִתָּ֑ם כֹּ֖ל
כְּלִ֥י מַעֲשֶֽׂה: וַיְהִ֣י ׀ כָּל־זְהַ֣ב הַתְּרוּמָ֗ה אֲשֶׁ֤ר הֵרִ֨ימוּ֙ לַֽיהוָ֔ה שִׁשָּׁ֨ה
עָשָׂ֥ר אֶ֛לֶף שְׁבַע־מֵא֥וֹת וַחֲמִשִּׁ֖ים שָׁ֑קֶל מֵאֵת֙ שָׂרֵ֣י הָאֲלָפִ֔ים
וּמֵאֵ֖ת שָׂרֵ֣י הַמֵּאֽוֹת: אַנְשֵׁי֙ הַצָּבָ֔א בָּזְז֖וּ אִ֥ישׁ לֽוֹ: וַיִּקַּ֨ח מֹשֶׁ֜ה
וְאֶלְעָזָ֣ר הַכֹּהֵ֗ן אֶת־הַזָּהָ֔ב מֵאֵ֛ת שָׂרֵ֥י הָאֲלָפִ֖ים וְהַמֵּא֑וֹת וַיָּבִ֤אוּ
אֹתוֹ֙ אֶל־אֹ֣הֶל מוֹעֵ֔ד זִכָּר֥וֹן לִבְנֵֽי־יִשְׂרָאֵ֖ל לִפְנֵ֥י יְהוָֽה:

וּמִקְנֶ֣ה ׀ רַ֗ב הָיָ֞ה לִבְנֵ֧י רְאוּבֵ֛ן וְלִבְנֵי־גָ֖ד עָצ֣וּם מְאֹ֑ד וַיִּרְא֞וּ
אֶת־אֶ֤רֶץ יַעְזֵר֙ וְאֶת־אֶ֣רֶץ גִּלְעָ֔ד וְהִנֵּ֥ה הַמָּק֖וֹם מְק֥וֹם מִקְנֶֽה:
וַיָּבֹ֥אוּ בְנֵֽי־גָ֖ד וּבְנֵ֣י רְאוּבֵ֑ן וַיֹּאמְר֤וּ אֶל־מֹשֶׁה֙ וְאֶל־אֶלְעָזָ֣ר הַכֹּהֵ֔ן
וְאֶל־נְשִׂיאֵ֥י הָעֵדָ֖ה לֵאמֹֽר: עֲטָר֤וֹת וְדִיבֹן֙ וְיַעְזֵ֣ר וְנִמְרָ֔ה וְחֶשְׁבּ֖וֹן
וְאֶלְעָלֵ֤ה וּשְׂבָם֙ וּנְב֣וֹ וּבְעֹ֔ן: הָאָ֗רֶץ אֲשֶׁ֨ר הִכָּ֤ה יְהוָה֙ לִפְנֵי֙ עֲדַ֣ת

מט) וְלֹא נִפְקַד. לֹא נֶחְסַר. וְתַרְגּוּמוֹ: "וְלָא שְׁגָא", אַף הוּא בִּלְשׁוֹן חֶסְרוֹן חַכְמֵי חֲסָרוֹן, כְּמוֹ: "אָנֹכִי אֲחַטֶּנָּה" (בראשית לא, לט), תַּרְגּוּמוֹ: "דַּהֲוַת שָׁגְיָא מִמִּנְיָנָא", וְכֵן: "כִּי יִפָּקֵד מוֹשָׁבֶךָ" (שמואל א׳ כ, יח), יִחְסַר מְקוֹם מוֹשָׁבְךָ, אִישׁ הֶרָגִיל לֵישֵׁב שָׁם. וְכֵן: "וַיִּפָּקֵד מְקוֹם דָּוִד" (שם פסוק כז), נֶחְסַר מְקוֹמוֹ וְאֵין אִישׁ יוֹשֵׁב שָׁם:

נ) אֶצְעָדָה. אֵלּוּ צְמִידִים שֶׁל רֶגֶל: וְצָמִיד. שֶׁל יָד: עָגִיל. נִזְמֵי אֹזֶן: וְכוּמָז. דְּפוּס שֶׁל בֵּית הָרֶחֶם, לְכַפֵּר עַל הִרְהוּר הַלֵּב שֶׁל בְּנוֹת מִדְיָן:

פרק לב

ג) עֲטָרוֹת וְדִיבֹן וְגוֹ'. מֵאֶרֶץ סִיחוֹן וְעוֹג הָיוּ:

מטות | 456   פרק לב | במדבר

יִשְׂרָאֵל אֶרֶץ מִקְנֶה הִוא וְלַעֲבָדֶיךָ מִקְנֶה: וַיֹּאמְרוּ   ה
אִם־מָצָאנוּ חֵן בְּעֵינֶיךָ יֻתַּן אֶת־הָאָרֶץ הַזֹּאת לַעֲבָדֶיךָ לַאֲחֻזָּה
אַל־תַּעֲבִרֵנוּ אֶת־הַיַּרְדֵּן: וַיֹּאמֶר מֹשֶׁה לִבְנֵי־גָד וְלִבְנֵי רְאוּבֵן   ו
הַאַחֵיכֶם יָבֹאוּ לַמִּלְחָמָה וְאַתֶּם תֵּשְׁבוּ פֹה: וְלָמָּה תְנִיאוּן אֶת־   ז
לֵב בְּנֵי יִשְׂרָאֵל מֵעֲבֹר אֶל־הָאָרֶץ אֲשֶׁר־נָתַן לָהֶם יְהוָה: כֹּה   ח
עָשׂוּ אֲבֹתֵיכֶם בְּשָׁלְחִי אֹתָם מִקָּדֵשׁ בַּרְנֵעַ לִרְאוֹת אֶת־הָאָרֶץ:
וַיַּעֲלוּ עַד־נַחַל אֶשְׁכּוֹל וַיִּרְאוּ אֶת־הָאָרֶץ וַיָּנִיאוּ אֶת־לֵב בְּנֵי   ט
יִשְׂרָאֵל לְבִלְתִּי־בֹא אֶל־הָאָרֶץ אֲשֶׁר־נָתַן לָהֶם יְהוָה: וַיִּחַר־אַף   י
יְהוָה בַּיּוֹם הַהוּא וַיִּשָּׁבַע לֵאמֹר: אִם־יִרְאוּ הָאֲנָשִׁים הָעֹלִים   יא
מִמִּצְרַיִם מִבֶּן עֶשְׂרִים שָׁנָה וָמַעְלָה אֵת הָאֲדָמָה אֲשֶׁר נִשְׁבַּעְתִּי
לְאַבְרָהָם לְיִצְחָק וּלְיַעֲקֹב כִּי לֹא־מִלְאוּ אַחֲרָי: בִּלְתִּי כָּלֵב בֶּן־   יב
יְפֻנֶּה הַקְּנִזִּי וִיהוֹשֻׁעַ בִּן־נוּן כִּי מִלְאוּ אַחֲרֵי יְהוָה: וַיִּחַר־אַף   יג
יְהוָה בְּיִשְׂרָאֵל וַיְנִעֵם בַּמִּדְבָּר אַרְבָּעִים שָׁנָה עַד־תֹּם כָּל־הַדּוֹר
הָעֹשֶׂה הָרַע בְּעֵינֵי יְהוָה: וְהִנֵּה קַמְתֶּם תַּחַת אֲבֹתֵיכֶם תַּרְבּוּת   יד
אֲנָשִׁים חַטָּאִים לִסְפּוֹת עוֹד עַל חֲרוֹן אַף־יְהוָה אֶל־יִשְׂרָאֵל: כִּי   טו
תְשׁוּבֻן מֵאַחֲרָיו וְיָסַף עוֹד לְהַנִּיחוֹ בַּמִּדְבָּר וְשִׁחַתֶּם לְכָל־הָעָם
הַזֶּה: וַיִּגְּשׁוּ אֵלָיו וַיֹּאמְרוּ גִּדְרֹת צֹאן נִבְנֶה לְמִקְנֵנוּ   טז

תְּנִיאוּן

ו) הַאַחֵיכֶם. לְשׁוֹן תְּמִיהָה הוּא:

ז) וְלָמָּה תְנִיאוּן. תָּסִירוּ וְתַמְנִיעוּ לִבָּם "מֵעֲבֹר",
שֶׁיִּהְיוּ סְבוּרִים שֶׁאָתֶּם יְרֵאִים לַעֲבֹר מִפְּנֵי הַמִּלְחָמָה
וְחֹזֶק הֶעָרִים וְהָעָם:

ח) מִקָּדֵשׁ בַּרְנֵעַ. כָּךְ שְׁמָהּ, וּשְׁתֵּי קָדֵשׁ הָיוּ:

יב) הַקְּנִזִּי. חוֹרְגוֹ שֶׁל קְנַז הָיָה, וְיָלְדָה לוֹ אִמּוֹ שֶׁל
כָּלֵב אֶת עָתְנִיאֵל:

יג) וַיְנִעֵם. וַיְטַלְטְלֵם, מִן "נָע וָנָד" (בראשית ד, יב):

יד) לִסְפּוֹת. כְּמוֹ: "סְפוּ שָׁנָה עַל שָׁנָה" (ישעיה כט, א),
"עוֹלוֹתֵיכֶם סְפוּ וְגוֹ'" (ירמיה ז, כא), לְשׁוֹן תּוֹסֶפֶת:

במדבר | פרק לב

יז פֹּה וְעָרִים לְטַפֵּנוּ: וַאֲנַחְנוּ נֵחָלֵץ חֻשִׁים לִפְנֵי בְּנֵי יִשְׂרָאֵל עַד אֲשֶׁר אִם־הֲבִיאֹנֻם אֶל־מְקוֹמָם וְיָשַׁב טַפֵּנוּ בְּעָרֵי הַמִּבְצָר מִפְּנֵי

יח יֹשְׁבֵי הָאָרֶץ: לֹא נָשׁוּב אֶל־בָּתֵּינוּ עַד הִתְנַחֵל בְּנֵי יִשְׂרָאֵל

יט אִישׁ נַחֲלָתוֹ: כִּי לֹא נִנְחַל אִתָּם מֵעֵבֶר לַיַּרְדֵּן וָהָלְאָה כִּי בָאָה נַחֲלָתֵנוּ אֵלֵינוּ מֵעֵבֶר הַיַּרְדֵּן מִזְרָחָה:

שביעי /רביעי/

כ וַיֹּאמֶר אֲלֵיהֶם מֹשֶׁה אִם־תַּעֲשׂוּן אֶת־הַדָּבָר הַזֶּה אִם־תֵּחָלְצוּ

כא לִפְנֵי יְהוָה לַמִּלְחָמָה: וְעָבַר לָכֶם כָּל־חָלוּץ אֶת־הַיַּרְדֵּן לִפְנֵי

כב יְהוָה עַד הוֹרִישׁוֹ אֶת־אֹיְבָיו מִפָּנָיו: וְנִכְבְּשָׁה הָאָרֶץ לִפְנֵי יְהוָה וְאַחַר תָּשֻׁבוּ וִהְיִיתֶם נְקִיִּים מֵיְהוָה וּמִיִּשְׂרָאֵל וְהָיְתָה

כג הָאָרֶץ הַזֹּאת לָכֶם לַאֲחֻזָּה לִפְנֵי יְהוָה: וְאִם־לֹא תַעֲשׂוּן כֵּן הִנֵּה חֲטָאתֶם לַיהוָה וּדְעוּ חַטַּאתְכֶם אֲשֶׁר תִּמְצָא אֶתְכֶם: בְּנוּ־לָכֶם

כד

כה עָרִים לְטַפְּכֶם וּגְדֵרֹת לְצֹנַאֲכֶם וְהַיֹּצֵא מִפִּיכֶם תַּעֲשׂוּ: וַיֹּאמֶר בְּנֵי־גָד וּבְנֵי רְאוּבֵן אֶל־מֹשֶׁה לֵּאמֹר עֲבָדֶיךָ יַעֲשׂוּ כַּאֲשֶׁר אֲדֹנִי

טז] **נִבְנֶה לְמִקְנֵנוּ פֹּה.** חָסִים הָיוּ עַל מָמוֹנָם יוֹתֵר מִבְּנֵיהֶם וּבְנוֹתֵיהֶם, שֶׁהִקְדִּימוּ מִקְנֵיהֶם לְטַפָּם. אָמַר לָהֶם מֹשֶׁה: לֹא כֵן, עֲשׂוּ הָעִקָּר עִקָּר וְהַטָּפֵל טָפֵל, בְּנוּ לָכֶם תְּחִלָּה עָרִים לְטַפְּכֶם וְאַחַר כָּךְ גְּדֵרוֹת לְצֹאנְכֶם (להלן פסוק כד):

יז] **וַאֲנַחְנוּ נֵחָלֵץ חֻשִׁים.** מְזֻיָּנִין מְהִירִים, כְּמוֹ: "מַהֵר שָׁלָל חָשׁ בַּז" (ישעיה ח, ג), "יְמַהֵר יָחִישָׁה" (שם ה, יט): [**לִפְנֵי בְּנֵי יִשְׂרָאֵל.** בְּרָאשֵׁי גְּסָיוֹת, מִתּוֹךְ שֶׁגִּבּוֹרִים הָיוּ, שֶׁכֵּן נֶאֱמַר בְּגָד: "וְטָרַף זְרוֹעַ אַף קָדְקֹד" (דברים לג, כ). וְאַף מֹשֶׁה חָזַר וּפֵרֵשׁ לָהֶם בְּחֵלֶק הַדְּבָרִים: "וְאֵת אֶתְכֶם בָּעֵת הַהִוא וְגוֹ' חֲלוּצִים תַּעַבְרוּ לִפְנֵי אֲחֵיכֶם בְּנֵי יִשְׂרָאֵל כָּל בְּנֵי חָיִל" (דברים ג, יח), וּבִירִיחוֹ כְּתִיב: "וְהֶחָלוּץ הֹלֵךְ לִפְנֵיהֶם" (יהושע ו, יג), זֶה רְאוּבֵן וְגָד שֶׁקִּיְּמוּ תְּנַאי. - תּוֹסֶפֶת מַרְבִּיעַ שֶׁמַּעְיָא שֶׁהֵעִיד:

"עוֹנִי רַבִּי לְהַגִּיהַּ"] וְיָשַׁב טַפֵּנוּ. בְּעוֹדֵנוּ אֵצֶל אַחֵינוּ: **בְּעָרֵי הַמִּבְצָר.** שֶׁנִּבְנֶה עַכְשָׁיו:

יט] **מֵעֵבֶר לַיַּרְדֵּן וְגוֹ'.** בָּעֵבֶר הַמַּעֲרָבִי. **כִּי בָאָה נַחֲלָתֵנוּ.** כְּבָר קִבַּלְנוּהָ בָּעֵבֶר הַמִּזְרָחִי:

כד] **לְצֹנַאֲכֶם.** תֵּבָה זוֹ מִגִּזְרַת "צֹנֶה וַאֲלָפִים כֻּלָּם" (תהלים ח, ח), שֶׁאֵין בּוֹ מֶלֶךְ מַפְסִיק בֵּין עַיִ"ן לַדָּלֶ"ת, וְחָלָ"ף שֶׁפָּת כָּאן אַחַר הָעַיִ"ן, בִּמְקוֹם הֵ"א שֶׁל "צֹנֶה" הוּא. מִיסוֹדוֹ שֶׁל רַבִּי מֹשֶׁה הַדַּרְשָׁן לָמַדְתִּי: **וְהַיֹּצֵא מִפִּיכֶם תַּעֲשׂוּ.** לַגָּבוֹהַּ, שֶׁקִּבַּלְתֶּם עֲלֵיכֶם לַעֲבֹר לַמִּלְחָמָה עַד כִּבּוּשׁ וְחִלּוּק, שֶׁמֹּשֶׁה לֹא בִּקֵּשׁ מֵהֶם אֶלָּא "וְנִכְבְּשָׁה וְאַחַר תָּשֻׁבוּ" (לעיל פסוק כב), וְהֵם קִבְּלוּ עֲלֵיהֶם "עַד הִתְנַחֵל" (לעיל פסוק יח), הֲרֵי הוֹסִיפוּ לְהִתְעַכֵּב שֶׁבַע שֶׁחִלְּקוּ, וְכֵן עָשׂוּ:

כה] **וַיֹּאמֶר בְּנֵי גָד.** כֻּלָּם כְּאִישׁ אֶחָד:

מִצְוֶה: טַפֵּנוּ נָשֵׁינוּ מִקְנֵנוּ וְכָל־בְּהֶמְתֵּנוּ יִהְיוּ־שָׁם בְּעָרֵי הַגִּלְעָד: כו
וַעֲבָדֶיךָ יַעַבְרוּ כָּל־חֲלוּץ צָבָא לִפְנֵי יהוה לַמִּלְחָמָה כַּאֲשֶׁר כז
אֲדֹנִי דֹּבֵר: וַיְצַו לָהֶם מֹשֶׁה אֵת אֶלְעָזָר הַכֹּהֵן וְאֵת יְהוֹשֻׁעַ כח
בִּן־נוּן וְאֶת־רָאשֵׁי אֲבוֹת הַמַּטּוֹת לִבְנֵי יִשְׂרָאֵל: וַיֹּאמֶר מֹשֶׁה כט
אֲלֵהֶם אִם־יַעַבְרוּ בְנֵי־גָד וּבְנֵי־רְאוּבֵן ׀ אִתְּכֶם אֶת־הַיַּרְדֵּן כָּל־
חָלוּץ לַמִּלְחָמָה לִפְנֵי יהוה וְנִכְבְּשָׁה הָאָרֶץ לִפְנֵיכֶם וּנְתַתֶּם
לָהֶם אֶת־אֶרֶץ הַגִּלְעָד לַאֲחֻזָּה: וְאִם־לֹא יַעַבְרוּ חֲלוּצִים אִתְּכֶם ל
וְנֹאחֲזוּ בְתֹכְכֶם בְּאֶרֶץ כְּנָעַן: וַיַּעֲנוּ בְנֵי־גָד וּבְנֵי רְאוּבֵן לֵאמֹר לא
אֵת אֲשֶׁר דִּבֶּר יהוה אֶל־עֲבָדֶיךָ כֵּן נַעֲשֶׂה: נַחְנוּ נַעֲבֹר חֲלוּצִים לב
לִפְנֵי יהוה אֶרֶץ כְּנָעַן וְאִתָּנוּ אֲחֻזַּת נַחֲלָתֵנוּ מֵעֵבֶר לַיַּרְדֵּן:
וַיִּתֵּן לָהֶם ׀ מֹשֶׁה לִבְנֵי־גָד וְלִבְנֵי רְאוּבֵן וְלַחֲצִי ׀ שֵׁבֶט ׀ מְנַשֶּׁה לג
בֶן־יוֹסֵף אֶת־מַמְלֶכֶת סִיחֹן מֶלֶךְ הָאֱמֹרִי וְאֶת־מַמְלֶכֶת עוֹג
מֶלֶךְ הַבָּשָׁן הָאָרֶץ לְעָרֶיהָ בִּגְבֻלֹת עָרֵי הָאָרֶץ סָבִיב: וַיִּבְנוּ לד
בְנֵי־גָד אֶת־דִּיבֹן וְאֶת־עֲטָרֹת וְאֵת עֲרֹעֵר: וְאֶת־עַטְרֹת שׁוֹפָן לה
וְאֶת־יַעְזֵר וְיָגְבֳּהָה: וְאֶת־בֵּית נִמְרָה וְאֶת־בֵּית הָרָן עָרֵי מִבְצָר לו
וְגִדְרֹת צֹאן: וּבְנֵי רְאוּבֵן בָּנוּ אֶת־חֶשְׁבּוֹן וְאֶת־אֶלְעָלֵא וְאֵת לז
קִרְיָתָיִם: וְאֶת־נְבוֹ וְאֶת־בַּעַל מְעוֹן מוּסַבֹּת שֵׁם וְאֶת־שִׂבְמָה לח

כח | וַיְצַו לָהֶם. כְּמוֹ 'עֲלֵיהֶם', וְעַל תְּנָאָם מִנָּה אֶלְעָזָר וִיהוֹשֻׁעַ, כְּמוֹ: "ה' יִלָּחֵם לָכֶם" (שמות יד, יד):

לב | וְאִתָּנוּ אֲחֻזַּת נַחֲלָתֵנוּ. כְּלוֹמַר, בְּיָדֵנוּ וּבִרְשׁוּתֵנוּ תְּהִי מָחֻזַת נַחֲלָתֵנוּ מֵעֵבֶר הַזֶּה:

לו | עָרֵי מִבְצָר וְגִדְרֹת צֹאן. זֶה סוֹף פָּסוּק מוּסָב עַל תְּחִלַּת הָעִנְיָן, "וַיִּבְנוּ בְנֵי גָד" אֶת הֶעָרִים הַלָּלוּ לִהְיוֹת "עָרֵי מִבְצָר וְגִדְרֹת צֹאן":

לח | וְאֶת נְבוֹ וְאֶת בַּעַל מְעוֹן מוּסַבֹּת שֵׁם. נְבוֹ וּבַעַל מְעוֹן שְׁמוֹת עֲבוֹדָה זָרָה הֵם, וְהָיוּ הָאֱמוֹרִיִּים קוֹרִים עָרֵיהֶם עַל שֵׁם עֲבוֹדָה זָרָה שֶׁלָּהֶם, וּבְנֵי רְאוּבֵן הֵסֵבּוּ אֶת שְׁמָם לְשֵׁמוֹת אֲחֵרִים, וְזֶהוּ: "מוּסַבֹּת שֵׁם", נְבוֹ וּבַעַל מְעוֹן מוּסַבּוֹת לְשֵׁם אַחֵר: וְאֶת שִׂבְמָה. בָּנוּ שִׂבְמָה, וְהִיא שְׂבָם הָאֲמוּרָה לְמַעְלָה (פסוק ג):

במדבר | פרק לג | מסעי

לט וַיִּקְרְא֣וּ בְשֵׁמֹ֔ת אֶת־שְׁמ֖וֹת הֶעָרִ֣ים אֲשֶׁ֣ר בָּנ֑וּ: וַיֵּלְכ֣וּ בְּנֵ֣י מָכִ֣יר
מ בֶּן־מְנַשֶּׁ֛ה גִּלְעָ֖דָה וַֽיִּלְכְּדֻ֑הָ וַיּ֥וֹרֶשׁ אֶת־הָאֱמֹרִ֖י אֲשֶׁר־בָּֽהּ: וַיִּתֵּ֤ן מפטיר
מא מֹשֶׁה֙ אֶת־הַגִּלְעָ֔ד לְמָכִ֖יר בֶּן־מְנַשֶּׁ֑ה וַיֵּ֖שֶׁב בָּֽהּ: וְיָאִ֣יר בֶּן־מְנַשֶּׁ֗ה
מב הָלַ֛ךְ וַיִּלְכֹּ֖ד אֶת־חַוֹּתֵיהֶ֑ם וַיִּקְרָ֥א אֶתְהֶ֖ן חַוֹּ֥ת יָאִֽיר: וְנֹ֣בַח הָלַ֔ךְ
וַיִּלְכֹּ֥ד אֶת־קְנָ֖ת וְאֶת־בְּנֹתֶ֑יהָ וַיִּקְרָ֧א לָ֦ה נֹ֖בַח בִּשְׁמֽוֹ:

פרק לג

א אֵ֣לֶּה מַסְעֵ֣י בְנֵֽי־יִשְׂרָאֵ֗ל אֲשֶׁ֥ר יָצְא֛וּ מֵאֶ֥רֶץ מִצְרַ֖יִם לְצִבְאֹתָ֑ם ל מסעי
ב בְּיַד־מֹשֶׁ֥ה וְאַהֲרֹֽן: וַיִּכְתֹּ֨ב מֹשֶׁ֜ה אֶת־מוֹצָאֵיהֶ֛ם לְמַסְעֵיהֶ֖ם עַל־
ג פִּ֣י יהו֑ה וְאֵ֥לֶּה מַסְעֵיהֶ֖ם לְמוֹצָאֵיהֶֽם: וַיִּסְע֤וּ מֵֽרַעְמְסֵס֙ בַּחֹ֣דֶשׁ
הָרִאשׁ֔וֹן בַּחֲמִשָּׁ֥ה עָשָׂ֛ר י֖וֹם לַחֹ֣דֶשׁ הָרִאשׁ֑וֹן מִֽמָּחֳרַ֣ת הַפֶּ֗סַח
ד יָצְא֤וּ בְנֵֽי־יִשְׂרָאֵל֙ בְּיָ֣ד רָמָ֔ה לְעֵינֵ֖י כָּל־מִצְרָֽיִם: וּמִצְרַ֣יִם מְקַבְּרִ֗ים
אֵת֩ אֲשֶׁ֨ר הִכָּ֧ה יהו֛ה בָּהֶ֖ם כָּל־בְּכ֑וֹר וּבֵאלֹהֵיהֶ֕ם עָשָׂ֥ה יהו֖ה
ה שְׁפָטִֽים: וַיִּסְע֥וּ בְנֵֽי־יִשְׂרָאֵ֖ל מֵֽרַעְמְסֵ֑ס וַיַּחֲנ֖וּ בְּסֻכֹּֽת: וַיִּסְע֖וּ

לט) וַיּוֹרֶשׁ. כְּתַרְגוּמוֹ: "וְתָרֵיךְ", שֶׁתֵּיבַת 'רֵישׁ' מְשַׁמֶּשֶׁת שְׁתֵּי מַחְלוֹקוֹת: לְשׁוֹן יְרֻשָּׁה וּלְשׁוֹן הוֹרָשָׁה, שֶׁהוּא טֵרוּד וְתָרוּךְ:

מא) חַוֹּתֵיהֶם. כְּפַרְגְּנֵיהוֹן: "וַיִּקְרָא אֶתְהֶן חַוֹּת יָאִיר." לְפִי שֶׁלֹּא הָיוּ לוֹ בָּנִים קְרָאָם בִּשְׁמוֹ לְזִכָּרוֹן:

מב) וַיִּקְרָא לָה נֹבַח. "לָה" אֵינוֹ מַפִּיק ה"א, וְרָאִיתִי בִּיסוֹדוֹ שֶׁל רַבִּי מֹשֶׁה, לְפִי שֶׁלֹּא נִתְקַיֵּם לָהּ שֵׁם זֶה לְפִיכָךְ הוּא רָפֶה, שֶׁמַּשְׁמָעוּתוֹ מִדְרָשׁוֹ כְּמוֹ 'לֹא'. וְתָמַהְנִי, מַה יִּדְרֹשׁ בִּשְׁתֵּי תֵבוֹת הַדּוֹמוֹת לָהּ, "וַיֹּאמֶר לָה בֹּעַז" (רות ב, יד), "לִבְנוֹת לָה בָיִת" (זכריה ה, יא):

פרק לג

א) אֵלֶּה מַסְעֵי. לָמָּה נִכְתְּבוּ הַמַּסָּעוֹת הַלָּלוּ? לְהוֹדִיעַ חֲסָדָיו שֶׁל מָקוֹם, שֶׁאַף עַל פִּי שֶׁגָּזַר עֲלֵיהֶם לְטַלְטְלָם וְלַהֲנִיעָם בַּמִּדְבָּר, לֹא תֹאמַר שֶׁהָיוּ נָעִים וּמְטֻלְטָלִים מִמַּסָּע לְמַסָּע כָּל אַרְבָּעִים שָׁנָה וְלֹא הָיְתָה לָהֶם מְנוּחָה, שֶׁהֲרֵי אֵין כָּאן אֶלָּא אַרְבָּעִים וּשְׁתַּיִם מַסָּעוֹת, צֵא מֵהֶם אַרְבַּע עֶשְׂרֵה שֶׁכֻּלָּם הָיוּ בַּשָּׁנָה הָרִאשׁוֹנָה לִתְחִלָּתָם, שֶׁמַּשֶּׁנָּסְעוּ מֵרַעְמְסֵס עַד שֶׁבָּאוּ לְרִתְמָה, שֶׁמִּשָּׁם נִשְׁתַּלְּחוּ הַמְרַגְּלִים, שֶׁנֶּאֱמַר: "וְאַחַר נָסְעוּ הָעָם מֵחֲצֵרוֹת וְגוֹ'" (לעיל יב, טז), "שְׁלַח לְךָ אֲנָשִׁים וְגוֹ'" (שם יג, ב), וְכָאן הוּא אוֹמֵר: "וַיִּסְעוּ מֵחֲצֵרוֹת וַיַּחֲנוּ בְּרִתְמָה" (להלן פסוק יח), לָמַדְתָּ שֶׁהִיא בַּמִּדְבָּר פָּארָן. וְעוֹד הוֹצֵא מִשָּׁם שְׁמוֹנֶה מַסָּעוֹת, שֶׁהָיוּ לְאַחַר מִיתַת אַהֲרֹן, מֵהֹר הָהָר עַד עַרְבוֹת מוֹאָב בִּשְׁנַת הָאַרְבָּעִים, נִמְצָא שֶׁכָּל שְׁמוֹנֶה וּשְׁלֹשִׁים שָׁנָה לֹא נָסְעוּ אֶלָּא עֶשְׂרִים מַסָּעוֹת: זֶה מִיסוֹדוֹ שֶׁל רַבִּי מֹשֶׁה. וְרַבִּי תַּנְחוּמָא דָּרַשׁ בּוֹ דְּרָשָׁה אַחֶרֶת: מָשָׁל לְמֶלֶךְ שֶׁהָיָה בְּנוֹ חוֹלֶה וְהוֹלִיכוֹ לְמָקוֹם רָחוֹק לְרַפְּאוֹתוֹ. כֵּיוָן שֶׁהָיוּ חוֹזְרִין, הִתְחִיל אָבִיו מוֹנֶה כָּל הַמַּסָּעוֹת. אָמַר לוֹ: כָּאן יָשַׁנּוּ, כָּאן הוּקַרְנוּ, כָּאן חָשַׁשְׁתָּ אֶת רֹאשְׁךָ וְכוּ' (תנחומא ג):

מִסְכֹּת וַיַּחֲנוּ בְּאֵתָם אֲשֶׁר בִּקְצֵה הַמִּדְבָּר: וַיִּסְעוּ מֵאֵתָם וַיָּשָׁב ז
עַל־פִּי הַחִירֹת אֲשֶׁר עַל־פְּנֵי בַּעַל צְפוֹן וַיַּחֲנוּ לִפְנֵי מִגְדֹּל: וַיִּסְעוּ ח
מִפְּנֵי הַחִירֹת וַיַּעַבְרוּ בְתוֹךְ־הַיָּם הַמִּדְבָּרָה וַיֵּלְכוּ דֶּרֶךְ שְׁלֹשֶׁת
יָמִים בְּמִדְבַּר אֵתָם וַיַּחֲנוּ בְּמָרָה: וַיִּסְעוּ מִמָּרָה וַיָּבֹאוּ אֵילִמָה ט
וּבְאֵילִם שְׁתֵּים עֶשְׂרֵה עֵינֹת מַיִם וְשִׁבְעִים תְּמָרִים וַיַּחֲנוּ־שָׁם:
וַיִּסְעוּ מֵאֵילִם וַיַּחֲנוּ עַל־יַם־סוּף: וַיִּסְעוּ מִיַּם־סוּף וַיַּחֲנוּ בְּמִדְבַּר־ יא שני
סִין: וַיִּסְעוּ מִמִּדְבַּר־סִין וַיַּחֲנוּ בְּדָפְקָה: וַיִּסְעוּ מִדָּפְקָה וַיַּחֲנוּ יב יג
בְּאָלוּשׁ: וַיִּסְעוּ מֵאָלוּשׁ וַיַּחֲנוּ בִּרְפִידִם וְלֹא־הָיָה שָׁם מַיִם לָעָם יד
לִשְׁתּוֹת: וַיִּסְעוּ מֵרְפִידִם וַיַּחֲנוּ בְּמִדְבַּר סִינָי: וַיִּסְעוּ מִמִּדְבַּר סִינַי טו טז
וַיַּחֲנוּ בְּקִבְרֹת הַתַּאֲוָה: וַיִּסְעוּ מִקִּבְרֹת הַתַּאֲוָה וַיַּחֲנוּ בַּחֲצֵרֹת: יז
וַיִּסְעוּ מֵחֲצֵרֹת וַיַּחֲנוּ בְּרִתְמָה: וַיִּסְעוּ מֵרִתְמָה וַיַּחֲנוּ בְּרִמֹּן פָּרֶץ: יח יט
וַיִּסְעוּ מֵרִמֹּן פָּרֶץ וַיַּחֲנוּ בְּלִבְנָה: וַיִּסְעוּ מִלִּבְנָה וַיַּחֲנוּ בְּרִסָּה: כ כא
וַיִּסְעוּ מֵרִסָּה וַיַּחֲנוּ בִּקְהֵלָתָה: וַיִּסְעוּ מִקְּהֵלָתָה וַיַּחֲנוּ בְּהַר־ כב כג
שָׁפֶר: וַיִּסְעוּ מֵהַר־שָׁפֶר וַיַּחֲנוּ בַּחֲרָדָה: וַיִּסְעוּ מֵחֲרָדָה וַיַּחֲנוּ כד כה
בְּמַקְהֵלֹת: וַיִּסְעוּ מִמַּקְהֵלֹת וַיַּחֲנוּ בְּתָחַת: וַיִּסְעוּ מִתָּחַת וַיַּחֲנוּ כו כז
בְּתָרַח: וַיִּסְעוּ מִתָּרַח וַיַּחֲנוּ בְּמִתְקָה: וַיִּסְעוּ מִמִּתְקָה וַיַּחֲנוּ כח כט
בְּחַשְׁמֹנָה: וַיִּסְעוּ מֵחַשְׁמֹנָה וַיַּחֲנוּ בְּמֹסֵרוֹת: וַיִּסְעוּ מִמֹּסֵרוֹת ל לא
וַיַּחֲנוּ בִּבְנֵי יַעֲקָן: וַיִּסְעוּ מִבְּנֵי יַעֲקָן וַיַּחֲנוּ בְּחֹר הַגִּדְגָּד: וַיִּסְעוּ לב לג
מֵחֹר הַגִּדְגָּד וַיַּחֲנוּ בְּיָטְבָתָה: וַיִּסְעוּ מִיָּטְבָתָה וַיַּחֲנוּ בְּעַבְרֹנָה: לד
וַיִּסְעוּ מֵעַבְרֹנָה וַיַּחֲנוּ בְּעֶצְיֹן גָּבֶר: וַיִּסְעוּ מֵעֶצְיֹן גֶּבֶר וַיַּחֲנוּ לה

יח| וַיַּחֲנוּ בְּרִתְמָה. עַל שֵׁם לָשׁוֹן הָרַע שֶׁל מְרַגְּלִים, שֶׁנֶּאֱמַר: "מַה יִּתֵּן לְךָ וּמַה יֹּסִיף לָךְ לָשׁוֹן רְמִיָּה, חִצֵּי גִבּוֹר שְׁנוּנִים עִם גַּחֲלֵי רְתָמִים" (תהלים ק״כ, ג-ד):

לז בְּמִדְבַּר־צִן הִוא קָדֵשׁ: וַיִּסְעוּ מִקָּדֵשׁ וַיַּחֲנוּ בְּהֹר הָהָר בִּקְצֵה
לח אֶרֶץ אֱדוֹם: וַיַּעַל אַהֲרֹן הַכֹּהֵן אֶל־הֹר הָהָר עַל־פִּי יהוה וַיָּמָת שָׁם בִּשְׁנַת הָאַרְבָּעִים לְצֵאת בְּנֵי־יִשְׂרָאֵל מֵאֶרֶץ מִצְרַיִם בַּחֹדֶשׁ
לט הַחֲמִישִׁי בְּאֶחָד לַחֹדֶשׁ: וְאַהֲרֹן בֶּן־שָׁלֹשׁ וְעֶשְׂרִים וּמְאַת
מ שָׁנָה בְּמֹתוֹ בְּהֹר הָהָר: וַיִּשְׁמַע הַכְּנַעֲנִי מֶלֶךְ עֲרָד
מא וְהוּא־יֹשֵׁב בַּנֶּגֶב בְּאֶרֶץ כְּנָעַן בְּבֹא בְּנֵי יִשְׂרָאֵל: וַיִּסְעוּ מֵהֹר
מב הָהָר וַיַּחֲנוּ בְּצַלְמֹנָה: וַיִּסְעוּ מִצַּלְמֹנָה וַיַּחֲנוּ בְּפוּנֹן: וַיִּסְעוּ מִפּוּנֹן
מג וַיַּחֲנוּ בְּאֹבֹת: וַיִּסְעוּ מֵאֹבֹת וַיַּחֲנוּ בְּעִיֵּי הָעֲבָרִים בִּגְבוּל מוֹאָב:
מד וַיִּסְעוּ מֵעִיִּים וַיַּחֲנוּ בְּדִיבֹן גָּד: וַיִּסְעוּ מִדִּיבֹן גָּד וַיַּחֲנוּ בְּעַלְמֹן
מה דִּבְלָתָיְמָה: וַיִּסְעוּ מֵעַלְמֹן דִּבְלָתָיְמָה וַיַּחֲנוּ בְּהָרֵי הָעֲבָרִים לִפְנֵי
מז נְבוֹ: וַיִּסְעוּ מֵהָרֵי הָעֲבָרִים וַיַּחֲנוּ בְּעַרְבֹת מוֹאָב עַל יַרְדֵּן יְרֵחוֹ:
מח וַיַּחֲנוּ עַל־הַיַּרְדֵּן מִבֵּית הַיְשִׁמֹת עַד אָבֵל הַשִּׁטִּים בְּעַרְבֹת
מט מוֹאָב: וַיְדַבֵּר יהוה אֶל־מֹשֶׁה בְּעַרְבֹת מוֹאָב עַל־
נ יַרְדֵּן יְרֵחוֹ לֵאמֹר: דַּבֵּר אֶל־בְּנֵי יִשְׂרָאֵל וְאָמַרְתָּ אֲלֵהֶם כִּי אַתֶּם
נא עֹבְרִים אֶת־הַיַּרְדֵּן אֶל־אֶרֶץ כְּנָעַן: וְהוֹרַשְׁתֶּם אֶת־כָּל־יֹשְׁבֵי

שלישי/
חמישי/

לח) **עַל פִּי ה׳.** מְלַמֵּד שֶׁמֵּת בִּנְשִׁיקָה:

מ) **וַיִּשְׁמַע הַכְּנַעֲנִי.** לְלַמֶּדְךָ שֶׁמִּיתַת אַהֲרֹן הִיא הַשְּׁמוּעָה, שֶׁנִּסְתַּלְּקוּ עַנְנֵי כָבוֹד, וּכְסָבוּר שֶׁנִּתְּנָה רְשׁוּת לְהִלָּחֵם בְּיִשְׂרָאֵל, לְפִיכָךְ חָזַר וּכְתָבָהּ:

מד) **בְּעִיֵּי הָעֲבָרִים.** לְשׁוֹן חֳרָבוֹת וְגַלִּים, כְּמוֹ: ״לְעִי הַשָּׂדֶה״ (מיכה א, ו), ״שָׂמוּ אֶת יְרוּשָׁלַ͏ִם לְעִיִּים״ (תהלים עט, א):

מט) **מִבֵּית הַיְשִׁמֹת עַד אָבֵל הַשִּׁטִּים.** כָּאן לִמֶּדְךָ שִׁעוּר מַחֲנֵה יִשְׂרָאֵל שְׁנֵים עָשָׂר מִיל, דְּאָמַר רַבָּה בַּר בַּר חָנָה: לְדִידִי חֲזִי לִי הַהוּא אַתְרָא וְכוּ׳. **אָבֵל הַשִּׁטִּים.** מִישׁוֹר שֶׁל שִׁטִּים ״אָבֵל״ שְׁמוֹ:

נא-נב) **כִּי אַתֶּם עֹבְרִים אֶת הַיַּרְדֵּן וְגוֹ׳. וְהוֹרַשְׁתֶּם וְגוֹ׳.** וַהֲלֹא כַמָּה פְעָמִים הֻזְהֲרוּ עַל כָּךְ! אֶלָּא כָּךְ אָמַר לָהֶם מֹשֶׁה: כְּשֶׁאַתֶּם עוֹבְרִים בַּיַּרְדֵּן בַּיַּבָּשָׁה, עַל מְנָת כֵּן תַּעַבְרוּ, וְאִם לָאו, בָּאִים מַיִם וְשׁוֹטְפִין אֶתְכֶם. וְכֵן מָצִינוּ שֶׁאָמַר לָהֶם יְהוֹשֻׁעַ עוֹדָם בַּיַּרְדֵּן (יהושע ד, י). בְּמַסֶּכֶת סוֹטָה (לב ע״א) וּבְתוֹסֶפְתָּא דְּסוֹטָה (ח, ה):

נב) **וְהוֹרַשְׁתֶּם. וְגֵרַשְׁתֶּם. מַשְׂכִּיֹּתָם.** כְּתַרְגּוּמוֹ: ״בֵּית סִגְדָּתְהוֹן״, עַל שֵׁם שֶׁהָיוּ מְסוֹכְכִין אֶת הַקַּרְקַע בְּרִצְפַת אֲבָנִים שֶׁל שַׁיִשׁ לְהִשְׁתַּחֲווֹת עֲלֵיהֶם בְּפִשּׁוּט יָדַיִם וְרַגְלַיִם, כְּדִכְתִיב: ״וְאֶבֶן מַשְׂכִּית... לְהִשְׁתַּחֲוֹת עָלֶיהָ״ (ויקרא כו, א): **מַסֵּכֹתָם.** כְּתַרְגּוּמוֹ: ״מַתְּכָתְהוֹן״:

הָאָ֖רֶץ מִפְּנֵיכֶ֑ם וְאִבַּדְתֶּ֗ם אֵ֚ת כָּל־מַשְׂכִּיֹּתָ֔ם וְאֵ֨ת כָּל־צַלְמֵ֤י מַסֵּֽכֹתָם֙ תְּאַבֵּ֔דוּ וְאֵ֥ת כָּל־בָּמוֹתָ֖ם תַּשְׁמִֽידוּ: וְהוֹרַשְׁתֶּ֥ם אֶת־ נג הָאָ֖רֶץ וִֽישַׁבְתֶּם־בָּ֑הּ כִּ֥י לָכֶ֛ם נָתַ֥תִּי אֶת־הָאָ֖רֶץ לָרֶ֥שֶׁת אֹתָֽהּ: וְהִתְנַחַלְתֶּם֩ אֶת־הָאָ֨רֶץ בְּגוֹרָ֜ל לְמִשְׁפְּחֹֽתֵיכֶ֗ם לָרַ֞ב תַּרְבּ֤וּ אֶת־ נד נַחֲלָתוֹ֙ וְלַמְעַט֙ תַּמְעִ֣יט אֶת־נַחֲלָת֔וֹ אֶל֩ אֲשֶׁר־יֵ֨צֵא ל֥וֹ שָׁ֛מָּה הַגּוֹרָ֖ל ל֣וֹ יִהְיֶ֑ה לְמַטּ֥וֹת אֲבֹתֵיכֶ֖ם תִּתְנֶחָֽלוּ: וְאִם־לֹ֨א תוֹרִ֜ישׁוּ נה אֶת־יֹשְׁבֵ֣י הָאָרֶץ֮ מִפְּנֵיכֶם֒ וְהָיָה֙ אֲשֶׁ֣ר תּוֹתִ֣ירוּ מֵהֶ֔ם לְשִׂכִּים֙ בְּעֵ֣ינֵיכֶ֔ם וְלִצְנִינִ֖ם בְּצִדֵּיכֶ֑ם וְצָרֲר֣וּ אֶתְכֶ֔ם עַל־הָאָ֕רֶץ אֲשֶׁ֥ר אַתֶּ֖ם יֹשְׁבִ֥ים בָּֽהּ: וְהָיָ֗ה כַּאֲשֶׁ֥ר דִּמִּ֛יתִי לַעֲשׂ֥וֹת לָהֶ֖ם אֶֽעֱשֶׂ֥ה נו לָכֶֽם:

וַיְדַבֵּ֥ר יְהֹוָ֖ה אֶל־מֹשֶׁ֥ה לֵּאמֹֽר: צַ֞ו אֶת־בְּנֵ֤י יִשְׂרָאֵל֙ וְאָמַרְתָּ֣ לא לד אֲלֵהֶ֔ם כִּֽי־אַתֶּ֥ם בָּאִ֖ים אֶל־הָאָ֣רֶץ כְּנָ֑עַן זֹ֣את הָאָ֗רֶץ אֲשֶׁ֨ר תִּפֹּ֤ל לָכֶם֙ בְּנַחֲלָ֔ה אֶ֥רֶץ כְּנַ֖עַן לִגְבֻלֹתֶֽיהָ: וְהָיָ֨ה לָכֶ֧ם פְּאַת־נֶ֛גֶב ג

נג. **וְהוֹרַשְׁתֶּם אֶת הָאָרֶץ.** וְהוֹרַשְׁתֶּם אוֹתָהּ מִיּוֹשְׁבֶיהָ, וְאָז "וִישַׁבְתֶּם בָּהּ" – תּוּכְלוּ לְהִתְקַיֵּם בָּהּ, וְאִם לָאו – לֹא תוּכְלוּ לְהִתְקַיֵּם בָּהּ:

נד. **אֶל אֲשֶׁר יֵצֵא לוֹ שָׁמָּה.** מִקְרָא קָצָר הוּא זֶה, אֶל מָקוֹם אֲשֶׁר יֵצֵא לוֹ שָׁמָּה הַגּוֹרָל לוֹ יִהְיֶה: **לְמַטּוֹת אֲבֹתֵיכֶם.** לְפִי חֶשְׁבּוֹן יוֹצְאֵי מִצְרַיִם. דָּבָר אַחֵר, בִּשְׁנֵים עָשָׂר גְּבוּלִין כְּמִנְיַן הַשְּׁבָטִים:

נה. **וְהָיָה אֲשֶׁר תּוֹתִירוּ מֵהֶם.** יִהְיוּ לָכֶם לְרָעָה: **לְשִׂכִּים בְּעֵינֵיכֶם.** לִיתֵדוֹת הַמְנַקְּרוֹת עֵינֵיכֶם. תַּרְגּוּם שֶׁל יְתֵדוֹת: "סִכַּיָּא": **וְלִצְנִינִם.** פּוֹתְרִים בּוֹ הַפּוֹתְרִים לְשׁוֹן מְשׂוּכַת קוֹצִים הַסּוֹכֶכֶת אֶתְכֶם, לִסְגֹּר וְלִכְלֹא אֶתְכֶם מֵאֵין יוֹצֵא וָבָא: **וְצָרֲרוּ אֶתְכֶם.** כְּתַרְגּוּמוֹ:

פרק לד

ב. **זֹאת הָאָרֶץ אֲשֶׁר תִּפֹּל לָכֶם וְגוֹ'.** לְפִי שֶׁהַרְבֵּה מִצְוֹת נוֹהֲגוֹת בָּאָרֶץ וְאֵין נוֹהֲגוֹת בְּחוּצָה לָאָרֶץ, הֻצְרַךְ לִכְתֹּב מַצְרָנֵי גְבוּלֶיהָ סָבִיב, לוֹמַר לְךָ מִן הַגְּבוּלִים הַלָּלוּ וְלִפְנִים הַמִּצְוֹת נוֹהֲגוֹת: **תִּפֹּל לָכֶם.** עַל שֵׁם שֶׁנֶּחְלְקָה בְגוֹרָל נִקְרֵאת חֲלֻקָּה לְשׁוֹן נְפִילָה. וּמִדְרַשׁ אַגָּדָה אוֹמֵר: עַל יְדֵי שֶׁהִפִּיל הַקָּדוֹשׁ בָּרוּךְ הוּא שָׂרֵיהֶם שֶׁל שִׁבְעָה אֻמּוֹת מִן הַשָּׁמַיִם וּכְפָתָן לִפְנֵי מֹשֶׁה, אָמַר לוֹ: רְאֵה אֵין בָּהֶם עוֹד כֹּחַ:

ג. **וְהָיָה לָכֶם פְּאַת נֶגֶב.** רוּחַ דְּרוֹמִית אֲשֶׁר מִן הַמִּזְרָח לַמַּעֲרָב: **מִמִּדְבַּר צִן.** אֲשֶׁר אֵצֶל אֱדוֹם, מַתְחִיל מִקְצוֹעַ דְּרוֹמִית מִזְרָחִית שֶׁל אֶרֶץ תִּשְׁעַת הַמַּטּוֹת. כֵּיצַד? שָׁלֹשׁ אֲרָצוֹת יוֹשְׁבוֹת בִּדְרוֹמָהּ שֶׁל אֶרֶץ יִשְׂרָאֵל זוֹ אֵצֶל זוֹ: קְצָת אֶרֶץ מִצְרַיִם, וְאֶרֶץ אֱדוֹם כֻּלָּהּ, וְאֶרֶץ מוֹאָב כֻּלָּהּ. אֶרֶץ מִצְרַיִם בְּמִקְצוֹעַ דְּרוֹמִית מַעֲרָבִית, שֶׁנֶּאֱמַר בְּפָרָשָׁה זוֹ: "מֵעַצְמוֹן נַחְלָה מִצְרַיִם וְהָיוּ תוֹצְאֹתָיו הַיָּמָּה" (להלן פסוק ה),

מִמִּדְבַּר־צִן עַל־יְדֵי אֱדוֹם וְהָיָה לָכֶם גְּבוּל נֶגֶב מִקְצֵה יָם־הַמֶּלַח
קֵדְמָה: וְנָסַב לָכֶם הַגְּבוּל מִנֶּגֶב לְמַעֲלֵה עַקְרַבִּים וְעָבַר צִנָה
וְהָיָה תּוֹצְאֹתָיו מִנֶּגֶב לְקָדֵשׁ בַּרְנֵעַ וְיָצָא חֲצַר־אַדָּר וְעָבַר
עַצְמֹנָה: וְנָסַב הַגְּבוּל מֵעַצְמוֹן נַחְלָה מִצְרַיִם וְהָיוּ תוֹצְאֹתָיו
הַיָּמָּה: וּגְבוּל יָם וְהָיָה לָכֶם הַיָּם הַגָּדוֹל וּגְבוּל זֶה־יִהְיֶה לָכֶם
גְּבוּל יָם: וְזֶה־יִהְיֶה לָכֶם גְּבוּל צָפוֹן מִן־הַיָּם הַגָּדֹל תְּתָאוּ לָכֶם

וְנַחַל מִצְרַיִם הָיָה מְהַלֵּךְ עַל פְּנֵי כָּל חֹרַן מִצְרַיִם, שֶׁנֶּאֱמַר: "מִן הַשִּׁיחוֹר אֲשֶׁר עַל פְּנֵי מִצְרַיִם" (יהושע יג, ג), וּמַפְסִיק בֵּין אֶרֶץ מִצְרַיִם לְאֶרֶץ יִשְׂרָאֵל. וְאֶרֶץ אֱדוֹם מֻנַּחַת לְצַד הַמִּזְרָח, וְאֶרֶץ מוֹאָב אֵצֶל אֶרֶץ אֱדוֹם, בְּסוֹף הַדָּרוֹם לַמִּזְרָח. וּכְשֶׁיָּצְאוּ יִשְׂרָאֵל מִמִּצְרַיִם, אִם רָצָה הַמָּקוֹם לְקָרֵב אֶת כְּנִיסָתָם לָאָרֶץ, הָיָה מַעֲבִירָם אֶת הַנִּילוּס לְצַד צָפוֹן וּבָאִין לְאֶרֶץ יִשְׂרָאֵל, וְלֹא עָשָׂה כֵן, וְזֶהוּ שֶׁנֶּאֱמַר: "וְלֹא נָחָם אֱלֹהִים דֶּרֶךְ אֶרֶץ פְּלִשְׁתִּים" (שמות יג, יז) שֶׁהֵם יוֹשְׁבִים עַל הַיָּם בְּמַעֲרָבָה שֶׁל אֶרֶץ כְּנַעַן, כָּעִנְיָן שֶׁנֶּאֱמַר בַּפְּלִשְׁתִּים: "יוֹשְׁבֵי חֶבֶל הַיָּם גּוֹי כְּרֵתִים" (צפניה ב, ה), וְלֹא נָחָם אוֹתָם הַדֶּרֶךְ, אֶלָּא הַסֵּבָן וְהוֹצִיאָם דֶּרֶךְ דְּרוֹמָה אֶל הַמִּדְבָּר, וְהוּא שֶׁקְּרָאוֹ יְחֶזְקֵאל "מִדְבַּר הָעַמִּים" (יחזקאל כ, לה) לְפִי שֶׁהָיוּ כַּמָּה אֻמּוֹת יוֹשְׁבִים בְּצִדּוֹ. וְהוֹלִיכָן אֵצֶל דְּרוֹמָה מִן הַמַּעֲרָב כְּלַפֵּי מִזְרָח תָּמִיד, עַד שֶׁבָּאוּ לִדְרוֹמָה שֶׁל אֶרֶץ אֱדוֹם, וּבִקְּשׁוּ מִמֶּלֶךְ אֱדוֹם שֶׁיַּנִּיחֵם לַעֲבֹר דֶּרֶךְ אַרְצוֹ וּלְהִכָּנֵס לָאָרֶץ דֶּרֶךְ רָחְבָּהּ, וְלֹא רָצָה, וְהֻצְרְכוּ לִסְבֹּב אֶת כָּל דְּרוֹמָה שֶׁל אֱדוֹם עַד בּוֹאָם לִדְרוֹמָה שֶׁל אֶרֶץ מוֹאָב, שֶׁנֶּאֱמַר: "וְגַם אֶל מֶלֶךְ מוֹאָב שָׁלַח וְלֹא אָבָה" (שופטים יא, יז), וְהָלְכוּ כָּל דְּרוֹמָהּ שֶׁל מוֹאָב עַד סוֹפָהּ, וּמִשָּׁם הָפְכוּ פְּנֵיהֶם לַצָּפוֹן עַד שֶׁסָּבְבוּ כָּל מֶצֶר מִזְרָחִי שֶׁלָּהּ לְרָחְבָּהּ, וּכְשֶׁכִּלּוּ אֶת מִזְרָחָהּ מָצְאוּ אֶת אֶרֶץ סִיחוֹן וְעוֹג שֶׁהָיוּ יוֹשְׁבִין בְּמִזְרָחָהּ שֶׁל אֶרֶץ כְּנַעַן, וְהַיַּרְדֵּן מַפְסִיק בֵּינֵיהֶם, וְזֶהוּ שֶׁנֶּאֱמַר: "וַיֵּלֶךְ בַּמִּדְבָּר וַיָּסָב אֶת אֶרֶץ אֱדוֹם וְאֶת אֶרֶץ מוֹאָב וַיָּבֹא מִמִּזְרַח שֶׁמֶשׁ לְאֶרֶץ מוֹאָב" (שם פסוק יח), וְכָבְשׁוּ אֶת אֶרֶץ סִיחוֹן וְעוֹג שֶׁהָיְתָה בִּצְפוֹנָהּ שֶׁל אֶרֶץ מוֹאָב, וְקָרְבוּ עַד הַיַּרְדֵּן, וְהוּא כְּנֶגֶד מִקְצוֹעַ צְפוֹנִית מַעֲרָבִית שֶׁל אֶרֶץ

מוֹאָב. נִמְצָא שֶׁאֶרֶץ כְּנַעַן שֶׁבְּעֵבֶר הַיַּרְדֵּן לַמַּעֲרָב, הָיָה מִקְצוֹעַ דְּרוֹמִית מִזְרָחִית שֶׁלָּהּ אֵצֶל אֱדוֹם:

וְנָסַב לָכֶם הַגְּבוּל מִנֶּגֶב לְמַעֲלֵה עַקְרַבִּים. כָּל מָקוֹם שֶׁנֶּאֱמַר: 'וְנָסַב' אוֹ 'וְיָצָא', מְלַמֵּד שֶׁלֹּא הָיָה הַמֶּצֶר שָׁוֶה, אֶלָּא הוֹלֵךְ וְיוֹצֵא לַחוּץ, יוֹצֵא הַמֶּצֶר וְעוֹקֵם לְצַד צְפוֹנוֹ שֶׁל עוֹלָם בַּאֲלַכְסוֹן לַמַּעֲרָב, וְעוֹבֵר הַמֶּצֶר בִּדְרוֹמָהּ שֶׁל מַעֲלֵה עַקְרַבִּים, נִמְצָא מַעֲלֵה עַקְרַבִּים לִפְנִים מִן הַמֶּצֶר. **וְעָבַר צִנָה.** אֵל צִן, כְּמוֹ: 'מִצְרַיְמָה'. **וְהָיוּ תוֹצְאֹתָיו.** קְצוֹתָיו, בִּדְרוֹמָהּ שֶׁל קָדֵשׁ בַּרְנֵעַ: **וְיָצָא חֲצַר אַדָּר.** מִתְפַּשֵּׁט הַמֶּצֶר מַרְחִיב לְצַד צָפוֹן, וְנִמְשָׁךְ עוֹד בַּאֲלַכְסוֹנוֹ לַמַּעֲרָב, וּבָא לוֹ לַחֲצַר אַדָּר וּמִשָּׁם לְעַצְמוֹן וּמִשָּׁם לְנַחַל מִצְרַיִם. וּלְשׁוֹן 'וְנָסַב הַגְּבוּל' כָּאן, לְפִי שֶׁכָּתַב: "וְיָצָא חֲצַר אַדָּר", שֶׁהִתְחִיל לְהַרְחִיב מֵעֵבֶר אֶת קָדֵשׁ בַּרְנֵעַ, וְרֹחַב אוֹתָהּ רְצוּעָה שֶׁבָּלְטָה לְצַד צָפוֹן הָיְתָה מִקָּדֵשׁ עַד עַצְמוֹן, וּמִשָּׁם וְהָלְאָה נִתְקַצֵּר הַמֶּצֶר וְנָסַב לְצַד הַדָּרוֹם וּבָא לוֹ לְנַחַל מִצְרַיִם, וּמִשָּׁם לְצַד הַמַּעֲרָב אֶל הַיָּם הַגָּדוֹל, שֶׁהוּא מֶצֶר מַעֲרָבָהּ שֶׁל כָּל אֶרֶץ יִשְׂרָאֵל, נִמְצָא שֶׁנַּחַל מִצְרַיִם בְּמִקְצוֹעַ מַעֲרָבִית דְּרוֹמִית:

ה) וְהָיוּ תוֹצְאֹתָיו הַיָּמָּה. אֶל מֶצֶר הַמַּעֲרָב, שֶׁאֵין עוֹד גְּבוּל נֶגֶב מַאֲרִיךְ לְצַד הַמַּעֲרָב מִשָּׁם וְהָלְאָה:

ו) וּגְבוּל יָם. וּמֶצֶר מַעֲרָבִי מַהוּ? **וְהָיָה לָכֶם הַיָּם הַגָּדוֹל.** לִמֶצֶר. **וּגְבוּל.** הַנִּסִּין שֶׁבְּתוֹךְ הַיָּם אַף הֵם מִן הַגְּבוּל, וְהֵם אִיִּים שֶׁקּוֹרִין אישל"ש:

ז) וּגְבוּל צָפוֹן. מֶצֶר צָפוֹן: **מִן הַיָּם הַגָּדֹל תְּתָאוּ לָכֶם הֹר הָהָר.** שֶׁהוּא בְּמִקְצוֹעַ צְפוֹנִית מַעֲרָבִית,

פרק לד | במדבר   מסעי | 464

ח הֹר הָהָר: מֵהֹר הָהָר תְּתָאוּ לְבֹא חֲמָת וְהָיוּ תּוֹצְאֹת הַגְּבֻל
ט צְדָדָה: וְיָצָא הַגְּבֻל זִפְרֹנָה וְהָיוּ תוֹצְאֹתָיו חֲצַר עֵינָן זֶה־יִהְיֶה
י לָכֶם גְּבוּל צָפוֹן: וְהִתְאַוִּיתֶם לָכֶם לִגְבוּל קֵדְמָה מֵחֲצַר עֵינָן
יא שְׁפָמָה: וְיָרַד הַגְּבֻל מִשְּׁפָם הָרִבְלָה מִקֶּדֶם לָעָיִן וְיָרַד הַגְּבֻל
יב וּמָחָה עַל־כֶּתֶף יָם־כִּנֶּרֶת קֵדְמָה: וְיָרַד הַגְּבוּל הַיַּרְדֵּנָה וְהָיוּ
תוֹצְאֹתָיו יָם הַמֶּלַח זֹאת תִּהְיֶה לָכֶם הָאָרֶץ לִגְבֻלֹתֶיהָ סָבִיב:
יג וַיְצַו מֹשֶׁה אֶת־בְּנֵי יִשְׂרָאֵל לֵאמֹר זֹאת הָאָרֶץ אֲשֶׁר תִּתְנַחֲלוּ
אֹתָהּ בְּגוֹרָל אֲשֶׁר צִוָּה יְהוָה לָתֵת לְתִשְׁעַת הַמַּטּוֹת וַחֲצִי
יד הַמַּטֶּה: כִּי לָקְחוּ מַטֵּה בְנֵי הָראוּבֵנִי לְבֵית אֲבֹתָם וּמַטֵּה
בְנֵי־הַגָּדִי לְבֵית אֲבֹתָם וַחֲצִי מַטֵּה מְנַשֶּׁה לָקְחוּ נַחֲלָתָם: שְׁנֵי
טו הַמַּטּוֹת וַחֲצִי הַמַּטֶּה לָקְחוּ נַחֲלָתָם מֵעֵבֶר לְיַרְדֵּן יְרֵחוֹ קֵדְמָה
מִזְרָחָה:

וְרָחֲבוֹ מַשְׁפִּיעַ וְנִכְנָס לְתוֹךְ הַיָּם, וְיֵשׁ מֵחֲלַב הַיָּם לְפָנִים הֵימֶנּוּ וְחוּצָה הֵימֶנּוּ. תְּתָאוּ. תַּשְׁפִּיעוּ לָכֶם לִנְטוֹת מִמַּעֲרָב לְצָפוֹן אֶל הֹר הָהָר: תְּתָאוּ. לְשׁוֹן סִבָּה, כְּמוֹ: "אֶל תָּו הָרָאשִׁים" (דברי הימים א' כ, יז), "וְתָאֵי הַשַּׁעַר" (יחזקאל מ, י), הַיָּצִיעַ שֶׁקּוֹרִין אפנדי"ץ, שֶׁהוּא מוּסָב וּמֻשְׁפָּע:

ח מֵהֹר הָהָר. תָּסֹבּוּ וְתֵלְכוּ אֶל מֵצֶר הַצָּפוֹן לְצַד הַמִּזְרָח, וְתִפְגְּעוּ בִּ"לְבֹא חֲמָת", זוֹ אַנְטוֹכְיָא: תּוֹצְאֹת הַגְּבֻל. סוֹפֵי הַגְּבוּל. כָּל מָקוֹם שֶׁנֶּאֱמַר 'תּוֹצְאוֹת הַגְּבוּל', אוֹ הַמֵּצֶר כָּלֶה שָׁם לְגַמְרֵי וְאֵינוֹ עוֹבֵר לְהָלָן כְּלָל, אוֹ מִשָּׁם מִתְפַּשֵּׁט וּמַרְחִיב וְיוֹצֵא לַאֲחוֹרָיו לְהִמָּשֵׁךְ לְהָלָן בַּאֲלַכְסוֹן יוֹתֵר מִן הָרֹחַב הָרִאשׁוֹן, וּלְעִנְיַן לְחַב הַמִּדָּה הָרִאשׁוֹן קְרָאוֹ 'תּוֹצָאוֹת', שֶׁשָּׁם כָּלְתָה אוֹתָהּ מִדָּה:

ט-יב וְהָיוּ תוֹצְאֹתָיו חֲצַר עֵינָן. הוּא הָיָה סוֹף הַמֵּצֶר הַצְּפוֹנִי, וְנִמְצָא חֲצַר עֵינָן בְּמִקְצוֹעַ צְפוֹנִית מִזְרָחִית, וּמִשָּׁם "וְהִתְאַוִּיתֶם לָכֶם" אֶל מֵצֶר

הַמִּזְרָחִי: וְהִתְאַוִּיתֶם. לְשׁוֹן הֲסִבָּה וּנְטִיָּה, כְּמוֹ: "תִּתְאוּ": שְׁפָמָה. בַּמֵּצֶר הַמִּזְרָחִי, וּמִשָּׁם הָרִבְלָה מִקֶּדֶם לָעָיִן. שֵׁם מָקוֹם, וְהַמֵּצֶר הוֹלֵךְ בְּמִזְרָחוֹ, נִמְצָא הָעַיִן לְפָנִים מִן הַמֵּצֶר, וּמֵאַרְצָם שֶׁל יִשְׂרָאֵל הוּא: וְיָרַד הַגְּבֻל. כָּל שֶׁהַגְּבוּל הוֹלֵךְ מִצָּפוֹן לַדָּרוֹם, הוּא יוֹרֵד וְהוֹלֵךְ: וּמָחָה עַל כֶּתֶף יָם כִּנֶּרֶת קֵדְמָה. שֶׁיְּהֵא יָם כִּנֶּרֶת תּוֹךְ לַגְּבוּל בַּמַּעֲרָב, וְהַגְּבוּל בְּמִזְרַח יָם כִּנֶּרֶת, וּמִשָּׁם יוֹרֵד אֶל הַיַּרְדֵּן, וְהַיַּרְדֵּן מוֹשֵׁךְ וּבָא מִן הַצָּפוֹן לַדָּרוֹם בַּאֲלַכְסוֹן, נוֹטֶה לְצַד מִזְרָח, וּמִתְקָרֵב לְצַד אֶרֶץ כְּנַעַן כְּנֶגֶד יָם כִּנֶּרֶת, וּמוֹשֵׁךְ לְצַד מִזְרָחָהּ שֶׁל אֶרֶץ יִשְׂרָאֵל כְּנֶגֶד יָם כִּנֶּרֶת, עַד שֶׁנּוֹפֵל בְּיָם הַמֶּלַח, וּמִשָּׁם כָּלֶה הַגְּבוּל בְּתוֹצְאוֹתָיו אֶל יָם הַמֶּלַח, שֶׁמִּמֶּנּוּ הִתְחַלְתָּ מֵצֶר דְּרוֹמִית מִזְרָחִית, הֲרֵי סָבַבְתָּ אוֹתָהּ לְאַרְבַּע רוּחוֹתֶיהָ:

טו קֵדְמָה מִזְרָחָה. אֶל פְּנֵי הָעוֹלָם שֶׁהֵם בַּמִּזְרָח, שֶׁרוּחַ מִזְרָחִית קְרוּיָה פָּנִים וּמַעֲרָבִית קְרוּיָה אָחוֹר, לְפִיכָךְ דָּרוֹם לַיָּמִין וְצָפוֹן לַשְּׂמֹאל:

רביעי
/שישי/

טז וַיְדַבֵּ֥ר יְהוָ֖ה אֶל־מֹשֶׁ֥ה לֵּאמֹֽר: אֵ֚לֶּה שְׁמ֣וֹת הָֽאֲנָשִׁ֔ים אֲשֶׁר־
יז יִנְחֲל֥וּ לָכֶ֖ם אֶת־הָאָ֑רֶץ אֶלְעָזָר֙ הַכֹּהֵ֔ן וִיהוֹשֻׁ֖עַ בִּן־נֽוּן: וְנָשִׂ֥יא
יח אֶחָ֛ד נָשִׂ֥יא אֶחָ֖ד מִמַּטֶּ֑ה תִּקְח֖וּ לִנְחֹ֥ל אֶת־הָאָֽרֶץ: וְאֵ֖לֶּה שְׁמ֣וֹת
יט הָֽאֲנָשִׁ֑ים לְמַטֵּ֣ה יְהוּדָ֔ה כָּלֵ֖ב בֶּן־יְפֻנֶּֽה: וּלְמַטֵּה֙ בְּנֵ֣י שִׁמְע֔וֹן
כ שְׁמוּאֵ֖ל בֶּן־עַמִּיהֽוּד: לְמַטֵּ֣ה בִנְיָמִ֔ן אֱלִידָ֖ד בֶּן־כִּסְלֽוֹן: וּלְמַטֵּ֥ה
כא בְנֵי־דָ֖ן נָשִׂ֑יא בֻּקִּ֖י בֶּן־יָגְלִֽי: לִבְנֵ֣י יוֹסֵ֔ף לְמַטֵּ֥ה בְנֵֽי־מְנַשֶּׁ֖ה נָשִׂ֑יא
כב חַנִּיאֵ֖ל בֶּן־אֵפֹֽד: וּלְמַטֵּ֥ה בְנֵֽי־אֶפְרַ֖יִם נָשִׂ֑יא קְמוּאֵ֖ל בֶּן־שִׁפְטָֽן:
כג וּלְמַטֵּ֥ה בְנֵֽי־זְבוּלֻ֖ן נָשִׂ֑יא אֱלִיצָפָ֖ן בֶּן־פַּרְנָֽךְ: וּלְמַטֵּ֥ה בְנֵֽי־יִשָּׂשכָ֖ר
כד נָשִׂ֑יא פַּלְטִיאֵ֖ל בֶּן־עַזָּֽן: וּלְמַטֵּ֥ה בְנֵֽי־אָשֵׁ֖ר נָשִׂ֑יא אֲחִיה֖וּד בֶּן־
כה שְׁלֹמִֽי: וּלְמַטֵּ֥ה בְנֵֽי־נַפְתָּלִ֖י נָשִׂ֑יא פְּדַהְאֵ֖ל בֶּן־עַמִּיהֽוּד: אֵ֕לֶּה
כו אֲשֶׁ֥ר צִוָּ֖ה יְהוָ֑ה לְנַחֵ֛ל אֶת־בְּנֵֽי־יִשְׂרָאֵ֖ל בְּאֶ֥רֶץ כְּנָֽעַן:

חמישי

לה א וַיְדַבֵּ֧ר יְהוָ֛ה אֶל־מֹשֶׁ֖ה בְּעַֽרְבֹ֣ת מוֹאָ֑ב עַל־יַרְדֵּ֥ן יְרֵח֖וֹ לֵאמֹֽר:
ב צַו֮ אֶת־בְּנֵ֣י יִשְׂרָאֵל֒ וְנָֽתְנ֣וּ לַלְוִיִּ֗ם מִֽנַּחֲלַ֛ת אֲחֻזָּתָ֖ם עָרִ֣ים לָשָׁ֑בֶת
ג וּמִגְרָ֕שׁ לֶעָרִ֖ים סְבִיבֹֽתֵיהֶ֑ם תִּתְּנ֖וּ לַלְוִיִּֽם: וְהָי֧וּ הֶֽעָרִ֛ים לָהֶ֖ם
ד לָשָׁ֑בֶת וּמִגְרְשֵׁיהֶ֣ם יִהְי֔וּ לִבְהֶמְתָּ֖ם וְלִרְכֻשָׁ֖ם וּלְכֹ֥ל חַיָּתָֽם: וּמִגְרְשֵׁי֙ הֶֽעָרִ֔ים אֲשֶׁ֥ר תִּתְּנ֖וּ לַלְוִיִּ֑ם מִקִּ֤יר הָעִיר֙ וָח֔וּצָה אֶ֥לֶף

יז| אֲשֶׁר יִנְחֲלוּ לָכֶם. בִּשְׁבִילְכֶם. כָּל נָשִׂיא וְנָשִׂיא אַפּוֹטְרוֹפּוֹס לְשִׁבְטוֹ, וּמְחַלֵּק נַחֲלַת הַשֵּׁבֶט לַמִּשְׁפָּחוֹת וְלַגְּבָרִים, וּבוֹרֵר לְכָל אֶחָד וְאֶחָד חֵלֶק הָגוּן, וּמַה שֶּׁהֵם עוֹשִׂים יִהְיֶה כְּאִלּוּ עֲשָׂאוּם שְׁלוּחִים. וְלֹא יִתָּכֵן לְפָרֵשׁ 'לָכֶם' זֶה בִּכְלַל 'לָכֶם' שֶׁבְּמִקְרָא, שֶׁאִם כֵּן הָיָה לוֹ לִכְתֹּב: יַנְחִילוּ לָכֶם, 'יִנְחֲלוּ' מַשְׁמַע שֶׁהֵם נוֹחֲלִים לָכֶם בִּשְׁבִילְכֶם וּבִמְקוֹמְכֶם, כְּמוֹ: "ה' יִלָּחֵם לָכֶם" (שמות יד, יד):

יח| לִנְחֹל אֶת הָאָרֶץ. שֶׁיְּהֵא נוֹחֵל וְחוֹלֵק אוֹתָהּ בִּמְקוֹמְכֶם:

כז| לִנְחֹל אֶת בְּנֵי יִשְׂרָאֵל. שֶׁהֵם יַנְחִילוּ אוֹתָהּ לָהֶם לְמַחְלְקוֹתֶיהָ:

פרק לה

ב| וּמִגְרָשׁ. רֶוַח מָקוֹם חָלָק לָעִיר חוּץ לָעִיר סָבִיב לִהְיוֹת לְנוֹי לָעִיר, וְאֵין רַשָּׁאִין לִבְנוֹת שָׁם בַּיִת וְלֹא לִנְטֹעַ כֶּרֶם וְלֹא לִזְרֹעַ זְרִיעָה:

ג| וּלְכֹל חַיָּתָם. לְכָל צָרְכֵיהֶם:

ד| אֶלֶף אַמָּה סָבִיב. וְאַחֲרָיו הוּא אוֹמֵר: "אַלְפַּיִם בָּאַמָּה" (פסוק ה), הָא כֵּיצַד? אַלְפַּיִם הוּא נוֹתֵן לָהֶם

ה אַמָּה סָבִיב: וּמַדֹּתֶם מִחוּץ לָעִיר אֶת־פְּאַת־קֵדְמָה אַלְפַּיִם בָּאַמָּה וְאֶת־פְּאַת־נֶגֶב אַלְפַּיִם בָּאַמָּה וְאֶת־פְּאַת־יָם ׀ אַלְפַּיִם בָּאַמָּה וְאֵת פְּאַת צָפוֹן אַלְפַּיִם בָּאַמָּה וְהָעִיר בַּתָּוֶךְ זֶה יִהְיֶה לָהֶם מִגְרְשֵׁי הֶעָרִים: ו וְאֵת הֶעָרִים אֲשֶׁר תִּתְּנוּ לַלְוִיִּם אֵת שֵׁשׁ־עָרֵי הַמִּקְלָט אֲשֶׁר תִּתְּנוּ לָנֻס שָׁמָּה הָרֹצֵחַ וַעֲלֵיהֶם תִּתְּנוּ אַרְבָּעִים וּשְׁתַּיִם עִיר: ז כָּל־הֶעָרִים אֲשֶׁר תִּתְּנוּ לַלְוִיִּם אַרְבָּעִים וּשְׁמֹנֶה עִיר אֶתְהֶן וְאֶת־מִגְרְשֵׁיהֶן: ח וְהֶעָרִים אֲשֶׁר תִּתְּנוּ מֵאֲחֻזַּת בְּנֵי־יִשְׂרָאֵל מֵאֵת הָרַב תַּרְבּוּ וּמֵאֵת הַמְעַט תַּמְעִיטוּ אִישׁ כְּפִי נַחֲלָתוֹ אֲשֶׁר יִנְחָלוּ יִתֵּן מֵעָרָיו לַלְוִיִּם:

ששי לב /שביעי/

ט וַיְדַבֵּר יְהוָה אֶל־מֹשֶׁה לֵּאמֹר: דַּבֵּר אֶל־בְּנֵי יִשְׂרָאֵל וְאָמַרְתָּ אֲלֵהֶם כִּי אַתֶּם עֹבְרִים אֶת־הַיַּרְדֵּן אַרְצָה כְּנָעַן: יא וְהִקְרִיתֶם לָכֶם עָרִים עָרֵי מִקְלָט תִּהְיֶינָה לָכֶם וְנָס שָׁמָּה רֹצֵחַ מַכֵּה־נֶפֶשׁ בִּשְׁגָגָה: יב וְהָיוּ לָכֶם הֶעָרִים לְמִקְלָט מִגֹּאֵל וְלֹא יָמוּת הָרֹצֵחַ עַד־עָמְדוֹ לִפְנֵי הָעֵדָה לַמִּשְׁפָּט: יג וְהֶעָרִים אֲשֶׁר תִּתֵּנוּ שֵׁשׁ־עָרֵי מִקְלָט תִּהְיֶינָה לָכֶם: יד אֵת ׀ שְׁלֹשׁ הֶעָרִים תִּתְּנוּ מֵעֵבֶר לַיַּרְדֵּן וְאֵת שְׁלֹשׁ הֶעָרִים תִּתְּנוּ בְּאֶרֶץ כְּנָעַן עָרֵי מִקְלָט

סָבִיב, וּמֵהֶם חֶלֶק הַפְּנִימִיִּים לְמִגְרָשׁ וְהַחִיצוֹנִיִּים לְשָׂדוֹת וּכְרָמִים:

יא | וְהִקְרִיתֶם. אֵין הַקְרָיָה אֶלָּא לְשׁוֹן הַזְמָנָה, וְכֵן הוּא אוֹמֵר: "כִּי הִקְרָה ה' אֱלֹהֶיךָ לְפָנָי" (בראשית כז, כ).

יב | מִגֹּאֵל. מִפְּנֵי גּוֹאֵל הַדָּם שֶׁהוּא קָרוֹב לַנִּרְצָח:

יג | שֵׁשׁ עָרֵי מִקְלָט. מַגִּיד שֶׁאַף עַל פִּי שֶׁהִבְדִּיל מֹשֶׁה בְּחַיָּיו שָׁלֹשׁ עָרִים בְּעֵבֶר הַיַּרְדֵּן, לֹא הָיוּ קוֹלְטוֹת עַד שֶׁנִּבְחֲרוּ שָׁלֹשׁ שֶׁנָּתַן יְהוֹשֻׁעַ בְּאֶרֶץ כְּנָעַן:

יד | אֵת שְׁלֹשׁ הֶעָרִים וְגוֹ'. אַף עַל פִּי שֶׁבְּאֶרֶץ כְּנַעַן תִּשְׁעָה שְׁבָטִים וְכַאן אֵינָן אֶלָּא שְׁנַיִם, הִשְׁוָה מִנְיַן עָרֵי מִקְלָט שֶׁלָּהֶם, מִשּׁוּם דְּבַגִּלְעָד נְפִישֵׁי רוֹצְחִים, דִּכְתִיב: "גִּלְעָד קִרְיַת פֹּעֲלֵי אָוֶן עֲקֻבָּה מִדָּם" (הושע ו, ח):

במדבר | פרק לה

טו תִּהְיֶינָה: לִבְנֵי יִשְׂרָאֵל וְלַגֵּר וְלַתּוֹשָׁב בְּתוֹכָם תִּהְיֶינָה שֵׁשׁ־
הֶעָרִים הָאֵלֶּה לְמִקְלָט לָנוּס שָׁמָּה כָּל־מַכֵּה־נֶפֶשׁ בִּשְׁגָגָה:
טז וְאִם־בִּכְלִי בַרְזֶל ׀ הִכָּהוּ וַיָּמֹת רֹצֵחַ הוּא מוֹת יוּמַת הָרֹצֵחַ:
יז וְאִם בְּאֶבֶן יָד אֲשֶׁר־יָמוּת בָּהּ הִכָּהוּ וַיָּמֹת רֹצֵחַ הוּא מוֹת
יוּמַת הָרֹצֵחַ: יח אוֹ בִּכְלִי עֵץ־יָד אֲשֶׁר־יָמוּת בּוֹ הִכָּהוּ וַיָּמֹת
רֹצֵחַ הוּא מוֹת יוּמַת הָרֹצֵחַ: יט גֹּאֵל הַדָּם הוּא יָמִית אֶת־הָרֹצֵחַ
בְּפִגְעוֹ־בוֹ הוּא יְמִתֶנּוּ: כ וְאִם־בְּשִׂנְאָה יֶהְדֳּפֶנּוּ אוֹ־הִשְׁלִיךְ עָלָיו
בִּצְדִיָּה וַיָּמֹת: כא אוֹ בְאֵיבָה הִכָּהוּ בְיָדוֹ וַיָּמֹת מוֹת־יוּמַת הַמַּכֶּה
רֹצֵחַ הוּא גֹּאֵל הַדָּם יָמִית אֶת־הָרֹצֵחַ בְּפִגְעוֹ־בוֹ: כב וְאִם־בְּפֶתַע
בְּלֹא־אֵיבָה הֲדָפוֹ אוֹ־הִשְׁלִיךְ עָלָיו כָּל־כְּלִי בְּלֹא צְדִיָּה: כג אוֹ
בְכָל־אֶבֶן אֲשֶׁר־יָמוּת בָּהּ בְּלֹא רְאוֹת וַיַּפֵּל עָלָיו וַיָּמֹת וְהוּא
לֹא־אוֹיֵב לוֹ וְלֹא מְבַקֵּשׁ רָעָתוֹ: כד וְשָׁפְטוּ הָעֵדָה בֵּין הַמַּכֶּה וּבֵין

טז) **וְאִם בִּכְלִי בַרְזֶל הִכָּהוּ.** אֵין זֶה מְדַבֵּר בְּהוֹרֵג בְּשׁוֹגֵג אֶלָּא בְּהוֹרֵג בְּמֵזִיד, וּבָא לְלַמֵּד שֶׁהַהוֹרֵג בְּכָל דָּבָר צָרִיךְ שֶׁיְּהֵא בּוֹ שִׁעוּר כְּדֵי לְהָמִית, שֶׁנֶּאֱמַר בְּכֻלָּם: "אֲשֶׁר יָמוּת בּוֹ", כְּדִמְתַרְגְּמִינָן: "דְּהִיא כְּמִסַּת דִּימוּת בַּהּ", חוּץ מִן הַבַּרְזֶל, שֶׁגָּלוּי וְיָדוּעַ לִפְנֵי הַקָּדוֹשׁ בָּרוּךְ הוּא שֶׁהַבַּרְזֶל מֵמִית בְּכָל שֶׁהוּא, אֲפִלּוּ מַחַט, לְפִיכָךְ לֹא נָתְנָה בּוֹ תּוֹרָה שִׁעוּר לִכְתֹּב בּוֹ: "אֲשֶׁר יָמוּת בּוֹ". וְאִם תֹּאמַר בְּהוֹרֵג בְּשׁוֹגֵג הַכָּתוּב מְדַבֵּר, הֲרֵי הוּא אוֹמֵר לְמַטָּה: "אוֹ בְכָל אֶבֶן אֲשֶׁר יָמוּת בָּהּ בְּלֹא רְאוֹת וְגוֹ'" (להלן פסוק כג), לַמֵּד עַל הָאֲמוּרִים לְמַעְלָה שֶׁהוֹרֵג בְּמֵזִיד הַכָּתוּב מְדַבֵּר:

יז) **בְּאֶבֶן יָד.** שֶׁיֵּשׁ בָּהּ מְלֹא יָד: **אֲשֶׁר יָמוּת בָּהּ.** שֶׁיֵּשׁ בָּהּ שִׁעוּר לְהָמִית, כְּתַרְגּוּמוֹ. לְפִי שֶׁנֶּאֱמַר: "וְהִכָּה

אִישׁ אֶת רֵעֵהוּ בְּאֶבֶן" (שמות כא, יח), וְלֹא נָתַן בָּהּ שִׁעוּר, יָכוֹל כָּל שֶׁהוּא? לְכָךְ נֶאֱמַר: "אֲשֶׁר יָמוּת בָּהּ":

יח) **אוֹ בִּכְלִי עֵץ יָד.** לְפִי שֶׁנֶּאֱמַר: "וְכִי יַכֶּה אִישׁ אֶת עַבְדּוֹ אוֹ אֶת אֲמָתוֹ בַּשֵּׁבֶט" (שם פסוק כ), יָכוֹל כָּל שֶׁהוּא? לְכָךְ נֶאֱמַר בְּעֶזְרָא: "אֲשֶׁר יָמוּת בּוֹ", שֶׁיְּהֵא בּוֹ כְּדֵי לְהָמִית:

יט) **בְּפִגְעוֹ בוֹ.** אֲפִלּוּ בְּתוֹךְ עָרֵי מִקְלָט:

כ) **בִּצְדִיָּה.** כְּתַרְגּוּמוֹ: "בְּכַמְנָא", בְּמַאֲרָב:

כב) **בְּפֶתַע.** בְּחִנָּם, וְתַרְגּוּמוֹ: "בִּתְכֵיף", שֶׁהָיָה סָמוּךְ לוֹ, וְלֹא הָיָה לוֹ שָׁהוּת לְהִזָּהֵר עָלָיו:

כג) **אוֹ בְכָל אֶבֶן אֲשֶׁר יָמוּת בָּהּ. הִכָּהוּ. בְּלֹא רְאוֹת.** שֶׁלֹּא רָאָהוּ: **וַיַּפֵּל עָלָיו.** מִכָּאן אָמְרוּ, הַהוֹרֵג דֶּרֶךְ יְרִידָה – גּוֹלֶה, דֶּרֶךְ עֲלִיָּה – אֵינוֹ גּוֹלֶה:

גֹּאֵל הַדָּם עַל הַמִּשְׁפָּטִים הָאֵלֶּה: וְהִצִּילוּ הָעֵדָה אֶת־הָרֹצֵחַ כה
מִיַּד גֹּאֵל הַדָּם וְהֵשִׁיבוּ אֹתוֹ הָעֵדָה אֶל־עִיר מִקְלָטוֹ אֲשֶׁר־נָס
שָׁמָּה וְיָשַׁב בָּהּ עַד־מוֹת הַכֹּהֵן הַגָּדֹל אֲשֶׁר־מָשַׁח אֹתוֹ בְּשֶׁמֶן
הַקֹּדֶשׁ: וְאִם־יָצֹא יֵצֵא הָרֹצֵחַ אֶת־גְּבוּל עִיר מִקְלָטוֹ אֲשֶׁר כו
יָנוּס שָׁמָּה: וּמָצָא אֹתוֹ גֹּאֵל הַדָּם מִחוּץ לִגְבוּל עִיר מִקְלָטוֹ כז
וְרָצַח גֹּאֵל הַדָּם אֶת־הָרֹצֵחַ אֵין לוֹ דָּם: כִּי בְעִיר מִקְלָטוֹ יֵשֵׁב כח
עַד־מוֹת הַכֹּהֵן הַגָּדֹל וְאַחֲרֵי־מוֹת הַכֹּהֵן הַגָּדֹל יָשׁוּב הָרֹצֵחַ
אֶל־אֶרֶץ אֲחֻזָּתוֹ: וְהָיוּ אֵלֶּה לָכֶם לְחֻקַּת מִשְׁפָּט לְדֹרֹתֵיכֶם כט
בְּכֹל מוֹשְׁבֹתֵיכֶם: כָּל־מַכֵּה־נֶפֶשׁ לְפִי עֵדִים יִרְצַח אֶת־הָרֹצֵחַ ל
וְעֵד אֶחָד לֹא־יַעֲנֶה בְנֶפֶשׁ לָמוּת: וְלֹא־תִקְחוּ כֹפֶר לְנֶפֶשׁ לא
רֹצֵחַ אֲשֶׁר־הוּא רָשָׁע לָמוּת כִּי־מוֹת יוּמָת: וְלֹא־תִקְחוּ כֹפֶר לב
לָנוּס אֶל־עִיר מִקְלָטוֹ לָשׁוּב לָשֶׁבֶת בָּאָרֶץ עַד־מוֹת הַכֹּהֵן:

כה **עַד מוֹת הַכֹּהֵן הַגָּדֹל.** שֶׁהוּא בָּא לְהַשְׁרוֹת שְׁכִינָה בְּיִשְׂרָאֵל וּלְהַאֲרִיךְ יְמֵיהֶם, וְהָרוֹצֵחַ בָּא לְסַלֵּק אֶת הַשְּׁכִינָה מִיִּשְׂרָאֵל וּמְקַצֵּר אֶת יְמֵי הַחַיִּים, אֵינוֹ כְדַאי שֶׁיְּהֵא לִפְנֵי כֹּהֵן גָּדוֹל. דָּבָר אַחֵר, לְפִי שֶׁהָיָה לוֹ לְכֹהֵן גָּדוֹל לְהִתְפַּלֵּל שֶׁלֹּא תֶאֱרַע תַּקָּלָה זוֹ לְיִשְׂרָאֵל בְּחַיָּיו: **אֲשֶׁר מָשַׁח אֹתוֹ בְּשֶׁמֶן הַקֹּדֶשׁ.** לְפִי פְשׁוּטוֹ, מִן הַמִּקְרָאוֹת הַקְּצָרִים הוּא שֶׁלֹּא פֵּרַשׁ מִי מְשָׁחוֹ, אֶלָּא כְּמוֹ: אֲשֶׁר מְשָׁחוֹ הַמּוֹשֵׁחַ אוֹתוֹ בְּשֶׁמֶן הַקֹּדֶשׁ. וְרַבּוֹתֵינוּ דְּרָשׁוּהוּ בְּמַסֶּכֶת מַכּוֹת (דף יא ע"ב) לְרַבּוֹת דָּבָר, לְלַמֵּד שֶׁאִם עַד שֶׁלֹּא נִגְמַר דִּינוֹ מֵת הַכֹּהֵן הַגָּדוֹל וּמִנּוּ אַחֵר תַּחְתָּיו, וּלְאַחַר מִכָּאן נִגְמַר דִּינוֹ, חוֹזֵר בְּמִיתָתוֹ שֶׁל שֵׁנִי, שֶׁנֶּאֱמַר: "אֲשֶׁר מָשַׁח אֹתוֹ", וְכִי הוּא מְשָׁחוֹ לַכֹּהֵן, אוֹ הַכֹּהֵן מָשַׁח אוֹתוֹ? אֶלָּא לְהָבִיא אֶת הַנִּמְשָׁח בְּיָמָיו שֶׁמַּחֲזִירוֹ בְּמִיתָתוֹ:

כו **אֵין לוֹ דָּם.** הֲרֵי הוּא כְהוֹרֵג אֶת הַמֵּת, שֶׁאֵין לוֹ דָּם:

כט **בְּכֹל מוֹשְׁבֹתֵיכֶם.** לָמַד שֶׁתְּהֵא סַנְהֶדְרִין נוֹהֶגֶת בְּחוּצָה לָאָרֶץ כָּל זְמַן שֶׁנּוֹהֶגֶת בְּאֶרֶץ יִשְׂרָאֵל:

ל **כָּל מַכֵּה נֶפֶשׁ וְגוֹ'.** הַבָּא לְהָרְגוֹ עַל שֶׁהִכָּה אֶת הַנֶּפֶשׁ: **לְפִי עֵדִים יִרְצַח.** שֶׁיְּעִידוּ שֶׁבְּמֵזִיד וּבְהַתְרָאָה הֲרָגוֹ:

לא **וְלֹא תִקְחוּ כֹפֶר.** לֹא יִפָּטֵר בְּמָמוֹן:

לב **וְלֹא תִקְחוּ כֹפֶר לָנוּס אֶל עִיר מִקְלָטוֹ.** לְמִי שֶׁנָּס אֶל עִיר מִקְלָט, שֶׁהָרַג בְּשׁוֹגֵג, אֵינוֹ נִפְטָר מִגָּלוּת בְּמָמוֹן לִתֵּן כֹּפֶר "לָשׁוּב לָשֶׁבֶת בָּאָרֶץ" בְּטֶרֶם יָמוּת הַכֹּהֵן: **לָנוּס.** כְּמוֹ 'לָנָס', כְּמוֹ: "שׁוּבִי מִלְחָמָה" (מיכה ב, ח), שֶׁשָּׁבוּ מִן הַמִּלְחָמָה, "עֻזִּי מִמּוֹעֵד" (צפניה ג, יח), "כִּי מֻלִים הָיוּ" (יהושע ה, ה), כַּאֲשֶׁר תֹּאמַר 'שׁוּב' עַל מִי שֶׁשָּׁב כְּבָר, וּ'מוּל' עַל שֶׁמָּל כְּבָר, כֵּן תֹּאמַר 'לָנוּס' עַל מִי שֶׁנָּס כְּבָר, וְקוֹרְאֵהוּ 'נוּס' — מִבְרָח. וְאִם תֹּאמַר 'לָנוּס' — לִבְרֹחַ, וּתְפָרְשֵׁהוּ: לֹא תִקְחוּ כֹפֶר

במדבר | פרק לו | מסעי

לג וְלֹא־תַחֲנִיפוּ אֶת־הָאָרֶץ אֲשֶׁר אַתֶּם בָּהּ כִּי הַדָּם הוּא יַחֲנִיף אֶת־הָאָרֶץ וְלָאָרֶץ לֹא־יְכֻפַּר לַדָּם אֲשֶׁר שֻׁפַּךְ־בָּהּ כִּי־אִם בְּדַם שֹׁפְכוֹ: לד וְלֹא תְטַמֵּא אֶת־הָאָרֶץ אֲשֶׁר אַתֶּם יֹשְׁבִים בָּהּ אֲשֶׁר אֲנִי שֹׁכֵן בְּתוֹכָהּ כִּי אֲנִי יְהוָה שֹׁכֵן בְּתוֹךְ בְּנֵי יִשְׂרָאֵל:

שביעי

לו א וַיִּקְרְבוּ רָאשֵׁי הָאָבוֹת לְמִשְׁפַּחַת בְּנֵי־גִלְעָד בֶּן־מָכִיר בֶּן־מְנַשֶּׁה מִמִּשְׁפְּחֹת בְּנֵי יוֹסֵף וַיְדַבְּרוּ לִפְנֵי מֹשֶׁה וְלִפְנֵי הַנְּשִׂאִים רָאשֵׁי אָבוֹת לִבְנֵי יִשְׂרָאֵל: ב וַיֹּאמְרוּ אֶת־אֲדֹנִי צִוָּה יְהוָה לָתֵת אֶת־הָאָרֶץ בְּנַחֲלָה בְּגוֹרָל לִבְנֵי יִשְׂרָאֵל וַאדֹנִי צֻוָּה בַיהוָה לָתֵת אֶת־נַחֲלַת צְלָפְחָד אָחִינוּ לִבְנֹתָיו: ג וְהָיוּ לְאֶחָד מִבְּנֵי שִׁבְטֵי בְנֵי־יִשְׂרָאֵל לְנָשִׁים וְנִגְרְעָה נַחֲלָתָן מִנַּחֲלַת אֲבֹתֵינוּ וְנוֹסַף עַל נַחֲלַת הַמַּטֶּה אֲשֶׁר תִּהְיֶינָה לָהֶם וּמִגֹּרַל נַחֲלָתֵנוּ יִגָּרֵעַ: ד וְאִם־יִהְיֶה הַיֹּבֵל לִבְנֵי יִשְׂרָאֵל וְנוֹסְפָה נַחֲלָתָן עַל נַחֲלַת הַמַּטֶּה אֲשֶׁר תִּהְיֶינָה לָהֶם וּמִנַּחֲלַת מַטֵּה אֲבֹתֵינוּ יִגָּרַע נַחֲלָתָן: ה וַיְצַו מֹשֶׁה אֶת־בְּנֵי יִשְׂרָאֵל עַל־פִּי יְהוָה לֵאמֹר כֵּן מַטֵּה בְנֵי־יוֹסֵף דֹּבְרִים: ו זֶה הַדָּבָר אֲשֶׁר־צִוָּה יְהוָה לִבְנוֹת צְלָפְחָד לֵאמֹר לַטּוֹב בְּעֵינֵיהֶם תִּהְיֶינָה לְנָשִׁים אַךְ לְמִשְׁפַּחַת מַטֵּה אֲבִיהֶם תִּהְיֶינָה

לְמִי שֶׁיֵּשׁ לוֹ לִבְרֹחַ לְמָטְרוֹ מִן הַגָּלוּת, לֹא יָדַעְתִּי הֵיאַךְ יֹאמַר: "לָשׁוּב לָשֶׁבֶת בָּאָרֶץ", הֲרֵי עֲדַיִן לֹא נָס, וּמֵהֵיכָן יָשׁוּב?

לג | וְלֹא תַחֲנִיפוּ. וְלֹא תַּרְשִׁיעוּ, כְּתַרְגּוּמוֹ: "וְלָא תְחַיְּבוּן":

לד | אֲשֶׁר אֲנִי שֹׁכֵן בְּתוֹכָהּ. שֶׁלֹּא תַּשְׁכִּינוּ אוֹתִי בְּטֻמְאָתָהּ: כִּי אֲנִי ה' שֹׁכֵן בְּתוֹךְ בְּנֵי יִשְׂרָאֵל. אַף בִּזְמַן שֶׁהֵם טְמֵאִים, שְׁכִינָה בֵּינֵיהֶם:

פרק לו

ג | וְנוֹסַף עַל נַחֲלַת הַמַּטֶּה. שֶׁהֲרֵי בְּנָהּ יוֹרְשָׁהּ, וְהַבֵּן מִתְיַחֵס עַל שֵׁבֶט אָבִיו:

ד | וְאִם יִהְיֶה הַיֹּבֵל. מִכָּאן הָיָה רַבִּי יְהוּדָה אוֹמֵר: עָתִיד הַיּוֹבֵל שֶׁיִּפְסֹק. וְאִם יִהְיֶה הַיֹּבֵל. כְּלוֹמַר, אֵין זוֹ מְכִירָה שֶׁחוֹזֶרֶת בַּיּוֹבֵל, שֶׁהֲיֻרְשָׁה אֵינָהּ חוֹזֶרֶת, וַאֲפִלּוּ אִם יִהְיֶה הַיּוֹבֵל לֹא תַּחֲזוֹר הַנַּחֲלָה לַשֵּׁבֶט, וְנִגְרְעָה שֶׁנּוֹסְפָה "עַל נַחֲלַת הַמַּטֶּה אֲשֶׁר תִּהְיֶינָה לָהֶם":

ז לְנָשִׁ֑ים וְלֹֽא־תִסֹּ֤ב נַחֲלָה֙ לִבְנֵ֣י יִשְׂרָאֵ֔ל מִמַּטֶּ֖ה אֶל־מַטֶּ֑ה כִּ֣י
ח אִ֗ישׁ בְּנַחֲלַת֙ מַטֵּ֣ה אֲבֹתָ֔יו יִדְבְּק֖וּ בְּנֵ֥י יִשְׂרָאֵֽל׃ וְכָל־בַּ֞ת יֹרֶ֣שֶׁת
נַחֲלָ֗ה מִמַּטּוֹת֮ בְּנֵ֣י יִשְׂרָאֵל֒ לְאֶחָ֗ד מִמִּשְׁפַּ֛חַת מַטֵּ֥ה אָבִ֖יהָ תִּֽהְיֶ֣ה
ט לְאִשָּׁ֑ה לְמַ֗עַן יִֽירְשׁוּ֙ בְּנֵ֣י יִשְׂרָאֵ֔ל אִ֖ישׁ נַחֲלַ֥ת אֲבֹתָֽיו׃ וְלֹֽא־תִסֹּ֧ב
נַחֲלָ֛ה מִמַּטֶּ֖ה לְמַטֶּ֣ה אַחֵ֑ר כִּי־אִישׁ֙ בְּנַ֣חֲלָת֔וֹ יִדְבְּק֕וּ מַטּ֖וֹת בְּנֵ֥י
מפטיר י יִשְׂרָאֵֽל׃ כַּאֲשֶׁ֛ר צִוָּ֥ה יְהוָ֖ה אֶת־מֹשֶׁ֑ה כֵּ֥ן עָשׂ֖וּ בְּנ֥וֹת צְלָפְחָֽד׃
יא וַתִּהְיֶ֜ינָה מַחְלָ֣ה תִרְצָ֗ה וְחָגְלָ֧ה וּמִלְכָּ֛ה וְנֹעָ֖ה בְּנ֣וֹת צְלָפְחָ֑ד לִבְנֵ֥י
יב דֹדֵיהֶ֖ן לְנָשִֽׁים׃ מִֽמִּשְׁפְּחֹ֛ת בְּנֵֽי־מְנַשֶּׁ֥ה בֶן־יוֹסֵ֖ף הָי֣וּ לְנָשִׁ֑ים וַתְּהִי֙
יג נַחֲלָתָ֔ן עַל־מַטֵּ֖ה מִשְׁפַּ֥חַת אֲבִיהֶֽן׃ אֵ֣לֶּה הַמִּצְוֺ֞ת וְהַמִּשְׁפָּטִ֗ים
אֲשֶׁ֨ר צִוָּ֧ה יְהוָ֛ה בְּיַד־מֹשֶׁ֖ה אֶל־בְּנֵ֣י יִשְׂרָאֵ֑ל בְּעַֽרְבֹ֣ת מוֹאָ֔ב עַ֖ל
יַרְדֵּ֥ן יְרֵחֽוֹ׃

ח׀ וְכָל בַּת יֹרֶשֶׁת נַחֲלָה. שֶׁלֹּא הָיָה בֵן לְאָבִיהָ:
יא׀ מַחְלָה תִרְצָה וְגוֹ'. כָּאן מְנָאָן לְפִי גְדֻלָּתָן זוֹ מִזּוֹ
בְּשָׁנִים, וְנִשְּׂאוּ כְּסֵדֶר תּוֹלְדוֹתָן, וּבְכָל הַמִּקְרָא מְנָאָן
לְפִי חָכְמָתָן, וּמַגִּיד שֶׁשְּׁקוּלוֹת זוֹ כָּזוֹ:

הפטרות וקריאות נוספות
HAFTAROT AND SPECIAL READINGS

HAFTARAT BEMIDBAR

On erev Rosh Ḥodesh Sivan read the haftara on page 501.

2 1 Yet the children of Israel will number like the sands of the sea, not measurable or HOSEA
countable, and rather than being told, "You are Not My People," they will be told, "You
2 are the sons of the living God." Then the children of Yehuda and the children of Israel
will gather together; they will designate one leader and escape from the land, for the
3 day of Yizre'el will be a great one. Say then to your brothers "People," and to your sisters
4 "Loved." Berate your mother, for she is not my wife, nor I her husband. Let her remove
5 her prostitute's rouge from her face, her adulterous acts from between her breasts, lest I
strip her naked as the day she was born and make her as a desert wilderness. I will make
6 her into parched wasteland and let her die from thirst. As for her sons, I will have no
7 mercy, for they are the sons of a harlot, for their mother has whored; she has conceived
them in shame. She said, "I will follow after my lovers; it is they who give me bread and
8 water, keep me in wools and linens, lotions and wines," so I will obstruct her path with
9 prickly shrubs; I will fence her in with walls; her way will be lost to her. She will pursue
her lovers but not catch them; she will search them out but never find them. Then she
10 will say, "I will go and return to my first husband, for I fared better then than now." But
she did not care to know that it was I who furnished her with grain, wine, and oil, I who
11 lavished silver upon her and gold which they used for Baal. Hence I will take back My
grain as it ripens in its season, My wine as it ages; I will seize My wools and My linens
12 meant to cover her nakedness. And now I will expose her indecency for her lovers to
13 see, and there will be no one to rescue her from My hand. I will put an end to all her
joyous occasions – her holidays, her New Moons, her Sabbaths, and all her festive
14 seasons. I will ravage her vines and fig trees, of which she once said, "These are my
harlot's favors, given to me by my lovers." I will make them into abandoned woodlands,
15 and wild animals will feed on them. I will revisit upon her the days of the Baalim,
for whom she burned incense and adorned herself with earrings and
jewels, how she followed after her lovers and forgot Me. So declares the
16 Lord.   Behold, now I will coax her, I will lead her back to the open desert, and
17 I will speak to her heart. Then and there I will give her vineyards to her, and the Valley
of the Scourge will be a doorway to hope; she will return to Me in song as in the first
18 days of her youth, as on the day when she came up out of the land of Egypt.   It
will be on that day, says the Lord: you will call Me "my Husband"; no longer will you
19 call Me "my Master." I will eradicate the names of the Baalim from her mouth; no more
20 will they be mentioned by name. On that day I will make a covenant with them: with
the beasts of the fields, and the birds of heaven, and the crawling creatures of the ground.
I will break the bow and the sword; I will crush conflict out from the land, and you will
21 rest in safety. I will betroth you to Me forever; I will betroth you to Me in righteousness
22 and justice, in kindness and compassion. I will betroth you to Me in faithfulness, and
you will know the Lord.

הפטרת במדבר

On ערב ראש חודש סיון read the הפטרה on page 501.

הושע ב א וְֽהָיָ֞ה מִסְפַּ֣ר בְּנֵֽי־יִשְׂרָאֵ֗ל כְּח֣וֹל הַיָּ֔ם אֲשֶׁ֥ר לֹֽא־יִמַּ֖ד וְלֹ֣א יִסָּפֵ֑ר וְֽ֠הָיָ֠ה בִּמְק֞וֹם
ב אֲשֶׁר־יֵאָמֵ֤ר לָהֶם֙ לֹֽא־עַמִּ֣י אַתֶּ֔ם יֵאָמֵ֥ר לָהֶ֖ם בְּנֵ֥י אֵֽל־חָֽי: וְ֠נִקְבְּצ֠וּ בְּנֵֽי־יְהוּדָ֤ה
וּבְנֵֽי־יִשְׂרָאֵל֙ יַחְדָּ֔ו וְשָׂמ֥וּ לָהֶ֛ם רֹ֥אשׁ אֶחָ֖ד וְעָל֣וּ מִן־הָאָ֑רֶץ כִּ֥י גָד֖וֹל י֥וֹם יִזְרְעֶֽאל:
ג אִמְר֥וּ לַאֲחֵיכֶ֖ם עַמִּ֑י וְלַאֲחֽוֹתֵיכֶ֖ם רֻחָֽמָה: רִ֤יבוּ בְאִמְּכֶם֙ רִ֔יבוּ כִּי־הִיא֙ לֹ֣א אִשְׁתִּ֔י
ד וְאָנֹכִ֖י לֹ֣א אִישָׁ֑הּ וְתָסֵ֤ר זְנוּנֶ֨יהָ֙ מִפָּנֶ֔יהָ וְנַאֲפוּפֶ֖יהָ מִבֵּ֥ין שָׁדֶֽיהָ: פֶּן־אַפְשִׁיטֶ֣נָּה עֲרֻמָּ֔ה
ה וְהִ֨צַּגְתִּ֔יהָ כְּי֖וֹם הִוָּלְדָ֑הּ וְשַׂמְתִּ֣יהָ כַמִּדְבָּ֗ר וְשַׁתִּ֨הָ֙ כְּאֶ֣רֶץ צִיָּ֔ה וַהֲמִתִּ֖יהָ בַּצָּמָֽא:
ו וְאֶת־בָּנֶ֖יהָ לֹ֣א אֲרַחֵ֑ם כִּֽי־בְנֵ֥י זְנוּנִ֖ים הֵֽמָּה: כִּ֤י זָֽנְתָה֙ אִמָּ֔ם הֹבִ֖ישָׁה הֽוֹרָתָ֑ם כִּ֣י
ז אָמְרָ֗ה אֵלְכָ֞ה אַחֲרֵ֤י מְאַהֲבַי֙ נֹתְנֵ֣י לַחְמִ֣י וּמֵימַ֔י צַמְרִ֣י וּפִשְׁתִּ֔י שַׁמְנִ֖י וְשִׁקּוּיָֽי: לָכֵ֛ן
ח הִנְנִי־שָׂ֥ךְ אֶת־דַּרְכֵּ֖ךְ בַּסִּירִ֑ים וְגָֽדַרְתִּי֙ אֶת־גְּדֵרָ֔הּ וּנְתִיבוֹתֶ֖יהָ לֹ֥א תִמְצָֽא: וְרִדְּפָ֤ה
אֶת־מְאַהֲבֶ֙יהָ֙ וְלֹֽא־תַשִּׂ֣יג אֹתָ֔ם וּבִקְשָׁ֖תַם וְלֹ֣א תִמְצָ֑א וְאָמְרָ֗ה אֵלְכָ֤ה וְאָשׁ֙וּבָה֙
ט אֶל־אִישִׁ֣י הָרִאשׁ֔וֹן כִּ֣י ט֥וֹב לִ֛י אָ֖ז מֵעָֽתָּה: וְהִיא֙ לֹ֣א יָֽדְעָ֔ה כִּ֤י אָֽנֹכִי֙ נָתַ֣תִּי לָ֔הּ הַדָּגָ֖ן
י וְהַתִּיר֣וֹשׁ וְהַיִּצְהָ֑ר וְכֶ֨סֶף הִרְבֵּ֥יתִי לָ֛הּ וְזָהָ֖ב עָשׂ֥וּ לַבָּֽעַל: לָכֵ֣ן אָשׁ֗וּב וְלָקַחְתִּ֤י דְגָנִי֙
יא בְּעִתּ֔וֹ וְתִירוֹשִׁ֖י בְּמֽוֹעֲד֑וֹ וְהִצַּלְתִּי֙ צַמְרִ֣י וּפִשְׁתִּ֔י לְכַסּ֖וֹת אֶת־עֶרְוָתָֽהּ: וְעַתָּ֛ה אֲגַלֶּ֥ה
יב אֶת־נַבְלֻתָ֖הּ לְעֵינֵ֣י מְאַהֲבֶ֑יהָ וְאִ֖ישׁ לֹֽא־יַצִּילֶ֥נָּה מִיָּדִֽי: וְהִשְׁבַּתִּי֙ כָּל־מְשׂוֹשָׂ֔הּ חַגָּ֥הּ
יג חָדְשָׁ֖הּ וְשַׁבַּתָּ֑הּ וְכֹ֖ל מֽוֹעֲדָֽהּ: וַהֲשִׁמֹּתִ֗י גַּפְנָהּ֙ וּתְאֵ֣נָתָ֔הּ אֲשֶׁ֣ר אָמְרָ֔ה אֶתְנָ֥ה הֵ֨מָּה֙
יד לִ֔י אֲשֶׁ֥ר נָֽתְנוּ־לִ֖י מְאַהֲבָ֑י וְשַׂמְתִּ֣ים לְיַ֔עַר וַאֲכָלָ֖תַם חַיַּ֥ת הַשָּׂדֶֽה: וּפָקַדְתִּ֣י עָלֶ֗יהָ
אֶת־יְמֵ֤י הַבְּעָלִים֙ אֲשֶׁ֣ר תַּקְטִ֣יר לָהֶ֔ם וַתַּ֤עַד נִזְמָהּ֙ וְחֶלְיָתָ֔הּ וַתֵּ֖לֶךְ אַחֲרֵ֣י מְאַהֲבֶ֑יהָ
טו וְאֹתִ֥י שָׁכְחָ֖ה נְאֻם־יְהוָֽה: לָכֵ֗ן הִנֵּ֤ה אָֽנֹכִי֙ מְפַתֶּ֔יהָ וְהֹֽלַכְתִּ֖יהָ הַמִּדְבָּ֑ר
טז וְדִבַּרְתִּ֖י עַל־לִבָּֽהּ: וְנָתַ֨תִּי לָ֤הּ אֶת־כְּרָמֶ֨יהָ֙ מִשָּׁ֔ם וְאֶת־עֵ֥מֶק עָכ֖וֹר לְפֶ֣תַח תִּקְוָ֑ה
יז וְעָ֤נְתָה שָּׁ֨מָּה֙ כִּימֵ֣י נְעוּרֶ֔יהָ וּכְי֖וֹם עֲלוֹתָ֥הּ מֵאֶֽרֶץ־מִצְרָֽיִם: וְהָיָ֤ה בַיּוֹם־
יח הַהוּא֙ נְאֻם־יְהוָ֔ה תִּקְרְאִ֖י אִישִׁ֑י וְלֹֽא־תִקְרְאִי־לִ֥י ע֖וֹד בַּעְלִֽי: וַהֲסִרֹתִ֛י אֶת־שְׁמ֥וֹת
יט הַבְּעָלִ֖ים מִפִּ֑יהָ וְלֹֽא־יִזָּכְר֥וּ ע֖וֹד בִּשְׁמָֽם: וְכָרַתִּ֨י לָהֶ֤ם בְּרִית֙ בַּיּ֣וֹם הַה֔וּא עִם־חַיַּ֤ת
כ הַשָּׂדֶה֙ וְעִם־ע֣וֹף הַשָּׁמַ֔יִם וְרֶ֖מֶשׂ הָאֲדָמָ֑ה וְקֶ֨שֶׁת וְחֶ֤רֶב וּמִלְחָמָה֙ אֶשְׁבּ֣וֹר מִן־הָאָ֔רֶץ
כא וְהִשְׁכַּבְתִּ֖ים לָבֶֽטַח: וְאֵרַשְׂתִּ֥יךְ לִ֖י לְעוֹלָ֑ם וְאֵרַשְׂתִּ֥יךְ לִי֙ בְּצֶ֣דֶק וּבְמִשְׁפָּ֔ט וּבְחֶ֖סֶד
כב וּבְרַחֲמִֽים: וְאֵרַשְׂתִּ֥יךְ לִ֖י בֶּאֱמוּנָ֑ה וְיָדַ֖עַתְּ אֶת־יְהוָֽה:

HAFTARAT NASO

13 2 There was a man of Tzora whose name was Manoaḥ, from the family of Dan. His wife JUDGES
3 was barren and had never given birth. An angel of the Lord appeared to the woman and said to her: "Look! Though you have been barren and have never given birth, you
4 shall conceive and bear a son. Take care: drink neither wine nor strong drink, and eat
5 nothing unclean. For indeed, you shall be with child; you shall bear a son. Let no razor touch his head, for the boy shall be a nazirite to God from the womb. He will begin to
6 save Israel from the hands of the Philistines." The woman went and told her husband, "A man of God came to me; he looked like an angel of God – dazzling, awe-inspiring.
7 I did not ask him where he was from, and he did not tell me his name. He said to me, 'You shall be with child, and you shall bear a son; drink neither wine nor strong drink and eat nothing unclean, for the boy will be a nazirite to the Lord from the womb until his dying day.'"
8 Then Manoaḥ appealed to the Lord. "Please, my Lord," he said, "let the man of God whom
9 You sent come to us again and teach us what to do with the boy who will be born." God heard Manoaḥ's voice, and God's angel came to the woman once more. She was sitting in the
10 field, her husband Manoaḥ not with her. The woman rushed to tell her husband. "Look!"
11 she said to him. "The man who came to visit me that day has appeared!" Manoaḥ rose and followed his wife. When he reached the man, he said to him, "Are you the man who
12 spoke to this woman?" "I am," he said. "Now," said Manoaḥ, "may your words come to
13 pass. How should the boy be properly dealt with?" The Lord's angel replied to Manoaḥ,
14 "The woman must be kept from all that I said to her. She must eat nothing derived from the grapevine, drink neither wine nor strong drink, and eat nothing unclean; she must
15 follow all my instructions." Manoaḥ said to the Lord's angel, "Please let us detain you,
16 and we will prepare a young goat for you." "Even if you detain me, I will not eat your food," the Lord's angel said to Manoaḥ, "but if you prepare a burnt offering, offer it to
17 the Lord." For Manoaḥ did not realize that he was an angel of the Lord. "What is your name," Manoaḥ asked the Lord's angel, "so that when your words come to pass, we may
18 honor you?" "Why should you ask my name?" the Lord's angel replied to him. "For
19 it is wondrous." Manoaḥ took the young goat and the grain offering and offered them up on the rock to the Lord. As Manoaḥ and his wife were watching, He performed
20 wonders: as the flames flared up from the altar to the heavens, the Lord's angel ascended in the altar's flames while Manoaḥ and his wife were watching. They threw themselves
21 down with their faces to the ground. When the Lord's angel did not appear again to
22 Manoaḥ and his wife, Manoaḥ realized that he had been an angel of the Lord. "We
23 will surely die!" Manoaḥ said to his wife, "for it was God we saw!" "Had the Lord wanted to kill us," his wife said to him, "He would not have accepted burnt offerings or grain offerings from us. And He would not have shown us all that we saw or made this

הפטרת נשא

שופטים יג ב וַיְהִי אִישׁ אֶחָד מִצָּרְעָה מִמִּשְׁפַּחַת הַדָּנִי וּשְׁמוֹ מָנוֹחַ וְאִשְׁתּוֹ עֲקָרָה וְלֹא יָלָדָה:
ג וַיֵּרָא מַלְאַךְ־יְהֹוָה אֶל־הָאִשָּׁה וַיֹּאמֶר אֵלֶיהָ הִנֵּה־נָא אַתְּ־עֲקָרָה וְלֹא יָלַדְתְּ וְהָרִית
ה וְיָלַדְתְּ בֵּן: וְעַתָּה הִשָּׁמְרִי נָא וְאַל־תִּשְׁתִּי יַיִן וְשֵׁכָר וְאַל־תֹּאכְלִי כׇּל־טָמֵא: כִּי הִנָּךְ הָרָה וְיֹלַדְתְּ בֵּן וּמוֹרָה לֹא־יַעֲלֶה עַל־רֹאשׁוֹ כִּי־נְזִיר אֱלֹהִים יִהְיֶה הַנַּעַר מִן־הַבָּטֶן וְהוּא יָחֵל לְהוֹשִׁיעַ אֶת־יִשְׂרָאֵל מִיַּד פְּלִשְׁתִּים: וַתָּבֹא הָאִשָּׁה וַתֹּאמֶר לְאִישָׁהּ לֵאמֹר אִישׁ הָאֱלֹהִים בָּא אֵלַי וּמַרְאֵהוּ כְּמַרְאֵה מַלְאַךְ הָאֱלֹהִים נוֹרָא מְאֹד וְלֹא
ז שְׁאִלְתִּיהוּ אֵי־מִזֶּה הוּא וְאֶת־שְׁמוֹ לֹא־הִגִּיד לִי: וַיֹּאמֶר לִי הִנָּךְ הָרָה וְיֹלַדְתְּ בֵּן וְעַתָּה אַל־תִּשְׁתִּי ׀ יַיִן וְשֵׁכָר וְאַל־תֹּאכְלִי כׇּל־טֻמְאָה כִּי־נְזִיר אֱלֹהִים יִהְיֶה הַנַּעַר מִן־הַבֶּטֶן עַד־יוֹם מוֹתוֹ:

ח וַיֶּעְתַּר מָנוֹחַ אֶל־יְהֹוָה וַיֹּאמַר בִּי אֲדוֹנָי אִישׁ הָאֱלֹהִים אֲשֶׁר שָׁלַחְתָּ יָבוֹא־נָא עוֹד
ט אֵלֵינוּ וְיוֹרֵנוּ מַה־נַּעֲשֶׂה לַנַּעַר הַיּוּלָּד: וַיִּשְׁמַע הָאֱלֹהִים בְּקוֹל מָנוֹחַ וַיָּבֹא מַלְאַךְ
י הָאֱלֹהִים עוֹד אֶל־הָאִשָּׁה וְהִיא יוֹשֶׁבֶת בַּשָּׂדֶה וּמָנוֹחַ אִישָׁהּ אֵין עִמָּהּ: וַתְּמַהֵר הָאִשָּׁה וַתָּרׇץ וַתַּגֵּד לְאִישָׁהּ וַתֹּאמֶר אֵלָיו הִנֵּה נִרְאָה אֵלַי הָאִישׁ אֲשֶׁר־בָּא בַיּוֹם
יא אֵלָי: וַיָּקׇם וַיֵּלֶךְ מָנוֹחַ אַחֲרֵי אִשְׁתּוֹ וַיָּבֹא אֶל־הָאִישׁ וַיֹּאמֶר לוֹ הַאַתָּה הָאִישׁ אֲשֶׁר־
יב דִּבַּרְתָּ אֶל־הָאִשָּׁה וַיֹּאמֶר אָנִי: וַיֹּאמֶר מָנוֹחַ עַתָּה יָבֹא דְבָרֶיךָ מַה־יִּהְיֶה מִשְׁפַּט־
יג הַנַּעַר וּמַעֲשֵׂהוּ: וַיֹּאמֶר מַלְאַךְ יְהֹוָה אֶל־מָנוֹחַ מִכֹּל אֲשֶׁר־אָמַרְתִּי אֶל־הָאִשָּׁה
יד תִּשָּׁמֵר: מִכֹּל אֲשֶׁר־יֵצֵא מִגֶּפֶן הַיַּיִן לֹא תֹאכַל וְיַיִן וְשֵׁכָר אַל־תֵּשְׁתְּ וְכׇל־טֻמְאָה אַל־תֹּאכַל כֹּל אֲשֶׁר־צִוִּיתִיהָ תִּשְׁמֹר: וַיֹּאמֶר מָנוֹחַ אֶל־מַלְאַךְ יְהֹוָה נַעְצְרָה־נָּא
טז אוֹתָךְ וְנַעֲשֶׂה לְפָנֶיךָ גְּדִי עִזִּים: וַיֹּאמֶר מַלְאַךְ יְהֹוָה אֶל־מָנוֹחַ אִם־תַּעְצְרֵנִי לֹא־אֹכַל בְּלַחְמֶךָ וְאִם־תַּעֲשֶׂה עֹלָה לַיהֹוָה תַּעֲלֶנָּה כִּי לֹא־יָדַע מָנוֹחַ כִּי־מַלְאַךְ יְהֹוָה
יח הוּא: וַיֹּאמֶר מָנוֹחַ אֶל־מַלְאַךְ יְהֹוָה מִי שְׁמֶךָ כִּי־יָבֹא דְבָרְךָ וְכִבַּדְנוּךָ: וַיֹּאמֶר דברך
יט לוֹ מַלְאַךְ יְהֹוָה לָמָּה זֶּה תִּשְׁאַל לִשְׁמִי וְהוּא־פֶלִאי: וַיִּקַּח מָנוֹחַ אֶת־גְּדִי הָעִזִּים וְאֶת־הַמִּנְחָה וַיַּעַל עַל־הַצּוּר לַיהֹוָה וּמַפְלִא לַעֲשׂוֹת וּמָנוֹחַ וְאִשְׁתּוֹ רֹאִים: וַיְהִי בַעֲלוֹת הַלַּהַב מֵעַל הַמִּזְבֵּחַ הַשָּׁמַיְמָה וַיַּעַל מַלְאַךְ־יְהֹוָה בְּלַהַב הַמִּזְבֵּחַ וּמָנוֹחַ
כא וְאִשְׁתּוֹ רֹאִים וַיִּפְּלוּ עַל־פְּנֵיהֶם אָרְצָה: וְלֹא־יָסַף עוֹד מַלְאַךְ יְהֹוָה לְהֵרָאֹה אֶל־
כב מָנוֹחַ וְאֶל־אִשְׁתּוֹ אָז יָדַע מָנוֹחַ כִּי־מַלְאַךְ יְהֹוָה הוּא: וַיֹּאמֶר מָנוֹחַ אֶל־אִשְׁתּוֹ
כג מוֹת נָמוּת כִּי אֱלֹהִים רָאִינוּ: וַתֹּאמֶר לוֹ אִשְׁתּוֹ לוּ חָפֵץ יְהֹוָה לַהֲמִיתֵנוּ לֹא־לָקַח

	24	announcement." The woman bore a son and named him Shimshon. The boy grew up and
	25	the Lord blessed him. The spirit of the Lord first stirred him in the Dan encampment between Tzora and Eshtaol.

HAFTARAT BEHAALOTEKHA

ZECHARIAH

2:14 Shout out and be joyful, daughter Zion, for I am coming, and I will dwell in your midst – the Lord has spoken. Many nations will join themselves to the Lord on that day, and they will be My people. I will dwell in your midst, and you will know that the Lord of Hosts sent me to you. The Lord will take possession of Yehuda as His portion of holy ground, and He will choose Jerusalem once again. Hush, all flesh, before the Lord, for He has stirred from His holy abode. 3:1 Then He showed me Yehoshua the High Priest standing before an angel of the Lord with the Adversary on his right to oppose him. The Lord said to the Adversary: The Lord drives you away, Adversary. The Lord, who has chosen Jerusalem, drives you away. Yes, this is a firebrand saved from the fire. And Yehoshua, wearing filthy clothing, was standing before the angel, who spoke and said to those standing before him, "Take those filthy clothes off him." Then the angel said to him, "See, I have removed your guilt from you and dressed you in finery." I said, "Place a pure turban on his head," and they placed a pure turban on his head. They dressed him in clothing. The angel of the Lord remained standing. Then that angel of the Lord testified regarding Yehoshua: "So says the Lord of Hosts: If you walk in My ways, if you keep My watch, if you judge My House, and guard My courtyards, then I will give you walkers among these who are standing. Listen, Yehoshua the High Priest, you and your friends who sit before you, for they are men of wonders: Behold, I am bringing My servant Tzemaḥ. Upon the stone that I set before Yehoshua, one stone with seven eyes, I will engrave its inscription, and I will wipe away the guilt of this land in one day. On that day – the Lord of Hosts has spoken – you will call one to another: Come under the shade of the vine; come under the shade of the fig." 4:1 Then the angel with whom I had spoken returned and roused me like a man stirring from his sleep. He said to me, "What do you see?" I said, "I see a candelabrum of pure gold, its bowl at the top. It has seven lamps – seven – and seven indentations for the lamps, which are at the top. Next to it are two olive trees, one to the right of the bowl and one to its left." I spoke and said to the angel with whom I spoke, "What are these, my lord?" And the angel with whom I spoke replied and said, "You know what these are." I said, "No, my lord." Then he spoke and said to me, "This is the word of the Lord to Zerubavel: Not with valor and not with

מִידָּנוּ עֹלָה וּמִנְחָה וְלֹא הֶרְאָנוּ אֶת־כָּל־אֵלֶּה וְכָעֵת לֹא הִשְׁמִיעָנוּ כָּזֹאת: וַתֵּלֶד כד
הָאִשָּׁה בֵּן וַתִּקְרָא אֶת־שְׁמוֹ שִׁמְשׁוֹן וַיִּגְדַּל הַנַּעַר וַיְבָרְכֵהוּ יהוה: וַתָּחֶל רוּחַ יהוה כה
לְפַעֲמוֹ בְּמַחֲנֵה־דָן בֵּין צָרְעָה וּבֵין אֶשְׁתָּאֹל:

הפטרת בהעלתך

רָנִּי וְשִׂמְחִי בַּת־צִיּוֹן כִּי הִנְנִי־בָא וְשָׁכַנְתִּי בְתוֹכֵךְ נְאֻם־יהוה: וְנִלְווּ גוֹיִם רַבִּים אֶל־ ב יד זכריה
יהוה בַּיּוֹם הַהוּא וְהָיוּ לִי לְעָם וְשָׁכַנְתִּי בְתוֹכֵךְ וְיָדַעַתְּ כִּי־יהוה צְבָאוֹת שְׁלָחַנִי
אֵלָיִךְ: וְנָחַל יהוה אֶת־יְהוּדָה חֶלְקוֹ עַל אַדְמַת הַקֹּדֶשׁ וּבָחַר עוֹד בִּירוּשָׁלָםִ: טו
הַס כָּל־בָּשָׂר מִפְּנֵי יהוה כִּי נֵעוֹר מִמְּעוֹן קָדְשׁוֹ: וַיַּרְאֵנִי אֶת־יְהוֹשֻׁעַ ג א
הַכֹּהֵן הַגָּדוֹל עֹמֵד לִפְנֵי מַלְאַךְ יהוה וְהַשָּׂטָן עֹמֵד עַל־יְמִינוֹ לְשִׂטְנוֹ: וַיֹּאמֶר ב
יהוה אֶל־הַשָּׂטָן יִגְעַר יהוה בְּךָ הַשָּׂטָן וְיִגְעַר יהוה בְּךָ הַבֹּחֵר בִּירוּשָׁלָםִ הֲלוֹא
זֶה אוּד מֻצָּל מֵאֵשׁ: וִיהוֹשֻׁעַ הָיָה לָבֻשׁ בְּגָדִים צוֹאִים וְעֹמֵד לִפְנֵי הַמַּלְאָךְ: ג
וַיַּעַן וַיֹּאמֶר אֶל־הָעֹמְדִים לְפָנָיו לֵאמֹר הָסִירוּ הַבְּגָדִים הַצֹּאִים מֵעָלָיו וַיֹּאמֶר ד
אֵלָיו רְאֵה הֶעֱבַרְתִּי מֵעָלֶיךָ עֲוֺנֶךָ וְהַלְבֵּשׁ אֹתְךָ מַחֲלָצוֹת: וָאֹמַר יָשִׂימוּ צָנִיף ה
טָהוֹר עַל־רֹאשׁוֹ וַיָּשִׂימוּ הַצָּנִיף הַטָּהוֹר עַל־רֹאשׁוֹ וַיַּלְבִּשֻׁהוּ בְּגָדִים וּמַלְאַךְ
יהוה עֹמֵד: וַיָּעַד מַלְאַךְ יהוה בִּיהוֹשֻׁעַ לֵאמֹר: כֹּה־אָמַר יהוה צְבָאוֹת אִם־ ו
בִּדְרָכַי תֵּלֵךְ וְאִם אֶת־מִשְׁמַרְתִּי תִשְׁמֹר וְגַם־אַתָּה תָּדִין אֶת־בֵּיתִי וְגַם תִּשְׁמֹר
אֶת־חֲצֵרָי וְנָתַתִּי לְךָ מַהְלְכִים בֵּין הָעֹמְדִים הָאֵלֶּה: שְׁמַע־נָא יְהוֹשֻׁעַ ׀ הַכֹּהֵן ח
הַגָּדוֹל אַתָּה וְרֵעֶיךָ הַיֹּשְׁבִים לְפָנֶיךָ כִּי־אַנְשֵׁי מוֹפֵת הֵמָּה כִּי־הִנְנִי מֵבִיא אֶת־
עַבְדִּי צֶמַח: כִּי ׀ הִנֵּה הָאֶבֶן אֲשֶׁר נָתַתִּי לִפְנֵי יְהוֹשֻׁעַ עַל־אֶבֶן אַחַת שִׁבְעָה ט
עֵינָיִם הִנְנִי מְפַתֵּחַ פִּתֻּחָהּ נְאֻם יהוה צְבָאוֹת וּמַשְׁתִּי אֶת־עֲוֺן הָאָרֶץ־הַהִיא
בְּיוֹם אֶחָד: בַּיּוֹם הַהוּא נְאֻם יהוה צְבָאוֹת תִּקְרְאוּ אִישׁ לְרֵעֵהוּ אֶל־תַּחַת גֶּפֶן וְאֶל־ י
תַּחַת תְּאֵנָה: וַיָּשָׁב הַמַּלְאָךְ הַדֹּבֵר בִּי וַיְעִירֵנִי כְּאִישׁ אֲשֶׁר־יֵעוֹר מִשְּׁנָתוֹ: ד א
וַיֹּאמֶר אֵלַי מָה אַתָּה רֹאֶה וַיֹּאמַר רָאִיתִי ׀ וְהִנֵּה מְנוֹרַת זָהָב כֻּלָּהּ וְגֻלָּהּ עַל־רֹאשָׁהּ וָאֹמַר ב
וְשִׁבְעָה נֵרֹתֶיהָ עָלֶיהָ שִׁבְעָה וְשִׁבְעָה מוּצָקוֹת לַנֵּרוֹת אֲשֶׁר עַל־רֹאשָׁהּ: וּשְׁנַיִם ג
זֵיתִים עָלֶיהָ אֶחָד מִימִין הַגֻּלָּה וְאֶחָד עַל־שְׂמֹאלָהּ: וָאַעַן וָאֹמַר אֶל־הַמַּלְאָךְ ד
הַדֹּבֵר בִּי לֵאמֹר מָה־אֵלֶּה אֲדֹנִי: וַיַּעַן הַמַּלְאָךְ הַדֹּבֵר בִּי וַיֹּאמֶר אֵלַי הֲלוֹא יָדַעְתָּ ה
מָה־הֵמָּה אֵלֶּה וָאֹמַר לֹא אֲדֹנִי: וַיַּעַן וַיֹּאמֶר אֵלַי לֵאמֹר זֶה דְּבַר־יהוה אֶל־זְרֻבָּבֶל ו

7 strength, but with My spirit, says the Lord of Hosts. Who are you, great mountain before Zerubavel? Surely it will become a level plain. He will remove the re-foundation stone with clamor: Favor, favor to her!"

HAFTARAT SHELAḤ

2 1 Yehoshua son of Nun had sent two men as spies from Shitim, in secret: "Go forth and survey the land and the region of Yeriḥo." So the men had set out, arriving at the house
2 of a harlot named Raḥav, where they lay down for the night. And word reached the king
3 of Yeriḥo: "Listen, people have come here tonight – Israelites – to probe the land." The king of Yeriḥo sent word to Raḥav: "Bring out those men who came to you, who arrived
4 at your house, for they have come to probe the land." Now, the woman had taken the two men and hidden them, and she replied, "Yes, men came to me, but I did not know
5 where they were from. Just as the gate was being closed at nightfall, the men left, and I
6 do not know where they went. Go after them quickly, for you can overtake them." She had taken the spies up to the roof and hidden them amongst the stalks of flax she had
7 laid out on the roof. The king's men ran after them toward the Jordan route, over the
8 river fords; and the moment the pursuers left, the gate was closed behind them. They
9 were not yet asleep when she went up to them on the roof. "I know that the Lord has given you the land," she said to the men, "and that dread of you has fallen upon us; for
10 all the inhabitants of the land quake before you. For we have heard that the Lord dried up the waters of the Sea of Reeds before you when you left Egypt, and we have heard what you did to the two Amorite kings across the Jordan – how you utterly destroyed
11 Siḥon and Og. We heard it and our hearts dissolved; no one has the spirit to face you, for
12 the Lord your God is God of heaven above and earth below. Now, please swear to me by the Lord – for I have shown you loyalty – that you, too, will be loyal to my father's
13 house. Give me a true sign that you will spare my father and mother and my brothers
14 and sisters and all that is theirs. Please, save our souls from death!" The men replied to her, "We pledge to die in your place, if you speak no word of this, and when the Lord
15 gives us the land, we will show you true loyalty." She let them down by a rope through
16 the window, for her house was built into the city wall; she lived inside the wall. "Flee toward the hills," she said to them, "lest the pursuers run into you. Hide there for three
17 days until the pursuers have returned; only then be on your way." They said to her, "We
18 will be free of this oath you have sworn us to unless, when we come back to the land, you tie this scarlet thread in the window you let us down from. Bring your father, your

JOSHUA

לֵאמֹ֑ר לֹ֤א בְחַ֙יִל֙ וְלֹ֣א בְכֹ֔חַ כִּ֣י אִם־בְּרוּחִ֔י אָמַ֖ר יהו֥ה צְבָאֽוֹת: מִֽי־אַתָּ֧ה הַֽר־הַגָּד֛וֹל לִפְנֵ֥י זְרֻבָּבֶ֖ל לְמִישֹׁ֑ר וְהוֹצִיא֙ אֶת־הָאֶ֣בֶן הָרֹאשָׁ֔ה תְּשֻׁא֕וֹת חֵ֥ן חֵ֖ן לָֽהּ:

הפטרת שלח

יהושע ב

א וַיִּשְׁלַ֣ח יְהוֹשֻֽׁעַ־בִּן־נ֠וּן מִֽן־הַשִּׁטִּ֞ים שְׁנַֽיִם־אֲנָשִׁ֤ים מְרַגְּלִים֙ חֶ֣רֶשׁ לֵאמֹ֔ר לְכ֛וּ רְא֥וּ אֶת־הָאָ֖רֶץ וְאֶת־יְרִיח֑וֹ וַיֵּ֨לְכ֜וּ וַ֠יָּבֹ֠אוּ בֵּית־אִשָּׁ֥ה זוֹנָ֛ה וּשְׁמָ֥הּ רָחָ֖ב וַיִּשְׁכְּבוּ־שָֽׁמָּה:

ב וַיֵּ֣אָמַ֔ר לְמֶ֥לֶךְ יְרִיח֖וֹ לֵאמֹ֑ר הִנֵּ֣ה אֲנָשִׁ֗ים בָּ֣אוּ הֵ֤נָּה הַלַּ֙יְלָה֙ מִבְּנֵ֣י יִשְׂרָאֵ֔ל לַחְפֹּ֖ר אֶת־הָאָֽרֶץ:

ג וַיִּשְׁלַח֙ מֶ֣לֶךְ יְרִיח֔וֹ אֶל־רָחָ֖ב לֵאמֹ֑ר ה֠וֹצִ֠יאִי הָאֲנָשִׁ֨ים הַבָּאִ֤ים אֵלַ֙יִךְ֙ אֲשֶׁר־בָּ֣אוּ לְבֵיתֵ֔ךְ כִּ֛י לַחְפֹּ֥ר אֶת־כָּל־הָאָ֖רֶץ בָּֽאוּ:

ד וַתִּקַּ֧ח הָֽאִשָּׁ֛ה אֶת־שְׁנֵ֥י הָאֲנָשִׁ֖ים וַֽתִּצְפְּנ֑וֹ וַתֹּ֣אמֶר ׀ כֵּ֗ן בָּ֤אוּ אֵלַי֙ הָֽאֲנָשִׁ֔ים וְלֹ֥א יָדַ֖עְתִּי מֵאַ֥יִן הֵֽמָּה:

ה וַיְהִ֨י הַשַּׁ֜עַר לִסְגּ֗וֹר בַּחֹ֙שֶׁךְ֙ וְהָֽאֲנָשִׁ֣ים יָצָ֔אוּ לֹ֣א יָדַ֔עְתִּי אָ֥נָה הָלְכ֖וּ הָאֲנָשִׁ֑ים רִדְפ֥וּ מַהֵ֛ר אַחֲרֵיהֶ֖ם כִּ֥י תַשִּׂיגֽוּם:

ו וְהִ֖יא הֶעֱלָ֣תַם הַגָּ֑גָה וַֽתִּטְמְנֵם֙ בְּפִשְׁתֵּ֣י הָעֵ֔ץ הָעֲרֻכ֥וֹת לָ֖הּ עַל־הַגָּֽג:

ז וְהָאֲנָשִׁ֗ים רָדְפ֤וּ אַחֲרֵיהֶם֙ דֶּ֣רֶךְ הַיַּרְדֵּ֔ן עַ֖ל הַֽמַּעְבְּר֑וֹת וְהַשַּׁ֣עַר סָגָ֔רוּ אַחֲרֵ֕י כַּאֲשֶׁ֛ר יָצְא֥וּ הָרֹדְפִ֖ים אַחֲרֵיהֶֽם:

ח וְהֵ֖מָּה טֶ֣רֶם יִשְׁכָּב֑וּן וְהִ֛יא עָלְתָ֥ה עֲלֵיהֶ֖ם עַל־הַגָּֽג:

ט וַתֹּ֙אמֶר֙ אֶל־הָ֣אֲנָשִׁ֔ים יָדַ֕עְתִּי כִּֽי־נָתַ֧ן יהו֛ה לָכֶ֖ם אֶת־הָאָ֑רֶץ וְכִי־נָֽפְלָ֤ה אֵֽימַתְכֶם֙ עָלֵ֔ינוּ וְכִ֥י נָמֹ֛גוּ כָּל־יֹשְׁבֵ֥י הָאָ֖רֶץ מִפְּנֵיכֶֽם:

י כִּ֣י שָׁמַ֗עְנוּ אֵ֠ת אֲשֶׁר־הוֹבִ֨ישׁ יהו֜ה אֶת־מֵ֤י יַם־סוּף֙ מִפְּנֵיכֶ֔ם בְּצֵאתְכֶ֖ם מִמִּצְרָ֑יִם וַאֲשֶׁ֣ר עֲשִׂיתֶ֡ם לִשְׁנֵי֩ מַלְכֵ֨י הָאֱמֹרִ֜י אֲשֶׁ֨ר בְּעֵ֤בֶר הַיַּרְדֵּן֙ לְסִיחֹ֣ן וּלְע֔וֹג אֲשֶׁ֥ר הֶחֱרַמְתֶּ֖ם אוֹתָֽם:

יא וַנִּשְׁמַע֙ וַיִּמַּ֣ס לְבָבֵ֔נוּ וְלֹא־קָ֨מָה ע֥וֹד ר֛וּחַ בְּאִ֖ישׁ מִפְּנֵיכֶ֑ם כִּ֚י יהו֣ה אֱלֹהֵיכֶ֔ם ה֤וּא אֱלֹהִים֙ בַּשָּׁמַ֣יִם מִמַּ֔עַל וְעַל־הָאָ֖רֶץ מִתָּֽחַת:

יב וְעַתָּ֗ה הִשָּֽׁבְעוּ־נָ֥א לִי֙ בַּֽיהו֔ה כִּי־עָשִׂ֥יתִי עִמָּכֶ֖ם חָ֑סֶד וַעֲשִׂיתֶ֨ם גַּם־אַתֶּ֜ם עִם־בֵּ֤ית אָבִי֙ חֶ֔סֶד וּנְתַתֶּ֥ם לִ֖י א֥וֹת אֱמֶֽת:

יג וְהַחֲיִתֶ֞ם אֶת־אָבִ֣י וְאֶת־אִמִּ֗י וְאֶת־אַחַי֙ וְאֶת־אחותי [אַחְיוֹתַ֔י] וְאֵ֖ת כָּל־אֲשֶׁ֣ר לָהֶ֑ם וְהִצַּלְתֶּ֥ם אֶת־נַפְשֹׁתֵ֖ינוּ מִמָּֽוֶת:

יד וַיֹּ֧אמְרוּ לָ֣הּ הָאֲנָשִׁ֗ים נַפְשֵׁ֤נוּ תַחְתֵּיכֶם֙ לָמ֔וּת אִ֚ם לֹ֣א תַגִּ֔ידוּ אֶת־דְּבָרֵ֖נוּ זֶ֑ה וְהָיָ֗ה בְּתֵת־יהו֥ה לָ֙נוּ֙ אֶת־הָאָ֔רֶץ וְעָשִׂ֥ינוּ עִמָּ֖ךְ חֶ֥סֶד וֶאֱמֶֽת:

טו וַתּוֹרִדֵ֥ם בַּחֶ֖בֶל בְּעַ֣ד הַֽחַלּ֑וֹן כִּ֤י בֵיתָהּ֙ בְּקִ֣יר הַֽחוֹמָ֔ה וּבַחוֹמָ֖ה הִ֥יא יוֹשָֽׁבֶת:

טז וַתֹּ֤אמֶר לָהֶם֙ הָהָ֣רָה לֵּ֔כוּ פֶּֽן־יִפְגְּע֥וּ בָכֶ֖ם הָרֹדְפִ֑ים וְנַחְבֵּתֶ֨ם שָׁ֜מָּה שְׁלֹ֣שֶׁת יָמִ֗ים עַ֚ד שׁ֣וֹב הָרֹדְפִ֔ים וְאַחַ֖ר תֵּלְכ֥וּ לְדַרְכְּכֶֽם:

יז וַיֹּאמְר֥וּ אֵלֶ֖יהָ הָאֲנָשִׁ֑ים נְקִיִּ֣ם אֲנַ֔חְנוּ מִשְּׁבֻעָתֵ֥ךְ הַזֶּ֖ה אֲשֶׁ֥ר הִשְׁבַּעְתָּֽנוּ:

יח הִנֵּ֛ה אֲנַ֥חְנוּ בָאִ֖ים בָּאָ֑רֶץ אֶת־תִּקְוַ֡ת חוּט֩ הַשָּׁנִ֨י הַזֶּ֜ה תִּקְשְׁרִ֗י בַּֽחַלּוֹן֙ אֲשֶׁ֣ר הוֹרַדְתֵּ֣נוּ ב֔וֹ וְאֶת־אָבִ֨יךְ וְאֶת־

19 mother, your siblings, and all your father's household into your home. If anyone ventures outside the doors of your house, his blood will be upon his own head – we will be free of blame – while if a hand is laid on anyone who remains in the house with you, his
20 blood shall be upon ours. But if you speak a word of this, we shall be free of the oath we
21 swore to you." "As you say, so be it," she said, and she sent them away. They left, and she
22 tied the scarlet thread in the window. They set out and arrived at the hills. They stayed there for three days until the pursuers turned back, for the pursuers had searched the
23 entire route but failed to find them. The two men then went back, descended the hills, and crossed over. They came to Yehoshua son of Nun and reported all that had befallen
24 them. "The Lord has delivered the whole land into our hands," they said to Yehoshua, "and what is more, all the people of the land quake before us."

HAFTARAT KORAḤ

On Rosh Ḥodesh Tamuz read the haftara on page 497.

11 14 And Shmuel said to the people, "Come, let us go to Gilgal, and we will renew the   I SAMUEL
   15 kingship there." All the people went to Gilgal, and they crowned Sha'ul king there at Gilgal before the Lord. They sacrificed peace offerings before the Lord, and Sha'ul
12 1 rejoiced greatly along with all the men of Israel.   Then Shmuel addressed all of Israel. "Now, I have heeded your voices in all you said to me, and I have crowned a king
    2 over you – and now, here is the king, walking before you. I have grown old and grey, but my sons are here with you; I have been walking before you from my youth until this day.
    3 Here I am – testify against me in front of the Lord and in front of His anointed – whose ox have I seized, and whose donkey have I seized? Whom have I cheated, and whom have I oppressed, and from whose hand have I taken a bribe and averted my eyes
    4 from him? Let me repay you." And they said, "You have not cheated us,
    5 nor oppressed us, nor taken anything from anyone." "The Lord is witness against you," he said to them, "and His anointed is witness on this day, that you have found nothing
    6 in my possession." And it was declared, "The witness is…   the Lord," Shmuel said to the people, "who appointed Moshe and Aharon and brought your ancestors
    7 out of the land of Egypt. Now take your stand, and I will plead my case with you before the Lord: all the Lord's acts of loyalty that He has done for you and your ancestors.
    8 When Yaakov arrived in Egypt and your ancestors cried out to the Lord, the Lord sent
    9 Moshe and Aharon to take them out of Egypt, and they settled them in this place. But they forgot the Lord their God, and He sold them into the hands of Sisera, the general of Ḥatzor, and into the hands of the Philistines, and into the hands of the king of Moav,
   10 who attacked them. Then they cried out to the Lord. 'We have sinned,' they said, 'for we left the Lord and served the Baalim and the Ashterot – oh, save us from the hands

יט אִמֵּ֣ךְ וְאַחַ֗יִךְ וְאֵת֙ כׇּל־בֵּ֣ית אָבִ֔יךְ תַּאַסְפִ֥י אֵלַ֖יִךְ הַבָּ֑יְתָה וְהָיָ֡ה כֹּ֣ל אֲשֶׁר־יֵצֵא֩ מִדַּלְתֵ֨י בֵיתֵ֧ךְ ׀ הַח֛וּצָה דָּמ֥וֹ בְרֹאשׁ֖וֹ וַאֲנַ֣חְנוּ נְקִיִּ֑ם וְכֹ֠ל אֲשֶׁ֨ר יִֽהְיֶ֤ה אִתָּךְ֙ בַּבַּ֔יִת דָּמ֥וֹ
כ בְרֹאשֵׁ֖נוּ אִם־יָ֥ד תִּֽהְיֶה־בּֽוֹ׃ וְאִם־תַּגִּ֖ידִי אֶת־דְּבָרֵ֣נוּ זֶ֑ה וְהָיִ֣ינוּ נְקִיִּ֔ם מִשְּׁבֻעָתֵ֖ךְ אֲשֶׁ֥ר
כא הִשְׁבַּעְתָּֽנוּ׃ וַתֹּ֨אמֶר֙ כְּדִבְרֵיכֶ֣ם כֶּן־ה֔וּא וַֽתְּשַׁלְּחֵ֖ם וַיֵּלֵ֑כוּ וַתִּקְשֹׁ֛ר אֶת־תִּקְוַ֥ת הַשָּׁנִ֖י
כב בַּחַלּֽוֹן׃ וַיֵּלְכוּ֙ וַיָּבֹ֣אוּ הָהָ֔רָה וַיֵּ֤שְׁבוּ שָׁם֙ שְׁלֹ֣שֶׁת יָמִ֔ים עַד־שָׁ֖בוּ הָרֹדְפִ֑ים וַיְבַקְשׁ֧וּ
כג הָרֹדְפִ֛ים בְּכׇל־הַדֶּ֖רֶךְ וְלֹ֥א מָצָֽאוּ׃ וַיָּשֻׁ֜בוּ שְׁנֵ֤י הָֽאֲנָשִׁים֙ וַיֵּרְד֣וּ מֵהָהָ֔ר וַיַּעַבְרוּ֙ וַיָּבֹ֔אוּ
כד אֶל־יְהוֹשֻׁ֖עַ בִּן־נ֑וּן וַיְסַ֨פְּרוּ־ל֔וֹ אֵ֥ת כׇּל־הַמֹּצְא֖וֹת אוֹתָֽם׃ וַיֹּאמְרוּ֙ אֶל־יְהוֹשֻׁ֔עַ כִּֽי־נָתַ֧ן יְהֹוָ֛ה בְּיָדֵ֖נוּ אֶת־כׇּל־הָאָ֑רֶץ וְגַם־נָמֹ֛גוּ כׇּל־יֹשְׁבֵ֥י הָאָ֖רֶץ מִפָּנֵֽינוּ׃

הפטרת קרח

On הפטרה read the ראש חודש תמוז on page 497.

שמואל א׳

יד וַיֹּ֤אמֶר שְׁמוּאֵל֙ אֶל־הָעָ֔ם לְכ֖וּ וְנֵלְכָ֣ה הַגִּלְגָּ֑ל וּנְחַדֵּ֥שׁ שָׁ֖ם הַמְּלוּכָֽה׃ וַיֵּלְכ֨וּ כׇל־הָעָ֜ם
טו הַגִּלְגָּ֗ל וַיַּמְלִ֩כוּ֩ שָׁ֨ם אֶת־שָׁא֜וּל לִפְנֵ֤י יְהֹוָה֙ בַּגִּלְגָּ֔ל וַיִּזְבְּחוּ־שָׁ֛ם זְבָחִ֥ים שְׁלָמִ֖ים לִפְנֵ֣י
יב א יְהֹוָ֑ה וַיִּשְׂמַ֨ח שָׁ֥ם שָׁא֛וּל וְכׇל־אַנְשֵׁ֥י יִשְׂרָאֵ֖ל עַד־מְאֹֽד׃ וַיֹּ֤אמֶר שְׁמוּאֵל֙ אֶל־כׇּל־יִשְׂרָאֵ֔ל הִנֵּה֙ שָׁמַ֣עְתִּי בְקֹלְכֶ֔ם לְכֹ֥ל אֲשֶׁר־אֲמַרְתֶּ֖ם לִ֑י וָאַמְלִ֥יךְ עֲלֵיכֶ֖ם
ב מֶֽלֶךְ׃ וְעַתָּ֞ה הִנֵּ֥ה הַמֶּ֣לֶךְ ׀ מִתְהַלֵּ֣ךְ לִפְנֵיכֶ֗ם וַאֲנִי֙ זָקַ֣נְתִּי וָשַׂ֔בְתִּי וּבָנַ֖י הִנָּ֣ם אִתְּכֶ֑ם
ג וַאֲנִי֙ הִתְהַלַּ֣כְתִּי לִפְנֵיכֶ֔ם מִנְּעֻרַ֖י עַד־הַיּ֣וֹם הַזֶּ֑ה הִנְנִ֣י עֲנ֣וּ בִ֡י נֶ֩גֶד֩ יְהֹוָ֨ה וְנֶ֣גֶד מְשִׁיח֡וֹ אֶת־שׁוֹר֩ ׀ מִ֨י לָקַ֜חְתִּי וַחֲמ֣וֹר מִ֣י לָקַ֗חְתִּי וְאֶת־מִ֤י עָשַׁ֙קְתִּי֙ אֶת־מִ֣י רַצּ֔וֹתִי וּמִיַּד־מִי֙
ד לָקַ֣חְתִּי כֹ֔פֶר וְאַעְלִ֥ים עֵינַ֖י בּ֑וֹ וְאָשִׁ֖יב לָכֶֽם׃ וַיֹּ֣אמְר֔וּ לֹ֥א עֲשַׁקְתָּ֖נוּ וְלֹ֣א רַצּוֹתָ֑נוּ וְלֹֽא־
ה לָקַ֥חְתָּ מִיַּד־אִ֖ישׁ מְאֽוּמָה׃ וַיֹּ֨אמֶר אֲלֵיהֶ֜ם עֵ֧ד יְהֹוָ֣ה בָּכֶ֗ם וְעֵ֤ד מְשִׁיחוֹ֙ הַיּ֣וֹם הַזֶּ֔ה כִּ֣י
ו לֹ֧א מְצָאתֶ֛ם בְּיָדִ֖י מְא֑וּמָה וַיֹּ֥אמֶר עֵֽד׃ וַיֹּ֤אמֶר שְׁמוּאֵל֙ אֶל־הָעָ֔ם יְהֹוָ֗ה אֲשֶׁ֤ר עָשָׂה֙ אֶת־מֹשֶׁ֣ה וְאֶֽת־אַהֲרֹ֔ן וַאֲשֶׁ֧ר הֶעֱלָ֛ה אֶת־אֲבֹתֵיכֶ֖ם מֵאֶ֥רֶץ מִצְרָֽיִם׃
ז וְעַתָּ֗ה הִֽתְיַצְּב֛וּ וְאִשָּׁפְטָ֥ה אִתְּכֶ֖ם לִפְנֵ֣י יְהֹוָ֑ה אֵ֚ת כׇּל־צִדְק֣וֹת יְהֹוָ֔ה אֲשֶׁר־עָשָׂ֥ה
ח אִתְּכֶ֖ם וְאֶת־אֲבוֹתֵיכֶֽם׃ כַּֽאֲשֶׁר־בָּ֥א יַעֲקֹ֖ב מִצְרָ֑יִם וַיִּזְעֲק֤וּ אֲבוֹתֵיכֶם֙ אֶל־יְהֹוָ֔ה וַיִּשְׁלַ֨ח יְהֹוָ֜ה אֶת־מֹשֶׁ֣ה וְאֶֽת־אַהֲרֹ֗ן וַיּוֹצִ֤יאוּ אֶת־אֲבֹֽתֵיכֶם֙ מִמִּצְרַ֔יִם וַיֹּשִׁב֖וּם בַּמָּק֥וֹם הַזֶּֽה׃
ט וַֽיִּשְׁכְּח֖וּ אֶת־יְהֹוָ֣ה אֱלֹהֵיהֶ֑ם וַיִּמְכֹּ֣ר אֹתָ֡ם בְּיַ֣ד סִֽיסְרָא֩ שַׂר־צְבָ֨א חָצ֜וֹר וּבְיַד־פְּלִשְׁתִּ֗ים
י וּבְיַד֙ מֶ֣לֶךְ מוֹאָ֔ב וַיִּֽלָּחֲמ֖וּ בָּֽם׃ וַיִּזְעֲק֤וּ אֶל־יְהֹוָה֙ וַיֹּ֣אמַ֔ר חָטָ֕אנוּ כִּ֤י עָזַ֙בְנוּ֙ אֶת־יְהֹוָ֔ה

11 of our enemies, and we will serve You.' So the Lord sent Yerubaal and Bedan and Yiftaḥ
and Shmuel and saved you from the hands of the enemies around you, and you dwelled
12 in safety. But when you saw that King Naḥash of the Amonites came upon you, you
told me, 'No, we must have a king to reign over us,' though the Lord your God is your
13 King. And now, here is the king that you yourselves have chosen – that you yourselves
14 demanded – here, the Lord has set a king over you! If you fear the Lord, then serve
him and heed his voice, and do not spurn the word of God; both you and the king who
15 reigns over you must follow the Lord your God. But if you do not heed the Lord's
voice and rebel against the Lord's word, then the Lord's hand shall bear down against
16 you and your ancestral houses. And now, stand by and see what a tremendous feat the
17 Lord is about to perform before your very eyes: Is it not the wheat harvest today? I
will call out to the Lord, and He will unleash thunder and rain. Then you will know,
and then you will see, how great an evil you have committed in the eyes of the Lord by
18 asking for a king for yourselves." Then Shmuel called out to the Lord, and the
Lord unleashed thunder and rain on that day. All the people were struck with terror
19 of the Lord, and of Shmuel as well. And all the people said to Shmuel, "Pray on your
servants' behalf to the Lord your God so that we will not die; for we have added yet
20 another evil to all our offenses by asking for a king for ourselves." "Do not fear,
though you have done all this evil," Shmuel said to the people, "so long as you do not
21 turn away from the Lord; serve the Lord with all your heart. But do not turn away
22 to follow futilities that neither help nor save, for they are futile. For the Lord will not
desert His people for the sake of His great name, because the Lord has undertaken to
make you His people.

HAFTARAT ḤUKAT

When Ḥukat and Balak are read together read the haftara on page 487.
On Rosh Ḥodesh Tamuz read the haftara on page 497.

11 1 Yiftaḥ the Gileadite was a valiant warrior. He was the son of a harlot; Gilad sired Yiftaḥ, JUDGES
2 but Gilad's wife bore him sons as well. When the wife's sons grew up, they drove Yiftaḥ
away, telling him, "You shall have no share in our father's estate, for you are the son of
3 another woman." So Yiftaḥ fled from his brothers; he settled in the land of Tov. Worthless
4 men were drawn to him and went out raiding with him. Time passed, and the
5 Amonites waged war upon Israel. When the Amonites attacked Israel, the elders of Gilad
6 set out to bring Yiftaḥ back from the land of Tov. "Come with us," they said to Yiftaḥ,
7 "and be our commander, so that we can fight against the Amonites." "But you despised
me," Yiftaḥ said to the elders of Gilad, "and drove me away from my father's house. Why

יא וַנַּעֲבֹד אֶת־הַבְּעָלִים וְאֶת־הָעַשְׁתָּרוֹת וְעַתָּה הַצִּילֵנוּ מִיַּד אֹיְבֵינוּ וְנַעַבְדֶךָּ: וַיִּשְׁלַח
יְהֹוָה אֶת־יְרֻבַּעַל וְאֶת־בְּדָן וְאֶת־יִפְתָּח וְאֶת־שְׁמוּאֵל וַיַּצֵּל אֶתְכֶם מִיַּד אֹיְבֵיכֶם
יב מִסָּבִיב וַתֵּשְׁבוּ בֶּטַח: וַתִּרְאוּ כִּי־נָחָשׁ מֶלֶךְ בְּנֵי־עַמּוֹן בָּא עֲלֵיכֶם וַתֹּאמְרוּ לִי לֹא
יג כִּי־מֶלֶךְ יִמְלֹךְ עָלֵינוּ וַיהֹוָה אֱלֹהֵיכֶם מַלְכְּכֶם: וְעַתָּה הִנֵּה הַמֶּלֶךְ אֲשֶׁר בְּחַרְתֶּם
יד אֲשֶׁר שְׁאֶלְתֶּם וְהִנֵּה נָתַן יְהֹוָה עֲלֵיכֶם מֶלֶךְ: אִם־תִּירְאוּ אֶת־יְהֹוָה וַעֲבַדְתֶּם אֹתוֹ
וּשְׁמַעְתֶּם בְּקֹלוֹ וְלֹא תַמְרוּ אֶת־פִּי יְהֹוָה וִהְיִתֶם גַּם־אַתֶּם וְגַם־הַמֶּלֶךְ אֲשֶׁר מָלַךְ
טו עֲלֵיכֶם אַחַר יְהֹוָה אֱלֹהֵיכֶם: וְאִם־לֹא תִשְׁמְעוּ בְּקוֹל יְהֹוָה וּמְרִיתֶם אֶת־פִּי יְהֹוָה
טז וְהָיְתָה יַד־יְהֹוָה בָּכֶם וּבַאֲבוֹתֵיכֶם: גַּם־עַתָּה הִתְיַצְּבוּ וּרְאוּ אֶת־הַדָּבָר הַגָּדוֹל
יז הַזֶּה אֲשֶׁר יְהֹוָה עֹשֶׂה לְעֵינֵיכֶם: הֲלוֹא קְצִיר־חִטִּים הַיּוֹם אֶקְרָא אֶל־יְהֹוָה וְיִתֵּן
קֹלוֹת וּמָטָר וּדְעוּ וּרְאוּ כִּי־רָעַתְכֶם רַבָּה אֲשֶׁר עֲשִׂיתֶם בְּעֵינֵי יְהֹוָה לִשְׁאוֹל לָכֶם
יח מֶלֶךְ: וַיִּקְרָא שְׁמוּאֵל אֶל־יְהֹוָה וַיִּתֵּן יְהֹוָה קֹלֹת וּמָטָר בַּיּוֹם הַהוּא
יט וַיִּירָא כָל־הָעָם מְאֹד אֶת־יְהֹוָה וְאֶת־שְׁמוּאֵל: וַיֹּאמְרוּ כָל־הָעָם אֶל־שְׁמוּאֵל
הִתְפַּלֵּל בְּעַד־עֲבָדֶיךָ אֶל־יְהֹוָה אֱלֹהֶיךָ וְאַל־נָמוּת כִּי־יָסַפְנוּ עַל־כָּל־חַטֹּאתֵינוּ
כ רָעָה לִשְׁאֹל לָנוּ מֶלֶךְ: וַיֹּאמֶר שְׁמוּאֵל אֶל־הָעָם אַל־תִּירָאוּ אַתֶּם
עֲשִׂיתֶם אֵת כָּל־הָרָעָה הַזֹּאת אַךְ אַל־תָּסוּרוּ מֵאַחֲרֵי יְהֹוָה וַעֲבַדְתֶּם אֶת־יְהֹוָה
כא בְּכָל־לְבַבְכֶם: וְלֹא תָּסוּרוּ כִּי אַחֲרֵי הַתֹּהוּ אֲשֶׁר לֹא־יוֹעִילוּ וְלֹא יַצִּילוּ כִּי־תֹהוּ
כב הֵמָּה: כִּי לֹא־יִטֹּשׁ יְהֹוָה אֶת־עַמּוֹ בַּעֲבוּר שְׁמוֹ הַגָּדוֹל כִּי הוֹאִיל יְהֹוָה לַעֲשׂוֹת
אֶתְכֶם לוֹ לְעָם:

הפטרת חקת

When חקת and בלק are read together read the הפטרה on page 487.
On ראש חודש תמוז read the הפטרה on page 497.

יא א וְיִפְתָּח הַגִּלְעָדִי הָיָה גִּבּוֹר חַיִל וְהוּא בֶּן־אִשָּׁה זוֹנָה וַיּוֹלֶד גִּלְעָד אֶת־יִפְתָּח: שופטים
ב וַתֵּלֶד אֵשֶׁת־גִּלְעָד לוֹ בָּנִים וַיִּגְדְּלוּ בְנֵי־הָאִשָּׁה וַיְגָרְשׁוּ אֶת־יִפְתָּח וַיֹּאמְרוּ לוֹ לֹא־
ג תִנְחַל בְּבֵית־אָבִינוּ כִּי בֶּן־אִשָּׁה אַחֶרֶת אָתָּה: וַיִּבְרַח יִפְתָּח מִפְּנֵי אֶחָיו וַיֵּשֶׁב בְּאֶרֶץ
ד טוֹב וַיִּתְלַקְּטוּ אֶל־יִפְתָּח אֲנָשִׁים רֵיקִים וַיֵּצְאוּ עִמּוֹ: וַיְהִי מִיָּמִים וַיִּלָּחֲמוּ
ה בְנֵי־עַמּוֹן עִם־יִשְׂרָאֵל: וַיְהִי כַּאֲשֶׁר־נִלְחֲמוּ בְנֵי־עַמּוֹן עִם־יִשְׂרָאֵל וַיֵּלְכוּ זִקְנֵי גִלְעָד
ו לָקַחַת אֶת־יִפְתָּח מֵאֶרֶץ טוֹב: וַיֹּאמְרוּ לְיִפְתָּח לְכָה וְהָיִיתָה לָּנוּ לְקָצִין וְנִלָּחֲמָה
ז בִּבְנֵי עַמּוֹן: וַיֹּאמֶר יִפְתָּח לְזִקְנֵי גִלְעָד הֲלֹא אַתֶּם שְׂנֵאתֶם אוֹתִי וַתְּגָרְשׁוּנִי מִבֵּית

8 do you come to me now, when you are in trouble?" "For that reason we ourselves have come back to you now," the elders of Gilad said to Yiftaḥ. "You shall march out with
9 us and fight the Amonites, and you shall be the leader of all the people of Gilad." "If you bring me back to fight against the Amonites," Yiftaḥ replied to the elders of Gilad,
10 "and the Lord delivers them to me, then I shall be your leader." The elders of Gilad said to Yiftaḥ, "The Lord shall bear witness between us if we do not comply with your
11 words." So Yiftaḥ went with the elders of Gilad, and the people made him their head and
12 commander. Yiftaḥ repeated all his terms before the Lord at Mitzpa.   Yiftaḥ sent messengers to the king of the Amonites: "What do you have against us, that you
13 came to attack our land?" The king of the Amonites replied to Yiftaḥ's messengers, "Israel seized my lands when they came out of Egypt – from the Arnon to the Yabok and up
14 to the Jordan. Now hand them back peacefully." Once again Yiftaḥ sent messengers to
15 the king of the Amonites. "Thus says Yiftaḥ," they said. "Israel did not seize the land of
16 Moav nor the land of the Amonites. For when they came out of Egypt, Israel trekked
17 through the wilderness to the Sea of Reeds, then they arrived at Kadesh. And Israel sent messengers to the king of Edom, saying, 'Please let us pass through your land,' but the king of Edom would not listen; they also reached out to the king of Moav, but he would
18 not comply. So Israel remained in Kadesh. They trekked through the wilderness, making their way around the land of Edom and the land of Moav until they reached the eastern side of the land of Moav, where they encamped across the Arnon. They did not enter
19 Moabite territory, for the Arnon is the Moabite border. Then Israel sent messengers to Siḥon, king of the Amorites, the king of Ḥeshbon. Israel said to him, 'Please, let us pass
20 through your land to our own place.' But Siḥon did not trust Israel to pass through his territory. And Siḥon assembled all his troops, encamped at Yahtza, and attacked Israel.
21 The Lord, God of Israel, delivered Siḥon and all of his people into Israel's hands; they defeated them, and the Israelites took possession of the entire land of the Amorites,
22 who lived in that land. They took possession of all the Amorite territory from Arnon
23 to the Yabok, and from the wilderness to the Jordan. Now, the Lord, God of Israel,
24 dispossessed the Amorites before His people, Israel – why should you possess it? You take possession of what Kemosh, your god, grants you, and we will take possession of
25 everything the Lord, our God, grants us. Now, are you any better than Balak son of Tzipor, king of Moav? Did he pick a quarrel with Israel? Did he wage war against them?
26 Israel has been dwelling in Ḥeshbon and its boroughs, Aroer and its boroughs, and in all the towns near Arnon, for three hundred years – why have you not reclaimed them all
27 this time? I have never offended you, yet you do me wrong by fighting against me. May
28 the Lord, who judges, judge between the Israelites and the Amonites today." But the
29 king of the Amonites did not listen to the words Yiftaḥ delivered to him.   The spirit of the Lord settled upon Yiftaḥ, and he crossed through Gilad and Menashe; he

הפטרת חקת

ח אָבִי וּמַדּוּעַ בָּאתֶם אֵלַי עַתָּה כַּאֲשֶׁר צַר לָכֶם: וַיֹּאמְרוּ זִקְנֵי גִלְעָד אֶל־יִפְתָּח לָכֵן עַתָּה שַׁבְנוּ אֵלֶיךָ וְהָלַכְתָּ עִמָּנוּ וְנִלְחַמְתָּ בִּבְנֵי עַמּוֹן וְהָיִיתָ לָּנוּ לְרֹאשׁ לְכֹל יֹשְׁבֵי גִלְעָד:
ט וַיֹּאמֶר יִפְתָּח אֶל־זִקְנֵי גִלְעָד אִם־מְשִׁיבִים אַתֶּם אוֹתִי לְהִלָּחֵם בִּבְנֵי עַמּוֹן וְנָתַן יְהוָה אוֹתָם לְפָנָי אָנֹכִי אֶהְיֶה לָכֶם לְרֹאשׁ: וַיֹּאמְרוּ זִקְנֵי־גִלְעָד אֶל־יִפְתָּח
י יְהוָה יִהְיֶה שֹׁמֵעַ בֵּינוֹתֵינוּ אִם־לֹא כִדְבָרְךָ כֵּן נַעֲשֶׂה: וַיֵּלֶךְ יִפְתָּח עִם־זִקְנֵי גִלְעָד
יא וַיָּשִׂימוּ הָעָם אוֹתוֹ עֲלֵיהֶם לְרֹאשׁ וּלְקָצִין וַיְדַבֵּר יִפְתָּח אֶת־כָּל־דְּבָרָיו לִפְנֵי יְהוָה בַּמִּצְפָּה:
יב וַיִּשְׁלַח יִפְתָּח מַלְאָכִים אֶל־מֶלֶךְ בְּנֵי־עַמּוֹן לֵאמֹר מַה־לִּי וָלָךְ כִּי־בָאתָ אֵלַי לְהִלָּחֵם בְּאַרְצִי: וַיֹּאמֶר מֶלֶךְ בְּנֵי־עַמּוֹן אֶל־מַלְאֲכֵי יִפְתָּח כִּי־
יג לָקַח יִשְׂרָאֵל אֶת־אַרְצִי בַּעֲלוֹתוֹ מִמִּצְרַיִם מֵאַרְנוֹן וְעַד־הַיַּבֹּק וְעַד־הַיַּרְדֵּן וְעַתָּה הָשִׁיבָה אֶתְהֶן בְּשָׁלוֹם: וַיּוֹסֶף עוֹד יִפְתָּח וַיִּשְׁלַח מַלְאָכִים אֶל־מֶלֶךְ בְּנֵי עַמּוֹן:
יד
טו וַיֹּאמֶר לוֹ כֹּה אָמַר יִפְתָּח לֹא־לָקַח יִשְׂרָאֵל אֶת־אֶרֶץ מוֹאָב וְאֶת־אֶרֶץ בְּנֵי עַמּוֹן:
טז כִּי בַּעֲלוֹתָם מִמִּצְרָיִם וַיֵּלֶךְ יִשְׂרָאֵל בַּמִּדְבָּר עַד־יַם־סוּף וַיָּבֹא קָדֵשָׁה: וַיִּשְׁלַח
יז יִשְׂרָאֵל מַלְאָכִים ׀ אֶל־מֶלֶךְ אֱדוֹם ׀ לֵאמֹר אֶעְבְּרָה־נָּא בְאַרְצֶךָ וְלֹא שָׁמַע מֶלֶךְ אֱדוֹם וְגַם אֶל־מֶלֶךְ מוֹאָב שָׁלַח וְלֹא אָבָה וַיֵּשֶׁב יִשְׂרָאֵל בְּקָדֵשׁ: וַיֵּלֶךְ בַּמִּדְבָּר
יח וַיָּסָב אֶת־אֶרֶץ אֱדוֹם וְאֶת־אֶרֶץ מוֹאָב וַיָּבֹא מִמִּזְרַח־שֶׁמֶשׁ לְאֶרֶץ מוֹאָב וַיַּחֲנוּן בְּעֵבֶר אַרְנוֹן וְלֹא־בָאוּ בִּגְבוּל מוֹאָב כִּי אַרְנוֹן גְּבוּל מוֹאָב: וַיִּשְׁלַח יִשְׂרָאֵל מַלְאָכִים
יט אֶל־סִיחוֹן מֶלֶךְ־הָאֱמֹרִי מֶלֶךְ חֶשְׁבּוֹן וַיֹּאמֶר לוֹ יִשְׂרָאֵל נַעְבְּרָה־נָּא בְאַרְצְךָ עַד־
כ מְקוֹמִי: וְלֹא־הֶאֱמִין סִיחוֹן אֶת־יִשְׂרָאֵל עֲבֹר בִּגְבֻלוֹ וַיֶּאֱסֹף סִיחוֹן אֶת־כָּל־עַמּוֹ וַיַּחֲנוּ בְּיָהְצָה וַיִּלָּחֶם עִם־יִשְׂרָאֵל: וַיִּתֵּן יְהוָה אֱלֹהֵי־יִשְׂרָאֵל אֶת־סִיחוֹן וְאֶת־כָּל־
כא עַמּוֹ בְּיַד יִשְׂרָאֵל וַיַּכּוּם וַיִּירַשׁ יִשְׂרָאֵל אֵת כָּל־אֶרֶץ הָאֱמֹרִי יוֹשֵׁב הָאָרֶץ הַהִיא:
כב וַיִּירְשׁוּ אֵת כָּל־גְּבוּל הָאֱמֹרִי מֵאַרְנוֹן וְעַד־הַיַּבֹּק וּמִן־הַמִּדְבָּר וְעַד־הַיַּרְדֵּן: וְעַתָּה
כג יְהוָה ׀ אֱלֹהֵי יִשְׂרָאֵל הוֹרִישׁ אֶת־הָאֱמֹרִי מִפְּנֵי עַמּוֹ יִשְׂרָאֵל וְאַתָּה תִּירָשֶׁנּוּ:
כד הֲלֹא אֵת אֲשֶׁר יוֹרִישְׁךָ כְּמוֹשׁ אֱלֹהֶיךָ אוֹתוֹ תִירָשׁ וְאֵת כָּל־אֲשֶׁר הוֹרִישׁ יְהוָה אֱלֹהֵינוּ מִפָּנֵינוּ אוֹתוֹ נִירָשׁ: וְעַתָּה הֲטוֹב טוֹב אַתָּה מִבָּלָק בֶּן־צִפּוֹר מֶלֶךְ מוֹאָב
כה הֲרוֹב רָב עִם־יִשְׂרָאֵל אִם־נִלְחֹם נִלְחַם בָּם: בְּשֶׁבֶת יִשְׂרָאֵל בְּחֶשְׁבּוֹן וּבִבְנוֹתֶיהָ
כו וּבְעַרְעוֹר וּבִבְנוֹתֶיהָ וּבְכָל־הֶעָרִים אֲשֶׁר עַל־יְדֵי אַרְנוֹן שְׁלֹשׁ מֵאוֹת שָׁנָה וּמַדּוּעַ לֹא־הִצַּלְתֶּם בָּעֵת הַהִיא: וְאָנֹכִי לֹא־חָטָאתִי לָךְ וְאַתָּה עֹשֶׂה אִתִּי רָעָה לְהִלָּחֶם
כז בִּי יִשְׁפֹּט יְהוָה הַשֹּׁפֵט הַיּוֹם בֵּין בְּנֵי יִשְׂרָאֵל וּבֵין בְּנֵי עַמּוֹן: וְלֹא שָׁמַע מֶלֶךְ בְּנֵי
כח עַמּוֹן אֶל־דִּבְרֵי יִפְתָּח אֲשֶׁר שָׁלַח אֵלָיו: וַתְּהִי עַל־יִפְתָּח רוּחַ יְהוָה
כט

30 crossed Mitzpeh Gilad; and from Mitzpeh Gilad he crossed over to the Amonites. Then Yiftaḥ swore a vow to the Lord. He said, "If You deliver the Amonites into my hand,
31 then whatever comes out of the doors of my home to meet me when I return safely from the Amonites shall be for the Lord, and I shall offer it up as a burnt offering."
32 Yiftaḥ crossed over to the Amonites and attacked them, and the Lord delivered them
33 into his hand. He defeated them from Aroer to Minit, twenty towns, all the way to Avel Keramim – a crushing defeat – and the Amonites were conquered by the Israelites.

HAFTARAT BALAK

When Ḥukat and Balak are read together read this haftara.

MICAH

5 6 And the remnant of Yaakov will be found amid countless peoples as dew brought down from the Lord, as ample rains shower upon grass; they will not look to any man,
7 nor place their hopes in humankind. The remnant of Yaakov will be among nations, amid countless peoples, like a lion among wild beasts of the forest, like a young lion among flocks of sheep whom, as they pass, he tramples and rips to pieces; there is no
8 one to save them. Your hand shall be raised over your foes; your enemies will be cut
9 down.   On that day, so says the Lord: I will cut out the horses from among
10 you, I will destroy your chariots, and I will cut down the fortified cities of your land
11 and demolish all your fortresses. I will cut out all practice of witchcraft, and there will
12 be no more fortune-tellers among you. I will cut down your idols, the worship pillars
13 from your midst; no longer will you bow down to the craft of your hands. I will rip out
14 the Ashera from your midst, and I will destroy your cities. I will lash out with My anger
6 1 and wrath in vengeance against nations who did not heed My words.   Hear now what the Lord says: Arise; argue your case before the mountains; let the hills hear your
2 plea. Hear, O mountains, the Lord's dispute – you, earth's everlasting foundations. For
3 the Lord has a dispute with His people; He will contend with Israel: My people! How
4 have I wronged you? How have I worn you down? Bear witness against Me, for I brought you up from the land of Egypt; I redeemed you from the house of slavery; I sent Moshe,
5 Aharon, and Miriam to lead you. My people, remember now how Balak, king of Moav, schemed, and how Bilam son of Beor responded; remember from Shitim to Gilgal so
6 that you may come to realize the righteous ways of the Lord. What then can I offer the Lord when I bow low to the God Most High? Should I come before Him with burnt
7 offerings, with year-old calves? Would the Lord want a thousand rams, untold rivulets of oil? Should I offer my firstborn as payment for my crimes, the fruit of my womb for

וַיַּעֲבֹר אֶת־הַגִּלְעָד וְאֶת־מְנַשֶּׁה וַיַּעֲבֹר אֶת־מִצְפֵּה גִלְעָד וּמִמִּצְפֵּה גִלְעָד עָבַר בְּנֵי
עַמּוֹן: וַיִּדַּר יִפְתָּח נֶדֶר לַיהוה וַיֹּאמַר אִם־נָתוֹן תִּתֵּן אֶת־בְּנֵי עַמּוֹן בְּיָדִי: וְהָיָה
הַיּוֹצֵא אֲשֶׁר יֵצֵא מִדַּלְתֵי בֵיתִי לִקְרָאתִי בְּשׁוּבִי בְשָׁלוֹם מִבְּנֵי עַמּוֹן וְהָיָה לַיהוה
וְהַעֲלִיתִהוּ עוֹלָה:

וַיַּעֲבֹר יִפְתָּח אֶל־בְּנֵי עַמּוֹן לְהִלָּחֶם בָּם וַיִּתְּנֵם יהוה בְּיָדוֹ: וַיַּכֵּם מֵעֲרוֹעֵר וְעַד־
בּוֹאֲךָ מִנִּית עֶשְׂרִים עִיר וְעַד אָבֵל כְּרָמִים מַכָּה גְּדוֹלָה מְאֹד וַיִּכָּנְעוּ בְּנֵי עַמּוֹן מִפְּנֵי
בְּנֵי יִשְׂרָאֵל:

לא

לב
לג

הפטרת בלק

When בלק and חקת are read together read this הפטרה.

מיכה
ה

וְהָיָה ׀ שְׁאֵרִית יַעֲקֹב בְּקֶרֶב עַמִּים רַבִּים כְּטַל מֵאֵת יהוה כִּרְבִיבִים עֲלֵי־עֵשֶׂב
אֲשֶׁר לֹא־יְקַוֶּה לְאִישׁ וְלֹא יְיַחֵל לִבְנֵי אָדָם: וְהָיָה שְׁאֵרִית יַעֲקֹב בַּגּוֹיִם בְּקֶרֶב
עַמִּים רַבִּים כְּאַרְיֵה בְּבַהֲמוֹת יַעַר כִּכְפִיר בְּעֶדְרֵי־צֹאן אֲשֶׁר אִם עָבַר וְרָמַס
וְטָרַף וְאֵין מַצִּיל: תָּרֹם יָדְךָ עַל־צָרֶיךָ וְכָל־אֹיְבֶיךָ יִכָּרֵתוּ: וְהָיָה בַיּוֹם־
הַהוּא נְאֻם־יהוה וְהִכְרַתִּי סוּסֶיךָ מִקִּרְבֶּךָ וְהַאֲבַדְתִּי מַרְכְּבֹתֶיךָ: וְהִכְרַתִּי עָרֵי
אַרְצֶךָ וְהָרַסְתִּי כָּל־מִבְצָרֶיךָ: וְהִכְרַתִּי כְשָׁפִים מִיָּדֶךָ וּמְעוֹנְנִים לֹא יִהְיוּ־לָךְ:
וְהִכְרַתִּי פְסִילֶיךָ וּמַצֵּבוֹתֶיךָ מִקִּרְבֶּךָ וְלֹא־תִשְׁתַּחֲוֶה עוֹד לְמַעֲשֵׂה יָדֶיךָ: וְנָתַשְׁתִּי
אֲשֵׁירֶיךָ מִקִּרְבֶּךָ וְהִשְׁמַדְתִּי עָרֶיךָ: וְעָשִׂיתִי בְּאַף וּבְחֵמָה נָקָם אֶת־הַגּוֹיִם אֲשֶׁר
לֹא שָׁמֵעוּ: שִׁמְעוּ־נָא אֵת אֲשֶׁר־יהוה אֹמֵר קוּם רִיב אֶת־הֶהָרִים
וְתִשְׁמַעְנָה הַגְּבָעוֹת קוֹלֶךָ: שִׁמְעוּ הָרִים אֶת־רִיב יהוה וְהָאֵתָנִים מֹסְדֵי אָרֶץ כִּי
רִיב לַיהוה עִם־עַמּוֹ וְעִם־יִשְׂרָאֵל יִתְוַכָּח: עַמִּי מֶה־עָשִׂיתִי לְךָ וּמָה הֶלְאֵתִיךָ עֲנֵה
בִי: כִּי הֶעֱלִתִיךָ מֵאֶרֶץ מִצְרַיִם וּמִבֵּית עֲבָדִים פְּדִיתִיךָ וָאֶשְׁלַח לְפָנֶיךָ אֶת־מֹשֶׁה
אַהֲרֹן וּמִרְיָם: עַמִּי זְכָר־נָא מַה־יָּעַץ בָּלָק מֶלֶךְ מוֹאָב וּמֶה־עָנָה אֹתוֹ בִּלְעָם בֶּן־
בְּעוֹר מִן־הַשִּׁטִּים עַד־הַגִּלְגָּל לְמַעַן דַּעַת צִדְקוֹת יהוה: בַּמָּה אֲקַדֵּם יהוה אִכַּף
לֵאלֹהֵי מָרוֹם הַאֲקַדְּמֶנּוּ בְעוֹלוֹת בַּעֲגָלִים בְּנֵי שָׁנָה: הֲיִרְצֶה יהוה בְּאַלְפֵי אֵילִים

ו
ז

ח
ט

י

יא

יב

יג

יד

ו א

ב

ג

ד

ה

ו

ז

8 the sins of my being? Man, God has told you what is good and what the Lord seeks from you: only to do justice, love goodness, and walk modestly with your God.

HAFTARAT PINḤAS

If this parasha falls before the 17th of Tamuz, read this haftara.
If it falls afterwards, read the haftara on page 491.

I KINGS

18:46 The hand of the Lord settled on Eliyahu, and he hitched up his tunic and ran
19:1 before Aḥav until he reached Yizre'el. When Aḥav told Izevel all that Eliyahu had
2 done and how he had put all the prophets to the sword, Izevel sent a messenger to Eliyahu: "So may the gods do to me and more if by this time tomorrow,
3 I have not treated your life like one of theirs." Frightened, he understood and fled for his life at once, and he reached Be'er Sheva of Yehuda and left
4 his servant boy there. But he continued a day's journey into the wilderness, then came and sat under a certain broom tree and prayed that he might die. "Enough!" he said. "O Lord, take my life now, for I am no better than my ancestors."
5 Then he lay down and fell asleep beneath that broom tree. Suddenly, an angel was
6 touching him, urging him, "Get up; eat." He looked up and there, at his head, was a
7 stone-baked cake and a flask of water. He ate and drank and lay back down. The angel of the Lord came back a second time and touched him. "Get up; eat," it said, "or the long
8 journey will prove too much for you." He got up and ate and drank, and by the strength
9 of that food, he walked forty days and forty nights to the mountain of God, Ḥorev. There he reached a cave, and there he spent the night. Suddenly, the word of the Lord came to
10 him and said to him, "Why are you here, Eliyahu?" "I acted out of fervor, out of passion for the Lord, God of Hosts," he said, "for the Israelites have abandoned Your covenant, destroyed Your altars, and put Your prophets to the sword. I am the only one left, and
11 they seek to take my life." "Go out and stand on the mountain before the Lord," He said, "for the Lord is about to pass by." And a great, powerful wind split mountains and shattered rocks before the Lord – but the Lord was not in the wind. And after the wind,
12 an earthquake – but the Lord was not in the earthquake. And after the earthquake,
13 fire – but the Lord was not in the fire. And after the fire – a faint sound of silence. And when Eliyahu heard, he wrapped his face in his cloak and went out and stood by the entrance of the cave. And suddenly a voice came to him and said, "Why are you here,
14 Eliyahu?" "I acted out of fervor, out of passion for the Lord, God of Hosts," he said, "for the Israelites have abandoned Your covenant, destroyed Your altars, and put Your
15 prophets to the sword. I am the only one left, and they seek to take my life." And the Lord answered him, "Set back out on your way to the Wilderness of Damascus.

במדבר | הפטרת פינחס   הפטרות וקריאות נוספות | 489

ח בְּרִבְבוֹת נַחֲלֵי־שָׁמֶן הַאֶתֵּן בְּכוֹרִי פִּשְׁעִי פְּרִי בִטְנִי חַטַּאת נַפְשִׁי: הִגִּיד לְךָ אָדָם מַה־טּוֹב וּמָה־יהוה דּוֹרֵשׁ מִמְּךָ כִּי אִם־עֲשׂוֹת מִשְׁפָּט וְאַהֲבַת חֶסֶד וְהַצְנֵעַ לֶכֶת עִם־אֱלֹהֶיךָ:

הפטרת פינחס

If this פרשה falls before the 17th of תמוז, read this הפטרה.
If it falls afterwards, read the הפטרה on page 491.

מלכים א׳ יח וַיַד־יהוה הָיְתָה אֶל־אֵלִיָּהוּ וַיְשַׁנֵּס מָתְנָיו וַיָּרָץ לִפְנֵי אַחְאָב עַד־בֹּאֲכָה יִזְרְעֶאלָה:
יט א וַיַּגֵּד אַחְאָב לְאִיזֶבֶל אֵת כָּל־אֲשֶׁר עָשָׂה אֵלִיָּהוּ וְאֵת כָּל־אֲשֶׁר הָרַג אֶת־כָּל־הַנְּבִיאִים בֶּחָרֶב: ב וַתִּשְׁלַח אִיזֶבֶל מַלְאָךְ אֶל־אֵלִיָּהוּ לֵאמֹר כֹּה־יַעֲשׂוּן אֱלֹהִים וְכֹה יוֹסִפוּן כִּי־כָעֵת מָחָר אָשִׂים אֶת־נַפְשְׁךָ כְּנֶפֶשׁ אַחַד מֵהֶם: ג וַיַּרְא וַיָּקָם וַיֵּלֶךְ אֶל־נַפְשׁוֹ וַיָּבֹא בְּאֵר שֶׁבַע אֲשֶׁר לִיהוּדָה וַיַּנַּח אֶת־נַעֲרוֹ שָׁם: ד וְהוּא־הָלַךְ בַּמִּדְבָּר דֶּרֶךְ יוֹם וַיָּבֹא וַיֵּשֶׁב תַּחַת רֹתֶם אֶחָת וַיִּשְׁאַל אֶת־נַפְשׁוֹ לָמוּת וַיֹּאמֶר ׀ רַב עַתָּה אֶחָד יהוה קַח נַפְשִׁי כִּי־לֹא־טוֹב אָנֹכִי מֵאֲבֹתָי: ה וַיִּשְׁכַּב וַיִּישַׁן תַּחַת רֹתֶם אֶחָד וְהִנֵּה־זֶה מַלְאָךְ נֹגֵעַ בּוֹ וַיֹּאמֶר לוֹ קוּם אֱכוֹל: ו וַיַּבֵּט וְהִנֵּה מְרַאֲשֹׁתָיו עֻגַת רְצָפִים וְצַפַּחַת מָיִם וַיֹּאכַל וַיֵּשְׁתְּ וַיָּשָׁב וַיִּשְׁכָּב: ז וַיָּשָׁב מַלְאַךְ יהוה ׀ שֵׁנִית וַיִּגַּע־בּוֹ וַיֹּאמֶר קוּם אֱכֹל כִּי רַב מִמְּךָ הַדָּרֶךְ: ח וַיָּקָם וַיֹּאכַל וַיִּשְׁתֶּה וַיֵּלֶךְ בְּכֹחַ ׀ הָאֲכִילָה הַהִיא אַרְבָּעִים יוֹם וְאַרְבָּעִים לַיְלָה עַד הַר הָאֱלֹהִים חֹרֵב: ט וַיָּבֹא־שָׁם אֶל־הַמְּעָרָה וַיָּלֶן שָׁם וְהִנֵּה דְבַר־יהוה אֵלָיו וַיֹּאמֶר לוֹ מַה־לְּךָ פֹה אֵלִיָּהוּ: י וַיֹּאמֶר קַנֹּא קִנֵּאתִי לַיהוה ׀ אֱלֹהֵי צְבָאוֹת כִּי־עָזְבוּ בְרִיתְךָ בְּנֵי יִשְׂרָאֵל אֶת־מִזְבְּחֹתֶיךָ הָרָסוּ וְאֶת־נְבִיאֶיךָ הָרְגוּ בֶחָרֶב וָאִוָּתֵר אֲנִי לְבַדִּי וַיְבַקְשׁוּ אֶת־נַפְשִׁי לְקַחְתָּהּ: יא וַיֹּאמֶר צֵא וְעָמַדְתָּ בָהָר לִפְנֵי יהוה וְהִנֵּה יהוה עֹבֵר וְרוּחַ גְּדוֹלָה וְחָזָק מְפָרֵק הָרִים וּמְשַׁבֵּר סְלָעִים לִפְנֵי יהוה לֹא בָרוּחַ יהוה וְאַחַר הָרוּחַ רַעַשׁ לֹא בָרַעַשׁ יהוה: יב וְאַחַר הָרַעַשׁ אֵשׁ לֹא בָאֵשׁ יהוה וְאַחַר הָאֵשׁ קוֹל דְּמָמָה דַקָּה: יג וַיְהִי ׀ כִּשְׁמֹעַ אֵלִיָּהוּ וַיָּלֶט פָּנָיו בְּאַדַּרְתּוֹ וַיֵּצֵא וַיַּעֲמֹד פֶּתַח הַמְּעָרָה וְהִנֵּה אֵלָיו קוֹל וַיֹּאמֶר מַה־לְּךָ פֹה אֵלִיָּהוּ: יד וַיֹּאמֶר קַנֹּא קִנֵּאתִי לַיהוה ׀ אֱלֹהֵי צְבָאוֹת כִּי־עָזְבוּ בְרִיתְךָ בְּנֵי יִשְׂרָאֵל אֶת־מִזְבְּחֹתֶיךָ הָרָסוּ וְאֶת־נְבִיאֶיךָ הָרְגוּ בֶחָרֶב וָאִוָּתֵר אֲנִי לְבַדִּי וַיְבַקְשׁוּ אֶת־נַפְשִׁי לְקַחְתָּהּ: טו וַיֹּאמֶר יהוה אֵלָיו לֵךְ שׁוּב לְדַרְכְּךָ מִדְבַּרָה דַמָּשֶׂק וּבָאתָ

16 When you arrive, anoint Ḥazael as king over Aram. As for Yehu son of Nimshi, anoint him as king over Israel; and as for Elisha son of Shafat of Avel Meḥola, anoint him as
17 a prophet in your place. Whoever escapes the sword of Ḥazael will be killed by Yehu,
18 and whoever escapes the sword of Yehu will be killed by Elisha. I will leave but seven thousand of Israel: every knee that has not bowed to Baal and every mouth that has
19 not kissed him." He set out from there and found Elisha son of Shafat. He was plowing with twelve pairs of oxen before him, and he was with the twelfth. When
20 Eliyahu reached him, he tossed his cloak over him. He left the oxen and went running after Eliyahu. "Let me just kiss my father and mother," he said, "and I will follow you." "Go back, then," he said to him. "What have I done
21 to you?" He turned back from him and took the pair of oxen; he slaughtered them, and, using the oxen gear, he boiled their meat and gave it out to the people to eat. Then he set out and followed Eliyahu and became his attendant.

HAFTARAT PINḤAS OR MATTOT

Read this haftara on the first Shabbat after the 17th of Tamuz.

1 1 The words of Yirmeyahu, son of Ḥilkiyahu, one of the priests who were in Anatot in   JEREMIAH
2 the land of Binyamin, to whom the word of the Lord came in the days of Yoshiyahu
3 son of Amon, king of Yehuda, in the thirteenth year of his reign, and continued during the days of Yehoyakim son of Yoshiyahu, king of Yehuda, until the end of the eleventh year of Tzidkiyahu son of Yoshiyahu, king of Yehuda – until the exile of Jerusalem in
4 the fifth month: The word of the Lord came to me: "Before I formed you
5 in the womb I knew you. Before you were born I consecrated you. I placed you as a
6 prophet to the nations." I said, "Please, Lord God, I am not capable of speaking, for I am
7 still only a boy." The Lord replied to me, "Do not say, 'I am a boy,' for you shall go to all
8 to whom I send you, and you shall speak as I instruct you. Do not fear them, for I am with
9 you to rescue you, declares the Lord." The Lord extended His hand and touched my
10 mouth and the Lord said to me, "Look, I have placed My words in your mouth. I have appointed you this day against the kingdoms and against the nations to uproot and tear
11 down, to destroy and demolish, to build and to plant."   The word of the Lord came to me: "What do you see, Yirmeyahu?" I replied, "I see the branch of an almond
12 tree." And the Lord said to me: "You have seen well, for I am watchful about keeping
13 My word."   The word of the Lord came to me a second time: "What do you
14 see?" I answered, "I see a boiling cauldron facing the north." And the Lord said to me:
15 "From the north disaster shall burst forth upon all the inhabitants of the land, for I am about to summon all the tribes of the kingdoms of the north," declares the Lord. "They shall come; each shall set up a throne at the entrance of the gates of Jerusalem against

הפטרת מטות

טז וּמָשַׁחְתָּ אֶת־חֲזָאֵל לְמֶלֶךְ עַל־אֲרָם: וְאֵת יֵהוּא בֶן־נִמְשִׁי תִּמְשַׁח לְמֶלֶךְ עַל־
יז יִשְׂרָאֵל וְאֶת־אֱלִישָׁע בֶּן־שָׁפָט מֵאָבֵל מְחוֹלָה תִּמְשַׁח לְנָבִיא תַּחְתֶּיךָ: וְהָיָה
יח הַנִּמְלָט מֵחֶרֶב חֲזָאֵל יָמִית יֵהוּא וְהַנִּמְלָט מֵחֶרֶב יֵהוּא יָמִית אֱלִישָׁע: וְהִשְׁאַרְתִּי בְיִשְׂרָאֵל שִׁבְעַת אֲלָפִים כָּל־הַבִּרְכַּיִם אֲשֶׁר לֹא־כָרְעוּ לַבַּעַל וְכָל־הַפֶּה אֲשֶׁר לֹא־
יט נָשַׁק לוֹ: וַיֵּלֶךְ מִשָּׁם וַיִּמְצָא אֶת־אֱלִישָׁע בֶּן־שָׁפָט וְהוּא חֹרֵשׁ שְׁנֵים־עָשָׂר צְמָדִים לְפָנָיו וְהוּא בִּשְׁנֵים הֶעָשָׂר וַיַּעֲבֹר אֵלִיָּהוּ אֵלָיו וַיַּשְׁלֵךְ אַדַּרְתּוֹ אֵלָיו:
כ וַיַּעֲזֹב אֶת־הַבָּקָר וַיָּרָץ אַחֲרֵי אֵלִיָּהוּ וַיֹּאמֶר אֶשְּׁקָה־נָּא לְאָבִי וּלְאִמִּי וְאֵלְכָה אַחֲרֶיךָ וַיֹּאמֶר
כא לוֹ לֵךְ שׁוּב כִּי מֶה־עָשִׂיתִי לָךְ: וַיָּשָׁב מֵאַחֲרָיו וַיִּקַּח אֶת־צֶמֶד הַבָּקָר וַיִּזְבָּחֵהוּ וּבִכְלִי הַבָּקָר בִּשְּׁלָם הַבָּשָׂר וַיִּתֵּן לָעָם וַיֹּאכֵלוּ וַיָּקָם וַיֵּלֶךְ אַחֲרֵי אֵלִיָּהוּ וַיְשָׁרְתֵהוּ:

הפטרת פינחס או מטות

Read this הפטרה on the first שבת after the 17th of תמוז.

ירמיה

א א דִּבְרֵי יִרְמְיָהוּ בֶּן־חִלְקִיָּהוּ מִן־הַכֹּהֲנִים אֲשֶׁר בַּעֲנָתוֹת בְּאֶרֶץ בִּנְיָמִן:
ב אֲשֶׁר הָיָה דְבַר־יְהֹוָה אֵלָיו בִּימֵי יֹאשִׁיָּהוּ בֶן־אָמוֹן מֶלֶךְ יְהוּדָה בִּשְׁלֹשׁ־עֶשְׂרֵה שָׁנָה לְמָלְכוֹ:
ג וַיְהִי בִּימֵי יְהוֹיָקִים בֶּן־יֹאשִׁיָּהוּ מֶלֶךְ יְהוּדָה עַד־תֹּם עַשְׁתֵּי־עֶשְׂרֵה שָׁנָה לְצִדְקִיָּהוּ
ד בֶן־יֹאשִׁיָּהוּ מֶלֶךְ יְהוּדָה עַד־גְּלוֹת יְרוּשָׁלַ͏ִם בַּחֹדֶשׁ הַחֲמִישִׁי: וַיְהִי דְבַר־

אֶצָּרְךָ

ה יְהֹוָה אֵלַי לֵאמֹר: בְּטֶרֶם אֶצָּרְךָ בַבֶּטֶן יְדַעְתִּיךָ וּבְטֶרֶם תֵּצֵא מֵרֶחֶם הִקְדַּשְׁתִּיךָ
ו נָבִיא לַגּוֹיִם נְתַתִּיךָ: וָאֹמַר אֲהָהּ אֲדֹנָי יֱהֹוִה הִנֵּה לֹא־יָדַעְתִּי דַּבֵּר כִּי־נַעַר אָנֹכִי:
ז וַיֹּאמֶר יְהֹוָה אֵלַי אַל־תֹּאמַר נַעַר אָנֹכִי כִּי עַל־כָּל־אֲשֶׁר אֶשְׁלָחֲךָ תֵּלֵךְ וְאֵת
ח כָּל־אֲשֶׁר אֲצַוְּךָ תְּדַבֵּר: אַל־תִּירָא מִפְּנֵיהֶם כִּי־אִתְּךָ אֲנִי לְהַצִּלֶךָ נְאֻם־יְהֹוָה:
ט וַיִּשְׁלַח יְהֹוָה אֶת־יָדוֹ וַיַּגַּע עַל־פִּי וַיֹּאמֶר יְהֹוָה אֵלַי הִנֵּה נָתַתִּי דְבָרַי בְּפִיךָ: רְאֵה הִפְקַדְתִּיךָ ׀ הַיּוֹם הַזֶּה עַל־הַגּוֹיִם וְעַל־הַמַּמְלָכוֹת לִנְתוֹשׁ וְלִנְתוֹץ וּלְהַאֲבִיד
יא וְלַהֲרוֹס לִבְנוֹת וְלִנְטוֹעַ: וַיְהִי דְבַר־יְהֹוָה אֵלַי לֵאמֹר מָה־אַתָּה רֹאֶה
יב יִרְמְיָהוּ וָאֹמַר מַקֵּל שָׁקֵד אֲנִי רֹאֶה: וַיֹּאמֶר יְהֹוָה אֵלַי הֵיטַבְתָּ לִרְאוֹת כִּי־שֹׁקֵד
יג אֲנִי עַל־דְּבָרִי לַעֲשֹׂתוֹ: וַיְהִי דְבַר־יְהֹוָה ׀ אֵלַי שֵׁנִית לֵאמֹר מָה אַתָּה
יד רֹאֶה וָאֹמַר סִיר נָפוּחַ אֲנִי רֹאֶה וּפָנָיו מִפְּנֵי צָפוֹנָה: וַיֹּאמֶר יְהֹוָה אֵלַי מִצָּפוֹן תִּפָּתַח
טו הָרָעָה עַל כָּל־יֹשְׁבֵי הָאָרֶץ: כִּי ׀ הִנְנִי קֹרֵא לְכָל־מִשְׁפְּחוֹת מַמְלְכוֹת צָפוֹנָה נְאֻם־יְהֹוָה וּבָאוּ וְנָתְנוּ אִישׁ כִּסְאוֹ פֶּתַח ׀ שַׁעֲרֵי יְרוּשָׁלַ͏ִם וְעַל כָּל־חוֹמֹתֶיהָ סָבִיב

16 her ramparts roundabout and against all the cities of Yehuda. Thus will I pronounce My judgment upon them on account of their wickedness: they abandoned Me, sacrificed to
17 other gods, and worshipped the works of their own hands. As for you, be courageous; stand up and speak to them as I will instruct you. Do not break down because of them
18 lest I break you down before them. I have made you today a fortress city, an iron column, and walls of bronze against the entire land – against the kings of Yehuda, its princes,
19 its priests, and the people of the land. They will wage battle against you, but they will
2 1 not prevail, for I am with you," declares the Lord, "to rescue you."   The word
2 of the Lord came to me: "Go and proclaim to the people of Jerusalem: 'This is what the Lord has said: I recall on your behalf the devotion of your youth, your bridal love,
3 when you followed Me into the wilderness, a land unseeded. Israel is a treasure to the Lord, His choice harvest. All who eat of it will be held to account. Evil will befall them, declares the Lord.'"

HAFTARAT MASEI

Read this haftara even on Rosh Ḥodesh Av.

1 4 Listen to the word of the Lord, House of Yaakov and all the tribes of the House of   JEREMIAH
5 Israel. This is what the Lord said: What fault did your forefathers find with Me that they distanced themselves from Me? They followed nothingness and became nothing.
6 They did not say, "Where is the Lord who lifted us up from the land of Egypt, who guided us in the wilderness, a land of deserts and pits, an arid land, deathly dark, a land
7 never traversed by man, where no one ever dwelt?" I brought you to a fertile land, to eat its fruits and bounty, but you came and defiled My land, and made My heritage an
8 abomination. The priests did not say, "Where is the Lord?" The teachers of the Torah did not know Me. The shepherds betrayed Me. The prophets prophesied in the name of
9 Baal. They pursued that which was useless. Therefore, I will continue to contend with
10 them, declares the Lord. I will contend with their children's children. Cross over to the islands of the Kittites and observe. Send emissaries to Kedar and ponder well. See
11 if anything like this ever happened before. Has a people ever exchanged its gods, and
12 they are non-gods? Yet my nation exchanged its glory for something useless. Heavens, be
13 astounded by this. Storm and become utterly desolate, declares the Lord. For My nation has performed two wrongs: they have forsaken Me, the source of living waters, to dig
14 wells, broken wells that cannot hold water. Is Israel a slave? Is he born to a maidservant?
15 Why has he become an object of plunder? Young lions roar at him. They voiced their
16 cries. They laid waste to his land. His cities have been set afire, with no inhabitants. Even
17 the men of Nof and Taḥpanḥes crush your skull. This has been done to you because you
18 deserted the Lord your God during the time He guided you upon the journey. Now of what use is it to you to approach Egypt to drink the waters of Shiḥor? Of what use is it

במדבר | הפטרת מסעי

טז וְעַל כָּל־עָרֵי יְהוּדָה: וְדִבַּרְתִּי מִשְׁפָּטַי אוֹתָם עַל כָּל־רָעָתָם אֲשֶׁר עֲזָבוּנִי וַיְקַטְּרוּ
יז לֵאלֹהִים אֲחֵרִים וַיִּשְׁתַּחֲווּ לְמַעֲשֵׂי יְדֵיהֶם: וְאַתָּה תֶּאְזֹר מָתְנֶיךָ וְקַמְתָּ וְדִבַּרְתָּ
יח אֲלֵיהֶם אֵת כָּל־אֲשֶׁר אָנֹכִי אֲצַוֶּךָּ אַל־תֵּחַת מִפְּנֵיהֶם פֶּן־אֲחִתְּךָ לִפְנֵיהֶם: וַאֲנִי הִנֵּה
נְתַתִּיךָ הַיּוֹם לְעִיר מִבְצָר וּלְעַמּוּד בַּרְזֶל וּלְחֹמוֹת נְחֹשֶׁת עַל־כָּל־הָאָרֶץ לְמַלְכֵי
יט יְהוּדָה לְשָׂרֶיהָ לְכֹהֲנֶיהָ וּלְעַם הָאָרֶץ: וְנִלְחֲמוּ אֵלֶיךָ וְלֹא־יוּכְלוּ לָךְ כִּי־אִתְּךָ אֲנִי
ב א נְאֻם־יְהוָה לְהַצִּילֶךָ: וַיְהִי דְבַר־יְהוָה אֵלַי לֵאמֹר: הָלֹךְ וְקָרָאתָ בְאָזְנֵי
ב יְרוּשָׁלַםִ לֵאמֹר כֹּה אָמַר יְהוָה זָכַרְתִּי לָךְ חֶסֶד נְעוּרַיִךְ אַהֲבַת כְּלוּלֹתָיִךְ לֶכְתֵּךְ
ג אַחֲרַי בַּמִּדְבָּר בְּאֶרֶץ לֹא זְרוּעָה: קֹדֶשׁ יִשְׂרָאֵל לַיהוָה רֵאשִׁית תְּבוּאָתֹה כָּל־
אֹכְלָיו יֶאְשָׁמוּ רָעָה תָּבֹא אֲלֵיהֶם נְאֻם־יְהוָה:

הפטרת מסעי

Read this הפטרה even on ראש חודש אב.

ירמיה ב ד שִׁמְעוּ דְבַר־יְהוָה בֵּית יַעֲקֹב וְכָל־מִשְׁפְּחוֹת בֵּית יִשְׂרָאֵל: כֹּה ׀ אָמַר יְהוָה מַה־
ה מָּצְאוּ אֲבוֹתֵיכֶם בִּי עָוֶל כִּי רָחֲקוּ מֵעָלָי וַיֵּלְכוּ אַחֲרֵי הַהֶבֶל וַיֶּהְבָּלוּ: וְלֹא אָמְרוּ
ו אַיֵּה יְהוָה הַמַּעֲלֶה אֹתָנוּ מֵאֶרֶץ מִצְרָיִם הַמּוֹלִיךְ אֹתָנוּ בַּמִּדְבָּר בְּאֶרֶץ עֲרָבָה
ז וְשׁוּחָה בְּאֶרֶץ צִיָּה וְצַלְמָוֶת בְּאֶרֶץ לֹא־עָבַר בָּהּ אִישׁ וְלֹא־יָשַׁב אָדָם שָׁם: וָאָבִיא
אֶתְכֶם אֶל־אֶרֶץ הַכַּרְמֶל לֶאֱכֹל פִּרְיָהּ וְטוּבָהּ וַתָּבֹאוּ וַתְּטַמְּאוּ אֶת־אַרְצִי וְנַחֲלָתִי
ח שַׂמְתֶּם לְתוֹעֵבָה: הַכֹּהֲנִים לֹא אָמְרוּ אַיֵּה יְהוָה וְתֹפְשֵׂי הַתּוֹרָה לֹא יְדָעוּנִי וְהָרֹעִים
ט פָּשְׁעוּ בִי וְהַנְּבִיאִים נִבְּאוּ בַבַּעַל וְאַחֲרֵי לֹא־יוֹעִלוּ הָלָכוּ: לָכֵן עֹד אָרִיב אִתְּכֶם
י נְאֻם־יְהוָה וְאֶת־בְּנֵי בְנֵיכֶם אָרִיב: כִּי עִבְרוּ אִיֵּי כִתִּיִּים וּרְאוּ וְקֵדָר שִׁלְחוּ וְהִתְבּוֹנְנוּ
יא מְאֹד וּרְאוּ הֵן הָיְתָה כָּזֹאת: הַהֵימִיר גּוֹי אֱלֹהִים וְהֵמָּה לֹא אֱלֹהִים וְעַמִּי הֵמִיר
יב כְּבוֹדוֹ בְּלוֹא יוֹעִיל: שֹׁמּוּ שָׁמַיִם עַל־זֹאת וְשַׂעֲרוּ חָרְבוּ מְאֹד נְאֻם־יְהוָה: כִּי־שְׁתַּיִם
יג רָעוֹת עָשָׂה עַמִּי אֹתִי עָזְבוּ מְקוֹר ׀ מַיִם חַיִּים לַחְצֹב לָהֶם בֹּארוֹת בֹּארֹת נִשְׁבָּרִים
יד אֲשֶׁר לֹא־יָכִלוּ הַמָּיִם: הַעֶבֶד יִשְׂרָאֵל אִם־יְלִיד בַּיִת הוּא מַדּוּעַ הָיָה לָבַז: עָלָיו
טו יִשְׁאֲגוּ כְפִרִים נָתְנוּ קוֹלָם וַיָּשִׁיתוּ אַרְצוֹ לְשַׁמָּה עָרָיו נִצְּתָה מִבְּלִי יֹשֵׁב: גַּם־בְּנֵי־ נִצְּתוּ
טז נֹף וְתַחְפַּנְחֵס יִרְעוּךְ קָדְקֹד: הֲלוֹא־זֹאת תַּעֲשֶׂה־לָּךְ עָזְבֵךְ אֶת־יְהוָה אֱלֹהַיִךְ בְּעֵת וְתַחְפַּנְחֵס
יז מוֹלִיכֵךְ בַּדָּרֶךְ: וְעַתָּה מַה־לָּךְ לְדֶרֶךְ מִצְרַיִם לִשְׁתּוֹת מֵי שִׁחוֹר וּמַה־לָּךְ לְדֶרֶךְ

19 to you to approach Assyria to drink the waters of the river? Your own evil will discipline you; your own waywardness will rebuke you. Know and see that your abandonment of the Lord your God has been bad and bitter. There is no fear of Me in you, says the
20 Almighty, Lord of Hosts. I broke your yoke long ago. I tore your restraints asunder. You said, "I will never again transgress!" Yet on every high hilltop and under every leafy
21 tree you recline like a harlot. I planted you as a choice grape: perfect and genuine seed.
22 How did you change on Me into a weed? Rotten grapes of a strange vine! Although you scrub yourself with natron and heap soap on yourselves, your guilt is stained before
23 Me, declares the Lord God. How can you say that you were never defiled? That you never followed the Be'alim? Look back upon your path in the valley. Recognize what
24 you did, like a young she-camel clinging to her wild ways. Like a wild ass accustomed to the wilderness; inhaling wind as she pleases, her wailing cannot be silenced. Yet those
25 who seek her need not be weary. In her month they will find her. Spare your foot from becoming bare and your throat from suffering thirst! But you said, "Never mind. No. I
26 have loved strangers; it is them whom I will follow." Like the shame of a thief when he is found out, so will the House of Israel be shamed: They, their kings, their noblemen,
27 their priests, and their prophets. They say to the tree, "You are my father!" And to the stone, "You gave birth to me!" They have turned their backs to me, not their faces but
28 in their time of trouble they say, "Arise and save us!" Where are the gods that you have crafted for yourself? Let them rise if they can save you in your time of trouble. For your gods, Yehuda, are as numerous as your cities.

3 4 By now, you should have called Me: "Father! You were my childhood companion!" *Ashkenazim add*

4 1 If you, Israel, return to Me, declares the Lord, I will welcome your return. If *Sepharadim add* you remove your abominations from My presence, you shall not suffer exile.
 2 You will utter oaths – exclaiming "as the Lord lives" truthfully, justly, and righteously – so that other nations will bless themselves by Him and come to take pride in Him.

במדבר | הפטרת מסעי — הפטרות וקריאות נוספות

יט אַשּׁוּר לִשְׁתּוֹת מֵי נָהָר: תְּיַסְּרֵךְ רָעָתֵךְ וּמְשֻׁבוֹתַיִךְ תּוֹכִחֻךְ וּדְעִי וּרְאִי כִּי־רַע וָמָר
כ עָזְבֵךְ אֶת־יהוה אֱלֹהָיִךְ וְלֹא פַחְדָּתִי אֵלַיִךְ נְאֻם־אֲדֹנָי יֱהוִֹה צְבָאוֹת: כִּי מֵעוֹלָם
אֶעֱבוֹר שָׁבַרְתִּי עֻלֵּךְ נִתַּקְתִּי מוֹסְרוֹתַיִךְ וַתֹּאמְרִי לֹא אֶעֱבוֹד כִּי עַל־כָּל־גִּבְעָה גְּבֹהָה
כא וְתַחַת כָּל־עֵץ רַעֲנָן אַתְּ צֹעָה זֹנָה: וְאָנֹכִי נְטַעְתִּיךְ שׂוֹרֵק כֻּלֹּה זֶרַע אֱמֶת וְאֵיךְ
כב נֶהְפַּכְתְּ לִי סוּרֵי הַגֶּפֶן נָכְרִיָּה: כִּי אִם־תְּכַבְּסִי בַּנֶּתֶר וְתַרְבִּי־לָךְ בֹּרִית נִכְתָּם עֲוֺנֵךְ
כג לְפָנַי נְאֻם אֲדֹנָי יֱהוִֹה: אֵיךְ תֹּאמְרִי לֹא נִטְמֵאתִי אַחֲרֵי הַבְּעָלִים לֹא הָלַכְתִּי רְאִי
כד דַרְכֵּךְ בַּגַּיְא דְּעִי מֶה עָשִׂית בִּכְרָה קַלָּה מְשָׂרֶכֶת דְּרָכֶיהָ: פֶּרֶה ׀ לִמֻּד מִדְבָּר בְּאַוַּת
נַפְשָׁהּ נַפְשׁוֹ שָׁאֲפָה רוּחַ תַּאֲנָתָהּ מִי יְשִׁיבֶנָּה כָּל־מְבַקְשֶׁיהָ לֹא יִיעָפוּ בְּחָדְשָׁהּ יִמְצָאוּנְהָ:
כה וּגְרוֹנֵךְ מִנְעִי רַגְלֵךְ מִיָּחֵף וגרונך וּגְרֹנֵךְ מִצִּמְאָה וַתֹּאמְרִי נוֹאָשׁ לוֹא כִּי־אָהַבְתִּי זָרִים וְאַחֲרֵיהֶם
כו אֵלֵךְ: כְּבֹשֶׁת גַּנָּב כִּי יִמָּצֵא כֵּן הֹבִישׁוּ בֵּית יִשְׂרָאֵל הֵמָּה מַלְכֵיהֶם שָׂרֵיהֶם וְכֹהֲנֵיהֶם
כז יְלָדְתָּנוּ וּנְבִיאֵיהֶם: אֹמְרִים לָעֵץ אָבִי אַתָּה וְלָאֶבֶן אַתְּ ילדתני יְלִדְתָּנוּ כִּי־פָנוּ אֵלַי עֹרֶף וְלֹא פָנִים
כח וּבְעֵת רָעָתָם יֹאמְרוּ קוּמָה וְהוֹשִׁיעֵנוּ: וְאַיֵּה אֱלֹהֶיךָ אֲשֶׁר עָשִׂיתָ לָּךְ יָקוּמוּ אִם־
יוֹשִׁיעוּךָ בְּעֵת רָעָתֶךָ כִּי מִסְפַּר עָרֶיךָ הָיוּ אֱלֹהֶיךָ יְהוּדָה:

Ashkenazim add
ג ד הֲלוֹא מֵעַתָּה קָרָאת קראתי לִי אָבִי אַלּוּף נְעֻרַי אָתָּה:

Sepharadim add
ד א אִם־תָּשׁוּב יִשְׂרָאֵל ׀ נְאֻם־יהוה אֵלַי תָּשׁוּב וְאִם־תָּסִיר שִׁקּוּצֶיךָ מִפָּנַי וְלֹא תָנוּד:
ב וְנִשְׁבַּעְתָּ חַי־יהוה בֶּאֱמֶת בְּמִשְׁפָּט וּבִצְדָקָה וְהִתְבָּרְכוּ בוֹ גּוֹיִם וּבוֹ יִתְהַלָּלוּ:

READINGS AND HAFTAROT FOR SPECIAL SHABBATOT

MAFTIR FOR SHABBAT ROSH ḤODESH

NUMBERS 28

9 On the Sabbath day: two yearling lambs without blemish and two-tenths of a measure
10 of fine flour as a grain offering, mixed with oil, and its libation. This is the burnt offering for every Sabbath, to be brought in addition to the regular daily burnt offering and its libation.
11 On your New Moons you shall present a burnt offering to the Lord: two young bulls,
12 one ram, and seven yearling lambs, all without blemish. There shall be a grain offering of three-tenths of a measure of fine flour mixed with oil for each bull, a grain offering of
13 two-tenths of fine flour mixed with oil for each ram, and a grain offering of one-tenth of fine flour mixed with oil for each lamb. This shall be a burnt offering of pleasing aroma, a
14 fire offering to the Lord. Their libations shall be half a hin of wine for a bull, a third of a hin of wine for a ram, and a quarter of a hin of wine for a lamb. This is the monthly burnt
15 offering for each New Moon of the year. One male goat shall be brought as a purification offering to the Lord, in addition to the regular burnt offering and its libation.

HAFTARAT SHABBAT ROSH ḤODESH

ISAIAH 66

1 Thus speaks the Lord: The heavens are My throne; the world, My footstool. What
2 house, then, would You build for Me, where could I rest? All this – My own hands made, all these are Mine, so says the Lord. And these are the ones I look toward: the poor, of
3 humbled spirit, who tremble at My words. While he, killing his ox is like a murderer of men, the one who offers up a lamb might so well behead a dog; the offering brought may just as well be pigs' blood; and his remembrance incense is a blessing of iniquity.
4 These men, they choose their paths, their souls desire their disgusting things, and so I too will choose – will choose their torments, and bring to them what they most fear. I called out – no one answered; I spoke, but none was listening. They did what was evil
5 in My sight, and chose what I never desired.   You who tremble to hear His word, listen to the Lord's word: Your brothers said, the ones who hated you, who cast you out, "Because of my name, the Lord is honored." We will see your joy, and they
6 will be shamefaced. A voice roaring out from the city, a voice, out of the Sanctuary, a
7 voice – it is the Lord's, as He repays His enemies. Before she had writhed in labor she
8 gave birth; before the agonies took her she was delivered of a boy. Who ever heard of

קריאות והפטרות לשבתות מיוחדות

מפטיר לשבת ראש חודש

במדבר כח ט וּבְיוֹם֙ הַשַּׁבָּ֔ת שְׁנֵֽי־כְבָשִׂ֥ים בְּנֵֽי־שָׁנָ֖ה תְּמִימִ֑ם וּשְׁנֵ֣י עֶשְׂרֹנִ֗ים סֹ֧לֶת מִנְחָ֛ה בְּלוּלָ֥ה בַשֶּׁ֖מֶן וְנִסְכּֽוֹ: י עֹלַ֥ת שַׁבַּ֖ת בְּשַׁבַּתּ֑וֹ עַל־עֹלַ֥ת הַתָּמִ֖יד וְנִסְכָּֽהּ: יא וּבְרָאשֵׁי֙ חָדְשֵׁיכֶ֔ם תַּקְרִ֥יבוּ עֹלָ֖ה לַיהוָ֑ה פָּרִ֨ים בְּנֵֽי־בָקָ֤ר שְׁנַ֙יִם֙ וְאַ֣יִל אֶחָ֔ד כְּבָשִׂ֧ים בְּנֵֽי־שָׁנָ֛ה שִׁבְעָ֖ה תְּמִימִֽם: יב וּשְׁלֹשָׁ֣ה עֶשְׂרֹנִ֗ים סֹ֤לֶת מִנְחָה֙ בְּלוּלָ֣ה בַשֶּׁ֔מֶן לַפָּ֖ר הָאֶחָ֑ד וּשְׁנֵ֣י עֶשְׂרֹנִ֗ים סֹ֤לֶת מִנְחָה֙ בְּלוּלָ֣ה בַשֶּׁ֔מֶן לָאַ֖יִל הָֽאֶחָֽד: יג וְעִשָּׂרֹ֤ן עִשָּׂרוֹן֙ סֹ֣לֶת מִנְחָ֔ה בְּלוּלָ֥ה בַשֶּׁ֖מֶן לַכֶּ֣בֶשׂ הָאֶחָ֑ד עֹלָה֙ רֵ֣יחַ נִיחֹ֔חַ אִשֶּׁ֖ה לַיהוָֽה: יד וְנִסְכֵּיהֶ֗ם חֲצִ֣י הַהִין֩ יִהְיֶ֨ה לַפָּ֜ר וּשְׁלִישִׁ֧ת הַהִ֣ין לָאַ֗יִל וּרְבִיעִ֥ת הַהִ֛ין לַכֶּ֖בֶשׂ יָ֑יִן זֹ֣את עֹלַ֥ת חֹ֙דֶשׁ֙ בְּחָדְשׁ֔וֹ לְחָדְשֵׁ֖י הַשָּׁנָֽה: טו וּשְׂעִ֨יר עִזִּ֥ים אֶחָ֛ד לְחַטָּ֖את לַיהוָ֑ה עַל־עֹלַ֧ת הַתָּמִ֛יד יֵעָשֶׂ֖ה וְנִסְכּֽוֹ:

הפטרת שבת ראש חודש

ישעיה סו א כֹּ֚ה אָמַ֣ר יְהוָ֔ה הַשָּׁמַ֣יִם כִּסְאִ֔י וְהָאָ֖רֶץ הֲדֹ֣ם רַגְלָ֑י אֵי־זֶ֥ה בַ֙יִת֙ אֲשֶׁ֣ר תִּבְנוּ־לִ֔י וְאֵי־זֶ֥ה מָק֖וֹם מְנוּחָתִֽי: ב וְאֶת־כָּל־אֵ֙לֶּה֙ יָדִ֣י עָשָׂ֔תָה וַיִּהְי֥וּ כָל־אֵ֖לֶּה נְאֻם־יְהוָ֑ה וְאֶל־זֶ֣ה אַבִּ֔יט אֶל־עָנִי֙ וּנְכֵה־ר֔וּחַ וְחָרֵ֖ד עַל־דְּבָרִֽי: ג שׁוֹחֵ֣ט הַשּׁ֗וֹר מַכֵּה־אִישׁ֙ זוֹבֵ֣חַ הַשֶּׂ֔ה עֹ֣רֵֽף כֶּ֔לֶב מַעֲלֵ֤ה מִנְחָה֙ דַּם־חֲזִ֔יר מַזְכִּ֥יר לְבֹנָ֖ה מְבָ֣רֵֽךְ אָ֑וֶן גַּם־הֵ֗מָּה בָּֽחֲרוּ֙ בְּדַרְכֵיהֶ֔ם וּבְשִׁקּוּצֵיהֶ֖ם נַפְשָׁ֥ם חָפֵֽצָה: ד גַּם־אֲנִ֞י אֶבְחַ֣ר בְּתַעֲלֻלֵיהֶ֗ם וּמְגֽוּרֹתָם֙ אָבִ֣יא לָהֶ֔ם יַ֤עַן קָרָ֙אתִי֙ וְאֵ֣ין עוֹנֶ֔ה דִּבַּ֖רְתִּי וְלֹ֣א שָׁמֵ֑עוּ וַיַּעֲשׂ֤וּ הָרַע֙ בְּעֵינַ֔י וּבַאֲשֶׁ֥ר לֹֽא־חָפַ֖צְתִּי בָּחָֽרוּ: ה שִׁמְעוּ֙ דְּבַר־יְהוָ֔ה הַחֲרֵדִ֖ים אֶל־דְּבָר֑וֹ אָמְרוּ֩ אֲחֵיכֶ֨ם שֹׂנְאֵיכֶ֜ם מְנַדֵּיכֶ֗ם לְמַ֤עַן שְׁמִי֙ יִכְבַּ֣ד יְהוָ֔ה וְנִרְאֶ֥ה בְשִׂמְחַתְכֶ֖ם וְהֵ֥ם יֵבֹֽשׁוּ: ו ק֤וֹל שָׁאוֹן֙ מֵעִ֔יר ק֖וֹל מֵֽהֵיכָ֑ל ק֣וֹל יְהוָ֔ה מְשַׁלֵּ֥ם גְּמ֖וּל לְאֹיְבָֽיו: ז בְּטֶ֥רֶם תָּחִ֖יל יָלָ֑דָה בְּטֶ֨רֶם יָב֥וֹא חֵ֛בֶל לָ֖הּ וְהִמְלִ֥יטָה זָכָֽר: ח מִֽי־שָׁמַ֣ע כָּזֹ֗את מִ֤י רָאָה֙ כָּאֵ֔לֶּה הֲי֤וּחַל אֶ֙רֶץ֙ בְּי֣וֹם אֶחָ֔ד אִם־יִוָּ֥לֵֽד

anything like this? Who ever saw such happenings as these? Can the land give birth in a day? Can a nation be born at a single step? Yet Zion has labored, and has birthed her
9 children. Would I bring on the labor and not deliver? So the Lord speaks: Would I who
10 fathered close the womb? So your God speaks. Bring Jerusalem joy, exult in
11 her, all of you who love her; celebrate her joy with her, all of you who mourned her. That you may suck your fill from the bosom of her comforting; may suckle, take delight in
12 the brilliance of her glory. For thus says the Lord: See Me make peace flow to her like a river, and the substance of nations – like a rushing brook – and you shall
13 suckle. You will be borne upon hips, playing upon loving laps; as a man is consoled by
14 his mother, just so shall I comfort you, and in Jerusalem, you shall be consoled. You shall look on, your heart rejoicing, while your bones grow vigorous, like grass, and the hand
15 of the Lord becomes known to His servants, and His rage known to all His foes. For see: the Lord is coming in fire, His chariots a storm wind, to slake His fury in rage, His
16 rebuke in flames of fire. For in fire, the Lord comes to judgment, and by the sword, to
17 all flesh, and many are those the Lord will execute. Those in the gardens, sanctifying and cleansing themselves, one after the other in the midst of it, while eating the flesh of pigs and pests and mice, they will all be gathered in together: so the Lord has spoken.
18 For I – I know their works, their thoughts; and time will come, to gather all nations
19 and tongues, and they will come, and look upon My glory. I shall place a sign among them, send out survivors from them to all nations, to Tarshish, Pul, and Lud, to the great archers, Tuval, Yavan, to the distant coastlands where none ever heard tell of Me
20 or saw My glory, and they will tell of My glory to the nations. And they will bring back all your brothers from among all other nations, an offering to the Lord, on horseback and on chariot, on camels, mules, dromedaries, to My holy mount, Jerusalem – so says the Lord – just as the children of Israel would bring up their offerings in pure vessels,
21 to the Lord's House, and from among them also I shall take priests and Levites, so
22 says the Lord. For just as the new heavens, the new earth that I am now forming, will
23 stand forever before Me, so says the Lord, so will stand your children, your name. And it will be – every New Moon, every Sabbath – all flesh will come to worship Me, so says
24 the Lord. Going out, they will see bodies of those people who sinned against Me, for the worms will not die nor the fire be quenched, and they will be repugnant to all flesh.

And it will be – every New Moon, every Sabbath – all flesh will come to worship Me, so says the Lord.

When a two-day Rosh Ḥodesh falls on Shabbat and Sunday, Sepharadim add the first and last verses of the haftara for erev Rosh Ḥodesh, on the following page.

במדבר | הפטרה וקריאות נוספות | הפטרה לשבת ראש חודש

ט גּוֹי פַּעַם אֶחָת כִּי־חָלָה גַּם־יָלְדָה צִיּוֹן אֶת־בָּנֶיהָ: הַאֲנִי אַשְׁבִּיר וְלֹא אוֹלִיד יֹאמַר
י יְהוָה אִם־אֲנִי הַמּוֹלִיד וְעָצַרְתִּי אָמַר אֱלֹהָיִךְ: שִׂמְחוּ אֶת־יְרוּשָׁלַ͏ִם וְגִילוּ
בָהּ כָּל־אֹהֲבֶיהָ שִׂישׂוּ אִתָּהּ מָשׂוֹשׂ כָּל־הַמִּתְאַבְּלִים עָלֶיהָ: לְמַעַן תִּינְקוּ וּשְׂבַעְתֶּם
יא מִשֹּׁד תַּנְחֻמֶיהָ לְמַעַן תָּמֹצּוּ וְהִתְעַנַּגְתֶּם מִזִּיז כְּבוֹדָהּ: כִּי־כֹה ׀ אָמַר יְהוָה
יב הִנְנִי נֹטֶה־אֵלֶיהָ כְּנָהָר שָׁלוֹם וּכְנַחַל שׁוֹטֵף כְּבוֹד גּוֹיִם וִינַקְתֶּם עַל־צַד תִּנָּשֵׂאוּ
וְעַל־בִּרְכַּיִם תְּשָׁעֳשָׁעוּ: כְּאִישׁ אֲשֶׁר אִמּוֹ תְּנַחֲמֶנּוּ כֵּן אָנֹכִי אֲנַחֶמְכֶם וּבִירוּשָׁלַ͏ִם
יג תְּנֻחָמוּ: וּרְאִיתֶם וְשָׂשׂ לִבְּכֶם וְעַצְמוֹתֵיכֶם כַּדֶּשֶׁא תִפְרַחְנָה וְנוֹדְעָה יַד־יְהוָה
יד אֶת־עֲבָדָיו וְזָעַם אֶת־אֹיְבָיו: כִּי־הִנֵּה יְהוָה בָּאֵשׁ יָבוֹא וְכַסּוּפָה מַרְכְּבֹתָיו לְהָשִׁיב
טו בְּחֵמָה אַפּוֹ וְגַעֲרָתוֹ בְּלַהֲבֵי־אֵשׁ: כִּי בָאֵשׁ יְהוָה נִשְׁפָּט וּבְחַרְבּוֹ אֶת־כָּל־בָּשָׂר וְרַבּוּ
טז חַלְלֵי יְהוָה: הַמִּתְקַדְּשִׁים וְהַמִּטַּהֲרִים אֶל־הַגַּנּוֹת אַחַר אַחַד בַּתָּוֶךְ אֹכְלֵי בְּשַׂר אַחַת
יז הַחֲזִיר וְהַשֶּׁקֶץ וְהָעַכְבָּר יַחְדָּו יָסֻפוּ נְאֻם־יְהוָה: וְאָנֹכִי מַעֲשֵׂיהֶם וּמַחְשְׁבֹתֵיהֶם
יח בָּאָה לְקַבֵּץ אֶת־כָּל־הַגּוֹיִם וְהַלְּשֹׁנוֹת וּבָאוּ וְרָאוּ אֶת־כְּבוֹדִי: וְשַׂמְתִּי בָהֶם אוֹת
יט וְשִׁלַּחְתִּי מֵהֶם ׀ פְּלֵיטִים אֶל־הַגּוֹיִם תַּרְשִׁישׁ פּוּל וְלוּד מֹשְׁכֵי קֶשֶׁת תֻּבַל וְיָוָן הָאִיִּים
הָרְחֹקִים אֲשֶׁר לֹא־שָׁמְעוּ אֶת־שִׁמְעִי וְלֹא־רָאוּ אֶת־כְּבוֹדִי וְהִגִּידוּ אֶת־כְּבוֹדִי
כ בַגּוֹיִם: וְהֵבִיאוּ אֶת־כָּל־אֲחֵיכֶם ׀ מִכָּל־הַגּוֹיִם ׀ מִנְחָה ׀ לַיהוָה בַּסּוּסִים וּבָרֶכֶב
וּבַצַּבִּים וּבַפְּרָדִים וּבַכִּרְכָּרוֹת עַל הַר קָדְשִׁי יְרוּשָׁלַ͏ִם אָמַר יְהוָה כַּאֲשֶׁר יָבִיאוּ בְנֵי
כא יִשְׂרָאֵל אֶת־הַמִּנְחָה בִּכְלִי טָהוֹר בֵּית יְהוָה: וְגַם־מֵהֶם אֶקַּח לַכֹּהֲנִים לַלְוִיִּם אָמַר
כב יְהוָה: כִּי כַאֲשֶׁר הַשָּׁמַיִם הַחֳדָשִׁים וְהָאָרֶץ הַחֲדָשָׁה אֲשֶׁר אֲנִי עֹשֶׂה עֹמְדִים לְפָנַי
כג נְאֻם־יְהוָה כֵּן יַעֲמֹד זַרְעֲכֶם וְשִׁמְכֶם: וְהָיָה מִדֵּי־חֹדֶשׁ בְּחָדְשׁוֹ וּמִדֵּי שַׁבָּת בְּשַׁבַּתּוֹ
כד יָבוֹא כָל־בָּשָׂר לְהִשְׁתַּחֲוֺת לְפָנַי אָמַר יְהוָה: וְיָצְאוּ וְרָאוּ בְּפִגְרֵי הָאֲנָשִׁים הַפֹּשְׁעִים
בִּי כִּי תוֹלַעְתָּם לֹא תָמוּת וְאִשָּׁם לֹא תִכְבֶּה וְהָיוּ דֵרָאוֹן לְכָל־בָּשָׂר:

והיה מדי חדש בחדשו ומדי שבת בשבתו

יבוא כל בשר להשתחות לפני

אמר יהוה

When a two-day ראש חודש *falls on* שבת *and Sunday, Sepharadim add the first and last verses of the* הפטרה *for* ערב ראש חודש, *on the following page.*

HAFTARAT SHABBAT EREV ROSH ḤODESH

20 **18** Yehonatan then said to David, "Tomorrow is the New Month, and you shall be missed,   I SAMUEL
19 for your seat will be empty. Now wait three days, then on the day people go back to work,
20 make your way swiftly down to your hiding place, and stay close to the Ezel Stone. As
21 for me – I will shoot three arrows to its side, as though aiming at a target. Now, when I send the boy off to find the arrows, if I say to him, 'Look, the arrows are just past you, come take them,' then come, for all is well with you, and there is nothing wrong – as
22 the Lord lives. But if I say to the boy, 'Look, the arrows are far past you,' then go, for
23 the Lord has sent you away. As for the matter we spoke of, you and I – the Lord is
24 between me and you forever."   David hid out in the field. The New Month
25 came around, and the king sat down at the feast to eat. When the king sat in his usual seat by the wall, Yehonatan rose, and Avner sat by Sha'ul's side while David's seat remained
26 empty. Sha'ul did not mention anything that day. "It must be by chance that he is not
27 clean," he thought; "he must be unclean."   But the next day, on the second day of the New Month, David's seat was still empty, and Sha'ul asked Yehonatan, his son,
28 "Why did the son of Yishai fail to come to the feast – both yesterday and today?" "David
29 urgently asked me for leave to Beit Leḥem," Yehonatan answered Sha'ul. "He said, 'Please let me go, for we have a family feast in the city, and my brother has bid me – so now, if I have gained your favor, please let me get away to see my brothers.' That is why he
30 has not come to the king's table."   Sha'ul burst into a rage at Yehonatan. "Son of a perverse, wayward woman!" he said. "Oh, I knew you would side with the son of
31 Yishai – to your own disgrace and the disgrace of your mother's nakedness! But as long as the son of Yishai lives on this earth, you and your kingship will not endure – so
32 bring him to me now, for he is a dead man!"   But Yehonatan answered Sha'ul,
33 his father. "Why should he be killed?" he said to him. "What has he done?" And Sha'ul hurled the spear toward him to strike him down, and Yehonatan realized that his father
34 was determined to kill David.   Furious, Yehonatan rose up from the table; he ate no food on the second day of the New Month out of anguish for David, for his father
35 had humiliated him.   In the morning, Yehonatan went out to the field for the
36 rendezvous with David, a young boy with him. He said to his boy, "Now, run and find
37 the arrows I am about to shoot." The boy ran off, and he shot the arrows past him. When the boy reached the place where Yehonatan's arrows had fallen, Yehonatan called out after the boy, "Oh – the arrows are far past you." Then Yehonatan called out after the boy,
38 "Quick – hurry, do not linger." When Yehonatan's boy gathered up the arrows and came
39 back to his master – the boy knew nothing; only Yehonatan and David knew about the
40 arrangement – Yehonatan gave his gear to his boy and said to him, "Go – bring these back

הפטרת שבת ערב ראש חודש

שמואל א׳
כ

יח וַיֹּאמֶר־לוֹ יְהוֹנָתָן מָחָר חֹדֶשׁ וְנִפְקַדְתָּ כִּי יִפָּקֵד מוֹשָׁבֶךָ: וְשִׁלַּשְׁתָּ תֵּרֵד מְאֹד וּבָאתָ אֶל־הַמָּקוֹם אֲשֶׁר־נִסְתַּרְתָּ שָּׁם בְּיוֹם הַמַּעֲשֶׂה וְיָשַׁבְתָּ אֵצֶל הָאֶבֶן הָאָזֶל:
כא וַאֲנִי שְׁלֹשֶׁת הַחִצִּים צִדָּה אוֹרֶה לְשַׁלַּח־לִי לְמַטָּרָה: וְהִנֵּה אֶשְׁלַח אֶת־הַנַּעַר לֵךְ מְצָא אֶת־הַחִצִּים אִם־אָמֹר אֹמַר לַנַּעַר הִנֵּה הַחִצִּים ׀ מִמְּךָ וָהֵנָּה קָחֶנּוּ ׀ וָבֹאָה כִּי־שָׁלוֹם לְךָ וְאֵין דָּבָר חַי־יְהֹוָה: וְאִם־כֹּה אֹמַר לָעֶלֶם הִנֵּה הַחִצִּים מִמְּךָ וָהָלְאָה
כב
כג לֵךְ כִּי שִׁלַּחֲךָ יְהֹוָה: וְהַדָּבָר אֲשֶׁר דִּבַּרְנוּ אֲנִי וָאָתָּה הִנֵּה יְהֹוָה בֵּינִי וּבֵינְךָ עַד־עוֹלָם:
כד וַיִּסָּתֵר דָּוִד בַּשָּׂדֶה וַיְהִי הַחֹדֶשׁ וַיֵּשֶׁב הַמֶּלֶךְ אֶל־הַלֶּחֶם לֶאֱכוֹל: אֶל־
כה וַיֵּשֶׁב הַמֶּלֶךְ עַל־מוֹשָׁבוֹ כְּפַעַם ׀ בְּפַעַם אֶל־מוֹשַׁב הַקִּיר וַיָּקׇם יְהוֹנָתָן וַיֵּשֶׁב אַבְנֵר מִצַּד שָׁאוּל וַיִּפָּקֵד מְקוֹם דָּוִד:
כו וְלֹא־דִבֶּר שָׁאוּל מְאוּמָה בַּיּוֹם הַהוּא כִּי אָמַר מִקְרֶה הוּא בִּלְתִּי טָהוֹר הוּא כִּי־לֹא טָהוֹר: וַיְהִי מִמׇּחֳרַת הַחֹדֶשׁ הַשֵּׁנִי
כז וַיִּפָּקֵד מְקוֹם דָּוִד וַיֹּאמֶר שָׁאוּל אֶל־יְהוֹנָתָן בְּנוֹ מַדּוּעַ לֹא־בָא בֶן־יִשַׁי גַּם־תְּמוֹל גַּם־הַיּוֹם אֶל־הַלָּחֶם:
כח וַיַּעַן יְהוֹנָתָן אֶת־שָׁאוּל נִשְׁאֹל נִשְׁאַל דָּוִד מֵעִמָּדִי עַד־בֵּית לָחֶם:
כט וַיֹּאמֶר שַׁלְּחֵנִי נָא כִּי זֶבַח מִשְׁפָּחָה לָנוּ בָּעִיר וְהוּא צִוָּה־לִי אָחִי וְעַתָּה אִם־מָצָאתִי חֵן בְּעֵינֶיךָ אִמָּלְטָה נָּא וְאֶרְאֶה אֶת־אֶחָי עַל־כֵּן לֹא־בָא אֶל־שֻׁלְחַן הַמֶּלֶךְ:
ל וַיִּחַר־אַף שָׁאוּל בִּיהוֹנָתָן וַיֹּאמֶר לוֹ בֶּן־נַעֲוַת הַמַּרְדּוּת הֲלוֹא יָדַעְתִּי כִּי־בֹחֵר אַתָּה לְבֶן־יִשַׁי לְבָשְׁתְּךָ וּלְבֹשֶׁת עֶרְוַת אִמֶּךָ:
לא כִּי כׇל־הַיָּמִים אֲשֶׁר בֶּן־יִשַׁי חַי עַל־הָאֲדָמָה לֹא תִכּוֹן אַתָּה וּמַלְכוּתֶךָ וְעַתָּה שְׁלַח וְקַח אֹתוֹ אֵלַי כִּי בֶן־מָוֶת הוּא:
לב וַיַּעַן יְהוֹנָתָן אֶת־שָׁאוּל אָבִיו וַיֹּאמֶר אֵלָיו לָמָּה יוּמַת מֶה עָשָׂה:
לג וַיָּטֶל שָׁאוּל אֶת־הַחֲנִית עָלָיו לְהַכֹּתוֹ וַיֵּדַע יְהוֹנָתָן כִּי־כָלָה הִיא מֵעִם אָבִיו לְהָמִית אֶת־דָּוִד:
לד וַיָּקׇם יְהוֹנָתָן מֵעִם הַשֻּׁלְחָן בׇּחֳרִי־אָף וְלֹא־אָכַל בְּיוֹם־הַחֹדֶשׁ הַשֵּׁנִי לֶחֶם כִּי נֶעֱצַב אֶל־דָּוִד כִּי הִכְלִמוֹ אָבִיו: וַיְהִי בַבֹּקֶר
לה וַיֵּצֵא יְהוֹנָתָן הַשָּׂדֶה לְמוֹעֵד דָּוִד וְנַעַר קָטֹן עִמּוֹ: וַיֹּאמֶר לְנַעֲרוֹ רֻץ מְצָא נָא
לו אֶת־הַחִצִּים אֲשֶׁר אָנֹכִי מוֹרֶה הַנַּעַר רָץ וְהוּא־יָרָה הַחֵצִי לְהַעֲבִרוֹ: וַיָּבֹא הַנַּעַר
לז עַד־מְקוֹם הַחֵצִי אֲשֶׁר יָרָה יְהוֹנָתָן וַיִּקְרָא יְהוֹנָתָן אַחֲרֵי הַנַּעַר וַיֹּאמֶר הֲלוֹא הַחֵצִי מִמְּךָ וָהָלְאָה:
לח וַיִּקְרָא יְהוֹנָתָן אַחֲרֵי הַנַּעַר מְהֵרָה חוּשָׁה אַל־תַּעֲמֹד וַיְלַקֵּט נַעַר
לט יְהוֹנָתָן אֶת־הַחֵצִי וַיָּבֹא אֶל־אֲדֹנָיו: וְהַנַּעַר לֹא־יָדַע מְאוּמָה אַךְ יְהוֹנָתָן וְדָוִד יָדְעוּ הַחִצִים אֶת־הַדָּבָר:
מ וַיִּתֵּן יְהוֹנָתָן אֶת־כֵּלָיו אֶל־הַנַּעַר אֲשֶׁר־לוֹ וַיֹּאמֶר לוֹ לֵךְ הָבֵיא הָעִיר:

41 to town." When the boy had left, David emerged from the southern side of the stone, flung his face to the ground, and bowed three times. And they kissed each other and
42 wept with each other until David's sobs reached a crescendo. "Go in peace," Yehonatan said to David, "for the two of us have sworn in the name of the Lord, 'May the Lord be between me and you, and between my seed and your seed, forever.'"

מא הַנַּעַר בָּא וְדָוִד קָם מֵאֵצֶל הַנֶּגֶב וַיִּפֹּל לְאַפָּיו אַרְצָה וַיִּשְׁתַּחוּ שָׁלֹשׁ פְּעָמִים וַיִּשְּׁקוּ ׀
מב אִישׁ אֶת־רֵעֵהוּ וַיִּבְכּוּ אִישׁ אֶת־רֵעֵהוּ עַד־דָּוִד הִגְדִּיל: וַיֹּאמֶר יְהוֹנָתָן לְדָוִד לֵךְ לְשָׁלוֹם אֲשֶׁר נִשְׁבַּעְנוּ שְׁנֵינוּ אֲנַחְנוּ בְּשֵׁם יהוה לֵאמֹר יהוה יִהְיֶה ׀ בֵּינִי וּבֵינֶךָ וּבֵין זַרְעִי וּבֵין זַרְעֲךָ עַד־עוֹלָם:

MEGILLAT RUTH

1 1 Once, in the days when the judges ruled, there was a famine in the land. One man set out from Beit Leḥem of Yehuda and journeyed to live for a while in the land of Moav,
2 and his wife and two sons came with him. This man's name was Elimelekh, his wife's was Naomi, and his two sons' names were Maḥlon and Kilyon, all Efratites from Beit
3 Leḥem of Yehuda. They duly arrived in the fields of Moav, and there they stayed. But
4 then Elimelekh, Naomi's husband, died, and she was left there with her two sons. Both of them married Moabite women – the first was called Orpa, the second Ruth – and
5 they lived on there for some ten years. After that, the two of them – Maḥlon and Kilyon – died as well, and the woman was left bereaved of both her children and her
6 husband. She got up, her daughters-in-law with her, to return from the land of Moav, for word had reached her in the land of Moav that the Lord had brought His people to
7 mind and granted them bread. So she left the place where she had been, both of her
8 daughters-in-law with her, and set off along the way back to the land of Yehuda. But to her two daughters-in-law she said, "Go on now, turn back, each to your mother's home,
9 and may the Lord show you that kindness that you have shown the dead and me. The Lord grant that you find a place of rest, each in your husband's home." As she kissed
10/11 them, they wept aloud and said, "No. We shall return with you to your people." Said Naomi, "Turn back, daughters; why would you come with me? Have I still sons in my
12 womb who could be husbands to you? Turn back, my daughters – go; I am too old to be with a man. Even were I to say, 'There is hope for me still,' were I even this night to
13 be married, even if I could bear sons again, are you to wait for them as they grow? Would you be chained to them, never to be with another man? No, daughters, for your presence
14 is most bitter to me now, for the hand of the Lord has beaten me." Aloud they wept still
15 more, then Orpa kissed her mother-in-law – but Ruth clung to her. And Naomi said, "Your sister-in-law has turned back to her people, to her gods. Turn back after your
16 sister-in-law." But Ruth replied, "Do not entreat me to leave you, to turn back, not to walk after you. For wherever you walk, I shall walk, and wherever you stay, there I stay.
17 Your people is my people; your God is my God. Wherever you die, there I die, and there shall I be buried. So may the Lord do to me – and more – for death alone will separate
18 me from you." Naomi saw that Ruth was determined to come with her, and she spoke
19 to her no more. The two of them walked on until they came to Beit Leḥem, and when they arrived at Beit Leḥem, the whole town crowded around as the women asked, "Can
20 this be Naomi?" She said to the women, "Call me not Naomi. Call me Mara, for Shaddai
21 has made my life bitter beyond words. I was full when I left this place, and empty has the Lord returned me. Why call me, 'Naomi'? the Lord has spoken up against me;
22 Shaddai has ruined me." This is how Naomi, returning from the land of Moav with her daughter-in-law, Ruth the Moabite, returned. They arrived at Beit Leḥem just as the

מגילת רות

א וַיְהִי בִּימֵי שְׁפֹט הַשֹּׁפְטִים וַיְהִי רָעָב בָּאָרֶץ וַיֵּלֶךְ אִישׁ מִבֵּית לֶחֶם יְהוּדָה לָגוּר
ב בִּשְׂדֵי מוֹאָב הוּא וְאִשְׁתּוֹ וּשְׁנֵי בָנָיו: וְשֵׁם הָאִישׁ אֱלִימֶלֶךְ וְשֵׁם אִשְׁתּוֹ נָעֳמִי
וְשֵׁם שְׁנֵי־בָנָיו ׀ מַחְלוֹן וְכִלְיוֹן אֶפְרָתִים מִבֵּית לֶחֶם יְהוּדָה וַיָּבֹאוּ שְׂדֵי־מוֹאָב
ג וַיִּהְיוּ־שָׁם: וַיָּמָת אֱלִימֶלֶךְ אִישׁ נָעֳמִי וַתִּשָּׁאֵר הִיא וּשְׁנֵי בָנֶיהָ: וַיִּשְׂאוּ לָהֶם
ד נָשִׁים מֹאֲבִיּוֹת שֵׁם הָאַחַת עָרְפָּה וְשֵׁם הַשֵּׁנִית רוּת וַיֵּשְׁבוּ שָׁם כְּעֶשֶׂר שָׁנִים:
ה וַיָּמֻתוּ גַם־שְׁנֵיהֶם מַחְלוֹן וְכִלְיוֹן וַתִּשָּׁאֵר הָאִשָּׁה מִשְּׁנֵי יְלָדֶיהָ וּמֵאִישָׁהּ: וַתָּקָם
ו הִיא וְכַלֹּתֶיהָ וַתָּשָׁב מִשְּׂדֵי מוֹאָב כִּי שָׁמְעָה בִּשְׂדֵה מוֹאָב כִּי־פָקַד יְהוָה אֶת־
ז עַמּוֹ לָתֵת לָהֶם לָחֶם: וַתֵּצֵא מִן־הַמָּקוֹם אֲשֶׁר הָיְתָה־שָּׁמָּה וּשְׁתֵּי כַלֹּתֶיהָ עִמָּהּ
ח וַתֵּלַכְנָה בַדֶּרֶךְ לָשׁוּב אֶל־אֶרֶץ יְהוּדָה: וַתֹּאמֶר נָעֳמִי לִשְׁתֵּי כַלֹּתֶיהָ לֵכְנָה
שֹּׁבְנָה אִשָּׁה לְבֵית אִמָּהּ יַעַשׂ יְהוָה עִמָּכֶם חֶסֶד כַּאֲשֶׁר עֲשִׂיתֶם עִם־הַמֵּתִים יַעַשׂ
ט וְעִמָּדִי: יִתֵּן יְהוָה לָכֶם וּמְצֶאןָ מְנוּחָה אִשָּׁה בֵּית אִישָׁהּ וַתִּשַּׁק לָהֶן וַתִּשֶּׂאנָה
י קוֹלָן וַתִּבְכֶּינָה: וַתֹּאמַרְנָה־לָּהּ כִּי־אִתָּךְ נָשׁוּב לְעַמֵּךְ: וַתֹּאמֶר נָעֳמִי שֹׁבְנָה
יא בְנֹתַי לָמָּה תֵלַכְנָה עִמִּי הַעוֹד־לִי בָנִים בְּמֵעַי וְהָיוּ לָכֶם לַאֲנָשִׁים: שֹׁבְנָה בְנֹתַי
יב לֵכְןָ כִּי זָקַנְתִּי מִהְיוֹת לְאִישׁ כִּי אָמַרְתִּי יֶשׁ־לִי תִקְוָה גַּם הָיִיתִי הַלַּיְלָה לְאִישׁ
יג וְגַם יָלַדְתִּי בָנִים: הֲלָהֵן ׀ תְּשַׂבֵּרְנָה עַד אֲשֶׁר יִגְדָּלוּ הֲלָהֵן תֵּעָגֵנָה לְבִלְתִּי הֱיוֹת
יד לְאִישׁ אַל בְּנֹתַי כִּי־מַר־לִי מְאֹד מִכֶּם כִּי־יָצְאָה בִי יַד־יְהוָה: וַתִּשֶּׂנָה קוֹלָן
טו וַתִּבְכֶּינָה עוֹד וַתִּשַּׁק עָרְפָּה לַחֲמוֹתָהּ וְרוּת דָּבְקָה בָּהּ: וַתֹּאמֶר הִנֵּה שָׁבָה
טז יְבִמְתֵּךְ אֶל־עַמָּהּ וְאֶל־אֱלֹהֶיהָ שׁוּבִי אַחֲרֵי יְבִמְתֵּךְ: וַתֹּאמֶר רוּת אַל־תִּפְגְּעִי־
בִי לְעָזְבֵךְ לָשׁוּב מֵאַחֲרָיִךְ כִּי אֶל־אֲשֶׁר תֵּלְכִי אֵלֵךְ וּבַאֲשֶׁר תָּלִינִי אָלִין עַמֵּךְ
יז עַמִּי וֵאלֹהַיִךְ אֱלֹהָי: בַּאֲשֶׁר תָּמוּתִי אָמוּת וְשָׁם אֶקָּבֵר כֹּה יַעֲשֶׂה יְהוָה לִי וְכֹה
יח יוֹסִיף כִּי הַמָּוֶת יַפְרִיד בֵּינִי וּבֵינֵךְ: וַתֵּרֶא כִּי־מִתְאַמֶּצֶת הִיא לָלֶכֶת אִתָּהּ וַתֶּחְדַּל
יט לְדַבֵּר אֵלֶיהָ: וַתֵּלַכְנָה שְׁתֵּיהֶם עַד־בּוֹאָנָה בֵּית לָחֶם וַיְהִי כְּבוֹאָנָה בֵּית לֶחֶם
כ וַתֵּהֹם כָּל־הָעִיר עֲלֵיהֶן וַתֹּאמַרְנָה הֲזֹאת נָעֳמִי: וַתֹּאמֶר אֲלֵיהֶן אַל־תִּקְרֶאנָה
כא לִי נָעֳמִי קְרֶאןָ לִי מָרָא כִּי־הֵמַר שַׁדַּי לִי מְאֹד: אֲנִי מְלֵאָה הָלַכְתִּי וְרֵיקָם
הֱשִׁיבַנִי יְהוָה לָמָּה תִקְרֶאנָה לִי נָעֳמִי וַיהוָה עָנָה בִי וְשַׁדַּי הֵרַע לִי: וַתָּשָׁב
כב נָעֳמִי וְרוּת הַמּוֹאֲבִיָּה כַלָּתָהּ עִמָּהּ הַשָּׁבָה מִשְּׂדֵי מוֹאָב וְהֵמָּה בָּאוּ בֵּית לֶחֶם

2 1 barley harvest began. Naomi had a relative from her husband Elimelekh's family, a man
2 of substance and great strength: his name was Boaz. Ruth the Moabite said to Naomi, "I shall go to the field and gather the fallen grains, and follow after anyone who should
3 show me favor." Naomi said, "Go, then, my daughter," and so she went. She came and started to gather in the field after the harvestmen, and it chanced to be the field plot of
4 Boaz that she came to – that man of Elimelekh's family. And there came Boaz himself, arriving from Beit Leḥem and saying to the harvestmen, "The Lord be with you." "The
5 Lord bless you," they replied. "Whose is that young woman over there?" asked Boaz
6 of his servant in charge of the harvestmen. "That is some Moabite girl," replied the servant in charge of the harvestmen, "the one who came back with Naomi from the land
7 of Moav. She said, 'Let me come gleaning, gathering among the sheaves where the harvestmen have been,' and so she came. She has been standing out here from early
8 morning until now and hardly sat at all in the shelter." Boaz went to Ruth and said, "Daughter, take heed. Do not go gleaning in any other field, and do not leave this one;
9 cling close by my young women. Keep your eyes on the field they are harvesting from and follow after them. I have instructed the young men by no means to touch you. When
10 you are thirsty, go to the jugs and drink of the water the young men have drawn." Ruth fell upon her face, bowing low, and she asked him, "Why is it that I have found favor in
11 your eyes, that you give me recognition such as this when I am a stranger?" Boaz said, "I have heard of all you have done for your mother-in-law ever since your husband died, of how you left your father, your mother, the land of your birth, and came to a people
12 you knew not the day before. May the Lord repay your labors; may your reward be full at the hand of the Lord, God of Israel, under whose mantle you come to take shelter."
13 "Sir," she said, "I hope to find favor in your eyes, for you give me solace, for you have
14 spoken to your servant's heart though I am not fit to be your servant." When the time came for eating, Boaz said to her, "Come here; eat of this food and dip your bread in the vinegar." She sat down beside the harvestmen, and he served her roasted grains, and she
15 ate and had her fill with more left over. And when she stood up to begin gleaning again, Boaz instructed his workers, "Let her glean among the sheaves as well; do not disgrace
16 her. Drop some ears from the bundles as well; leave them, let her glean them, and do
17 not reproach her." Ruth carried on gleaning in the field until evening, then threshed
18 what she had gleaned; it was almost an ephah of barley. She lifted it up and came into the town. Her mother-in-law saw what she had gleaned; she produced all that was left
19 after she had eaten her fill and gave it to her. "Where did you gather today," she asked, "and where did you work? Bless whoever recognized you so." So Ruth told her mother-in-law under whose patronage she had worked: "The man's name is Boaz, with whom I
20 worked today." Said Naomi to her daughter-in-law, "The Lord bless him, for he has not abandoned his kindness to the living or the dead," and Naomi told her, "The man is our

א וּלְנׇעֳמִ֣י מידע לְאִישָׁ֔הּ אִ֚ישׁ גִּבּ֣וֹר חַ֔יִל מִמִּשְׁפַּ֖חַת מוֹדַ֑ע אֱלִימֶ֑לֶךְ וּשְׁמ֖וֹ בֹּֽעַז׃ בִּתְחִלַּ֖ת קְצִ֥יר שְׂעֹרִֽים׃
ב וַתֹּ֩אמֶר֩ ר֨וּת הַמּוֹאֲבִיָּ֜ה אֶֽל־נׇעֳמִ֗י אֵֽלְכָה־נָּ֤א הַשָּׂדֶה֙ וַאֲלַקֳטָ֣ה בַשִּׁבֳּלִ֔ים אַחַ֕ר אֲשֶׁ֥ר אֶמְצָא־חֵ֖ן בְּעֵינָ֑יו וַתֹּ֥אמֶר לָ֖הּ לְכִ֥י בִתִּֽי׃
ג וַתֵּ֤לֶךְ וַתָּבוֹא֙ וַתְּלַקֵּ֣ט בַּשָּׂדֶ֔ה אַחֲרֵ֖י הַקֹּצְרִ֑ים וַיִּ֣קֶר מִקְרֶ֔הָ חֶלְקַ֤ת הַשָּׂדֶה֙ לְבֹ֔עַז אֲשֶׁ֖ר מִמִּשְׁפַּ֥חַת אֱלִימֶֽלֶךְ׃
ד וְהִנֵּה־בֹ֗עַז בָּ֚א מִבֵּ֣ית לֶ֔חֶם וַיֹּ֥אמֶר לַקּוֹצְרִ֖ים יְהֹוָ֣ה עִמָּכֶ֑ם וַיֹּ֥אמְרוּ ל֖וֹ יְבָרֶכְךָ֥ יְהֹוָֽה׃
ה וַיֹּ֤אמֶר בֹּ֙עַז֙ לְנַעֲר֔וֹ הַנִּצָּ֖ב עַל־הַקּוֹצְרִ֑ים לְמִ֖י הַנַּעֲרָ֥ה הַזֹּֽאת׃
ו וַיַּ֗עַן הַנַּ֛עַר הַנִּצָּ֥ב עַל־הַקּוֹצְרִ֖ים וַיֹּאמַ֑ר נַעֲרָ֤ה מֽוֹאֲבִיָּה֙ הִ֔יא הַשָּׁ֥בָה עִֽם־נׇעֳמִ֖י מִשְּׂדֵ֥י מוֹאָֽב׃
ז וַתֹּ֗אמֶר אֲלַקֳטָה־נָּא֙ וְאָסַפְתִּ֣י בָעֳמָרִ֔ים אַחֲרֵ֖י הַקּוֹצְרִ֑ים וַתָּב֣וֹא וַֽתַּעֲמ֗וֹד מֵאָ֤ז הַבֹּ֙קֶר֙ וְעַד־עַ֔תָּה זֶ֛ה שִׁבְתָּ֥הּ הַבַּ֖יִת מְעָֽט׃
ח וַיֹּ֩אמֶר֩ בֹּ֨עַז אֶל־ר֜וּת הֲל֧וֹא שָׁמַ֣עַתְּ בִּתִּ֗י אַל־תֵּֽלְכִי֙ לִלְקֹט֙ בְּשָׂדֶ֣ה אַחֵ֔ר וְגַ֛ם לֹ֥א תַעֲבוּרִ֖י מִזֶּ֑ה וְכֹ֥ה תִדְבָּקִ֖ין עִם־נַעֲרֹתָֽי׃
ט עֵינַ֜יִךְ בַּשָּׂדֶ֤ה אֲשֶׁר־יִקְצֹרוּן֙ וְהָלַ֣כְתְּ אַחֲרֵיהֶ֔ן הֲל֥וֹא צִוִּ֛יתִי אֶת־הַנְּעָרִ֖ים לְבִלְתִּ֣י נׇגְעֵ֑ךְ וְצָמִ֗ת וְהָלַכְתְּ֙ אֶל־הַכֵּלִ֔ים וְשָׁתִ֕ית מֵאֲשֶׁ֥ר יִשְׁאֲב֖וּן הַנְּעָרִֽים׃
י וַתִּפֹּל֙ עַל־פָּנֶ֔יהָ וַתִּשְׁתַּ֖חוּ אָ֑רְצָה וַתֹּ֣אמֶר אֵלָ֗יו מַדּ֩וּעַ֩ מָצָ֨אתִי חֵ֤ן בְּעֵינֶ֙יךָ֙ לְהַכִּירֵ֔נִי וְאָנֹכִ֖י נׇכְרִיָּֽה׃
יא וַיַּ֤עַן בֹּ֙עַז֙ וַיֹּ֣אמֶר לָ֔הּ הֻגֵּ֨ד הֻגַּ֜ד לִ֗י כֹּ֤ל אֲשֶׁר־עָשִׂית֙ אֶת־חֲמוֹתֵ֔ךְ אַחֲרֵ֖י מ֣וֹת אִישֵׁ֑ךְ וַתַּֽעַזְבִ֞י אָבִ֣יךְ וְאִמֵּ֗ךְ וְאֶ֙רֶץ֙ מֽוֹלַדְתֵּ֔ךְ וַתֵּ֣לְכִ֔י אֶל־עַ֕ם אֲשֶׁ֥ר לֹא־יָדַ֖עַתְּ תְּמ֥וֹל שִׁלְשֽׁוֹם׃
יב יְשַׁלֵּ֥ם יְהֹוָ֖ה פׇּעֳלֵ֑ךְ וּתְהִ֨י מַשְׂכֻּרְתֵּ֜ךְ שְׁלֵמָ֗ה מֵעִ֤ם יְהֹוָה֙ אֱלֹהֵ֣י יִשְׂרָאֵ֔ל אֲשֶׁר־בָּ֖את לַחֲס֥וֹת תַּֽחַת־כְּנָפָֽיו׃
יג וַ֠תֹּ֠אמֶר אֶמְצָא־חֵ֨ן בְּעֵינֶ֤יךָ אֲדֹנִי֙ כִּ֣י נִֽחַמְתָּ֔נִי וְכִ֥י דִבַּ֖רְתָּ עַל־לֵ֣ב שִׁפְחָתֶ֑ךָ וְאָנֹכִי֙ לֹ֣א אֶֽהְיֶ֔ה כְּאַחַ֖ת שִׁפְחֹתֶֽיךָ׃
יד וַיֹּ֩אמֶר֩ לָ֨הֿ בֹ֜עַז לְעֵ֣ת הָאֹ֗כֶל גֹּ֤שִֽׁי הֲלֹם֙ וְאָכַ֣לְתְּ מִן־הַלֶּ֔חֶם וְטָבַ֥לְתְּ פִּתֵּ֖ךְ בַּחֹ֑מֶץ וַתֵּ֙שֶׁב֙ מִצַּ֣ד הַקֹּצְרִ֔ים וַיִּצְבׇּט־לָ֣הּ קָלִ֔י וַתֹּ֥אכַל וַתִּשְׂבַּ֖ע וַתֹּתַֽר׃
טו וַתָּ֖קׇם לְלַקֵּ֑ט וַיְצַו֩ בֹּ֨עַז אֶת־נְעָרָ֜יו לֵאמֹ֗ר גַּ֣ם בֵּ֧ין הָעֳמָרִ֛ים תְּלַקֵּ֖ט וְלֹ֥א תַכְלִימֽוּהָ׃
טז וְגַ֛ם שֹׁל־תָּשֹׁ֥לּוּ לָ֖הּ מִן־הַצְּבָתִ֑ים וַעֲזַבְתֶּ֥ם וְלִקְּטָ֖ה וְלֹ֥א תִגְעֲרוּ־בָֽהּ׃
יז וַתְּלַקֵּ֥ט בַּשָּׂדֶ֖ה עַד־הָעָ֑רֶב וַתַּחְבֹּט֙ אֵ֣ת אֲשֶׁר־לִקֵּ֔טָה וַיְהִ֖י כְּאֵיפָ֥ה שְׂעֹרִֽים׃
יח וַתִּשָּׂא֙ וַתָּב֣וֹא הָעִ֔יר וַתֵּ֥רֶא חֲמוֹתָ֖הּ אֵ֣ת אֲשֶׁר־לִקֵּ֑טָה וַתּוֹצֵא֙ וַתִּתֶּן־לָ֔הּ אֵ֥ת אֲשֶׁר־הוֹתִ֖רָה מִשָּׂבְעָֽהּ׃
יט וַתֹּ֩אמֶר֩ לָ֨הּ חֲמוֹתָ֜הּ אֵיפֹ֨ה לִקַּ֤טְתְּ הַיּוֹם֙ וְאָ֣נָה עָשִׂ֔ית יְהִ֥י מַכִּירֵ֖ךְ בָּר֑וּךְ וַתַּגֵּ֣ד לַחֲמוֹתָ֗הּ אֵ֤ת אֲשֶׁר־עָשְׂתָה֙ עִמּ֔וֹ וַתֹּ֗אמֶר שֵׁ֤ם הָאִישׁ֙ אֲשֶׁ֨ר עָשִׂ֧יתִי עִמּ֛וֹ הַיּ֖וֹם בֹּֽעַז׃
כ וַתֹּ֨אמֶר נׇעֳמִ֜י לְכַלָּתָ֗הּ בָּר֥וּךְ הוּא֙ לַיהֹוָ֔ה אֲשֶׁר֙ לֹא־עָזַ֣ב חַסְדּ֔וֹ אֶת־הַחַיִּ֖ים וְאֶת־הַמֵּתִ֑ים וַתֹּ֧אמֶר לָ֣הּ נׇעֳמִ֗י קָר֥וֹב לָ֛נוּ הָאִ֖ישׁ מִגֹּאֲלֵ֥נוּ הֽוּא׃ וַתֹּ֖אמֶר ר֑וּת

21 relative, one of our redeemers." "He said to me as well," said Ruth the Moabite, "'Cling
22 by my young men until they finish all my harvest,'" and Naomi told her daughter-in-law Ruth, "That is well, my daughter. Go out with his young women; do not go and come
23 to harm in other fields." So it was that she clung by Boaz's young women to glean until the barley harvest was over, and then the wheat, and after that she sat at home with her

3 1 mother-in-law. "Daughter," said her mother-in-law Naomi to her, "do I not wish I could
2 find you a resting place that would be good for you? Now there is Boaz, our relative, whose young women you were with, and he will be doing his winnowing at the threshing
3 floor tonight. You are going to wash yourself and anoint yourself and put on your dress and go down to that threshing floor. Do not let the man know that you are there until
4 he has finished eating and drinking. And when he lies down, take note of the place where he lies, and afterward go there, uncover his feet, and lie down also – he will tell you what
5
6 to do next." "I shall do," said Ruth, "all that you tell me to do." She went down to the
7 threshing floor and did exactly as her mother-in-law had instructed her. Boaz ate and drank and was happy, and he went and lay down beside the heap of grain. Then she came
8 to him silently, uncovered his feet, and lay herself down. At midnight the man started
9 and turned over – there was a woman lying at his feet! "Who are you?" he said, and she answered, "I am your maidservant Ruth – spread your mantle over your maidservant,
10 for you are a redeemer." And he replied, "The Lord bless you, daughter, for this last kindness is yet greater than your first, for you have not gone after the young men, poor
11 or rich. Now, daughter, do not be afraid. I shall do all that you ask, for all within my
12 people's gate know well that you are a woman of great strength, and I am indeed a
13 redeemer to you, but there is a redeemer still closer than me. Stay on here tonight, and in the morning, if he wishes to redeem you, good: let him redeem. And if he cares not
14 to redeem you, I shall redeem you myself, as the Lord lives – stay until morning." So she lay at his feet until morning and left before one person could recognize another. "Let
15 not a soul know there was a woman at the threshing floor," said he. And then, "Give me the wrap that you are wearing; hold it out." She did, and he measured six measures of
16 barley into it; he placed it upon her and went out into the city. She came to her mother-in-law, "Who are you, my daughter?" she said. And Ruth told her all that the man had
17 done for her. "He gave me these six measures of barley," she said. "He said to me, 'Do
18 not go back to your mother-in-law empty-handed.'" Said Naomi, "Sit down now, daughter, until you find out how the matter will fall, for that man will not rest unless the

4 1 matter is settled today." Boaz went up to the city gate and sat down, and the very redeemer of whom he had spoken passed by. "Peloni Almoni," said Boaz, "come here
2 and be seated," and he turned aside and sat down. Then Boaz took ten men from among
3 the elders of the city, "Be seated here," he said, and they too sat. Then he said to the redeemer, "Naomi, who came back from the land of Moav, must sell the field plot of our
4 kinsman Elimelekh. I said I would let you know of it, inviting you to buy it in the presence of those sitting here, in the presence of the elders of my people. If you wish to

מגילת רות

הפטרות וקריאות נוספות

כא הַמּוֹאֲבִיָּה גַּם ׀ כִּי־אָמַר אֵלַי עִם־הַנְּעָרִים אֲשֶׁר־לִי תִּדְבָּקִין עַד אִם־כִּלּוּ אֵת
כב כָּל־הַקָּצִיר אֲשֶׁר־לִי: וַתֹּאמֶר נָעֳמִי אֶל־רוּת כַּלָּתָהּ טוֹב בִּתִּי כִּי תֵצְאִי עִם־
כג נַעֲרוֹתָיו וְלֹא יִפְגְּעוּ־בָךְ בְּשָׂדֶה אַחֵר: וַתִּדְבַּק בְּנַעֲרוֹת בֹּעַז לְלַקֵּט עַד־כְּלוֹת
קְצִיר־הַשְּׂעֹרִים וּקְצִיר הַחִטִּים וַתֵּשֶׁב אֶת־חֲמוֹתָהּ:

ג א וַתֹּאמֶר לָהּ נָעֳמִי חֲמוֹתָהּ בִּתִּי הֲלֹא אֲבַקֶּשׁ־לָךְ מָנוֹחַ אֲשֶׁר יִיטַב־לָךְ: וְעַתָּה
ב הֲלֹא בֹעַז מֹדַעְתָּנוּ אֲשֶׁר הָיִית אֶת־נַעֲרוֹתָיו הִנֵּה־הוּא זֹרֶה אֶת־גֹּרֶן הַשְּׂעֹרִים
ג הַלָּיְלָה: וְרָחַצְתְּ ׀ וָסַכְתְּ וְשַׂמְתְּ שִׂמְלֹתַיִךְ עָלַיִךְ וְיָרַדְתִּי הַגֹּרֶן אַל־תִּוָּדְעִי לָאִישׁ שִׂמְלֹתַיִךְ וְיָרַדְתְּ
ד עַד כַּלֹּתוֹ לֶאֱכֹל וְלִשְׁתּוֹת: וִיהִי בְשָׁכְבוֹ וְיָדַעַתְּ אֶת־הַמָּקוֹם אֲשֶׁר יִשְׁכַּב־שָׁם
ה וּבָאת וְגִלִּית מַרְגְּלֹתָיו וְשָׁכָבְתִּי וְהוּא יַגִּיד לָךְ אֵת אֲשֶׁר תַּעֲשִׂין: וַתֹּאמֶר אֵלֶיהָ וְשָׁכַבְתְּ אֵלַי
ו כֹּל אֲשֶׁר־תֹּאמְרִי אֶעֱשֶׂה: וַתֵּרֶד הַגֹּרֶן וַתַּעַשׂ כְּכֹל אֲשֶׁר־צִוַּתָּה חֲמוֹתָהּ:
ז וַיֹּאכַל בֹּעַז וַיֵּשְׁתְּ וַיִּיטַב לִבּוֹ וַיָּבֹא לִשְׁכַּב בִּקְצֵה הָעֲרֵמָה וַתָּבֹא בַלָּט וַתְּגַל
ח מַרְגְּלֹתָיו וַתִּשְׁכָּב: וַיְהִי בַּחֲצִי הַלַּיְלָה וַיֶּחֱרַד הָאִישׁ וַיִּלָּפֵת וְהִנֵּה אִשָּׁה שֹׁכֶבֶת
ט מַרְגְּלֹתָיו: וַיֹּאמֶר מִי־אָתְּ וַתֹּאמֶר אָנֹכִי רוּת אֲמָתֶךָ וּפָרַשְׂתָּ כְנָפֶךָ עַל־אֲמָתְךָ
י כִּי גֹאֵל אָתָּה: וַיֹּאמֶר בְּרוּכָה אַתְּ לַיהוה בִּתִּי הֵיטַבְתְּ חַסְדֵּךְ הָאַחֲרוֹן מִן־
יא הָרִאשׁוֹן לְבִלְתִּי־לֶכֶת אַחֲרֵי הַבַּחוּרִים אִם־דַּל וְאִם־עָשִׁיר: וְעַתָּה בִּתִּי אַל־
תִּירְאִי כֹּל אֲשֶׁר־תֹּאמְרִי אֶעֱשֶׂה־לָּךְ כִּי יוֹדֵעַ כָּל־שַׁעַר עַמִּי כִּי אֵשֶׁת חַיִל אָתְּ:
יב וְעַתָּה כִּי אָמְנָם כִּי אִם גֹאֵל אָנֹכִי וְגַם יֵשׁ גֹּאֵל קָרוֹב מִמֶּנִּי: לִינִי ׀ הַלַּיְלָה וְהָיָה
יג בַבֹּקֶר אִם־יִגְאָלֵךְ טוֹב יִגְאָל וְאִם־לֹא יַחְפֹּץ לְגָאֳלֵךְ וּגְאַלְתִּיךְ אָנֹכִי חַי־יהוה
יד שִׁכְבִי עַד־הַבֹּקֶר: וַתִּשְׁכַּב מַרְגְּלוֹתָו עַד־הַבֹּקֶר וַתָּקָם בִּטְרוֹם יַכִּיר אִישׁ אֶת־ בְּטֶרֶם
טו רֵעֵהוּ וַיֹּאמֶר אַל־יִוָּדַע כִּי־בָאָה הָאִשָּׁה הַגֹּרֶן: וַיֹּאמֶר הָבִי הַמִּטְפַּחַת אֲשֶׁר־
טז עָלַיִךְ וְאֶחֳזִי־בָהּ וַתֹּאחֶז בָּהּ וַיָּמָד שֵׁשׁ־שְׂעֹרִים וַיָּשֶׁת עָלֶיהָ וַיָּבֹא הָעִיר: וַתָּבוֹא
אֶל־חֲמוֹתָהּ וַתֹּאמֶר מִי־אַתְּ בִּתִּי וַתַּגֶּד־לָהּ אֵת כָּל־אֲשֶׁר עָשָׂה־לָהּ הָאִישׁ:
יז וַתֹּאמֶר שֵׁשׁ־הַשְּׂעֹרִים הָאֵלֶּה נָתַן לִי כִּי אָמַר אַל־תָּבוֹאִי רֵיקָם אֶל־חֲמוֹתֵךְ: אֵלַי
יח וַתֹּאמֶר שְׁבִי בִתִּי עַד אֲשֶׁר תֵּדְעִין אֵיךְ יִפֹּל דָּבָר כִּי לֹא יִשְׁקֹט הָאִישׁ כִּי־אִם־
כִּלָּה הַדָּבָר הַיּוֹם:

ד א וּבֹעַז עָלָה הַשַּׁעַר וַיֵּשֶׁב שָׁם וְהִנֵּה הַגֹּאֵל עֹבֵר אֲשֶׁר דִּבֶּר־
ב בֹּעַז וַיֹּאמֶר סוּרָה שְׁבָה־פֹּה פְּלֹנִי אַלְמֹנִי וַיָּסַר וַיֵּשֵׁב: וַיִּקַּח עֲשָׂרָה אֲנָשִׁים מִזִּקְנֵי
ג הָעִיר וַיֹּאמֶר שְׁבוּ־פֹה וַיֵּשֵׁבוּ: וַיֹּאמֶר לַגֹּאֵל חֶלְקַת הַשָּׂדֶה אֲשֶׁר לְאָחִינוּ
ד לֶאֱלִימֶלֶךְ מָכְרָה נָעֳמִי הַשָּׁבָה מִשְּׂדֵה מוֹאָב: וַאֲנִי אָמַרְתִּי אֶגְלֶה אָזְנְךָ לֵאמֹר

5 redeem this, redeem; and if you will not redeem it, tell me: let me know, for there is none before you to redeem, and I am next in line to you." "I shall redeem," he said. "On the day you buy that field from Naomi," said Boaz, "and from Ruth the Moabite, you will have bought the wife of a dead man with it, to restore the dead man's name on his estate."
6 Said the redeemer, "Such a redemption I could not perform; it could be the ruin of my
7 estate. You redeem in my place; I cannot redeem." In those long-ago days in Israel, a redemption or exchange – anything to be officially enacted – was completed as follows. One man would take off his shoe and would hand it to the other: that was the bond then
8 recognized among Israel. Now this redeemer said to Boaz, "Take possession," and he
9 took off his shoe. "You are my witnesses this day," said Boaz to the elders and to all the people present, "that I take possession of all that was Elimelekh's and all that was Kilyon's
10 and Maḥlon's, from Naomi's hand. And with it I take Ruth the Moabite, Maḥlon's wife, to be mine, to rebuild the name of the dead on his estate. And the dead man's name will not be cut off from among his brothers, from the gate of his own city – you are my
11 witnesses this day." And all the people at the gate and the elders said, "We bear witness. May the Lord make the woman who is joining your house like Raḥel and like Leah, who together built the House of Israel; may you go from strength to strength in Efrata
12 and your name be ever spoken in Beit Leḥem. May your house be as the house of Peretz, whom Tamar bore to Yehuda, growing from the seed that the Lord will give you from
13 this young woman." And so it was that Boaz took Ruth, and she became his wife, and
14 he came to her; the Lord granted her conception, and she bore a son. And the women said to Naomi, "Blessed be the Lord, who has not withheld your redeemer on this
15 day – may the child's name be spoken in all Israel. May he restore your spirit and sustain your old age, for your daughter-in-law, who loves you, she has borne him, she who is
16 better to you than seven sons could be." Naomi took the child and placed him in her
17 bosom and became his nurse. And her neighbors named him, saying, "A son is born for Naomi!" They called him Oved. And that was Oved the father of Yishai the father of David.
18
19 This is the line of Peretz: Peretz was the father of Ḥetzron. Ḥetzron was the father of
20 Ram; Ram was the father of Aminadav. Aminadav was the father of Naḥshon; Naḥshon
21
22 was the father of Salma. Salma was the father of Boaz; Boaz was the father of Oved. Oved was the father of Yishai – and Yishai was the father of David.

קָנֵה נֶגֶד הַיֹּשְׁבִים וְנֶגֶד זִקְנֵי עַמִּי אִם־תִּגְאַל גְּאָל וְאִם־לֹא יִגְאַל הַגִּידָה לִּי
וְאֵדַע כִּי אֵין זוּלָתְךָ לִגְאוֹל וְאָנֹכִי אַחֲרֶיךָ וַיֹּאמֶר אָנֹכִי אֶגְאָל: וַיֹּאמֶר בֹּעַז ה
בְּיוֹם־קְנוֹתְךָ הַשָּׂדֶה מִיַּד נָעֳמִי וּמֵאֵת רוּת הַמּוֹאֲבִיָּה אֵשֶׁת־הַמֵּת קָנִיתִי לְהָקִים
שֵׁם־הַמֵּת עַל־נַחֲלָתוֹ: וַיֹּאמֶר הַגֹּאֵל לֹא אוּכַל לִגְאָל־לִי פֶּן־אַשְׁחִית אֶת־ ו
נַחֲלָתִי גְּאַל־לְךָ אַתָּה אֶת־גְּאֻלָּתִי כִּי לֹא־אוּכַל לִגְאֹל: וְזֹאת לְפָנִים בְּיִשְׂרָאֵל ז
עַל־הַגְּאֻלָּה וְעַל־הַתְּמוּרָה לְקַיֵּם כָּל־דָּבָר שָׁלַף אִישׁ נַעֲלוֹ וְנָתַן לְרֵעֵהוּ וְזֹאת
הַתְּעוּדָה בְּיִשְׂרָאֵל: וַיֹּאמֶר הַגֹּאֵל לְבֹעַז קְנֵה־לָךְ וַיִּשְׁלֹף נַעֲלוֹ: וַיֹּאמֶר בֹּעַז ח ט
לַזְּקֵנִים וְכָל־הָעָם עֵדִים אַתֶּם הַיּוֹם כִּי קָנִיתִי אֶת־כָּל־אֲשֶׁר לֶאֱלִימֶלֶךְ וְאֵת
כָּל־אֲשֶׁר לְכִלְיוֹן וּמַחְלוֹן מִיַּד נָעֳמִי: וְגַם אֶת־רוּת הַמֹּאֲבִיָּה אֵשֶׁת מַחְלוֹן קָנִיתִי י
לִי לְאִשָּׁה לְהָקִים שֵׁם־הַמֵּת עַל־נַחֲלָתוֹ וְלֹא־יִכָּרֵת שֵׁם־הַמֵּת מֵעִם אֶחָיו
וּמִשַּׁעַר מְקוֹמוֹ עֵדִים אַתֶּם הַיּוֹם: וַיֹּאמְרוּ כָּל־הָעָם אֲשֶׁר־בַּשַּׁעַר וְהַזְּקֵנִים יא
עֵדִים יִתֵּן יְהוָה אֶת־הָאִשָּׁה הַבָּאָה אֶל־בֵּיתֶךָ כְּרָחֵל ׀ וּכְלֵאָה אֲשֶׁר בָּנוּ שְׁתֵּיהֶם
אֶת־בֵּית יִשְׂרָאֵל וַעֲשֵׂה־חַיִל בְּאֶפְרָתָה וּקְרָא־שֵׁם בְּבֵית לָחֶם: וִיהִי בֵיתְךָ יב
כְּבֵית פֶּרֶץ אֲשֶׁר־יָלְדָה תָמָר לִיהוּדָה מִן־הַזֶּרַע אֲשֶׁר יִתֵּן יְהוָה לְךָ מִן־הַנַּעֲרָה
הַזֹּאת: וַיִּקַּח בֹּעַז אֶת־רוּת וַתְּהִי־לוֹ לְאִשָּׁה וַיָּבֹא אֵלֶיהָ וַיִּתֵּן יְהוָה לָהּ הֵרָיוֹן יג
וַתֵּלֶד בֵּן: וַתֹּאמַרְנָה הַנָּשִׁים אֶל־נָעֳמִי בָּרוּךְ יְהוָה אֲשֶׁר לֹא הִשְׁבִּית לָךְ גֹּאֵל יד
הַיּוֹם וְיִקָּרֵא שְׁמוֹ בְּיִשְׂרָאֵל: וְהָיָה לָךְ לְמֵשִׁיב נֶפֶשׁ וּלְכַלְכֵּל אֶת־שֵׂיבָתֵךְ כִּי טו
כַלָּתֵךְ אֲשֶׁר־אֲהֵבַתֶךְ יְלָדַתּוּ אֲשֶׁר־הִיא טוֹבָה לָךְ מִשִּׁבְעָה בָּנִים: וַתִּקַּח נָעֳמִי טז
אֶת־הַיֶּלֶד וַתְּשִׁתֵהוּ בְחֵיקָהּ וַתְּהִי־לוֹ לְאֹמֶנֶת: וַתִּקְרֶאנָה לוֹ הַשְּׁכֵנוֹת שֵׁם יז
לֵאמֹר יֻלַּד־בֵּן לְנָעֳמִי וַתִּקְרֶאנָה שְׁמוֹ עוֹבֵד הוּא אֲבִי־יִשַׁי אֲבִי דָוִד:
וְאֵלֶּה תּוֹלְדוֹת פָּרֶץ פֶּרֶץ הוֹלִיד אֶת־חֶצְרוֹן: וְחֶצְרוֹן הוֹלִיד אֶת־רָם וְרָם יח יט
הוֹלִיד אֶת־עַמִּינָדָב: וְעַמִּינָדָב הוֹלִיד אֶת־נַחְשׁוֹן וְנַחְשׁוֹן הוֹלִיד אֶת־שַׂלְמָה: כ
וְשַׂלְמוֹן הוֹלִיד אֶת־בֹּעַז וּבֹעַז הוֹלִיד אֶת־עוֹבֵד: וְעוֹבֵד הוֹלִיד אֶת־יִשַׁי וְיִשַׁי כא כב
הוֹלִיד אֶת־דָּוִד:

APPENDIX
THE CLASSIC COMMENTATORS

Rabbi Yitzḥak Abarbanel (1437–1508) wrote an extensive commentary on most of Tanakh. His commentary does not flow verse by verse, but is divided into sections that cover several verses. He is famous for opening each section with an extensive list of questions, followed by an essay in which he answers them all. Abarbanel's commentary is based on rational analysis, and he often disagrees with many of the traditional commentators who preceded him. Abarbanel served as finance minister to King Ferdinand of Spain until the expulsion of the Jews from Spain in 1492.

Rabbi Aharon Ibn Alrabi (14th to 15th century) was a prominent scholar in Sicily. He was involved in many public religious debates with Karaites, Muslims, and Christians, and was invited to present his opinions to Pope Marvin V. He was known for his strong and critical opinions and was an independent, rationalist thinker who did not hesitate to write commentary which disagreed with midrash or rabbis who preceded him. Of all his writings, the only one that has survived is a commentary he wrote on Rashi.

Rav Moshe Alshikh (16th-century France and Israel) was a well-known kabbalist. When Rabbi Yosef Karo wanted to renew the institution of the Sanhedrin, Alshikh was one of his appointees. His commentary to the Torah is largely based on kabbala.

Rabbi Eliyahu ben Amozegh (1822–1900) was an Italian rabbi, kabbalist, philosopher, and scholar. His commentary to the Torah draws from a wide range of disciplines, and he was known for his universalist thinking. His commentary was printed only once and is not readily available.

Rabbi Yitzḥak Arama (1420–1494) wrote a complex commentary to the Torah known as *Akedat Yitzḥak*. He was a contemporary of Abarbanel, and upon his expulsion from Spain he moved to Italy. He was an original thinker who blended Kabbala and philosophy with deep human insights in his Torah commentary.

Rabbeinu Baḥya ben Asher (1255–1340) was a Spanish commentator. He frequently cites commentators who came before him, and his original insights are mostly in the realm of mysticism, especially as he tries to explain the mystical comments of Ramban.

Rabbi Eliezer Ashkenazi (1513–1586) served as a rabbi in Egypt, Cyprus, Italy, Prague, and Poland. He was fiercely independent in his ideas and did not hesitate to argue with the leading of his time or of those in previous generations.

Rabbi Moshe Yitzḥak Ashkenazi (1821–1898) was an Italian rabbi. His commentary, *Ho'il Moshe*, which is not very well-known, spans all the books of Tanakh. Like many of the Italian commentaries, his approach was grounded in trying to appreciate the meaning of the text as written, and diverges from both the Ashkenazi and the Sephardic traditions.

Rabbi Ḥayyim Ibn Attar (1696–1743) was a Moroccan rabbi known primarily for his commentary on the Torah, *Or HaḤayyim*. His commentary focuses heavily on spiritual and mystical understandings of the Torah, and he is often referred to (especially in Ḥasidic circles) as the Or HaḤayyim Hakadosh – the Holy Or HaḤayyim.

◂ Rabbi Yaakov

APPENDIX – THE CLASSIC COMMENTATORS

Rabbi Yaakov Baal Haturim (1269–1343) is most famous for his halakhic masterpiece, the Tur, which eventually served as the foundation for the *Shulḥan Arukh*. He was born in Ashkenaz and moved to Spain, so that he was aware of the two main halakhic traditions. He wrote a brief Torah commentary which focuses on gematria and finding rare occurrences of words – this commentary is printed in many editions of the *Mikraot Gedolot*. Lesser known is a longer commentary which is largely based on Rashi, Ramban, and his father, Rabbeinu Asher (Rosh).

Rabbi Yosef Bekhor Shor (12th century) was a French rabbi and talmudic scholar who studied with Rabbeinu Tam and is cited frequently in Tosafot as "Ri of Orleans." His commentary on the Torah relies heavily on rational thinking and focuses on understanding the literal meaning of the text. It is filled with original ideas.

Rabbi Naftali Tzvi Yehuda Berlin (Netziv, 1816–1893) was head of the Volozhin Yeshiva. His commentary on the Torah, *Haamek Davar*, crosses many boundaries – he was interested in both a *peshat* reading of the text and deeper exploration drawing on the Gemara and halakha. Surprisingly for a Lithuanian rosh yeshiva, he sometimes makes reference to scientific discoveries as they impact our understanding of the Torah.

Daat Zekenim is a collection of comments written by an assortment of the authors of *Tosafot* on the Talmud. These were mostly Rashi's students. Most of their comments are grounded in the Talmud, but they sometimes feature original insights.

Rabbi Avraham Ibn Ezra (1089–1172) was a prominent commentator focusing primarily on *peshat*, the literal meaning of the text, and logic. Born in Muslim Spain, he moved extensively throughout his life, spending time in Portugal, Italy, France, and England (where he died). Ibn Ezra had extensive secular learning, having studied medicine and other sciences, and was an acclaimed Hebrew poet. He is also known for his sharp wit and his disputes with the Karaite sect. While respectful of the rabbinic tradition, he did not feel bound to accept all of rabbinic commentary, especially on the non-halakhic portions of the Torah.

Rabbi Levi ben Gershon, aka Gersonides (Ralbag, 1288–1344), was a French Jewish philosopher, talmudist, mathematician, physician, and astronomer. His commentary on the Torah is divided into two parts – one is an explanation of the words, the other is an exploration of the big ideas and messages he derives from the Torah.

Rabbi Pinḥas HaLevi (13th century) is thought to be the author of the *Sefer Haḥinukh*. The book is not a Torah commentary but rather follows the order of the Torah and presents a list of the 613 mitzvot with a brief explanation for each. As part of those explanations, the author occasionally discusses the Torah text. The author, who lived in Spain, chose to be anonymous, and is the brother of the more well-known Rabbi Aharon HaLevi, who wrote a commentary on the Talmud.

Rabbi Moshe Ḥafetz (17th century), an Italian commentator wrote *Melekhet Maḥashevet*. Very little is known about this author.

Rabbi Avraham ben Harambam (1186–1237), the Rambam's son, was for many years the head of the Jewish community in Cairo, succeeding his father. He continued his father's rationalist methodology, while adding on his own mystical approach to Judaism. He too was a prominent medical doctor. His commentary on the Torah puts its primary focus on understanding the literal meaning of the words and then moves on to explore their significance.

Rabbi Samson Raphael Hirsch (1808–1888) was a German rabbi often credited with having saved German Orthodoxy from the challenges of the Reform movement. He believed in integrating traditional Jewish learning with modern German life, an approach which he termed Torah *Im Derekh Eretz*, and served in the Moravian parliament when he was chief rabbi. Hirsch wrote extensively, including many works of philosophy, but mostly in German. Rabbi Hirsch's commentary on the Torah, translated from German, combines a careful look at the text of the Torah, details of halakha, creative grammar, psychology, and philosophy. His commentary is considered both modern and

◀ traditional

traditional, and it was an important weapon in his battle with the Reform movement as he tried to demonstrate the unbreakable bond between the Oral Torah and the Tanakh.

Rabbi David Tzvi Hoffman (1843–1921) was a rabbi in Germany who also earned a doctorate and was eventually head of the Hildesheimer Rabbinical Seminary in Berlin. He was considered a leading authority in halakha, and in addition to his halakhic writings he authored a commentary on the Torah which incorporated elements of the new academic study of Tanakh, including history, archaeology, and linguistic analysis. He believed that the modern methods of study, which many were using to challenge the authority of the Torah, could and should be used to enhance our Torah study and deepen our understanding.

Rabbi Moshe Isserles (aka Rama, 16th-century Poland) wrote *Torat HaOlah*, a book of philosophy. Rama is best known for his halakhic works which recorded Ashkenazi customs and halakhic norms contrasting with the Sephardic ones written in the *Shulhan Arukh*.

Rabbi Yosef Kara (c. 1050–1130) was a student and colleague of Rashi in northern France. He was an older colleague of Rashbam, and he is recognized as a creative and innovative commentator who was one of the champions of the approach to try to find the simple reading of the text. He dedicated many of his efforts to refuting challenges from and debating with the Christian church.

Rabbi Yosef Ibn Kaspi (1280–1345) was a philosopher in Spain and Provence. His commentary on the Torah is aimed very much at a rational understanding of the *peshat*, and he was influenced by rational thinkers such as the Rambam as well as by *peshat* commentaries like those of Rashbam and Ibn Ezra. Like many in his circle, he held that the search for *peshat* should take precedence over accepting traditional rabbinic explanations to Tanakh in non-halakhic matters.

Rabbi Shlomo Ephraim Luntschitz (1550–1619) was a rabbi and rosh yeshiva in Prague. In his commentary, *Keli Yakar*, he cites frequently from Rashi, Ramban, Sforno, Abarbanel, and others, and says that he is interested in trying to "get close" to the *peshat*, or plain reading of the text. In addition to his desire to figure out what the text actually means, his commentary is filled with moral teachings and ideas for deeper meaning.

Rabbi Moshe ben Maimon (Rambam, 1135–1204), was known primarily for his great works of halakha (*Mishneh Torah*) and philosophy (*Moreh Nevukhim*). He did not write a commentary on the Torah, but within his two major works, especially *Moreh Nevukhim*, there are many passages in which he explains various passages from the Torah. The Rambam's approach is rationalist and often has philosophical grounding.

Rabbi Ḥizkiya ben Manoaḥ (13th century) was a French rabbi. His commentary, *Ḥizkuni*, is based largely on Rashi, but he draws from others as well and adds some of his own ideas. He builds on Midrash and rabbinic commentary to try to arrive at a closer reading of the Torah text.

Rabbi Yaakov Tzvi Mecklenburg (1785–1865), who was a rabbi in eastern Prussia, wrote *HaKetav VehaKabbala*. His commentary was intended to demonstrate the link between the Written Torah and its literal meaning on the one hand, and the Oral Torah and the halakha on the other. Along with those of Malbim and Rabbi Hirsch, his commentary was an important defense against the challenges of the growing Reform movement.

Rabbi Shmuel ben Meir (Rashbam, 1085–1158) was a well-known talmudic scholar in France. He was both a student and a grandson of Rashi, and he is quoted frequently in the Tosafot on the pages of the Talmud. He also wrote his own commentary to parts of the Talmud where Rashi's commentary was missing. Rashbam's commentary on the Torah was focused almost exclusively on what the verses mean and has many original insights, including those which are dramatically different from those of the rabbis of the Talmud. Rashbam is famous for his polite but firm disagreements with his grandfather Rashi, especially about Rashi's reliance on midrash.

◀ Rabbi Meir

APPENDIX – THE CLASSIC COMMENTATORS

Rabbi Meir Leibush ben Yeḥiel Mikhel (Malbim, 1809–1879) was a rabbi who taught in Romania and other European countries. In his commentary, which covers most of Tanakh, he argues that no two Hebrew words are exact synonyms, and that each has a unique meaning. Malbim draws heavily on earlier commentaries like Ramban and Abarbanel and tries to demonstrate the connection between the Oral Torah and the Written Torah. Malbim dedicated many of his efforts, including a significant part of his Torah commentary, to debate with the Reform movement.

Rabbi Moshe ben Naḥman, aka Nahmanides (Ramban, 1194–1270), was a leading Spanish rabbi, philosopher, and kabbalist. Aside from his extensive commentary on the Talmud, he wrote a very rich commentary on the Torah, which includes a literal understanding of the text, discussion of context and broad themes, analysis of Midrash (especially those cited by Rashi), and Jewish mysticism. Ramban frequently quotes both Rashi and Ibn Ezra, and often disagrees with both. He was most fierce in his disagreements with the Rambam's writings on the Torah.

Rabbi Isaac Samuel Reggio (1784–1855) was an Italian rabbi, linguist, and mathematician. His commentary aims to understand the literal reading of the Torah while being aware of and sensitive to traditional rabbinic interpretations. He has many novel and creative ideas in understanding the big picture in the Torah.

Rabbi Ovadya Sforno (1475–1550) lived in Italy, where he studied Hebrew, mathematics, and medicine, in addition to his primary interest, Torah. In his commentary to the Torah, he often paraphrases Rashi, Ibn Ezra, Rashbam, and Ramban, but he adds many original thoughts. His primary interest is understanding what the verses mean, but he also tries to derive meaning for contemporary life.

Rabbi Meir Simḥa Hakohen (*Meshekh Ḥokhma*, 1843–1926) was a prominent rabbi in Latvia who spent his entire rabbinical career in Dvinsk. He was best known as a great talmudic scholar, but he wrote a fascinating commentary on the Torah which blends talmudic thinking, halakhic analysis, and original and creative readings of the Torah text.

Rabbi Shlomo Yitzḥaki (Rashi, 1040–1105) was a French rabbi considered by many to be the father of all the commentaries. Aside from his comprehensive commentary on the Talmud, he wrote an extensive commentary on all of Tanakh. Rashi's commentary on the Torah was distributed widely during his own lifetime and was embraced by both scholars and non-scholars. His commentary focuses on his unique understanding of what *peshat*, or the simple reading of the text is, but is based mostly on Midrash. Rashi's commentary also includes many educational messages, and his commentary is so popular that many people do not know whether some of the stories they have learned are in the Torah itself or in Rashi's commentary on the Torah.

In Appreciation

We feel fortunate to be involved in a publication partnering with Rabbi Shlomo Einhorn, who embodies the impactful teachings and Torah values crucial for today's Jewish youth.

Rabbi Einhorn understood the priority our father, Jack M. Nagel z"l, placed on Torah Education and Religious Zionism. In addition to a weekly shiur that they shared, he became his cherished teacher, spiritual leader and close friend.

We gratefully acknowledge and thank Rabbi Shlomo for his insightful commentary and vision as Executive Editor of The Koren Lev Ladaat Ḥumash.

May he and his dear Rebbitzen Shira be blessed to continue to lead and inspire the greater Los Angeles community and see much happiness and nachas from their wonderful family.

THE NAGEL, LERER & PARKER FAMILIES

NOTES

NOTES

NOTES

NOTES

NOTES

NOTES

NOTES

NOTES

NOTES